Microsoft® Office 2000

2000

DEPLOYMENT AND ADMINISTRATION

Microsoft® Office 2000

2000

DEPLOYMENT AND ADMINISTRATION

Bill Camarda

Microsoft® Office 2000 Deployment and Administration

International Standard Book Number: 0-7897-1931-2

Library of Congress Catalog Card Number: 98-88239

Printed in the United States of America

First Printing: March 2000

02   01   00   4   3   2   1

Trademarks

Warning and Disclaimer

ASSOCIATE PUBLISHER
Greg Wiegand

ACQUISITIONS EDITOR
John Pierce

DEVELOPMENT EDITOR
Susan Cohen

MANAGING EDITOR
Thomas F. Hayes

TECHNICAL EDITORS
Mark Hall
Bill Bruns

PROJECT EDITOR
Lori A. Lyons

COPY EDITORS
Kay Hoskin
Nancy Albright
Audra McFarland

INDEXER
Sandy Henselmeier

PROOFREADER
Maribeth Echard

TEAM COORDINATOR
Sharry Lee Gregory

INTERIOR DESIGNER
Ruth Lewis

COVER DESIGNERS
Dan Armstrong
Ruth Lewis

COPYWRITER
Eric Borgert

EDITORIAL ASSISTANT
Angela Boley

LAYOUT TECHNICIANS
Darin Crone
Liz Johnston

Contents at a Glance

Table of Contents

II Customizing Office to Your Organization's Needs

6 Customizing Word to Your Organization's Needs   121

7 Customizing Excel to Your Organization's Needs   167

21 Integrating Office Documents with Desktop Publishing Systems   579

VI Superior Techniques for Managing Office

About the Author

Bill Camarda has nearly 20 years' experience as a writer and technology consultant serving the needs of leading computing, Internet, networking, and financial services companies, including IBM, AT&T, Bell Atlantic, Lucent Technologies, MCI/WorldCom, Viacom, Met Life, and many others. His copywriting and consulting experience encompass a broad range of work—from white papers and brochures to video, audio, and Web-site development—serving a wide range of audiences, from executive-level corporate decision-makers to technical professionals, from entrepreneurs to end users. He is also author of 13 computer books, most of them targeted at expert PC users, including these recent Macmillan titles: *Special Edition Using Word 2000, Microsoft Office Administrator's Desk Reference, Special Edition Using Word 97 Bestseller Edition*, and *Windows Sources Word 97 for Windows SuperGuide*.

Dedication

This one is for my wife, my love, Barbara.

Acknowledgments

I'd like to thank some very talented, knowledgeable, and *patient* coauthors: Gordon Padwick, Michael Larson, Brady Merkel, Deb Shinder, Laura Stewart, Daryl Lucas, Steve Kern, Paul Kimmel, Chris Negus, and Bo Williams. And, as always, the alchemists at Que who turn raw manuscripts into world-class books, led by John Pierce. That includes my development editor, Susan Cohen, plus all these folks and a few I've no doubt missed: Susan Hobbs, Lori Lyons, Maribeth Echard, Kay Hoskin, Sandy Henselmeier, and Liz Johnston.

Most important, thanks to *you*, my reader.

Into the millennium!

Tell Us What You Think!

As the reader of this book, *you* are our most important critic and commentator. We value your opinion and want to know what we're doing right, what we could do better, what areas you'd like to see us publish in, and any other words of wisdom you're willing to pass our way.

As an Associate Publisher for Que, I welcome your comments. You can fax, email, or write me directly to let me know what you did or didn't like about this book—as well as what we can do to make our books stronger.

Please note that I cannot help you with technical problems related to the topic of this book, and that due to the high volume of mail I receive, I might not be able to reply to every message.

When you write, please be sure to include this book's title and author as well as your name and phone or fax number. I will carefully review your comments and share them with the author and editors who worked on the book.

Fax: 317-581-4666
Email: consumer@mcp.com
Mail: Greg Wiegand
          Que
          201 West 103rd Street
          Indianapolis, IN 46290 USA

Introduction

There are plenty of books for the casual Office user. But what about a comprehensive, independent, up-to-date guide for people who are responsible for *managing* Office? People whose livelihoods depend on Office working the way it's supposed to? People, in short, like *you?*

There's only one book like that, and you're holding it.

Que's *Microsoft Office 2000 Deployment and Administration* is the objective guide to all the critical Office management issues you care about:

- Getting Office 2000 (and Office 98 for the Macintosh) installed and configured as cost-effectively as possible
- Integrating Office in a real-world environment that probably isn't 100-percent Microsoft-based
- Leveraging Office's powerful workgroup capabilities to support today's fast-moving virtual teams
- Learning how to manage Office 2000's powerful new Web collaboration, intranet, and HTML features
- Customizing Office so that it supports your business goals— instead of shoehorning your business into Office's default limitations
- Helping your colleagues use Office to create documents that are consistent, accurate, professional, and reflect your organization's image
- Mastering the management tools, enhancements, and third-party solutions that can make Office more valuable to you

- Ensuring that your colleagues know how to use Office as effectively as possible—and showing them where to get fast answers when they don't

- Troubleshooting those tough problems with Microsoft Office that your users can't solve—or the ones they create for themselves

If you're like most people who manage Office, no two days are alike. Monday, you're troubleshooting damaged Normal.dot templates in Word. Tuesday, you're deploying an intranet using Office Server Extensions. Wednesday, you're testing third-party Excel add-ins. Thursday, you're figuring out how to use Access data on the Web. To be successful, you need a wide range of information, much of which can't be pigeonholed into traditional "computer book" topics.

Accordingly, this book covers a lot of territory—bringing together a lot of information that's never been brought together before (if it even existed).

From customizing your Office installation across the network, to exporting Word files into other programs, you'll find it here. You'll discover strategies for managing the development and review of large documents and presentations by multiple authors. You'll learn how to access worksheets on your intranet—even if Netscape Communicator is your standard browser, instead of Internet Explorer.

It's an eclectic mix—but you have an eclectic job!

Who Should Read This Book?

This book is for you, if

- You're a system administrator or other technology professional who manages Office on a network or in a mobile environment.

- You're an office manager or other business professional who needs to help your colleagues work and collaborate more effectively with Office

- You provide Office support or training, either formally (through a help desk or training department) or informally.

- You oversee a publishing organization or other production environment that uses Word and Office to produce large documents and might use Office with desktop publishing software.

- You're in a cross-platform organization with users working on both Windows or Macintosh systems.

- You are deploying or managing a corporate intranet or Web site that uses documents created in Microsoft Office.

- You're an Office "power user" who often finds yourself helping other Office users throughout your company or organization.

- You're an Office Visual Basic for Applications (VBA) developer who needs information on deploying your custom applications effectively.

How This Book Is Organized

Microsoft Office 2000 Deployment and Administration is organized into seven parts:

Part I: Managing Installation and Deployment

The book begins with a close look at what it takes to install and configure Office so that it best meets the needs of your organization. You walk through the planning process and master Office 2000's extensive new tools and options for streamlining installation, hands-on. You find a full chapter on installing Office 2000 using Microsoft's System Management Server (SMS) 2; another chapter on deploying Microsoft Office 98 for the Macintosh; and still another chapter on troubleshooting and fixing failed installations.

Part II: Customizing Office to Your Organization's Needs

In Part II, you learn specific ways to customize each of Office's most widely used applications to your organization's needs: Word, Excel, PowerPoint, Access, Outlook, and FrontPage. You learn how to customize user interfaces and toolsets to make important features more accessible and eliminate features you don't want to support.

You learn how to customize Office applications at startup via Autoexec macros and how to deploy productivity options, such as custom dictionaries and AutoText lists. Finally, you take a close look at Outlook 2000, arguably the most malleable personal information manager ever created—and understand your options for customizing Outlook (with and without Microsoft Exchange).

Part III: Using Office to Support Teams and Workgroups

Nowadays, few documents, worksheets, or presentations are created solely by a single individual. In Part III, you learn how to help Office users work together as teams. You learn how to organize and streamline the work of creating and reviewing documents, worksheets, presentations, and databases; and how to share schedules and corporate address books built with Microsoft Outlook 2000. There's also a full chapter on managing VBA in the enterprise, including tips for making the most of the new VBA programming environment, the COM add-in architecture for custom solutions, and VBScript.

Part IV: Integrating Office in Your Heterogeneous Environment

Notwithstanding the hype, few organizations use 100-percent Microsoft technology. And even those organizations often face the challenge of managing multiple versions of Office applications—with their multiple file formats. Part IV shows how to integrate Office into your real-world environment.

Whether you're introducing Word files into a law office that has used WordPerfect 5.1 for DOS since Ronald Reagan was President, trying to figure out why RTF files suddenly don't import into PageMaker properly, managing mixed Windows/Macintosh environments, or using Excel worksheets with Lotus Notes, you find practical solutions here. You also learn about Microsoft and third-party enhancements that can help you solve problems Office won't solve by itself.

Part V: Office, the Internet, and Intranets

More than ever before, organizations distribute the bulk of their information electronically—internally via intranets and externally via Web sites. Microsoft Office 2000 offers extensive new features designed to make it as easy to create documents for intranets and Web sites as it is to create them for print—for example:

- Most documents can be saved to HTML—and HTML documents can be saved to native Office formats—with remarkable fidelity and very few lost features; rich formatting such as charts and revision marks are stored using a combination of HTML and Extensible Markup Language (XML). Microsoft says that it now provides "equal support for HTML as a companion file format."

- Microsoft's Save to the Web feature and Web Folders make it easy to save files directly to an intranet or a Web site, without complex FTP uploads.

- New Web discussion features enable users to review and annotate documents on a corporate intranet.

- PowerPoint 2000 presentation broadcasts enable users to deliver live presentations over intranets and Web sites.

- Office 2000 integration with Microsoft NetMeeting enables users to hold videoconferences concerning documents they are working on; the conferences can be impromptu or scheduled in advance using Outlook 2000.

These capabilities are powerful, but they must be managed in new ways, and they introduce new challenges along with the benefits. In this section, you learn what these features can do, how they work, and the best ways to deploy and manage them. You also learn how to avoid the "gotchas" that can easily trip you up if you're not careful.

Part VI: Superior Techniques for Managing Office

Microsoft Office doesn't exist in a vacuum. It exists in real organizations with real challenges, opportunities, risks, schedules, and budgets. In Part VI, you learn techniques that can make Office 2000 a better "citizen" of the organization. You learn how to use Office 2000's extensive new features for reducing total cost of ownership (and decide which features are actually appropriate for your organization). You learn techniques for making Office more secure; resisting macro virus infections; and raising productivity by providing better support without spending more.

You learn new techniques for supporting your increasingly mobile base of Office users—and master Office's powerful multilingual features for international organizations.

Part VII: Troubleshooting and Optimizing Office

Part VII brings together detailed, up-to-date troubleshooting information for each major Office application: Word, Excel, PowerPoint, Access, Outlook, and FrontPage. You find just enough "theory" to help you understand how each Office application is designed and structured so you can "reason out" solutions to the problems that aren't covered here. The book wraps up with a detailed look at additional resources—Microsoft and otherwise—that can help you identify and troubleshoot even more problems.

Finally, because it's likely that you'll be called upon to customize Office installations, Appendix A gives you handy information about Microsoft's defaults: which features are installed by default, which are typically installed only the first time someone tries to use them, which are typically run from the CD-ROM or network, and which are typically not installed at all.

How This Book Is Designed

Que works hard to ensure its books deliver the quickest possible access to the most relevant information—and this book is no exception. At the back of the book, you find an exceptionally detailed index. Throughout the book, you find icons flagging several types of information designed to add value:

TIP Tips point out shortcuts, ideas, and techniques for managing Office that you might not discover on your own.

N O T E Notes offer a closer look at some Office features or issues you might want to know more about—without distracting you from the fast answers you're looking for. ■

CAUTION

Cautions help you avoid Microsoft Office management and feature pitfalls that can cost your organization both time and money.

Conventions Used in This Book

Most Que books share typographical conventions that make them easy to understand—after you've read one, you're right at home with all the others.

For example, you might read about key combinations such as Ctrl+Y, Office's standard shortcut for repeating the last command. Ctrl+Y means: Hold down the **Control** key, press **Y**, and then release both keys.

Here is other special formatting you'll see:

■ Internet addresses are specified in a `monospaced boldface`—for example, `www.microsoft.com`. If a Web address is too long to fit on a single line, the address will be divided at the backslash. This indicates that the address should be treated as a single line; you should not press **Enter** or add spaces partway through. You can see this in the following example: `http://www.microsoft.com/office/2000/Office/Documents/entpwkbk.htm`

- Terms introduced and defined for the first time are formatted in *italic*.

- Terms formatted in `monospaced boldface` may also represent type that should be entered verbatim, as in the following example:

  Type the following command line:

  ```
  setup.exe /q1 /b1
  ```

- Finally, text formatted in monospace type represents code listings, such as VBA program listings, as in the following example:

```
Sub Macro7()
'
' Macro7 Macro
' Macro recorded 05/26/99 by Bill Camarda
'
    Selection.Font.Bold = wdToggle
End Sub
```

As an Office professional, you're responsible for the software tools your colleagues depend on most. You have unique leverage within your organization: You can dramatically improve everyone's productivity by managing Office more effectively. This book will show you how. ●

Managing Installation and Deployment

Planning Your Office 2000 Installation

by Bill Camarda

If you're responsible for deploying Microsoft Office 2000 for Windows or Office 98 for the Macintosh, your success depends in large part on your initial planning.

In this chapter, you walk through the planning steps that you consider prior to implementing Office in your organization, and identify resources you can use to streamline the process.

Evaluating Your Goals for Office

In determining how (and whether) to deploy the latest versions of Office, begin by considering what you hope to achieve from the upgrade. Potential reasons to upgrade to Office 2000 for Windows include the following:

- **Better productivity and ease-of-use.** Office 2000 continues Office's long-term goal of making features more accessible to users. Improved New and Open dialog boxes; command menus that display only features that users need; and new easy-to-use graphics tools such as Publisher 2000 desktop publishing software and PhotoDraw 2000 graphics software might enable your users to accomplish more, in less time, with fewer requirements for specialized skills.

  According to Ziff-Davis' *PC Computing* Magazine, Office 2000 users were 24% more productive than users performing similar tasks in previous versions of Office. However, because the set of features your users work with (as well as their sophistication) can affect your productivity dramatically, these figures cannot be accepted at face value.

- **Better collaboration.** Office 2000's Web features—including Web discussions, online presentations, and much improved saving to HTML—are intended to make intranets a far more powerful day-to-day tool for users throughout the organization. They might also make Office 2000 a publishing tool of choice, even for simpler Web sites and intranets that do not focus on sophisticated collaborative applications.

- **Lower total cost of ownership.** Microsoft has delivered an unprecedented range of tools and features designed to lower the cost of deploying and managing Office. These include a dramatically improved Custom Installation Wizard for across-the-network installation; Detect and Repair to automatically fix damaged Office applications; support for custom and intranet-based Help; improved Office Assistant natural language Help; and much more. Of course, for many companies the real cost comparison is not between Office 2000 and competitive suites, but between deploying Office 2000 and leaving an already-deployed version of Office in place—and to this end, Office 2000 must demonstrate not only lower deployment costs, but also higher business value.

- **Stronger international support.** International organizations might find Office 2000's single global executable and language-customizable user interfaces easier to manage in complex worldwide environments. Even smaller organizations might appreciate Office 2000's out-of-the-box support for French and Spanish, in addition to English. Other improvements, such as the new Unicode format used by the Access 2000 database, might also prove valuable to global firms.

- **The "knowledge desktop."** Microsoft promotes the "Outlook Today" feature in the Outlook 2000 personal information manager (see Figure 1.1) as providing a digital dashboard that gives users quick access (and better control over) both their goals and their tools. Other features, such as the improved data analysis features in the Excel 2000 spreadsheet program, might make it easier to transform raw data into knowledge for decision making.

FIGURE 1.1
Outlook Today, a
custom startup page for
each individual user.

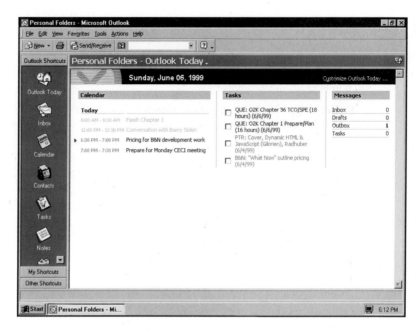

- **Better support for custom application development.** An improved Visual Basic for Applications development environment, VBScripting in Outlook (and a new object model that exposes more of Outlook's capabilities to customization), and the enhanced Internet Explorer 5 all provide a more robust environment for building custom applications.

To a lesser degree, similar points might be made in support of upgrading to Office 98 for the Macintosh:

- **Better productivity and ease-of-use.** Compared with previous versions of Office for the Macintosh, Office 98 provides a more robust feature set and a more Mac-like user experience.

- **Better support.** Microsoft Office 98 is the first version of Office for the Macintosh that includes Microsoft's natural language Help (though Help does not reflect enhancements made in Office 2000 for Windows).

- **Better collaboration.** Although Office 98 does not contain Office 2000's extensive Web-centered capabilities, it does offer features, such as Excel workbook sharing and PowerPoint presentation conferencing, which can promote collaboration.

- **Better Web support.** Although Office 98 does not contain Office 2000's round-trip HTML capabilities, it does contain the first version of Word for the Macintosh that can save Word files to HTML format for use on simple intranets and Web sites.

- **More centralized control.** Office 2000 enables administrators to assert stronger control over Office throughout the entire life cycle, including finely grained control over the features that are installed and used, and how Office fits into the enterprise's computing architecture.

Evaluating Possible Disadvantages of Upgrading to Office

Perhaps none of the arguments described in the previous section provide compelling reasons to upgrade from the version of Office you are already running. Your organization might be reluctant to upgrade if any of the following situations apply to you:

- Your users have barely scratched the surface of the features available in their current version of Office (the 32-bit Office 95 or Office 97 suite, or even the 16-bit Office 4.x suite).

- You handle Web or intranet publishing through a specialized group of employees; you do not need or want to provide HTML publishing tools to all your users.

- You are still running Windows 3.x or an early version of the Mac OS on some of your workstations, and you have an extensive base of 16-bit custom applications that you're not prepared to upgrade.

- Your installed base of hardware does not support Office 2000 or Office 98 (see the "Inventorying Workstations and Servers" section later in this chapter).

- Your organization has other IT projects of higher priority than upgrading Office, such as Y2K upgrades or ERP implementation.

N O T E   Microsoft Office has its own Y2K issues. Earlier versions of Word and PowerPoint are not strictly year 2000 compatible, but unless you make extensive use of WordBasic macros, you're unlikely to have too many problems continuing to use these packages past the year 2000. You need to carefully evaluate Excel macros, however, on an individual basis, and Access 2.0 is simply not Y2K compatible. ■

Even if you are planning to upgrade, timing might be an issue. There are two primary concerns:

- **Coordinating with the rest of your IT strategy.** For example, some organizations will roll out Office 2000 and Windows 2000 (expected in late 1999) concurrently, thereby lowering the cost of deployment by performing only a single rollout. You might also want to time your upgrade to correlate with new hardware purchases or leases so that you can deploy Office at the same time that you deploy your hardware. This also gives you the option of deploying Office first on the hardware most capable of running it well.

- **Gauging the experiences of early adopters.** While Office 2000's retail release date was June 1999, large corporations have been eligible to deploy it since April 1999. You might want to evaluate their experiences, as reported in the trade press and other forums, before committing to deployment. Some companies have a policy to wait for at least one service pack to appear prior to deploying a major Office suite or operating system. At press time, Microsoft has not yet announced any plans for an Office 2000 service pack.

Reviewing the Costs of Deployment

If deploying Office 2000 appears to offer significant financial or competitive benefits to your organization, your next step is to evaluate the costs associated with deployment. These include the following:

- **Office software.** Take into account participation in corporate volume discount programs, such as Microsoft Open License Program, which is available for companies purchasing software for 25 or more desktops; or Microsoft Select, which offers tiered, volume discounts based on your organization's total two-year forecast of acquisitions within a category of products.

- **Third-party software that must also be updated.** This might include foreign language dictionaries and vertical market add-in products. Microsoft also recommends upgrading antivirus software to newer versions that support the antivirus API built into Office 2000, which allows for automatic scanning of files between the time a user selects a file for opening and the time an Office application actually opens it.

- **Costs for planning and deployment.** Includes costs of setting up a test lab, trial rollouts, and managing the rollout process.

- **Additional hardware requirements.** For example, memory, processor upgrades, and the cost of visiting the desktop to perform those upgrades.

- **Costs associated with updating custom software.** These are a factor, especially if you are upgrading from 16-bit applications.

- **Additional server and bandwidth capacity if Office 2000 is to be run from the network.** Includes the costs of deploying these (over and above network enhancements you would have made anyway).

- **Costs of training and support, especially for Office 2000's new intranet/Web features.** Includes in-person training, computer-based training, Microsoft and third-party books and videos, retraining of help desk personnel, and communication with users. If you plan to make use of Office 2000's Web and intranet capabilities, you should plan for extensive training to ensure your users use these features efficiently and in a way consistent with your corporate policies.

▶ For more information about supporting Microsoft Office, **see** Chapter 35, "Deploying and Using Office 2000's Web-Collaboration Components," on **p. 895**.

After you've compared costs and benefits, you can make the decision to deploy or not, based on these questions:

- Based on your comparison of costs and benefits, how quickly will Office 2000 pay for itself?

- How does that payoff compare with the other IT projects competing for your limited time and resources?

- Actually install Office 2000 on test systems, and get yourself familiar with it. What do your instincts tell you? Which of these features do you envision your users working with? Are other features impractical for your organization? What do your best help desk people think about it?

- Finally, what (if any) are the costs of not upgrading—costs in lost productivity and potential competitive disadvantage?

Planning Office Deployment for Your Enterprise

If you've concluded that deploying Office 2000 (or Office 98 for the Macintosh) makes sense, the next step is to plan the deployment.

Microsoft uses the acronym *SMART* to describe the goals of planning. Your plan should be *specific, measurable, achievable, results-based* (with realistic outcomes), and *time-oriented* (with realistic schedules and milestones). Your plan should also

- Reflect a risk assessment that identifies potential obstacles, the likelihood of these obstacles causing problems, and contingency/fallback plans.

- Specify which resources will be available to handle each step.

- Be thoroughly documented, with feedback mechanisms in place to improve future roll-outs. The documentation should be in a form that can be used to support future roll-outs as well—for instance, a Systems Management Server equipment database that can also be leveraged in operating systems upgrades.

Gathering Resources for Deployment Planning

Microsoft has published a number of documents that can help you avoid reinventing the wheel as you plan your Office 2000/98 rollout. These resources are all accessible from the Microsoft Office Deployment Resources page, `www.microsoft.com/office/enterprise/deployment/default.htm`. Highlights include

- **Office 2000 Resource Kit.** An online book that reviews key issues associated with deploying and managing Office 2000. The Office 2000 Resource Kit is accompanied by a downloadable software toolkit containing utilities and other resources for deployment, such as the Custom Installation Wizard for centralizing installation over a network; the Office Profile Wizard for storing standard or custom Office settings; and an updated version of the System Policy Editor and Office 2000 system policy templates for controlling access to certain features. The Office 2000 Resource Kit can be reached directly at `www.microsoft.com/office/ork`.

- **Deployment and Maintenance White Paper.** A review of the features built into Office 2000 that are designed to reduce the cost of ownership across the entire life cycle. Many of these features are covered in depth in this book; for example, Chapter 2, "Automating and Customizing Office Installations Across the Network," walks through using the Office Profile Wizard and Custom Installation Wizard; Chapter 37, "Reducing Office 2000's Total Cost of Ownership," reviews system policies in depth.

- **Customer Deployment Scenario.** Shows how a fictitious organization might make decisions about how to deploy Office and then use Office 2000's deployment tools to translate those decisions into reality. (A series of case studies from companies such as J.D. Edwards, Turner Broadcasting System, and Unisys is also available in the Early Experiences area of the Deployment Resources page.)

- **Deploying Office 2000 with Microsoft Systems Management Server.** Shows how to use SMS 2.0 to deploy and centrally manage systems running Office 2000. SMS 2.0 deployment is also covered in Chapter 3, "Using Systems Management Server 2 to Install Office."

- **Running Microsoft Office 2000 with Windows Terminal Server Fast Facts.** Briefly describes issues you might face in deploying Office 2000 on Windows terminals, where Office itself is being run from Microsoft Windows NT Server 4.0 Terminal Edition. Running Office 2000 on Terminal Server is also covered in Chapter 23, "Running Office on Windows Terminal Server."

- **Office 2000 Guided Tours for IT Professionals.** Three guided tours that show how Office 2000 can simplify the user experience, reduce cost of ownership, and increase integration with the Web and other enterprise resources.

- **Deploying and Maintaining the Workgroup Web.** A white paper that shows how to make the most of the intranet workgroup Webs that Office 2000 enables, thereby creating a more collaborative workplace. Many of these issues are also covered in this book, in Chapters 31, 32, 33, 35, and 36.

- **Microsoft Office 2000 and File Sharing in a Heterogeneous Environment.** This document describes your options for running Office 2000 in an organization that also uses earlier versions of Microsoft Office. For an independent look at these issues, see Chapter 19 of this book. For a review of issues surrounding integration with non-Microsoft business applications, which are largely ignored in Microsoft's paper, see Chapter 18 of this book.

- **Converting Files Between Different Versions of Office Software.** This is a file format matrix showing various Office document formats, the application versions they correspond with, and the converters (if any) that must be installed to facilitate coexistence.

- **Extending Office 2000.** This white paper describes the integration between Office 2000 and other Microsoft products, including Microsoft BackOffice and Microsoft Internet Explorer.

- **Office Server Extensions FAQ.** Information about the Office Server Extensions, which must be installed on a Web server in order for workgroups and organizations to take full advantage of Office 2000's Web-based collaboration capabilities.

- **Enterprise Planning Workbook.** This is a fill-in-the-blanks Microsoft Word workbook that helps you define the issues and steps associated with deploying Office 2000 in your company.

- **Office 2000 Sample Plan.** This is a detailed sample plan for deploying Office, as developed by an actual company, a large financial institution. This sample plan is available at `www.microsoft.com/office/enterprise/deployment/sampplan.htm`.

■ **Deploying Microsoft Office 2000: Notes from the Field.** This is an online version of the Microsoft Press book by the same name, sharing the experiences and best practices of Microsoft Consulting Services in deploying Office 2000.

■ **The Office 2000 Deployment Template.** This is a Microsoft Project template containing detailed steps and timeframes associated with deploying Office 2000. You can adapt this template to your specific needs. The template is shown in Figure 1.2. If you do not have Microsoft Project, you can download a 60-day trial version from **www.microsoft.com/office/98/project/trial/info.htm**.

■ **The Custom Maintenance Wizard.** Microsoft says this Wizard simplifies staged rollouts and ongoing maintenance, and makes it easy to change Office features and settings from a centralized location after deployment. As of late September 1999, however, this Wizard had not yet been released, even in a beta version.

FIGURE 1.2

The Microsoft Office 2000 Deployment Template, running in Microsoft Project 98.

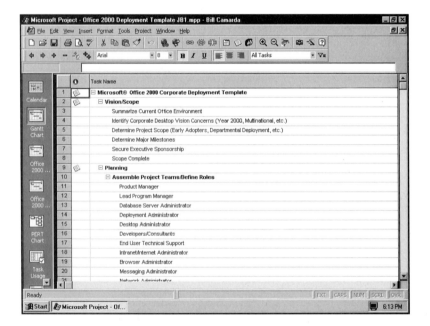

Establishing an Office Deployment Team

In a sizable organization, you need to establish a team with clear individual responsibilities, led by a project manager with clear authority and the support of management. This team should include most or all of the following:

■ IT experts familiar with the organization's enterprise computing architecture

■ Microsoft Office and Microsoft operating system platform specialists

■ Members of user organizations

■ Support and training specialists

■ Network administrators

- Web/intranet administrators and designers
- Security specialists
- Internal custom software developers

Don't neglect to provide any up-front training that your team members need to be effective participants in Office planning and implementation.

Inventorying Workstations and Servers

When your team is in place, begin the process of inventorying the workstations and servers you expect to run Office 2000. Are they powerful enough? Do some need to be upgraded with more memory? Do any still run Windows 3.1? If so, should these be upgraded, discarded, or configured as clients running Office 2000 from Windows Terminal Server? Do other systems need to be replaced? Establish a testing lab with representative computers and software, and begin evaluating the performance you can actually expect.

 TIP   Consider using the Office 2000 and/or Windows 2000 rollout as an opportunity to standardize hardware, limiting the number of vendors and technologies your IT organization must support.

N O T E   Office 2000 is more than a desktop application: It is a network application.

- It encourages not only the construction of intranets, but also their constant use in more ways than ever.
- It typically relies on the network heavily for rollout, and then on an ongoing basis, to install new features as individual users need them, and to host shared resources, such as templates, workbooks, and clip media.
- It can be configured to run on Windows terminals that depend heavily on Windows Terminal Server and network infrastructure to deliver acceptable performance.

Although it is difficult to accurately evaluate the impact Office 2000 will have on your network infrastructure, you should make best efforts to do so, and plan for network enhancements where they appear to be needed. For example:

- Will you overstress the network by allowing users to pick the time when Office is installed, or should you push installation via Systems Management Server at night or on the weekend?
- Are certain segments of the network overstressed; might they need to be moved from 10Mbps Ethernet to 100Mbps, or onto switched infrastructure?
- Is your external Internet connection sufficient to support Office 2000's built-in Web features, such as Help or Office on the Web? Or should you temporarily or permanently disable those features pending the availability of more bandwidth?
- Are your intranet servers maxing out? If so, you might want to upgrade or supplement them if you plan to use Office 2000 features, such as Web folders, or offload functions, such as print sharing, to other servers. (In some organizations, Linux servers configured with Samba and running on old hardware might be worth considering, because they provide a way to add capacity and reuse existing resources without purchasing new NT Server software licenses.) ▓

Table 1.1 presents Microsoft's stated system requirements for Office 2000, along with a more realistic view of what you need to achieve decent performance with Office. Of course, these estimates are only a starting point. Take into account issues that are specific to your organization, such as

- The complexity of work your users do
- Any custom applications that must integrate with Office
- Your network's performance, especially if you are planning to deploy some or all of Office on network servers instead of client workstations

Table 1.1   Office 2000 for Windows System Requirements

Requirement	Minimum (Official Microsoft)	Realistic
Processor	Pentium 75 (Professional, Small Business, Standard Edition) Pentium 166 (Premium, if running PhotoDraw)	Pentium 166 (Professional, Small Business, Standard Edition) Pentium 233 (Premium, if running PhotoDraw)
Operating system	Windows 95, 98, or NT Workstation 4.0, SP3 or higher	Windows 95, 98, or NT Workstation 4.0, SP3 or higher
RAM (Win95/98)	16MB for operating system plus 4MB RAM for each application running simultaneously (except 8MB for Outlook, Access, or FrontPage; 16MB for PhotoDraw); 8MB additional to run Office email	32MB for operating system plus 8MB RAM for each application running simultaneously (except 16MB for Outlook, Access, FrontPage, or PhotoDraw); 8MB additional to run Office email
RAM (Windows NT Workstation 4.0)	32MB for operating system plus 4MB RAM for each application running simultaneously	64MB for operating system plus 8MB RAM for each application running simultaneously
Disk space (Default Installation)	Premium edition: 526MB for all applications Professional: 391MB for all applications Standard: 189MB for all applications Small Business Edition: 360MB for all applications	Premium: 526MB for all applications Professional: 391MB for all applications Standard: 189MB for all applications Small Business Edition: 360MB for all applications
CD-ROM drive	Yes	Yes
Monitor	VGA or Higher, SuperVGA Recommended	SuperVGA

Requirement	Minimum (Official Microsoft)	Realistic
Mouse	Microsoft Mouse, IntelliMouse or compatible	Microsoft Mouse, IntelliMouse or compatible
Internet connection/modem	For Internet features, Internet connection and 9,600 baud (or higher) modem, 14,400 recommended	For Internet features, Internet connection and 28,800 baud modem

Table 1.2 presents Microsoft's stated minimum and practical system requirements for Office 98 Macintosh Edition. Microsoft's estimates seem fairly realistic, except that some users have noted that individual Office applications seem to run better with more memory assigned to them than these estimates might permit, especially when creating large, complex documents, worksheets, or presentations.

Table 1.2   Office 98 for Macintosh System Requirements

Requirement	Minimum	Realistic
Processor	Any PowerPC	PowerPC 120 MHz
Operating system	Mac OS 7.5	Mac OS 7.5.5 preferably Mac OS 8.1
Memory	16MB	32MB
Hard disk space	49–120MB	100–120MB
CD-ROM drive	Yes (or install from network)	Yes (or install from network)
Monitor	16 grays or 256 colors, 640×400	16 grays or 256 colors, 640×400

Specifying Client Configurations

At this stage, you can begin to identify the appropriate version of Office 2000/98 for each workgroup or constituency in your organization. Currently, seven versions of Office are targeted to a variety of audiences, from small business people to developers. Table 1.3 lists the products included in each edition.

Table 1.3   Versions of Office 2000 and Office 98, and Their Components

Component	Premium Edition	Prof. Edition	Standard Edition	Small Bus. Ed.	Devel. Edition	Office 98/Mac
Word 2000	X	X	X	X	X	X
Excel 2000	X	X	X	X	X	X
Outlook 2000	X	X	X	X	X	
Publisher 2000	X	X		X	X	X
Small Business Tools	X	X		X	X	

continues

Table 1.3   Continued

Component	Premium Edition	Prof. Edition	Standard Edition	Small Bus. Ed.	Devel. Edition	Office 98/Mac
Access 2000	X	X			X	
PowerPoint 2000	X	X	X		X	X
FrontPage 1.019	2000				2000	1.0
PhotoDraw 2000	X				X	
Internet Explorer	5.0	5.0	5.0	5.0	5.0	4.0 (upgradable to 4.5)
Office Development Tools					X	
Outlook Express	X	X	X	X	X	X
Encarta 98 Deluxe						
Bookshelf 98						

Keep in mind opportunities to reduce costs. For instance, in many organizations, relatively few users need access to Microsoft Access databases; these companies might save money by purchasing more Standard Edition licenses and fewer Professional Edition licenses.

Beyond specifying the correct version of Office, you can also make preliminary choices about the features your users do and do not need. Microsoft Office 2000 provides the finest control ever of which features you deploy. Features might also be deployed as Install on First Run, meaning that they are installed locally across the network only when a user first seeks to use them.

The Appendix lists the components of an Office 2000 Premium Edition install, and their default settings (Installed Locally, Install on First Run, Run from CD, or Not Installed).

Some opportunities to reduce the size of an Office installation are shown in the following list:

- Install fewer standard wizards and templates.
- Do not install FrontPage tutorials or samples.
- Do not install querying tools and drivers.
- Install fewer graphics filters.
- Do not install optional applications, such as Microsoft Photo Editor.
- Do not install the Clip Gallery.
- Do not install international support files.

- Do not install Office Server Extensions support.
- Choose the Not Available option for features you do not want to be used, even through Install on First Run. (In some cases, you can use the System Policy Editor to disable menu commands, so the features do not even appear in the user interface.)

Choosing the Best Installation Approach

Office 2000 provides a variety of installation options, including the following:

- Local installation on each client workstation from CD-ROM
- Customized installation across the network using the Custom Installation Wizard and Office Profile Wizard
- Installation so that most components of Office 2000 run from a network server instead of a local workstation (or, the closely related Windows Terminal Server installation)
- Installation that integrates with System Policies to customize and limit how users can work with Office applications
- Installation with Microsoft Systems Management Server or another desktop management tool

NOTE If you are deploying Office 2000 on a set of brand-new Windows workstations, another option might make sense: cloning copies of hard drives to contain all the applications, data, and configuration settings you want, prior to placing the new computers in the field. This works best with Windows 95/98 workstations that are configured identically or nearly identically.

If you are deploying computers running Windows NT 4 Workstation, be doubly careful to ensure the underlying hardware is truly identical, because even minor variations can cause problems. Also take care to use your cloning software's feature for changing the unique IDs that are created with each new NT installation. ■

At this stage, your team should decide which of these options are the most cost-efficient, the least disruptive, and the easiest to use—given the technical and financial resources available to you.

▶ For more information about the Custom Installation Wizard, **see** Chapter 2, "Automating and Customizing Office Installations Across the Network," on **p. 27**.

▶ For more information about deploying Office 2000 using Systems Management Server, **see** Chapter 3, "Using Systems Management Server 2 to Install Office," on **p. 63**.

You should also begin carefully documenting the process you are developing, and continue to document every change you make through formal rollout and beyond. Document problems and the responses you choose. Also, invite feedback, preferably early enough in the process to reflect it.

Considering Additional Important Issues in Planning Your Pilot Rollout

Prior to your pilot rollout, consider how you will handle issues such as these, and make tentative (or if possible, firm) decisions:

- How, if at all, will you provide international features to your users? For instance, will you purchase the Multi-Language Pack? Will you provide French and Spanish proofing tools? (For more information about using Office 2000 in multilingual environments, see Chapter 42, "Using Office in a Global Environment.")

- What Web features will you provide? Will you deploy Internet Explorer 5? (For more information about deploying Internet Explorer 5, see Chapter 36, "Deploying Internet Explorer 5 with the Internet Explorer Administration Kit.")

- What levels of security will you establish for your macros and other macros that might need to be run? (For more information about Microsoft Office 2000 security, see Chapter 38, "Maximizing Office 2000 Security.")

- Will you use system policies to restrict user access to specific tools and features? (For more information about working with system policies, see Chapter 37, "Reducing Office 2000's Total Cost of Ownership.")

- Will you use profiles to support users who roam among workstations? (For more information about working with Office profiles, see Chapter 37, "Reducing Office 2000's Total Cost of Ownership.")

- What custom applications are you planning, and when will they be ready for testing and rollout? (For more information about managing your Visual Basic for Applications code resources, see Chapter 17, "Managing Office Programmability.")

- How will you support coexistence among multiple versions of Office, multiple document formats, and third-party office software? Do you need to update third-party software that works with Office, such as templates, add-ins, voice-recognition software, and antivirus software? (For more information about managing diverse environments incorporating legacy software and earlier versions of Office, see Chapter 18, "Migrating from or Coexisting with Legacy Applications," and Chapter 19, "Managing Multiple Versions of Office.")

Testing Office in the Lab

Now that you have a fairly good idea of how you would like to deploy Office to your users, put your plan to the test on representative hardware in your lab before you try it out on real users. Here are some of the elements to test thoroughly in the lab first:

- Test the installation process on both servers and representative client workstations.
- Test the customizations you make using Custom Installation Wizard and Office Profile Wizard.

- Test the uninstall process on representative workstations.

- Test existing macros and add-ins. (Now might also be a good time to test for Y2K compliance in custom macros and VBA code, as discussed in Chapter 38. You might also discover macros that are no longer used, and can be retired.)

- Test workstation, notebook PC, and server performance working with representative files.

- Test the integration of the Microsoft Outlook client with your email system.

- Test Internet Explorer 5's compatibility with your Web applications and sites (if you have not already deployed it and are considering doing so).

- Test the Internet Explorer installation process, via the Internet Explorer Administration Kit Wizard (or whatever process you choose).

- Thoroughly test the system policies you plan to deploy, if any.

- Test a representative sample of documents that need to be converted to newer Office formats (keeping in mind that, except for Access, there have been no significant format changes since Office 97).

The goal of all this testing is to demonstrate a technical approach to deploying Office 2000 that should work in the real world. After you've done so, you're ready to find out whether the plan really will work, through a pilot rollout.

Planning and Running a Pilot Rollout

At this point, you're ready to pilot your Office 2000 rollout. Working with your user representatives, identify a workgroup or department that

- Is at least moderately receptive to new technology (but it's best not to use the IT organization itself, which is rarely representative of the user base)

- Is not facing an unusually challenging business deadline

- Has management willing to support the pilot rollout

N O T E Some organizations run prepilot rollouts with even smaller groups. ▪

Keep in mind that word spreads quickly within a company, and even though your pilot is a shakedown cruise, if it becomes apparent that you did not plan the pilot well, word will get out—and you will face a more skeptical organization when the real rollout arrives.

Before installing Office 2000 on pilot systems, do the following:

- Communicate clearly and specifically with the users who will be affected.

- Develop plans for training the users and providing help desk support. (Unfortunately, many companies neglect this step until the enterprisewide rollout—causing many more problems during the pilot process than are necessary.)

- Determine who will be responsible for each aspect of the pilot rollout.

■ Be sure the department's systems are ready to accept Office 2000. For example, if you intend to use Install on First Run capabilities of Office 2000, the Active Desktop must be installed (although it can be switched off, as most companies have chosen to do). Active Desktop is built intoWindows 98 and Internet Explorer 4.0 or later.

■ Schedule the pilot rollout to minimize business disruption.

After the rollout, carefully evaluate the results, asking the following:

■ Did your systems for automated installation work? In other words, did Office install properly, with the proper features, at the correct times?

■ Did your systems for support and training work? Did you get more (or fewer) support calls than you expected?

■ How did the time and cost of the pilot rollout compare to what you expected?

■ What else should have gone more smoothly from your perspective as an administrator? What can you do about it?

■ What did your users like (and dislike) about the rollout process?

■ What do theylike (and dislike) about Office 2000 now that they're running it?

Learning Lessons for the Enterprisewide Rollout

Based on the answers to these questions, adjust your plans for your enterprisewide rollout as follows:

■ Revise your budgets and staffing to reflect what you now know about schedules, support, and rollout costs.

■ Revise network installation scripts and other key customization.

■ Finalize your enterprise communications plans so that users will know exactly what to expect.

■ Establish a final-phase deployment plan for the business units that you intend to upgrade, based on business constraints, receptiveness to technology, and other issues—who should be upgraded first, next, last, or not at all?

■ Update your policies and procedures guidelines to reflect the forthcoming rollout.

■ Make arrangements to purchase and take delivery of the software and hardware you need.

■ Prepare and communicate a detailed schedule with milestones and timelines that take into account contingencies and holidays.

■ Get final management approvals, as needed.

Rolling Out Office 2000 Enterprisewide

Finally, you're ready to roll out Office 2000 enterprisewide. Start by running administrative installations on each of your servers, as explained in detail in Chapter 2.

Next, communicate with users, telling them the following:

- What to expect
- Where to get more information if they need it
- When the upgrade will happen, and what impact it might have on them
- Whether there are steps that the users need to perform, such as logging onto a server and running the installation from the desktop

If individual workstations must be upgraded, or if incompatible software must be removed from them, do so—either centrally, through Systems Management Server or another desktop management package, or locally at each client workstation. Check to be sure that all network permissions are in place. Finally, install Office using whichever techniques you've chosen and tested.

Of course, rolling out Office 2000 doesn't end the process; you need to closely monitor its impact, both to improve future phases of the rollout and to enhance user support and productivity. Check the following:

- Is your feedback process working to ensure that users and managers can communicate problems and opportunities for improvement? Similarly, do you have a way to replicate successes with Office throughout the enterprise?
- With which features are users having trouble? Can more computer-based (or other) training be provided to support these features?
- Are there features, such as workgroup features, where you expected more widespread usage than you're seeing? If so, what communications methods are available to promote these features?
- What additional templates and sample documents can you provide?
- Can you improve coordination with departmental and workgroup managers in later phases of the rollout, or later rollouts?
- Finally, have you documented your own successes and failures in terms of automating rollout processes with system policies, user profiles, installation scripts, and Systems Management Server?

N O T E Microsoft's forthcoming Office 2000 Custom Maintenance Wizard promises to provide an easy way to make changes to Office on users' workstations even after you've completed deployment. This makes careful documentation and follow-up even more important. You will have an opportunity to fix the problems that users report by providing new functionality and tools or changing Office behaviors—all from a central location. ■

CHAPTER 2

Automating and Customizing Office Installations Across the Network

by Bill Camarda

Now that you've done the high-level planning associated with deploying Microsoft Office 2000, you're ready to plan and run the installation process itself. In this chapter, you walk through automating and running a networked installation using Office 2000's powerful new tools for customization. The process consists of five key steps:

1. **Download and install the Office 2000 Resource Kit.** You will depend heavily on two of the tools included there:
   - The Custom Installation Wizard
   - The Office Profile Wizard

2. **Install and customize Office 2000 on a client workstation.** At this stage, you can customize Office 2000 much as a user would, except your customizations are then rolled out to all similar users.

3. **Run the Office Profile Wizard.** This stores your customized settings in an Office Profile Settings (OPS) file.

4. **Customize your network setup using the Custom Installation Wizard.** At this stage, you can choose which features to install, as well as incorporate the OPS customizations you've already made.

5. **Run setup on each user's computer.** You can have users do this themselves, or you can perform the installation centrally, using System Management Server or another desktop management tool.

In the following sections, you walk through all five steps of the process, in-depth.

Downloading and Installing the Office 2000 Resource Kit

For Office administrators, Microsoft's Online Office 2000 Resource Kit is an essential resource. The Resource Kit's online book is regularly updated by Microsoft and can be found at **www.microsoft.com/office/ork**.

The accompanying Microsoft Office Resource Kit Toolbox brings together all Microsoft's software for administering and managing Office 2000.

N O T E If you have used the Office Resource Kit before, you will find three surprises in the new edition:

1. According to Microsoft, although the Office 2000 Resource Kit is available in book form, it has been revamped to function best as an online resource, with short content blocks and extensive hyperlinks.

2. The content of the Resource Kit has been refocused entirely on system requirements, upgrading strategies, and techniques for deploying and maintaining Office 2000. Broader coverage in the previous editions has been eliminated.

3. The Office administration tools provided with Office 2000 have been dramatically improved to streamline both deployment and maintenance. ■

Even if you have purchased the Microsoft Office 2000 Resource Kit, you should visit the Toolbox page at **www.microsoft.com/office/ork/2000/appndx/toolbox.htm**. (See Figure 2.1 to ensure that you have the latest versions of these tools, including new tools Microsoft released after the release of Office 2000.)

Many, but not, all the tools you need are in the Office Resource Kit Toolbox (Orktools.exe), currently a 9MB download. To download Orktools.exe, click the **Download Now** button next to it.

As of late September 1999, the page also contained several other optional software tools that you might find useful, as listed in Table 2.1.

Table 2.1   Optional Tools Available in the Office 2000 Resource Kit Toolbox

Tool	What It Does
Answer Wizard Builder (AWBuild.exe)	Answer Wizard Builder for creating custom Answers that can be accessed through Office 2000 Help.
Converter Pack (convpack.exe) and Converter Pack 16 (cnvpck16.exe)	A set of less commonly used text and image converters for Office 2000. Cnvpck16.exe contains versions for Office 4.x under Windows 3.1, as well as an extraction utility you can use to customize the converters you install with Office 2000.
Custom Maintenance Wizard	A new tool that allows administrators to centrally change or update the Office 2000 features already installed on client workstations.

Tool	What It Does
Customizable Alerts (CustAlrt.exe)	Sample HTML and ASP pages that can help you create ASP scripts for handling custom error messages in Office 2000.
Enhanced Setup.exe (SetupChn.exe)	A new and improved version of Setup.exe that allows you to chain a second installation (such as Microsoft Publisher 2000) at the end of an automated Office 2000 installation.
Help on the Web Sample Files (Msoffice.css,Office.css)	Samples you can use to customize the Office 2000 Help on the Web feature.
HTML Help Workshop Sample Files (Hlponweb.exe)	Cascading style sheets for use with HTML Help Workshop.
Index Server HTML Filter	Updates the HTML filter built into Index Server. (NLHTML.exe)
International information (Internat.exe)	Documents listing Office 2000 language settings and components.
Keypath workbook (keypath.exe)	An Excel worksheet with detailed technical information about the components of Office, including Registry values and ComponentID Global Unique Identifiers (GUID) that can be used for troubleshooting purposes.
Migrated settings workbook (Settings.xls)	An Excel worksheet with detailed information about settings that migrate from previous versions of Office.
Migration Guides for Office 2000	Separate Word documents covering migration to Access 2000, Excel 2000, PowerPoint 2000; migration from WordPerfect; and Y2K issues in Excel 2000.
Office 2000 Command Translator (Cmdlang.exe)	Installs the Command Translator, which assists users who need to know the names of Office commands as they appear in other languages. (Requires Access and Excel.)
Office 2000 Transforms Error Messages (Errors.mst)	Provides more descriptive error messages for Setup that can help you troubleshoot problem installations.
Office 2000 Transforms for Windows Installer Shortcuts (09WIS_1.mst and 09WIS_2.mst)	Provides enhancements that enable administrators to deploy Office 2000 on client workstations with only a single client system restart.
Office Information (Offinfo.exe)	Documents details and settings for Office 2000 components.
Office Information (Offinfo.exe)	Documents details and settings for Office 2000 components.
Office Server Extensions Migration Utility (Migrate.msi)	Updates the Office Server Extensions database settings page to provide support for backup and restore.

Part

I

Ch

2

continues

Table 2.1 Continued

Tool	What It Does
Online Broadcasting Service (OnLBroad.exe)	Installation files for Microsoft's new Online Broadcasting Service.
Outlook Administration Tools	Tools for modifying Outlook profiles; evaluating Outlook 2000 total cost of ownership; managing Outlook 2000 forms; and converting existing items.
Outlook Bar Reference Information (OutlookBar.doc)	Information about customizing the Outlook Bar, the column of shortcuts on the left side of the Outlook window.
Outlook Information (Outlook.prf)	Sample Outlook profile.
Outlook Today Information Sample Files	Information and tools for and customizing the Outlook Today page that appears by default when users run Outlook.
Publisher Information (PubInfo.exe)	Spreadsheet files containing support information for Microsoft Publisher.
Readme.doc (Readme.doc)	Updated Readme.doc file for the Office Resource Kit.
Systems Management Server Sample Files (SMSInfo.exe)	Package Definition Files for remote installation of Office 2000 with Systems Management Server 1.2 and 2.0.

FIGURE 2.1
The Microsoft Office
Resource Kit Toolbox
page.

Download Now button

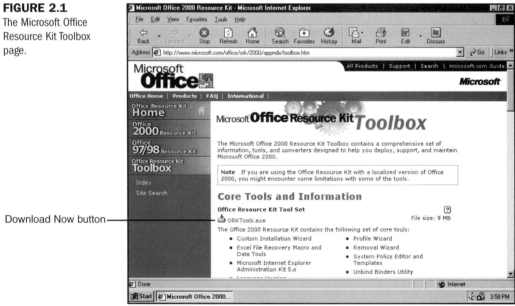

After you download Orktools.exe, double-click the file to install it. The Office Resource Kit tools install as a folder on the Start menu. To display them, choose **Start**, **Programs**, **Microsoft Office Tools**, **Microsoft Office Resource Kit Tools**.

N O T E Install the Office Resource Kit Tools on the server you intend to use for networked installation. If you want to create customizations with the Office Profile Wizard, also install the tools on the client workstation where you prepare these customizations. ■

N O T E To read the online Resource Kit, choose **Start**, **Programs**, **Microsoft Office Tools**, **Microsoft Office Resource Kit Documents**. The first page of the Office Resource Kit appears in your browser window (see Figure 2.2). ■

Part

I

Ch

2

FIGURE 2.2
The Office 2000 Resource Kit document file, displayed by Internet Explorer 5.

N O T E The Office Removal Wizard is a tool that you can use to remove previous installations of Office (but not user data associated with them). Although the Office Setup program contains a routine to remove previous versions of Office if you choose to, the Office Removal Wizard is more thorough.

If you find in test systems that Setup is leaving components that should not be left in place, or that older components are causing conflicts with newer components, you might want to run the Office Removal Wizard on all computers before you install Office 2000 on them. ■

Installing Office 2000 on a Client Workstation

If you want to prepare an OPS file for use in a custom installation, first install Office on a client workstation using the standard procedure (run Setup; then choose the options you want to install). Then, open each application and customize it as you want. You can customize more than 1,500 elements throughout Office, including

- Settings in <u>T</u>ools, <u>O</u>ptions dialog boxes
- Toolbar settings
- Custom templates stored in the Application Data folder
- Locations of shared templates
- Custom dictionaries
- File locations
- Registry keys

As you can imagine, this can take some planning. Chapters 6 through 11 of this book contain in-depth coverage of customizations you might want to consider, including techniques for customizing templates in Word, Excel, and PowerPoint.

N O T E   If you want to include only custom templates, you don't need to create an OPS file: You can add the templates directly through the Custom Installation Wizard. ■

Running the Office Profile Wizard

Now that you've painstakingly customized Office, you want to capture the customizations so you can use them on all the workstations you install. To do so, run the Office Profile Wizard, a component of the Office 2000 Resource Kit. Assuming you've installed the Resource Kit Tools on this client workstation, as discussed earlier in this chapter, follow these steps:

1. Choose **Start, <u>P</u>rograms, Microsoft Office Tools, Microsoft Office 2000 Resource Kit Tools, Profile Wizard**. The Office Profile Wizard opens (see Figure 2.3).

FIGURE 2.3
The opening window of the Office Profile Wizard.

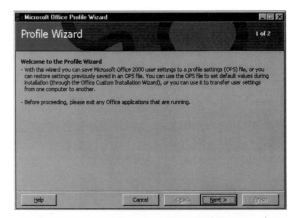

2. Click **Next**. The **Save or Restore Settings** dialog box opens (see Figure 2.4).

3. Click **Browse** to specify the location where you want to save your OPS file. You can save the file anywhere you want, but before you deploy Office, you want to place a copy of it to the root folder of the administrative installation point.

FIGURE 2.4
Saving settings in the Office Profile Wizard.

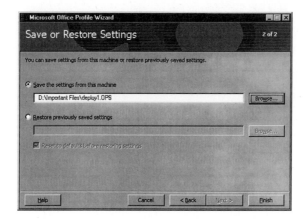

Part

I

Ch

2

4. Click **Finish**. The Office Profile Wizard compiles a binary file with all the data and files it needs. When it finishes, it displays a report, as shown in Figure 2.5.

FIGURE 2.5
The Office Profile Wizard displays a report describing what it has done.

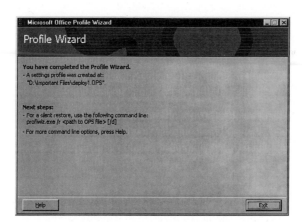

TIP Store copies of your OPS files; these can be used later to restore damaged settings, or to copy customizations from one computer to another (for example, from a desktop to a notebook, or to a new, faster computer).

Creating an Administrative Installation Point

In previous versions of Office, it was necessary to create complex scripts defining which elements of Office to install, and which feature states (behavior) Office should start with—if you could create these customizations at all. In Office 2000, you can accomplish the same goals visually—and far more simply.

First, create a new folder on your network server, on a drive that contains at least 550MB free space. Name the folder in a way that makes it recognizable as an Office 2000 installation folder; in this procedure, we've used INSTLO2K. Be sure that the folder (or the drive the folder is on) can be shared by the users who have to install Office. If necessary, create a new share, as follows:

1. Right-click the folder name in Windows Explorer.

2. Choose **Sharing** from the shortcut menu. The Sharing tab of the Properties dialog box opens (see Figure 2.6).

FIGURE 2.6

Ensuring the administrative installation location is shared on the network.

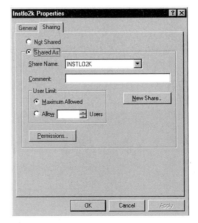

3. Click the **Shared As** button.

4. If necessary, click **Permissions**, and establish appropriate permissions in the Access Through Share Permissions. You need to provide read/write access for at least one workstation—the one you create the administrative install from. However, users who will install from your administrative installation location thereafter should have only read access.

CAUTION

Keep in mind that users need ongoing access to this folder, both to install additional features via Office 2000's Install on First Run feature, and to run Detect and Repair to fix damaged files.

Now that you've created the share, access it from a workstation, and run an administrative installation of Office, as follows:

1. At a computer running either Windows NT Workstation, Windows 2000, Windows 98, or Windows 95, connect to the server share and be sure you can read and copy files from that location.

2. Map the network share with a drive name. Right-click the network share folder, and choose **Map Network Drive** from the shortcut menu; then select a drive name in the Map Network Drive dialog box (see Figure 2.7).

FIGURE 2.7

Mapping a share so it can be accessed from a client workstation.

3. Place your Office 2000 CD-ROM (Disk 1) in the CD-ROM at the client workstation.

4. Click **Start**, **Run**, **Browse**.

5. Browse to the Setup.exe file on your CD-ROM drive. Select it, and click **Open**.

6. The Run dialog box appears, with the filename and path in it. Edit the command line, adding

```
/a data1.msi
```

For instance, if your CD-ROM drive is Drive L, the line should read

```
L:\Setup.exe /a data1.msi
```

as shown in Figure 2.8.

Data1.msi is the Office setup package file you create containing the base settings you will work from when customizing Office.

7. Click **OK**.

FIGURE 2.8

The Run dialog box, set to begin an administrative installation.

The Administrative Setup begins; if this is the first software package you install with the new Windows installer, the Windows Installer is installed before you continue. The opening Administrative Installer window appears, as shown in Figure 2.9. Follow these steps:

1. Enter the company or organization name you want to appear on all copies of Office installed from this administrative installation point.

2. Enter your 25-character CD-ROM key, if prompted to do so.

3. Click **Next**. The Microsoft license agreement appears.

4. Read the license agreement, and click **I Accept the Terms in the License Agreement**.

N O T E Of course, now is not the time to determine whether Microsoft's terms are acceptable;
you will want to review the license agreement as you evaluate Office 2000, as one key
aspect of estimating the cost of deploying Office throughout your organization. ■

5. Click **Next**.

6. In the next window (see Figure 2.10), you're asked to identify the location you've specified as your administrative installation point. Click **Browse**. The Select a Destination
Folder window appears (see Figure 2.11).

7. In the Look In drop-down box, select the drive corresponding to the network share you
created.

8. Click **OK**.

9. Click **Install Now**. Windows Installer copies Office 2000's files to the administrative
installation point. Expect this to take at least 5–10 minutes, possibly more, depending
on the speed of your workstation's CD-ROM (and possibly on network congestion).

TIP Whether you are running a large network with many users, or whether you expect to make extensive
use of the Install on First Use feature, consider creating multiple administrative installation points. As
you'll see later, in the "Identifying Additional Servers" section, you can specify as many locations as you
want, and Windows Installer searches these locations in the order you prefer to find the files it needs.

If you want more than one administrative installation point, you have two choices. You can run administrative install again, installing in a new administrative installation point either on another drive or
another server elsewhere in the company.

Or you can simply copy the top-level folder (and all subfolders) to the new administrative installation
location. If you do this, users who work from the second location will create installations that contain
the same default organization name as you established in the original administrative installation.

FIGURE 2.10
Identifying the location of your administrative installation point.

Part

I

Ch

2

FIGURE 2.11
Browsing to the location in the Select a Destination Folder dialog box.

TIP If you intend to install a second part of Office, such as Microsoft Publisher 2000, run an administrative setup for this program as well, placing the files in the same folder as for Office disk 1. Use the appropriate Setup command, including the correct MSI filename. For instance, to install Publisher from Disk 2 on a network drive mapped as Drive L, use the following command:

```
L:\setup.exe /a data2.msi
```

Replacing the Original Setup.exe

After the release of Office 2000, Microsoft released an updated version of Setup.exe, version 9.0.2720. To find out whether you have the most recent version of Setup.exe, follow these steps:

1. Right-click **Setup.exe** in the root folder of the Administrative Installation Point (or in the root folder of the CD-ROM disk you installed·from).

2. Choose **Properties** from the shortcut menu.

3. Click the **Version** tab.

4. In the Item Name box, click **Product Version**; the product version displays at right.

If the value is 9.0.2611 (or any other value lower than 9.0.2720), you should replace your Setup.exe file with Microsoft's latest version. The new version contains three significant improvements:

- It provides a new */chained* command-line option, which enables you to set up a second Windows Installer-based program, such as Microsoft Publisher 2000, at the same time you set up Office 2000 Disk 1. (You cannot, however, chain more than two installations.)

- It increases the size of the security buffer, solving a problem that early corporate users of Setup.exe encountered: When installing on Windows NT, administrators who were members of large numbers of groups sometimes were not recognized with appropriate administrative privileges.

- It supports more complex Setup settings (INI) files.

You can download Setupchn.exe at **www.microsoft.com.office/ork/2000/appndx/toolbox.htm**.

▶ For more information on downloading components of the Office Resource Kit Toolkit, **see** the section "Downloading and Installing the Office 2000 Resource Kit," earlier in this chapter on **p. 28**.

After you've downloaded SetupChn.exe, double-click it to install the file. By default, the new Setup.exe is installed at c:\Program Files\ORKTools\Download\Tools\Setup. You can use the new Setup.exe with the following programs, either in standalone installations, networked installations, or installations via Microsoft Systems Management Server such as

- Microsoft Office 2000
- Microsoft Publisher 2000
- Microsoft Office Server Extensions (see the following important caution)
- Versions of Word, Excel, PowerPoint, Access, Outlook, and Publisher sold individually
- Microsoft Office 2000 MultiLanguage Pack
- Microsoft Office 2000 English Language Pack (available as an option with some international versions of Office)

N O T E   You cannot use this version of Setup with programs that use the older Acme Setup installer, such as Microsoft PhotoDraw. ■

To substitute the new version for the existing version, copy it over each existing Setup.exe you want to replace, except for Office Setup Extensions (OSE), as discussed in the following Caution.

CAUTION

If you want to use the new Setup.exe to install OSE, you must follow a different procedure, because the setup program for these extensions is named Setupse.exe.

After downloading the new setup program, rename it Setupse.exe, and copy it over the Setupse.exe program in the OSE folder.

Do not replace the Setup.exe file that also appears in the OSE folder.

Customizing Network Setup Using the Custom Installation Wizard

By now, you've already done the following:

Part

I

Ch

2

- Installed the Office Resource Kit Toolbox on the server you intend to use for network installation, and on a client workstation you will use for creating a custom OPS file

- Optionally, installed Office 2000 on a client workstation, customized it, and ran the Office Profile Wizard to save an OPS file that contains the customizations

- Created an administrative installation point on your network server, and ensured users have appropriate access to it

- Ran an administrative install from a client workstation, placing Office 2000 files in the administrative installation point

- Optionally, ran a second administrative install to copy additional Office components into the administrative installation point, such as Microsoft Publisher 2000

- If necessary, copied Microsoft's updated Setup.exe file to the locations in the administrative installation point that will use it

You're now ready to create custom installation files using the Custom Installation Wizard.

N O T E   Set aside some time to work with the Custom Installation Wizard. The precise number of steps might vary, and many steps require careful consideration and double-checking. ■

For even more information on the custom installation wizard, including forms you can use to plan each step, download Microsoft's Enterprise Planning Workbook for Office 2000 Deployment (entpwkbk.doc) at **www.microsoft.com/office/enterprise/deployment/default.htm**.

Understanding What the Custom Installation Wizard Does

The new Windows installer relies on two files to perform an Office installation. The first is an MSI *package* file, such as data1.msi, the file that controls setup on Disk 1 of the Office 2000 CD-ROM. This file contains the standard settings used by Setup, and is never changed.

A second file, an MST *transform* file, contains all the changes you make; in other words, all the variations between the standard Setup and the customized setup you want to run. When a user runs Setup from the administrative installation point, Windows Installer works from both the MSI package file and the MST transform file. You can create many different MST transform files for different installation scenarios; they all work with the same, unchanged MSI package file.

The Custom Installation Wizard is Microsoft's new tool for creating MST transform files. As you'll see in the following sections, the Custom Installation Wizard walks you through the process, step-by-step, including

■ Setting a location on users' hard drives where Office will be installed

■ Deciding whether to remove previous versions of Office, and if so, which applications to remove

■ Setting feature installation states

■ Including an OPS file

■ Adding more custom files, Registry entries, and shortcuts

■ Setting additional properties

N O T E Some of the settings you can establish through the Custom Installation Wizard might also be established in one of two other ways:

● By running Setup from the command line with a specific switch or parameter. (Setup command line switches are covered later in this chapter, in the "Deploying Office with Your Customized MST File" section.)

● By including a custom property in the Setup settings file (Setup.ini). (The Setup settings file is covered later in this chapter, in the "Customizing a Setup.ini Settings File" section.

If Windows Installer finds conflicting information in any of these locations, it follows these priorities: Setup command line options take precedence over Setup.ini values, which take precedence over MST transform file settings. This enables you to customize an MST file but use the command line or settings file to override a customization, such as file locations, when you need to do so. ■

Running the Custom Installation Wizard

To start the Custom Installation Wizard on the server containing your administrative installation point, choose **Start, Programs, Microsoft Office Tools, Microsoft Office 2000 Resource Kit Tools, Custom Installation Wizard**. The Custom Installation Wizard opens, as shown in Figure 2.12.

The Wizard gives you many of the options common to most Microsoft wizards: navigation buttons such as Back and Next; and a Help button you can use to get information about the current window. Each screen also tells you what step you are on; this information appears at the top right. After you've made it through the first few steps, the Wizard is also able to tell you how many steps remain, based on the information you've already provided.

Choosing MSI and MST Files to Work With To begin working with the Wizard, follow these steps:

1. Click **Next**. You're now asked which MSI file to open (see Figure 2.13).

2. **Browse** to your administrative installation point and choose the MSI file you want to use. For example, if you are installing Disk 1 of Office 2000, browse to the root folder of the administrative installation point, and select data1.msi.

FIGURE 2.12
The first window of the Custom Installation Wizard.

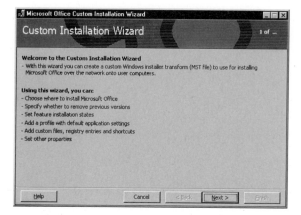

FIGURE 2.13
The Open the MSI File window of the Custom Installation Wizard.

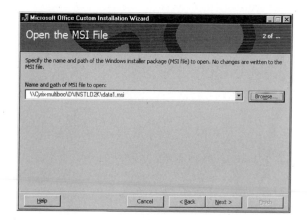

 TIP Each window of the Custom Installation Wizard has its own Help, accessible by clicking **Help** at the lower-left corner.

3. Click **Next**. You're now asked whether you want to modify an existing MST file (see Figure 2.14). If you have an MST file to modify, browse to it and select it. Otherwise, leave **Do Not Open an Existing MST File** selected, and click **Next**.

4. In the **Select the MST File to Save** window (see Figure 2.15), enter a name and path for your new MST file. The default setting is New Custom Setup File.mst, and the default file location is the root folder of your administrative installation point.

FIGURE 2.14

The Open the MST File window of the Custom Installation Wizard.

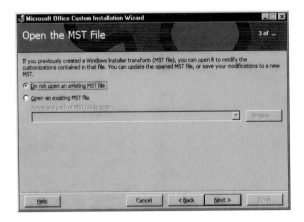

 TIP After you reach this stage, you can move to any page on the Custom Installation Wizard not only by clicking **Back** and **Next**, but also by choosing the page from the drop-down list of pages and descriptions at the top right of the Wizard screen.

FIGURE 2.15

The Select the MST File to Save window of the Custom Installation Wizard

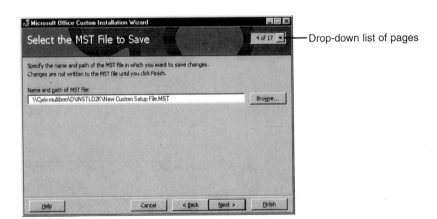

———Drop-down list of pages

 TIP If you plan to create several MST files for different scenarios, use descriptive names for each, such as Marketing.mst.

Specifying a Default Installation Path and Organization Name   To continue to the next steps in the Wizard, do the following:

1. Click **Next**. You're now asked to Specify Default Path and Organization (see Figure 2.16).

FIGURE 2.16
The Specify Default Path and Organization window of the Custom Installation Wizard.

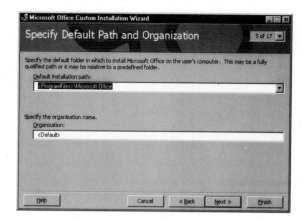

For some folders, you can specify either a fully qualified path or a *relative* path that defines a location, which is relative to a user's Windows or Office folders. You can also use bracketed keywords for several important folders, such as the <Windows> and <Favorites> system folders that apply to all users on a computer, and the <My Documents|Personal> and <StartMenu> folders that apply only to specific users, and are stored in those users' profiles.

N O T E   For more information about using this syntax to set custom folder locations, click **Help** on the Specify Default Path and Organization window. ▪

2. On the same window, you can also specify an organization name up to 52 characters in length—including spaces. When you do, your organization's name appears in the Help, About dialog box, and in the splash screen that appears as each Office application loads.

3. When you're finished specifying filenames, click **Next**.

Controlling Which Previous Versions of Office to Remove   In the screen shown in Figure 2.17, specify which previous versions of Office applications you want to remove. The Default Setup behavior prompts the user about whether to remove all previous applications or none; the user might not choose individual applications.

If you prefer, you can specify exactly which versions to remove, by checking the **Remove the Following Versions of Microsoft Office Applications** button. You can then select boxes for each program you want to remove; and clear boxes for each program you want to leave intact. If you choose which applications to remove yourself, users do not get a choice in the matter. In fact, the Remove Previous Versions window does not even appear when they run Setup.

You can also select or clear the **Obsolete Microsoft Office Files** check box, which removes old files, Registry settings, Start menu shortcuts, and INI file settings used by Office applications that already have been removed.

FIGURE 2.17
The Remove Previous Versions window of the Custom Installation Wizard.

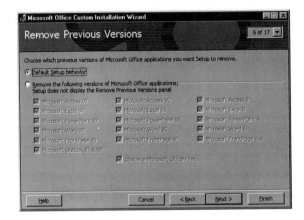

CAUTION

Note that Outlook 2000 and Outlook 97/98 cannot coexist. If you choose not to remove the previous version of Outlook, you must not install Outlook 2000. In the following window of the Custom Installation Wizard, Set Feature Installation States, mark Outlook 2000 as Not Available, so it does not install, and users are not able to install it themselves.

When you're finished making selections here, click **Next**.

Setting Feature Installation States   In the screen shown as Figure 2.18, choose which Office 2000 features and applications to include in your default installation, and whether to give users any chance to override your selections.

FIGURE 2.18
The Set Feature Installation States window of the Custom Installation Wizard.

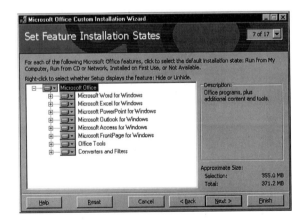

If you've installed Disk 1, you can now make selections that encompass Word, Excel, PowerPoint, Access, FrontPage, shared Office Tools, and Converters and Filters.

N O T E   This window corresponds to the Microsoft Office 2000: Select Features window in stand-alone Office 2000 installations. ■

For most features and applications, you have some or all the following options, available by clicking the drop-down box to the left of the item:

- **Run from My Computer.** Installs the application or feature locally on the user's computer. Provides the best local performance, and is essential if your network connections are not reliable or constant.

- **Run from Network.** Requires the user to run the application or feature from the administrative installation point on the network. Minimizes local storage space required; but runs more slowly, and the component becomes unavailable when the network connection is unavailable.

- **Run from CD-ROM.** Requires the user to run the feature from an original Office 2000 CD-ROM. Rarely, if ever, used in a networked business environment.

- **Installed on First Use.** Installs the application or feature locally across the network the first time the user attempts to use it. Helps you balance limited local storage against the needs of specific users, but requires a reliable network connection.

- **Not Available.** Does not install the application or feature, and prevents the user from installing it later. Note, however, that some references to the feature might remain. For instance, whether you make PowerPoint Pack and Go features unavailable, this does not eliminate PowerPoint's File, Pack and Go menu item. In many cases, however, you can use system policies to eliminate the menu item, so users won't call you to ask why the feature doesn't work, or wonder why you didn't permit them to use it.

In some cases, when you change the state of one feature, the Custom Installation Wizard changes other features to match. For example, if you choose to make Microsoft PowerPoint Content Templates unavailable, the Wizard also makes the subordinate components (called *child features)* unavailable—in this case, Typical Content Templates and Additional Content Templates.

Preventing Users from Overriding Your Feature Selections   By default, the settings you establish in this window appear as Office 2000's default settings when users run Setup from their workstations. Users can override these settings unless you take further action.

You can prevent users from overriding the settings in one of two ways:

- You can have users run Setup in *Quiet mode* (setup /qn), which automatically installs your default settings without displaying each window of the Setup wizard. Quiet mode is covered in the section "Understanding Setup Command Line Switches," later in this chapter.

- You can allow users to run Setup, and permit them to make certain customizations but not others. To do so, *hide* the feature selections you don't want users to change, as described next.

To hide an application or feature so users cannot see or change it when they run Setup:

1. Set the feature or application to the state you want (for example, **Installed on First Use**, **Run from Network**, **Not Available**).

2. Right-click the feature or application icon.

3. Choose **Hide** from the shortcut menu (see Figure 2.19). The item now appears in bold-face with a bracketed **[H]** to indicate that it is hidden from users.

FIGURE 2.19
Hiding a feature.

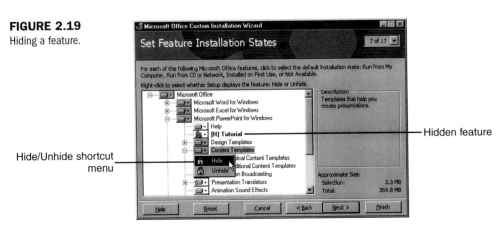

- Hide/Unhide shortcut menu
- Hidden feature

4. To unhide a feature you've hidden, right-click the icon and choose **Unhide** from the shortcut menu.

5. When you've finished setting features and hiding any that you do not want users to access, click **Next**.

N O T E   If you choose not to install a feature or application now, but later decide to install it, check **www.microsoft.com/office/ork** for the Custom Maintenance Wizard, a new tool Microsoft promises will simplify the maintenance and updating of existing Office 2000 applications. ■

Customizing Default Application Settings   In the window shown as Figure 2.20, specify which settings accompany each application.

- If you want to use Microsoft's default values—as you might if you are installing Office for the first time, and do not care much about customizing it—choose **Do not customize; use Microsoft default values**.

FIGURE 2.20

The Customize Default Application Settings window of the Custom Installation Wizard.

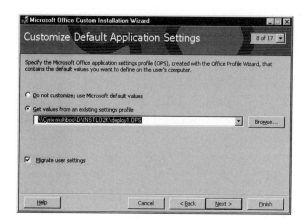

■ If you have created an OPS file with customizations you want to use, click **Browse**. Then, browse to and select the OPS file you want to use. Creating an OPS file is discussed earlier in this chapter, in the "Running the Office Profile Wizard" section.

■ If your users are upgrading and you want to migrate their existing user settings, be sure the **Migrate user settings** check box is checked.

■ If you migrate user settings, but a user's settings conflict with the OPS file you develop, Setup uses the OPS file to create initial settings, but changes these settings to reflect the user's preferences the first time each Office application is run.

When you're finishedspecifying how you want to customize application settings, click **Next**.

Adding Files to the Installation   In the window shown as Figure 2.21, specify additional files you want to be deployed with Office 2000, such as custom templates you've created. Follow these steps:

1. Click **Add**.

2. Choose one or more files to include.

3. Click **Add** again. You're then asked where you want to store these files on users' computers; be careful to choose the correct folder from the drop-down list. For example, if you've customized the template folder you want to use, be sure you choose the same folder for the custom templates you want to store in it.

> **NOTE**   If you've already added files to an OPS file you've included, you can skip this step—but if you haven't used an OPS file, this gives you another opportunity to add files. ■

4. Click **OK** when you've finished setting paths for your custom files.

5. Click **Next**. Your custom files are copied into the MST file.

FIGURE 2.21

The Add Files to the Installation window of the Custom Installation Wizard.

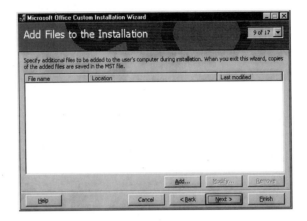

Adding Registry Entries to the Installation   In the window shown as Figure 2.22, specify additional Registry entries you want to include with your Office 2000 installation.

FIGURE 2.22

The Add Registry Entries window of the Custom Installation Wizard.

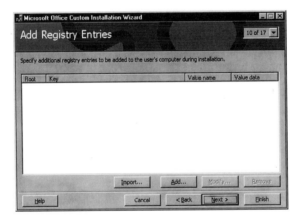

CAUTION

This is your obligatory "don't mess with the Registry if you're not careful or you don't know what you're doing, because you could foul up Office and Windows utterly beyond repair" caution!

In most scenarios, you will already have provided for the Registry entries you need by choosing features and application states, and by importing an OPS file that contains Registry entries from an existing Office 2000 installation. However, you might need a Registry entry that isn't stored by the Office Profile Wizard, such as the Office setting that establishes the system short date for Year 2000 compliance. If so, you can add it here.

This window offers two methods for incorporating a Registry entry:

- You can click **Add**, and enter the Registry entry directly in the Add/Modify Registry Entry dialog box, first choosing the correct **Root** and **Data type** keys (see Figure 2.23). However, you run the risk of entering a Registry entry incorrectly, causing Office to run improperly (or not at all).

- You can import the key(s) you need from an existing Registry file. This is usually safer.

FIGURE 2.23

Adding a Registry entry manually, through the Add/Modify Registry Entry dialog box.

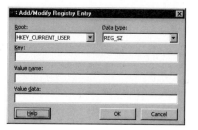

To import an existing Registry key, run Office on a client workstation, and establish the settings you want from within Office, or through system policies. (See Chapter 37, "Reducing Office 2000's Total Cost of Ownership," for a detailed discussion of system policies.) Next, export the REG Registry key you need, as follows:

1. Choose **File, Run**.

2. Enter `regedit` in the Run dialog box, and click **OK**. The Registry Editor opens.

3. Select the Registry key or selected branch of the Registry you want to export.

4. Choose **Registry, Export Registry File**. The Export Registry File dialog box opens (see Figure 2.24).

FIGURE 2.24

Exporting Registry entries through the Export Registry File dialog box of the Registry Editor (Regedit).

5. Type a filename, and click **Save**. The Registry entries you selected are saved in a file with the REG extension.

Now, return to the Custom Installation Wizard, and follow these steps:

1. Click **Import**.

2. Browse to the Registry file you want, and click **Open**. All the Registry entries now appear in the Add Registry Entries window.

3. To remove one, click **Remove**.

> **CAUTION**
>
> If you aren't sure what a custom registry entry does, remove it from the list, and rely on the defaults built into Office, or those in your OPS file—at least you're sure those work.

4. When you're finished adding or importing registry entries, click **Next**.

Adding, Modifying, or Removing Shortcuts   In the next window (see Figure 2.25), the Custom Installation Wizard shows Office's default shortcut keys and where they appear. These shortcuts cover not only the Start Menu and its submenus, but also the Office Shortcut Bar.

You can make changes here. For example, if you don't like the fact that Office places New Office Document and Open Office Document in privileged locations at the top of the Start menu, you can remove them by clicking each one and clicking **Remove**.

Conversely, if you aren't deploying the Office Shortcut Bar but you want some of its shortcuts, such as New Appointment, you can place them on the Start menu instead. Or you can add new desktop shortcuts. For example, you can place Word, Excel, and PowerPoint shortcuts on users' desktops, making the programs easier to find for users who aren't comfortable working from the Start menu.

FIGURE 2.25

The Add, Modify, or Remove Shortcuts window of the Custom Installation Wizard.

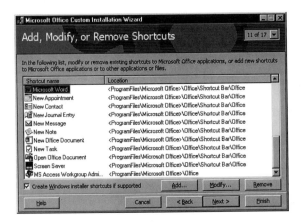

To modify a shortcut, select it and click **Modify**. Or, to add a new shortcut, click **Add**. The Add/Modify Shortcut Entry dialog box appears (see Figure 2.26). Next, follow these steps:

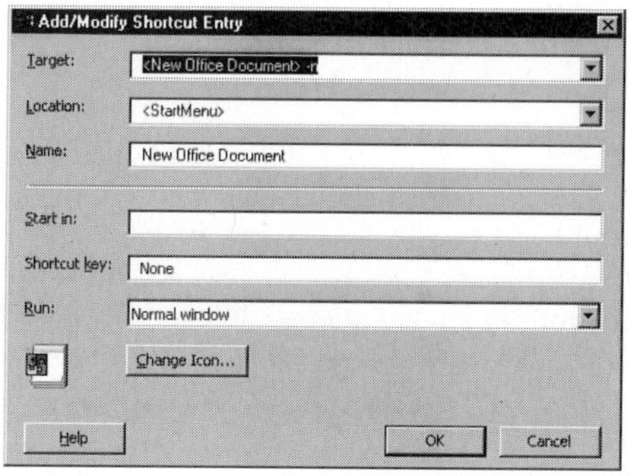

FIGURE 2.26
The Add/Modify
Shortcut Entry window
of the Custom
Installation Wizard.

1. If you clicked **Add**, select the shortcut you want to create from the Target drop-down box. If you clicked **Modify**, the correct shortcut is already created. You can now customize several aspects of how this shortcut looks and acts.

2. To customize where the shortcut is placed, click the **Location** drop-down box, and choose a new location. For example, if you want the shortcut on the desktop, click **Desktop**.

3. To change the name of the shortcut, edit it in the **Name** text box. (Editing the name doesn't change the shortcut's behavior.)

4. To change the path the application should start in, enter a new path in the **Start in** text box.

5. To establish a Windows keyboard shortcut, enter it in the **Shortcut key** text box. You must use Microsoft's virtual key codes, as listed in Table 2.2:

Table 2.2   Virtual Key Codes for Creating Windows Shortcuts

These Virtual Key Codes	Correspond to These Keyboard Keys
VK_0 through VK_9	0 through 9
VK_A through VK_Z	A through Z
VK_F1 through VK_F12	F1 through F12 function keys

Combine these virtual key codes with the modifiers SHIFT, CTRL and/or ALT to increase the number of valid keyboard combinations. For example, CTRL+SHIFT+VK_F1 tells Windows installer to establish the keyboard combination Ctrl+Shift+F1. A shortcut might have only one keyboard combination associated with it.

6. By default, applications run in a normal window, but if you want them to run minimized or maximized, choose the option you want from the Run drop-down box.

7. If you want to change the icon associated with a shortcut, click **Change Icon** and choose a new icon from the library in the Change Icon dialog box.

8. Choose **OK** twice.

9. Click **Next**.

TIP If the Custom Installation Wizard warns you that some icons are missing, you can disregard the warning if you are working with an MSI file on your local hard drive, or in the root folder of the networked administration installation point.

Identifying Additional Servers Office 2000 relies heavily on the network for installation, application updates, and automated maintenance. Therefore, it is essential that a networked source of Office files remain available to users at all times. One way to ensure this is to provide multiple administrative installation points. After you've done so, when Windows Installer needs to access a server, it can keep looking until it finds one that is up and running.

In Figure 2.27, you can identify additional administrative installation points. After you've done so, you can use the Move Up and Move Down buttons to specify the order in which Windows Installer should search these servers.

FIGURE 2.27
The Identify Additional Servers window of the Custom Installation Wizard.

To add an administrative installation point, follow these steps:

1. Click **Add**. The Add Network Server Entry dialog box opens.
2. Either enter a path to the additional administrative installation point, or click **Browse** to browse the network for it.
3. Click **OK**.
4. To add yet another location, click **Add** again, and repeat the process.
5. When you're finished adding administrative installation points, click **Next**.

Adding Additional Installations That Run After Setup If you want to automatically run additional installations after Office setup is finished—such as third-party programs that customize Office with additional templates, tools, or features—you can do so in the Add Installations and Run Programs window (see Figure 2.28).

FIGURE 2.28

The Add Installations and Run Programs window of the Custom Installation Wizard.

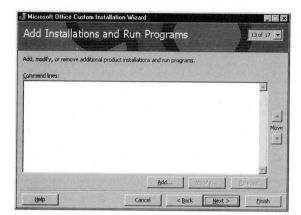

Unfortunately, there's a big catch: You can automate installation of only one additional Office component that relies on the new Windows Installer. (This includes Microsoft Publisher and many of the programs Microsoft will release in the future.) To install even *one* of those programs, you must use the special version of Setup.exe covered in the section "Replace the Original Setup.exe," earlier in this chapter.

That restriction aside, you can insert command lines that install a wide variety of third-party software; run batch files; perform system cleanup—almost anything you can imagine.

To add a command, follow these steps:

1. Click **Add**.
2. Enter the command line manually in the Add/Modify Program Entry window, or click **Browse** to select a program executable you want to run.
3. Click **OK**.

To add a second command, repeat the process.

TIP

If you have the new Setup.exe and you want to chain a second Windows Installer installation to the one you're customizing, follow these steps:

1. Click **Add**.
2. **Browse** to the Setup.exe file associated with the second installation, and click **OK**.
3. In the Command line text box, after setup.exe, enter the command-line option:

   ```
   /chained
   ```

Again, this works only if you are using the updated version of Setup.

If you insert several commands, you can use the Move Up and Move Down buttons to specify the order in which they run. A command is not executed until the previous command is completed; however, Setup does not check to ensure the command completed successfully!

CAUTION

Be sure to test Add Installations and Run Programs carefully before you deploy it. Many installations require reboots and make other system changes that can interrelate in unexpected ways.

TIP

If your systems vary, you might want to use relative paths in the command lines you create. See the Help page for an explanation of how to do so.

When you're finished adding installations and programs to run at the end of Setup, click **Next**.

Customizing Outlook Installation Options   By default, the first time a user runs Outlook, he or she is prompted to enter profile and account information. However, you can specify this information in advance through the Customize Outlook Installation Options window (see Figure 2.29).

FIGURE 2.29
The Customize Outlook Installation Options window of the Custom Installation Wizard.

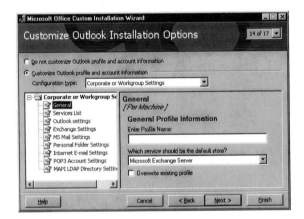

▶ For more information about customizing Outlook options, **see** "Customizing Outlook to Your Organization's Needs," Chapter 10, on **p. 265**.

First, choose which Configuration type you want to use:

- Corporate or Workgroup Settings
- Internet Only

Depending on your choice, the appropriate list of options appears in the folder below. You can then customize each option.

For example, if you choose Corporate or Workgroup Settings, you can define whether to rely on Microsoft Exchange Server or Personal Folders as the user's default information store. If you choose Internet Only Settings, you can specify whether to create POP3 email or LDAP directory accounts, or both.

When you've finished setting Outlook options, click **Next**.

Customizing Internet Explorer 5 Installation Options   In the window shown in Figure 2.30, you can customize how you want to handle (or not handle) Internet Explorer 5 installation.

Certain Office 2000 features, such as NetMeeting and Web Discussions, assume the presence of Internet Explorer. Some features require the latest version of Internet Explorer to work; others, such as NetMeeting, settle for Internet Explorer 4.0 or even Internet Explorer 3.0. However, some organizations do not want to run any version of Internet Explorer: They might have established Netscape Navigator as their default browser. Whatever decisions your company has made, you can implement them here.

FIGURE 2.30
The Customize IE 5 Installation Options window of the Custom Installation Wizard.

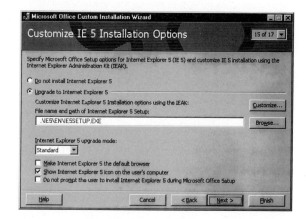

By default, the Custom Installation Wizard is set to run the standard Internet Explorer 5 upgrade, if Internet Explorer 5 isn't already installed. It displays the Internet Explorer 5 icon, but does not change an existing default browser. You can change each of these behaviors.

- To not install Internet Explorer 5, click **Do not install Internet Explorer 5.**

- To install Internet Explorer 5 from a different source (as you might if you have downloaded a more recent version of Internet Explorer 5 than the one provided with Office 2000), enter the new path (or click **Browse** to find the newer version's setup file, which is always named IE5Setup.exe).

- To install only a minimum version of Internet Explorer 5 (browser only, no Outlook Express, Microsoft Media Player, or other add-ons), choose **Minimum** from the Internet Explorer 5 Upgrade Mode drop-down box.

- To make Internet Explorer 5 a user's default browser, check the **Make Internet Explorer 5 the default browser** check box.

- To not display the Internet Explorer 5 icon on the desktop after installation, clear the **Show Internet Explorer 5 icon on the user's computer** check box.

- To hide the setup dialog box that would enable users to override your choices about Internet Explorer 5, check the **Do not prompt the user to install Internet Explorer 5 during Microsoft Office Setup** check box.

You can also customize Internet Explorer 5 more thoroughly, by clicking **Customize**. This runs the Internet Explorer Administration Kit (see Figure 2.31), where you can customize Internet Explorer 5 to include

- Links and Favorites lists that are relevant to your organization
- Predefined Internet connection settings that meet your specific needs
- Faster setup with less user involvement
- Security, content, and other restrictions that users cannot override

▶ For more information about deploying Internet Explorer 5, **see** "Deploying Internet Explorer 5 with the Internet Explorer Administration Kit," Chapter 36, on **p. 929**.

FIGURE 2.31
The opening window of the Internet Explorer Administration Kit.

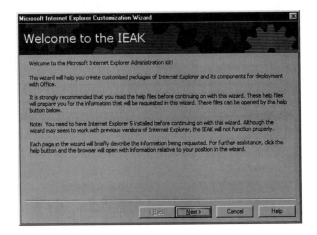

N O T E Before running the Internet Explorer Administration Kit, read its online help thoroughly.

When you're finished customizing Internet Explorer 5 installation options, click **Next**.

Modifying Setup Properties In the Modify Setup Properties screen (see Figure 2.32), you can modify several aspects of Setup's behavior. For instance, you can change the text Setup uses to describe the installation to users.

CAUTION

Before making changes to any of these items, click **Help** and read the detailed description of these elements and the syntax they require. You will find that it's easy to make a mistake that causes Setup to look or run incorrectly.

When you've finished making changes to Setup, click **Next**.

FIGURE 2.32

The Modify Setup Properties window of the Custom Installation Wizard.

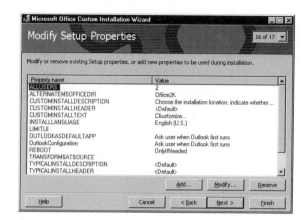

Part

I

Ch

2

Saving Your Completed MST File You've now—finally—reached the end of the Custom Installation Wizard (see Figure 2.33). You can now click **Back** or choose pages from the drop-down list at the top right to check your work. After you're satisfied, return to the Save Changes page, and click **Finish**. The Custom Installation Wizard builds your MST file.

FIGURE 2.33

The Save Changes window of the Custom Installation Wizard.

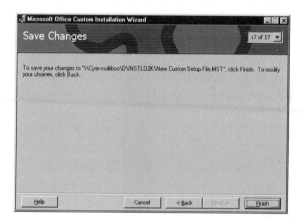

After your MST file is created, the Custom Installation Wizard displays a dialog box explaining what has been done. The dialog box includes the setup command line that can be used to run a setup based on this MST file (see Figure 2.34). This command includes the /qn+ switch for running Setup in quiet mode with no user involvement.

You can select and copy this command line for inclusion in batch files, messages to users, or links that can be embedded in email messages to run Setup automatically when they are clicked on. If you're not ready to proceed with Office installation on client workstations, copy the command line to a file, so you have a record of it to use when you are ready.

FIGURE 2.34

The Custom Installation Wizard concludes by providing the Setup.exe command that runs Setup with this MST file, in quiet mode.

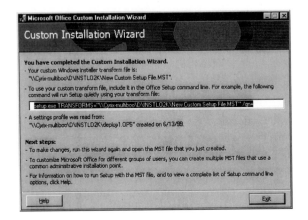

 TIP If you realize later that you need to change some settings, run the Custom Installation Wizard again, and choose this MST file in window #3 (Open the MST File).

N O T E If you've incorporated an OPS file or extensive templates and other files, it might take several minutes to create your MST file, which might be several megabytes in size.

Deploying Office with Your Customized MST File

Now that you have created your customized MST file, how do you actually use it in deploying Office? You have three choices. The simplest is to copy the command line created in the last step of the Custom Installation Wizard, and provide it to users, along with detailed instructions such as the following:

1. Choose **Start**, **Run**.
2. Paste the command line the Custom Installation Wizard provided into the Run dialog box. If necessary, edit the command line to reflect any changes you need, such as a different file location or different setup switches.
3. Click **OK**, and Office sets itself up. This might take 15–20 minutes, depending on the speed of your computer.

If you do not want your users messing with command-line syntax—even simply to copy it from one location to another—you can include this command line in a batch file that runs when they log onto your network.

If you choose to have users run setup via a command line, you might want to customize the command line you use. For instance, the default command line uses the switch /qn+, which specifies an absolutely silent installation that gives the user no choices, but displays a message when it completes (unless a reboot is required to complete installation).

However, what if you do want to give users some options? Table 2.3 lists the most commonly used options available from the Setup command line. A more detailed list is available in the

Excel file Setupref.xls, which is installed along with the Office Resource Kit Documents (Start, Programs, Microsoft Office Tools, Microsoft Office 2000 Resource Kit Documents, Office Information folder).

Table 2.3   Most Commonly Used Setup Switches

Setup Parameter	Does This
/a msifile	Creates a new administrative installation point using the MSI file you specify (the package file that contains Office's default settings). The MSI file and Setup.exe must be in the same folder.
/foption msifile	Repairs a damaged MSI file, using the MSI file you specify. The MSI file must be the one you originally installed with, and it must be in the same folder as Setup.exe.

Several options are available:

/fp Reinstalls only missing files

/fo Reinstalls only missing or outdated files

/fe Reinstalls missing files or files where an older version or version with the same date is present

/fd Reinstalls missing files, or any files present in different versions

/fc Reinstalls missing or corrupt files

/fa Reinstalls all files regardless of whether they are missing or corrupt

/fu Rewrites all essential user Registry entries

/fm Rewrites all essential local machine Registry entries

/fs Reinstalls shortcuts, overwriting any that already exist

/fv Runs setup from the source package, recaching the local package |
| /i msifile | Chooses an MSI file to install with. The MSI file and Setup.exe must be in the same folder. |
| /qoption | Specifies which Setup interface users will see

/n None (Silent/quiet installation)

/b Basic (only progress indicators and error messages)

/r Reduced (collects no user information, but provides full progress indicators and all error messages)

/f Full (displays the full setup user interface, subject to any choices you made in your MST transform file, which contains all your customizations)

Adding a + symbol to any of these options tells Setup to display a completion message, but only if no reboot is needed after installation |

Part

I

Ch

2

continues

Table 2.3   Continued

Setup Parameter	Does This
/x msifile	Uninstalls Office, using the MSI file you specify. The MSI file must be the one you originally installed with, and it must be in the same folder as Setup.exe.
property=value	Specifies a property you want to customize, and a value you want to use. For example, "TRANSFORMS=New Custom Setup File.MST" specifies that you want to use the New Custom Setup File.MST transform file. (If your value contains spaces, as in this example, surround the entire property switch with quotation marks.)

Customizing a Setup.ini Settings File

Perhaps the best solution for customizing Setup's behavior is to customize the Setup.ini file that appears in the same folder as Setup.exe. This file is self-documenting, and a detailed list of commands appears in the Setupref.xls file that installs with the Office 2000 Resource Kit (Start, Programs, Microsoft Office Tools, Microsoft Office 2000 Resource Kit Documents, Office Information folder).

When Setup is run from an administrative installation point, it automatically looks for Setup.ini in the same folder, and uses any Setup instructions it finds there. A typical Setup.ini file contains the sections shown in Table 2.4.

Table 2.4   Most Commonly Used Setup Switches

Setup.ini Section	Does This
[MSI]	Specifies an MSI file to use. The MSI file must be in the same folder as setup.exe.
[MST]	Specifies an MST (transform) file to use, with path information; for instance: MST1=d:\InstlO2K\marketing.mst
[Options]	Specifies properties; for instance: USERNAME=Robert Smith
[Display]	Specifies user interface level (same as /q command line switches). Options include Display=None (silent/quiet installation) Display=Basic (only progress indicators and error messages) Display=Reduced (collects no user information, but provides full progress indicators and all error messages)

Setup.ini Section	Does This
	Display=Full (displays the full setup user interface, subject to any customizations in your MST file)
	Adding a separate line with the statement
	CompletionNotice=Yes
	Tells Setup to display a completion message, but only if no reboot is needed after installation
[Logging]	Specifies what, if anything, to include in a log file that is created as setup proceeds

Part

I

Ch

2

CHAPTER 3

Using Systems Management Server 2.0 to Install Office 2000

by Deb Shinder

Systems Management Server 2.0 (SMS) is an enterprise management software package that you can use to speed the delivery of Office 2000 to all the desktops in your organization. SMS enables the administrator to investigate all facets of his network, including the ability to conduct hardware inventory, software inventory, network bandwidth analysis, software metering, Year 2000 compliance assessments, and system status updates.

This chapter will focus on the software distribution features of SMS 2.0 that help streamline the process of distributing Office 2000 to all the machines in your network.

 N O T E This chapter does not cover installation of the SMS software itself. Check the SMS 2.0 product documentation for details regarding the setup and deployment of SMS 2.0 in your organization.

SMS 2.0 takes advantage of a new technology available for the first time in Office 2000: the Windows Installer. The Windows Installer was introduced with Office 2000 and allows for an automated deployment of the software. Windows Installer technology also makes use of many of the new administrative features available with Office 2000, including these two:

- Self-Repairing Programs
- Install on Demand

Combined, the features of the new Windows Installer service and the power of SMS 2.0 allow the Office administrator a great deal of flexibility in how Office 2000 is distributed and enhance his or her ability to customize Office 2000 distributions.

This chapter covers these important topics:

- Office 2000 installation requirements
- SMS 2.0 software distribution process
- Special considerations for the Office 2000 administrator when using SMS 2.0 for automated distribution and installation
- Planning issues that need to be considered prior to rolling out Office 2000
- Implementing an Office 2000 distribution using SMS 2.0

If you are not acquainted with SMS 2.0, you should work closely with a trained SMS administrator. Together, the Office 2000 administrator and the SMS administrator can develop a well-thought-out deployment schedule.

Preparing to Deploy Office 2000 Using SMS

The first step in deploying Office 2000 is ensuring that the hardware meets minimum requirements.

Reviewing Office 2000 Installation Requirements

Hardware requirements vary with the type of installation required. Office 2000 offers a great deal of flexibility in product installation. You can install a single application from the suite, all the applications, or even a few selected applications with the option of installing others at a later time. Table 3.1 provides information on the installation requirements for various modes of Office 2000 installations.

Table 3.1 Office 2000 Hardware Requirements

Operating System	Office 2000 Features Installed	RAM Requirements	Hard Disk Space Requirement
Windows 95/98	Word, Excel, and PowerPoint	16MB RAM, and 4MB RAM for each application that will be running simultaneously	252MB to run the entire suite (Word, PowerPoint, Excel, Access, and FrontPage)
	Outlook	8MB required on top of the base 16MB of RAM	
	Access	8MB	
	FrontPage	8MB	
	PhotoDraw	16MB	100MB in addition to the 252MB for the basic suite
	Publisher and Small Business Tools		174MB in addition to the 252MB for the basic suite
	Temp file storage		100MB (on system partition)*
Windows NT 4.0 (Requires Service Pack 3 or greater)	Word, Excel, and PowerPoint	32MB plus 4MB for each application running	252MB for the basic Office 2000 suite
	Outlook	8MB	
	Access	8MB	
	FrontPage	8MB	
	PhotoDraw	16MB	100MB hard disk space
	Publisher and Small Business Tools		174MB hard disk space

Operating System	Office 2000 Features Installed	RAM Requirements	Hard Disk Space Requirement
	Temp file storage space		100MB (on boot partition)*

The boot partition on Windows NT system is defined as the partition that contains the operating system files. The system partition on a Windows 9x machine is defined as the partition containing the operating system files.

Setting Up an Administrative Installation Point

After you review the hardware requirements and make any necessary upgrades, the next step in using SMS 2.0 is to set up an *"Administrative Installation Point."* This is a shared folder on an SMS 2.0 computer that contains the Office 2000 installation files. Depending on the type of distribution you are planning, you will need varying amounts of disk space available on the server that houses the Administrative Installation Point. Table 3.2 describes the hard disk space requirements for the different Office 2000 distribution types.

Part
I
Ch
3

Table 3.2   Hard Disk Space Requirements for Administrative Installation Point

Office 2000 Version	PDF (Package Definition File) in Office 2000 Resource Kit	Hard Disk Space Required for Administrative Installation Point*
Office Premium	Off9pre.sms	554MB
Office Professional	Off9pro.sms	530MB
Office Small Business Edition	Off9sbe.sms	407MB
Office Standard	Off9std.sms	484MB
Office Disk 2	Pff9cd2.sms	555MB
Publisher	Pub2000.sms	

Disk space requirements vary depending on the size of the partition. Larger partitions have larger cluster sizes, which increase the required amount of disk space.

A Package Definition file drives the installation process. The Office 2000 Resource Kit CD-ROM also contains PDF files for the entire Office 2000 suite, as well as for the standalone versions of each of the members of the Office 2000 suite. However, you can't mix the standalone version PDF files with those used for the entire Office 2000 suite installation.

N O T E   Don't confuse the PDF file used here with the PDF (Portable Document Format) files used for Adobe Acrobat documents. ■

If you want to customize your installation to include only parts of the Office suite, you should create "Transform" files, which are saved with the file extension .mst. These MST files contain information that the Windows Installer uses to customize an Office 2000 installation.

You can create your own MST file from scratch or use the Custom Installation Wizard (CIW), which is included in the Office Resource Kit. The CIW is easier and less error-prone than the "handmade" approach and is the recommended method for creating custom installations.

To obtain the Office 2000 Resource Kit tools, you can purchase the Office 2000 Resource Kit, which includes valuable documentation as well as the tools, or you can download the tools from the following Web site:

`www.microsoft.com/office/ork/2000/appndx/toolbox.htm#09wis`

Using SMS to Distribute Software

Before we get into the details of how to use SMS 2.0 to deploy Office 2000, we need to learn some new vocabulary and a bit about how SMS 2.0 carries out the software distribution process.

Using Packages, Installation Programs, and Program Advertising

Key concepts in a software rollout using SMS 2.0 include package creation, installation programs, and the advertising of programs to client computers, as well as the concept of "administrative context."

Creating Packages   A *package* is the core collection of information that SMS 2.0 uses to coordinate the distribution of software. A package contains information about the location of installation source files and how to install the source files after they are located. All software installations begin with the creation of a package for the application to be installed.

A "Package Definition File," or PDF, defines the package. Previous versions of SMS used Package Definition Files that ended with the .pdf file extension. SMS 2.0 Package Definition Files end with the .sms file extension.

The application's distribution points are defined in the package. These distribution points are shared folders on servers that participate in an SMS 2.0 Site hierarchy. By including several servers as distribution points, the administrator can more precisely control the effects of application distribution on network bandwidth and can optimize access by client machines during the installation process.

You can create your own packages by using the SMS 2.0 console, but the Office 2000 Resource Kit contains many Package Definition Files that will meet the needs of most administrators. Microsoft recommends that you use these files because they have been tested in a variety of situations and are well proven. There is an import utility that enables you to import new Package Distribution Files.

The new Create Package from Definition Wizard, shown in Figure 3.1, simplifies the package creation process. We will use this wizard later to create a new package from one of the Package Definition Files included in the Office 2000 Resource Kit.

FIGURE 3.1
The Create Package
from Definition Wizard.

Packages include complete instructions on how to install the software on a target machine. After it's defined and created in SMS, a package can be modified at a later time. The source installation files can also be included in the package. A key component of a package is the "program" it contains.

Creating a Program   In SMS 2.0, a *program* typically refers to the setup.exe command, which is used to launch the installation of the application(s). One package can contain multiple programs. Each program can contain different command-line switches that are used to customize installation. Different programs can be used to call alternate MST files, which are used to create complex customized installations.

Advertising the Package   After the package is created and sent to distribution servers, it must be *advertised*. An advertisement distributes a program, contained within a package, to the computers that should receive the package.

The advertisement is aimed at a target audience, such as computers in the Sales department. Or, the package can be advertised to a group of users based on Windows NT security groups. Advertising *Agent* software on the client computers check for advertisements to see whether any new software needs to be installed.

Information contained in the advertisement determines when the program will be installed. For example, the client machines might receive an advertisement that says the program can be installed whenever the user wants, or the administrator might configure the software to mandate an installation at a specific time without the user's intervention.

Understanding When and Why to Use the SMS Administrative Context   Installing Office 2000 with SMS on Windows 95/98 machines is simple because of the weak security model in those operating systems. A user does not have to have any special permission to install programs or alter the configuration of the operating system. However, using SMS with Windows NT machines is more complex.

Understanding Windows NT Security Issues   Windows NT client computers pose a special problem. Security is an integral component of Windows NT operating systems. The "user rights" conferred to a typical user limit what that user can do to the operating system.

Office 2000 installation requires that the logged-on user have administrative privileges. If the user does not have administrative privileges, the installation will fail.

Circumventing Windows NT Security Problems by Using Administrative Context   You can get around this problem by using the SMS 2.0 *Administrative Context*. You can create a temporary account that has administrative privileges on the user's machine to allow for successful installation.

Because Office 2000 uses the Windows Installer, the installation can "survive" a reboot, which is sometimes required to complete the installation. The Windows Installer allows the installation to continue with administrative rights. The temporary account is deleted from the machine when the installation is complete.

N O T E   This doesn't work for non-Windows Installer programs. Internet Explorer 5.0 is a non-Windows Installer application. We will look later at how to work around this problem of Internet Explorer 5.0 not being able to "survive" the reboot. ■

Using Administrative Context in an Unattended Installation   Office 2000 can be installed with or without user intervention. An *attended* installation is done when the user can interact with the installation program. An *unattended* installation is done when user input is not desired.

The Administrative Context must be used with unattended installations when Windows NT is the operating system. If you schedule an Office 2000 rollout after-hours, when the user has logged out, there is *no* user context. The Administrative Context enables you to continue the installation on an NT system without a logged-on user.

Understanding How the Software Is Distributed

The following steps are involved in the software distribution:

1. SMS 2.0 copies the application files to the assigned distribution points. Clients then access the installation files from those installation points.

2. The advertisement is copied to computers called *client access points*. The actual SMS 2.0 Site server computer is much too important to handle jobs such as advertising. The SMS 2.0 Site server hands off this duty to other computers. These "ad men," or *Client Access Points* (CAPs), are the points of contact for the client computers. Each client computer contacts the CAPs to determine whether any applications advertised for that computer.

3. The client machines have an "agent" working for them; it is known as the *Advertised Programs Client Agent*. It is this agent that actually goes out looking for jobs (applications to install). The Advertised Programs Client Agent resides on the client computers and can be configured to check for advertisements on a scheduled basis, as shown in Figure 3.2.

FIGURE 3.2

Configuring the time period for the Agent to check for new programs.

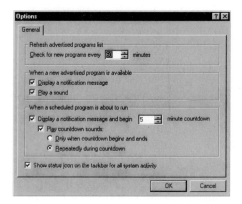

4. Advertised programs can be either mandatory or optional. Mandatory Programs must be run, and the user cannot intervene in the process. Optional programs can be run at the user's leisure. The user can access advertised programs via the Advertised Programs Control Panel applet.

5. The CAP tells the client computer where to find the installation files and installation instructions (the package). Information about what program to run in the package is also distributed to the client. Different clients might run different command lines, depending on the user or group machine is associated with. The client will be presented with a list of Distribution Servers and will select from that list to access the package.

Reviewing Special Considerations for Distributing Office 2000

Each application distributed with SMS will have its own specific issues that need to be researched before deployment. The most significant issues affecting Office 2000 include the Microsoft Transform file, "Install on Demand," and the concept of resilient resources.

Using the MST Files

Transform files are used to customize an Office 2000 installation. You might not want to install the entire suite of applications. If not, use a Transform file that is saved with the .mst file extension.

MST files act as modifiers for the instructions that are contained in a Microsoft Installation file (MSI). They contain all the instructions required by the Windows Installer to install the specified application. The MSI file included with Office 2000 is named data1.msi.

The Transform file enables you to customize the following aspects of installation:

- Which Office 2000 applications and features are installed
- What shortcuts will be installed and where they are placed
- Removal of any previous versions of Office applications

■ Running the application from the user's computer

■ Running the application from the server

■ Installing the application on demand

An MST file is a text file, which can be created or edited by hand using any text editor.

> **CAUTION**
>
> Microsoft recommends that you do not edit the file manually because of the potential for errors.

Microsoft provides a tool that enables the Office 2000 administrator to create a custom installation via a Transform file, using the Custom Installation Wizard. Figure 3.3 shows the CIW option for removing previous versions of Office.

FIGURE 3.3
The Custom Installation Wizard lets you remove previous versions of Office.

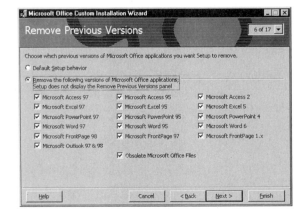

Figure 3.4 shows the Set Feature Installation States dialog box, from which the administrator configures which applications to install and whether they should be run from the server, installed on the client machine, or installed on demand. You can also choose to not install a selected application.

FIGURE 3.4
Selecting installation states with the Custom Installation Wizard.

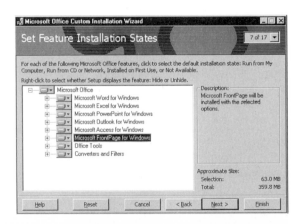

When you're choosing whether to install Internet Explorer 5, keep in mind that most of the collaborative features included in Office 2000 depend on Internet Explorer 5 being installed. Figure 3.5 shows the Customize IE 5 Installation Options dialog box, which lets you specify whether to make Internet Explorer 5.0 the default browser.

FIGURE 3.5
Customizing the Internet Explorer 5.0 installation options.

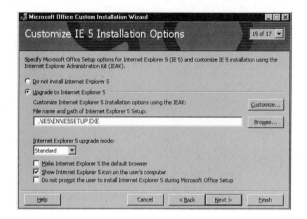

After you create the MST, it is included in the command-line arguments for a "program" that is contained in the SMS 2.0 package. For example, if you made a transform and saved it as marketing.mst, the program command-line argument would be as follows:

```
Setup.exe transforms=marketing.mst
```

This would start the installation process, and the customizations in the marketing.mst file would be applied during the setup.

TIP More details on how to create transforms and command-line arguments are included in the Office 2000 Resource Kit.

Using the Install on Demand Feature

With Windows Installer, you can install just shortcuts to an application instead of the entire application. When the user clicks on the shortcut, the installation process begins.

The *Install on Demand* feature enables you to randomly distribute bandwidth demand over time. This asynchronous approach to software distribution is less likely to lead to network bottlenecks than a single "push" distribution is. This is because all users are unlikely to use the same programs at once. When the installation process is randomized over time, you minimize the potential for traffic bottlenecks on the network.

Install on Demand is dependent on the availability of the installation source files. To ensure availability, the program can contain a command-line argument that includes the SOURCELIST parameter. This enables you to include a number of distribution servers that a client can choose from when Install on Demand is initiated.

Part
I

Ch
3

Planning an Office 2000 Distribution

You should develop a plan prior to actual deployment. Office 2000 is a hardware-intensive application, and you must know beforehand whether your machines can handle the applications. The Office 2000 administrator needs to work closely with the network administrator during the software distribution process to address the following bandwidth issues:

- You should decide whether Internet Explorer will be installed on all machines, even those not used for Web browsing. Many of Office 2000's Intranet collaborative functions depend on the installation of Internet Explorer 5.

- Decide whether you want users to participate in the installation process. This can make your life easier or more difficult, depending on the reliability and expertise of the users.

- If your network includes Windows NT client machines, consider whether the users have administrative rights. If not, you must take special action to customize the software distribution process.

Using the SMS Inventory Component

Before you can install Office 2000, the machines must meet minimum hard disk space, processor, and RAM requirements. You also must know what operating system each computer is running. You can use SMS 2.0 to collect hardware information about client systems on your network. Then, you can create an Office 2000 Readiness Report detailing which computers are and which are not ready for the upgrade to Office 2000.

To collect this information, install the Hardware Inventory Client Agent on the target computers. Then, you can schedule the data collection process, as shown in Figure 3.6. Similar data collection mechanisms are available for running a software inventory.

FIGURE 3.6
Configuring the
Hardware Inventory
Client Agent's schedule.

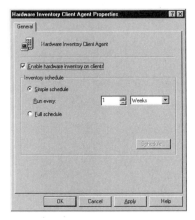

After the hardware data is collected, you can construct queries to identify machines that are not Office 2000-ready or create reports using the SMS Crystal Info reporting tool.

Contact Microsoft for preconstructed queries and reports for Office 2000 readiness.

Addressing Network Bandwidth Issues

You need an assessment of the network's capabilities and limitations prior to the Office 2000 deployment. You want to answer the following questions before beginning the software distribution:

1. When are the periods of highest network usage?
2. When is the network least used?
3. Where are the bottlenecks in the network design?
4. What are the maximum and minimum network transfer rates, and where are these found?

You will use this information to plan the locations of the distribution servers and the timing of a rollout. The type of Office 2000 installation you perform depends on your network's capabilities. SMS 2.0 includes a network discovery tool and a network analyzer to assist you in assessing the network's capabilities.

Upgrading Microsoft Internet Explorer

Microsoft recommends that all users upgrade to Internet Explorer 5.0 to take full advantage of all Office 2000 collaborative features. The SMS 2.0 software inventory tool can help you assess which machines will require the Internet Explorer 5.0 upgrade. After collecting the inventory information, you can create a report on what browsers the machines are currently running.

 TIP For those machines that will require the Internet Explorer 5.0 upgrade, you need to know whether any are running Windows NT and whether the users on those Windows NT machines have administrative privileges. If not, you must use the special procedures described next to install Internet Explorer 5.0.

Selecting the Type of Installation

The package file included in the Office 2000 Resource Kit includes programs for four types of installations:

- Typical
- Custom
- Manual
- Uninstall

Each includes a program in the package file. You can edit and customize these programs or add programs of your own.

The *Typical* program is used for unattended installations without an MST file. The user is presented with dialog boxes and a progress bar to inform him that an installation is taking place.

The *Custom* program is used for unattended installations that include an MST file. The user gets status dialog boxes and a progress indicator in this instance as well.

The *Manual* program enables full user intervention during the setup process.

The *Uninstall* program enables you to automatically uninstall Office 2000.

Addressing Office Upgrade Issues

The software inventory tells you which computers are running previous versions of Microsoft Office software. If you want to allow the users to keep previous versions of Office software, Office 2000 and Office 97 can both run on the same computer. Allowing the use of both suites for a period lets users compare and contrast the capabilities of the two versions.

Determining Who Gets What Applications

Plan the components of the Office suite you will distribute based on group, computer, or segment memberships. User requirements are typically based on job function. For example, members of the marketing group might need only Word, Excel, and PowerPoint. Members of the Accounting group might require Excel and Access.

Plan the user scenarios, and then create Transform files based on the different installation scenarios.

If you have a group of sophisticated users, you can plan an attended installation for them. The users in this group will be able to choose which components they prefer to install.

Using Scripts with Windows NT Client Machines

Remember that Office 2000 must be installed on Windows NT machines by an account that has administrative rights. This is because Office 2000 must have access to components of the operating system that typical users do not have access to. Using a special script included in the Office 2000 Resource Kit can solve this problem.

Applications that do not use the Windows Installer service and that require a reboot will fail to complete installation during the post-reboot phase. This can pose a challenge if you want to install Internet Explorer 5.0 during the Office 2000 distribution.

To retain administrative privileges after the reboot, you will need to use the O2ksetup.ipf script and then compile that script to create a program that will be included in the SMS 2.0 Package Definition File. This script will allow the installation of Internet Explorer 5.0 to complete after the required reboot, by allowing the installation process to continue with administrative rights.

CAUTION

The mouse and keyboard will not be functional after the reboot, so they are to be used only for completely unattended installations. Let users know that for a period of time they might not be able to use the keyboard or mouse but that the situation is only temporary. Users who do not understand the process might turn the computer off and then on again.

N O T E A certain rollback procedure allows the installation to continue if the user cycles the computer's power. However, at particular points during the installation, this can corrupt the installation and potentially require administrative support. Reinstalling the operating system might be the only solution in some cases. ■

Implementing the Office 2000 Distribution Using SMS

You need to complete three steps prior to actually creating the package:

1. Create the Administrative Installation share.
2. Make required updates to the SMS 2.0 server, depending on the release number of the SMS 2.0 software.
3. Compile the O2Ksetup script in a program that is included in the SMS 2.0 Package.

Creating the Administrative Install Share

To create the Administrative Installation share, follow these steps:

1. Click **Start, Run**.
2. At the **Run** command, type:

   ```
   <drive_letter>:\<setup_folder>\SETUP.EXE /a
   ```

   The <setup_folder> is the folder that contains the Office 2000 setup.exe program. This starts the setup program that places the installation files in a shared folder of your choice.
3. The first dialog box looks like that in Figure 3.7. Enter the CD-ROM key in the text boxes and the company name at the bottom.

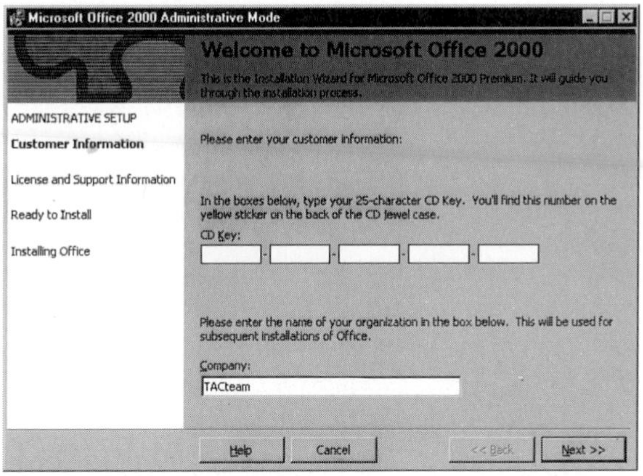

Part

I

Ch

3

FIGURE 3.7
Beginning the administrative installation.

4. Click **Next**, and the setup program asks for the setup location. Enter a UNC path and not a local path. Be sure that you have created this folder in advance and that you have shared that folder before you attempt to complete this step. The Location dialog box appears (see Figure 3.8).
5. Click the **Install Now** button to begin moving the source files to the Administrative share. You see a progress indicator, as shown in Figure 3.9.

FIGURE 3.8
Defining the
Administrative
Installation share.

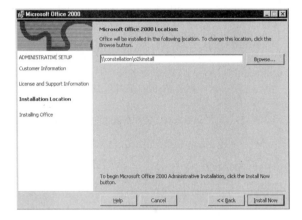

FIGURE 3.9
The Administrative
share installation
progress bar.

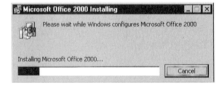

Updating the SMS Program

You might need to update client components of SMS 2.0. You can check by going to a client machine and doing the following:

1. Open the **Control Panel**.
2. Double-click on the **Systems Management** applet, and then click on the **Components** tab. The dialog box shown in Figure 3.10 appears.

FIGURE 3.10
Checking the version of
the Available Programs
Manager Win32.

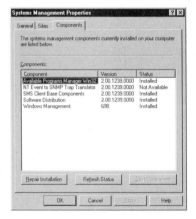

3. If the version of the Available Programs Manager Win32 is earlier than 100.1239.003, you need to update this program.

The best way to update the program is to upgrade the version of SMS 2.0 to Service Pack 1. You can download SMS 2.0 Service Pack 1 from the following Web site:

`http://www.microsoft.com/smsmgmt`

You need the original CD-ROM in order to complete the upgrade process.

If you need to upgrade the program and cannot install SMS 2.0 Service Pack 1, do the following:

1. Search for the **sms2oo2k.exe** file on your hard drive. The file's location might vary from computer to computer. The best approach is to use the Windows NT **Find** command.

2. Copy this file to the SMS 2.0 Site server, and then double-click on the file to begin the installation process. The file decompresses and automatically updates the outdated files.

Because this is a client-based program, the update does not take effect immediately. The new files must be distributed to the client machines that are members of the SMS 2.0 Site Hierarchy. Depending on how site replication is configured, this could take from several hours to a day.

Customizing and Compiling the O2kSetup Script

Editing and compiling the O2kSetup script enables Internet Explorer 5 to continue the installation process with administrative rights after the reboot.

You must first perform two procedures:

1. Edit the O2kSetup.ipf file to include entries specific to your domain and administrative context.

2. Compile the edited O2Ksetup.ipf script to create an .exe file, which will be the basis of a new program you will add to the SMS 2.0 package that will be subsequently distributed.

Use the SMS 2.0 Installer for both tasks. You can find it on the SMS 2.0 CD-ROM. Do a search for the file smsinstl.exe on the SMS 2.0 CD-ROM, and then double-click it to install the program.

 TIP Before you start the SMS Installer script editor, search your hard disk to find the location of the O2ksetup.ipf file and write down its location. You will need to know the path to the file to open it in the script editor.

From the **Start** menu, select **Programs, Microsoft SMS Installer, Microsoft SMS Installer 32**. This will start the script editor.

To edit the O2ksetup.ipf file, follow these steps:

1. With the SMS Installer script editor open, click the **File** menu and select **Open**. In the **File Name** box, type the path to the O2ksetup.ipf file. This opens the script for editing. You should see something that looks like Figure 3.11.

Part

I

Ch

3

FIGURE 3.11

You can now edit the O2ksetup.ipf script.

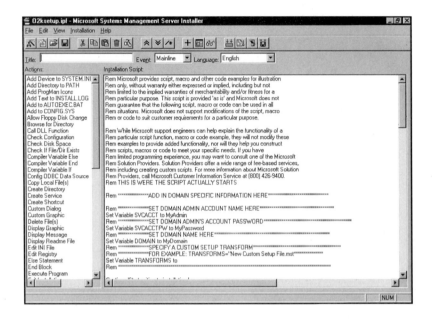

2. This file is just a plain text file, which can be edited with any text editor. However, you take the risk of not being able to compile it properly if you manually edit the file. The script editor provides a safe GUI interface in which you can edit individual entries in the script.

   You need to edit four variables:

DOMAIN	The domain the client is located on
SVCACCT	The administrative account used for installation
SVCACCTPW	The password of the chosen administrative account
TRANSFORMS	Any customized MST Transform files you want to include in the installation process

3. Double-click on the following line:

   ```
   Set Variable SVCACCT to MyAdmin
   ```

   You should see the dialog box shown in Figure 3.12.

FIGURE 3.12

The Set Variable dialog box.

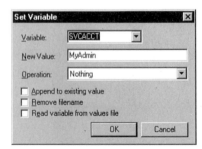

4. Enter the name of the account that provides the administrative context for installation. This account must have administrative rights on all the target machines. If all Windows NT machines have the same password for the local administrators account, you can use the administrator for the **New Value**. However, if there are different passwords, it is best to name a user that is a member of the DomainAdmins group. The DomainAdmins group is automatically placed in the local administrators group on each client machine in the domain.

CAUTION

You should give this account a strong password for security reasons.

---

5. Repeat step 4 for the lines that include the DOMAIN, SVCACCTPW, and TRANSFORMS entries. Replace the default variable with the names of your domain, the password on the administrative account, and the name of any Transform file you want to include. The syntax for the TRANSFORMS entry is

   `TRANSFORMS=custom2.mst`

   where *custom2* represents a Transform file containing customizations to the installation process.

6. Click the **File** menu and select **Save As** to save it to a secure location. Click the **Installation** menu, and then click **Compile**. You will see a quick progress dialog box, and then the compilation will be complete. You will then see an O2ksetup.exe file in the directory where the O2ksetup.ipf file is located.

7. Copy the O2ksetup.exe file and also the SHUTDOWN.EXE file (located in the same folder as the original O2ksetup.ipf script) to the top-level folder of your administrative installation share.

Now you can create the installation package.

Creating and Distributing the Office 2000 Package

Open the SMS 2.0 administrative console and follow these steps:

1. Right-click on the **Packages** node in the left pane, move to the **New** command, and then click the **Package from Definition** command.

2. This starts the Create Package from Definition Wizard. Click **Next** to continue.

3. The Package Definition dialog box appears. Click the **Browse** button and locate the Off9pre.sms Package Definition File. Select that file and click **Open**. Your dialog box should look like the one shown in Figure 3.13. Click **Next**.

4. The Source Files dialog box asks you how to handle the source files. Choose **Always Obtain Files from a Source Directory**, and then click **Next**.

5. The Source Directory dialog box requests the location of the administrative installation share you created earlier. In the **Source Directory** text box, enter the UNC path as shown in Figure 3.14. Then click **Next**.

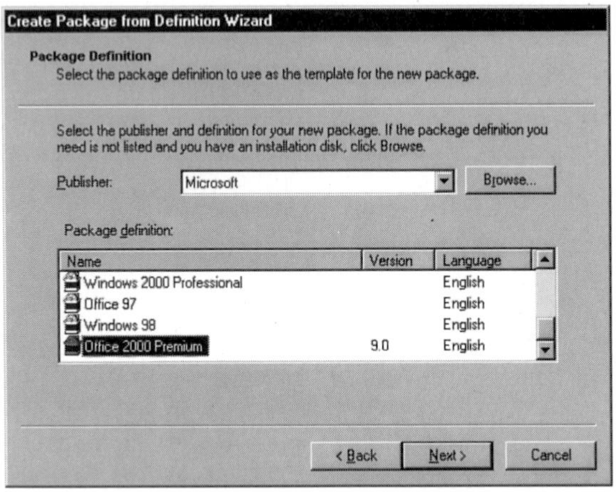

FIGURE 3.13

The Off9pre.sms Package Definition File imported in SMS.

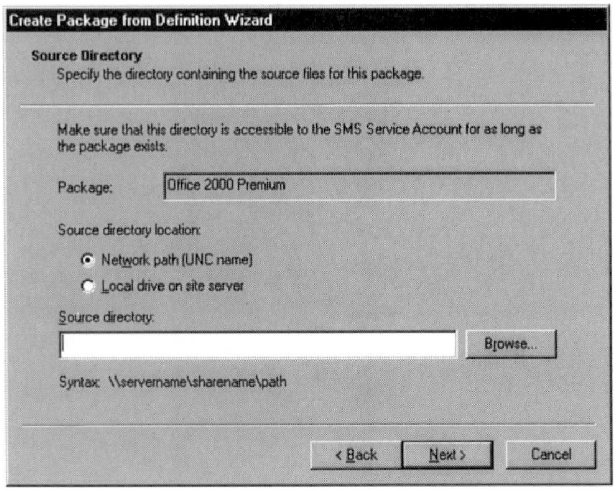

Create Package from Definition Wizard

Package Definition
Select the package definition to use as the template for the new package.

Select the publisher and definition for your new package. If the package definition you need is not listed and you have an installation disk, click Browse.

Publisher: `Microsoft` ▼ `Browse...`

Package definition:

Name	Version	Language	
Windows 2000 Professional		English	▲
Office 97		English	
Windows 98		English	
Office 2000 Premium	9.0	English	▼

`< Back` `Next >` `Cancel`

FIGURE 3.14

The Source Directory dialog box.

Create Package from Definition Wizard

Source Directory
Specify the directory containing the source files for this package.

Make sure that this directory is accessible to the SMS Service Account for as long as the package exists.

Package: `Office 2000 Premium`

Source directory location:
- ⦿ Network path (UNC name)
- ○ Local drive on site server

Source directory:
`_____` `Browse...`

Syntax: \\servername\sharename\path

`< Back` `Next >` `Cancel`

6. Review the package characteristics. If everything looks good, click **Finish**.

After completing the procedure, right-click the **Packages** node and click **Refresh**. The new package will then show up in the SMS 2.0 administrative console.

Expand the **Packages** node, and then click the **Programs** node. Your screen should look like Figure 3.15.

Note that this package contains four programs. These programs were defined in the Package Definition File you imported earlier.

Right-click on the **Custom** program in the right pane, and then click on the **Properties** command. Note the command-line entry on the **General** tab, as it appears in Figure 3.16.

FIGURE 3.15
Programs in the package.

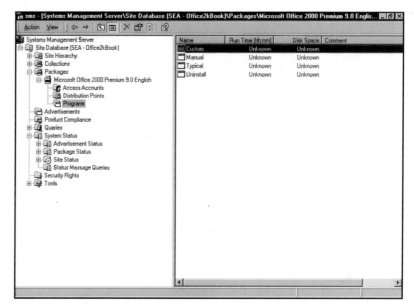

FIGURE 3.16
Properties of the Custom program.

Some common command-line arguments include the following:

/qn   Provides no user interface during installation.

/qr   Provides basic dialog boxes and progress bars during installation.

/qb-   Provides only a progress bar during installation.

/jm   Executes an Install on Demand installation. Only shortcuts will be added to the user's desktop.

none   Standard installation with complete installation dialog boxes and user interaction.

SOURCELIST=<*UNC_or_Local_Path*>   Instructs the installation program to use resilient locations for installation and Install on Demand. You can include multiple paths and separate the paths with semicolons.

Part

I

Ch

3

TRANSFORMS=*<name_of_transform_file>*   Instructs the installation to use the specified Transform file.

These command-line arguments can be used in any program you include in your package.

In the special case of the O2ksetup.EXE program, you do not need to specify the Transform file on the command line because it was included with the script itself.

> **CAUTION**
>
> Regardless of what program you are executing, always test it before implementing it on your live network.

Defining a New Program Using the O2ksetup.exe File

Now you will use the O2ksetup.EXE file you created earlier to install Internet Explorer 5 on Windows NT computers that do not have users logged on with administrative rights. The O2ksetup.EXE program was not included in the Package Definition File you imported, so you must define this new program yourself.

To do this, perform the following steps:

1. Right-click on the **Programs** node in the left pane of the SMS 2.0 administrative console, and then select **New** and click **Program**.

2. You see a dialog box similar to the one in the preceding figure. In the **Name** text box, type the name of the program, such as **O2ksetup Program**. Add a comment. Then, click the **Browse** button to find the O2ksetup.EXE file and select it. Leave the default entries in the **Run** and **After running** text boxes.

3. Click on the **Requirements** tab. Select the option button for **This Program Can Run Only on Specified Platforms**. Then, select **All x86 Windows 2000 Clients** and **x86 NT 4.0 Service Pack 4 Clients**.

4. Click the **Environment** tab. In the **Program Can Run:** drop-down box, select **Whether or Not a User Is Logged On**. In the **Drive Mode** frame, select **Runs with UNC Name**.

You have completed the procedure for creating new programs within a package. Repeat this procedure whenever you need to create a new program that might customize the setup routine.

Designating Software Distribution Points

To distribute the software, you must tell SMS 2.0 where the software will be located. In the SMS 2.0 administrative console, right-click on the new package you created, point to the **All Tasks** command, and then click the **Distribute Software** command.

Then, follow these steps:

1. You start with the Welcome screen for the Distribute New Software Wizard. Click **Next** to move past this screen.

2. You will see a dialog box like that shown in Figure 3.17. Select the **Distribute an existing package** option button and be sure **Office 2000 Premium** is selected. Then, click **Next**.

FIGURE 3.17
Selecting the package
to distribute.

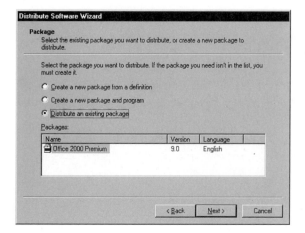

3. In the next screen, select the server or servers that will act as distribution points for the package. Then click **Next**.

4. At this point, you choose to advertise a program in your package. In this case, advertise the O2ksetup program you just created. Configure the dialog box so that it looks like that shown in Figure 3.18.

FIGURE 3.18
Choosing to advertise
a program.

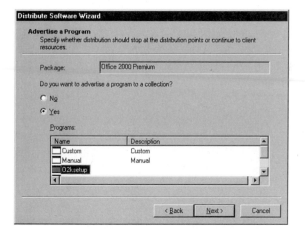

5. This dialog box asks whom you want the program to be advertised to. In SMS 2.0, you can create *collections* of computers based on parameters of your choice. After completing the Office 2000 Readiness Query, you can create a collection based on those results. Or, you might want to create a collection of users from certain groups. If you have not made a collection, you can create one now. Select a collection, and then click **Next**.

6. Either type in a name or use the default name in the Advertisement Name dialog box. You should enter a comment for the users who have the choice of whether to install it or not. Click **Next**.

Part

I

Ch

3

7. Choose to advertise to subcollections, and then click **Next**.

8. In the dialog box that appears (see Figure 3.19), choose a time to start advertising the program and whether you want the advertisement to expire and not be available after a certain point in time. Then click **Next**.

FIGURE 3.19

Scheduling the advertisement.

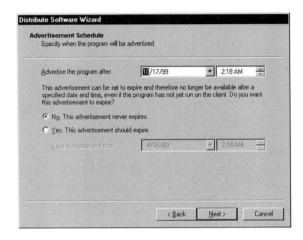

9. Choose to assign the program, as shown in Figure 3.20. You can choose not to assign the program, or you can choose to assign the program and set availability time, assignment time, and expiration date. Click **Next**.

FIGURE 3.20

Assigning the program.

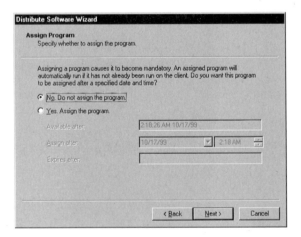

10. Examine the choices, and then click **Finish**.

You have completed the steps required to have SMS 2.0 install Office 2000 to the systems of your choice.

CHAPTER 4

Managing Macintosh Office 98 Installations and Deployments

by Bill Camarda

Microsoft Office 98 represents one of the most important fruits of the resurrected working relationship between Microsoft and Apple Computer. Instead of porting the Windows version of the Office applications directly to the Mac OS, Office 98 for Macintosh was written independently of the Windows version and reflects the strengths of the Macintosh user interface much more closely than the previous version, Office 4.2.

As its name implies, Office 98 was released after Office 97 for Windows, and Microsoft took care to ensure that the Mac OS and Windows versions could coexist peacefully. Most importantly, for Microsoft Word, Excel, and PowerPoint, document formats are the same in each platform (there are no Macintosh versions of Access or Outlook).

NOTE The release of Office 2000 for Windows has complicated document exchange in a few minor ways, and in one major way: At press time, documents saved by Office 2000 as Web pages cannot easily be read by Office 98 for the Macintosh. These and other document exchange issues are covered in detail in Chapter 26, "Managing Mixed Macintosh/Windows Office Environments." ■

Given the reasonable similarities between the Macintosh and Windows versions of Office, the more significant issues in deploying Office 98 for the Macintosh are often human and organizational, not just technical.

Assessing the Human-Related Issues for Office 98 Deployment

The following generalizations might or might not apply to your organization, but they do apply to many others:

Challenge: Many Macintosh users view Microsoft and Bill Gates the way Princess Leia viewed Darth Vader in *Star Wars*: They are extremely skeptical of Microsoft products. Traditionally, the concerns were sometimes well founded. Office 4.2 for the Macintosh ran poorly on many of the Macintosh systems on which it was deployed, in part because it was a straight port from the Windows version, not written from the ground up to reflect the technical strengths and limitations of the Macintosh platform. Similarly, Office 4.2 looked and felt like a Windows application, alienating many Macintosh users who are strongly attached to the Macintosh look and feel.

Solution: Office 98 addresses many of these problems: Its applications look and feel like Macintosh applications; they support Macintosh technologies such as Publish-and-Subscribe; and they were built from the ground up as Macintosh applications, so they deliver better performance than might be expected. You might want to share some of the positive reviews from the Macintosh press with your users; these are thoughtfully compiled by Microsoft at `www.microsoft.com/macoffice/newsroom/awards.htm`. More to the point, you might want to demonstrate Office 98 for the Macintosh to some or all the most influential Macintosh users in your organization, if they haven't already worked with it. Focus on ways in which Office 98 for the Macintosh solves their problems more effectively. This leads to the next challenge.

Challenge: In many organizations, Macintosh computers are used primarily in specific departments, such as graphics design. The needs and workflows of these departments are often unique, and not always well understood by the IT professionals responsible for deploying Office.

Solution: As with any major deployment, but especially in this case, begin by understanding the needs of your users. How do they currently use Office? How can Office 98 for the Macintosh help them become more efficient? (If you can't answer this question, there's little point in upgrading.) What problems do they envision? For example, will they need to install new desktop publishing software filters to deal with Office 98's new file formats? If so, will those filters work as well as the ones they are using now? Will they have to spend time developing new workarounds for problems they've already solved? Be prepared to ask these questions, and to help your users develop answers to them, before proceeding with an Office 98 deployment.

▶ For more information about importing Word documents into desktop publishing systems, **see** Chapter 21, "Integrating Office Documents with Desktop Publishing Systems," on **p. 579**.

This book seeks to assist with one additional challenge facing the Office professional who wants to deploy on Macintosh: There is simply much less information available—less information from Microsoft, less information from Apple (which has focused many of its resources outside the traditional corporate market), and less information from the traditional Macintosh user community, which (as discussed earlier) is skeptical of Microsoft. Fortunately, this problem is partly counterbalanced by the relative simplicity of Office 98 for the Macintosh installation, even across the network.

Reviewing Macintosh Hardware Requirements for Office 98

Although Office 98's performance on current Macintosh systems is solid, be sure your installed base of Macintosh computers is powerful enough to handle it. Office 98's hardware requirements are as follows:

- **Processor.** Any Macintosh or Macintosh-compatible system that uses a PowerPC chip can run Office 98, but Microsoft recommends that your computer CPU have a clock speed of at least 120MHz. This eliminates the first two generations of Power Macintosh computers.

- **RAM.** You need at least 16MB of RAM to run any of the Office applications separately. It's often advantageous, however, to run several Office applications simultaneously, in which case you need more RAM. Microsoft recommends 32MB of RAM if you run the Office applications simultaneously.

- **Hard Drive.** Set aside 50 to 120MB of your hard disk for your Office installation—and be sure the resulting installation leaves enough room for data and virtual memory. Later in this chapter, you learn how to customize your installation to include as many, or as few, of the Office accessories included in the installation. If you want to store all Office 98's clip art locally, add another 50MB. If you plan to upgrade to Microsoft Internet Explorer 4.5 and the latest version of Outlook Express, set aside another 12MB.

- **Mac OS Version.** You need Mac OS 7.5 or later, but System 7.5.5 is recommended. Office 98 works with Mac OS 8.51, but see the "Running the Combined Updater for Office 98" section of this chapter for information about a patch Microsoft has provided to solve several reported problems.

- **Monitor.** Your monitor should display 16 levels of gray or 256 colors with a resolution of at least 640×400 pixels.

- **Peripherals.** You need a CD-ROM drive to install the software; in an office environment, you might need a network connection to install the software from an office LAN. Microsoft also recommends that you have some sort of connection to the Internet, which, of course, must be provided separately. Such a connection enables you to make use of Office 98's Internet features and to access updates on the Microsoft Web site.

Part

I

Ch

4

Preparing for Your Office 98 Installation

Before you install Microsoft Office 98, take the following steps:

- If you are using Symantec Antivirus for the Macintosh (SAM) version 4.52 or earlier, update to SAM Intercept version 4.5.3 prior to installing Office; this update is available at `http://www.symantec.com/techsupp/files/sam/symantec_antivirus_for_macintosh.html`.

- If you create documents for use in international environments, be aware that the fonts installed with Microsoft Office 98 do not include the Euro character. If this is a concern, consider not including the default fonts. Better yet, download and install the replacement Macintosh TrueType fonts, available at no cost from Microsoft's Typography Web site, **www.microsoft.com/typography**.

■ If you are using RAM Charger, upgrade to version 8.1 or later; later, if you find that you still have problems traceable to RAM Charger, such as broken or flashing dialog boxes, open the RAM Charger Control Panel and instruct RAM Charger not to manage the memory it allocates to Microsoft Office programs. Information on RAM Charger is available at Jump Development Group's Web site, **www.ramcharger.com**.

■ If you plan to provide custom Word templates, Excel add-ins, or other resources to your users, prepare and gather them now.

■ Download Microsoft's Combined Updater for Office 98 (**www.microsoft.com/ macoffice/productinfo/98dl/combinedupdate.htm**), covered later in this chapter. This updater brings together several fixes for Office 98 problems. You'll want to apply this Updater to your Macintosh computers as soon as you finish installing Office 98, especially if you intend to run Office under System 8.5.

TIP Although the Office 98 CD-ROM contains uncompressed files that need no special utilities, if you customize your installation with files Microsoft provides at its **www.microsoft.com/macoffice** Web site, you might need two additional tools:

● The latest version of the StuffIt Expander engine, which might not be included with the version of StuffIt Expander provided on your Macintosh (a trial version is available from Aladdin Systems at **www.aladdinsys.com**).

● Apple's free Disk Copy utility, which enables you to mount disk images on your desktop, and convert disk images between formats (available from Apple at **http://asu.info.apple.com/ swupdates.nsf/artnum/n11162**).

Installing Office 98

Installing Office 98 for Macintosh is somewhat different from installing its Windows counterpart. In this section, you learn some of the mechanics of the installation process, as well as some of the tools provided in the installation. Three approaches to installation are covered:

■ **The Easy Install**, in which you simply drag a folder from the Office 98 CD-ROM onto the desktop, and Office 98 installs all the most commonly used Office 98 features.

■ **The Full Install**, in which you drag a folder to the desktop that contains all Office 98's features (excluding optional tools stored in the Value Pack), not just the most common features. The Full Install requires 14MB more disk space than the Easy Install.

■ **The Custom Install**, in which you use a conventional installer utility, Microsoft's Custom Installer, to choose exactly which features to install.

Understanding the Contents of the Office 98 CD-ROM

Open the CD-ROM containing Office 98 and you see the folders displayed in Figure 4.1.

FIGURE 4.1
When you display the contents of the Microsoft Office 98 CD-ROM, you see all the instructions you need to get started.

Note that four main folders are visible containing the following items:

■ **Microsoft Office 98 for Macintosh files.** In traditional Mac or Windows installations, the applications are stored in compressed formats. In the Office 98 installation, however, the files are uncompressed and appear much as they will on your hard drive.

■ **Value Pack.** Contains small tools and accessories that complement the Office applications.

■ **Microsoft Internet.** Contains the Internet Explorer Web browser and the Outlook Express email client.

■ **Office Custom Install.** Contains the conventional installation files familiar to Macintosh users.

Using Local Drag-and-Drop Installation

To run an Easy Install of Microsoft Office 98, simply drag the Microsoft Office 98 folder from the Office 98 CD-ROM (or wherever you've stored it) to the hard disk from which you want it to run.

To run a Full Install of Microsoft Office 98, double-click the **Office Custom Install** folder. You'll see three items (see Figure 4.2); one of them is another folder called Microsoft Office 98. Drag that folder to the hard disk from which you want to run Office.

FIGURE 4.2
When you double-click Office Custom Install, you see another Microsoft Office 98 folder consisting of the entire Full Install.

Part

I

Ch

4

Understanding First Run Installation

Many Mac OS applications use additional files called extensions or preferences. These files reside in the System Folder on your local hard drive and are essential to running your applications. Office 98 for Macintosh makes extensive use of these types of files; however, extensions and preference files are not installed directly during the drag-and-drop installation.

When you start the software for the first time after a drag-and-drop installation, Office 98 transfers the necessary system extensions and other pertinent files into Macintosh's System Folder. This process, referred to as *First Run Installation (FRI)*, delays the startup of the Office applications as these files are copied into their necessary locations. This startup delay occurs only the first time that you use Office 98 after a drag-and-drop installation.

One useful feature of the drag-and-drop installation is that FRI checks your System Folder for any files that might be needed but are not present, such as QuickTime or any other software libraries. Also, FRI protects against inadvertent removal of any important files from the System Folder. If you accidentally delete a relevant extension, FRI senses this the next time you launch an Office application and replaces that file.

Furthermore, FRI is beneficial when you upgrade to newer versions of the Mac OS. If you perform a clean system install that creates a new System Folder, FRI can reinstall the Office system files you need in the new System Folder the first time you launch an Office application after you upgrade.

N O T E   After you install Office, you can change the name of your hard disk or move the entire Office folder to another folder or drive without preventing FRI from working properly. However, you cannot change the folder structure within the Microsoft Office 98 folder. ■

Running the Office 98 Custom Installer Utility

If you want more control over your Office installation than the Easy and Full Installs provide, you can use the Office Custom Install utility. If you've installed Office for the Macintosh (or Windows) before, you'll find this utility familiar. It enables you to select specific features and capabilities for each major Office application, Word, Excel, and PowerPoint; and also to choose which shared tools to install.

To run Office Custom Install, double-click the **Office Custom Install** folder, and double-click the **Installer** icon. The Custom Installer runs. It first searches your hard disk for previous installations of Office or individual Office applications.

N O T E   If you are installing from a CD-ROM purchased as an upgrade, Office 98 will not install unless it finds evidence of a previous Office application. However, you don't have to have the entire suite installed; for instance, it would be sufficient to have the Microsoft Word 4.0 or Excel 4.0 application file installed, with none of the supporting files. ■

You're asked whether you want to remove previous copies of Office from your hard drive, including old extensions and preference files.

TIP As you'll see later in this chapter, you can also use the Custom Installer to prepare a folder on your server for centralized installation across your network.

To use the Custom Installer program, follow these steps:

1. Open the **Office Custom Install** folder on your CD.

2. Launch the Installer application by double-clicking the **Installer** icon. If the Installer detects earlier versions of Microsoft Office applications, it asks whether you want to remove those applications.

 TIP If you have the space on your hard drive, keep your earlier version of Office intact while installing Office 98. Although Office 98 can read and write earlier versions of the software, you can eliminate any possible conversion problems by keeping your old software around until you're ready to delete it.

3. Following that, you're prompted with the dialog box you see in Figure 4.3. You can pick and choose which elements of the various applications you want to include in your Office 98 installation.

TIP To get more information about an item, click the button in the right column.

Part
I

Ch
4

FIGURE 4.3
The Office 98 Custom Installer enables you to pick and choose which capabilities to include in your Office 98 applications.

4. After clicking the **Office** tools to include in the installation, click the **Install** button. You're prompted for your name and organization, which are used to personalize your Office applications. Insert them, and choose **OK**.

5. The Custom Installer runs, copying appropriate files to your hard disk.

Choosing Value Pack Components

Along with your Office 98 applications, the installation CD contains a variety of complementary applications. You can drag and drop some of these components from the Value Pack folder on the CD; you need to install other components using the Value Pack Installer (see Figure 4.4), an installer program that works very much like the Office Installer discussed earlier. To install the Value Pack components onto your hard drive, you must have already installed a copy of Microsoft Office.

FIGURE 4.4

The Value Pack Installer enables you to pick and choose which options to add to your Office 98 installation.

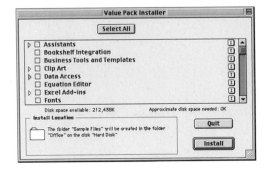

The Value Pack components are as follows:

- **Assistants.** In an attempt to humanize its Help, Office 98 provides help through a series of animated characters, called Assistants. Installing some or all the 13 Assistants on the CD-ROM enables users to choose which animated character to use.

- **Bookshelf Integration.** Microsoft Bookshelf is Microsoft's separate multimedia reference application, containing a dictionary, thesaurus, book of quotes, maps, and a concise encyclopedia. If you install Bookshelf Integration, users can search Bookshelf from within any Office application.

- **Business Tools and Templates.** The Value Pack contains templates, checklists, and short guides focused on helping small businesses create documents more quickly and manage themselves more effectively.

- **Clip Art.** The Clip Art component contains hundreds of PICT images files, organized in 20 categories, including Business, People, Industry, and Travel. It also contains small libraries of JPEG photos, QuickTime movies, and audio files; Web page backgrounds; and Screen Beans silhouetted cartoon characters well suited for informal newsletters and other publications.

- **Data Access.** This folder contains the Microsoft Query application and ODBC drivers needed to access external databases, such as Microsoft Access for Windows, and to utilize their data in Office 98 for the Macintosh applications.

- **TrueType Fonts.** This folder contains a library of 58 TrueType fonts. Many organizations that use Macintosh prefer to utilize only PostScript fonts for consistency; if you are in one of those organizations, do not install these fonts. Also, as mentioned earlier in this chapter, this font library does not support the Euro character.

- **Microsoft Movie.** This application enables you to embed a QuickTime movie into one of your Office documents. Note that this application runs only from within Office or another Macintosh application that supports Microsoft's Object Linking and Embedding. Relatively few Macintosh applications other than Microsoft's do. One exception is PageMaker, but only to the extent that PageMaker is primarily used to create print documents (not multimedia).

- **Mac OS System Updates.** This folder contains a series of minor system updates that Apple has released. These include System 7.5 Update 2.0, 7.55 Update, 7.6.1 Update, and 8.1 Update. Microsoft has provided these as a convenience, and to eliminate bugs and conflicts that might arise on systems that have not had the updates applied. If you are running System 7.51, System 7.52, 7.53, 7.6, or 8.1, you might want to apply one of these updates before installing Office 98. At present, no update is included for System 8.5.

- **Microsoft Office Manager.** The Manager enables you to launch the different Office applications or switch between active applications by using the keyboard. It appears as both a Macintosh control panel and an icon in the menu bar. "MOM" is similar to the Microsoft Office Shortcut Bar in Office 2000 for Windows.

- **Programmability.** This folder contains one Word template and one Excel template that each contains several sample Visual Basic macros designed to solve a variety of problems Office users often face. For instance, one of the Word macros enables users to create footnotes in the MLA or *Chicago Manual of Style* format; another one provides more detailed information about the current document. The folder also contains the Excel Analysis Toolpack, a set of worksheet analysis tools.

- **Proofing Tools.** This folder contains spelling dictionaries, thesauri, and hyphenation instructions for several languages. You'll find partial or complete sets of proofing tools for Danish, Dutch, French, German, Italian, Norwegian, Portuguese, Spanish, and Swedish. You'll also find the Set Language Excel add-in, which gives Excel the same capability to switch languages as Word already has "out of the box."

- **PowerPoint Translators.** This folder contains translators that can be installed in PowerPoint 4.0, an older version of PowerPoint, enabling that version to read PowerPoint 98 presentations (with certain limitations). Separate versions are provided for PowerPC and 68×00-based Macintosh computers.

- **Sample Files.** This folder contains an Excel worksheet with samples of data formatted for use with Excel's Solver feature.

- **Support.** This folder contains several files, each containing the Microsoft Office logo in a different graphics format. You can use it to test and compare the capabilities of Office's programs and graphics filters.

- **Templates.** This component contains an extensive library of templates for PowerPoint, Word, and Excel documents. Although you might not want to use the templates as they are, they might serve as an excellent foundation for later customization.

- **Text Converters.** The text converters in this component enable you to import files from previous versions of Word for Windows, WordPerfect, Word for Macintosh, and other formats into your Office 98 documents.

- **Textures.** These are backgrounds that you can use in Web pages (and also in Word documents intended to be read onscreen).

- **Unbinder.** Microsoft Binder for Windows is an application that enables you to combine PowerPoint, Excel, and Word documents into a single file. Unfortunately, you cannot work on files while they're in a binder. This component unbinds these documents so that you can work on the elements of the bound files separately.

- **Word Speak.** This component enables Office to speak the contents of your Word documents out loud.

The following components are installed with the full Office Installation. If you perform an Easy option, however, either by using the Installer or the drag-and-drop method, you need to add these components separately. You can do this with the Value Pack Installer.

- **More Help.** This folder contains Help files for Visual Basic for Applications, the programming language used by Word 98 and Excel 98.
- **Wizards.** Wizards guide you step-by-step through sophisticated document creation.
- **Microsoft Excel Add-ins.** These files are a collection of macros and wizards that add functionality to your Excel application. Such capabilities include autosaving and file conversion, as well as statistical and analytical tools.
- **Genigraphics.** This folder contains the GraphicsLink application, which streamlines the process of uploading PowerPoint presentations for conversion into 35mm slides.
- **Equation Editor.** This component enables you to incorporate sophisticated equations into your Word and PowerPoint documents.

Running Office 98 from a CD-ROM or a Network Drive

You can run Office 98 from the installation CD-ROM or a remote network drive rather than installing it on your local hard drive. Each time you run Office 98 from either a CD-ROM or a network drive, however, there is a performance hit as the Mac OS loads the shared libraries into memory. This same process occurs when Office is on your hard drive, but information travels much more slowly over a network or CD-ROM drive than from a local hard drive.

As in the drag-and-drop installation, FRI runs the first time you activate an Office application from a CD-ROM or network drive, at which time you incur a startup delay. Successive launches do not have the FRI delay.

Installing Office 98 from a Server

If you manage multiple Macintosh computers, you can avoid tediously installing Office 98 at every workstation. You can set up a central installation folder on your central file server—either AppleShare, Novell NetWare, or Microsoft Windows NT Server will do, as long as it has a volume that supports a Macintosh file system—and installs to individual workstations from there.

Your deployment strategy is similar to the installation process described in the section "Using the Office 98 Installer Program," except that you first install Office to your network hard drive. Of course, you must have write privileges to the folder you intend to use. Follow these steps:

1. Launch the **Office Installer** program and select a desired location on the remote hard drive.
2. Using the Installer sequence described earlier, select the **Office** capabilities and **Value Pack** components that you want to include in the installation. Complete the selection process and allow the installation to occur.
3. Use the Value Pack Installer to add a desired set of components.

4. Add any custom templates you might have to the appropriate Templates folders in the Office 98 folder on the remote hard drive.

5. Optionally, clear the name and organization information from the installation point by copying the Microsoft Office 98 file from Microsoft Office 98:Office folder on the CD-ROM to the new Microsoft Office 98:Officefolder on the network hard drive.

6. Transfer the Microsoft Office folder to each workstation hard drive.

7. Optionally, run one Office application, thereby initiating the First Run Installation process. If you do so, users won't encounter the unusually slow program loading that would otherwise occur the first time that they ran an Office 98 application.

Let's cover these steps in more detail.

Installing Office 98 on a Remote Hard Drive   In the Office Custom Install folder on the installation CD-ROM, run the Installer program and select an appropriate place on the network hard drive. This process works the same as the installer process described earlier in the section "Using the Office 98 Installer Program."

Selecting Desired Office 98 Accessories and Value Pack Components   Using the installation process described earlier, select the accessories you want to add to your Office installation. Click the **Install** button and complete the installation.

When you've finished, you can use the separate Value Pack installer to install on your network server any Value Pack Components you want to include on your Office 98 client systems.

Customizing Your Network Office 98 Folder   If you want to include custom templates for all your colleagues to use, place them in the Templates folder in the Microsoft Office 98 folder on your network hard drive. You can add Excel Add-ins to the Microsoft Office 98:Office:Excel Add-ins folder. You can even insert documents you want displayed at each user startup by inserting these documents in the Microsoft Office 98:Office:Startup folder.

Clearing the Personalization Information   When you installed the software on the network hard drive, the Installer prompted you for your name and organization. By default, if you proceed to install to users' workstations from the server, they will see your name and organization each time they launch their Office applications. To let users customize their own Office applications, you can remove this personalization information. To do this, go to the following folder on the installation CD-ROM:

```
Office Custom Install:Microsoft Office 98:Office
```

From this folder, drag the file Microsoft Office 98 from the CD-ROM into the Microsoft Office 98:Office folder on the network drive. Now, when your users launch an Office application for the first time, they will be prompted for their name and organization.

Transferring the Office 98 Folder to Local Hard Drives   You can transfer the new Office 98 folder on the network hard drive to your users' hard drives in several ways:

- Assuming you have write access to your users' hard drives, you can push the folder onto each workstation hard drive where you want it installed. Simply drag the Microsoft Office 98 folder to your users' hard drives using the Mac OS' built-in file sharing. This is the most labor-intensive option, but might be your best choice if your users turn their computers off during off-hours, and it is your only choice if your network privileges prohibit you from writing to local hard drives.

■ You might be able to automate push installs by writing a custom script using Frontier, AppleScript, or another Macintosh-compatible scripting language. Such a script would launch the Custom Installer from each user's desktop. If you place it in each user's System Folder:Startup Items folder, it then launches automatically when each user restarts his computer.

■ If you have access to a desktop management tool, you can automate the process to run unattended (or largely unattended). Two products especially worth considering are FileWave 3.2 from Wave Research (**www.filewave.com**), which comes with templates for deploying Microsoft Office 98 and Internet Explorer 4.0; and Apple's own Apple Network Assistant (**www.apple.com**).

■ Finally, the most low-tech option is to simply inform your users where the network installation folder can be found, and instruct them to drag and drop the folder themselves. Of course, this assumes your users are familiar enough with your Macintosh network to do so reliably; and will understand (and be willing to follow) your instructions.

Running the Combined Updater for Office 98

After you've installed Office 98 successfully, you should update it to reflect Microsoft's latest bug fixes. The most convenient way to do so is to run the Combined Updater for Office 98 (see Figure 4.5) from each individual workstation.

FIGURE 4.5
Running the Microsoft Office 98 Combined Updater.

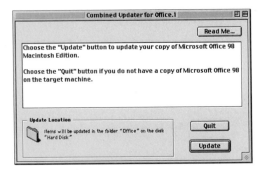

This software, downloadable at **www.microsoft.com/macoffice/users/issues.htm#comb**, addresses two privacy issues and several software compatibility issues:

■ Fixes a bug in the original Office 98 which allowed deleted, unwanted data to remain in files where the data could sometimes be read by a text editor (although not from within the Office application that created it).

■ Changes Microsoft Office so that when files are written, they do not contain a Unique Identifier that could trace a file back to a user based on the serial number of the Ethernet card in her computer.

- Fixes a bug in Visual Basic for Applications (VBA) that caused some G3 Macintosh computers to crash when running any of the following templates, wizards, and add-ins: Word's built-in Memo and Report templates; the Value Pack Newsletter, Calendar, and Agenda Wizards; and potentially other templates and Excel add-ins that use compiled VBA code.

- Fixes Fast Save problems in Word 98 that occasionally corrupt long documents.

- Fixes several problems affecting Macintosh computers running Office 98 under Mac OS 8.5, including

  - Fixes bugs that caused minor changes in page layout when documents created under earlier versions of the Mac OS were opened under Mac OS 8.5

  - Updated Office 98 to take advantage of built-in Euro support in Mac OS 8.5

  - Fixes bugs that sometimes caused menus to drop-down slowly and appear in white instead of Mac OS 8.5's platinum appearance

N O T E   If you do not want to eliminate the Unique Identifier from your Office documents, or if you are not planning to run Mac OS 8.5, you can download and run individual updaters instead of the Combined Updater. If you do so, however, you must run them in the following order (skipping any you don't need to install):

1. Unwanted Data

2. Mac OS 8.5

3. Unique Identifier ■

Before you run the Combined Updater, close any Office programs you might have running, as well as Internet Explorer. (If you don't, your Macintosh will restart after you run the updater.)

When the Combined Updater finishes, it creates a SimpleText log file named MS Office 98 Updater Log that lists the updates it has made (see Figure 4.6). If certain updates are unnecessary, these are not included in the log. It makes sense to check this log for any problems or surprises.

N O T E   If you are running Office 98 from a network server, search the Microsoft Knowledge Base for article Q189542, which explains how to make the appropriate updates on both the server and individual workstations.

If you are running Office 98 from a CD-ROM (Run from CD), search the Microsoft Knowledge Base for article Q189544, which explains how to make the appropriate updates. ■

Part

I

Ch

4

FIGURE 4.6

The MS Office 98 Updater Log tells you exactly which updates it made.

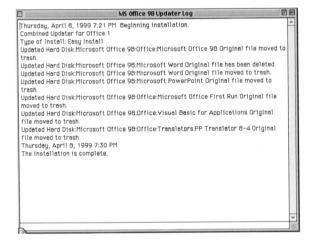

Introducing Internet Explorer 4.5 and Outlook Express 4.5

Recent Macintosh computers and Microsoft Office 98 each ship with Internet Explorer 4.0; Office also includes Outlook Express, a mail and news reader that is superior to the Microsoft Internet Mail and News software included with Internet Explorer 4.0. More recently, Microsoft has updated both programs. The new Internet Explorer 4.5 and Outlook Express 4.5 have several advantages, many of them focused on making the tools more usable and more Mac-like. These include

- Greatly improved printing of Web pages.
- AutoFill that automates filling in Web forms based on profiles you create in advance (such as your name, address, and so on; but keep in mind the security implications in a corporate environment).
- The Page Holder feature (which makes it easier to switch between a Web site and the links it references).
- Integration with Sherlock, Apple's Mac OS 8.5 tool for finding information on your computer or on the Web.
- Drag-and-drop images: See an image on a Web page that you like? Just drag it to the desktop.
- Stronger support for AppleScript in Outlook Express.

Internet Explorer 4.5 and Outlook Express 4.5 are shown in Figures 4.7 and 4.8, respectively.

N O T E   Internet Explorer 4.5 supports only PPC (PowerPC) Macintosh computers; it does not run on older Macintosh computers with 68×00 processors.

FIGURE 4.7
Internet Explorer 4.5.

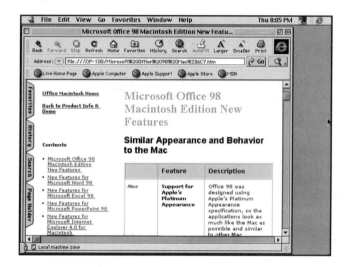

FIGURE 4.8
Outlook Express 4.5.

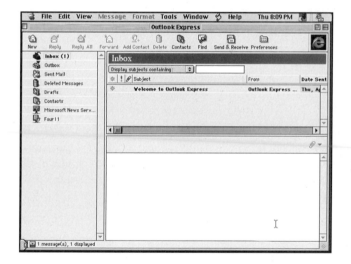

Part

I

Ch

4

CAUTION

Before upgrading to Internet Explorer 4.5, test it on a Macintosh comparable to those your users work with. Some early users have reported that Internet Explorer 4.5 might reduce performance of other applications even when it is only running in the background, because (more than most Macintosh applications) it is set to constantly be polled by the Mac OS looking for new activity.

You should also be aware that Microsoft Internet Explorer 4.5, unlike previous versions of Internet Explorer, relies on Apple's own version of Java rather than Microsoft's. This is fallout from the Sun versus Microsoft Java lawsuit; Microsoft has abandoned further development of Java for the Macintosh. Unfortunately, Apple's Java Virtual Machine has traditionally been buggier than Microsoft's, so it's conceivable that you might encounter more problems with Web sites that run Java applets.

Internet Explorer and Outlook Express install as easily as Office 98: You simply drag a folder from your CD-ROM (or other device) to the hard disk you want to store your files on (see Figure 4.9).

FIGURE 4.9
Installing Internet Explorer 4.5 and Outlook Express 4.5.

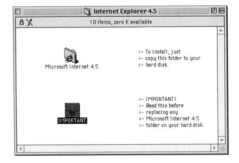

CAUTION

If you have already installed Internet Explorer 4.5 or Outlook Express 4.5, you cannot reinstall them by simply dragging the folder from the CD-ROM to your hard drive: Doing so will destroy existing message data stored in the OE User(s) folder. To preserve existing messages while reinstalling Microsoft's Internet 4.5 folder, double-click the **IMPORTANT** icon that appears beneath the Microsoft Internet 4.5 folder, and follow the detailed instructions there.

Understanding Internet Explorer Administration Kit 4.5

If you plan to roll out Internet Explorer 4.5 and/or Outlook Express 4.5 to a large number of users, you might be interested in the Internet Explorer 4.5 Administration Kit (IEAK) (see Figure 4.10), available at no charge from Microsoft at **www.microsoft.com/windows/ieak/en/download/bits/mac45.asp**.

FIGURE 4.10
The Internet Explorer 4.5 Administration Kit Wizard.

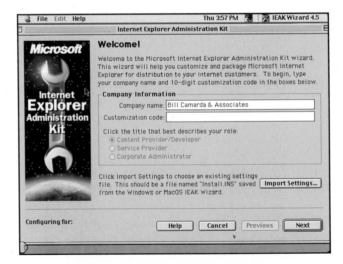

IEAK 4.5 contains a Wizard that enables you to create a custom version of Internet Explorer, including network settings, default home and search page, mail and news settings, proxy settings, and default URL Favorites bookmarks. The IEAK can also establish locked-down security and Ratings preference panels, helping you enforce restrictions on how your users work on the Internet. (You can also manually customize the HTML help pages that accompany your version of Internet Explorer.)

Before you use IEAK 4.5, be aware of the following:

- It requires a 25MB download from Microsoft, decompression with the latest version of StuffIt, and access to the Disk Copy utility for creating disk images.

- You'll need a 10-digit customization code from Microsoft. This is available at no charge, but without it, the IEAK Wizard will not run.

- Microsoft strongly recommends that all your Macintosh computers run Open Transport 1.1.1 or later as their TCP/IP networking software, and Open Transport PPP 1.0 (OT/PPP) as their PPP software. (These upgrades are included with IEAK.) Third-party versions of PPP, such as FreePPP, aren't supported; in fact, IEAK disables them.

N O T E It might not be obvious how to license IEAK for the Macintosh, because all the licensing screens refer only to IEAK for Windows, and an IEAK 5.x for Windows license does not work when you run IEAK 4.x for the Macintosh. To license the Macintosh version correctly, follow these steps:

1. At **http://ieak.microsoft.com/en/license/newlicensee.asp** accept the IEAK license agreement. Your IEAK account profile is displayed.

2. Scroll down to Licenses, and select **Get 4.x Code**.

3. Click **Submit**. Microsoft sends your IEAK 4.x customization code via email.

Part

I

Ch

4

Troubleshooting Office 2000 Installations

by Deb Shinder

The new Windows Installer, which replaces the Acme Setup program used to install previous versions of Office, has improved the ease and reliability of the installation process in many ways. It enables administrators to customize the installation process to a much greater degree than before.

However, introducing new software into your system always creates the potential for something to go wrong. Although the installation process offers added flexibility, it also entails added complexity—which, unfortunately, can increase the chance of problems.

You can prevent many of those potential problems by properly planning and carefully carrying out the deployment of Office 2000 in your organization. This chapter discusses typical installation pitfalls, how to avoid them, and how to resolve those you can't prevent.

Planning Your Office 2000 Installation to Avoid Pitfalls

The best way to deal with software installation problems is to *not* have to deal with them at all. Many administrators take a reactive approach to problem solving; they wait for the problem to occur and then try to "fix it." A better method is the proactive approach: Take steps to prevent the problem from occurring in the first place. This chapter covers a few ways in which proper planning can serve as your first line of defense in the troubleshooting process. For more information on planning, see Chapter 1, "Planning Your Office 2000 Installation," for detailed guidelines on overall planning issues.

Earlier chapters stressed the importance of planning prior to your Office 2000 deployment or upgrade. That process should include anticipating potential problems and "heading them off at the pass."

Any software package that is as large and feature-rich as Office 2000 has the potential to tax your system's resources or cause a conflict with some other program installed on your computer. The first step toward preventing installation problems is to select your installation options carefully. To do so, you might need to do some research.

Locating Microsoft and Third-Party Resources

Many good resources are available from Microsoft and third parties, both in print and online, including. Here are some suggestions you should follow:

- Obtain, read, and use the Office 2000 Resource Kit. The print version contains valuable information and tips on installing and troubleshooting Office 2000, and it comes with a CD-ROM that includes many useful tools. You can access an electronic version of the Resource Kit on the Web at **http://www.microsoft.com/office/ork/2000/default.htm**.
- Consult the Knowledge Base on Microsoft's Technet CD or Web site for known installation issues before you deploy Office 2000. You can subscribe to Technet or access its resources online at **http://technet.microsoft.com/cdonline/default.asp**.

Reviewing General Preinstallation Guidelines

This section contains some general guidelines that will reduce the likelihood of problems during your Office 2000 installation.

If you plan to upgrade an operating system (from Windows 95 to 98, Windows NT to Windows 2000, or whatever), do it before you install Office 2000. Thoroughly test the operating system upgrade before you deploy a new, major software package such as Office 2000. Otherwise, it might be difficult to determine whether problems that arise are related to Office 2000 itself or to the new operating system installation.

Determine that all network components are working properly and that network connections are established before you start the Office 2000 installation. Again, this helps to isolate the sources of problems, and it is a crucial step if you will be deploying Office 2000 over the network.

Assess other programs that will be running on the computer(s), especially earlier applications. Some earlier word processing programs, for instance, use a nondynamic method of flagging RAM and will take all available RAM when loaded, leaving none for Office. You might want to remove earlier programs that you no longer need.

Consider the advantages of running Office 2000 locally instead of from an application server. This eliminates the element of network traffic from running Office applications and speeds performance—both the performance of Office on that system and the performance of a congested network.

Addressing Hardware Issues

One of the best ways to minimize installation problems is to install Office 2000 on machines that exceed minimum hardware requirements.

This means, first and foremost, that the system must have plenty of physical memory (RAM). Microsoft's official recommendation for desktop machines running Office 2000 is 16MB of RAM for the operating system (Windows 95/98; or 32MB for Windows NT), plus an additional 4MB for each application running simultaneously (8MB for Microsoft Outlook). For practical purposes, your desktop computers should have at least 64MB of RAM if you're going to install and run Office 2000 properly in a multitasking environment. Having 128MB or even 256MB is better.

If all your company's desktop machines don't meet these recommendations and upgrading the hardware isn't feasible at this time, don't despair. There are still ways you can effectively deploy Office 2000:

- **Install fewer features and applications.** If a user needs only the word processing capability, install only Word 2000. Customize the installation process and leave out applications that are not needed.

- **Install all applications, but instruct users to open only a minimal number of programs at one time.** Remember that the memory requirements are based on applications running simultaneously. If a user closes Word before opening Access, RAM requirements will be reduced.

- **Run Office 2000 on a Windows terminal server.** This enables even the "thinnest" of client machines to get all the benefits of the Office 2000 applications by connecting as terminal clients and running individual instances of Office on the server. See Chapter 23, "Running Office 2000 with Microsoft Terminal Services," for more information about using Office 2000 with Windows terminal services.

Processing power is less of an issue than memory (although it's important if you are doing complex calculations). Microsoft's minimum is only a Pentium 75MHz or higher, but Office 2000 will install and run more efficiently if you have at least a 166MHz processor.

An often-overlooked hardware item is the hard disk. Office makes extensive use of the hard drives, and if you are running applications across the network, the server should have fast SCSI disks.

Part
I

Ch
5

Finally, be sure you have enough disk space on the drive to which you choose to install Office 2000. Installation will not proceed if the Windows Installer finds insufficient disk space. Microsoft specifies that 189MB of free space is needed to install Office 2000 Disc 1 (Excel, Outlook, PowerPoint, and Word). Office 2000 Premium Edition might require more than 400MB in a custom installation.

Setting Up a Test (Prototype) Environment

Setting up a prototype environment, or test lab, can be your best troubleshooting tool. In this situation, you can test different installation procedures and options before deploying Office 2000 to your production machines, which will help you accurately predict any problems that might occur and find solutions to them.

There are two keys to setting up a prototype environment:

1. It should be completely independent of your company LAN.
2. It should be as nearly identical as possible to the company LAN environment.

To create a realistic test environment, you should have one server that runs the same operating system and other software as your production server(s) and one or more client computers using the same operating system that is used on your network desktop systems (again with all the same software installed). The hardware for the prototype and production machines should also be as close to the same as possible.

In this environment, you can go through all the steps of installing Office 2000, testing any installation scripts, using Systems Management Server or the Windows 2000 IntelliMirror software distribution features, and selecting different installation options to determine the effect on stability and performance.

Prototyping enables you to uncover problems that might occur in an actual installation scenario and to address them beforehand. This prevents the employees' loss of productivity and inconvenience that would result if they were to encounter "surprise" problems during the actual installation.

The test lab is useful long after you've completed the deployment of Office 2000. It can be used for troubleshooting problems that occur later, in a controlled and "safe" environment that won't affect the network's productivity. It can also be used to plan future upgrades and as a training ground where administrators can familiarize themselves with the new software and its features.

Troubleshooting Installation Problems on Standalone Systems

Most problems that occur during the installation of Office 2000 on a standalone system can be traced to obsolete files left on the system or conflicting Registry settings made by other programs or older installations of Office. The most likely troublemakers are files that were installed by previous versions of Office. The best way to avoid installation problems is to install Office 2000 to as clean a system as possible.

It might not be feasible for you to format the hard disk, reinstall the operating system, and put Office 2000 on a completely fresh system, but this is the surest way to a successful installation. Luckily, you have other alternatives.

Using the Office Removal Wizard

Office 2000 includes the Office Removal Wizard for removing components from previous versions of Office. The Removal Wizard makes it easy to remove unneeded or obsolete files and settings from users' computers in preparation for the installation of Office 2000.

The Removal Wizard consists of the following files:

Offcln9.opc specifies files, Registry, and INI file settings, and shortcuts associated with a particular language version of Office to be removed.

Oclean9.dll carries out instructions in Offcln9.opc to clean up the user's hard disk.

Offcln9.exe provides the user interface that lets you run the wizard as a standalone utility.

Administrators can customize the OPC file to remove all the components you specify. This can include non-Office applications as well.

The Removal Wizard runs automatically during the setup of Office 2000. When you install Office 2000, the Setup program detects unneeded files, settings, and shortcuts from previously installed versions of Office and removes them.

N O T E   The removal feature in Setup is part of the Windows Installer package, which runs Setup with administrative permissions. This means prior versions of Office can be removed even if the user running Setup doesn't have administrative permissions. ■

The Removal Wizard can detect the following components from earlier versions of Office:

- ■ Microsoft Office 4.x, Office 95, and Office 97
- ■ Microsoft Team Manager 97
- ■ Microsoft Outlook 97 and Outlook 98 (does not include Outlook Express)
- ■ Microsoft FrontPage 1.1, FrontPage 97, FrontPage 98
- ■ Microsoft Publisher 2.0, Publisher 95, Publisher 97, and Publisher 98
- ■ Microsoft Project 4.0, Project 95, Project 97, Project 98

The Removal Wizard can also detect and remove standalone applications such as Word and shared components such as the Office Binder.

Setup will also detect incompletely installed or uninstalled components that leave unusable files on the hard disk and will remove them.

The Removal Wizard, which can be run as a standalone utility, is installed as one of the core tools when you install the Office 2000 Resource Kit. Figure 5.1 shows the standalone Removal Wizard.

FIGURE 5.1

You can run the Office Removal Wizard in one of three modes.

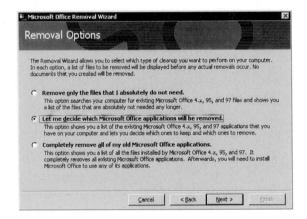

When you run the wizard, you can choose from three modes, depending upon just how much file cleanup you desire.

- **Aggressive mode (Completely remove all...).** In this mode, the wizard removes all Office-related components, including components shared by more than one Office application. If your users are upgrading from many different version of Office, you might choose to run the wizard in aggressive mode to thoroughly clean their hard disks.

- **Safe mode (Remove only the files...).** In this mode, the wizard removes only those components that are no longer needed. Safe mode removes only components that are not being used by any application.

- **Safe mode with user discretion (Let me decide...).** This is a form of safe mode that lets you choose which detected applications you want to keep and which ones to delete.

The wizard shows you a list of files that can be safely removed, as shown in Figure 5.2.

N O T E If you have standalone Office applications from a previous version, or if you had the Professional or Developer's version of Office 95 or 97 installed and are now installing the Standard or Small Business version of Office 2000, you should run the Removal Wizard in the safe mode with user discretion so you can be sure you retain all applications from the earlier versions that you want to keep. ■

Before the files are removed from your system, you will see a prompt like the one shown in Figure 5.3. You can permanently remove the old Office files from your system by clicking **Finish** in the wizard's Remove Now dialog box.

FIGURE 5.2
The Removal Wizard lists the detected files or applications that can be safely removed.

FIGURE 5.3
You must confirm that you want to remove the files.

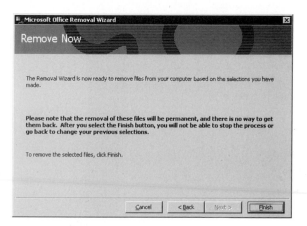

Restoring the Inbox After Removing Office

If you run the Microsoft Office 2000 Setup program in Maintenance mode and click Remove Office, you will not have an Inbox icon on your Windows 95 or Windows NT desktop. This is because Office 2000 replaces the Inbox icon on the desktop with the Microsoft Outlook icon, and when you remove Office, Outlook and all its icons will also be removed.

To restore the Inbox on your Windows 95 or Windows NT desktop, you must reinstall the Windows Messaging client to restore the icon. To reinstall Windows Messaging, open the **Add/Remove Programs** applet in Control Panel, select the **Windows Setup** tab, and add the **Windows Messaging Component**.

Correcting Inaccurate Display of Available Disk Space During Setup

If you are performing a custom installation of Office 2000, the "Available Space on Local Hard Disks" list might not display the correct hard disk space information (see Figure 5.4). This sometimes happens if you manually type a path in the Installation Location box instead of using the Browse button to select a destination folder.

FIGURE 5.4
If you type a path into the "Install Office 2000 at" box instead of using the Browse button, the hard disk information that appears might be incorrect.

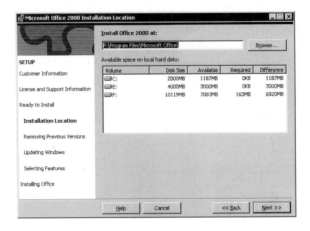

You can fix the problem by clicking the **Next** button in the Installation Location dialog box and then clicking the **Back** button to update the Available space on local hard disks list.

Overcoming Internet Explorer 5 Installation Problems

Microsoft Internet Explorer 5 does not install if there is less than 5MB of free space on the drive where your operating system is installed, regardless of the location you choose to install the Office 2000 files.

You can free some space on the drive and install MSIE 5.0 by itself by following these steps:

1. On the Windows **Start** menu, click **Run**.
2. In the **Open** box, click **Browse**.
3. Insert the first Office 2000 compact disc in your CD-ROM drive.
4. Open the **\Ie5\en** folder and double-click **Ie5setup.exe**.
5. Follow the instructions on your screen to complete setup.

Troubleshooting Problems with Office 2000 Application Shortcuts

If you attempt to install Office 2000 into a folder other than the default location and the destination folder has a very long total path length, you might get the following message:

```
"Warning 1909. Could not create shortcut <filename>.lnk. Verify that the desti-
nation folder exists and that you can access it."
```

This might occur several times as Setup tries to create shortcuts to all the Office 2000 applications. After Setup is complete, you find that you cannot use the shortcuts on the Programs menu to open the Office 2000 applications, but that if you use Windows Explorer to navigate to the \Microsoft Office\Office folder and double-click on the actual program file (such as Winword.exe), you can open and use the program.

The solution is to uninstall Office 2000 using the Add/Remove Programs applet in Control Panel and then run Setup again, choosing the default installation location or selecting a shorter path.

This problem might also occur even though you installed Office 2000 to the default location, if your Windows file associations have become corrupted. In that case, perform the following steps:

1. Uninstall Office using the **Add/Remove Programs** Control Panel applet.
2. Click **Start**, point to **Find**, and click **Files or Folders**.
3. In the **Named** box, type **Shell.inf** and click **Find Now**.
4. Right-click the **Shell.inf** file and click **Install**.
5. Wait approximately one minute, depending on the speed of your hard disk.
6. Click **Start**, **Shutdown**, **Restart**, and then click **OK** to restart the computer.
7. Run the Office 2000 Setup again.

Identifying and Addressing Internal Error Messages

Some Setup problems might result in a not-very-helpful "internal error" message, directing you to contact Product Support for assistance. Some common causes of this are listed in the following sections.

Internal Errors 2336 and 2755: File Permissions   If you are installing Office 2000 on Windows NT and the operating system partition is formatted as NTFS, you might receive one of the following error messages:

```
Internal error 2336: Please contact Product Support for assistance.

Internal error 2755: Please contact Product Support for Assistance.
```

Both of these are caused by NTFS permissions problems. These messages indicate that the user performing the installation does not have full access permissions to the *<system root>* folder (usually named winnt) or to the winnt\Installer subfolder.

You can solve the problem by changing the permissions on the \Installer folder to Full Control for the appropriate account or by assigning Full Control permissions on the folder to the Everyone group.

Internal Error 2893: Long Company Name   If Internal Error 2893 occurs during the installation of Office 2000, one of the following things has happened: A company name that is more than 52 characters long has been entered in the Custom Installation Wizard or via the COMPANYNAME property in the Options section of Setup.ini, or the COMPANYNAME property was added to the command line when Setup was being run from the Run dialog box.

When this error occurs, click **OK**, and Setup will finish without any problems, and the company name will be truncated when it appears in the "About" box in Office 2000.

Internal 2343: Lotus Notes Registry Entries   If you have unistalled Lotus Notes prior to installing Office 2000, or if you have incorrect entries for Lotus Notes in the Registry, you might receive the following message when you attempt to install Office 2000:

Part

I

Ch

5

```
Internal Error 2343: Please contact Product Support for assistance.
```

followed by this message, shown in Figure 5.5:

```
Installation ended prematurely because of an error.
```

FIGURE 5.5
Installation will not proceed if Office 2000 Setup encounters a fatal error.

NOTE This happens only if you have uninstalled Lotus Notes or it is installed incorrectly. When it's installed correctly, Lotus Notes does not interfere with Office 2000 installation.

If this occurs, you should download the Err2343.exe file from **http://support.microsoft.com/download/support/mslfiles/**. This is a utility provided by Microsoft to correct the problem.

Internal Error 2344: Missing Imagehlp.dll   If you have uninstalled McAfee VirusScan from your computer, it might have removed the Imagehlp.dll file, and you might get the following message when you attempt to install Office 2000:

```
Internal Error 2344: Please contact Product Support for assistance
```

followed by this message:

```
Installer ended prematurely because of an error.
```

To correct this problem, perform the following steps:

1. Copy **Extract.exe** from the \system folder on the Office 2000 Disc 1 to your desktop.

2. From the **Start** menu, select **Programs**, **MS-DOS Prompt** (on Windows 95/98) or **Command Prompt** (on Windows NT). Or, choose **Start**, **Run** and type **cmd**.

3. Enter the command for your operating system, press **Enter**, and then enter the **extract** command (see the following example):

```
Windows 95/98:<ENTER>
extract d:\ie5\en\setupw95.cab imagehlp.dll /L c:\windows\system
```

NOTE In this example, the CD-ROM drive is d:, and Windows is installed in the default path (C:\Windows). If you are using Windows NT 4.0, the default path would be C:\Winnt, and you would extract the file to the system32 folder.

4. Close the DOS window after the extraction is complete. This should solve the problem.

Internal Error 1500: Another Installation in Progress   You might receive the following message when you try to run the Office 2000 Setup program:

```
Error 1500. Another installation is in progress. You must complete that instal-
lation before continuing this one.
```

First, check to make certain you haven't inadvertently double-clicked on the Setup icon a second time and opened another instance of the Windows Installer. If not, and you get the same message when you click **Retry**, you might have to edit the Registry to solve the problem.

> **CAUTION**
>
> Editing the Registry incorrectly can cause serious problems, including making your system unstable or unbootable. Follow all directions exactly and always back up the Registry before you edit it. If you are using Windows NT, update your Emergency Repair Disk as well.

Follow these steps to edit the Registry to solve this problem:

1. From the **Start** menu, select **Run**. In the **Open** box, type **regedit** if you are using Windows 95/98 or **regedt32** if you are using Windows NT/2000.
2. In the left pane of the Registry Editor, select the **HKEY_LOCAL_MACHINE\ SOFTWARE\Microsoft\Windows\CurrentVersion\Installer** key.
3. Right-click on the folder named **InProgress**, and then delete it.
4. Close the Registry Editor and restart the computer.

You should now be able to install Office 2000.

Troubleshooting Installation Problems on Networked Systems

The first step in troubleshooting networked installations of Office 2000 is to determine whether Microsoft lists your network operating systems and client software as supported. The following network servers and clients are listed in the Microsoft Knowledge Base as having been tested with Microsoft Office 2000:

- Network operating system (server)
- Microsoft Windows 2000 Server and Advanced Server Networks
- Microsoft Windows NT 4.0 Server Networks
- Microsoft Windows NT 4.0 Workstation Peer-to-Peer networks
- Microsoft Windows 95/98 Peer-to-Peer networks
- Novell Netware 3.x and 4.x networks

Part
I

Ch
5

N O T E Novell NetWare 5 was released late in the Microsoft Office 2000 development cycle, and according to Microsoft, it was not tested for full support. Novell made significant changes to version 5, so you should test Office 2000 in the NetWare 5 environment, as discussed in the earlier section "Setting Up a Test (Prototype) Environment." ■

- Banyan VINES 6 and 7 networks (with the latest patches)
- UNIX NFS networks
- Artisoft LANtastic 6.x or later networks
- DEC Pathworks 5.0d or later networks
- IBM LanServer 4.0 networks

N O T E Microsoft warns that although these networks have been tested, you could still encounter problems when you install or use Microsoft Office 2000 with any of these networks. Issues that arise and are reported to Microsoft will be addressed in Knowledge Base articles, accessible on the Web at **www.microsoft.com/technet/support/searchkb.htm**. ■

Correcting Errors Associated with Security Settings

On a Novell NetWare network or a Windows NT Server network or Windows 2000 domain, each user logs on to the network with a unique username and password and is authenticated by the server. Each user account has permissions to access certain resources (files and folders).

Setup problems might be caused by incorrect security settings, and after Office 2000 is set up successfully, some users might be unable to run Office applications over the network because their accounts do not have the necessary permissions. Check to be sure that full Read/Write permissions have been granted to those users for the folders Office 2000 uses.

In a Windows 95/98 peer-to-peer network, sharing problems are less likely to occur. But be sure users have full Read and Write permissions to the Microsoft Office folder (stored by default in the Program Files directory on the C: drive).

Correcting the Error Associated with Quitting Office 2000 in a NetWare Network

If you are running Office 2000 on a Novell IntranetWare 4.11 network, you might get the following message when you attempt to shut down an Office 2000 application:

```
This connection must be maintained for Novell Directory Services use on tree <tree
name>. It can only be removed after logging out of Directory Services on the tree.
Do you wish to log out of directory services on the tree <tree name> now?
```

This is known to occur when you use the Novell IntranetWare client version 2.2 for Windows 95. You must contact Novell for an updated version of the Novellnp.dll file in order to correct this situation.

Identifying the Source of Error Messages When Running Office 2000 from a Network Source

If you have installed Office 2000 to run from the network and your computer is disconnected from the network, you will receive the following message when you start Windows:

```
The drive or network connection that the shortcut 'Microsoft Office.lnk' refers
to is unavailable.  Make sure that the disk is properly inserted or the network
resource is available, and then try again.
```

This happens because a shortcut to the Microsoft Office startup file is located in the Windows Startup folder, which runs automatically whenever you boot into the operating system. When the network connection is restored, you will no longer get the error message.

N O T E The same error message is displayed if you have installed Office 2000 to run from a CD-ROM and the correct CD-ROM is not in the CD-ROM drive. ■

Pinpointing Setup Problems in a Networked Environment

Tracking down problems in a network installation is always more complex than tracking them on a standalone machine because there are more possible sources of the trouble. If you are unable to pinpoint the cause of your Office 2000 setup problems in a network environment, do the following:

1. Run diagnostic utilities for the Netware, Windows NT, or Windows 2000 server to determine whether the problem is in the networking connection (as opposed to Office 2000).
2. Be sure the desktop machines are running updated versions of the network client software, and then check the Knowledge Base to ascertain whether the client software (such as Novell Client32 or the Microsoft Client Services for NetWare) has been tested and found to be compatible with Office 2000.
3. Check other computers on the network to see whether they have the same problems. This will help you determine whether the problem is related to the server.
4. Try to re-create the problem in the test lab environment if you have one; try it first on a standalone machine and then on a networked machine.

Part

I

Ch

5

Using Log Files for Troubleshooting Installation Problems

Office 2000 creates two log files during Setup and stores them in your \Temp folder. Both are text files, with names similar to "Office 2000 Professional Setup (0002).txt" and "Office 2000 Professional Setup (0002)_MsiExec.txt." The first is created for Setup.exe and the second for the Windows Installer.

NOTE The numbers in parentheses distinguish between multiple instances of running Setup, so "(0002)" would be the log time for the second time you ran Setup. ■

If during installation you receive an error message that indicates a problem with the Windows Installer (such as An error occurred when installing or upgrading the Windows Installer), you should look at the Setup log. Problems with command-line properties and switches are also shown in the Setup log file.

If the Setup log doesn't indicate any errors and its last entry is successfully launched MsiExec, you need to examine the Windows Installer log.

If you received an error message during the installation, such as Internal Error 2343, look for a reference to the error number in the log file. This particular error message would contain a log entry that says SetNotesDir, which indicates that you have uninstalled Lotus Notes, as discussed earlier in this chapter in the section on common internal error messages.

For more information about interpreting the log files, see Microsoft Knowledge Base article Q237957.

Identifying Systemwide Problems That Impact Office 2000 Setup

Setup problems might be caused by any of several systemwide problems, including the following:

- **Lost clusters and other disk errors.** Run ScanDisk in Windows 95/98 or Chkdsk if you are using Windows NT, and then repair any disk problems that are found.

- **Fragmented drive.** Run the Windows 95/98 or 2000 Defragmentation utility; or, if you are using Windows NT, run a third-party defragger such as Diskeeper.

- **Corrupted swap file.** In Windows 95/98, delete the Win386.swp file and create a new swap file.

- **Viruses or TSR virus detectors.** Scan for viruses before running Setup, and then turn off any TSR virus-detection programs.

Getting Help with Setup Problems

Many sources offer help for your Office 2000 installation problems. A Web search for "Office 2000 setup" will yield numerous sites, and more are popping up each day. You can also use the following resources:

- **Local user groups.** In many cities, you can find Office user groups that meet on a regular basis. You might be able to get support with Office 2000 problems by contacting your local Windows user group. Look in your local telephone directory or see www.wugnet.com/ on the Web for more information about user groups.

- **Newsgroups.** Microsoft hosts a public newsgroup devoted exclusively to Office setup issues. Configure your newsreader to connect to the `msnews.microsoft.com news` server, and then subscribe to the `microsoft.public.office.setup` newsgroup. You can post questions to the group and read others' responses to installation problems.
- **Mailing lists.** `Office2000@onelist.com` is a mailing list devoted to discussion of Office 2000. To subscribe, point your Web browser to `www.onelist.com/community/Office2000` or send email to `Office2000-owner@onelist.com` for more information.

Contacting Microsoft

Before you call Microsoft, you should check the Knowledge Base and other Web resources as mentioned earlier. Telephone technical support can be expensive, as well as time-consuming.

If you do find that you need to call, you can minimize frustration by having the following information in hand when you call:

- Your product ID number
- The version and build of your operating system
- The exact error message(s) you received
- Your account number, if you have a technical support contract with Microsoft ●

Part

I

Ch

5

PART II

Customizing Office to Your Organization's Needs

CHAPTER 6

Customizing Word to Your Organization's Needs

by Bill Camarda

Microsoft might have created Word, but with Office 2000 you can *re*-create it to best serve the word processing needs of your organization. A relatively small investment of time in customizing Word can significantly improve the productivity of your workgroup and company. And, as you'll soon see, if you're prepared to invest yet a little more time, you can have an even greater impact.

This chapter gets you to the heart of customizing Word, showing you how to turn nearly any task your users perform into a one-step process accessible from a toolbar, menu, or keyboard. First, you review templates, which enable you to customize Word not only to the needs of individual users, but also to specific documents. You then take a close look at new and existing techniques for customizing the interface and personalizing the menus and toolbars that Word offers (including an objective look at whether you want them and techniques for turning them off).

Then, you walk through the Options dialog box to discover which customizations offer the most potential in your organization. Finally, you learn about Word Startup options that can get your people working a little bit sooner every day.

CAUTION

Some customizations, such as changing keystroke commands or moving menu items, can confuse users who are relying on standard books and training materials. Other customizations should at least be briefly explained to your users, so they aren't surprised by differences between their customized version of Word and the standard version they might use at home, or learn about in books and other training materials.

Using Templates to Customize Word

Templates are critical tools for customizing Word, so it's important that you understand them. Chances are that you already know one role Word templates play: They contain patterns of text, formats, and graphics that determine the basic structure of each Word document. This aspect of working with templates is covered in detail in Chapter 12, "Standardizing Document Production with Word and Excel." This chapter focuses on a less familiar role of templates— *as storage locations for Word customizations.*

Word templates can store a wide range of elements that can enable you to customize your document, including the following:

- Styles
- AutoText entries (boilerplate text, graphics, and other document elements)
- Macros (whether recorded using the Word Macro Recorder or written from scratch in Visual Basic for Applications [VBA])
- Toolbars and buttons that you can add to any toolbar
- Menus and commands that you can add to any menu
- Keyboard shortcuts

TIP

In Word 2000 and Word 97, styles, macros, and custom toolbars can also be stored in documents. However, AutoText boilerplate text entries—an important component of many Word customizations—are still stored only in templates.

Unless you have a specific need to provide customizations for an individual document (for example, you're sending a customized document to a recipient who can't be relied upon to install a separate Word template properly), it still makes sense to maintain all your customizations in templates. For one reason, templates are typically stored only in assigned templates folders, whereas documents can be stored anywhere—making customizations in documents potentially much harder to track.

Later in this chapter, you learn how to add the preceding elements to a template. First, however, you take a closer look at how templates work in Word, so that you can plan a strategy for using them most effectively.

Using the Normal Template

Whenever you open a Word document, you're already using the most important template that Word offers: the Normal template. In Windows, this template is stored as Normal.dot in your Templates folder, typically C:\Windows\Application Data\Microsoft\Templates or C:\Winnt\ Profiles\Username\Application Data\Microsoft\Templates. On the Macintosh, it is typically stored at Microsoft Office 98:Office:Templates:Normal.

All default styles for Word (heading styles, fonts, and so on) are collected in the Normal template, in addition to built-in AutoText entries for letters and business documents. Whenever a user clicks the **New** button on the Standard toolbar, or chooses **Blank Document** in the File, New dialog box, the user creates a document based on the Normal template.

What's more, the styles and other settings stored in the Normal template are always available to *all* Word documents, so any changes made to a user's Normal template can affect new documents created with it later. A template, such as Normal, that is available to all documents is called a *global template*. By default, Normal is the only global template, but you or your colleagues can add others through the Tools, Templates and Add-Ins dialog box.

When users customize their own version of Word with new AutoText entries or macros, they most commonly store the changes in the Normal template (although they can choose to store them in a different template, as you'll see later). Out of the box, the Normal template is 27K, but in the hands of an active user, it can balloon to several hundred kilobytes or more.

N O T E If you delete or rename the Normal template, intentionally or inadvertently, Word restores it to the original settings it had when you first installed Word. This means that deleting or renaming the Normal template is a last resort for salvaging it if you have hopelessly damaged it.

After you delete or rename the Normal template and restart Word, Word looks for the Normal template in the locations where it would typically be found: in the Templates folder, the Workgroup Templates folder if you've set one up, or in a different User Templates folder you might have specified in the User Information tab of the <u>T</u>ools, <u>O</u>ptions dialog box.

When Word cannot find the Normal template in these locations, it assumes the file is not present and creates a new one with standard Word settings. Of course, this restored Normal template does not have any of the customizations contained in the previous Normal template—either customizations you provided or customizations your user added afterward. ▪

Using Other Templates to Create Specialized Documents

Beyond the Normal template, Word also enables you to create and use additional templates—templates built into Word and those that you can create yourself.

If you choose **File**, **New**, click the **Reports** tab, and double-click on **Contemporary Report**, for example, Word creates a new report document based on its built-in Contemporary Report template. Although the Normal template is still available and open, the styles contained in this document are based on the styles contained in the Contemporary Report document. Similarly, any user interface settings that might be stored in the Contemporary Report template (as it happens, there aren't any) are also available for use.

Attaching a New Document Template to an Existing Document   Assuming that you stay with consistent style names, *especially those that the Word built-in styles use*, you can change the look and feel of a document instantly, by attaching a different template to it. This works best if you select a new template that contains style names similar to the ones in the currently attached template. If you are working with a document based on the Contemporary Report template, for example, you could quickly change the document's look by attaching the Professional Report template instead. To attach a new template to your document, follow these steps:

1. Choose **Tools**, **Templates and Add-ins** to display the Templates and Add-ins dialog box (see Figure 6.1).

Part

II

Ch

6

2. Click **Attach**.

3. In the Attach Template dialog box, browse to the template you want to use and click **OK**.

4. In the Templates and Add-ins dialog box, select the **Automatically update document styles** check box.

5. Click **OK**.

FIGURE 6.1

You can change the template attached to a document through the Templates and Add-ins dialog box.

If you've been careful about structuring your templates, this makes it extremely easy to update all your corporate documents in the wake of a company merger or graphic redesign. Create and deploy a new template with revised styles and then attach it to your documents. Or, better yet, copy the updated version of the template *over* the previous version. If **Automatically update document styles** is selected, the documents update themselves automatically.

Making Multiple Global Templates Available to Open Documents You can open as many templates as you need at any given time, although loading a large number of templates slows down the program's performance. As mentioned earlier, Word provides for global templates whose settings are available to all open Word documents. To make a template global, follow these steps:

1. Choose **Tools, Templates and Add-ins**.

2. Click **Add**.

3. In the Add Template dialog box, browse to the template you want to use and click **OK**.

4. The template appears in the Global Templates and Add-ins box with a check mark next to it.

5. Click **OK**.

The template is now globally available to all documents in the current session. If a user exits Word and restarts it again, however, the template is not available unless the user displays this dialog box and reselects the check box associated with the template.

Although a global template's user interface settings and AutoText entries are available for use in any Word document, its styles are not. Even after you open a global template, each document continues to use the styles in the template to which it is attached.

TIP If you want a template to load as a global template automatically every time Word starts, copy it into the Word startup folder. In Windows, this is typically C:\Program Files\Microsoft Office\Office\Startup. On the Macintosh, it is typically Microsoft Office 98:Office:Startup:Word. The Word startup folder is covered in the section "Customizing the Word Startup Folder" at the end of this chapter.

Setting a Strategy for Customizing Templates

Until now, you've been reviewing the basic techniques for loading and working with templates that already exist in Word. Now, briefly consider how you might approach using customized templates to improve productivity in your organization.

If you are deploying Word 2000 for the first time, or if you are confident that your users have not already personalized their Normal templates with AutoText entries or other changes, consider replacing the Word built-in Normal template with one adapted to your company's needs. Your company's Normal template can include all the customizations that the majority of your users can benefit from, as in the following examples:

- Suppose that your department routinely publishes long documents with Word. You might create a special Long Document toolbar with shortcuts for indexing, cross-referencing, building tables of contents, and so on.

- Suppose that you have a series of forms that all your people use—vacation request forms, requisition forms, and so on. You might create a Company menu with commands that load these forms from specialized templates (or, possibly, commands that run Internet Explorer and display an intranet page containing the appropriate form).

In addition to these companywide templates, you can also build specialized templates that address the needs of subsets of your users: specific workgroups or users in many different departments who perform the same tasks. For example:

- Suppose that you're called upon to support the needs of a sales department. You might create a Sales template with toolbar buttons and macros that run your custom mail merge routine for sales letters; and provide access to AutoText boilerplate text for proposal documents.

- Suppose that you support clerical staff who uses Word exclusively to prepare pre-designed letters, memos, and reports. You could create a Clerical Support template that displays a dialog box at startup that allows the user to choose which kind of document to create.

If you support sophisticated users who have already customized their own Normal templates extensively, you can place your companywide customizations in a second template (perhaps Normal2) and copy it to each user's Word startup folder. Now, Word loads two templates at startup: the Normal template each user has customized and the Normal2 template that includes your companywide customizations.

N O T E   Many users do customize their own systems, but *not* in ways that affect the Normal template. For example, they might add words to their custom spelling dictionaries. These dictionaries are separate DIC files, which are available to all Office applications on a specific computer.

Similarly, new text-only AutoCorrect entries are stored in ACL files available to all Office applications. If Word users create formatted AutoCorrect entries, or entries that contain graphics, however, these are stored in the Normal template and are eliminated if you replace the user's Normal template with your own. ■

Creating a New Template for Your Company

If you want to store your custom settings in the Normal template, you need only open a document based on the Normal template and start creating your settings; they are automatically stored in the Normal template.

If, as is more likely, you want to store your customizations in a different template, follow these steps to create a new blank template:

1. Choose **File**, **New**.
2. Select **Blank Document** in the General tab, if it is not already selected.
3. Click **Template** in the Create New area.
4. Click **OK**.

You now have a new template where you can store customized text and graphics, styles, AutoText entries, custom toolbar and menu settings, macros, and other elements.

TIP   If you already have a document you want to use as a basis for your template, save the document as a template by following these steps:

1. Choose **File**, **Save As**.
2. Choose **Document Template** (*.dot) from the **Save as type** drop-down box. Word switches folders to display your current template folder, typically C:\Windows\Profiles\ *username*\Application Data\Microsoft\Templates.
3. Click **Save**.

Modifying Styles in the New Template   A key element of many templates is a set of consistent, distinctive styles that help users build consistently formatted, attractive documents.

▶ For more information about building templates with consistent styles, **see** Chapter 12, "Standardizing Document Production with Word and Excel," on **p. 311**.

When you create a new template, it contains the styles that appeared in the template that you based it on. Word provides several ways to change these styles. Following are two approaches that are especially worth discussing:

■ With Style by Example, you can format text manually and transform that formatted text into a style. Style by Example is extremely easy to use and enables you to see exactly how your text will look. The styles you modify are stored in the document you have open—in this case, the new template you've just created. Also, you cannot change the Normal style using this feature.

■ Through the Word Style dialog box (accessible through Format, Style), you can create all your styles, optionally basing one style on another to ensure consistency. The Style dialog box is less intuitive, but it is more systematic, enabling you to see all the style options available to you.

Each approach is covered in the following sets of steps. You can choose the one that's most convenient or use them both together. To create a new style using Style by Example, follow these steps:

1. Enter a paragraph of text in the template you've created. This is dummy text that you can use to simply give you something to format. Any amount of text is sufficient, as long as you end it with a paragraph mark.

2. Format the paragraph the way you want it.

3. Select the paragraph.

4. In the Style box at the left end of the Formatting toolbar, type the style name you want to use. If you use a custom style name that already exists—other than one built into Word—the Modify Style dialog box opens, as shown in Figure 6.2. Word then asks whether you want to reformat the style or reformat the text using the existing style. Choose to reformat the style.

5. Click **OK**.

FIGURE 6.2
The Modify Style dialog box asks whether you want to change the style or reformat the text using the existing style.

Style box

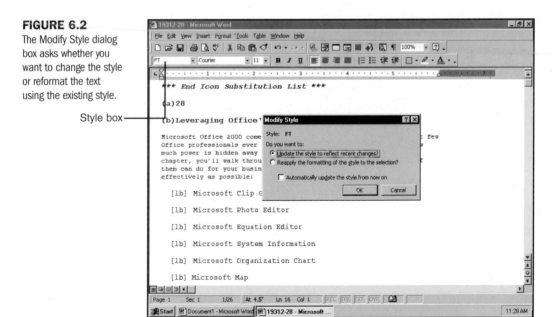

To create a new style using the Style dialog box, follow these steps:

1. Choose **Format**, **Style**.

2. In the **Styles** scroll box, choose **Normal**, if it isn't already selected (see Figure 6.3).

3. Click **New**. The New Style dialog box appears.

4. Enter a new style name in the Name text box.

TIP

Because you chose **Normal** in the preceding step 2, your new style is based on the Normal style, which means that it contains all of the Normal style's attributes, except where you override them. As you build a set of styles, you might find it convenient to base some of these new styles on one another. If you want all your newsletter headlines to use the same font, for example, create a basic Headline style and then create additional styles based on it—changing font size and adding italic, boldface, or effects as desired.

---

5. Click **Format** to display a list of formatting categories, as shown in Figure 6.4. When you choose one of these categories, its standard dialog box appears. If you choose **Font**, for example, the Font dialog box appears.

6. When you finish changing the formats in a formatting dialog box, click **OK** to return to the New Style dialog box.

7. Repeat steps 5 and 6 to add all of the desired formatting to the style.

8. Select the **Add to template** check box and click **OK** in the New Style dialog box.

9. Click **Close** in the Style dialog box.

FIGURE 6.3
In the Style dialog box, choose **Normal** as the style you want to modify.

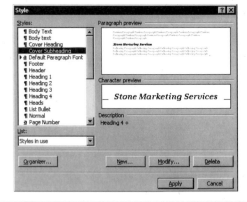

CAUTION

If you want to stay in control of the styles you create, you might want to turn off the Word automatic style creation feature, which creates new styles as you format text, even if you don't ask it to do so. To turn this feature off, follow these steps:

1. Choose **Tools**, **AutoCorrect**.

2. Click the **AutoFormat As You Type** tab.

3. Clear the **Define Styles Based on Your Formatting** check box.

4. Click **OK**.

FIGURE 6.4
Click **Format** to choose the category of formatting you want to change.

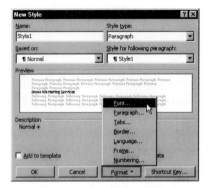

Adding AutoText Entries to the New Document Template   AutoText entries are blocks of boilerplate text (and other document elements) that you can insert into any document by typing a few characters of the entry's name and pressing **Enter** as soon as a ScreenTip appears, offering to replace text you've typed with the corresponding AutoText entry.

▶ AutoText entries are covered in detail in Chapter 12, "Standardizing Document Production with Word and Excel," on **p. 311**.

To incorporate an AutoText entry into a custom template, making it available to all documents based on that template, follow these steps:

1. Open the custom template or a document based on it.
2. Select the material that you want to incorporate into an AutoText entry.
3. Choose **Insert**, **AutoText**, **AutoText**. The AutoText tab of the AutoCorrect dialog box opens.
4. In the Look In dialog box, choose the name of your custom template, instead of Normal.
5. In the **Enter AutoText Entries Here** text box, edit the name of your AutoText entry.
6. Click **Add**.

Adding Macros to the New Template   VBA macros, covered in more detail in Chapter 17, "Managing Office Programmability," are a key element of many custom Word templates. You can record or write VBA macros that automate complex procedures and then perform the following tasks:

■ Attach those macros to toolbar buttons, menu commands, and/or keyboard shortcuts, giving users fast access to them.

■ Run macros automatically at specific times, without any user intervention.

All the macros stored in the Normal template are available to all the documents a user creates. All the macros stored in other templates loaded as global templates are available to all documents, as long as those templates are still loaded as global templates. In addition, macros stored in a custom template are available to any document attached to that template.

N O T E   In Word 97, Microsoft changed the way macros are stored, and the new approach is retained in Word 2000. This is discussed later in this chapter, in "Using the Word Organizer to Copy Elements Between Templates," p. 141. ▨

Recording Macros to Store in Your New Template   By default, when you record a new macro, it is stored in the Normal template. To store a macro in another template when you record it, however, follow these steps:

1. Choose **Tools**, **Macro**, **Record New Macro**.
2. Enter a name and description for the macro in the **Macro Name** and **Description** text boxes.
3. In the **Store Macro In** drop-down box, choose the custom template where you want to store the macro. (The template must already be loaded.)
4. Click **OK**.
5. Record the macro.
6. Click the **Stop Recording** button on the Stop Recording toolbar when you're finished.

Defining Macros to Run Automatically   As listed in Table 6.1, Word reserves five macro names for automatic macros intended to run at specific times during a Word session. Word looks for macros using these names and runs them automatically, without user intervention.

Table 6.1   Automatic Macros Available in Word

Macro Name	What It Does
AutoExec	If stored in the Normal template, runs when Word starts. If stored in another global template, loads whenever that global template is loaded.
AutoExit	Runs when Word exits.
AutoNew	Runs whenever you create a new document based on the template containing the AutoNew macro.
AutoOpen	Runs whenever you open a document based on the template containing the AutoOpen macro.
AutoClose	Runs whenever you close a document based on the template containing the AutoClose macro.

You can use the following automatic macros in a wide variety of ways:

- You might use an AutoExec macro to automatically open a specific document, such as a tracking sheet, or to open the last document the user was working on.
- You could use an AutoNew macro to display a dialog box giving the user choices about what should be entered in a document and then inserting text into the document based on the user's selections. Some companies use AutoNew to display the Summary tab of the File, Properties dialog box, encouraging the user to enter information that can be used later to track documents.

- You could write an AutoOpen macro to check whether the document being opened was written by the individual opening it. If not, it might ask whether the reader wants to turn on the Track Changes feature to mark revisions.

- You might use an AutoClose macro to automatically create a backup copy of the file in a different folder or location on the network.

- You could create an AutoExit macro to restore the Word user interface to the settings it had when the session began.

If you're careful, you can store multiple AutoNew, AutoClose, AutoExec, or AutoOpen macros on the same computer, as long as they are stored in different templates. This can come in handy. For example, it enables you to define a set of actions that should occur whenever a run-of-the-mill document is created, but a different set of actions that take place when a *specialized* document is created using a custom template.

Customizing the Word Interface

This section focuses on changing your toolbars and menus to best suit the needs of your business. You can store these changes in templates, which enables you to customize the appearance of Word for all your users (via the Normal template or another global template) or only for specific users creating their own documents (via custom document templates attached to specific documents).

NOTE Later in this chapter, you learn how to create additional customizations in the Tools, Options dialog box, which are stored in the Registry. ■

Word enables you to not only create your own toolbars and menus, but also add virtually anything to any new or existing toolbar or menu, whether you created it or not. For example, you can create toolbar buttons or menu items corresponding to the following:

- Any of the hundreds of Word buttons already assigned to specific tasks. (Many of these already appear on one or another of the toolbars in Word, but quite a few don't.)

- Any individual VBA command corresponding to an individual task that Word can perform. These commands include every Word menu item, most Word formatting options, and even obscure commands such as **GoToNextFootnote** or **DrawInsertMoon** (which switches you into Page Layout view and transforms your mouse pointer into a moon-shaped drawing tool).

- Any macro you've recorded or written in VBA.

- Any font available on your computer. (In other words, you can create a button that reformats text in whatever font you specify.)

- Any AutoText entry you've created. (In other words, when a user clicks your customized toolbar button, Word inserts the text, graphics, or field codes associated with the entry.)

- Any style you've created or any built-in Word style.

Part
II

Ch
6

You can add customized menus, toolbars, and keyboard shortcuts to the Normal template—in which case, all documents will have access to these shortcuts unless you specify otherwise. Or, you can customize a specific template, creating different working environments for different situations. Imagine that the following three people share a computer:

- Joe has poor eyesight. Joe's template automatically displays enlarged toolbar buttons and text magnified to 150 percent.

- Diane is the part-time office manager. Diane's template includes toolbar buttons for sending email, creating purchase orders, and completing quarterly reports on office activity.

- Kevin is a salesperson who's on the road most of the time. Kevin's template duplicates the customized template in his notebook PC, providing the tools he needs to build customized sales documents fast.

You could write an AutoNew macro to display a dialog box asking who is using the computer (or checking who most recently logged on to Windows). Based on this information, the macro would automatically load the appropriate template, thereby customizing Word to the needs of the specific user.

Personalizing Your Menus and Toolbars

Because many users find the Word interface quite complex, Word and the rest of Office 2000 contains personalized menus and more easily customized toolbars. When users first display Word, they see abbreviated menus that contain only those commands Microsoft expects them to use most. If a user selects a menu and pauses for a moment, the remaining commands appear.

As the user works with additional commands, these become part of the set that always appears. In this way, Word attempts to personalize itself for individual users, showing them the commands they use while eliminating clutter associated with commands they never use.

Word also displays abbreviated versions of the Standard and Formatting toolbar on the same line, including only those buttons Microsoft expects you to use most. You can remove buttons (and add selected buttons) directly from the toolbar, instead of using the traditional customization tools in Word. As you see later, however, the Customize dialog box remains available for all customizations, including those that can't be performed directly from the toolbar.

Evaluating Personalized Menus and Toolbars for Your Organization

As with most Microsoft products nowadays, personalized menus and toolbars are the outgrowth of extensive market and usability testing—and Microsoft's good-faith attempt to retain features while improving simplicity. For many organizations, these features are likely to achieve the goals Microsoft has set for them.

But you should evaluate carefully whether these features are necessarily right for your organization. For instance, organizations whose users are relatively experienced with Office might find personalized menus and toolbars distracting. They might wonder where their familiar menu commands and toolbar buttons have gone. In organizations like this, the new features might lead to more support calls, not less. These features might also complicate the use of standardized training materials, which assume that every user has access to essentially the same menus and toolbars.

Turning Off Personalized Menus and Toolbars for Your Organization

If you decide you do not care to use these features, you can turn them off on a single workstation—or use system policies to turn off personalized menus on many workstations at once.

> **CAUTION**
>
> If you turn these features off in Word (or in any other Office application), you've turned them off in *all* Office 2000 applications.

To turn personalized menus and toolbars off on a single, local workstation, run Word and follow these steps:

1. Choose **Tools, Customize**.
2. Click the **Options** tab.
3. Clear the **Standard and Formatting Toolbars Share One Row** check box.
4. Clear the **Menus Show Recently Used Commands First** check box.
5. Click **Close**.

You can also use the System Policy Editor to turn off personalized menus and toolbars on any workstation subject to your system policies. However, you cannot turn off the Standard and Formatting Toolbars Share One Row setting.

NOTE The System Policy Editor enables you to control a wide range of Office features centrally through *system policies*, which are applied when a user logs on to the network. The System Policy Editor is part of the Office 2000 Resource Kit Toolbox, downloadable at

`http://www.microsoft.com/office/ork`

When working with system policies for Office 2000, use this version of the System Policy Editor, not the previous versions that were included with Windows 95/98 or Windows NT 4.0. ■

▶ For more information about working with the System Policy Editor, **see** "Using System Policies with Office 2000," in Chapter 37, on **p. 970**.

To create a system policy that turns off personalized menus, follow these steps:

1. Run the System Policy Editor. Assuming that you have installed System Policy Editor as part of the Office 2000 Resource Kit Toolbox, choose **Start, Programs, Microsoft Office Tools, Microsoft Office 2000 Resource Kit Tools, System Policy Editor**.
2. Choose **Options, Policy Template**.

Part
II

Ch
6

3. Select the Office9.adm policy template (if necessary, first browse to it and add it to the list); click **OK.**

4. Click the **New** button and double-click **Default User**.

5. Go to **Microsoft Office 2000, Tools, Customize Options**.

6. Select the **Menus Show Recently Used Commands First** check box.

7. At the bottom of the dialog box, leave the **Check to Enforce Setting On** check box cleared.

8. Choose **OK.**

9. Choose **File, Save** to save the POL policy file you just created.

10. Copy the policy file to a location on your network where it can be added to the network logon script for users who are affected by it.

Changing the Contents of a Word Toolbar

Often, you might want to change the contents of a Word toolbar—possibly to simplify Word's interface or to simplify access to custom features you've created. Word 2000 provides the following two ways to make changes to a toolbar:

■ If you want to remove toolbar buttons, or add toolbar buttons that are closely related to those which are already displayed, use the Add or Remove Buttons feature.

■ If you want to make more extensive changes, such as adding buttons to a toolbar for custom features, use the Add or Remove Buttons feature, discussed next in the section "Customizing Word Toolbars More Thoroughly."

If you wish one of your toolbars had slightly different buttons, Word 2000 makes it easier than ever to do something about it. Click the down arrow at the far right of any Word toolbar and click **Add or Remove Buttons**. An extensive list of buttons appears (see Figure 6.5).

If you want to add a button that doesn't currently appear, click a place to select it. If you want to remove a button, click the button to clear its check mark. To reset the toolbar to its original buttons, choose **Reset Toolbar**. To customize the toolbar more thoroughly than you can do here, click **Customize**. (The next section covers customizing toolbars more thoroughly.)

On the Add or Remove Buttons list associated with the Standard toolbar, Microsoft provides buttons for three widely used features, some of which have appeared on the Standard toolbar in one or another previous version of Word: Close, Envelopes and Labels, and Find. Similarly, Microsoft makes available Formatting toolbar buttons for *these* commonly used features: Single Spacing, 1.5 Spacing, Double Spacing, Superscript, Subscript, and Language.

Customizing Word Toolbars More Thoroughly

Although the Add or Remove Buttons lists are extremely convenient, you might find you need to add buttons that aren't included there or create an entirely new toolbar. To more thoroughly customize your toolbars, choose **Tools, Customize, Toolbars**. The Customize dialog box shown in Figure 6.6 appears.

FIGURE 6.5
Adding related buttons to a toolbar.

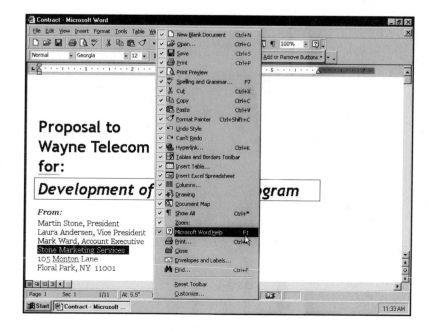

FIGURE 6.6
From the Customize dialog box, you can customize toolbars, menus, and keyboard commands.

Toolbars that are already open are selected with check boxes; you can display any other toolbar for customization by marking its check box.

Creating a New Toolbar   To create a new toolbar, follow these steps:

1. Click the **Toolbars** tab in the Customize dialog box if necessary and then click **New**; the New Toolbar dialog box opens (see Figure 6.7).

2. In the **Toolbar name** text box, enter a brief descriptive name for your toolbar.

3. In the **Make toolbar available to** drop-down box, choose the template where you want to store your new toolbar. The template must already be open.

4. Click **OK**. A small toolbar containing no buttons appears on the screen. You might want to move it out of the way by dragging its title bar.

Part

II

Ch

6

FIGURE 6.7
Enter the name of the new toolbar and the open template where you want to store it.

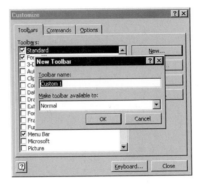

Adding a Command to a Toolbar   Now that you have displayed the toolbars you want to customize, click the **Commands** tab in the Customize dialog box (see Figure 6.8).

FIGURE 6.8
The Commands tab of the Customize dialog box.

Word displays the commands available to be added to a toolbar, organized into the following categories:

- **File, Edit, View, Insert, Format, Tools, Table, and Window and Help.** These categories correspond to the commands on each Word menu, with many additions. The File menu, for example, contains commands such as Close All and Save All.

- **Web, Drawing, AutoShapes, Borders, Mail Merge, Forms, and Control Toolbox.** These categories correspond to commands available on specialized Word toolbars—again, with many additions. The Drawing category, for example, contains specialized tools such as Shadow On/Off and Disassemble Picture, which aren't included on the standard Drawing toolbar.

- **All Commands.** This lists the methods available to VBA—in other words, virtually anything you can do to anything in Word is here—more than 1,200 commands in all.

- **Macros.** This lists all the recorded macros currently available to Word—in other words, in global templates that are currently loaded.

- **Fonts.** This lists all fonts installed on the computer.

- **AutoText.** This lists all AutoText entries currently available to Word.

- **Styles.** This lists all styles in use in the document that is currently open (but not necessarily all styles available to Word).

- **Built-in Menus.** This includes copies of each menu built into Word. Note that you can add menus not only to Word's menu bar but also to toolbars. Also note that the Work and Font menus are included here. This means you can customize Word for Windows to include all the menus contained in Word 98 for the Macintosh—simplifying the transition for Macintosh users who are moving to Windows.

- **New Menu.** This enables you to add a new menu to either the menu bar or any toolbar.

To add a button to a toolbar, select it from the **Commands** scroll box and drag it to the position on the toolbar where you want it. As you move the button onto a toolbar, a thick crosshatch marking appears to help you see where your mouse pointer is. When you release the mouse button, the new button appears on the toolbar.

Changing a Button's Text or Image   In many cases, the commands you add to toolbars already have ready-made icons attached to them. This is not always the case, however. If you drag a custom macro to a toolbar, for example, Word inserts the entire macro name, including its project name (for example, Normal.NewMacros.NameOfMacro). This takes up a lot of real estate. To solve the problem, right-click on the button to display the Customize shortcut menu.

If you can abbreviate the macro's name to a reasonable length (three to five characters, for example), edit it in the Name text box. If not, click **Change Button Image**; Word displays 42 generic buttons available for you to use (see Figure 6.9).

FIGURE 6.9
Choosing a button in the Customize shortcut menu.

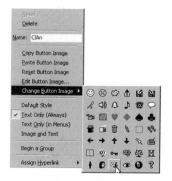

If none of these buttons fit the bill, you can create your own button by choosing Edit Button Image from the shortcut menu. The Word Button Editor appears (see Figure 6.10). In this dialog box, you can edit your button one pixel at a time—an excruciatingly slow task.

Part

II

Ch

6

FIGURE 6.10
The Word Button Editor.

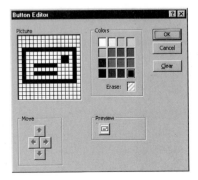

Unless you're an artist blessed with patience, you might find that creating your own button image from scratch with the Button Editor is difficult—to put it charitably. You do have an alternative: You can import an image from a clip art library or graphics program.

Unfortunately, relatively few clip art images, including those in Word, were designed to be clear at 1/4-inch square. But if you want to try to import art, follow these steps:

1. Open the application containing the artwork.
2. Copy the artwork into the Clipboard. If you have a choice, copy it as a bitmap.
3. Switch back to Word.
4. Be sure the toolbar button you want to change is visible.
5. Choose **Tools, Customize**.
6. With the dialog box open, right-click on the button you want to change to display the Customize shortcut menu.
7. Choose **Paste Button Image**.

Resetting Toolbars to Their Original Settings   If you decide you've gone too far in changing a toolbar, you can restore it to its original settings by performing the following steps:

1. Choose **Tools, Customize**.
2. In the **Toolbars** scroll box, select the toolbar you want to reset.
3. Click **Reset**.
4. Click **Close**.

Making Toolbars Easier to Work With   Earlier in this chapter, you saw that the Options tab of the Customize dialog box enables you to turn off the Office 2000 new personalized menus and toolbars. The same tab also contains four options that can make Word toolbars a bit easier for users to work with (see Figure 6.11).

One of these options, **Show ScreenTips on toolbars**, is turned on by default. With this option turned on, when a user hovers the mouse pointer over a toolbar button, Word displays the button's title. You can help users learn hard-to-remember keyboard shortcuts by turning on a complementary option: **Show shortcut keys in ScreenTips**. With this option checked, Word displays the keyboard shortcut that is equivalent to the toolbar button, along with the button's name.

FIGURE 6.11
The Options tab of the
Customize dialog box.

As the resolution of computer monitors has increased to 800×600 and beyond, Word's toolbar
buttons have grown increasingly tiny. You can compensate by checking the Large Icons
option. As you can see in Figure 6.12, these icons are *very* large.

FIGURE 6.12
A toolbar with the
Large Icons setting
turned on.

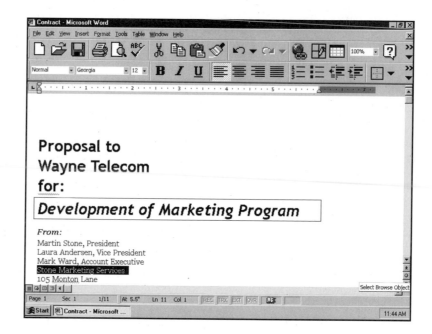

▶ For more information about making Office and Windows easier to use for physically challenged
individuals, **see** Chapter 43, "Making Office More Accessible to People with Disabilities," on
p. 1093.

Finally, if your colleagues make extensive use of fonts, you can help them see what specific
fonts will look like, by selecting the **List font names in their font** check box. Now, when a
user clicks the down arrow next to the **Font** drop-down box, all the font names appear in the
fonts themselves (see Figure 6.13).

Part

II

Ch

6

FIGURE 6.13
Displaying font names
in their fonts.

Customizing Menus

You can also create or customize menus from the Customize dialog box. To create a new menu, follow these steps:

1. Choose **Tools**, **Customize**.
2. Click the **Commands** tab.
3. In the **Categories** scroll box, select **New Menu**.
4. Click **New Menu** in the Commands scroll box.
5. Drag New Menu from the Commands scroll box to the menu bar, dropping it where you want the new menu to appear. You now have a new menu named *New Menu*.
6. Right-click **New Menu** in the menu bar; the Customize shortcut menu appears.
7. In the **Name** text box, enter the name that you want to use for your new menu.

 TIP To specify a keyboard shortcut, place the & (ampersand) symbol before the letter to use as the shortcut. Don't use the following letters, which are already shortcuts for other menus: F, E, V, I, O, T, A, W, or H.

8. Press **Enter**. The edited menu name appears on your menu bar.

Adding a Menu to a Toolbar   In Word 2000, menus can also be added to toolbars. While some users find it disconcerting to find menu items scattered among toolbar buttons, this can be helpful for organizing extensive numbers of custom commands. For example, you might create a custom toolbar that contains buttons that run complex macros together with a menu listing custom documents you've created. The user might choose a reporting document from the menu and then click a button to run a macro that retrieves certain types of data.

To add a menu to a toolbar, follow these steps:

1. Be sure the toolbar you want to place the menu on is visible. Either display it using **View**, **Toolbars** or by choosing it in the Toolbars tab of the Customize dialog box.
2. If you are adding a custom menu, create the menu, following the steps in the previous section, "Customizing Menus."
3. After you've placed your custom menu on the menu bar, with the Customize dialog box still open, drag the custom menu from the menu bar to the toolbar location you want.

Adding a Command to a Menu   Whether you want to add a command to a built-in menu or a new menu, the procedure is the same. With the Commands tab of the Customize dialog box displayed, follow these steps:

1. Select the category of commands you want.

2. Select the specific command from the **Commands** scroll box.

3. Drag the command to the desired menu, which can be located on the menu bar or on a toolbar.

4. With the mouse button still pressed, drag down the menu to the location where you want to place the new command.

5. Release the mouse button. The new menu item remains displayed and selected.

6. If you want to edit the command—either to shorten it or change the keyboard shortcut associated with it—right-click on it and click inside the **Name** text box on the Customize shortcut menu.

7. Edit the command name and press **Enter**.

Removing a Command from a Menu   To remove a command from a menu, display the Customize dialog box, select the command from the menu, and drag it off the menu. You can drag commands off any menu, including Word's built-in menus. You can also drag entire menus off the menu bar.

Using the Word Organizer to Copy Elements Between Templates

You've now walked through creating a custom template and adding styles, AutoText entries, macros, toolbars, and menus to that template. But what happens if one of your colleagues has built a macro you'd like to incorporate in a custom template for wider use? Or what if you need to reorganize your library of AutoText entries, combining entries stored in multiple templates? Or how about if you want to copy customizations into a specific document, for use by a colleague who doesn't want to bother with installing templates?

When you need to copy elements between templates (or between templates and documents), use the Organizer.

To display the Organizer, follow these steps:

1. Choose **Tools**, **Templates and Add-ins**.

2. Click the **Organizer** button. The Organizer appears (see Figure 6.14).

You can copy elements in either direction, as follows:

1. Click the tab containing the element that you want to copy. (Because you can't store AutoText entries in a document, if you click the **AutoText** tab, Word displays the template to which your document is attached.)

2. In either the left or right pane, click the element that you want to copy.

3. Click **Copy**.

Part

II

Ch

6

FIGURE 6.14
In the Organizer, you can copy styles, toolbars, and macro project items between templates and documents; and copy AutoText entries between templates.

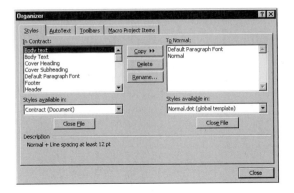

 TIP   You can delete a template element by selecting it, clicking **Delete**, and clicking **Yes** to confirm. You can rename a template element by selecting it, clicking **Rename**, entering a new name in the Rename dialog box, and clicking **OK**.

By default, the Organizer displays the elements stored in your current document in the left pane, and elements stored in the Normal template in the right pane. If you want to change which two templates (or documents) are displayed, see the following procedure:

1. Click **Close File** on either side of the Organizer dialog box. The template or document's elements disappear, and the name of the button you clicked changes to Open File.

2. Click **Open File**.

3. Browse to and select the template (or document) you want to open.

4. If necessary, repeat the process in the opposite pane, so the Organizer displays both of the templates (or documents) you want to work with.

If you are creating a custom template, be careful to copy all the elements into it that you need. In particular, if you create a toolbar with buttons that run macros, be sure you also copy the macros.

In Word 6.0 and Word 95, the Organizer copied individual macros, and Word 2000 still copies individual macros that have been converted from older WordBasic versions. For macros created in Word 2000, for example, the Organizer only moves *macro project items*, in other words, modules that might contain multiple individual macros all stored together within a specific template. As a result, you might not see the names of the VBA macros you expect to see.

If this happens, choose **Tools**, **Macro**, **Visual Basic Editor** to open the Visual Basic Editor, and then browse the Project window to identify the module containing the macros you need. (If you've recorded the macro as part of the Normal template, for example, you'll find it in **Normal\Modules\NewMacros**.) Then use the Organizer to move that module.

Keep in mind that the Visual Basic Editor displays modules contained only in templates that are currently in use, so you might have to open additional templates in Word before you find the macro you're looking for.

Customizing Word Options

In Word, the Options dialog box (**Tools**, **Options**) brings together ten categories of Word features that can easily be customized. By default, users can control these settings; however, you can also control many of these centrally—either by setting them during the installation process (see Chapter 2, "Automating and Customizing Office Installations Across the Network") or later via System Policies. Following are the ten groups of features that can be customized:

- **View.** These options control how users view their documents.
- **General.** This category includes options that don't fit anywhere else.
- **Edit.** These options control how Word reacts when users edit a document.
- **Print.** These options control how and what Word prints.
- **Save.** These options control how Word saves documents, including how and when Word saves files and what gets saved in each file.
- **Spelling & Grammar.** These options control how Word checks spelling and grammar.
- **Track Changes.** These options control the way Word represents revisions as it tracks them. (These options are covered in Chapter 13, "Using the Workgroup Revision Tools in Word and Excel.")
- **User Information.** These options store the information Word uses whenever it needs a user's name, initials, and mailing address.
- **Compatibility.** These options make it easier to use documents created in other formats and work with the users who created those documents.
- **File Locations.** These options specify where Word looks for documents, images, templates, and other files it needs.

In the following sections, you learn what each option offers you, the Office administrator, and which offers the most potential in your environment.

N O T E   There are a few settings that you cannot control centrally from the System Policy Editor—primarily settings that apply to a single document. There are also a few settings that users cannot control via the Options dialog box, but you can control centrally. Several of these are designed to help Word work more effectively in global environments. ■

▶ For more information about working with system policies, **see** Chapter 37, "Reducing Office 2000's Total Cost of Ownership," on **p. 963**.

Part

II

Ch

6

Customizing View Options

You've already learned that Word 2000 offers new ways to control and simplify the user interface—and the user experience. You can control many other aspects of how Word looks through the View tab of the Options dialog box. In the following two sections, you review controlling these settings locally, at a user workstation, and then centrally via system policies.

Controlling View Options Locally Through the Options Dialog Box   The default settings for
View options are shown in Figure 6.15.

FIGURE 6.15

The View tab of the
Options dialog box
brings together a
variety of changes to
how Word looks.

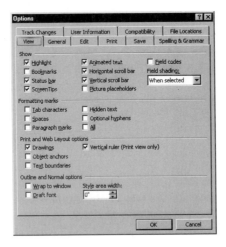

The selections in the first category of View options, **Show**, control features in both your document and user interface. For example, to make more space in your editing window, you can clear check boxes that control the display of the following:

- The **Status bar** at the bottom of the Word editing window.
- The **Horizontal scroll bar** that is used to scroll left and right. (If you use the **Wrap to window** option, you'll rarely need the **Horizontal scroll bar**.)
- The **Vertical scroll bar** that scrolls up and down through documents.

To make a heavily marked-up document more readable, you can temporarily hide highlighting by clearing the **Highlight** check box.

Selecting the **Bookmarks** check box adds gray brackets at the beginning and end of any text you've bookmarked. Displaying bookmarks can make it easier to build index entries, cross-references, and other automated features based on them.

To make Word run a bit faster, especially when you're focused on editing text and don't care about images, you can select **Picture placeholders**. This instructs Word to display an empty box wherever you've inserted an image. When **Picture placeholders** is turned off, Word spends time processing images for display, even if you're merely scrolling past them to another destination. The more images your document contains, the slower Word becomes.

N O T E   Because the placeholder boxes are the same size as the original images, you can use
Picture placeholders in Print Layout view to evaluate layouts more quickly when you
don't need to view the pictures themselves. ■

Selecting the **Animated text** check box enables Word to display animation created in the Animation tab of the Format, Font dialog box, such as sparkle text. When this box is cleared, the animation disappears and the text appears as it will when printed (that is, without animation).

Clearing the **ScreenTips** check box turns off ScreenTips that appear when you hover the mouse pointer over a comment, tracked change, footnote, or endnote.

> **N O T E** To turn off the AutoComplete ScreenTips that appear when you start typing text that matches an AutoText entry, clear the **Show AutoComplete Tip for AutoText and Dates** check box in the AutoText tab of the AutoCorrect dialog box. To turn off ScreenTips that appear on toolbar buttons, choose **Tools**, **Customize**, **Options**, and clear the **Show ScreenTips on Toolbars** check box. ▪

Selecting the **Field codes** check box causes field codes to be displayed throughout documents, rather than the results they generate. Users might prefer this option when troubleshooting fields, such as cross-references or index entries that aren't delivering the results they expect.

> **N O T E** Whether this box is selected or not, users can still toggle field codes on and off by selecting them and pressing Shift+F9. However, as long as the check box is selected, when a user enters new fields, they appear as field codes rather than results. ▪

In the **Field shading** drop-down box, you can tell Word how to keep you posted about the presence of field codes in your document. The default option, when selected, tells Word to display field codes in gray only when you've selected or clicked within them.

The **Always** option tells Word to show field codes and field results in gray *all* the time. Marking field codes in gray shows you where they begin and end and reminds you which information is being generated in your document automatically. However, you (or a colleague unfamiliar with Word field codes) might find the gray formatting distracting. If so, choose **Never**.

> **CAUTION**
>
> If this option is set to **Never**, users might inadvertently manually edit field codes that are later automatically reset to their original text when the field codes are updated.

Controlling the Display of Nonprinting Characters By default, when users click the **Show/Hide Paragraph** button on the Standard toolbar, Word displays much more than paragraph marks. Word also shows the following:

- Tab characters
- Spaces (places a dot everywhere a space was typed)
- Hidden text (displays all hidden text, including hidden fields)
- Optional hyphens (shows where hyphens might appear in an automatically hyphenated document)

At times, this might give users more information than they want. For example, users might want to see all the paragraph marks in their documents to help them manage important paragraph formatting. However, they might not want to see an obtrusive dot between every single word on your page.

You can control whether each type of formatting mark appears by clearing the **All** check box and then selecting or clearing its check box in the **Formatting Marks** area of the **View** tab.

TIP   Clicking the **Show/Hide Paragraph Marks** button does the same thing as checking the **All** box in the View tab of the Options dialog box.

All supersedes any other check boxes. This is a convenience; you can set up Word to display the nonprinting characters you want to see most of the time, and then simply toggle **All** on or off when you need to see the rest of them, rather than adjusting each setting individually.

Controlling Print and Web Layout Options   Print and Web Layout options controls four elements that can help you manage the way your document appears in print or when displayed in a Web browser. Following are the available choices:

- Clearing the **Drawings** check box hides any drawings a user has placed in the drawing layer of a document: AutoShapes, WordArt, clip art, callouts, and text boxes. (Drawings are already hidden in Normal or Outline view.)
- Selecting the **Object anchors** check box displays object anchors, so you can see how drawings and other document elements are linked to specific paragraphs or other elements on your page.
- Selecting the **Text boundaries** check box displays your current margins with a thin dotted line. It also places dotted lines at column and object borders—giving you more visual feedback about where text can be placed.
- Finally, in Print Layout view, clearing the **Vertical ruler** hides the rulerthat appears to the left of the editing window.

Using Wrap to Window   In documents with narrow left and right margins, users might find that some text stretches past the far-right edge of the screen—requiring them to scroll back and forth on every line. **Wrap to window** tells Word to make sure all text appears within the width of your screen. Although this slightly reduces the what-you-see-is-what-you-get accuracy of the display, it eliminates the horizontal scrolling.

Because **Wrap to window** tells Word to display widths inaccurately, it's unavailable in Page Layout and Web Layout views.

Displaying Text in Draft Font   **Draft font** enables you to display all the text in your document using a Windows 12-point typewriter font. Spacing and paragraph indents are correct.

If you have a slower computer, **Draft font** can significantly improve the program's performance. Some users turn on draft font for original writing and then turn it off when they need to work with formatting.

Controlling Style Area Width   Style area width enables users to display the styles associated with each paragraph in a column to the left of their document text (see Figure 6.16). This makes it more convenient to identify and work with heavily styled documents. By default, this is set to 0"—in other words, no **Style area width**. If you set it to a higher number, such as 0.8", the style information becomes visible.

FIGURE 6.16
This figure shows a document displaying styles in use at the left edge of the editing window.

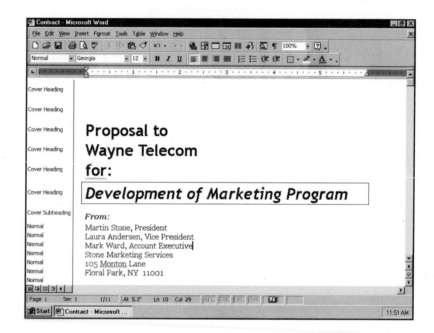

Controlling View Options Centrally from the System Policy Editor   Every setting in the View tab can be controlled from the System Policy Editor. To find these settings, open the Default User tab and go to **Microsoft Word 2000, Tools | Options, View**. Note that two additional options can be set here that are unavailable in the View options dialog box:

- If you turn on the **Show, Left Scroll Bar** policy setting, users see a left scroll bar and a right vertical ruler.

- If you turn on the **Formatting Marks, Optional Breaks** policy setting, Word displays optional hyphenation breaks that show where words would be broken with hyphens if a document were hyphenated and printed now.

Customizing General Options

Quite simply, the General tab of the Options dialog box is where Word collects the options that don't fit anywhere else. In the following two sections, you review controlling these settings locally, at a user workstation, and then centrally via system policies.

Part
II

Ch
6

Controlling General Options Locally Through the Options Dialog Box   Each of the General options can be controlled locally from a user workstation through the General tab of the Options dialog box. The default settings are shown in Figure 6.17. The settings are listed and discussed in the following:

FIGURE 6.17

The default settings for the General tab of the Options dialog box.

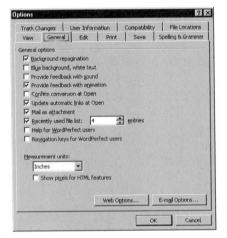

- **Background repagination.** This option controls whether Word keeps track of page numbering continuously while you work. By default, it does. Like all of the Word automatic, on-the-fly features, this one takes a little bit of processing power. So, if you're finding that Word 2000 runs too slowly on your computers, you might try turning off Background repagination. (**Background pagination** is always on in Print Layout and Web Layout views.)

- **Blue background, white text.** This option is designed to help WordPerfect users feel at home. It displays text in white against a blue, WordPerfect for DOS-like background. Some people who have never used WordPerfect still find this to be softer on their eyes; it's a matter of personal taste.

- **Provide feedback with sound.** This option tells Word to play sounds in response to specific actions or events, such as error messages. To play sounds, users' computers must have a sound card, speakers, and the sound files themselves, which are typically installed in the \Windows\Media\Microsoft Office 2000 folder.

- **Provide feedback with animation.** This option is turned on by default and uses special animated pointers to tell users that automated procedures are in progress, such as AutoFormatting, background saves, and background printing. If you are running Word on Windows NT Terminal Server, or on an older computer with a 486 processor or a low-end Pentium (for example, a Pentium 60 or 90), turning this option off can slightly enhance system performance.

- **Confirm conversion at Open.** This is an option that might come in handy for users who often work with files in other formats. In general, Word is capable of recognizing the source of a document and using the appropriate converter. For example, Word recognizes WordPerfect 5.1 documents and uses the WordPerfect import filter, even if those documents have a Word-like DOC extension. However, in rare instances, Word might choose the wrong filter or you might want to choose the filter you use. If you discover that this might occur in your environment, check this box. When you open a file in a different format, Word asks the user to choose which converter to use.

■ **Update automatic links at Open.** This option is turned on by default and tells Word to automatically update any information in a document that is based on other files linked to that document. In general, you should leave this enabled. However, if you prefer to see your documents with the content they had the last time you worked with them, or if you suspect that source documents are no longer available, you can clear this check box to turn off automatic updating.

■ **Mail as attachment.** This next option relates to the way Word integrates with MAPI-compatible email software (such as Microsoft Outlook) that might be installed on your computer. With this option turned on, if you choose **File**, **Send to**, **Mail Recipient**, Word opens an email message window and includes the formatted text of the document as the message. If you choose **Mail Recipient (As Attachment)**, Word creates a new email message and attaches a copy of the current document to it. If you clear the **Mail as attachment** check box, Word no longer offers a **Mail Recipient (As Attachment)** option; instead it offers **Mail Recipient (as Text)** which, as the name implies, copies the text of the document to the email message.

■ **Recently used file list.** By default, Word displays the last four files you worked on at the bottom of the File menu. If you work on a great many files, you might want to increase the number of files displayed in this list. Conversely, if you have added custom items to the File menu, you might not even have room for four files. To make a change, click in the **entries** scroll box and type a number from 1 to 9. This box is often cleared for security purposes; otherwise, it's obvious which files your users have been working on.

■ **Help for WordPerfect users.** When this option is turned on, Word's parallel Help system for users transitioning from WordPerfect for DOS is also enabled. When you type a keyboard combination that corresponds to a WordPerfect feature, WordPerfect Help tells you how to perform the same task in Word and, in some cases, even demonstrates the feature.

■ **Navigation keys for WordPerfect users.** When this option is turned on, Word's Page Up, Page Down, Home, End, and Esc keys start behaving the way they would if you were running WordPerfect. For example, you would use Home, Home, Left-Arrow to move the insertion point to the beginning of the current line.

■ **Measurement units.** Settings in this box tell Word which measurement system to use in its rulers and in some of its dialog boxes: Inches, Centimeters, Points, or Picas. Note that not every measurement changes when you change this setting. For example, font size is still measured in points no matter which setting you choose.

■ **Show pixels for HTML features.** This option tells Word to display measurements in screen pixels rather than inches.

Part

II

Ch

6

Controlling General Options Centrally from the System Policy Editor Except for **Background repagination**, every setting in the General tab can be controlled from the System Policy Editor. To find nearly all of these settings, open the Default User tab and go to **Microsoft Word 2000, Tools | Options, General**. To find **Provide feedback with sound**, go to **Microsoft Office 2000, Miscellaneous**.

Three additional options are accessible only from the System Policy Editor, not the Options dialog box. These are for users in a global environment and are as follows:

- Asian fonts also apply to Latin text
- Use character units
- English Word 6.0/95 options (allows you to specify whether Word 6.0/95 documents should be opened normally or opened as if they contain Asian text)

Customizing Edit Options

If your users have been working with Word for quite some time, you've probably become very comfortable with Word's default editing settings. If they are relatively new to Word, they might find some of these settings uncomfortable. In the following two sections, you review controlling Edit settings locally, at a user workstation, and then centrally via system policies.

Controlling Edit Options Locally Through the Options Dialog Box Edit settings are controlled through the Edit tab of the Options dialog box. The default settings are shown in Figure 6.18. These settings are listed and discussed in the following:

FIGURE 6.18
The Edit tab controls how Word responds as you enter and edit text.

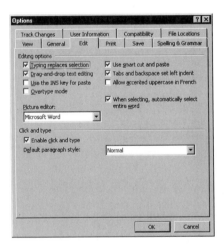

- **Typing replaces selection.** This option is on by default, which means that you can replace text by selecting it and typing over it. That makes editing faster, and most people like it. Others find themselves deleting text they meant to keep. If you find that happening, clear the check box.

- **Drag-and-drop text editing.** This option, which is also on by default, activates Windows' drag-and-drop feature. With this feature turned on, you can select text, click, and drag the text to a new location. Some people find drag-and-drop editing an especially intuitive way of moving text. Others find that they accidentally move text when drag-and-drop editing is enabled. If you want to turn it off, clear the check box.

- **Use the INS key for paste.** If this option is checked, the Insert key pastes text from your Clipboard into your document. In Word 95 and previous versions, INS normally toggled Overtype mode on and off unless you checked this box. However, Microsoft has disabled that toggle. As a result, checking this box gives you another convenient way to insert text without losing any capabilities that aren't already gone. In Insert mode, Word inserts text as you type and moves existing text to its right. In Overtype mode, Word instead replaces existing text, one character at a time, as you type "into it." You can turn on Overtype mode by double-clicking **OVR** in the status bar, or you can do it here by checking the **Overtype Mode** check box.

- **Use smart cut and paste.** Checking this option tells Word to eliminate any extra spaces you might leave when you delete text, or extra spaces you might insert when you paste text. In effect, smart cut and paste ensures there is exactly one space between each word in a sentence. It's another way in which Word acts as if it knows better than you do. The fact is, Word is almost always right, but some people find features like these a little presumptuous.

- **Tabs and backspace set left indent.** This option is turned on by default; it enables you to increase and decrease left indents at the beginning of a paragraph by pressing the Tab and Backspace keys.

- **Allow accented uppercase in French.** This option tells Word it can suggest accented uppercase characters as corrections when proofing, or as options in the Change Case dialog box. This works only for text formatted as French, and it works only if you have French proofing tools installed.

- **When selecting, automatically select entire word.** This option is a shortcut designed to make it easier to select large blocks of text. You don't have to precisely start at the beginning of a word to select the whole word. Rather, as soon as you select the space after a word, the program assumes you intended to select the whole word. It works backward, too; with this box checked, Word selects the word ahead of the selection if you have already selected one word and are starting to select another. Some people don't like Word to make assumptions about what they intend to select. If that's you, clear the check box.

- **Picture editor.** This drop-down box enables you to choose which drawing or image-editing program opens when you double-click an image in your document. Typically, the choices are Microsoft Word (in other words, Word's built-in picture-editing feature) or Microsoft Photo Editor 3.0 (if you have installed it). Other imaging tools registered as OLE applications might appear as well.

Part

II

Ch

6

■ **Enable click and type.** Checking this option enables you to choose whether you want to use Word's new feature, which enables you to double-click anywhere on a page and start typing there. Click and type sets a tab wherever you use it. The feature is turned on by default; if you don't want stray tabs in your document, or if you find it confusing, clear the check box.

■ **Default paragraph style.** This option enables you to choose which style Word should use for new paragraphs that are created when you use Word's click-and-type feature. (Existing paragraphs aren't changed.) For example, if you start with a new blank document and double-click in the middle of the document, the first paragraph will remain in Normal style, but all the paragraphs inserted by the click-and-type feature—including the one that includes the insertion point—will be formatted with the style shown in this box.

TIP The **Default paragraph style** drop-down box does not automatically display every built-in style available to a document. Instead, it shows Normal, Heading 1, every style that's being used in the document, and any user-defined styles that are available. (To see a list of user-defined styles, choose **Format**, **Style**, and in the **List** drop-down box, pick **User-Defined Styles**.)

Controlling Edit Options Centrally from the System Policy Editor   Except for **Overtype mode** and **Default paragraph style**, every setting in the Edit tab can be controlled from the System Policy Editor. To find nearly all of these settings, open the Default User tab and go to **Microsoft Word 2000**, **Tools | Options**, **Edit**.

Two additional options are accessible only from the System Policy Editor, not the Options dialog box. These control Input Method Editors, which are text entry front-ends for users working in Asian languages:

■ IME Control Active

■ IME TrueInLine

Customizing Print Options

Word enables you to control a variety of printing behaviors, including whether fields and links update before printing; whether you can print more quickly using draft output and background printing; which of your printer's paper trays are used by default; and which information is included with your print jobs. In the following two sections, you review controlling Editing settings locally, at a user workstation, and then centrally via system policies.

Controlling Print Options Locally Through the Options Dialog Box

Print settings are controlled through the Print tab of the Options dialog box; the default settings are shown in Figure 6.19. These settings are listed and discussed in the following:

FIGURE 6.19
Use this dialog box to
set special printing
options.

- **Draft output.** Users occasionally might want to print a document with extensive graphics and formatting, but don't need to see the graphics or formatting right now—only the text. If so, they can often print more quickly by using Word's Draft Output feature.

- **Update fields; Update links.** These settings tell Word to update fields and/or links before printing a document, ensuring that the document is up-to-date.

CAUTION

Although you'll often want users to update fields and links before you print, sometimes they shouldn't. For instance, to accurately track a project (or for legal reasons), you might need to print a memo precisely as it appeared several months ago, with old dates and old numbers. Before users print such a document, they should clear the **Update fields** and **Update links** check boxes.

- **Allow A4/Letter paper resizing.** Word enables users to switch automatically between the standard 8 1/2"×11" paper size used in the United States and the slightly longer, narrower A4 size that is widely used elsewhere. To enable this automatic switching feature, select the **Allow A4/Letter paper resizing** check box. With this box selected, Word adjusts page layout and margins automatically to compensate for changes in paper size when the document is about to be printed. These changes are not stored permanently and do not affect the document as it appears onscreen. In the future, if a user instructs Word to print the document at 8 1/2"×11" again, Word will do so.

- **Background printing.** By default, Word prints *in the background*, so users can return to work in your document more quickly, but print jobs run a bit more slowly. If you find that Word prints too slowly, try disabling background printing. Display the Print tab of the Options dialog box and clear the **Background printing** check box. Word now prevents users from working in their files until it has sent all pages to your printer (or Windows print spooling file).

- **Print PostScript over text.** While running Word 2000 for Windows, you might occasionally need to accommodate watermarks or other surprinted text created in Word for the Macintosh. The **Print PostScript over text** option enables PostScript code that might have been placed in a Macintosh Word document to be printed above text, not beneath it.

■ **Reverse print order.** Instructs your printer to print your pages backward. Some printers, including Hewlett-Packard DeskJet inkjet printers, have this feature built in to their drivers. However, others, such as Canon and Lexmark inkjet printers, do not. With these printers, using this Word option is the only way to print pages backward.

■ **Document properties.** Instructs your printer to print information about the document that is stored in Word's File, Properties dialog box.

■ **Field codes.** Instructs your printer to print field codes instead of field results.

■ **Comments.** Instructs your printer to print all comments about a document, starting on a new page at the end of the document.

■ **Hidden text.** Instructs Word to print hidden text in a document (the dotted underline that appears onscreen does not print). If you are especially concerned about security, you might want to permanently clear this check box using the System Policy Editor.

■ **Drawing objects.** Instructs your printer to include drawing objects; if this box is cleared, empty boxes appear where the graphics would have, and printing might run a little faster.

■ **Print data only for forms.** Instructs your printer to print only the data a user entered in a form, not the surrounding form elements.

Controlling Print Options Centrally from the System Policy Editor   Except for **Print PostScript over text** and **Print data only for forms**, which are typically used only with occasional documents, every setting in the Print tab can be controlled from the System Policy Editor. To find these settings, open the Default User tab and go to **Microsoft Word 2000, Tools | Options, Print**.

Two additional options are accessible only from the System Policy Editor, not the Options dialog box. These control duplex printing and apply only if you have a printer that can print on both sides of a sheet.

Customizing Save Options

Word enables you to control several aspects of how it saves files. In the following two sections, you review controlling Save settings locally, at a user workstation, and then centrally via system policies.

Controlling Save Options Locally Through the Options Dialog Box

Save settings are controlled through the Save tab of the Options dialog box; the default settings are shown in Figure 6.20. These settings are listed and discussed in the following:

FIGURE 6.20
Use the Save tab of the Options dialog box to control save options in Word.

- **Always create backup copy.** Checking this box tells Word to rename the previous version of your document with a BAK extension in the same folder as the new version it is saving.

- **Allow fast saves.** Checking this option enables Word to save time on most saves by recording all the changes to your document together, at the end of the document file. On occasion, even when Fast Saves is turned on, Word performs a full save, integrating all the changes throughout your document. Be sure to clear **Allow fast saves** before saving a document file that will be used in another program, such as QuarkXPress or PageMaker. If you often export Word files to other programs, consider using the System Policy Editor to turn this feature off permanently.

> **CAUTION**
>
> Also turn Fast Saves off if you're concerned about document security. With Fast Saves turned on, it's possible to use a text editor such as Notepad to read fragments of text that you thought you had deleted from your documents.

- **Prompt for document properties.** Selecting this option causes the Properties dialog box to open whenever a user saves a document for the first time. Turning this option on might slightly inconvenience your users, but it can help you capture a great deal of valuable information about the documents they create—for both tracking and automation purposes.

- **Prompt to save normal template.** With this box checked, users are given a chance to abandon changes to default settings, AutoText entries, and macros before Word saves them to the Normal template at the end of an editing session.

- **Embed TrueType fonts.** Checking this box tells Word to embed the TrueType fonts that have been used in a document. Select this box if you suspect your file's recipients won't have access to the fonts you used to create your document. Keep a few things in mind, however. First of all, embedding fonts can dramatically increase font size. It's probably not a good option if your documents have many fonts and you're planning to send multiple copies across a network. Second, not all TrueType fonts can be embedded; font manufacturers have the power to prevent their fonts from being embedded as an antipiracy measure, and some companies such as Émigré have exercised that option. Third, PostScript fonts can't be embedded with this feature.

■ **Embed characters in use only.** Occasionally, you might want to embed a font you've used in only one or two document headlines. To save space, Word 2000 now provides this option, which enables you to embed up to 32 individual characters from a font without embedding the entire font. If you've used more characters than this, Word embeds the entire font. Stay away from this option if you expect your recipients to edit the headline, because they will not have access to other characters they might need.

 You can find out whether fonts you own can be embedded—and learn quite a bit more about your TrueType fonts—by using Microsoft's free Font Properties Extension, downloadable at **www.microsoft.com/ typography/property/property.htm**.

 If your organization creates complex, heavily formatted documents that you want others to read but not edit, consider using Adobe Acrobat to save relatively compact versions of your file, which can then be read and printed with fonts and formatting largely intact.

■ **Save data only for forms.** With this option checked, Word saves only the text entered by the person filling out the electronic form, not the surrounding form itself. This information is stored in a tab-delimited, text-only format that is easy to import into databases.

■ **Allow background saves.** Checking this option enables Word to save in the background as users work. While Word is saving, a pulsating disk icon is displayed in the status bar.

■ **Save AutoRecover info every.** The entry in this scroll box tells Word how often to create a document recovery file. You can set intervals from 0 to 120 minutes—if it's set to 0, Word saves AutoRecover information every time you pause typing.

CAUTION

Remind your users that AutoRecover does *not* substitute for saving files regularly, and that it is not *100 percent* reliable.

■ **Save Word files as.** In this box, you can specify a default format other than Word 2000 in which to save your files. You can choose any format for which you have installed an export filter. This is an invaluable option for organizations that are migrating to Office 2000 in stages or are intending to utilize multiple word processing packages indefinitely.

- **Disable features not supported by Word 97.** Checking this box enables you to save files in Word 2000/Word 97 format without saving features that cannot be displayed properly in Word 97. For example, if you select this box, Word does not save nested tables. This option is helpful in ensuring that all your documents are consistent and accessible to all your users, even as you migrate to Office 2000 in stages.

- **File sharing options.** Finally, these options enable you to specify a password users need to open a document or a password they need to modify it. You can also select **Read-only recommended**. If you do, when a user opens the file, a dialog box appears to discourage him or her from opening your document in a way that permits modification, without actually preventing him or her from doing so.

Controlling Save Options Centrally from the System Policy Editor   Most of the settings in the Save tab can be controlled from the System Policy Editor. To find these settings, open the Default User tab and go to **Microsoft Word 2000, Tools | Options, Save**. Three options cannot be controlled through policies: **Embed TrueType fonts, Save data only for forms**, and **Passwords**.

One additional option is accessible only from the System Policy Editor, not the Options dialog box: **Add bi-directional marks when saving text files**. This instructs Word to add bidirectional marks to text files it saves, when those files are in bidirectional languages such as Hebrew or Arabic.

Customizing Spelling and Grammar Options

Word enables you to control several aspects of how it checks spelling and grammar. In the following three sections, you review controlling Spelling & Grammar settings locally at a user workstation, providing custom dictionaries that enable Word to recognize the specialized words and names your company uses, and customizing spelling and grammar centrally via system policies.

Controlling Spelling & Grammar Options Locally Through the Options Dialog Box

Spelling and grammar settings are controlled through the Spelling & Grammar tab of the Options dialog box; the default settings are shown in Figure 6.21. These settings are listed and discussed in the following:

- **Check spelling as you type.** When turned on, Word continually checks users' spelling and places wavy red underlines under any words it cannot find in its dictionary.

- **Hide spelling errors in this document.** When turned on, Word continues to check spelling as a user types, but does not display wavy red underlines. However, when a user runs the spelling checker feature, it works faster, because the checking has already been done.

FIGURE 6.21

Use the Spelling & Grammar tab of the Options dialog box to control the Word spelling check and grammar check options.

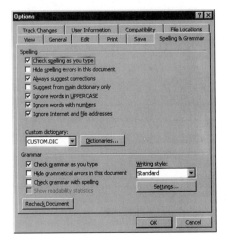

- **Always suggest corrections.** Word's spelling suggestions are often inaccurate in highly technical documents or documents that contain a lot of arcane jargon. For such documents, in the interest of time, you might want to disable Word's suggested spellings to make the spelling checker run faster.

- **Suggest from main dictionary only.** By default, Word looks in all open dictionaries to make suggestions about spelling changes. This can take time. It also means that Word might recognize as correct certain words that are not correct in the context in which you're working. If you're sure your current document won't benefit from words you added to your custom dictionaries, select this box.

- **Ignore words in UPPERCASE.** No spell checker understands all acronyms. Because most acronyms are all caps, you can tell Word not to flag words that are all caps. (This feature is turned on by default.)

- **Ignore words with numbers.** Some product names combine words and numbers. Suppose that you sell a 686MX computer, a DX677 CD player, and a KFE100 fire extinguisher. Word might flag each of these as incorrect—a real problem if you're proofing a long price list. Therefore, by default, Word ignores word/number combinations.

- **Ignore Internet and file addresses.** Until recently, most spell checkers have incorrectly flagged Internet file addresses such as the Web address **www.microsoft.com** or the filename c:\windows\system.dat. If you leave this check box checked, Word doesn't spell-check addresses such as these.

- **Check grammar as you type.** When turned on, Word continually checks users' grammar and places wavy green underlines under any words or sentences it believes to be incorrect.

- **Hide grammatical errors in this document.** When turned on, Word continues to check grammar as a user types, but does not display wavy green underlines. However, when a user runs a grammar check, it works faster, because the checking has already been done.

- **Check grammar with spelling.** When turned on, Word automatically checks grammar at the same time it checks spelling. If your users do not like Word's grammar feature, you might want to turn this off.

- **Show readability statistics.** When turned on, Word displays a set of Readability Statistics after each grammar check is complete. Among other things, these statistics purport to estimate how much education a user requires to understand the current document.

N O T E The Spelling & Grammar tab can control one additional aspect of Word spell checking: custom dictionaries. These are covered in the following section. ▪

Providing Custom Spelling Tools   The Word spelling checker is a blessing—except when it identifies hundreds (or thousands) of words as possible errors when you know better— perhaps those words are really product names or names of your company's senior executives.

In Chapter 12, "Standardizing Document Production with Word and Excel," you learn how to customize AutoCorrect to fix some of these errors automatically. But what if you want to include a custom dictionary specific to your organization? Follow these steps:

1. Open a new document.
2. Enter all the words you want to include, one on each line. If you're adding names, consider importing the last name field from an Outlook or Access database and then eliminating the duplications by hand or with a macro.
3. Save the file as Text Only, using the DIC extension.
4. Copy the file to the folder containing Microsoft Office's dictionaries (typically C:\Windows\Profiles\Username\Application Data\Microsoft\Proof in Windows; Microsoft:Custom Dictionary on the Macintosh).
5. Choose **Tools, Options**.
6. Click the **Spelling & Grammar** tab.
7. Click **Dictionaries**. The Custom Dictionaries dialog box opens, listing all dictionaries stored in that folder (see Figure 6.22).

N O T E Typically, the Custom Dictionaries dialog box already lists CUSTOM.DIC, the file where Word stores all the words that users add to the spelling dictionary. If you've copied another DIC file there, this should also be listed. ▪

8. Select the check box next to the dictionary you just created.
9. Click **OK**.

▶ For more information about controlling the Word spelling and grammar settings, **see** "Customizing Spelling and Grammar Options," earlier in this chapter on **p. 157**.

FIGURE 6.22
Adding a custom
dictionary.

Controlling Spelling & Grammar Options Centrally from the System Policy Editor   Several
of the settings in the Spelling & Grammar tab can be controlled from the System Policy
Editor. To find these settings, open the Default User tab and go to **Microsoft Word 2000,
Tools | Options, Spelling & Grammar**.

The following options cannot be controlled through policies: **Hide spelling errors in this
document, Hide grammatical errors in this document**, individual grammar settings, or
dictionaries.

The following options, primarily intended for international environments, can be set in the
System Policy Editor, but not through the Options dialog box:

- Use German Post Reform Rules (new German spellings)
- Combine Aux Verb/Adj.
- Use Auto-Change List
- Process Compound Nouns
- Hebrew
- Arabic modes

Customizing User Information

Word utilizes users' names, initials, and addresses in a variety of ways. It stores users' names
in the Author field of the Properties dialog box whenever they create a new document. It
includes names automatically in letters and envelopes created with the Word wizards and
templates; initials are also included in letters. It also attaches users' names and initials to any
changes or comments they insert using the Word Track Changes or Comments features.

To set or change a user's name, initials, or address, display the User Information tab of the
Options dialog box (see Figure 6.23). Enter the **Name, Initials**, and **Mailing address** as you
want them to appear when Word uses them. (For example, your initials don't have to correspond precisely to the name you enter in the name box—it's up to you.)

FIGURE 6.23

Use the User Information tab of the Options dialog box to change your personal information settings.

User Information cannot be set using system policies. You can, however, set a Company Name during centralized deployment with the Custom Installation Wizard, as is covered in Chapter 2, "Automating and Customizing Office Installations Across the Network." This can help you protect both the hardware and software assets that belong to your firm.

N O T E Word tracks the Company Name as it was entered during installation, but this information is stored as a binary value in the Registry (HKEY_CURRENT_USER\Software\Microsoft\Office\9.0\Common\UserInfo\Company) and cannot be permanently changed from inside Word. ■

Customizing Compatibility Options

You might be accustomed to working with a different version of Word or a different brand of word processor, such as WordPerfect. Or, you might have documents that originated on a different system, such as a Macintosh running Microsoft Word 5.1. These programs differ subtly in the ways they display text.

These subtleties are almost all minor, but they can occasionally cause significant problems. For example, Microsoft 5.1 for the Macintosh uses larger Small Caps than Word 2000. This minor difference can conceivably affect where lines, or even pages, break—throwing off carefully created page layouts.

Using the Compatibility tab of the Options dialog box (see Figure 6.24), you can adjust Word to display your document as it would look if opened in a different program. Compatibility can be set for each document individually and is not centrally controllable via system policies.

N O T E These Compatibility settings don't actually change the contents of an existing file. They change only its appearance, so that you can accurately format your document to reflect the software and computer from which it eventually is used and printed. ■

FIGURE 6.24

In the Compatibility tab, you can adjust Word 2000 settings to match that of earlier versions of Word for Windows, DOS, and Macintosh, as well as WordPerfect.

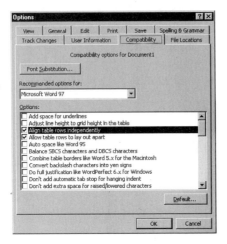

If you know the program that created a file, the quickest way to ensure compatibility is to choose that program name in the **Recommended options for** drop-down list box. Word 2000 has built-in options designed to reflect differences in appearance for the following:

- Word 97
- Word 6.0/95
- Word for Windows 1.0
- Word for Windows 2.0
- Word for the Macintosh 5.x
- Word for MS-DOS
- WordPerfect 5.x for DOS
- WordPerfect 6.x for Windows
- WordPerfect 6.0 for DOS

You can also choose **Custom** to create custom settings if you need them.

N O T E If you're upgrading from Word 97, Word 2000 provides Compatibility options that affect these features:

- How Word 2000 adjusts line height to grid height in tables
- How Word 2000 lays out AutoShapes
- How Word 2000 breaks lines for Asian text
- How Word 2000 lays out footnotes

▶ For more information about compatibility with other word processing software and about font substitution, **see** Chapter 18, "Migrating from or Coexisting with Legacy Applications," on **p. 481**.

Customizing File Locations

Word enables you to control where it looks for the files your users need. In the following two sections, you review controlling File Locations settings locally, at a user workstation, and then centrally via system policies.

Controlling File Location Options Locally Through the Options Dialog Box

File Location settings are controlled through the File Locations tab of the Options dialog box; the default settings are shown in Figure 6.25. By default, on Windows computers that use profiles, the Word settings are as shown in Table 6.2.

Table 6.2   Where Word Looks for Files, Templates, and Other Resources

File Type	Location
Documents	C:\Windows\Profiles*Username*\Personal
Clipart	No default location
User Templates	\C:\Windows\Profiles*Username*\Application Data\Microsoft\Templates
Workgroup Templates	No default location
User Options	No default location
AutoRecover Files	C:\Windows\Profiles*Username*\Application Data\Microsoft\Word
Tools	C:\Program Files\Microsoft Office\Office
Startup	C:\Windows\Profiles*Username*\Application Data\Microsoft\Word\Startup

FIGURE 6.25
The File Locations tab enables you to change where Word looks for documents, templates, and tools.

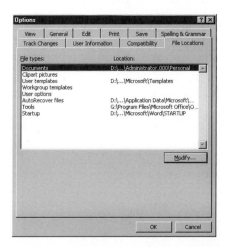

You can change these settings, either locally at the user workstation or centrally through system policies. To change the locations locally, follow these steps:

1. Select the row containing the file type and location you want to change.

2. Click **Modify**. The Modify Location dialog box opens (see Figure 6.26).

3. Browse to the folder you want and click **OK** twice.

FIGURE 6.26
The Modify Location dialog box enables you to set a new location for whatever file type you've chosen.

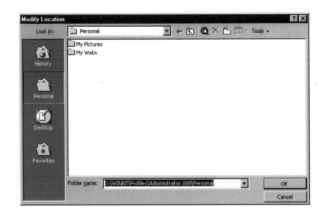

Controlling File Locations Options Centrally from the System Policy Editor   File Locations settings can all be controlled from the System Policy Editor. Some are controlled for Office as a whole; others are controlled specifically for Word.

User Templates and Shared (Workgroup) Templates are set for Office 2000 as a whole, from the following location in the Default User tab of System Policy Editor: **Microsoft Office 2000, Shared Paths**.

Documents, Clipart Pictures, AutoRecover Files, Tools, and Startup are set for Word from the following location in the Default User tab of System Policy Editor: **Microsoft Word 2000, Tools | Options, File Locations**.

Customizing How Word Starts in Windows

You have extensive control over how Word starts up—including control over *when* it starts up. If your users nearly always work with Word, you can set Windows 95/98 or Windows NT to run Word automatically at startup. To do so, copy a shortcut to Word into your computer's startup folder. Assuming that you haven't customized your system, or created system profiles that point to a startup folder on a network server, follow these steps:

1. Choose **Start, Programs, Windows Explorer** (or, in Windows NT, Windows NT Explorer).

2. Browse to **c:\windows\start menu\programs** (or, in Windows NT, **c:\winnt\start menu\ programs**).

N O T E If a user has a roaming profile on a Windows NT domain, the Start menu items reside on a server in that domain, and on the local Windows NT Workstation in a folder named c:\winnt\profiles*username*\start menu\programs. Because roaming profiles are synched on the work-station from the server upon login, you should edit them at the server. In Windows 98, they might be stored locally in a folder named c:\windows\profiles*username*\start menu\programs. ■

3. In the right pane, right-click on the Microsoft Word shortcut and choose **Copy** from the shortcut menu.

4. In the left pane, click **Startup** to display the contents of your computer's startup folder.

5. Right-click inside the right pane and choose **Paste** from the shortcut menu.

6. Shut down and restart Windows. Word starts automatically.

The Properties dialog box for a Windows shortcut (accessible by right-clicking the shortcut and choosing **Properties**) contains a command corresponding to the shortcut's target (a program, folder, or file). This command is displayed in the **Target** text box of the Shortcut tab. Typically, the command for a shortcut to Word is the following:

```
C:\Program Files\Microsoft Office\Office\WINWORD.EXE
```

If you want, you can edit this command to include a Word startup switch or to follow Winword.exe with the path and name of a document or template you always want to load.

Table 6.3 lists some Word startup switches.

Table 6.3   Commonly Used Word Startup Switches

This Switch	Does This
/a	Loads Word without loading add-ins or global templates.
/l<addin name>	Loads Word with a specific add-in. (Follow /l with the add-in's file-name and complete path.) Be sure not to include a space between the l and the add-in name.
/m	Loads Word without running any automatic macros (AutoExec and so on). (Follow /m with a macro name, and Word runs that macro rather than AutoExec.) Be sure not to include a space between the m and the macro name.
/n	Starts Word without opening a blank document.
/t<template name>	Starts Word and opens a document *based on a specific template*. (Follow /t with the name of the template, as in the following example: C:\Program Files\Microsoft Office\Office\Winword.exe" /t"C:\My Documents\Test.dot.)

You can use these startup switches in the Start, <u>R</u>un dialog box to specify how Word runs at any time, not just at startup. You can also create a separate shortcut that loads Word with specific switches and copies it to the Desktop alongside a standard Word shortcut. This way, users can choose which way they want to start Word in any given session.

Part

II

Ch

6

On the Macintosh, you can make an alias and copy it into the Startup folder, as follows:

1. Click to select the **Microsoft Word** program icon (typically in the Microsoft Office 98 folder).

2. Choose **File**, **Make Alias**.

3. Drag the alias into the Startup Items folder within the System Folder.

4. Choose **Special**, **Restart** to restart the Macintosh. Word starts automatically.

Customizing the Word Startup Folder

Like Windows, Word also has a startup folder. In Windows, the Word startup folder is typically C:\Program Files\Microsoft Office\Office\Startup. (The typical Macintosh location is Microsoft Office 98:Office:Startup:Word.)

Anything placed in this startup folder—documents, templates, or (in Windows) Word add-ins—is loaded when Word starts. You can even place shortcuts in the Word Startup folder; the files they point to are loaded into Word.

A template placed into the Word Startup folder loads as a global template. This means that the macros, AutoText entries (boilerplate text), toolbars, menus, and keyboard shortcuts contained in it are available to all documents no matter which template is attached to those documents. Although the new resources are available, each document a user opens is still attached to its original template and retains the formatting and settings found in that template. ●

7

Customizing Excel to Your Organization's Needs

by Bill Camarda

Excel is flexible enough to meet an extraordinary range of user needs. In this chapter, you'll learn techniques for customizing Excel, with the following goals:

- To help your users become more productive
- To improve the quality of your worksheets and analysis of your data
- To make Excel easier for you to manage

You'll find coverage of these and other techniques for customizing Excel:

- Using templates to provide a consistent framework for custom workbooks
- Changing the default settings
- Changing the user interface
- Controlling how Excel works locally or centrally via system policy settings
- Changing what happens to Excel at startup

Using Templates to Customize Excel

Templates are fundamental to customizing Excel, so it's critical that you understand them. As in Word, Excel templates can include patterns of text, formulas, values, formats, and graphics that form the basis of new worksheets and workbooks. More specifically, templates can include the following:

- Any worksheet or cell formatting that you can create using commands on the Format menu
- Page formatting
- Print area settings
- Cell styles, similar to styles in Word, except that they can also contain number formatting and protection
- Multiple worksheets, including worksheet names
- Protected and hidden workbook areas, including columns, rows, and sheets
- Text, including both labels and page headers/footers
- Cell formulas
- Cell values
- Charts, maps, graphics, audio or video clips, and other workbook elements

Templates can also store Excel customizations, enabling you to change how Excel works, based on the needs of a specific workbook, project, or user. Excel templates can be used to create the following customizations:

- Macro procedures (whether recorded using the Excel Macro Recorder or written from scratch in Visual Basic for Applications [VBA])
- Custom toolbars and buttons that you can add to any toolbar
- Custom menus and commands that you can add to any menu
- Custom keyboard shortcuts
- ActiveX controls, such as form controls
- Workbook calculation options (discussed later, in the "Customizing Calculation Options" section)
- Window display options (discussed later, in the "Customizing View Options" section)

Creating a New Excel Template

Excel makes creating a new template easy. Create a workbook that includes all the boilerplate information, formatting, macros, customizations, and settings that you want to store in your template. (Or, if you already have such a workbook, make a copy and delete all the "live data" from it, leaving only formulas and other boilerplate information.)

After you've done so, choose **File, Save As**; the Save As dialog box opens. Choose **Template** (*.XLT) from the **Save as Type** drop-down box. Excel automatically switches folders to display the local folder containing your existing templates. Enter a new filename and click **Save**. Excel saves the workbook as a template, using the XLT extension.

N O T E   Custom templates affect only new workbooks you create with them after you deploy them. Deploying or editing a template has no impact on any workbook that already exists, even if that workbook was created based on the template. ■

Simple as this is, there are a couple of points you should be aware of. First, if you simply rename a file manually with an XLT extension, without browsing to your Office Template folder, the file remains a workbook, not a template. Conversely, if you save an XLS workbook in a folder set aside for templates, it behaves as a template.

Second, by default, the templates are stored in your local template folder. This location can vary depending on the version of Windows you are using, but on typical systems with user profiles enabled, you can find Excel templates at

`C:\Windows\Profiles\username\Application Data\Microsoft\Templates`

On Windows NT 4.0 systems, typically substitute `c:\Winnt` for `c:\Windows`.

In Excel 98 for the Macintosh, templates are typically stored at

`Microsoft Office 98:Office:Templates`

Templates that you save in this default folder appear in the General tab of the New dialog box when you choose **File**, **New**. If you choose, you can also create subfolders below the Templates folder and store your templates there. As long as each subfolder contains at least one Excel template or workbook, the subfolders appear as separate tabs within the New dialog box, as shown in Figure 7.1.

FIGURE 7.1
A custom subfolder
containing custom
Excel templates.

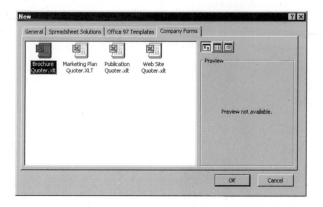

TIP   To display a picture of the first page of a custom template in the Preview area of the New dialog box, open the template, choose **File**, **Properties**, click the **Summary** tab, and select the **Save Preview Picture** check box.

Making Templates Available to Your Workgroup

Excel for Windows provides several solutions for providing centralized access to shared templates. In each case, you first set up a folder in a network location that all your authorized users can access and copy your shared templates there.

After you create your startup folder and place your templates there, you can then do only one of the following:

- Create a shortcut to the template; then email each user a copy of the shortcut (LNK) file, with instructions on how and where to store the file (for example, copy it to the same folder as the user's local templates).

- Ask users to specify the networked location as an alternate startup file location in the General tab of the Tools, Options dialog box.

- Specify the alternate startup file location centrally via system policies, using the System Policy Editor. (Run the System Policy Editor; be sure the Excel9.adm policy template is loaded; click **New**; choose **Default User**; go to **Microsoft Excel 2000, Tools | Options, General**; select the **Alternate startup file location** check box; and enter the startup file location below. Save the template and place it in the users' logon folder.) For more detailed information about working with the System Policy Editor, see the "Using System Policies with Office 2000" section in Chapter 37, p. 970.

N O T E If you specify an alternate startup file location, Excel attempts to open every file in that folder. Be sure your alternate startup file location contains only files that Excel can open. In addition to templates, this folder might contain charts and workspace files.

Note that templates placed in a user's local XLstart startup folder supersede templates with the same name stored in the Alternate Startup File Location. ■

As you might suspect, it's easiest to set up a shared template folder before you deploy Office 2000. You can then either deploy the shortcut file or specify the alternate startup file location using the Office Profile Wizard and the Custom Installation Wizard; users are then forced to do nothing and, as a result, cannot make mistakes that lead to increased support costs.

N O T E Microsoft has promised to release a Custom Maintenance Wizard (CMW) that allows settings, such as Alternate Startup File Locations, to be changed centrally after deployment; but as this is written, the CMW has not yet been released. Before you implement an alternate startup file location, check

`http://www.microsoft.com/office/enterprise`

to see whether the CMW has been released, and if so, whether it will serve your needs. ■

▶ For more information about Network installation using the Office Profile Wizard and Custom Installation Wizard, **see** Chapter 2, "Automating and Customizing Office Installations Across the Network," on **p. 27**.

Changing the Default Workbook Settings with the Book.xlt Template

Whenever a user opens an Excel workbook, he is using default settings built in to the program itself. For instance, by default, text entered into a cell is formatted as 10 point Arial. You can control the standard font and font size from the General tab of the Tools, Options dialog box, but there are many other elements you might like to control that do not have easily accessible settings. Excel provides a solution: the Book.xlt template.

Book.xlt is not a file that comes with Excel; however, if you create a Book.xlt template file and store it in the appropriate location, that template can be used to customize how the program works. Whenever Excel starts, it looks for Book.xlt in its XLStart startup folder and then the alternate startup folder (if one exists; by default, there is no alternate startup folder). (On the Macintosh, the local startup folder is located at System Folder:Preferences:Excel Startup Folder, and the default template file is named Workbook instead of Book.xlt.)

If Book.xlt cannot be found, Excel displays a blank workbook using its built-in defaults. If, however, Excel *does* find Book.xlt, it displays a workbook containing whatever settings (and text, graphics, formats, headers and footers, macros, or other elements) are built in to that Book.xlt template.

To create a new default workbook template, do the following:

1. Create or open a template with the formatting options you want.
2. Choose **File, Save As**.
3. In the **Save as type** drop-down box, select **Template**.
4. In the **File name** text box, type **Book**.
5. In the **Save in** box, locate your startup or alternate startup folder. The startup folder, named XLStart, can typically be found at C:\Windows\Profiles\USERNAME\Application Data\Microsoft\Excel\XLStart. The alternate startup folder is set in the **General** tab of the Tools, Options dialog box.
6. Click **Save**. By storing Book.xlt in the XLStart folder, you ensure that Excel knows where to find it and uses its settings whenever a user creates a new default workbook.

N O T E If you have established an alternate startup file location network folder, as discussed in the previous section, you can place Book.xlt there. This simplifies upgrades—you simply place the new Book.xlt in the alternate startup file location, and all users are automatically upgraded.

The downside: This can slightly degrade performance as users must connect to a networked folder whenever they create a new workbook. And if the network connection fails or the server goes down, users lose access to your customized defaults. ■

Changing Default Worksheet Settings with the Sheet.xlt Template

Just as Excel searches for Book.xlt when asked to create a new default workbook template, it also searches for Sheet.xlt when asked to create a new worksheet within an existing workbook. This enables you to customize the appearance of every worksheet—for example, to include consistently formatted headings or to ensure that a consistent summary graph appears on every new worksheet.

To create a Sheet.xlt file and specify that Excel use it every time it creates a new worksheet, follow these steps:

1. Create a workbook with one worksheet that includes the formatting and other information that you want to appear on all new worksheets.
2. Choose **File, Save As**.
3. In the **Save as type** drop-down box, select **Template**.
4. In the **File name** text box, type **Book**.
5. In the **Save in** box, locate your startup or alternate startup folder.
6. Click **Save**.
7. Click **Save**.

N O T E If you delete or rename Book.xlt or Sheet.xlt intentionally or inadvertently, Excel restores the original settings it used when you first installed the program. It does, however, reflect changes to the default font and font size that might have been made in the Options dialog box. ■

Setting a Strategy for Customizing Templates

In this section, you'll briefly consider ways you might use customized templates to enhance productivity throughout your organization. First, create a custom Book.xlt template that includes elements you want all your workbooks to include by default, including the following:

- Corporate logo.
- Consistent headers and footers.
- Standard formatting you want to apply on all your worksheets. For instance, Excel 97 and Excel 2000 no longer default to printing gridlines (or displaying them in Print Preview). If you still want gridlines to print by default with your company's future workbooks, you can include that setting in Book.xlt.
- VBA macros that can incorporate certain blocks of cells, retrieve data from databases, or perform other functions, or that run automatically when a workbook is opened or closed.

 TIP To create a macro that runs automatically when a workbook is opened, name it Workbook_Open or Auto_Open. To create a macro that runs automatically before a workbook is closed, name it Workbook_BeforeClose or Auto_Close.

To write a macro that runs whenever a user switches worksheets—possibly to change the user interface to reflect the different requirements of the other worksheet—use the Visual Basic Editor to set the VBA SheetActivate or SheetDeactivate property associated with the Application object or sheet object.

- Customized toolbars and buttons that provide access to custom macros (as discussed later in this chapter).

Create Book.xlt first, so you can build your specialized custom templates around the company-wide settings you establish here. Next, if necessary, create Sheet.xlt (although many organizations do not need a standard worksheet template if they have carefully designed Book.xlt).

After you've created your default templates, you can build custom templates—or adapt existing workbooks into templates consistent with the formatting you've specified. Templates are ideal for forms, such as requisition forms that include calculations.

 TIP Consider using the Excel Template Wizard with Data Tracking add-in to create a companion database for your Excel form and to automatically capture data entered in each new copy of the form. If installed, this add-in can be activated by selecting its check box in the Tools, Add-Ins dialog box.

In addition to these companywide templates, you can also build specialized templates that address the needs of subsets of your users: either specific workgroups or users in many different departments who perform the same tasks. For example:

- Suppose that you're called upon to support the needs of a sales department. You might work with Sales to create a Proposal template that automates the pricing of complex bids and RFPs.

- Suppose that you support clerical staff who use Excel exclusively for data entry. You could create a Clerical Support template that displays a dialog box at startup, enabling the user to choose which kind of form to use.

Other opportunities for centralizing and standardizing workbooks include the following:

- Return on investment analyses for new products and services
- Marketing planning and other what-if forecasting
- Project management (if you do not use a formal project management package such as Microsoft Project)

Maximizing Worksheet Accuracy Throughout Your Organization

Surveys have shown that user-developed worksheets and workbooks in many organizations are riddled with inaccuracies. These inaccuracies can lead directly to incorrect analyses and poor decisions. Remember when Fidelity Investments announced a $2.3 billion gain for their flagship Magellan Fund and had to admit later there was really a loss? The reason: Someone switched a minus and a plus sign.

Centralizing worksheet development wherever possible can mitigate this problem, but only if you carefully plan for accuracy throughout the entire development process. Centrally deploying inaccurate workbooks and requiring their use only makes matters worse—and the fingers will point at you.

Part

II

Ch

7

Raymond R. Panko, a professor at the University of Hawaii's College of Business Administration, has systematically reviewed the extensive research that now exists on spreadsheet accuracy, and his findings are worth quoting in depth:

> Every study that has attempted to measure errors, without exception, has found them at rates that would be unacceptable in any organization. These error rates, furthermore, are completely consistent with error rates found in other human activities. With such high cell error rates, most large spreadsheets will have multiple errors, and even relatively small "scratch pad" spreadsheets will have a significant probability of error.
>
> **Despite the evidence, individual developers and organizations appear to be in a state of denial** (writer's emphasis). They do not regularly implement even fairly simple controls to reduce errors, much less such bitter pills as comprehensive code inspection. One corporate officer probably summarized the situation by saying that he agreed with the error rate numbers but felt that comprehensive code inspection is simply impractical. In other words, he was saying that the company should continue to base critical decisions on bad numbers.
>
> A major impediment to implementing adequate disciplines, of course, is that few spreadsheet developers have spreadsheeting in their job descriptions at all, and very few do spreadsheet development as their main task. In addition, because spreadsheet development is so dispersed, the implementation of policies has to be left to individual department managers. While organizations might identify critical spreadsheets and only impose hard disciplines on them, this would still mean that many corporate decisions would continue to be made on the basis of questionable analyses.

Now that you're scared, what can you do about it? The following sections offer some help in ensuring the accuracy of the templates you provide to your colleagues.

Planning Your Workbooks Carefully

Although spreadsheets are infinitely malleable, and you will often find that your understanding of the problem evolves over time, most spreadsheets benefit from much more advanced planning than they receive. You can avoid many problems later if you start by considering the following four points in the planning stage:

- **Understand the problem.** Spend some time thinking through the problem you are trying to analyze. Write a brief summary of the problem and its key elements as you understand them; better yet, include that summary in your workbook. Many spreadsheet experts set aside the entire first worksheet for a detailed explanation of the workbook, along with tracking information, such as lists of revisions and the dates they were made.

- **Understand the analysis issues.** For example, where will you get the data? If you are importing data from an external source, how will you ensure its reliability? Will you have to worry about "cleaning" or reformatting that data? Will the data you have really support the analysis you want to make? If not, where can you get additional data? If your workbook will include links, how will those links be maintained over time?

- **Envision the finished workbook.** What might it look like? Will it have many worksheets or just one? How might it best be organized? What reporting capabilities will be needed? Which Excel features, such as an outlining, PivotTables, and charts, might be useful? Do you have the skills to use these features? Should you use multiple workbooks connected by a workspace?

- **Understand the user.** Who will use your workbook? Who owns it? What skill levels do they have—Excel skills, business skills, domain knowledge? What help and guidance will they need? How will you protect your workbook against unauthorized change? Conversely, how will users be given the flexibility they need to meet changing business requirements? What processes will you put in place to ensure the spreadsheet continues to work correctly—and serve your business goals—over time?

Organizing Your Workbooks for Clarity and Accuracy

Here are some general rules for organizing worksheets to improve their clarity and reduce the risk of error:

- Wherever possible, separate different elements of your analysis into different worksheets.

- Separate data that must be input from the resulting output. Consider formatting input cells differently, perhaps with a lightly shaded color that does not interfere with printing.

- Avoid repetition of data within your model—especially input data.

- If you have a choice between creating a formula and using an existing, tested Excel function, use the function.

- Where an input cell contains data that is used extensively throughout your workbook, place that cell in an especially visible location.

- To make the workbook easier to understand, use range names extensively.

- Document your workbook extensively. Use the Excel 2000 in-cell Comments feature liberally to explain the assumptions that underlie your formulas and data. As discussed previously, consider setting aside the first worksheet for documentation. You might want to place information about the workbook in the Properties dialog box.

- If you include VBA code that provides dialog boxes and other user interface elements, consider providing a custom Help file as well.

- Now that you can insert hyperlinks in Excel workbooks, consider linking your workbook to an easily updated Help page on your intranet.

- Be sure to lock every cell that users should not be permitted to change; after doing so, check the workbook to be sure you haven't prevented changes to a cell that needs changing.

- Be sure you hide the cells and formulas you don't want your users to see. (Remember, you can hide cells only on protected worksheets.)

- Include a header or footer specifying the security level of the workbook—for example, "Confidential: Not to Be Used Outside Acme Corporation."

- Where input is required, use the Excel Data, Validation dialog box to eliminate obvious user-entry problems (text instead of numbers and so on).

- Download Microsoft's free Excel add-ins for Y2K compliance, the Date Fix Wizard, Date Migration Wizard, and Date Watch Wizard.

- Wherever possible, insert drop-down boxes and other controls that enable users to select among predefined choices instead of entering data from scratch.

- To help users track key trends and data faster, use the Excel 2000 new Conditional Formatting feature to add formatting that appears only when cells are displaying values in a range you specify.

- Format the workbook for maximum readability, making judicious use of clearly written headings and subheadings, and graphs carefully designed to illuminate analysis. Be careful, however, not to add clutter—unnecessary fonts, multiple type font sizes, graphs and maps that don't add actionable information, and so on.

Testing and Auditing Your Workbooks

Nothing personal, but human beings are imperfect. As noted earlier, humans make roughly the same percentage of worksheet errors as they make in other tasks of similar complexity. Even if you follow all the steps listed previously, errors can still occur. The following shows how to catch them:

- **Use the tools Bill Gates gave you.** Use the Auditing toolbar to trace precedents, descendants, and formulas that display error messages. As mentioned earlier, use data validation.

- **Review every formula for common errors.** Here are some easy-to-miss errors that appear repeatedly in Excel workbooks:

  - **Incorrect order of calculation.** As you probably remember from your math classes, formulas must be read in the correct order to calculate properly. Excel reads formulas in the following order: Parentheses, Exponents, Multiplication, Division, Addition, and Subtraction. For instance, Excel calculates the formula
    =20*3+6
    as 66—spoken aloud, 20 times 3 is 60, plus 6 is 66. But
    =20*(3+6)
    is 180, because Excel now calculates the values between the parentheses before it multiplies by 20.

    In legacy workbooks created in Lotus 1-2-3, you can encounter differences in the way each program calculates the same data. (See "Customizing Transition Options," later in this chapter.)

  - **Using absolute instead of relative cell references, or vice versa.** If you use absolute cell references (containing $ symbols before row and/or column names), these cell references don't adjust automatically when copied into new cells. Absolute cell references are often necessary, but if you forget you've used them, you can easily generate incorrect data when you copy them.

- **Have you used the right function in the right place?** Are you sure you meant IRR (Internal Rate of Return), not MIRR (Modified Internal Rate of Return)? Are you positive you wanted ABS to strip that minus sign off the value it returns? Are your IF statements in the right order (if not, True is returned as False, and everything that depends on this cell goes haywire).

- **Are your cell references pointing to the right cell(s)?** It's so easy to slip your mouse pointer or type incorrectly and miss by a cell or two. Also, as your workbook includes more and more data, will your cell references capture it all? Or are they limited to a specific range that you will one day exceed?

- **Are all your range and cell names unique?** Excel permits you to use the same range or cell name on different sheets within the same workbook, but this can lead formulas based on those names to calculate incorrectly.

■ **Stress your formulas with the most extreme data they might have to handle.** Will the formulas deliver the results you expect if one division loses money or if sales plummet or soar? Will they work in a short month, like February? Will they work if you add more than 10,000 data points?

■ **Get out your calculator and test formulas by hand.** You should test *all* of them, but most people simply refuse to do this. At absolute minimum, test a representative sample—for example, a few dozen formulas scattered across your workbook. If you find problems, hunker down and test all of them.

■ **Ask others to thoroughly review your work.** Have others peer-review your workbooks, in detail, before you deploy them—and build sufficient time into your schedule for a serious review, not just a cursory signoff.

Using Custom Views

If you are distributing templates or workbooks, as you develop them, you might find specific display and print settings that work best. For example, you might have saved specific print areas, or the workbook might best be viewed in full-screen view. In some cases, there might be two or more views that work best while users are performing a specific task, or at different times in the spreadsheet review process.

You can save each set of display and print settings as a custom view, allowing users to easily toggle quickly among them. To create a custom view, set up your workbook exactly how you want users to see it, with settings for the following:

■ Column widths

■ Display options, such as Zoom or Full screen

■ Window sizes and positions onscreen (keeping in mind that these can be affected by the size and resolution of your colleagues' monitors)

■ Split windows or frozen panes

- Active sheets
- Selected cells on each sheet
- Hidden rows and columns
- Filter settings
- Print areas
- Other print settings

Next, choose **View**, **Custom Views** (see Figure 7.2). Click **Add** to display the Add View dialog box (see Figure 7.3). Name the view and specify whether you want to include **Print settings** or **Hidden rows, columns and filter settings**. Then, click **OK**. The View is now stored with the workbook or template. To use it, choose **View**, **Custom Views**, select it from the list of **Views**, and choose **Show**.

FIGURE 7.2

The Custom Views dialog box.

FIGURE 7.3

The Add View dialog box.

Organizing a Project with Workspace Files

Often, projects you create for users contain multiple workbooks. To streamline the process of working with these workbooks, you might want to create a workspace file; when users open this file, all the related workbooks open and are arranged onscreen as you want.

Workspace files contains information on all the workbooks for a given project, including the following:

- Which workbooks you want to open
- The location of each file
- The size and position of each workbook in the Excel window

To create a workspace file, follow these steps:

1. Open the workbooks that you want to include. If the workspace file is shared, be sure the workbooks are located on a network drive or in a shared folder.

2. Position and size the workbooks.

3. Choose **File**, **Save Workspace** (see Figure 7.4).

4. If you want the workspace file to open automatically each time you start Excel, specify the Excel startup folder or your networked alternate startup file location in the **Save in** box.

5. Give the workspace file a name and click **Save**. The file is saved in the Excel XLW workspace format.

FIGURE 7.4
The Save Workspace dialog box.

 TIP The drive and path information for each workbook is saved in the workspace file. If you move the workbook files, Excel cannot find them when you open the workspace file. To avoid possible problems, save the workspace file in the same networked folder as the workbook files.

Customizing the Excel User Interface

Excel's user interface is highly malleable and can be adjusted to serve the needs of a wide variety of users. These adjustments are covered in the following sections.

NOTE With every version of Office, there is more similarity between the interfaces of the individual applications. Some of the Excel user interface adjustments that are common throughout Office are covered briefly in the following sections and in much greater depth in Chapter 12, "Standardizing Document Production with Word and Excel."

▶ For information about customizing Excel to eliminate excess elements of the user interface, **see** "Using System Policies to Disable Elements of the Excel User Interface," later in this chapter on **p. 185**.

Giving Users More Display Space to Work In

As workbooks grow faster than screen real estate, your users might find themselves wanting to view more rows or columns at the same time. Excel provides several user interface customizations that make this possible. Some of these options also give you, the manager, a benefit: better control over how users work with Excel.

Part
II
Ch
7

Displaying and Hiding the Formula Bar

Excel's *formula bar* (see Figure 7.5) enables users to see (and edit) the formulas that underlie a worksheet's results. Some users do not need to see these formulas; others *should* not see them. Hiding the formula bar makes it a bit more difficult for the casual user to see formulas, while at the same time providing a bit more space for viewing the worksheet. To hide the formula bar, click the **View** menu and clear the check box next to **Formula bar**.

FIGURE 7.5
The Excel formula and status bars.

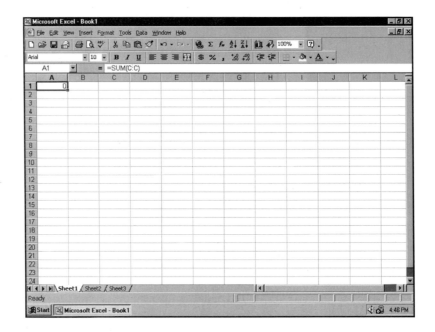

 TIP You can also hide the formula bar by choosing **Tools**, **Options**, **View** and clearing the **Formula bar** check box.

If you never want your users to have access to the formula bar, you can prevent access through system policies. In the System Policy Editor, open the **Excel9.adm** template; go to **Default User, Microsoft Excel 2000, Tools | Options**; and set restrictions for both **Show Formula Bar in Normal view** and **Show Formula bar in Full view**.

▶ For more information on using the System Policy Editor, **see** the "Using System Policies with Office 2000" section of Chapter 37, on **p. 970**.

Personalizing Excel Menus and Toolbars

In Office 2000, Word, Excel, PowerPoint, Access, and Outlook share several identical customization features for menus and toolbars. In each program, you can do the following:

- Add or remove commonly used buttons from each toolbar by clicking the down arrow at the right edge of the toolbar, clicking **Add** or **Remove** buttons, and clearing or selecting individual button icons.

- Specify whether to use Office 2000's new personalized menus, which attempt to display only the commands users need (**T**ools, **C**ustomize, **O**ptions, **M**enus Show Recently Used Commands First).

- Add toolbars through **Tools, Customize, Toolbars**.

- Add commands to toolbars and menus through **Tools, Customize, Commands**.

- Create new icons and add them to your buttons.

▶ Each of these features is covered extensively in Chapter 6, "Customizing Word to Your Organization's Needs," beginning with the section "Personalizing Your Menus and Toolbars" on **p. 132**.

Displaying and Hiding the Status Bar

The status bar (refer to Figure 7.5) can be used to provide custom messages to users and occasionally provides useful instructions or information about a command. But for many users, the status bar spends most of its time simply reporting "Ready." To hide the status bar, click the **V**iew menu, and clear the check box next to **Status bar**.

If you never want your users to have access to the status bar, you can prevent access through system policies. In the System Policy Editor, open the **Excel9.adm** template; go to **Default User, Microsoft Excel 2000, Tools | Options | View**; and set restrictions for both **Show Status Bar in Normal View** and **Show Status Bar in Full View**. For more information on using the System Policy Editor, see the "Using System Policies with Office 2000" section of Chapter 37, p. 970.

Displaying and Hiding Toolbars

Excel 2000 displays two built-in toolbars: the Standard and Formatting toolbars. Some users might want to take advantage of Excel 2000's new option to display abbreviated versions of the Standard and Formatting toolbar on the same line, including only those buttons most users work with most often. To set this option, choose **Tools, Customize, Options**, and select the **Standard and Formatting Toolbars Share One Row** check box.

To display additional built-in Excel toolbars, right-click any toolbar and select the toolbar you want to show from the shortcut menu. The shortcut menu lists the most commonly used toolbars. If you do not see the toolbar you want on the shortcut menu, do the following:

1. Right-click any toolbar and select **Customize** from the shortcut menu to display the Customize dialog box.

2. Click the **Toolbars** tab.

3. Select the check box for the toolbar you want to display.

Part

II

Ch

7

Moving and Resizing Toolbars

By default, Excel displays the Standard toolbar and the Formatting toolbar docked (attached) at the top of the program window, just below the title bar. You can dock any toolbar at the top of the program window or at the left, right, or bottom edge of the window.

A toolbar that is not docked is a *floating* toolbar. You can easily resize and move floating toolbars around the program window as you work on your spreadsheet. Figure 7.6 shows the difference between a docked and floating toolbar.

FIGURE 7.6
The difference between a docked toolbar and a floating toolbar.

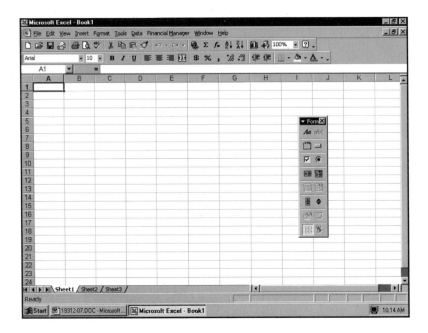

To move a floating toolbar, simply click the title bar and drag the toolbar to a new location. If you want to dock a floating toolbar, drag the toolbar to the top, left, right, or bottom edge of the program window. When you drag the toolbar to the edge of the program window, you notice that the toolbar outline snaps into place.

The docked Forms toolbar now has two small lines at the top of the toolbar. This is the move handle. To create a floating toolbar out of a docked toolbar, simply click the move handle and drag the toolbar out over your spreadsheet. To dock a toolbar in another location, click the move handle and drag the toolbar to a different edge of the program window.

After a toolbar is docked, it cannot be resized. You need to undock it first and create a floating toolbar. To resize a floating toolbar, position the mouse pointer over any edge until it changes into a double-headed arrow and then drag the edge of the toolbar. To hide a floating toolbar, click the **Close** button (x) on the toolbar. To hide a docked toolbar, right-click it and click the toolbar in the shortcut menu that appears.

Displaying Excel Worksheets in Full Screen View

Sometimes hiding the formula bar, status bar, and excess toolbars still isn't enough—users want to see more of their worksheets. They can, using **View**, **Full Screen** (see Figure 7.7). This view shows only the menus, and if the user has specified it, also the formula bar.

FIGURE 7.7
The Full Screen view in
Microsoft Excel.

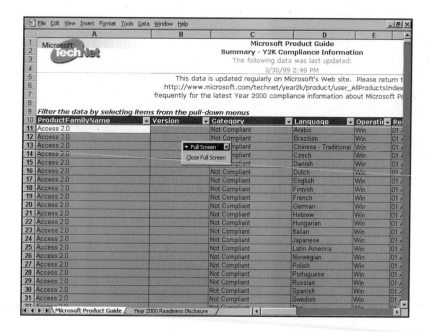

TIP   Another solution is **View**, **Zoom**, which allows users to shrink the worksheet as much or as little as they want to view more of it at once.

Establishing Office-Wide Customizations That Affect Excel

Excel shares several elements with the rest of Office. The result: Some customizations made in Excel affect the entire Office suite, and some customizations made elsewhere in Office affect Excel. For instance:

- Text added to the CUSTOM.DIC custom dictionary in any Office application is automatically reflected in the Excel spelling checker. (However, entries in additional Word custom dictionaries are not available to Excel.)

Part

II

Ch

7

■ Unformatted text added to the Word and PowerPoint AutoCorrect lists is available to Excel and is also used by the PowerPoint AutoCorrect feature. Formatted text added to the Word AutoCorrect list is not available to Excel. Similarly, several AutoCorrect settings are set for Excel, PowerPoint, and Access at the same time and can be established centrally via system policies. The settings are Correct Two Initial Capitals, Capitalize First Letter of Sentences, Capitalize Names of Days, Correct Accidental Use of Caps Lock Key, and Replace Text As You Type. The centralized system policies can be found through the System Policy Editor at Default User\Microsoft Office 2000\Tools|AutoCorrect (Excel, PowerPoint, and Access). Word AutoCorrect settings are established separately.

■ Customizations made in the Options tab of the Tools, Customize dialog box are applied throughout Office, not just in Excel. For example, by default, Excel 2000 displays abbreviated Standard and Formatting toolbars, combined on a single line—a change in behavior from previous versions of Excel. Users who prefer full Standard and Formatting toolbars can get them by choosing **Tools**, **Customize**, **Options**, and clearing the **Standard and Formatting Toolbars Share One Row** check box. Having done so, the full menus appear in each Office application. Other settings in this category include the following:

- Menus Show Recently Used Commands First
- Show Full Menus After a Short Delay
- Large Icons
- List Font Names in Their Font
- Show ScreenTips on Toolbars
- Show Shortcut Keys in ScreenTips
- Menu Animations

These settings can also be established centrally by system policies, found in System Policy Editor at Default User\Microsoft Office 2000\Tools|Customize|Options.

■ Excel Help shares the same assistants and behaviors as the rest of Office. If, for example, you turn off the Office Assistant in Excel, it doesn't appear in Word, either: Rather, the large Help dialog box appears. (You can control three categories of Assistants centrally: General settings such as which Assistant you want to use, Options settings such as whether the Assistant appears when users press F1, and Help on the Web settings such as the URL where user feedback is sent. These settings can be established centrally by system policies, through the System Policy Editor at Default User\Microsoft Office 2000\Assistant.

■ Most Web Options (accessible by choosing **Tools**, **Options**, **General**, **Web Options**) are Office-wide. These include options such as whether to use cascading style sheets for font formatting in HTML documents, whether to support PNG graphics, and whether to encode pages for a specific international character set. You can control four categories of Web options centrally:

- General settings such as whether to rely on Cascading Style Sheets for font formatting.
- Files settings such as whether supporting graphics and other files should be saved in a separate folder when a Web page is saved.

- Pictures settings such as whether to create PNG graphics files that older browsers cannot read.

- Encoding settings controlling the international encoding scheme Web pages are saved with (in the U.S., this is typically the default "Western Alphabet (Windows)."

These settings can be established centrally by system policies, through the System Policy Editor at Default User\Microsoft Office 2000\Tools|Options|General|Web Options. Certain Web options are PowerPoint-specific; these are covered in the next chapter, in the section "Establishing Office-Wide Customizations That Affect PowerPoint, on p. 204."

■ Excel shares Office-wide applets such as Microsoft Graph, WordArt, and MS Organization Chart 2.0 and shares the same library of patterns and textures as the rest of Office.

Using System Policies to Disable Elements of the Excel User Interface

If you have installed the System Policy Editor along with the Office 2000 Resource Kit Toolbox, you can use the System Policy Editor to disable Excel commands and shortcut keys you do not want your users to access. To do so, follow these steps:

1. Choose **Start, Programs, Microsoft Office Tools, Microsoft Office 2000 Resource Kit Tools, System Policy Editor**.

2. Choose **Options, Policy Template** and be sure the appropriate policy template files are present (Access9.adm, Excel9.adm, Frontpg9.adm, Office9.adm, and so on).

3. Click the **New** button to create a new policy file.

4. Double-click **Default User**.

5. In the Default User dialog box, double-click **Microsoft Excel 2000**.

6. Go to **Disable Items in User Interface** and then to **Predefined**.

7. Select the **Disable Command Bar Buttons and Menu Items** check box. A list of predefined menu items appears below.

8. Select the commands you want to disable.

9. Select the **Disable Shortcut Keys** check box. A list of predefined menu items appears below.

10. Select the shortcut keys you want to disable.

11. Choose **File, Save** to save the policy file.

12. Include the Policy file in your users' network logon script.

Tables 7.1 and 7.2 show which commands and shortcut keys can be disabled through the System Policy Editor.

Part

II

Ch

7

Table 7.1   Excel Commands and Menus That Can Be Disabled

File, Open, Tools, Find	Tools, Macro, Visual Basic Editor
File, Save As Web Page	Tools, Macro, Script Editor
File, Web Page Preview	Tools, Add-Ins
File, Send to Mail Recipient	Tools, Customize
Insert, Hyperlink	Tools, Options
Tools, Protection	Help, Office on the Web
Tools, Protection, Protect Sheet	Help, Detect and Repair
Tools, Protection, Protect Workbook	Web, Start Page
Tools, Protection, Protect and Share Workbook	Web, Search the Web Page
Tools, Online Collaboration	Web, Favorites
Tools, Macro, Macros	Web, Go
Tools, Macro, Record New Macro	Web, Address

Table 7.2   Excel Commands and Menus That Can Be Disabled

Shortcut Key	What It Does
Ctrl+F	Find
Ctrl+K	Insert, Hyperlink
Alt+F8	Tools, Macro, Macros
Alt+F11	Tools, Macro, Visual Basic Editor
Alt+Shift+F11	Tools, Macro, Microsoft Script Editor

Customizing Excel Options

The Options dialog box (Tools, Options) enables you to adjust settings that control how you view and work with Excel files. These settings are saved to the Windows Registry and are read when Excel starts. When two or more users open a shared workbook or template, each user's individual settings are applied to the file.

Nearly all of the settings available in the Excel 2000 for Windows Options dialog box are also available in the Tools, Preferences dialog box in Excel 98 for the Macintosh.

N O T E   Throughout the following sections, we discuss using the System Policy Editor to establish centralized policies for using Excel. The System Policy Editor is part of the Office 2000 Resource Kit Toolbox, downloadable at www.microsoft.com/office/ork. When installed, the System Policy Editor can be opened by choosing **Start, Programs, Microsoft Office Tools, Microsoft Office 2000 Resource Kit Tools, System Policy Editor**. Unless otherwise specified, the system policies covered in this chapter can be found in the Excel9.adm template, at Default User\Microsoft Excel 2000. When working with system policies for Office 2000, use the version of the System Policy Editor included in the Office 2000 Resource Kit Toolbox, not the previous versions that were included with Windows 95, 98, or Windows NT 4.0. ■

▶ For more information about working with the System Policy Editor, **see** the "Using System Policies with Office 2000" section of Chapter 37, on **p. 970**.

Customizing View Options

You've already learned that Excel 2000 offers new ways to control and simplify the user interface —and the user experience. You can control many other aspects of how Excel looks through the View tab of the Options dialog box. These include color, comments, column and row headings, gridlines, and sheet tabs. In the following two sections, you review controlling these settings locally, at a user workstation, and then centrally via system policies.

Controlling View Options Locally Through the Options Dialog Box

The default settings for View options are shown in the View tab of the Options dialog box (see Figure 7.8). Disabling the formula bar and status bar was discussed earlier in this chapter; the remaining items are discussed in the following list:

FIGURE 7.8
The View tab of the Excel Options dialog box.

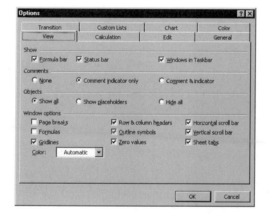

■ **Windows in Taskbar.** According to Microsoft's Help files, selecting this box specifies a *single document interface* (SDI) like that of Word 2000, where each open workbook gets its own taskbar entry. However, the feature does not seem to work in the original release of Office 2000. If it did, you might consider using it if your users find the inconsistency between Word's SDI and Excel's multiple document interface confusing. This seems unlikely, however; based on early feedback, users would prefer to switch Word back to its older multiple document interface to resolve the discrepancy—but unfortunately, this cannot be done. (The **Windows in Taskbar** option is not available in Excel 98 for the Macintosh.)

■ **Comments.** By default, any cell with an attached comment is flagged by a tiny red triangle at the top right called the *comment indicator*. The comment itself becomes visible when a user clicks on the cell or hovers over it. If you prefer comments to remain invisible, perhaps for security reasons, you can choose **None**. This can be enforced on a specific user's computer through a system policy; otherwise, the user is free to change the setting. Conversely, at times users might want to see all comments visible at once. This can be done by selecting the **Comment & indicator** button.

Part

II

Ch

7

■ **Objects.** Often, users don't need to view graphics and other objects in a worksheet as they work; they might need to view them only when the worksheet is complete and ready to be printed. By choosing **Show placeholders** or **Hide all**, users can make Excel run more quickly by eliminating the need to redraw graphics as they scroll. It's likely that users will want to toggle this setting on and off, but if you are running Excel 2000 on slow hardware, you might consider making your default setting **Show placeholders** when you customize installation using the Office Profile Wizard.

■ **Window options.** These settings allow you to choose which worksheet elements appear onscreen. You can turn the following elements on and off: **Page breaks**, **Formulas** in cells (instead of their results), **Gridlines**, **Row & column headers**, **Outline symbols**, **Horizontal scroll bar**, **Vertical scroll bar**, and **Sheet tabs** that enable navigation between worksheets.

You can also specify whether zero values are shown. If you clear the **Zero values** check box, wherever a cell would normally display the value 0, it instead appears blank. This is ideal for blank invoices and other forms that might otherwise display endless rows of zeros until they are filled out. Unlike many of the settings in Excel's Options dialog box, Zero values can be set individually for each *worksheet*, not each workbook.

■ **Color.** This setting lets you choose a color for gridlines. The default, **Automatic**, uses the text color set by Windows, typically black.

Controlling View Options Centrally from the System Policy Editor

The Windows in Taskbar and Comments options discussed in the preceding section can also be customized centrally using the System Policy Editor. With the Excel9.adm template open, go to **Default User**, **Microsoft Excel 2000**, **Tools | Options**, **View** and establish the policy setting you want.

▶ For more information on using the System Policy Editor, **see** the "Using System Policies with Office 2000" section of Chapter 37, on **p. 970**.

Customizing Calculation Options

Calculation Options control how Excel worksheets calculate. By default, Excel automatically calculates values for formulas entered into cells as soon as they are entered, and immediately any time they change. In the following two sections, you review when you might want to change these settings and then how to control them locally at a user workstation. Calculation options are set individually for each workbook and cannot be controlled centrally through system policies.

Sometimes you might not want Excel to automatically recalculate your workbooks as soon as you make changes to them. For example, you might have a workbook that queries an external database for quarterly sales data. Depending on the time it takes to perform the query, you might want to manually recalculate your workbook at a time when network traffic is minimal.

Figure 7.9 shows the Calculation tab of the Options dialog box, with its default settings. If you want to stop Excel from calculating automatically, choose **Manual**; Excel then calculates only when you manually ask it to do so.

You can also choose **Automatic except tables** to allow Excel to keep calculating, except where it relates to data retrieved from external database tables.

You can also control how efficiently Goal Seek and Solver functions arrive at solutions from this tab. By default, if you create a worksheet that requires iterations, Excel stops calculating after 100 iterations or as soon as all values change by less than 0.001, whichever comes sooner. If you want to change this, select the **Iteration** box and specify a different value. The more iterations and the smaller the change between calculation results, the more time Excel needs to calculate a worksheet—but the more accurate the final result is likely to be.

FIGURE 7.9

The Calculation tab of the Options dialog box.

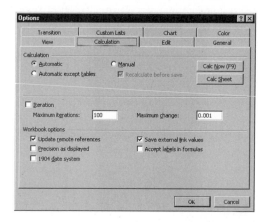

Following is an explanation of several more calculation settings:

- **Update remote references.** Remote references are references to data stored in other applications. Selecting this box recalculates and updates formulas that use this data. Clearing this box prevents the recalculation and is sometimes called locking links.

- **Precision as displayed.** By default, Excel stores values to 15 digits of precision, but rounds off the values it displays. In the worst case, this can lead to situations where 1+1 is shown as equaling 3, because the underlying data is actually 1.49+1.49. One solution, of course, is to increase the number of decimal points displayed in a worksheet. Sometimes, however, this can be quite disconcerting to those viewing the information, and you might be willing to sacrifice a bit of accuracy to avoid the problem. To do so, select **Precision as displayed**, and Excel calculates based on the data as displayed, rather than the underlying data. The underlying, more accurate data is still stored in your worksheet, so if you clear this check box later, Excel recalculates to reflect it.

- **1904 date system.** In Excel for Windows, every date carries its own serial number; serial number 1 corresponds to January 1, 1900. However, by default, Excel for the Macintosh uses a different date system, where serial number 1 corresponds to January 1, 1904. This was because early Macintosh computers did not support dates prior to 1904. Although this is no longer the case, the 1904 date system has been carried forward as the Macintosh default setting, for backward compatibility.

Part

II

Ch

7

As a result, the same date can carry two different serial numbers 1,462 numbers apart, depending on the platform used to create the workbook. This can cause inaccurate or failed calculations when workbooks are moved between platforms. To fix the problem, Excel 2000 for Windows enables you to specify the Macintosh's 1904 date system workbook by workbook; conversely, Excel 98 for the Macintosh enables you to choose the 1900 system.

Your choice of date system can be different for each workbook. However, if legacy spreadsheets do not prevent this, it is best to choose one date system for both platforms and stick with it. You cannot do this using System Policies. However, you *can* establish the setting in Book.xlt (Windows) or Workbook (Mac)—the templates where Excel stores default settings for new workbooks. For more information on this issue, see Knowledge Base article Q180162.

- **Save external link values.** Checked by default, this setting saves copies of values Excel gets from external documents. If you maintain links to large blocks of data from external documents, you might want to clear this check box to reduce your file size and the time it takes to load the file.

- **Accept labels in formulas.** Checked by default, this permits you to use label names in formulas if the ranges on your worksheet contain row or column labels.

In Excel 98 for the Macintosh, **Calc Now** and **Calc Sheet** buttons also appear on the Calculation tab.

Customizing Edit Options

Excel enables you to control several aspects of the editing process, including cell drag-and-drop editing, Excel's AutoComplete feature, and other data entry and editing features. In the following two sections, you review controlling editing settings locally, at a user workstation, and centrally via system policies.

Controlling Edit Options Locally Through the Options Dialog Box

Excel's default Edit settings are displayed in the Edit tab of the Options dialog box, as shown in Figure 7.10, and explained in detail as follows:

- **Edit directly in cell.** Checked by default, this allows users to edit within a cell, not just in the formula bar. If you want to prevent editing, you can hide the formula bar *and* clear this setting. Conversely, if you hide the formula bar but want to permit editing, be sure this box remains selected.

- **Allow cell drag-and-drop.** Selected by default, this turns on the Windows drag-and-drop feature.

- **Alert before overwriting cells.** Selected by default, this displays a warning message if you try to superimpose copied cells over locations that already contain data.

- **Extend list formats and formulas.** Selected by default, this tells Excel to automatically format new items in a list just like the items that preceded it.

- **Enable automatic percent entry.** By default, if you enter a number in a cell formatted as a percentage, Excel multiplies the number by 100. If you select this check box, which is *not* checked by default, Excel does this only with numbers below 1.

- **Move selection after Enter.** By default, when you press Enter in a cell, Excel moves down one cell. You can change the direction Excel moves or clear the **Move selection after** Enter check box, in which case Excel does not change the highlighted cell after you press **Enter**.

- **Fixed decimal.** If you want all the values in your workbook to use the same number of decimal places, select the **Fixed decimal** check box and specify the number in the **Places** scroll box.

- **Cut, copy, and sort objects with cells.** Selected by default, this selects graphics, buttons, text boxes, and other objects whenever users select the cells associated with them.

- **Ask to update automatic links.** Selected by default, this displays a confirmation message before updating data in linked items.

- **Provide feedback with animation.** Cleared by default, this setting animates the movement of surrounding cells to their new location whenever cells, rows, or columns are inserted or deleted. It can make movement easier to see, but can also reduce video performance—and is definitely not recommended for slower systems or Windows Terminal Server systems.

- **Enable AutoComplete for cell values.** Selected by default, this turns on Excel's AutoComplete feature, which can often fill in the remaining text in a cell when it recognizes that the first few letters match text in another cell within the same column.

FIGURE 7.10
The Edit tab of Excel's
Options dialog box.

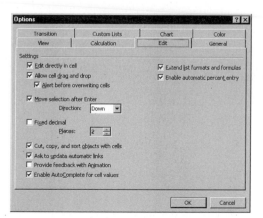

Controlling Edit Options Centrally from the System Policy Editor

All the settings discussed in the previous section can also be customized centrally using the System Policy Editor. With the Excel9.adm template open, go to Default User, Microsoft Excel 2000, Tools | Options, Edit and establish the policy setting you want. For more information on using the System Policy Editor, see the "Using System Policies with Office 2000" section of Chapter 37, page 970.

Part

II

Ch

7

Customizing General Options

The General tab of the Options dialog box contains Excel settings that don't fit anywhere else, including default file and alternate startup folder locations, user names, cell reference styles, and other settings. In the following two sections, you review controlling these settings locally, at a user workstation, and centrally via system policies.

Controlling General Options Locally Through the Options Dialog Box

Excel's default General settings are displayed in the General tab of the Options dialog box, as shown in Figure 7.11, and explained in detail as follows:

FIGURE 7.11

The General tab of Excel's Options dialog box.

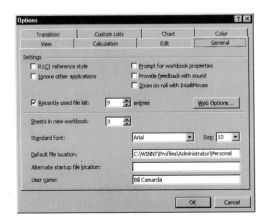

- **R1C1 reference style.** By default, Excel uses the A1 reference style, in which the first cell in row and column 1 is named A1, and other cells in the same column are named A2, A3, and so forth. Some users, especially users with a background as programmers, might be more familiar with another style, called R1C1. In this style, both rows and columns are referred to with numbers, preceded by the letter R for row and C for column. R1C1 is the first cell in the first row and column; R2C1 is equivalent to A2; R3C1 is equivalent to A3. Selecting the **R1C1 reference style** check box allows users to work with this reference style.

- **Ignore other applications.** Not selected by default, this prevents Excel from exchanging data with other applications.

- **Prompt for workbook properties.** Not selected by default, this causes the Properties dialog box to open whenever a user saves a workbook for the first time. Turning this option on can slightly inconvenience your users, but it can help you capture a great deal of valuable information about the workbooks they create—for both tracking and automation purposes.

■ **Provide feedback with sound.** This option tells Excel to play sounds in response to specific actions or events, such as error messages. To play sounds, users' computers must have a sound card, speakers, and the sound files themselves, which are typically installed in the \Windows\Media\Microsoft Office 2000 folder.

■ **Zoom on roll with IntelliMouse.** With this option selected, the wheel button of the Microsoft IntelliMouse (and compatible mice) zooms instead of scrolls. This option is unavailable on Excel 98 for the Macintosh, because Macintosh mice do not have wheel buttons.

■ **Recently used file list.** By default, Excel displays the last four workbooks you worked on at the bottom of the File menu. If you work on a great many files, you might want to increase the number of files displayed in this list. Conversely, if you have added custom items to the File menu, you might not evenhave room for four files. To make a change, click in the **entries** scroll box and type a number from 1 to 9. This box is often cleared for security purposes; otherwise, it's obvious which workbooks users have been working on.

■ **Sheets in new workbook.** By default, when users create a new workbook, Excel places three worksheets in it. You can change this value here. The maximum number of worksheets in an Excel workbook is now 255.

■ **Standard font/Standard size.** As discussed earlier in this chapter, you can use these settings to change the standard font and font size from the default setting of 10-point Arial (9-point Geneva on the Macintosh).

■ **Default file location.** By default, Excel stores files in the following folder: c:\Windows\Profiles\username\Personal. No default file location is set on the Macintosh. If you want to use a different folder, such as a network folder, you can change this setting.

■ **Alternate startup file location.** As discussed earlier in this chapter, Excel automatically makes available any files that appear in the XLStart folder. If you want, you can specify a networked alternate startup file location with templates, add-ins, chart files, and other resources that are also made available.

■ **User name.** This setting personalizes workbooks with the user's name. By default, the name that appears is the one written to the Registry upon installation, but the name can be changed here by the user. This name is used by Comments, Tracked Changes, Shared Workbooks, the Properties dialog box, Online Collaboration, and other Excel features. Changes made here affect all Office applications. Before finishing deployment of Office, or reassigning computers, check that each user's name is set correctly.

On the Macintosh, another setting appears: **Macro Virus Protection**. This is similar to the macro virus protection setting in Excel 98 for Windows. It displays a warning when workbooks containing macros are about to be opened. Excel 98 does not support signed code. (See Chapter 37 for more information on macro virus protection.)

Part

II

Ch

7

Controlling General Options Centrally from the System Policy Editor

All the settings on the General tab except for **Provide feedback with sound** and **User name** can be customized centrally using the System Policy Editor. With the Excel9.adm template open, go to Default User, Microsoft Excel 2000, Tools | Options, General, and establish the policy setting you want.

Customizing Transition Options

Excel's Transition options make it easy for users of Lotus 1-2-3 to switch to Excel. Years ago, this was an enormous issue, as Lotus 1-2-3 was the world's dominant spreadsheet program for nearly a decade. If you are transitioning from an older version of Excel, however, you can ignore most of the settings on this tab, with one exception: **Save Excel files as**, which allows you to choose an older Excel format as your standard.

Settings here allow you to enable help for Lotus 1-2-3 users, choose which file format to save your files in by default, and change the way data is entered and manipulated to follow Lotus 1-2-3's conventions. In the following two sections, you review controlling these settings locally, at a user workstation, and centrally via system policies.

Controlling Transition Options Locally Through the Options Dialog Box

Excel's default Transition settings are displayed in the Transition tab of the Options dialog box, as shown in Figure 7.12, and explained as follows:

FIGURE 7.12

The Transition tab of Excel's Options dialog box.

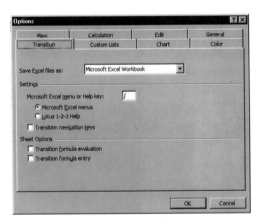

- **Save Excel files as.** This allows you to choose a standard format for saving files. You can choose any export filter you want. As always, saving in an older format means that you lose newer features you might have included in your workbook. For more information on older Excel formats, see Chapter 19. For more information on exchanging data with Lotus 1-2-3, see the "Moving from Competitive Worksheets to Excel 2000" section in Chapter 18.

■ **Microsoft Excel menu or Help key.** By default, when you press the / (forward slash) key, Excel highlights the menus, allowing users to make a selection using keyboard shortcuts. In 1-2-3 for DOS, pressing the slash displays a set of command options. If you prefer, you can set the / key (or any other key) to display help for Lotus 1-2-3 users that corresponds to the command lists they are used to seeing (see Figure 7.13).

FIGURE 7.13
1-2-3 transition help Excel can offer when users press the / key.

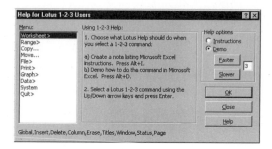

■ **Transition navigation keys.** Selecting this box allows users familiar with 1-2-3 to keep using 1-2-3's navigation keys.

■ **Transition formula evaluation.** Selecting this box tells Excel to evaluate formulas using 1-2-3's conventions. These include evaluating text strings as zero, evaluating Boolean expressions as 0 or 1, and following 1-2-3's rules for database sorting. This option is unavailable in Excel 98 for the Macintosh.

■ **Transition formula entry.** Selecting this box converts Lotus 1-2-3 Release 2.2 formulas to Excel syntax and adjusts the behavior of Excel range names to match the behavior of 1-2-3 range names. This option is unavailable in Excel 98 for the Macintosh.

Controlling Transition Options Centrally from the System Policy Editor

All these settings except for **Transition formula evaluation** and **Transition formula entry** can also be customized centrally using the System Policy Editor. With the Excel9.adm template open, go to **Default User, Microsoft Excel 2000, Tools | Options, Transition** and establish the policy setting you want. For more information on using the System Policy Editor, see the "Using System Policies with Office 2000" section of Chapter 37, page 970.

Customizing Custom List Options

Excel comes with four standard lists that allow it to automatically fill in days of the week and months of the year. However, this only scratches the surface of the lists you might need.

For example, let's say that you often need to perform analyses on each of your product lines. If the analyses were always identical, you could store a worksheet template and copy it whenever you need a new worksheet. But often the analyses aren't identical each time. At one time, you might be looking at sales growth in each product line; the next time, you might be analyzing each product line's R&D costs or contribution to overhead. In these cases, what you really want is a custom list, so that when you type Baseball and choose a fill series, Excel realizes you want to add Football, Hockey, and Soccer.

In the Custom Lists tab of the Options dialog box (see Figure 7.14), you can specify sets of data that Excel can automatically fill in whenever needed. You can either add entries manually in the **List entries** scroll box or click **Import** to select cells that already contain the entries you want to save as a custom list.

Custom Lists can include text or a mixture of text and numbers. If you want to create a custom list that contains only numbers, you can do so, but you must use the following workaround. Format cells in your worksheet as text, enter the values there and choose **Tools**, **Options**, **Custom List**. Click **Import** to select them.

FIGURE 7.14

The Custom Lists tab of Excel's Options dialog box.

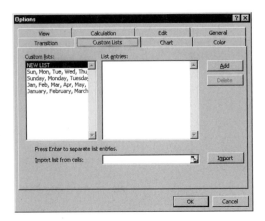

None of the settings on this tab can be customized centrally via the System Policy Editor. In fact, in Excel 97 and 2000 for Windows, custom lists can be maddeningly difficult to share, because they are stored in the Registry, not in a separate file (as in previous versions of Excel). The best solution is to create them before deploying Office, save them with the Office Profile Wizard, and deploy them centrally using the Custom Installation Wizard.

If it is too late to do that, Microsoft has published a detailed procedure for exporting the Excel 97 Registry key containing custom lists (Microsoft Knowledge Base article Q155208). This procedure can be adapted fairly easily for Excel 2000—instead of searching the HKEY_CURRENT_USER\Software\Microsoft\Office\8.0\Excel\Microsoft Excel key, search the HKEY_CURRENT_USER\Software\Microsoft\Office\9.0 key.

CAUTION

As always, be extremely careful editing the Registry—and be equally careful that you do not overwrite existing Registry keys that you do not want to change.

When Microsoft releases the Custom Maintenance Wizard for Office 2000, it is possible that there might be a more convenient way to deploy new custom lists from a central location.

Customizing Chart Options

Excel enables you to customize settings for individual charts, such as how tips are displayed and how zero values are plotted. Most of the settings in this tab are active only when a chart is selected. In the following two sections, you review controlling these settings locally, at a user workstation, and centrally via system policies.

Controlling Chart Options Locally Through Tools, Options

Excel's default Chart settings are displayed in the Chart tab of the Options dialog box, as shown in Figure 7.15, and are explained as follows:

- **Plot empty cells as.** By default, Excel leaves gaps in charts to correspond with empty cells. You might prefer that Excel interpolate (**Interpolated**) a value based on the surrounding cells or insert a **Zero** value.

- **Plot visible cells only.** By default, Excel does not plot cells you have marked as hidden, for security reasons. If you want it to plot these cells, clear this check box.

- **Chart sizes with window frame.** If you want charts to always fill the window containing them, and to grow or shrink as you enlarge or reduce the size of the window, check this box.

- **Show names.** Selected by default, this setting displays the name of any chart item when you hover the mouse above it.

- **Show values.** Selected by default, this setting displays the value associated with any data point in a chart when you hover the mouse above it.

Setting Chart Options Centrally from the System Policy Editor

Show names and **Show values** can also be customized centrally using the System Policy Editor. With the Excel9.adm template open, go to Default User, Microsoft Excel 2000, Tools | Options, Chart and establish the policy setting you want. For more information on using the System Policy Editor, see Chapter 37.

Customizing Color Options

In the Color tab (see Figure 7.16), you can customize color palettes and specify chart line and fill colors.

Part

II

Ch

7

FIGURE 7.15

The Chart tab of Excel's Options dialog box, shown with a chart active.

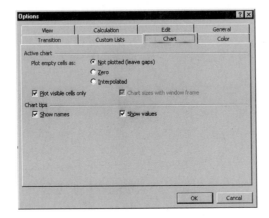

FIGURE 7.16

The Color tab of Excel's Options dialog box.

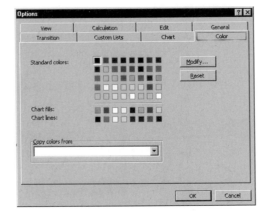

You can choose a different Standard color from the default Black text, working from a palette of 40 standard colors plus 16 colors Excel typically sets aside for chart fills and chart lines. You can also copy color palettes between active workbooks by choosing them from the **Copy colors from** drop-down box.

In Windows, these settings cannot be customized centrally using the System Policy Editor. They can, however, be modified in Book.xlt, the standard template that contains default settings for all new workbooks on a specific computer.

Note that the same options are available in Excel 98 for the Macintosh, but the color palette can vary, leading to slight changes in the appearance of colors as you move between platforms.

Customizing How Excel Starts in Windows

You can control how Excel starts up and when it starts up. If your users nearly always work with Excel, you can set Windows 95/98 or Windows NT to run Excel automatically at startup. To do so, copy a shortcut to Excel into your computer's startup folder. Assuming that you haven't customized your system, or created system profiles that point to a startup folder on a network server, follow these steps:

1. Choose **Start**, **Programs**, **Windows Explorer** (or, in Windows NT, **Windows NT Explorer**).

2. Browse to C:\Windows\Profiles\All Users\Start Menu\Programs).

3. In the right pane, right-click the Microsoft Excel shortcut and choose **Copy** from the shortcut menu.

4. In the left pane, browse to your computer's Startup folder (typically, C:\Windows\Profiles\UserName\Start Menu\Startup).

5. Right-click inside the right pane and choose **Paste** from the shortcut menu.

6. Shut down and restart Windows. Excel starts automatically.

Using Excel Startup Switches

Excel startup switches contain parameters that are passed to the application when you start Excel, customizing how you want the application to start. To use startup switches, do the following:

1. Right-click the **Start** button and select **Open** in the shortcut menu.

2. If you used the default location to install Excel, double-click the program's icon.

3. Locate the Excel shortcut icon.

4. Right-click the Excel shortcut icon and select **Properties** in the shortcut menu to display the Microsoft Excel Properties dialog box.

5. Click the **Shortcut** tab, as shown in Figure 7.17.

FIGURE 7.17
Customizing how Excel starts using startup switches.

Part

II

Ch

7

6. In the **Target** text box, type a space after the path to the Excel program and then type one of the switches listed in Table 7.3. Switches are *not* case sensitive. If you use two switches at the same time, separate them with spaces.

Table 7.3   Excel Startup Switches

Switch	Function
`"workbook path\`*`filename`*`"`	Starts Excel and opens a specific workbook.
`/r "workbook path\`*`filename`*`"`	Starts Excel and opens a specific workbook as read-only.
`/e`	Starts Excel and prevents the display of a new blank workbook.
`/i`	Starts Excel maximized regardless of its previous window settings.
`/m`	Starts Excel and creates a new workbook with one Excel 4.0 macro sheet.
`/o`	Reregisters Excel in the Windows Registry, writing default information in keys within HKEY_ CURRENT_USER\Software\Microsoft\Office\9.0\ Excel that have missing values. Does *not* fix incorrect values.
`/p "folder path\`*`folder name`*`"`	Starts Excel and specifies the working folder, overriding settings in the General tab of the Options dialog box.
`/regserver`	Reregisters Excel, overwriting all existing Registry entries and reassociating Excel with Excel files, such as workbooks, templates, and add-ins. After reregistering, exits Excel.
`/s`	Starts Excel without loading any files in the XLstart or Alternate Startup Files folder; a valuable troubleshooting tool when Excel crashes at startup and you suspect a template or other startup file is at fault. If you don't want to run any macros or add-ins either, use /automation instead.
`/unregserver`	Unregisters Excel, removing all existing Registry entries and disassociating Excel with Excel files, such as workbooks, templates, and add-ins. After unregistering, exits Excel.

You can use these startup switches in the Start, Run dialog box to specify how Excel runs at any time, not just at startup. You can also create a separate shortcut that loads Excel with specific switches and copy it to the desktop alongside a standard Excel shortcut. This way, users can choose which way they want to start Excel in any given session.

On the Macintosh, you can run Excel at startup by making an alias of the Excel 98 program icon and copying it into the Startup folder, as follows:

1. Click to select the Microsoft Excel program icon (typically in the Microsoft Office 98 folder).

2. Choose **File**, **Make Alias**.

3. Drag the alias into the Startup Items folder within the System Folder.

4. Choose **Special**, **Restart** to restart the Macintosh. Excel starts automatically.

Working with Add-Ins

An add-in is a hidden, read-only file in which Visual Basic, XLM, or C code has been compiled to provide supplemental and specialized functionality to Excel workbooks. By default, Excel installs these files in the Microsoft Office\Office\Library folder or one of its subfolders. You can recognize add-in programs by the common file extensions of DLL, XLL, or XLA. The following are descriptions of the add-ins that are available with Excel 2000:

- Use the AccessLinks Add-In to import Excel 2000 data into Access 2000 and use Access forms and reports. You must have Access 2000 installed to use this add-in.

- Use the Analysis ToolPak to add financial, statistical, and engineering analysis functions. The accompanying Analysis ToolPak—VBA adds VBA functions for the Analysis ToolPak.

- Use the AutoSave add-in to automatically save workbooks at specified intervals.

- Use the Conditional Sum Wizard to create a formula that adds data in lists according to specified criteria.

- Use the Euro Currency Tools to convert and format currency data to the new Euro. If you install this add-in on Windows 98 or Windows 2000, or on a Windows 95 or Windows NT 4.0 system that has been updated with Euro support, you are able to view and use Excel 2000 worksheets with Euro values and formulas and use the new EUROCONVERT worksheet function. If you install this add-in on a Windows system without Euro support, the EUROCONVERT function still works, but a square box appears in place of the Euro symbol.

- Use the Internet Assistant VBA add-in to convert worksheet data and charts to HTML.

- Use the Lookup Wizard to create a formula to look up data in a list, based on a known value in the list.

- Use the MS Query Add-In to support older macros designed to call MS Query 1.0 or 2.0, instead of the current version.

- Use the Open Database Connectivity (ODBC) Add-in to connect to ODBC external SQL-based data sources.

- Use the Report Manager to quickly create reports based on different print areas, custom views, and scenarios within a workbook.

- Use the Solver Add-In to calculate what-if scenarios based on adjustable variables and constraints.

- Use the Template Utilities add-in to manage Excel's built-in templates.

- Use the Template Wizard with Data Tracking to create a template that enters worksheet data into a database and tracks changes.

Part

II

Ch

7

■ Use the Update Add-In Links to convert links that called add-ins in earlier versions of Excel so they instead take advantage of corresponding built-in features of Excel 2000.

To load any of the Excel add-ins or a third-party add-in, do the following:

1. Choose **Tools**, **Add-Ins** to display the Add-Ins dialog box shown in Figure 7.18.

FIGURE 7.18
Loading Excel add-in programs.

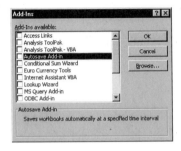

2. If you want to use an Excel add-in, select the check box in the **Add-Ins available** box. To install a third-party add-in, click the **Browse** button and locate the add-in program on your hard disk.

3. Click **OK**.

After the add-in is loaded, associated commands are available through the appropriate menu. Typically, specialized functions appear as menu items on the Tools menu, or the add-in is available in the Tools, Wizard menu. To conserve memory, you should unload add-ins that you don't use. Unloading an add-in removes its features and commands from Excel, but does not remove it from your computer. To unload an add-in, do the following:

1. Choose **Tools**, **Add-Ins** to display the Add-Ins dialog box.

2. In the **Add-Ins available** box, clear the check box next to the add-in you want to unload. ●

CHAPTER 8

Customizing PowerPoint to Your Organization's Needs

by Bill Camarda

Microsoft PowerPoint, once an afterthought for most users of the Microsoft Office suite, has become an enormously popular resource for millions of users worldwide, including many who never attempted to create formal presentations before. Meanwhile, the features have expanded, now including not only multimedia but also powerful Web/intranet-based presentation delivery.

The result: It is now more important than ever for you to ensure that your colleagues are using PowerPoint as effectively as possible and that they are using it in ways consistent with your company's goals. In this chapter, you review the following several techniques for customizing PowerPoint 2000 to ensure that it truly does meet the business goals you set for it:

- Customizing the PowerPoint interface, including how PowerPoint starts
- Controlling PowerPoint options, locally through the Options dialog box and centrally via system policies
- Creating custom presentation templates for your business
- Recording PowerPoint Visual Basic for Applications (VBA) macros

Introducing the PowerPoint Three-Pane Interface

In PowerPoint 2000, Microsoft introduces a new three-pane interface that enables users to see slides, text outlines, and notes pages at the same time (see Figure 8.1). Most users will appreciate this enhancement: They can now organize all the elements of their presentation concurrently. Gone are the days when users overlook major PowerPoint tools such as notes pages simply because they're invisible.

If, however, some of your users are working on smaller monitors (or are simply accustomed to the old slide-only interface), they can display it as Slide view.

FIGURE 8.1
PowerPoint enables you to see three elements of your presentation on the same screen.

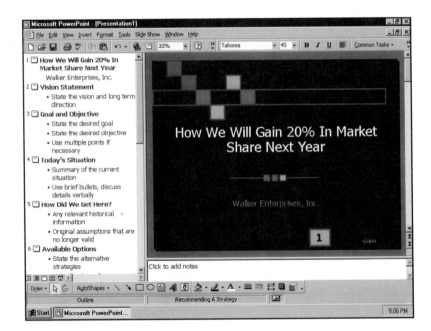

Establishing Office-Wide Customizations That Affect PowerPoint

PowerPoint shares several elements with the rest of Office. The result: Some customizations made in PowerPoint affect the entire Office suite, and some customizations made elsewhere in Office affect just PowerPoint. For instance:

- Text added to the CUSTOM.DIC custom dictionary in any Office application is automatically reflected in the PowerPoint spelling checker. (However, entries in additional Word custom dictionaries are not available to PowerPoint.)

- Unformatted text added to the Word or Excel AutoCorrect list is also used by the PowerPoint AutoCorrect feature, and any AutoCorrect entries you create in PowerPoint are available to other Office applications with AutoCorrect. Similarly, several AutoCorrect settings are set for Excel, PowerPoint, and Access at the same time and can be established centrally via system policies. The settings are **Correct Two Initial Capitals**, **Capitalize First Letter of Sentences**, **Capitalize Names of Days**, **Correct Accidental Use of Caps Lock Key**, and **Replace Text As You Type**. The centralized system policies can be found through the System Policy Editor at Default User\ Microsoft Office 2000\Tools|AutoCorrect (Excel, PowerPoint, and Access). Word AutoCorrect settings are established separately.

■ Customizations made in the Options tab of the Tools, Customize dialog box are applied throughout Office, not just in PowerPoint. For example, by default, PowerPoint 2000 displays abbreviated Standard and Formatting toolbars, combined on a single line— a change in behavior from previous versions of PowerPoint. Users who prefer full Standard and Formatting toolbars can get them by choosing **Tools**, **Customize**, **Options** and clearing the **Standard and Formatting Toolbars Share One Row** check box. Having done so, the full menus appear in each Office application. Other settings in this category include the following:

- Menus Show Recently Used Commands First
- Show Full Menus After a Short Delay
- Large Icons
- List Font Names in Their Font
- Show ScreenTips on Toolbars
- Show Shortcut Keys in ScreenTips
- Menu Animations

These settings can also be established centrally by system policies, found in the System Policy Editor at Default User\Microsoft Office 2000\Tools|Customize|Options.

■ PowerPoint Help shares the same assistants and behaviors as the rest of Office. If, for example, you turn off the Office Assistant in Word, it doesn't appear in PowerPoint either; rather, the large Help dialog box appears. You can control three categories of Assistants centrally: General settings such as which Assistant you want to use, Options settings such as whether the Assistant appears when users press F1, and Help on the Web settings such as the URL where user feedback is sent. These settings can be established centrally by system policies, through the System Policy Editor at Default User\Microsoft Office 2000\Assistant.

■ Most Web Options (accessible by choosing **Tools**, **Options**, General, **W**eb Options) are Office-wide. These include options such as whether to use cascading style sheets for font formatting in HTML documents, whether to support PNG graphics, and whether to encode pages for a specific international character set. You can control the following four categories of Web options centrally:

- General settings such as whether to rely on Cascading Style Sheets for font formatting.
- Files settings such as whether supporting graphics and other files should be saved in a separate folder when a Web page is saved.

- Picture settings such as whether to create PNG graphics files that older browsers cannot read.

- Encoding settings controlling the international encoding scheme Web pages are saved with (in the U.S., this is typically the default "Western Alphabet (Windows)").

  These settings can be established centrally by system policies, through the System Policy Editor at Default User\Microsoft Office 2000\Tools|Options| General|Web Options. Certain Web options are PowerPoint-specific; these are covered later in this chapter, in the section "Setting PowerPoint-Specific Web Options."

- PowerPoint shares Office-wide applets such as Microsoft Graph, WordArt, and MS Organization Chart 2.0 and shares the same library of patterns and textures as the rest of Office.

Customizing Toolbars and Menus

PowerPoint 2000 shares the same menu and toolbar customization capabilities as Word and Excel. Briefly, here are some of the ways you can customize PowerPoint menus and toolbars:

- PowerPoint 2000 makes it easy to subtract buttons from any toolbar—or to add selected buttons corresponding to widely-used related tools. Each toolbar has a down arrow at its right edge; click it and choose **Add or Remove Buttons** to display a list of buttons that can be displayed or hidden.

- As in Word and Excel (and PowerPoint 97), more extensive customizations can be made through the Tools, Customize dialog box. For instance, you can add menus or toolbars, and you can add commands corresponding to any built-in command, VBA macro, font, and virtually any dialog box setting.

▶ For more detailed discussion, **see** "Personalizing Your Menus and Toolbars," on **p. 132**.

Customizing PowerPoint Options

As with all Office programs, PowerPoint contains an Options dialog box that brings together a wide variety of settings for locally controlling how the program works. Many of these settings can also be established centrally, using the System Policy Editor. These settings, which are discussed in detail in the following sections, fall into six categories:

- **View settings.** These include settings that affect what PowerPoint displays when it starts and how it displays slideshows.

- **General settings.** These include settings that fit in no other category.

- **Edit settings.** These control how PowerPoint edits and formats text.

- **Print settings.** These control how PowerPoint prints presentations. This tab includes options that can be set locally or centrally for all presentations, as well as options that apply only to the current presentation.
- **Save settings.** These control how PowerPoint saves presentation files.
- **Spelling and Style settings.** These control how PowerPoint checks spelling, as well as presentation style and consistency.

N O T E Throughout the following sections, we discuss using the System Policy Editor to establish centralized policies for using PowerPoint. The System Policy Editor is part of the Office 2000 Resource Kit Toolbox, downloadable at **www.microsoft.com/office/ork**. When installed, the System Policy Editor can be opened by choosing **Start, Programs, Microsoft Office Tools, Microsoft Office 2000 Resource Kit Tools, System Policy Editor**. Unless otherwise specified, the system policies covered in this chapter can be found in the PPOINT9.ADM template at Default User\Microsoft PowerPoint 2000.

When working with system policies for Office 2000, use the version of the System Policy Editor included in the Office 2000 Resource Kit Toolbox, not the previous versions that were included with Windows 95/98 or Windows NT 4.0. ▓

▶ For more information about working with the System Policy Editor, **see** "Running System Policy Editor," in Chapter 37, on **p. 973**.

Customizing View Options

PowerPoint 2000 offers new ways to control and simplify its user interface. Many of these options can be adjusted, enabled, or disabled through the View tab of the Options dialog box. In the following sections, you review controlling these settings locally, at a user workstation, and centrally via system policies.

Customizing How PowerPoint Starts Locally Through the Options Dialog Box

By default, PowerPoint starts with an opening Startup Dialog box designed for introductory users (see Figure 8.2). The dialog box presents the following four options:

- **AutoContent Wizard.** AutoContent Wizards walk the user through a series of questions to help build a skeletal presentation that instructs the user about what content to add.
- **Design Template.** Choosing this option displays a list of consistently designed presentations that contain no text, but do contain backgrounds, text formatting, bullets, and other elements.
- **Blank presentation.** Choosing this option displays an empty presentation that uses PowerPoint's default settings for text and color. Unless you or the user has changed these defaults, this results in a simple black-and-white presentation with no backgrounds or custom bullets. This option is preferred by some users who like to build the content of their presentations before worrying about the look-and-feel.

FIGURE 8.2
The PowerPoint opening
screen for introductory
users.

■ **Open an existing presentation.** This option displays a list of presentations a user has
recently worked on. The user can choose one or click **More Files** to display the Open
dialog box.

For many experienced users, this screen is simply an obstacle to getting work done. They
might prefer to access existing presentations directly from the Open dialog box or from the
Most Recently Used list on the File menu. For those times when they want to create a new
presentation, the AutoContent Wizard, Design Templates, and library of Presentations are all
easily accessible through the File, New Presentation dialog box.

To stop this screen from appearing, you can select the **Don't show this dialog box again**
check box, or you can choose **Tools**, **Options**, **View**, clear the **Startup Dialog** check box,
and choose **OK**.

Removing the Startup Dialog Box Centrally from the System Policy Editor   The Startup
dialog box can be enabled or disabled centrally with the following system policy from the
PPOINT9.ADM policy template (Microsoft PowerPoint 2000, Tools | Options, View, Startup
dialog).

Removing the New Slide Dialog Box Locally Through the Options Dialog Box   When a user
clicks the **New** button or chooses **Insert**, **New Slide**, PowerPoint displays the New Slide
dialog box (see Figure 8.3). Many experienced users prefer not to see this dialog box, especially because the default slide it offers to insert is a title slide they only need occasionally.
Even if this feature is turned off, the same options are available when a user really needs
them: the user can choose **Format**, **Slide Layout** or click **Common Tasks**, **Slide Layout**
on the Formatting toolbar.

If the New Slide dialog box is more of a hindrance than a help to your users, you can turn it
off. To turn the feature off locally, either select the **Don't show this dialog box again** check
box in the New Slide dialog box or choose **Tools**, **Options**, **View** and clear the **New Slide
Dialog** check box.

FIGURE 8.3

The New Slide dialog box.

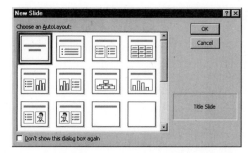

Removing the New Slide Dialog Box Centrally from the System Policy Editor   The Startup dialog box can be enabled or disabled centrally with the following system policy from the PPOINT9.ADM policy template (Microsoft PowerPoint 2000, Tools | Options, View, New slide dialog).

Controlling Other View Options Locally Through the Options Dialog Box   In addition to the Startup dialog box and New slide dialog box, you can control several other elements of the PowerPoint interface locally through the View tab of the Options dialog box (see Figure 8.4).

FIGURE 8.4

The View tab of the PowerPoint Options dialog box.

These elements include the following:

- Whether a status bar appears.

- Whether a vertical ruler also appears whenever the user displays a horizontal ruler through **View**, **Ruler**.

- Whether PowerPoint displays separate open presentations as separate items on the Windows taskbar. (In other words, does PowerPoint use a single document interface or a multiple document interface? This is a choice many Word 2000 users would welcome, but are denied!) With **Windows in taskbar** selected, each open presentation gets its own taskbar item.

Controlling Other View Options Centrally from the System Policy Editor The user interface elements discussed in the previous section can all be controlled centrally by using system policies stored in the PPOINT9.ADM policy template (Default User, Microsoft PowerPoint 2000, Tools | Options, View).

Controlling Slideshow Options Locally Through the Options Dialog Box The PowerPoint Tools, Options, View tab also enables you to control settings that apply to the slideshows that your users create. These three settings are especially useful if you run slideshows in environments that you can't completely control, such as trade-show kiosks. The settings are as follows:

- **Popup menu on right mouse click.** Determines whether users access a menu to control slideshows by right-clicking a mouse.

- **Show popup menu button.** Determines whether a semi-transparent button appears at the lower-left corner of a slideshow, giving users access to slideshow controls.

- **End with black slide.** Determines whether a black slide appears at the end of a slideshow. If this is cleared, users return to PowerPoint immediately at the end of a slideshow.

Controlling Slideshow Options Centrally from the System Policy Editor The slideshow options discussed in the preceding section, "Controlling Slideshow Options Locally Through the Options Dialog Box," can all be controlled centrally by using system policies stored in the PPOINT9.ADM policy template (Default User, Microsoft PowerPoint 2000, Tools | Options, View).

Customizing General Options

The General tab of the Options dialog box contains PowerPoint options that don't fit anywhere else. In the following two sections, you review controlling these settings locally, at a user workstation, and centrally via system policies.

Controlling General Options Locally Through the Options Dialog Box Each General option can be controlled locally from a user workstation through the General tab of the Options dialog box. The default settings are shown in Figure 8.5 and are explained as follows:

- **Provide feedback with sound to screen elements.** Selecting this check box tells PowerPoint to play sounds in response to specific actions or events, such as error messages. You need three things to play sounds: a sound card, speakers, and the sound files themselves.

- **Recently used file list.** By default, PowerPoint displays the last four presentations a user worked on at the bottom of the File menu. If your users work on many files concurrently, you might want to increase the number of files displayed in this list. Conversely, this check box is often cleared for security purposes; you might not want it to be so obvious which presentations your users have been working on.

- **Link sounds with file size greater than.** This check box enables you to set a threshold file size for audio files. If the files are smaller, they are embedded in the presentation; if they are larger, they are linked from their original source. Increasing or decreasing this setting can help you control presentation file size and network traffic. Remember, however, that if a linked audio file becomes unavailable (as, perhaps, it might on a notebook PC disconnected from your LAN), the audio part of the presentation will be lost, and error messages might be displayed.

FIGURE 8.5

The General tab of PowerPoint's Options dialog box.

Controlling General Options Centrally from the System Policy Editor

Each General option discussed in the previous section can also be controlled centrally with system policies from the PPOINT9.ADM policy template (Microsoft PowerPoint 2000, Tools | Options, General). Two additional options not discussed in the preceding, the user's **Name** and **Initials**, do not have corresponding system policies, because they are set at each computer individually; whereas system policies are generally used for many computers and users at once.

Controlling PowerPoint-Specific Web Options Locally Through the Options Dialog Box

Most Web Options that affect PowerPoint are set for Office as a whole, as discussed earlier, in the section "Establishing Office-Wide Customizations That Affect PowerPoint." However, three options are specific to PowerPoint. These can be controlled locally by choosing **Tools, Options, General**, clicking **Web Options**, and displaying the **General** tab (see Figure 8.6).

FIGURE 8.6

Setting PowerPoint Web Options dialog box General tab.

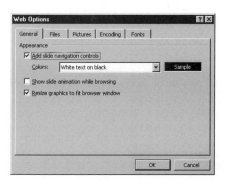

Following are the options on the Web options General tab:

- **Add slide navigation controls.** With this option selected, notes pages and presentation outlines are visible from within a Web browser; you can choose among several color schemes from the **Colors** drop-down box.

- **Show slide animation while browsing.** This option, cleared by default, displays slide animation and transition effects in Web browsers. This option requires more bandwidth, however, and is compatible only with Internet Explorer 4.0 and 5.

- **Resize graphics to fit browser window.** This option resizes graphics to stay in proportion with the rest of a Web page, but is compatible only with Internet Explorer 4.0 and 5.0.

Controlling PowerPoint-Specific Web Options Centrally from the System Policy Editor

The three Web General Options discussed in the previous section can also be controlled centrally with system policies from the PPOINT9.ADM policy template (Microsoft PowerPoint 2000, Tools, Options, Web Options, General). Other Web General Options are set for Office as a whole and can be set through the System Policy Editor at Default User\Microsoft Office 2000\Tools|Options|General|Web Options. These options are discussed in greater detail earlier in this chapter, in the section "Establishing Office-Wide Customizations That Affect PowerPoint."

Customizing Edit Options

PowerPoint enables you to control several aspects of the editing process. Several of PowerPoint's Edit settings are familiar to experienced Word users. They resemble the settings that Word provides for AutoFormatting and AutoCorrect; however, they are set separately. Changes made to the Word equivalent settings do not affect how PowerPoint behaves. In the following two sections, you review controlling editing settings locally, at a user workstation, and centrally via system policies.

Controlling Edit Options Locally Through the Options Dialog Box
PowerPoint's default Edit settings are displayed in the Edit tab of the Options dialog box, as shown in Figure 8.7, and are described in the following:

- **Replace straight quotes with smart quotes.** With this box checked, PowerPoint replaces straight up-and-down quotation marks and apostrophes with curly ones that look better. If you're exporting your document for use by another program, especially if you're crossing platforms (let's say, to the Macintosh or a UNIX workstation), be sure the other program can display smart quotes properly before using them.

TIP

If your organization prepares presentations for many companies, you might find that you have one client that requires smart quotes and another that prohibits them. Sometimes, you realize partway through a presentation that PowerPoint has been adding undesired smart quotes. Yes, you can turn smart quotes off through the **AutoFormat as you type** tab of the AutoCorrect dialog box, but what about the ones that are already in your document? Use Find & Replace to get rid of them.

First, choose **Edit, Replace**. Then, place a straight quotation mark (") in the **Find** box and another straight quotation mark (") in the **Replace** box. Choose **Replace All**. PowerPoint searches for *both* curly and straight quotation marks and replaces them all with straight quotation marks. Repeat the process for curly and straight single quotation marks (apostrophes). You might want to automate this process with a macro.

FIGURE 8.7
The Edit tab of the PowerPoint Options dialog box.

- **When selecting, automatically select entire word.** PowerPoint provides this shortcut to make it easier to select large blocks of text. With this box checked, users don't have to precisely start at the beginning of a word to select the whole word. Rather, as soon as they select the space after a word, PowerPoint assumes they intended to select the whole word. If you suspect your users will find this inconvenient, clear the check box.

- **Use smart cut and paste.** Checking this box tells PowerPoint to eliminate any extra spaces users might inadvertently leave when deleting or pasting text—ensuring there is exactly one space between each word in a sentence.

- **Drag-and-drop text editing.** With this feature turned on (as it is by default), users can select text, right-click, and drag the text to a new location. Some people find this especially intuitive; others find drag-and-drop text editing leads them to accidentally move text they didn't intend to move.

- **Auto-fit text to text placeholder.** If a user enters more text in a placeholder text box than will fit, PowerPoint can shrink the text to make it fit—but PowerPoint doesn't shrink the text past the size specified in the **Visual Clarity** tab of the Style Options dialog box (which is covered later in "Customizing Spelling and Style Settings").

- **AutoFormat as you type.** With this check box selected, PowerPoint automatically formats headings, bulleted and numbered lists, borders, numbers, and symbols as you work. It's all or nothing—you can't specify which of these elements you want PowerPoint to AutoFormat, as you can in Word.

- **New charts take on PowerPoint font.** This option specifies that the text in new charts will be 18-point Arial. If you've established a different standard for your charts, and you want your standard to override PowerPoint's defaults, clear this check box.

■ **Maximum number of undos.** This scroll box specifies how many actions your users can reverse—in other words, how many actions must be stored in memory. The default setting is 20; users can undo up to 20 actions and then redo up to 20 actions. If your systems are relatively short on memory, reducing this value is one way to extend the memory you have.

Controlling Edit Options Centrally from the System Policy Editor   Each of the Edit options discussed in the previous section can also be controlled centrally with system policies from the PPOINT9.ADM policy template (Microsoft PowerPoint 2000, Tools, Options, Edit).

Customizing Print Options

PowerPoint enables you to control a variety of printing behaviors, including aspects of printing that apply to every presentation and that apply only to a specific presentation. Both categories of settings can be controlled locally from user workstations; only settings that apply to every presentation can be controlled centrally via system policies. In the following two sections, you review controlling Print settings locally and then centrally.

Controlling Print Options Locally Through the Options Dialog Box   Print settings are controlled through the Print tab of the Options dialog box; the default settings are shown in Figure 8.8. The settings of primary interest to Office administrators are described in detail in the following:

FIGURE 8.8
The Print tab of
PowerPoint's Options
dialog box.

■ **Background printing.** By default, PowerPoint prints *in the background* so that users can return to work in their presentations more quickly, but print jobs run a bit more slowly. If you find that PowerPoint prints too slowly, try disabling background printing. PowerPoint now prevents users from working in their presentations until it has sent all pages to your printer (or Windows print spooling file).

■ **Print TrueType fonts as graphics.** This setting is a workaround for a variety of printing problems, notably error messages that you are sending too many fonts to your printer. The problem is most common with older printers and was more common in earlier versions of Windows, such as Windows 3.x.

■ **Print inserted objects at printer resolution.** Checking this box instructs PowerPoint to print at your printer's default resolution; you should rarely need to check this box.

Controlling Print Options Centrally from the System Policy Editor The three Print options discussed in the previous section—but *not* the Print tab's other options for individual presentations—can also be controlled centrally with system policies from the PPOINT9.ADM policy template (Microsoft PowerPoint 2000, Tools | Options, Print).

Customizing Save Options

PowerPoint enables you to control several aspects of how it saves files. In the following two sections, you review controlling Save settings locally, at a user workstation, and centrally via system policies.

Controlling Save Options Locally Through the Options Dialog Box Save settings are controlled through the Save tab of the Options dialog box; the default settings are shown in Figure 8.9 and detailed in the following:

FIGURE 8.9

The Save tab of PowerPoint's Options dialog box.

■ **Allow fast saves.** This feature enables PowerPoint to save time on most saves by recording all the changes to a presentation at the end of the file, rather than integrating them one by one throughout the file. When a sufficient number of changes have been made, PowerPoint performs a full save.

N O T E In Chapter 6, we discouraged you from using Fast Saves with Microsoft Word, because Fast Saved files cannot be reliably understood by other software that may import them. However, this is unlikely to be an issue with PowerPoint, because it is much less likely that you'll be exchanging presentations with users of other presentation software. ■

■ **Prompt for file properties.** This option opens the Properties dialog box whenever you save a presentation for the first time. Turning this option on might slightly inconvenience your users, but it can help you capture valuable information about the presentations they create.

- **Save AutoRecover info every.** This scroll box tells PowerPoint how often to create an AutoRecover file for open presentations. You can set intervals from 1 to 120 minutes; the default is 10 minutes. As has been mentioned elsewhere, AutoRecover files are no substitute for saving regularly, and they are far from 100 percent reliable, but they do afford some modest protection against file loss.

- **Convert charts when saving as previous version.** With this box selected, if you save to a previous version of PowerPoint, your charts are also converted so that they can be edited in that version of PowerPoint.

- **Save PowerPoint files as.** Here, you can specify a default format to save all your files in the following:

  - PowerPoint Presentation (PowerPoint 2000 and 97)
  - PowerPoint 97-2000 & 95 Presentation (a single file containing presentations readable in both formats)
  - PowerPoint 95 Presentation
  - PowerPoint 4.0 Presentation
  - Web Page (a mixture of HTML, XML, CSS, and JavaScript that is compatible with Internet Explorer 5.0, largely compatible with Internet Explorer 4.0, and generally—but not entirely—compatible with Netscape 4.0 and later browsers)

▶ For more information about managing PowerPoint presentation formats in environments where users are working with multiple versions of PowerPoint, **see** "Managing Multiple Versions of Office," on **p. 517**.

- **Default File Location.** Here you can set the default folder where PowerPoint saves files and where it looks first when users choose File, Open. The default setting is c:\windows\Profiles*username*\Personal; however, you might want to change this to your user's network location or possibly to a centralized folder where you store all presentations.

N O T E Don't confuse Default File Location with the location where PowerPoint presentation templates are stored. This is typically c:\Program Files\Microsoft Office\Templates\Presentations. Again, you might want to change this to a network location; this time, consider changing it to a read-only folder if you don't want users to change your standard shared presentations. ■

Controlling Save Options Centrally Through System Policies   The Save options discussed in the preceding can also be controlled centrally with system policies from the PPOINT9.ADM policy template (Microsoft PowerPoint 2000, Tools, Options, Save).

Using system policies, you can also set a Shared Templates path for Word, PowerPoint, and Excel at the same time. The policies you need are available in the OFFICE9.ADM Policy Template (Microsoft Office 2000, Shared Paths, Shared Templates).

▶ For more details on using the System Policy Editor, **see** Chapter 37, "Reducing Office 2000's Total Cost of Ownership," **p. 963**.

Customizing Spelling and Style Settings

PowerPoint's Spelling and Style options enable you to control the way PowerPoint checks spelling and its powerful new style checking feature. The options include several that are also available in Word; however, the settings are independent. Changes you make here do not affect the Word settings. In the following sections, you review controlling Spelling and Style settings locally, at a user workstation, and centrally via system policies.

Controlling Spelling Options Locally Through the Options Dialog Box

Spelling settings are controlled through the Spelling and Style tab of the Options dialog box; the default spelling settings are shown in Figure 8.10 and explained in the following list:

FIGURE 8.10
The Spelling and Style tab of the PowerPoint Options dialog box.

- **Check spelling as you type.** When turned on, PowerPoint continually checks users' spelling and places wavy red underlines under any words it cannot find in its dictionary.

- **Hide spelling errors in this document.** When turned on, PowerPoint continues to check spelling as a user types, but does not display wavy red underlines. However, when a user runs the spelling checker feature, it works faster, because the checking has already been done.

- **Always suggest corrections.** PowerPoint's spelling suggestions are often inaccurate in highly technical presentations that contain a lot of arcane jargon. For such presentations, in the interest of time, you might want to disable the suggested spellings to make the spelling checker run faster.

- **Ignore words in UPPERCASE.** No spelling checker understands all acronyms. Because most acronyms are all caps, you can tell PowerPoint not to flag words that are all caps. (This feature is turned on by default.)

- **Ignore words with numbers.** Some product names combine words and numbers and might wrongly be flagged by a typical spell checker. Therefore, by default, PowerPoint ignores word/number combinations.

■ **Check style.** This turns on PowerPoint's new style checking feature. If you turn this feature on (or leave it on; it is turned on by default), you might also want to review and control the Style Options discussed in the following section.

Controlling Spelling Options Centrally Through the System Policy Editor   The spelling options and Check Style option discussed in the previous section can also be controlled centrally with system policies from the PPOINT9.ADM policy template (Microsoft PowerPoint 2000, Tools | Options, Spelling and Style).

Controlling How PowerPoint 2000 Checks Presentation Styles Locally Through the Options Dialog Box   With PowerPoint 2000, Microsoft continues on its long-term goal of helping users build better presentations. Previous versions introduced Design Template to make presentations look good and Content Wizards to help users structure their ideas more effectively. PowerPoint 2000 adds Style Checking to help make sure their presentations are punctuated and capitalized consistently and are legible and uncluttered.

To control PowerPoint's Style Options settings, choose **Tools, Options, Spelling and Style**; then click **Style Options** (see Figure 8.11). The Visual Clarity tab of the Style Options dialog box opens.

FIGURE 8.11

The Visual Clarity tab of the Style Options dialog box.

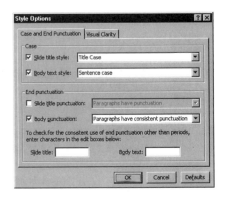

Here, you can control settings for

■ **Standardizing the case of Slide Titles and Body Text.** The default settings are **Title Case** for slide titles and **Sentence case** for body text.

■ **Standardizing the end punctuation of Slide Titles and Body Text.** The default settings are to ignore the punctuation of slide titles, but standardize each body text bullet to end with a period. If you want to standardize punctuation for either titles or body text, you can specify any punctuation character you want. For example, you can standardize titles to end with a colon.

PowerPoint automatically changes the case or punctuation of text that is not consistent with the settings you establish. This can be a powerful tool for adding a professional finish and consistency to your company's presentations. You might be tempted to mandate strict settings and prevent users from changing them. But before you do, be aware that there are inevitably times when users need to violate those settings—and if you lock them down, they might have no way to do so. Be careful, or you might find yourself being called for support every time a user can't capitalize a word in the middle of a body text bullet.

Controlling How PowerPoint 2000 Checks Presentation Styles Centrally Through the System Policy Editor The Presentation Style options discussed in the previous section can also be controlled centrally with system policies from the PPOINT9.ADM policy template (Microsoft PowerPoint 2000, Tools | Options, Spelling and Style, Visual Clarity).

Controlling Settings for Visual Clarity Locally Through the Options Dialog Box How many times have you seen a presentation where the presenter was so wordy, the text on the slides became too small? PowerPoint 2000 provides Visual Clarity settings designed to help prevent this from occurring. To control these settings, choose **Tools**, **Options**, **Spelling and Style**; then click **Style Options** and the **Visual Clarity** tab (see Figure 8.12).

FIGURE 8.12
The Visual Clarity tab
of the Style Options
dialog box.

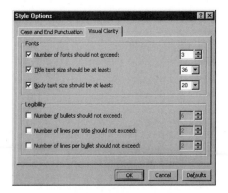

The settings include the following:

- **Number of fonts should not exceed.** The default is three. This seems a good rule of thumb, but be sure it corresponds to the requirements of your corporate design guidelines, if you have them.

- **Title text size should be at least.** The default is 36 point. There might be a little give in this value, but you should rarely reduce it below 32 points.

- **Body text size should be at least.** The default is 20 point. Again, you should rarely reduce this below 18 point. Keep in mind that some fonts are more readable at smaller sizes than others, and that optimal type size can vary depending on how you make your presentations. For instance, if you are presenting 35mm slides in a large room, err on the side of larger text.

- **Number of bullets should not exceed.** By default, PowerPoint does not check this setting, but if you turn it on, PowerPoint flags users when they enter more than six bullets on a slide.

■ **Number of lines per title should not exceed.** By default, PowerPoint does not check this setting, but if you turn it on, PowerPoint flags users when they write a slide title that uses more than two lines.

■ **Number of lines per bullet should not exceed.** By default, PowerPoint does not check this setting, but if you turn it on, PowerPoint flags users when they write a bullet point that uses more than two lines.

The settings on this tab are purely advisory. When a user violates a rule you set, PowerPoint doesn't actually change their work; rather, it gently notifies them that they've exceeded a reasonable limit, as shown in Figure 8.13.

FIGURE 8.13
PowerPoint Help gently guides users toward better visual clarity.

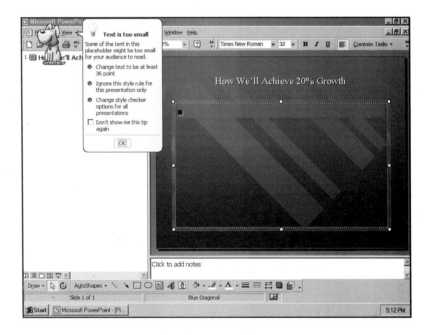

Controlling How PowerPoint 2000 Checks Visual Clarity Centrally from the System Policy Editor The Presentation Style options discussed in the previous section can also be controlled centrally with system policies from the PPOINT9.ADM policy template (Microsoft PowerPoint 2000, Tools | Options, Spelling and Style, Visual Clarity).

Creating Custom Presentations for Your Users

You've already seen that PowerPoint provides extensive prefabricated resources for presenters: more than 40 design templates, 24 detailed presentations, automated options for building onscreen presentations, overheads, 35mm slides, and even Web presentations.

But at some point, generic isn't enough. In the following sections, you learn how to build and deploy custom presentations that cover the specific material your presenters need to deliver, save them huge amounts of time, and help ensure that all the presentations your company makes are of high quality.

PowerPoint offers the following two primary techniques for customization:

- **Building your own design template.** Starting either from scratch or with a built-in template, you create a new presentation and then edit the slide master to include your logos, text formatting, color schemes, backgrounds, and any other visual elements you need. You then save the file, choosing **Design Template** (*.pot) in the Save As dialog box. By default, PowerPoint saves the template in the folder specified for User Templates, and when you next create a new file, the new template appears in the **General** tab of the File, New dialog box.

- **Building your own content template.** To build a content template, you follow all the steps listed in the preceding bullet and then add boilerplate text to as many slides as you can. For instance, if you are creating a content template that helps users summarize the financial results in each division of your company, create separate boilerplate slides for each region. When you've finished, save the file as a **Design Template** (*.dot)—both the built-in designs and boilerplate slides are saved.

 TIP Borrow from PowerPoint's built-in tools wherever possible. For example, you might build a presentation using PowerPoint's built-in *Financial Overview* or *Reporting Progress or Status* presentation, trim it down to the bare essentials, reformat them as needed, and then duplicate the remaining slides to create a separate section of the presentation for each division in your company.

You might want to go a step further and make your content template available through the AutoContent Wizard. To do so from a local workstation, follow these steps:

1. Choose **File**, **New**.
2. Display the **General** tab and double-click on the **AutoContent Wizard**.
3. Click **Next** to display the Presentation Type window (see Figure 8.14).
4. Click the category of presentation where you want to store your custom presentation (**General**, **Corporate**, **Projects**, or **Sales/Marketing**; you cannot choose **All** or **Carnegie Coach**).
5. Click **Add**. The Select Presentation Template dialog box opens.
6. Browse to and select the presentation you want and choose **OK**.
7. Click **Finish**.

 TIP The best time to customize presentations is before you deploy Office, because you can include your custom presentations as part of your centralized installation process. At the same time, you can also remove any standard presentations and design templates you believe are inconsistent with your corporate image. You can use the Custom Installation Wizard and Office Profile Wizard to do this; these are covered in Chapter 2, "Automating and Customizing Office Installations Across the Network."

FIGURE 8.14
Choosing the category in which you want the custom presentation to appear.

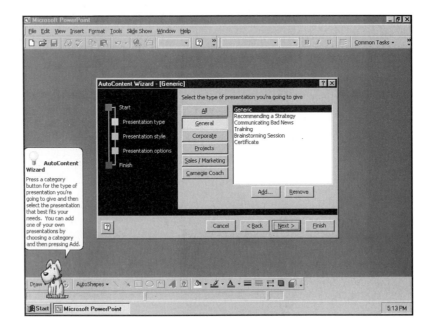

Changing PowerPoint's Default Blank Presentation

One brute-force technique for customizing your presentations is to simply substitute a design template of your own for PowerPoint's black-and-white Blank Presentation.POT. To do so, use either of these methods:

■ Rename the selected template to `Blank Presentation.pot`. Before renaming it, rename the real blank to `Blank Presentation.pxx`, to preserve it should you want to restore it later. After your selected template is set up as the Blank, it will be the template that appears whenever the user selects Blank Presentation from the first dialog box.

■ Combine a simple procedure with a macro. Establish a procedure wherein all users start with the Blank Presentation (the original Blank), and as soon as the presentation opens, run a macro that applies a particular template to the presentation.

CAUTION

Renaming the Blank Presentation template is somewhat risky. If the real Blank presentation is lost or if you forget to rename it before renaming your selected template, you might have to reinstall the software to reestablish a true Blank Presentation template. Also, any users who want a real Blank will not be able to use it, unless your new name retains the .pot extension and you move it to the Presentation Designs folder. In either case, you've removed some of the PowerPoint flexibility.

Presenting Guidelines for Successful Custom Presentations

So far, we have largely focused on the techniques and technology associated with deploying custom presentations. But it's worth remembering that a bad presentation, widely deployed and given repeatedly, will damage your company more than any individual unqualified presenter ever could have.

If you intend to take responsibility for customizing presentations on behalf of your workgroup or company, here are some guidelines for ensuring you give them presentations that reflect well on you:

- **Understand the expectations and needs of the people who will view your presentations.** How can your presentations serve those needs? Here's your chance to cut out the slides that pat your company on the back for 100 years of excellence! If your presentations are used in international environments, be conscious of cultural differences in the way viewers respond to both visual and content cues.

- **Focus on your presenters.** What kinds of presentations do they give? What media do they work in? Are they comfortable as presenters? Do they tend to use barebones presentations that simply provide a loose structure for ad libbing, or do they need tools for building extremely detailed presentations? Are they comfortable with PowerPoint and related tools? What complementary resources, such as visually consistent clip art, do you have to deliver to help them finish the job?

- **Focus on the business and physical environment where your presentations are given.** This helps drive the look-and-feel decisions you make. For example, your presentation should use hotter colors and more multimedia if it must cut through the clutter of a loud, crowded trade-show booth. The same presentation would be disastrous, given one-on-one in an executive's office.

- **Understand the technical environment your presentations must thrive in.** If presented on the Internet, they might face the same slow download times as other Web pages. If presented onscreen by your sales force, they are subject to the color and speed limitations of your installed base of notebook PCs. If sent to customers, are you sure your customers use PowerPoint 2000? If not, which versions do they use? Should you provide the PowerPoint viewer? Will your presentations include handouts? If so, be sure the handouts print clearly. Will your presentations be output to 35mm slides? If so, test the process to ensure the slides look as you expect them to, with the appropriate fonts and colors.

- **Consider your corporate image.** Is it staid, cutting-edge, or somewhere in between? Do you have corporate design standards that should be followed? Are there rules for how you use your logo? Standard color schemes that all external materials must conform to?

- **Provide instructions.** Include detailed instructions, either in the presentation itself or, perhaps better, in an attached Word memo.

CAUTION

It might be better to attach the memo because careless users can easily leave the instructions embedded in presentations they deliver to customers—an embarrassing mistake.

N O T E In reading this checklist, it might have occurred to you to hire a professional graphics designer to create your presentations. This makes quite a lot of sense—*if you can find the right designer.*

Be aware that many designers have little experience with PowerPoint and don't care much for it, because its design tools lack the precision of many professional graphics design tools. For example, PowerPoint has traditionally had relatively poor color-matching capabilities and relatively poor support for EPS graphics.

Also be aware that the majority of designers still work on the Macintosh; and colors and fonts used on the Macintosh do not always translate as intended if displayed on Windows computers. Finally, many designers who do run PowerPoint still run earlier versions such as PowerPoint 4.0x for the Macintosh. (In fact, there is no PowerPoint 2000 for the Macintosh, although PowerPoint 98 for the Macintosh uses essentially the same format and offers many of the same features.) If your designer uses an obsolete version of PowerPoint, he might not have access to the features you want in your presentations.

Bottom line: Ask lots of questions and test the files you get! ■

Improving Productivity with VBA Macros

Macros are programs that you create by recording a series of frequently performed steps. VBA is the programming language that Office uses to create these macros, although the user need not know VBA to create a macro—the code is inserted by Office as the person records their steps. The user can execute the program at any time, thus automating the steps contained in the macro. Macros can be written for just about any activity you perform in PowerPoint. Although many tasks that previously required macros are now automated directly through the software itself—such as AutoCorrect or inserting Word Tables—there are still several processes that can be automated to save time and support consistency. Following is a list of those automated processes:

- **Starting a presentation.** Build a macro that opens a new presentation, chooses a particular template, selects a specific layout, and leaves the user at their first blank slide, after having only clicked a toolbar button. The macro could also include the creation of a title slide, should your title slides have consistent content.

- **Opening toolbars.** Create a macro that opens specific toolbars for specific tasks, such as opening the Drawing and Picture toolbars when a piece of clip art is inserted. By creating a macro that inserts a particular piece of clip art and then opens the desired toolbars, three tasks are converted to one simple keystroke or mouse-click.

- **Formatting changes.** A macro that opens the Slide Master in PowerPoint and inserts, moves, and resizes your company logo on the slide can save a lot of steps and assure consistent placement of your logo on any presentation template. Of course, if a specific presentation template has been chosen for everyone to use and a macro created to apply it, the master should have already been set up for that template.

- **Printing.** If every presentation created must be printed in a particular format for hardcopy storage, create a macro that initiates the print job, selects the output format, and prints the file. By making a macro for this task, you can be assured that all your presentation hard copies are, for example, three-slide-per-page handouts and that two sets are made.

- **Running a slideshow.** Create a macro that selects a particular slideshow, starts on a particular slide, and runs the show. This saves the audience from having to see the file selected and the Slideshow command invoked. If timings and a recorded narration are part of the show, the macro becomes even more powerful by invoking built-in automation.

Recording a VBA macro is simple and doesn't require knowledge of VBA. If, however, you are familiar with VBA, the editing and enhancement of macros are much easier for you.

To record a PowerPoint macro, follow these steps:

1. Before recording, be sure that you have set the stage so that the macro begins at the point that its user will be when he invokes it later. For example, if the user will already have the presentation open when the macro is invoked, have the presentation open when you begin to build the macro.

2. Choose **Tools**, **Macro**, **Record New Macro**. The Record Macro dialog box opens, as shown in Figure 8.15.

3. Give the macro a name (no spaces) and choose which presentation the macro is stored in (and thus available to). Type a description, if needed.

NOTE If you store a macro in the active presentation, it is available only from within that presentation. If, however, you store it in a presentation created purely for the use of macros, you have access to the macro whenever that presentation is open. You can store all your general-use macros in a macro presentation and distribute it to your colleagues (call it Macro.ppt, for example).

To access these macros, your users can open that presentation and then invoke any macro they want. If the macro presentation is empty (of any text or graphic content), it will be a small file and not create any problems in terms of system resources if you have it open while working on other presentations.

4. Click **OK** to close the Record Macro dialog box. Your macro is now recording, signified by a small floating toolbar onscreen, with a **Stop** button on it.

5. Record your macro. Perform each step in the exact order you want it performed each time the macro is run.

6. When your steps are completed, click the **Stop** button.

FIGURE 8.15

Recording a new
PowerPoint macro.

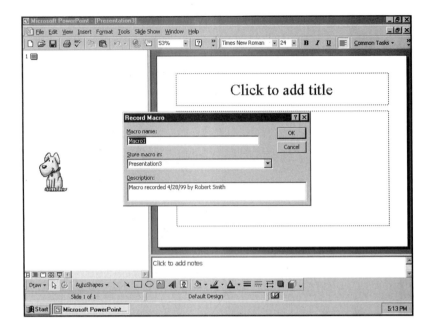

After you've created your macro, you can use the **Tools**, **Customize** command to assign it to a toolbar button. To invoke a macro, click the button assigned to it. ●

Customizing Access to Your Organization's Needs

by Gordon Padwick

Customizing the Access interface is an essential part of building a multiuser database. The commands and options in Access that make it easy to develop a database are the very same tools you don't want end users to be able to access. Without a customized interface, it is far too easy for an inexperienced user to wreak havoc on a database.

So, while customizing the other Office applications is beneficial, it is not necessary. However, with Access, it is a crucial part of planning your database and ensuring the integrity of your data.

Customizing the Access Interface

One of the easiest ways to customize an Access database, is to customize the interface—how the database appears onscreen to the end users. You can accomplish this in several ways:

- You can tailor the menu bars and toolbars to display only those commands users of the database will need. If people find it difficult to ascertain what a toolbar button is used for, you can alter the appearance of the buttons to display a text description instead of (or as well as) the button image.

- The settings in the Options dialog box can be changed to customize the Access interface and default settings of Access objects, such as tables, queries, and forms.

- A new object in Access 2000 is the Data Access Page (DAP). This object is a special type of Web page you can create to display or gather information on an intranet or the Internet.

- You can design a Switchboard Form, to provide users with a starting point when they open the database, from which they can access the other forms, queries, and reports you have created for the database.

- Using startup switches, you can modify the settings that start Access. This includes the ability to automatically start access and display a particular database, or to troubleshoot startup problems.

- Although recommended only for advanced users, another way to customize Access is by adjusting the Registry settings. You can alter the settings for the Jet 4.0 Database Engine, as well as the ODBC (Open Database Connectivity) driver settings through the Registry.

- The final section in this chapter discusses how macros and VBA code can be used to customize Access.

Customizing Access Menu Bars and Toolbars

In the other Office applications, you will probably initially customize the menu bar and toolbars 1for your organization's needs, and then rarely adjust those custom settings. However, in Access, you're more likely to customize the menu bar and toolbars for each database you create.

Toolbars in Access operate differently than they do in the other Office applications. In Word, Excel, and PowerPoint, two toolbars (Standard and Formatting) are displayed by default. However, in Access, a single toolbar is displayed, based on the object and view that are active. For example, if the Database window is active, the Database toolbar displays. When you display the Design view for a table, the Table Design toolbar appears. When you display a table in the datasheet view, the Table Datasheet toolbar appears. You can tweak these toolbars to customize them for your database, or you can create new custom toolbars from scratch.

One reason for creating a custom toolbar is to limit the commands to which end users have access. For instance, you might want to create a toolbar that has buttons for accessing only certain tables, queries, and reports, previewing, printing, and exiting the application.

You accomplish this by specifying the custom toolbar in the Startup dialog box (Tools, Startup) and designating a switchboard as the opening form. You will need to clear the Display Database Window check box. The end user now has an interface they can navigate through, but with limited options (and no way to modify the Access objects). Figure 9.1 shows this type of startup window with a custom toolbar and switchboard.

FIGURE 9.1
Use the settings in the Startup dialog box to designate the default menu bar and startup form in this figure.

The way you customize menu bars and toolbars in Access is similar to the way you customize these items in Word, Excel, and PowerPoint. In each application, you can

- Add to or remove buttons from each toolbar by clicking the down arrow at the right edge of the toolbar and clicking Add or Remove Buttons, or by using the Customize dialog box (**Tools**, **Customize**, **Commands**) to drag buttons on and off active toolbars.

- Specify whether to use Office 2000's new personalized menus, which attempt to display only the commands users need (**Tools**, **Customize**, **Options**, **Menus Show Recently Used Commands First**).

- Create new toolbars through **Tools**, **Customize**, **Toolbars**.

- Modify the existing button images or create new images and add them to your toolbar buttons.

▶ Each feature listed previously is covered extensively in Chapter 6, beginning with the section "Personalizing Your Menus and Toolbars," on **p. 132**.

The next few sections focus on customizing features that are unique to Access.

Customizing Toolbar Properties

To customize the Access menu bar and toolbars, choose **Tools**, **Customize**. There are three tabs in the Customize dialog box: Toolbars, Commands, and Options. On the **Toolbars** tab of the Customize dialog box (shown in Figure 9.2), you'll see a list of all the toolbars available in Access. New toolbars that you create appear at the bottom of the list.

FIGURE 9.2
You cannot delete the built-in toolbars, only the custom toolbars you create.

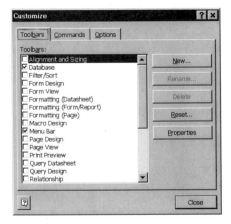

One toolbar feature unique to Access is toolbar properties. By selecting the Properties button, you can change the toolbar name and options the in the Properties dialog box (see Figure 9.3). You can change only some of the properties for the built-in Access toolbars; you are not allowed to change the name or type of the built-in toolbars.

FIGURE 9.3
If you don't want users to change the placement of the toolbar, change the Docking option to Can't Change.

Designating a Toolbar Type When you create a custom toolbar, you can designate the toolbar type in the properties dialog box. There are three types of toolbars you can create in Access: menu bars, toolbars, and pop-ups. Although *menu bars* traditionally contain drop-down menus, and *toolbars* traditionally display command button icons, you can place command buttons on a menu bar and drop-down menus on a toolbar. *Pop-ups* are text commands on shortcut and drop-down menus.

Customizing Command Buttons and Menus

The Commands tab on the Customize dialog box lists the various command buttons (and menus) available in Access. Categories are listed on the left, with the commands in each category on the right. There are also categories listing the built-in menus, Access objects (such as queries and forms), macros, and ActiveX controls.

You can select a command then click the **Description** button to see what action each command performs (see Figure 9.4). It is from this tab that you add commands (and menus) to the toolbars.

Part

II

Ch

9

FIGURE 9.4
The Commands tab not only lists all the menu commands, but gives you the option to list individual objects, such as specific tables within the database.

Although the basic steps for adding and removing toolbar buttons are addressed in Chapter 6 in the section "Adding a Command to a Toolbar," it is important to note that you can add any command available through the menus to a toolbar. Although Microsoft places what it thinks are the most frequently used commands on the toolbars, you invariably have commands your users want to work with that are not on the toolbar. An example of one of these might be the Filter by Form command located under the Records category. Placed on a toolbar for use with a form, it enables the user to filter the database using a blank copy of their data entry form.

▶ For more information about toolbar buttons, **see** Chapter 6, "Customizing Word to Your Organization's Needs," on **p. 121**.

Setting General Toolbar and Menu Bar Options

From the Options tab of the Customize dialog box, you select the behavior of the toolbars, change the appearance of toolbar icons, and select the options associated with ScreenTips. Suppose you don't like the default behavior of the Personalized Toolbars and Menus, which initially show only the most recently used commands on the menu and the full list after a short delay. You can force Access to always show the full menu by clearing the check from the **Menus Show Recently Used Commands First** option.

TIP   If your advanced users prefer the personalized menus, teach your less experienced users to double-click the menus. This forces the full menus to appear. As users become more experienced, you can introduce the personalized menu concept to them.

Creating New Toolbars, Menu Bars, and Pop-Ups

To create a new toolbar, menu bar, or pop-up, you first must access the Customize dialog box (choose **Tools**, **Customize**). After you have the dialog box displayed, follow these steps:

1. Select the **Toolbars** tab and click **New**.

2. Type the name for the new toolbar, menu, or pop-up and click **OK**.

3. To the side of the Customize dialog box a small gray box appears with a close button (an X) in the upper-right corner. This is the new toolbar you have created.

N O T E   The default is to create a toolbar. To change this new item to a menu bar or pop-up, click the **Properties** button and change the type (as described earlier in the section "Customizing Toolbar Properties"). The remainder of these steps will use the term toolbar to refer to all three types. ▪

4. On the Commands tab, find the first button or menu you want to place on the new toolbar. When you drag the item over the new toolbar, a copy is placed on the new toolbar (see Figure 9.5). Continue to drag each item until all the desired buttons and menus are on new toolbar. If you need to rearrange the order of the items on the new toolbar, simply drag and drop them to the correct position. The Customize dialog box must be open for you to modify toolbars.

FIGURE 9.5
The "I" indicator shows where the command will be placed on the toolbar.

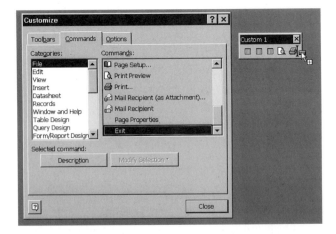

5. While the Customize dialog box is open, you can right-click the items on the toolbar and modify them. For example, you can display both the image and text (refer to Figure 9.1), you can edit the existing button image, pick a new image altogether (see Figure 9.6), or alter the properties (which enables you to alter the button ScreenTip).

FIGURE 9.6
You can also create your own image by selecting Edit Button Image instead.

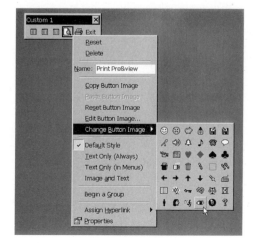

Customizing Access Options

The Options dialog box offers customization that affects the Access program and databases in general. The changes you make in the Options dialog box are not specific to each database; rather, they are global changes. Using the Options dialog box, you can control how the Access interface is viewed, including the editing features, keyboard functionality, datasheet settings, form and report settings, as well as query and table-design settings. You display the Options dialog box by choosing **Tools**, **Options** (see Figure 9.7).

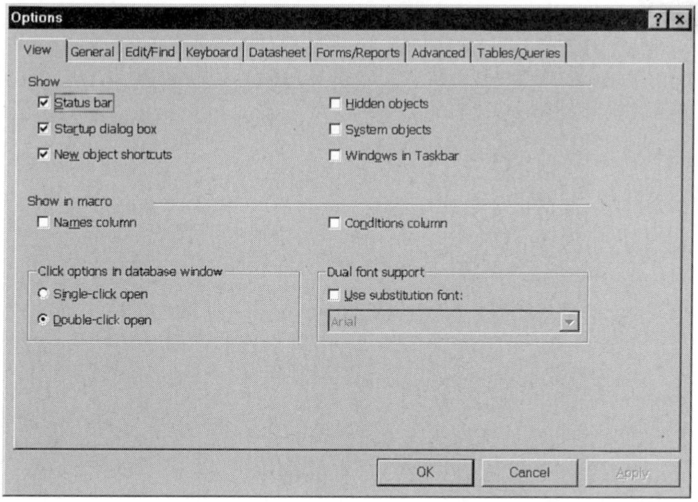

FIGURE 9.7
The Options dialog box enables you to customize the look, feel, and behavior of the Access environment.

Access has eight tabs in the Options dialog box (**Tools**, **Options**). These tabs organize the options that you can customize. Users can control these settings; however, you can also control many of these centrally—either by setting them during the installation process (see Chapter 2, "Automating and Customizing Office Installations Across the Network") or later, via System Policies.

N O T E The System Policy Editor enables you to control a wide range of Office features centrally through *system policies*, which are applied when a user logs onto the network. The System Policy Editor is part of the Office 2000 Resource Kit Toolbox, downloadable at

`http://www.microsoft.com/office/ork`

When working with system policies for Office 2000, use this version of the System Policy Editor, not the previous versions that were included with Windows 95/98 or Windows NT 4.0. ▓

▶ For more information about working with the System Policy Editor, **see** "Using System Policies with Office 2000," on **p. 970**.

- ▓ **View.** These options determine the elements users will see in the database window, the single- and double-click options, and font substitution options.
- ▓ **General.** This category includes options that logically don't fit into the other option categories, such as four-digit year formatting, Web options, and print margins.
- ▓ **Edit/Find.** These options control the find/replace and filter settings, along with the editing actions that require confirmation.
- ▓ **Keyboard.** The options on this tab set the actions of the Enter and Arrow keys, as well as the action to be taken when you activate a field.
- ▓ **Datasheet.** Use these options to change the appearance of the datasheet view. You can set the color, font, gridline, and cell effect (flat, raised, sunken).
- ▓ **Forms/Reports.** From this tab, you can change the action taken when you drag to select controls in forms or reports, and change the default template used for forms and reports.
- ▓ **Advanced.** This tab contains a variety of options for multiuser environments including the Dynamic Data Exchange (DDE) settings, database shared, and record locking.
- ▓ **Tables/Queries.** These options control the default settings for table and query design. You can choose the default table field type and size, and whether AutoJoin is enabled in multitable queries.

The most significant options are discussed in the next few sections. To learn about an option not discussed here, click the **What's This?** button (question mark) in the Options dialog box and then click the option you are interested in. A pop-up appears describing the option.

Customizing View Options

Access 2000 offers new ways to control and simplify the user interface—and the user experience. You can control many other aspects of how Access looks through the View tab of the Options dialog box.

The items found on the View tab control the display of various elements of the Access interface. For example, you can choose not to display the Startup dialog box each time Access starts by removing the check next to the Startup Dialog Box option. If you want to suppress the Startup dialog box only periodically, you can use command-line switches (discussed in the later section, "Modifying Startup Settings").

New in Access 2000 are the options New Object Shortcuts and Windows in Taskbar (refer to Figure 9.7). Let's assume you even allow end users to access the database window. Deactivating the New Object Shortcuts option prevents users from creating new objects (such as new queries or reports) from the shortcuts in the database window by hiding those shortcuts. When the Windows in Taskbar option is selected, it displays an item on the Windows taskbar for each database object you have open. For instance, if you have a form and a query open, the taskbar displays three objects: the database window, the form window, and the query window. Generally with databases, you want to avoid any confusion for end users by suppressing the display of window objects on the taskbar. When suppressed, the windows can still be viewed through the Window menu command.

Another new feature in Access 2000 is Use Substitution Font. This option enables you to display characters in a datasheet, form, or report that are not supported by the default font. Dual font support is useful when your data consists of both English-language characters and characters in another language, and the default font does not support the characters in that language. By indicating a substitution font, Microsoft Access will use the substitution font whenever it encounters characters that the default does not support.

Customizing General Options

The General tab (shown in Figure 9.8) contains settings that apply to the operation of Access in general, rather than to specific objects created in Access (such as queries or forms). The general options are particularly useful for controlling features in a multiuser environment. For example, you can assign the default margins used for printed documents, and set the default database folder from which users retrieve forms, queries, and reports.

A powerful new feature in Access 2000 is Name AutoCorrect. In previous versions of Access, if you renamed a field in a table, objects based on that field (such as forms or queries) no longer display the data from that field. Microsoft Access 2000 automatically corrects common side effects that occur when you rename objects or controls in a Microsoft Access database.

When you open an object, Access automatically looks for and fixes discrepancies between the object and the other items that reference the object. For example, if you open a form that is bound to a query, Access compares the date/time stamps for the query and the form. If they are different, Access performs a Name AutoCorrect.

By default, Name AutoCorrect is active for databases that are created with Access 2000. However, for databases converted to Access 2000 from previous versions, you must turn on the Name AutoCorrect option. To use the Name AutoCorrect feature, users must have write and exclusive access to the database. The Name AutoCorrect makes the changes each time that the object is opened, but can't save the changes until someone with permissions to modify the design opens and saves the object.

FIGURE 9.8
Apply general database and Web options in this dialog box.

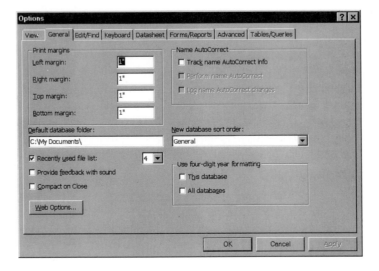

N O T E   Name AutoCorrect does not work in every situation. It cannot change references in an invalid SQL statement, fix references in Visual Basic code, or fix references in a linked table when the table or fields have been renamed in the back end of a front-end/back-end database.

Name AutoCorrect does not work in a replicated database. When you replicate a database, Access turns Name AutoCorrect off. You cannot turn on Name AutoCorrect in a database Design Master or replica.

It cannot repair references to macros in a toolbar or menu. Nor does it work with Microsoft Access Projects. ■

Another new feature on the General tab is <u>W</u>eb Options, which enables you to customize the colors associated with hyperlinks.

Customizing Edit/Find Options

The Edit/Find tab contains three sets of options: Default Find/Replace Behavior, Confirm, and Filter by Form Defaults. These options are used for establishing the default search types, confirmation settings, and filter-by-form value list defaults.

The Default Find/Replace Behavior options let you choose from three types of searches: Fast Search, General Search, and Start of Field Search. Fast Search is the default. It searches the current field looking for whole word matches. To search all fields matching any part of the field, use the General Search option. The Start of Field Search option searches the current field looking for matches with the first few characters in the field. No matter what search type you choose as the default, users can change the criteria in the Find in Field dialog box.

Through this tab, you can also select when confirmation messages appear. Depending on what you have selected, Access asks for confirmation when deleting documents, changing records, and performing action queries. The default is for all three check boxes to be selected.

The Filter by Form options relate to the list of field entries, called a *value list*, that appears for you to choose from. In other words, when you create a filter using a form, you can select the criteria for your filter from a list of values that currently exist in the database.

Customizing Keyboard Options

One area that you might elect to customize for the end user is keyboard behavior. Using this tab, you can control which field is active in a table or recordset when you press **Enter**. You can also control how the keyboard arrow keys behave—whether they move from character to character or field to field. Depending on the type of data entry performed, you might want to change the setting for what action is taken when you enter a field. As a default, this is set to select entire field, which is fine if the existing value is typically replaced upon entering the field. However, if you typically add to the existing information in a field, then you might want to change this setting to go to the end of the field.

Customizing Datasheet Options

The Datasheet tab enables you to control the colors, fonts, default column width, gridlines, and cell appearance in Datasheet views for tables, queries, and forms. Several common Datasheet customizations include changing the default font and hiding gridlines.

Typically, the datasheet is the default view used to look directly at the data in a table in your database. Most organizations prefer not to give users access directly to the tables, but develop forms through which users can display and edit data. Although you can display data in a form in a datasheet layout, it is less common than the columnar, justified, and tabular layouts. So, unless you are planning to use the datasheet view in your forms (or the users working with the table datasheet view threaten to revolt if you don't change the appearance of the screen), it is unlikely you will alter these settings.

Customizing Forms/Reports Options

From the Forms/Reports tab, you can specify a default form or report template other than the Normal template. Access then uses the specified template when you create a form or report from scratch (without using the wizard). So, if you want to create new forms or reports using a custom company template, designate the template on the Forms/Reports tab.

The Forms/Reports tab also contains an option for how objects are selected in forms and reports. When you drag the mouse to select objects, you can require that the objects must be entirely within the selection. The default option is set to select objects that are only partially within the selection.

Customizing Advanced Options

The Advanced tab contains many settings: DDE (Dynamic Data Exchange), timeout intervals, record-locking behavior, open mode, command-line arguments, and error trapping. The most important of these is open mode—whether only one person at a time can access the database (exclusive) or whether the database can be shared by many users simultaneously (shared). Because most databases are designed for multiuser environments, the shared mode is common. However, there might be situations in which you want only one person at a time to open and use a particular database.

Customizing Tables/Queries Options

The settings on the Tables/Queries tab control the table and query design. Several settings you might want to change include the default field type and field size. When you install Access, the field type is Text. If you find that when you design tables the majority of fields are of another type, such as Number, you might want to change your default field type to save time when creating tables. Likewise, the default field size should be decreased or increased based on your needs. Most tables don't require 50 characters for the majority of the text fields.

The Tables/Queries tab also lists several options for defining queries. For example, you might want the queries to display table names (a handy feature if your queries are designed from multiple tables). The Enable AutoJoin feature creates an inner join between two tables when fields with the same name and data type are in both tables, and one is a primary key.

The permissions setting in the Tables/Queries tab affects only new queries. The default is User's. A user with Administer permissions for the query can save changes to the query, or change its ownership. Owner's permissions allows other users to view data returned from a query or (in some cases) to run a query (even if they are restricted from seeing the underlying table). When Owner's is selected, only the query owner can save changes to the query and change the ownership of the query.

Designing a Data Access Page for Your Access Database

Data access pages are Web pages that you can build in Access 2000. While they can be accessed on the Web or on your company intranet site, data access pages are stored in Access (and can be used in Access), or can just as easily be saved on your file system in HTML.

With Data Access Page, Microsoft has brought HTML one level closer to the graphical Access development environment. Now an object type exists that can be developed directly in Access without exporting and conversion. Data access pages support a rich set of tools, including a dozen or so controls (such as list boxes, option buttons, and scrolling text boxes), relatively precise positioning of those controls, sorting, grouping, filtering, and the capability to take advantage of event execution in the pages developed.

Access 2000 also includes a graphical Web page editor—it's not as good as the better commercial editing environments (including FrontPage and even Word), but it's functional and customized for use in Access. With Access, you can create and edit any HTML page, regardless of whether it was generated from within Access or not.

Evaluating Data Access Pages

Data access pages are implemented via Microsoft's proprietary ActiveX object model. That means that data access pages will appear correctly only in version 5 or later of Microsoft's Internet Explorer Web browser. It's impossible to tell how many Internet Explorer 5 browsers will be deployed at any point in time, but the distribution curve has shown that it takes a year or so for a majority of users in the general public to migrate to a new version. Even then, the market saturation will probably be far less than you'll need to generate pages that most people can use. On the other hand, at least you don't need to install the ASP extensions on the Web server anymore, so maybe this is a step in the right direction.

Other shortcomings exist, such as the almost unbelievable absence of a tool that enables you to convert an existing form into a data access page in this release of Access 2000. You can, however, create data access pages based on another Web page—a nice feature. When working with data access pages, you'll be alternatively amazed at how intriguing this idea is—to view an Access data object from a browser—but equally nagged by the feeling that this isn't quite ready for prime time yet.

One of the things that makes data access pages so difficult to get accustomed to is that they do things that the Web just hasn't been used for before. Where have you ever seen an Access-type record navigation bar on the Web? How about expanding and collapsing sections of a Web page based on the data underlying it? Experienced Web developers recognize that these tricks aren't part of standard HTML and must be done with complicated coding behind the scenes.

They're right. But because you haven't seen them before or been involved in writing the code, the Data Access Page development environment is a little like a toy chest filled with baubles written in Visual C++. You won't know what the toys do until you play with them.

In any case, Data Access Page is the first really new feature in Access in several versions and has a whole new learning curve associated with it. Adding controls, manipulating controls, handling grouping and sorting options, properties, and so on—it's all new. Even the venerable Field List window has changed for DAPs.

Creating a Data Access Page

So much is new in Data Access Page that you'll need to try a few and examine how they are built before you can really understand just how different this technique is from creating the other Access objects. Creating your first data access page is likely to be a frustrating experience as you discover all the new controls and techniques available to you, especially if you already have experience writing Web pages or creating Access forms and reports. It's a whole new world. A good place to start is the Page Wizard, which exposes you to some of the features at your disposal. The wizard generates passable data access pages that you can modify easily (unlike most wizard-created objects, which might generate difficult-to-read code).

N O T E Data Access Page does not work in Access 2000 unless you have Internet Explorer 5 installed on your system. The Data Access Page features are then grayed out in the Pages tab. Internet Explorer 5 or later is required to create or modify data access pages. ■

CAUTION

Data Access Page saves representations of your pages in both the Database window and on the file system. If you delete or move the page in the file system, however, the icon in the Database view is not updated, causing an error should you try to edit or open the page later from within Access. Access gives you the option of trying to find a moved data access page on the file system, but if you delete the HTML file, the remaining icon in the Pages tab of the Database window is then useless.

Surprisingly, if you try to delete the icon in the Database window, you are given the option of deleting the HTML files as well, if you desire.

N O T E   If you create data access pages using the Page Wizard and intend to apply a decorative theme to the page (see steps 4 and 5 as follows), you'll need to be sure you have the Theme Wizard installed before beginning the design process. Unlike most Office 2000 add-ins, you can't install the Theme Wizard after you've already started the Page Wizard. You can, however, install more themes in the middle of the process. ◾

To create a data access page using the Page Wizard, click **Pages** in the list of objects in the Database window and follow these steps:

1. Double-click **Create Data Access Page by Using Wizard**. The Page Wizard opens, asking which fields you want on your page, as shown in Figure 9.9. The statement **You can choose from more than one table or query** is no different from forms or reports, but the way this is implemented in Data Access Page is a little different (as you'll soon see). Select a data source and some fields. Click **Next** to continue. Figure 9.9 shows fields selected from the Customers table and Order Details Extended query in the Northwind database.

FIGURE 9.9
The first dialog box of the Page Wizard looks just like the first step in a form or report wizard.

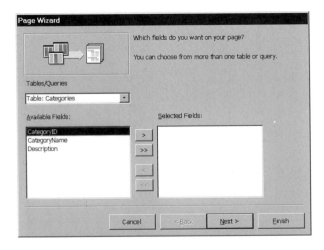

2. The second dialog box of the Page Wizard, offers the option of adding another group header, but advises that this option, if chosen, creates a read-only page. Press **Next** to continue.

3. You're asked to select a sort order for the detail records in the third dialog box, shown in Figure 9.10. You can reverse the default order, if desired, by clicking the button to the right of the field name. Notice that Access enables you to select sorting options only for the data fields in the detail section of the page. Press **Next** to continue.

FIGURE 9.10
Choose sort order for the data access page.

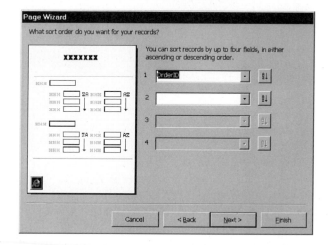

4. The final dialog box of the Wizard, like most, offers to name the page and to let you open it in Design view or in its default state, as do most wizards. Additionally, this Wizard offers the option of applying a theme to your page. Most wizards don't offer the option of applying formatting at this point, although other ways exist to include custom formatting in forms and reports. Using themes creates a professional look for your data access page, so check the option **Do You Want to Apply a Theme to Your Page?** and click **Finish**.

5. After a slight pause, Access creates your data access page and minimizes it; while it's minimized, a new dialog box appears (see Figure 9.11) for you to use in selecting a theme for your page. The nearly 70 themes listed are borrowed from Microsoft FrontPage 2000. They contain information on the default background for pages, font styles and colors, and field defaults. Most reside on the Office Premium Edition CD-ROM and are not installed by default, so have your CD-ROM (and a big hard drive) ready if you want to go through all of them. Select a theme and click **OK**.

FIGURE 9.11
The Theme dialog box enables you to choose a prepackaged look for your data access page.

6. You return to Design view to edit your page and add finishing touches. Typical data access pages include modifiable labels ("Click here and type title text") that are invisible in the final product if ignored. You can add more controls or HTML elements in this view, if required. Save your work (**File, Save**); you'll notice that the data access page is saved in two places: in the Page tab of the Database window and outside of the database in an HTML file. You can switch to Page view in Access (**View, Page View**) to get a preview of the page (see Figure 9.12), or view your page in Internet Explorer (**File, Open**), as shown in Figure 9.13.

FIGURE 9.12
Switch to Page view to see the finished data access page.

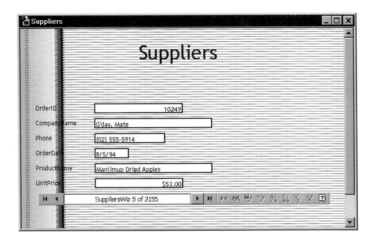

FIGURE 9.13

The same data access page in Internet Explorer 5. This works correctly even if no Web server is installed on your PC.

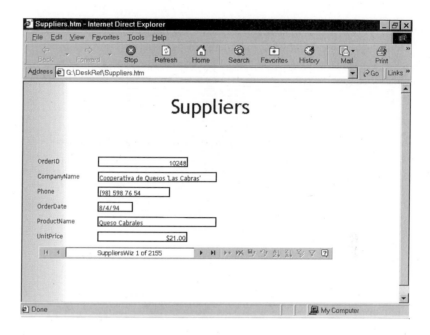

After your page is finished, you can modify it extensively by reopening it in Design view from the Database window and applying additional controls, editing the HTML, and so on. You have full control over the size and properties of each data element control, but some techniques you might have used in the Form or Report Design views might not work in the HTML Editor (such as selecting multiple objects with the Ctrl key, for example). A number of new properties are available for Data Access Page controls; these are adequately described in Help.

NOTE You can also create a data access page from scratch in the Design view. This is the best way to become intimate with the design elements required to successfully complete a task such as this. The Design view is also the view in which you modify the data access page. ■

The Design View contains the following elements:

- The Page window acts as the design canvas on which you place, move, resize, and modify page objects.

- The Field List presents a hierarchical view of the data objects in the database (including related objects) for you to drag and drop onto the Page window.

- The Property Sheet contains all the modifiable properties for each object on the page (and the Page itself). Note that some object features, such as a hyperlink associated with a label, can't be changed with the Property Sheet—they must be changed in the GUI.

- The Alignment and Sizing window contains standard alignment controls for making your page elements line up.

N O T E Some of these windows might not be visible, depending on the way Access was closed last time. If you can't see any of the default windows (and want to), click **View** and the name of the window you want to see. Windows that are already visible have check marks next to them. ■

The default toolbox is somewhat different for data access pages than for forms.

Designing a Switchboard Form for Your Database

One way to customize a database is to use the Access Switchboard Manager to create a simple front end for your forms and reports, enabling end users to get to them with one or two mouse clicks. You can even nest switchboards, so that a main switchboard includes a button that opens a second switchboard, and so on.

Understanding Switchboards

A switchboard consists of a switchboard form and switchboard pages. The *switchboard form* is the actual form the end user sees. This form contains buttons and text and any other objects you put on it. The buttons on the form perform actions you define on the *switchboard pages*. The pages and action items are stored in a table called Switchboard Items.

You can use the Switchboard Manager to edit switchboards that you've already created, and because the switchboards are implemented as one form with attributes modified in code, it's probably best that you do. Any modifications you make to the Switchboard form (adding controls, pictures, and so on) risks making the underlying code inoperable.

The Northwind sample database does not include a switchboard, but all the included database wizards create customized switchboards for their applications. As an example, the Inventory Control Wizard (**File**, **New**, **Databases**, **Inventory Control**) creates the simple switchboard shown in Figure 9.14. It has been slightly modified from the default Switchboard Manager version by adding a bitmap graphic on the left.

FIGURE 9.14
A sample switchboard created by a database wizard. You can enhance the plain switchboards created with the wizards by adding graphics.

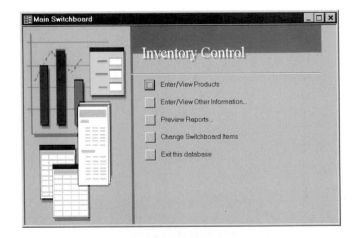

Creating a Switchboard by Using the Switchboard Manager

Follow these steps to create a switchboard for your database:

1. From Database View, select **Tools**, **Database Utilities**, **Switchboard Manager**. If the Database Utilities command is not visible, double-click the **Database Utilities** command to see the entire list of options.

2. If this is the first time you've run the Switchboard Manager in your database (including Northwind), then you are asked to confirm that you want to create a new switchboard. Click **Yes** to continue.

3. Access creates a form called Switchboard in the background and the Switchboard Manager window appears. The Main Switchboard page (really the Switchboard form) appears in the list of valid Switchboard Pages, and five buttons appear on the right:

    - **Close** makes the Switchboard Manager disappear. This isn't a cancellation, because the Main Switchboard form has now been created.

    - **New** creates a new switchboard page in the list.

    - **Edit** opens an existing switchboard form for editing in a view of the Switchboard Manager called Edit Switchboard (not in Design view).

    - **Delete** removes a page from the switchboard. Because switchboard pages are not physically separate forms in the database (and the Delete button won't remove the default switchboard page), you're not deleting database objects with this button. Of course, if you delete a switchboard page, you cannot get it back.

    - **Make Default** makes the currently selected switchboard page the main page for the application.

4. To add buttons to the Main Switchboard, select Make Default and click **Edit**. The Edit Switchboard Page opens. Until you create some buttons for this page, your only options are **C**lose and **N**ew; Close returns to the Switchboard Manager, and New opens the Edit Switchboard Item dialog box as shown in Figure 9.15. Click **New** to add an item.

5. Three boxes are in the Edit Switchboard Item dialog box; the first two are always labeled **T**ext and **C**ommand. The third field appears, disappears, and changes depending on the selection you make in the Command field. Enter the text you want to appear next to the command button in the Text box and choose a Command from the drop-down list (refer to Figure 9.15). Commands available include

    - **Go to Switchboard.** Opens the switchboard named in the third field.

    - **Open Form in Add Mode.** Opens the form named in the third field with its Data Entry property set to Yes, so records in it can be added, but not edited or viewed.

    - **Open Form in Edit Mode.** Opens the form named in the third field with its Data Entry property set to No, so records in it can be viewed, edited, or added.

    - **Open Report.** Opens the report named in the third field in Print Preview view.

    - **Design Application.** Creates a button that opens the Switchboard Manager.

    - **Exit Application.** Closes the current database.

    - **Run Macro.** Runs the macro named in the third field.

- **Run Code.** Executes the function named in the third field. Note that you can't enter a Sub procedure name here—only functions work. The return value (all functions return values) is ignored.

FIGURE 9.15

The Edit Switchboard Item dialog box lets you configure the buttons on a switchboard page.

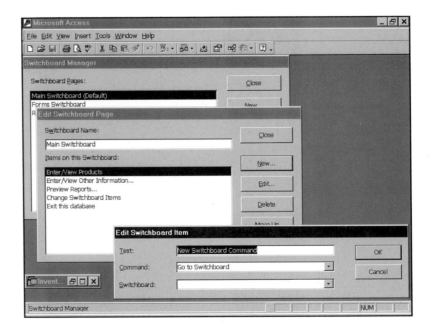

For example, if you want to edit employee information, you can enter Edit Employees in the Text field, select **Open Form** in Edit Mode from the Command field, and select **Employees** in the Form field that appears. Click **OK** after you've made your selections to return to the Edit Switchboard Page window.

 TIP As with menu buttons, entering an ampersand (&) character in the text field will make it appear underlined in the Switchboard and it will act as a hotkey in your application. For example, entering "E&xit" will make the "x" appear underlined, and a user pressing **Alt+X** will make the code behind the "Exit" button execute.

6. Repeat step 5 for as many buttons as you want on your switchboard. When you've added all the buttons you need, click **Close** to return to the Switchboard Manager.

7. If you want to add additional switchboard pages, click **New** on the Switchboard Manager and repeat steps 5 and 6 until the page is complete. For example, you can create a page containing only reports (call it Reports) and add a button (using the Go to Switchboard command) on the Main Switchboard to open it. This creates a cascade of switchboard pages as deep as you like. Don't forget to include navigation on each page to return to the previous page and/or the main switchboard page.

TIP Creating menu structures more than three deep is not a good idea. The navigation quickly becomes too difficult for users to follow.

8. Open each of your switchboard pages (using the Edit button) and arrange the buttons in a sensible order by selecting each button and clicking either Move Up or Move Down as necessary. Alphabetical order is best if no other arrangement seems right. After closing the pages to return to the Switchboard Manager, select **Close** to return to the Database Window.

Your switchboard exists in the database as a generic form called Switchboard, with quite a bit of code underlying its On Current and On Open properties. Each generic button calls a function in the class modules generated by the Switchboard manager. Editing this code is not for the squeamish. However, you can modify the design of the Switchboard form itself if you're careful not to delete any of the elements the code requires to execute. Figure 9.16 shows a default switchboard form and Figure 9.17 shows one that's enhanced a bit.

FIGURE 9.16

The default Switchboard form is legible and usable but not particularly interesting.

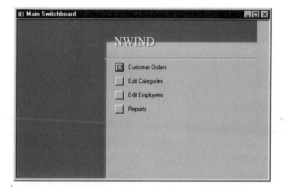

FIGURE 9.17

You can move and add elements in a standard switchboard to make your application a little less conventional.

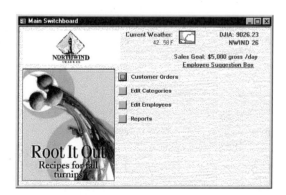

Customizing How Access Starts

Starting Access is no great mystery. You double-click the Access icon on the desktop or you start Access from the Start menu. Access starts and the Startup dialog box displays. But what if you want a particular database to automatically open for you? Or what if you don't like using the Startup dialog box?

You can modify the startup in several ways. Access provides a dialog box from which you can control several options: the application title, the default menu bar, and whether or not the Database window appears.

Customizing the Startup Dialog Box

The Startup dialog box lets you specify options that are applied when the database is opened. You can view the Startup dialog box by choosing **Tools**, **Startup**. You can display the name of your database in the upper-left corner of the Access window, next to the Access icon (the key) by entering the name in the Application Title text box (see Figure 9.18). If no application title is specified, the title bar displays the name Microsoft Access.

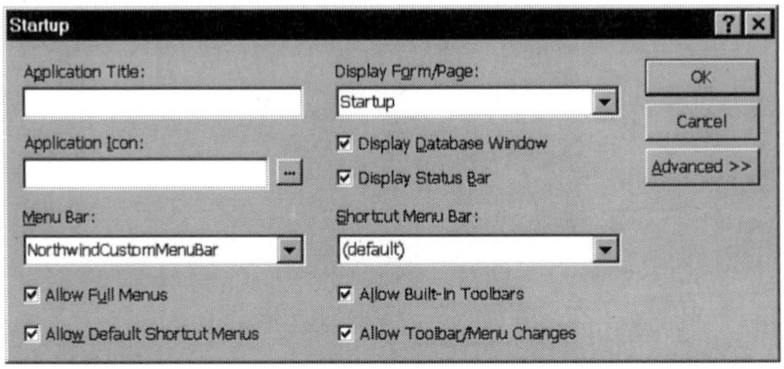

FIGURE 9.18
To display a database without the startup settings, hold down the Shift key as the database opens.

You can also specify a different icon to display instead of the Access (key) icon. Enter the full path of the icon in the **Application Icon** field, or click the adjacent ellipsis (...) button to browse for icons.

Other powerful options in the Startup dialog box are **Menu Bar** and **Shortcut Menu Bar**. You can specify a custom menu bar and/or shortcut menus (displayed when you right-click) for use with your database, instead of using the default Access menus. Creating custom menu and shortcut bars is discussed in the section "Customizing the Toolset" later in this chapter.

If you would like a form (such as a switchboard) to appear on startup, choose the form in the **Display Form** field. You can display other forms instead of switchboards on startup, but a switchboard is particularly appropriate because its purpose is to provide an easy way to navigate through the database.

If you clear the Display Database Window check box, end users will not see the window containing the tables, queries, reports, and so on. After the database is open, the database window can be displayed by choosing **Window**, **Unhide**. This provides a nice subtle way to hide the database window from most end users and quick access to it when database administrators or power users need to create or modify database objects.

TIP You can open a database without enabling these startup options by holding down the Shift key while the database is opening.

Using Switches to Modify Startup

Access, like most Office applications, has a series of command-line switches that are used to control how Access starts. For example, you can use a command-line switch to open a particular database when you start Access (which you can't do from the Tools, Startup dialog box). This can be useful when end users do the majority of their work in the same database, and you can have more than one shortcut on the desktop for each database they need access to. You can also control how the database opens. You can open a database, using switches, for exclusive use or read-only use.

And the use of switches isn't limited to the control of databases. Using switches, you can control what dialog boxes appear when Access opens. For example, you can use a switch to hide the Startup dialog box.

Command-line switches are set through your Access shortcut property window by using the following steps:

1. Add a shortcut for Access to your desktop.

 TIP To create a shortcut, right-click your desktop. From the menu, select **New**, **Shortcut**. The Create Shortcut dialog box displays. Select the **Bro̲wse** button. From the Browse dialog box, locate and select the application for which you want to create a shortcut and click **Open**. Click the **N̲ext** button. Click **F̲inish**.

2. Right-click the Access shortcut to display the context menu.
3. Select **P̲roperties** to display the Microsoft Access Properties.
4. Select the **Shortcut** tab. The Target text box setting determines the way Access will start. The target is the complete path of the application. The switches go after the complete path of the application. The current contents of your Target text box might have quotes around the database name. These quotes are required if a space exists anywhere in the database or path name.

On the Shortcut tab, you see the Target text box. The Target setting determines Access' startup behavior. The following sections discuss the switches you can enter for the Target text box.

Opening a Database When You Start Access If users work primarily with one database, you can expedite opening the database by adding the database to the command-line switch. To open a database automatically, use the following syntax in the Target text box:

```
"\path\msaccess.exe" "\path\database_name"
```

`"\path\msaccess.exe"` is the path and executable filename for the Access application. This information is automatically added to the Target field when you create the shortcut. At the end of that text enter the path and name of the database file in quotes. `"\path\database_name"` is the complete path and name of the database you want to open when starting Access. Be sure to place a space between the existing text in the Target text box and your entry for "\path\ database_name" entry. If you want to open the Northwind database with a switch, you would create the following entry for the Target field:

```
"C:\Program Files\Microsoft Office\Office\MSAccess.exe"
➡"C:\Program Files\Microsoft Office\Office\Samples\Northwind.mdb"
```

TIP If you work with two or three databases frequently, you might want to create multiple shortcuts and set their Targets to different databases. Be sure to include the name of the database in the shortcut's name to avoid confusion.

Opening a Database As Exclusive by Using a Switch

Certain database tasks are best done in *exclusive access* for performance reasons. When a database is opened with exclusive access, you prevent other users from opening that database. If you are deleting large numbers of records, adding several rows to a large, indexed table, or updating key information, you might find that it is more efficient to be the only person using a particular database. You can open a database for exclusive use when starting Access by using the /excl switch after the name of the database. If you created a shortcut to Access with the Target set to open Northwind, you would have the following value:

```
"C:\Program Files\Microsoft Office\Office\MSAccess.exe"
➡"C:\Program Files\Microsoft Office\Office\Samples\Northwind.mdb"
```

To open Northwind with exclusive access, you would add /excl as shown:

```
"C:\Program Files\Microsoft Office\Office\MSAccess.exe"
➡"C:\Program Files\Microsoft Office\Office\Samples\Northwind.mdb" /excl
```

TIP If you sometimes need to open your startup database for exclusive use and other times you don't need exclusive use, you can create two shortcuts, each with the appropriate Target setting.

Opening a Database for Read-Only Access by Using a Switch   If you are setting up a database for use by less-experienced users who shouldn't do anything but read from a database, consider setting the database to open as read-only by using the /ro switch. For example, to open the Northwind database for read-only access by using the /ro switch, you would enter the following for the Target:

```
"C:\Program Files\Microsoft Office\Office\MSAccess.exe"
➡"C:\Program Files\Microsoft Office\Office\Samples\Northwind.mdb" /ro
```

Obviously, this isn't the most secure way to open a database for read-only access. Operating system, network, and Access' security are much more sophisticated and secure, but the /ro switch does provide a quick way to automatically open a database for read-only access.

TIP There are other reasons to open the database as read only. If you put a database on a read-only medium, you open the database as read only and exclusive to prevent Access from trying to write a lock file. This is often used to ship access databases on CD-ROMs.

Using Switches with Database Security   If you have elected to use Access' built-in security features to secure a database, you can still use switches to open the database. Two switches that come in handy when security has been implemented are /user and /pwd. The /user switch enables you to pass your username to Access for the database you are opening. The /pwd switch is used to provide the appropriate password for the database. If you needed to open the Northwind database and you had a username of *smith* and a password of *apple,* you would use the following value for the Target:

Part

II

Ch

9

> **CAUTION**
>
> The /pwd switch does not work with the database password. This switch is for user-level security only.

```
"C:\Program Files\Microsoft Office\Office\MSAccess.exe"
➥"C:\Program Files\Microsoft Office\Office\Samples\Northwind.mdb"
➥/user smith /pwd apple
```

N O T E   If you used the Security Wizard to set up your security, you probably need to include the /WRKGRP switch. For example, if you created a database named *expenses1* and set up security using the Security Wizard, you would need to use the following command line to log on as a user named *smith* with a password of *apple*:

```
"C:\Program Files\Microsoft Office\Office\msaccess.exe"
➥"C:\expenses1.mdb" /WRKGRP "C:\Secured.mdw" /user smith /pwd apple ▦
```

Performing Database Maintenance with Switches

Some switches enable you to perform maintenance tasks such as compacting, repairing, and converting databases. Two approaches are available for using these specialized switches. One is to create a separate shortcut that is used only to perform these tasks. Another is to create a batch file that accesses the database and executes the desired switch. One of these switches is /compact *databasename.* This switch compacts and repairs the Access database. Another switch is /convert *databasename.* The /convert switch converts a previous-version Access database to an Access 2000 database with a new name, and then closes Access.

Optimizing Access by Altering the Windows Registry

In the previous section, you saw how to customize Access by using command-line switches. Although command-line switches control the startup behavior of Access, there are a couple of ways to control the overall Access environment.

One way is to use the Access Options dialog box. Another way is to modify the settings for Access found in the Windows Registry. The Registry is the single location where all system and application settings are stored. When you make a change to Access by using the Options dialog box, you are actually making a change to the Registry.

CAUTION

Before you start modifying the entries in the Registry, you should know that incorrectly modifying the Registry can mean that you might damage Access, or your Windows installation to the point of not being able to run it. And, in some cases, uninstalling and reinstalling Access doesn't always correct the problem. Always use extreme care when working with the Registry!

If you find a way to set an option by using the Options or other dialog box, do it that way. The Registry is not something to play with just for fun!

For an advanced user, modifying the Registry does provide a benefit over the settings available through the Options dialog box. You are able to directly work with the settings of the database engine. To state it simply, you can optimize the database engine for your environment. In large organizations with large amounts of data moving across networks, engine optimization can become important. If, for example, your users are complaining of not being able to open records and you determine that it is because of a record-locking issue, you can adjust the record-locking settings.

You are probably wondering how to edit the Registry. You use the Registry Editor. Use the following steps to start the Registry Editor:

1. Click the **Start** button on the taskbar.

2. Select **Run**. The Run dialog box displays.

3. Enter **regedit** and press **Enter**. The Registry Editor starts as shown in Figure 9.19.

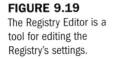

FIGURE 9.19
The Registry Editor is a tool for editing the Registry's settings.

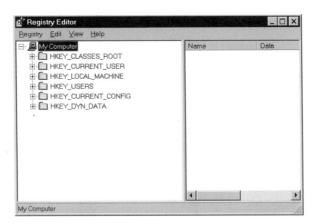

In the left pane of the Registry Editor, you see a series of folders. These folders are called *keys*. The Registry's information is divided by type of information into the keys that you see listed. Traversing a key's structure is just like maneuvering through a directory listing in the Windows Explorer. When you click the expand button (+ sign) for a key, you'll see a list of subfolders. You'll continue to open folders until you get to your final destination.

You are now ready to make changes to the Registry. When you make a change, it does not take effect until the next time you start Access.

> **CAUTION**
>
> Before you begin editing the Registry, it is highly recommended that you back it up. To do this, select **Export Registry File** from the Registry Editor's Registry menu.

N O T E To learn more about working with the Windows Registry, we recommend reading a copy of *Using the Windows 98 Registry* or *Special Edition Using the Windows 95 Registry*, both published by Que. ▨

Customizing Jet 4.0 Database Engine Settings

The majority of users access their data in one of two ways when working with Access: either with the Jet engine or by using Open Database Connectivity (ODBC). Using the Registry, you can control the way the Jet engine performs by adding entries. Typically, on a machine that has recently had Access installed, you might not find the actual subkey that you need and you might have to add it yourself. Complete the following steps to add the needed subkey:

1. Click the expand button for HKEY_LOCAL_MACHINE.
2. Continue through the key structure until you are at \HKEY_LOCAL_MACHINE\ SOFTWARE\Microsoft\Office\9.0\Access\Jet\4.0\Engines.
3. With the Engines key selected, select **Edit**, **New**, **Key**. A new key is added.
4. Type **Jet 4.0** and press **Enter** to name the key (see Figure 9.20).

FIGURE 9.20
The newly added key is listed in the Registry.

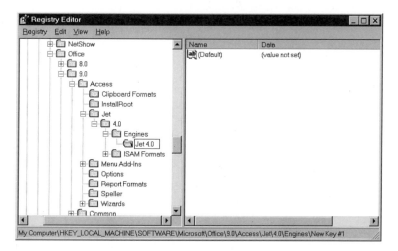

N O T E Making changes to this subkey affects only Access. On your machine, you might have several programs that use the Jet 4.0 database engine, including Microsoft Excel and Visual Basic 6.0. If you want the changes you make to affect all applications that use the Jet 4.0 database engine, make changes to the settings in the \HKEY_LOCAL_MACHINE\SOFTWARE\ Microsoft\Jet\4.0\Engines\Jet 4.0 subkey. ■

After you have the Jet 4.0 key added to the Registry, you can add values to it. To add a value, use the following steps:

1. Select the key to which you want to add values.
2. Select **Edit**, **New**.
3. Select the type of value you want to add: string, binary, or DWORD.
4. Enter a name for the value and press **Enter**.
5. Double-click the value. A dialog box displays.
6. Enter the appropriate data for the value and press **Enter**.

Table 9.1 lists some of the values you set for the Jet 4.0 database engine. This table doesn't list all the available values but lists the ones you are most likely to use. Remember, Access works fine without setting any of these values. Set these values only if you are having performance issues. Another word of caution—I highly recommend that you set one value, exit the Registry Editor, start Access, and be sure it works before setting another value. I know that it is tedious to set one value at a time and test Access after each value, but it is a lot easier to troubleshoot by using this method. If you enter ten values and Access won't start, then you would have ten places to look for errors.

 TIP Changes to the Registry apply to all databases all the time. If you want to change Registry settings just for a single session, you can use the `Application.DBEngine.SetOption` method in a VBA procedure. The values set using the `Application.DBEngine.SetOption` method remain in effect until either the `Application.DBEngine.SetOption` method is executed again or until the current session is closed.

Table 9.1   Jet 4.0 Database Engine Registry Values

Value Name	Value Type	Description
LockRetry	DWORD	This value sets the maximum number of times Jet should attempt to access a locked page before returning a lock-conflict message. The default setting for this value is 20. You might want to increase this if you have a high-volume database and users are frequently receiving lock-conflict messages.

Value Name	Value Type	Description
MaxLocksPerFile	DWORD	You might want to set this value if you are running Access on a NetWare 3.1 network. If the locks in a Jet transaction attempt to exceed the assigned value, the transaction is split into two or more parts and then each part is committed. Refer to your NetWare documentation for information on NetWare's lock limit. You might also notice a performance increase in Access when setting this value if you are running Access on a NetWare network.
PagesLockedToTableLock	DWORD	If you perform bulk insert, delete, or update operations to your tables, you might want to consider setting this value to a nonzero value. The default setting for this value is 0. When set to 0, Jet never automatically changes from page locking to table locking. You can specify the maximum number of pages that are locked before Jet escalates to table locking. In a multiuser environment, it is recommended that you use this setting carefully because when a table is locked, your users are not able to use it. I recommend using this value only if your bulk operations are always performed after hours.
Threads	DWORD	The Threads value is used to control the number of background threads available to the Jet database engine. By increasing the number of available threads, you can gain performance. However, assigning more threads to Access can decrease the performance of other applications running on the same machine. The default setting for this value is 3. If you are running Access on a dedicated machine or if you are running Access on a Windows NT machine with multiple processors, you might want to use this value. You might also want to change this value if Access is running in the foreground.

Part

II

Ch

9

Customizing ODBC Driver Settings

In the previous section, ODBC was mentioned as one of the more common data access methods used with Access. And, like Jet 4.0, ODBC can be customized via the Registry. The subkey you'll be working with in this case is \HKEY_LOCAL_MACHINE\SOFTWARE\Microsoft\Office\9.0\Access\Jet\4.0\Engines\ODBC. You might find that the ODBC subkey does not exist and needs to be created using the technique described in the previous section.

After you have navigated to this subkey, you are ready to set the values found in Table 9.2. This table doesn't list all the available values, but it does list the ones you are most likely to use.

N O T E Making changes to this subkey affects only Access. On your machine, you might have several programs that use the ODBC driver, including Microsoft SQL Server and Visual FoxPro. If you want the changes you make to affect all applications that use the ODBC, make changes to the settings in the \HKEY_LOCAL_MACHINE\SOFTWARE\Microsoft\Jet\4.0\Engines\ODBC subkey. ■

TIP The `Application.DBEngine.SetOption` method discussed in a previous tip can be used to set ODBC driver Registry values for a single session.

Table 9.2   Jet 4.0 Database Engine Registry Values (ODBC)

Value Name	Value Type	Description
ConnectionTimeout	DWORD	This value controls how long a connection can be idle before it is timed out. The default setting for this value is 600. If your users are frequently being timed out, you might want to increase this value. On the other hand, if you have the problem of people staying logged on when they are not using the connection, then decrease this number.
DisableAsync	DWORD	This value is used to control the type of query execution used. The default setting for this value is 0, meaning the asynchronous execution is to be used if possible. Setting `DisableAsync` to 1 forces synchronous query execution. Setting this to 1 can increase speed when performing query execution but is recommended only for single-user environments, not for multiple-user environments. Basically, what this value does is increase query performance at the expense of processor cycles on the local machine.
QueryTimeout	DWORD	The meaning of this value is dependent on the setting of the `DisableAsync` value. If `DisableAsync` is set to 0, then the `QueryTimeout` value is the number of seconds to wait for a response from the server between query-completion polls. If `DisableAsync` is set to 1, then the `QueryTimeout` value is the number of seconds of total processing time that a query can run before timing out. The default setting for this value is 60. If users are frequently getting timed out while performing queries, increase the setting for this value.

Value Name	Value Type	Description
TraceSQLMode	DWORD	By default, this value is set to 0. When set to 0, Jet does not trace SQL statements to the ODBC data source in the SQLOUT.txt file. If this is set to 1, then it writes the statements to SQLOUT.txt. The advantage of setting this to 1 is that it performs an audit trail of SQL statements that are performed through Jet to an ODBC data source. The downside of setting this value to 1 is that you are increasing the overhead associated with these operations and can degrade performance. This is also a debugging flag.

Remember that any changes you make do not take effect until the next time you start Access.

Enhancing User Productivity with Macros and VBA

A normal progression occurs as organizations gain experience working in Access. The first element most people learn to work with is the Access table. Next come queries and forms. Reports follow, and macros come into vogue at about the same time the organization starts to control the state of the application—it becomes desirable to make the application perform differently depending on some variable or condition in the database.

Forms, queries, and so forth all behave the same regardless of what else is happening in the custom application, but macros impart some intelligence to the database, permitting you to force certain things to happen depending on other things happening.

Access is different from other Office applications, however, in that its implementation of macros is independent of its programming language, Visual Basic for Applications (VBA). In Word, Excel, and PowerPoint, macros (now) are really VBA procedures that can be generated automatically from the interface, usually by recording keystrokes. In those applications, you can record a macro without any knowledge of VBA, but the macro is stored as VBA code, and it's edited in the VBA Editor. In Access, macros are unrelated to VBA except in function (see Figure 9.21). And they're probably doomed for just that reason.

Starting with Access 95, the Access programming language (used for modules) began to be called VBA, even though it was somewhat incompatible with the VBA in other Office applications. Because Microsoft has long made its intentions clear—that the Office applications should share a common programming interface—it seems reasonable to expect that it won't be long until Access macros, those white elephants of the Office community, are no longer supported. In fact, since Access 97, anything you can do in a macro you can also do in VBA, but VBA does a lot of things macros can't handle.

So, why use a macro for anything at all? For one thing, the macro interface is somewhat simpler than that of VBA, because so many fewer options exist. For people with no programming experience, the macro-coding environment might seem friendlier and less overwhelming.

FIGURE 9.21

A macro library from Northwind, showing names, conditions, actions, and comments. Access macros have nothing in common with macros in the other Office applications.

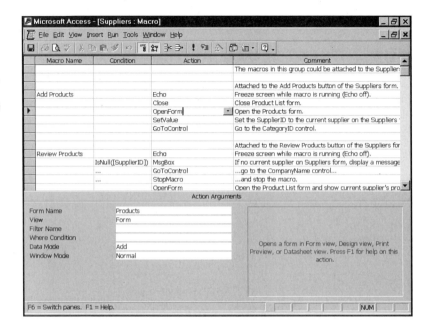

Creating Macros in Access

A macro contains a list of actions and arguments that automate a series of tasks that would otherwise have to be performed individually. Access provides a Design window for creating macros.

An example of a macro that would be useful to end users is one that runs a query, opens a report, and displays a message box that allows the user to print the report. You can create a macro to accomplish this by following these steps (which assume you have already created the query and the report):

1. Click **Macro** in the Objects list of the Database Window and select **New**.
2. Display the drop-down list under the Action column heading in the Macro Window, and select **OpenQuery**.
3. The fields that appear at the bottom of the Macro window are dynamic; they change depending on the action you select. When you select **OpenQuery**, you get three fields: Query Name, View, and Data Mode. Select the query to run in the **Query Name** field.
4. Select the desired **View Option**—Datasheet, Design, or Print Preview. Datasheet runs the query and displays the result in a datasheet. Design opens the query in the Design view. Print Preview displays a preview of the query results as they will appear when printed.
5. Select the desired **Data Mode** option—Add, Edit, or Read Only. Add enables users to add new records. Edit enables users to modify existing records or add records. Read Only does not allow any modifications, additions, or deletions of records.

6. Optionally, type a comment about the OpenQuery action in the Comment field to the right of the action. Figure 9.22 shows the macro so far.

FIGURE 9.22

A description of the actions you can take in each field appears in the lower-right corner of the window.

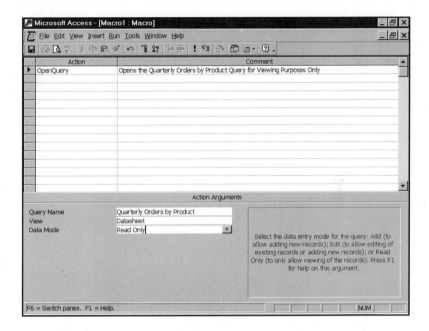

Part

II

Ch

9

When you have the OpenQuery action completed, you then add the OpenReport action, following these steps:

1. Under the OpenQuery action, add the OpenReport action. This action displays four fields at the bottom of the Macro window: Report Name, View, Name, and Where Condition.

2. Choose the name of the report to open in the Report Name field.

3. In the **View** field, select **Print**, **Design**, or **Print Preview**. Print opens the report and prints it. Design opens the report in the Design view. Print Preview opens the report in Print Preview.

4. Optionally, specify a filter in the Filter Name field to restrict or sort the records used in the report.

5. Optionally, specify a Where condition in the **Where Condition** field. A Where condition is similar to a filter; it is an SQL statement that determines which records are selected from the underlying tables or queries.

6. Optionally, type a comment in the **Comment** field for the OpenReport action.

Now that you have the OpenReport action completed, it is time to add the message box action, following these steps:

1. Under the OpenReport action, add the MsgBox action. This action displays four fields at the bottom of the Macro window: **Message**, **Beep**, **Type**, and **Title**.

2. Type the message to be displayed in the **Message** field. The message can be a maximum of 255 characters.

3. Choose Yes or No in the **Beep** field to specify whether you went the computer to beep when the message box is displayed.

4. In the **Type** field, type the text you want to appear in the title bar of the message box. Your choices are None, Critical, Warning?, Warning!, and Information.

5. In the **Title** field, type the text you want to appear in the title bar of the message box.

6. Optionally, type a comment next to the MsgBox action.

7. The macro is now complete (see Figure 9.23). Save it and close the Macro window.

FIGURE 9.23
The Design view of this macro shows the actions and comments.

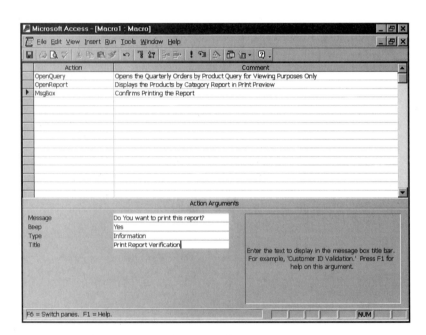

You can't run a macro before saving it. If you make changes to a macro, you also have to save it before running the macro again. To modify a macro, select **Macro** from the list of objects in the Database window and click the **Design** button.

You can implement the macro in several ways; it can be assigned to a button on a toolbar or form, or assigned to a keyboard shortcut.

NOTE Although the macro environment might seem friendlier, Microsoft is strongly encouraging people to use VBA and ultimately, the option to create macros in Access will disappear altogether. Also, becoming a good macro programmer doesn't ease the transition to VBA at all. The Office object model and terminology can be confusing, as can any programming language, but insulating yourself from it by encouraging the development of macros is often counterproductive because the learning curve is just as great when you need to use VBA later. Macros can't perform error handling; they can't make use of variable scope; and whole planets of the VBA object environment are unavailable to the macro programmer to manipulate. Last, they're usually slower executing than VBA modules. ▪

Importing, Exporting, and Linking with VBA

To use data from other applications from within Access, you need to either import it or link to it. Importing data makes a copy, so any changes you make in Access don't affect the original data source; linking data maintains it in its original application and location, so any changes you make to the data in Access are actually made in the serving application. When you link external data, Access acts as a client, a front end, to the remote data source.

You will discover that it is usually convenient to set up this kind of relationship between applications from the Access graphical interface, where you can use the menu commands and follow the step-by-step instructions Access provides to create the linkages you need. But at times, it's more convenient to use VBA, such as when the remote data source might not be known during the design of the application or might change during execution.

The key to using VBA to connect to remote data sources is the use of the Transfer set of VBA methods: `TransferDatabase`, `TransferSpreadsheet`, and `TransferText`. Depending on the source and format of the data to be imported or linked to, one of these methods should suffice.

TransferDatabase   The `TransferDatabase` method of the `DoCmd` object takes the following syntax:

```
DoCmd.TransferDatabase [transfertype], databasetype, databasename[, objecttype],
➥source, destination[, structureonly][, saveloginid]
```

The only required arguments are the `databasetype`, `source`, and `destination`. Valid `databasetypes` are strings representing recognized external databases, such as "Microsoft Access," "dBASE III," "ODBC Databases," and several more listed in VBA Help for the `TransferDatabase` method. Be sure the filter for any `databasetype` you choose has been installed on the client machine before executing this code, or an error condition will be generated.

The source and destination arguments are string expressions that name the source and destination database and/or table. Note that the method for exporting a database object is the same as the method for importing one, except that the source and destination names are reversed and the optional `transfertype` argument `acExport` is used.

In this command more than most, the optional arguments are practically required to eliminate ambiguity in the command. The `transfertype` argument determines whether the desired action is an import (the default), export, or link. The `objecttype` argument is useful only when working with two Access databases; otherwise, you can transfer only table-type objects. The `structureonly` argument is convenient if you're interested in copying the table structure, not the included data.

The following simple example illustrates the basic use of this command:

```
DoCmd.TransferDatabase , "Microsoft Access",  "Nwind.mdb", , "Employees",
"Employees"
```

Note the use of the commas to mark the places of arguments not used; they're required if you don't specify optional arguments in the middle of the command. You should omit the extra commands at the end, however. This command imports the Employees table from the file `Nwind.mdb` in the current directory into the current database.

The use of `TransferDatabase` can get quite complicated, as in this example:

```
DoCmd.TransferDatabase acLink, "ODBC Database",
"ODBC;DSN=OracleDBs;UID=marlowe;PWD=mypassword;
LANGUAGE=us_english;DATABASE=myDB", acTable,
"sourceTable", "destTable"
```

Here, we connect to a pre-existing Oracle database (called `'myDB'`) via ODBC and link the local table `'destTable'` in Access to the source table `'sourceTable'`. Changes made to data in `'destTable'` will actually change values in `'sourceTable.'`

TransferSpreadsheet   `TransferSpreadsheet` is a little less complicated than `TransferDatabase`; its syntax is

DoCmd.TransferSpreadsheet `[transfertype][, spreadsheettype], tablename, filename[, hasfieldnames][, range]`

The only required arguments are the name of the table to be imported to or exported from and the spreadsheet filename. The `transfertype` argument, as in the `TransferDatabase` method, specifies whether this is an import, export, or link (import is the default). The `spreadsheettype` argument assumes that the spreadsheet in question is Excel, but several variants of Excel and Lotus 1-2-3 are supported (with some limitations for linking to 1-2-3 spreadsheets) through the use of various constants for this argument. The `hasfieldnames` argument specifies whether the names of fields are to be imported or replicated as the headers of columns in the spreadsheet, and the range is a valid range of cells to be imported (you can't specify a range to export to).

N O T E   Worth noting is the fact that the `spreadsheettype` argument in the `TransferSpreadsheet` method uses integer constants (which Access predefines as `acSpreadsheetTypeLotusWK1`, `acSpreadsheetTypeExcel8`, and some others), but the `databasetype` argument in `TransferDatabase` requires a string ("`Microsoft Access`," "`dBASE III`," and so on). ■

The following example imports the range A1 through J400 (which includes fieldnames) of the Excel 2000 spreadsheet stored in the file `Products.xls`:

```
DoCmd.TransferSpreadsheet acImport, acSpreadsheetTypeExcel9,  "Products",
"products.xls", True, "A1:J400"
```

TransferText   The `TransferText` command reads or writes data that is stored in a flat text file. The syntax is

```
DoCmd.TransferText [transfertype][, specificationname],
tablename, filename[, hasfieldnames][, HTMLtablename][, codepage]
```

The required arguments `tablename` and `filename` refer to the table and file to be imported, linked, or exported, as desired. Various `transfertypes` support importing or exporting delimited, fixed-width HTML tables or lists, or mail-merge files; note that linking to a text file doesn't permit writing to it, but changes in the text file are reflected in Access. The `specificationname` argument is used to name an import or export specification that was created with the Import/Export Wizard in Access (selecting File, Get External Data, Import or Link, and then selecting a file starts the wizard, which permits the saving of a specification). Using a specification is required when working with a fixed-width file.

The `hasfieldnames` argument works the same as in the `TransferSpreadsheet` method, specifying whether columns of text should have field names at the top. The `HTMLtablename` argument specifies the name of a table or list in the HTML file referenced, and the `codepage` argument represents a language `codepage` pertinent to the file in question.

An example illustrates how a flat text file can be imported into an Access table:

```
DoCmd.TransferText acImportDelim, , "Employees", "employees.csv"
```

Improving Module Performance

Access loads modules on demand, that is, when procedures in those modules are requested by the application. Because this loading almost always occurs during application execution (while users are sitting in front of the screen, waiting for something to happen), sluggish modules can cause the appearance of a sluggish application (and programmer, by extension). You can take some positive steps, however, to be sure that your VBA code is as speedy as possible:

- **Write efficient code.** Try to keep related statements in one procedure and/or module if possible. You might find it helpful to write modularly, but that doesn't mean that every module should have three or four lines of code; each procedure call is another executable statement that must be run to continue. Use SELECT statements instead of nested IF statements, if possible, because IF statements are notorious CPU hogs (and IIF statements are doubly so). Use SQL aggregate functions (DLookup, DCount, and so on) instead of DoCmd.RunSQL commands, which have to be interpreted at runtime.

- **Compile your code.** Access doesn't really compile code in the way a C or FORTRAN compiler does—it doesn't convert the text-programming language to machine-language object code. But it does perform a one-pass optimization and reduction to an intermediate form called *p-code*, and p-code runs a whole lot faster than uncompiled VBA. Compiling your code at design time (by selecting Debug, Compile) does two useful things: It error-checks your code for obvious errors and it takes care of the first step of interpretation, performing the p-code conversion while you watch it instead of while your user watches it.

- **Dimension your variables.** It takes time to figure out what data type your variables should be, and that time is expended while the code is running if you haven't declared them earlier. Using the Option Explicit command (or setting the VBA Require Variable Declaration option by clicking Tools, Options, Editor, Require Variable Declaration) not only improves database performance, but it lessens the chance that a misspelled variable name will wreak havoc in your application.

- **Help VBA out.** Use techniques that lessen the amount of work the engine has to do. Use the Me keyword to refer to controls in and properties of the current form or report to prevent VBA from searching the whole application for the referenced object. Declare and use constants (typed appropriately) instead of variables that never change value. Remember that calculations performed on integers are much faster than calculations on floating-point numbers, so declare your variables as integers (Int or Long) if possible. You can implement a more efficient two-decimal floating-point number by declaring it as Currency. Finally, be sure the HasModule property of forms and reports is set to No if they have no class modules; this makes them lightweight and allows the runtime interpreter to avoid inspecting the form or report's properties looking for any modules that might be there.

One other technique that you might consider is intentionally controlling when your modules execute. If you need to do a lot of back-end calculation and setup (creating temporary tables), it might be advantageous to create a module that runs immediately after the application is started, rather than after the user has begun working in it. Forcing a startup delay is often more forgivable (look at how long it takes to boot Windows) than interrupting the user as she works. ●

CHAPTER 10

Customizing Outlook to Your Organization's Needs

by Gordon Padwick

Before the introduction of Outlook, people used one program for managing contacts, another for scheduling, and yet another for email. Although these programs were often excellent, it was difficult to share information between them, which made it hard to take full advantage of their functionality.

By combining these functions into an integrated application, Outlook improves on the individual applications. With Outlook 2000, you can search through your contacts for an email address and then automatically send a message to that person. If you want to plan a meeting with several colleagues, you can use the shared calendar capabilities to search for a time when everyone is available and then send out invitations and keep track of the responses.

Outlook combines the following areas of functionality into one program, replacing multiple individual applications for many users:

- **Email.** The most widely used feature of this program, Outlook provides the tools necessary to create, send, and respond to email messages. As an email *client*, Outlook doesn't actually deliver the email messages, but it works with existing email systems including Microsoft Exchange Server, Microsoft Mail, Hewlett-Packard OpenMail, Lotus cc:Mail, and CompuServe that perform many of the communication functions. Outlook can also send and receive Internet email by way of an Internet service provider (ISP) and intranet email by way of a mail server that supports Internet protocols.

NOTE Microsoft doesn't support Lotus Notes/Domino email. However, Lotus offers an Outlook add-in that provides this capability.

- **Fax.** Outlook makes it possible for you to send and receive faxes using fax information services supplied with Outlook (such as WinFax Starter Edition and Microsoft Fax) or fax add-ins available from third parties (such as Symantec WinFax Pro).

- **Contacts.** Outlook keeps track of the names, addresses, phone and fax numbers, and other information about your business and personal contacts. You can use Outlook to keep a record of activities for each contact.

- **Calendar.** Outlook helps you manage your personal schedule, keeping track of meetings, appointments, and events. You can also use the calendar to schedule meetings at times when attendees and resources are available.

- **Journal.** Outlook can keep a diary of your activities, ranging from phone calls and client meetings, to the history of working with Office and Office-compatible documents.

- **Tasks.** You can keep a list of the things you have to do, with or without deadlines, and request other people to accept tasks you need them to perform. Outlook can provide automatic reminders and track the status and completion of your tasks.

- **Notes.** This feature is for all the little bits of information that otherwise end up as sticky notes on your computer, desk, or refrigerator. You can use Outlook to keep these notes electronically.

- **Sharing information.** You can use Outlook to share information with other people. If you're using Outlook as a client for Microsoft Exchange Server, public folders are used for this purpose. Otherwise, you can use Net folders to share information by way of the Internet or an intranet.

N O T E Public folders reside on the server and can be accessed by users who have appropriate permissions. Net folders reside on individual users' computers; Outlook automatically distributes Net folders between users at predetermined intervals by way of the Internet or an intranet to keep those folders synchronized. In effect, Net folders function very much like public folders. ■

Although Outlook contains several areas of functionality, it is important to remember that Outlook is essentially a messaging, or email, application. As such, its data is stored in the message storage files provided by the email system. If you are using Outlook as a client for Microsoft Exchange on a network, your Outlook data (including email messages, contact data, calendar items, and so on) is usually stored in the Exchange message store on your organization's Microsoft Exchange Server. This has the advantage of centralizing the data, making it easy to share information and making it available for regular backups by the Exchange administrator or network administrator. If you are using Outlook on a standalone computer, your data can be stored in a personal storage file (PST) or offline storage file (OST).

▶ For more information on personal storage files and offline storage files, **see** Chapter 48, "Troubleshooting and Optimizing Outlook," **p. 1183**.

Introducing Outlook 2000

First introduced as Outlook 97, Outlook was upgraded separately from the rest of Office 97 in early 1998. Outlook 98 retained the functionality of Outlook 97 but offered improvements in the user interface, along with new features for messaging and collaboration. Still more enhancements are available in Outlook 2000. Many of the capabilities covered in this chapter are available in Outlook 97, Outlook 98, and Outlook 2000.

Some of the most significant new features introduced in Outlook 98 and Outlook 2000 are described here:

- **Outlook Today window.** Provides an overview of email, calendar, and tasks. New in Outlook 98; enhanced in Outlook 2000.

- **Customizable menu bars and toolbars.** New in Outlook 98.

- **Background archiving.** New in Outlook 98.

- **Support for a wide variety of Internet standards,** including POP3/SMTP, IMAP4, LDAP, and NNTP. New in Outlook 98.

- **Internet message disposition receipts.** New in Outlook 2000.

- **Support for HTML and Multipurpose Internet Mail Extensions (MIME).** This feature enables you to send messages that are formatted as Web pages, including images and links to Internet sites. Messages sent as HTML can be read by HTML-based browsers and email clients, as well as by Outlook. New in Outlook 98.

- **Security for email messages.** Supported through Secure Multipurpose Internet Mail Extensions (S/MIME). Digital signing enables you to send secure messages to users with other browsers that support S/MIME. New in Outlook 98.

- **vCard and vCalendar.** Standards that enable you to exchange business information over the Internet. vCards contain personal information such as names, addresses, phone numbers, and email addresses. vCalendars contain meeting and appointment information. New in Outlook 98.

- **iCalendar.** Standard for group scheduling by way of the Internet. New in Outlook 98; enhanced in Outlook 2000.

- **Options available as add-ins in Outlook 97,** such as a preview pane for viewing email messages and the Rules Wizard for automating the processing of messages, are now built in. The Rules Wizard is also supplemented with tools for filtering junk and adult-content messages. Enhanced in Outlook 2000.

- **Net folders** enable people to share message folders by way of the Internet or an intranet. You can use Net folders to share information as a series of email messages. New in Outlook 98; enhanced in Outlook 2000.

- **Saving a personal or group calendar as a Web page.** New in Outlook 2000.

- **Direct booking of resources** without the need for resource computers. New in Outlook 2000.

- **Distribution lists can be maintained within a Contacts folder** instead of requiring a personal address book. New in Outlook 2000.

- **Contact activity tracking** allows tracking of email, tasks, appointments, and documents by contact. New in Outlook 2000.

- **Automatic detection of duplicate contacts.** You can choose whether to create a duplicate contact item or merge new information into an existing contact item. New in Outlook 2000.

■ **Shortcuts in the Outlook Bar** can be created to any file, folder, or Web page. New in Outlook 2000.

■ **Folder home pages** can be used to associate Web pages with Outlook folders. New in Outlook 2000.

■ **The Outlook object model** is substantially enhanced in Outlook 2000.

■ **Visual Basic for Applications (VBA)** can now be used to programmatically access the Outlook object model and other Office applications' object models from within Outlook. New in Outlook 2000.

Installing Outlook 2000

Like Outlook 98, Outlook 2000 can be installed in one of three ways, known as *service options,* depending on a user's needs. Outlook 97 did not offer service options. The service options available in Outlook 98 and Outlook 2000 include the following:

■ **Corporate or Workgroup (C/W).** The primary service option for corporate users. Outlook functions as the client for email systems, such as Microsoft Exchange Server, Microsoft Mail, or cc:Mail, and can be used with Internet and intranet email and to send and receive faxes. This option provides all the Outlook personal information management capabilities (contacts, calendar, journal, tasks, and notes).

■ **Internet Mail Only (IMO).** This option provides access to Internet and intranet email, provides all the Outlook personal information management capabilities, and can be used to send and receive faxes.

■ **No E-mail Support.** This option provides all the Outlook personal information management capabilities, but no email or fax support.

When you install Outlook 2000 (either as part of Office 2000 or separately), the installation process automatically detects whether a previous version of Outlook has been installed on the computer. If Outlook 98 was previously installed, Outlook 2000 is installed with the same service option Outlook 98 had. If Outlook 97 was previously installed, the Corporate or Workgroup Outlook 2000 option is installed.

N O T E   After you've installed Outlook 2000, it's much easier to switch from one service option to another than it was in Outlook 98. ■

If you're installing Outlook 2000 on a computer on which Outlook hasn't previously been installed, the installation process offers a choice of service options. Also, if the installation process finds an application, such as Netscape Communicator or Outlook Express, you are asked whether you want to import information from one of those applications.

Understanding How Outlook Relates to Other Microsoft Email Clients and Internet Products

Because email is one of the key strategic capabilities of Outlook, it is important for you to understand the role Outlook plays within Microsoft's family of email clients and messaging services. Microsoft provides the following programs you can use as email clients and to work on the Internet:

- **Microsoft Exchange client.** This email client, also known as *Windows Messaging*, is automatically installed on most Windows 95 and Windows NT computers. Outlook is designed as an upgrade to the Exchange client. When you install Outlook 98, the Exchange client is removed from the desktop.

- **Outlook 97.** This is the initial version of Outlook that was distributed with Office 97. Outlook 97 is also included with recent releases of Microsoft Exchange Server, so that it can function in its role as a client to Exchange.

- **Outlook 98.** This is the updated version of Outlook that was released independently from the rest of Office 97 in early 1998. Both Outlook 97 and Outlook 98 run on 32-bit Windows (Windows NT, Windows 95, and Windows 98).

- **Outlook for 16-bit Windows and Macintosh.** These versions of Outlook are designed to provide a consistent messaging platform for organizations that must support Windows 3.*x* and Macintosh platforms along with 32-bit Windows.

- **Outlook Express.** This is the email client and Internet newsreader that is included as part of Microsoft Internet Explorer 4.0, 4.01, and 5.0. Despite its similar name, it is a completely separate product from Outlook, not a subset of Outlook. Both Outlook 98 and Outlook 2000 rely on Outlook Express to provide newsreader services.

- **Internet Explorer.** Internet Explorer provides essential services used by Outlook for accessing the Internet. When you install Outlook 2000, Internet Explorer 5.0 is automatically installed if it's not already present on the computer.

- **Outlook Web Access.** Available as an installation option for Microsoft Exchange 5.5, Outlook Web Access enables users to gain secure access to their email, calendar, group scheduling, and Exchange public folder information using a Web browser such as Internet Explorer. This enables mobile users to get their messages and other information even if they are working on another platform, such as UNIX.

Corporate users who are connected to a network and a mail service typically use Outlook for its messaging and information-management features and use Internet Explorer to browse the Internet. To participate in Internet newsgroups, they can use Outlook Express, unless the Exchange administrator has set up newsgroup support in Exchange public folders. In that case, Outlook can be used for reading and contributing to the newsgroups.

Independent users usually choose the IMO Outlook service option and use the Internet for email. Although the C/W option provides facilities for using Internet email, the IMO option is superior in this regard because it allows monitoring of email messages as they are sent and

Part

II

Ch

10

received. Also, Outlook with the IMO option opens and closes considerably faster than Outlook with the C/W option. Outlook uses Internet Explorer facilities for surfing the Web and Outlook Express facilities for participating in newsgroups.

People who require fast and reliable Internet email and newsgroup functionality but who don't need any of the information-management features of Outlook can choose to use Outlook Express and Internet Explorer instead. This is a good solution for many home and small business users and for Office for Macintosh users.

Understanding How Outlook Relates to Microsoft Exchange

Of all the ways you can use Outlook, one of its key strategic roles is as a client to Microsoft Exchange. Microsoft Exchange is a client/server messaging system that is built around Microsoft Exchange Server, a powerful application that runs under Windows NT server on an organization's network. Individual users on the network run client software to create, edit, send, and read messages, while Exchange Server provides the centralized storage, delivery, and collaboration services for the network.

Many users in an Exchange Server environment work at computers that are physically connected to the Exchange Server through a Windows NT network. When users log on to the Windows NT network, they gain access to the resources of the network, including their Exchange Server accounts, which are secured by their network logons and passwords. Exchange can also be used by remote users, who connect to the Exchange Server either using a dial-up connection and a modem or by way of the Internet.

Individual users of C/W Outlook have one or more *Windows email profiles*. Each profile contains one or more *information services*, which enables a user to communicate with different email systems, such as Microsoft Exchange Server, Microsoft Mail, and Lotus cc:Mail. By customizing a profile, a user can select one or more mail services to be used.

Users can configure their Windows email profiles by using the Mail applet in the Windows Control Panel or by issuing commands within Outlook. With C/W Outlook installed but not configured for use as a client for Exchange Server, follow these steps to add the Exchange Server information service to a profile.

1. In C/W Outlook, choose **Tools**, **Services** to display the Services dialog box, shown in Figure 10.1. Any information services already installed are listed.
2. Click **Add** to display the Add Service to Profile dialog box, shown in Figure 10.2.

FIGURE 10.1

Use the Services dialog box to install additional information services in a profile.

FIGURE 10.2

Select the information service you want to add to your profile.

3. Select **Microsoft Exchange Server** and click **OK** to configure the service.

4. The Microsoft Exchange Server dialog box appears. Use the options in the **General** tab (shown in Figure 10.3) to identify your Exchange Server and your Exchange mailbox. Enter the name of your Exchange Server and your mailbox name, and then click **Check Name**. Outlook verifies the names of the server and the mailbox and, if successful, underscores both names. To be connected to the Exchange Server each time you start Outlook, select the **Automatically detect connection state** option button. If you will be working remotely, select the **Manually control connection state** option button and choose the connection state that best matches your working pattern.

FIGURE 10.3

Use the General tab to enter your Exchange Server account information.

Part

II

Ch

10

5. Use the options in the **Advanced** tab (shown in Figure 10.4) to select additional mailboxes to open when you start Outlook. You can open only the mailboxes of users who have given you the appropriate permissions. You can also choose to encrypt your messages to provide extra security.

FIGURE 10.4

Use the Advanced tab to select additional mailboxes for which you want to set security options.

6. To set up offline folder files, click the **Offline Folder File Settings** button to display the dialog box shown in Figure 10.5. (If you will be using your computer remotely and connecting to Exchange Server using a modem, Outlook stores a copy of your messages in the offline folders and keeps the originals in your online folders on the Exchange Server.) Select or type the name of the file that you will use to store your offline messages, and then select the encryption settings you want to use. You can't change the encryption settings after you have created the offline folders. When you click **OK** to return to the Advanced tab, the **Enable offline use** check box is selected. You can clear the box if you don't want to work offline.

N O T E After you've begun to use your offline folders, you can return to this dialog box and click **Compact Now** to recover unused space from the offline folder file. You can also click **Disable Offline Use** if you will no longer be working offline. ▪

FIGURE 10.5

Use the Offline Folder File Settings dialog box to identify your offline folder file and to select the encryption setting for the file.

7. Use the options in the **Dial-Up Networking** tab (shown in Figure 10.6) to select or configure a Dial-Up Networking connection for working over a modem. You can select an existing connection from the drop-down list, or you can click **New** to create a new Dial-Up Networking connection. Enter the username, password, and domain name you use to log on to your network with the dial-up connection. You can also choose whether you want to access a specific account when you log on by dial-up networking and whether to select an account when you log on.

FIGURE 10.6

Select an existing Dial-Up Networking connection or create a new one.

8. Use the options in the **Remote Mail** tab (shown in Figure 10.7) to configure your computer for working remotely. When working remotely, you can choose to select the messages individually that you want to download, or you can apply a filter to control which messages are downloaded. You might, for example, want to download all messages from a specific author or all messages that contain certain text in the Subject line. You can also schedule connections on a periodic schedule, such as every hour.

FIGURE 10.7

Use the Remote Mail tab to select your options for working remotely with Microsoft Exchange and to schedule periodic connections.

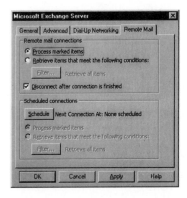

9. Click **OK** to complete your changes and close the Microsoft Exchange Server dialog box. Outlook displays a message reminding you that you must close and restart Outlook to make the new information service available.

Customizing the Outlook Interface

Outlook provides a flexible user interface that users can customize to meet their preferences and requirements.

Personalizing Your Menus and Toolbars

Outlook shares the capability to personalize menus and toolbars with the other major Office applications. For detailed information about this, see "Personalizing Your Menus and Toolbars" in Chapter 6. By default, personalized menus and toolbars are enabled. Refer to Chapter 6 for information about disabling these features on individual computers and about disabling them using a system policy.

> **N O T E** You can't enable and disable personalized menus and toolbars for individual Office applications. When you enable the capability, it is enabled for all Office applications; likewise, when you disable the capability, it is disabled for all Office applications. ▪

By default, Outlook displays the Standard toolbar but can also display an Advanced toolbar. As in other Office applications, you can customize these toolbars by adding and removing toolbar buttons. You can also create custom toolbars. See "Changing the Content of a Word Toolbar," "Customizing Word Toolbars More Thoroughly," "Creating a New Toolbar," "Changing a Button's Text or Image," "Resetting Toolbars to Their Original Settings," and "Making Toolbars Easier to Work With" in Chapter 6 for information about customizing toolbars.

You can also customize Outlook's menu bar (by adding and removing menus) and the individual menus (by adding and removing menu items). See "Customizing Menus," "Adding a Menu to a Toolbar," "Adding a Command to a Menu," and "Removing a Command from a Menu" in Chapter 6.

Using Outlook Today

In Outlook 2000, you can display the Outlook Today screen, shown in Figure 10.8, to summarize your activities in Outlook. Outlook Today enables you to see at one time whether you have any new email messages, any items on your calendar, or any outstanding tasks.

> **N O T E** The Outlook Today screen shown in Figure 10.8 is the default. You can choose **Customize Outlook Today** to display the information differently. ▪

To display the Outlook Today window, choose **View**, move the pointer onto **Go To**, and choose **Outlook Today**.

All the information in the Outlook Today window contains hyperlinks to the underlying Outlook items of information. You can click any information displayed in Outlook Today to see its details in an Outlook form.

FIGURE 10.8
The Outlook Today screen summarizes your current activities.

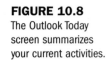
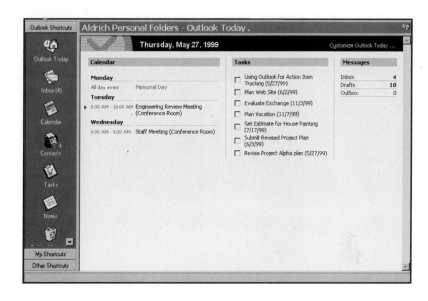

Click **Customize Outlook Today** in the Outlook Today window to control whether to go directly to Outlook Today each time you start Outlook, to customize the display of the Messages, Calendar, and Tasks lists, and to choose among several styles for displaying the Outlook Today window.

The Outlook Today window is defined by HTML code to which you have access and that you can modify. You can customize the Outlook Today window to present any information that's available to your computer, including Outlook items and information in files accessible on the network and available on the Internet or an intranet.

N O T E For detailed information about customizing Outlook Today, see the 26-page document *Customizing the Outlook Today Page,* which you can download from
http://www.microsoft.com/office/ork/2000/Appndx/toolbox.htm.

Viewing Messages

Outlook saves incoming messages in the Inbox folder. You can display the headers of messages in the Inbox folder in an Information viewer, as shown in Figure 10.9. The viewer shows who sent each message, the subject of the message, and the date and time the message was received. Click the column heading that you want to use to sort message headers in the viewer. For example, click the **From** heading to display message headers alphabetically by the sender's name, or click the **Received** heading to sort message headers by the date they were received. Use the toolbar at the top of the message window to print, reply to, or forward messages, and so on.

If you prefer to read an email message in a Message form, double-click its message header.

FIGURE 10.9

The Inbox Information viewer lists the headers of the email messages you have received.

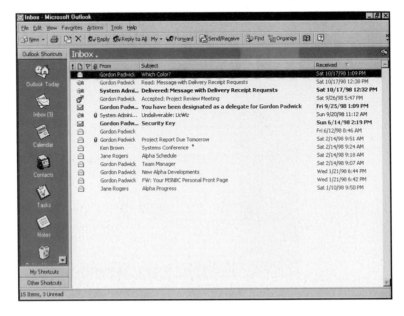

Using AutoPreview Although the message window is useful, it can be time-consuming to open your messages and read them one at a time, especially if you often receive a lot of messages.

To alleviate this problem, you can activate AutoPreview to display the first three lines of each message as part of the header, as shown in Figure 10.10. This makes it easier to select which messages you want to read. In the case of short messages, you might even see the entire message in the AutoPreview display.

FIGURE 10.10

AutoPreview displays up to three lines of each message in your Inbox.

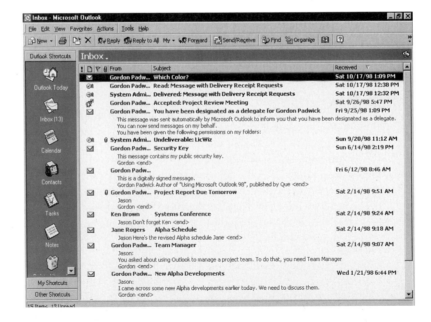

To activate AutoPreview, select the **Inbox** folder or any other folder that contains messages. Then, choose **View**, **AutoPreview**. To turn off the AutoPreview feature, select the same command.

Using the Preview Pane   You can use the Preview pane to display the contents of a message in a resizable pane that takes up as much of the screen as you want. Figure 10.11 shows a message whose contents are displayed in the Preview pane. This enables you to see much more of the message than you would see if you used AutoPreview. The Preview Header (the gray bar at the top of the Preview pane) lists the sender, the subject, and the addresses to which the message was sent. You can resize the Preview pane by dragging the border that separates it from the pane that displays message headers.

FIGURE 10.11
The Outlook 98 Preview pane displays a large portion of the currently selected message.

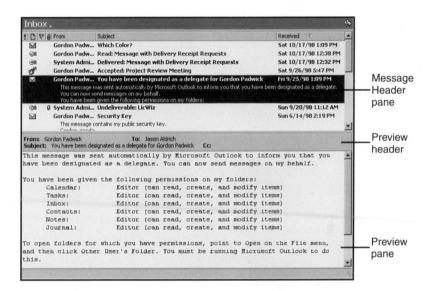

To display the Preview pane, activate a folder that contains messages and choose **View**, **Preview Pane**. To close the Preview pane, select the same command.

> **N O T E**   If the Preview pane doesn't have a header on your screen, move the pointer onto the top border of the Preview pane, right-click to display a context menu, and choose **Header Information**. ▪

You can control the appearance and actions of the Preview pane with the Preview Pane dialog box shown in Figure 10.12. To display the dialog box, right-click the **Preview Pane** header, and then select **Preview pane options** from the shortcut menu that appears.

If you select **Mark messages as read in preview window**, Outlook considers a message as having been read after it has been displayed in the Preview pane for the number of seconds listed in the **Wait x seconds before marking item as read** box. You can also choose to mark an item as read when you move away from it by selecting another message or folder. If you select **Single key reading using space bar**, you can move from message to message by pressing the spacebar.

Part

II

Ch

10

FIGURE 10.12
Use the Preview Pane dialog box to control the Preview pane's appearance and functions.

 Click **Font** to select the font to be used in the Preview pane header.

Using the Outlook Bar and Folder List

The Outlook Bar and Folder List, shown in Figure 10.13, provide two ways to navigate among your Outlook folders. You can display either pane, neither, or both according to your preferences.

FIGURE 10.13
The Outlook Bar and Folder List provide two ways to display the contents of Outlook folders.

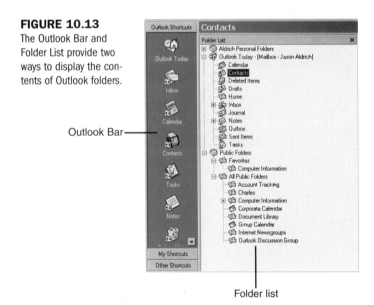

Folder list

The Outlook Bar contains icons representing the various folders in which Outlook saves information. By default, the Outlook Bar contains three groups of icons: Outlook Shortcuts, My Shortcuts, and Other Shortcuts. Click a group name to display the icons in that group. Click a shortcut to access a folder and open an Information viewer that displays information about items in that folder.

The Folder List displays all your Outlook and Exchange folders in an Explorer-style tree. You can navigate the folder list by clicking on the folders. To expand/collapse a branch of the list, double-click it. The Folder List generally displays more folders in the same amount of space as the Outlook Bar.

To display the Outlook Bar, choose **View**, **Outlook Bar**. Select the same command to hide the Outlook Bar.

To activate the Folder List, choose **View**, **Folder List**. To hide the Folder List, select the same command, or click the **Close** button in the upper-right corner of the Folder List.

Customizing Outlook

Outlook has many customizable options, which you can select on individual computers or by creating system policies in the Outlook 2000 Policy Template. The following sections describe setting options on an individual computer.

▶ For information about using system policies to set Outlook options, **see** "Using System Policies with Office 2000," on **p. 970**.

You set Outlook options for individual computers by making selections in the Options dialog box. Most of the options are organized according to functional areas: E-mail, Calendar, Task, Contact, Journal, and Note. To display the Options dialog box, choose **Tools**, **Options**. Then, click the tab that contains the options you want to customize.

NOTE The options described in this section are for C/W Outlook. Some of the options available in IMO Outlook are slightly different. ▉

After making changes in any of the tabs in the Options dialog box, click **Apply** if you want to activate the changes and keep the dialog box open. To close the dialog box, click **OK**.

Setting Preferences

The Preferences tab, shown in Figure 10.14, enables you to control the default reminder time for new Calendar and Task items. By selecting any of the Options dialog box buttons, you can select from a wide variety of additional options for each major function of Outlook.

Selecting E-mail Options The E-mail Options dialog box, shown in Figure 10.15, enables you to choose how Outlook handles messages and how replies and messages you forward are formatted.

Clicking **Advanced E-mail Options** or **Tracking Options** leads to more detailed dialog boxes.

Advanced E-mail Options Use the Advanced E-mail Options dialog box, shown in Figure 10.16, to specify how messages are sent and received in more detail. The Save messages section controls how Outlook saves copies of the messages you send.

Part
II

Ch
10

FIGURE 10.14

The Preferences tab of the Options dialog box leads to more detailed options for each major function of Outlook.

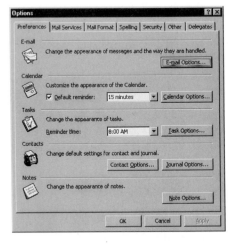

FIGURE 10.15

The E-mail Options dialog box enables you to choose options for sending and receiving messages.

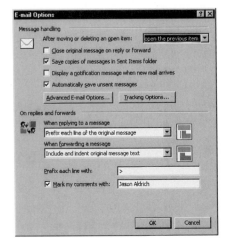

NOTE Outlook provides a Drafts folder to save messages in progress. If you close a message before you are ready to send it, it is automatically saved in the Drafts folder so you can finish the message and send it later. ■

You can also specify when and how incoming messages are received, as well as the default importance and sensitivity settings for each new message you send.

FIGURE 10.16

The Advanced E-mail Options dialog box enables you to control the details of sending and retrieving messages.

Tracking Options   Use the Tracking Options dialog box to set the default method that Outlook uses to track the messages you send (see Figure 10.17). You can also change the tracking for an individual message using the **Options** toolbar button while you are creating the message. Select **Request a read receipt for all messages I send** if you want to be notified when recipients open, and presumably read, messages you send. Select **Request a delivery receipt for all messages I send** to be notified when messages have been successfully transferred to the recipient's email server. Select **Delete blank voting and meeting responses after processing** if you don't want to keep those items in your Inbox.

FIGURE 10.17

Use the Tracking Options dialog box to set the default tracking for all future messages.

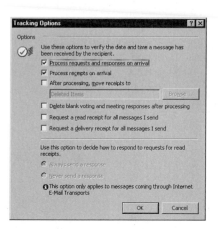

Selecting Calendar Options   You can use the Calendar Options dialog box, shown in Figure 10.18, to specify the days in your workweek and the starting and ending time of the workday. You can also use this dialog box to set your time zone, national holidays, and options for resource scheduling, and you can select a background color for Outlook to use when displaying calendars.

FIGURE 10.18
Use the Calendar Options dialog box to control the display of the Calendar window.

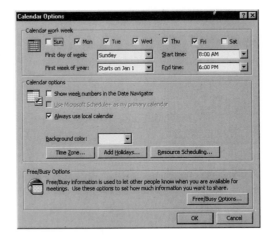

Selecting Task Options The Task Options dialog box, shown in Figure 10.19, controls the display color of overdue and completed tasks.

FIGURE 10.19
Use the Task Options dialog box to control the colors in which overdue and completed tasks are displayed.

Selecting Contact Options Use the Contact Options dialog box, shown in Figure 10.20, to select how you want Outlook to save a contact's full name based on the information you enter for a new contact. Also, use this dialog box to select how you want Outlook to construct a File As name for each contact.

FIGURE 10.20
Use the Contact Options dialog box to indicate how you want Outlook to handle names for new contacts.

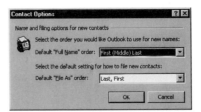

Selecting Journal Options The Journal Options dialog box, shown in Figure 10.21, enables you to select which items you want Outlook to automatically add to the Journal. Select the boxes next to the items that you want to be recorded in the journal. Click next to the name of a contact to record all items that you either sent to or received from that contact. Select one or more Office 2000 applications to record the history of your work with any documents from those applications.

FIGURE 10.21
Use the Journal Options dialog box to select the Outlook items you want Outlook to record, including correspondence or documents you have exchanged with specific email contacts.

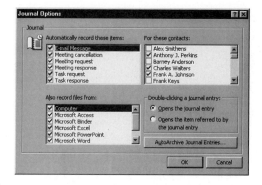

Use the **AutoArchive Journal Entries** button to determine how often you want to copy items from the Journal folder to an archive file.

Selecting Note Options   Use the Notes Options dialog box, shown in Figure 10.22, to customize the default color, size, and font for new notes.

FIGURE 10.22
Use the Notes Options dialog box to control the appearance of notes.

Setting Mail Services Options

The Mail Services tab of the Options dialog box, shown in Figure 10.23, controls how Outlook selects a mail profile at startup. If you use more than one profile, you can have Outlook prompt you for the profile to use each time you start Outlook. Otherwise, select the profile that you want Outlook to use as the default.

FIGURE 10.23
Use the Mail Services tab to select your startup profile and to control how Outlook checks for mail.

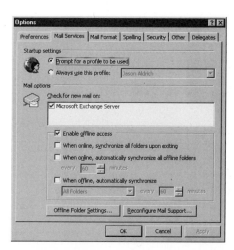

Select one or more mail services that you want to check for mail. All mail services that you have installed in your profile are displayed in the **Check for new mail on** list.

Also, use this tab to determine whether you will allow offline access in this profile and how folders will be synchronized when working offline.

> **N O T E** The section of the dialog box that deals with offline access is visible only if you have the Microsoft Exchange Server information service in your profile. Furthermore, the section is enabled only if you enabled offline use when you set up the Microsoft Exchange Server information service. ▪

You can click the **Reconfigure Mail Support** button to switch from the C/W service option to the IMO option. Similarly, when you are using the IMO option, you can click this button to switch to C/W.

> **N O T E** When you switch from one service option to another, Outlook needs to read some files from your Office 2000 CD-ROM (if you installed from that) or from your server (if Office was installed from the server). ▪

Setting Mail Format Options

Use the Mail Format tab, shown in Figure 10.24, to select the message format—**HTML, Microsoft Outlook Rich Text**, or **Plain Text**. By default, Outlook uses its built-in editor for creating messages. If you prefer to use Word as your editor, select **Use Microsoft Word to edit e-mail messages**. You can also select your default font and stationery for HTML messages and a signature that is automatically added to your new messages. Use the **Signature Picker** button to select from existing signatures or to create new ones.

FIGURE 10.24

The Mail Format tab lets you select the message format, appearance, and a default signature for the messages you create.

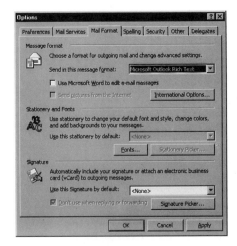

Setting Spelling Options

Use the Spelling tab, shown in Figure 10.25, to set preferences for spell checking messages, including the special cases that you want the spelling checker to ignore. You can also use this tab to edit the contents of your custom dictionary and to select a dictionary if you have installed a dictionary in more than one language.

FIGURE 10.25

Use the Spelling tab to select your preferences for the spelling checker and to manage your spelling dictionaries.

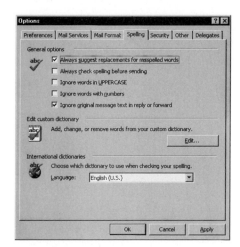

Setting Security Options

The Security tab lets you modify your settings for secure email. As you can see in Figure 10.26, these options are unavailable unless your email administrator has enabled security features at the server level or, if you're using Internet email, unless you've obtained a certificate (Digital ID).

FIGURE 10.26

Use the Security tab to select secure email options and to control the execution of scripts in messages you receive.

You can also use this tab to customize the security settings for the Internet, your intranet, restricted sites, and trusted sites. Adjusting these settings can help protect you from potentially dangerous viruses and unwanted programs or scripts that might be included with messages you receive.

Setting Other Options

The Other tab, shown in Figure 10.27, enables you to specify whether you want to automatically empty your Deleted Items folder when you exit Outlook. If you check this box, you will not be able to recover items that were in your Deleted Items folder at the time you exited Outlook.

You can also use this tab to set more advanced options or to customize AutoArchive and the Preview pane.

FIGURE 10.27

The Other tab of the Options dialog box leads to more advanced options, as well as to AutoArchive and Preview pane settings.

Selecting Advanced Options   Clicking the **Advanced Options** button in the Other tab displays the Advanced Options dialog box, shown in Figure 10.28. You can use this dialog box to specify which folder should be active when you start Outlook. If you select **Warn before permanently deleting items**, Outlook asks for confirmation before completely deleting items, including the automatic deletion of items in your Deleted Items folder. The Appearance Options section controls the display in the Calendar and Notes folders. Additional buttons are described here:

- **Reminder Options.** Choose whether you want to display or hear reminders, or both. Also, if you choose to hear reminders, you can select the sound file that's played.

- **Add-In Manager.** Enables you to install, configure, or remove add-in components that are available from Microsoft and third-party suppliers.

- **Advanced Tasks.** Choose whether or not you want Outlook to provide reminders about tasks with due dates, and also whether you want to keep copies of tasks you assign to someone else and to receive status reports when those tasks are completed.

- **Custom Forms.** Enables you to manage forms by copying them from one forms library to another (available only in C/W Outlook), to set Outlook so that it will use your browser to display forms that Outlook itself doesn't understand, and to create a link to a forms library on a Web page.

- **COM Add-Ins.** Use this to install COM add-ins to and remove COM add-ins from Outlook. You can also use this to load (make active) and unload (make inactive) installed COM add-ins.

FIGURE 10.28

The Advanced Options dialog box enables you to control several details of Outlook operation.

Selecting AutoArchive Options   Click the **AutoArchive** button in the Other tab to display the AutoArchive dialog box, shown in Figure 10.29. This dialog box enables you to control the frequency of the AutoArchive process, which periodically moves older items to a separate storage file so that your primary storage file doesn't get too large.

FIGURE 10.29

The AutoArchive dialog box controls the schedule and behavior of AutoArchive operations.

In Outlook 98 and Outlook 2000, AutoArchive executes in the background, so you can continue working while the archiving occurs. In Outlook 97, you can't do other work in Outlook while the folders are being archived.

Selecting Preview Pane Options   Click the **Preview Pane** button in the Other tab to display the Preview Pane dialog box shown in Figure 10.30. See the section "Using the Preview Pane" earlier in this chapter for a description of this dialog box.

FIGURE 10.30

Use the Preview Pane dialog box to control how the Preview pane works and to select the font to be used in the Preview pane header.

Setting Delegates Options

The Delegates tab (available only in C/W Outlook), shown in Figure 10.31, enables you to select other users who are authorized to act on your behalf. You must be logged on to your Exchange Server to use this feature. After adding users to the delegates list, you can set individual permissions, such as which of your folders the users can see and open and whether they can create new items or just read existing ones.

FIGURE 10.31

The Delegates tab enables you to select other users whom you want to allow to send Outlook items on your behalf.

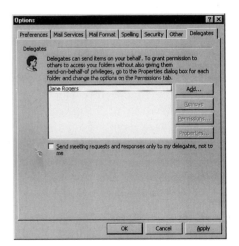

Selecting Internet E-mail Options

If you have one or Internet email information services in your profile, the Options dialog box also has an **Internet E-mail** tab, shown in Figure 10.32.

In some cases, the Options dialog box has additional tabs if you have installed certain Outlook add-ins.

FIGURE 10.32

The Internet E-mail tab enables you to select how your Internet email is encoded, as well as whether and how frequently you want Outlook to automatically connect to your email server.

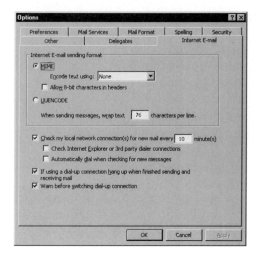

Creating Custom Views

Outlook provides Information viewers that offer various views of the information in folders. When you are using an Information viewer to look at the items in one of your Outlook folders (such as the Inbox, Calendar, or Contacts folder), you see the items as the result of a *view*. Outlook installs a variety of views by default, giving you different ways of organizing and working with data. Each view displays specified fields in a folder and displays those fields in a certain format.

For example, the Messages view of the Inbox folder shows only message headers, whereas the Messages with AutoPreview view activates AutoPreview to show the first three lines of each message under the header. The Last Seven Days view shows only those messages received in the last week, and the By Sender view groups messages according to who sent those messages.

You can select the view you want to use by choosing **View**, moving the pointer onto **Current View**, and selecting the view you want from the submenu that appears.

N O T E In Outlook 97, the Standard toolbar contains a list of the currently available views for each folder, and the quickest way to switch between views is to select a view from the list.

In Outlook 98 and Outlook 2000, the Current View list moved from the Standard toolbar to the Advanced toolbar. To display the Advanced toolbar, choose **View**, move the pointer onto **Toolbars**, and choose **Advanced**. ■

You can change the settings for a view or create your own custom views. To edit the view that you currently have open, choose **View**, move the pointer onto **Current View**, and choose **Customize Current View**. The View Summary dialog box appears, as shown in Figure 10.33.

FIGURE 10.33
Use the View Summary dialog box to display a description of the current view and to change its attributes.

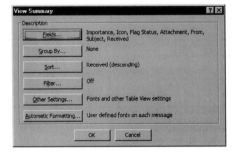

This dialog box shows the following settings for the current view in six categories:

- **Fields.** Select which item fields should appear in the view.

- **Group By.** Select an optional grouping expression. For example, grouping your email messages by the From field puts all the messages from each sender together.

- **Sort.** Select one or more fields to use to determine the order in which the items are displayed. For example, you might want a view of the Contacts folder to be sorted alphabetically by last name or by zip code.

- **Filter.** Select a condition that limits which items should appear. You might want to show only the Calendar items with a certain keyword in the Categories field, or only those that are more than one day in duration.

- **Other Settings.** Change display attributes such as fonts, shading, border lines, and whether the Preview pane is displayed.

- **Automatic Formatting.** Define rules for automatic formatting, such as using red text for high-priority items or using a different font for completed tasks.

To change any of these attributes for the current view, click the appropriate button and use the dialog box that appears to customize your settings.

To create new views or to make a copy of a view, choose **View**, move the pointer onto **Current View**, and choose **Define Views**. The Define Views dialog box for the folder appears, as shown in Figure 10.34.

Click **New** to create and name a new view for the current folder. To make a copy of an existing view, select the view in the list, and then click **Copy**.

After you create a view or copy an existing one, you can modify the new view's properties to meet your needs.

FIGURE 10.34
Use the Define Views dialog box to select a view to modify or to create a new view.

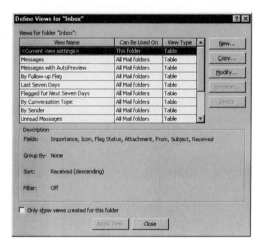

Taking Advantage of Templates

Instead of creating every Outlook item from scratch, you can create templates and subsequently base new items on those templates. For example, suppose you have to create monthly reports in a standard format. Each report probably contains boilerplate text that doesn't change much from month to month. Instead of creating the report from scratch each month, you can create it once and save that report as a template. Subsequently, you can create reports based on the template and just fill in the blanks. This technique can be a great timesaver.

Outlook saves templates as files in the Windows file system. Each template is a separate file with .oft as its filename extension.

The following sections describe how you can use templates for email messages. You can use similar templates for other types of Outlook items.

Creating an Email Template

Start by creating a skeleton email message that contains such things as boilerplate text, section headings, and empty tables. If you want to assign the same categories to each message, assign those categories to the initial message, and then you don't have to remember to assign categories to each individual message.

After you've created the skeleton message, instead of choosing Send in the toolbar to send it, open the **File** menu and choose **Save As** to open the Save As dialog box. The dialog box opens with the subject of the message as the proposed filename; you can change the filename if necessary. Open the **Save As Type** list at the bottom of the dialog box, and select **Outlook Template**. Then, choose **Save** to save the template.

Part

II

Ch

10

Using an Email Template

When it comes time to create a message based on the template, follow these steps:

1. Click the **Inbox** icon in the Outlook Bar to open the Inbox Information viewer.

2. Choose **Tools** in the menu bar, move the pointer onto **Forms**, and choose **Choose Form** to display the dialog box shown in Figure 10.35.

FIGURE 10.35
The Choose Form dialog box opens with the Standard Forms Library selected.

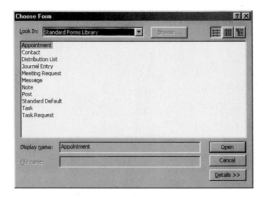

3. Open the **Look In** drop-down list and select **User Templates in File System**. Outlook displays a list of templates you have previously created and saved in the default Templates folder. If necessary, navigate to the folder in which you saved the template you want to use.

4. Select the appropriate template, and then choose **Open** to display a message form based on the template.

5. Finish creating the message and send it in the usual way.

Using Templates for Other Types of Outlook Items

Templates are useful for more than just sending messages. Some examples of other uses are listed here:

- **Sending meeting requests.** If you regularly send meeting requests to people, you can create a template for a meeting request. After creating the template, open it, fill in the details, and send the request.

- **Creating similar contact items.** Perhaps you want to create contact items for many people in an organization, most of whom have the same street address, share some phone numbers, and perhaps have the same Web site address. Create a contact template that contains all the shared information and use it to create individual contact items.

- **Assigning tasks to a team.** As a team manager, you might want to assign similar tasks to several team members. The task items you need to create for each team member contain text that's the same for everyone. Create a task item that contains the shared information, save it as a template, and use the template to create individual task items.

Modifying a Template

After you've created templates, you'll probably want to modify them from time to time. That's quite easy to do.

1. In the Outlook Bar, click the icon you would normally choose if you were creating an Outlook item from scratch.

2. Choose **Tools**, move the pointer onto **Forms**, and choose **Choose Form** to display the Choose Form dialog box.

3. Open the **Look In** list and select **User Templates in File System** to display a list of existing templates.

4. Double-click the name of the template you want to modify. Outlook opens the template in a template form, which is similar to the form in which you originally created the template.

5. Make any necessary changes to the template, choose **File**, **Save** to save the modified template, and then close the template. ●

Part

II

Ch

10

CHAPTER 11

Customizing FrontPage to Your Organization's Needs

by Brady P. Merkel

Whether you use FrontPage 2000 to personally develop a Web site for your intranet, or collaborate in a team to develop a site on the Internet, you can customize FrontPage 2000 to meet your needs. For starters, FrontPage includes features that enable you to target specific server and browser environments—so that you can avoid using Web technologies that aren't generally in use by your site's intended audience, or are not available on your Web server. You can also use the FrontPage built-in security and collaboration tools that permit multiple Webmasters to simultaneously develop Web content for the same site at the same time.

To enhance individual productivity, FrontPage 2000 adopts the same familiar Office interface features, such as customizable toolbars and menus. Choose **Tools**, **Customize** to adjust your toolbars and menus to your preferences.

Defining Browser and Server Compatibility for Your Web Site

When you create a Web site, avoid using features that are not supported by either your Web server or the browser your intended audience uses. For example, if you are developing content for an Internet Web site that users of the Netscape Communicator browser will visit, avoid using client-side VBScript programs and ActiveX controls, as these technologies are supported only by Internet Explorer. Similarly, if you are developing your Web content on a laptop using Windows 98 and the Personal Web Server, but you intend to publish the Web to a UNIX-based Web server, you should avoid using Active Server Pages (ASP).

> **NOTE** Previous versions of FrontPage required a Web server to develop Web sites offline—such as the Personal Web Server for Windows 98. With FrontPage 2000, you no longer must use a Web server—you can develop Web sites in folders on your disk drive. Do not despair—if you have Web content hosted under Personal Web Server now, FrontPage 2000 will work with it as expected. ∎

FrontPage enables you to customize the specific technologies (see Figure 11.1) to avoid while you author your Web content—changing the commands available during page development so that you use only the features supported by your target environments.

To define the browser and server environments that you want to target, choose **Tools**, **Page Options**, and then click the **Compatibility** tab, as shown in Figure 11.1. Depending on the needs of your Web site, you can also choose the technologies you want to employ in your Web content.

FIGURE 11.1
Choose the intended browser and server capabilities for your Web site.

For example, when you choose to target the Microsoft WebTV browser environment, all technologies are disabled except for ASP. In this case, FrontPage disables all the menu and toolbar selections for ActiveX controls, VBScript, JavaScript, Java Applets, Dynamic HTML, Frames, and Cascading Style Sheets (CSS) versions 1.0 and 2.0, as these technologies are not supported by WebTV (as of late March of 1999). Disabling these features in FrontPage restricts you from using them, and any related capabilities (such as Page Transitions when JavaScript is disabled, or database connections when ASP is disabled).

When you use a technology that you later disable with the Compatibility tab, FrontPage does not remove or change any Web content that you already have—FrontPage changes only the user interface so that you don't use the technology from this point forward.

Also, you should choose the client-side scripting language used in your pages, such as for form validation scripts. Client-side scripts are programs that run within a Web page at the browser, rather than at the server. When FrontPage writes the page with the embedded script, it can use JavaScript, VBScript, or no script at all (for Web TV-targeted Web sites, for example). Because VBScript is supported only in Microsoft browsers, you might prefer to use JavaScript, which is supported by both Microsoft and Netscape browsers. To select your client-side script preference, choose **Tools**, **Web Settings**, and click the **Advanced** tab, as shown in Figure 11.2. For the **Default Scripting Language**, select the **Client** language you want to use, or choose **<None>** if you do not want to use client-side scripts.

FIGURE 11.2
Select the default scripting language for client-side scripts.

Customizing Your Web Site Theme

As you begin to build your Web site, and perhaps invite other Webmasters to help, one of your immediate challenges is to establish a consistent page layout and design for all your Web pages. Using Themes, you can choose or develop the style you want and apply it to all pages within your Web site. If you later want to modify the site's theme, use FrontPage's integrated theme designer to tweak the settings and apply the improvements to every page—all without having to re-edit a single page.

When you install Office 2000, you can choose to install several predefined themes—where each theme provides a coordinated look and feel for your content, including text styles, graphics, buttons, and colors. To select the best theme for your Web site, think creatively and free-associate to find a suitable metaphor for your content. For example, a telecommunications company could use pictures of antique phones, phone keypads, or simply numbers as their metaphor. For fun, the company could also associate DTMF dial tones to their buttons for further emphasis to the metaphor.

After you decide on the appropriate metaphor for your Web site, use FrontPage 2000's integrated theme designer to build it. To build your own theme, start by choosing a current theme that best fits your metaphor—choose **Format, Theme** and peruse the list of themes. Select a theme that best suits your metaphor's graphics, as the graphic images are the most time-consuming to create. You'll find that it is easier to alter the colors and styles first and then change the graphic images when you have more time. After you choose a theme, click **Modify** to display the theme designer customization buttons.

Modifying Theme Colors

To change the color scheme for your theme, choose **Format, Theme, Modify,** and click **Colors**. Be aware, each theme has two color modes—one to use when you choose **Vivid Color** and another to use for **Normal Colors**. For completeness, be sure to select colors for both modes.

In the **Modify Theme** dialog box , select a new scheme from the current **Color Schemes** tab, as shown in Figure 11.3, or build your own new scheme using the **Color Wheel** tab, as shown in Figure 11.4. To assign colors at the individual HTML element level, use the **Custom** tab, as shown in Figure 11.5.

TIP In the Color Wheel tab, press and hold the spacebar while you click to choose from other interesting color schemes using the spiral pattern, as shown in Figure 11.6.

FIGURE 11.3
Select a color scheme for your new theme.

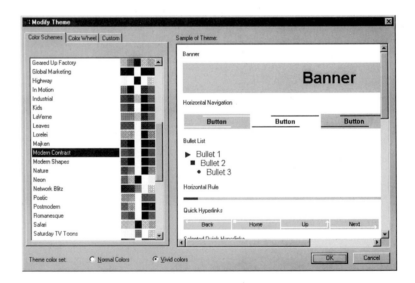

FIGURE 11.4
Generate a new color scheme using the color wheel.

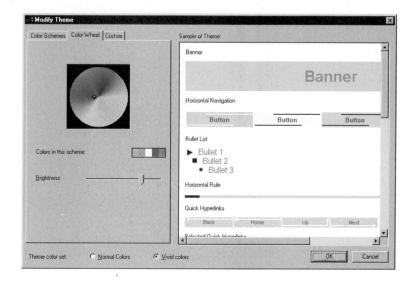

FIGURE 11.5
Designate specific color choices for individual HTML tags.

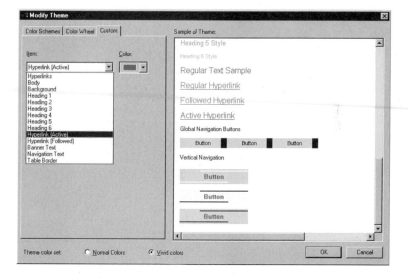

FIGURE 11.6
Generate other color schemes using a spiral pattern in the color wheel.

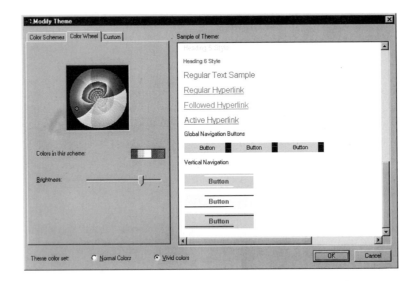

Modifying Theme Graphics

To customize a theme that best fits your metaphor, select the individual graphics for the background, bullets, banners, horizontal rules, and buttons. Similar to color schemes, there are two sets of theme graphics—Normal and Active Graphics. Creating images for the Active Graphics set can be more time-consuming than that for Normal, because you must create new images. For example, you need three images for navigational buttons—one when not selected, another when the mouse pointer hovers over the button, and a third when the button is clicked. To save time, you can choose the same file for each, and return later when you have more time to create distinctive versions.

To customize the graphics for your theme, choose **Format, Theme**. Click **Modify** to display the row of customization buttons, and click **Graphics** to display the Modify Theme dialog box. Click the **Picture** tab to modify the image elements to your theme. Choose the graphic item you want to work on in the **Item** list, and for each file listed in the Picture tab (see Figure 11.7), click **Browse** to select the appropriate image file. Remember to choose the image files for both the **Normal Graphics** set and the **Active Graphics** set.

Modifying the Style of Text in Your Graphics

FrontPage 2000 can overlay text on many of the graphic images available in your theme. Use the theme designer to choose the style for the text, so that the graphic elements are consistent with your overall page style.

To customize the text formatting for the graphics in your theme, choose **Format, Theme**, and click **Modify** to display the row of customization buttons. Click **Graphics** to display the Modify Theme dialog box and click the **Font** tab, as shown in Figure 11.8.

FIGURE 11.7
Select image files for both the Normal and Active Graphics sets.

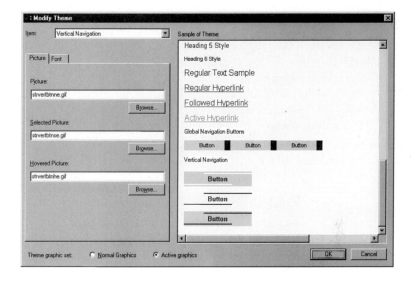

FIGURE 11.8
For a consistent look, use the same style for text in your images as on your page.

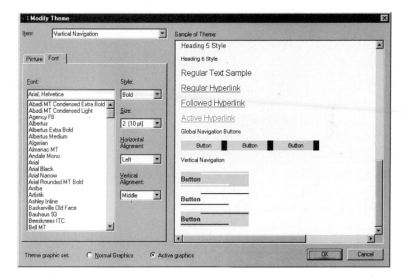

Select the graphical element from the **Item** option list and choose the preferred font name from the **Font** list. Also set the font's style, size, and horizontal and vertical alignments. Be sure to make your font changes for both the **Normal Graphics** and **Active Graphics** sets.

TIP
To produce the same font effect with Web browsers on other platforms, type additional font names, delimited by commas. When a browser cannot find the first font listed, it looks for the second, and so on. Otherwise, it displays the default font, which is usually Times New Roman.

Modifying the Style of HTML Text in Your Document

To modify the HTML text formatting for your Web pages, choose **Format**, **Theme**, and click **Modify** to display the row of customization buttons. Click **Text** to display the Modify Theme dialog box, as shown in Figure 11.9. Select the HTML text element from the **Item** option list at the top of the dialog box. Then, select the font name from the **Font** list. Click **More Text Styles** if you want to add CSS style information to a theme item, such as a border around text or background shading.

▶ To learn more about CSS, **see** Chapter 33 "Managing HTML/XML As Your Primary File Format," on **p. 867**.

FIGURE 11.9
Choose the font and assign CSS styles for a consistent look within your Web pages.

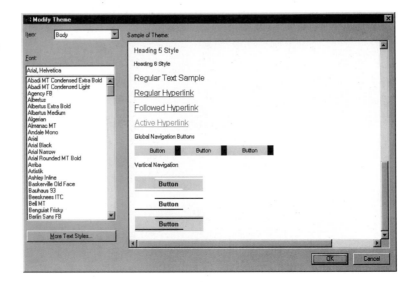

Defining a Standard HTML Format

As you author Web content and share it with other team members, you'll find that a standard format for the HTML pages goes a long way toward readability. If all team members adopt the same HTML formatting constructs, then making adjustments and understanding document structure becomes easier.

If the team members all use FrontPage to create the Web content, then customize FrontPage to save pages using the same preferred HTML formatting. Choose **Tools**, **Page Options**, and click the **HTML Source** tab, as shown in Figure 11.10. Choose **Reformat Using the Rules Below**, and if you want, customize the individual settings for each HTML tag.

FIGURE 11.10
Customize the HTML formatting of your pages.

Similarly, if the Web content developers use the same editors (image editing, Office applications, and so on), then the goal of page consistency is more readily achieved. To edit Office documents in their native application (rather than the FrontPage Editor environment), choose **Tools** and then **Options** to display the Options dialog box. Click the **Configure Editors** tab, as shown in Figure 11.11, and check the **Open Web Pages** in the Office application that created them.

▶ For more information on using Office 2000 applications to edit Web content, **see** Chapter 33, "Managing HTML/XML As Your Primary File Format," on **p. 867**.

FIGURE 11.11
Define external editors using the Configure Editors tab.

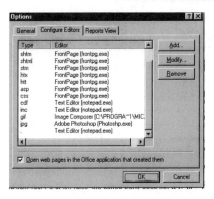

Also, you can associate specific file types with different editors within FrontPage. For example, you can associate .jpg files to open in Adobe Photoshop whenever you choose to edit a Joint Photographic Experts Group (JPEG) file.

Part

II

Ch

11

Securing Your Web

FrontPage enables you to control the security of your Web site—defining who can view the pages, who can author content, and who can administer it (such as change permissions or add other users). FrontPage defines the following levels of security:

- **Browse.** Users with Browse permission can view your Web content through their browser.

- **Author.** Users with Author permission can both browse and modify content using FrontPage or other Office 2000 applications.

- **Administer.** Users with Administer permission can browse, author, add, and remove users, and adjust user permissions.

 TIP If you want to set different user and permission levels for separate areas of your Web site, convert those areas to subwebs and assign the subwebs separate permissions. When inside a subweb, choose **Tools**, **Security**, and click the **Permissions** tab. Choose **Use Unique Permissions** and click **Apply**. Now, you can designate separate user and group permissions.

To define the user permissions for your Web site, choose **Tools**, **Security**, **Permissions**, and click the **Users** tab, as shown in Figure 11.12. If you want all users to have browse permission, choose **Everyone has browse access**. If you choose **Only registered users have browse access**, then the Web server requires users to authenticate when they first connect to the Web site—requiring them to enter a username and password. If the user is not permitted to browse, then the Web server does not allow him or her to view the Web content.

FIGURE 11.12
Define users and their
security levels in the
Users tab.

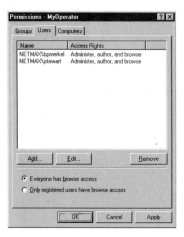

To add new users for your Web site, click **Add**. The Add Users dialog box displays, as shown in Figure 11.13. If your Web site is hosted on a Windows NT network, select the Windows NT domain in the **Obtain list from** list. Choose **Browse this web**, select each user to grant Browse permission, and click **Add**. Then click **OK**. Repeat this procedure for each user to whom you want to grant **Author and Administer Permission**.

FIGURE 11.13
Add users with your
preferred permissions.

To edit a specific user's permission, select the user in the Users tab, and click **Edit**. The Edit Users dialog box appears, as shown in Figure 11.14. Change the permission level, and click **OK**.

FIGURE 11.14
Change a user's per-
mission in the Edit
Users dialog box.

Part

II

Ch

11

Similarly, use the Groups tab to grant permissions to entire groups of users.

Collaborating in FrontPage

FrontPage 2000 includes a set of collaboration tools that enables you to manage an approval workflow, assign individuals to files and tasks, and perform check-in and check-out source control. FrontPage collaboration capabilities help you and content authors track the progress of your content, and maintain accountability for tasks and files.

▶ You can use the Office Server Extensions to provide additional collaboration capabilities. **See** Chapter 35, "Deploying and Using Office 2000's Web-Collaboration Components," on **p. 895**.

Managing Workflow and Approvals

If you work within a team of content authors, you can use the FrontPage 2000 integrated workflow tools to track the status of Web site files. You assign files to specific individuals, and as the people perform their duties, they affix an updated status to the file.

To manage your Web site files' workflow, use the Review Status report, as shown in Figure 11.15. The report enables you to assign an individual and initial status to the files.

FIGURE 11.15

Assign an individual and a review status to Web files in the Review Status Report.

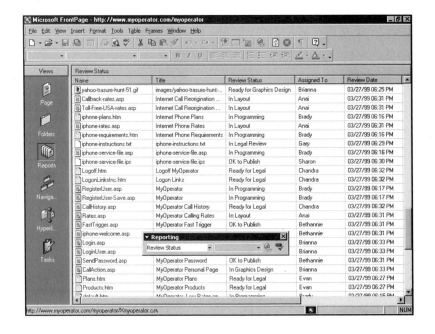

Assigning Individuals   To assign an individual to a file, select the file in the Review Status Report and click once in the **Assigned To** column, pause, and then click again. The field changes to a drop-down menu where you can select from the list of users. To update the list of users, right-click the file, and choose **Properties**. Click the **Workgroup** tab, as shown in Figure 11.16, and click **Names**. The Usernames Master List dialog box appears, as shown in Figure 11.17. To add a new name, type the name in the **New Username** text box and click **Add**.

FIGURE 11.16

Use a file's Workgroup tab to identify a responsible individual and review status for a file.

TIP   In addition to people's names, add entries for your separate workgroups, such as Graphics, Programming, Page Layout, and Management. Assign tasks and files to the workgroup name, such that each workgroup manager can then assign the particular task or file to the appropriate person within their workgroup.

FIGURE 11.17
Use the Usernames
Master List dialog box
to add and remove
individuals' names.

Setting the Review Status   To set the review status of a file, select the file and click once in the Review Status column, pause, and then click again. The field changes to a drop-down menu where you can select the status. To update the list of status levels, right-click the file and choose **Properties**. Click the **Workgroup** tab (refer to Figure 11.16) and click **Statuses**. The Review Status Master List dialog box appears, as shown in Figure 11.18. To add a status level, type it into the **New review status** text box, and click **Add**.

FIGURE 11.18
Use the Review Status
Master List dialog box
to add your own status
levels.

Using Source Control

New in FrontPage 2000 are integrated source control tools. The term *source control* refers to the capability to check in and check out files. If you work within a team of content authors, use source control to prevent two or more authors from editing the same file at the same time—the first person who checks out a file can modify it, and others can only obtain a read-only version until the file is checked back in. If the author who checked out a file prefers not to save the changes, he or she can undo a checkout.

To enable FrontPage source control, close all open files and choose **Tools and Web Settings**. Click the **General** tab and choose **Use Document Check-in and Check-out**. Click **Yes** to confirm that you want to do the operation now, as it might take a few minutes to recalculate the Web depending on the size of content.

Checking Out a File   To check out a file, double-click the filename in the Folder List. Click **Yes** to confirm that you want to check out the file for editing. The file opens in Page View or the assigned editor, and you can edit it normally. If you click **No**, then FrontPage allows you to open a read-only version of the file. If you try to save the file, FrontPage prevents you from doing so, warning you that the file is read-only. To save your changes, save the file to a new filename.

You can also check out a file without opening it—useful when you know you need to check out the file anyway. For example, you might need to work on an HTML form and the associated form handler at the same time. Right-click the file in the Folder List and choose **Check Out**.

To undo a checkout of a file, right-click the file in the Folder List and choose **Undo Check Out**. Click **Yes** to confirm when FrontPage warns you that your changes will be lost.

Checking In a File   Check in a file when you finish editing it and want to allow other authors to modify it. To check in a file, close it from Page View, or right-click the file in the Folder List and choose **Check In**. If the file is currently open for editing, click **Yes** to save your changes up to that point. After an open file is checked in, FrontPage treats the file as read-only until you check the file out again. ●

PART III

Using Office to Support Teams and Workgroups

Standardizing Document Production with Word and Excel

by Bill Camarda

Even the most traditional companies are increasingly becoming "virtual": Their most important work is done by cross-functional teams that might include not only members of different departments, but also freelancers, outsourcers, suppliers, and even customers.

With the walls of the corporation becoming so permeable, it can be a challenge to present your company as a single integrated entity capable of serving customers and making decisions. Of course, the challenge goes beyond appearances: How can you actually *be* a coherent entity under these circumstances?

If you manage Microsoft Office well, you can make a significant contribution toward maintaining a coherent corporate image—and even grounding that image in reality. Conversely, if you fail to manage Microsoft Office, you can easily find yourself publishing documents that look as if they came from different planets, not just different companies. Worse yet, you can find yourself making decisions based on inconsistent information and assumptions.

In this chapter, you learn practical techniques and Office features that can help you standardize and organize your document production companywide, while improving productivity. In particular, you learn about the following topics:

- How to deploy templates that enable users to share the latest styles and shortcuts for building consistent documents
- How to set up and standardize AutoCorrect lists that make it easier for your users to create accurate documents
- How to use AutoText boilerplate entries to streamline document production and make it more consistent
- How to create standardized charts and graphs that present the same image in all your documents

Planning to Standardize Your Company's Documents

To gain the maximum benefit from standardization, invest some up-front effort in planning. Ask yourself these questions: What types of documents ought to be standardized first, and which aspects of those documents are worth standardizing? Which documents are worth standardizing later—and which ones are unlikely to ever be worth the effort? The following section helps you establish priorities that make sense for your organization.

Deciding Where to Start

In most organizations, common sense dictates that you focus attention on the documents that best accomplish the following:

- Represent you to your customers
- Offer the greatest potential gain in quality and/or productivity
- Are created most often

Although organizations differ, you might want to use Table 12.1 as a starting point.

Table 12.1   Identifying Documents for Standardization

Type	Priority	Role	Program
Customer	High	External	PowerPoint presentations
Estimates	High	Internal	Excel/Access
Expense reports	Middle	Internal	Word
Fax cover sheets	Middle	Internal	Word
Forms	High	Internal	Word
Internal	Low	Internal	PowerPoint presentations
Letters	High	Int./Ext.	Word
Manuals	Middle	Internal	Word
Memos	Low	Internal	Word
P&Ls	High	Internal	Excel
Product sheets	High	External	Word
Proposals	High	External	Word
Purchase orders	Middle	Internal	Word
Reports	Middle	Internal	Word/Access

Later in this chapter, you find some tips that can help you extend customization beyond the standard document types listed in the preceding table to other documents such as intranet pages, product catalogs, and meeting agendas.

Understanding What You Can Standardize

Within the document types listed in Table 12.1, the following elements are ripe for standardization:

- Fonts, typically to match corporate standards
- Graphics, especially logos
- Color schemes, again to match corporate standards
- Charts
- Design layouts
- Formulas, to ensure accuracy and consistency
- Fields (in Word), to automate documents without requiring all users to understand complex Word features
- Links among documents, again to ensure accuracy and consistency
- Form elements such as drop-down boxes and list boxes

When pursuing document standardization, consider the following issues:

- **Does your organization already have graphic design standards that cover some of the documents you intend to standardize?** Ask your corporate communications or marketing department (if your company has one). If graphics standards do exist, be sure your organization's computers have the fonts needed to implement them. Deploying a specialized font companywide can be expensive; you might want to work with your designers to choose a reasonable alternative that is already installed on most users' systems.

- **Do you need to take any production constraints into account?** For example, if you're designing a letter, be sure it accommodates your corporate stationery. Before you deploy a customized color scheme for slides, be sure the colors reproduce well in both 35mm and overhead formats if necessary.

- **Do any legal constraints affect your documents?** If you want to standardize product sheets, for example, you might need to include standard disclaimers or trademark language. Ask your legal department (if you have one).

- **How can you involve the people who will be using the documents you develop?** Ideally, you should involve your colleagues from start to finish, using whatever resources are available, including sample documents that already exist.

Using Templates to Standardize Word

With these management basics in mind, let's look at the most powerful Office tool for standardization: the template, which is available in Word, Excel, and PowerPoint. Templates let you predefine and standardize virtually any content, formatting, or elements that can appear in an Office document. For example, Office templates can contain the following items:

- **Boilerplate text.**
- **Manual text formatting.** Boldface, italic, font size, and so on.

Part
III

Ch
12

- **Paragraph formatting (in Word).** Indentation, spacing before and after paragraphs, line spacing, tab settings, and so on.
- **Document formatting.** Margins, page breaks, backgrounds, and so on.
- **Styles.** For headings, headers, footers, tables of contents, and so on.
- **Images.** Logos, photographs, clip art, and so on.
- **Tables (in Word and PowerPoint).**
- **Multiple worksheets (in Excel).**
- **Protected/hidden areas of worksheets (in Excel).**
- **Slide show settings and Notes pages (in PowerPoint).**
- **Formulas and functions.** These can perform calculations, insert current dates, build tables of contents (in Word), or automate links to other Office data anywhere on your network (such as current information stored in an Excel worksheet).
- **Form controls.** For creating electronic forms that users can fill out online. (In Word, these are called *form fields*.)

Word and Excel templates also enable you to build specialized tools into your documents—including custom macros, toolbars, menus, keyboard shortcuts, and (in Word) AutoText entries—that are relevant to only a specific type of document.

▶ For in-depth discussion of techniques for using these tools, **see** Chapter 6, "Customizing Word to Your Organization's Needs," on **p. 121**.

TIP If you choose to customize your templates this way, be sure to educate your users, who might otherwise find it disconcerting that tools "appear" and "disappear" depending on the document they are working on.

By providing templates to your users, you make it much easier for them to create standardized documents. In effect, you've done most of the formatting work for them in advance—and in many cases, you've done much of the work of structuring the documents for them as well. Of course, your custom templates also significantly improve productivity: Users no longer have to "reinvent the wheel" each time they create a document; instead, they can focus more of their efforts on the value-added thinking associated with their work.

Although templates work slightly differently in each Office program, the same four-step process applies: You create the template, save it, test it, and deploy it.

N O T E Outlook 2000 also provides a feature called a template that functions essentially as a pad of electronic forms you can use to track contacts, send email, or perform other personal information management tasks. This feature is covered in Chapter 10, "Customizing Outlook to Your Organization's Needs."

This chapter focuses primarily on Word and Excel templates; you take a closer look at PowerPoint templates in Chapter 14, "Using PowerPoint in a Team Setting." ▪

Creating a Boilerplate Document to Use As a Template

Your first step in creating a template is to create a boilerplate document that looks and works the way you want it to and includes all the components that can reasonably be standardized. You do this using the same editing and formatting tools that Word, Excel, and PowerPoint make available for creating any document.

As was already mentioned, it's best to involve the individuals who will be using the documents. You might be able to use their existing documents as a starting point; you might also have professionally designed materials that can serve as a starting point.

Before you save your template, spell-check it. In addition, if it is a Word document, consider running Word's grammar tools on it. Although the grammar tools flag many sentences that are perfectly acceptable, they might flag some errors you did not catch.

 TIP In Word and Excel, you can also record or write VBA macros that are stored within your templates. Macros are discussed in several places throughout this book, including later in this chapter. (In PowerPoint, macros are stored within individual presentations.)

Saving Templates

After you edit your document to include all the contents you need, save it as a template by performing the following steps:

1. Choose **File, Save As**.
2. Type the name of the template in the **File Name** text box.
3. In the **Save As Type** drop-down box, specify that you want to save the file as a template. In Word 2000, choose Document Template (.dot); in Excel 2000, choose Template (.xlt); in PowerPoint 2000, choose Presentation Template (.pot).
4. Click **Save**.

Testing Templates

After you save your document as a template, open a new document based on that template. Be sure the document looks and works the way you intended it to. If possible, test the template on a representative sample of the systems that will run it, not just your own computer. Table 12.2 contains a template-testing checklist.

Table 12.2	Template-Testing Checklist
Category	**Tasks**
Accuracy	Do the documents created by your template *look* the way they're supposed to? Have any spelling or grammatical errors crept in? Are calculations consistently accurate when a wide variety of values are plugged in? In Word, do fields (especially date and time fields) report accurate results that are formatted appropriately?

continues

Table 12.2   Continued

Category	Tasks
Availability	Does the template have access to all the resources it needs, no matter where you run it from? For example, does it depend on fonts that are unavailable on some computers? Does it link to documents that some users will not have rights to access?
Usability	Is the template easy to use and understand? Does it contain the features users need most? Does it accommodate the needs of users? For example, does a fax cover sheet template include sufficient room for users to enter notes? Does a form's drop-down box contain the options users are most likely to need? Will the document look good in print as well as onscreen?
Macro Correctness	Do macros run properly on all systems, or do they report error messages users will find confusing? If you are deploying in a cross-platform environment, have you tested them on Macintosh and Windows systems? Have you added help to your macro where appropriate? Has the template been checked for macro viruses with an up-to-date virus scanner before even a test deployment?

Involving Your Team in the Template-Testing Process

While you're developing a complex Word or Excel template, such as a proposal document or an estimate worksheet, you might receive extensive feedback on content—both your boilerplate text and the assumptions you've built into your calculations. To streamline testing, use Office's tools for tracking changes.

Invite each of your testers to create a new document based on the template. Have each person turn on Word's or Excel's Track Changes tool (**Tools, Track Changes, Highlight Changes**) and make his or her recommended changes.

Then use Word's Merge Documents feature (**Tools, Merge Documents**) or Excel's Share Workbook feature (**Tools, Share Workbook**) to combine all the reviewers' changes into a single document. After you resolve any issues that were raised, you can save the revised file as a template again. (For more information about the Track Changes and Merge Documents features, see Chapter 13, "Using the Workgroup Revision Tools in Word and Excel.")

Deploying Your Templates

After you create and test your templates, the next step is to deploy them so that all users have access to them. You have two decisions to make: *where* to deploy them, and *how* to deploy them.

Choosing Where to Install Custom Templates

You can deploy your custom templates *locally* or *centrally*. Locally, you can place a copy of each custom template on each workstation where Word, Excel, or PowerPoint is installed.

With this option, the templates are available even if the network is not. Updating the templates, however, can be challenging.

In small, informal organizations, copying templates to individual workstations is often sufficient. Given a choice, however, most Office administrators prefer to store custom templates centrally, on a network server, typically in a read-only folder that only the administrator has rights to change. When the time comes to update your templates—as it certainly will—you have to do it only once, on the server.

CAUTION

Whichever method you choose, be sure you keep a separate backup of your custom templates in case the server crashes or you encounter a macro virus infection.

Installing Custom Templates on Each Workstation   If you have to copy templates to individual workstations, it's helpful for you to understand the folder structure Office uses to display templates. In Windows 95 or 98, Office stores all local *custom* templates in the \Windows\Application Data\Microsoft\Templates folder, or in a subfolder within that folder. In Windows NT, the templates are typically stored in the \Winnt\Profiles*username*\Application Data\Microsoft\Templates folder, where *username* corresponds to the name you log in with.

N O T E   Built-in templates are stored elsewhere. In the United States and English-speaking Canada, they are stored in the \Program Files\Microsoft Office\Templates\1033 folder. In local versions of Office that use other languages, the 1033 folder is replaced by a four-digit code representing that language. For more information about how Office works in international environments, see Chapter 42, "Using Office in a Global Environment." ▪

Custom templates stored in the top-level Templates folder appear in the **General** tab of the New dialog box whenever a user chooses **File**, **New**. In addition, the New dialog box displays a separate tab for every folder within the Templates folder that contains at least one template or wizard available for use by the application you are working in. By default, the folders include the following:

- Databases (Access)
- Design Templates (PowerPoint)
- Legal Pleadings (Word)
- Letters & Faxes (Word)
- Memos (Word)
- Other Documents (Word)
- Presentations (PowerPoint)
- Publications (Word)
- Reports (Word)
- Spreadsheet Solutions (Excel)
- Web Pages (Word)

Part
III

Ch
12

N O T E The folders displayed in the New dialog box are nothing more than ordinary subfolders you can create in Windows Explorer. Therefore, you can easily create your own subfolders for specialized categories of documents, such as proposals, estimates, or reports. To do so, perform the following steps:

1. Choose **Start**, **Programs**, **Windows Explorer**.
2. Browse to and select the folder where your templates are stored.
3. Choose **File**, **New**, **Folder**. A new folder appears.
4. ype the name of the folder as you want it to appear on a tab in the New dialog box.
5. Press **Enter**.

The folders are not visible from within Office applications if they are empty. You must add one template to each folder in order for it to appear in the New dialog box. ▨

TIP All these folders are available when a user opens a new Office document from the Desktop by choosing **Start**, **New Office Document**.

Whenever you copy a template into any of these folders—via the Windows Explorer, from the command line, or via any other technique—the template appears the next time a user opens the New dialog box on that workstation.

Deploying Word 2000 Templates on Word 98 for the Macintosh If you create Word templates on a Word 2000 system and deploy them in a cross-platform environment, you need to perform a few extra steps to make your Windows-based templates work with Word 98 for the Macintosh.

N O T E The following procedure also applies to moving templates from Word 6 or Word 95 on a Windows platform to Word 6 on the Macintosh. ▨

1. Copy the file to the Macintosh, either across the network or by opening it from a DOS-formatted floppy disk. Most current Macintosh computers can read DOS-formatted floppy disks, but if you are using an older Macintosh, you might need to install Apple File Exchange or a third-party equivalent.
2. Optionally, rename the file, removing the .dot filename extension.
3. Open Word 98 for the Macintosh.
4. Choose **File**, **Open**.
5. In the Open dialog box, browse to wherever you copied the template, and then select it.
6. Click **Open**. The template opens.
7. Choose **File**, **Save**. Word saves the template with a Macintosh file Resource Fork, enabling the file to be recognized as a Word for the Macintosh template.
8. Close the template.

9. Quit Word.

10. Move your template into the Microsoft Office 98\Templates folder.

11. Run Word again. The template should now work properly.

NOTE Word 2000 templates that contain Web features (such as Web pages created in Word 2000 and then saved as templates in Word's .dot format) might not convert well to Word 98 for the Macintosh. One workaround is to save the file in Word 97-2000 & 6.0/95 - RTF format, open it as a document in Word 98, and then resave the document as a Word template.

For more information on conversion issues between Word 2000 and Word 98, see Chapter 26, "Managing Mixed Macintosh/Windows Office Environments." ■

Customizing the Office 2000 Template Folder Structure   You have nearly complete flexibility in how you customize the Office template folders and the template files they contain. For example, you might not want to give users access to *any* of Word's standard templates, especially if you've provided carefully customized alternatives. In that case, you can use Windows Explorer to delete these templates, as well as the folders they're stored in.

Deploying Custom Templates Along with Office

If you are deploying custom templates to individual workstations at the same time you are installing Office on those workstations, you can build the custom templates into the Office installation process. Office 98 for the Macintosh makes this quite easy. A detailed explanation appears in Chapter 4, "Managing Macintosh Office 98 Installations and Deployments," but the basic steps are quite simple, as outlined here:

1. Run a custom installation on a network drive, as discussed in Chapter 4.

2. Copy your custom templates to folders within the Microsoft Office 98\Templates folder.

3. Drag the entire Microsoft Office 98 folder to each workstation you want to install. The custom templates are installed along with the rest of Office.

With Office 2000 for Windows, including custom templates in the installation process is a bit more challenging. You'll need to customize your installation using the Microsoft Office Custom Installation Wizard and the Office Profile Wizard. This process is described in detail in Chapter 4.

Deploying Custom Templates After Office Is Installed

Even if you've had the time to create custom templates prior to rolling out Office, it's still likely you'll want to add more templates later. When the time comes, you can deploy templates to individual workstations in any of the following ways:

■ By copying the files to one workstation at a time through Windows Explorer. (Each connected PC is listed under the Network Neighborhood icon.)

■ Through a maintenance installation of Office that simply adds the templates to the individual workstation folders that already exist, as discussed in Chapter 2, "Automating and Customizing Office Installations Across the Network."

Part

III

Ch

12

■ By setting up a new job or "advertisement" in Microsoft Systems Management Server (as discussed in Chapter 3, "Using Systems Management Server 2.0 to Install Office 2000") or via another network software distribution program.

On large networks, however, there's a better alternative: distributing templates to a single location on a network server and then giving users access to them there. Then, when you make changes to a template, you need to copy it to only one location, and everyone is automatically updated.

Centralizing Templates on a Network Server

To centralize templates on a network server, begin by creating a folder and ensuring that users have full read rights to the folder but no rights to make changes. In Windows NT Server, you can do this by providing a network share. Follow these steps after you create the folder in Windows NT Explorer:

1. Right-click on the folder to display the shortcut menu.

2. Choose **Sharing**. The folder's Properties dialog box appears (see Figure 12.1).

FIGURE 12.1
Establishing a network share for a folder in Windows NT Server.

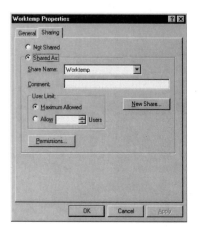

3. Click **Shared As**. The **Share Name** text box becomes active. You can edit it or leave the default name that Windows NT provides, which matches the name of the folder (or the last part of the folder name if it contains multiple words). Although share names can include blanks and be up to 12 characters, limiting them to eight characters with no blanks helps you avoid potential problems, especially if you're providing access to non-Windows systems.

4. Click the **Permissions** button. The Access Through Share Permissions dialog box appears (see Figure 12.2).

5. In the **Type of Access** drop-down list, choose **Read**.

6. Click **OK** twice.

FIGURE 12.2
Setting the shared
folder as read only.

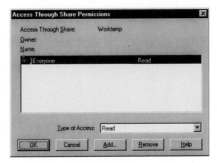

Sharing a folder as described here is the simplest method of providing access on a Windows NT Server network. If you have formatted your network drive to use the NTFS file system, however, you can get finer control by using NT folder and file permissions. These enable you to specify which users and groups of users can access a folder or even a specific file (in this case, a template).

Permissions are accessible through the **Security** tab of the Properties dialog box associated with each folder or file—but *only* if the drive is formatted with NTFS. You can use permissions in conjunction with folder sharing to "layer" on additional security where it's needed. For example, you can share the entire Templates folder (which automatically shares all subfolders within it). Then, you can restrict individual subfolders.

Suppose, for example, that only your Sales department should have access to proposal templates. First, you create a Proposals subfolder and store the templates there. Next, create a Sales group of users with the Windows NT Server User Manager for Domains utility, and then limit access to the Proposals subfolder to include only members of the Sales group. When the folder has been shared and you've restricted access as needed, you need to instruct your Office applications to look for templates there.

In the next section, you'll learn how to establish a location for Word workgroup templates from within Word. In the section after that, you'll learn how to specify a network location for all Office workgroup templates when you install Office.

You can also use System Policies to define a common Office-wide location for templates at any time. See Chapter 37, "Reducing Office 2000's Total Cost of Ownership," for an extensive discussion of how to establish Microsoft Office System Policies, which enable you to centrally define a path to shared templates for all the users on your Windows NT network every time they log on to the network.

Follow the detailed instructions in Chapter 37 for establishing a System Policy using the System Policy Editor. You will find the setting for Shared Templates in the System Policy Editor under the following heading: Default User\Microsoft Office 2000\Shared Paths\Shared Templates Path (see Figure 12.3).

Part
III

Ch

12

FIGURE 12.3
Setting a path for shared templates in the System Policy Editor.

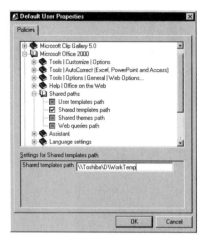

Establishing a Workgroup Template for Word from an Individual Workstation

In Word, a feature called *Workgroup Templates* enables you to establish a location for shared templates without using the System Policy Editor. You can set up Word to look in a networked Workgroup Template folder at the same time it looks in the local template folder on the user's workstation—in other words, whenever the user chooses **File**, **New**. Then, if it finds any templates in the workgroup folder, it displays them in the **General** tab of the New dialog box alongside templates stored locally.

To specify a Word Workgroup Template folder on a single workstation, do the following:

1. Choose **Tools**, **Options**.
2. Click the **File Locations** tab (see Figure 12.4).
3. In the **File types** scroll box, double-click on **Workgroup Templates**. The Modify Location dialog box opens (see Figure 12.5).
4. From the **Look in** drop-down list, choose **Network Neighborhood**.
5. Browse to the computer and folder you've set up for this purpose.
6. Click **OK** twice.

FIGURE 12.4
The File Locations tab tells you where your workgroup templates are (if they've been established).

FIGURE 12.5
In the Modify Location dialog box, you can browse to the shared folder you want to use for your workgroup templates.

If you prefer not to set Workgroup Templates or System Policies on each computer, you do have an alternative. You can store the template centrally, create a shortcut to it, and copy the shortcut into each user's Templates folder. When the user chooses the shortcut, Word finds the original template on your server (assuming the server is available). To use this method, follow these steps:

1. In Windows Explorer (or Windows NT Explorer), right-click on the file and choose **Create Shortcut** from the shortcut menu. A shortcut to the template appears.

2. Press **Ctrl+C** to copy the shortcut file.

3. Using Network Neighborhood, paste the shortcut into the Office 2000 Templates folder on each computer on which you want to use it. (Typically, this folder is C:\Program Files\Microsoft Office\Templates.)

Part
III

Ch
12

Discovering Additional Ways to Use Templates for Standardization

As you become increasingly familiar with the work your colleagues are doing, you might be able to identify additional opportunities for standardizing documents. Here are a few quick tips to make the job easier.

Using Templates to Standardize Intranet Pages   In Word 2000, you can save any HTML page as a document template. As you'll see, this feature has significant limitations. But it does give you a relatively easy way to let your people publish simple standardized pages on your corporate Intranet, such as the following:

■ Internal résumés for your company skills database

■ Project updates and information

■ Simple product sheets

To create a document template from a Word Web document, perform the following steps:

1. Create the Web page using Word's editing and formatting tools.
2. Choose **File**, **Save As**.
3. In the **Save As Type** drop-down list, choose **Document Template**.
4. If you want to store your Web page template with Word's other Web page templates, double-click on the **Web Pages** folder.
5. Click **Save**.

Word assumes that new documents created with a template are .doc files (not HTML files) unless you specifically save these new documents as Web pages. If you've created a template with the intention of creating new Web pages, you can solve this problem by adding a macro named AutoNew that runs whenever you create a new document from this template. The AutoNew macro performs one function: It displays the Save As dialog box with Web Page selected; the user only has to add the name of the file and click Save. The AutoNew macro is shown here:

```
Sub AutoNew()
' AutoNew Macro
    Application.Run MacroName:="FileSaveAsWebPage"
End Sub
```

Using Other Templates That Can Serve As the Foundation for Custom Documents   Many Office professionals are familiar with basic Word templates such as the Letter and Memo templates, but other templates and wizards also make excellent starting points for custom documents. In Office 97, these were installed only as part of the ValuPack. Now, however, they can be installed through the standard setup process.

Consider running the following wizards to create documents based on the settings your colleagues will use most. Then customize the styles and appearance of the resulting documents and resave each of them as a new template:

■ The Agenda Wizard

■ The Award Wizard

- The Brochure Wizard
- The Calendar Wizard
- The Weekly Time Sheet Template

Using Custom AutoCorrect Lists to Enforce Consistent Spelling

Are your users often called upon to accurately spell unusual names of people or products? Do they find it difficult to get the spellings correct? Then, it might be worth your time to modify Office so that it automatically fixes these spelling mistakes before you're embarrassed by them. To do so, you need to understand the AutoCorrect feature that's built into Office 2000.

When AutoCorrect's Replace Text As You Type setting is enabled, all the major Office programs except Outlook can automatically fix errors based on a database of mistakes and corrections that Office creates the first time you run any of these programs. This database of AutoCorrect revisions is stored in the following two locations:

- Formatted text and graphics are stored in each user's Normal.dot template (and are accessible to Microsoft Word only).
- Other text corrections are stored in an .acl file accessible to all major Office applications except Outlook. The .acl file is typically located in one of the following locations:

  For Windows 95 or 98:
  `c:\Windows\Application Data\Microsoft\Office`
  For Windows NT:
  `c:\Winnt\Profiles\username\Application Data\Microsoft\Office`

In Office 2000, there is a separate .acl file for each language you have enabled. The English Language file is named MSO1033.acl; others are named using the four-digit language code assigned by Windows.

To create a standardized .acl file, manually add all the custom entries you want by following this procedure:

1. In Word, Excel, PowerPoint, or Access, choose **Tools, AutoCorrect**. The AutoCorrect dialog box opens (see Figure 12.6).
2. Enter an incorrect usage in the **Replace** text box.
3. Enter a correct usage in the **With** text box.
4. Click **Add**.
5. Repeat the process until you're finished.

Part
III

Ch
12

FIGURE 12.6

You can create a standardized AutoCorrect file by adding entries in the AutoCorrect dialog box.

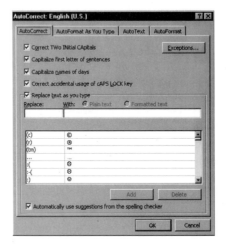

 TIP

You already learned that in Word, users can store not just corrections but also blocks of formatted text and graphics as AutoCorrect entries. This gives your sophisticated users a great way to quickly place repeated images (such as manual icons) and formatted text blocks into their documents.

To create a Word AutoCorrect entry that includes a graphic or formatted text, first select a block that includes the text and image. (You can't select an image by itself; you must include surrounding text or a table as well.) Then, select the block of text and graphics and choose **Tools, AutoCorrect**. Enter the text shortcut of your choice in the **Replace** box, and then click **Add**.

While you're editing your AutoCorrect file, you might also want to subtract a few AutoCorrect entries from your customized Office .acl file. In particular, if you often create documents with manual subheadings such as "(c)," you might want to remove the entry that automatically replaces "(c)" with the copyright symbol ©. Similarly, Word 2000 automatically replaces three dots (...) with an ellipsis (…), which is slightly more attractive but cannot be understood by many email programs and does not convert properly when transferred to non-Windows PCs. To remove an AutoCorrect entry, select it in the AutoCorrect window and click **Delete**.

When you have a standardized AutoCorrect file, copy it to the appropriate Windows folder on each computer where you want to use it. Rename the existing .acl file on each computer, and then rename the file you just copied there, giving it the name the original .acl file had.

CAUTION

AutoCorrect, AutoText, and most of Word's other automatic features (such as Check Spelling As You Type, Check Grammar As You Type, AutoFormat As You Type, and AutoComplete) might significantly reduce the performance of voice dictation systems such as Dragon's Naturally Speaking and IBM's ViaVoice families of software products.

AutoCorrect can also trigger unexpected events in Microsoft Access form controls (for more information, see Knowledge Base Q165480, available at **support.microsoft.com/support/kb/articles/ q165/4/80.asp**). You can either turn off AutoCorrect completely or set the individual form control's Allow AutoCorrect property to **No**.

Using Word Custom AutoText Entries to Provide Standard Copy Blocks

Word's AutoText feature is designed to help users manage and quickly insert boilerplate text. As an Office administrator, you can use it to build a boilerplate library and make it available to all the users on your network at once. These AutoText libraries can be very useful, so it's worth a little time to plan them carefully.

Planning Your AutoText Library

Start by giving some thought to how you'll name your AutoText entries. Be sure your entry names have an internal logic to them and will be easy for your colleagues to remember. Also try to keep them relatively short so they can be entered quickly.

Review a selection of representative documents your organization creates to look for language that might be reused. You might want to edit your existing language before storing it as an AutoText entry. In some cases, you might find entire documents that can be reused and saved as separate templates, as discussed earlier in this chapter.

In addition, look for other document elements that can be saved as AutoText entries: logos, signatures, formatted tables, and so on. And think about other AutoText entries that would be of value, such as proposal language that would assist the sales force; disclaimers and certifications; corporate capabilities language; the company history, experience, and mission statement; and so on.

Consider ways to make the AutoText entries more accessible to inexperienced users. For example, you might create a custom toolbar or menu that contains the AutoText entries your colleagues are likely to use most (refer to Chapter 6, "Customizing Word to Your Organization's Needs").

Give people hard copy listings of all the AutoText entries you're providing them. To print a list of AutoText entries, perform the following steps:

1. Create or open a new document based on the template containing the entries you want to print.
2. Choose **File**, **Print**.
3. In the **Print What** drop-down list, choose **AutoText Entries**.
4. Click **OK**.

Creating Your AutoText Library

After you decide which AutoText entries you want to create, you can begin the process of creating them. All AutoText entries are stored in templates, so create a new, empty template where you can store your entries, by performing the following steps:

1. Choose **File**, **New**.

2. Select **Blank Document** and click the **Template** option button in the Create New area.

3. Click **OK**. You now have a new template file.

4. Choose **File**, **Save As**.

5. Enter a name for your template in the **File Name** box.

6. Click **Save**. Word saves the template in your Templates folder.

Now, create a document based on that template by performing the following steps:

1. Choose **File**, **New**.

2. Select the template you just created.

3. Click **OK**.

Next, you have to tell Word to store the entries in the new template, not in Normal.dot (where it would normally store them). This is important: If you copy your Normal.dot template into other users' Templates folders, you'll overwrite all their custom settings. To tell Word to store AutoText settings in the template you just created instead of in Normal.dot, follow these steps:

1. Choose **Insert**, **AutoText**, **AutoText**. The AutoText tab of the AutoCorrect dialog box opens (see Figure 12.7).

2. From the **Look In** drop-down list, choose the name of the template you just created. (This option doesn't just tell Word where to look for AutoText entries, it also tells Word where to place new ones.)

3. Click **OK**.

FIGURE 12.7
Specifying the template your AutoText entries will go into.

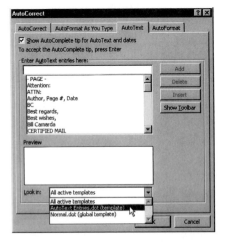

You're finally ready to start adding custom AutoText entries of your own. To add an AutoText entry, perform the following steps:

1. Type the text into your document (or if you prefer, copy it there from another document).

2. Select the text.

3. Choose **Insert**, **AutoText**, **New**. The Create AutoText dialog box opens (see Figure 12.8).

4. In the **Please name your AutoText entry** text box, type the abbreviation users will use to invoke the AutoText entry.

5. Click **OK**.

6. Repeat the process for each new entry.

FIGURE 12.8
Creating a new AutoText entry.

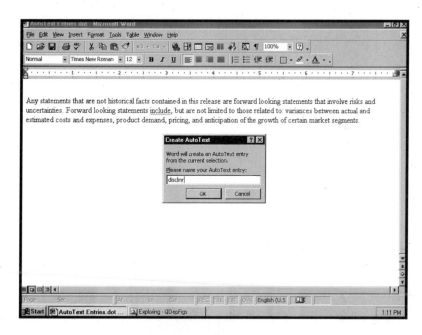

Now, all that's left is to make your AutoText-filled template available to all the users in your workgroup. There are several ways to do so. Here's one of the best.

1. Store the template on your server in a location that is accessible to all your users.

2. In Windows Explorer (or Windows NT Explorer), right-click on the file and choose **Create Shortcut** from the shortcut menu. A shortcut to the template appears.

3. Press **Ctrl+C** to copy the shortcut file.

4. Using Network Neighborhood, paste the shortcut into the Office 2000 Startup folder on every computer on which you want to use it. (Typically, this folder is C:\Program Files\Microsoft Office\Office\Startup. Don't confuse it with the Windows 95 or Windows NT Startup folder.)

After you do this, Word searches for the template and loads it at startup along with Normal.dot, making all your custom AutoText entries available to users. Because the template itself is still stored on your server, however, it's easy to update.

Part

III

Ch

12

Using Excel's Custom Chart Gallery Files to Standardize Charts

When it comes to creating charts, Microsoft Excel provides literally millions of combinations of chart type, colors, titles, axes, legend placement, data labels, gridlines, backgrounds, and so on. That's great. But all this flexibility can make it very challenging to standardize the look of all your charts so they look like they came from the same organization. You might not care much about variations in internal documents, as long as your users generate charts that are readable, accurate, and not misleading. Charts created for customers are another story, however. For those, it's important to be sure all your charts are consistent—and of consistently high quality.

Excel 2000 (and Excel 98 for the Macintosh) enables you to do this with a feature called User-Defined Charts. With this feature, you create one or more charts with the exact settings that you want to be reflected in all your users' charts. You might, for example, define "official" pie charts, bar charts, line charts, and area charts. After you've perfected your charts, you can store them as custom chart types and distribute them to all the users in your workgroup. Here's how it works.

First, create the chart by following these steps:

1. In an Excel worksheet, select sample data you want to build your chart with.

2. Choose **I**nsert, **Chart** to display the Chart Wizard (see Figure 12.9).

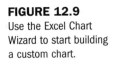

FIGURE 12.9
Use the Excel Chart Wizard to start building a custom chart.

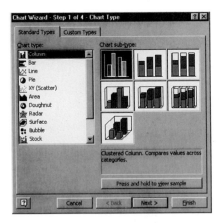

3. Select the chart type and subtype you want to create, and then click **Next**.

4. Walk through the remaining screens of the Chart Wizard, creating settings for data ranges, series, titles, axes, gridlines, legends, data labels, data tables, and other chart elements. (The elements will vary depending on the type of chart you're working with.)

5. Click **Finish**, and the chart appears.

6. Now, refine the chart to more precisely reflect the design you want to use. You can edit individual elements of your chart by right-clicking on them and choosing the **Fo**rmat

command from the top of the shortcut menu. For example, to change the way an individual data series is formatted, right-click on one data point and choose **Format Data Series**. You can then control a wide variety of settings associated with that data series, including color, patterns, and borders; whether each data point is labeled with a name or value; the order in which data series are presented; and much more.

7. When you finish, right-click on the edge of the chart to select the entire chart (not a specific chart element).

8. Choose **Chart Type** from the shortcut menu.

9. Click the **Custom Types** tab. An approximate sample of your chart appears in the Sample window (see Figure 12.10).

FIGURE 12.10

A rough preview of your custom chart. (Note that fonts might not be correct.)

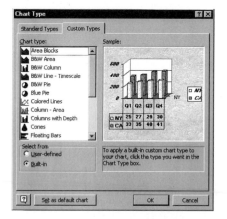

10. In the Select From area, click **User-defined**.

11. Click **Add**. The Add Custom Chart Type dialog box appears (see Figure 12.11).

FIGURE 12.11

Name and describe your custom chart in the Add Custom Chart Type dialog box.

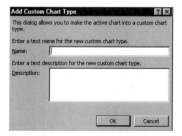

12. In the **Name** text box, enter a text name for your new custom chart type.

13. If you want, describe your custom chart in the **Description** text box.

14. Click **OK** twice. Your custom chart now appears as a user-defined chart type in the **Custom Types** tab of the Chart Types dialog box.

Part
III

Ch
12

Each custom chart type you create is stored in a separate Excel file that can be distributed or shared. In Excel 2000 for Windows, the file is called Xlusrgal.xls and is normally found in C:\Windows\Application Data\Microsoft\Excel. In Excel 98 for the Macintosh, the file is called Excel Chart User Gallery and is found in System Folder:Preferences. You have two options for distributing this file:

- You can copy it to the appropriate folder on each workstation.

- You can store the file on a network server and use the System Policy Editor to define where Excel should look for it. The System Policy Editor is discussed at length in Chapter 33, "Managing HTML/XML As Your Primary File Format." You will find the setting for User-Defined Chart Galleries under the following heading: Default User\Excel 2000\Miscellaneous\Chart Gallery.

N O T E   The custom chart types are available only from within Excel. However, you can create a chart within Excel using a custom chart type and then paste it (or link to it) in Word or PowerPoint. ■

CHAPTER 13

Using the Workgroup Revision Tools in Word and Excel

by Bill Camarda

Word and Excel have extensive features that make it easier for members of workgroups to share documents, review them, organize and resolve everyone's comments, gain approval, and take action. Very few users start working with these features on their own, however. Most need training, coordination, encouragement, and guidance. As your organization's Office administrator, you are tasked with providing this assistance—and if you do so, you can make your organization substantially more productive. That's what this chapter is about: helping you understand the most widely used workgroup features in Word and Excel so that you can help your colleagues make the most of them.

In addition to the workgroup features covered in this chapter, Office 2000 introduces new Web-collaboration features. Deploying and managing these features is covered in depth in Chapter 35, "Deploying and Using Office 2000's Web-Collaboration Components."

For more information about the Outlook workgroup features, see Chapter 15, "Workgroup Scheduling and Collaboration in Outlook 2000." To learn about the Access features for sharing databases, see Chapter 16, "Sharing Database Resources with Access 2000." For a discussion of the PowerPoint workgroup features, see Chapter 14, "Using PowerPoint in a Team Setting."

Using the Word 2000 Reviewing Toolbar

Word 2000 contains several powerful tools for managing the revisions process:

- The *Comments* feature (formerly called "Annotations") enables you and other reviewers to mark a document with comments that don't appear when the document is printed. Because it's easy to find and read comments, this feature makes it easy to respond to the comments of reviewers.

- The *Track Changes* feature (formerly called "Revisions") enables you to propose specific changes in a document's text (and in some cases, formatting), which can then be accepted or rejected. You can also use a closely related feature, Compare Documents, to check changes made between two versions of a document, so you can determine where a problem arose or whether a change requested by a team member was disregarded when a new draft was created.

- *Highlighting* is the electronic equivalent of that transparent yellow pen you might have used in high school. It provides a simple way to mark questionable text in color.

- *Versioning* enables you to save multiple documents in the same file. That means no more worrying about finding multiple files to compare—or about keeping track of changes that mysteriously disappear.

The following sections review these tools. Then, in the section titled "Establishing and Managing a Review Process for Complex Documents," you walk through using these tools as part of an end-to-end process for managing large-document development with multiple authors. The process defined there can be adapted for a wide variety of projects, including product manuals, sales and marketing guides, customer proposals, intranet/Web site development, and many others.

In Word 2000, Word's revision tools are kept together on a single Reviewing toolbar (see Figure 13.1). To display the Reviewing toolbar (or any other toolbar), choose **View**, **Toolbars** and select it from the list. Although there are other ways to access these tools, your colleagues will usually find it most convenient to work with them from the toolbar.

FIGURE 13.1
Word's revision tools are all accessible from the Reviewing toolbar.

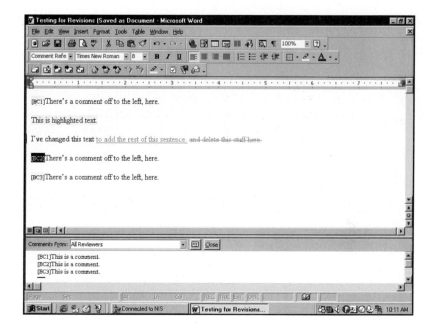

Using the Word Comments Tool

How can Word users make comments on one another's documents without adding text that might have to be deleted manually at some point? How do they make comments throughout an entire document in a way that makes those comments easy to manage and resolve? The solution is the Comments feature.

Inserting a comment places a comment mark in the document and opens a separate Comments pane where users can type comments and others can read them (see Figure 13.2).

To insert a comment, perform the following steps:

1. Place the insertion point where you want the comment to appear, or select the text you want to comment on.

2. Click the **Insert Comment** button on the Reviewing toolbar or choose **Insert**, **Comment**. Your initials and the comment number appear in the document as hidden text. At the same time, the Comments pane opens.

N O T E   Word uses the user's initials as stored in the Registry. These initials are typically set when Office is installed but can be changed in the **User Information** tab of the dialog box accessible with the **Tools**, **Options** command.

Part
III

Ch
13

FIGURE 13.2

The Comments pane, with comments displayed.

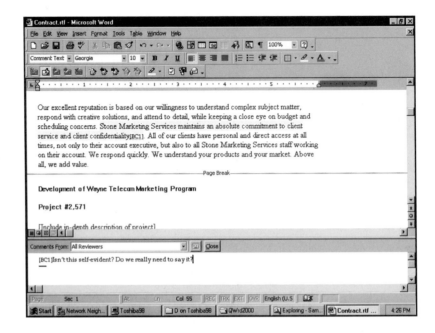

3. Type and format your comments in the Comments pane.

4. To close the Comments pane, click on **Close** or press **Alt+Shift+C**. To create another comment, click in the editing pane, place your insertion point where you want the next comment, and repeat steps 1 through 3.

Users can enter just about anything in a Comments pane, including graphics, sound annotations, and most fields (with a few exceptions, such as table of contents and index entries). They can also copy text or graphics from the editing window to the Comments pane, and vice versa.

The comment number that appears in the document reflects the sequence in which comments appear in the document. Word does not number each individual's comments separately. When comments are inserted, moved, copied, or deleted, all other comments are automatically renumbered accordingly.

Numbered comment marks are visible in the editing pane whenever the Show/Hide button (the ¶ symbol on the Standard toolbar) is toggled on.

Reviewing Comments Already Inserted in a Document

Word uses pale yellow highlighting to mark text in a document that has a comment associated with it. In Word 2000, you can view the contents of a comment instantly by positioning your mouse pointer above text that has been highlighted to indicate a comment. The comment appears as a ScreenTip.

To edit a comment or to review many comments at once, open the Comments pane by double-clicking on any comment in the document. The Comments pane shows all the comments in a document, and you can scroll through them. When you position your insertion point on a comment in the Comments pane, Word scrolls the document to the matching position.

The easiest way to move between comments is to click the **Next Comment** or **Previous Comment** button on the Reviewing toolbar.

If you want to review only the comments made by a specific reviewer, press **F5** to open the Go To dialog box. Then, select **Comment** from the **Go to What** box. You can then choose the name of the reviewer from the **Enter Reviewer's Name** drop-down list. To move to the next comment, click **Next**; to move to the previous comment, click **Previous**.

Deleting Comments from Your Document

After you respond to a comment in your document, you might want to delete it. To delete a comment, select the entire comment mark in your document (but don't include the highlighted text associated with it). Then, click the **Delete Comment** button on the Reviewing toolbar or delete the comment mark as you would any other text in your document.

Limiting Reviewers to Only Making Comments

The Comments feature gives reviewers a way to comment about a document without actually changing the text. That way, the author or editor maintains control over what actually makes it into the document. You can go one step further and prevent reviewers from making any changes to a document except for comments. Follow these steps to protect the document for comment:

1. Choose **Tools**, **Protect Document**. The Protect Document dialog box opens (see Figure 13.3).

FIGURE 13.3
In the Protect Document dialog box, you can prevent reviewers from making changes, except as comments.

2. Choose **Comments**.
3. Type a password in the **Password** text box, and then click **OK**.
4. When the Confirm Password dialog box opens, retype the password and click **OK**. (As always, remember to store your password in a secure location.)

Inserting Audio Comments

With audio and voice recognition becoming more widespread in business PCs, more of your users might be comfortable speaking to their PCs via microphone. If so, they might want to use Word's Comments feature to insert spoken comments. The following steps explain how to do so:

1. Click where you want to insert the spoken comment.

2. Click the **Insert Comment** button on the Reviewing toolbar (or choose **I**nsert, **Co**mment).

3. Click the **Insert Sound Object** icon at the top of the Comments pane (it looks like a cassette tape). A cassette tape icon appears next to the comment mark in the Comments pane.

4. The Windows Sound Recorder opens, as shown in Figure 13.4. Click the **Record** button and record your comment.

FIGURE 13.4

Recording a comment using the Windows Sound Recorder.

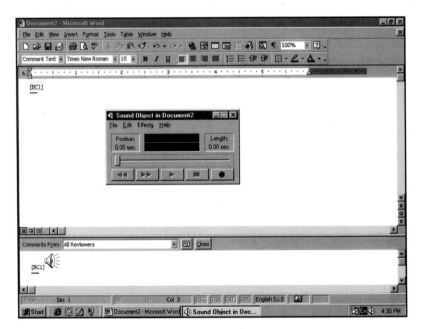

5. If you're asked to update the object, do so.

6. Close the Comments pane.

Because you're using the standard Windows Sound Recorder, you have access to all of its features. For example, you can choose **I**nsert File from the Sound Recorder's **E**dit menu and include a sound file you've already recorded or stored elsewhere. You might use this feature to provide access to a sound clip copied from your intranet or a recent speech by one of your company's executives.

You can listen to a comment that has been inserted in a document by following these steps:

1. Choose **V**iew, **C**omments to display the Comments pane.

2. Double-click on the microphone icon that appears next to the comment you want to hear.

3. Close the Comments pane when you finish.

N O T E Users cannot make voice comments if their computers are not equipped with a sound card and microphone; however, they can still attach .wav audio files that might have been created elsewhere. ■

> **CAUTION**
>
> Be aware that the routine use of voice comments can enlarge document files and increase the strain on your network. If hard drive space or network bandwidth are at a premium, you might want to discourage the use of voice comments.

Printing Comments

Often, you might find it convenient to print the comments in a document. There are two ways to do so. First, you can print the document with its comments. This method prints the comment marks in the text so you can see the locations that correspond to each comment. (Because comment marks are hidden text, this means other hidden text also appears.) The comments themselves appear on a separate page.

To print the document with comments, perform the following steps:

1. Choose **File**, **Print**.
2. Click **Options**.
3. Select the **Comments** check box. The **Hidden Text** check box is automatically selected as well.
4. Click **OK**.
5. In the Print dialog box, select any other print settings you want and click **OK**.

Alternatively, you can print only the comments by performing the following steps:

1. Choose **File**, **Print**.
2. Select **Comments** from the **Print What** drop-down list.
3. Click **OK**.

Working with the Word Track Changes Feature

Comments are well-suited for observations about a document, but they are less well-suited for specific corrections. For this, Word offers another feature: Track Changes.

With Track Changes, you can propose inserted text, which appears underlined, and all your proposed insertions appear in the same color. You can also propose deletions. The text that you delete does not disappear; it appears in color with strikethrough formatting. These underlined insertions and the deletions marked as strikethrough are collectively known as *revision marks*. If several users suggest revisions, each user's changes are automatically marked in a different color. After all changes have been proposed, the original author can decide whether to accept or reject the revisions either one at a time or all at once.

To turn on the Track Changes feature, double-click the **TRK** button in the status bar. The letters TRK become darkened, and all changes you make after that are marked as revisions. (You can also turn on Track Changes by clicking the **Track Changes** button on the Reviewing toolbar.) You can turn off Track Changes whenever you want either by double-clicking the **TRK** box in the status bar or by clicking the **Track Changes** button in the Reviewing toolbar again to toggle it off.

CAUTION

If you reorganize your document by cutting and pasting large blocks of text, these blocks will appear as large deletions and insertions. Within the blocks of pasted (inserted) text, you won't be able to tell whether additional copy edits were made.

N O T E With Track Changes turned on, you might occasionally be surprised to see change marks showing up where no new text has been entered. These change marks might be updated fields.

Here's a common example. If you enter a date in a document using **Insert**, **Date and Time** and leave the **Update Automatically** check box selected in the Date and Time dialog box, when you update the fields in your document, the new date is marked as a text change. This was a deliberate design decision (the alternative was to ignore that any change occurred), but many users find it disconcerting. ■

Viewing and Hiding Revisions Within a Document

Figure 13.5 shows a sample document with revisions marked. To the far left, vertical lines called *change lines* appear next to each line of text that contains a revision. This makes it easier to tell where revisions have been made.

FIGURE 13.5
A sample document, including revision marks.

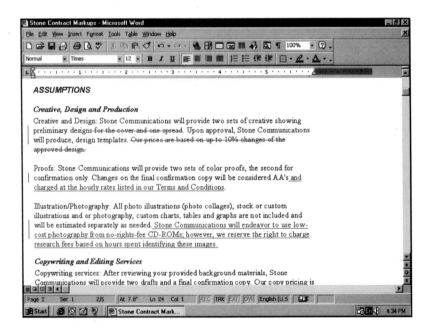

Many editors and writers find it distracting to watch all the colored text, underlines, and strikethroughs pile up as they revise a document. If that bothers you, you can have Word track revisions without showing them onscreen. By doing so, you can work with the document as if the Track Changes feature weren't turned on. However, because Word is still invisibly tracking your changes, you or your colleagues can accept or reject them later. To track changes without displaying them on the screen, perform the following steps:

1. Right-click on the **TRK** button in the status bar and choose **Highlight Changes** from the shortcut menu. (Or, if you prefer, choose **Tools**, **Track Changes**, **Highlight Changes**.) The Highlight Changes dialog box appears (see Figure 13.6).

FIGURE 13.6
The Highlight Changes dialog box controls whether tracked changes appear on the screen or in print.

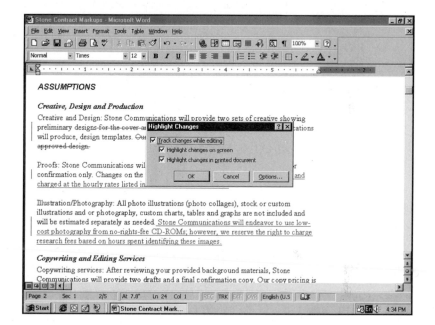

2. Clear the **Highlight changes on screen** check box.
3. Click **OK**.

Hiding Revision Marks When You Print

By default, the changes you enter in a document are shown in any printouts you make. If those changes are highlighted on the screen, change lines appear as well. You might not want that. For example, perhaps you're proposing revisions, but it hasn't been decided whether to accept them. If you want Word to print the original unrevised copy, do the following:

1. Right-click on the **TRK** button in the status bar and choose **Highlight Changes** from the shortcut menu (or, if you prefer, choose **Tools**, **Track Changes**, **Highlight Changes**).
2. Clear the **Highlight Changes in Printed Document** check box.
3. Click **OK**.

Part
III

Ch
13

Controlling How Track Changes Works

Word 2000 gives you nearly complete control over how Track Changes works. For example, as you've learned, text that you insert while Track Changes is turned on appears in your document with an underline; text that you delete appears with strikethrough.

As mentioned earlier, Word automatically assigns a color to each document reviewer. Word also marks lines that have been changed with vertical bars on the outside border of each page—in other words, in the left margin of even-numbered pages and the right margin of odd-numbered pages. You can change these behaviors and others as well. To do so, right-click on **TRK** in the status bar and choose **Options** from the shortcut menu. (You can reach the same dialog box by choosing **Tools, Options, Track Changes**.) The Track Changes tab of the Options dialog box appears, as shown in Figure 13.7.

FIGURE 13.7

The Track Changes tab of the Options dialog box controls how changes appear in your documents.

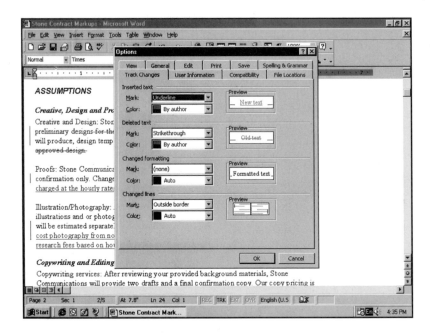

Controlling How Inserted and Deleted Text Is Displayed   To change the way inserted text is marked, choose **Underline**, **Bold**, **Italic**, **Double Underline**, or **(none)** in the **Mark** drop-down list, located in the Inserted text area. Whenever you make a change, its effects are displayed in the Preview box to the right of the drop-down box you've changed.

You can control the way deleted text appears in the same way. In the Deleted Text area of the dialog box, choose an option from the **Mark** drop-down box.

Controlling How Word Assigns Colors to Reviewers   In most organizations, it's common for several people to review one document. Whenever a reviewer turns on Track Changes, Word searches Tools, Options, and User Information Registry settings to identify the reviewer. If this reviewer hasn't worked on the document before, his or her revisions appear in a color that has not been used before.

Fifteen colors are available in Word's Color drop-down boxes, but it automatically assigns colors to only the first eight reviewers. If more than eight reviewers will work on a document, the revisions can still be tracked separately, but some reviewers have to share a color. If you prefer that all revisions appear in the same color, choose the color yourself in each **Color** drop-down box.

> **N O T E** Word provides less control over colors than you might want. For example, if you specify a color for inserted text or deleted text, every reviewer's changes will appear in that color. You *cannot*, for example, set aside a specific color for each individual or each job task (blue for copy editor, red for legal reviewer, and so on). ▪

TIP If you review a document twice, you might want to display each reviewing "pass" in a different color. To do so, before you review the document for the second time, change the name stored in the User Information tab of the Options dialog box (accessible through **Tools**, **Options**, **User Information**). If your name is John Doe, for example, you might change the name to "John Doe 2nd Review" or something equally descriptive.

> **CAUTION**
>
> Before users start working with Track Changes (or adding comments with the Comments feature), either you or they should be certain their correct name and initials appear in the User Information tab of the Options dialog box. If your company frequently reassigns PCs, this dialog box might contain the name of a previous user.

Controlling How Changed Lines Appear   As you've learned, Word flags changes in a document by displaying vertical lines along the outside border of the page on every line containing a change. In the Changed Lines area of the Track Changes dialog box, you can control where these lines appear and how they look.

In the **Mark** drop-down box, you can specify that they always print along the left border, the right border, or not at all. By default, the color of these lines is Auto, which is typically black; you can specify another color manually if you prefer.

> **N O T E** If you encounter anomalies in which changed lines appear in Word 2000, see Microsoft Knowledge Base article Q160113. ▪

Controlling How Formatting Changes Are Marked   In versions of Word through Word 95, there was no way to track formatting changes. If you changed formatting while Word was tracking revisions, the change would not be marked in any way.

Word 2000 does track formatting changes. By default, however, formatting changes are not marked in your document, even though vertical lines do appear in the margins next to them. This can be very confusing: When you review a document that includes tracked formatting changes, you'll see that changes have been made to the line, but you'll have no idea what those changes were.

The Track Changes dialog box enables you to specify a mark for changed formatting: Bold, Italic, Underline, or Double Underline. (You'll probably want to use a mark that isn't used for a different kind of tracked change. If you haven't customized your other settings, Double Underline might be your best bet.)

Limiting Reviewers to Making Only Tracked Changes

Earlier in this chapter, you learned how to protect a document to accept only comments, which prevents reviewers from making any permanent changes to the document. You can do the same thing with Tracked Changes. When the Protect Document for Tracked Changes option is turned on, no editing is allowed unless it is made with Track Changes turned on (unless the reviewer enters the correct password). To protect your document for Tracked Changes, perform the following steps:

1. Choose **Tools**, **Protect Document**. The Protect Document dialog box opens (refer to Figure 13.3).
2. Choose **Tracked Changes**.
3. Type a password in the **Password** text box and click **OK**.
4. When the Confirm Password dialog box opens, retype the password and click **OK**.

Marking Tracked Changes Automatically with Compare Documents

Many people don't know Word well, and even more people don't follow directions well. Suppose you've given a colleague a lengthy document for review, and he or she has neglected to use the Track Changes feature as you requested. The document comes back full of changes—but what has actually been changed? How can the changes be evaluated?

Or, perhaps you have two drafts of a document, and you need to know which specific changes were made between them, perhaps to help you determine which version is newer? (File date stamps aren't always conclusive in this respect.)

Using Word's Compare Documents feature, you can automatically compare the two files and use Tracked Changes to mark all the differences between two files. To do so, perform the following steps:

1. Open the document where you want the change marks to be placed—commonly, the most recent version.
2. Choose **Tools**, **Track Changes**, **Compare Documents**. The Select File to Compare with Current Document dialog box appears.
3. Browse to and select the file you want to compare with the file that's already open.
4. Click **Open**.

Word moves through the document, adding change marks wherever additions or deletions were made in the document. In a long document, this can take some time. In the status bar, Word tells you what percentage of the document has been compared. When Word finishes, you can work with these change marks the same way you would if you had created them using the Track Changes feature.

TIP In a long document with many changes, using Track Changes can slow down Word. Instead of using Track Changes, you might deliberately choose to use Compare Documents, which marks all your changes at once after you've edited the document.

Note that this shortcut can lead to a few minor discrepancies. For example, Compare Documents cannot mark some changed field results with change marks, if the field results are longer than 750 characters.

Merging Revisions from Multiple Reviewers

If you've been handed revisions from several reviewers, each of whom has saved his or her file separately, you can merge these separate files into a single document, where you can then decide how to resolve all their concerns at once. Follow these steps:

1. Open the file where you want all your colleagues' changes to be placed.
2. Choose **Tools**, **Merge Documents**.
3. The Select File to Merge into Current Document dialog box appears.
4. Browse to and select the file that you want to merge into your current file.
5. Click **OK**.

One by one, you can repeat this process with each set of revisions; all revisions then appear in the same document, with each reviewer's changes appearing in a different color.

Resolving Proposed Changes to a Document

Now that you (and your colleagues) have marked up a document with change marks, the next step is to resolve the changes.

To walk through a document containing Tracked Changes, first open the document, and then display the Reviewing toolbar. Click the **Next Change** button, and Word selects the first change in your document. To accept the change, click **Accept Change**. To reject it, click **Reject Change**; the change disappears from the document, and the original text is restored. (Of course, you always have the option of accepting or rejecting a change and then editing the text to reflect the reviewer's concerns in your own way.)

Sometimes, you might want to see who made a change: For example, you might have to pay more attention if the change came from the CEO than if it came from someone in the next cubicle. Place your mouse pointer over the change, and Word displays a ScreenTip showing who made the change, when the person made it, and what kind of a change he or she made.

It's not essential that you resolve all changes at the same time; you can simply leave the revision marks that you cannot yet resolve. When you have resolved all the changes in the document, clicking **Next Change** displays a dialog box saying that Word found no tracked changes.

Controlling How to View a Document You Are Reviewing

As you review changes, you might want to see what the document would look like if *all* changes were accepted, or what it looked like before *any* changes were made. If so, right-click

Part
III

Ch
13

on the **TRK** icon on the status bar and choose **Accept or Reject Changes** from the shortcut menu. The Accept or Reject Changes dialog box appears, as shown in Figure 13.8.

FIGURE 13.8
The Accept or Reject Changes dialog box.

To view changes with Word's underline, strikethrough, or other markings, select the **Changes with Highlighting** option button. To view the document as it would look if all changes had been accepted, select the **Changes Without Highlighting** option button. To view the document as it would look if all changes were rejected, select **Original**. If you want, you can keep working with this dialog box open, toggling back and forth to see how the document would look "before and after" potential changes were made.

Accepting or Rejecting All Changes at Once

Occasionally, you might want to accept or reject all of a reviewer's changes at the same time instead of reviewing them individually. To do so, perform the following steps:

1. Choose **Tools**, **Track Changes**, **Accept or Reject Changes**. The Accept or Reject Changes dialog box opens.

2. To accept all changes, click **Accept All**. (To reject all changes, click **Reject All**.)

3. In the confirmation dialog box that appears, click **OK**.

If you change your mind immediately, you can reverse your decision by clicking **Undo** within the Accept or Reject Changes dialog box or by using the **Undo** button on the Standard toolbar afterward. All the change marks reappear in your document, and you have the opportunity to review them one at a time.

Emphasizing Text with the Highlighter

A low-tech substitute for Track Changes and Comments is the Word or Excel Highlighter tool, which allows users to select text in yellow (or any of 15 other colors), just as they might have done in their high school textbooks.

To use the Highlighter in Word or Excel, just select a block of text and click the Highlight button in the Standard toolbar. The text then appears in color. In Word, you can also click the Highlight button and then drag across the text you want to highlight.

Because the Highlighter is extremely easy to use, many users use it in place of other revision tools. From a management standpoint, however, the Highlighter leaves much to be desired.

First of all, it's clumsy to move among highlights in a document (although this can be done from within the Find and Replace dialog box; users can search for the next highlight). In addition, because there's no easy way to add comments to highlighted text without adding it to the document, many users simply highlight text without explaining their concerns about that text. Finally, few users know a quick way to get rid of all the highlights in a document; as a result, stray highlights are often left in a document after they're no longer necessary.

TIP There is a shortcut for eliminating all highlighting, but you have to know where to look:

1. Press **Ctrl+A** to select the entire document.

2. Click the drop-down arrow next to the **Highlight** button on the Standard toolbar, and then choose **None**.

Using the Word Versioning Feature

In business environments, you're commonly faced with the challenge of locating an old version of a document, tracking the process by which a document was changed, or discovering who was responsible for a specific change. As the Office administrator, you might be called upon to come up with a solution that simplifies the process. Word 2000's Versioning feature might be what you need.

With Versioning, Word can store all versions of a document together, in the same file. Because Word stores only the changes among versions, the file sizes remain smaller than they would if you had saved separate files.

> **CAUTION**
>
> Versioning is one of the few Word 2000 features that cannot be used when creating Web pages. If you need to manage versions of Web pages, consider using the source control features built into Microsoft FrontPage 2000.

To use Versioning, click the **Save Version** button on the Reviewing toolbar. The Save Version dialog box opens, as shown in Figure 13.9. You're asked to make comments about the version you're saving; for example, why the draft was created or whose input it reflects. Word automatically records the date and time the draft was created and who created it.

Part

III

Ch

13

FIGURE 13.9
The Save Version
dialog box.

If you want more control, choose **File**, **Versions**. The Versions dialog box opens, as shown in Figure 13.10. You have several options here. You can choose **Save Now** to save a separate version immediately. If you do, the Save Versions dialog box opens, and you are invited to make a comment that will accompany the saved version.

FIGURE 13.10

The Versions dialog box.

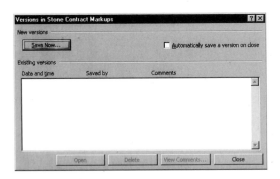

If you don't want to worry about saving versions manually, you can tell Word to save a new version whenever you save the file after making changes. In the Versions dialog box, select the **Automatically save a version on close** check box. Word inserts the comment *Automatic version* whenever you save a version using this automatic save feature.

N O T E If you choose to close a file and then ask Word to save the changes, these are likewise saved in a new version when the **Automatically save a version on close** check box is selected. This option does *not* automatically save a new version when you close a file if you did not make changes. (In other words, the feature is incorrectly named: It automatically saves *changes* in a new version, regardless of whether the file is closed.) ▪

Displaying an Older Version of a File

By default, Word assumes you want to work with the most recent version of your file, preventing you from inadvertently editing older versions. Sometimes, you'll want to view an older version, however, perhaps to retrieve some language that had been deleted but is now useful again. To view an older version of a file, follow these steps:

1. Choose **File**, **Versions**.

2. Choose the version from the Existing Versions window.

3. Click **Open**.

Word opens the second version in a separate window and tiles the two windows as shown in Figure 13.11. In the title bar of the window containing the older version of the file, Word displays the date and time that version was saved.

FIGURE 13.11
Displaying a current and older version of a file at the same time.

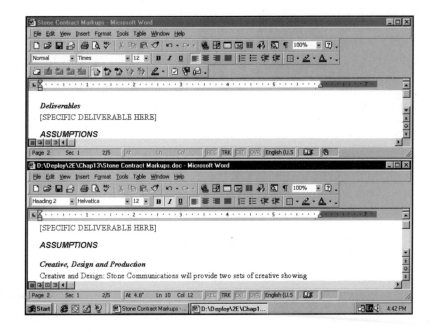

You can open additional versions only while you're working in the window containing your most current version. Word can open several versions at once, but it displays only two versions in the editing window. You can reorganize the screen so all versions are visible by choosing **Arrange All** from the **Window** menu.

Viewing Comments About a File Version

If you've stored comments about a version, the first few words of those comments are visible in the Versions dialog box. If you need to read a comment that's longer than the space available, however, click the **View Comments** button. The View Comments dialog box opens, as shown in Figure 13.12. Notice that comments on older drafts can only be read—not edited. This is a security precaution to help prevent your colleagues from "rewriting history." It's less than airtight, however; someone who is determined to do so could export each version to a separate Word file and create a new file containing all the versions, along with the comments of their choice.

Part III

Ch 13

FIGURE 13.12
The View Comments dialog box.

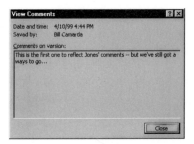

CAUTION

Be cautious about using Versioning in an environment in which multiple versions of Word are in use. Saving a Word 2000 file to Word 95, Word 6, or an earlier version eliminates all the versions except the current one.

Before you export a document for use in desktop publishing or other software, make a backup copy and eliminate the earlier versions from the file you export.

Using the Word Master Documents Feature

As the Office administrator, you might be asked to coordinate team efforts to build large documents with many chapters or other document elements. You can streamline the process with master documents.

A *master document* is a container that holds hyperlink pointers to individual documents. The individual documents referenced within a master document are called *subdocuments*. (A master document can also contain anything else a regular document can, including text, graphics, and formatting.)

Master documents closely resemble Word outlines, except that the material being organized and integrated can come from many different documents and locations. Master documents help you do the following:

- Quickly see where elements appear in a large document.
- Reorganize a large document, even though its components are in different files.
- Be sure that all parts of your document are formatted consistently, even if they're in different files.
- Create cross-references, tables of contents, and other tables that encompass multiple documents.
- Send one command that prints the entire document, even though the document is split into several files.
- Create pagination and headers and footers that work across subdocuments, making it easier to build consistent large documents.

Master documents also can speed up Word, because extremely large individual documents tend to be cumbersome to work with.

CAUTION

In versions of Word prior to Word 97, master documents were not consistently reliable enough for production use. But master document reliability is much improved in Word 2000, 98, and 97. Keep in mind the following constraints:

- The total size of a master document and its subdocuments together cannot exceed 32MB.
- On Word 98 for the Macintosh, the size of a master document and its subdocuments is limited by free memory available between the system memory and the applications (and can be reduced by misbehaving Macintosh applications that do not load where they're supposed to).

You can create a master document in two ways: by starting from the ground up or by merging existing documents into a master document, which transforms the existing documents into *subdocuments*. When edited within the context of a master document, subdocuments behave much like Word document sections. They can have their own headers, footers, margins, page size, page orientation, and page numbers. But you can also override differences in sectional formatting by editing and printing from the master document, where the formatting follows a single consistent template.

Creating a New Master Document

To create a new master document, choose **View**, **Outline**. Word displays the Outlining toolbar on the left and the Master Document toolbar on the right (see Figure 13.13). Table 13.1 describes the buttons in the Master Document toolbar.

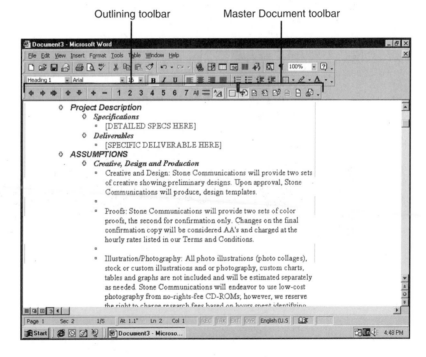

FIGURE 13.13
At left is the Outlining toolbar; at right is the Master Document toolbar.

Outlining toolbar   Master Document toolbar

Table 13.1   Word's Master Document Toolbar

Button	What It Does
Expand/Collapse Subdocuments	Toggles the display of subdocuments on and off
Create Subdocument	Turns selected outline items into individual subdocuments
Remove Subdocument	Removes a subdocument from a master document

continues

Table 13.1   Continued

Button	What It Does
Insert Subdocument	Opens a subdocument and inserts it into the current master document
Merge Subdocument	Combines two or more adjacent subdocuments into one subdocument
Split Subdocument	Splits one subdocument into two
Lock Document	Locks master document or subdocument so that it cannot be edited

Most experienced Word users prefer to begin creating master documents using Word's out-lining tools, finishing the outline for the entire large document—and getting it approved, if necessary—before breaking the outline into subdocuments. Whether or not you choose this route, it makes sense to use consistent heading styles (Heading 1, Heading 2, and so on) throughout your document before you break it into subdocuments.

Creating a Subdocument

After you outline (or otherwise organize your document), your next step is to specify which text should be placed in subdocuments.

To transform a portion of a large document into a subdocument, select it and click the **Create Subdocument** button. A small document icon appears in the upper-left corner of the selected area, and a light gray box appears around the text (see Figure 13.14).

FIGURE 13.14
Viewing a subdocu-ment within a master document.

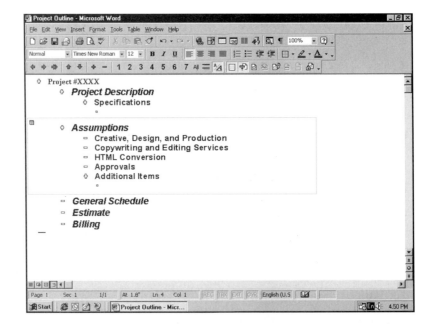

If you've used Word's heading styles (or, in Word 2000, the Outline Level feature), you can create many subdocuments at once by displaying the Word outline level where you want the headings to break. For example, if you have a large document, and you want to break it into subdocuments that begin at each second-level heading, follow these steps:

1. Click the **2** icon on the Outlining toolbar to display only first- and second-level headings.

2. Press **Ctrl+A** to select the entire document.

3. Click the **Create Subdocument** button.

Word creates a separate subdocument that starts at each second-level heading and contains all the text beneath that heading.

Transforming an Existing Document into a Master Document

If you already have a large document that you want to transform into a master document, it's easy to do so, as long as you've used Word's built-in heading styles (or in Word 2000, the Outline Levels available in the Paragraph dialog box). However, if you have not used those features, depending on how your document was formatted, it might be worth the time to add styles by using one or more of the following techniques:

■ Search for manual formatting that corresponds to document headings and replace that formatting with Word's built-in heading styles, such as Heading 1, Heading 2, and so on.

■ Carefully use the AutoFormat feature to make these style changes for you.

■ Use Word 2000's new Outline Levels feature to connect custom styles (which do not use the built-in heading style names) with outline levels, which Word can use as the top-level elements in subdocuments.

NOTE Regarding this last method, in previous versions of Word, the only way to assign outline levels for use in automatic numbering or in master documents was to use Word's heading styles (Heading 1, Heading 2, and so on). This is no longer the case. Now when you create a style, you can also specify an outline level from 1 to 9.

So, for example, you could create a style called *Main Heading* that included an outline level of 1. Then in outlines and master documents and when you use AutoFormatting, Word treats paragraphs formatted with this style exactly as it would treat paragraphs formatted with the built-in Heading 1 style.

Do the following to create custom styles for your headings that include outline levels:

1. Format a paragraph of text (typically, one of your headings) the way you want that heading level to appear.

2. Be sure the insertion point is in the paragraph, and choose **Format**, **Paragraph**. The Paragraph dialog box opens.

3. In the **Indents and Spacing** tab, choose an outline level from the **Outline Level** drop-down box.

4. Click **OK**.

Part

III

Ch

13

continues

continued

5. Click in the **Style** box on the Formatting toolbar.

6. Type the name of your new style and press **Enter**.

7. Repeat these steps to create styles for the remaining heading levels in your document, including the appropriate outline level in each style. ■

Saving a Master Document

When you save a master document, Word also saves all its individual subdocuments. If these subdocuments don't have names yet, Word assigns names to them based on the first letters contained in them and adds numbers if the filenames would otherwise be identical—for example, Chapter1.doc, Chapter2.doc, Chapter3.doc, and so on.

After you save a subdocument, its text is contained in that subdocument, not in the master document. This has two important implications. First, you can edit subdocuments individually as if they were regular documents. In fact, you can even use them in other master documents. Second, if you delete a subdocument or move it, its text disappears from the master document.

If you want to edit a subdocument in a way that affects the master document, open the subdocument from within the master document. To add elements that reference the contents of other subdocuments, such as fields, a table of contents, or an index, for example, edit your subdocument from within the master document. Unless the master document is open, the subdocument does not have access to the other files it needs, and error messages are likely to be displayed in place of the information you want.

You can rename or move a subdocument—even to another workstation or server—as long as you open it from within the master document by double-clicking on its subdocument icon, and as long as the master document is still open when you resave it with its new name or location.

Opening a Subdocument

You can edit subdocuments in three ways. First, you can edit them within the master document. Second, from within the master document, you can double-click on the subdocument icon to display a file that contains only the subdocument. Third—and usually least desirable—you can open the subdocument without opening the master document and edit it the same way you edit any other document.

Using Styles in Master Documents and Subdocuments

If you open a subdocument from within the master document, it uses the master document's styles. If you open the subdocument separately using Word's **File**, **Open** command, it uses any styles associated with the subdocument.

Some users are surprised at changes in a subdocument's formatting from one editing session to the next—this is usually the explanation. In general, it makes the most sense to work on your subdocuments from within the master document whenever that's practical, and consistent formatting and styles are all managed from the master document rather than individual documents.

Printing Master Documents and Subdocuments

To print all the contents of a master document, switch to Normal view and print from there. To print only selected contents or an outline at only specified levels, use Word's Outline view tools. You also can print individual subdocuments by double-clicking on them and then printing them as you would any other document.

N O T E If you print from Normal view, Word places a section break between subdocuments. By default, this is a next page section break, meaning that it functions as a section break and a page break combined.

If you want the next subdocument to start printing on the same page as the previous one, delete the next page section break, select **Insert**, **Break**, and use the Break dialog box to insert a continuous section break instead. ▪

Adding an Existing Document to a Master Document

Suppose you need to create a master document largely from scratch, but you have one existing document you would like to incorporate into it. Follow these steps to incorporate an existing document as a subdocument in a master document:

1. Open the master document. The Outlining and Master Document toolbars appear.
2. Place the insertion point where you want to insert the new document.
3. Click the **Insert Subdocument** button. The Insert Subdocument dialog box appears.
4. Find and select the document you want to insert and click **OK**. The document appears in a box in your master document.
5. To open the subdocument you've inserted, double-click on its subdocument icon.

When Word saves a file that has been turned into a subdocument, the file retains its original name. If you import a subdocument that uses a template other than the master document, the master document's template applies if you open or print the subdocument from within the master document. If you open your document without using the master document, the individual file's template takes effect.

Adding an Index, Table of Contents, or Other Table

Master documents make it possible to build indexes, tables of contents, figures, or authorities that encompass multiple documents. To do so, perform the following steps:

1. Open the master document. (Be sure that all subdocuments are present and accounted for.)
2. Switch to Normal view (choose **View**, **Normal**).
3. Place the insertion point where you want the index or table.
4. Choose **Index and Tables** from the **Insert** menu, and then follow the same steps you normally would to create indexes or tables of contents.

Working with Others on the Same Master Document

Because master documents are likely to be used by many people—each of whom is responsible for a component—Word makes special provisions for sharing the master document.

When you open a master document, you can edit any subdocument that you created in the first place. You can read all subdocuments that others created, but you can't edit them without unlocking them first.

To unlock a subdocument, place the insertion point inside it and click on the **Unlock Document** toolbar button. You cannot retrieve and edit a file that someone else is currently editing.

To determine who created a file, Word checks the **Author** text box in the **Summary** tab of the file's Properties dialog box (**File**, **Properties**). If you change the Author information, you can change the subdocument's read/write behavior.

Managing Read/Write Privileges

Normally, you can't write to a document if someone else is using it—even if he or she is viewing it as read-only. If you have to be able to edit a file at all times, you can reserve read-write privileges by setting a password. You can accomplish this by performing the following steps:

1. Open the master document or subdocument and choose **File**, **Save As**.
2. In the Save As dialog box, click **Tools** and choose **General Options** from the menu.
3. If you want to prevent others from writing changes to the file, type a password in the **Write Reservation Password** text box. Type the password again to confirm it. (And, as always, store the password in a secure place where you can gain access to it.)
4. Press **Enter**. Word asks you to confirm any passwords you've added.
5. Type the password again and click **OK**.

If you want to discourage, but not prevent, changes by others, you can check **Read-Only Recommended**. When the file is opened, Word encourages users to open the file as read-only, but it doesn't require them to do so.

Reorganizing Your Master Document

All Word's outlining tools work in master documents as well after you click the Expand Subdocuments toolbar button to see your detailed document outline. You can move body text or headings within a subdocument or between subdocuments. You can promote or demote headings. You can select and move large blocks of copy by displaying only high-level headings and cutting and pasting those.

You can also move all the contents of a subdocument. To do so, first click its subdocument icon to select it, and then drag it wherever you want.

Merging and Splitting Subdocuments

You can combine two subdocuments into one. Or, perhaps you would rather split one subdocument into two when it gets too big or when you want to delegate parts of it to another author. To combine two subdocuments, perform the following steps:

1. Move both subdocuments next to each other in the master document.
2. Select both subdocuments.
3. Click the **Merge Subdocument** button.
4. Save the master document. When Word saves the merged subdocument, it uses the name of the first subdocument contained in it.

NOTE You can also select several subdocuments that are not adjacent. Click the first subdocument icon, hold down the **Shift** key, and click the icons of each other subdocument that you want to select. ■

To split one subdocument into two, follow these steps:

1. Place the insertion point where you want the subdocument to split.
2. Click the **Split Subdocument** toolbar button.
3. Save the master document.

Removing a Subdocument

To remove a subdocument but retain its text in the master document, click the subdocument icon and click the **Remove Subdocument** toolbar button.

To remove the subdocument and also remove its text, click its subdocument icon and press **Delete**. The document file remains on the disk, but it is no longer attached in any way to the master document.

Troubleshooting Master Documents

Because master documents are typically used on large projects that involve quite a bit of effort, when they run into problems, there's a lot at stake.

If Word reports that a master document might be corrupt, select all the contents of your master document (including subdocument contents) and copy them to a new document. You might have to copy the contents of subdocuments individually, or you can create a new master document that incorporates the existing subdocuments, which are rarely if ever damaged.

If Word won't save a master document, it might be out of memory. If that happens, try this:

1. Cancel the save, close other programs and files, and try again.
2. If this fails, convert some subdocuments into text within the master document by selecting them and clicking the **Remove Subdocuments** toolbar button. Then try saving again.

TIP Also be sure that the version of Word 2000 you're using has been updated at least to SR-1, which contains some master document bug fixes.

If you're still having problems saving a large master document, consider the following alternatives:

- Use Word's **Insert**, **File** feature, which enables you to insert the entire contents of a file into your document. This is just like pasting the text into your document and creates no links with the source file.

- Use the {INCLUDETEXT} field, which incorporates an entire Word document or a bookmarked selection from a document. By default, {INCLUDETEXT} enables you to edit the text in your new document and save changes back to the source document by pressing **Ctrl+Shift+F7**.

- Use the Office 2000 Binder feature, which enables you to group many documents together for printing and distribution, but doesn't offer the editing or management capabilities of Word's master documents. Note that the Office 2000 Binder is not included in the default Office installation (in other words, it does not even install on first run). To use Binder, you must either add it to the original installation or run the Windows Installer later to add the feature.

Establishing and Managing a Review Process for Complex Documents

Word's revision tools can and should be used as part of an overall plan for managing document production effectively. In this section, you walk through using these features to coordinate a complex business writing project that includes multiple coauthors and reviewers.

You can use this "skeleton framework" to develop a wide variety of large projects, including product manuals, sales and marketing guides, customer proposals, intranet/Web development, and many others.

Plan the Review Process

Start by identifying your document's audience, goals, schedule, format, and other requirements. You can use the accompanying Document Planning Form (see Figure 13.15) as a starting point.

TIP You might want to adapt this paper form into an electronic form using Word's Forms feature (available through **View**, **Toolbars**, **Forms**). Then, you can save the electronic form as a template so it will be easy to create a new copy of the form every time you start planning a new document project.

FIGURE 13.15
A sample Document Planning Form you can use as a starting point.

Document Planning Form

Name of Document:	

Type of Document:	☐ Sales/Marketing Guide ☐ Documentation/Manual ☐ Sales Proposal/Presentation ☐ Business Plan/Business Case ☐ Mgmt. Proposal/Presentation ☐ Other: _____

Goals of Document:	

Audience(s) for Document:	☐ Customers ☐ Sales Force ☐ Internal Management ☐ Customer Service Representatives/Telemarketers ☐ Stockholders/Industry Analysts ☐ Other (provide details below)

Subject Matter Resources	Name	Title	Phone	Email
#1				
#2				
#3				
#4				

Schedule		
	Project Starts:	
	Research/Interviews:	
	First Draft Delivered:	
	Preliminary Review Complete:	
	Subject Matter Review Complete:	
	Second Draft Delivered:	
	All Content Review Complete:	
	Confirmation Draft Delivered:	
	Executive/Legal Review Complete:	
	Final Document Files Delivered:	
	Publication Date:	

Executive/Legal Reviewers	Name	Title	Phone	Email
#1				
#2				
#3				

Notes on Executive/Legal Reviewer Schedule/Availability:

Other Resources		
	Style guidelines:	
	Word design template to be used:	
	Previous document to use as a model:	

Special Issues/Concerns Affecting This Project:

N O T E Be sure you understand whether there will be additional uses for your document later. For example, knowing that a printed manual will be repurposed as online Help might lead you to create a document with more subheads, more "bite-sized" text blocks, and more cross-references in the form of hyperlinks. Knowing that a document will be translated for international markets might lead you to avoid informal usage that might not be reliably translated. ▣

Take into account all theconstituencies and subject matter experts you'll need to involve:

▪ Subject matter reviewers in each relevant area

▪ Marketing and/or sales executives with responsibility for the product or service

▪ Legal reviewers, if necessary

Consider building a flowchart of the review process using the Word drawing tools or the MS Organization Chart 2.0 applet that comes with Word 2000 (see Figure 13.16). Or, if the project is especially complex, consider using Microsoft Project's project management tools.

FIGURE 13.16
Building a review flow-chart with Word's drawing tools.

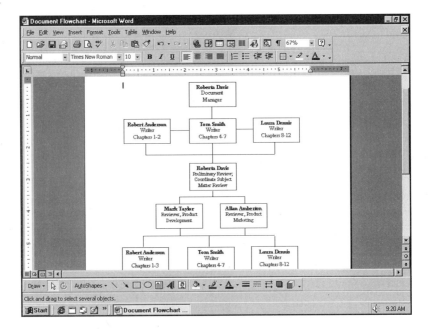

Choose the Most Appropriate Reviewing Tools for Your Process

Define which reviewing tools are used at each stage of the process, and then be sure your reviewers know how to use them. For instance, you might decide in advance to do the following:

- Use the Comments feature for comments that require high-level guidance.

- Make backup copies of all submitted first drafts, and turn on the Track Changes feature on the copy that is your working draft so that all changes, including comments, are marked with the name of the individual making them.

- Use Word's Protect Document feature to prevent reviewers from making changes without using either the Comments or Track Changes tool (see the following Note).

- Instruct all reviewers to avoid using the Highlighter tool.

N O T E Sometimes, you need to allow reviewers to make detailed text changes. For instance, a product manager is likely to understand the subtleties of her product much better than the author of a product marketing guide or manual does, and the manager might find it necessary to make text changes in virtually every sentence. In cases like these, use Word's Protect Document for Tracked Changes feature.

In other cases, you really don't want your reviewers to make detailed text changes; you do need to hear their comments, however. A good example is legal review. You almost certainly do *not* want your corporate attorney making line-by-line edits in your document, but you *do* need to be made well aware of her legal concerns so you can evaluate them in the context of the organization's overall goals and respond with the best possible solution. In these cases, use Protect Document for Comments, which limits reviewers to inserting comments in the Comments pane. ▪

Outline Your Document and Create Master Documents

First, create a rough high-level chapter outline and assign responsibilities for writing each chapter—as well as the responsibility of coordinating the entire manuscript. An example is shown in Figure 13.17.

FIGURE 13.17
A high-level chapter outline.

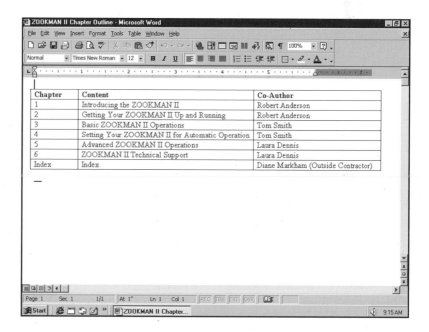

Next, create a more detailed outline and divide it into subdocuments using Word's master document toolbar. If you have a template that serves as the basis for this document, create your new document based on that template. Then, do one of the following:

- ▪ If you *haven't* used a template, create (or copy in via The Organizer) all the styles you want your users to work with. If you *have* used a template, add any new styles that aren't already part of the template. (See Chapters 6 and 7 for detailed explanations of styles and templates.)

- ▪ Insert a first-level heading for the title of each chapter. Format these first-level headings with styles that use Outline Level 1. The *Title* or *Heading 1* style is a good choice, or you can create your own. (See Chapter 15 for a detailed explanation of outline levels.)

Part

III

Ch

13

Name your first-level headings carefully because your names will be reflected in the filenames of the subdocuments. A good system is to start with phrases such as *Chapter 1, Chapter 2,* and so forth.

CAUTION

Only use first-level headings for document elements you want to appear at the beginning of new subdocuments, such as the names of chapters.

- Add any boilerplate text you want to use in every chapter.
- Add any instructions you want to give the writer.
- If you have a more detailed outline, switch to Outline view and insert the other outline elements between the first-level headings.
- Create headers and footers for the entire document, including chapter-and-page numbering if necessary.
- Save your document.

CAUTION

Give the master document a separate name; don't let Word simply borrow the name of the first chapter. If it does, all your chapter numbers might wind up misnumbered. (For instance, if you allow Word to name the master document Chapter 1, it will name the Chapter 1 subdocument "Chapter 2.doc," and so forth.)

Before you create subdocuments, make a backup copy of the master document.

Figure 13.18 shows how the document might look before being divided into subdocuments.

Next, copy or resave your document into the shared folder you want everyone to use.

Why copy the file *now* instead of waiting until after you've created your subdocuments? Because Word inserts each subdocument's full pathname into the hyperlink it inserts when you create your subdocument. That hyperlink includes drive and folder names that will no longer work if you move the master document later.

N O T E   Be sure the folder you use will be accessible to all the individuals who need to work on your master document or subdocuments. ▪

To transform each first-level heading into a separate subdocument, follow these steps:

1. If you aren't already in Outline view, switch to it to display the document as an outline. Your first-level headings should appear furthest to the left, with lower level headings and body text to the right. Make any necessary adjustments.
2. Press **Ctrl+A** to select the entire document.

FIGURE 13.18
The document before subdocuments are created, as shown in Outline view.

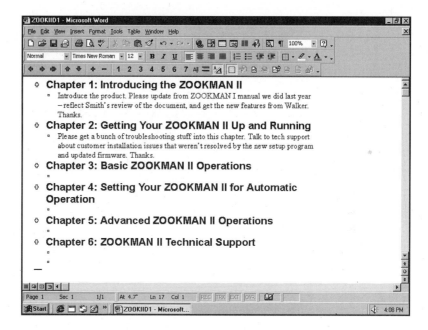

3. On the Master Document toolbar, click **Create Subdocument**. Word divides the document into multiple subdocuments, as shown in Figure 13.19.

4. Save the document. Word saves each subdocument as a separate file.

FIGURE 13.19
The document after subdocuments have been created, as shown in Outline view.

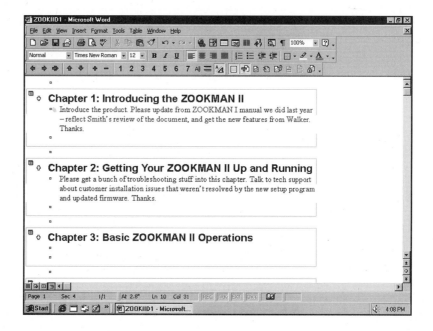

Part

III

Ch

13

After you've organized your subdocuments, give your colleagues instructions on which documents to use, where to find them, and when they are expected back. If you use Microsoft Outlook and Microsoft Exchange Server, you can delegate tasks to your colleagues with Outlook's Assign Task feature.

Distribute Subdocuments to Your Reviewers

First, assign an author to each subdocument. By doing so, you can give each subdocument's primary author priority in getting access to the file. Of course, this also means you might have to wait for the author to finish before you can gain access—so you might not think it's worth the trouble. If you choose to assign coauthors to each subdocument, do so by using the following steps:

1. Double-click on the subdocument icon next to the first chapter you want to assign. The subdocument opens in a separate editing window.

2. Choose **File**, **Properties** and display the **Summary** tab (see Figure 13.20).

3. In the **Author** box, type the author's name.

FIGURE 13.20
Changing a subdocument's author in the Summary tab of the Properties dialog box.

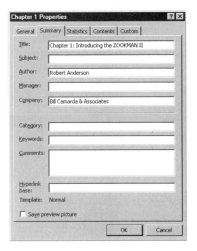

4. Choose **OK**.

5. Save and close the subdocument.

6. Repeat the process with each subdocument.

Next, give each coauthor specific instructions. This part of the process is critical! Figure 13.21 shows a covering memo (designed with Word's built-in Professional Memo template), which you can use as a starting point to help your coauthors understand what you expect of them. You can, of course, use email instead if you prefer.

FIGURE 13.21
Sample guidance you might provide to a document's coauthors.

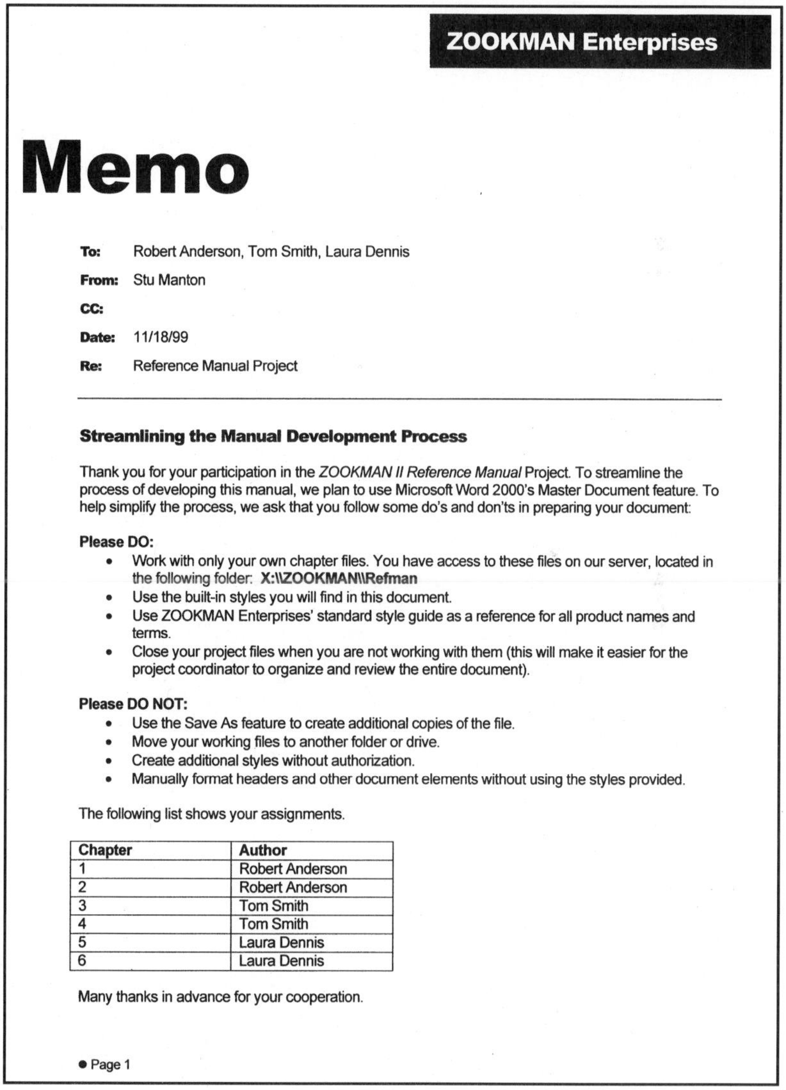

ZOOKMAN Enterprises

Memo

To: Robert Anderson, Tom Smith, Laura Dennis

From: Stu Manton

CC:

Date: 11/18/99

Re: Reference Manual Project

Streamlining the Manual Development Process

Thank you for your participation in the *ZOOKMAN II Reference Manual* Project. To streamline the process of developing this manual, we plan to use Microsoft Word 2000's Master Document feature. To help simplify the process, we ask that you follow some do's and don'ts in preparing your document:

Please DO:
- Work with only your own chapter files. You have access to these files on our server, located in the following folder: **X:\\ZOOKMAN\\Refman**
- Use the built-in styles you will find in this document.
- Use ZOOKMAN Enterprises' standard style guide as a reference for all product names and terms.
- Close your project files when you are not working with them (this will make it easier for the project coordinator to organize and review the entire document).

Please DO NOT:
- Use the Save As feature to create additional copies of the file.
- Move your working files to another folder or drive.
- Create additional styles without authorization.
- Manually format headers and other document elements without using the styles provided.

The following list shows your assignments.

Chapter	Author
1	Robert Anderson
2	Robert Anderson
3	Tom Smith
4	Tom Smith
5	Laura Dennis
6	Laura Dennis

Many thanks in advance for your cooperation.

● Page 1

After you distribute your files, review your coauthors' progress periodically. Occasionally, open the master document and see how far along your authors have come with their chapters. You'll be able to tell at a glance who hasn't started yet! Follow these steps to check progress:

1. Choose **File**, **Open**.

2. Browse to the master document and click **Open**.

3. Switch to Outline view if you aren't there already.

4. Click the **Expand Subdocuments** button on the Master Document toolbar to view the contents of all your subdocuments.

5. Use Word's navigation and outlining tools to move throughout each subdocument.

N O T E   You won't see the changes another user might be making while you have the master document open. To see the latest changes your colleague has saved to disk, close the master document and reopen it.

Review Your Coauthors' Submissions

You can review all coauthors' first submissions by displaying the entire document as a master document. At this stage, you might want to make edits for consistency and fix obvious problems that should not be seen by subject matter experts—such as errors in product names, incorrect formatting or styles, and so forth. If necessary, return the drafts to the individual writers, with revisions made using the Track Changes feature and comments inserted with the Comments feature.

Most revisions and comments of this nature should be resolved before the chapters are forwarded to subject matter experts for review, leaving only queries related to subject matter.

Make another set of backup files before redistributing the document for second review.

Be sure the document is set up for review. For example, if you want users to work with Track Changes, be sure the feature is already turned on. (TRK should appear in black in the status bar.) If you want to protect the document from users making changes in other ways, be sure Protect Document is turned on, along with the appropriate settings and passwords. (If the Protect Document command appears in the Tools menu, Protect Document is not yet turned on.)

Again, you might be able to simply specify a networked location where reviewers can find the file. If this is not possible, send the file as an attachment using **File**, **Send To**, **Mail Recipient as Attachment** (covered in Chapter 4). If the document must be reviewed by one individual before another can see it, use Word's routing feature (**File**, **Send To**, **Routing Recipient**).

Distribute a simple reviewer's instruction sheet or copy brief instructions into your cover email message—including when you expect the files back.

You might want your cover note to specify the precise scope of the review so that product development executives do not begin copy editing your document when you simply want them to ensure that their products have been described accurately.

Complete the Review Process

If each reviewer worked from the live subdocument in your master document folder, simply reopen the master document and start reviewing the changes and comments (or have the document's coauthors review them) using the Revisions toolbar.

If you sent files as attachments, *first* use **Tools**, **Track Changes**, **Compare Documents** to incorporate each reviewer's changes into the subdocument that is part of your master document. *Then* resolve the comments and changes one by one.

If the document needs to be reviewed again—either by the original subject matter experts or by company executives and lawyers—distribute it again as described earlier.

 TIP By this time, you should have a reasonable sense of whether you're still on schedule. If the schedule has slipped, notify the people who are to receive your final files; for instance, your printer, your graphic designers, or your Web/intranet content coordinator.

Create a Final Document

Here's a checklist of some things to consider before delivering finished text:

- Are all queries resolved, including Comments?

- Have all Comment marks and other internal notes been removed from the document?

- Have all last-minute changes been reflected? For example, if a product has been renamed, is the new name used throughout?

- Have the index and table of contents been created and updated?

- Have all other fields in the document been updated? If the document is being exported to another format, must fields be unlinked (replaced with text)? If so, be sure you store a copy of the entire document that still contains the fields.

- Are page numbering, headers, and footers correct, especially where document section breaks occur?

- Does the document contain a blank page that shouldn't be there? (This sometimes happens when copy is slightly longer than will fit on a page and when the last paragraph on a page consists of a blank paragraph mark.)

- Is all company-related "backmatter" in place? For example, is there an official document number that must be included?

- Are all graphics in place, accurate, and updated? Are captions accurate and numbered properly? Are references to figures in text accurate and numbered properly?

- Are copyrights and trademarks—yours and those of your competitors—recognized appropriately? In particular, are they marked with a ™ or ® in the document on first reference?

- Has the document been spell checked again and manually proofed for the types of errors the spelling checker misses?

- Finally, has the document been saved in the format its recipients need? For instance, if your graphic designers use desktop publishing software that does not have a reliable filter for importing Word 2000/Word 97 files, you might need to save the document in Word 6 format.

Part
III

Ch
13

Using the Excel Workgroup Tools

So far, you've learned about the Word 2000 features for organizing a document in a workgroup. But in many organizations, the key workgroup tool for organizing and planning is Excel. Excel 2000 and 98 also include the following powerful features for workgroups:

- **The Comments feature,** much like Word's, which enables one or more reviewers to comment on individual cells
- **The Share Workbook feature,** which enables more than one individual to work in an Excel workbook at the same time
- **The Merge Workbook feature,** which enables you to integrate and reconcile data from differing versions of the same workbook

Adding Comments in Excel

Often, you might want to make a comment on a value (or other element) in a cell in an Excel worksheet. To do so, select the cell you want to comment on and choose **Insert**, **Comment**. A yellow "sticky tag" appears, pointing to the cell. You can enter your comment beneath your name.

If you plan to make several comments at once, choose **View**, **Toolbars**, **Reviewing** to display Excel's Reviewing toolbar (see Figure 13.22). From there, you can click the **New Comment** button each time you want to make a comment.

FIGURE 13.22

Inserting comments with the Reviewing toolbar.

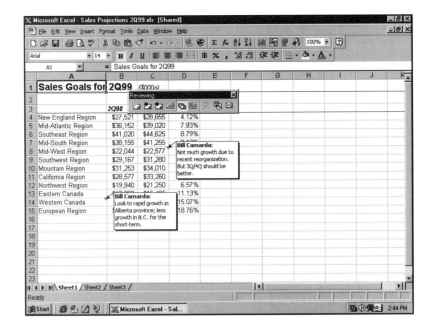

To systematically review comments in a workbook, display the Reviewing toolbar and click **Next Comment**. Read the comment, make any necessary changes to the workbook, and then (if you want) click **Delete Comment** to eliminate the comment.

Sharing a Workbook in Excel

Using shared workbooks, several members of a workgroup can edit the same Excel 2000 or 98 workbook at the same time. Excel tracks the changes each user makes and provides a mechanism for reconciling potential conflicts that might be introduced.

Shared workbooks have many applications. You can use them to provide information that many salespeople or telephone representatives need at the same time, while storing and updating it centrally. Or, you might allow individual managers to update worksheets in their areas of responsibility, while maintaining control over a summary worksheet that shows how the company as a whole is doing.

To set up a workbook for sharing, perform the following steps:

1. Choose **Tools**, **Share Workbook**. The Share Workbook dialog box opens, showing who currently has the workbook open (see Figure 13.23).

FIGURE 13.23
In the Share Workbook dialog box, you can set up a workbook to be shared throughout your workgroup.

2. Mark the **Allow changes by more than one user...** check box.
3. Click **OK**.

> **CAUTION**
>
> Sharing a workbook opens it to any user who can reach it—in other words, any user who has rights to access the file on the network. Use Excel's separate password features, covered in Chapter 35, "Deploying and Using Office 2000's Web-Collaboration Components," to determine who can open or modify your shared workbooks.

> **⸰ CAUTION**
>
> Excel 2000 might crash with an invalid page fault if you use shared workbooks containing more than 98 worksheets or slightly fewer than 98 worksheets if they contain an unusually large amount of data.

Updating Workbooks to Reflect Your Colleagues' Changes

Changes that others make to a workbook are not instantly reflected in the workbook. By default, you see them only when you save the workbook. If this is insufficient, you can force regular updates as outlined here:

1. Choose **Tools**, **Share Workbook**. The Share Workbook dialog box opens.

2. Be sure the workbook is already shared, and then click the **Advanced** tab (see Figure 13.24).

FIGURE 13.24

In the Advanced tab, you can control how Excel manages the shared workbook.

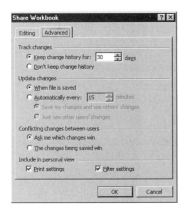

3. In the Update Changes area, mark the **Automatically Every** option button and use the scroll box to specify how frequently you want the changes updated. The default setting is 15 minutes. By default, Excel saves your file whenever it displays new changes; if you prefer not to save after each update, mark the **Just see other users' changes** option button.

4. Click **OK**.

When you save a shared workbook in which one of your colleagues has made a change, Excel notifies you that a change has been made and marks the cell. If you select the cell (or hover the mouse pointer over it), Excel displays a ScreenTip showing who made the change and which change he or she made (see Figure 13.25).

FIGURE 13.25
When you select a cell that a colleague has changed, Excel tells you the details of the change.

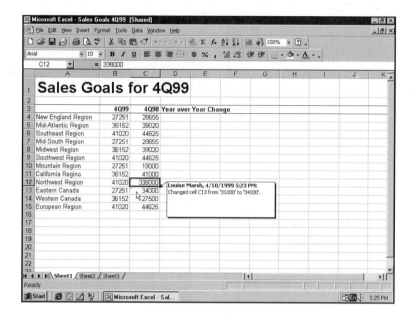

Resolving Conflicts Between Changes

What if you enter a value in a shared workbook, and a few minutes later, a colleague enters a conflicting value in the same cell? By default, Excel displays a dialog box showing the conflict, as shown in Figure 13.26. You can then choose which value to accept, yours or someone else's.

FIGURE 13.26
In the Resolve Conflicts dialog box, you can choose between your value and conflicting values set by one or more colleagues.

If you don't even want to review a colleague's conflicting changes, you can set Excel to disregard them by performing the following steps:

1. Choose **Tools, Share Workbook**. The Share Workbook dialog box opens.
2. Be sure the workbook is already shared, and then click the **Advanced** tab.
3. Select the **The changes being saved win** option button.
4. Click **OK**.

Now whenever you save, Excel saves your changes and discards anyone else's conflicting changes without ever displaying the Resolve Changes dialog box.

Part

III

Ch

13

N O T E As Office administrator, you might be called upon to ensure that only authorized individuals set Excel to disregard conflicting changes without even reviewing them. ■

Systematically Reviewing Changes

By default, you see your colleagues' changes marked in your workbook only until the next time you save them. However, you can view all the changes that have been made since the workbook was shared and then systematically review them, accepting or rejecting them one at a time. To change the way you view colleagues' revisions in a shared workbook, follow these steps:

1. Choose **Tools**, **Track Changes**, **Highlight Changes**. The Highlight Changes dialog box opens (see Figure 13.27).

FIGURE 13.27
In the Highlight
Changes dialog box,
you can control which
changes you want to
view.

2. In the **When** drop-down box, choose which changes you want to view: changes made since you last saved, changes you haven't reviewed, changes since a specific date, or all changes.

3. If you want to review changes made by a specific individual, select the **Who** check box and choose the individual whose changes you want to review. Another alternative, Everyone But Me, enables you to ignore the changes you made in the workbook and to focus on the changes made by your colleagues.

4. If you want to view changes to a specific range of cells, select the **Where** check box. Then, click in the worksheet and drag the mouse pointer to select a range of cells you want to review.

5. By default, Excel highlights all changes on the screen. You can also have the changes summarized on a separate new sheet in your workbook. If this sounds helpful, mark the **List changes on a new sheet** check box.

6. Click **OK**.

In addition to viewing changes, someone in your workgroup will be called upon to resolve them. Here's how that's done:

1. Choose **Tools**, **Track Changes**, **Accept or Reject Changes**. The Select Changes to Accept or Reject dialog box opens (see Figure 13.28).

FIGURE 13.28
Specifying which
tracked changes you
want to resolve.

2. Using the **When**, **Who**, and **Where** boxes, specify which changes you want to resolve, as described in the previous steps.

3. Click **OK**. Excel selects the first change in your workbook and offers you the chance to accept or reject it (see Figure 13.29). At that time, you can also choose **Accept All** or **Reject All** to accept or reject all the changes at once.

FIGURE 13.29
Excel tells you about
the tracked change
and gives you the
opportunity to accept
or reject it.

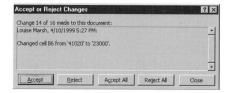

If you choose to accept or reject the changes one at a time, Excel continues through the workbook, flagging proposed changes one at a time. You can stop at any time by clicking **Close**.

Tracking the History of a Shared Workbook

By default, Excel tracks all the changes made to a shared workbook for 30 days. You can adjust this setting—or stop Excel from tracking changes—in the Advanced tab of the Share Workbook dialog box (refer to Figure 13.24). If you want to track *all* changes made to your workbook—even at the risk of slowing down Excel a bit—you can reset the value as high as 32,767 days (nearly 90 years).

> **CAUTION**
>
> As soon as you stop sharing a workbook, all shared workbook histories disappear. If you believe you might want to archive the decision-making process that went into a workbook, make a backup copy before you turn off workbook sharing.

Limitations of Shared Workbooks

Several of Excel's features are off-limits in a shared workbook. You cannot do the following:

- Assign, change, or remove passwords
- Delete worksheets
- Insert or delete blocks of cells (except that you can insert or delete rows and columns)

- Insert or revise charts, pictures, objects, hyperlinks, or drawings that use Excel's drawing tools
- Merge cells
- Create or apply conditional formats
- Set up or change data validation
- View, change, or save scenarios
- Group or outline data
- Insert automatic subtotals
- Create data tables
- Create PivotTables or change their layout
- Change dialog boxes or menus
- Create, edit, or assign macros within the shared workbook (although you can record a macro and save it to a workbook that isn't shared)

Limiting Excel Reviewers to Making Only Tracked Changes

Earlier in this chapter, you saw how to protect a Word document so that no edits could be made without Track Changes turned on. You can do the same thing in Excel with a shared workbook.

To protect a shared workbook so that all changes are tracked and nobody can turn off tracking without a password, follow these steps *before* you share the workbook:

1. Choose **Tools**, **Protection**, **Protect and Share Workbook**. The Protect Shared Workbook dialog box opens (see Figure 13.30).

FIGURE 13.30
The Protect Shared Workbook dialog box.

2. Select the **Sharing with track changes** check box.
3. Enter a password and click **OK**. The Confirm Password dialog box opens.
4. Enter the password again and click **OK**.

Merging Workbooks in Excel

In some cases, your team members might need to create separate copies of the same shared workbook as they work. For example, one of your team members might need to work on a notebook PC while traveling; she might use **File**, **Save As** to save a copy of the workbook you've been sharing. You can merge multiple copies of the same workbook, to create a workbook that looks the same as it would if all changes were made to the same shared workbook.

CAUTION

For the Merge Workbooks feature to work, you must do the following *before* you make copies of the workbook.

1. Share the workbook.

2. Be sure the **Track Changes (history)** feature is turned on.

You must also merge the workbooks within the time period you specified in Track Changes.

To merge multiple copies of a workbook, perform the following steps:

1. Open the shared workbook into which you want to import changes.

2. Choose **Tools**, **Merge Workbooks**. (This menu item is available only if you have a shared workbook open.) The Select Files to Merge into Current Workbook dialog box appears.

3. Browse to and select the workbook (or workbooks) you want to incorporate. (You can merge several workbooks at the same time by using **Shift+click** if each of those files began life together as the same shared workbook.)

4. Click **OK**.

CHAPTER 14

Using PowerPoint in a Team Setting

by Bo Williams

You can streamline your office's use of PowerPoint by developing and implementing presentation standards—a standard template, approved graphics, and animation files—that can create a common look for all your company's presentations. The PowerPoint design templates make it easy to create consistency without limiting creativity; you can build your own templates and control user access to them. Also, you can make presentation development a team effort with PowerPoint tools, such as Online Collaboration, Meeting Minder and presentation conferencing, and the Office NetMeeting feature.

Establishing Presentation Standards for Your Workgroup

PowerPoint offers more than 40 Design Templates to help you create presentations, signs, and flyers, alone or with others on the Web, that best meet your needs, as shown in Figure 14.1. Within any company, department, or workgroup, it is often desirable for presentations to have a standard appearance.

FIGURE 14.1
The Design Templates tab in PowerPoint 2000 includes more than 40 templates, plus any new templates that users have created and saved in a template format.

Although too much standardization can stifle creativity, setting some basics—background colors, text formats, and so on—often enhances productivity, and might even free your designers to be more creative. They can then turn their attention to more powerful features, such as graphics, photographs, video, sound, and animation effects.

Establishing Levels of Standardization

When standardizing a presentation format, it's best to decide the level of standardization you want to impose, such as the following:

- **Complete control.** Standardize the template, fonts, number of bullets per slide, colors for charts, acceptable clip art images, and the level of multimedia to be used, if appropriate for your output methods.
- **General control.** Choose a template, select font styles and colors, but otherwise let users add presentation content and extra elements as they see fit.
- **Bare minimum.** Choose a template, but beyond that take a hands-off approach to presentation content.

The more control you impose, the more consistent your presentations will be. However, too much consistency can be boring. At a long meeting with many presentations, the audience is likely to lose interest if all the presentations look exactly alike.

A hands-off approach encourages creativity. Presentations from different departments and divisions can have a lot more variety—in the choices of fonts, colors, and the use of animation and sound. However, too much variation might prove distracting. This strategy might accentuate the varying skill levels in different departments—one department might give a sharp, high-tech presentation, whereas another gives a more simplistic show because they're less familiar with the common PowerPoint features.

Implementing Your Standardization Level

Regardless of the level of control you seek, imposing that control is the next step, as in the following:

- To control the entire look of a presentation, you must fine-tune your design template and save it to the Presentation Designs folder with all fonts, colors, layouts, and master elements, such as title placeholders and graphics.

- If you want to standardize only a few features, be sure these attributes are set and saved as part of the design template file. Although the presentation contains default fonts and colors, your developers have the freedom to change them.

To ensure that your staff uses these approved design templates, you can take one of the following actions:

- Create a macro that users are instructed to invoke as soon as they open a new presentation. The macro can close the existing presentation and open a new one, using the standardized template. Another macro approach might be to record the process of applying the standardized design template to the open presentation, thus overriding the open presentation's formats. This latter approach does not control anything more than the content of a template—colors, fonts, and any graphics inserted on the master.

- For ultimate control, remove all the other design templates from the Presentation Designs folder, moving them to a folder not within the Templates folder. Although they are still on the system if anyone wants to use them, they're not in plain sight to tempt anyone. Your users have no choice but to use either the blank presentation or the standardized design template.

Customizing Your Office Presentations

When creating your standardized template, remember the following PowerPoint features that are at your disposal for customizing a presentation:

- You can place items on the slide master so that they appear on every slide in the presentation. Any formatting applied to the master is applied to all slides that are based on that master. You might do this with your company logo or an approved graphic.

  You open the master by choosing b, b, and **Slide Master** (or **Title Master**). Figure 14.2 shows the slide master for the Dad's Tie.pot template. If the presentation is saved as a template (.pot extension), the master content applies to all presentations created using the template.

Part
III

Ch
14

FIGURE 14.2

Format text and insert graphics on the master to control the content of all the slides in the presentation.

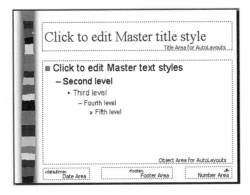

- You can create your own presentation design templates for use as the basic structure for new presentations. To create an entire presentation—titles and most text included—choose **File**, **Save As**, and use the **Save as type** option to create a design template (.pot). Figure 14.3 shows the Save As dialog box with the Design Template format selected.

FIGURE 14.3

To create a custom template, choose the Design Template format and save the file to the Presentation Designs folder.

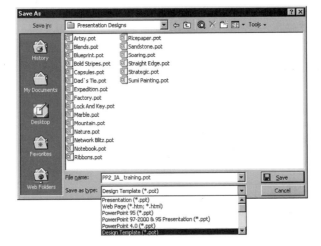

- You can choose **Tools**, and then **Options** to work with the PowerPoint defaults that control the way the software works. Figure 14.4 shows the Options dialog box with the Save tab on top.

▶ For more information on standardizing the user interface, including Options dialog box settings, **see** Chapter 8, "Customizing PowerPoint to Your Organization's Needs," on **p. 203**.

FIGURE 14.4
Choose a default file location for all saved presentations in the Options dialog box.

Collaborating Online with Your Workgroup

PowerPoint takes advantage of Office features that make presentation building a true team effort. These tools enable two or more users to watch, work on, and comment on a presentation in progress. This process is completely interactive—all members of the group can see the other members' comments and view the show simultaneously. You can also use Meeting Minder to designate action items during a conference.

Using the Online Collaboration Tool

Online Collaboration is a tool that enables two or more users on a network to watch a presentation simultaneously. One member of the workgroup must act as host and control the progress of the show. The other members watch the show and make their own comments on a given slide for the whole group to see. As the show progresses, the host can tweak the show, such as adjusting the timing per slide and adding other comments to the slide for improvements. The host can also give another user control of the presentation at any time.

Before you begin collaborating online, it's a good idea to make some decisions, such as

- Who will be the host? The host should be someone who everyone trusts to take notes, be objective, and pay attention as the team works together, watching and making suggestions for improving the presentation.
- What will be your connection method? If you're on a network in your office, write a list of each team member's computer name/number as they're seen on the network. If you'll be connecting over the Internet, get a list of their Internet addresses.
- Which slides are you going to see? Will you see the whole slideshow or just a section of it? Set this up by choosing **Set Up Show** from the **Slide Show** menu. Enter the **From and To** slide numbers, and click **OK**.

Part

III

Ch

14

To set up and run an Online Collaboration, choose **Online Collaboration**, and then **Schedule Meeting** from the **Tools** menu. A dialog box opens that shows the configuration involved in setting up the meeting (see Figure 14.5).

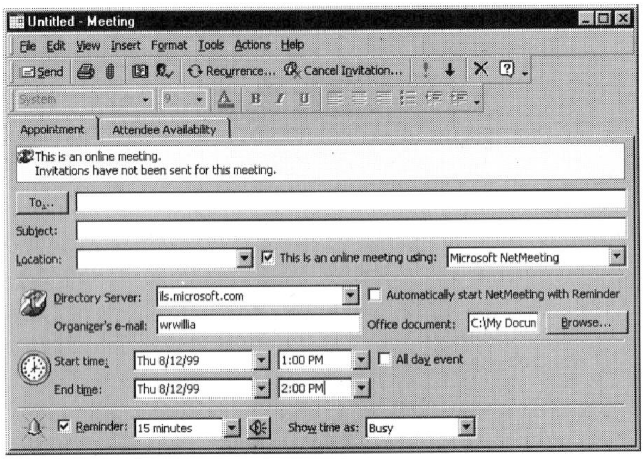

FIGURE 14.5
The dialog box shows the general meeting configuration involved.

After the meeting begins, the team members watch the show as the host controls it. Any team member can place comments on slides that appear onscreen merely by clicking on them. The mouse pointer turns into a pen, and that team member can write on the slide. The rest of the team can see the comments and then respond with their own, as needed.

The host controls the show. He or she adds comments by right-clicking the screen and choosing **Speaker's Notes** from the shortcut menu. The host also reviews the timing of the slides and the ongoing comments of the audience. If an idea or problem arises that requires action, the host can invoke the Meeting Minder by right-clicking the screen and choosing **Meeting Minder** from the shortcut menu.

N O T E   If you and a co-worker want to review a presentation simultaneously, connect your two computers with a null modem cable (available at most computer stores or office supply superstores). Choose **View on Two Screens** from the **Slide Show** menu. Your screen and that of the connected computer show the presentation simultaneously. ▪

Using the Meeting Minder

The Meeting Minder is a meeting management tool that you can use to record meeting minutes in an online meeting and assign action items to any of the participants. You can use Meeting Minder in conjunction with the Online Collaboration tool or on its own during a discussion or formal meeting. To use the Meeting Minder to assign tasks to the team members, invoke the Meeting Minder by right-clicking the active slide and choosing **Meeting Minder** from the shortcut menu. To invoke it on its own (not during a meeting), choose **Meeting Minder** from the **Tools** menu. A two-tabbed dialog box appears (see Figure 14.6).

FIGURE 14.6
The Meeting Minder enables you to take meeting notes and/or set up action items and assign them to members of your presentation team.

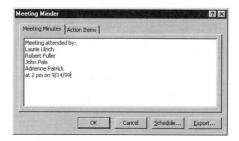

- **Meeting Minutes.** Simply type your comments into this box during the meeting. The box holds more than 50 lines of text, and word wrap is in effect. If you want to use your comments in a printable (and more editable) Word document, click **Export**. Click **Schedule** to open Outlook and enter an appointment or task related to the meeting minutes.

- **Action Items.** As presenter in a meeting, or in a managerial role in a meeting, you can assign tasks to different members of the team. Click this tab to enter a task description, assign the task to someone, and enter a completion date. Click **Add** to add it to the list of tasks (see Figure 14.7). Click **Export** to send the task list to Word for printing or editing, or to Outlook for scheduling.

FIGURE 14.7
Set up action items and assign them to a team member. Click **Add** to build the list of tasks.

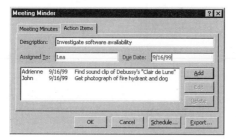

Make your entries into one or both of the tabs, and click **OK**. This saves your entries and closes the dialog box.

Your Meeting Minder notes and tasks accrue for this presentation. When you choose Meeting Minder again (during a subsequent online meeting or in another meeting) with this particular presentation open, the previous meetings' notes and tasks appear, and you can add to them. To save separate meeting notes and/or tasks, click the **Export** button (in either tab) to send the content to Word and save them as a document. You can do this for each meeting, generating a separate Word document in each case. It's a good idea to save these files with a name that reflects the meeting date—this makes specific documents easier to track down later. ●

Part

III

Ch

14

CHAPTER 15

Workgroup Scheduling and Collaboration in Outlook 2000

by Gordon Padwick

In this chapter, you learn about the Outlook collaboration features for planning and scheduling meetings, which include the ability to check for available time on other people's calendars. Also, you find out how people who use Outlook as a client for Exchange Server can create and use public folders to share information. Finally, you learn to customize Outlook forms, changing how Outlook looks and acts while you work with Outlook items.

One of Outlook's most useful collaboration features is the capability to automate, at least to some extent, the process of scheduling meetings. Although this takes a little getting used to, it's certainly worth the effort.

Suppose you need to schedule a meeting with several members of your organization. Traditionally, you might call each person to inquire about availability or even send each person an email message. Comparing everyone's obligations and free time to find the best opportunity for a meeting is quite a chore.

Outlook makes the scheduling process faster and more reliable, taking advantage of the Outlook Calendar and email. As long as everyone in your organization is diligent in keeping an up-to-date calendar, you can find out quickly when people are available and then send them invitations to your meeting.

Later in this chapter, you learn how to check for available times on other people's schedules before you send them a meeting request. If you can't rely on the accuracy of other people's calendars, you might prefer to just send the meeting request and wait for their responses.

Scheduling Meetings with Other People

Outlook uses your organization's email system with Outlook's Calendar and Contact features so that you can schedule meetings and manage contacts within your organization. In this section, you go beyond tracking your own calendar and learn how to share this information with members of your workgroup.

Sending a Meeting Request

To send a meeting request to someone, follow these steps:

1. Open your calendar in any view.

2. Choose **Actions**, **New Meeting Request** to display the Meeting form (shown in Figure 15.1).

FIGURE 15.1
Use the Meeting form to schedule a meeting with your colleagues.

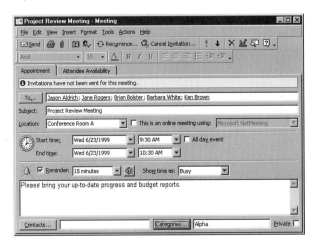

TIP   Outlook uses the term *form* to refer to the window (such as the one shown in Figure 15.1) that you use to work with items in an Outlook folder. For more information, **see** "Customizing Forms in Outlook," on **p. 401**, later in this chapter.

---

3. Click the **To** button to display the Select Attendees and Resources dialog box (shown in Figure 15.2). If you have more than one address book, select the address book you want to use from the **Show Names from The** drop-down list.

4. From the list at the left, select the names of the people you want to invite to the meeting and the resources you need at the meeting. Click **Required** or **Optional** to invite a person. Click **OK** when you have made all your selections.

5. Fill the remaining fields in the Meeting form, including the date and time of the meeting and any comments you want to send in the message.

6. Click **Send** to send the meeting request to each person or resource via email.

Outlook marks the meeting on your calendar and sends the meeting request to each person or resource you selected. You can double-click on the meeting item in your calendar to check the responses from the people you have invited.

FIGURE 15.2
Select the people you want to invite to the meeting.

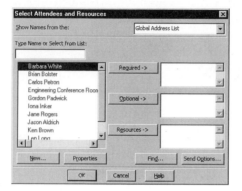

Receiving a Meeting Request

If you've been invited to a meeting, a message header like the one shown in Figure 15.3 appears in your Inbox. If you have the Preview pane enabled, you can select the message header to display the details of the message. Double-click the message header to open it in a form, as shown in Figure 15.4.

FIGURE 15.3
A new meeting request in your Inbox.

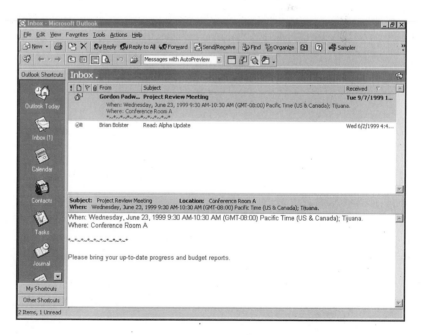

FIGURE 15.4
The Meeting form
shows the details of
the proposed meeting.

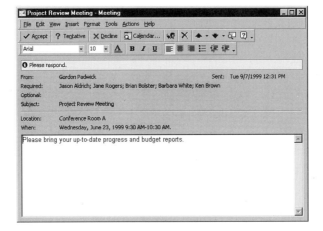

Notice that the Meeting form shows you who else has been invited to the meeting and asks
you to respond. The form also shows whether the meeting request conflicts with, or is adjacent to, something that's already on your calendar. If other people invited to the meeting have
already responded, the form tells you whether they have accepted or rejected the invitation.

You can respond to the meeting request by clicking **Accept**, **Tentative**, or **Decline** at the left
end of the form's toolbar. After you click one of the buttons, Outlook presents the following
response options, shown in Figure 15.5:

- If you select **Edit the response before sending**, Outlook displays a message form in
  which you can enter comments to go with your response.

- If you select **Send the response now**, Outlook immediately sends a message to the
  person who invited you to the meeting, indicating your response.

- If you select **Don't send a response**, Outlook doesn't send a message in response to
  the request.

FIGURE 15.5
Use this dialog box to
specify how you want
to respond to the
meeting request.

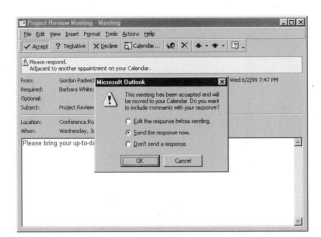

If you respond to the request by choosing **Accept** or **Tentative**, Outlook automatically adds the meeting to your calendar, marking the time as "Busy" if you accepted or "Tentative" if you tentatively accepted. Outlook doesn't add the meeting to your calendar if you decline the request.

Receiving Responses to a Meeting Request

When people respond to a meeting request you sent, the Outlook programs on their computers automatically send you email messages, which appear in your Inbox as shown in Figure 15.6. You can double-click a message to read its full details.

FIGURE 15.6

Replies to the meeting request appear in your Inbox.

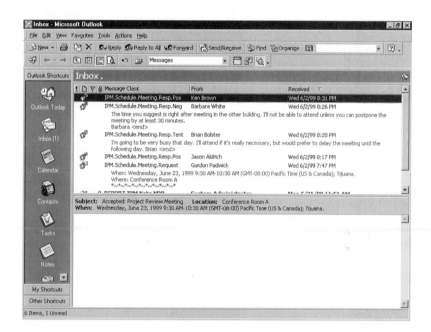

As you can see in Figure 15.7, the message window for a meeting response gives you information about how many people have accepted or declined your invitation.

Updating Information for a Meeting

After you've planned a meeting, you might need to send additional information, such as changes in the meeting time or location, to those who will be attending. To send updated information to all attendees, double-click the meeting on your calendar to display its Meeting form. Edit the details of the Meeting form and click **Send Update**. Outlook automatically sends updated meeting information to each person.

FIGURE 15.7

The meeting response includes details about the replies you have previously received.

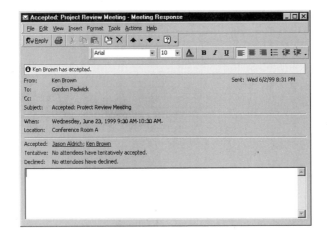

If you change the date or time of a previously scheduled meeting and you save the changes to the meeting, Outlook automatically asks whether you want to send an update to each of the attendees. If you just want to send a message to each of the attendees without changing the information about the meeting itself, choose **Actions**, **New Message to Attendees** while the Meeting form is open. Outlook displays a standard message window with the attendees already entered in the **To** text box. Fill out and send the message just as you would normally create and send an email message.

Cancelling a Meeting

To cancel a meeting, double-click the meeting on your calendar to open its Meeting form. Choose **Actions**, **Cancel Meeting**. Outlook displays the message box shown in Figure 15.8.

FIGURE 15.8

Outlook offers to notify the attendees when you cancel a meeting.

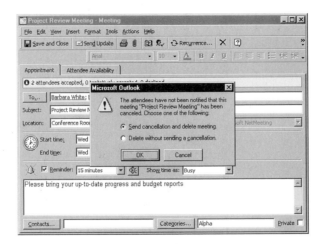

N O T E Figure 15.8 shows the response with the Office Assistant disabled. If you have the Office
Assistant enabled, the response appears in the Office Assistant window. ■

Choose **Send cancellation and delete meeting** to send a message to each attendee and
remove the meeting from your calendar. When each attendee opens the cancellation message, Outlook deletes the meeting from that person's calendar.

You can choose **Delete without sending a cancellation** to delete the message from your
calendar without sending a message to the attendees, although it's unlikely you would want to
do that.

Scheduling Recurring Meetings

Many organizations have meetings that occur on a regularly scheduled basis. You might, for
example, have a weekly staff meeting or a quarterly budget review. Outlook can automatically
schedule recurring meetings.

Follow these steps so Outlook can automatically schedule recurring meetings:

1. Open your calendar in any view.

2. Choose **Actions, New Recurring Meeting** to display the Appointment Recurrence
   dialog box shown in Figure 15.9. Fill out the fields in the dialog box to define the recurrence schedule of the meeting and click **OK**. Outlook displays a Message form you can
   use to send details about the meeting to the people who should attend.

FIGURE 15.9
Use the Appointment
Recurrence dialog box
to define how often a
meeting should occur.

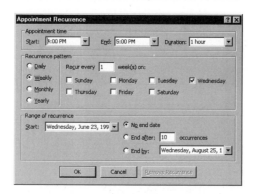

3. Select the attendees, and then fill out the rest of the meeting details.

4. Click **Send** to send the meeting request.

You can also convert a single meeting that you have scheduled into a recurring meeting.
Double-click the meeting item on your calendar to open the Meeting form and click the
Recurrence toolbar button. Fill out the Appointment Recurrence dialog box, and then send
the meeting request as usual.

Finding Available Time for a Meeting

The problem with sending meeting requests is that you have no guarantee that the attendees have the time available on their schedules. You can use Outlook to plan a meeting by finding available time on everyone's schedule. Of course, for this to work, all your colleagues have to maintain their schedules in Outlook meticulously.

To schedule a meeting when people are available, follow these steps:

1. Open your calendar and select the date and time on which you tentatively want to schedule the meeting.

2. Choose **Actions**, **Plan a Meeting**. The Plan a Meeting dialog box appears, as shown in Figure 15.10.

FIGURE 15.10

The Plan a Meeting dialog box initially shows your schedule for the selected day, including the tentative time for the meeting.

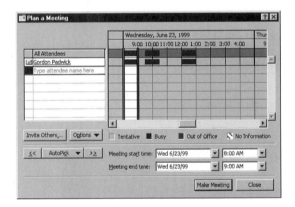

3. Choose **Invite Others** to select the names of the people and resources you want to attend the meeting. You can indicate whether each person's attendance is **Required** or **Optional**. After you make your selections, click **OK** to return to the Plan a Meeting form.

4. After a few seconds' delay in which Outlook retrieves schedules from the server, the form is updated to show the busy times on each person's schedule (see Figure 15.11). The form shows color-coded information for busy, tentative, and out-of-office commitments.

FIGURE 15.11

The Plan a Meeting form shows each person's current schedule and, at the top, summarizes the commitments of all the people you've invited, including your own.

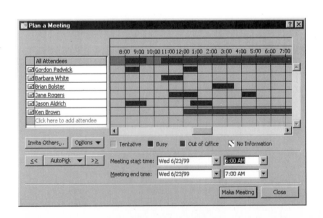

N O T E The summary line is particularly useful if you want to invite more people than can be shown at one time in the combined schedule. ■

5. Choose **AutoPick**, and Outlook searches for the first available block of time when all the people you have invited are available for the period you initially proposed. As shown in Figure 15.12, Outlook proposes the first time after the time you initially suggested when all the proposed participants are available.

FIGURE 15.12
AutoPick finds the first available time for the meeting.

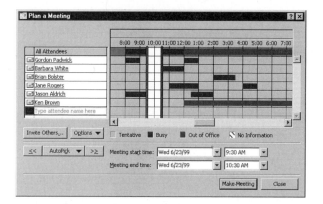

N O T E If there isn't a time-slot available on the day you proposed when all participants are available for the meeting duration you proposed, Outlook searches subsequent days until it finds a day when that amount of time is available for all participants. ■

6. Click **Make Meeting** to accept the proposed time for the meeting. Then, fill out the rest of the fields in the Meeting form and send it as usual.

Using Outlook with Public Folders

If you're using Outlook as a client for Exchange Server, you can use *public folders* to share messages and other Outlook items with other people in your organization. Public folders are stored on your organization's Exchange Server, where they can be made available to all the users on the network. They can function as electronic bulletin boards for the exchange of ideas and announcements, official company documents, and other common information. Storing shared information in public folders is more efficient than sending individual messages to each user, and it makes the information easy to find and use.

Because public folders is a capability of Exchange Server, you can't use them if you don't use Exchange Server as one of your messaging services. You can, however, use the Outlook Net Folders add-in to share information with other users by way of the Internet.

Understanding Public Folders

Public folders can contain Outlook items, such as email messages, contacts, appointments, and notes. Public folders can also contain other files, such as Word documents, Excel worksheets, PowerPoint presentations, and multimedia files.

The owner of a public folder controls who has access to the folder and the type of access each person has, and he or she can restrict the type of items that can be placed in a particular folder. If you have access to a folder that contains your company's client list, you might be allowed only to add items into the folder.

Most public folders are created to store email messages. You can use Outlook to read the messages in a public folder, to respond to those messages, and to create or post new messages.

> **N O T E** The Exchange administrator assigns permissions to individual users to create public folders on the Exchange Server. A person who creates a public folder owns that folder and controls who has access to it and whether each of those persons can only read items, add new items, edit existing items, and delete items. ■

Accessing Information in Public Folders

Accessing a public folder is similar to accessing your personal folders. You can open your Folder List and select one of the available public folders. Alternatively, you can create icons in the Outlook Bar for one or more public folders and then click a public folder icon. The following steps describe how to access a public folder from the Folder List.

1. Choose **View**, **Folder List**. Outlook displays the Folder List, similar to the one shown in Figure 15.13.

FIGURE 15.13

The Folder List contains the Public Folders item if you're using Outlook as a client for Exchange Server.

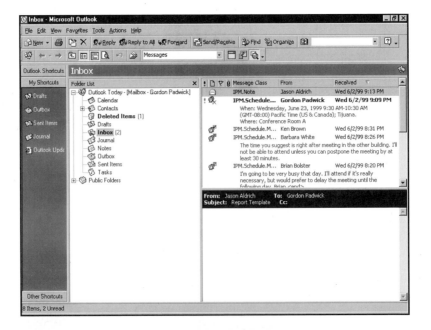

2. Expand the Public Folders item by clicking the plus sign. Outlook shows two items within Public Folders: Favorites and All Public Folders. Expand **All Public Folders** to display a list of individual public folders, such as those shown in Figure 15.14.

FIGURE 15.14
Individual public folders may contain other public folders. In this figure, the plus sign at the left of Computer Information indicates the presence of other folders.

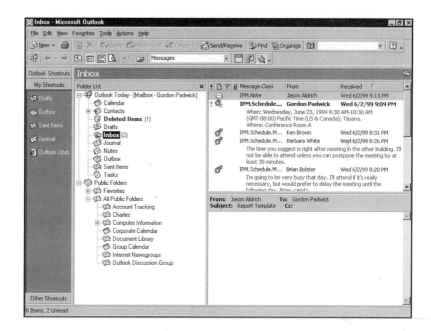

3. Select a public folder to display headers of the individual items it contains, in much the same way as email items in your Inbox are displayed. You can double-click an item's header to open it in the default form for the selected item.

You can create an icon for any public folder in one of the Outlook Bar groups. To do so, perform these steps:

1. Open the Outlook Bar group in which you want to create an icon for a public folder.

2. Drag the name of a public folder from the Folder List into the Outlook Bar.

Subsequently, you don't have to open the folder list to access the public folder. Instead, simply click the icon in the Outlook Bar.

Public folders work very much like your Inbox and other personal folders. The following list shows that you can use many of the same Outlook capabilities for viewing public folders as you use with your other folders:

■ Choose **View**, **AutoPreview** to activate the automatic preview of unread items in a public folder.

■ Choose **View**, **Preview Pane** to open the Preview pane, displaying a larger amount of the content of each item in the folder.

■ Choose **View**, **Current View** and select a view from the list of available views.

Sometimes, you might find an item in a public folder that you want to copy to your own folders. For example, you might want to copy an event from the company's calendar to your personal calendar. In such a case, you can add your own comments or notes to the calendar item without sharing them in the public folder.

To copy an item from a public folder, select the item you want to copy and choose **Edit**, **Copy to Folder**. Select the destination folder in the dialog box that appears and click **OK**. Alternatively, you can drag an item from a public folder either to the name of one of your folders in the Folder List or to the icon that represents that folder in the Outlook Bar.

Posting Information in Public Folders

If the owner of a public folder has given you permission to create items in that folder, you can post information to that folder. Posting an item is much like sending an email message, but the item's destination is the public folder, not an email recipient.

The person who created the folder—the folder's owner—can grant a variety of permissions to other users of that folder. You might have permission to post items in some folders, but not in others. For example, your organization's personnel department might have created a folder for posting job openings within the company. You would probably have the right to read those messages, but not to post your own items.

Your organization might have folders for posting product ideas, special events, complaints, or other information that might come from anyone in the organization. In this case, you have probably been granted the permissions to create items, as well as to read them.

The owner of a public folder can grant permission to delete items from that folder. Usually an owner grants other people permission to delete items those people have posted, not items other people have posted.

Beginning a New Conversation

Outlook users can respond to the items other people have posted in a public folder. Other people can respond to those responses, and so on, creating a related set of items. The set is known as a *conversation* or *thread*.

To begin a conversation by posting a message in a public folder, follow these steps:

1. Select the public folder in which you want to post an item.
2. Choose **File**, move the pointer onto **New**, and choose **Post in This Folder**. The Discussion form appears for your use.
3. Fill in the subject and text of the message, and then select a category. The Post To and Conversation lines are filled in automatically with the name of the folder and the subject of the message (see Figure 15.15).

FIGURE 15.15
The form for posting information to a public folder is similar to a Message form.

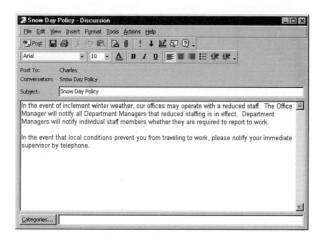

4. Click the **Post** button to close the form and save the item in the selected public folder.

Posting a Response to an Item

After you read an item in a public folder conversation, you can post a response to that item for others to read.

N O T E The subject of the item that begins a conversation becomes the name of that conversation. When people respond to the original item, or to other responses, those responses automatically have the same conversation name. Responses can, though, have a different subject name. ■

Follow these steps to post a response:

1. Double-click an item in a public folder to read it.
2. Click the **Post Reply** toolbar button. The Discussion form appears with the original item displayed and with space for your response above the original item.
3. Enter the subject and the text of your response. The Post To and Conversation lines, which can't be changed, contain the name of the folder and the name of the conversation.
4. Click the **Post** button to close the form and post the new message in the discussion.

Viewing Messages by Conversation

A public folder can contain messages from many conversations. As with any other folder, you can select from a variety of Outlook views for displaying the contents of the folder. The most useful view for reading messages in a conversation is the By Conversation Topic view. Choose **View**, **Current View**, **By Conversation Topic**. Figure 15.16 shows the appearance of the public folders when viewed by conversation topic. Notice that Outlook displays the total number of items in each conversation, as well the number you haven't read.

FIGURE 15.16
This public folder contains several conversations whose individual messages are collapsed.

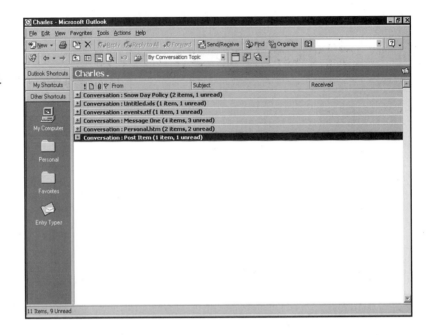

By clicking the plus sign at the left of a conversation heading, you can expand the conversation to see all its messages, as shown in Figure 15.17.

FIGURE 15.17
One conversation has been expanded to reveal the individual items.

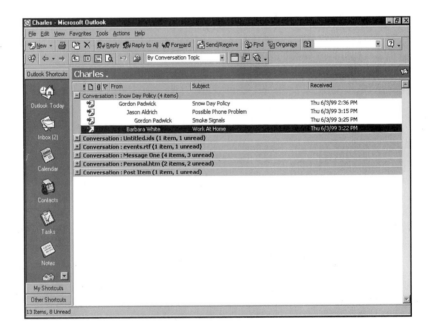

Sending an Email Response to a Discussion

Sometimes, you might want to send a response directly to the person who posted an item in a public folder, without posting the response for everyone to see. Additionally, you might want to forward or copy an item to another user, even someone who doesn't have access to the public folders.

To reply to the person who posted the item, simply select the item and click the **Reply** button. Outlook creates a message addressed to the sender of the original item. As with any email message, you can select additional To, Cc, and Bcc addresses.

To forward an item to another person without replying to the sender, select the item and click the **Forward** button. Outlook creates a new message for you to forward. In this case, you have to provide the To address before sending the message.

Creating a Public Folder

If your Exchange administrator has given you permission to create public folders, you create a public folder just as you would any other folder. After you create the folder, you are automatically the owner; you have the capability to designate the permissions of other users to view the folder and to read, create, edit, and delete items in the folder.

Just like personal folders, public folders can contain subfolders, so the steps for creating a public folder start with selecting its parent folder. To do so, follow these steps:

1. In the Folder List, select the parent folder of the new public folder.
2. Right-click on that folder to display the shortcut menu.
3. Choose **New Folder** to create the folder.
4. Type the name for the new folder and press **Enter**.

Understanding Forms and Public Folders

When you create a new public folder, you and the other users on your network can use the same forms for viewing, editing, and creating items in the folders as you would use in your personal folders. For example, if a public folder is designed to hold email items, you can use the usual forms for creating and reading email messages. By default, a new public folder can contain email messages, but the folder's owner can change the default item type for the folder.

Because public folders are often used for special purposes within an organization—such as a discussion of product ideas or information about company policies—you might want to use custom forms for working with items in a public folder. Outlook lets you associate one or more forms with a folder and to designate a default form for that folder.

To view and modify the forms associations for a public folder that you own, follow these steps:

1. Display the Folder List.
2. Right-click the folder name whose properties you want to modify and choose **Properties** in the shortcut menu.

3. Select the **Forms** tab in the Properties dialog box (see Figure 15.18). This tab is not available for public folders you don't own.

4. In the Allow these forms in this folder area, select your preference for which forms are available to this folder. In the example in Figure 15.18, the folder has been restricted to allow the use of only the form named CorpInfo.

FIGURE 15.18

The Forms tab of the Properties dialog box for a folder shows which custom forms you can use with the folder.

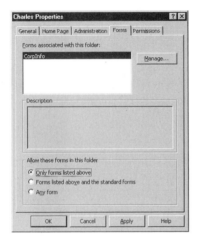

5. Click **Apply** to apply your changes, and click **OK** to close the dialog box.

In this example, all items created in this folder are edited using the custom form you selected.

Making a Public Folder Available Offline

Normally, public folders are available only when your computer is connected to the Exchange Server. However, you might need to access a public folder while you're working offline. In order to do that, you must copy a public folder to the Favorites item in the Folder List and then synchronize that copy of the folder with the original public folder.

1. Open the Folder List and, if necessary, expand the **All Public Folders** section.

2. Drag the public folder that you want to have available offline from the All Public Folders section of the Folder List to the Favorites section.

3. Expand the **Favorites** section and right-click the folder you just copied to display its context menu.

4. Choose **Properties** in the context menu and select the **Synchronization** tab to see the options shown in Figure 15.19.

5. In the This folder is available section of the dialog box, select **When offline or online**.

FIGURE 15.19
Use the Synchronization tab of a public folder to make the folder available for offline use.

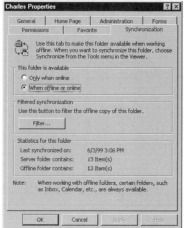

Now, you have a copy of the public folder available for offline use. Depending on Outlook's synchronization settings, the copy of the public folder is automatically synchronized with the original folder whenever you connect to the Exchange Server. At any time while you're working with Outlook, you can select the copy of the public folder, choose **Tools,** move the pointer onto **Synchronize**, and choose **This Folder** to resynchronize the folders.

Customizing Forms in Outlook

Outlook uses forms as a way of displaying the different types of items that are stored in Outlook folders, one item at a time. When you create a new item such as an email message or open an existing item for editing, you are using a form to view the information. A *form* is a window in Outlook that contains controls such as text boxes, check boxes, lists, and buttons.

Outlook's built-in forms provide an easy and convenient method for entering and editing data. A well-designed form enables you to see many fields on the screen at one time. The Table view, in contrast, can be difficult to use, because you can see only a few fields at a time. However, a Table view has the advantage that you can display information about many items at a time.

You can customize the forms that come with Outlook to create forms that are personalized or that perform specific functions within an organization. The next section reviews the forms that come with Outlook and then shows how to customize forms for your own use.

Reviewing Outlook's Standard Forms

Outlook comes with a standard set of forms for creating, reading, and editing the items in Outlook folders. You usually don't even have to think very much about using forms. When you double-click an item, such as a contact, Outlook automatically opens the item using the default form for the active folder. Many people simply use the default forms that come with Outlook and have no need to create custom forms.

N O T E Outlook doesn't let you create custom forms from scratch for creating, viewing, and editing items. Instead, you have to base custom forms on Outlook's standard forms. Although this might, perhaps, sound like a limitation, in fact it offers the advantage of automatically providing all the functionality that's built into the standard forms.

In addition to forms for use with Outlook items, Outlook 2000 (but not prior versions of Outlook) allows you to create UserForms that you can use to create custom dialog boxes.

You might want to customize a form in Outlook simply to make cosmetic changes, such as modifying the form's background color, font, or the arrangement of the controls. (Controls are the items on the form that enable you interact with the form, such as text boxes, check boxes, buttons, and list boxes.) Maybe you have created one or more custom fields. If so, you can display those fields on a built-in form if you customize it.

You can also modify a blank page of an existing form as though you were creating a form from scratch. This is particularly useful if you have designed a custom application in a public folder in which you're using many custom fields.

To build a form in Outlook, you begin by modifying an existing form. Therefore, it's a good idea to start by reviewing the following built-in Outlook forms:

- Use the Message form to create and edit email messages and faxes.
- Use the Contact form to work with contact items.
- Use the Appointment form to work with appointments and meetings in the Calendar folder.
- Use the Journal Entry form for creating journal entries.
- Use the Meeting Request form to send a meeting request to another person via email.
- Use the Note form for creating and editing notes.
- Use the Post form for posting messages to a folder. This form is most often used for posting messages in a public folder, although you can use it to post a message in one of your personal folders as well.
- Use the Task form to create a task in your Tasks folder.
- Use the Task Request form to send an email message to someone requesting that a person accept a task.

Outlook includes two additional special-purpose forms:

- Outlook uses the Standard Default form when it's unable to load the specific form associated with a message or folder.
- Use the Security Key Exchange form for sending secure message keys to another user so you can send encrypted messages. This form is available only if the Exchange administrator has enabled advanced security.

You can use Office documents as templates for items to be posted to an Outlook folder. If you choose **File**, **New**, **Office Document**, the New Office Document dialog box is displayed. Select the Office application you want to use and click **OK**. You can either post the document to a folder or send the document as an email message.

Understanding a Form's Anatomy

To create and modify forms, you need to know about the form's structure. Two concepts that are essential to understanding a form are tabs and controls. By customizing these two elements, you can create a unique and distinctive form to suit your needs.

Tabs   Many of the standard forms in Outlook have several pages. Each of these pages is identified by a *tab*, a button at the top of the page that identifies it. Within a form, each page must have a unique name, which should be descriptive of the function of that page. Some forms, such as the Notes form and the Journal Entry form, have only one page and, therefore, have no tabs.

Controls   Outlook has several controls you can use on your forms, including text boxes, list and combo boxes, check boxes, and command buttons. You can move the controls around on a form, change the text that appears on a label, and change the font for a control. You can also add new controls to a form and delete controls you don't need.

Creating New or Modified Forms

To create a new form or to modify an existing one, you work with the form in Design view. Outlook's Design view provides a set of tools for adding controls to and modifying controls on a form and for modifying the properties of the form. These design tools are similar to the tools that are available in Visual Basic (VB) and in Visual Basic for Applications (VBA), which is used to create automated applications in Word, Excel, PowerPoint, and Access.

Outlook 2000, but not previous versions of Outlook, uses VBA to allow you to control the overall Outlook environment as well as to access and control other Office applications from within Outlook. However, Outlook uses Visual Basic Scripting Edition (VBScript) within forms.

N O T E   Outlook 2000 comes with updated versions of VBA and VBScript. ▪

To customize an existing form, open the form as usual, either by opening an existing item using that form or by creating a new item with the form. For example, to customize the Contact form, you can begin by creating a new contact—by displaying the Contact Information viewer and choosing **New**. Alternatively, with any Information viewer displayed, you can choose **File**, move the pointer onto **New**, and choose **Contact**.

After you have the form open, switch into Design view by choosing **Tools**, moving the pointer onto **Forms**, and choosing **Design This Form**. Outlook displays the form in Design view, as shown in Figure 15.20.

FIGURE 15.20
A form's design view
shows the form's con-
trols superimposed on
a grid.

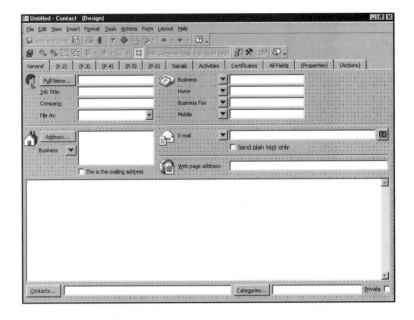

In Design view, you can make changes to the pages used in the standard Outlook form, such
as the General, Details, Activities, Certificates, and All Fields pages of the standard Contact
form. You can make any of the following changes:

- Change the size and position of controls
- Delete controls you don't need
- Add new controls

You can also activate and rename form pages that aren't used in a standard form. Unused
pages are shown in Design view, with tab names enclosed in parentheses, such as (P.2), (P.3),
(P.4), (P.5), and (P.6) in the Design view shown in Figure 15.20. You can place whatever controls you need on these pages.

To create a new form, open any Outlook Information viewer. Then choose **Tools**, move the
pointer onto **Forms**, and choose **Design a Form**. The Design Form dialog box appears, as
shown in Figure 15.21.

Open the **Look In** drop-down list and select the forms library that contains the form you
want to use. Select a form as a model for your new form and click **Open**. The form opens in
Design view.

Saving and Publishing Forms

After you make changes to a form's design, you need to save the new form. If you opened an
existing form for modification and you want to save your changes and update the form,
choose **File**, **Save** or press **Ctrl+S**.

Part

III

Ch

15

FIGURE 15.21
You can use the
Design Form dialog
box to select a form to
use as a starting point
for a new form.

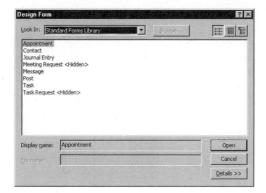

To save the form as a new form, you need to publish the form. Publishing a form saves it in a folder or a forms library. Publishing a form in a folder makes that form available in that folder. Publishing a form in a forms library makes the form available to be opened at a later time or to be shared with other users.

To publish a form, choose **Tools**, move the pointer onto **Forms**, and choose **Pu̲blish Form As**. The Publish Form As dialog box appears, as shown in Figure 15.22.

FIGURE 15.22
The Publish Form As
dialog box enables you
to publish a form in a
folder or form library.

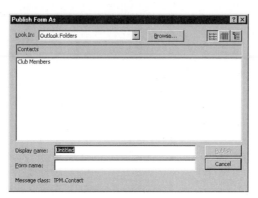

Type a name in the **Display n̲ame** text box. Outlook automatically uses this name as the form name. If you want to use a different name for the form, enter that name in the **Form name** text box.

The **L̲ook In** list determines where the form will be saved. If you select an individual folder, Outlook saves the form in that folder, and the form is available for use in that folder. If you select **Outlook Folders**, the form is made available to any of your Outlook folders. If you want to use this form in other folders, select **Personal Forms Library**. Later, you can copy the form from the library to any folder. You can also select the **Organizational Forms Library** to make forms available to anyone in your organization.

NOTE The Organizational Forms Library is available only if the Exchange administrator has created it. ■

Click **Publish** to close the dialog box and publish the form.

Setting a Default Form for a Folder

If you've published a form, you can select it as the default form for a folder. Then, any new items you create in the folder are created using the custom form.

In the Folder List, right-click the folder you want to customize and choose **Properties** from the shortcut menu. The Properties dialog box appears with the **General** tab displayed, as shown in Figure 15.23. Select the form you want to use from the **When posting to this folder, use** drop-down list. If you published the form to this folder, its name appears in the list.

FIGURE 15.23
You can use the Contacts Properties dialog box to set the default form for a folder.

If the form you want to use is not on the drop-down list, click **Forms** to display the Choose Form dialog box, shown in Figure 15.24. In the **Look In** drop-down list, select **Personal Forms Library** to find any forms you have published in your personal library. To use one of Outlook's standard forms, select **Standard Forms Library**. Select the form you want to use and click **Open**.

Using a Forms Library

You can use a forms library to store forms that you want to reuse in many different folders. Click the **Forms** tab of the Properties dialog box and click **Manage Forms**. The Forms Manager dialog box appears (see Figure 15.25). You can use the Forms Manager to copy a form from a library (such as your Personal Forms Library) into a folder.

FIGURE 15.24
Use the Choose Form dialog box to select a form from the Standard Forms Library.

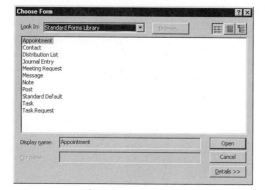

FIGURE 15.25
Use the Forms Manager to copy forms from a library to a folder.

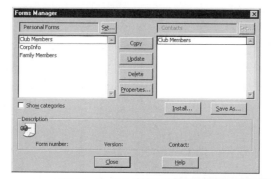

To select a library, click the **Set** button. The Set Library To dialog box appears, as shown in Figure 15.26. To use a form from your Personal Forms Library, select **Personal Forms** in the **Forms Library** drop-down box and click **OK**. When you return to the Forms Manager, all forms in your Personal Forms Library are displayed. To copy a form from the library to the current folder, select the form you want to copy and click the **Copy** button. Click **Close** when you finish managing your forms.

FIGURE 15.26
Use the Set Library To dialog box to choose the Forms Library with which you want to work.

Adding and Deleting Controls

You can add controls to a form by using the Toolbox. The Toolbox, shown in Figure 15.27, is available when you are using the form Design view. You can show or hide the Toolbox by clicking the Control Toolbox toolbar button or by choosing **Form, Control Toolbox**.

FIGURE 15.27

Use the Toolbox to add controls to a form.

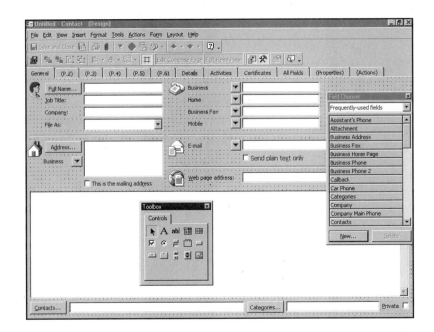

The Toolbox contains these controls:

- **Label.** Used to display text on a form. Labels are used for instructions or to identify different areas of a form.

- **TextBox.** A box that can display the contents of a field within an Outlook item and can be used to enter data into a field. Text boxes come in a single-line variety (such as the Subject box on many forms) and a multiline variety (such as the Notes area of most forms).

- **ComboBox and ListBox.** Used to display lists of information on a form. ListBox controls take up a set amount of space on the form, whereas ComboBox controls can be set up as drop-down lists, which display their lists only when a user clicks on them.

- **Checkbox.** Used for true/false or yes/no questions. Users can change the value of the check box by clicking it.

- **OptionButton.** Used to select one option out of a short list. When you have a group of option buttons working together, selecting one option button automatically turns the other options buttons off.

- **ToggleButton.** Looks like a push button, but has two states or *values*. Clicking the button once leaves it pushed in, which represents true (or on). Clicking it again makes the button appear raised, representing false (or off).

- **Frame.** Used as a container for other controls. If you place two or more option buttons within a frame, they are automatically treated as a group so that only one button in the group can be selected at a time. The Frame control can also be used to create rectangles and lines on a form.

- **CommandButton.** Creates a push button on the form. Clicking the button causes an event to occur. In order for something to happen when a button is clicked, you must create an event procedure in VBScript.

- **Image.** Can be used to add images to your form. You can insert the contents of an image file in several different formats, including Windows bitmaps (BMP), Windows metafiles (WMF), enhanced metafiles (EMF), icons (ICO or CUR), GIF, and JPEG (JPG).

- **Tabstrip and Multipage.** Enables you to create the dynamic effect of multiple pages or multiple sets of controls within a form. VBScript programming is required to make effective use of these controls.

- **Scrollbar and SpinButton.** Provide graphical controls that a user can click to set or change numeric values. VBScript programming is used to transfer these values to other controls.

- **Select Objects.** This is not a control, but just a button that enables you to select controls on the form by clicking on them.

Adding a Control   To place a control on a form, click the button on the toolbox that represents the control you want to use. Then, click the location on the form where you want the control to appear. The control is placed with its upper-left corner at the location where you clicked. If you prefer, instead of just clicking the location of the corner, you can click and drag a rectangle to indicate the initial size of the control.

Selecting Controls   Many operations on controls require you to select one or more controls first. You can select a control by clicking it. A group of white buttons, called *selection handles*, appear around the selected control.

You can select more than one control at a time so that you can reposition the controls as a group or edit the properties of the controls as a group. After selecting one control, **Ctrl+click** the additional controls you want to select. The most recently selected control shows white selection handles, and the previously selected controls show black selection handles.

Another method for selecting multiple controls is to drag a rectangle around the controls. To do this, begin by clicking a location on the background of the form where there are no controls. Then, drag a rectangle from that point to surround or touch any controls you want to select.

If you have several controls selected and you want to reduce the selection to just one control, click on a control that is not selected to remove the current selection. Then, you can select the control you want.

Deleting Controls   To delete a control, select the control, and then press the **Delete** key or click the **Delete** toolbar button. Be sure you have not selected more controls than you want to delete. If you accidentally delete too much, use **Edit, Undo** to restore the controls.

Adding Fields

Many of the controls you place on a form are used to work with the fields for items in Outlook folders. For example, a Contacts form usually has controls to edit the name, title, and phone numbers of the contact, as well as many others.

Not every available field is displayed on the standard Outlook forms. (To include all of them would create some very crowded forms.) You might want to add one of these standard fields (or a user-defined field) to a built-in or custom form.

To display the list of available fields, click the **Field Chooser** toolbar button. The Field Chooser window appears (see Figure 15.28). To add a field to the form, drag the desired field from the Field Chooser onto the form. A control that represents the field appears on the form. You can drag the control to a new location if you don't like its position on the form.

FIGURE 15.28
Use the Field Chooser to add standard and user-defined fields to a form.

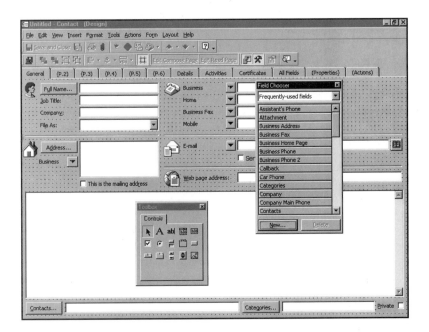

The Field Chooser initially displays a list of frequently used fields. You can open the drop-down list to display other selections of fields.

Controlling a Form's Appearance

Outlook forms, and the controls on the forms, are objects. This is most important to VBScript programmers because VBScript works with the properties, methods, and events of objects. Objects are used throughout Office applications to represent elements such as documents, workbooks, database tables, and many other items.

N O T E The word "object" can be loosely defined within the Office environment to mean some-thing that is accessible to program code. Some objects, such as forms and controls, are visible. Other objects, such as the Application object, aren't visible but represent a structure. ■

To control an object's appearance, you can modify the properties of the object with VBScript programming or by using the Properties toolbar button, as described in this section.

When you're designing an Outlook form, you work with the properties of the form and the controls on the form. Properties are attributes that describe the appearance and nature of the form or control. Some properties are very simple. For example, a form has ForeColor and BackColor properties, which control the foreground and background color. Label controls have a Font property (which controls the appearance of the text of the label) and a Caption property (which defines the text that appears on the label).

There are many properties and, in most cases, you can leave the properties unchanged from their original values. Sometimes, however, you might need to change the properties of a control or form.

To view the properties of a control, right-click the control to display its context menu, and then choose **Properties**. The Properties dialog box shown in Figure 15.29 appears. You can use the **Display** tab to change the name of the control, as well as its appearance properties.

FIGURE 15.29
The Display tab of the Properties dialog box shows the name and other attributes of a control.

You can use the **Value** tab, shown in Figure 15.30, to bind (connect) the control to one of the fields for the items you will be editing with the form.

You can use the **Validation** tab, shown in Figure 15.31, to declare that a field is required for this item and to set a validation rule guaranteeing that appropriate data is entered in the control.

The Properties dialog box provides access to only the most frequently used properties of controls. To see a complete list of a control's properties, right-click a control to display its context menu, and then choose **Advanced Properties** to display the properties sheet, such as that shown in Figure 15.32. You can scroll through the list of properties and change the values of any of them. You can leave the properties sheet open as you move from one control to another, and the window updates to display the properties of the currently selected control.

FIGURE 15.30
The Value tab of the Properties dialog box shows how the control gets its value.

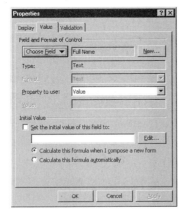

FIGURE 15.31
You can use the Validation tab of the Properties dialog box to create a validation rule, ensuring accurate data entry.

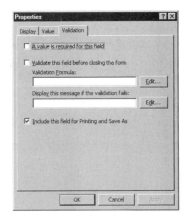

FIGURE 15.32
The properties sheet shows all the available properties of a control.

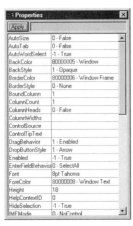

CHAPTER 16

Sharing Database Resources with Access 2000

by Laura Stewart

This chapter focuses on forms for data entry and manipulation, and how to use subforms in a data-entry environment. You also learn how to use forms for other purposes, such as a database switchboard and as an input box for criteria for reports or queries, or a subform.

This chapter also covers using Access in a multiuser environment. The purpose of a database is to store related information in one location. Access enables several users to access the same database simultaneously and make changes, while different users can retrieve and update the data from different locations.

This chapter also explains client/server databases—a database that is split between a *client* (often referred to as the front-end part of the database) and a *server* (the back-end part of the database).

Using Forms to Streamline Workgroup Communication Within Access Databases

In a workgroup setting, forms are convenient tools to permit multiple users to view and update records in your Access database. Forms also enable you to control exactly what the users can view and edit, and, also, make data entry more user friendly for people who have little or no experience in Access. By using a form, you can add or delete records, as well as search for, modify, and print records. Each of these functions can be customized for your specific business situation.

For example, adding drop-down menus to the form can make adding records quicker and easier by automatically populating certain fields or prompting the user for specific data. You can also customize a search engine to facilitate locating records. All these things can be accomplished by customizing a data entry form. This section focuses on how to create a basic form using the Form Wizard (the best way to get started quickly), and how to customize forms to meet your specific needs.

▶ For additional information, **see** "Customizing Access to Your Organization's Needs," on **p. 227**.

Forms generally have an underlying data source from which it pulls and in which it stores data. Because these forms are used for data entry and manipulation, a table should be the data source. The table needs to be created before you create the form. If necessary, you can modify the table if you need more fields as the form is created. In this chapter, you create a customer information form using the Northwind database that comes with Access.

N O T E You can also use queries as data sources for forms, but queries don't let you modify or add new records, which defeats the purpose of using forms for data entry. ■

Creating Data Entry Forms Using the Form Wizard

You can create a form for any existing table. For illustration purposes in this chapter, we use the Customer table in the Northwind database (that comes with Access) as the source for a form. Figure 16.1 shows the Customers: Table in the Design view, which contains the following fields:

CustomerID	Address	Country
CompanyName	City	Phone
ContactName	Region	Fax
ContactTitle	Postal Code	

FIGURE 16.1
The Design view of the Customer table shows the field names, data types, and description.

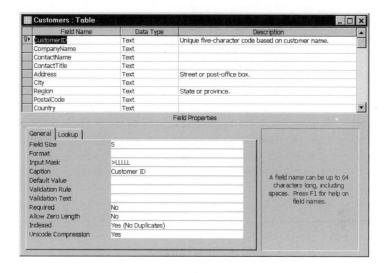

To create a new form, start by clicking **Forms** in the list of objects in the Database window. From here, there are three ways you can create forms in Access: AutoForm, Form Wizard, and Design View.

■ Use *AutoForm* if you're in a real hurry. In a few mouse clicks, a basic form is instantly created. All the table fields are displayed on the form. This is a great option if you need a simple form based on only one table or if you intend to do a lot of customization and just want a starting point to work with.

■ With a few more steps, the *Form Wizard* gives you several very useful options: You can choose the fields to include in the form (you don't have to include them all), you can add fields from other tables (such as order information for each customer), and you can select from several themes to format the appearance of the form. Once created, you can leave the form as is, or customize it to fit your organization's specific needs.

■ The *Design View* can be used to create a form from scratch, or to modify a form created using the AutoForm or Form Wizard.

To create an AutoForm, click the **New** button in the Database window, choose **AutoForm: Columnar**, select the table for the data source, and click **OK**. The completed form appears. To customize the form, skip ahead to the section "Customizing a Form in the Design View," later in this chapter.

To create a form using the Form Wizard, double-click **Create Form by Using Wizard from the list of Form** options in the Database window. On the first step of the Form Wizard, you select the source of the data for the form. From the list of Available Fields for that source, you choose which fields you want on the form by adding them to the Selected Fields column. In Figure 16.2, the CustomerID, CompanyName, and ContactName have been added to the Selected Fields list.

FIGURE 16.2
Use the arrow buttons to add to or remove fields from the Selected Fields column.

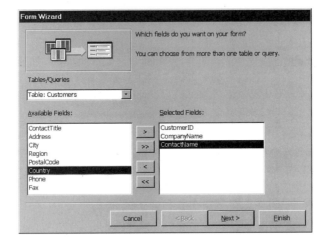

One of the advantages of the Form Wizard is it enables you to include fields from other tables, such as information about the orders each customer has placed. To accomplish this, a primary key must link the tables. A *primary key* is a field (or fields) in the main table that uniquely identifies each record. That same field must appear in the table you want to link to. For example, in the Customer table, the CustomerID field is the primary key field. Each customer has one and only one ID. The CustomerID field is also in the Orders table (and might be listed several times if a customer has placed several orders).

You must identify the other data source in the first step of the Form Wizard and include those fields in the Selected Fields list (refer to Figure 16.2). A *subform* (a form embedded in the main form) will be added to the main form to display the related data.

For the example we are constructing, we'll use fields from both the Customer and the Orders table. The Orders table contains the CustomerID field, which enables us to display the order information for each customer. In this example, the OrderID and OrderDate fields are included from the Orders table.

TIP

You can use more than two tables in your form. In the Northwind database example, it would make sense to have product information, such as the specific names of the products ordered, display in the form. Because of the way the Northwind database is structured, this requires four tables: Customers, Orders, Order Details, and Products. The Orders table lists the CustomerID and the OrderID (the primary key for the Orders table). The Order Details table lists the OrderID and the ProductID (which combined together make the primary key field for the Order Details table). The Products table lists the ProductID (the primary key) and the ProductName. Using multiple tables is not difficult; however, you must understand the relationships between the tables in your database.

A new feature in Access 2000 enables you to print the relationships window. Display the relationships window by choosing **Tools**, **Relationships**. Then, choose **File**, **Print Relationships**.

When you use multiple tables, the next step in the Wizard gives you the choice of how you want to represent the data from the tables; if you choose data from only one table, you won't see this step.

The data from different tables can be represented on a form in any of three ways. The first is through a subform (see Figure 16.3). The form shows the fields from the first table, with the fields from the second table in a subform. This is the default setting—the option button **Form with subform(s)** is marked.

FIGURE 16.3
A subform is one option for representing multiple tables on a form.

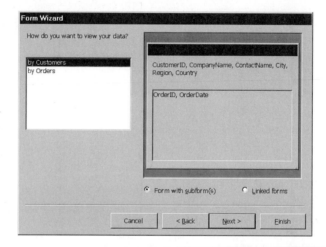

An alternative to a subform is to have the data pop up when a button is pushed. This is called a linked or pop-up form (see Figure 16.4) and is set by selecting the **Linked forms** option button.

FIGURE 16.4
When the main form already has a lot of fields, using a pop-up linked form conserves form real estate. In this example, pressing a button on the form will display the information from the Orders table.

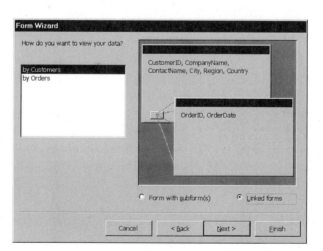

If you want all the data displayed in a single form, click the name of the second table in the upper-left corner of the Form Wizard window (see Figure 16.5). Fields from both tables are combined in the list. If you select the name of the first table, the Linked forms option becomes active.

FIGURE 16.5
You can also combine fields from multiple tables into one form.

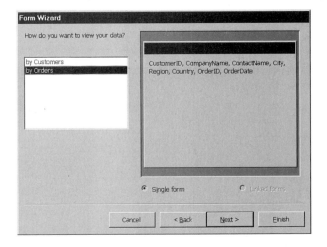

The option you choose for displaying the linked data dictates the options that appear when you click **Next**. For the subform option, you are asked what format you want the subform data to be displayed in. If you use the single form, you can indicate the layout of the form.

In the next step, you select the style of the form, which sets the background colors, font colors, and label and text box styles. Select a style that suits your organization, and click **Next**.

In the final step of the Wizard, you enter a title for the form (and subform if applicable), which appears at the top of the form when it's displayed. You can also open the form in the Design view (to make modifications) or display it in the Form view to see how it will look to end users. Figure 16.6 shows the finished form in the Form view.

FIGURE 16.6
The form title is Customers Information and the subform title is Order Information Subform.

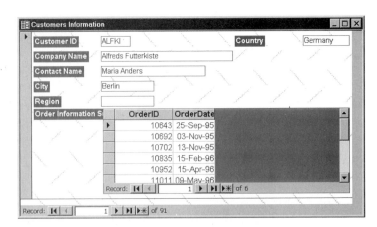

You can modify forms in the Design view. You might want to move or resize fields, add sub-forms, add graphic pictures (such as a company logo, product photo or sketch, or employee picture), or change the styles and colors used with the form. You can also customize fields by adding drop-down list boxes from which end users can pick items. These types of customizations are discussed in the next section.

Customizing a Form in the Design View

You can create a form from scratch, adding and formatting each object you need. However, it can save you a lot of time if you start with either an AutoForm or a form generated by the Form Wizard, using the methods described in the previous section.

> **N O T E**   You can create a form from scratch by double-clicking the **Create Form in Design View** option from the list of Form objects in the Database window. ▓

When you first enter the Design view, you see your form and the Toolbox. The *Toolbox* is a floating toolbar (which you can move, resize, or dock like any toolbar) containing a number of common tools you use to add objects to your forms. The graphical objects on forms are called *controls*, the usual type is a text box (typically with a corresponding label).

When you display a form created by the Form Wizard in the Design view, the form typically has several *sections*. The sections are delineated by thick gray banners and labeled on the far-left side of the screen. Figure 16.7 shows the Customer Information Form with the Form Header, Detail, and Form Footer sections.

FIGURE 16.7

The Form Header/ Footer sections, although available on the form, are collapsed and not being used.

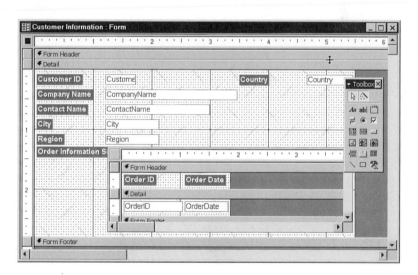

All forms have a Detail section, and you might also see Form Header and Form Footer sections. If needed, you can add Page Header and Page Footer sections as well. The Details section is typically where the data source fields are, including any subforms. Form Footers are often used to hold the form navigation buttons, such as Next Record, New Record, and so on.

Items on the Form Header and Footer are static. They remain displayed regardless of which record you have displayed. The data displayed in the items in the Details section are dynamic; as the user navigates through the records, the data changes. In Figure 16.7, the Form Header and Footer sections are collapsed and not being used. You expand a section by placing the cursor at the bottom of the section banner. The mouse pointer changes into a plus sign with arrows up and down (as shown in Figure 16.7). Drag down to expand the section.

Modifying Form Properties   Double-clicking the Form Selector box (refer to Figure 16.7) in the upper-left corner of the form displays the properties for the form. Here, you can change the form caption (the text that appears in the title bar), choose the views allowed (whether users will be able to see the form in the Form view, the Design view, or both), decide what items should be shown (such as scrollbars and navigation buttons), change the data source, and change the form formatting. To edit a property, click in the appropriate property text box. With some properties, such as Caption, you simply type the new text. For other properties, such as Views Allowed, a drop-down list appears from which you can select an option.

Adding Fields   If you did not include all the fields from your data source table, you can add any of those missing fields to the form. Choose **View**, **Field List** to display a list of the available fields from your table. Drag and drop the fields you want onto the form. In Figure 16.8, the Address field is being added to the form. Once added, you can then move, resize, or format the field's label and text box.

FIGURE 16.8
Resize the window containing the field list to see more of the field names.

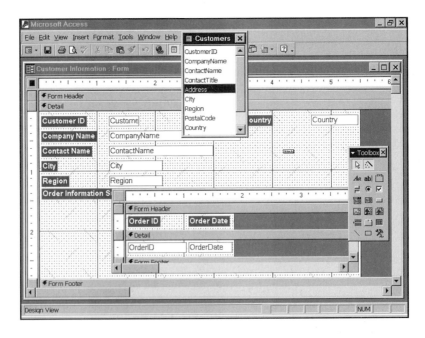

N O T E   Only fields from the table used as the data source for the main form appear on the Field List. To add fields to a subform, you must first make the subform the active object and then choose **View**, **Field List**. Alternatively, you can display the subform separately to modify the fields.

Adding Subforms   You can add a subform to a form to display related records from another table. You can include a subform while creating a form using the Form Wizard, or add a subform in the Design View. Before you add a subform to a form, be sure you have enlarged the Details section to allow sufficient space to create the subform the size you need. If you need to create a subform inside another subform, you need to resize both the main form Details section and the subform Details section.

You're not limited to just one subform. Forms can have multiple subforms. Although in some cases these might be additional subforms to main form, the more likely scenario is to need a subform to a subform, or *nesting subforms*. For example, we created a form (called Customer Information) in the section "Creating Data Entry Forms Using the Form Wizard," that is based on the Customer table and has a subform (called Order Information Subform) showing information from the Orders table. The Order Information subform, however, shows only the OrderID and the OrderDate fields. It does not identify the products ordered, because that data is stored in another table. Because of the way the Northwind database is structured, we would need to add a subform to the Order Information Subform, linking it to the Order Details table (which stores both the OrderID and ProductID fields).

Instead of doing this manually, it is much easier to do this with the Form Wizard (which will create the subforms for you). The key is knowing that you want to display this data ahead of time and understanding the relationships structure among your database tables.

In this example, the main form has a one-to-many relationship with the first subform, and the first subform has a one-to-many relationship with the second subform.

There are several ways to display the data in a nested subform. If the properties are set to view the form as a Datasheet, you will see plus signs (new in Access 2000) in front of the records that contain links to the nested subform. As in a table datasheet view, you can click the plus sign to view the linked data. You can change the property for the first subform to view the data as a single form. The Datasheet shows you all the order records from the customer and you have to click to see the details of each order. The Single Form option shows you one order (and the details) at a time. The focus is on the individual items in an order rather than all the orders.

CAUTION

Unfortunately, the Northwind database supplied as a sample database from Microsoft contains a few errors. The ProductID field in the Order Details table actually contains the ProductName information. Although this makes it possible to see the product names by linking only three tables, it is structurally not correct. When you check the linking relationship among the tables (Tools, Relationships), the ProductID field in the Order Details table is linked to the ProductID field in the Products table. When you attempt to create a form that links these three tables, you see a compile error message and are placed in the Visual Basic Editor window.

To add a subform to a form, click the subform/subreport icon on the Toolbox. Move the mouse pointer to the starting point for the subform and drag to create the subform. A Subform Wizard appears and walks you through the steps necessary to add the subform. You can either choose to use an existing form as the subform, or you can use an existing table or query as the basis for the subform. If you decide on this second option, leave the option Use Existing Tables and Queries selected and click **Next**.

TIP When the Control Wizards button (in the upper-right corner of the Form Design Toolbox) is active, it launches wizards when you add controls to forms. By default, this button is active. However, if you add a control and a Wizard does not appear, it is probably because the Control Wizards' button is not active. If this button is not active, you will have to set all parameters and options in the properties box for the control. Using the Control Wizards saves you time and effort.

Choose the table and fields you want on the subform. For example, in the form being built in this chapter, the Order Details table and the ProductID field would be selected. Click **Next**.

In the next step, you must choose how the subforms are linked, so the form knows which fields to pull from the other table. The Wizard guesses the link (see Figure 16.9) or you can define your own link by identifying exactly which field in the data source for main form is linked to the field in the data source for the subform. For this example, the Wizard had guessed correctly. If it hadn't, the OrderID field would have been identified for both the Orders table and the Order Details table.

FIGURE 16.9
If you choose the **Define my own** option, another screen appears from which you can select the appropriate fields.

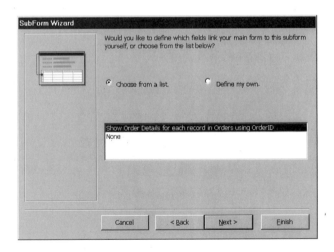

Click **Next**. On the final step of the Wizard, you enter a name for the form and click **Finish**. The subform is added to the main form.

The Forms tab of the database window should now show the subform you created. You can go to Design view and make any changes to that subform, or you can double-click the subform in the Design view of the main form to make changes to the form properties.

N O T E You can see the linked fields by looking at the Data tab on the property sheet. The *parent link* is the main table, and the *child link* is the field from the subform data source. You can also change other properties for the subform on the subform property sheet (see Figure 16.10). ■

FIGURE 16.10

The source object and linked fields can be changed on the sub-form property sheet.

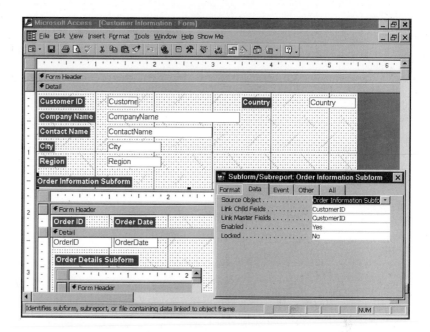

Adding List Boxes and Combo Boxes Use list boxes or combo boxes to provide users with a list of data from which to choose, instead of requiring them to enter the data. These types of controls are particularly handy when you have a list of typical or known entries. For example, you can use one of these boxes for a list of State abbreviations, a list of product names, a list of customer and client names, and similar lists.

- ■ A *list box* displays the multiple items in the list, and users can choose only from the items on the list. List boxes are a good choice when the list of items is relatively short.

- ■ A *combo box* displays only one item from the list; users click a drop-down button to see other entries in the list. Combo boxes take up less space on the form and can be set up to enable users to enter values not on the list.

Suppose your company is focused in a tristate area—Virginia, Tennessee, and North Carolina—but you have a few customers in other states. You can set up your state field as a combo box with the choices VA, TN, and NC and also enable users to enter other state prefixes.

N O T E If you are replacing an existing text box field with a combo or list box, first delete the existing field on the form. Then, add the new control (as described later). ■

To add a list or combo box to a form, click the desired icon on the Toolbox and draw the box where you want it on the form. You can move and size the box later. A Wizard appears asking you where the box should get its values (see Figure 16.11). The values can come from an existing table, you can type the values, or you can find a record on the form based on the combo box value.

FIGURE 16.11

The Combo Box and List Box Wizards have exactly the same options.

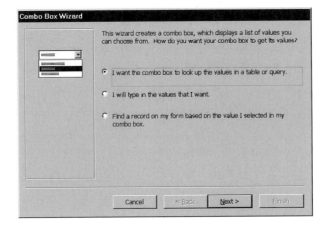

 TIP The last option (Find a record on my form based on the value I selected in my combo box) is useful for searches. This option creates a combo box containing data from the data source. The form displays the corresponding records, based on the selection in the combo box. For example, if the combo box contains the Cust_ID entries, the record shown matches the chosen Cust_ID entry.

Make a selection and click **Next**. The next screen that appears depends on the option you select. If you select the first option, you identify the table or query source on the next screen. If you select the second option, you are asked to enter the values. If you select the last option, you identify the field you want as the source for the box.

In Figure 16.12, the second option (where you enter the values) was selected and several State codes have been entered. With this option, you can size columns on this screen by placing your cursor at the end of a column and expanding or shrinking the column to the desired width. Because state abbreviations are small, it would make sense to shrink the column width.

After you complete the screen, click **Next**.

When a value is selected from the list, Access can either remember the value for later use or store the selected value in a field in your table. Remembering the value for later use retains the value while you are working in the form. When the form is closed, the value is removed. The value is not permanently stored as it would be in a table. The second option actually enables you to edit the field to make permanent changes to the underlying table. After you make your choice, click **Next**.

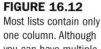

FIGURE 16.12
Most lists contain only one column. Although you can have multiple column lists, they are rare.

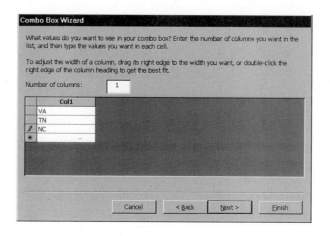

In the final step of the Wizard, you choose a label for the control; this is the label that appears in the form next to the control. After you enter the label, click **Finish**.

By default, combo boxes accept values that are not on the list. You can change this behavior by changing the Limit To List property to **Yes**. You can also set the AutoExpand feature to choose values based on one or two characters entered. For example, if you set AutoExpand to one character, when someone types **V**, it automatically expands to VA.

Adding Option Groups   Another control useful on data entry forms is the option group—a box that contains a list of items from which users can select the appropriate value. Suppose your customer contacts are usually Account Managers, Sales Reps, or Purchasing Agents. You can set up an option group with these three options, plus Other.

Once again, if you have a field on the form that currently contains the values you want to use in the option group, delete the field before you create the option group.

To add an option group to a form, select the Option Group icon on the Toolbox and draw the control where you want it on the form. The Option Group Wizard appears. The first step is to enter the labels for each option. In Figure 16.13, the labels Account Manager, Sales Rep, Purchasing Agent, and Other have been entered. After you have entered the labels, click **Next**.

At this point, you can choose a default value, or you can identify a default value after you complete the Wizard.

The next step is to assign a value to each option. The default is incremental numbers beginning with 1, which will work for the example. Click **Next**.

You have the choice of saving the option values for later use in the form or storing them in a field in your source table. If you choose to save the value, Access remembers the value only while the form is active. When the form is closed, the value is removed. The value is not permanently stored. If you decide to store the value in a field, the number replaces the data in that field. In other words, if the first record has the position listed as Account Manager, it now displays the number 1 to correspond to the option box number.

FIGURE 16.13
Type the values that
you want displayed in
the option group.

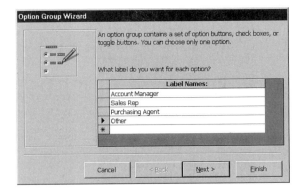

CAUTION

The value of an option group can be only a number, not text. If you want to be able to edit the field from the form, a number replaces the text in the table field (see Figure 16.14). If you want text to appear in the field instead, you can create a separate table for the field data (for example, called Positions), and then make the Position field in the Customer table a Lookup field that looks up data in the Position table. This also gives you an accurate list that corresponds to each option value.

The next screen is where you can format the Option Box. Choose from option buttons, check boxes, or toggle buttons for each of the items that are listed in the Option Box. The box itself can appear etched, flat, shadowed, sunken, or raised. Use the Sample on the left side of the screen to preview the appearance of the your choices. After you've made your selections, click **Next**.

The final step of the Wizard is to add a caption to label the Option Box, and then click **Finish**. Figure 16.14 shows the form (in the Form View) and the underlying main data source, the Customers table.

Checking Tab Order and Record Navigation   Because you have added, deleted, and moved fields around, you will want to check the *tab order* of your form (the order in which the focus goes from field to field as the user presses the Tab key). In data entry, the tab order needs to make sense and the default tab order is the order in which the fields were added to the form. To view the current tab order, choose **View**, **Tab Order**. To change the order, select the field to change and drag it to the new location. When you have the fields in the desired order, click **OK**.

Forms have built-in navigation buttons on the bottom, but users unfamiliar with Access might not understand how they work. You can create larger navigation buttons to facilitate data entry. Typically, these types of buttons are placed in either the Form Header or Form Footer section. Before you add a navigation button, it might be necessary to expand the section. Position the mouse pointer at the bottom of the gray section banner. The pointer changes into a plus sign with arrows pointing up and down. Drag down about an inch to expand the section area.

Part

III

Ch

16

FIGURE 16.14
The form contains an option box, a combo box, and a subform.

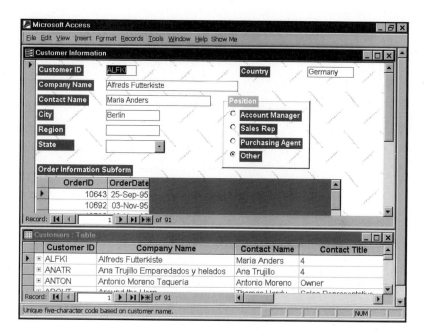

Click the **Command Button** icon on the Toolbox and click in the section area; the Command Button Wizard appears. With the Record Navigation category selected, choose the type of command you want for the button, such as Goto Previous Record, and click **Next**. You have the option of displaying text on the button or selecting a picture. The pictures listed are related to the action you selected. So, if the action selected is Goto Previous Record, you then have a choice of triangles, arrows, or a hand pointing left. After you've picked what you want displayed on the button, click **Next**. In the next step, enter a name for the button and click **Finish**. Add other buttons (such as next record, deleting record, add record, and exit from the database) as necessary.

If you've added navigation buttons on the Form Header, you can change the properties of the form to conceal the default navigation buttons, hide the scrollbars, or the Minimize and Maximize buttons—change Navigation Buttons to No, Scrollbars to Neither, Record Selectors to No, Min Max Buttons to None. Figure 16.15 shows the finished form.

Changing the Action of Your Control Option   You do not have to just choose action options from the Command Button Wizard. You can potentially assign your own macro, expression, or code to every control on the form, with commands that execute on enter, on exit, on lost focus, on got focus, on click, on double-click, on mouse up, on mouse down, on mouse move, on key down, on key up, on key press, after update, and before update.

To change the action of a control, select the control in Design view. Right-click and choose **Properties** from the shortcut menu. Click the **Event** tab to view all the possible actions. In each of these fields, you can choose to assign a macro, build an expression, or develop code. For example, suppose you want the Delete button to verify whether the user really wants to delete the record. On the Event tab, you see [Event Procedure] for the On Click event. When you click in this property, an ellipsis (…) appears. Click the ellipsis to view the code, which controls the event. When you created the button, the Command Button Wizard generated the code. You can modify the code to prompt the user with an input box and perform only the other action (in this example, delete the record) if the response is **Yes**. Here is the necessary code:

```
Private Sub Delete_Click()
Dim Message, Title, Result, buttons
Message = "Are you sure you want to delete this record?"
Title = "Delete Check" 'This line sets the title
Buttons = vbYesNo 'This line sets the buttons that will appear
Result = MsgBox(Message, buttons, Title)
If Result = 6 Then '6 is the value assigned to Yes
     DoCmd.DoMenuItem acFormBar, acEditMenu, 8, , scMenuVer70
     DoCmd.DoMenuItem acFormbar, acEditMenu, 6, , acMenuVer70
Else If Result = 7 Then
     MsgBox ("The record was not deleted")
End If
EndSub
```

FIGURE 16.15

The form shown in Figure 16.14 now has navigation buttons.

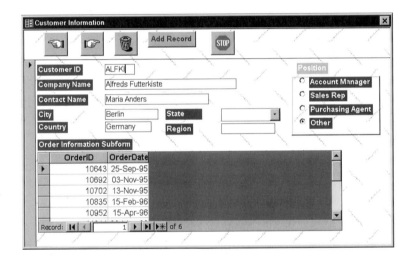

N O T E You can have as many events for controls as you like. You can have fields populate when focus is lost on a field (that is when the field is no longer active), reports can run on the click of a button, forms can open on the double-click of a button, and so on. Just choose the control that runs the action, choose the command (such as On Click or On Focus), and assign a macro or code. ■

Using Message Boxes Records are added when you move to the next record unless otherwise specified. One way to provide a confirmation to the user that the data has been added to the database is to display a message box when the last field loses focus. To do this, create a new macro with the macro action MsgBox that displays the message "Your record has been added." Save your macro and name it Messagebox. In Design view, select the last field to have data entered. On the Event tab in the Properties dialog box, click the **On Lost Focus** field and choose the macro **Messagebox**. Now, when a user moves from that field, the message box appears.

Using Form Modes   Forms can be opened in two modes. In the *Add mode*, the user does not see the other records but only a blank form for data entry. In the *Edit mode*, the user sees all entries and can also add and modify records. Depending on the situation, you can have the form open in the mode that suits your needs. If the form is to be opened from a switchboard, you can assign the mode in which the form opens. (A switchboard is Access's database navigation device. Switchboards are covered in detail in Chapter 9.)

▶ For additional information, **see** "Designing a Switchboard Form for Your Database," on **p. 244**.

Using Access in Multiuser Environments

The purpose of a database is to store related information in one location. Unlike Excel, Word, or PowerPoint, Access enables several users to access the same database simultaneously and make changes. In other words, Access is a multiuser environment.

The advantage of a multiuser environment is that many users can maintain one consistent set of data, and different users can retrieve and update the data from different locations. One problem with a multiuser environment is that other users are locked out of a record when one user is applying updates.

Understanding Record Locking

With several people updating the same record, locking can occur, causing data to be lost or corrupted. Because others could be using the same record as you, you can protect records by choosing a record-locking strategy. Record-locking gives one user exclusive rights to the record being edited. Three record-locking strategies are available:

- **No Locks.** As the name implies, no locks occur on the records. If two or more people are editing a record at the same time, Access informs them that another person has changed the record. You can then choose to overwrite the other user's changes, copy your changes to the Clipboard, or ignore your changes.

- **Edited Records.** This strategy locks all records being edited, preventing others from making changes.

- **All Records.** This strategy locks the records in the table or tables you are editing until you close the table or tables. Avoid this strategy unless you are the only person who will update records. If many people will be updating records, this strategy is unproductive, because users will often have to wait for records to be unlocked. Users might find themselves wasting time attempting to update records that cannot be updated.

To set the record-locking strategy for the open database, choose **Tools**, **Options**, and click the **Advanced** Tab.

If you use a record-locking strategy other than No Locks, Access provides symbols to help users know the record status. The symbols are displayed in the current record selector. A *forward arrow* indicates that the record is active but has not been edited. A *pencil* indicates that the record has been edited but not saved; when this symbol is displayed, others cannot edit

Part III

Ch 16

the record or view your changes. As soon as a record is saved, other users can see the changes. A *circle with a line through it* appears if another person locked the record. If you try to edit this record, you see a message indicating that the record is locked and who has it locked.

The Advanced tab in the Options dialog box provides four settings that help prevent locking conflicts:

- **Refresh Interval.** The number of seconds between which records are updated. You can choose a value between 0 and 32,766 seconds, with the default being 60 seconds. If you are doing extensive data entry and others need to see the data quickly, decrease this interval.

- **Update Retry Interval.** The number of milliseconds between the attempts Access makes to save a locked record. You can choose values between 0 and 1,000; the default is 250.

- **Number of Update Retries.** The number of times Access tries to save the locked record. The default is 2, but you can choose values between 0 and 10.

- **OBDC Refresh Interval.** If you are using ODBC, this sets the interval for refresh. As with the Refresh Interval option, you can choose anywhere between 0 and 32,766 seconds. The default is 1,500 seconds.

Because Access is a multiuser environment, you should open the database exclusively if you are going to make extensive changes to the database. This helps eliminate conflict errors and avoids confusing other users. Opening a database exclusively means only you can make changes; all other users will be opening the database in read-only mode.

TIP When updating objects, you should also update all dependent objects. If all dependent objects are not updated, discrepancies can result in the objects and data.

N O T E If you make changes to an object another person has open, they have to close that object before they will see the modifications. ▪

Understanding Client/Server Databases A client/server database is a database that is split between *client* (often referred to as the front-end part of the database) and a *server* (the back-end part of the database). A client/server database is actually two databases: One database stores all the tables (the back-end server) and the other database contains the queries, forms, reports, macros, and modules (the front-end client). The back-end database is usually located on a network. The front-end database is typically on individual workstations. The objects (queries, forms, and so forth) in the front-end database are linked to the back-end database (tables).

N O T E The terms *client* and *front-end* are synonymous here; just as are *server* and *back-end*. ▪

Here are some of the reasons for having a client/server database:

- **Size.** Having two databases decreases the size of files, which reduces the chance of data corruption.
- **Manageability.** If you have all the tables on the network, they can be backed up frequently, which wards off data loss.
- **Customization.** If several users want the same underlying information but want to do different things with it, they can have different front-end applications.
- **Security.** Linked tables cannot be modified; the records can be changed, but the design cannot. This prohibits front-end users from manipulating the design of the tables.

Part
III
Ch
16

To create a front-end/back-end application, you can either create two different databases (when you initially create the database) or use the Database Splitter (to convert an existing database).

Knowing When to Split a Database   Most beginning Access programmers create their databases as if they were building a skyscraper: It's one enormous structure with a bunch of interconnecting pieces, all or most of which need to be present for the thing to work as a whole. Unfortunately, databases aren't buildings, and sometimes it makes a lot of sense to separate like functions from their cousins to improve performance or maintainability.

It's easy to see, for example, how it is probably better to place several VBA procedures with similar functions (mathematical, string manipulation, database utility, and so forth) in one code module to make managing them less arduous. It's harder to see how *splitting* a perfectly good database into two can improve its performance. But it certainly can, given the right environment. Furthermore, the capability in Access to decouple the interface (forms, reports, queries) from the data store (tables) makes it an unusually versatile application, well suited to use in office networks and in prototyping.

When you create a database that includes tables and at least one of the interface elements mentioned previously, you create a *monolithic* database—one that can stand alone. For developing code and for learning, this is certainly the best structure for a database. It's extremely fast because all the data is stored on the local file system, and it's easy to manage because little or no possibility exists that someone else will alter any of the database while you're developing it.

But after a database is ready for release to the general public, a monolithic design begins to present problems. For example, Access can support up to 30 concurrent users. If you save an all-in-one database to a network server and tell the entire company where it is, you risk bringing your network to a screeching halt, depending on the network and the size of the company.

Every time someone on the office network loads your database, a significant portion is transported over the network lines—the data tables, the forms, everything. As users make changes to the data, only the changes are sent back (so they're really sharing a central data store). So, network traffic isn't really an issue at that point.

Understanding How a Split Database Works   A better answer exists for network-enabled databases. If you can detach the data store (the tables) from everything else, store the tables alone on the network, and let users install the interface components alone on their local hard drives, the network traffic becomes limited to data passing back and forth. In the case of the Northwind database, the data alone comprises about 800KB, but not all that is sent over the network. If the remote tables are linked in the distributed interfaces to the centralized data store, only the data requested is sent, limiting traffic somewhat.

As the number of users and the size of the database increase, the amount of traffic increases as well, but adding code to a local copy of the interface (new reports, forms, and so on) has almost no direct effect on network traffic. At this point, you'll probably need to use a dedicated database server running Microsoft SQL Server or a similar server-based database. These databases have the capability to process some queries themselves, without sending all the data across the network.

TIP   If the front-end application is the same for everyone, splitting the database might not be the best choice. If you change any of the objects other than the tables, you will have to update all the front-end databases individually. In such a case, you should use database replication (which is covered later in this chapter).

Creating a New Front-End/Back-End Application   To create a new front-end/back-end application, first create a new database with the tables that will be used for the front-end application. Then, create another new database, and link the tables from the first database.

To link tables:

1. Choose **File**, **Get External Data**, **Link Tables**.
2. Choose the database containing the tables and click **Link**.
3. A list of the available tables appears. Choose one, multiple, or all the tables to link.

You can now create queries, forms, reports, macros, and modules in the front-end database. You can create several front-end databases that all link to the same back-end database. Be sure you always link to the back-end database, because you cannot link to a linked table.

Using the Database Splitter to Split a Database   You can convert an existing database to a front-end/back-end application by using the Database Splitter.

CAUTION

Always back up your database before performing a split.

Choose **Tools**, **Database Utilities**, **Database Splitter**. The Database Splitter Wizard appears. A confirmation window appears, advising you to save a copy of your database first (which hopefully you have already done). Click **Split Database** to continue.

A standard Open/Save dialog box appears asking for the location and name of the back-end database. Access recommends using the same name except adding _be to identify that this database is the back-end. If you want to place the back-end (the data store) on a network, now would be a good time to save it to the fully qualified UNC network path where it will reside, so the links in the interface point to the correct path. After the file is saved, click **Split**. A message box appears indicating that the database has been split. The name of your existing database remains the same but you will notice that the tables are now linked. If you saved the back-end to a network path, you can now distribute the front-end (the interface) to anyone on your local network (assuming their permissions are appropriate), and the linked tables will point to the correct data source.

Managing Database Replication

Another way to take advantage of a multiuser environment is through replication. Database replication consists of a design master database and replica database(s). If not everyone can get to the main database, you can create replica sets of the master database. When you synchronize, changes between the master and the replica sets are applied to all the databases.

A few changes occur to a database when it is replicated. Three additional fields are added to each table:

- s_GUID is a unique identifier for each record.
- s_Lineage is a binary field that stores information about changes to each record.
- s_Generation stores information about groups of changes.

Several tables might also be added to the database. If a conflict occurs during replication, MsysSidetables is added, containing information regarding the conflicts. MsysErrors contains information regarding where and why errors occurred during synchronization. It identifies the table, record, and replica affected and states the last change to the record, the type of operation that failed, and the reason for the failure. MsysSchemaProb is created if an error occurs while updating the design of a replica. MsysExchangeLog stores information about the synchronizations.

These tables are system tables, which do not have to be viewable. To change whether the tables are viewable, choose **Tools**, **Options** and use the Show System Objects option on the View tab.

TIP

Changes occur to any AutoNumber fields in a replicated database. AutoNumber fields in existing records do not change, but AutoNumber values for inserted records are random. If you have any applications that rely on incremental numbers, change the AutoNumber field to a Date/Time field before replicating.

You can use Briefcase replication, replication from the Tools menu, or the Microsoft Replication Manager. The Microsoft Replication Manager is available only if you have Office 2000, Developer Edition.

Briefcase replication involves dragging a database from a shared folder onto My Briefcase in Windows Explorer. When you do this, the database is converted to a design master and a replica is created in My Briefcase. You're most likely to use Briefcase replication when you are moving between a laptop and a desktop computer. You can have the same database in both places, can make changes to both, and can synchronize these changes. To synchronize the databases, click the **My Briefcase** icon and then click the database file. Select **Update Selection** and then **Update**.

> **N O T E** If you do not have Briefcase installed, click the Windows **Start** button and choose **Settings**. Click **Control Panel**, click **Add/Remove Programs**, and double-click **Accessories** on the Windows Setup tab. To install Briefcase replication, run the Access Setup program. ■

To create a replica, choose **Tools, Replication, Create Replica**. If you have the database open, Access tells you it is going to close the database and convert it to the design master. It also prompts you to make a backup copy of the database before replicating. This is recommended—if you do not like what the replication does to your database, you can delete it and use the backup copy.

The next dialog box prompts you for a location for the new replica. Choose a location and name and click **OK**. All the objects in the design master database now show they are replicated. The circle icons (with bidirectional arrows) next to the objects indicate replicated objects.

Changes to the design can be made only to the design master, but changes to the records in tables can be made to the replicas and the design master. For changes to be applied to all databases, you must synchronize the databases.

To synchronize, choose **Tools, Replication, Synchronize Now**. Access asks you which database to synchronize with. If you have several replicas, you will have to repeat this step for each one. On this screen, you can also choose to switch the design master. If there are no conflicts, you get a message box indicating the synchronization is complete. If there are conflicts, a message indicates that you need to resolve the conflicts. You can choose to do so now or later. If you do not resolve the conflicts, this message occurs every time any of the databases is opened. When you resolve the conflicts, a list appears with the conflicting records of each table, so you can choose which table's record to accept.

If you have *Microsoft Access Developer's Edition*, you can use the Replication Manager. This provides a visual interface for making changes to the replication set as well as scheduling synchronization.

 TIP Any objects you add to the design master can be local or replicable. If you do not want the objects to replicate to other databases, make them local. By choosing **View**, **Properties** on an object, you can choose whether the object is replicable.

If the design master becomes damaged or deleted, you can make a new design master from one of the replicas. Open the replica you want to use for the design master and choose **Tools**, **Replication**, **Synchronize Now**. Select the replica in the list and click **OK**. Repeat this process for each remaining replica in the set. Then, choose **Tools**, **Replication**, **Recover Design Master**.

You can remove a replica by deleting it in Windows Explorer.

Customizing Views for Each User

You can specify which views a user can have. As mentioned earlier, you can have a form open in either Add or Edit mode. You can also limit whether a user can switch among Datasheet, Design, or Form views. Limiting views is useful when you want users to be able to see only certain forms or enter data on certain forms.

Choosing which views are allowed can be done in several places. One place is in Properties of the form. Alternatively, if you are opening a form by using a macro, you can specify in the macro the view in which the form is opened. Through Visual Basic commands, you can use the ViewsAllowed command.

Another way to customize views is by using the Workgroup Administrator. If users belong to a workgroup, you can set permissions for each user. Users' permissions will not determine the views they can see but will limit the type of changes they can make. User and Group accounts and permissions are found under **Tools**, **Security**.

You can use Visual Basic along with permissions to change views for users. The code looks at users to determine which group they belong to. You can then use Case...Select statements or If...Then statements to determine how a form is opened. This code can be assigned to a button on the switchboard so that pressing a button opens the form in a predetermined view. ●

CHAPTER 17

Managing Office Programmability

by Daryl Lucas

More and more organizations are coming to rely on Microsoft Office programmability for business-critical functions. After all, no application works exactly the way you want it to right out of the box, including the user interface. Surely you have found yourself writing the same kind of document over and over and wanted to automate its monotony, at least to some degree. Or, perhaps you have built up databases of information in all kinds of sources (from Access tables to mainframe stores) that end users—whether employees, customers, or business partners—want and need to see in human-readable forms. Or, perhaps you need PowerPoint to do something it doesn't normally do with a point and a click, but can be made to do with a little bit of coaxing.

Welcome to the world of Office programming.

Understanding Office Programmability

You cannot use Office for long without bumping into its programmability—macro viruses have made sure of that. But even apart from that infamy, Office programmability is hard to miss. Right-click over a toolbar, and it's there (Customize). Open a document from someone you once knew, and it might be there (Enable Macros? What difference does it make?). Almost every Office feature relates in some way to its built-in capability to be programmed.

Leveraging Office Through Programmability

Even if you, yourself, do not need to program Office, just about every organization does. It is also likely that your co-workers, boss, friends, spouse, and other users will, too. Sooner or later, they will ask, "How can I make Word do a mail merge with the contact info in Outlook?" or, "How can I make the Save As command default to a different filename?" They ask because they know that Office is programmable.

This means much more than it used to, though. In the early days (the 1980s), *application programmability* meant *keyboard playback.* The popular term, *macro,* was not a synonym for *program.* Those days are over. If you still think of application programmability as macro recording, forget it. This is not your father's Microsoft Office.

With the release of Office 2000, every application in the suite fully supports the most powerful and ubiquitous application programming language ever pressed into widespread use—Visual Basic for Applications (VBA). This is a language with few limits.

The mildly curious will therefore find more than just a Macros command on every Tools menu—much more. Even a small bit of Office programming opens two key doors:

■ Extend the functionality of individual applications. You can make simple tools do very power things.

■ Integrate disparate applications and the data they contain.

Extending applications means making the applications do more of what you want them to do, and making them do it better, faster, and more accurately. For example,

■ From Word, create a report for a customer based on data stored in a corporate database. Produce a PowerPoint presentation and a Word document that includes an Excel chart.

■ From Excel, publish a set of documents on the corporate intranet that displays monthly sales data in a chart that employees can manipulate and display as they like.

■ Create an Access database front end that works directly with data stored in an Oracle database.

Integrating applications means sharing data among applications with minimal effort, using data from one in another, and using the features of one application to do work in another.

Understanding COM, the Heart and Soul of Office

Many years ago, Microsoft tried to get the world excited about Object Linking and Embedding (OLE). Forget what OLE meant at the time—what matters is that many people ignored this attempt to "enhance" their work because it was slow, made their files very large, had lots of problems, and served little use. But something special happened along the way to perfecting this stillborn technology: programs discovered one another. The language used to let programs link or embed turned into a standard way for them to communicate with one another and share one another's data. It also turned into a way for programs to break their functionality into smaller pieces—the "object" part of the ill-fated OLE term.

Microsoft's further work on this technology went way beyond OLE's original goals and eventually came under the umbrella term Component Object Model (COM). You can get along in life without knowing much about the inner workings of COM, but if you are going to manage Office programmability, you need at least to get acquainted with it. COM lies at the center of everything you do with Office. Windows is built on it, all of Microsoft's Windows applications are built on it, and all of Office's functionality requires it.

Think of it this way: Office is a collection of applications. Each application is itself a collection of mini-applications. And each mini-application is itself a collection of micro-applications. If you drill all the way down to the smallest level, you will eventually stop at the tiniest application of all and not be able to drill any further. But what you will have is a huge collection—a huge web, if you will—of interconnected pieces, each one an application in itself.

More to the point, however, is the fact that they all speak the same language. Each one can tell the others what it can do and will let the others give it orders. Each and every piece can ask for services from the others, provide services to the others, and participate in work that the others do. This is part of their agreement to be COM players.

It is this COM-based agreement that makes Office programmable. At the highest level, Office tells the outside world what it can do and lets the outside world give it orders. By going through Office, the outside world can use the services of the pieces inside Office.

We call the pieces *component objects*, or simply *objects*.

Understanding Office's Object Models

Everything in Office is an object. Everything you program involves objects.

The most important objects in Office are the applications themselves. For example, Microsoft Access, the application, is an object called `Access`, with at least one property, the `Application` object. In VBA code, you refer to it in the following way:

```
Access.Application
```

You can think of this as an address in reverse, in the form of State, City. Access is the larger location; Application is the specific place where Access and all its kids live. If you want to meet the Access objects, you first must travel to `Access.Application`. The same is true of all of the Office applications.

This implies that you will find many more smaller, local objects inside `Access.Application`, and this is exactly what you do find. `Access.Application` is a lot like the State of Access, with smaller municipalities, streets, and avenues all within its borders—a land of places to visit and things to do.

In other words, every object has a place in a hierarchy of objects. Figure 17.1 shows a very simple object model diagram depicting the Access `Application` object and its relationship to the many objects that live inside it (there are too many to show all at once). Figure 17.2 shows a much simpler object model, Forms 2.0. The VBA Forms object model describes the UserForms that provide the user interface for VBA solutions. The diagram lets you see how the objects in the model are organized.

FIGURE 17.1

The Access `Application` object holds so many objects that you need a very large diagram to show them all at once.

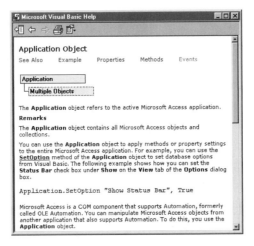

FIGURE 17.2

The Forms 2.0 object model is just one of the many object models available to Office 2000 developers.

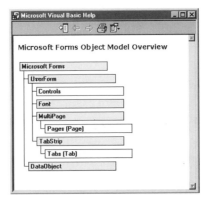

Office has many other object hierarchies as well. Even VBA itself has an object model all its own. See Figure 17.3 for the VBA map.

FIGURE 17.3

VBA is available to Office users through the Visual Basic Editor, as shown in this object model diagram.

As implied by the size of the `Access.Application` object model, by far the most significant objects in Office 2000 are the applications themselves. In all Office applications, you can often use the `Application` object to gain access to other object models, including the Visual Basic Editor, but also including most of the application's specific features. Figure 17.4 shows how the `Word.Application` object opens the door to the `ActiveDocument`—one of Word's most important objects.

FIGURE 17.4

Each Office *Application* object, like that in Word, serves as a gateway to the application's entire feature set.

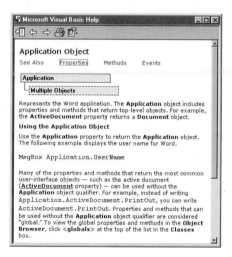

Not all the object models available to you require entry through an `Application` object. Many other object models exist independently of the `Application` object or have global scope and can be accessed outside of it, even though they are contained inside the application. Table 17.1 shows some of the most important object hierarchies you will come across.

Part
III
Ch
17

Table 17.1 Important Object Models in Office 2000

Object	Type Library	Filename
CommandBars	Office	mso9.dll
Scripts	Office	mso9.dll
FileSearch	Office	mso9.dll
Assistant	Office	mso9.dll
COM Add-ins	Office	mso9.dll
Workbooks	Excel 9.0	excel.exe
Documents	Word 9.0	winword.exe
Presentations	PowerPoint 9.0	powerpnt.exe
CurrentProject	Access 9.0	msaccess.exe
ADO	ADO 2.1	msado15.dll
ADOX	ADO 2.1 for DDL and Security	msadox.dll
JRO	Jet and Replication Objects 2.1	msjro.dll
VBA	Visual Basic for Applications 6.0	vbe6.dll
FileSystemObject	Windows Scripting Host	scrrun.dll

N O T E The Windows Scripting Host is not included with Office, but it is an important object model and one with which you will want to become familiar. See **http://msdn. microsoft.com/scripting/** for more information. ■

If you are going to take advantage of Office programmability, you need to learn Office's object models. You can get more information on all of these object models in the VBA Help file. From the Visual Basic Editor, press **F1**, or click **Help**, **Microsoft Visual Basic Help** from the menu. Display the Answer Wizard tab, type in the object name, and then click **Search**. You can also navigate the object models by using the Object Browser (**F2** in the Visual Basic Editor). Finally, you can also see object model diagrams for all the Office applications and their various parts in the *Microsoft Office 2000/Visual Basic Programmer's Guide*.

Understanding VBA's Role in Office

VBA is the Office 2000 programming language, but what exactly is it? What is its relationship to the various applications? And how is it related to Visual Basic, the development tool?

Understanding the Architecture VBA is much more than a programming language; it is a COM component—specifically, a COM server, a type library available to COM clients. That is what makes it available to the Office applications—Word, Excel, PowerPoint, Access, Outlook, and FrontPage *host* VBA.

Another way of saying this is that by itself, VBA can do nothing but inside an Office application, it can do plenty. What it needs is a COM-compliant host that knows what to do with it. In Office 2000, all the applications act as VBA hosts. The host gets to specify what commands are available to you, the programmer, and what those commands can do. The host runs the VBA code.

You can see how this works in the Visual Basic Editor (VBE). In any Office 2000 application, press **Alt+F11** (or click **Tools, Macro, Visual Basic Editor**). In the VBE, choose **Tools, References** to see the list of available type libraries. Visual Basic for Applications will be at the top of the list. That is a programmatic way of referencing the VBA 6.0 type library. All Office VBA projects get a reference to this type library by default.

How does Visual Basic, the product, relate to all of this? Visual Basic also uses VBA, but it is an entirely different kind of host. It is a platform for creating hosts. There are some differences between Visual Basic's implementation of VBA and Office's implementation, but those differences get fewer and fewer each time Office comes out in a new version. In fact, Microsoft has stated in so many words that they want Office to be a development platform all its own, with the full power of a real-live programming environment such as VB.

▶ For more on this topic, **see** the section "Going the Extra Mile with Microsoft Office Developer," on **p. 471**, later in this chapter.

Extending Office with VBA Projects   Office 2000 hosts VBA code through two mechanisms. The first of these is the *VBA project*.

Whenever you create a VBA solution in Office 2000, you store the code in a project. The exact definition of a project differs from application to application, but, in general, a project corresponds to an application file or template—that is, a file specific to that application. Table 17.2 lists the Office 2000 applications and the application files that can hold VBA project code.

Table 17.2   Where Office 2000 Applications Store VBA Project Code

Word	Documents, `Normal.dot`, other templates (`*.dot` files), add-ins (`*.wll` files)
Excel	Workbooks, `Personal.xls`, other templates (`*.xlt` files), add-ins (`*.xla` files)
PowerPoint	Presentations, templates (`*.ppt` files), add-ins (`*.ppa` files)
Outlook	`Vbaproject.otm`
Access	Databases
FrontPage	Microsoft `FrontPage.fpm`

Inside every project is a set of *modules*. In general, all Office project files can store VBA code in five kinds of modules:

- Standard Modules
- Class Modules
- Document Modules
- UserForms (Microsoft Forms)
- ActiveX Designers

Each Office application has its own implementation of this model. Every Word project, and only Word, for example, has a `ThisDocument` object that can store VBA code. Every Excel project has a `ThisWorkbook` object. Rather than a `ThisDatabase` object, Access databases have `Form_<name>` document objects and `Report_<name>` document objects. (Access does not have a UserForm command on its Insert menu, but you can import UserForms that you created in other Office applications. They show up in the Access VBE as Forms.)

Figure 17.5 shows how all of this is organized and displayed in the Visual Basic Editor.

FIGURE 17.5

An Office 2000 project file stores all its code in modules, including these Access Forms and Reports, which are Document Modules.

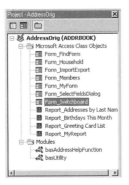

The final piece of the VBA project is the code inside every module, which is usually divided into two sections: *declarations* and *procedures*. You write all commands that apply to the entire module in the declarations section, and you place all procedures in the code section. A procedure is simply a Sub or a Function—the most basic unit of executable code. Function procedures always return a value; Sub procedures do not.

In summary, you write and store all code, forms, and modules in project files, which in most cases correspond to templates, documents, presentations, workbooks, and database files (Outlook and FrontPage are the two exceptions). You use the Visual Basic Editor to create, edit, and manage all code.

Extending Office with Add-Ins   The second mechanism you can use to extend Office 2000 is *add-ins*. Add-ins promise to be a significant part of your programmability program, so they deserve a thorough treatment. But Office's whole add-in model has changed in a big way, so a more detailed discussion appears in the "COM Add-Ins" section later in this chapter.

For now, suffice it to say that Office 2000 lets you extend its functionality with external files that can be loaded invisibly, without intervention from the user and separately from the application's project files. Previous versions of Office supported this kind of extensibility, but with much less flexibility. Word, Excel, PowerPoint, Access, and Outlook all had their own idea of what an add-in was, how it should be created, and how it could be loaded. Office 2000 replaces them all that with one consistent add-in model called *COM add-ins*.

Taking Advantage of Office 2000's Developer Features

The user interfaceof Office 2000 closely resembles that of Office 97; some of the most significant changes involve its programming environment. What has changed?

Anyone who programs Office has a lot to digest with this new version. The list of new features is not long, but the changes go a lot deeper than a simple list would indicate. Just the fact that every major Office application—Access, Excel, FrontPage, Outlook, PowerPoint, and Word—now works essentially the same way, programmatically speaking, takes some getting used to. Office 2000 is, in most ways, the fulfillment of Microsoft's old promise of a universal programming language. With the lone exception of Outlook's need for VBScript in its Forms Designer, VBA now handles all programming tasks for all the Office applications.

In short, VBA now permeates the entire suite. What was left of application-specific programming languages has all but disappeared. In its place is a single language usable and accessible to all Office applications equally.

That short, potent list of new features looks like the following:

- Visual Basic for Applications 6.0
- COM Add-Ins
- The Visual Basic Editor
- Microsoft Script Editor
- Office Web Components
- New Events
- VBA in Outlook
- Digital signing of VBA code

For more information on general enhancements to Office programming, see "What's New for Microsoft Office Developers" in Visual Basic Help.

Programming for Real with VBA 6.0

Office 97 shipped with VBA 5.0, but not every application used it, nor did the VBA-aware applications use it consistently. Office 2000, which includes VBA 6.0, gets more power from this new version of the language and lets all the applications access it. The biggest news is that the general procedure for creating VBA solutions is the same for all applications, even though each application has its own special implementation as well.

Significant new features in the language include the following:

- Support for the Implements keyword
- Enumerated constants
- More ActiveX controls

Developing Office-Wide Solutions with COM Add-Ins

COM add-ins are COM components that support the IDTExtensibility2 interface and work specifically to extend the functionality of Office 2000 applications. They fill the same role that Word templates, Excel add-ins, and PowerPoint add-ins have filled in the past, but with a different interface to the application. In Word 97, for example, you might develop your solution code in a template, and then distribute the template to users. Users would place the template in the Startup folder, a Templates folder, or some other location. In PowerPoint, you would create your solution in a PowerPoint presentation template, and then save it as an add-in. Users would load the add-in through the Tools menu. Excel had a slightly different model as well.

COM add-ins change all that. Instead of using a template for Word and an add-in for PowerPoint, you use a DLL for both, and both install the same way. They do not take away your ability to use the old approach; they just add a new method.

Anyone who is unfamiliar with COM components or with their development might ask, "Why this approach?" COM add-ins have several advantages over their predecessors:

- **Consistency of installation.** In all previous versions of Office, each application had its own add-in model. You had to use one way of installing add-ins for Word, another for Excel, and still another for PowerPoint. Some methods were relatively easy, others were relatively hard, but none could be called consistent with the others. By contrast, COM add-ins all install the same way. If you know how to create or install a COM add-in, you know how to extend every application in the Office suite.

- **Transparency to the user.** If the programmer creates and distributes the add-in properly, the user might never see it. Many users will not even have to load it.

- **Suitewide use.** You do not have to make a COM add-in work with all Office applications, but you can. You can code the add-in in such way that it can be loaded and used by Word, Excel, Access, Outlook, FrontPage, and PowerPoint. That was never possible before. You no longer have to develop separate add-ins for each application.

- **Ability to be machine-specific or user-specific.** Depending on where you register the add-in, you can make it available to all users or only to specific users.

Using COM Add-Ins To use COM add-ins, two things have to happen:

1. Someone has to create the add-in.
2. Someone has to install the add-in on a user's system.

   You might also need to follow a third step:

3. Someone has to load the add-in in the Office application.

Whether step 3 is necessary depends on how the add-in is installed. Steps 1 and 2 make it available to the application, but do not necessarily load it.

Creating the Add-In COM add-ins must support the IDTExtensibility2 interface, which is included in the Microsoft Add-In Designer type library. This type library is shipped with Office 2000 and is stored in `msaddndr.dll`, which is installed with other "designer" DLLs in `C:\Program Files\Common Files\designer` by default. (You can create COM add-ins in any programming language that supports COM—Visual Basic 5.0 or later, Visual C++, Delphi, Visual J++, and many other products. The news for Office developers is that you can now create COM components in Microsoft Office Developer as well.) To add support for the IDTExtensibility2 interface, simply add a reference to the Microsoft Add-In Designer.

Installing the Component   This involves copying the DLL to the user's system, registering it as an ActiveX control, and registering it as an Office add-in. The programmer who creates the add-in will have to create a Setup to handle this. Users of MOD can use the Package and Deployment Wizard to create this Setup.

To register the DLL as an Office add-in, add it to one of the two Registry keys shown in Table 17.3, depending on whether you want it to be available to all users or just the current user. All entries are the same except for the root level. If you use the MOD Package and Deployment Wizard to handle the Setup, the Wizard will make these entries for you.

Part
III

Ch
17

Table 17.3   Registry Keys You Must Add to *HKLM | HKCU\Software\ Microsoft\Office\<appname>\Addins\<add-in object.class>* to Register a COM Add-In

Key	Value Type	Valid Values	Explanation
FriendlyName	String (REG_SZ)	Any null-terminated string	"Invoice Creator."
Description	String (REG_SZ)	Any null-terminated string	"Creates new invoices."
LoadBehavior	Long integer (DWORD)	0	Unloaded.
		2	Load at startup after user enables.
		3	Load at startup.
		8	Load on demand.
		9	Same as 8, but COM Add-Ins dialog box shows load status.
		16	Load at next startup, and then load on demand.

The two keys are identical except for the root level. Add-ins available for use by all users are registered in HKEY_LOCAL_MACHINE; add-ins available only to one user are registered in HKEY_CURRENT_USER.

N O T E   If a component does not appear on the list, be sure it has been added to the Registry. ■

Loading the Add-In   After the add-in is installed and properly registered on the system, you load it in the Office application. All Office 2000 applications support the use of COM add-ins. To load a COM add-in, use the COM Add-Ins dialog box (see Figure 17.6).

FIGURE 17.6
You can manage COM add-ins from the COM Add-Ins dialog box.

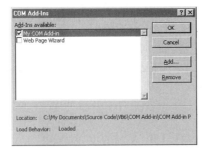

Because this command does not appear on any menus or toolbars by default, you will need to add it. Use the **Tools**, **Customize** command to place it wherever you prefer; it is listed in the **Tools** category of **Commands** in the Customize dialog box (see Figure 17.7).

FIGURE 17.7
Adding the COM Add-Ins dialog box is a simple matter of adding it to a menu, toolbar, or keyboard shortcut.

Writing Office-Wide Code: COM Add-Ins' Advantage   COM add-ins have one very big advantage over earlier add-in models: They can be loaded and used by any Office application (if you code carefully enough). This won't automatically happen—you have to be careful not to use application-specific code. But at least this is possible. With previous versions of Office, it was impossible—there was no way to load a Word template in PowerPoint, for example. VBA solutions in previous versions were tied inextricably to the application in which they were developed, even if the code was application-neutral.

Example: `Application.Run "MacroName"` would be the same syntactically in Word and Excel, but you could not load the template across applications.

Steering Clear of the Disadvantages   COM add-ins do not make sense in all situations because they have more complexity. In most cases, they have two downsides:

■ **More work.** It's harder to write and often harder to distribute a COM add-in than simply to copy a template to a user's machine. Writing a COM add-in requires a tool that can create COM components. Even in its most basic form, that's more involved than simply typing code into a Word template's code module. A COM add-in also has to be distributed with a Setup program that will register it properly (or it has be registered manually). While neither of these requirements is fatal, both do make your list of things to do longer.

■ **More can go wrong with installation.** If you do not create an appropriate Setup (or register the add-in with regsvr32), it simply will not work. This can be a problem if you do not have a good setup tool. It can also cause problems in networked environments that have locked-down workstation registries. At the very least, you have to test installation on a variety of systems before you can be sure that your add-in setup is going to work.

Creating Solutions with the Visual Basic Editor

You now use the VBE to write and edit VBA code in all applications (see Figure 17.8). Press **Alt+F11** to open the VBE from any application or to toggle between the VBE and its host. Closing the host closes the VBE as well.

Part III

Ch 17

Project   Declarations area   Procedure

FIGURE 17.8
All office 200 applications use the Visual Basic Editor for code writing and editing. The project/module/procedure/declarations/area model is readily visible in this example from Access.

Module

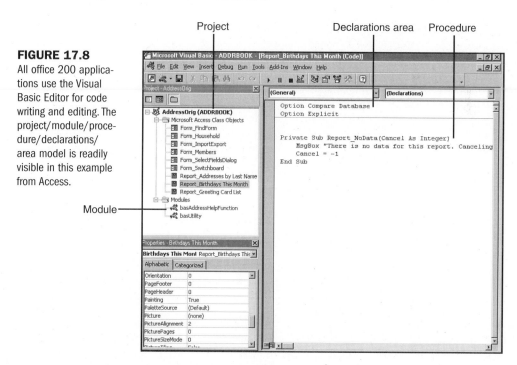

Putting Code in the Right Place   Every VBA solution you code has four organizational units: the project itself, modules, procedures, and a declarations area. If you understand what each unit is, making your way around the Visual Basic Editor will be easy. The following definitions explain how each fits into the whole.

- **Project.** The basic storage unit for VBA code. In Word, projects include documents and templates. In Excel, projects include workbooks and templates. In Access, projects include databases. In PowerPoint, projects include presentations.

- **Module.** A storage location for VBA code. There are five kinds of modules: Standard Modules, Class Modules, Document Modules, ActiveX Designers, and Microsoft Forms. You code custom objects in Class Modules. You code most other kinds of code in Standard Modules.

- **Procedure.** A Sub or Function block. Functions return a value; Subs do not.

- **Declarations Area.** The part of a code module before any procedures. Module-level variable and constant declarations always go in the Declarations Area.

Note that you can have more than one VBE open at once, one for each host. Thus, if you have Word, PowerPoint, and Access all open at once, you can also have the VBE hosted by each application all open at the same time. But only one VBE will serve each host at any one time.

Speeding Your Work with Keyboard Shortcuts Some of the work you do in the VBE will reoccur time and time again. To help streamline your use of often-used features, Microsoft has provided keyboard shortcuts for each of them. Table 17.4 lists them.

Table 17.4	Keyboard Shortcuts in the Visual Basic Editor
Alt+F11	Toggle between application and VBE
F1	Help
F2	Open the Object Browser
F3	Find Next
F4	Open Properties Window
F5	Run Macro
F7	View Code
F8	Step Into
Shift+F7	View object
Ctrl+S	Save project

Navigating the Object Browser A key component of the VBE is the Object Browser.

To see all the objects available to your VBA code, press **F2**. This will open the Object Browser (see Figure 17.9). The Object Browser lets you navigate the entire object model of all the libraries available to your project. If you want to learn about the objects you can program, spend some time with the Object Browser.

By default, the Object Browser lists all objects in all libraries, but you can also filter the list by library or by search term. Figure 17.10 shows how the list appears when you select a specific library (in this case, the Office library) in the Project/Library drop-down list.

FIGURE 17.9
By selecting a specific object in the Project/Library drop-down, you can view a subset of the objects available to your project, such as the Office library.

FIGURE 17.10
Sometimes, you might want to limit the Object Browser's display of objects to a specific type library.

To search for a particular term, type the term in the Search drop-down box and click the **Search** button. A list of objects that include that term will be listed in the Search Results list box (see Figure 17.11).

For an overview of VBA in Office 2000, see "Office 2000 and Visual Basic for Applications" in the Office Resource Kit.

Sharing Data with Office Web Components

Office Web Components are ActiveX controls that you can place in HTML pages to access Excel spreadsheet and Access database data. Because they are ActiveX controls, you can host them in any client that supports ActiveX controls—most notably Internet Explorer 4.01 or later and Visual Basic forms.

Part

III

Ch

17

FIGURE 17.11
Searching for a particular keyword, object name, method, constant, or property can help you locate the item in the haystack of type libraries.

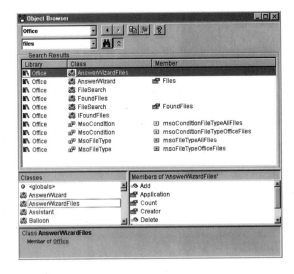

The Office Web Component object models are extensive, so programming them gives you a lot of power. The Msowcvba.chm Help file gives extensive instructions on using them. This file is installed in the \Office\<LanguageID> folder by default (\Office\1033 for U.S. English). You will find links to Help files for each Web Component in this topic; see Table 17.5 for a list of the components and their Help files.

Table 17.5   The Office Web Components

Component	Associated Help File
Spreadsheet Component	Msowcdss.chm
PivotTable List	Msowcdpl.chm
Chart Workspace	Msowcdch.chm
Data Source Control	Msowcrdp.chm

Office Web Components have several significant advantages and disadvantages.

Leveraging Web Components' Advantages   Office Web Components have the following advantages:

- **Interactivity.** Office Web Components give you full access to the data to which they are bound. Users can view, manipulate, and even change the data right from the host.

- **Scriptability.** You can write VBScript and program against the Component's object model the same way you can program any other COM server. This is ideal on an intranet.

- **Distribution.** Users do not have to have Excel or Access installed to use Web Components. Each component is fully functional all by itself. This is great for office intranets that need to get the data out to the users but do not want to roll out the Office upgrade all at once. As soon as you buy the licenses, you can make this data available to end users, even if they do not yet have Office 2000.

Avoiding Web Components' Disadvantages   Office Web Components have the following disadvantages:

- **Licensing.** Even though they are called *Web* Components, they are *not* suitable for the World Wide Web. Users of Web Components *must* have an Office 2000 license. They do not have to have the host application actually installed on their machines, but you cannot deploy Web Components to any users who do not have an Office license. This makes them useful only on corporate intranets and in certain standalone VB applications.

- **Browser dependence.** Only Internet Explorer hosts ActiveX components, so if you are not an IE shop, you basically cannot use the Web browser as the host. You can still distribute a Visual Basic application to host them, but you will have to create the application.

▶ For more information on any of these new technologies, **see** "What's New for Microsoft Office Developers" in Visual Basic Help.

Editing Scripts with the Microsoft Script Editor

Because XML/HTML is now a companion file format for Office 2000, and because some editions of Office 2000 now include FrontPage, all Office 2000 applications except Outlook include the Microsoft Script Editor (MSE). The MSE provides two main functions:

- Direct editing of HTML/XML tags and content in Web pages and Office documents
- Creation of scripting code in both VBScript and JavaScript

The MSE resembles the Visual Basic Editor in some ways, but it is tailored for editing Web pages and has more in common with Visual InterDev. In fact, you might think of the MSE as Visual InterDev Lite. You do not have to have access to a Web server to use MSE.

▶ For more information on using HTML/XML as a primary file format, **see** "Managing HTML/XML As Your Primary File Format," on **p. 867**.

To launch the Microsoft Script Editor from any application (but Outlook), press **Alt+Shift+F11** (see Figure 17.12) or click **Tools**, **Macro**, **Microsoft Script Editor**. The MSE is not installed by default, so you might be prompted to install it.

Coding Against New Events

New Events have found their way into all the Office applications and several companion object models. In Office 97, Excel had the lion's share of useful Events. Word, PowerPoint, and FrontPage now share the riches. In addition, all Events fire at the application level, to give the programmer a consistent way of accessing them. Even Document events are available from the Application object.

The CommandBar (and its collection) was introduced in Office 97, but it lacked one critical feature: Events. Office 2000 CommandBar objects have three new Events (see Table 17.6):

FIGURE 17.12
The Microsoft Script Editor lets you edit HTML/XML code and script.

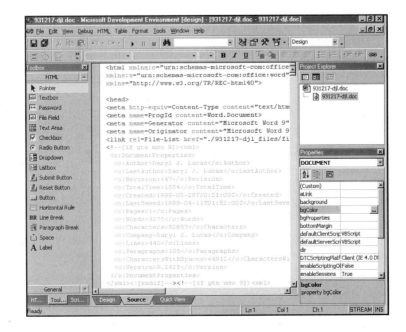

Table 17.6   New *CommandBar* Events

Object	Event
CommandBarButton	Click
CommandBarComboBox	Change
CommandBars (collection)	Update

Enhancing Security with Digital Signatures

Having a High security setting is a good way to protect against unwanted code, but it also forces you to dispense with unsigned code—*all* unsigned code, even your own. That's fine if you have a certificate to pass out to all your developers. But what if you do not? Or, what if you have a corporate certificate, but you do not want to use it on code that has not been released? Or, what if you are just one or two users who need to develop and use Office VBA solutions without having to answer a Security dialog box with the opening of every template and add-in?

You have three options:

- Buy a public certificate from a certificate authority such as VeriSign. This is the most secure solution, but it is also the most expensive.
- Use Windows NT Certificate Services to create certificates that your developers can use. This is a good option for secure networks in corporate settings where a network Administrator or a team leader can create certificates for use by a workgroup.

■ Use the Selfcert.exe tool to let developers self-certify their own code. This is the least secure solution, but it does let developers avoid the Security dialog box when opening their own code while also benefiting from a High security setting.

The Selfcert.exe tool ships with Office 2000, but it is not installed by default. To install the tool, run Office Setup, and then select **Office Tools**, **Digital Signature for VBA projects**, as shown in Figure 17.13. The file is on Office CD-ROM1 under \Pfiles\Msoffice\Office.

FIGURE 17.13
Install the Selfcert.exe tool to create your own digital signatures for VBA projects.

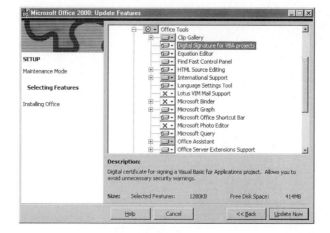

To use the Selfcert.exe tool, simply run it. You will be prompted to give your name (see Figure 17.14).

FIGURE 17.14
The Selfcert.exe tool lets you sign your own VBA code.

After you have created the certificate, you need to add it to your list of Trusted Sources. To do so, you need to have Internet Explorer 4.0 or later installed. If you do, add it to one of the VBA projects you have developed, and perform the following steps:

1. In the VBE, select the project you want to sign in the Project Explorer.
2. Click **Tools**, **Digital Signature**. The Digital Signature dialog box appears.
3. Click **Choose**. The Select Certificate dialog box appears.
4. Select the certificate you just created and click **OK** twice.

5. Save the project.

6. Open the project in the application. If this is a template file that loads on startup, you can close and restart the application instead. You will see a Security Warning dialog box (see Figure 17.15). To add yourself (actually, the certificate you just created) to the list of Trusted Sources, check the **Always trust macros form this source** check box, and then click **Enable Macros**.

FIGURE 17.15
The Security Warning dialog box lets you add a certificate to the list of Trusted Sources.

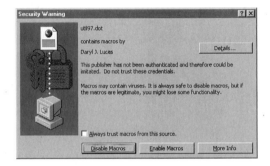

If you choose to do this, keep in mind that you will have to re-sign the project every time you change the code within it. (You do not need to re-sign it if you change other objects stored in it, such as CommandBar buttons.)

▶ To install your certificate into the Certificate Store and for other information on using digital certificates to sign VBA projects, **see** Chapter 38, "Maximizing Office 2000 Security," on **p. 981**.

Programming Word

Word 2000, like PowerPoint, has several new objects, properties, and methods, and can now fire many Events at the application level. Table 17.7 lists the new Events.

Table 17.7   Word Programming at a Glance

New Event	Description
Where code is stored	Documents, Normal.dot, other templates (*.dot files), Word add-ins (*.wll files)
Application Events	DocumentBeforeClose, DocumentBeforePrint, DocumentBeforeSave, DocumentOpen, NewDocument, WindowActivate, WindowBeforeDoubleClick, WindowBeforeRightClick, WindowDeactivate, WindowSelectionChange
Document Events	New, Open, Close

The list of new objects, properties, and methods is much too long to include here. For more information on these new language elements and other new features in Word's implementation of VBA, see "What's New for Microsoft Word 2000 Developers" in Word Visual Basic Help (see Figure 17.16). In Word, press **Alt+F11**, and then press **F1**, display the Answer Wizard, and search on the topic title.

FIGURE 17.16
The Word VBA Help file is loaded with detailed information on improvements to Word language elements.

For more information on Word VBA programming in general, see "Frequently Asked Visual Basic Questions" in Word Visual Basic Help.

Programming Excel

The Excel 2000 object model has seen many changes and improvements over Excel 97. Some of the more significant changes include the following:

- **ADO (the ADODB object model).** This is now the preferred method for all data access in Excel.

- **Unit labels for charts.** In code, you can assign labels to individual data units in charts.

- **Office Web Components.** Excel components are the stars of this show, with the PivotTable List control, the Chart Workspace control, and the Spreadsheet control providing three out of the four.

As in Word 2000, Excel 2000 supports all Excel 97 VBA language elements by including discontinued elements as hidden members (see Table 17.8).

Table 17.8 Excel 2000 Programming at a Glance

Event	Object
Where code is stored	Workbooks, `Personal.xls`, other templates (`*.xlt` files), Excel add-ins (`*.xla` files)
Workbook Events	`Activate, AddinInstall, AddinUninstall, BeforeClose, BeforePrint, BeforeSave, Deactivate, NewSheet, Open, SheetActivate, SheetBeforeDoubleClick, SheetBeforeRightClick, SheetCalculate, SheetChange, SheetDeactivate, SheetFollowHyperlink, SheetSelectionChange, WindowActivate, WindowDeactivate, WindowResize`
Worksheet Events	`Activate, BeforeDoubleClick, BeforeRightClick, Calculate, Change, Deactivate, FollowHyperlink, SelectionChange`
Application Events	`NewWorkbook, SheetActivate, SheetBeforeDoubleClick, SheetBeforeRightClick, SheetCalculate, SheetChange, SheetDeactivate, SheetFollowHyperlink, SheetSelectionChange, WindowActivate, WindowDeactivate, WindowResize, WorkbookActivate, WorkbookAddinInstall, WorkbookAddinUninstall, WorkbookBeforeClose, WorkbookBeforePrint, WorkbookBeforeSave, WorkbookDeactivate, WorkbookNewSheet, WorkbookOpen`

For more information on new features in Excel's implementation of VBA, see the two topics, "What's New for Microsoft Excel 2000 Developers" and "Changes to the Microsoft Excel 97 Object Model" in Excel Visual Basic Help. In Excel, press **Alt+F11**, and then press **F1**, display the Answer Wizard, and search on the topic title you want to read.

Programming PowerPoint

From a programming perspective, PowerPoint 2000 has undergone five significant changes:

- `PowerPoint.Application` now fires Events
- Supports COM add-ins
- Has a Tables collection (part of the Shapes collection)
- Lets you work with panes and views programmatically
- Lets you publish to the Web from the object model

Table 17.9 lists all of the Events fired by various PowerPoint objects.

Table 17.9 PowerPoint Programming

Event	Object
Where code is stored	Presentations, templates (*.ppt files), add-ins (*.ppa files)
Application Events	NewPresentation, PresentationClose, PresentationNewSlide, PresentationOpen, PresentationPrint, PresentationSave, SlideShowBegin, SlideShowEnd, SlideShowNextBuild, SlideShowNextSlide, WindowActivate, WindowBeforeDoubleClick, WindowBeforeRightClick, WindowDeactivate, WindowSelectionChange

For more information on new features in PowerPoint's implementation of VBA, see "What's New for Microsoft PowerPoint 2000 Developers" in PowerPoint Visual Basic Help (see Figure 17.17). In PowerPoint, press **Alt+F11**, and then press **F1**, display the Answer Wizard, and search on the topic title.

FIGURE 17.17
PowerPoint 2000's upgraded object model has a lot to offer VBA developers.

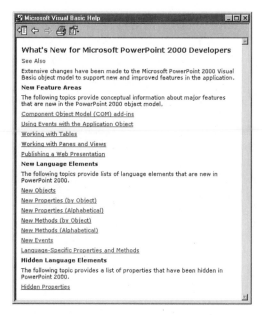

Programming Access

Access is the one Office application that has always been synonymous with programming because it is a database management system. The following are some of the new features that Access 2000 brings to the programming table:

- **Jet 4.0.** This latest version of Access' native database engine supports row-level locking, transactions, and Unicode.
- **JRO.** Jet and Replication Objects lets you set up and use replicas of Jet databases.

■ **ADO.** ActiveX Data Objects is an object model that uses OLE DB as a universal data access layer. Using ADO lets you access data sources of all kinds, whether they be Access tables, SQL Server sources, or even nonrelational sources, from a very flat, simple object hierarchy.

▶ For more information on using data providers in ADO, **see** "Using Providers with ADO" in Visual Basic Help.

■ **MSDE.** The Microsoft Data Engine is an alternative to Jet. It lets you create desktop data stores that are compatible with SQL Server, enabling you to scale up with little hassle.

■ **Support for Unicode.**

Table 17.10 lists all the Events fired by various Access objects.

Table 17.10   Access Programmability at a Glance

Event	Object
Form Events	Activate, AfterDelConfirm, AfterInsert, AfterUpdate, ApplyFilter, BeforeDelConfirm, BeforeInsert, BeforeUpdate, Click, Close, Current, DblClick, Deactivate, Delete, Dirty, Error, Filter, GotFocus, KeyDown, KeyPress, KeyUp, Load, LostFocus, MouseDown, MouseMove, MouseUp, Open, Resize, Timer, Unload
Report Events	Activate, Close, Deactivate, Error, NoData, Open, Page
Where code is stored	Database files
Data access object models	ADO through OLE DB, DAO

Programming Outlook

Outlook 97 and 98 supported only VBScript. Now you can use Outlook 2000 as an Automation client just as you can the other applications, and you can use full-powered VBA to code your Outlook solutions. You also can use the Visual Basic Editor to create and edit VBA code. You cannot, however, store your modules in separate project files. You are limited to the ThisOutlookSession object, which stores code in a file on disk.

VBA does not replace all your Outlook 2000 coding chores, however. You still must use VBScript to program custom Forms. You also must use Outlook's Script Editor (see Figure 17.18)—*not* the Microsoft Script Editor that you use to write and edit HTML documents and script in other applications—to write and edit the code; in fact, you cannot use the MSE in Outlook at all—it is not supported.

▶ For more information on creating custom Outlook Forms, **see** Chapter 15, "Workgroup Scheduling and Collaboration in Outlook 2000," on **p. 385.**

FIGURE 17.18
You must use Outlook's Script Editor to automate custom Outlook forms

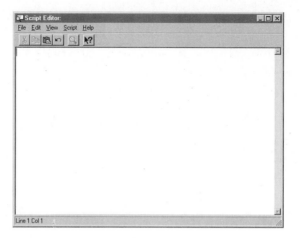

Unlike Word, PowerPoint, and Excel, Outlook stores all project code in one file, Vbaproject.otm. By default, this file is located in the C:\Windows\Application Data\Microsoft\Outlook folder on Windows 95 and 98 machines that do not have profiles enabled. On Windows NT 4.0 machines and 95/98 machines that have user profiles enabled, \Application Data is preceded by \<username>.

Outlook has the richest Event set of all of the Office applications. Table 17.11 lists all the Events fired by various Outlook objects.

Table 17.11   Outlook 2000 Programming at a Glance

Event	Object
Where code is stored	C:\Windows\<username>\Application Data\Microsoft\ Outlook\Vbaproject.otm
Application Events	ItemSend, NewMail, OptionsPagesAdd, Quit, Reminder, Startup
NameSpace Events	OptionsPagesAdd
Item Events (AppointmentItem, ContactItem, DocumentItem, and so on)	AttachmentAdd, AttachmentRead, BeforeAttachmentSave, BeforeCheckNames, Close, CustomAction, CustomPropertyChange, Forward, Open, PropertyChange, Read, Reply, ReplyAll, Send, Write
Explorer Events	Activate, BeforeFolderSwitch, BeforeViewSwitch, Close, Deactivate, FolderSwitch, SelectionChange, ViewSwitch
Explorers Events	NewExplorer
Folders Events	FolderAdd, FolderChange, FolderRemove
Inspector	Activate, Close, Deactivate
Inspectors	NewInspector

continues

Table 17.11   Continued

Event	Object
Items	ItemAdd, ItemChange, ItemRemove
OutlookBarGroups	BeforeGroupAdd, BeforeGroupRemove, GroupAdd
OutlookBarPane	BeforeGroupSwitch, BeforeNavigate
OutlookBarShortcuts	BeforeShortcutAdd, BeforeShortcutRemove, ShortcutAdd
SyncObject	OnError, Progress, SyncEnd, SyncStart

Like Access and FrontPage, Outlook has a purpose and programming model that is full-featured and unique. For example, many Outlook programming tasks involve Microsoft Exchange and can be understood only in that context.

For more information on what is new for Outlook 2000 developers, see "What's New for Microsoft Outlook 2000 Developers" in Outlook Visual Basic Help.

Programming FrontPage

As a Web site development tool, most FrontPage 2000 programming chores have always involved HTML scripting. This version retains that role but improves on it and extends it in several key ways:

- Uses the Microsoft Script Editor for creation and editing of all script, including VBScript and JavaScript.
- Leaves existing HTML code alone when importing existing pages or pages created in other editors.
- The entire FrontPage object model is exposed through VBA, including the Application, Documents, and Web objects, and FrontPage itself can serve as an Automation client.
- New source control feature lets you protect code you are developing from being used by others.
- Supports all Office Web Components.
- Supports creation of Webs without connection to a Web server.
- WordPerfect-style "Reveal Codes" in WYSIWYG view of Web pages, so you can see the HTML tags that create the effects you see.

Table 17.12 lists all the Events fired by various FrontPage objects.

Table 17.12   FrontPage Programming at a Glance

Event	Object
Where code is stored (default location)	C:\Windows\<*username*>\Application Data\Microsoft\ FrontPage\Macros\MicrosoftFrontPage.fpm

Event	Object
Application Events	OnAfterPageSave, OnAfterWebPublish, OnBeforePageSave, OnBeforeWebPublish, OnPageClose, OnPageNew, OnPageOpen, OnWebClose, OnWebNew, OnWebOpen, WindowActivate, WindowDeactivate
Document Events (FPHTMLDocument)	onafterupdate, onbeforeupdate, onclick, ondblclick, ondragstart, onerrorupdate, onhelp, onkeydown, onkeypress, onkeyup, onmousedown, onmousemove, onmouseout, onmouseover, onmouseup, onreadystatechange, onrowenter, onrowexit, onselectstart
Page Element Events (FPHTMLAnchorElement, FPHTMLAreaElement, and so on)	onafterupdate, onbeforeupdate, onblur, onclick, ondataavailable, ondatasetchanged, ondatasetcomplete, ondblclick, ondragstart, onerrorupdate, onfilterchange, onfocus, onhelp, onkeydown, onkeypress, onkeyup, onmousedown, onmousemove, onmouseout, onmouseover, onmouseup, onrowenter, onrowexit, onselectstart

Part

III

Ch

17

▶ For more information on the Microsoft Script Editor, **see** the "Microsoft Script Editor" section earlier in this chapter.

Changes to the FrontPage feature set include many more details than can be explained here. For more information on FrontPage 2000's new programmability features, see "What's New for Developers in FrontPage" in FrontPage Visual Basic Help. In FrontPage, press **Alt+F11**, press **F1**, and search on the topic title in the Answer Wizard.

For more information on using Events to control the creation of Webs and for control of Page elements, see "Using Events to Control Actions" in FrontPage Visual Basic Help.

Migrating Code from Earlier Versions

The good news is that the core implementation of VBA has not changed. For the most part, the VBA in Word 97, PowerPoint 97, and Excel 97 run without modification in their 2000 counterparts. The bad news is that individual object models have undergone extensive changes in some cases, and so it pays to be paranoid. Some code in version 97 projects that started out in earlier versions might not make the transition to VBA 6.0.

One of the key techniques Office 2000 uses to preserve backward compatibility is through the use of hidden language elements. Microsoft has replaced some of the objects, properties, and methods that were in earlier versions of Office with new ones. Rather than removing the discontinued elements from the language altogether and breaking existing code, these elements now exist as hidden parts of the model. VBA still supports them, but they do not show up in the Object Browser.

Another common theme is the conversion process. In general, to convert code, you open the old file in the new application. But there are many variations on this theme. Some detail on how this works out in individual applications follows.

Migrating Word Code

Most of the conversion issues you must manage in Word involve WordBasic, not Word 97 VBA. Word 2.0, Word 6.0, and Word 95 store all WordBasic code in macros, which in turn are always stored in templates. Word 2000 converts all WordBasic macros whenever you do any of the following to a Word 6.0 or Word 95 template:

- Open it directly
- Create a new document based on it
- Attach it to a document

Code written in previous versions of Word will run in Word 2000 as long as it meets a few conditions.

- WordBasic code written in Word 2.0 needs to be upgraded to Word 6.0 or 95 before it can be converted to VBA.
- WordBasic code written in Word 6.0 or 95 must be converted by Word 2000 to be guaranteed proper conversion.
- VBA code written in Word 97 will run unmodified.
- Word 97 modules that contain converted WordBasic code will *not* be converted to Word 2000 equivalents.

> **CAUTION**
>
> If you have any converted WordBasic code in Word 97 projects, be aware that the WordBasic calls might not work in Word 2000 because some of the WordBasic calls have changed. To ensure proper conversion of WordBasic code, you must convert from Word 6.0 or Word 95 format.

To convert any WordBasic code, simply open the template that contains it or open a document that is based on that template. For example, the following Word 95 WordBasic code is a Sub procedure that adjusts the width of a table column. It takes three numbers as arguments and assumes that the selection is in a table.

```
Sub AdjustColumnOneRows(lngWidth, intStartRow, intEndRow)

    If TableLib.GotoRow(intStartRow) = PsTrue Then
        For iCounter = intStartRow To intEndRow
            StartOfRow
            EditGoTo .Destination = "\Cell"
            TableColumnWidth \
                .ColumnWidth = lngWidth, \
                .RulerStyle = wdAdjustProportional
            LineDown
        Next iCounter
    End If
End Sub
```

When the template that contains this code is opened in Word 2000, it becomes the following:

```
Private Sub AdjustColumnOneRows(lngWidth, intStartRow, intEndRow)

Dim iCounter
    If WordBasic.Call("TableLib.GotoRow", intStartRow) = PsTrue Then
        For iCounter = intStartRow To intEndRow
            WordBasic.StartOfRow
            WordBasic.WW7_EditGoTo Destination:="\Cell"
            WordBasic.TableColumnWidth _
                ColumnWidth:=lngWidth, _
                RulerStyle:=wdAdjustProportional
            WordBasic.LineDown
        Next iCounter
    End If
End Sub
```

If written from scratch in pure VBA, the procedure would look more like the following:

```
Private Sub AdjustColumnOneRows( _

        ByVal lngWidth As Long, _
        ByVal intStartRow As Integer, _
        ByVal intEndRow As Integer)
    With selection.Tables(1)
        Dim iCounter As Integer
        For iCounter = intStartRow To intEndRow
            .Cell(Row:=iCounter, Column:=1).SetWidth _
                ColumnWidth:=lngWidth, _
                rulerstyle:=wdAdjustProportional
        Next iCounter
    End With
End Sub
```

Part

III

Ch

17

N O T E Word 2000 makes a big assumption about procedure scope when it converts your macros into modules. Word 2000 assumes that the macro's only public entry point is Sub MAIN. It therefore declares all other procedures Private when converting the macro. (This is why the list of macros in converted WordBasic templates (**Tools**, **Macro**, **Macros**) shows everything as ModuleName.MAIN.) This will work as long as all outside calls to your non-MAIN procedure use the syntax WordBasic.Call "ModuleName.ProcedureName" to call them. It will *not* work if you use the normal VBA syntax of ModuleName.ProcedureName, because only Public procedures can be called from outside the module. In migrating your WordBasic code to VBA, you will need to change Private to Public for any procedures you want to be callable from outside the module. ■

For more information on converting WordBasic code, see "Visual Basic Equivalents for WordBasic Commands" in the Word Visual Basic Editor.

If you have nothing but Word 97 projects to convert, you should have few problems. Only two properties have been hidden in Word 2000, the BrowseToWindow property of the Pane object and the VirusProtection property of the Options object. For more information on other changes to the Word object model, see "What's New for Microsoft Word 2000 Developers" in Word Visual Basic Help.

Migrating Excel Code

For backward compatibility, many, many objects, properties, and methods from earlier versions of Excel have been hidden in the Excel 2000 object model. They are still available and Excel will still run them, but they do not show up in the Object Browser and Microsoft says you should not write new code that uses them.

Excel continues to support the following:

- Excel 4.0 and 5.0 macro sheets and dialog sheets
- Excel 4.0 and 5.0 macro code
- Excel 5.0, 95, and 97 VBA objects, methods, and properties that have been removed or modified

Most of the hidden objects, methods, and properties have been replaced by objects, methods, and properties in four shared object libraries:

- Shapes
- UserForms
- ActiveX
- CommandBars

For more information on hidden language elements, including a list of them and what to code in their place, see "Changes to the Microsoft Excel 97 Object Model" in Excel Visual Basic Help. In Excel, press **Alt+F11**, press **F1**, display the Answer Wizard, and search on the topic title.

For more detailed discussion of changes to Excel 95 VBA, see "Changes to Visual Basic in Microsoft Excel for Windows 95" in Excel Visual Basic Help.

Migrating PowerPoint Code

PowerPoint programming made its debut in version 97, so you should expect a clean migration of any code you have stored in presentations, templates, or add-ins. The PowerPoint 2000 object model has some new objects, properties, and methods, but you will not need to convert any old code. Only one language element has been hidden, the `Visible` property of the `BulletFormat` object, a property now handled by the `Type` property.

Also, PowerPoint 2000 code will run in PowerPoint 97 as long as it does not require the use of new features, and as long as the project file is not digitally signed.

For more information on new VBA features in PowerPoint 2000, see "What's New for Microsoft PowerPoint 2000 Developers" in PowerPoint Visual Basic Help.

Migrating Access Code

Upgrading database code from Access 95 and 97 should go fairly smoothly because VBA made its debut in Access 95. For all such cases, you can eliminate most problems by following a few general rules:

■ Save a backup of the original before converting it. Assume that something will go wrong, even if it is unlikely, because it is much more difficult to replace a database from scratch than to go back to the original.

■ Before converting, compile the database and all modules in it. If you do not, you cannot be sure that it is free of compile errors to begin with, and a code set that starts out with compile errors will certainly not survive a format conversion. For example,

- When you install Office 2000, it upgrades DAO to version 3.6, and any code that uses DAO will retain the use of this object model but use its upgraded form. Precompiling makes it easier for Access to convert this code accurately.

- If a library dependency is broken in the original database, it will be difficult to repair it in the converted database unless you can run the code.

■ If Access encounters a compile problem during conversion, it will display an error (see Figure 17.19). Rather than working with this database in Access 2000, go back and try to fix the problem in the original first. Then, recompile and reconvert the database.

■ If you want to migrate Access 95 VBA code, eliminate keywords that were introduced in Access 97: `AddressOf`, `Assert`, `Decimal`, `DefDec`, `Enum`, `Event`, `Friend`, `Implements`, `RaiseEvent`, `WithEvents`.

Part
III

Ch
17

FIGURE 17.19
Avoid this message by fixing all compile errors in the original database file before converting it to Access 2000.

If you need to convert Access 1.0 or 2.0 code, you will need to do some manual tuning and watch out for some issues specific to Access Basic and to 16-bit Windows. For help with these issues, see the Access Visual Basic "Convert Access Basic Code to Visual Basic" Help topic.

You will also find an extensive set of documents on general Access programming topics in the main Access Help file under the top-level topic, "Programming Information" (see Figure 17.20).

Avoiding the Pitfalls of "Backward Compatibility"   Be careful how much you rely on the promise of backward compatibility. According to the VBA Help, VBA 6.0 ensures compatibility by hiding—rather than simply removing—language elements that are no longer supported in the object model. In theory, this means that your old code will run even if you cannot (easily) write new code using the old functions or macros.

But this is not always true. For example, the following code works in Word 97 but not in Word 2000:

```
WordBasic.CopyFile ActiveDocument.FullName, "C:\Backup\" & ActiveDocument.Name
```

FIGURE 17.20

Save yourself some grief—read the instructions *before* diving in.

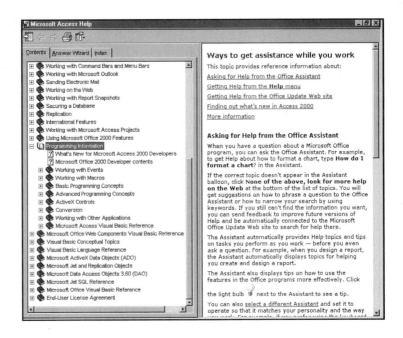

If you run this in Word 2000, the line will fail with `Error 438, Object does not support this property or method`. What happened? `WordBasic.CopyFile` has been replaced with `WordBasic.CopyFileA`. If you convert a Word 6.0 or Word 95 template that has the WordBasic `CopyFile` command, Word 2000 will convert this call correctly. But if you have already converted this call to VBA in Word 97 and then convert it to Word 2000, `WordBasic.CopyFile` will not be converted to `WordBasic.CopyFileA`. Your code will not run. In such a case, relying on backward compatibility dies after just one generation.

If you are one to ask why anyone would rely on old WordBasic commands in VBA code, consider the alternatives. VBA has no equivalent for `CopyFile` because `CopyFile` will work on open documents whereas VBA's replacement, `FileCopy`, will not. What is more, many people who have come to rely on converted code have had no compelling reason (until now) to change it. In any organization that has lots of solution code, rewriting old code can be a huge chore. Why rewrite it if it works? The truth is, many organizations rely heavily on backward compatibility.

On the other hand, if you are one who faces the prospect of rewriting hundreds or thousands of lines of code just to climb onto the latest bandwagon, you might be quite frustrated. To some degree, that frustration is justified, but you can minimize the impact by doing two things:

- **Realize that most migration of code can happen gradually.** Most of your code will probably be backward-compatible. Because it runs, change it one piece at a time, rather than wholesale. This is a good strategy for many situations.

- **Focus your energy on conversion of forms.** This is where most of the work really lies. WordBasic custom dialog boxes and Excel Dialog Sheets were replaced with VBA

UserForms, but there was no easy way to convert one into the other. Now the same prospect holds true for Access and Outlook as well. Although painful, moving forward will be easiest in the long run if you start re-creating these forms in VBA now.

Many organizations are tempted to avoid this agony by ignoring it. Why? They assume that the application will soon be replaced with something better anyway, so why bother?

But software—especially vertical, custom solutions developed in-house—strongly resists retirement. It has a way of sticking around. (That is one reason, by the way, that we had a Y2K problem—many early developers assumed that their code would soon be replaced with newer applications, but it was not.) The WordBasic, Access Basic, and Excel 4.0 macro code that you have come to rely on will probably still be in service long after the sun sets on Office 2000. Rather than leave these applications vulnerable to a discontinuation of backward compatibility, migrate the code to VBA now, while you still have time.

Besides, it is great practice.

Protecting Against Macro Viruses

Part
III

Ch
17

Thanks to macro viruses, Office's programming power is very well-known, even by people who normally wouldn't care whether Office is programmable. Office's greatest strength is therefore one of its greatest weaknesses. What can you do about it?

- **Enable virus protection in all Office applications.** All of the applications that support VBA also have security settings that let you control the execution of VBA code. If you run these applications on a standalone machine, you can keep VBA from running altogether if you so choose. If you administer a site of many machines, you can specify how easy it is for macro code to run by setting these up in your MSI and MST files.

- **Use very recent antivirus software.** There are several excellent vendors of antivirus software, including Symantec, Trend Micro, Network Associates, and others. All of them update their virus definition files on a regular basis.

▶ For more information on Office 2000 security, **see** Chapter 38, "Maximizing Office 2000 Security," on **p. 981**.

The Office 2000 Resource Kit also has information on protecting against macro viruses. See the topic "Managing Security."

Enabling Virus Protection in All Office Applications

To enable virus protection in any Office application, perform the following steps:

1. Click **Tools**, **Macro**, **Security**. The Security dialog box displays (see Figure 17.21).

FIGURE 17.21
You can prevent the running of all macro code except in trusted sources by choosing **High**.

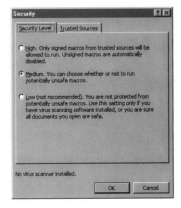

2. Click the **Security Level tab**.

3. To enable virus protection, select the **Medium** or **High** setting.

Office 2000 has stricter rules about what Medium security means than earlier versions. For example, Word 97 prompts you with the macro warning dialog box if you open a template or document that contains macros, but not for any templates loaded from the Startup folder. The same is true of Excel 97. Word 2000 and Excel 2000 will behave the same way only if you tell to do so; otherwise, the macro warning dialog box will display for each and every template that loads on startup, even `Normal.dot` and `Personal.xls`. To disable prompting for startup templates, check the **Trust all installed add-ins and templates** check box in the Trusted Sources tab of the Security dialog box (see Figure 17.22).

FIGURE 17.22
You can get the benefit of the High security setting if you can take advantage of digitally signed code.

Please remember: Barring all unsigned code from running on your machines cannot protect you from all malicious code. Most organizational security breaches—in some cases, over 70 percent—start *inside* the organization, where trusted sources work freely. Just because a macro comes from a trusted source does not mean that the source should be trusted. Enable High security setting if you must, but do not expect it to save you from all traps.

Adding an Additional Layer of Protection

Although it will not do anything to stop virus writers from writing viruses, Microsoft has made it easier for antivirus software vendors to access Office files by creating an antivirus Application Programming Interface (API). This API gives vendors a consistent way to check files for macro viruses and clean them without damaging the infected file.

To take advantage of this new technology, be sure you are using a recent version of a leading antivirus package. Later versions detect and remove VBA-based infections much more easily than earlier versions.

Also remember to update the virus definition files as often as they are posted, daily if necessary. This is the only way you can be sure of having protection from known viruses that can, and sometimes do, spread very quickly through email or other means. (Remember Melissa?)

In the end, third-party antivirus software is your best protection against macro viruses because it can protect you from code that is known to be malicious, whether it comes from a trusted source or not.

Part
III

Ch
17

Going the Extra Mile with Microsoft Office Developer

If you need to develop solutions for others or are a network Administrator responsible for deploying and administering Office, you would do well to consider having at least one copy of Microsoft Office Developer (MOD). This version of Office 2000 has everything that the Premium Edition has plus several features and tools that help you write, distribute, and maintain solution code.

Unlike previous editions of the developer edition of Office, MOD is not aimed at Access developers only. This version meets the needs of all VBA developers. It extends the usefulness of the VBE and helps you create VBA-based solutions in the following ways:

- Royalty-free Access runtime, including MS Graph, for distribution of database solutions to non-Office users
- Replication Manager, a database helper tool for setting up and maintaining database replicas
- Visual SourceSafe 6.0, for version control of all VBA projects (not just Access)
- More ActiveX controls for use in applications and forms
- Windows API Viewer, a tool to help you create API Declares
- Data Environment, a helper for establishing connections to database sources
- Ability to create COM Add-Ins, with templates for targeting specific applications
- Package and Deployment Wizard, a tool that helps you create sets of Setup files for distribution to users, including registration of COM add-ins and components
- Code Librarian, a tool for storing, filing, organizing, and retrieving VBA code
- HTML Help Workshop Software Development Kit, for help creating Help files and extending the Help engine; includes the Help runtime

- Agent SDK, for customization of Office Agents
- WebBot Components, programmable DHTML components you can embed in Office documents
- Office 2000 edition of MSDN library, a set of CD-ROM–based documentation
- Hard-copy editions of the Microsoft Office 2000/Visual Basic Programmer's Guide and Object Model diagrams

Programming Defensively

Using VBA to customize Office has some dangers and limitations. Like most other kinds of dangers, these hazards stay hidden from view until you least expect them and then strike with ruthless, painful consequences. Taking a few precautions will protect you from all of them. This section explains how to defend against some of the most common.

Always Specify Object Qualifiers

Some objects available to your Office VBA code have *global* scope. That is, regardless of what object contains them (usually the Application object), they have such universal use that they do not have to be qualified with the Application object when you reference them. You can see a list of global objects in the Object Browser of the Visual Basic Editor; click **<globals>** in the Classes list, and then note the items in the Members of list.

This can shorten your code a lot whenever specifying the context might seem unnecessary.

For example, the following command will display the number of add-ins loaded:

```
MsgBox AddIns.Count
```

But this can be a problem. Many Office applications have access to the same object models. Both Word and Excel, for example, have an AddIns collection. How do you know which application is supplying the count of add-ins? Unless you know where the code is executing, you don't. This might be what you want, but then again, it might not.

The rule of thumb therefore is this: *Always use object qualifiers unless you have a good reason not to.* That is, when you reference the object in VBA code, qualify it. Use

```
MsgBox Word.Application.AddIns.Count
```

rather than the unqualified call.

When would you use MsgBox AddIns.Count? Whenever you want your code to run in any Office application. But if you do this, make the decision consciously. Don't leave it to chance or to a careless assumption.

Protect Against Damaged Documents

Office documents can and do get damaged from time to time. If you have code in a document or template that gets damaged, you will lose your code unless you can recover it. The best defense against this is to have a recent backup of your work. You can be reasonably sure of achieving this if you do the following:

- Keep recent backups of every template you create.
- Make text copies of every module you write.
- Have original graphics files centrally stored and available for active duty if their copies inside templates gets lost.

Avoid Distribution Mistakes

Some of the code you can write for Office applications makes use of shared components that do not ship with standalone versions of the same product. These shared components all come with the Microsoft Office 9.0 Object Library, a type library referenced by default in all new Office VBA projects. (You can explicitly include it in a VBA project by setting a reference to this library in the Visual Basic Editor.) This library lives in `mso9.dll`, a file you are not allowed to distribute. In other words, the issue is not a technical limitation but a licensing one.

Shared Office components include the following object models:

- `CommandBars`
- Shapes
- ActiveX
- Scripts
- `FileSearch`
- Assistant
- COM Add-Ins

`mso9.dll` also contains constants that you should not use if you are targeting standalone installations. These constants are all prefixed with `mso`, as in `msoThisThat`. If you cannot distribute `mso9.dll`, the `mso` constants will not work.

As a simple example, suppose you write a Word macro that uses the `FileSearch` component. You can freely distribute the template or document that uses it, but you cannot distribute the file (`mso9.dll`) that does the file search. Users of standalone Word will not be able to use your code.

What to do? If you write any code that might run on a system that lacks an Office license, clear the reference to the Office 9.0 Object Library in your project file. Know what the forbidden features are and either carefully avoid using them, work around them, or write error-handling routines to deal with resulting failures gracefully. If your code does require the use of these components, be sure to list the Office suite, not just the relevant application, as a system requirement. Above all, be aware that if you set a reference to the Office 9.0 object library, you are targeting Office users, not Word users, Excel users, or Access users.

Knowing Where to Go for More Information

VBA takes a long time to master, despite its relative ease. Do not feel put out if you get stuck on a programming task. Some VBA objects do not do what you think they should do; at other times, you just need more information to move ahead with your solution. The good news is that you have a lot of good resources close by. This section highlights some of them.

The Visual Basic Help File

In the VBE, display Help, click the Contents tab, and select the **Visual Basic Conceptual Topics** topic. You will find a very long list of specific, detailed subtopics on many basic VBA concepts. If you go nowhere else for any other information, this alone will take you most of the way toward mastering the basics.

The Office Resource Kit and Tools

Consider the Office Resource Kit (ORK) the owner's manual that did not come in the box. It has many useful pieces of information about Office in general but also some advice and tools related to VBA. Like the Boy Scout who brought his pocket knife, you will save yourself a lot of time in the long run if you take the time early to read it and become familiar with its utilities.

Two Office Resource Kit tools relate to Office programming and might be useful to you.

- **The HTML Help Workshop.** This tool lets you build HTML help files that you can include in your VBA solutions. The tool includes an image editor for creating hyperlinked graphics files.

- **The Microsoft Office Converter Pack.** This tool enables users to install file converters so Office users can share files with users of other Office versions and users of other applications. You might find this tool useful for batch conversion of documents, workbooks, presentations, and databases that contain code that needs to be converted.

If you do not have the ORK in book form, you can download the tools from the ORK Web site at `http://www.microsoft.com/office/ork/`. Click the **Toolbox** sidebar for download instructions. Remember that if you want these tools to be available to multiple users on your network, you will need to make them available at a distribution point.

▶ For more information on Office installation, **see** "Planning Your Office 2000 Installation," on **p. 9** and "Automating and Customizing Office Installations Across the Network," on **p. 27**.

Online Sources of Training and Information

We've already mentioned the Office Resource Kit; you can find a great deal more Office 2000–related information on Microsoft's Web site and public newsgroups. Table 17.13 summarizes them.

Table 17.13   Online Sources of Information

Microsoft Office Developer Forum	`http://msdn.microsoft.com/officedev/`
Microsoft Scripting Technologies (Windows Scripting Host)	`http://msdn.microsoft.com/scripting/`
Office Resource Kit Web site	`http://www.microsoft.com/office/ork/`
Microsoft Office	`http://msdn.microsoft.com/officedev/tech`
Product Documentation	`nical/documentation.asp`
Microsoft public newsgroups	`news://msnews.microsoft.com`

Spend at least a day learning your way around each of these sources so you know what they have to offer. Then, return to them as you need to. You will often find useful updates and sources of help.

The Office Developer Forum, for example, is Microsoft's main place for Office developers. For the most part, you will find the information relevant and helpful.

The Product Documentation site has the full text of several useful books: *Getting Results with Office 2000 Developer*, the *Microsoft Office 2000 Developer Object Model Guide*, the *Microsoft Office 2000/Visual Basic Programmer's Guide*, the *Microsoft FrontPage 2000 Software Developer's Kit*, and the *Microsoft Office HTML and XML Reference*.

The Microsoft Office newsgroups are another important source of help. Microsoft maintains hundreds of newsgroups on its `msnews.microsoft.com` server. As of this writing, it maintains over a dozen groups that relate directly to VBA programming. The following is a partial list of these newsgroups.

Access:

- `microsoft.public.access.activexcontrol`
- `microsoft.public.access.commandbarsui`
- `microsoft.public.access.dataaccess.pages`
- `microsoft.public.access.developers.toolkitode`
- `microsoft.public.access.devtoolkits`
- `microsoft.public.access.formscoding`
- `microsoft.public.access.interopoledde`
- `microsoft.public.access.macros`
- `microsoft.public.access.modulesdaovba`
- `microsoft.public.access.modulesdaovba.ado`

Part
III

Ch
17

Excel:

- ◼ microsoft.public.excel.interopoledde
- ◼ microsoft.public.excel.programming
- ◼ microsoft.public.excel.sdk
- ◼ microsoft.public.excel.templates
- ◼ microsoft.public.excel.worksheet.functions

FrontPage:

- ◼ microsoft.public.frontpage.client

Office:

- ◼ microsoft.public.office.intranets
- ◼ microsoft.public.officedev

Outlook:

- ◼ microsoft.public.outlook.interop
- ◼ microsoft.public.outlook.program_addins
- ◼ microsoft.public.outlook.program_forms
- ◼ microsoft.public.outlook.program_vba

PowerPoint:

- ◼ microsoft.public.powerpoint

HTML, XML, Scripting:

- ◼ microsoft.public.scripting.debugger
- ◼ microsoft.public.scripting.jscript
- ◼ microsoft.public.scripting.vbscript
- ◼ microsoft.public.scripting.wsh
- ◼ microsoft.public.xml

Word:

- ◼ microsoft.public.word.oleinterop
- ◼ microsoft.public.word.vba.addins
- ◼ microsoft.public.word.vba.beginners
- ◼ microsoft.public.word.vba.classes
- ◼ microsoft.public.word.vba.customization
- ◼ microsoft.public.word.vba.general
- ◼ microsoft.public.word.vba.userformsmicrosoft.public.word.word6-7macros
- ◼ microsoft.public.word.word97vba

Although the names of these newsgroups might change, and although new ones are often being added, these resources are available 24 hours a day, 7 days a week. It is a good idea to be aware of them and to take advantage of them. Unlike some Internet newsgroups, most of these groups are quite active and full of useful posts. Even if you never post a question, it pays to visit on a regular basis and read the ongoing threads. You will surely learn something. ●

Part
III

Ch
17

PART IV

Integrating Office in Your Heterogeneous Environment

CHAPTER 18

Migrating from or Coexisting with Legacy Applications

by Bill Camarda

Office 2000's breathtaking range of features can help your organization accomplish virtually anything. But if you are migrating to Office from other business applications, such as WordPerfect, Lotus 1-2-3, or dBASE—or trying to coexist in environments where some users continue to work with products from other vendors—you'll have significant hurdles to overcome before you can benefit from the new Office 2000 features. This chapter addresses both scenarios:

- **Migration.** You have existing collections of databases, documents, spreadsheets, and the like that you want to convert into a form Office 2000 can use so the original work spent on this data is not lost.

- **Coexistence.** You plan to continue using non-Microsoft applications along with Office 2000, and you need for the two sets of programs to cooperate when exchanging data files back and forth.

Planning for Document Conversions

Earlier in this book, we stressed the importance of proper planning before introducing Office 2000 into your company. Planning is doubly important if you intend to migrate from or coexist with competitive business applications.

Keep in mind that converting small and large batches of documents or worksheets represents two entirely different management challenges. Users who must convert only a single document can often simply open that document in the new Office application of their choice and let the application handle the conversion "automatically." Having done so, they can personally "clean up" minor formatting problems they might encounter in the converted document.

Users and administrators who must convert a folder full of documents can turn to a tool for file conversion, such as the Microsoft Word Batch Conversion Wizard, which can automate small-scale conversions with relative simplicity. In addition, these users and administrators can use the same import and export filters Word provides for single-document conversion.

> **N O T E** If you expect users to perform conversions manually, be sure to include the appropriate filters as part of their installations. At minimum, specify **Install on First Run** for these filters, and be sure that they remain available from a network installation point.

As an Office administrator, however, you might face a larger challenge: converting all the documents in a department or company. Problems that seem minor in individual documents can quickly become overwhelming when dozens, hundreds, or thousands of people with varying computer skill levels encounter them all at once. The following checklist walks you through some of the issues to consider before embarking on a large-scale document conversion project:

1. **Invest sufficient time in planning.** Give yourself time—preferably at least a few months—to develop and execute your conversion plan. That gives you time to perform the following tasks:

   - Evaluate your hardware and software to ensure that the migration or coexistence will not overwhelm any of your computers.

   - Identify data files that must be converted to new formats or must coexist with Office 2000. Make copies of these files for testing.

   - Identify conversion tools or third-party resources if you decide you need them. Be aware that Microsoft solutions are not the only solutions available, nor are they always the best solutions. In certain instances, filters or other tools provided by your legacy software vendor (such as Corel or Lotus) might do a better job exporting files to Office than Microsoft's tools do importing them.

   - Thoroughly identify any unique issues you might face, such as macros in existing documents, international characters, special symbols, images, layout anomalies, and so forth.

   - Test various approaches. For example, if you cannot consistently import documents well in the Word 2000/Word 97 format, perhaps RTF or Word 6.0/95 will work.

- Build a process that works consistently well (preferably a centralized process that you can control tightly), and then document that process thoroughly.

2. **Test thoroughly.** Test your converted documents thoroughly, and test your complex documents the most thoroughly. Testing should involve users and should cover the entire document development process, including printing and unexpected changes to file sizes (for example, small files that become inexplicably huge when imported into Word). Be especially careful with documents that must be "round-tripped" from Office to third-party software and back. To the extent it's practical, discourage this practice; such documents are notorious for developing problems.

3. **Provide consistent documents.** To the extent possible, every document you provide to your users should behave in the same way. You're asking for trouble if you decide that *some* documents in *some* folders should continue to be saved as WordPerfect 5.1 files without consistent extensions, whereas other folders are permanently converted to Word and stored as .doc files.

4. **Be realistic.** Do not overestimate how many documents you can convert in a given period of time. Even more important, do not assume that your converted documents will be perfect the first time or that you can rely on them instantly in situations where perfect formatting is crucial. To whatever extent is possible, assume that it will take users a little more time to deliver converted documents than it would for "native" documents, and schedule your deadlines accordingly.

5. **Know your resource and expertise limits.** If you must convert thousands of documents reliably, consider outsourcing the task to a consultant with extensive experience in similar document conversions. One such company is Microsystems (www.microsystems.com, 1-630-261-0611), which sells extremely high-end software to automate conversions or will take full responsibility for large-scale conversion projects at a price of roughly 20 cents per document.

Converting WordPerfect Documents into Word

WordPerfect has existed in many versions and has been owned by many companies: first WordPerfect Corporation, then Novell, and currently Corel. At one time, WordPerfect ruled the word processing field and was the standard by which other programs were measured. However, Word now holds that distinction, and it is very common for offices to convert from WordPerfect to Word.

Software in Law Offices

In the legal field, conversions from WordPerfect to Word are especially common now, as law offices (where WordPerfect remains a stronghold) attempt to work with corporate clients (who have nearly universally standardized on Word).

Law firms with large document libraries might want to discuss their conversion requirements with consultants who specialize in the unique formatting and document management issues they face. One such consulting group, Payne Consulting (www.payneconsulting.com), maintains a Web site with resources specific to law firms.

continues

continued

The American Bar Association has a strong technology section that studies the integration of popular software packages into law offices. Office 2000 is one of the most popular choices. The most common migration path for law firms recently has been from WordPerfect, formerly the preferred package for law work, to Word and Office 2000.

In addition, a variety of third-party software companies produce templates, macros, and other support packages for Office 2000 to make it more suitable for the work demands of a law office. For example, Eidelman Associates' LawOffice 97 is a suite of add-ins for Microsoft Office 97 that can be highly tailored through targeted consulting to meet the objectives of a particular law department or law firm. Its components include document management add-ins that enhance Word, extensive integration with Outlook and Microsoft Exchange, and more.

To learn about additional Microsoft and third-party resources for Office users in the legal field, visit Microsoft's Industry Solutions for the Legal Industry site: **www.microsoft.com/industry/legal/**. While you're at this site, you might want to download Microsoft's Life After Reveal Codes white paper, which offers techniques for WordPerfect users who have come to depend heavily on that program's Reveal Codes feature and find themselves at a disadvantage without it.

In the following sections, you learn how to approach exchanging files with WordPerfect.

Opening Individual WordPerfect Documents in Word 2000

Word 2000 contains built-in support for opening documents created in the following versions of WordPerfect. The following two converters are included in the default Word 2000 installation and are typically placed in the Program Files\Common Files\Microsoft Shared\Textconv folder.

- **Wpft532.cnv.** Supports opening and saving WordPerfect 5.x files (both DOS and Windows).

- **Wpft632.cnv.** Supports opening, but not saving, WordPerfect 6.0 for DOS and 6.1 for Windows files.

N O T E Corresponding filters are included in the default Word 98 for the Macintosh installation and are placed in the Microsoft Office 98:Shared Applications:Text Converters folder on the Macintosh. ▧

▶ For information about installing additional filters, including an optional WordPerfect 4.0 for DOS filter, **see** "Downloading and Installing the Office 2000 Resource Kit," on **p. 28**.

Corel retained the WordPerfect 6.x for Windows document format in WordPerfect 7.x, 8.x, and 9.x for Windows (including the version of WordPerfect included in WordPerfect Office 2000, which is the same as WordPerfect 9.x). If you are using WordPerfect 7.x or 8.x, try using the WordPerfect 6.x for Windows filter. Because Word's filter is designed for WordPerfect 6.x only, however, features specific to WordPerfect 7.x and 8.x are unlikely to convert properly. WordPerfect 9.x includes a Word 97/2000 export and import filter.

CAUTION

If you convert a file from Word to WordPerfect format, be sure you open, paginate, and save the file in WordPerfect before you reopen the same file in Word. Otherwise, fonts, justification, styles, mail merge, and some other features might not work properly.

For single documents created with WordPerfect, the easiest method for migrating a single file is typically to open Word and then open the target file. Choose **File, Open**. The Open dialog box that appears contains a drop-down list of file formats (see Figure 18.1). If you used a common extension for your legacy files (for example, .doc), the drop-down list of files limits what is displayed in the Open file window. This makes file selection easier.

FIGURE 18.1
In the Open dialog box, you can select the type of file formats to import and the conversions to maintain or change.

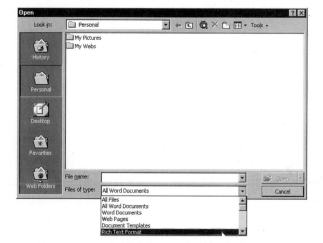

Understanding the Limits of WordPerfect Converters in Word

Because WordPerfect files usually open in Word, it's easy to overlook the limitations of Word's conversion filters (unless you're responsible for helping users overcome them). In this section, you take a closer look at Word's converters—what they can and cannot do.

NOTE Certain inherent differences in the way Word and WordPerfect structure documents make it difficult for Microsoft (or anyone else) to implement a perfect converter. For example, WordPerfect places style definitions in a prefix for every document file, even if users don't specify styles. Word's conversion filter picks up these style definitions, sometimes using them in troublesome ways.

For example, WordPerfect style definitions that have the same name as Word's existing built-in style definitions override the Word definitions. So, different documents with the same styles will look different depending on where they were created. ■

Table 18.1 lists the limitations of Word 2000/97's conversion to and from WordPerfect 5.x. Table 18.2 lists additional limitations that apply to Word's filter for opening WordPerfect 6.x files.

Part
IV

Ch
18

Table 18.1   Limitations of Word's WordPerfect 5.x Filter

Feature	Word 2000/97 Conversion to WordPerfect 5.x	WordPerfect 5.x Conversion to Word 2000/97	Notes
Alignment	Yes, but see note	Yes, but see note	You might have to reposition centering codes manually after you convert your documents.
All caps	Yes	Not supported	Text using All Caps formatting is converted to capital letters.
Center and flush right codes	Not supported	Yes, but see note	In conversions to Word, center and flush-right codes are converted to center and right-align tab stops.
Comments	Yes	Not supported	In conversions to WordPerfect, Comments become Comment Text.
Date/Time Fields	Yes, but see note	Yes, but see note	Only default formats are converted.
Decimal Table Cell Alignment	Not supported	See note	In conversions to Word, decimal table cell alignments are converted to right paragraph alignments; these might have to be adjusted manually.
Default Tab Stops	No	Yes	
Document Titles/ Descriptive Names	See note	See note	In conversions to Word, WordPerfect Descriptive Names are converted into information stored in the Title document property. In conversions to WordPerfect, information in the Title document property is converted to Descriptive Names.
Equations	No	No	
Extended Characters	Yes	See note	Some WordPerfect characters are converted to reflect the Unicode values Word uses; others, such as ©, ½, and £, do not convert properly.

Feature	Word 2000/97 Conversion to WordPerfect 5.x	WordPerfect 5.x Conversion to Word 2000/97	Notes
First Line Indents	Yes	Yes	Converted to first-line tabs.
Footnotes	Yes, but see note	Yes, but see note	In conversions to WordPerfect, endnotes that were placed at the end of a section are moved to the end of a document because WordPerfect does not have a sections feature. Word's restarted numbers and custom footnote marks will not convert, nor will custom separators.
Formulas	No	No	
Gutter Margins	Yes	Yes	
Hidden Text	Yes	Not Supported	Word Hidden Text becomes WordPerfect Comment Text; depending on WordPerfect document settings, this might be visible.
Kerning	Yes	Yes	
Leading	Not supported	No	
Line Draw	Yes, but see note	Yes, but see note	In conversions to Word, line spacing might change; you might have to adjust it to the current font point size to eliminate undesirable gaps.
Macros	No	No	
Margins	Yes, but see note	Yes, but see note	Conversions adjust margin values to reflect the different ways Word and WordPerfect measure margins. Word measures from the paper's edge to body text; WordPerfect measures from the paper's edge to headers/footers.
Mirror Pages	No	No	

Part

IV

Ch

18

continues

Table 18.1 Continued

Feature	Word 2000/97 Conversion to WordPerfect 5.x	WordPerfect 5.x Conversion to Word 2000/97	Notes
Newspaper columns	Yes	Yes	
Outlining	Yes	Yes	In conversions to Word, WordPerfect paragraph numbers are converted to Word numbering SEQ fields that serve the same purpose—but are not consistent with the numbering that users apply from within Word.
Page Break Before Paragraph	Yes, but see note	Not supported	Places a hard page break in the approximately correct location.
Parallel Columns	Not supported	Yes, but see note	In conversions to Word, WordPerfect parallel columns are changed to tables. In layouts containing page-anchored boxes, the full parallel column layout is converted to use Word's Columns feature (as in newspaper columns).
Print Merge/ Mail Merge	Yes	Yes, but see note	In conversions to Word, conditional print merge constructs and macros are lost. Word data sources must be either tab- or comma-delimited or in table format in order to be translated to WordPerfect secondary files.
Revision Marks	Yes, but see note	Yes, but see note	Converted to redlining.
Space Before/ After Paragraph	Yes, but see note	Not supported	Places additional blank paragraph lines before or after paragraphs.

Feature	Word 2000/97 Conversion to WordPerfect 5.x	WordPerfect 5.x Conversion to Word 2000/97	Notes
Spacing (condensed or expanded text)	No	Not supported	
Strikethrough	Yes, but see note	Yes, but see note	WordPerfect strikethrough converts to Word strikethrough; WordPerfect redlining converts to Word Tracked Changes.
Styles	Yes	Yes, but see note	In conversions to Word, WordPerfect styles that contain paragraph formatting codes are translated to Word paragraph styles. WordPerfect styles containing only character formatting codes are translated to Word character styles. Text contained in a style becomes Normal text; tables, graphics, and some other features are translated but are not assigned Word styles.
Subdocuments (INCLUDE field)	Yes	Yes	
Tab Leaders	Yes	Yes, but see note	In conversions to Word, the dot, minus sign, and underscore leaders convert accurately; other WordPerfect leaders become Word dot leaders.
Tables	Yes, but see note	Yes	Word cells that have been merged vertically are not converted properly.
Text Boxes and Lines	Yes	Yes, but see note	In conversions to Word, some text boxes and lines become Word drawing layer objects.
Underlining	Yes	Yes	Type of underlining sometimes changes in unexpected ways.

Part

IV

Ch

18

continues

Table 18.1   Continued

Feature	Word 2000/97 Conversion to WordPerfect 5.x	WordPerfect 5.x Conversion to Word 2000/97	Notes
Widow Control	Yes	Yes	In conversions to Word, this becomes a paragraph property.
Word Numbered Lists	Yes, but see note	Yes, but see note	Word numbered lists convert to WordPerfect paragraph numbers.

Table 18.2   Additional Limitations

Feature	WordPerfect 6.x for DOS and Windows Conversion to Word 2000/97
ADVANCE Codes	Converted to advance fields; not all are converted properly.
Back Tabs	If preceded by text, lost.
Bookmarks	Converted properly.
Borders/Fill for Columns and Pages	Lost.
Captions	Lost.
Center and Flush-Right Codes	Converted to center and right-align tab stops.
Chapter/Volume Numbers	Lost.
Comments	Comments in body text convert properly; those in headers/footers or footnotes/endnotes are lost.
Contour Wrap Around Graphics Boxes	Converted to Square Wrap.
Cross-References	Converted to Hyperlinks.
Drop Caps	Lost.
Equations	In Windows, converted as editable equation objects. On Macintosh, result is retained but editable equation is lost.
Footnotes	Custom footnote marks converted to automatic numbered marks; if Notes numbering format has been changed, Notes numbered with the new format become custom Notes.
Indexes/Lists	Converted to plain text.
Insert File Name	Lost.
Labels/Bar Codes	Label text preserved; bar codes lost.

Feature	WordPerfect 6.x for DOS and Windows Conversion to Word 2000/97
Leading Adjustment Between Lines and Baselines	Lost.
Line Numbers	Lost.
Macros	Lost.
Margins	Adjusted to preserve page layout; users might be prompted to adjust margins manually.
Merge Codes	Lost.
Outlining, Paragraph Numbers, Counters	Converted to Word SEQ fields, which work, but can lead to serious inconsistencies later when Word users use the outline numbering feature in the same document because Word itself no longer uses SEQ fields for this purpose.
Page Features (Center Page, Page Binding, Subdivide Pages)	Lost.
Paragraph Margins	Converted to left/right paragraph indents.
Redlining	Converted to comments.
Spacing Between Paragraphs	Converted to Spacing After settings in Format, Paragraph dialog box.
Strikeout	Converted to strikethrough character formatting.
Tab Leaders	Dot, minus-sign, and underscore tab leaders convert properly; others are converted to dot leaders.
Table Vertical Cell Merge/Cell Alignment	Lost.
Text Boxes, Graphics Boxes, Lines	Some are converted to OfficeArt objects; graphics lines are converted to solid lines.
Trailing Default Tabs	Lost.
Word/Letter spacing	Lost.
WordPerfect Characters	Converted if WordPerfect fonts containing the characters are installed on the computer.

Part
IV

Ch
18

In documents that are converted to Word, { PRIVATE } field codes are added to store formatting data that Word cannot translate. Don't edit the contents of these fields, and don't delete them if you think the document might ever be converted back to a WordPerfect format.

TIP   For even more detailed coverage of this issue, read Microsystems' white paper, "Making the Change from WordPerfect to Word in a Legal Environment," which you can download from `http://www.microsystems.com/expert.htm`.

Microsystems lists the following Word features as especially trouble-prone in a conversion from WordPerfect to Word. (Microsystems' list is similar but not identical to Microsoft's; you should study both lists before proceeding.)

- Back tabs
- Conditional EOP
- Courier request forms
- Cross references
- Delayed headers and footers
- Document type
- Empty paragraphs (Paragraph Marks with No Text)
- Endnotes
- Fax cover sheet
- Fonts
- Footnotes
- Graphic lines
- Graphics
- Horizontal and vertical advance codes
- Indents
- Labels
- Landscape and portrait on same page
- Leading
- Letters
- Line numbering
- Merge codes
- Multiple headers & footers
- Newspaper or parallel columns
- Numbering
- Pleadings
- Printer command function
- Private codes
- Redlining (track changes)
- Special font attributes (such as small, large, very large, and so on)
- Special page features
- Special paper size/type specifications
- Special symbols
- Styles
- Tables
- Tables of authorities
- Tables of contents
- Text boxes

Converting WordPerfect Macros to Word

Suppose your old WordPerfect documents contain macros; they cannot be automatically converted to Word VBA macros. However, if you have the Office 95 Resource Kit, that kit's Supplemental Converters includes a utility called WPIMPORT.DOT that enables you to copy WordPerfect macros into text documents so you can understand what they do and (presumably) reproduce their capabilities in Word's programming environment.

In many cases, you might discover that Word has a built-in feature that does essentially the same job WordPerfect once required a macro for. For instance, AutoCorrect can be used to expand abbreviations and insert special characters, tasks for which WordPerfect users often wrote macros.

Converting WordPerfect Graphics to Word

If you open a WordPerfect 5.x or 6.x document that contains graphics in the WordPerfect Graphics (WPG) format, the WordPerfect converter calls upon Word's WPG graphics filter to convert those graphics. (This converter installs on first run, so you might be called upon to insert your original CD-ROM or connect to your original network installation point.)

Word eliminates any background colors from the WPG image to improve its clarity in Word. However, you might not want this behavior. If you want Word to retain the colors, you can edit the behavior of Word's converter. Browse to your Office Macros folder (typically, \Program Files\Microsoft Office\Office\Macros) and double-click on **Support9.dot**. If you are asked whether you want to enable macros, do so.

The Macros toolbar opens. From the **Sample Macros** list, choose **Edit Conversion Options**. The Edit Converter and Filter Options dialog box opens, as shown in Figure 18.2. Choose **WordPerfect Graphics** from the **Conversion** drop-down box and be sure **RetainBackground=** is highlighted. In the **Setting** text box, enter **Yes**. Then, click **Set** and **OK**.

FIGURE 18.2
Adjusting the WordPerfect filter to retain WPG graphics backgrounds.

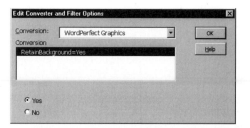

 TIP You might find that you want to make other adjustments while you have the Edit Converter and Filter Options dialog box open. For example, as mentioned earlier, Word's WordPerfect import filter uses { SEQ } fields to convert WordPerfect paragraph numbering. If you would like to use Word's "true" paragraph numbering feature, choose **WordPerfect 5.x** from the **Conversion** drop-down box and set **FavorSequenceFields=No**.

Converting to and from Lotus Word Pro

After Word and WordPerfect, today's number-three-selling word processor is Lotus Word Pro. Word Pro is part of Lotus SmartSuite, which competes with Microsoft Office. Because Lotus is a division of IBM, SmartSuite is installed on most IBM home and small business PCs; it is also relatively popular in organizations that consider Lotus Notes a strategic product. Some businesses that had standardized years ago on Lotus Ami Pro followed Lotus' recommendations to move to Word Pro. In short, although Lotus Word Pro hasn't achieved the marketshare Lotus might like it to, it's entirely possible that you'll encounter it in your "travels" as an Office administrator.

N O T E The following discussion is applicable to SmartSuite R9.x Millennium Edition (Word Pro 9.x). ▪

Because Microsoft does not provide a Word Pro filter, the entire responsibility for document conversion and coexistence falls on the Word Pro side of the fence. You have two options for saving Word Pro files so they are readable in Word: You can save in "MS Word" format or "RTF" (Rich Text Format). Files saved in MS Word format use the Word 6.0/95 format. To save an individual Word Pro file as MS Word, open the file in Word Pro and follow these steps:

1. In Word Pro, choose **File**, **Save As**.
2. In the **Save As Type** drop-down box, choose **MS Word**.
3. Click **Yes** to confirm that you want to save the file in Word.
4. Click **Save**.

To open a Word file in Word Pro, follow these steps:

1. Choose **File**, **Open**.
2. In the **Files of type** drop-down box, choose **MS Word**.
3. Browse to and select the file you want to open.
4. Click **Open**.

Much as Microsoft Word provides templates, Word Pro offers SmartMasters that enable you to create documents with formatting, text, and behavior already set. In an environment that encompasses Word and Word Pro, you can use a SmartMaster to specify a standard default format that Word can read (such as MS Word or RTF). When you do so, all files are saved as Word files by default. To establish MS Word as Lotus Word Pro's default Save format, first follow these steps to create a SmartMaster that saves to MS Word:

1. In Word Pro, choose **File**, **New Document**.
2. Select **default.mwp** from the list of SmartMasters, and then click **OK**.
3. Choose **File**, **Save As**.
4. In the **Save As Type** drop-down box, choose **Lotus SmartMaster**.
5. In the **File name** box, rename the SmartMaster (as **msword.mwp**, for instance).
6. Browse to where you want to save the SmartMaster.
7. Choose **Save**. The Save As SmartMaster Options dialog box opens.
8. In the **Initial Save Format** box, choose the Microsoft file type you want Word Pro to use by default.

Next, set this SmartMaster as your default—the one you want Word Pro to use when you create a new file. Follow these steps:

1. In Word Pro, choose **File**, **User Setup**.
2. Choose **Word Pro Preferences**.
3. Click the **Default Files** tab.
4. In the **Plain Document SmartMaster** box, choose the SmartMaster you just created.
5. Click **OK**.

Word Pro Release 9 does not contain a Word 2000 or Word 97 filter, but you might be able to get the results you need by exporting from Word Pro to RTF. Table 18.3 lists Word Pro's support for importing and exporting RTF files.

Table 18.3   Lotus Word Pro's Import/Export RTF Capabilities

Feature	Import into Word Pro R9	Export to RTF	Comments
Alternating header/ footer	Yes	Yes	
Basic page numbering	Yes	Yes	Might become misaligned.
Boldface text	Yes	Yes	
Bullets - in text	Yes	Yes	Bullet alignment lost if you switch styles.
Cell attributes	Yes	Yes	
Cell patterns	Yes	Yes	Patterns might vary when exported to RTF.
Centered text	Yes	Yes	
Column balance	Yes	Yes	Lost.
Column breaks	Yes	Yes	Lost.
Column width	Yes	Yes	
Connected cells	Yes	Yes	
Date	Yes	Yes	
Double-underlined text	Yes	Yes	
Drop caps	Yes	Yes	Drop caps might become misaligned or "cut off" at the top when exported from Word Pro to RTF.
Fonts	Yes	Yes	
Footnote options	Yes	Yes	
Footnote text	Yes	Yes	Duplicate numbers might appear in an exported footnote.
Frame line	Yes	No	Word Pro's "designer borders" are lost.
Frame placement	Yes	Yes	
Frame shadows	No	No	Shadows might change appearance.

continues

Part

IV

Ch

18

Table 18.3   Continued

Feature	Import into Word Pro R9	Export to RTF	Comments
Frame size	Yes	Yes	
Graphics	Yes	Yes	
Gutter width	Yes	Yes	
Headings	Yes	Yes	
Hidden text	Yes	Yes	
Indent all	Yes	Yes	
Indent first	Yes	Yes	
Indent rest	Yes	Yes	
Indent right	Yes	Yes	
Initial header/ footer	Yes	Yes	
International characters	Yes	Yes	
Italic text	Yes	Yes	
Justified text	Yes	Yes	
Left-aligned text	Yes	Yes	
Line spacing	Yes	Yes	Line spacing might vary from original.
Lines	Yes	No	Lines and designer borders are lost.
Lines	Yes	Yes	Designer lines lost.
Lowercase text	Yes	Yes	
Margins	Yes	Yes	
Nonbreaking space	Yes	Yes	
Page breaks	Yes	Yes	
Page orientation	Yes	Yes	Word Pro files with Landscape orientation revert to Portrait when exported to RTF.
Page size	Yes	Yes	
Protected text	No	No	
Protection	No	No	
Revision marking	Yes	Yes	Might not properly mark page numbers as revised when importing from RTF to Word Pro.
Right-Aligned Text	Yes	Yes	
Row height	Yes	Yes	To preserve row height in Word Pro, choose **Exactly** in the Paragraph dialog box when specifying row height in Word.
Shading	Yes	Yes	

Feature	Import into Word Pro R9	Export to RTF	Comments
Small caps text	Yes	Yes	
Special characters			
Strikethrough text	Yes	Yes	
Styled page numbering	Yes	Yes	
Superscript/ subscript text	Yes	Yes	Subscript lost on import to Word Pro.
Tab center	Yes	Yes	
Tab left	Yes	Yes	
Tab numeric	Yes	Yes	
Tab right	Yes	Yes	
Tab rulers	Yes	Yes	
Table creation	Yes	Yes	
Text wrap around	Yes	Yes	Text might not wrap on every side.
Text, before and after	Yes	Yes	
Underlined text	Yes	Yes	
Uppercase text	Yes	Yes	
Watermarks	N/A	No	Lost.
Word underlined text	Yes	Yes	

TIP If you set it up correctly, Word Pro will go even further toward coexisting with Word: You can customize its menus so they resemble Word's. This might be a useful strategy if you plan to transition Word Pro users to Word, or if you find your users must switch back and forth between programs.

To customize Word Pro's menu sets, choose **File**, **Menu Customization**. Then, choose the **Microsoft Word** menu set and click **Make Default**. If the Word menu set is not present, the MSWord.mnu file must be installed into the \WordPro\Menus\ folder. You can also establish a centralized network location for your menu sets, as outlined in these steps:

1. Choose **File**, **Setup**, **Word Pro Preferences**.
2. Click the **Locations** tab.
3. Click in the **Menus** edit box and edit the path to reflect the network folder you want to use.
4. Click **OK**.

Running Batch Conversion of Documents into Word

You can convert batches of legacy word processing files using Word's *Batch Conversion Wizard*. With the Batch Conversion Wizard, you can create Word 2000 documents from files in the following formats:

- Lotus 1-2-3
- Microsoft Excel
- Microsoft Word Template
- Microsoft Works 3.0 for Windows
- Microsoft Works 4.0 for Windows
- MS-DOS Text with Layout
- Outlook Address Book
- Personal Address Book
- Rich Text Format (RTF)
- Schedule+ Contacts
- Text
- Text with Layout
- Unicode Text
- Windows Write
- Word 4.0–5.1 for Macintosh
- WordPerfect 5.x
- WordPerfect 6.x

Similarly, you can convert documents from Word 2000 *to* the following formats:

- Lotus 1-2-3
- Microsoft Excel Worksheet
- Microsoft Works 3.0 or 4.0
- MS-DOS Text, MS-DOS Text with Line Breaks, or MS-DOS Text with Layout
- Rich Text Format (RTF)
- Text Only, Text with Layout, or Text with Line Breaks
- Unicode Text
- Windows Write
- Word 2.x for Windows
- Word 2000 Template
- Word 4.0 for Macintosh
- Word 5.0 for Macintosh
- Word 5.1 for Macintosh
- Word 6.0/95 for Windows and Macintosh
- WordPerfect 5.0 (including Secondary Files)

- WordPerfect 5.1 for DOS
- WordPerfect 5.1 or 5.2 Secondary File
- WordPerfect 5.x for Windows

The Batch Conversion Wizard can convert all files in a specific folder. Before you use it, either place all the files you want to convert in the same folder or, if you want to convert files in their current folders, list the folders you want to convert and run the Batch Conversion Wizard separately in each folder.

By default, the Batch Conversion Wizard installs on first run; alternatively, you can copy Convert9.Wiz from the CD-ROM (\Pfiles\Msoffice\Template\1033\) to the folder where your Word 2000 templates are stored. To run the Wizard, choose it from the **Other Documents** tab of the New dialog box (or double-click on it in Windows Explorer). If you're asked to do so, confirm that you want to open it with macros enabled. The preliminary Conversion Wizard dialog box appears.

TIP If you plan to use the Conversion Wizard often, select the file and click the **Add to Favorites** button in the Open dialog box. Then you can access it directly from the Favorites folder.

After you've displayed the Conversion Wizard, follow these steps:

1. Click **Next**. The From/To screen appears (see Figure 18.3).
2. If you want to convert files stored in another format into Word 2000 files, click **Convert from another format to Word**. Then, choose the format from the highlighted drop-down box. If you want to convert Word 2000 files into another format, click **Convert from Word to another format**. A drop-down box becomes active beneath that button. From this drop-down box, select the format you want.
3. Click **Next** to move to the next window.
4. From the Folder Selection window (see Figure 18.4), click **Browse** (next to Source Folder) to specify the folder where your existing files are.

Part IV

Ch 18

FIGURE 18.3
On the From/To page of the Conversion Wizard, you specify which format you want to convert your file to (or from).

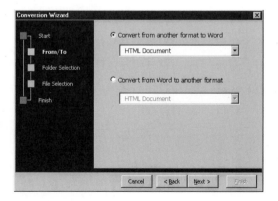

FIGURE 18.4
From the Folder Selection page, you can choose both a source and a destination folder.

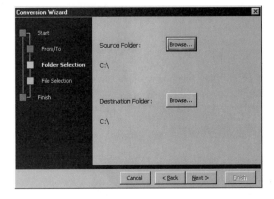

5. The Browse for Folder dialog box appears (see Figure 18.5). Select a folder and click **OK**.

6. Click the **Browse** button located next to the words "Destination Folder."

7. In the Browse for Folder dialog box, select a destination folder and click **OK**.

FIGURE 18.5
From the Browse for Folder dialog box, you can choose a specific folder as either your source or destination folder.

8. Click **Next** to display the File Selection window (shown in Figure 18.6). From here, you can select the specific files you want to convert.

FIGURE 18.6
In the File Selection window, you can choose to convert all or some files in a folder.

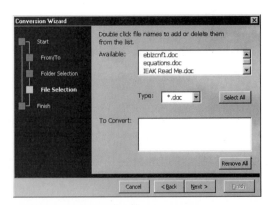

9. To convert all the files in the selected folder, click **Select All**. All the files now appear in the To Convert box.

 TIP If no files appear in the Available box, click the arrow next to the **Type** drop-down box to choose a different file extension, or click inside the box and type the extension you want.

10. To prevent a file from being converted, double-click it in the **To Convert** box.

11. When you finish selecting files, choose **Next**.

12. Click **Finish** to perform the file conversions. A progress bar appears on the screen showing how far along in the conversion process the Conversion Wizard is. When the process finishes, the Conversion Wizard offers you an opportunity to run another conversion. If you click **Yes**, the Wizard runs again.

N O T E If you choose the same folder for input and output and you've chosen a conversion where the file extension does not change (such as converting Word 6 to Word 2000 files), the old files are overwritten in the new format. Be careful to ensure this is what you want to happen before you run the conversion. ▢

N O T E Don't assume the entire process will run unattended: Check in every few minutes. The conversion process might occasionally stop to report an error message or, in some cases, to attempt to load a Web page included in a file being converted. ▢

Using Font Substitution During Document Conversion

When you convert files from another word processing program, if Word 2000 cannot find some or all of the fonts used by the original program, Word automatically substitutes fonts it *does* have.

In some cases, these font substitutions are no-brainers. For example, many Macintosh documents are created with PostScript fonts such as Times Roman and Courier. On standard Windows PCs that don't have Adobe fonts installed, Word substitutes the TrueType equivalents Times New Roman and Courier New.

Note that the substituted fonts are similar *but not identical* to the originals; so, you might find unwelcome changes in line and page breaks. Also note that the original font names still appear in the **Font** drop-down box on the Formatting toolbar. So, if you return the document to its source, the original fonts will automatically be in use.

Occasionally, you'll want to control the way Word substitutes fonts. For example, perhaps you've been handed a document formatted with the Eras Bold ITC font. You don't own Eras Bold ITC, and Word substitutes Lucida Sans Unicode, which looks quite different. However, you *do* have one of the many competitive "knockoff" fonts that resemble Eras Bold ITC. Your font has a name that Word doesn't recognize as being equivalent to Eras. You can tell Word to use *that* font instead of Lucida Sans Unicode whenever it comes across text formatted as Eras Bold ITC.

To specify font substitution, choose **Tools**, **Options** and click the **Compatibility** tab. Then, click **Font Substitution** to open the Font Substitution dialog box (see Figure 18.7).

FIGURE 18.7

In the Font Substitution dialog box, you can control which fonts are used when you don't have the fonts with which your document was formatted.

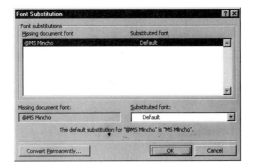

N O T E　If your document has no substituted fonts, Word won't display the Font Substitution dialog box. Rather, it displays a message telling you no font substitution is necessary. ▪

The Font Substitution dialog box lists all the missing document fonts it has found and the font it has substituted for each. (Often, it simply substitutes a default font, typically Times New Roman.) To change a font substitution, select the row containing the missing document font and the font Word has substituted. Then, in the **Substituted font** drop-down box, select the font you want to use.

As you've already learned, when you substitute a font, Word displays and prints the document using the font you chose. However, the original font is still shown in the Font drop-down box. This is obviously welcome for documents that might be returned to their source at a later time. In other cases, however, it can be confusing. After all, the font you see on the screen no longer matches the font with which Word "says" the text has been formatted.

It's easy to reformat the document using the fonts you've already chosen as substitutes. In the Font Substitution box, choose **Convert Permanently**. Click **OK** to confirm the change. Wherever Word finds a substituted font in your document, it converts the document to call for the substituted font name instead of the original one.

Using the Font Mapping File to Export Fonts Correctly

When Word exports files to WordPerfect 5.1 format, it uses default font mapping that translates Windows font names into font names typically available to WordPerfect 5.1 for DOS. If this font mapping is incorrect, you can adjust it. To do so, edit the Rtf_wp5.txt file provided with Word 2000, rename it RTF_WP5.DAT, and save it in the same folder as the files you want to export (being sure to save it as pure ASCII text, not a Word file).

The file itself contains instructions for editing, but briefly you must use each font's precise name (the precise names of common Windows TrueType fonts are provided in the file) and use the following syntax:

```
WinFontName;WPFontName
```

For instance, to convert Windows' Century Schoolbook TrueType font to WordPerfect for DOS' Courier New (TT) font, you would include the following line in your RTF_WP5.DAT file:

```
Courier New;Courier New (TT)
```

 TIP You might want to edit this file using Notepad.

Converting from Other Spreadsheet Software to Excel 2000

Excel includes built-in converters for most (but not all) competitive spreadsheets you're likely to encounter. If you are converting only a small number of simple spreadsheets, these tools are likely to be all you need. But if your spreadsheets are more numerous or complex, so is your management challenge.

In this section, you'll focus primarily on techniques for converting 1-2-3 files—including limitations and workarounds you need to know about in order to be successful. First, however, here is a list of the formats Excel 1-2-3 can open:

- Files from any previous version of Excel (see Chapter 19 for coverage of managing multiple versions of Excel)
- Web pages
- Comma- or tab-delimited text files
- Microsoft Query database query files
- Lotus 1-2-3 for DOS files
- Lotus 1-2-3 for Windows files through Release 5 (WK1, WK3, WK4) but *not* 1-2-3 97 or 1-2-3 Millennium Edition .123 files
- Quattro Pro for DOS files
- Quattro Pro for Windows files, Release 1.0 through 8.0, but *not* Quattro Pro 6 files
- Microsoft Works 2.0 files
- dBASE files
- Data Interchange Format (DIF) files
- SYLK files

To import a single spreadsheet file into Excel from another program or format on this list, first be sure the file is not password protected. If you do not clear password protection using the source program, Excel cannot open the file.

Next, run Excel and choose **File, Open**. Browse to the folder where the spreadsheet file is located, and choose the appropriate format from the **Files of type** drop-down box. Select the file you want to open. (If you want to select several files in the same folder, hold down **Ctrl** and select each one.) Click **Open**. The legacy spreadsheet (or spreadsheets) are loaded into Excel.

CAUTION

Files are not saved in Excel format until the first time you manually save them, and then only if you change the **Files of type** option to **Excel** in the Open dialog box.

Reviewing Your Converted Worksheets

Before you place converted worksheets into production, be sure you review the items in the list that follows. Better yet, review the entire list prior to conversion, so you can make plans to avoid or manage these issues wherever possible.

- **Formulas.** In some cases, Excel calculates the elements of a formula in different order than other spreadsheets do. If you've imported files from 1-2-3 and prefer to retain 1-2-3's rules, choose **Tools, Options, Transition**; then, select the **Transition Formula Evaluation** check box in the Sheet Options area. Also watch out for formulas that Excel might have converted to their results. This occurs when Excel encounters operators or functions it cannot translate.

- **Functions.** As discussed later in this chapter, although Excel has equivalents for most functions used by competitive worksheets, in some cases Excel's functions use different calculation rules, especially when evaluating text in formulas, evaluating some logical operators, and using criteria in database queries. See Table 18.4 (in the next section) for lists of 1-2-3 and corresponding Excel functions.

- **Numbers converted as text.** Excel sometimes converts numbers as strings of text, which can, of course, cause formulas that depend on those numbers to fail. You can often notice these incorrect numbers because they are left-aligned (like most text), whereas surrounding values are right-aligned (like most numbers). To convert a text string to a numeric value, copy it; then, choose **Edit, Paste Special**, choose **Multiply**, and click **OK**. (This multiplies the text string by 1 and places the resulting numeric value in the cell where the text had been.)

- **Dates.** Dates might be reformatted or converted improperly, and you should also check legacy worksheets for Y2K compliance.

- **Currency formats.** For example, Lotus reports that Excel sometimes converts cells formatted in Yen to dollars without informing the user of the change.

- **Special characters.** This can especially be a problem if you are importing DBF files. Excel's filter always uses the ASCII character set, even if the original dBASE file was created with a different character set. You might have to replace special characters manually after file conversion.

- **What-if scenarios.** Excel cannot import scenarios created with Lotus 1-2-3's Version Manager or Quattro Pro's Scenario Manager.

- **Charts/graphs.** Excel does not import these; they must be rebuilt manually.

- **External data links.** Excel can import data links only if they are compatible with Open Database Connectivity (ODBC) or Microsoft Query; otherwise, the links must be rebuilt manually. Among the links that cannot be imported: 1-2-3 Release 4 database records and Quattro Pro for Windows Hot Links to external database tables or to the Data Modeling Desktop.

- **Macros.** Excel can read and run most Lotus 1-2-3 2.01 for DOS macros, but all other spreadsheet macros must be rewritten using Visual Basic for Applications.

- **Formatting.** Minor formatting anomalies are common; for instance, Excel translates 1-2-3 gradient fills as solid colors. Also, note that 1-2-3 can apply formatting from an associated FMT, FM3 or ALL file, but in order for Excel to do so, you must place the formatting in the same folder as the spreadsheet before you perform the conversion.

- **Embedded OLE objects.** For example, Excel cannot directly import maps created with the Lotus Maps feature, although you might be able to copy them into Excel worksheets as images.

- **Recent features.** If you needed to "downsave" a worksheet to an older Excel-compatible file format, which features were lost in the transition?

Finally, did all worksheets convert, or only the first worksheet? This is a more serious problem when you export Excel files to other spreadsheet formats because many formats do not support multiple worksheets. These single-worksheet formats include the following:

- Formatted text (space-delimited)
- Text (tab-delimited)
- CSV (comma-delimited)
- Microsoft Excel 4.0 Worksheet
- Microsoft Excel 3.0 Worksheet
- Microsoft Excel 2.2 Worksheet (Macintosh)
- Microsoft Excel 2.1 Worksheet
- WK1, FMT (1-2-3)
- WK1, ALL (1-2-3)
- WKS (1-2-3)
- WQ1 (Quattro Pro/DOS)
- DBF 4 (dBASE IV)
- DBF 3 (dBASE III)
- DBF 2 (dBASE II)
- CSV (Windows, Macintosh, DOS, or OS/2)
- DIF (Data Interchange Format)
- SYLK (Symbolic Link)

Part
IV
Ch
18

When reading the preceding sections, you likely came to one inescapable conclusion: *You must carefully review converted spreadsheet files before you use them for decision making.*

As in the discussion of WordPerfect-to-Word conversion (earlier in this chapter), careful planning and testing are key, and depending on your specific worksheets, you *might* find that you achieve more accurate conversions if you export to Excel in the program you're leaving—such as 1-2-3 or Quattro Pro—rather than importing to Excel using Microsoft's import filters.

Comparing 1-2-3 and Excel Functions

Most, but not all, of the @functions built into 1-2-3 have equivalents in Excel. Table 18.4 lists the functions as they appear in each program, with notes about differences as necessary.

Table 18.4   Functions Within Applications

1-2-3 Function	Excel Function	Notes on Differences
@@	INDIRECT	
@ABS	ABS	
@ACOS	ACOS	
@ASIN	ASIN	
@ATAN	ATAN	
@ATAN2	ATAN2	
@AVG	AVERAGE	
@CELL	CELL	
@CELLPOINTER	CELL	If you use the Excel CELL function without a second argument, CELL returns information about the current selection.
@CHAR	CHAR	
@CHOOSE	CHOOSE	
@CLEAN	CLEAN	
@CODE	CODE	
@COLS	COLUMNS	
@COS	COS	
@COUNT	COUNTA	
@CTERM	NPER	Excel's NPER function specifies periodic payment, not future value.
@DATE	DATE	
@DATEVALUE	DATEVALUE	
@DAVG	DAVERAGE	
@DAY	DAY	

1-2-3 Function	Excel Function	Notes on Differences
@D360	DAYS360	@D360 is not available in versions of 1-2-3 earlier than Release 3.
@DCOUNT	DCOUNTA	
@DDB	DDB	
@DGET	DGET	
@DMAX	DMAX	
@DMIN	DMIN	
@DSTD	DSTDEVP	
@DSTDS	DSTDEV	@DSTDS is not available in versions of 1-2-3 earlier than Release 3.
@DSUM	DSUM	
@DVAR	DVARP	
@DVARS	DVAR	@DVARS is not available in versions of 1-2-3 earlier than Release 3.
@ERR	None	In Excel, you can enter error values directly into formulas and cells.
@EXACT	EXACT	
@EXP	EXP	
@FALSE	FALSE	
@FIND	FIND	
@FV	FV	
@HLOOKUP	HLOOKUP	To calculate HLOOKUP the same way 1-2-3 does, choose **Tools, Options, Transition, Transition Formula Evaluation**.
@HOUR	HOUR	
@IF	IF	Unlike 1-2-3, Excel allows the last two arguments of the IF function to be any value, not just numbers or strings.
@INDEX	INDEX	Excel's INDEX function also contains a form that lets you choose from an array of values.
@INT	TRUNC or INT	
@IRR	IRR	In Excel, the arguments are rearranged.
@ISERR	ISERR	In Excel, ISERR detects any of six Excel error values.
@ISNA	ISNA	
@ISNUMBER	ISNONTEXT or ISNUMBER	
@ISRANGE	ISREF	@ISRANGE is not available in versions of 1-2-3 earlier than Release 3.

Part

IV

Ch

18

continues

Table 18.4   Continued

1-2-3 Function	Excel Function	Notes on Differences
@ISSTRING	ISTEXT	
@LEFT	LEFT	
@LENGTH	LEN	
@LN	LN	
@LOWER	LOWER	
@LOG	LOG	
@MAX	MAX or MAXA	
@MID	MID	
@MIN	MIN or MINA	
@MINUTE	MINUTE	
@MOD	MOD	To calculate MOD the same way 1-2-3 does, choose **Tools, Options, Transition, Transition Formula Evaluation**.
@MONTH	MONTH	
@N	N	
@NA	NA	
@NOW	NOW	
@NPV	NPV	
@PI	PI	
@PMT	PMT	In Excel, the arguments are rearranged.
@PROPER	PROPER	
@PV	PV	In Excel, the arguments are rearranged.
@RAND	RAND	Excel's version of RAND changes values with every recalculation; 1-2-3's version changes them only once per work session.
@RATE	RATE	In Excel, the arguments are rearranged.
@REPEAT	REPT	
@REPLACE	REPLACE	
@RIGHT	RIGHT	
@ROUND	ROUND	
@ROWS	ROWS	
@S	S	
@SECOND	SECOND	
@SIN	SIN	
@SLN	SLN	
@SQRT	SQRT	

1-2-3 Function	Excel Function	Notes on Differences
@STD	STDEVP or STDEVPA	
@STDEV	STDEV or STDEVA	
@STDEVP	STDEVP	
@STDS	STDEV or STDEVPA	@STDS is not available in versions of 1-2-3 earlier than Release 3.
@STRING	FIXED	
@SUM	SUM	
@SYD	SYD	
@TAN	TAN	
@TERM	NPER	In Excel, the arguments are rearranged.
@TIME	TIME	
@TIMEVALUE	TIMEVALUE	
@TODAY	TODAY	
@TRIM	TRIM	
@TRUE	TRUE	
@UPPER	UPPER	
@VALUE	VALUE	
@VAR	VARA	
@VARP	VARPA	
@VARS	VAR or VARA	@VARS is not available in versions of 1-2-3 earlier than Release 3.
@VDB	VDB	
@VLOOKUP	VLOOKUP	To calculate VLOOKUP the same way 1-2-3 does, choose **Tools**, **Options**, **Transition**, **Transition Formula Evaluation**.
@YEAR	YEAR	

Converting Old Database Files into Access

First, the good news: Access accepts the file formats of many popular database programs, including those listed here:

- dBASE III, III+, IV, and 5.0
- FoxPro 2.x and 3.0
- Paradox 3.x, 4.x, and 5.0
- Text-based data files, both delimited and fixed-width fields
- Lotus 1-2-3 worksheets

Part
IV

Ch
18

- Excel worksheets
- HTML documents and ODBC files
- Outlook and Exchange data

With databases, you might find that you have to work in stages. Start with a small and commonly used database. Attempt your conversions and see what happens. To be sure the conversion was successful, you should examine the resulting Access database and ensure the following steps were actually completed:

- All records were transferred.
- Information ended up in the correct fields.
- All information is present; nothing was clipped, and no extraneous characters were added.
- Relations in relational databases were preserved.
- Created tables can be searched.
- Report formats are intact.

The actual sampling plan and testing methods should be noted in a work instruction; the database specialists can use this to confirm the success of your conversions.

TIP

When converting an existing database to Access, use the field names from your legacy database for the new receiving database in Access. Conversions are much more successful when field names are the same in the two databases.

Another important step to take before attempting conversions and exchanges is to know exactly how the data is used and what is planned for the new database. A couple of examples can illustrate how this can be beneficial.

Converting in One Step

Take the example of a company that sells and fulfills magazine subscriptions. Its database has been kept in dBASE IV format. The database has the subscriber's name, address, phone number, and email address. To this, you add the magazines they purchased, the date of payment, the date the subscription ends, the amount of money still owed, and so on.

This database is very large, but it is in a simple flat format. The company wants to convert this to Access so that it can eventually be linked to Excel for fast reports on cash flow.

With this information, you would know that the existing database must be converted, the existing data would continue to be manipulated and edited in Access, and new subscribers would be added after conversion. Therefore, you need a rapid conversion during the night so that subscription-data-entry people can use the new database the next day. You cannot move in stages because all the information has to stay together.

Therefore, you would attempt a full conversion with a copy of the database to work out any problems before the official conversion. This would include testing how well data entry people can cope with Access and the new database.

Converting in Stages

In a second example, a company has been using Approach to create a multilevel relational database to track all operations. This includes order entry, customer complaints, quality-assurance inspections, production planning, and the like. In this situation, different parts of the database will be linked to the new Access database in stages. In other words, conversion will take place one department at a time.

One of the major problems will be the lack of a conversion utility for Approach. Therefore, the Approach file will be translated to a format Access can accept. Then, the separate data tables will be linked, and new relationships will be defined within Access. This will involve a lot of planning and work if it's to be carried out successfully.

We should note here that Access can bring in sets of data in two different methods:

- **Importing.** The data file and many of its characteristics are directly converted to Access format.
- **Linking.** The old data file can be linked as a table inside of an Access database.

Importing tends to be used when you want to convert a database to Access format without really changing the size, scope, or function of the database. Linking is used in cases when you are building a coalition of databases. Linking is also used when you want to continue to use the legacy database program. Linking leaves the data in its original format and allows Access users to access the data fields.

 TIP Linked tables in Access can accept queries without any problem.

Importing a Legacy Database into Access

To import a legacy DBF (dBASE-compatible) database, first create a new database or open an existing database where you plan to import the data. Then, follow these steps:

1. Choose **File, Get External Data, Import**. The Import dialog box opens (see Figure 18.8).
2. In the **Files of type** drop-down box, choose the file type you want to open.
3. Browse to and select the file you want to import, and then click **Import**. If you're connecting to a file across a network, use a universal naming convention path, not a mapped drive name. Access creates a table named after the file you imported and places the data there.
4. To import more dBASE information, repeat steps 1–3.

FIGURE 18.8

Importing data into an Access database.

Now that you've imported the DBF file as a table, you can set field properties and a primary key for the table.

To import a text file, such as a CSV file, first create a new database or open an existing database where you plan to import the data. Then follow these steps:

1. Choose **File**, **Get External Data**, **Import**. The Import dialog box opens.

2. In the **Files of type** drop-down box, choose the file type you want to open.

3. Browse to and select the file you want to import, and then click **Import**. If the source file was extremely simple, Access might automatically import it into a new table within the current database. Otherwise, Access will display the Import Text Wizard, which walks you through the process of ensuring the table accurately reflects your data (see Figure 18.9). You'll have to make a series of decisions, such as how the data fields are delimited, the widths of columns, the original format of the data, and so forth. Answering these questions correctly ensures a successful conversion. If you experience problems, try other answers in the Wizard and retest your results.

FIGURE 18.9

The Import Text Wizard appears when you are trying to import text-based databases, such as those with comma-delimited data.

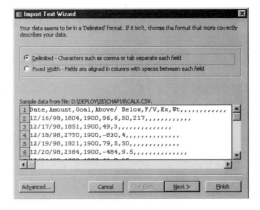

If you find errors, go back and double-check the field settings, indexes, and relations of the original database versus the new Access database. You need to correct and repeat the process until you have a successful conversion. It is not unusual to have to do this several times. However, if it takes more than several tries, you should consider an alternative—such as looking for third-party conversion tools or translating your legacy data into a different format before testing it again.

Importing and Exporting with Outlook

As Table 18.5 shows, Outlook 2000 can import several types of Personal Information Manager (PIM) files, address books, and other data files. As you can also see from the table, Microsoft provides fewer options for directly exporting data files into competitive applications, but most PIMs accept the comma-separated values (CSV) format that Outlook offers.

Table 18.5   Importing and Exporting with Outlook 2000

Source Program	Extension	Import to Outlook 2000?	Export from Outlook 2000?
Microsoft Schedule+ 1.0	.cal	Yes	No
Microsoft Schedule+ 7x	.scd	Yes	No
Microsoft Schedule Plus Interchange	.sc2	Yes	No
Microsoft Personal Folder File	.pst	Yes	Yes
Microsoft Exchange Personal Address Book	.pab	Yes	Yes
Microsoft Internet Mail (IE 3.02)	.pst	Yes	No
Microsoft Outlook Express		Yes	No
ACT! 2.0, 3.0, or 4.0 for Windows	.dbf	Yes	No
ECCO 3.0, 3.01, 3.02, or 4.00	.eco	Yes	No
Eudora Light (1.54 or 3.0.1)		Yes	No
Eudora Pro 2.2, 3.0, or 3.0.1		Yes	No
Netscape Mail 2.02, 3.0, or 3.01		Yes	No
Netscape Messenger 4.0		Yes	No
SideKick 1.0/95 and 2.0	.skcard	Yes	No
Lotus Organizer 1.0, 1.1, 2.1, and 97	.org, .or2, .or3	Yes	No
Comma Separated Values (MS-DOS)	.csv	Yes	Yes
Comma Separated Values (Windows)	.csv	Yes	Yes
Tab Separated Values (MS-DOS)	.txt	Yes	Yes
Tab Separated Values (Windows)	.txt	Yes	Yes
vCalendar	.vcs	Yes	No

Part

IV

Ch

18

continues

Table 18.5   Continued

Source Program	Extension	Import to Outlook 2000?	Export from Outlook 2000?
vCard	.vcf	Yes	No
Microsoft Access	.mdb	Yes	Yes
Microsoft Excel	.xls	Yes	Yes
Microsoft FoxPro	.dbf	Yes	Yes
dBASE	.dbf	Yes	Yes

These can be added to the converters already in Outlook. To import the schedule and contact information from a SideKick file (.skcard), perform the following steps:

1. In Outlook, choose **File**, **Import and Export**. This brings up the Import and Export Wizard (see Figure 18.10).

FIGURE 18.10
Outlook has an Import and Export Wizard to help you load legacy data.

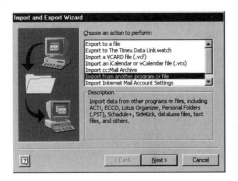

2. Click **Import from Schedule+ or another program or file**.
3. Follow the wizard's instructions. First select the file type and browse until you locate and highlight the target file. At that point, you also have to decide whether to create duplicate data. If you are importing into an existing Outlook file that already has some of the information you are importing, don't duplicate.
4. If you are asked to, enter the password for the file.
5. Map the fields to be transferred between the two programs. This is the only way to ensure the correct transfer of information.

The wizard now completes the importation. Naturally, you should double-check the imported data to ensure that the transfer was successful and the data landed in the correct fields.

Not all PIMs are fully compatible with Outlook. That means the wizard asks you questions on how to handle specific pieces of information in your legacy PIM database. For example, in SideKick the following situations occur:

- The contact log in SideKick is treated as an extended Notes field in Outlook.

- Recurring appointments become individual appointments in Outlook, and you need to restore the recurring feature manually.

- SideKick tasks, calls, and goals are all converted to tasks in Outlook.

- The field names in the contact, task, and appointment fields have different names in many cases, and these need to be mapped manually in the Wizard.

As you have learned about the other programs in the Office suite, test your conversion carefully before you place converted files into production.

Converting with Third-Party Filters

You might encounter situations where Microsoft Office does not provide an adequate import or export filter, and neither does the program you are migrating away from. Or you might no longer have access to such a program; for example, many users have lost their original copies of DOS word processing software that was once quite popular, such as WordStar, Volkswriter, or EasyWriter. In situations like these, the best option might be third-party software. Some examples are covered in this section.

Conversions Plus from DataViz (and the comparable MacLinkPlus for the Macintosh) offer the following converters:

Part IV

Ch 18

- Ami Pro 1.2 (Read Only), 2.0x, 3.x

- ClarisWorks 1.0, 2.x, 3.0, 4.0 (Windows and Macintosh; word processing, spreadsheet, database)

- dBASE II, III, IV (DBF)

- DCA/RFT

- Excel 4.0, 5.0, 7.0, 97, 98

- FoxBASE/FoxPro

- Lotus 1-2-3 (WKS, WK1, WK3, WK4, 97, 98)

- MacWrite II

- MacWrite Pro 1.0, 1.5

- MS Word for the Macintosh 4.0, 5.0, 5.1, 6.0, 98

- MS Word for Windows 2.0, 6.0, 7.0, 97

- MS Word for DOS 5.5

- MS Works 2.0 (Read Only), 3.0, 4.0 (Windows and Macintosh; word processing, spreadsheet, database)

- Multimate 3.x, 4.0

- Multimate Advantage 1.0 (Read Only)

- PerfectWorks 2.1 (word processing, spreadsheet, database)
- Quattro Pro (DOS) 4.0
- Quattro Pro (Windows) 1.0, 5.0, 6.0, 7.0, 8.0
- RTF
- Text
- Word Pro 96, 97, 98
- WordPerfect for DOS 2.0, 2.1, 3.x
- WordPerfect for DOS 5.0 (Read Only), 5.1, 6.x
- WordPerfect Windows 5.x, 6.x, 7.0, 8.0
- WordPerfect Works 2.0 (word processing, spreadsheet, database)
- WordStar (DOS) 5.5, 6.0, 7.0

DataViz also offers the similar MacLink Plus for the Macintosh.

If you need to view older files, and it is sufficient to cut and paste their data into Office applications, consider Quick View Plus 5.1 Enterprise Edition from Inso Software. This utility can display more than 200 file formats, covering virtually every common DOS, Windows, and Macintosh format—including Office 2000 formats.

Quick View Plus can also integrate with your email and browser software, allowing users to view formatted documents even if they do not have the original source applications. To learn more about QuickView Plus, visit `http://www.inso.com/qvp/index.htm`. If you need a copy of QuickView Plus for small office or home office use, contact Jasc Software at `http://www.jasc.com/qvp.html`.

Advanced Computer Innovations, Inc. produces a utility called WordPort that can convert to and from many different word processing programs. Its strength lies in its capability to preserve advanced formatting features. It can be run in batch mode for translating up to thousands of files in one pass. The ACI Web site is located at `www.acii.com/conv.htm`. ACI also offers R-Doc/X for the conversion of very old (in computer years) word processors, such as Spellbinder, PeachText, Leading Edge WP, and Word Marc. Also available from ACI is ListPort, which converts flat data between most database programs. This includes options for reordering the data, breaking up data fields, and combining fields, as well as other options that can be quite helpful when migrating to Access.

And, finally, there is HiJaak Pro for the capture and conversion of graphic files—a migration question that has not yet been addressed. Many of the applications in Office 2000 enable you to incorporate graphics into forms, documents, spreadsheets, and the like. Often, however, corporations forget that they have a collection of logos, illustrations, drawings, and photos that also have to migrate into Office 2000. For the earlier formats or for Macintosh-to-PC conversions, a third-party utility such as HiJaak Pro is necessary. HiJaak is currently sold by IMSI (`www.imsisoft.com`).

In summary, a wide variety of third-party options are available. As with any software program, you should first test their capabilities with actual sets of your data to ensure that they work properly. ●

CHAPTER 19

Managing Multiple Versions of Office

by Daryl Lucas

Good news: The Office 2000 versions of Word, Excel, and PowerPoint have the same file format as their Office 97 cousins. In fact, their file formats have been renamed to "97-2000" to reflect their dual identity. This means that you can open Office 2000 files in Office 97 applications without invoking file converters or hassling with file viewers.

Unfortunately, the good news has an asterisk. Users of Office 97 can open 97-2000 files, but they do not have access to many of the new features hidden inside. And speaking of Access, the 97-2000 file format used by that powerhouse application has undergone a change, and that means you will have to convert databases. None of these blows will kill your rollout, but they do bring challenges.

This chapter discusses ways to make the process of managing these differing Office versions as smooth as possible.

Managing Changes in Word File Formats

Word 2000 has the same file format that Word 97 (for Windows) and Word 98 (for the Macintosh) have. This means that Word 97 and 98 do not have to convert a Word 2000 file to open and display it. You can share your Word 2000 files with users of these earlier versions without the need to distribute a file viewer or file converters.

However, Word 2000 introduces new features that Word 97 and 98 do not have, and the distance from Word 95 is even greater. As soon as you upgrade to Word 2000, you have two tasks to do:

■ Upgrading existing documents to the new format

■ Enabling users of the earlier software to open and edit converted documents

▶ Upgrading files to Word 2000 also involves conversion of macro code. For information on this issue, **see** "Migrating Code from Earlier Versions," on **p. 437**.

Converting Files to Word 2000 Format

Word 2000 ships with a large number of import filters. These filters let you open text files in a variety of formats so you can save them in Word's native format. Table 19.1 lists the text import filters included with Word 2000.

These built-in filters do not require any installation; they come with Word 2000. They represent your most portable file formats because Word can both read and write them.

Table 19.1   Text File Formats for Which Word 2000 Has Import Filters

File Format	Built-In	Included in Office Setup	Included in Converter Pack	Allows Export
HTML/XML	x		For all but Word 6.0	x
Lotus Ami Pro 2.x			Word 6.0 only	x
Lotus Ami Pro 3.x		x	For all but Word 6.0	x
Microsoft Works 3.x, 4.x/95 (Windows)		For all but Word 6.0	For all but Word 6.0	For all but Word 6.0
MS-DOS text	x			x
MS-DOS text with layout		x	x	x
MS-DOS text with line breaks	x			x
Recover Text		x	x	n/a
Revisable-Form-Text Document Content Architecture (RFT-DCA)		x	x	x

File Format	Built-In	Included in Office Setup	Included in Converter Pack	Allows Export
Rich Text Format (RTF)	x			x
Text only	x			x
Text with layout		x	x	x
Text with line breaks	x			x
Unicode text	x			x
Windows Write 3.x		x	x	x
Word 1.0, 2.x (Windows)	x			
Word 3.x–6.0 (DOS)		x	x	x
Word 4.0, 5.x (Macintosh)	x		x	x
Word 6.0, 95 (Windows) (native format)	Import only	x	x	Word 97 only
WordPerfect 4.x (DOS)		x	x	x
WordPerfect 5.x (DOS, Windows)		x	x	x
WordPerfect 6.0 (DOS, Windows)		For all but Word 6.0	For all but Word 6.0	
WordStar 1.0, 2.0 (Windows)		x	x	
WordStar 3.3, 3.45, 4.0, 5.0, 5.5, 6.0, 7.0 (DOS)		x	x	4.0, 7.0 only

Some of the other filters require installation from Office Setup. If you have them set to Run on First Use, Office Setup prompts you the first time you use them. Otherwise, you can install them manually by running Setup. Figure 19.1 shows the item to choose in the Setup dialog box.

For the most part, the filters available in the Microsoft Office Converter Pack mirror those available in Office Setup. However, you can deploy the Converter Pack to users of earlier versions of Word, including Word 6.0, 95, and 97, so they can install the filters as well. You can also use it to manage the rollout of HTML/XML converters for the sharing of HTML documents.

▶ For more information on using the Converter Pack, **see** the "The Microsoft Office Converter Pack" section, later in this chapter.

▶ For more information on using HTML/XML as a primary file format, **see** Chapter 33, "Managing HTML/XML As Your Primary File Format," on **p. 867**.

Part

IV

Ch

19

FIGURE 19.1
Office Setup lets you
install some additional
Word file filters.

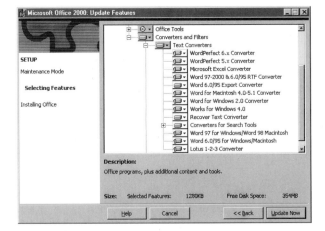

Word includes filters for other kinds of files as well as text documents. Word uses these filters to enable the inclusion of spreadsheet, database, and graphics data in word processing files. Table 19.2 lists some of the additional filters available to Word 2000.

Table 19.2   Nontext File Formats for Which Word 2000 Has Import Filters

File Format	Common File Extension	Built-In	Included in Office Setup	Included in Converter Pack
AutoCAD 1–12 (2-D graphics only) (DOS, Windows)	DXF			X
Computer Graphics Metafile (CGM:1992 1.0)	CGM		X	X
CorelDRAW 3.0, 4.0, 5.0, 6.0	CDR		X	X
dBASE II, III, III+, IV	DBF		X	X
Device-independent Bitmap	DIB	X	X	
Encapsulated PostScript	EPS		X	X
Enhanced Metafile	EMF	X	X	X
Excel 2.x, 3.0, 4.0, 5.0, 95, 97, 98, 2000	XLS		X	X
FlashPix	FPX		X	X
FoxPro 2.6	DBF		X	X
Graphics Interchange Format	GIF	X	X (87a, 89a)	X
JPEG (Joint Photographic Experts Group)	JPG	X	X (6.0)	X
Kodak Photo CD 3.0	PCD		X	X

File Format	Common File Extension	Built-In	Included in Office Setup	Included in Converter Pack
Lotus 1-2-3 2.x, 3.x, 4.0	WK1		X	X
Macintosh PICT	PCT	X	X	X
Micrografx Designer 3.x, Charisma 2.1, Draw	DRW			X
PC Paintbrush (all versions through ZSoft 3.0)	PCX		X	X
PictureIt!	MIX		X	
Portable Network Graphics	PNG	X	X (Tenth Spec)	X
Run-length Encoded	RLE	X	X	
Standard Windows bitmap	BMP	X	X	X
TIFF (Tagged Image File Format) 5.0, 6.0	TIF		X	X
Truevision Targa	TGA			X
Windows Metafile	WMF	X	X	X
WordPerfect Graphics 1.0, 1.0e, 2.0	WPG		X	X

Graphics are a special case because they include no text. When Word opens files that contain graphics or links to graphics, it uses graphics filters to display and store their data. If the graphics are in a format built into Word, it preserves the format. If the graphics are in a format for which Word has a filter, Word converts the graphics to a built-in format. If the graphics are in a format for which Word has no converter, Word displays a message and does not import the image. Table 19.2 lists the graphics formats for which Word 2000 has import filters built in.

Part IV

Ch 19

N O T E It is important to note that Word cannot create graphics files. Although Word can create some kinds of text files, such as WordStar 4.0 or Ami Pro 3.0 files, with the appropriate filter, Word cannot create PNG files, even though the PNG filter used by Office applications is an import/export filter. To create graphics files, you need a graphics program such as Microsoft PhotoDraw. You also can export PowerPoint slides as individual graphics files in any format for which PowerPoint has an export filter. ■

▶ For more information on using PowerPoint to create graphics files, **see** the "Saving PowerPoint 2000 Files in Other Formats" section later in this chapter.

Sharing Files with Word 97 Users

Some of the features introduced in Word 2000 cannot be displayed in Word 97 or 98 and will be lost if saved by the earlier version. The following is a list of the features that suffer from this limitation:

- Decorative underline formatting
- 24-bit color text formatting
- Text-wrapping breaks
- Top-page gutters
- Many types of graphic (shapes) positioning
- Asian text formatting
- Nested tables and nested table cells
- Spacing between table cells and cell margins
- Diagonal table cell borders
- Page breaks within tables
- Floating graphics within tables

If you need these features, you will not be able to share Word 2000 files with Word 97/98 users. Word 97/98 users will be able to open your Word 2000 files, but they will not be able to edit the files and save their changes without causing the new features to be lost.

If you want to share 97-2000 files with users of Word 97/98 and are willing to make some compromises, you have at least four options:

- Avoid using features that might suffer in the transition.
- Disable Word 2000 features that Word 97 does not support.
- Use Word 6.0/95 format as your default format.
- Use HTML/XML as a primary file format.

Sharing by Avoiding Incompatible Features   Most of the new features in Word 2000 affect esoteric uses of the product, not basic or even moderately sophisticated word processing tasks. If you know you will rarely need these features, you might not need a rigorous plan for avoiding incompatibilities at all. Just give a list of the trouble spots to the appropriate Word users and be done with it.

Sharing by Disabling Word 2000 Features   If you want to leave nothing to chance, you can cripple Word 2000 so that it keeps new features out of your documents entirely. Click **Tools, Options, Save**, and select the option to **Disable features not supported by Word 97**. (You cannot disable features not supported by Word 98.) This prevents you from accidentally using a format or feature that would be lost if saved in Word 97.

NOTE   You also can set this option in the system Policy Editor.

NOTE   You cannot prevent Word 97 users from saving 97-2000 files unless you prevent them from saving all documents.

Sharing by Using Word 6.0/95 As Default File Format   It was possible in Word 97 to use the Word 6.0/95 file format as the default; it is possible to do so in Word 2000 as well. If this is what you have been doing, you could continue to do so. However, you also continue to forfeit the new features available in the later versions.

Sharing by Using HTML/XML As Default File Format   You can, in a sense, bypass the issue of file format compatibility altogether by changing the default file format that everyone uses to HTML/XML. Keep in mind, however, that this option is available for users of Word 95, 97, and 98 only—it is not an option for users of Word 1.0, 2.0, or 6.0.

▶ For more information on using HTML/XML for the purpose of sharing files with users of Word 6.0/95 and 97/98, **see** the "Using HTML/XML As a Default Format" section later in this chapter.

Sharing Word 2000 Files with Word 6.0/95

Word 2000 supports two file formats created specifically for users of Word 6.0 and Word 95:

- Word 97-2000 & 6.0/95—RTF dual format
- Word 6.0/95 binary format

Both of these options represent a compromise. Users of Word 6.0 and Word 95 cannot save files in 97-2000 format. Although the dual format lets Word 6.0 and 95 users open the file, it does not let them preserve the 97-2000 data stream. If you use these formats to share data back and forth between users, remember that the sharing goes one way. Users cannot pass the files back and forth transparently.

In addition to the features that Word 97 does not support, Word 95 loses the following list of features as well:

- Embedded fonts
- Page borders and backgrounds
- All the following character formats: shading, double strikethrough, borders, engraving, embossing, animated text, and horizontal scaling
- Decorative paragraph borders
- Table of Contents one-click hyperlinks
- Floating graphics with text wrap
- Floating OLE objects
- Tracked changes for properties, paragraph numbers, and display fields
- All document passwords (open, tracked changes, comments, and forms)
- Functionality of ActiveX controls
- All Visual Basic for Applications (VBA) project code (UserForms, Modules, Class Modules, Designers, and Document Objects)
- Versioning
- AUTOTEXTLIST fields
- Decorative line styles (drawing)

Part
IV

Ch
19

- EMF, PNG, GIF, JPEG graphics (converted to WMF)
- Tight and Through text wrapping around graphics
- WordArt
- Automatic numbering in table cells
- Vertical text in tables
- Bottom-aligned and vertically centered text in tables

Word 6.0 loses the following features (introduced in Word 95):

- DOCVARIABLE fields
- Character highlighting
- Word 95 document properties

N O T E For more information on Word 2000 features not supported by Word 6.0 or Word 95 and what happens when they are converted, see "What Happens When I Save a Document As Word 6.0/95?" in Word 2000 Help. ■

N O T E The dual format saves two data streams: a 97-2000 portion and a 6.0/95 portion. However, the 6.0/95 portion is in Rich Text Format, not Word 6.0/95's native binary format. There is no dual format that includes Word 6.0/95's binary format. ■

Using the Batch Conversion Wizard

If you need to convert a large number of documents, the Batch Conversion Wizard can automate much of the work. This Wizard does the same thing you would do if you opened a document and then saved it in another format using the Save As command, but with an interface that lets you do the conversion with many documents at once.

To start the Wizard, choose **File, New, Other Documents, Batch Conversion Wizard** (see Figure 19.2).

Before you begin, simply identify where the source documents are and where you want to put the resulting (converted) documents. These locations can be the same if you specify different file extensions for each file type. Then, start the Conversion Wizard by choosing **File, New, Other Documents, Batch Conversion Wizard** (see Figure 19.3).

FIGURE 19.2

The Conversion Wizard is a Word template that you start by creating a new Batch Conversion Wizard document.

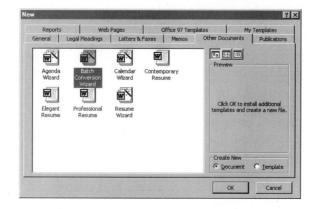

FIGURE 19.3

If you have a lot of documents to convert to or from Word 2000 format, you will want to become familiar with this tool.

Managing Changes in Excel File Formats

Excel 2000 has the same file format that Excel 97 (for Windows) and Excel 98 (for the Macintosh) have. This means that Excel 97 and 98 do not have to convert Excel 2000 files to open and display them. You can share Excel 2000 files with users of these earlier versions without the need to distribute file viewers or file converters.

But Excel 97 and 98 do not support all the features in Excel 2000, making smooth and painless shared use of files between versions impossible. If you have users who must share files between versions, the best you can do is be aware of the differences and try to minimize their impact.

Your options depend greatly on the version of Excel that represents the "backward" target. The following sections describe the options in detail.

Part

IV

Ch

19

Sharing Excel 2000 Files Using Excel 97-2000 Format

Excel 97/98 do a good job of supporting their more advanced host. Because the Excel 97/98 file format is the same as Excel 2000, most of the adjustments you must make involve limits on what you can see and do with the data in the earlier version. For the most part, you can share files between these earlier and later versions without trouble.

The biggest loss you incur is visibility of features in Excel 97/98. If you have an Excel 2000 file with a Web Component, a PivotChart, or a four-digit data type, you will either not be able to see the feature or not be able to use it in Excel 97/98. But you will not necessarily lose it when you save the file in Excel 97 or Excel 98.

N O T E For more information on saving files in other file formats, see the topic "Formatting and Features Not Transferred in File Conversions" in Excel help. ■

Table 19.3 Data, Features, and Formatting Lost or Replaced When Saved in Excel 97-2000 Format by Excel 97 or Excel 98

Feature	Lost	Modified
External data ranges		Auto-refresh, column formatting, filtering, and sorting do not work
PivotTable AutoFormat formatting	x	
OLAP PivotTable and PivotChart reports appear as read-only		Converted to read-only

You should also be aware that the Help file incorrectly reports the loss of some features. For example, PivotChart reports appear as regular charts in Excel 97/98, but saving the workbook does not delete or change their structure. Also, external data ranges might be fully functional; the Help file says that they are not. If you are concerned about your data at all, test the functionality thoroughly before you use it.

Sharing Excel 2000 Files with Excel 5.0/95

Excel 2000 supports two file formats created specifically for users of Excel 5.0/95:

- Excel 97-2000 & 5.0/95 dual format
- Excel 5.0/95 format

To create a file in either of these formats, click **File**, **Save As**, choose the appropriate format in the **Save as type** list box, and click **Save**.

N O T E The list of file formats available in the Save as type list box depends on what you have selected in the workbook. If you have a worksheet selected, you will see a list of file formats that can be created from a worksheet; if you have a chart selected, you will see a different list of formats. ■

Microsoft says that both "backward-compatible" file formats make ideal solutions for organizations that want to roll out their upgrades from Excel 5.0/95 gradually. However, the reality is a bit harsher than that. If you use them to share data back and forth between users, you will make some sacrifices.

The list of Excel 2000 features not supported in the Excel 5.0/95 format is quite long. To see a comprehensive list, display **Excel Help**, type "`Formatting and features not transferred in file conversions`" in the Answer Wizard, and click on the topic **Microsoft Excel 5.0/95 Workbook**. This topic goes into detail on how each feature is affected; see Table 19.4 for a summary.

Table 19.4 Summary List of Excel 2000 Features Crippled or Lost in Excel 5.0/95

Category	Features Crippled or Lost
Workbook properties and settings	Amount of data allowed per cell and per worksheet, data validation
Data formatting	Backgrounds, borders, text alignment, text rotation
Charting	PivotCharts, gradient fills, bubble charts, rotated labels, time-scale axes, data tables in charts
Analysis, PivotTable, and data access	New PivotTable features, new query types, new PivotTable and PivotChart report types, external data ranges, new worksheet functions
OLE objects and graphics	Excel 2000 features in the embedded object, WordArt objects, AutoShapes
Workgroup and Internet features	Comments, hyperlinks, change tracking, workbook sharing
Programmability	VBA Modules, Class Modules, and UserForms; Excel 97 and 2000 objects, properties, and methods; ActiveX controls

Part
IV

Ch
19

Sharing Excel 2000 Files Using HTML/XML

Another option is to use HTML/XML as your default file format. If you do so, you must also

- Use Cascading Style Sheets
- Have Internet Explorer 4.0 or later

Users of Excel 95, 97, and 98 must also install the HTML add-in, have Internet Explorer 4.0 or later, and use Cascading Style Sheets. You can use the Office Converter Pack to distribute the HTML add-in.

One more option is to use HTML/XML as your default file format and to publish worksheets and charts in Office Web Components. Users who need to edit, add to, and delete data as well as view it can do so in their browsers. They do not need to have Excel on their computers.

Working Around Other Excel File Conversion Issues

Before you deploy Excel 2000, you will want to think about three more file conversion issues: two-digit dates, conversion of hundred or thousands of files, and macro code. Moving from an earlier format to Excel 2000—even if from Excel 97—will require some attention to detail if you want to make the transition safely.

Converting Two-Digit Dates   Excel 97 changed the way Excel handles two-digit dates. If you have any workbooks from earlier versions of Excel that (1) include date functions, (2) use serial dates, or (3) use two-digit dates, you should check them for problems. The Office Resource Kit provides two add-ins to help with this chore:

■ The *Date Migration Wizard* scans folders for workbooks with date functions and flags the ones that might have problems (see Figure 19.4). This tool originally shipped with Excel 97, but is just as useful to Excel 2000 users.

FIGURE 19.4

The Date Migration Wizard ferrets out workbooks that use date functions and alerts you to possible problems.

■ The *Date Fix Wizard* provides three functions that help you manage serial dates (see Figure 19.5).

FIGURE 19.5

The Date Fix Wizard automates the process of changing date functions to four-digit format.

These add-ins are located in the \ork\pfiles\orktools\toolbox\tools\xltools folder of the Office Resource Kit. To install them in Excel 2000, click **Tools, Add-Ins, Browse**, open the appropriate file, and click **OK**. Excel adds a menu to the bottom of the Tools menu (see Figure 19.6). To use either tool, click the menu item you want to launch.

Converting in Batches   Excel 97 shipped with a batch conversion Wizard, much like Word. Excel 2000 does not include this tool.

FIGURE 19.6
When you load the Date add-ins, Excel adds them to your Tools menu.

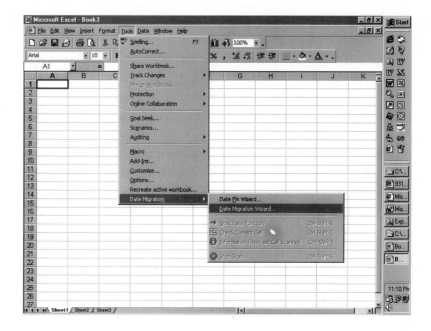

Converting Macro Code Excel was one of the first Office applications to adopt VBA as its native programming tongue, so you should be able to open most coded workbooks with little problem. You might, however, encounter errors when you try to compile your projects. In most cases, these errors arise out of changes in the Excel object model and can be fixed with some minor edits.

▶ For more information on upgrading Excel VBA code, **see** the "Migrating Code from Earlier Versions" section in "Managing Office Programmability," on **p. 463**.

Avoiding Pitfalls When Upgrading to Excel 2000

Assuming you are proceeding with a gradual rollout of Excel and must upgrade from earlier file formats, here are some steps you can take to lessen the negative impact:

■ If you must use an earlier version, use Excel 97. This leaves you with far fewer decisions to make about what to give up, fewer risks of data or formatting loss, and far more features intact than if you must share with Excel 95.

■ If possible, do not let Excel 97 users save 97-2000 files; make shared files read-only to users of the earlier version. Otherwise, the Excel 2000 features will be lost whenever one of these earlier versions saves the file. You can use System Policies to enforce this rule.

■ If you must share a particular workbook with an earlier version, avoid use of features unique to Excel 2000, such as Web Components, PivotCharts, and the new four-digit date formats. If you do not, users of earlier versions are not able to use them. Some of these features are also stripped from the file if it is saved in 97/98 format.

- Take advantage of the dual file format whenever you can put a read-only workbook to good use, such as in the publication of company handbooks, phone lists, and reference documents.

- You can always open earlier Excel files in Excel 2000. You can also use Excel 95 and 97 templates in Excel 2000.

- You can share an Excel 2000 template with users of Excel 97 and 98, but Excel 2000 features in the template will be lost.

▶ Upgrading files to Excel 2000 can involve conversion of macro code. For information on this issue, **see** the "Migrating Code from Earlier Versions" section in "Managing Office Programmability," on **p. 463**.

Managing Changes in PowerPoint File Formats

Like Excel and Word, PowerPoint 2000 has the same file format as its predecessor. PowerPoint 97 (for Windows) and PowerPoint 98 (for the Macintosh) do not have to convert PowerPoint 2000 presentations in order to open, display, and show them. You can share your PowerPoint 2000 files with users one generation behind without distributing file viewers or file converters.

But also like Word and Excel, PowerPoint 97 and 98 do not support the new PowerPoint 2000 features. You must therefore be aware of the challenges involved in upgrading.

Converting Presentations to PowerPoint 2000

PowerPoint 2000 can open presentations that originate in the following formats:

- PowerPoint 97 and 98
- PowerPoint 95
- PowerPoint 4.0
- Harvard Graphics 2.3, 3.0 (DOS)
- Freelance Graphics 4.0 (DOS)
- Freelance Graphics 1.0–2.1 (Windows)

N O T E Microsoft maintains a download site with updated filters for PowerPoint users at its Office Resource Kit Web site. Check `http://www.microsoft.com/office/ork` for updates.

To convert any of these formats to PowerPoint 2000, simply save the file as a PowerPoint presentation. It will be converted to PowerPoint 97-2000 format automatically.

N O T E The Harvard Graphics and Freelance Graphics filters come with the Converter Pack. Users of PowerPoint 97 and 95 can install these filters by running the Converter Pack setup. For more information on using the Office Converter Pack, **see** "Using The Microsoft Office Converter Pack" on **p. 545** later in this chapter.

Existing PowerPoint 97/98 files open with all data, formatting, and VBA code intact. However, you might need to edit some VBA code because of differences in the PowerPoint 97/98 and 2000 object models. PowerPoint displays a message whenever it comes upon a line that it cannot compile.

Sharing PowerPoint 2000 Presentations with Earlier Versions

PowerPoint 2000 takes roughly the same approach to backward compatibility taken by Word and Excel. You can convert PowerPoint 2000 presentations into two formats created specifically for users of earlier versions:

- PowerPoint 97-2000 & 95 dual format
- PowerPoint 95 format

Both of these formats are alternatives to the native PowerPoint 97-2000 format. You can convert presentations to these formats, or use one of them as a default format, if you want to share files with users of PowerPoint 95.

Each format gives you a different experience, however. The following sections go into greater detail.

Converting with the Dual Format   Here are some facts to consider when converting in the *dual* format:

- Even though the file contains data streams in both formats, PowerPoint 95 users cannot save dual-format files as dual-format files. They can view and edit the presentation, but they cannot save their changes without discarding the 97-2000 portion.

- PowerPoint 95 users might not be able to see features or effects specific to PowerPoint 97 or 2000. This can be a significant limitation depending on the extent to which you have used these features.

- VBA code does not run in PowerPoint 95. PowerPoint 95 does not support VBA, so all the code is left out of the version 95 data stream.

You can prevent PowerPoint 95 users from altering dual-format files by making the files read-only or by requiring a password to save (and not distributing the password).

The dual format is a good option for presentations that you need to distribute to a wide audience. You can publish the presentation without worrying about providing a separate file for each of three PowerPoint versions (although if you want to provide a file that is readable by PowerPoint 4.0 users, you have to provide a separate file).

Converting with the PowerPoint 95 Format   Whenever you save a PowerPoint 2000 file to PowerPoint 95 format, PowerPoint warns you that you might lose some data or features in the process. Because the list of possible losses is long, the warning also offers to take you to a Help file topic about the details of *what* might be lost (see Figure 19.7).

Part
IV

Ch
19

FIGURE 19.7
Saving a PowerPoint 2000 presentation in PowerPoint 95 format is a one-way trip to a barren land, so be sure you can afford to lose functionality in the resulting presentation before clicking **Yes**.

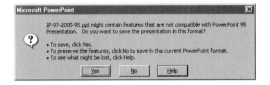

If you are not familiar with this list, click **Help** and read the description of the many features not supported by PowerPoint 95 (see Figure 19.8). It is very long.

FIGURE 19.8
Be aware of what you will lose before you use an earlier format.

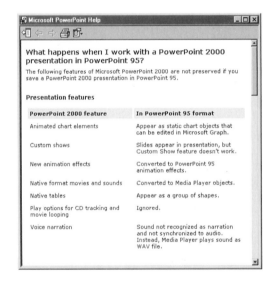

Table 19.5 summarizes the losses.

Table 19.5   Features Crippled or Lost in the Conversion to PowerPoint 95

Category	Features Crippled or Lost
Presentation features	Animated chart elements, new animation effects, custom shows, tables, new movie and sound features
Graphic features	3-D effects, animated GIFs, automatic numbered lists, AutoShapes, shape connectors, curves, graphic bullets, new fill effects, new line formatting options, new OLE object formatting options, WordArt drawings, new shadow effects
Workgroup and Internet features	Comments, embedded hyperlinks, compound hyperlinks, embedded action settings, e-mail message headers

Category	Features Crippled or Lost
Chart, macro, and character features	Embedded fonts, 97-2000 charts, VBA projects (UserForms, Modules, and Class Modules), Unicode character mappings
Internationalization features	Date format corrections, multilingual Kinsoku

Working with Earlier Formats via the PowerPoint Import Converter   The Microsoft Office Converter Pack includes two converters that let PowerPoint 95 users open PowerPoint 2000 presentations:

- The PowerPoint 97-2000 converter lets PowerPoint 95 users open and view PowerPoint 2000 presentations. This is a read-only filter.
- The HTML converter lets PowerPoint 95 users view and edit PowerPoint 2000 presentations saved as Web pages.

▶ For more information on using the Office Converter Pack, **see** "Using The Microsoft Office Converter Pack" later in this chapter.

Working with Newer Formats via the PowerPoint 2000 Viewer   The Office Resource Kit includes a PowerPoint Viewer, Pptvw32.exe, in the ork\pfiles\orktools\toolbox\tools\pptview folder. You are free to distribute this file to others who do not have PowerPoint but need to view PowerPoint 2000 presentations. As with all the Resource Kit tools, this file is available at the ORK Web site, `http://www.microsoft.com/office/ork`.

Saving PowerPoint 2000 Files in Other Presentation Formats

PowerPoint 2000 lets you save presentations in two other formats that might meet your data-sharing needs:

- Web Page (HTML/XML format)
- Graphics files (GIF, JPEG, DIB, WMF, PNG, TIFF)

The usefulness of these options depends on what you need to do with the output.

Saving As Web Pages   The method for savingand using presentations as Web Pages is the same as for Word and Excel. Click **File**, **Save as Web Page**, and give the presentation a name. Users who want to view or edit the converted presentations can open them either in a Web browser that supports XML or in PowerPoint. To open them in an earlier version of PowerPoint, they need to install the HTML/XML converter from the Converter Pack.

▶ For information on publishing PowerPoint presentations to a Web server, **see** Chapter 32, "Using Office 2000 Features to Enhance Your Web Site or Intranet," on **p. 819**.

Saving As Graphics Files   You can save PowerPoint slides as graphics files in any of the formats for which PowerPoint has an export filter. By default, PowerPoint has six such filters built in:

- Graphics Interchange Format (GIF)
- JPEG File Interchange Format (JPG)

- Portable Network Graphics (PNG)
- Device-independent bitmap (DIB, BMP)
- Windows Metafile (WMF)
- Tagged Image File Format (TIFF/TIF)

You can add WordPerfect Graphics (WPG) files to this list by installing the filter from Office Setup or from the Converter Pack.

To create graphics files in any of these formats, simply use the Save As command and choose the appropriate format in the Save as type drop-down list box. PowerPoint will ask whether you want to convert the entire presentation or just the selected slide. If you choose the entire presentation, each slide becomes a separate file; otherwise, only the selected slide is converted.

NOTE Graphics import filters are shared components, so it is a good idea to install them by default. If you use the Custom Installation Wizard or Systems Management Server to deploy Office, including all the graphics filters cuts down on the support calls and requests for additional filters you inevitably get.

Managing Changes in Access File Formats

Access is the only Office 2000 application with a new file format. Among other things, the new format enables Access databases to support Unicode, ActiveX Data Objects (ADO), and Web Components. However, you have some flexibility in moving back and forth between formats. Conversion to the 2000 format does not have to happen all at once, and it does not have to be a one-way street.

Managing the changes in Access' file format falls into two categories:

- How to do a sudden rollout
- How to do a gradual rollout

Preparing for Any Kind of Rollout

Before you convert any databases, you have two much more important questions to answer: Does *any* of them use *any* two-digit years in *any* tables, queries, reports, module code, or macro code? If they do not *use* two-digit years, do they *allow* two-digit years? If the answer to either of these questions is yes, change the database so that it uses and require four-digit years throughout. Do not convert it until you do.

The reason is simple: Different versions of Access treat two-digit years differently. Access 2.0 uses its own internal method, Access 95 uses an early version of the Oleaut32.dll system file, the Access 95 runtime uses a date-window version of Oleaut32.dll, and later versions of Access use date-window versions of Oleaut32.dll that allow the user to change the date window. Figure 19.9 shows the Windows 98 Control Panel applet that allows users to change the date window used by Oleaut32.dll.

FIGURE 19.9
The Regional Settings applet, available in Control Panel, allows the user to control how the operating system interprets two-digit dates—a nightmare for any database that uses two-digit dates.

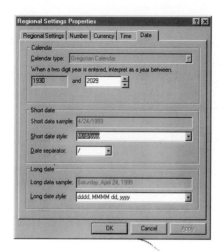

In other words, any database that has, uses, or allows two-digit dates can get corrupted three different ways:

- Merely by being converted or opened in a later version of Access. Dates interpreted one way in the earlier version are suddenly interpreted another way in the converted version, changing the data.

- Users using machines have different versions of Oleaut32.dll enter dates inconsistently.

- Users using machines on which they have changed the date window.

The easiest and best way to head off this problem is to remove two-digit years from all parts of the database—from forms to module code. If you do this, you need not fear data corruption from inconsistent use of date information; you can forge ahead with the rollout worry-free. If you do not, you cannot be sure that the date data, and the calculations on which they depend, are correct.

Rolling Out Access 2000 All at Once

In a sudden rollout, you convert all users and all databases to Access 2000 all at once. You do not need to make databases available to several versions at once because no one will be using an earlier version. You need only to move the files from the old format to the new one.

Before you convert an earlier-version database to Access 2000, you need to get ready:

- Back up the database. This might seem obvious, but it is the most important step. Keep a copy of the original before you try to change it.

- Replace references to the Microsoft DAO 2.5/3.x Compatibility Library with the Microsoft DAO 3.6 Object Library; the Access 2000 format does not support the DAO 2.5/3.x library. Then, edit your code so that it does not depend on any of the earlier objects. (You might need to remove the DAO 2.5/3.x reference manually after conversion.)

Part
IV

Ch
19

■ Compile the database and save it. If you get compile errors, fix them and continue recompiling until the errors are gone. If you do not fix compile errors now, Access 2000 is not able to save the converted database in a compiled state; you will get a warning when you convert it (see Figure 19.10), and you will continue to get compile errors in the converted database.

■ Close the database. If the database is shared, be sure all users have logged off.

FIGURE 19.10
This message displays when you convert a database to Access 2000 if you do not fix all compile errors first.

After you have finished preparing the database, follow these steps to convert it:

1. Open Access 2000 and be sure you have no databases open.

2. Click **Tools**, **Database Utilities**, **Convert Database**, **To Current Access Database Version**. Access will display the Database to Convert From dialog box (see Figure 19.11).

FIGURE 19.11
Choose the database you want to convert to Access 2000.

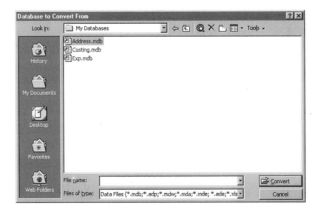

3. Click the database you want to convert, and then click **Convert**. Access prompts you to give the database a name.

4. Either give the database a new name or put the database in a different folder. You cannot overwrite an existing database with its converted version at this stage.

5. Click **Save**. Access converts the database and tries to compile it. If there are compile errors, Access tells you that the database remains in an uncompiled state. You need to fix these errors eventually.

Fixing Compile Errors   If you get a compile error upon opening a newly converted database, Access will tell you. If you are not sure what the error means, click **Help** for more information. Then, click **OK** in the error dialog box, and Access will open the Visual Basic Editor and highlight the line that contains the error. Click **Run, Reset** to stop execution and fix the error. Then, recompile the database.

If your previous-version database contained a reference to the Microsoft DAO 2.5/3.x Compatibility Library, you might need to remove it at this point, even if you did so before the conversion. Click **Tools, References**, and replace any reference to it with the Microsoft DAO 3.6 Object Library.

Converting a Secured Database   If you need to convert a secured database, convert its system database first, and then log on as an administrator and convert the member databases immediately afterward. (In Access 2000, the system database is called the Workgroup Information File.) You will need to log on with sufficient rights to open and run the database with Exclusive access, modify the design of tables, and administer permissions.

If you do not want to or cannot convert your databases to Access 2000 all at once, you can share them instead. The following section describes how to do this.

Rolling Out Access 2000 Gradually

In a gradual rollout, you convert some users and some databases to Access 2000. In addition, you want users of all versions, not just users of Access 2000, to have access to the data. You can do this with an earlier-version database in two ways: Enable it or split it.

Step 1: Enabling the Earlier-Version Database   To enable a database means simply to open it in Access 2000 rather than convert it. Click **File, Open**, choose an earlier-version database, and click **Open**; Access prompts you with the Convert/Open dialog box (see Figure 19.12). Choosing **Open Database** enables it.

Part IV

Ch

19

FIGURE 19.12
Choose **Open Database** if you want to enable, rather than convert, an earlier-version database.

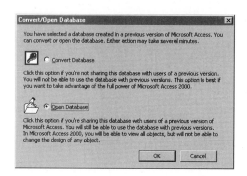

This gives the database a dual structure that allows users to view, add, change, and delete records in both old and new versions of Access.

Enabling has several limitations:

- It limits modifications of database objects to the version in which the database was created.
- Users cannot work directly with Access 2000 tables in the earlier version. The tables remain in the earlier format.

- Enabled databases are larger than converted databases.
- Module code that depends on the DAO 2.5/3.x Compatibility Library has to be modified to use DAO 3.6 before it can be enabled.

Access 95 toolbars and custom menus are converted on-the-fly to Office saved.

Step 2: Splitting the Database To split the database means to break it into two pieces, a front end and a back end. The back end contains the data tables, and the front end contains the user interface and its related forms, reports, queries, and code. For purposes of sharing databases among users of Access 2.0, 95, and 97, you convert the front end to Access 2000 while leaving the back end in the earlier format. This enables you to take advantage of Access 2000's wider feature set while also letting users of earlier versions access the data.

You can split a database whether it is in one file or already split into a front-end/back-end application. The basic process is as follows:

1. Convert the entire database to Access 2000.
2. Run the Database Splitter (Tools, Database Utilities, Database Splitter) on the converted database to split it into front-end and back-end pieces (see Figure 19.13).

N O T E Be sure to close all database objects before trying to split the database. If any forms, tables, or reports are open, the Database Splitter will fail. ▪

FIGURE 19.13
Run the Database Splitter to create a front-end/back-end application.

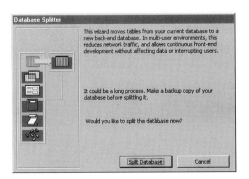

3. Delete the back-end piece created by the Database Splitter. By default, the back end is called <*databasename*>_be.mdb.
4. Use the Linked Table Manager to link to the back-end database, which is in the earlier format (see Figure 19.14).

N O T E Be sure to select the **Always prompt for new location** check box so you can browse to the earlier version of the back-end database. ▪

FIGURE 19.14
Use the Linked Table Manager to link an Access 2000 front end to an Access 2.0, 95, or 97 back end.

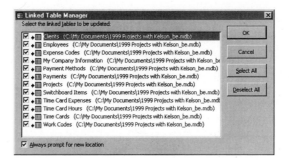

Converting an Access 2000 Database to Access 97 Format

Because of the change in the file format, you cannot open an Access 2000 database in any previous version of Access. (Hence, unlike Word, Excel, and PowerPoint, the Access 2000 file format is not dubbed "97-2000.") If you want to make an Access 2000 database available to users of earlier versions, you must convert it to Access 97 format.

To do so, click **Tools**, **Database Utilities**, **Convert Database**, **To Prior Access Database Version**. Type a new name for the database, or change its location, and click **Save**.

Take note of the following whenever you want convert an Access 2000 database to Access 97 format:

- You cannot convert a member of a replica set to an earlier version of Access.
- Module code that relies on Access 2000 add-ins or libraries (such as ADO 2.1 or later) needs to be modified.
- A database converted to Access 97 format loses
  - Data Access Pages. There is no workaround for this.
  - Unicode support. The resulting database uses a code page instead of a Unicode mapping. If you use any characters that do not map to the target code page, the resulting data will not convert correctly.
  - Support for the Decimal data type. Change FieldSize fields that use this data type to Single, Double, or Currency before converting.
  - Support for ADO. If you have module code that relies on ADO, it does not work. You need to use DAO or RDO instead.

Managing Outlook, Schedule+, and Personal Address Book Formats

Outlook 2000 has the same data storage formats as Outlook 98. This includes mail messages, address book, MAPI profiles, and PIM data. Outlook 97 is almost the same—prior to release 8.03, Outlook 97 had a different offline (OST) folder format. Otherwise, you can share

Outlook data files among users of these three versions of Outlook, and upgrading to Outlook 2000 does not require any conversion of files.

> **N O T E** Even though the file formats do not differ, you cannot have different versions of Outlook on the same computer. ▨

You can also use Microsoft Exchange Client email data with Outlook 2000 transparently. Exchange Client can read Outlook 2000 message folders, and Outlook 2000 can read Exchange Client message folders. You do not have to convert any files.

> **N O T E** Exchange Client cannot see Outlook 2000 custom forms or custom folder views saved in Outlook 2000 format. ▨

You cannot exchange data between Schedule+ and Outlook 2000. If you want to use Schedule+ data in Outlook 2000, you must import it.

> **N O T E** The exact procedure for switching to Outlook from another email client differs slightly from program to program. For detailed instructions on ten common scenarios, display **Outlook Help**, expand the **Getting Started** main topic, and choose **If you're switching from another e-mail or scheduling program**. ▨

Importing Data into Outlook

With the File, Import and Export command, Outlook 2000 lets you import five distinct kinds of data:

- ▨ Internet email account settings
- ▨ Internet email message stores and address books
- ▨ Calendar data (iCalendar, vCalendar)
- ▨ Contact information (vCard)
- ▨ Miscellaneous database data (database and proprietary email formats)

Each data type has its own unique structure and requires a different process for importing.

You can also export some types of data (see Table 19.6).

Importing Internet Email Account Settings   All Internet email clients (Outlook, Eudora, Netscape Messenger, and other Internet email clients) store account information. Outlook 2000 automatically uses any MAPI profiles that already exist on the client machine, including Internet mail accounts.

To import Internet email account information, click **File, Import and Export, Import Internet Mail Account Settings**. Outlook will offer to import mail accounts from email clients previously installed.

Importing Internet Email Message Stores and Address Books   Internet email clients have their own proprietary message and address book formats. Outlook 2000 lets you import messages from the following client formats:

- Eudora (Pro and Light) 2.x, 3.x, 4.x
- Netscape Mail 2.x, 3.x
- Microsoft Internet Mail 3.x
- Outlook Express 4.x, 5.0
- Netscape Messenger 4.0x

To import Internet email message stores or address book data, click **File, Import and Export, Import Internet Mail and Addresses**. Outlook prompts you to select the application from which you want to import data.

Importing Calendar Data (iCalendar, vCalendar)   iCalendar and vCalendar files are text files that specify the details of an appointment. You can use this format to send meeting requests to others as attachments in email messages. An iCalendar file is an Internet meeting request; a vCalendar file is an Outlook appointment.

To import iCalendar files, click **File, Import and Export, Import an iCalendar or vCalendar** file. Outlook prompts you for a filename.

Importing Contact Information (vCard)   A vCard is like a business card in electronic form. You can save Contact items as vCard files, and you can send these files as attachments to others. This is not a proprietary Outlook format; it is an Internet standard format.

To import a vCard file, click **File, Import and Export, Import a VCARD file**. Outlook prompts you for a filename.

Importing Miscellaneous Database Data   Your data does not have to fall into any of the preceding categories to be eligible for import. You can import plain text files, database files, and some proprietary email formats as well.

To import data in one of these miscellaneous formats, follow these steps:

1. Click **File, Import and Export, Import from another program or file**. Outlook prompts you for the file type (see Figure 19.15).

Part

IV

Ch

19

FIGURE 19.15
You can import almost any kind of data if you can get it into one of the formats Outlook imports.

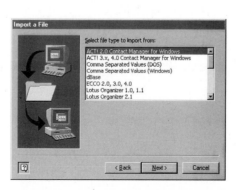

2. Click **Next**. Note: Because this feature is not installed by default, Outlook might ask whether you want to install it now. If so, click **Yes**. Outlook installs the feature and lets you proceed with the import.

3. When the Import a File dialog box appears, type or browse for a filename.

4. In the Options portion of the Import a File dialog box, specify whether Outlook should replace duplicates, create duplicates, or ignore duplicates (see Figure 19.16).

FIGURE 19.16
Tell Outlook what to do with duplicates should it encounter any in the process of importing.

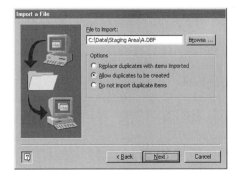

5. Click **Next**.

6. When Outlook prompts you to select a destination folder, navigate to the appropriate Outlook folder and click **Next**.

7. Outlook displays the next pane of the Wizard, which details the steps it is about to perform, tells you it might take a while and cannot be cancelled, and offers to let you change everything first.

8. To map imported fields to Outlook fields in the target folder, click **Map Custom Fields** and follow the instructions in the resulting dialog box.

9. To change the destination folder, click **Change Destination** and choose a new target folder.

10. When you are ready to do the import, click **Finish**.

You can use this method to import data from almost any source.

N O T E If you cannot import data from an email format you use, you can still import the data into Outlook if you can export it first into a format that Outlook *can* import. Just export the data, and then follow the preceding steps to map the data to the appropriate Outlook folder. ▪

Table 19.6 details the data import filters supplied with Outlook (including email filters). An x in the Allows Export column means that Outlook can create the file format using the File, Import and Export command.

Table 19.6   Data Import Converters Supplied with Outlook

Data Format	Common File Extensions	Allows Export
Comma-Separated Values (DOS, Windows)	CXV, TXT	x
dBASE	DBF	x
Eudora Light (1.54, 3.0.1)		
Eudora Pro (2.2, 3.0, 3.0.1)		
FoxPro	DBF	x
iCalendar	ICS	
Lotus Organizer 1.0, 1.1, 2.1, 97	ORG, OR2, OR3	
Microsoft Access	MDB	x
Microsoft Excel	XLS	x
Microsoft Exchange Personal Address Book	PAB	x
Microsoft Internet Mail	PST	x
Microsoft Mail	MMF	
Microsoft Outlook Express		x
Microsoft Schedule+ 1.0, 7.0/95	CAL, SCD	
NetManage ECCO Pro 2.0, 3.0, 3.01, 3.02, 4.0	ECO	
Netscape Mail 2.02, 3.0, 3.01		
Netscape Messenger 4.0		
Personal Folder File	PST	x
Schedule+ Interchange	SC2	
Starfish SideKick for Windows 2.0, 95	SKCARD	
Symantec ACT! 2.0, 3.x, 4.0	DBF	
Tab-Separated Values (DOS, Windows)	TXT	x
vCalendar	VCS	
vCard	VCF	

NOTE   Although Outlook 2000 does not introduce a new file format, it stores its data in a different location than its predecessors. Outlook 2000 puts Personal Store, Offline Store, Personal Address Book, and Offline Address Book files in the Application Data folder. Outlook 97 and 98 put these files in the Windows folder. ■

▶ For more information on upgrading to Outlook 2000, **see** Chapter 34, "Using Outlook As an Internet Mail and News Client," on **p. 881**.

Part
IV

Ch
19

Managing the Transition to Word, Excel, and PowerPoint 2000 by Choosing File Formats

No matter how you choose to deploy Office 2000, you should be aware of the file formats you choose to use. In particular, you should make a conscious decision about two things: specifying default formats, and whether to use HTML/XML as a default format.

Specifying Default Formats

You can specify the default file format used by Word, Excel, and PowerPoint. In Word and PowerPoint, click **Tools, Options, Save**, and select a file format in the **Save** *<application>* **files as** drop-down list box. In Excel, click **Tools, Options, Transition**, and select a file type.

You can also set these defaults in the System Policy Editor. Figure 19.17 shows how you would set the default Word file format to 97-2000 & 6.0/95 - RTF.

FIGURE 19.17
For backward compatibility during an upgrade transition, you can change default file formats for Word, PowerPoint, and Excel in the System Policy Editor.

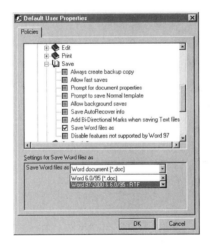

▶ For more information on using the System Policy Editor, **see** "Using System Policies with Office 2000," on **p. 970**.

Using HTML/XML As a Default Format

The fact that Word, PowerPoint, and Excel let you use HTML/XML as a default file format gives you a bit more flexibility than you had in the past. For example, you might need to create files in Word 2000 and share them with the entire organization, including users who do not have Word 2000. In the past, you had four main options:

- Save the file in an earlier format
- Distribute the WordViewer
- Upgrade everyone to Word 2000
- Save the file as a Web page

For a variety of reasons, all these options have significant drawbacks; using HTML/XML as a native file format solves most of them. It is not a cure-all, but it does make use of a nearly universal file format, and it eliminates the confusion of opening files with hidden or disabled features. Because most users in most organizations have a Web browser, you can make Office 2000 documents available to all just by publishing the file on a local Web server.

Even if you do not use HTML/XML as a primary file format, all Office 2000 users can save files as Web pages on Web folders. Although this does not solve every problem, it can be a good alternative to the other options.

▶ Using HTML/XML as a default file format does have tradeoffs. For more information on the pros and cons, **see** Chapter 33, "Managing HTML/XML As Your Primary File Format," on **p. 867**.

Using the Microsoft Office Converter Pack

The Microsoft Office Converter Pack is an Office Resource Kit tool with which you can install file converters for many versions of Word, Excel, and PowerPoint. For Office 2000 users, it supplies several text converters and graphics filters not included in default installations of Office. More importantly, it has a full set of converters and filters for users of earlier Office versions, enabling them to open files in Office 97-2000 format. It is especially handy for rolling out a standard set of file filters and converters for your entire organization, regardless of which version of Office any particular group or department is using, so you can all migrate to the newer formats.

To start the Converter Pack, run the Setup.exe file in \ork\pfiles\orktools\toolbox\tools\ocp to display the main dialog box (see Figure 19.18).

FIGURE 19.18
The Office Converter Pack lets users of recent Office versions install a long list of file converters.

The converters and filters that the Converter Pack makes available to users depends on which version of each application they have. The Convpack.ini file included with the converter specifies all the options. Here is a sample from the Word section:

```
; this file configures the Microsoft Office Converter Pack

[ConvPack]
Quiet=no
PreventUninstall=no
```

```
[Word6]
AmiPro2=yes
dBASE=yes
Lotus123=yes
Excel=yes
FoxPro=yes
Word97-2000=yes
DOSWord=yes
MacWord=yes
RFT-DCA=yes
Text=yes
Write=yes
WordPerfect4=yes
WordPerfect5=yes
WordStar=yes

[Word95]
AmiPro3=yes
dBASE=yes
HTML=yes
Lotus123=yes
Excel=yes
FoxPro=yes
Word97-2000=yes
DOSWord=yes
MacWord=yes
Works3=yes
Works95=yes
RFT-DCA=yes
Text=yes
Write=yes
WordPerfect4=yes
WordPerfect5=yes
WordPerfect6=yes
WordStar=yes

[Word97]
AmiPro3=yes
dBASE=yes
HTML=yes
Lotus123=yes
Excel=yes
FoxPro=yes
Word6-95=yes
DOSWord=yes
MacWord=yes
Works3=yes
Works95=yes
RFT-DCA=yes
Text=yes
Write=yes
WordPerfect4=yes
WordPerfect5=yes
WordPerfect6=yes
WordStar=yes
```

```
[Word2000]
AmiPro3=yes
dBASE=yes
FoxPro=yes
DOSWord=yes
Works3=yes
RFT-DCA=yes
Write=yes
WordPerfect4=yes
WordStar=yes
```

You specify converters and filters for each application version by editing the Convpack.ini file. Each converter has a Yes or No value; all options default to Yes. When choosing options for your users, keep in mind that the Converter Pack Setup program will skip *all* options for any application that is not properly installed on the target computer (merely copying executables does not do it). The Converter Pack does not display options for missing applications (see Figure 19.19).

FIGURE 19.19
Users of Office 95, 97, and 2000 can install many different kinds of file converters.

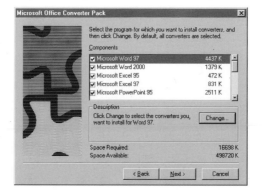

Part
IV

Ch
19

CHAPTER 20

Integrating Office Applications More Effectively

by Daryl Lucas

Far more Microsoft Office licenses sell than do licenses for the standalone Office applications. For most individuals and organizations in need of mainstream software, the package makes more sense than any one Office product alone because most people need to do more with their computers than perform just one narrowly defined task. As people have become more used to using data from Office's different applications, they have come to rely more on the Office suite as a whole.

What is more, business use of the suite is almost synonymous with network computing. Users are sharing data across the organization, making use of shared drive space, shared messaging, or shared output devices. They are also creating programmed solutions with Visual Basic for Applications (VBA) code, many of which involve automation of one Office application from another (an Excel macro that creates a Word report from a data set, for example).

In the end, this means users need to do more than just open a Word document now and then. They need to combine the document with a spreadsheet, a chart, or a slide. They need to use the Excel workbook as a piece of the database, not just as a private analytical tool. They need to publish the database to the intranet. They need to morph the presentation into a well-formatted report. They need to use applications and their data *together*. And they need to keep track of all this productivity.

More than anything else, they need to integrate their Office applications effectively.

Creating Rich Combinations of Office Data

One of the most powerful features of Office 2000 is the fact that it is a set of Windows applications. Because of the tools that Windows provides, you can place an Excel worksheet range into an Access table, a PowerPoint slide, or a Word document. You can transform a Word outline into a PowerPoint presentation. You can email any of these from Outlook. The ability to share information from such diverse sources is not required of Windows applications, but it is available, and Office 2000 takes advantage of it.

All 32-bit versions of Windows (95/98, NT, and 2000) provide three robust mechanisms for data sharing among applications: the Clipboard, Object Linking, and Object Embedding.

Understanding Data-Sharing Terminology

Let's clarify some terms before going any further. The following definitions apply to our discussion here, but not necessarily to all their possible nuances.

- **Object.** Structured data of a distinct file type, such as a Word document, an Excel worksheet, an Outlook message, or a PowerPoint slide. Only objects can be linked to or embedded in other documents.

 TIP To see a list of object types available on your system, click **Insert**, **Object**, **Create New** (in Word, PowerPoint, or Excel). The list of Object types includes all the types available from Office 2000 applications, as well as those available from other applications.

- **Host document.** The document or file into which you place an object.
- **Source file.** A file that provides the embedded or linked data (a file or file portion that you embed or to which you link).
- **Client application.** The host application; the application in which you embed or link the object; the application that creates the host document. Think of the client as the one that gives the orders. You can also think of it as the container—the application in which you assemble the master document.
- **Server application.** The application that created the object's data. If you create a slide in PowerPoint and embed it in Word, PowerPoint is the server application, and Word is the client application.
- **Linked object.** An object whose data is stored outside of its host document. When you change a linked object, all its hosts reflect the change. One piece of data can be linked to many objects in more than one host.
- **Embedded object.** An object whose data is stored entirely in its host document. An embedded object has no life outside of its host; it is part of the host. It is not a standalone file at all, and it has no links to any outside sources, not even to the application that created it.

Sharing Data the Simple Way: The Windows Clipboard

You can hardly use a Windows application without the Clipboard. Follow these steps to see how it works:

1. Select the data you want to move or copy and click **Edit**, **Cut** (**Ctrl+X**) or **Copy** (**Ctrl+C**).
2. Switch to the document where you want to put the data, and place the insertion point where you want the data to go.
3. Click **Edit**, **Paste** (**Ctrl+V**).

That's it. The Clipboard does the hard work for you. In Office 2000 applications, this process often takes the data from its native form and gives it a reasonably accurate approximation in its new home. An Excel worksheet range pasted into a Word document becomes a Word table, for example, and a PowerPoint slide looks just like a slide.

Sharing Data a Fancier Way: Object Embedding

If you select a slide in PowerPoint, copy it to the Clipboard, and paste it into a Word document, what do you expect to get? Do you expect a bona fide PowerPoint slide? By default, that is exactly what you get. But that worksheet range does not come in as a worksheet range—it comes in as a Word table. Why the difference?

The answer is the O part of OLE. Object Linking and Embedding refers to the fact that Windows can treat chunks of data as entire entities—*objects*—complete with information about what application created them and how they are structured. Thus, merely putting something on the Clipboard forces Windows to make a decision about what you copied and what you might want to paste. Because the data you copy to the Clipboard might or might not have any meaning apart from its native format, the application that executes the copy can tell Windows about the data, but it doesn't have to. So, when you copy (or cut) the object, Windows might not know what you copied.

But if it does, one of the paste options is often a so-called *embeddable object*. You can see how this works by repeating the copy/paste steps, this time using a slightly different method of pasting:

1. Follow Steps 1 and 2 as described previously.
2. Click **Edit**, **Paste Special**—not Edit, Paste (and not Ctrl+V). The Paste Special dialog box appears (see Figure 20.1). Notice the format that's selected by default.
3. Scroll through the available formats to see the description for each. Be sure **Paste** (not Paste Link) is selected.
4. In the **As** list box, select the **Object** format (if it is available).
5. Click **OK**.

When you Paste in this manner, you put an object in the document, not just an approximation of the original data. You get an independent data stream in its native format plus information about the application that created it and how to launch that application in the future—all inside the host document. Windows does not try to convert, approximate, translate, or change the data in any way. It gives you a file within a file.

FIGURE 20.1

When you choose Edit, Paste Special, you get to choose from the formats available for the data you copied. If you want to embed the data, choose the Paste option and the Object format at the top of the list, if it is available.

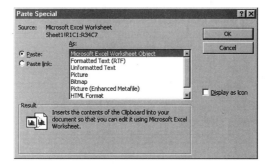

This process is called *embedding*. In Office 2000, you can embed several kinds of data in several other kinds of files.

TIP

Embedding an object makes the host file *much* larger than it would be if you were to link the object, because embedded objects exist entirely inside the host document and linked objects do not. If you cannot afford a large host file, do not use embedding; use linking. If you cannot afford to let the data change, lock the link.

▶ For more information on locking linked objects, **see** "Managing Linked Objects," on **p. 555** later in this chapter.

It is important to remember that when you embed an object, you do not create a link to any source. There is no source. The object is part of the file that hosts it. All the object's data exists inside the document that displays it, and if you delete the document, you delete the object as well. The only thing that makes it special is the fact that you can open another application to edit it.

Sharing Data the Fanciest Way: Object Linking

In the Paste Special dialog box, notice the Paste Link option below the Paste option. Choosing Paste Link, as the name suggests, pastes a link or a pointer to the data you're copying, not the data itself. This is entirely unlike embedding, because *none* of the data exists inside the host. The object contains an address, not a house.

But like the embedded object, the link contains more than just a path and filename; it contains information about the data's structure, the data's source application, and how to launch the source application. As with the embedded object, you can open another application to edit it.

Not all kinds of data can be linked. If you attempt to copy an Outlook message, for example, the Paste Link option is grayed out. But several types of bulwark Office data link just fine, including Word documents, Excel worksheets and charts, and PowerPoint slides.

Using Linking and Embedding to Create Rich Office Files

Word, Excel, and PowerPoint use two commands to create linked and embedded objects— Paste Special and Insert Object.

Using Paste Special   You use Paste Special to create linked or embedded objects from data that already exists, is easy to copy to the Clipboard, and consists of a file portion. To link or embed using Paste Special, follow these steps:

1. In the server application, cut or copy the data to the Clipboard.

N O T E   Windows is smart enough not to delete the data if you choose to create a link to data that you have placed on the Clipboard using the Cut command. It is better, though, to use Copy unless you are sure you will not need the data in its original document. ▪

2. Switch to the client application and place the insertion point where you want to create the object.

3. In the client application, click **Edit**, **Paste Special**. The Paste Special dialog box appears (see Figure 20.2).

FIGURE 20.2
The Paste Special command lets you create an embedded or linked object from Clipboard data.

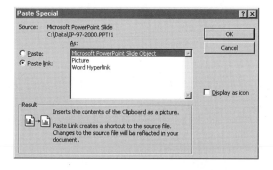

The Paste Special dialog box contains the following elements:

- **Source.** The name of the server application that placed the data on the Clipboard (if known), plus other optional details about the data. Depending on the server application, this can include the filename, the data range, or both.

- **Paste.** Creates an embedded object from the contents of the Clipboard and places it at the location of the insertion point.

- **Paste Link.** Creates an object linked to its source and places the object at the location of the insertion point.

Part
IV

Ch
20

N O T E   Unlike in past versions of Office, you can create a link even if you have not saved the source file. The link will be valid as long as the source file exists in its original state. ▪

N O T E   If it is not possible for an object to be linked, the Paste Link option will be grayed out. ▪

▪ **As.** Lists the formats in which the Clipboard has stored the data and can create an object. The formats available depend on both the data copied and the current target.

■ **Display as Icon.** Determines how the object will appear in the host document. If you do not check this box, the object will appear in its native form (a spreadsheet range, a paragraph, a slide, or whatever). If you check this option, the dialog box shows which icon will be used and displays the **Change Icon** button (see Figure 20.3).

FIGURE 20.3
If you want the object to take up as little space as possible, you can tell the program to display an icon—any icon—in its place.

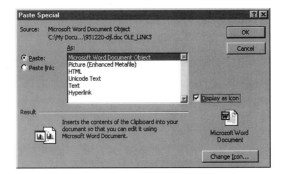

■ **Change Icon.** Lets you change the icon used to represent the object.

■ **Result.** Explains what kind of object will be created from the selected format (specified in the As list box). The explanation reflects how the Paste/Paste Link option will affect the result as well.

Using Insert Object   If the data you want to embed or link is difficult to copy to the Clipboard, exists as an entire file, or is registered on your system as an insertable object type, you can use Insert Object instead of Paste Special. (If the data does not yet exist, you *must* use Insert Object.)

N O T E   You cannot use Insert Object to create an object from a file portion that is not also an insertable object. Excel ranges and Word bookmarks are examples of data that cannot be created with Insert Object. ■

To create the object in a host document, follow these steps:

1. Click **Insert, Object**. The Object dialog box appears (see Figure 20.4).

FIGURE 20.4
You can create many kinds of OLE objects right from the host document. Just be sure to place the insertion point where you want the object to go before you click **OK**.

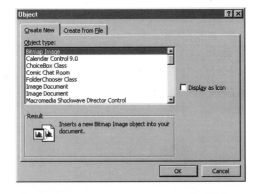

N O T E The Object dialog box looks slightly different in PowerPoint and Access, but it works the same as it does in Word and Excel. ▉

2. To create a new object from scratch, click **Create New**, select the type of object you want to create, and click **OK**. This creates an embedded object.

3. To create a new object from an existing file, click **Create from File**, type or browse for the filename, specify the link and icon options you want, and click **OK**. Link to file creates a linked object; otherwise, this creates an embedded object.

N O T E If you have more than a dozen or so insertable object types installed on your machine, or if you simply have a lot of software installed, you might notice a delay before the Object dialog box displays. This is because the list comes from the Class ID branch of the Registry, a branch that can get quite large if a lot of programs register classes. Insertable objects are only one type of class. ▉

Managing Linked Objects

Linked objects come with enough functionality to allow (and in some cases require) some housekeeping. For example, you might want to edit the object, control when it updates, or change a link that has gone awry.

Editing Linked Objects   You can edit a linked object at either end of the link (the source or the host), no matter how many hosts have links to it.

To edit the object at its source, simply edit is as you would any other file. Open it in the application that created it and make your changes. The changes are available to host documents as soon as you make them. (Whether the changes appear in the host document immediately might depend on options you can set in the host application.)

To edit the object from a host, follow these steps:

1. Right-click over the object and choose **Linked** *<objecttype>* **Object** from the shortcut menu.

N O T E If the object is an insertable object type, you can also double-click on it to open it in its server application. ▉

2. Choose either **Edit Link** or **Open Link** from the pop-up menu. In most cases, either choice opens the server application and displays the source file.

N O T E If the object is a link to a file portion, both editing and opening the link will open the entire file. ▉

3. In the server application, edit the data as you normally would. Your changes appear immediately in the host document, and you can switch between host and source as much as you want.

4. When you finish making changes to the object in the server application window, save and close the source. You are returned to the host file.

Part
IV

Ch
20

Updating Links   By default, Office 2000 clients update OLE links on their own. You do not have to tell them to do it. If a source to a link changes, you find out immediately.

To override this setting, follow these steps:

1. Open the document that contains the linked object and click **Edit, Links**. (If the document has no links, this command will be grayed out.)
2. Select the link you want to override in the **Source File** list.
3. Click the **Manual** update option.
4. If you want the object to reflect the source's current state, click **Update Now**.
5. Click **Close**, and then save the file to preserve the changes in the object.

From now on, this link reflects changes in the source only if you update the link by hand.

 TIP   You can disable both automatic and manual updating by *locking* the object. To do so, display the Links dialog box as described previously and check the **Locked** option. As long as this box is checked, the selected link cannot be updated.

Editing Links   If you need to change, fix, or break a link, you can use the Links dialog box to do so. To change or fix a link, follow these steps:

1. With the host file open, click **Edit, Links**. The Links dialog box appears (see Figure 20.5).

FIGURE 20.5
If you don't like the way a link is working, you can often change it with the Links dialog box.

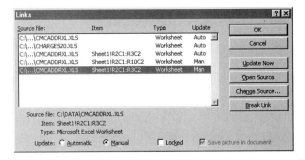

2. Select the link you want to edit in the **Source File** list.
3. To fix or change the link, click **Change Source**. The Change Source dialog box appears.
4. Choose the file you want to use as the new source. If you want to restrict the link to a file portion, click **Item** and type the Excel range (SheetName!RangeName), the Word bookmark name, or the PowerPoint slide number to which you want to link.
5. Click **OK** to close the Links dialog box, and then save the file to save the changes to the object.

To break a link, follow the previous Steps 1 and 2, and then click **Break Link**. Breaking a link converts the object to a picture.

Managing Embedded Objects

Managing embedded objects is very easy because they have no links to maintain. You can take the host document anywhere and not worry about breaking a link or having to protect the host from unwanted changes in the source.

You edit an embedded object in much the same way you edit a linked one, but a few subtle differences bear mentioning.

1. Right-click over the object and choose *<objecttype>* **Object** from the shortcut menu. (The word "Linked" is not part of the command.)

N O T E If the object is an insertable object type, you can also double-click on it to launch its server application. ■

2. Choose **Edit** or **Open** from the pop-up menu. (The word "Linked" is not part of either choice.) The server application's menus appear.

N O T E What is the difference between Edit and Open? Edit allows the server application to take over the client's menus and windows; Open starts a new instance of the server and opens the object there. When you choose Edit, the host document remains visible, and the object appears in a box inside it. When you choose Open, you don't see the host document any longer; you see the object in its server window. ■

3. Use the server application's commands to edit the data as you normally would.

4. When you finish editing the object, use the server's menu commands to save and close the object. You are returned to the host file.

 TIP If you chose Edit from the shortcut pop-up menu, you can return to the host document by clicking outside the object. If you chose Open, you must choose the appropriate menu command in the server application to save and close the file.

Using Excel Data in Word Documents

You most often benefit from using OLE between Word and Excel in two common scenarios. The first is when you need to report on data stored in a public data source. The second is when you need to include a spreadsheet or chart in a Word document.

Linking to Public Data

If you want to report on data in a worksheet that's stored or maintained elsewhere, Object Linking offers an ideal way to do it. Simply place the insertion point where you want the worksheet to appear, and then use Paste Special or Insert Object to create a linked object. The public worksheet then appears in the report.

For example, if you want to include a portion of a large worksheet in a Word document, follow these steps:

1. Select and copy the cells in Excel that you want to appear in the document.
2. Switch to Word and click **Edit**, **Paste Special**. The Paste Special dialog box appears.
3. In the **As** list box, select **Microsoft Excel Worksheet Object**.
4. Choose the **Paste Link** option.
5. Click **OK**.

Now, you have a worksheet in your report. Anytime the data in the worksheet changes, the report will reflect the new information.

Embedding External Data in Your Report

Another common use of OLE does not involve existing data at all but instead leverages the in-place editing allowed by object embedding. Suppose that inside the Word document, you need a complex table, a sophisticated chart, or a full-blown worksheet. However, you do not need or want any of this to be linked to anything else.

If you want to create such a compound document, follow these steps:

1. Position the insertion point where you want the Excel object to go.
2. Click **Insert**, **Object**. The Object dialog box appears.
3. Be sure **Create New** is selected.
4. In the **Object Type** list box, select **Microsoft Excel Chart** or **Microsoft Excel Worksheet**, depending on what you need.
5. If you want the user to control whether the object appears in its native form, check the **Display as icon** button.
6. Click **OK**.

Now, you have a fully functional Excel object inside your Word document.

 You can run Excel macros when you activate an embedded Excel object inside Word. Double-click the object, and then click **Tools**, **Macro**, **Macros**. The Macro dialog box that appears belongs to Excel, not Word. Select the macro you want to run and click **Run**. To return to Word, click outside the object.

Integrating Word, Excel, and PowerPoint with Outlook

Each of the major Office applications has a Send To option that enables you to easily share documents with others through public Exchange folders. In any of these applications, click **File**, **Send To**, **Exchange Folder**. Choose the folder you want and click **OK**. The application places a copy of the file in the folder. Users who want to view the file can open it from Outlook. This can be a handy way to collaborate on documents that several people need to edit.

Using OLE Objects in Access Databases

You can put both linked and embedded OLE objects in Access 2000 databases by means of the OLE Object field. This enables you to keep rich documentation together with highly structured data stores. You can use it to index or keep track of documents, workbooks, presentations, photos, drawings, media files, and other insertable object types.

To enable the inclusion of OLE objects in a database, start Microsoft Access, open the database, and follow these steps:

1. Identify the table in which you want to store the objects, and then open it in Design view.
2. Add a field and set its data type to **OLE Object**.
3. Switch to Datasheet view.
4. Identify a record (or create a new one) to which you want to add an OLE object, and then right-click over the **OLE Object** field.
5. Choose **Insert Object** from the shortcut menu. The Object dialog box appears.
6. Follow the steps for creating a linked or embedded object, described in the section "Using Insert Object," earlier in this chapter.

Although the Object dialog box lets you choose whether to display the object as an icon, Access uses this setting only in forms and reports. In tables and queries, Access always displays the object as a text description of its object type, not as an icon or in its native format. Figure 20.6 shows an example of this, an address list that includes an OLE Object field in which you can store maps or links to maps.

FIGURE 20.6

Access displays OLE objects as text descriptions of their object type so they take up a reasonable amount of room in the tight confines of a database table.

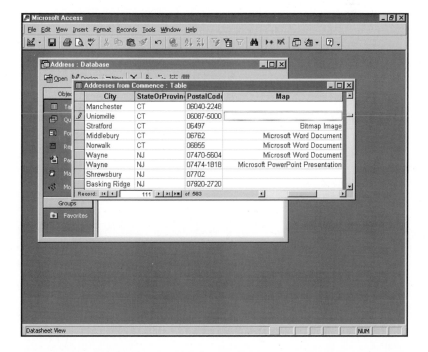

Part
IV

Ch
20

To see the object as an icon or as it appears in the server application, create a form or a report that includes the OLE Object field. Keep in mind that if the object is a document that has macro code, the server application's security settings will apply every time the database tries to display the object, which might mean answering queries about whether the document is safe to open.

TIP Displaying the object as an icon is handy if it is very large or if users do not need to see a preview before deciding whether to open it. But if you know how much room the object takes up, or if users need to see a preview of it in any case, using an icon can be frustrating. Just be aware that in most cases, some objects do not fit in the display window provided by the form or report, which means that the user does not see all of it.

Integrating Office Data into PowerPoint Presentations

Another common use of OLE involves supporting PowerPoint presentations with embedded documents. During the presentation, the presenter clicks on an embedded object displayed as an icon. The object opens and displays the object in a separate window.

Integrating Word, Excel, and PowerPoint Data into a PowerPoint Presentation

You can embed any kind of insertable object into a PowerPoint presentation, including Word documents, Excel worksheets, and other PowerPoint presentations.

To embed an object into a PowerPoint presentation, follow these steps:

1. Click **View**, **Normal** and navigate to the slide in which you want to embed the object.
2. Click **Insert**, **Object**. The Object dialog box appears.
3. Click the **Create from File** option.
4. Type or browse to the filename of the document or workbook you want to embed.
5. Be sure the **Link** option is not selected.
6. Select the **Display as icon** check box.
7. Click **OK**. An embedded object is inserted in the slide.
8. Click once on the object and drag it to where you want it to appear in the slide.
9. Right-click over the object and choose **Action Settings** from the shortcut menu. The Action Settings dialog box appears.

N O T E If you do not edit the Action Settings, the default action is in force. Clicking on the icon executes the Next Slide command instead of opening the document. ■

10. Select the **Mouse Click** tab.
11. Select the **Object Action** option and select **Open** from the drop-down list box.
12. Click **OK**.

TIP

Another way to achieve a similar result is to insert a hyperlink to the document instead of embedding it. Insert a shape, icon, or picture to serve as the jump-off point, and then display the Action Settings dialog box and choose the **Hyperlink To** option. In the drop-down list box, choose **Other File** and browse to the document you want to display. Keep in mind that this, like an OLE link, requires that the target file be available to the machine that is conducting the presentation because the document is not embedded.

The embedded object does not have to be a Word or Excel object; it can be another presentation as well. You can embed presentations in a host presentation. Launching supporting presentations from a host presentation is called *branching*.

To embed a PowerPoint presentation in a slide, follow the steps already described for embedding in Word and Excel.

Branching is a good way to set up training presentations and tutorials. The user gets to see an introductory slide or presentation and then gets to select the presentation that meets his or her needs. The user can click the preferred topic and follow the choice of slides.

Integrating Word Data into a PowerPoint Presentation

Both Word and PowerPoint offer several tools geared toward data integration. Using some simple menu commands, you can turn a Word outline into the skeleton of a PowerPoint presentation, and you can export a presentation to several kinds of Word documents.

The advantages are twofold. One, you can use Word's rich editing features to write the text of your presentation before adding graphics. Two, you can use Word's rich formatting to create handouts, reports, and other kinds of documentation from slideshows.

To create a PowerPoint outline in Word, follow these steps:

1. Create a new document.
2. Write the main points of your presentation and format them all with Word's built-in Heading 1 style. Each Heading 1 paragraph becomes its own slide.

TIP

Do not worry about the text's appearance at this point. You will probably modify it in PowerPoint later, anyway, when you can apply a design template or theme to the whole presentation. In fact, using a design template can save you a lot of labor-intensive formatting work.

3. Write all supporting points in similar fashion, formatting them as Heading 2, 3, or 4 paragraphs as appropriate.

TIP

You can quickly format any Word paragraph with a built-in heading style by pressing **Ctrl+Alt+number**. For example, to apply Heading 1, press **Ctrl+Alt+1**. To demote it one heading level, press **Alt+Shift+RightArrow**. To promote a heading one level, press **Alt+Shift+LeftArrow**.

4. When you are finished, click **File**, **Send To**, **Microsoft PowerPoint**. Word starts PowerPoint and creates a new presentation that consists of your outline, with one slide per Heading 1 paragraph.

5. In PowerPoint, click **Format, Apply Design Template**, and then select a template to format the entire presentation quickly.

You can use this technique to build presentations from any Word document that uses the built-in Heading styles. If you experiment with different combinations of heading levels, you will find that this method has a lot of flexibility and is easier than writing outlines in PowerPoint.

Integrating PowerPoint Data into a Word Document

To create a Word report from a PowerPoint presentation, follow these steps:

1. In PowerPoint, open the presentation that interests you.

2. Click **File, Send To, Microsoft Word**. The Write-Up dialog box appears (see Figure 20.7)

 TIP Think about the kind of output you intend to create before you export the presentation. If your slides include a lot of dark backgrounds or large color swaths and you want to print the reports on a color printer, you might want to lighten the backgrounds first. Or, if you intend to print on a laser printer, you can use the Grayscale Preview button on the Standard toolbar to see the effect of toning things down. Create a print-friendly version of the presentation before exporting it to a printer.

FIGURE 20.7
If you want to create handouts for your presentation, use PowerPoint's Send To command to create a Word document. You can export the presentation in several different formats, most of which can be linked to the original presentation.

3. Choose the page layout that best suits your needs: **Notes next to slides, Blank lines next to slides, Notes below slides, Blank lines below slides,** or **Outline only**.

4. Specify whether to **Paste** or **Paste link** the presentation in the target document. Paste creates an embedded object; Paste link creates a linked one.

N O T E If you choose **Outline only**, PowerPoint exports the outline as Rich Text; it does not create an embedded or linked object. ▦

▶ For more information on managing PowerPoint in workgroup settings, **see** Chapter 14, "Using PowerPoint in a Team Setting," on **p. 377**.

Performing a Mail Merge in Office

Word 2000 is your headquarters for performing mail merges, but you have a lot of flexibility in how to execute the details. For example, you can put mail merge source lists in Word tables, Excel worksheets, Access tables, and Outlook Contacts. What is more, you can start the mail merge process from any of these applications except Excel. You can also use non-Office data sources such as tab-delimited text files, dBASE files, Lotus 1-2-3 files, and any other data source for which you have an import filter.

Starting Mail Merges from Word

To start a mail merge from Word, follow these steps:

1. Click **Tools**, **Mail Merge**. The Mail Merge Helper dialog box appears (see Figure 20.8).

FIGURE 20.8
Word's Mail Merge Helper is your primary tool for integrating data from Word, Excel, Access, and Outlook contact lists.

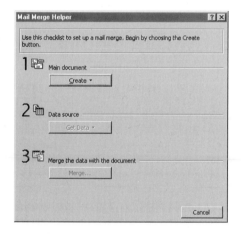

2. Click **Create** to specify what kind of merge you want—Form letters, Mailing labels, Envelopes, or a Catalog. Word asks whether you want to use the active document or a new document for the purpose. The document you choose to use becomes the *main document*.

> **N O T E** The main document is your template for the merged output. Insert merge fields that you want represented in every single merge result, and format it as you want the resulting documents to look. If you're not sure what you will want, experiment. ■

> **TIP** The Form letter and Envelope options place each record in a separate document section. The Label and Catalog options place records together, one after the other.

3. Click **Get Data** to specify the *data source*, the second half of the mail merge equation. You can create a new data source, open an existing one, use the Outlook Address Book, or specify a separate header file.

> **TIP**
> Choosing a data source involves so many choices and options that you might want to review some of Word's online Help on the topic. To do so, click **Help**, **Answer Wizard**, and then query on "mail merge data sources." Select the "Plan and organize a mail-merge data source" topic.

4. Choose **Open Data Source** and navigate to any file that contains a list that you want to use as a data source. After you specify a data source, Word prompts you to insert Merge fields and closes the Mail Merge Helper.

5. Back in the main merge document, click the **Insert Merge Fields** button on the Mail Merge toolbar to insert the fields you want represented in the resulting form letters, envelopes, labels, or catalog records.

6. When you have added all the fields you need, click **Tools**, **Mail Merge** again. The Mail Merge Helper dialog box appears, but this time it's filled with details about your main document (see Figure 20.9).

FIGURE 20.9
After you have specified a data source and added merge fields to the main document, you are ready to begin the merge.

7. To create the form letters, envelopes, labels, or catalog, click **Merge**. Word displays the Merge dialog box.

8. Specify any options you want, and then click **OK**. Word creates a new document using default settings that contains all the merged items from all the source records.

Performing the merge causes Word to merge the main document with the data source. The result is a new document that looks just like the main document but contains data from the data source in place of the merge fields. Each row of the data source produces a corresponding merge record, formatted as you specified in the main document. If the merge is a catalog or set of mailing labels, each entry or label matches the pattern you specified in the main document.

Starting Mail Merges from Outlook

You can start mail merges from both Outlook and Access in addition to Word. This can spare you from having to specify a data source, which is one of the most difficult parts of setting up mail merge main documents. In the case of Outlook, it also makes it a lot easier to merge to the Outlook Outbox.

To start a mail merge in Outlook, follow these steps:

1. Display the **Contacts** category.

2. Click **Tools**, **Mail Merge**. The Mail Merge Contacts dialog box appears (see Figure 20.10).

TIP Because you have already defined the data source (the Contacts folder), you need only specify the other options, such as the merge type and whether to create a main document from an existing document or a new one.

FIGURE 20.10
You can start a mail merge to a Word document from within Outlook.

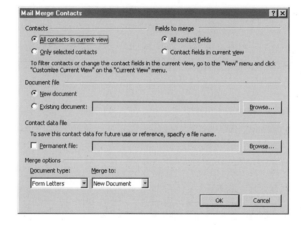

3. Specify the options you want and click **OK**. Outlook starts Word, creates a data source that contains all the relevant data, and creates a main document linked to it.

4. In Word, insert the mail merge fields as already described previously (if necessary) in addition to the message or other information you want to include in the merge.

5. When the main document is finished, click **Merge** on the Mail Merge toolbar. The Merge dialog box appears (see Figure 20.11).

FIGURE 20.11
If you start an email mail merge from Outlook, the Merge dialog box will be preset with Electronic Mail selected in the Merge to drop-down list. Click **Setup** to change the details.

6. Click **Merge** to perform the merge. If you specified a merge type of email, Word and Outlook create mail messages for each merged record and place them in the Outbox.

Starting Mail Merges from Access

To start a mail merge from Access, follow these steps:

1. Open the database that contains the merge source.

2. Click the down arrow next to the **Office Links** button on the Database toolbar and select **Merge It with MS Word**. The Microsoft Word Mail Merge Wizard appears (see Figure 20.12).

FIGURE 20.12
If you would rather not go through the agony of locating a data source for a mail merge, start with the data source itself.

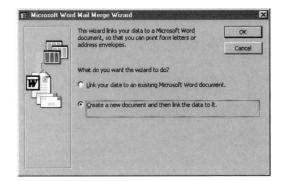

N O T E Although this is called a wizard, it has only one step. When you click **OK**, you are finished with it; switch to Word and begin crafting your mail merge main document. ▥

3. Choose whether to use an existing document or create a new one, and then click **OK**. Access starts Word and creates a mail merge main document for you.

The resulting Word document is a mail merge main document with the Access database as its data source. You can edit and format the main document as you would any other.

Using Excel As a Database Front End

Some organizations use Excel as a database front end. Doing this has at least three significant advantages:

- Users can leverage Excel's powerful analytical tools to filter, edit, and process data before it becomes part of the database.

- Users have a familiar software interface without having to learn or rely on a specialized database application.

- It is often a lot easier to develop data processing tools in Excel VBA than to modify or program a database.

In other words, it is a way to benefit from an n-tier architecture—separation of the user interface from the middle tier of business logic.

For example, imagine a company that sells products through a catalog. It has a customer database with names, addresses, and other information about customers. Several dozen employees work in accounting receiving payments from customers and posting this information to the database.

If the accounts receivable people shared a worksheet to enter payment information, they could enter, filter, and format the data before it ever affected the main database. This would protect the database from erroneous entries, let everyone use the same interface, and allow for changes to the entry point without any changes to the back-end database.

Evaluating the Import/Export Commands and Linking

There are two ways to use Excel as a database front end: importing/exporting and linking. Each option is much like (although not the same as) OLE linking and embedding. Import/export exports an Excel worksheet and imports it into an Access database. Linking places the worksheet in the database as a linked object, leaving a live connection between the worksheet and the database.

Each approach has its advantages and disadvantages. Import/export requires that the database often be out of date—indeed, almost always out of date, between imports of the source Excel data. It also requires that the database table that receives the import never be edited or changed by any other means. On the other hand, this method means that many users can work on the source worksheet, entering new data and modifying old records, without any drain on the database. This eliminates concurrency problems, many database access performance problems, and the need to reconcile updates.

Linking the worksheet to the database means that everyone always has up-to-date data. In certain situations, such as queries about order status, this can be a critical advantage. On the other hand, it reintroduces concurrency problems, as noted previously, as well as performance problems, whenever many people access the database at once.

Importing Excel Data into Access

To import worksheet data from Excel into an Access database, follow these steps:

1. Open the Access database.
2. Click **File**, **Get External Data**, **Import**. The Import dialog box appears.
3. Change **Files of type** to **Microsoft Excel (*.xls)** and select the workbook you want to import.
4. Click **Import**. Access displays the Import Spreadsheet Wizard (see Figure 20.13).

FIGURE 20.13

You can import any named range or whole worksheet. Just select the one you want, and a preview appears in the dialog box.

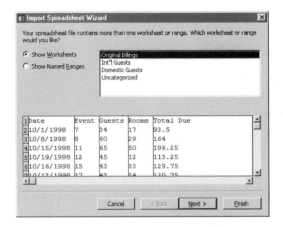

5. Specify whether to **Show Worksheets** or **Show Named Ranges**.

6. If the source workbook has more than one worksheet or named range, select the sheet or range you want to import. Then click **Next**.

7. If you want Access to create field names from the source's first row, check **First Row Contains Column Headings**. Then click **Next**.

8. Specify whether you want to put the data in a new table or an existing table, and then click **Next**.

9. If you want to change field names, tell Access whether to index specific fields or skip fields. Then, specify the options you want for each field (see Figure 20.14) and click **Next**.

FIGURE 20.14

To change the field data, click the field in the sample and then enter your changes in the Field Options area.

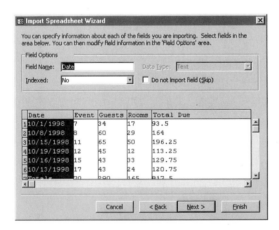

10. Specify whether to add a primary key to the table, and then click **Next**.

11. Name the table, specify whether Access should analyze it, and click **Finish**.

The list of database tables now includes a new table filled with the data you specified. This data table is not linked to the source Excel file in any way.

Linking Excel Data to Access

Linking an Excel data range to an Access database is much like inserting a linked OLE object. You place a new table in the database that has no data of its own yet reads all the data from the source at all times. This lets you place the data in the database and make it available to the database while also letting you read, access, and update the data from Excel.

You can link to Excel worksheets and to named ranges. To link an Excel worksheet or range to an Access database, follow these steps:

1. Open the Access database.

2. Click **File**, **Get External Data**, **Link Tables**. The Link dialog box appears.

3. Change **Files of type** to **Microsoft Excel (*.xls)** and select the workbook to which you want to link.

4. Click **Link**. Access displays the Link Spreadsheet Wizard (see Figure 20.15).

FIGURE 20.15
You can link to any worksheet or named range in the workbook you selected. Each becomes a new table in the database.

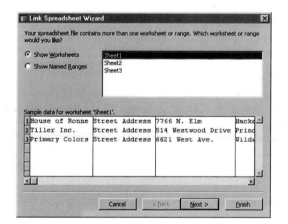

5. Specify whether to **Show Worksheets** or **Show Named Ranges**.

6. If the source workbook has more than one worksheet or named range, select the sheet or range to which you want to link. Then click **Next**.

7. If you want Access to create field names from the source's first row, check **First Row Contains Column Headings**. Then click **Next**.

8. Name the table and click **Finish**. The list of database tables now includes a linked Excel data object (see Figure 20.16).

Part
IV

Ch
20

FIGURE 20.16
Data sources to which you have linked appear in the list of tables with an arrow and an icon indicating their origin.

Using Internet Explorer As a Database Front End

Office 2000 introduces several new ways to view, edit, analyze, and report on database data. One of the most significant is Data Access Pages. Data Access Pages are HTML pages that use a Data Source Control Web Component to bind to and interact with back-end database data. You can use Data Access Pages with your data stores to publish databases to an intranet. In fact, with Data Access Pages, you can deploy any Access database to anyone who has an Office 2000 license, a copy of IE 4.01 or later, and access to your Web server. Users need only the browser to view, analyze, and edit the data.

▶ For more information on Office Web Components and some of the ways you can use them to share data, **see** Chapter 35, "Deploying and Using Office 2000's Web-Collaboration Components," on **p. 895**.

Data Access Pages are listed in the database object viewer under Pages (see Figure 20.17).

FIGURE 20.17
The Access list of database objects now includes Data Access Pages.

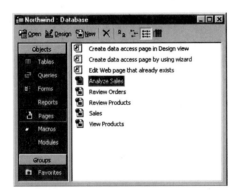

To create a Data Access Page in Access, follow these steps:

1. Open the database you want to share.

2. In the database object viewer, click **Pages**.

3. Double-click **Create data access page by using wizard**. The Page Wizard dialog box appears (see Figure 20.18). The initial screen looks exactly like the Forms Wizard, but the screens that follow differ significantly.

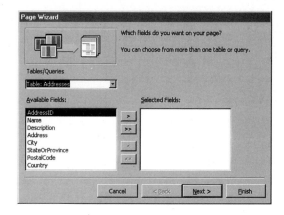

4. In the **Tables/Queries** drop-down list, select the table or query from which you want to create the page. From the **Available Fields** list, add the fields you want in the page. Then click **Next**.

5. If you want to add grouping levels, add the appropriate fields. Do not do this if you want the page to be used for data entry; grouping levels render the page read-only. Then click **Next**.

6. Specify the sort order you want to use, if any, and click **Next**.

7. Name the page. Unless you are just experimenting, check the option to modify the page and to apply a theme because you will need to do these things, anyway.

8. Click **Finish** to create the page and display it.

If you chose to modify the page, Access displays it in Design view (see Figure 20.19); if you checked the option to add a theme, Access also displays the Theme dialog box so you can pick one now. Otherwise, the page opens normally, and you can begin using it as a data entry form right away.

You edit the page in Design view, just as you do forms and reports. If you want the page to have a title, now is a good time to add it. You can also add additional controls, modify control properties, and write script code behind the page in the Microsoft Script Editor. None of these steps is necessary, however. After you save the page, it will be available to users who have been granted rights to the database.

When you save the page, Access prompts you for a filename and location. You can save the page to its public Web folder now, or you can save it in a working folder now and move it later. Either way, Access creates an *.HTM file plus a *<filename>*_Files subfolder below it to hold the associated Filelist.xml file, Cascading Style Sheet files, GIFs, and any other supporting files that are needed. Remember to move these along with the HTM file if and when you move the page.

FIGURE 20.19
Working with Data
Access Pages is a lot
like working with forms
and reports.

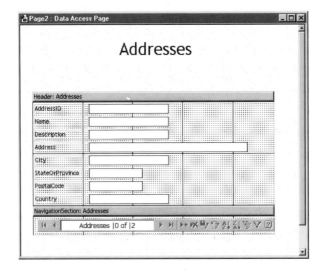

TIP

Be sure to close the database in Access before you deploy the page. If you leave it open, users will
not be able to view or edit the data.

Users open the Page in a Web browser the same way they open any other Web page, either
by double-clicking on the HTM file in Explorer or by browsing to it. Figure 20.20 shows a
simple Data Access Page in IE5.

FIGURE 20.20

With nothing but a
copy of Internet
Explorer 4.01 or later
and an Office 2000
license, any user can
view and edit database
data with a Data
Access Page.

▶ For more information on using Access (both as a data source and as a database front end), **see** Chapter 16, "Sharing Database Resources with Access 2000," on **p. 413**.

Keeping Track of Office Files with the Journal

If you use more than one Office application, and if you use these applications to integrate data, you work with a lot of data files. Outlook can keep an audit trail of all those files by means of the Journal. If you let Outlook do this, you can go back and find those documents if you ever forget where you placed them. It also enables you to track what you worked on when. Figure 20.21 shows an example—a set of journal entries for PowerPoint files opened during the month of April.

FIGURE 20.21
To open a Journal entry, double-click it. The entry shows you the time and date the file was open, how long it was open, and what kind of file it is. Double-click the shortcut to open the file again.

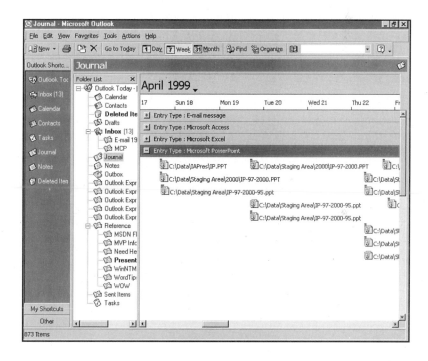

By default, Outlook logs a Journal entry every time you create, open, close, or save a data file in Word, Excel, PowerPoint, Access, or the Binder. You can override this setting by choosing **Tools**, **Options**, **Preferences**, **Journal Options**. In the Journal Options dialog box (shown in Figure 20.22), uncheck the relevant application in the **Also record files from** section.

You can also create Journal entries of your own. To do so, follow these steps:

1. Click **File**, **New**, **Journal Entry**.
2. Type a **Subject** (if desired) and select an **Entry Type**.
3. Place the insertion point in the notes area and click **Insert**, **Object**. The Insert Object dialog box appears.

Part
IV

Ch
20

4. Follow the steps for creating an embedded or linked object described in the section "Using Insert Object," on p. 554 earlier in this chapter.

5. Click **Save and Close**.

FIGURE 20.22
If you notice a significant delay in the saving of Office files, the Outlook Journal feature might be the reason.

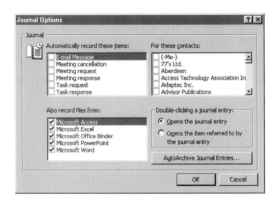

Finding Documents with Find Fast and Document Properties

Find Fast and Document Properties are either blessings or curses, depending on whom you ask. These powerful Office features can help you keep track of documents and find them much faster than you can by traditional means. But they can also be a source of trouble, or at least annoyance, if you let them. The key to using them wisely is to be aware of what they can do and modify them to suit your needs.

Using Find Fast

Find Fast indexes files so Office 2000 applications can find them quickly. It runs in the background while you work. The first time it runs, it creates indexes for all the files that match the criteria that have been set for it; from then on, it updates the indexes at some interval (every two hours by default).

N O T E Find Fast stores each set of indexes in four hidden files: ffastun.ffa, ffastun.ffl, ffastun.ffo, and ffastun0.ffx. ▪

To find out whether Find Fast is installed on your machine, display the Windows Control Panel and look for the telltale Find Fast applet. Its icon is a pair of binoculars accompanied by a lightning bolt (see Figure 20.23).

FIGURE 20.23
You can control how Find Fast works by changing its settings in Control Panel.

To change the Find Fast settings, launch the Find Fast applet from Control Panel. The main dialog box lists the indexes it is currently maintaining and their current status (see Figure 20.24).

FIGURE 20.24
You configure Find Fast through the Index menu of the main dialog box.

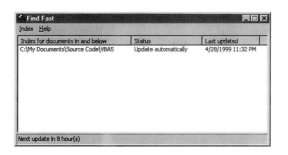

By default, Find Fast indexes your entire hard disk, but you can narrow the target significantly if you want. Click **Index, Create Index** to specify a target that is more to your liking. As you can see from Figure 20.25, you can limit the indexing to a deeply nested folder and a specific set of file types inside it.

TIP
You can also click **Index, Update Index** to change the folder being indexed. You do not have to create a new index.

FIGURE 20.25
To make searches as
fast as possible, check
**Speed up property dis-
play** and **Speed up
phrase searching**.

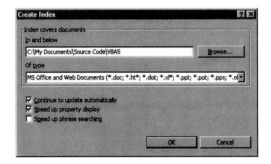

Another way to make Find Fast friendlier is to change an index's update interval. Although indexing occurs in the background, it does work the hard disk. If you use the computer all day, frequent updating can cause a noticeable drag on performance and become a bona fide annoyance. To change the update interval, just click **Index**, **Update Interval**, and then change the number to whatever you want. Keep in mind that if the computer is not on long enough for the interval to elapse, the update will not occur.

The rest of the options are self-explanatory.

Using the Document Properties

All Office applications include document properties in their data files. Document properties are a standard set of metadata (data about the file) stored in the file header. You can see the document properties by right-clicking over the file in Explorer and choosing **Properties**. Figure 20.26 shows a typical properties page for a Word document—underutilized as it is.

FIGURE 20.26
The more of these cate-
gories that are filled in,
the better the results
from Find Fast.

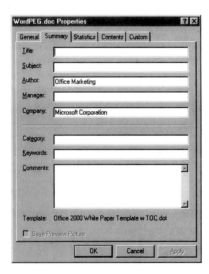

In Word, Excel, PowerPoint, FrontPage, and PhotoDraw, click **File**, **Properties** to edit a file's properties. In Access, click **File**, **Database Properties**.

TIP You do not have to settle for the predefined categories displayed on the Summary tab. You can create your own categories and use them to aid in indexing and finding files. To add your own categories, display the **Custom** tab and create as many as you need. As you can see from Figure 20.27, Microsoft took advantage of this feature for their Product Enhancement Guides, perhaps to make up for the absence of information in the Summary tab.

FIGURE 20.27
A few custom document properties can make your document searches that much easier.

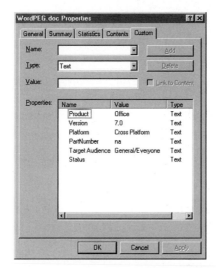

CHAPTER 21

Integrating Office Documents with Desktop Publishing Systems

by Bill Camarda

Although Microsoft Office has come a long way in enhancing its publishing capabilities, many organizations still find it necessary to integrate Office documents with specialized desktop publishing (DTP) software. This raises unique challenges for both Office users and publishing professionals, who must come up with solutions through trial and—all too often—error.

In this chapter, you'll explore the key issues that arise regarding the interface between Microsoft Office and the graphic arts department:

- Which documents should be "published" within Office, and which should be migrated into desktop publishing software?

- What are the best ways to convert Office files for use by the leading desktop publishing software packages?

- When does it make sense to use other alternatives, such as Adobe's Acrobat Exchange or Acrobat Distiller software to create platform-independent Portable Document Format (PDF) files for electronic distribution and viewing with the free Acrobat Reader?

The goal of this chapter is simple: to offer you the hard-to-find guidance you need to achieve the best possible results at the lowest cost.

N O T E In many organizations, document preparation is performed on Windows PCs, but desktop publishing is handled on the Macintosh. For additional information about managing key cross-platform issues, such as font substitutions, graphics formats, and filename incompatibilities, see Chapter 18, "Migrating from or Coexisting with Legacy Applications." ▨

Planning to Integrate Your Office Documents

At all too many companies, crucial decisions about publishing workflows are made by individuals who are familiar with only Office or with specific desktop publishing and graphics software, but not with both. Often, the result is that it takes longer than it should to produce documents—and they cost more than they should.

The solution is to objectively understand the advantages, disadvantages, and integration issues associated with Office and today's publishing software before you take on a large project or organize your department's workflow. In this section, you'll consider key issues that can make or break your next major publishing project.

Avoiding Multiprogram Workflows Wherever Possible

This is a fact of life in print publishing: Today's leading "industrial-strength" desktop publishing and graphics design tools, such as QuarkXPress, Adobe PageMaker, and Adobe Photoshop, are published by software companies other than Microsoft. And although more designers use PCs nowadays, these packages are still more likely to run well on Macintosh than on Windows platforms.

For the Office administrator, therefore, delivering Office documents to desktop publishing professionals usually means working in a cross-platform environment. In such an environment, Microsoft support—inconsistent as it can be—is largely absent. You might find yourself struggling with import file filters that are less than state-of-the-art and staffers who are unfamiliar with the foibles of Office (and who might be unforgiving of anything or anybody Microsoft-related).

Given these realities, the Office administrator will benefit from a clear understanding of when it is really necessary to move Office documents into a desktop publishing/graphics design environment—and when this can be avoided.

Choosing Which Documents Require Professional-Level Desktop Publishing It's usually still necessary to work with desktop publishing professionals and use professional-level software for documents that need to do the following:

- Print in full color—in other words, four-color or more—such as product and corporate brochures and most catalogs
- Reflect the highest possible design values, such as advertisements and annual reports, which require superb typography and state-of-the-art graphics
- Include high-quality photography that has to be "tweaked" to look as good as possible

- Require very complex multicolumn layouts (although Word is much better at this than it used to be, it is still not a full-fledged desktop publishing program)
- Call for specialized printing techniques such as die-cuts, duotones, or washes

Having said all this, for most organizations, the "meat-and-potatoes" of document production lie elsewhere, in the following:

- Newsletters, fliers, and data sheets that are either one-color or use a single additional "spot" color
- Most manuals, directories, and long-form documents

Many, if not most, of these documents can now be handled at least as effectively in Word and Office as in professional desktop publishing software, typically at lower cost.

Moreover, print publishing is increasingly shifting toward a "print-on-demand" model. In such a model, print runs are extremely short and can be customized to the needs of very narrow audiences, even an audience of one. Business software, such as Word and Access, lends itself to producing documents like these more effectively than most traditional desktop publishing and graphics software.

Devising Strategies to Keep More Documents in Office   Depending on how your company's workflow is organized, it might be a reasonable strategy to increase the percentage of documents that remain in Word and Office from conception through printing. This has the additional advantage of minimizing the number of hands that touch each document, potentially reducing cost and the likelihood of error. If this makes sense in your organization, take the following steps:

- Build relationships with printers who are willing to work with Microsoft Office files, especially printers using new on-demand reproduction systems such as Xerox Docutech high-volume printers, which integrate high-speed xerography with inputs from Windows or Macintosh computer files.
- Become proficient at creating PostScript files from Office documents. PostScript files can be used to create film for traditional printing, whereas native Office files typically cannot.(See the section "Creating PostScript Files from Office Documents" later in this chapter.)
- Hire or identify freelance graphics professionals who are willing to work in Word and Office when necessary. Alternatively, offer basic training in Office to the design professionals already on staff.
- As was discussed in Chapter 12, invest in well-designed Office document templates that "typical businesspeople" can use to build attractive documents with less involvement from professional designers.
- Consider using Microsoft Publisher for low-end publication projects. Publisher 2000, included in most versions of Microsoft Office 2000, integrates exceptionally well with Word 2000. For example, not only can Word 2000 files be imported into Publisher, but once imported, they can still be edited by Word. You simply select the text box you want to edit and choose **Edit, Edit Story in Microsoft Word**.

Part
IV

Ch

21

▶ For more information about Microsoft Publisher, **see** Chapter 27, "Managing Microsoft Publisher 2000," on **p. 703**.

Planning Your Document Conversion Process

In the previous section, you learned ways to keep documents within Office as long as possible—minimizing the need to worry about complex conversions and other problems. But often, this is not possible. Then, the question becomes this: How can you make the conversion process as simple and cost-effective as possible? Your goals in managing the interface between Office and desktop publishing/graphic design software should be the following:

■ To retain as much as possible of the intelligence you have built into your Office documents. That means trying to preserve formatting, links, automated fields, and so on. It means attempting to minimize the amount of work that must be done twice because it was lost in the conversion process.

■ To maximize accuracy by reducing the number of opportunities for error. This goal is closely related to the first. The more rework is needed, the more errors creep in—especially because few graphic design professionals are expert typists.

■ To transition documents from Office to desktop publishing software in the most cost-effective time possible—typically, as late in the process as possible, after all content revisions have been made.

■ To ensure that the individuals preparing documents in Office understand the software, production, and scheduling constraints that graphic designers face when transforming their "raw documents" into effective printed materials, and that they know how to provide Office documents that are "designer-ready."

■ Conversely, to ensure that the graphic designers understand the issues faced by other business professionals, including the messages they are trying to communicate, the occasional difficulty getting timely signoffs, and the need to find ways to accommodate text or design elements that cannot be imported smoothly from Microsoft Office.

Quite reasonably, most graphic designers are much more concerned with what "goes out the back end" (in other words, with the final printed or electronic product) than they are with what "comes in the front end" (from the business people and others who provide source material and copy). So, it falls to you, the Office administrator, to be concerned about those issues; if you aren't concerned, chances are nobody will be!

With these high-level goals in mind, the next section begins addressing the nuts and bolts of document conversion between Office and three leading desktop publishing software packages: QuarkXPress, Adobe PageMaker, and Adobe FrameMaker.

Using Word Documents with QuarkXPress

Among professional graphics designers, QuarkXPress is the market leader in desktop publishing software. The long-awaited latest version, QuarkXPress 4.0, offers some new tools, including some high-end illustration capabilities, new long-document features (such as indexing and tables of contents), and better color management. Many of the improvements in QuarkXPress 4.0x (currently 4.04), however, are incremental, so some design professionals have chosen to continue using the "tried-and-true" QuarkXPress 3.32.

Because QuarkXPress is so popular, it's likely that you'll be called upon to deliver Word documents to designers who use it. Therefore, this section contains detailed coverage on how to make QuarkXPress work better with Word documents. It also focuses primarily on the Macintosh version of QuarkXPress, which has by far the largest installed base.

N O T E When reading the following detailed discussion of importing Word files, you might wonder why linking and embedding Word documents is not discussed. Although QuarkXPress supports OLE 2.0 for Windows and the Macintosh equivalent, Publish and Subscribe, it does so only for image and graphics editing programs, not for word processing software.

In some organizations, the advantages of maintaining live links between your word processing documents and desktop publishing files might be compelling. If you need this capability, consider using Quark's leading competitor, Adobe PageMaker, as discussed later in this chapter in the section "Using Word Documents with Adobe PageMaker."

As it's installed "out of the box," neither version of QuarkXPress can import any Office 97 or Office 2000 files directly. QuarkXPress 4.0 ships with version 3.2 of Quark's Word filter, which recognizes Word documents in the following formats:

- Word 3.0 through Word 5.1 for the Macintosh
- Word 6.0/7.0 for Windows and Word 6.0 for the Macintosh

If your publishing professionals use QuarkXPress 3.32, chances are they are using Quark's Word filter 3.1, which can work with the same Word versions.

 TIP A beta of a Word 97/2000 filter has been posted on the QuarkXPress Web site at **www.quark.com/files/xtquarkxts_40.html**. Some users will want to experiment with it; most, however, will want to stick with the formally released Word 6.0 filters.

Among the acknowledged limitations of the beta Word 97/2000 filter are the following:

- No support for Word 97/2000 bullets
- No support for Word 97/2000 hidden text
- All default tabs are reset to .5"
- No support for embedded objects
- No support for tables
- No support for Fast Saves (as discussed later in this chapter)
- Exporting text from Quark to Word 97/2000 format on a Macintosh crashes the computer

In the next section, you'll walk through converting a Word 2000 document for use in QuarkXPress.

Part

IV

Ch

21

Preparing Word 2000 for Document Conversion to QuarkXPress

Unless you're prepared to try Quark's "beta" Word 97/2000 filter (which has been in beta for nearly two years as this is written), you'll want to save a copy of your Word document to Word 6.0/95 format before you import it into QuarkXPress. This presents no problem if you are using Word 98 for the Macintosh or either service release of Office 2000—or, of course, if you are using Word 6.0 or Word 95. (For information about the service releases of Office 2000, refer to Chapter 3, "Using Systems Management Server 2.0 to Install Office 2000.")

If you do want to experiment with Quark's Word 97 import filter, disable Word 2000 features before you save your file for export. Quark's Word 97 filter is unable to recognize nested tables and other features that are not supported in Word 97. To disable Word 2000 features, follow these steps:

1. Choose **Tools**, **Options** and click the **Save** tab.
2. From the **Save Word Files As** drop-down list, choose **Word Document (*.doc)**.

> **CAUTION**
>
> Do *not* use Word 2000's HTML format, which might include a variety of tags and scripts that QuarkXPress (and other desktop publishing software) cannot recognize.

3. Check the **Disable Features Not Supported By Word 97** check box.
4. Click **OK**.

 While you have this tab displayed, be sure the **Allow Fast Saves** check box is also cleared. QuarkXPress (and other desktop publishing software) cannot reliably read files with Fast Saves turned on. For more about this, see "Resaving with Fast Saves Turned Off," later in this chapter.

 If you're converting many files at once, use Word's batch converter.

Evaluating Your Word Document Prior to Conversion

The next step is to take stock of the document you want to convert. If your document is very simple, you can skip most of what follows. If your document contains elements such as styles, fields, indexes, tables, or bullets, however, it will be worth your time to read this.

> **N O T E** Although this discussion is presented in the context of importing to QuarkXPress, much of this information will be helpful if you need to prepare documents for importation to Adobe PageMaker or Adobe FrameMaker as well. ■

Preparing Styles for Conversion Your QuarkXPress (or PageMaker) designer can import Word styles and convert them automatically to reflect the formatting he or she chooses to use. Give your designer the opportunity to do so. Many designers claim the only reliable way to import a Word file is as ASCII text. *This is not true!*

Your Word styles can save your designer so much time that it's worth ensuring all your long documents contain them. If you have a document that doesn't contain styles but instead uses manual formatting for headings and other document elements, consider running AutoFormat to transform much of this manual formatting into styles your designer can use.

AutoFormat's default settings might make changes you won't want, and some of the changes it makes will be undone by Quark's import filter. The following steps show you how to limit AutoFormat to convert the elements that will be of value to your QuarkXPress designer:

1. In Word, choose **Format**, **AutoFormat**. The AutoFormat dialog box opens.

2. Click the **Options** button to display the AutoFormat tab of the AutoCorrect dialog box.

3. Select the following check boxes:

   Headings

   Other Paragraphs

   Ordinals (1st) with Superscript

   Bold and italic with real formatting

   Styles (selecting this check box ensures that you preserve any styles that might already be in your document)

4. Be sure all other check boxes are cleared.

5. Click **OK**.

6. In the AutoFormat dialog box, be sure **AutoFormat Now** is selected, and then click **OK**. (If you prefer to review every change individually, select **AutoFormat and Review Each Change** instead.)

Preparing Fields for Conversion   The QuarkXPress import filter doesn't handle fields properly. It inserts the raw field codes into its documents *instead of*, or in some cases, *alongside* the field results you would prefer to see displayed. As a result, QuarkXPress designers might see obscure text such as this scattered throughout their imported documents:

```
SUBJECT \* MERGEFORMAT
TIME \@ "M/d/yy h:mm:ss am/pm
```

If your document contains any of the following items, you have field codes that you need to deal with before you import the document into QuarkXPress:

- Automated times and dates
- Index entries or indexes
- Tables of contents
- Cross-references
- Bookmarks
- Formulas
- Hyperlinks
- Mail Merge Codes

Part

IV

Ch

21

You might want to make a backup copy of the document before you delete the fields so you still haveaccess to all the interactivity your fields provide (in case you're called upon to rework the document in Word later). Then, delete the fields as outlined in the following steps:

1. If the **Show/Hide** button (it shows a ¶ symbol) in the Standard toolbar is not selected, click it to display all the hidden text in your document. Doing this lets you easily locate and delete fields such as index entries that are hard to delete while they are invisible.

2. Press **Ctrl+A** to select the entire document.

3. Press **F9** to update all the fields in your document that can be updated, including such things as date/time fields and cross-references.

4. Be sure the entire document is still selected and press **Ctrl+Shift+F9**. This unlinks all the fields you've just updated, replacing the field codes with their current results.

   At this point, you've removed most types of fields, but some—such as index entry fields—remain. You'll need to get rid of those by using Word's Find and Replace feature. Continue with the remaining steps.

5. Choose **E̲dit**, **R̲eplace**.

6. In the **Fi̲nd What** text box, type **^d** (Word's shortcut for finding fields).

7. Be sure the **Replace Wit̲h** text box is blank.

8. Click **Replace A̲ll**.

9. Click **Close**.

10. Save the document.

Preparing Indexes for Conversion   As mentioned in the previous section, QuarkXPress cannot interpret Word index entries, which are fields. The procedure described in the previous section deletes index entries along with other fields so they do not appear as stray text in your designer's QuarkXPress file.

If someone has done all the hard work of building an index in Word, however, it seems a shame to start all over again in QuarkXPress. Moreover, Word contains some indexing automation features not available in QuarkXPress, such as the capabilities to index every appearance of a word or phrase at the same time or to build an index from a list of words you provide (available by choosing **Insert**, **Ind̲ex and Tables**, **AutoMark**). It's common for Word's automated features to handle as much as half of a large document's index automatically—often more. You'd hate to waste all these productivity features simply because the QuarkXPress Word filter isn't all it could be.

In this section, you learn two approaches for indexing Word documents and maintaining the indexes through the conversion to QuarkXPress 4.0. Each approach has its own advantages and disadvantages. First, however, it is helpful to understand how each program formats index entries.

Understanding Indexing Differences Between QuarkXPress 4.0 and Word 2000

■ Index entries in QuarkXPress 4.0 are formatted as follows:

The opening bracket and dollar sign ($) indicate the beginning of an index entry; the closing bracket indicates the end of the entry. When a semicolon appears, text after the semicolon is treated as a subentry. That is, it is listed beneath the original entry in the compiled index, as in the following example:

```
Brinkley, J.R.
      goat gland prostate surgery, 24
      medical license suspended, 32
      XER radio station, 27
```

■ Index entries in Word 2000 (and most previous versions) are formatted differently. In the following example, the curly brackets are actually field code brackets, and the information is stored in the document as a hidden field code:

```
{ XE "installing:Windows 95" }
```

As mentioned earlier, if you simply leave the field codes in your document, the QuarkXPress import filter will strip away the curly brackets but leave the remaining text, which will not be recognized as an index entry and will look like this:

```
XE "installing:Windows 95"
```

Creating Word Indexes That Can Be Retained in QuarkXPress 4.0   If you want to create your index entries in Word and retain them in QuarkXPress, you have two alternatives. The first is to create them in Word but use the format that Quark uses. For example, you might write a macro that places the following text in your document and then moves the cursor to a point after the tilde and before the greater than (>) symbol:

```
<$I~>
```

After you insert these characters into your document, enter your index entry manually. If you need to create a subentry (an entry that appears subordinate to another entry in the printed index), use the semicolon separator that QuarkXPress recognizes, not the colon that Word recognizes.

N O T E   By default, QuarkXPress uppercases all index entries automatically. By including the tilde in your macro (as shown previously), you work around this feature. You can then enter lowercase characters as needed and still alphabetize them in the order you want. ■

The advantage of this method: You don't have to do anything special to convert the index entries to a form Quark understands. When QuarkXPress imports the file, the entries are present and recognized.

Part
IV

Ch
21

The disadvantages of this method: You can't compile your index in Word, and your index entries are not automatically formatted as hidden text. (Instead, they appear in your document, potentially confusing reviewers.) In addition, you cannot use Word's built-in Mark Index Entry dialog box to create your entries or use automated features such as AutoMark because they insert index entries in Word format, not Quark format.

TIP If all or most of your indexed documents are exported to QuarkXPress, when you write your macro, you can specify **Alt+Shift+X** as the command that invokes it. This replaces the built-in keyboard shortcut that would normally display Word's Mark Index Entry dialog box.

A second approach to preserving your Word indexes in Quark is this: Enter them using Word's indexing tools as you would if you were not planning to export to QuarkXPress. Then write a macro that converts your XE field codes (but no other field codes) into document text Quark will recognize as index entries. The macro should delete the field brackets surrounding XE fields, adding **<$I** in place of the left bracket and **~>** in place of the right bracket. It should also replace colons with semicolons within index entries. Save a copy of your file and run the macro on the copy immediately before you export it to QuarkXPress.

The advantage of this method: You can use all Word's indexing features, including the automated features, and you can build interim indexes using Word's Index and Tables dialog box (by choosing **Insert, Index and Tables**).

The disadvantage of this method: You will have to check your document carefully to be sure that your macro has converted all your index entries and that it has not made changes to other fields or text in your document. Writing reliable macros to do this becomes even more difficult if your documents are created in a variety of formats or are indexed by multiple individuals with varying skills.

N O T E Only QuarkXPress 4.0 has built-in indexing capabilities, although add-on Quark XTensions are available to add indexing to Quark 3.3x.

To ensure QuarkXPress 4.0's indexing feature is available and working, choose **Utilities, XTensions Manager** and be sure a check mark appears next to the **Index** option (see Figure 21.1). If not, click to the left of the word *Index*, click **OK**, quit the program, and start it again. ■

Preparing Bullets and Numbering for Conversion Word's automatic numbers and bullets don't import into QuarkXPress, so you'll have to decide where it will be easier to replace them with manual bullets and numbering—in Word or in QuarkXPress. Although there's little difference in the work involved, adding them in Word reduces the chance that they'll be overlooked later. On the other hand, if you're moving from Word for Windows to QuarkXPress on the Macintosh, the manual symbols you insert (using **Insert, Symbol**) might not translate across platforms properly.

▶ For more information about which symbols will translate properly and which won't, **see** "Managing Font and Character Set Issues," on **p. 699.**

FIGURE 21.1
Checking that the
QuarkXPress 4.0
indexing feature is
active.

Missing check mark——

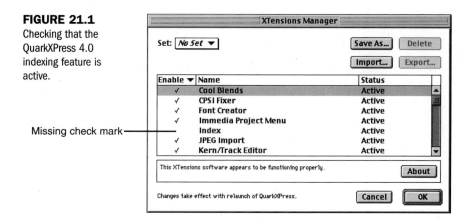

Preparing Tables for Conversion   QuarkXPress' Word import filters have never been very good at importing Word tables. At best, you'll get tab-delimited text, which might or might not line up accurately. QuarkXPress might also insert several lines of formatting, or it might ignore your table altogether, and in some cases, it ignores all the text that follows the table. In any case, Quark offers none of the table formatting Word can provide.

There are two solutions to this dilemma, neither of which is ideal. The first one preserves font formatting and approximate layout but sacrifices table formatting. The second option, available only on the Macintosh, preserves every bit of formatting and design but sacrifices print quality and prevents designers from making text changes to the table.

Preserving Table Text and Font Formatting   To retain the contents of your table, along with its font formatting (boldface, italic, and so on), perform the following steps:

1. Select the table.
2. Choose **Table, Convert Table to Text**.
3. In the Convert Table to Text dialog box, be sure **Tabs** is selected.
4. Click **OK**.

QuarkXPress imports your table as blocks of text separated by tabs. You'll lose table formatting such as borders, gridlines, and backgrounds.

If your document has many tables, you can move among them quickly by using Word 2000's Browse by Table feature, as outlined here:

1. Click the **Document Browser (Select Browse Object)** button in the lower-right corner of the Word interface (see Figure 21.2).

Part
IV

Ch
21

FIGURE 21.2
Setting Select Browse
Object to browse from
one table to the next.

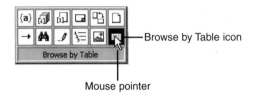

——Browse by Table icon

Mouse pointer

2. Click the **Browse by Table** icon in the grid that appears (the rightmost icon in the second row).

3. Click the blue double-down-arrow to move to the next table (see Figure 21.3).

FIGURE 21.3
Click the double-down-
arrow to browse to the
next table.

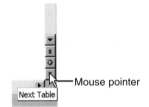

——Mouse pointer

Copying the Table As a Graphic (Macintosh Only)   If you're running Word 98 on the Macintosh, a second workaround is available that retains all the formatting in your table but might sacrifice some print quality. This procedure transforms your table into a PICT graphic and places it in a QuarkXPress document:

1. In any version of Word since 5.0, create and format the table.

2. Select the table by clicking inside it and choosing **Table**, **Select Table**.

3. Press **Command+Option+D**. Word copies the text to the Clipboard in Macintosh's PICT format.

4. Open or switch to QuarkXPress and display the document where you want to insert the table.

5. Click the **Rectangle Picture Box** tool on the Tool Palette, and then drag the mouse pointer to create a new picture box.

6. Choose **Edit**, **Paste**. QuarkXPress pastes the table into the picture box.

TIP   You could simulate this in Windows by using a screen-capture program to capture a picture of the table, opening it in a graphics program, copying it to the Clipboard, and pasting it into QuarkXPress.

Clearing Password Protection Prior to Conversion   When you password-protect a file in Word, it is encrypted—and therefore, no other program can read it properly. If you're working with a password-protected file, perform the following steps before you import it into *any* desktop publishing system:

1. Choose **File**, **Open**.

2. Browse to and select the password-protected file.

3. Click **Open**. The Password dialog box appears.

4. Enter the document's password. (Passwords are case sensitive.)

5. Click **OK**.

6. Choose **Tools**, **Options**.

7. Click the **Save** tab.

8. Clear the asterisks in the **Password to Open** text box. If there are asterisks in the **Password to Modify** text box, clear those as well.

9. Click **OK**.

10. Save the file.

This removes the encryption so that the file can be read by desktop publishing software.

Resaving with Fast Saves Turned Off   Word contains a shortcut feature, Fast Saves, which speeds up file saves by storing all changes at the end of the file instead of integrating them within the document where they belong. Occasionally, when you save a file, Word takes care of the "housekeeping" it deferred, but most of the time, your Fast Saved files contain text and other elements that aren't in the right order.

QuarkXPress (and other DTP) import filters might have trouble with Fast Saved files. (One symptom: Inexplicably, a file appears not to reflect the most recent set of changes you made, even though you know you saved them.)

Before you save a file for use in any desktop publishing program, do the following:

1. Choose **Tools**, **Options**.

2. Click the **Save** tab.

3. Clear the **Allow Fast Saves** check box.

4. Click **OK**.

5. Resave the file.

You've now gone a long way toward getting your files ready for QuarkXPress. (Your designer owes you dinner at the finest restaurant in town!)

Preparing QuarkXPress to Accept Your Files

Now it's time to be sure QuarkXPress is ready for your files. First, be sure you have the most recent Word file converters installed. On the Macintosh, look in QuarkXPress 4.00 Folder:Xtension. There should be a file called MS-Word Filter.

Select the file and choose **File**, **Get Info**. The MS-Word Filter Info window appears, displaying the date the file was created. In Windows, you can get the same information by checking the modified date for MS-Word Filter.xnt in the XTension folder in Windows Explorer.

Part

IV

Ch

21

N O T E You can visit Quark on the Web at **www.quark.com/files/xtquarkxts_40.html** to see whether newer filters are available. For example, the latest filter for QuarkXPress 4.0 for the Macintosh is named MS-Word 8 Filter 1.2 and is dated 7/22/99. This filter was designed to work with Word 97 for Windows files and Word 98 for the Macintosh files. Although it should work with most Word 2000 files, it might encounter troubles with some of the minor format changes Microsoft made to accommodate new features, and it will not handle files saved by Word 2000 in HTML format. ■

Next, run QuarkXPress. Choose **Utilities**, **XTensions Manager** and be sure a check mark appears next to **MS-Word Filter**. If not, add a check mark. Click **Save As** to create a new set of XTensions that includes MS-Word Filter. Name the set and click **OK**. If you did have to add the Word filter to your set of loaded XTensions, quit QuarkXPress and start it again.

Importing Your Word File into QuarkXPress

Finally, you're ready to import the file. In QuarkXPress, do the following:

1. Choose **File**, **New**, **Document** to open a new document in XPress. The New Document dialog box appears.

2. Be sure **Automatic Text Box** is selected and click **OK**. QuarkXPress displays an empty page.

3. Click inside the page.

4. Choose **File**, **Get Text**. The Get Text dialog box opens (see Figure 21.4).

FIGURE 21.4
The QuarkXPress 4.0 Get Text dialog box.

5. Be sure the **Include Style Sheets** check box is marked or QuarkXPress will disregard your Word styles.

6. Browse to the Word file you want and click **Open**.

7. QuarkXPress might ask you how to resolve conflicts between your style names and the ones it already contains. For example, both QuarkXPress and Word contain a Normal style. If you want to use the style already available in QuarkXPress, choose **Use Existing Style**. If you want to rename your styles so that their formatting specifications remain available to you, choose **Rename New Style**.

8. Quark imports the document.

TIP If you've transferred your file from Word for Windows and QuarkXPress for the Macintosh cannot find it, try one of the following fixes:

- If you are using QuarkXPress on the Macintosh, be sure you have Microsoft's OLE Extensions installed in your Macintosh system folder. If the computer isn't running any Microsoft software—and many designers' systems do not—you might have to download these files from the Quark Web site.

- Reopen and resave the file in Word 6.0 for the Macintosh, if you have the program available.

- Download and run the PC-Mac MS Word Script available at Quark's Web site (**www.quark.com/files/scripting.html**). This script changes the type and creator code of Word files so that QuarkXPress can recognize them as such. For more information on type and creator codes associated with Macintosh files, **see** "Ensuring Accurate Document Types on the Macintosh," on **p. 692**.

Exporting QuarkXPress Files to Word

Although text that finds its way into QuarkXPress tends to stay there, occasionally you might want to export text back to Word. You have four options for doing so:

- **ASCII Text.** This can be read in any editor from Windows Notepad to Word 2000.

- **MS Word 4.0.** The best available option if you plan to do extensive editing in Word, this option preserves a good deal of formatting (although far from all of it).

- **MS Word 3.0/MS Write.** This is an option you're not likely to ever need.

- **XPress Tags.** This is the best option if you expect to do only very light editing and don't want to force your designer to totally rework all of his or her pages. It saves an ASCII text file tagged with formatting codes in much the same way that HTML and RTF files are. If you use Word to edit the text file and then resave it in Text Only format, your designer can reimport it to QuarkXPress with design instructions relatively intact.

To export the text in a QuarkXPress document, perform the following steps:

1. Choose **File**, **Save Text**. The Save Text dialog box opens (see Figure 21.5).

FIGURE 21.5
Exporting text to Word from QuarkXPress.

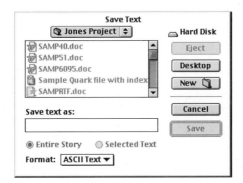

2. Enter a filename in the **Save text as** text box. If the file will be used in Windows, enter an 8.3 filename with an extension that Word can easily recognize, such as .doc for Word files or .txt for ASCII files.

3. In the **Format** drop-down list, choose the format you want to save the text in: ASCII Text (the default setting), XPress Tags, MSWord 3.0/Write, or MSWord 4.0.

4. Click **Save**.

Using Word Documents with Adobe PageMaker

PageMaker is the software that invented desktop publishing, but it rapidly fell behind QuarkXPress in winning the hearts and minds of designers. Recently, Adobe has worked hard to soup up PageMaker and make it competitive again.

Among the areas Adobe has worked hardest at improving is integration with Microsoft Office. In PageMaker 6.5 and PageMaker 6.5 Plus (the most current versions), you have remarkable flexibility in integrating Word and other Office documents into desktop publishing documents. For example, you can perform the following tasks:

- Place a document in PageMaker so that it can either be edited in PageMaker or be edited in Word and automatically updated in PageMaker

- Link or embed tables and spreadsheets up to 40 columns wide, as well as charts and other images

- Integrate database information from Microsoft Access or other applications, via the separate PageMaker Open Database Connectivity (ODBC) plug-in filter

If you're going to work with PageMaker and Office together, spend a few minutes looking over Chapter 11 of the PageMaker 6.5 manual, which contains admirably detailed coverage of PageMaker's many options for importing Office (and other) documents and graphics.

PageMaker's infrastructure for integrating with Microsoft Office is stronger than that of QuarkXPress. Like Quark, it relies on a filter that translates Word documents into information it can use. But that filter has many limitations. It will not, for example, import the following:

- Audio and video clips and other OLE objects

- Automatic bullets and numbering

- Backgrounds, borders, and shading

- Bookmarks

- Comments (in Word 6.0/95, called annotations)

- Emboss, engrave, or double-strikethrough character formatting

- Endnotes (footnotes do import)

- Equations built with earlier versions of Equation Editor (1.0 or 2.0)

- Form fields

- Graphics created with Word's Drawing toolbar

- Headers and footers

- Hidden text
- Hyperlinks (import as colored, unlinked text)
- Hyphenation, justification, character spacing (called letter spacing in most desktop publishing software), and kerning (PageMaker wants to do its own, and so will your designer)
- Page breaks
- Subdocuments in a master document (prior to importing, merge all subdocuments into a single document)
- Table formatting (except for tab-delimited text and character formatting, much like QuarkXPress)
- Vertical text
- WordArt images

Note that there are some elements you *can* import in PageMaker that you cannot import automatically in QuarkXPress and that could make a *big* difference in your productivity:

- Index entry fields for building an index
- Table of contents entry fields for building a table of contents

Updating Your PageMaker Word Filters

As with QuarkXPress, it's likely that you can find a more effective filter on the Web than in the shrink-wrapped CD-ROM you paid for. If you have an early copy of PageMaker 6.5, for example, you might not have a Word 97/2000 filter, or if you do, you might have an older version. As of press time, the latest version, Microsoft Word 97 Import Filter 1.4 (dated 1/13/98) was available at

www.adobe.com/supportservice/custsupport/LIBRARY/4d96.htm

This filter fixes some nagging problems in previous versions. In particular, it does the following:

- Imports graphics stored in Word documents as Portable Network Graphic (PNG) files if the free PNG filter is also installed. This is how Word stores both clipart graphics and WordArt images; however, WordArt images still do not import properly.
- Imports inline graphics in five other formats (JPEG, EMF, WMF, PICT, and BMP)— once again, assuming PageMaker's graphics filters are also installed.
- Imports text in Word text boxes, placing that text at the beginning of the PageMaker story.

TIP

If you find that the Word 97/2000 filter does not give you the results you expect, try these fallback methods for importing Word documents:

- Save in Word 6.0/95 format
- Save as RTF files with .rtf extensions (not .doc extensions)
- Save as WordPerfect 6.0 files

Part
IV

Ch
21

Getting Your Word Document Ready for PageMaker

Because PageMaker's filter has many of the same limitations as Quark's, you might want to follow some of the same steps for preparing your document that were discussed in the section "Preparing Your Word Document for Conversion," earlier in this chapter. Those include the following:

- Be sure your document uses styles consistently and as much as possible.
- Unlink fields in your document, except hidden index entry fields and table of contents entry fields. (PageMaker will take care of many common fields, such as date and time fields.)
- Consider the best way to handle tables, bullets, and numbering.
- Clear password protection from your document, if necessary.
- Save with Fast Saves turned off, in a format compatible with your installed PageMaker filters.

Importing Your Word Document into PageMaker

In this section, you'll walk through importing a Word 2000 document into PageMaker for the Macintosh; the steps to follow in Windows are extremely similar. With PageMaker already open, do the following:

1. Choose **File, New**. The Document Setup dialog box opens.
2. Click **OK**.
3. Choose **File, Place**. The Place document dialog box appears (see Figure 21.6).

FIGURE 21.6
Choosing a document to place in PageMaker 6.5 for the Macintosh.

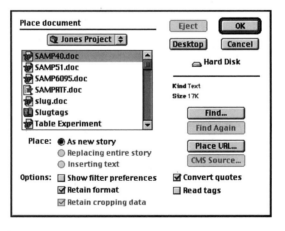

4. Browse to the document you want to place in your PageMaker document.
5. Mark the **Show filter preferences** check box.
6. Click **OK**. The Import filter dialog box appears (see Figure 21.7).

FIGURE 21.7
Controlling which elements of your Word document are imported into PageMaker.

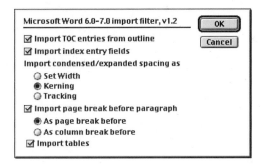

Microsoft Word 6.0–7.0 import filter, v1.2

OK

Cancel

☑ **Import TOC entries from outline**
☑ **Import index entry fields**
Import condensed/expanded spacing as
 ○ Set Width
 ◉ Kerning
 ○ Tracking
☑ **Import page break before paragraph**
 ◉ As page break before
 ○ As column break before
☑ **Import tables**

7. Be sure the settings are as you want them. To use Word's index entries, for example, be sure that **Import Index Entry Fields** is selected.

8. Click **OK**. The imported text appears in your document with PageMaker's text icon.

9. Click on the page where you want the text to be inserted.

TIP If PageMaker cannot recognize a Word file saved in Word 2000 or Word 98 format, try saving it to Word 6.0 format, reopening it in Word 6.0 for the Macintosh, and then resaving it.

Using Word Documents with Adobe FrameMaker

In many technical organizations, as well as other organizations where extremely large documents are routinely created, you might be asked to export Word documents to the publishing program Adobe FrameMaker.

The differences between FrameMaker's long document capabilities and Word's have narrowed dramatically in recent years. Many documents that once required FrameMaker can now stay within Word, at least from a technical standpoint. Moreover, for relative novices, Word is a much easier, more intuitive program to learn.

Having said that, established workflows and procedures might dictate that your organization continue to use FrameMaker. You might, for example, have a staff of publishing and editorial professionals with years of experience in FrameMaker and a preference for it. Or, you might have a large library of documents formatted with FrameMaker. And FrameMaker does represent more than a legacy solution: It offers the following advantages over Word even today:

■ A convenient one-step authoring environment for interactive Adobe PDF electronic documents

■ A cross-platform solution that encompasses not only Windows and Macintosh, but also a variety of UNIX workstation platforms

■ Precise, capable tools for publishing in Japanese

■ Conditional text that enables you to switch easily between multiple versions of the same document—in essence, a more elegant, capable version of Word 2000's Versions feature

■ Superior equation editing

Part
IV

Ch
21

- An optional version, FrameMaker+SGML 5.5, that supports the Standardized General Markup Language (SGML), a powerful tool for organizing and repurposing large documents

N O T E SGML is a complex language that makes it possible to build structure and intelligence into documents by tagging them with codes similar to those of HTML and writing Document Type Definitions (DTDs) that interact with these codes to present information in any number of ways. HTML, the language of World Wide Web documents, was derived from SGML.

SGML has traditionally been most widely used in high-volume production publishing organizations serving military and other government customers, where manuals run in the thousands of pages.

The idea at the heart of SGML, however, is a very powerful one with broad applicability. If you separate content from formatting and tag documents based on their structure, you make it possible to automate and streamline the option of reusing information in virtually any format.

Recently, a streamlined version of SGML, the Extensible Markup Language (XML), has emerged. XML eliminates some of SGML's complexity while maintaining its advantages, and many observers believe it will become a key delivery mechanism for electronic documents on the World Wide Web and intranets—supplanting HTML in many applications.

For the Office administrator interested in SGML or XML, two alternatives exist:

- Export Word and other documents to a program designed to handle them, such as FrameMaker+SGML (or even the latest version of WordPerfect).

- Purchase Microsoft's SGML Author for Word, version 1.2, a set of templates that add SGML capabilities to Word (at $595 per copy).

Understanding the FrameMaker Import Filter for Word

FrameMaker versions prior to 5.56 come with the import filters designed to accept Word files in the following formats:

- Word for Windows 1.*x*, 2.*x*, 6.0, and 95
- Word for the Macintosh 3.0, 4.0, 5.0, 5.1, and 6.0
- RTF

FrameMaker 5.56 also comes with a Word 97 import filter.

Like the other filters discussed in this chapter, FrameMaker's filters do quite a good job of importing manual character formatting and paragraph styles, but they do not handle embedded graphics well. Unlike QuarkXPress and PageMaker, they also can import Word tables intact, as long as you save your documents with Word 2000 features such as nested tables turned off. FrameMaker's filters also preserve some important long-document features, notably index entries.

Importing a Word Document into FrameMaker

To import a Word document into FrameMaker, follow these steps:

1. First, create a new document in FrameMaker. Choose **File**, **New**. FrameMaker's New dialog box opens (see Figure 21.8).

FIGURE 21.8
Creating a new document in FrameMaker.

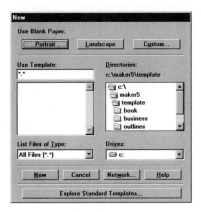

2. Browse to select a template that corresponds to the type of document you want to create.

3. Click **New**. The document opens.

4. Choose **File**, **Import**, **File**.

5. Select the **Copy into Document** check box to copy the Word document's text into your FrameMaker document.

6. Browse to and select the Word document you want to import.

7. Click **Import**.

8. If FrameMaker displays the Unknown File Type dialog box, choose **Microsoft Word** in the **Convert From** list, and then click **Convert**.

9. Click **Import**.

Creating PostScript Files from Office Documents

If you are planning to have your Office documents printed professionally, you might be called upon to create a PostScript file that your printer can use to make film for printing. To do so, perform the following steps:

1. Install the Apple LaserWriter II NT printer driver from your Windows or Mac OS disks. (This is the basic no-frills PostScript driver that virtually every printer can use—but check to see whether your printer prefers you to use a different driver.)

2. When you're ready to create a PostScript file, choose **File**, **Print**. The Print dialog box opens.

3. In the **Name** drop-down list, choose **Apple LaserWriter II NT**.

4. Select the **Print to File** check box.

5. Click **OK**.

6. The Print to File dialog box opens. Specify a name for your PostScript file. (Windows uses the .prn extension by default; some printers like to use the .ps extension.) Limit your filename to eight characters in case your printer is outputting from a Macintosh that does not recognize Windows' long filenames.

7. Click **OK**.

 In some cases, PostScript works better when your documents use PostScript fonts instead of the TrueType fonts that come with Windows and the Macintosh. Discuss this with your printer in advance.

Using Adobe's PDF to Publish Office Documents Electronically

Until now, this chapter has focused solely on print production with Office and desktop publishing systems. Increasingly, Office document professionals face the challenge of finding cost-effective ways to publish formatted documents electronically. Chapter 30 covers a variety of Web publishing solutions. However, one option for publishing Office documents electronically is important to mention here: Adobe Acrobat.

With Acrobat, you can create compact PDF files containing all images and formats, which you can then distribute electronically to anyone who has the free Acrobat Reader software. According to Adobe, more than 20 million copies of Acrobat Reader have been downloaded; you can be reasonably sure that any audience with Web access will have access to it. After opening the file in Acrobat Reader, you can print it or read it onscreen, and you can select and copy text from the file into other documents. You can also search Acrobat PDF files, which can contain internal links and tables of contents that make them quite convenient to use. (One drawback of PDF files: Text can be a little blurry on the screen, even though it prints exceptionally well.)

Although using Acrobat PDF files does nothing to improve the quality of your graphics design, it can streamline the production process from whatever software you work with. For example, you can create electronic documents that your recipients can print themselves on a color or black-and-white printer instead of hassling with conventional print production. Where conventional printing is still required, PDF files can be used by printers to double-check PostScript files that you send and to streamline prepress work.

To use Acrobat with Word, first install Acrobat, and then install PDFMaker, a set of macros for Word 97 and Word 2000. If you own Acrobat 4.0, PDFMaker comes with the product. If you own Acrobat 3.0, you can download PDFMaker as an add-on; you'll find it at **www.adobe.com/ supportservice/custsupport/LIBRARY/4d9e.htm**.

When you install PDFMaker, the Create Adobe PDF command is added to Word's File menu. Then, you can choose **File**, **Create Adobe PDF** to transform a Word 2000 file into PDF format. As you can see in Table 21.1, PDFMaker does a good job of maintaining the interactivity you build into your Word documents.

Table 21.1   How PDFWriter Converts Word Features

Word Feature	PDF Feature
Headings	PDF bookmarks
URLs	PDF Weblinks
Cross-references	PDF links
Page numbers	Links to destinations
Links to other documents	PDF links
Footnote/endnote citations	Links to the notes
Comments/annotations	PDF text notes
Text boxes	PDF article threads
Document properties	PDF document information

Although there are no "one-button macros" for creating PDF files from other Office applications, the task itself is easy. Like fax software, PDF behaves like a printer driver, showing up in the list of printers in your Print dialog box. You simply choose **PDF Writer** from the **Name** drop-down list instead of your current printer. The following steps walk you through the process:

1. Choose **File**, **Print**.
2. From the **Name** drop-down list in the Printer area, choose **PDF Writer**.
3. Click **OK**.
4. Windows prepares to create the PDF file. You're asked to enter a filename for the PDF file and a location where it will be stored.
5. Click **OK**. The PDF file is created and stored in the location you specified. ●

Part
IV

Ch
21

CHAPTER 22

Running Office with Multiple Versions of Windows

by Daryl Lucas

Technically, Office 2000 runs on four versions of Windows: Windows 95, Windows 98, Windows NT 4.0, and Windows 2000. Each of these versions has a distinct package, a retail price, and a Web site for support and news. That appears to give Office 2000 upgraders a reasonable range of options.

The practical truth is both a little more and a little less complicated than that. Windows 2000 has come to be known as "the Windows 2000 family," with five members at home including parents and children. Windows NT 4.0, meanwhile, has five service packs to its name. Windows 95 has two (one of which is not officially available), and Windows 98 has one. Does Office 2000 run on all of these? If so, that's more like 16 versions than four.

If you identify each version with its latest service pack, and if you consider the Windows 95/98 siblings to be as similar as the Windows NT/2000 sisters, you come up with more like two versions: Windows 9x and Windows NT/2000 with Service Pack X. Does Office 2000 run the same on each of these two generic platforms? Does it run the same on both of them?

This chapter answers those questions. The bottom line is that most features of Office 2000 work essentially the same way on all versions of Windows. But not all things are equal, not in every way. It pays to know the differences.

Understanding Office 2000 Features That Interact Directly with the Operating System

Office 2000 has extremely close ties to the operating system. It stores a lot of information in the Registry and in subfolders of the root Windows folder. It relies on the system for DDE, COM, and OLE services. It looks for, uses, and relies on services provided by the Windows Installer. It even uses Control Panel applets for management of some of its features.

This section looks in some detail at how Office 2000 works together with the operating system.

Understanding Setup and Maintenance

Office 2000 uses the Windows Installer for all setup and setup maintenance no matter what the underlying operating system. Windows Installer is also a core component of Windows 2000, so Office is using new technology that all other Windows applications (whether from Microsoft or not) will eventually *have* to use. Meanwhile, this technology is what enables Office 2000 to "run from source," "install on demand," and "repair on-the-fly." Although the Installer does not ship with Windows 9x or Windows NT, these earlier versions of Windows can use it as a component of the operating system. The Windows Installer ships with Office 2000.

N O T E Throughout this chapter, Windows 2000 refers to Windows 2000 Professional, the version of Windows formerly known as Windows NT 5.0. This version of Windows 2000 has inherited Windows NT's place and duties. ■

Setting User Preferences

Office 2000 applications store a lot of customization settings and user preferences. The location of these settings depends to some degree on the client operating system and how it is set up. The most significant differences come from whether user profiles are enabled, and whether a specific profile is roaming.

N O T E This chapter discusses *user profiles* in several places. In all cases, this term refers to *system* user profiles, configured in and maintained by the operating system. It does not refer to Office 2000 user profiles, which administrators can create with the Profile Wizard (an Office Resource Kit tool). Office 2000 user profiles contain settings that relate only to Office and do not have any dependencies on the operating system. System-level user profiles, on the other hand, depend entirely on the operating system.

When user profiles are enabled, most aspects of the Windows Desktop can change from user to user. This includes

- Background images
- Start menu programs
- Desktop colors
- Desktop shortcuts, icons, and icon placement
- Program groups
- Desktop themes ■

▶ For information on using Office 2000 user profiles, **see** Chapter 2, "Automating and Customizing Office Installations Across the Network."

All preferences are stored in one of two locations:

- Files
- Registry keys

▶ For information on enabling User Profiles on Windows 9x, **see** "Specifying Where Your Files Go," on **p. 613** later in this chapter.

Storing User Preferences in Files　In general, Office 2000 stores user-changeable files in the \Application Data\Microsoft folder of the client machine. On machines that have User Profiles enabled, the folder is C:\<*WindowsFolder*>\Profiles\<*UserName*>\Application Data\ Microsoft, where <*UserName*> corresponds exactly to the network logon name. On machines that do *not* have User Profiles enabled, the folder omits the \Profiles\<*UserName*> portion of the path. For the most part, specific settings are stored in subfolders of this main branch.

Table 22.1 lists the feature customizations that are stored in files and the subfolders they use.

Table 22.1　Location of User-Specific Settings Files

User-Specific Files	Subfolder of the \Application Data\Microsoft Folder
Add-ins	\AddIns
AutoCorrect lists	\Office
Custom dictionary	\Proof
Exclude dictionary	\Proof
Graph	\Proof
Office Shortcut Bar (if installed)	\Shortcut Bar
Personal information profiles (.pip files)	\Office
Shortcuts to most recently used files and folders	\Office\Recent
Templates (Word, Excel, PowerPoint)	\Templates
Queries (MS Query)	\Queries

N O T E　Office can store *startup* files, such as Excel's Personal.xls and Word's Normal.dot, in a machine-specific location rather than a user-specific location. For example, you can place global Word templates in C:\Program Files\Microsoft Office\Office\Startup, or Excel's Personal.xls in C:\Program Files\Microsoft Office\Office\XLStart. These locations are user-independent. But in most cases, this information can also be stored in the corresponding User Profiles location, enabling them to travel with the user. ■

Storing User Preferences in Registry Keys   Most of the settings stored in Registry keys correspond to options in the Tools, Options dialog boxes of each Office application. Registry keys also house all system policies, which likewise consist mainly of Tools, Options settings but reflect other settings as well. Although this seems like a short list, the sheer number of data items stored in the Registry far exceeds the number of check boxes you will ever click on any given day of heavy Office use. The Registry holds a *lot* of Office settings data.

Even though the Windows 9x Registry differs from the Windows NT and Windows 2000 Registries, Office 2000 stores all user- and application-specific settings in two general areas regardless of the Windows version:

- **User-independent** settings reside in the HKEY_LOCAL_MACHINE branch of the Registry. These keys do not change from user to user. They are associated with the machine, no matter who uses it.

- **User-specific** settings reside in the HKEY_CURRENT_USER branch of the Registry (and also in the Application Data folder). These keys change from user to user. They are stored on the server and copied to the client machine at logon.

Table 22.2 lists some of the settings that Office 2000 stores. This list represents the major categories; it does not list all or even most of them. The list appears here to give you a general idea of what the Registry contains, to point you to some of the most significant keys, and to illustrate the kinds of data Office tracks. It also illustrates the power of roaming profiles, as all of the HKCU entries are available to roaming users.

Table 22.2   Office 2000 Settings Stored in the Registry

Setting	Location
Application add-ins (COM add-ins)	HKCU\Software\Microsoft\Office\<*ApplicationName*>\Addins\<*Library.Class*> or HKLM\Software\Microsoft\Office\<*ApplicationName*>\Addins\<*Library.Class*>
Default program folder (used by Windows Installer)	HKLM\Software\Microsoft\Office\9.0\<*ApplicationName*>\InstallRoot
Find Fast	HKLM\Software\Microsoft\Office\9.0\Find Fast
Most Access options	HKCU\Software\Microsoft\Office\9.0\Access\Settings
Most Excel options	HKCU\Software\Microsoft\Office\9.0\Excel\Options
Most Outlook options	HKCU\Software\Microsoft\Office\9.0\Outlook\Preferences
Most PowerPoint options	HKCU\Software\Microsoft\Office\9.0\PowerPoint\Options
Most Publisher options	HKCU\Software\Microsoft\Office\9.0\Publisher\Tracking Data
Most Word options	HKCU\Software\Microsoft\Office\9.0\Word\Data
Office 2000 application settings	HKCU\Software\Microsoft\Office\9.0
Office Assistant options	HKCU\Software\Microsoft\Office\9.0\Common\Assistant

Setting	Location
Shared and common settings	HKCU\Software\Microsoft\Office\9.0\Common
System Policy settings	HKCU\Software\Policies\Microsoft
User Information	HKCU\Software\Microsoft\Office\9.0\Common\UserInfo
Word text converters	HKLM\Software\Microsoft\Office\9.0\Word\Text Converters

HKCU = HKEY_CURRENT_USER; HKLM = HKEY_LOCAL_MACHINE.

Office users benefit from this architecture in many ways, but two benefits stand out. The first is *location transparency*. If a user has a roaming profile, Office stores all of his or her customizations in a user-specific branch of the Registry. This enables the user to take his or her computer wherever necessary—without having to bring the hardware.

The second is *add-in universality*. If a network administrator needs to have a single Office 2000 add-in available to all users everywhere no matter who the user is, it can happen. All the user has to do is install the add-in in the HKLM Registry branch.

▶ For more information on how Windows 2000 leverages this flexibility, **see** "Running Office 2000 on Windows 2000," on **p. 617**, later in this chapter.

▶ For more information on installing COM add-ins, **see** Chapter 17, "Managing Office Programmability," on **p. 437**.

Setting System Policies

You can set system policies that control many specific Office 2000 features across the network no matter what operating system the client computers are using. In addition, you can set these policies for a single user, a specific group of users, or all users in a workgroup. As long as the clients log on to a Windows NT 4.0 Server or Windows 2000 Server, Office 2000 installations will use the policies you set.

For example, you can use a system policy to set default file formats for an entire workgroup. This can come in handy in organizations that need to upgrade a number of client machines gradually but want to keep everyone on the same file format during the transition.

Even though all Windows versions that support Office 2000 also support system policies, client computers must meet a few conditions before they can use the policies you set:

- **They must have User Profiles enabled.** This means altering the default for Windows 9x computers.
- **They must download the profile when logging on to the network.** Workstations that have specified Client for Microsoft Networks as the primary network logon client *and* that specify the domain download the profile automatically. Workstations that use a different network client need to be set up to download the policy in some other way, such as by means of a logon script.

■ **If they are to use group policies, they must have support for group policies installed.** No version of Windows installs support for group policies by default, so assume this will require an extra step on your part unless you have already taken care of it.

N O T E If you have been using system policies to manage previous versions of Office, you have to re-create them for Office 2000; they do not transfer automatically. Office 2000 moved the Registry location for policies and does not migrate them for you. Earlier versions stored their policies with the Software keys (such as Software\Microsoft\Office\9.0\Excel), whereas Office 2000 puts them all in a single HKCU\Software\Policies\Microsoft subkey. ■

N O T E System Policies give you a lot of control over client implementations of Office. For detailed information on creating and using system policies to manage a deployment of Office 2000, see "Using the System Policy Editor" in the Office 2000 Resource Kit. If you do not have the Office Resource Kit, you can access the entire text and all its software tools, including the System Policy Editor, at **http://www.microsoft.com/office/ork**. ■

The Office 2000 Resource Kit's System Policy Editor includes 10 policy templates (see Table 22.3). Setup installs the templates in C:\<*WindowsFolder*>\Inf by default.

Table 22.3   Policy Templates Included with the System Policy Editor

Template Name	Office 2000 Application
Office9.adm	Shared components
Access9.adm	Access
Excel9.adm	Excel
FrontPg4.adm	FrontPage
Outlk9.adm	Outlook
Pub6.adm	Publisher
Ppoint9.adm	PowerPoint
Word9.adm	Word
ClipGal5.adm	Clip Gallery
Instlr1.adm	Windows Installer

▶ For more information on using system policies to manage a workgroup of users, **see** Chapter 37, "Reducing Office 2000's Total Cost of Ownership," on **p. 963**.

Taking Advantage of Web Folders

Web Folders allow saving and opening of files to and from Web servers via HTTP as if they were ordinary files on an ordinary hard disk. Although this mainly results from the addition of extensions to the Web server (rather than the client machine), the Web Folders object appears in the Windows Explorer and appears to the users to be part of their machines. That's a significant pairing of Office functionality with the operating system.

Installation and use of Web Folders do not depend on client operating systems. As long as the Web server in question has the appropriate extensions installed, any workstation that has Office 2000 can also save files to Web Folders, collaborate on workgroup projects through Web Discussions, and open files from Web Folders.

N O T E A *Web Folder* is simply a shortcut to a Web Server. You do not need to do anything to "install" Web Folder functionality on client workstations. The functionality resides on the Web server, not on the client PC.

If you are not sure whether you have access to Web Folders, a simple experiment will tell you. With a file open in an Office application, such as Word or Excel, click **File**, **Save As**, and select the Web Folders item in the Places Bar. Navigate to any available Web folder on any server to which your computer has a connection. If you can save the file to one of these folders (or, by the same token, if you can open a file), you have access to Web Folders. If you still are not sure, ask your network administrator. ▓

 TIP If you want to be one of the ones who makes files available to Office 2000 users through Web Folders, you can add the functionality by installing Web server software on your PC. Any Office 2000 user can install Personal Web Server or Internet Information Server for the purpose of creating a Web server on the workstation. This makes it easy for individuals to share documents with others in a place and manner that does not require IS or network administrators to set up and maintain a site. *Caveat*: This is easier with Windows 98 than Windows 95, and easier with Windows NT 4.0 than with Windows 9x, and yet easier with Windows 2000 than with all others.

Taking Advantage of Find Fast

Office 2000 installs Find Fast by default and uses it to index Office documents for fast retrieval by File, Open operations. Although not a flashy or high-profile feature, it becomes part of the elite group of Control Panel applets (see Figure 22.1) and allows very flexible customization.

FIGURE 22.1
Find Fast is one of the many Office 2000 features that looks more like an operating system component than an Office application. You control it through Control Panel.

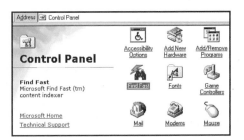

▶ For more information on Find Fast, including what it is and how it can help users, **see** "Finding Documents with Find Fast and Document Properties," on **p. 574**.

Understanding Multilanguage Support

Office 2000 is based on the Unicode standard and was designed for multilanguage use even without the use of Unicode fonts. Because of Office's architecture, you can type in any language supported by the operating system.

The way you manage this depends on the operating system. Windows 2000, for example, has support for all available languages, including Asian languages, without the need for a localized version of the operating system. Windows NT also lets you work with many languages that differ from that of the operating system (by setting the so-called *Input Locale*), but not with Asian languages. Windows 9x does not let you deviate from the localized version and requires the use of keyboard mapping.

▶ For more information on support for multiple languages in Office 2000, **see** Chapter 42, "Using Office in a Global Environment," on **p. 1079**.

Running Office 2000 on Windows 9x

Windows 95 represents the minimal platform on which you can run Office 2000. But because of the similarity between Windows 95 and Windows 98, Microsoft lists them together in the system requirements ("Windows 95/98").

▶ You can run Office 2000 on less powerful systems with Windows Terminal Server at the helm. For more information on the system requirements for such a setup and how to take advantage of this option, **see** Chapter 23, "Running Office 2000 with Microsoft Terminal Services," on **p. 623**.

> **N O T E** Online support for Windows 95 and Windows 98 is available at
> `http://support.microsoft.com/support/`. ▪

Retooling Your Operating System to Support Office 2000

As the oldest of the 32-bit OS quartet, Windows 95 requires the most retooling to support all of Office 2000's features. Windows 98 requires almost as much. The following paragraphs discuss some of the most significant tweaks confronting you.

Retooling the Keyboard   If you want to type in a language other than the operating system's language version, and if you want to avoid using a Unicode font, you must enable support for that language through Control Panel's Keyboard applet.

For example, to add additional keyboard mappings on a Windows 9x machine, follow these steps:

1. Start Control Panel.
2. Start the Keyboard applet.
3. Display the **Languages** tab.
4. Click **Add**.
5. Select the language you want to support, and then click **OK** twice.

If you want to type in supported Asian languages, you must also install an Input Method Editor (IME).

Retooling Windows 95 with Service Pack 1 For Office 2000 to work correctly in a networked environment, a Windows 95 machine must have Service Pack 1 (SP1) or later installed. SP1 upgrades the operating system kernel and several networking components on which Office applications rely. Be sure you have installed this upgrade before installing Office 2000 on Windows 95 clients.

You can get SP1 from the Windows support Web site: `http://support.microsoft.com/support/`.

SP2 (including 2.1 and 2.5) are not available for download; they require vendor installation.

Understanding Changes Made on Windows 95 Only Installing Office 2000 on a Windows 95 system upgrades the operating system. Several of the core components in Office's applications have the distinction of being system files, and the Installer will install them if they (1) do not already exist or (2) exist in an earlier version.

Table 22.4 lists the files that take part in an Office 2000 installation *only* if the target machine has Windows 95.

Table 22.4   Windows 95-Only Files Installed or Updated by Office 2000

Filename	Description
Office MSI files (2)	
eyedog.ocx	MSInfo ActiveX control (client container)
msisys.ocx	MSInfo ActiveX control (driver creator)
DCOM and Windows Installer Files (28)	
advpack.dll	Setup engine library (extracts .cab files and changes Registry keys)
asycfilt.dll	Core OLE 2.40 automation library
comcat.dll	Component Category Manager Library (OLE core library)
compobj.dll	OLE 2.3.1 16/32 Interoperability Library (DLL-to-EXE object binder)
dcom2w98.dll	Migration library for Windows 98 over DCOM98
dllhost.exe	COM EXE surrogate
imagehlp.dll	Image manipulation API
iprop.dll	OLE PropertySet Implementation
ole2.dll	OLE 2.1 16/32 interoperability library
ole32.dll	Core OLE library
oleaut32.dll	Core OLE 2.40 automation library
olecnv32.dll	Core OLE 2.1 library

continues

Table 22.4 Continued

Filename	Description
DCOM and Windows Installer Files (28)	
olepro32.dll	Core OLE automation library (compatibility shell; thanks to other OLE files)
olethk32.dll	Core OLE 2.1 library
rpcltc1.dll	Remote Procedure Call client support for Named Pipes (RPC support library)
rpcltc5.dll	Remote Procedure Call transport driver
rpcltccm.dll	Remote Process Control LTCCM library (RPC support library)
rpclts5.dll	Remote Procedure Call transport driver
rpcltscm.dll	Remote Procedure Call support library
rpcmqcl.dll	Remote Procedure Call message queue client
rpcmqsvr.dll	Remote Procedure Call message queue server
rpcns4.dll	RPC Name Service support library
rpcrt4.dll	Remote Procedure Call runtime
rpcss.exe	Distributed COM Services
secur32.dll	Win32 Security Services
stdole2.tlb	Standard OLE 2.40 automation type library
stdole32.tlb	Standard OLE 2.1 type library
storage.dll	OLE 2.3.1 16/32 Interoperability Library (document abstraction layer)

Dealing with Features That Are Less Effective on Windows 9x

Some of the system components that Office 2000 uses or relies on suffer from limitations under Windows 9x. The following sections summarize them.

Accepting a Limited Windows Installer   If an application or feature is set to Install on First Use and the Windows Installer does not find it, Windows prompts the user before installing it. This is unlike the Windows 2000 client, which does not prompt the user.

Getting DFS Shares to Work   Distributed File System (DFS) Shares allow multiple Windows NT Server 4.0 or Windows 2000 Server servers to share Install-on-demand duties. For example, in your Office 2000 deployment, you can point all your clients to \\Headquarters\Office2k, a DFS share that itself points to \\Outskirts\Office2k and \\Perimeter\Office2k. The effect is similar to the use of Windows Installer source lists—Office 2000 computers can install features and products from more than one network source without forcing the user to choose the source.

For this to work on a Windows 95 machine, you must install the DFS client software separately from Office Setup. To do so, follow these steps:

1. Get the DFS client from Microsoft's Web site; the compressed filename is Dfs-v41-win95client.exe.

2. Run the Dfs-v41-win95client.exe file on a DFS server to expand the CAB files to the *<systemroot>*\system32\dfs\win95 folder.

3. Share the *<systemroot>*\system32\dfs\win95 folder so client computers can connect to it. (You can also copy the CAB files to a floppy disk.)

4. On the Windows 95 workstation, run Control Panel's Network applet.

5. Click **Add**, double-click **Service**, and then click **Have Disk**.

6. Under Copy manufacturer's files from, browse to the network share on which you stored the CAB files and then click **OK**.

7. Select **DFS Services** for Microsoft Network Client in the Models dialog box and click **OK** twice.

8. Restart the computer when prompted.

N O T E If you have previously installed an earlier version of the DFS client and want to upgrade it to the latest version, remove the earlier version first. Then install the latest version. ▪

Addressing Other Windows 9x Issues and Problems

Microsoft designed Office 2000 to work best with Windows NT and Windows 2000. Users of Windows 9x do not necessarily suffer for this, but they can benefit from knowing about several issues that arise because of it.

Specifying Where Your Files Go   We noted in the "User Preferences" section that Office 2000 puts user-specific files in the C:*<WindowsFolder>*\Profiles*<UserName>*\Application Data\Microsoft folder if \Profiles*<UserName>* exists; otherwise it puts the files in C:*<WindowsFolder>*\Application Data\Microsoft. The \Profiles*<UserName>* folder exists only on machines that have User Profiles enabled. By default, all Windows NT 4.0 and Windows 2000 Professional machines use profiles; Windows 9x machines do not.

The reason is simple: Consider each platform's principal audience and purpose. User Profiles get most of their usefulness from networking environments, whereas Windows 9x has always been targeted mainly at the home market, where a logon procedure and a user profile is more of a nuisance than a help. Windows 9x has also never had a very secure networking model, making its appeal as a network client less than that of Windows NT. Hence, these operating systems do not use profiles by default.

Even if specific users have no immediate need for User Profiles, using profiles anyway has several advantages, especially in a corporate setting:

■ First, it makes the location of user settings consistent throughout the organization, no matter what client operating system is in place.

■ Second, it gives the user more flexibility; because it is relatively easy to add Users to the list of profiles, the user can have two or three Profiles tailored to specific duties.

■ Third, it allows more than one person to share a Windows 9x computer without any more intervention than having a User Profile for each person.

Part

IV

Ch

22

■ Fourth, it allows a user to roam from machine to machine, should the need ever arise, without a lot of extra work.

Enabling User Profiles on Windows 9x machines is not difficult. Simply run the Users applet in Control Panel (see Figure 22.2) and add the user for whom you want to add a profile.

FIGURE 22.2

To enable User Profiles on Windows 9x machines, run the Users applet in Control Panel.

NOTE Roaming User Profiles do not allow roaming across Windows 9x and Windows NT/2000 because of differences in their Registries. That is, if a user's main machine is a Windows 95 machine, that user's roaming profile enables him or her to use other Windows 95 and 98 machines, but not other Windows NT or Windows 2000 machines. ■

You do not have to enable User Profiles for Office 2000 to work correctly. Office will use the default C:\<*WindowsFolder*>\Application Data\Microsoft folder if no Profiles folder exists. But it is important to know that the difference affects where a lot of Office settings are stored. This can lead to confusion and makes management of the workstations a little more difficult as a result.

Automating Tasks with the Windows Scripting Host The Windows Scripting Host (WSH) is, in essence, a Windows replacement for the DOS batch language. You can use it to automate system tasks and work on system-level objects such as files, desktop shortcuts, and the Registry. It is COM-compliant and has a rich object model that is fully programmable by VBA programmers and other automation clients. If you need to leverage Office programmability, you will want to have it on client machines.

Windows 95 does not include WSH, but whether you need to install it depends on other decisions you have made. Internet Explorer 4.0 and later include WSH in their default installations, so if you have already upgraded client browsers, you can forego adding it now.

To check a client machine for the WSH, follow these steps:

1. Start Notepad.

2. Type this line (including the quotation marks):

   ```
   MsgBox "Hello from the Windows Scripting Host."
   ```

3. Save the file with a VBS extension.

4. Double-click the file.

If WSH is installed, you will see a message like the one shown in Figure 22.3.

FIGURE 22.3
You can test a client
machine for the
Windows Scripting
Host by trying to run
MsgBox "Hello" from a
plain-text VBS file.

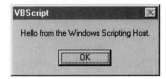

The WSH is available for download from **http://msdn.microsoft.com/scripting**.

▶ For more information on programming Office 2000, **see** Chapter 17, "Managing Office
Programmability," on **p. 437**.

Running Office 2000 on Windows NT 4.0

Office 2000 needs almost no special consideration to run well on Windows NT 4.0. In fact, the
only significant gotcha might involve administrator rights on the client machine; otherwise,
your detours will be short and brief.

N O T E Online support for Windows NT is available at **http://www.microsoft.com/
support/winnt**. ▧

Leveraging Windows NT's Foreign Language Support

If you want to type in a language other than the operating system's language version, you
need only add the appropriate Input Locale through Control Panel. You can use either the
Keyboard applet or the Regional Settings applet to add the locales you need.

For example, to add support for another language in which you need to type on a Windows
NT workstation, follow these steps:

1. Start Control Panel.
2. Start the Keyboard applet.
3. Display the Input Locales tab.
4. To add a new locale, click **Add**.
5. Select the language you want to support, and then click **OK** twice.

You can change the Locale through the Regional Settings applet as well. By changing the
locale, you are, in effect, changing the language version of the operating system.

N O T E This procedure works on Windows NT Server as well as Windows NT Workstation. ▧

Understanding Changes Made Only on Windows NT 4.0

Installing Office 2000 on a Windows NT system installs some files unique to that operating system, most notably a set of language files. The Installer installs these files if they (1) do not already exist or (2) exist in an earlier version.

Table 22.5 lists the Windows NT-only files that Office 2000 will install if necessary.

Table 22.5	Windows NT Files Installed or Updated by Office 2000
Filename	**Description**
big5.nls	Sorting table for Chinese (NLS file)
bopomofo.nls	Chinese IME support file (NLS file)
ctype.nls	Character type 1 Unicode translation data file
ksc.nls	Sorting table for Korean (NLS file)
msihwnfo.ocx	System Information plug-in
prc.nls	Core NLS sorting file
prcp.nls	Core NLS sorting file
setupdd.dll	NetMeeting display driver for NT Setup
sortkey.nls	Core NLS sorting file
sorttbls.nls	Core NLS sorting file
xjis.nls	Core NLS sorting file

NLS = National Language Support

Dealing with Features That Are Less Effective on Windows NT 4.0

Windows NT clients make no significant compromises in Office 2000 functionality except the lack of support for product-level on-demand installation. If an application is set to Install on First Use and the Windows Installer does not find it, Windows NT prompts the user before installing it. Windows 2000 does not prompt the user.

▶ For more information on the Install-on-demand features of the Windows Installer, **see** "Using Application Assignment and Publishing," on **p. 620** later in this chapter.

Addressing Other Windows NT Issues and Problems

You need to be aware of two important issues related to Office 2000 on Windows NT 4.0, covered next.

Retooling Windows NT with Service Pack 3   Office 2000 requires NT Service Pack 3 or later on networked machines. Although most users of Windows NT Workstation, especially in corporate settings, have already taken this step, not all have; if you have not, you *must* do so before installing Office 2000. Service Pack 3 fixes many known problems with Office 97 applications, with networking features, and with other problems identified long ago. Although Office 2000 is not Office 97, they share the same pedigree. For this reason, standalone machines should also have the Service Pack.

Handling Security Restrictions with the Pre-Installation Pack   If you are deploying Office to users who do not have Administrator privileges on their machines, you need the Microsoft Office 2000 Pre-Installation Pack for Windows NT, a Resource Kit tool. This tool enables the Installer to make the necessary changes to system folders and the Registry without having Administrator privileges.

Running Office 2000 on Windows 2000

It probably comes as no surprise that Microsoft would like you to run Office 2000 on Windows 2000. One was written with the other in mind. Office 2000 shines brightest in the Windows 2000 sky. Whereas the unique benefits do not rival fireworks, they do bear mentioning.

> **N O T E**   Online support for Windows NT is available at **http://support.microsoft.com/ support/**.

Understanding Windows 2000 Differences

This section outlines a few of the considerations unique to Windows 2000.

Adding Convenience with OLE Activation   OLE works differently in Windows 2000 from how it works in previous versions of Windows. OLE now calls the Windows Installer before launching server applications. If the server cannot be found or is missing a crucial file and the application is set to Install on First Use, the Windows Installer can retrieve the missing files transparently before returning the call to the server. If the application is not set to Install on First Use, OLE works as in earlier versions of Windows and returns an error.

▶ For more information on changes to OLE activation in Windows 2000, **see** "Transparently Installing and Repairing OLE Servers," on **p. 620** later in this chapter.

Understanding Changes Made Only on Windows 2000   Microsoft says only three files are unique to Office 2000 installations on Windows 2000 (see Table 22.6). In most other respects, the Windows 2000 file list looks very much like the one for Windows NT 4.0. Keep in mind, however, that other programs may install these files, so your Windows 9x and Windows NT clients may still have them.

Table 22.6   Files Installed Only on Windows 2000 Systems

Filename	Description
agtinst.inf	Microsoft Agent 2.0 uninstall information file
mlang.dat	Multilanguage Support file
mlang.dll	Multilanguage Support library

Leveraging Features Requiring Windows 2000 Professional

Most of the Windows 2000 features that Office 2000 can leverage require three pieces, not just one: Windows 2000 Professional on the client, Windows 2000 Server on the server, and *Active Directory*. Active Directory is an optional component of Windows 2000. Table 22.7 summarizes these pieces.

Table 22.7 Features That Require Both Windows 2000 Professional on the Client and Windows 2000 Server on the Server

Feature	Explanation
IntelliMirror	Comprises user data management, application installation and maintenance, and user and computer settings management.
Storage of roaming user data on the server	Must be stored in a location set to roam—the My Documents folder by default.
Application assignment to user	An application can be assigned to either a user or a computer. *Assigned to user* stores install-on-demand keys in the client machine's HKEY_CURRENT_USER Registry branch when the user logs on to a Windows 2000 computer. The next time the user tries to start the application, insert an OLE object of its type, or activate an object of its type, the application installs. Settings are stored in the HKEY_CURRENT_USER subkey and are specific to that user.
Application assignment to computer	Install-on-next-reboot keys in the client machine's HKEY_LOCAL_MACHINE branch of the Registry are set, and the application fully installs on next reboot. The application is available to all users.
Application publishing to user	Application settings are stored in the Active Directory, not in the client machine's Registry. The application is set to install-on-demand, but is also available in the Add/Remove Programs applet of Control Panel.

Making All Settings User-Specific: User-Specific OLE Registration   Windows 2000 allows storage of software application settings (such as file associations and class data) in a user-specific version of the HKEY_CLASSES_ROOT branch of the Registry. This is new. All previous 32-bit versions of Windows stored software application settings in the HKEY_LOCAL_MACHINE\Software\Classes branch of the Registry only (mirrored in HKEY_CLASSES_ROOT). Windows 2000 allows storage of software application settings in the HKEY_CURRENT_USER branch.

These settings are used by the Windows Installer service to install and repair Office 2000 features.

NOTE   This feature requires Windows 2000 on the client only. ▪

Copying, Moving, and Deleting HTML Files Intelligently   Office 2000 enables round-tripping of documents in HTML format. If you save an Office 2000 document as an HTML document, you lose none (or very little) of the formatting and features of the binary version of the file. You can later save it back to Office 2000's native format without any data loss or compromises.

One of round-tripping's ugly side effects is file proliferation. Whenever you create an HTML file from an Office document, the application saves a folder along with the file. The folder contains supporting files required to display the file properly in Web browsers. For example, if you save Goodbye.doc as Goodbye.htm, Word creates a Goodbye_files folder in the same location as Goodbye.htm and stores several additional files in Goodbye_files—files you need if you want to get the full functionality of the original.

Under Windows 2000, copying, moving, renaming, or deleting the Goodbye.htm file alone will cause its supporting folder to be copied, moved, renamed, or deleted as well. Likewise, copying, moving, renaming, or deleting the Goodbye_files folder will copy, move, or delete the Goodbye.htm file that goes with it.

N O T E   This feature requires Windows 2000 on the client only. ■

N O T E   This feature does not work inside the Web Folders object. It also does not work on files created in Microsoft FrontPage. ■

N O T E   You can turn this feature off. In the Windows 2000 Registry, open the HKEY_CURRENT_USER\Software\Microsoft\Windows\CurrentVersion\Explorer subkey, add an entry named NoFileFolderConnection, and set its value to 1 (DWORD). Setting this value to 0 or deleting the entry altogether restores the feature. ■

Rolling Back Failed Installations Automatically   Using Systems Management Server (SMS) under Windows 2000, the Windows Installer automatically rolls back an Office 2000 installation that fails.

N O T E   This feature requires Windows 2000 on both the client and server. ■

▶ For more information on using SMS to deploy Office 2000, **see** Chapter 3, "Using Systems Management Server 2.0 to Install Office 2000," on **p. 63**.

Taking Advantage of IntelliMirror-Based Features   IntelliMirror is a Windows 2000 technology that enhances use and maintenance of client applications and data from the server. IntelliMirror is so named because it allows the network file server to keep a copy of users' data files, application files, system files, and administrative settings for use in several different ways. It enables users to take their entire set of applications and data with them from computer to computer. It also enables the software repair of client machines that get damaged Registries, applications, or OLE servers.

All IntelliMirror technologies require Windows 2000 on both client and server machines, so all IntelliMirror-based features of Office 2000 require such a setup as well. The most significant IntelliMirror features that affect Office 2000 include these two:

- Application Assignment and Publishing
- Caching of run-from-network Office files

N O T E   These features require Windows 2000 on both the client and server. ▓

Using Application Assignment and Publishing   The Windows Installer allows two kinds of on-demand installation: *feature-level* and *product-level*. Feature-level installation relies on an Installer-aware application to install features not already present on the machine, so it can work on any 32-bit Windows PC. Product-level installation, on the other hand, relies on the operating system's intervention, so it requires Windows 2000. To deploy Office 2000 applications as install-on-demand, you must have Windows 2000 on the client.

Administrators can both assign and publish Office 2000 to users and computers. This enables users, through the use of roaming profiles, to access their Office applications and data at any computer on the network.

Caching Run-from-Network Office Files   When you install Office and set specific features to Run from Network, Setup leaves those files on the network server; it does not copy them to the client hard disk. When Office needs those files, it accesses them over the wire.

While this saves space on client hard disks, it also slows down program execution and increases network traffic. To speed up execution and cut down on network traffic, Windows 2000 Professional caches the code locally if it is connected to a Windows 2000 server. Thus, Office 2000 users who have Windows 2000 benefit directly from this by getting to compute faster, and everyone on the network benefits by getting to network faster.

Transparently Installing and Repairing OLE Servers   Object Linking and Embedding has always had a weakness: the location of the server. ("Server" in this context means *application that created the OLE object*, not a network file server.) If you embed an Excel chart in a Word document, activating the chart requires that the server application, Excel, is installed and registered properly on the workstation that opens it.

That is usually fine for the person who creates the document, but not if (1) the user deletes some files that Excel requires or (2) the user has moved Excel's location and not properly registered it or (3) the registration has become corrupted. For OLE activation to work correctly on Windows 95, Windows 98, and Windows NT 4,0, OLE servers have to be installed and registered properly.

Windows 2000 has a more robust architecture because it goes through the Windows Installer. When a user opens an OLE object, such as an embedded document or a linked presentation, the Windows Installer first handles the request to start the server. If any piece of the server is missing, the Installer can replace the missing piece on-the-fly, before handing the activation request to the OLE services, so the request will work.

Earlier versions of Windows can use the Windows Installer to repair broken OLE servers, but only by prompting the user first. Only on Windows 2000 Professional can the Installer install the missing files transparently.

This feature is called *OLE-level advertising*. It works on any Windows 2000 computer; it does not require Windows 2000 on the server unless the OLE server is located on a remote file server.

NOTE   This feature requires Windows 2000 on the client only. ▪

▶ For more information on Object Linking and Embedding, **see** "Using Linking and Embedding to Create Rich Office Files," on **p. 552**.

Leveraging DFS Shares   If you have Windows 2000 deployed throughout the network, you can use DFS Shares as an alternative to Windows Installer source lists without having to install any additional software on client machines. This gives you a single point of control over installation source information and is tied more closely to your network's organizational structure.

NOTE   This feature requires Windows 2000 on both the client and server. ▪

▶ For information on supporting DFS Shares on other Windows clients, **see** "Dealing with Features That Are Less Effective on Windows 9x," on **p. 612** earlier in this chapter.

Leveraging Enforceable System Policies   If you have Windows 2000 on the client, you can lock the machine's HKEY_CURRENT_USER\Software\Policies subkey to prevent users from changing the policies you have set. You do this through an ACL (Access Control List) at the server.

NOTE   This feature requires Windows 2000 on both the client and server. ▪

Dealing with Other Windows 2000 Issues and Problems

In your deployment of Office 2000, you really have only one limitation to work around: Windows 2000 does not support mandatory user profiles, a feature supported in Windows 9x and Windows NT 4.0. If you have been using mandatory user profiles, you need to replace them (or simply dispense with them).

Finding Additional Resources When You're Stuck

For the latest information on the technologies discussed in this chapter, see the relevant Web sites:

Office 2000: `http://www.microsoft.com/office/`

Office 2000 Resource Kit: `http://www.microsoft.com/office/ork/`

Windows 2000 Resource Kit:
`http://www.microsoft.com/windows2000/library/resources/reskit/default.asp`

Windows main page: `http://www.microsoft.com/windows/`

Windows 2000 Professional: `http://www.microsoft.com/windows/professional/`

Windows 2000 Server: `http: //www.microsoft.com/windows/server/`●

Running Office 2000 with Microsoft Terminal Services

by Deb Shinder

In many budget-conscious companies, hardware upgrades are slow to come to all desktop machines. Users may be working with older systems, which aren't capable of running Office 2000 properly, yet they may need its new features and functionality. This is one of the reasons the thin client concept is growing in popularity throughout the corporate world.

Running Office from a Microsoft Terminal Server is a viable alternative to buying new hardware. The application runs completely on the server, and only the client services run on the desktop machines. You can use a computer that doesn't meet minimum system requirements for Office 2000, and use the applications as if they were installed locally. Multiple users can log on and see only their individual session.

Unlike many other popular applications, Office 2000 was designed with specific features to take advantage of either Windows NT Terminal Server Edition or the Windows 2000 Server family, all of which come with terminal services built in.

Understanding Microsoft Terminal Services

Microsoft Terminal Services is designed to provide remote access to a server desktop through *thin client* software, which operates as a terminal emulator. The server transmits only the user interface of the program to the client, and the user at the client machine returns keyboard and mouse clicks, which are transferred across the network and processed by the server.

By installing Office 2000 on a terminal server, and installing the terminal services client software on the machines that need to use the Office applications, you can increase your users' productivity without spending money to upgrade their hardware. The administrator can control users' sessions to whatever degree is desired.

Users can customize their terminal desktops independently of other users, or the settings can be standardized and locked down by the administrator. Computer resources can be managed on a per-user basis, and users' documents are stored separately.

You can enable Terminal Services on the server in either *application server* or *remote administration* mode. The latter can be used only by administrators, and allows them to manage the server from any desktop running the client software. This chapter focuses on deploying Terminal Services in application server mode to distribute Office 2000 to client desktops throughout the organization.

Installing and Configuring Terminal Services on the Server

Terminal services are part of the Windows 2000 operating system. You need administrative privileges to install and configure its components. To allow your users to connect and run Office programs via terminal services, you must install the terminal services component on the server and configure the Terminal Server to run in application server mode.

Running the Windows Components Wizard

To install terminal services on a Windows 2000 server, start the Windows Components Wizard as follows:

1. Select **Start, Settings, Control Panel, Add/Remove Programs**.
2. Choose **Add Windows Components**.
3. Scroll down the list of Windows Components, and select the **Terminal Services** check box, as shown in Figure 23.1, and then click the **Next** button.
4. In Terminal Services Setup, choose **Application server mode**.
5. In Terminal Services Licensing Setup, select whether you want the license server to serve your entire enterprise or your domain/workgroup. Provide the directory location for the database.
6. Click **Next**, and then click **Finish**.
7. Restart the server, and the installation is complete.

FIGURE 23.1
Select the Terminal
Services check box in
Windows Components.

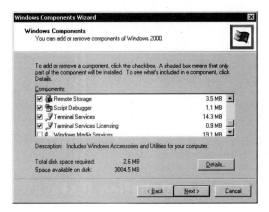

CAUTION

Generally, when Terminal Services runs in application server mode, each client computer that accesses the
server requires a separate Client Access License (CAL) . When you install Terminal Services in application
mode, you must also install the Licensing component, which you use to register and track licenses.

Configuring the Terminal Server Settings

The administrator can configure the terminal server settings by using the Configuration tool.
From the Start menu, select **Programs, Administrative Tools, Terminal Services
Configuration.**

Figure 23.2 shows the Configuration console, and the server settings that may be changed in
the right detail pane.

FIGURE 23.2
Administrators can
change terminal server
settings with the
Configuration tool.

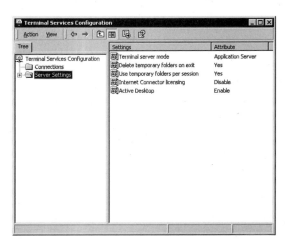

Installing the Terminal Services Client Software

The next step in setting up a terminal emulation environment for running Office 2000 is to install the client software on the desktop machines. You can create terminal services client disks for 16- or 32-bit Windows operating systems by using the Client Creator administrative tool included with Windows 2000 Server.

N O T E   You can use other operating system platforms' (such as Macintosh and UNIX) terminal server clients by using third-party software, such as Citrix Metaframe. ■

Making the Client Software Installation Disks

To make the client installation disks, you need four blank 3_-inch blank floppy disks (if they are not preformatted, you can choose to format them during the disk-creation process).

Access the Terminal Services client creator tool on the Windows 2000 server:

1. Select **Start**, **Programs**, **Administrative Tools**, **Terminal Services Client Creator**.

2. In the Create Installation Disk(s) dialog box , shown in Figure 23.3, choose the appropriate operating system platform.

FIGURE 23.3
Select the client platform for the installation disks.

3. Select **Terminal Services for 16-bit windows** if you will install the client software on the Windows 3.x platform, or **Terminal Services for 32-bit x86 windows** if you will install it on a machine running Windows 9598, Windows NT, or Windows 2000 Professional.

N O T E   If the disks on which you want to save the client software are not blank and formatted, select the **Format disk(s)** check box. ■

4. Place the first disk in the floppy drive and click **OK**. You are then prompted to insert subsequent disks.

Installing the Client Software

To install the 32-bit Terminal Services Client (for Windows 95/98, Windows NT or Windows 2000 machines), perform the following steps:

1. Insert the first disk created in the preceding step into your floppy drive. At a command prompt, type **a:setup** and press **ENTER**. The **Welcome to the Terminal Services Client installation** dialog box appears.

2. Click **Continue**.

3. In **Name**, type your full name. In **Organization**, type the name of your organization.

4. In the **Terminal Services Client Setup** dialog box, note the product ID number, and then click **OK**.

5. In the **License Agreement** dialog box, read the agreement and, if you accept the license agreement, click **I Agree**.

Part

IV

Ch

23

N O T E If you do not accept the license agreement, setup will stop and you will not be able to install the software. ▦

6. In the **Terminal Services Client Setup** dialog box, begin installation, and then click the large icon button.

7. If you want to install client software for all users, click **Yes**. To install the client only for the current user, click **No**.

8. In the **Terminal Services Client Setup** dialog box, click **OK**. This will finish the installation.

N O T E If you are installing the Terminal Services Client on a Windows 3.x machine, the process is almost identical, except that during the setup, you are asked to select a Program Group into which the Terminal Services Client should be placed. ▦

Configuring the Client Connection

After you install the client software, you can configure a new server connection by choosing **Start**, **Programs**, **Terminal Services Client**, **Client Connection Manager**. Figure 23.4 shows the Client Connection Manager with connections to several terminal servers already set up.

FIGURE 23.4
The Client Connection Manager is used to create and configure server connections.

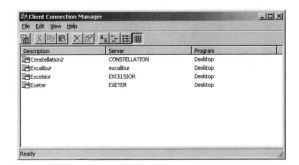

To make a new connection, follow these steps:

1. Click **File**, **New Connection**. This will start the Client Connection Manager Wizard.

2. After clicking **Next** on the Wizard's splash screen, you see the dialog box shown in Figure 23.5, where you are asked to type a name for the connection. Then, you must enter the name or IP address of the terminal server.

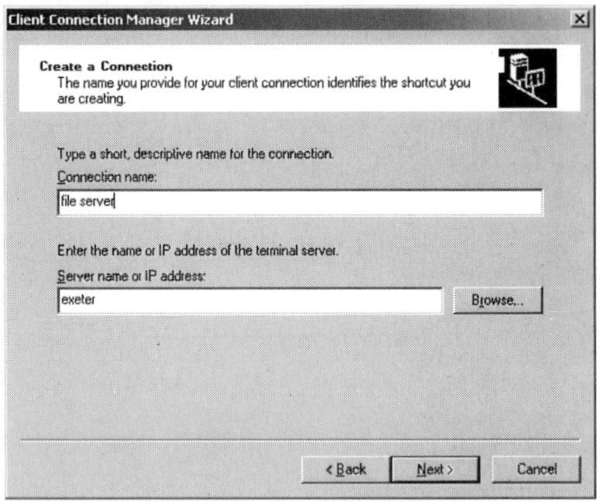

FIGURE 23.5

Enter a name for the
new connection and
server information.

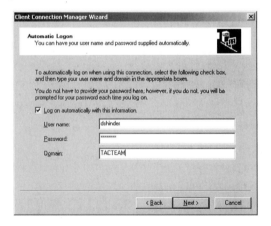

3. Click **Next**, and you have the option to enter username, password, and domain information to be used each time you connect, so you won't be prompted for it at the beginning of
   each session. If you want, enter this information in the dialog box shown in Figure 23.6.

FIGURE 23.6

Terminal Services will
enter your account
information automati-
cally each time you
connect.

N O T E The administrator must configure the user's account to allow the user to log on
automatically. ■

4. Click **Next**, and you are asked to choose a screen resolution for the terminal window.
   Alternatively, you can choose to display the terminal full screen.

5. Click **Next** again, and you have the option to enable **data compression**, and/or **cache
   frequently used bitmaps** to the local disk, to improve performance. Make your selections and click **Next**.

6. The next dialog box gives you the choice of running a specified program when you
   start the connection. To do so, type in the location of the program, and click **Next**.

7. You can change the icon used to represent the terminal services connection by clicking the **Change Icon** button and browsing for a new icon file. You can also select a program group into which the Terminal Services client programs are placed.

8. When you have made your selections, click **Next** to finish the configuration and end the Wizard.

Now you can use the new connection to establish a session with your terminal server.

Establishing and Ending a Terminal Connection

To connect to the terminal server:

1. From the **Start** menu, choose **Programs**, **Terminal Services Client**, and click the name you gave to the connection when it was created (alternativeely, you can open the **Client Connection Manager** and double-click on the connection name. You can also drag the connection icon to your desktop so it will be easily accessible).

2. The terminal window opens. Its size is dependent on the screen resolution you selected during creation of the connection. If you did not input username and password information to be entered automatically, you will see a Windows logon box as shown in Figure 23.7.

FIGURE 23.7
Enter your username and password in the terminal logon box.

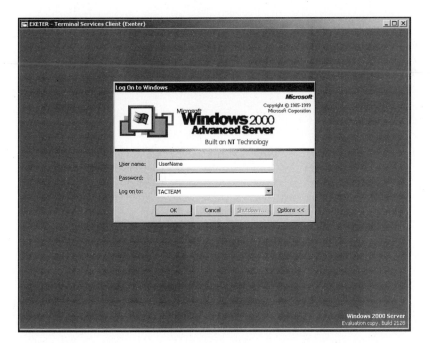

3. After a valid logon takes place, the server desktop appears. Figure 23.8 shows the terminal window with the server desktop displayed on the client desktop.

FIGURE 23.8

The server desktop is displayed in the terminal window on the client machine's desktop.

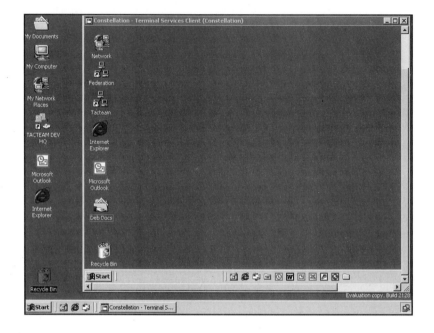

The terminal services user can run Word and other Office 2000 applications in the terminal window. Because Office is running as a multiuser application, other users can be connected to the terminal server and running Word at the same time, with no interference with one another. Each can customize the Office programs' settings with their preferences (unless the administrator has applied a policy prohibiting users from making such changes).

There are two ways to close a terminal session. You can either disconnect or log off.

- **Disconnecting** leaves the session running on the server. You can reconnect to the server and resume the session. To disconnect from a terminal session, simply close the terminal window on the client machine. A message box will be displayed, notifying you that any programs you did not close on the server will continue running. You can log back on later and reconnect to the same session.

  If you want to run a task on the server, such as a time-consuming database query, you can start the task and disconnect from the session, and then log back on later, and resume the task or check the results.

- **Logging off** ends the session that is running on the server. When you log off, applications running within the terminal session are closed and unsaved file changes might be lost. The next time you log on to the server, you will establish a new session, and cannot resume tasks you were engaged in previously.

The administrator can set the terminal server to disconnect client machines after a specified amount of idle time. If this happens, the client receives a message that the terminal server has disconnected the session. The administrator can also limit the amount of time a disconnected session is allowed to keep running on the server.

Using Office 2000 with Terminal Services

After the client has established a session with the terminal server, the user can run Office applications within the terminal windows as if they were open on the local desktop. Figure 23.9 shows Word 2000 running in a terminal window.

FIGURE 23.9
Word 2000 runs in the terminal window on the user's desktop.

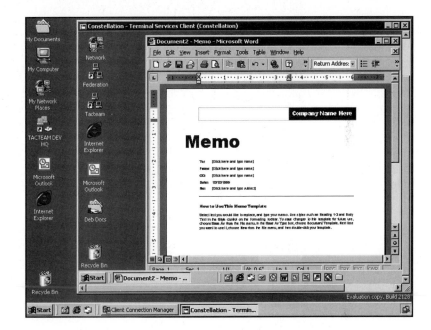

Part
IV
Ch
23

Windows 2000 Terminal Services also provides seamless Clipboard sharing. This means the contents of the Clipboard are available to applications locally on a user computer and within a Terminal Services session.

The shared Clipboard synchronizes its contents with the local Clipboard. You can copy text from a document that you have open on Word 2000 within a terminal session, and paste it into a document that is open on the desktop on your local computer. (You can't copy and paste files or folders, however—just data, such as text and graphics.)

The administrator can, if desired, disable the Clipboard-sharing feature on a per-connection basis. This is done using the Terminal Services Configuration tool on the terminal server.

Installing Office 2000 As a Multiuser Application

To install Office 2000 as a multiuser application on the terminal server and make it available to terminal services clients, you should first enable terminal services application server mode. If you install the application programs first and then change to application server mode, the programs might not work properly.

Now follow these steps:

1. Log on to the Terminal server as administrator and close all programs.

2. From the **Start** menu, select **Settings**, **Control Panel**, **Add/Remove Programs**.

3. In **Add/Remove Programs**, click **Add New Programs**.

N O T E Using the **Add/Remove Programs** applet, rather than running an application's setup pro-gram, ensures that applications are installed for use in a multisession environment. Another way to install programs to work in a multisession environment is to use the **change user** command. For more information on using the command-line utilities, see the Windows 2000 help files. **Add/Remove Programs** automatically runs the **change user** command, and is Microsoft's rec-ommended method.

4. Select the method to install the program (floppy, CD-ROM, or over the network) and follow the instructions in the Wizard. See Figure 23.10.

FIGURE 23.10
Use the Add/Remove Programs applet to install multisession applications on the terminal server.

5. The installation Wizard guides you through the rest of the installation process. For security purposes, the Office 2000 programs should be installed on a partition that is formatted with the NTFS file system.

If you are prompted to restart the computer to finish the installation, click **Finish** in **Add/Remove Programs** before accepting the prompt to restart the computer.

N O T E It might be necessary to log on again as the same user after the server has been rebooted in order to finish the application installation properly. Do not allow other users to log on before this step has been completed.

The Office 2000 applications are now available to terminal services clients.

> **CAUTION**
>
> Always ensure that there are no users logged on to the Terminal server before starting any program installation.

Improving Productivity in Office 2000

When a user is running the Microsoft Terminal Services client software, it behaves like any other application. The terminal window can be minimized while working on other applications, with the terminal session running in the background.

For the user, there are only slight differences between working on an Office application in a terminal window and using the same application on the local machine. Following are a few tips to help improve productivity and increase ease of use when Office 2000 is deployed in this way.

Saving a Document Created on the Terminal Server   Documents created by the user in Office applications can be saved on the terminal server or to the user's local hard drive. The default file location is set in the same way as when running the application on your local computer.

For example, in Word 2000, select **Tools**, **Options**, **File Locations** and then choose a path to the selected folder, as shown in Figure 23.11.

FIGURE 23.11
Use the Options sheet to set a default file save location.

To save the files on the user's local hard drive, browse to **My Network Places**, **Entire Network**, **Microsoft Network**, and choose the computer name and a share name on the local computer.

Using Terminal Services Client Shortcut Keys   Shortcut keys for Terminal Services client software can be used when working on the terminal desktop. Following is a list of available shortcut keys and their functions:

- **Alt+Page Up.** Switches between programs, left to right.
- **Alt+Page Down.** Switches between programs, right to left.
- **Alt+Home.** Displays the Start menu.
- **Ctrl+Alt+Break.** Switches between window and full screen.
- **Alt+Delete.** Displays the window's pop-up menu.
- **Ctrl+Alt+Minus (-).** Captures a screenshot of the active window within the client (same as Print Screen on the local computer).
- **Ctrl+Alt+Plus (+).** Captures entire client window (same as Alt+Print Screen on the local computer).

N O T E Screenshots captured to the terminal session Clipboard can be pasted into documents on the local computer. ■

Managing the Terminal Services Environment

Administrators have a great deal of flexibility in managing and controlling the terminal services environments of Office users.

With the Terminal Services Manager, you can view information about each user's session, what time the user logged on, the state of the session, and other properties. To view user information on a Terminal server, click the server or domain name in the **Terminal Services Manager** navigation pane, and then click the **Users** tab. Right-click the user's name, and then select **Status** to see the information, as shown in Figure 23.12.

FIGURE 23.12
The logon status box gives you information about an individual user's session.

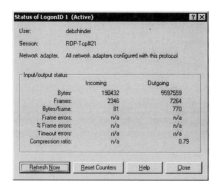

Implementing Security on the Terminal Server

The administrator controls how users and groups access a terminal server by setting permissions. The permissions you assign should reflect the level of access you want them to have. By default, there are three types of terminal services permissions: Guest, User, and Full Control.

The administrator can set permissions and policies to restrict particular users (or groups of users) from performing specified tasks. For instance, you can prevent a user from ending sessions.

Before users can log on to a terminal server, their Windows 2000 user accounts must be configured to enable them to do so.

N O T E You must have domain administrative privileges to configure domain user accounts.

Granting Users the Right to Log On to the Terminal Server   Follow these steps to allow a user to log on to Terminal Services running on a Windows 2000 server:

1. For a domain user account, open the Active Directory Users and Computers tool. From the **Start** menu, select **Programs**, **Administrative Tools**, **Active Directory Users and Computers**.
2. In the console tree, expand the domain node, and then click the Users folder.
3. For a local user account, right-click on **My Computer** and select **Manage**.
4. In the console tree, click **Users**.
5. Double-click the user for whom you want to change settings.
6. On the **Terminal Services Profile** tab, select the **Allow logon to terminal server** check box, and then click **Apply**. Figure 23.13 shows the Terminal Services Profile tab.

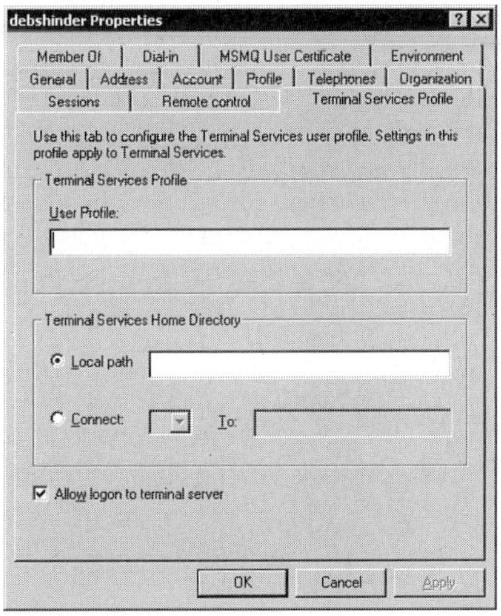

FIGURE 23.13

The logon to the terminal server must be enabled in the user account's properties sheet.

7. You can also specify a user profile here, which is applied only in the user's terminal sessions, and set a home directory locally or mapped to a network drive.

With both Windows NT Terminal Server Edition and Windows 2000 Server's built-in terminal services, policies can be set on terminal server sessions, which can be separate and different from the policies that govern the user's local workstation.

Limiting Access by Modifying the Desktop Environment   One effective security measure is to remove all icons and options from users' desktops for which they have no need. You can decide what they should have access to, and don't give them access to anything else.

You can use policies to disable access to the Run command and the command prompt, Control Panel, My Computer, Network Neighborhood, and/or Windows Explorer if your users do not need them.

N O T E   If users need terminal access to only one application (for instance, Word 2000), you can set the program to run when the user logs onto the system. When the user closes Word, the terminal session will be logged off. The user will not be able to access other applications or do anything else on the server. ■

Optimizing Performance

Office 2000 is designed to detect the Terminal Server environment and automatically optimize its behavior. For instance, when running on a thin client, it displays a splash screen that uses fewer system resources. There are additional settings you can configure for even better performance.

Remember that RAM and CPU requirements increase according to the number of terminal sessions that you expect to be running simultaneously.

In application server mode, Terminal Services is available for multisession use. Disabling unnecessary features that require the most resources can help to conserve server resources.

Disabling Active Desktop   Disabling Active Desktop in the server settings might improve performance if server resources are low. You must be an administrator to do this. You use the Terminal Services Configuration tool on the terminal server.

Restricting Access to Resource-Intensive Applications   Consider limiting access to such applications as Internet Explorer. Browsing the Web from the terminal server uses a great deal of server resources.

Customizing Default User Settings   On each individual Office 2000 application (Access, Excel, PowerPoint, and Word), perform the following:

Select **Tools**, **Customize**, **Options**. Select **None** for the Menu Animation option, as shown in Figure 23.14.

You might also want to ensure that **Provide feedback with sound** is disabled. Application features that are always on and running in the background by default (for instance, the automatic spelling and grammar checking in Microsoft Word) require more system resources, and you might want to disable them for optimal performance.

FIGURE 23.14
Disabling menu animation on Office applications helps to conserve resources and optimize performance.

Notifying Users of Terminal Server Shutdown

Microsoft recommends that when you shut down a Terminal server, you should use the **tsshutdn** command instead of the **Shut Down** option on the **Start** menu. This shuts down the server in a controlled manner.

The **Shut Down** option on the **Start** menu does not notify users before the ending users' sessions. Ending a user's session without warning can result in loss of data at the client.

The **tsshutdn** command is a utility that provides an administrator a way to remotely shut down or reboot a Terminal server from the command line.

The syntax for the command is

```
tsshutdn [wait_time] [/server:servername] [/reboot] [/powerdown]
[/delay:logoffdelay] [/v]
```

See Table 23.1 for an explanation of each parameter.

Table 23.1   Parameters for the tsshutdn Command

wait_time	After notifying users, specifies an amount of time (in seconds) to wait before logging off all users from their sessions. The default is 60 seconds.
/server:servername	Specifies the Terminal server to shut down. If unspecified, the current Terminal server is shut down.
/reboot	Reboots the Terminal server after user sessions are ended.
/powerdown	Turns off the Terminal server if the computer supports software control of AC power.
/delay:logoffdelay	After logging off users from their sessions, specifies the amount of time to wait before ending all processes and shutting down the Terminal server. The default is 30 seconds.
/v	Displays information about the actions being performed.

N O T E   Only administrators can use the **tsshutdn** command to shut down the terminal server. ■

When you use **tsshutdn** to shut down the terminal server, all users who are connected to terminal sessions will be notified that they are going to be shut down. If sessions have applications with open files, the system will prompt the user to save the files. The **tsshutdn** command does not cause the server to reboot unless you use the /reboot switch.

Configuring Advanced Administrative Options

The administrator can configure advanced settings, such as required encryption level, as well as disable user wallpaper and override other user-defined settings. To do so, in the Terminal Services Configuration tool on the server, double-click the connection you want to configure (RDP connection or, if you're using Citrix Metaframe, ICA connection). The properties sheet shown in Figure 23.15 will appear.

FIGURE 23.15
Administrators can configure advanced options for each connection using the connection Properties sheet.

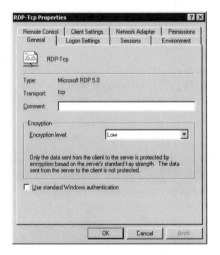

RDP and ICA are protocols used by the client and server to communicate with each other.

Troubleshooting Your Terminal Services

There are a number of resources available if you encounter problems with terminal server. One place to start is the Microsoft Web site at `www.microsoft.com`. You will find information there on both Windows 2000 terminal services and Windows NT 4.0 Terminal Server Edition.

Microsoft also provides public newsgroups for posting of questions and answers about terminal server issues. Check the `msnews.microsoft.com` news server, as newsgroups are added and renamed on a regular basis.

If you are using the Citrix products in conjunction with Microsoft terminal services, check `www.citrix.com` for additional information.

Finally, *Windows NT Magazine's* online edition at **www.winntmag.com** sponsors a Terminal Server community.

Resetting a Session

If a session malfunctions, the administrator can reset it, using the Terminal Services Manager on the terminal server, as shown in Figure 23.16.

FIGURE 23.16
Use the Terminal Services Manager to reset a malfunctioning terminal session.

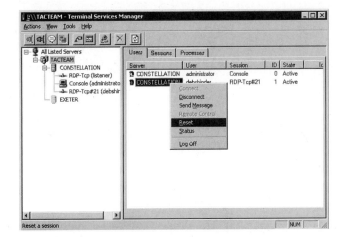

Administrators can also reset sessions from the command line, using the following syntax:

```
reset session {sessionname | sessionid} /server:servername]
```

> **CAUTION**
>
> Resetting a user's session without warning can result in loss of data at the session. Before resetting, you can use the Send Message selection in the right-click context menu to notify the user of your intentions.

CHAPTER 24

Distributing Office with Novell Z.E.N.works

by Chris Negus

In the old days, you could copy an application's executable file to a network file server (such as NetWare), and all your users could run it from the network without a hitch. Today, complex applications, such as Office 2000, require completely new tools to efficiently distribute software to its employees.

If your company supports Novell Directory Services (NDS), Novell NetWare, or IntraNetWare servers, the Novell Z.E.N.works product is an excellent way to distribute and manage Office 2000 (or any other software) across the enterprise.

The *Novell Application Launcher* (NAL) feature of Z.E.N.works provides tools for creating an exact image of an application on a workstation, storing that application in an NDS tree on a NetWare server as an *application object*, and distributing it on demand to any user with proper rights to that application.

By distributing a working image of an application, your users get not only the software, but also any preference changes or different configurations of the package you create. To the user, the NAL-deployed application appears as a local application in the NAL window or Windows Explorer. NAL also lets you automatically add icons for the application to the user's desktop, Start menu, or system tray.

 NOTE NAL was once a separate add-on to NetWare 4.11. For a complete description of what is in Z.E.N.works NAL, see "Understanding How Z.E.N.works NAL Works," later in this chapter. ∎

To take advantage of NAL, your organization must have its workstations connected to a NetWare server (4.11 or later) that supports NDS. From that server, you can distribute Office or other applications to Windows 95, Windows 98, Windows NT, and Windows 3.x client machines. The procedures in this chapter use Z.E.N.works version 1.1.

N O T E The version of Microsoft Office that you distribute must run on the target workstation. For example, because Office 2000 (a 32-bit application) doesn't run on Windows 3.x systems, it makes no sense to distribute it to your 3.x workstations. However, using the system requirements feature, the NAL can easily filter applications to avoid these types of problems. ■

This chapter describes

- Understanding how the Z.E.N.works NAL works
- Installing Office using NAL
- Distributing Office to the workstations

You'll also learn about other features of Novell's Z.E.N.works that support the process of managing software and hardware across your organization.

Understanding How Z.E.N.works NAL Works

Using the NAL feature of Z.E.N.works, you can distribute and manage applications so that they are available to every workstation in your enterprise. Applications can be packaged and tuned to the way you want them to look and act on every user's workstation. When you change or update a software package, those changes are automatically picked up by the user's workstation.

There are four basic components to the NAL. Two components are used by the administrator, and two are specific to the user workstations. Administrator components include snAppShot (for creating the application template) and a NAL snap-in component that works with NWAdmn32 (for creating the application object and setting its properties on the NetWare server). User components include the NAL window (for viewing and running distributed applications) and NAL Explorer (for having the NAL applications appear in the Windows Explorer).

TIP On top of the NAL components, you need a good understanding of NetWare (4.11 or later), NDS, and how Z.E.N.works fits together with them.

Using NAL Administrator Components

As administrator, you can use snAppShot to create an application template on a clean workstation. Then, you run NWAdmn32 to create the application object on the NetWare server. The next two sections describe what the two components do.

Using snAppShot The snAppShot program creates the application template that you use to create the application object. You run snAppShot from a clean computer and install the software you want to distribute. By a clean computer, we mean a computer that has just had the Windows operating system and a NetWare client installed (and nothing else). If this is not available, the computer should at least have never had Office 2000 installed.

Then, snAppShot gathers any file, Registry entry, or other component that has changed on your computer since before the installation and creates the application template from the differences. When running snAppShot, you can also automatically install the application template directly to the NetWare server from which it is distributed to users.

Using NetWare Administrator NAL Snap-In   The NAL NWAdmn32 snap-in adds features to the basic NetWare Administrator so that you can use the NetWare Administrator to manage application objects. Using NWAdmn32, you create the application object from the template of the application. Then, you can identify lots of properties for the application object, including the application's executable, the types of systems it runs on, how it is distributed, and other information.

Using NAL User Components

To the user whose workstation is properly configured to use NAL, applications that are ready to be distributed from the NetWare server simply look like application icons that are ready to run. Those icons can appear in either the NAL window or the Windows Explorer. As administrator, you can also add those icons to the desktop, Start menu, or system tray for each user. (See the section on working from client workstations later in this chapter for information on how to configure your workstation to use NAL.)

Using the NAL Window   The NAL window shows you the applications that are available to the user from the NDS tree on the NetWare server. The users open application folders from the NDS tree, and then select icons for the applications they want to run. If an application has not been installed yet to the user's workstation, it is installed and then launched on the workstation. If it has already been installed, it is simply launched.

Using Windows Explorer   Because many people use the Windows Explorer to navigate on their computers, NAL adds features that let users launch NAL applications from that window. An entry called *Application Explorer* appears in the Windows Explorer.

> **N O T E**   The Application Launcher does not yet integrate with Microsoft Internet Explorer. You must use Windows Explorer to launch NAL applications in Windows 98. ■

The NDS tree containing the applications appears under the Application Explorer folder. Users can select NAL applications as they would from the NAL Window.

Installing Office Using the Z.E.N.works NAL

Z.E.N.works stands for Zero Effort Networks. The Zero Effort part, however, applies to the end user and not the administrator. As an administrator, you have to do a bit more setup to get Office ready to install using NAL. Time and effort savings, however, quickly make up for your initial groundwork as the application is deployed throughout your enterprise.

As noted earlier, NAL relies on a NetWare Server and NDS infrastructure already being in place. Those prerequisites are detailed in the sections that follow. After everything is in place, however, deploying and installing Microsoft Office using NAL can be broken down into the following major steps:

Part
IV

Ch
24

■ Create the Microsoft Office application template. Run the snAppShot program from a clean workstation (the same kind that will eventually use the application). The snAppShot program discovers all the components on your workstation's hard disk, asks you to install the application (Microsoft Office), and then rechecks all components.

The differences between the two discoveries becomes the application template (consisting of the files, Registry entries, and other information that make up an installed Office application suite). You then copy the application template to a NetWare server (either as part of the snAppShot process or manually at a later time).

■ Create the Office application objects. Run the NWAdmn32 program from the NetWare server. This lets you create application objects from the application template you created for Office and set properties for those objects.

■ Distribute Office to the workstations. Set up each workstation to permit access to the application objects you created for Office. The user simply opens the icons representing the application objects. This installs the application and launches the program. The next time the user opens the icon, the installed copy runs on the local hard disk. This can be repeated for hundreds or thousands of workstations.

Figure 24.1 illustrates how NAL works to deploy Office to the workstations in your enterprise.

FIGURE 24.1
Use NAL to deploy Office to user workstations.

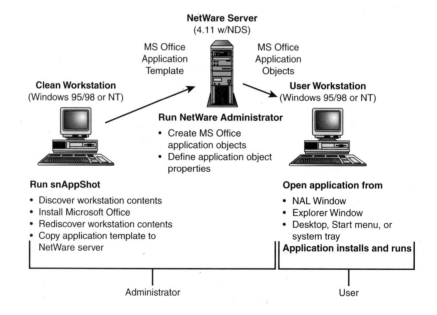

Deploying Microsoft Office with the Z.E.N.works NAL

> **CAUTION**
>
> You are about to create and distribute a replica of an installed application. This method of software distribution does not limit the number of workstations on which you can install the application. It is up to you to be sure that your company has obtained the proper number of licenses to use the application.

Prerequisites for Installing Office 2000 with NAL

The more copies of an application you need to install in your organization, the more efficient it is to use NAL. If you have only one or two workstations needing Microsoft Office, you probably won't want to go into the overhead associated with NAL. With a lot of users, however, you will gain tremendous time savings from using NAL to distribute software.

Before you can begin distributing applications with NAL, you need to have a NetWare infrastructure in place. That infrastructure includes having workstations connected to a NetWare network that has the right type of server and NDS configured. You also need to install the NAL. The next four sections describe what you need.

Configuring NetWare Server   Because NAL needs a recent version of NDS, your network must have access to a NetWare 4.11 (or more recent) server. An NDS tree must be configured so that you can associate the application objects with particular User, Group, Organization, or Organizational Units in the NDS tree.

> **N O T E**   For a complete description of NetWare servers, NDS, and other issues relating to setting up a NetWare network, refer to one of the many books available that describe NetWare. In particular, we recommend Que's *Special Edition Using NetWare 4.1.* ▓

The NetWare 4.11 server must have at least 70MB of available memory and 205MB of free disk space available for Z.E.N.works. On that server, as the administrator of NAL, you must have Administrator rights to the NetWare server and to the NDS container in which NAL is installed. You also need the rights to change the schema on the NDS tree. (To change or extend the schema on NDS, you must have Administrator rights to the root of the tree. After the schema has been changed, administrators with rights to lower contexts of the tree can make the changes they need.)

The workstations that are going to install applications using NAL must have access to the NetWare server. This includes both a physical network connection to the server, as well as having the correct rights configured for the workstations' users.

Working from Client Workstations   Client workstations are where applications are ultimately run. Workstations supported by NAL include those that use the following operating systems: Windows 95, Windows 98, Windows NT, and Windows 3.x. When you deploy an application to different types of workstations, each type will typically require that you create a different application object.

NOTE Although there is not yet a Windows 98 client with the Z.E.N.works Starter Pack, you can install the Windows 95 client on a Windows 98 machine and it should work fine. You can order the Z.E.N.works Starter Pack from Novell's Web site at `http://www.novell.com/products/clientscd`. ■

When you configure the properties for an application object, you identify the object as a Windows 95, NT, or 3.x compatible application when it is deployed. (Windows 95 application objects appear to Windows 98 computers.) A user at a NAL-enabled workstation won't even see an application that isn't noted as compatible with its operating system. (For example, an Office 2000 application object does not appear to a Windows 3.x or Windows NT pre-3.51 version.)

NOTE With a few minor modifications, the same Office application object can be deployed to both Windows 95 and Windows NT workstations. A procedure for doing this is available from the Z.E.N.works site (`www.zenworks.com`). Click **The Vault**, and then look for tips under the Office heading. ■

To the end user at the workstation, the application's icon appears in the locations defined by the administrator (such as the NAL window, Windows Explorer, Start menu, desktop, or system tray). The first time the user opens the icon, the software is automatically installed to the user's workstation and the application is launched. After that, opening the icon simply launches the application locally. Software is installed again only if the administrator changes the application object.

Maintaining Clean Administrative Workstations An Office application object that is distributed by NAL consists of the complete set of files, Registry entries, and other components that result from installing Office. That application object is created by

1. Discovering all components on the entire drive (or several drives) of a workstation.
2. Installing Office.
3. Rediscovering the contents of the drive.
4. Creating an application template from the differences between the first and second discoveries.

The template and the new files, Registry entries, and so on that make up the application are copied to a NetWare server. Using the NWAdmn32 command, you can then turn the template into an application object and set a variety of properties for it.

Novell highly recommends starting this process with a clean workstation: one with little more than the operating system installed and the network properly configured. The cleaner the computer is, the faster the drive can be scanned.

The workstation for creating the application object needs to match the workstation that uses the application. So, you might need clean Windows 95, Windows 98, Windows NT, and Windows 3.x workstations if you support all these configurations.

TIP To start with a clean computer each time you create an application object, you can use disk-image software to copy and restore a working image of your disk. Two products you might want to look into are PowerQuest Drive Image (**www.powerquest.com**) and Ghost (**www.ghost.com**).

Using Z.E.N.works Software Although NAL began as a free add-on product for NetWare 4, you can now purchase the Z.E.N.works Starter Pack directly from the following Web site: `http://www.novell.com/products/clientscd`

The Z.E.N.works Starter Pack contains two components, NAL and Novell Workstation Manager:

- **NAL.** NAL is used to deploy and manage applications across the enterprise. Information about how NAL works and how to use it to install Office is described in the rest of this chapter.
- **Novell Workstation Manager.** This component lets you gather information about the workstations in your enterprise and manage the users' desktops. With Workstation Manager features, you can manage user and system policies, store those policies in NDS, and schedule system actions.

The complete Z.E.N.works product contains these additional major features:

- **Remote Control.** This component lets you remotely manage your company's workstations based on information stored in NDS.
- **Help Requester.** This application provides utilities that help end users solve their workstation problems and allow them to troubleshoot their own problems on the network. It also helps create a database of contacts so that users can more easily determine whom to contact for their particular problem.
- **Hardware Inventory.** This utility enables you to associate actions with workstation objects that you gather in the NDS. For example, you can remotely determine which workstations need more memory, require changes to printer settings, or have an outdated BIOS. Often, you are able to correct the problem remotely.
- **Check 2000.** This is a five-user version of a product from Greenwich Mean Time that assesses and repairs Year 2000-related problems. It scans the software, hardware, and data on workstations to evaluate potential Y2K problems.
- **Software Metering.** This feature lets you track how many software licenses were distributed using the NAL.

Z.E.N.works is rich in administrative features and extremely flexible. For more information about Z.E.N.works, see the Z.E.N.works Cool Solutions page:

`www.novell.com/coolsolutions/zenworks`

Select the article titled "The Basics" for a description of what you need to know to use Z.E.N.works.

Part

IV

Ch

24

Before you can use NAL, you must install the following components from the Z.E.N.works Starter Pack:

- **Server software.** This includes the tools that are installed on the NetWare server. The install screen button is labeled Z.E.N.works (full version) components.

- **Client software.** This includes the tools that are installed on the client workstations that ultimately use the application object. There are different installation paths for Windows 95/98, Windows NT, and Windows 3.x clients.

To install Z.E.N.works server software, you must be logged in to the NDS tree as Admin from a Windows 95, Windows 98, or Windows NT workstation. After the software is installed, you can add a nwadmn32.exe icon to each administrative workstation from sys:public\win32 on the NetWare server.

More detailed instructions for setting up Z.E.N.works can be found in the help file that comes with Z.E.N.works. Look for the dmpolicy.hlp in the products\zenworks\public\win*\nls\english directory. Also, for information about how to design an NDS tree that can be used with Z.E.N.works, look for the zendsgn.htm document that comes with the Z.E.N.works Starter Pack.

Creating the Microsoft Office Application Template

If the prerequisites have been fulfilled (the NetWare server is accessible and Z.E.N.works has been installed), you are ready to create the application template for Microsoft Office. Start from the clean computer (running either Windows 95, Windows 98, or Windows NT), have your Microsoft Office CD-ROM ready to install.

N O T E   Remember that the workstation you use here must be the same as the type of workstation that runs the application later. For example, you cannot create an application template to run on Windows 3.1 from a Windows 95 workstation.

When you follow the procedure to create your Microsoft Office application template, the following components are installed on a NetWare server directory:

- All the files that make up an installed Microsoft Office application. (These files appear as numbered files with a .fil extension.)

- A filedef.txt file that identifies where all the files should be placed on the target system. (This is a text file that you can read if you are curious.)

- An Application Template file (binary version), given the name of the application and an .aot extension.

- An Application Template file (text version), given the name of the application and an .axt extension.

The AOT and AXT files contain identical information. Both contain the data needed to re-create the application on the user's workstation, including Registry entries, INI identifiers, and file changes. The differences are that you can read the AXT file with a text editor, the AOT is about half the size, and the AOT runs faster when you build the application object.

Later, when you use NWAdmn32 to create the application object from the application template, you are asked whether to use the AXT or AOT file. Use the AXT file only if you need to make some manual changes to the file. (Manual editing is not recommended, however, because it can cause errors.)

Here is the procedure to create an Office application template:

1. Start **snAppShot** (from products\zenworks\public\snapshot\snapshot.exe on the NetWare server).

   The snAppShot dialog box appears, as shown in Figure 24.2.

FIGURE 24.2

Create an application template from snAppShot.

2. Choose either **Standard**, **Custom**, or **Express** to discover the contents of your workstation. (This procedure assumes the Standard option.)

   - Standard uses default settings to discover the contents of the machine.
   - Custom lets you specifically choose the files and folders, INI files, system configuration files, Windows shortcuts, and Registry hives to include or exclude during discovery.
   - Express relies on a snAppShot Preferences file (created during a previous discovery) to use for comparison.

   A dialog box appears, asking you to name the application object and the title on the application's icon.

3. Type a name of the application object and a name to use on the application icon and click **Next**. (*MS Office 2000* was used for both in this example. Later, application names are changed to match each executable: Word, Excel, and so on.)

   A dialog box asks where to install the application files and NAL application template files that are output by snAppShot.

4. Browse for or enter the name of a folder to hold the files that make up the application object, and click **Next**. (I strongly recommend putting the files on the NetWare server where the application object is eventually installed. Otherwise, you have to copy them there later manually.)

   To identify the location for the application template files as the *sys\Snapshot\MS Office 2000* directory on a server named *madlad*, I typed **\\madlad\sys\Snapshot\MS Office 2000**.

   A dialog box asks you to name and provide a location for the application template file.

5. Type or browse for the location and name for the application and click **Next**. (You should use the same location entered in the previous step. So, in this example, I entered **\\madlad\sys\Snapshot\MS Office 2000\MS Office 2000.AOT**.)

   A dialog box asks which drives you want to scan.

6. Enter the drive you want to scan and click **Next**. (Typically, you simply enter **C:**. However, you need to enter any drive that the application is installed on.)

   A dialog box appears, showing you a summary of the settings you just entered.

7. Scroll through the settings, and then click **Next**. (You can also click **Save Preferences** to save the settings you just entered to use on another scan.)

   At this point, snAppShot scans your machine and drive to determine the current state of the components on your computer.

   When the scan is done, snAppShot asks you to install the application.

CAUTION

Don't change any files or settings on your computer from this point on except for those files that relate to the installation and configuration of the application (in this case, Microsoft Office). Files or settings you add or change before the entire snAppShot completes ends up as part of the application object that is distributed.

---

8. Close the snAppShot application and install Microsoft Office as you would on the local computer. (When you resume snAppShot later, it restarts automatically at this point.)

9. After Microsoft Office is installed, change any settings you like to suit your preferences. (For example, you might want to remove icons or change preferences for any of the Office applications.)

 As you are installing Microsoft Office, snAppShot is in a state where all information it needs is saved on the local hard disk. So, it is no problem if during this process you want to reboot the computer (as Office sometimes requests). When Windows is rebooted, snAppShot auto-starts and asks you whether you want to continue or restart snAppShot.

10. When Microsoft Office is configured exactly as you like it, you can reboot the computer. When the computer restarts, you should see a snAppShot dialog box (such as the one shown in Figure 24.3) asking whether you want to continue.

    Click **Yes** to resume the snAppShot process.

FIGURE 24.3
Resume snAppShot
after installing Office.

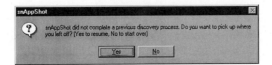

A dialog box appears, asking for the location of the application's install directory.

11. Type the location of the Office install directory. (For example, you might have used C:\Program Files.)

    Your computer is rescanned to gather the results from the installation of Office, and then it generates the application template. When the template is done, the snAppShot Completion Summary dialog box appears.

NOTE The rescan after installing Office takes a while (possibly several hours). Several hundred files need to be gathered and more than 38,000 changed Registry entries must be stored. Be patient. ■

12. Scroll through the Completion Summary dialog box to review where files are located and what the next steps are. (You should click the **Print** button to print out this information.)

13. Click **Finish** to complete the snAppShot process.

At this point, you should have all the application files (FIL) and template files (AOT and AXT) you need to create the application stored in a directory on the server. If for some reason you output these files to the local hard disk, you should go ahead now and copy them to a directory on the NetWare server from which the application object is created.

If you want to create an application object that you can use in either a Windows 95 or Windows NT workstation, some special modifications have to be made.

Now you are ready to create application objects for each of the applications in the Microsoft Office suite (Word, Excel, and so on) on the server.

Creating the Office Application Objects

Using the NetWare Administrator (NWAdmn32 command), with enhancements that are added when you install Z.E.N.works, you can make application objects out of the files and template you created for Microsoft Office using snAppShot. Because Microsoft Office consists of several applications, you should create one application object for at least each of the following applications:

■ Microsoft Word 2000

■ Microsoft Excel 2000

Part
IV
Ch
24

- Microsoft PowerPoint 2000
- Microsoft Outlook 2000
- Microsoft Access 2000
- Microsoft FrontPage 2000

To store these application objects, you can create *application containers* on the NetWare server. Rights to access these containers must be assigned. (Later, for each user who is granted access to an application through NAL, the application can appear in the user's NAL window, Explorer window, Start menu, desktop, or system tray, as you define.)

Each application object also has its own set of properties. The properties define such things as what workstation types it can run on, when the application is available, and the rights associated with the application (in other words, who can use it). Although most of the properties are the same for the Office application objects you create (for Word, Excel, and so on), you at least need to set a different icon name, icon, and executable file for each application object.

When all the Office application objects are complete, all these application objects need to be grouped together under one Global Unique Identifier (GUID). In this way, after a user has installed any Office application, running any of the other applications will simply cause it to run, without installing the entire Microsoft Office again from the server.

Using this GUID, NAL can track installation of the application. Even though each application runs a different program, the GUID is the same because all the same software is installed when any one of the applications is used.

NOTE The following procedure assumes you have already created an application template (using snAppShot) for Office and that the files associated with that template are available on your NetWare server. ▮

Follow these steps to create the Microsoft Office application objects:

1. Run NWAdmn32.

   The NetWare Administrator window appears.

2. Select an NDS container to be associated with the Office application objects.

NOTE If you want to create a new container to hold the Microsoft Office application objects, you may do so. To do this, right-click the object (such as an Organization Unit or Country) that you want to hold the new container and give a name to the container (such as MS Office 2000). ▮

3. Create an application object for the first Microsoft Office application, as follows:
   - Click the container you want to contain the application object.
   - Click **Object**, then **Create**, and then **Application**.

   A Create Application Object dialog box appears, as shown in Figure 24.4.

FIGURE 24.4
Create a Microsoft
Office application tem-
plate from NetWare
Administrator.

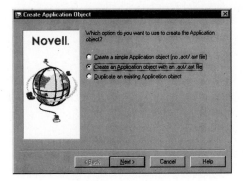

Part
IV
Ch
24

4. Select **Create an Application object with an .aot/.axt file** (as shown in the figure) and click **Next**.

A dialog box asks you for the path to the AOT or AXT file. (Figure 24.5 shows this dialog box with the location of the AOT file on the NetWare server used in an earlier procedure.)

FIGURE 24.5
Identify the location of
the application tem-
plate files you created.

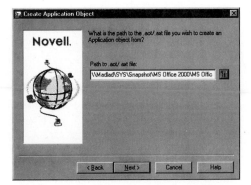

5. Type the full path to the AOT file (or AXT file) that is on the NetWare server and click **Next**. (Remember to precede the server name with two backslashes.)

A dialog box asks you to add customize information to the new application object.

6. Add the following customize information, and then click **Next**:

- **Object Name.** This name identifies the object in the folder. You should change this name to match the first application object you create, such as *MS Word 2000*.

- **SOURCE_PATH.** Type the location of the FIL files that were created with the application template. (This is probably the same folder that contains the AOT file.)

- **TARGET_PATH.** Enter the directory on the client workstation where the programs will appear. (You can probably take the default of %*WinSysDisk%\Program Files.)

An example of this window is shown in Figure 24.6.

FIGURE 24.6

Name the application object, source, and target paths.

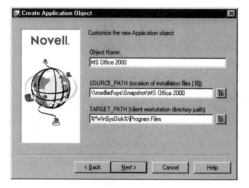

After selecting **Next**, a review of the application object information you created appears.

7. After you have reviewed the information, click **Create Another Application Object After This One**, and then select **Finish**.

   The new application object is created, and then a dialog box appears asking you how to create the next application object.

8. Click **Duplicate an Existing Application Object**, and then click **Next**.

   A dialog box asks you the name of the application you want to duplicate.

9. Type (or browse for) the name of the application object you just created. (For example, you might have called it MS Word 2000.)

   A dialog box appears, asking you to customize the new application object.

10. Return to step 6, but this time type the object name for the next application (For example, you might want to call this new application MS Excel 2000.)

CAUTION

Be sure you type a new object name. Problems can occur if you have two applications in the same folder with the same name. The source path and target path are probably the same as they were for the previous application object.

---

11. Repeat the remaining steps until you are finished with all the application objects (one for each of the Microsoft Office applications). For the last application object, just click **Finish** without creating another application object.

Adding Properties to Microsoft Office Application Objects

After you have created an application object for each program in the Microsoft Office suite, you need to change the properties of each of those objects. The application object properties define who has access to the object, what executable is run, what types of workstations can run the object, and a variety of other features.

The following procedure assumes you have already created an application object (using the NetWare Administrator) for each application in the Microsoft Office suite and you are now ready to set each object's properties.

Run NWAdmn32 to display the NetWare Administrator window, and then follow these steps to modify the properties pages of your application objects:

1. Find the first Microsoft Office application objects you created (for example, MS Word 2000), right-click the first one, and then select **Details**. The first application properties page appears (the Identification properties page), as shown in Figure 24.7.

FIGURE 24.7
Set the icon title, executable, and icon values on the Identification properties page.

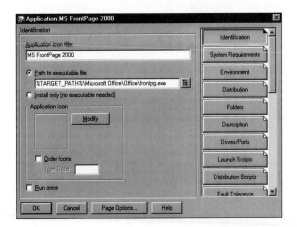

Part

IV

Ch

24

2. On the Identification properties page, you must set unique values for **Application icon title**, **Path to executable file**, and **Application Icon**. Table 24.1 shows examples of what you can use for applications in the Microsoft Office 2000 suite.

Table 24.1   Microsoft Office 2000 Applications

Application	Application Icon Title	Path to Executable File
Access	MS Access 2000	%TARGET_PATH%\Microsoft Office\Office\msaccess.exe
FrontPage	MS FrontPage 2000	%TARGET_PATH%\Microsoft Office\Office\frontpg.exe
Excel	MS Excel 2000	%TARGET_PATH%\Microsoft Office\Office\excel.exe
Outlook	MS Outlook 2000	%TARGET_PATH%\Microsoft Office\Office\outlook.exe
PowerPoint	MS PowerPoint 2000	%TARGET_PATH%\Microsoft Office\Office\powerpnt.exe
Word	MS Word 2000	%TARGET_PATH%\Microsoft Office\Office\winword.exe

3. Click the **System Requirements** button to set the properties associated with the types of workstations that can use the application object. Here is what you can change:

- **Operating System.** Select Windows 3.x, Windows 95, or Windows NT. The application object will appear only on workstations that are running the selected operating systems. You can also indicate that a particular major and minor version of the system be able to use the application.

> **CAUTION**
>
> An application object created on a Windows 3.x workstation can be used only on other Windows 3.x systems. Windows 95 and Windows NT applications can be shared between those two systems, but only if some modifications are made to the application template, as noted earlier in this chapter.

- **Display applications on machines that have at least X space.** You can require that an application be made available only to workstations that have at least a certain amount of RAM and free disk space.

4. Click the **Environment** button to set properties that change how the application is run.

   Typically, changes to these properties are not needed. You might, however, want to add command-line parameters to the executable, change the application to run as minimized or maximized (instead of normal), or define a file to enable error logging. (Clean Up Network Resources is particularly important if an application remaps drives or captures ports that must be released when all applications exit that use the resource.)

5. Click the **Distribution** button to set properties relating to how the application is distributed. You should mark Show Distribution Progress and Prompt Before Distribution, and Prompt User for Reboot Always. These settings keep the application from taking over the user's computer without asking first. For example, if a user casually opens an application icon and Prompt Before Distribution is not selected, the user gets no chance to prevent the application being downloaded to his or her workstation. Even a few minutes of interruption can be a bother.

6. Click the **Folders** button to set folder properties for the application object. This dialog box identifies the folder containing the application object and lets you add the application object to additional folders.

7. Click the **Description** button to add or change a description of the application object. This lets the administrator keep track of the services provided by the application object. This contains information that the user is prompted for just before the application is installed. It can include information about what will get installed, how long it will take, and whether or not the user's computer needs to be restarted.

8. Click the **Drives/Ports** button to add or modify drives that need to be mapped or ports that need to be captured for the application object. (If you map drives or capture ports, be sure that Clean Up Network Resources is selected on the Environment properties page so the resources are released when the application exits.)

9. Click the **Launch Scripts** button to add any scripts that should be run before launching or after terminating the application.

10. Click the **Fault Tolerance** button to add information to help ensure the application is always accessible, even when the server is not available. Essentially, these options offer alternatives when a requested application object is not available (such as when the server is down).

    Add load-balancing objects to ensure that if the application object is not available, another application object can be delivered, chosen randomly from the objects you enter. Add fault tolerance objects if you would like an application object that is not available to be replaced by objects in a specific order.

11. Click the **Contacts** button to add information on whom end users can contact if they have problems with this application object.

12. Click the **Associations** button to indicate which objects (such as an organizational unit, organization, country, user, or group) can use this application object. Click **Add**, and then browse for the object to be associated with the application object. (Although all applications are displayed to the user by default in either the NAL window or Explorer window, customizing an association enables you to add icons later to the user's Start menu, Desktop, or system tray.)

13. Click the **Administrator Notes** button to add notes about the application object that are available only to the administrator of the object. This is a way to track changes to the application object or add reminders of tasks you need to do with the object.

14. Click the **Macros** button to add macros that can help simplify items used in the creation of the application object, such as long pathnames. For example, this page will always include a definition of the SOURCE_PATH and TARGET_PATH macros to define where the application's source files and output files are placed, respectively. You can easily change all references to a macro value at once by changing it on the Macros properties page. To reference a macro, you need to surround it with percent signs (for example, %SOURCE_PATH%).

N O T E Macros are powerful features that let you customize many aspects of an application object. The help file that comes with the NAL contains helpful details for customizing applications with macros. ■

15. Click the **Registry Settings** button to view all the Registry settings that are modified by the application object. You can also make changes to or create additional Registry changes for the application object by using this page. Figure 24.8 shows an example of an application object's Registry settings.

FIGURE 24.8

Display and change Windows Registry settings for an application object.

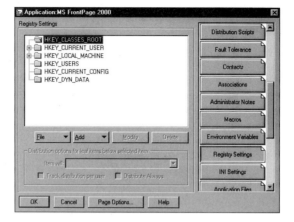

16. Click the **INI Settings** button to display and modify any INI file changes associated with the application object.

17. Click the **Application Files** button to display, add, modify, or delete files that make up the application object.

18. Click the **Text Files** button to add, modify, or delete additional text files to go with the application object. For example, you could import additional text files created with snAppShot into this page so that the new files can be distributed with the application object.

19. Click the **Schedule** button to schedule the application to be available only at particular times. Typically, you would want the application to be available to your users all the time. However, you can change the schedule to have the application available only during a range of days (such as Monday through Friday) or only at certain times (for example, making games available to run only after work hours).

20. Click the **Icons/Shortcuts** button to view, add, modify, or delete the icons and shortcuts that are associated with the application object.

21. Click the **File Rights** button to add rights to volume objects and paths that are associated with the application object. You can assign supervisor, read, write, create, erase, modify, file scan, and access control rights to the volume.

22. Click the **Termination** button if you want to define behavior that occurs when the administrator needs to terminate the application on the users' workstations. You can have messages of your choosing sent at set intervals, and then terminate the application after the time expires.

23. Click the **Application Site List** button to associate the application with different locations. The advantage of using this feature is that if a user travels to different offices in the company, the application object might be much more efficiently deployed from the location the user is currently visiting.

24. When you are satisfied with the properties changes you have made, click **OK**.

25. Repeat this procedure for each Microsoft Office application object that you have created. Then, proceed to the next section.

Synchronizing the Application Objects Under One GUID

To prevent the entire Microsoft Office suite from being installed each time an application is run, you need to sync together the application objects. To do this, you must have all the objects assigned to a single Global Unique Identifier (GUID).

After you sync the GUIDs, the first time a user executes any of the synched Office application objects, the whole Office distribution is installed. When a user later opens any of the other application objects, that application just runs without any additional installation.

Here's how you sync the GUIDs:

1. From the NetWare Administrator window, highlight all the application objects in the Microsoft Office distribution.
2. Click **Tools**, **Application Launcher Tools**, **Sync Distribution GUIDs**. The application objects are immediately synched together.

Assigning Where Icons Appear to Clients

The final steps in making Microsoft Office available to your users from NAL involves defining where the icons for the application objects will appear. By selecting the User, Group, Organization, or Organizational Unit object associated with the application objects, you can define where on the users' workstations the icons for each application will appear.

Here's how to assign launch options:

1. From the NetWare Administrator window, right-click the **User**, **Group**, **Organization**, or **Organizational Unit** container associated with the Microsoft Office application objects.
2. Select **Details**.
3. Click the **Applications** button.

   A dialog box listing the applications associated with the object is displayed.
4. Scroll to find the application objects you created for Microsoft Office.
5. Select any of the following to turn on icons on the workstations of members of this container.
   - Novell Application Launcher Window
   - Windows Start Menu
   - Windows Desktop
   - Windows System Tray
6. Click **OK**.

The icons are now available to appear in the selected location on the users' workstations.

Part

IV

Ch

24

Distributing Microsoft Office to the Workstations

After you have completed the administrative procedures for preparing the Microsoft Office application objects for deployment with NAL, users associated with the container can immediately use the applications from their workstations. For the user, it is easy.

As noted earlier, the users that are set up to use NAL will automatically see the application icons in one of several locations on their workstations (depending on how you defined it). From Windows Explorer, the NAL window, the Start menu, the Desktop, or the system tray, a user opens the NAL-delivered application, and it installs on the local workstation (if necessary) and then runs.

Launching Applications from Windows Explorer

In the standard Windows Explorer window (accessible by clicking Start, Programs, and Windows Explorer), an Application Explorer folder will appear. In that folder, the user will see the NDS tree that includes the application folders and application objects that are delivered by NAL.

A user simply double-clicks the icon for an application object to use the application. If the application is not yet installed on the user's computer, it will install at this point and then start up. If it is already installed, the application will run immediately.

> **CAUTION**
>
> The feature for adding NAL applications to Windows Explorer is not available in Windows 3.x operating systems. In those cases, users must run NAL applications from the NAL window.

To make the NAL features of Windows Explorer available to a user's workstation, you can add the following text to the user's login script:

```
if platform = "w95" then
        @\\server\sys\public\nalexpld.exe
    end
    if platform = "wnt" then
        if os_version = "v4.00" then
            @\\server\sys\public\nalexpld.exe
        end
end
```

where *server* is replaced by the name of the NetWare server that contains the nalexpld.exe command.

Launching Applications from the NAL Window

The Novell Application Launcher window is another way a user can view the applications that are made available from NAL.

Figure 24.9 shows the NAL window with the MS Office 2000 folder open and displaying the installed Microsoft Office application objects you have created.

FIGURE 24.9
Users can display
Novell-delivered appli-
cations from the NAL
window.

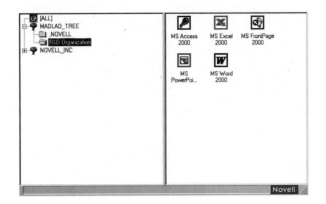

N O T E A change to NAL applications, such as adding an application icon, might not immediately
appear on a user's workstation. For a user to get the changes, have the user choose **View**,
Refresh in the NAL window. These changes are also picked up the next time the NAL window starts. ■

You can start the NAL window from sys:public\nal.exe on the server. However, the preferred
way is to run nal.exe from a user login script. You can do this by adding one of the following
lines to the user's login script:

```
#\\server\sys\public\nal.exe
```

or

```
@\\ server \sys\public\nal.exe
```

where *server* is replaced by the name of the NetWare server that contains the nal.exe command.

N O T E In the near future, ZENWorks 2.0 will be available, improving on many of the procedures
described in this chapter. Refer to the ZENWorks Web site at **www.zenworks.com** for
information on new features in the latest release. ■

CHAPTER 25

Using Office with Lotus Notes

by Steve Kern

What's a chapter on a Lotus product doing in a book on Microsoft Office? Aren't Lotus and Microsoft as diametrically opposed in the marketplace as they are on opposite sides of the country (Redmond, Washington versus Cambridge, Massachusetts)? As an administrator responsible for Microsoft Office applications, why should you care about Lotus Notes? To put it simply, with the sheer volume of Notes licenses in the marketplace, you are bound to encounter Notes at some point in your career. Believe it or not, Lotus and Microsoft do work together, as you'll see in this chapter.

Understanding Lotus Notes

Lotus Development Corporation introduced Lotus Notes in 1989. By the time Release 3 was introduced in 1994, there were approximately one million users. As of early 1999, Lotus Notes had more than 30 million messaging seats in the marketplace, and Notes is the premier group-ware application. Lotus has concentrated heavily on enabling Notes to work within almost any environment, including Microsoft Office applications. It is a client/server application—meaning that it uses a server, called the Domino server, to provide services to clients.

To cite just a few services, the Domino server hosts database applications, calendaring and scheduling, and email. Clients can be Web browsers or Lotus Notes clients. Notes clients and Domino servers are available for many platforms, from the PC to the AS/400, and even for the mainframe.

It is impossible to adequately describe Notes in a single chapter. Fortunately, Notes has extensive Help and reference databases that are installed with the product. There are also a number of very good books on Notes that you can turn to for more information: Que's *Special Edition Using Lotus Notes and Domino R5* by Randy Tamura, et al.; *Lotus Notes and Domino R5 Development Unleashed* by Debbie Lynd and Steve Kern, et al.; and *Sams Teach Yourself Lotus Notes R5 in 10 Minutes* by Jane Calabria and Dorothy Burke.

N O T E The terms Notes and Domino can be somewhat confusing. Technically speaking, Notes refers to the client, and Domino refers to the server. However, Notes is frequently used to refer to both the client and the server. ■

N O T E This chapter has been updated to include coverage of Notes R5. The screen shots of the Notes Client were taken from the new R5 client. Note that if you are using R4.x, your screens might look quite different. Where possible, the chapter covers both R4.x and R5. ■

Understanding Groupware

At the heart of the information age is knowledge. A business lives and dies by its capability to use, manage, and share information—turning raw data into knowledge. The term *groupware* (group information management software) is a loosely defined concept that refers to a type of application that lets groups of people collaborate to create, share, and use information more effectively. Since the inception and ensuing popularity of Lotus Notes, groupware has really caught on. Groupware promotes working together in teams. This fits in well with today's business climate, where teams are encouraged and heavily emphasized in almost every sector of business. These concepts have made their way into Microsoft Office as well—Microsoft has added version control, security, document routing, and so forth to Office applications to enable collaboration among team members.

Prior to the introduction of Lotus Notes, there were two principal methods of collaborating electronically. The first method, known as the *Share* model, consisted of posting information in a database that was accessible to all members of a workgroup. The second method, known as the *Send* model, consisted of routing documents via email. Both had serious limitations.

The most significant limitation of the Send model is that nobody knew where a particular document was at any point in time, because it wasn't stored in a centrally accessible location. The Share model solved that problem by storing information in a shared database. However, users had to visit the shared database to determine the status of a document or to perform a required action.

Because Lotus Notes combines email (the Send model) and data storage (the Share model), it overcomes the limitations of both models. Through the use of email, the information in a database can be brought to members of a workgroup. For example, a developer can design a database in such a way that when a new document, perhaps a requisition for supplies, is created, it is automatically routed to the correct approver via email. The email contains a link that the approver can click, which then opens the document. The approver can approve or deny the requisition on the spot.

Because the document is maintained in a centrally accessible database, members of the workgroup can always see the status of the requisition. This simple example illustrates the power inherent in groupware applications built with Lotus Notes and Domino.

Understanding Lotus Notes Databases

A Notes database (or Domino database) is not quite like other databases that you might be familiar with, such as FoxPro, SQL Server, or Sybase. Although some database applications in Notes might consist of more than one database, a database itself is self-contained: The file has all the code, as well as the data for the application. In this respect, it is similar to an Access database. Domino servers can literally host thousands of mail files, and at the same time host many discussions and other database applications. Notes clients and Web browsers can access applications and email on a Domino server.

In Release 4.6 or earlier, databases are represented on the Notes workspace by an icon. Although the traditional workspace is still available, in Release 5, Lotus has switched the paradigm for representing databases to bookmarks. The bookmarks appear in folders in a toolbar along the left side of the screen. The icons are similar to the database icons of earlier releases and display the title to the left of the icon.

Because the Notes client contains the "front end" of the application—the menus for printing, viewing, editing, and so on—the database files are relatively small. They contain only the code necessary for the functionality specific to that database application. Some applications involve more than one database. To address your email, the mail database looks up information in other databases, the Public Directory or Directories, and your Personal Directory.

In other databases, such as FoxPro or SQL Server, only the data resides in the database file. The application programs are completely separate files, and must be built from the ground up. For example, you have to create a menu system specifically for the application and program all the actions. As a consequence, these applications are generally made up of many files, and can be quite large in comparison to Notes databases.

Notes databases contain documents, which are roughly analogous to records in other database systems. Documents are presented to users in views and folders. Whereas Notes is similar to other database systems, it is not a relational database. Notes databases are unstructured, meaning that unlike a record in a relational database table, a document does not have a fixed set of fields. In addition, the fields themselves do not have a fixed length, and fields can be added or subtracted from a document. The unstructured character of Notes documents allows database designers to build powerful and sophisticated applications.

Notes comes with quite a few database templates, which you can use to create fully functional applications. Notes databases have the file extension .nsf (Notes Storage Facility) and templates have the extension .ntf (Notes Template Facility). These templates are an excellent way to put Notes into production quickly. Some commonly used templates are Discussion, TeamRoom, and Document Library. As a Notes database administrator or developer, you simply base the design of a new database on a template, and you have a fully functional application!

▶ For more information on building databases with templates, **see** "Using the Microsoft Office Document Library Database," on **p. 676** later in this chapter.

Using Office with Lotus Notes Mail

Notes Mail is really just a specialized Notes database application on the Domino server. Like Lotus cc:Mail, Microsoft Outlook, and Netscape Communicator, Notes Mail supports rich text. In other words, you can use different fonts, font sizes, and font colors in your messages. You can also embed files and images in the body of a mail message.

 TIP This chapter discusses the standard Notes client. However, depending on the release of your Notes server and what your Notes administrator is running on the server, you might be able to access Notes Mail using other clients as well. For example, you can access your mail database through clients that support POP3 and IMAP or a Web browser.

Figure 25.1 shows the Notes Mail interface. The Navigator pane in the upper-left corner of the window allows you to move through the various folders in your mail database. The View pane on the far right lists your message headers. The Preview pane at the bottom of the window displays the contents of your messages. You can turn the Preview pane on and off. When it's on, it displays the top portion of the current message. When it's off, the Navigator and View panes occupy the entire window. You can also open a message into a separate window by double-clicking its header in the View pane.

You can use Office with Notes Mail in two principal ways: You can use Word as an alternative mail editor and you can email Office documents with Notes Mail.

Using Word As Your Email Editor

With Notes 4.6, the option of using another mail editor on Win32 platforms became available. The Notes 4.6 and R5 Windows clients are 32-bit applications that can use Windows ActiveDoc technology to work with other mail editors. The mail editors that are currently certified are Lotus WordPro 97, Microsoft Word 95, and Microsoft Word 97. To enable Microsoft Word as the alternate mail editor, take these steps:

   1. Open the Notes client.

2. Choose **File**, **Tools**, **User Preferences** in the 4.6 client, or in R5, choose **File**, **Preferences**, **Notes Preferences**.

3. Click the Mail icon in the 4.6 Preferences dialog box or the Mail and News icon in the R5 Preferences dialog box.

4. Select Microsoft Word in the 4.6 Document Memo Editor or the R5 Alternate Document Memo drop-down box (see Figure 25.2).

5. Click **OK**.

FIGURE 25.1

You can use the Preview pane to view your messages.

Navigator pane

View pane

Preview pane

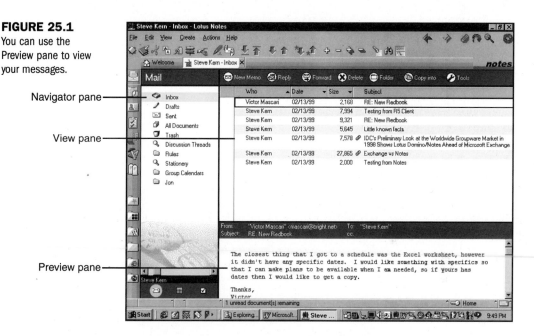

FIGURE 25.2

Switching the mail editor to Word.

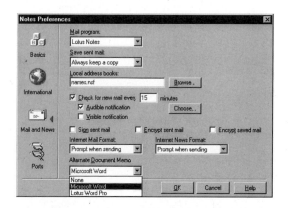

N O T E You must have a supported version of Word (or WordPro) installed on your computer for this procedure to work! ▓

After you complete these steps, you can create a mail message using Word as your editor by opening your mail database and choosing **Create**, **Word Memo** from your mailbox, or **Create**, **Mail**, **Word Memo** from outside your mailbox.

If you are familiar with the standard Notes mail editor, you will definitely notice some changes! As shown in Figure 25.3, the standard Notes toolbar is replaced with the Word toolbars. The memo itself is a blank Word document with rulers. (The rulers are there by default; you can hide them by choosing **View**, **Ruler**.)

N O T E In Notes 4.6, there is an Action button labeled Envelope and the address area is not present. Clicking the **Envelope** button opens a dialog box from which you choose recipients for your new memo. ▓

FIGURE 25.3

A mail memo composed using Word has the familiar Word toolbars.

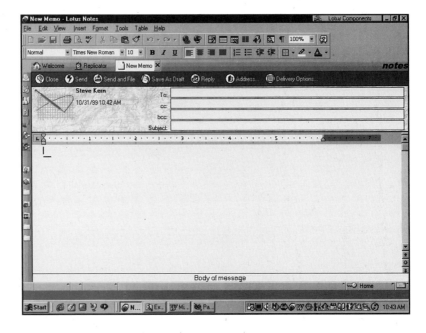

Using Word as an alternative mail editor lets you prepare your memos in an application that you might be more familiar with. Although the standard Notes editor is sufficient for most email messages, Word gives you more options for presenting your material because it is a full-featured word processor.

Sending Office Documents Through Notes Mail

You can send any type of file through Notes Mail by attaching the file to a mail memo. You can also copy a file, such as a Word document, Excel worksheet, or graphic image to the

Clipboard, and then paste it into the body of a Notes memo. You then address the memo, and send it. You can also send documents directly from an Office application.

Attaching Files to Your Email   To attach a file to a Notes mail memo, take these steps:

1. Open your mail database.
2. Click the **New Memo** button.
3. Address the memo, and enter a subject.
4. Choose **File**, **Attach**, and in the Create Attachment(s) dialog box, choose the file(s) you want to attach (see Figure 25.4).
5. Click the **Create** button.

FIGURE 25.4
You can select more than one file in the Create Attachment(s) dialog box.

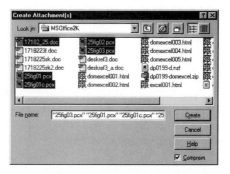

The file or files are now attached to your mail memo. Each attachment is represented by an icon in the body field (see Figure 25.5). If Notes recognizes the file type, it displays the appropriate icon.

FIGURE 25.5
The familiar Word icon represents an attached Word document.

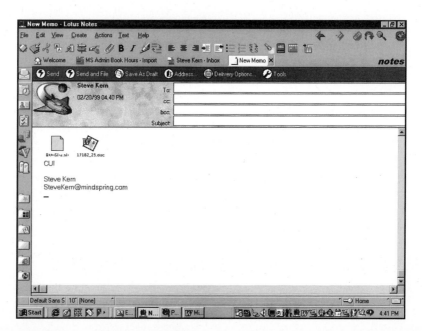

CAUTION

If the File, Attach command isn't available, it is probably because the insertion point is not in the body of the mail memo. You can embed file attachments only in a rich text field, which in a mail memo is the body field. The body field is not labeled, but it is immediately below the Address Header section (refer to Figure 25.5).

Opening a File Attachment   To open a file attachment, simply double-click the file icon. The Properties Box appears with three buttons: View, Launch, and Detach. Clicking **View** launches a universal viewer that is capable of viewing most, but not all, file types that you are likely to encounter. Clicking **Launch** opens the attachment in the appropriate application. For example, in Figure 25.5, clicking the **Word** icon and then clicking **Launch** opens the attached document in Word. The Launch button works only if the file type of the attachment is registered and you have a copy of the source application on your machine. Click **Detach** to copy the attached file to a local or network drive.

Pasting and Importing Office Files into a Mail Memo   Pasting an image, or part of a Word document or Excel spreadsheet, into a mail memo is very straightforward. Simply select the image, text, or range, and then copy it to the Clipboard. Switch to the Notes memo, click in the body field, and paste the contents of the Clipboard into the memo. You can also link a document to a mail memo using Object Linking and Embedding (OLE), OLE 2 (the most recent version of OLE), or Dynamic Data Exchange (DDE).

▶ For further discussion on attachments, **see** "Embedding Office Documents in Notes," on **p. 672** later in this chapter.

▶ You can also import certain file types directly into the body field of the memo. For more information, **see** "Importing Office Documents or Data into Lotus Notes," on **p. 673** later in this chapter.

Sending an Office File from its Application   If Notes is configured as your default mail application, you can send your Office file directly from the Office application! To do this, simply choose **File**, **Send To** from the Office application's menu. If no mail system has been configured to work with the Send To, the first time you choose Send To from the menu, a Wizard launches to help you configure a default mail system. In Windows 95 and Windows NT, you can configure your mail settings by clicking the **Start** menu, and then **Settings**. Next, choose **Mail** in the Control Panel folder. In Windows 98 and 2000, Microsoft did away with the Exchange client. To use the Send To, place a shortcut of the mail program in the SendTo folder in your profile.

Integrating Office Files with a Lotus Notes Database

The techniques that you use to integrate Office applications with Lotus Notes Mail are the same techniques that you use to integrate Office applications with other Lotus Notes databases. For example, because Notes Mail is just a specialized database application, the technique for attaching files to a Notes mail memo is exactly the same as the one that you use to attach a file to a discussion database or document library. In this section, you learn about embedding, linking, importing, and exporting. You also read about a special Notes database that is dedicated to the Microsoft Office suite, the Microsoft Office Document Library.

Using OLE with Office and Notes Databases

OLE and OLE 2 are technologies that let applications share information. OLE is available on Windows and Macintosh operating systems. OLE 2 is available on 32-bit Windows platforms: Windows 95/98 and Windows NT. OLE clients can exchange information with OLE servers. Notes can act as an OLE client, and Excel and Word can act as an OLE server. OLE objects can be Word documents, Excel spreadsheets, or OLE custom controls (OCXs). (An OCX is also referred to as an *applet*. These applets are small modules that can interact with the underlying document and are based on OLE 2.) To create an OLE object in a Notes document, you must have the document open in Edit mode and the insertion point must be in a rich text field. Objects can be linked or embedded.

Linking a Notes Document to an Office File   You can link a Notes document to a source file, such as a Word document. When you do this, Notes stores a pointer to the source file, and when the source file changes, Notes updates the view of it in the Notes document. The drawback to this use of OLE is that each user who needs to edit the linked object must be able to run the application (Word, for example). Furthermore, users must have access to the physical file. If the file is stored on a file server, the drive mappings must be identical, or else OLE will fail. When the source file is moved or deleted, the link will again fail.

To create an OLE link, follow these steps:

1. Open the source document and copy what you want to appear in Notes to the Clipboard.
2. Go to Notes, and open a document in Edit mode. Click in a rich text field.
3. Choose **Edit**, **Paste Special**.
4. In the Paste Special dialog box, select **Paste link to source** (see Figure 25.6).
5. Select the **Display as icon** check box, if you want.
6. Click **OK**, and save the document.

FIGURE 25.6
The Result area at the bottom of the dialog box changes with your selections.

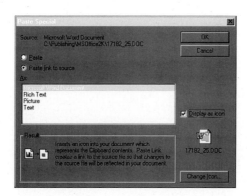

Whenever you open the document, Notes prompts you to refresh the linked document.

Embedding Office Documents in Notes   *Embedding* files gets around some of the limitations of linking because a copy of the source file is stored in the Notes file. If the source file is changed, however, the embedded file does not reflect the change. The user still has to be able to run the source file's application to edit the embedded object. Embedding a file is useful when you want to share a file with another Notes user who might not have access to the file server, or who might be working remotely via dial-up access to the Notes server. This is slightly different from attaching a file, because you can use the source document's application to edit the object in Notes. You can embed all or part of a file inside a Notes file.

Follow these steps to embed an entire file:

1. Open a Notes document in Edit mode, and place the insertion point in a rich text field.
2. Choose **Create**, **Object**.
3. In the Create Object dialog box, choose **Create new Object from a file** (see Figure 25.7).
4. Enter the path and filename, or click the Browse button and browse to the file.
5. Select the **Display as icon** check box if desired.
6. Click **OK**.

The object is now embedded in your Notes document.

FIGURE 25.7
Embedding an object in a Notes document is simple.

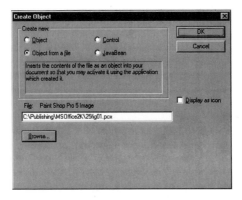

Follow these steps to embed part of a file:

1. Copy the part of the file that you want to embed to the Clipboard.
2. Open the Notes file in Edit mode and place the insertion point in a rich text field.
3. Choose **Edit**, **Paste Special**.
4. Select the **Paste** option button if necessary, and select the **Display as icon** check box if desired.
5. Click **OK**.

NOTE DDE is an earlier but similar technology that is also available on OS2. It is more restrictive because both the server application (such as Word) and Notes must be open for it to work. ▪

Importing Office Documents or Data into Lotus Notes

You can import information from applications external to Notes into two areas: documents and views. To import into a document, you must be in Edit mode, and the insertion point must be in a rich text field. You can import many different file types, from images (.bmp, .pcx, and so on) to Word documents (see Table 25.1). When you import into a view, the range of choices is limited to Structured Text, Tabular Text, and Lotus 1-2-3 Worksheet. You typically import into a view when you want to create multiple documents; for example, if you have a worksheet of timesheet information, after importing it into a view, all of the rows become documents.

Table 25.1   File Types for Importing and Exporting to and from Notes Documents

Windows and OS/2	Macintosh
Ami Pro	ANSI Metafile
ASCII Text	ASCII Text
Binary with Text	Lotus 1-2-3 Worksheet
BMP Image	Microsoft Word RTF
CGM Image	TIFF 5.0 Image
Excel 4.0/5.0 Spreadsheet	
GIF Image	
HTML File	
JPEG Image	
Lotus 1-2-3 Worksheet	
Lotus PIC	
Microsoft Word RTF	
PCX Image	
TIFF 5.0 Image	
WordPerfect 5.x/6.x	
Word for Windows 6.0/6.1	
WordPro 96/97	

Part
IV

Ch
25

To import a file into a document, follow this general procedure:

1. Be sure the document is in Edit mode, and that your insertion point is in a rich text field.

2. Choose **File**, **Import**.

3. Choose a file type to import, and select the file you want to import (see Figure 25.8).

4. Click **Import**.

FIGURE 25.8
Select the file type from the drop-down list and then select the file.

Importing data into a view is a little more complex. You can import structured text, tabular text, or worksheet (.wk1) files. You can also create a column descriptor (.col) file to massage the data while it is being imported. Column descriptor files can be used only with tabular text or worksheet files. They contain a list of column definitions followed by formulas (in the Notes Formula language) that define how the data is added to Notes—they are essentially field maps. Developers often create COL files to import existing data into Notes. Extensive discussion of this technique is beyond the scope of this chapter, but it is adequately documented in the Notes Designer Help database.

To import data into Notes views, you must have a form for the documents and a view. Each import option—tabular text, structured text, and worksheet—has a different dialog box, but the basic procedure is very similar (see Figure 25.9). It is often easiest to use a WK1 file, so if you want to import an Excel workbook, you have to save it as a WK1 file.

FIGURE 25.9
The Worksheet Import Settings dialog box. Note that the TimeSheet form has been selected.

The basic steps to import a spreadsheet into a Notes view are as follows:

1. Open the database to the view you want to use.

2. Choose **File**, **Import**.

3. Optionally, choose **Lotus 1-2-3 Worksheet** in the Files of Type drop-down list to display only WK1 files in the dialog box. Then, select the file and click the **Import** button.

4. Select the form that you want to use. In Figure 25.9, the form is called **TimeSheet**.

5. Choose the desired option under Column Format. See the Notes documentation for a full description of these choices.

6. Click **Import**.

When the import is complete, the rows of the spreadsheet become rows in the view (see Figure 25.10). Each row in the view represents a document in Notes.

FIGURE 25.10

The view after the import is complete displays the Notes documents that used to be rows in the spreadsheet.

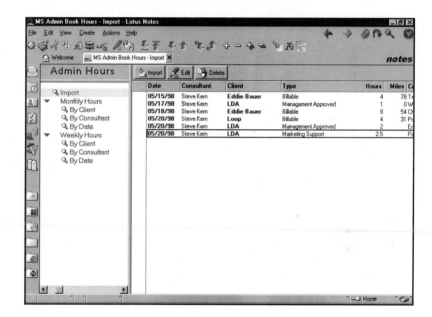

Exporting Data from Lotus Notes to Office

Exporting data is essentially the reverse of importing it. The dialog boxes that you use are the same (except for the Window Title), and the choices of file types for exporting documents and views are the same as those for importing. In other words, you can export documents from a view to the same three file types that you can import from structured text, tabular text, and worksheets.

 TIP

To export some, but not all, documents from a Notes view, click in the view selection margin to the left of the documents that you want to export. A check mark appears next to each document name. When you export, select **Selected documents**.

Exporting data from Notes views is an important technique because Notes has a fairly limited reporting facility. Other than views and documents, there is no built-in method to display Notes data, either printed or on the screen. This is discussed further in "Using Excel to Present Notes Data" later in this chapter.

To export data from a view to a worksheet, follow these steps:

1. Optionally, select the documents that you want to export.

2. Choose **File**, **Export**.

3. Choose **Lotus 1-2-3 Worksheet** as the file type, and supply a name.

4. Click **Export**.

5. Choose **Selected documents** (or **All documents** if you want to export the entire view), and select **Include View titles** if you want the titles of the view to show as column headers in the spreadsheet (see Figure 25.11).

6. Click **OK**.

FIGURE 25.11
Click Include View titles to convert the view column titles to column headers in the new worksheet.

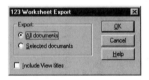

The file is created according to the choices you made. You can then open the file in Excel and use it in whatever way you want.

Using the Microsoft Office Document Library Database

To create a new database using the Microsoft Office Document Library template, you must have a Domino Designer license. If you want to place this database on a server, you must have the appropriate access level to the server. Take the following steps:

1. Choose **File**, **Database**, **New**.

2. Leave the server set to Local to create the new database on your local hard drive.

3. In the New Database dialog box, enter a filename and database title (see Figure 25.12).

4. From the templates list box, choose **Microsoft Office Library** (R4.6 or R5).

5. Click **OK**.

FIGURE 25.12
Creating a database based on the Microsoft Office Library template. The (R5) next to the template name indicates the Notes version.

CAUTION

If you enter the title first, the database title becomes the filename. Any spaces in the database title are transferred to the database filename. Therefore, it is a good practice to enter the filename first so that you can control how your new database is identified to the operating system. Bear in mind that some operating systems do not support long filenames, so you might want to consider using the standard 8.3 naming convention.

When creation of the new database is complete, which usually takes just a few moments, you will see a document describing the purpose of the database. This document is called the "About" document, and is always available from the Help menu when the database is selected or opened. To see the document at a later date, choose **Help**, **About This Database**. Additional information about this database is available by choosing **Help**, **Using This Database**.

This database features a built-in capability to embed documents based on Office applications using OLE and ActiveX. When you create a document based on an Office application, the server application takes over the interface. This is similar to what happens when you switch the mail editor to Word. Supported Office document types are: Excel Workbook, Paintbrush Picture, PowerPoint Presentation, and Word Document.

To create a document based on an object from one of these OLE server applications, choose **Create**, **MS Office** or in R5, click the **New MS Office Document** button. Figure 25.13 shows a Word document created in this manner. This allows you to edit these documents in place without leaving Notes.

Part
IV

Ch
25

FIGURE 25.13
A Word document created in the Microsoft Office Library has the familiar Word menus and toolbars, as well as additional buttons for Notes.

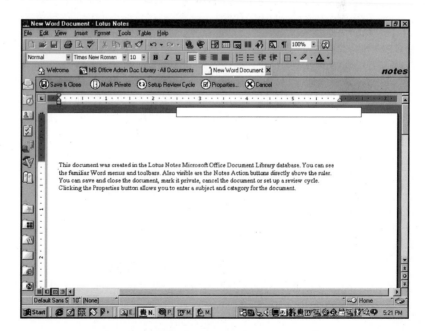

The document in Figure 25.14 was created in the Lotus Notes Microsoft Office Document Library database. You can see the Word menus and toolbars, as well as buttons from the Notes Action bar. The Action bar allows you to interact with Notes—you can click **Save & Close**, **Mark Private**, and **Setup Review Cycle**. Clicking **Properties** allows you to specify a subject and a category for the document.

This database takes advantage of the powerful workflow capabilities built into Notes and leverages your investment in Microsoft Office applications. You can set up review cycles for your documents, either serial or parallel. You can also maintain version control of the document so that the original remains intact. This database has many other capabilities as well, such as archiving and flagging documents as private (which locks the document and prevents others from reading it). This means that you can create documents, worksheets, and so forth in the familiar Office applications, and use Notes features to route them to other users for review.

Reporting on Notes Data Using Office Applications

Notes has no real reporting facility other than views to present documents in summary format. Views are quite powerful in their own right; you can create multiple lines per row, and add summary columns, average columns, percent columns, and group documents in nested categories. You can even create headers and footers when you print out the data in a view. However, many users prefer a more polished report. Lotus provides solutions to this in its own Lotus SmartSuite and in the Notes Reporter. Lotus Approach (a component of SmartSuite) is similar to Microsoft Access in its scope and use. The Notes Reporter is basically the reporting functions taken out of Approach. As an Office administrator, however, you'll be most interested in learning how to prepare reports using Access and Excel.

A typical view in a database that keeps track of hours is shown in Figure 25.14.

FIGURE 25.14
Note the summary columns and the nested categories in this view.

Closed twistie

Open twistie

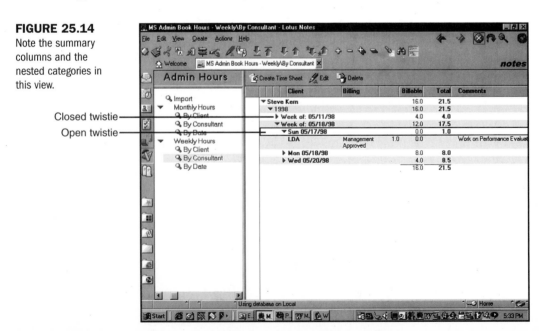

As you can see, views can be a very sophisticated means of presenting Notes data. You can click the *twisties* (small cyan triangles) beside each category to expand and collapse the category. This is great for onscreen display because it lets you go to the level of detail you want. You can select the categories and documents you want to print, and choose **File**, **Print**. When you click **Print View**, only the selected documents and categories will print.

Nonetheless, you might need to resort to another reporting tool to present data. You might want to sort the data differently, or total some columns that are not totaled in a view, or perform some sophisticated ad hoc calculations. There are a couple of options in Office that work. The first and simplest option is to export Notes data to a 1-2-3 Worksheet, as described in the section "Exporting Data from Lotus Notes to Office" earlier in this chapter. You can then open the WK1 file in Excel. The other option, discussed next, is to use Access to open Notes data.

Using Excel to Present Notes Data

Two methods of getting data into Excel work quite well. One is to export to a 1-2-3 Worksheet file, and the other is to export to a tabular text file. When the export is complete (see "Exporting Data from Lotus Notes to Office"), you can open the file in Excel. Opening a WK1 file is very straightforward (you simply open the file in Excel, and Excel recognizes it as a spreadsheet), but opening a tabular text file is a little more complex.

When you open a tabular text file in Excel, Excel detects it, and launches the Text Import Wizard. Excel's Text Import Wizard enables you to choose which columns to import and to set the data type (see Figure 25.15). If you've got a view that has six columns you want and four you don't need, now is the time to get rid of those extraneous columns by clicking the column, and selecting **Do not import column (skip)** in the Import Wizard.

FIGURE 25.15
Using Excel's Text Import Wizard is fairly simple. Note that column 1 is set to a date format.

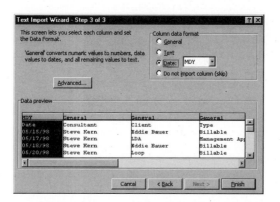

The Text Import Wizard is a three-step process. In the first step, you determine the row to start the import. Excel detects whether the file is fixed width or delimited; a tabular text file is fixed width. In the second step, you adjust the field widths. The third step lets you determine the type of data in each column, and whether to skip the column (refer to Figure 25.16). You can move back and forth among the three steps, and when you are satisfied, click **Finish**.

After you have the data in Excel, you can work with the cell borders, fonts, background colors, and so forth. You can also use Excel formulas to present data. If you have a report that you prepare frequently, you might consider writing a macro in Excel to automate the spreadsheet. You can store this macro in your Personal.xls file, which makes it available to any spreadsheet. Figure 25.16 shows a very simple application of cell formatting to present timesheet data.

FIGURE 25.16

Spicing up Notes data with an Excel worksheet is easy!

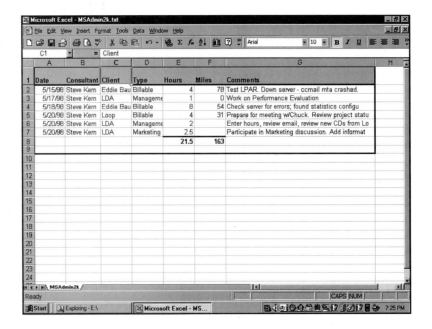

Using Access to Query Notes Data

Access, as its name implies, is often used to query data from other database applications. These other databases are often relational, such as Microsoft's SQL Server, Sybase, or Oracle. The database system is referred to as the *source* and there is usually some setup involved to configure your PC so that Access can open the database tables. The tools that allow you to get to these database sources are referred to as *drivers*. Access also supports opening any data source that is ODBC-compliant. *ODBC* is a widely used standard. You must set up an ODBC driver to get to an ODBC data source.

Notes databases are no exception to this, and Lotus provides its own driver, NotesSQL. NotesSQL enables you to get at Notes data using SQL statements. *SQL* (pronounced sequel) is an acronym that stands for Structured Query Language, which is a tool for querying databases. A description of SQL is beyond the scope of this chapter, but the basic syntax is pretty straightforward. The syntax is as follows:

```
SELECT <fields> FROM <tables> WHERE <conditions>
```

Despite this capability, don't forget that Notes is not a relational database! In fact, a Notes database is really just one large table. You can, however, set up pseudotables in a Notes database by creating views that contain the data you want to report against.

Setting Up ODBC with NotesSQL   Setting up NotesSQL is pretty straightforward. You can find NotesSQL on Lotus' Web site at **http://www.lotus.com**. Currently, it can be found listed under the Products link. After you download it, place the file (Nsqlw32.exe) in its own folder, and run it to extract the setup files. Next, run Setup.exe in the folder you've created for NotesSQL. Answer the Install Shield prompts, choosing **Typical** or **Custom**. When installation is complete, you are prompted to configure a data source for NotesSQL. You can also configure a data source at any time by following these steps:

1. Choose **Start**, **Settings**, **Control Panel**.
2. Open the 32bit ODBC manager.
3. Click the **System DSN** tab, and click the **Add** button.
4. Click **Lotus Notes SQL 2.0 (32-bit) ODBC Driver (.nsf)**, as shown in Figure 25.17.
5. Click **Finish**, and fill in the fields in the Lotus Notes ODBC 2.0 Setup dialog box (see Figure 25.18).
6. Specify a name for the data source, the server, and the filename, including the path. Leave the rest of the settings alone for now.
7. Click **OK** to return to the System DSN tab.
8. Click **OK** to close the ODBC manager.

Part

IV

Ch

25

FIGURE 25.17

It is usually best to configure a System DSN, especially if you are working on a network.

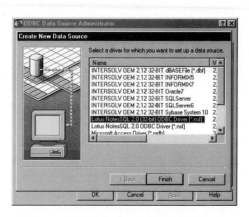

NOTE The text for the Notes ODBC driver in the Create New Data Source window does not reflect the current revision of NotesSQL. Even though the current release, as of this writing, is 2.05, the entry in the driver list still reads 2.0. ■

Now that you have a data source set up, you can open it with Access.

FIGURE 25.18
Leaving the server field
blank means that you
must have a copy
(called a *local Replica*)
of the database on
your hard drive. You can
also open a database
on a server.

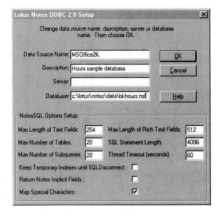

> **CAUTION**
>
> The ODBC driver treats all Notes fields as text, regardless of how Notes itself registers them. Furthermore, in some cases, all fields are the width that you specified in the Lotus Notes ODBC 2.0 Setup dialog box, which defaults to 254. If you are having difficulty with your queries, open the dialog box and change the default from 254 to a smaller value. You must keep this in mind when working with numbers because you will have to convert them from text in order to perform calculations.

Querying Notes Data with SQL   When you open your data source in Access, it will not look much like the relational databases that you are used to. Design elements such as forms and views are treated as tables. It is often best to use a view, but this means that the information you want to report on must be in a view column.

When you open an external data source in Access, you can either import the data or link to the tables. If you are going to report on Notes data that will be changing, it is a good idea to use the link option. To open the data source in Access, take these steps:

1. Create a new blank database in Access.
2. Choose **File**, **Get External Data**, **Link Tables**.
3. In the Link dialog box, choose **ODBC Databases ()** from the Files of type drop-down box (see Figure 25.19).
4. Click the **Machine Data Sources** tab in the Select Data Source dialog box, and choose the Notes ODBC source you defined (see Figure 25.20).
5. Click **OK**.

FIGURE 25.19
The Link dialog box enables you to specify the file type as ODBC.

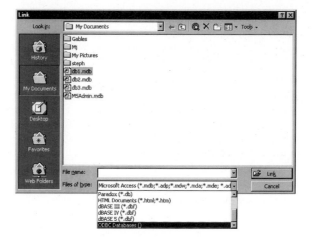

FIGURE 25.20
Click the Machine Data Source tab to select your Notes ODBC data source.

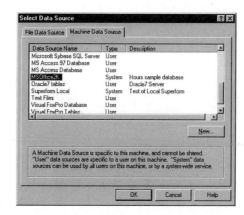

Part
IV

Ch

25

After you choose the Notes ODBC data source, the Link Tables dialog box appears with what may be a bewildering array of elements (see Figure 25.21). Here, you must have some knowledge of the internal design of the database in order to determine which element to choose.

FIGURE 25.21
Knowledge of the database's design will help you choose the correct design element for your report.

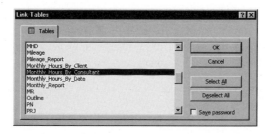

After you choose an element, Access prompts you to choose a field or fields to uniquely describe each record—again, you need to have some knowledge of the design of the Notes database. After this is completed, you can query the "table" (see Figure 25.22).

FIGURE 25.22
The Simple Query Wizard after several fields have been selected.

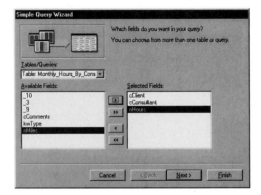

Now that you have a query, you can apply the selection criteria you need, and you can use any of the sophisticated reporting tools available in Access to present a polished report.

Using Office with Lotus Notes/FX

Lotus Notes/FX, or Field Exchange, is based on OLE technology, and enables Notes to exchange field-level information with other applications. Not all the Office applications or all versions are FX enabled. For example, none of the Office 95 applications work with Notes 4. Office has three applications that support Notes/FX: Excel, PowerPoint, and Word. Access does not support Notes/FX.

Information can be exchanged in one direction, or in both directions between a Notes document and an OLE server application. Notes/FX has to be set up by a Notes developer because the forms and/or actions are part of the database design.

> **N O T E** For both Notes/FX and NotesFlow (discussed in the section "Enabling Workflow with NotesFlow" later in this chapter) to work, the OLE Server application must be launched from within Notes. A Notes developer sets a property on the NotesFlow-enabled form to automatically launch the application. ■

All the OLE server applications that support Notes/FX provide help. For example, you can search Microsoft Word help for Notes FX and find several documents, including a table of fields. These fields are described as file properties and are available in each FX-enabled Office application. Some fields are the same throughout each FX-enabled application, and some are specific to the application. For example, common properties include items such as Title, Subject, Author, and Date Created; Multimedia Clips is a property in PowerPoint, but not in Word.

For Notes/FX to function, there must be corresponding fields in the OLE server application and in the Notes form. The tables in the server application list the names that the fields must have in Notes in order to function with Notes/FX. See Table 25.2 for a list of Notes/FX fields in Word.

Table 25.2   Notes/FX Fields in Word 97

Property Field	Notes Field Name	Notes Data Type
Title	Title	Text
Subject	Subject	Text
Author	Author	Text
Keywords	Keywords	Text
Comments	Comments	Text
Template	Template	Text
Manager	ManagerText	Text
Company	Company	Text
Category	Category	Text
Created	DateCreated	Time
Modified	LastSavedDate	Time
Last Saved By	LastSavedBy	Text
Size	NumberOfBytes	Text
Revision Number	NumberOfRevisions	Number
Total Editing	TotalEditingTime	Number
Time Printed	LastPrintedDate	Time
Pages	NumberOfPages	Number
Slides	NumberOfSlides	Number
Words	NumberOfWords	Number
Characters	NumberOfCharacters	Number
Characters (with spaces)	NumberOfCharacters WithSpaces	Number
Paragraphs	NumberOfParagraphs	Number
Lines	NumberOfLines	Number
Security	Security	Number
Document Class	DocumentClass	Text
Name of Application	NameOfApplication	Text

Part IV
Ch 25

Enabling Workflow with NotesFlow

Application developers in Lotus Notes can use special settings in Notes forms to publish a *NotesFlow action* to an OLE server application. An *action* is a scripted event attached to a form. For example, there might be an action titled *Submit for Review* that sends the document to others in your team for review.

In Office, Word, Excel, and PowerPoint, all recognize NotesFlow actions. NotesFlow actions appear in a special Action menu to the left of the Window menu. This corresponds to a similarly named menu in Notes. NotesFlow is available only in Release 4 or later of Notes. For NotesFlow to work, an application designer must create a Notes form that launches the OLE application.

Form Actions can be scripted and published using NotesFlow. When a form is used to create or open a document, the OLE application is opened, and the actions appear in the Action menu. ●

Managing Mixed Macintosh/Windows Office Environments

by Bill Camarda

Microsoft Office is a cross-platform product, available on both Microsoft Windows and Apple Macintosh platforms. Managing Office in both environments at once, however, brings its own challenges. Some of these challenges relate to differences in Office's features and behavior on each platform; others relate to connectivity; and still others relate to differences in the way the platforms themselves handle key tasks, such as fonts and printing.

In this chapter, you walk through the basics of managing Office in a cross-platform environment, identifying techniques and products that can make the process significantly easier.

Reviewing Office 2000 Components Not Included with Office 98 for the Macintosh

Although Office 98 for the Macintosh is a full-featured suite of productivity applications, it is missing some elements that exist on the Windows platform. If your custom solutions or business processes depend on these elements, you have to modify these functions accordingly. Office 98 for the Macintosh lacks the following features:

- **Web integration.** Office 98 for the Macintosh can create HTML files, and Internet Explorer 4.5 for the Macintosh can read files published from Office 2000. However, Office 98 lacks the extensive Web integration features built into Office 2000 for Windows. If you plan to exchange files for editing between platforms, use the native binary file formats, not the complex HTML/XML files created by Office 2000. Also, you cannot currently extend Office 2000's Web collaboration and discussion features to Macintosh users working with Office 98.

- **Microsoft Access.** There is no Macintosh version of Access; however, you can deliver database data to Macintosh users in several ways. You can build intranet-based applications with browser front ends. You can query Access (or other Windows databases) using ODBC drivers built into Office on both platforms. You can export static reports to Excel, RTF, HTML, and tab- or comma-delimited formats. You can build a cross-platform Microsoft FoxPro database and front-end it with FoxPro on the Macintosh and Access 2000 on a Windows PC. Finally, you can use Microsoft's new Office 98 FileMaker Pro Importer (**www.microsoft.com/mac/fmtools.htm**). This add-in steps you through the process of importing FileMaker data into Word or Excel, where it can be used in mail merges and for analysis.

- **Microsoft Outlook.** Outlook Express, a more limited Internet email and news client, is provided instead.

- **User profiles, System Policies, and other management tools.** The Macintosh does not support logon scripts, and Microsoft has not provided user profiles and System Policies. These limitations make it difficult to enforce restrictions on Macintosh Office users through the network, as you can do in Windows. Nor do you have as much flexibility customizing Help; for example, Microsoft does not provide tools for customizing the Answer Wizard on the Macintosh.

- **PhotoDraw 2000.** Microsoft's new drawing and photo editing program, included in most versions of Office 2000, is not available for the Macintosh.

- **Publisher 2000.** Similarly, Microsoft's business and home desktop publishing software, included in most versions of Office 2000, has no Macintosh version.

- **FrontPage 2000.** Microsoft's Office 98 for the Macintosh Gold Edition comes with FrontPage 1.0 for the Macintosh, a version of FrontPage that's considerably less sophisticated than the version that ships with most versions of Office 2000.

- **The Office Binder.** This feature enables users to pull together several Word, Excel, and PowerPoint files in a single file called a *binder*. For Office 98 users to work with the contents of an Office 2000 or Office 97 binder, they must run the Unbind Utility in the Office 98 ValuPack.

- **The Find Fast and Web Find Fast (for Windows NT) features.** In Windows, these features streamline the process of searching for documents on a local computer or corporate intranet.
- **The Excel Web Form Wizard.** In Windows, this feature simplifies the creation of intranet-based data entry forms from within Excel.
- **WordMail.** This feature enables Word to be used as the email editor for Microsoft Exchange clients.
- **Posting to public Microsoft Exchange folders.** In Office 2000 and 97, Outlook enables users to post Office documents to public Microsoft Exchange folders for easy companywide access. The Outlook Express email client does not provide this capability.
- **PowerPoint Web-based presentation conferencing.** In Windows, PowerPoint works with Microsoft's NetMeeting software to enable conferencing over the Web; this feature is not present on the Macintosh.
- **Other advanced PowerPoint features.** Features missing in Office 98 include Speaker Notes, AutoClipArt, and support for integration of Lotus Notes custom workflow (Lotus NotesFlow) commands.
- **Microsoft Photo Editor.** This image-editing applet is missing from Office 98 for the Macintosh. Microsoft might have assumed that most Macintosh users already have access to an image-editing program, such as Photoshop.

Conversely, Office 98 for the Macintosh contains the following features not available on Office 2000 for Windows:

- Balloon help
- Support for Apple Publish and Subscribe, Apple's method of integrating information across documents (Object Linking and Embedding is supported on both platforms)
- Support for Macintosh drag-and-drop editing
- QuickTime movie and QuickTime VR panorama support
- Optional Word 5.1 for the Macintosh menus, designed to simplify migration for Word 5.1/Mac users
- Word Speak, a Word add-in that works with MacInTalk to convert text to speech

Other differences between the platforms include the following:

- Additional components are significantly different on the two platforms; Office 98 contains the ValuPack, but Office 2000 does not.
- Web access works differently from within Office 98 applications. Instead of opening a Web browser from within Word, for example, Word opens a separate copy of Internet Explorer.
- Microsoft provides different software for enabling one-click access to Office applications. Office 98 provides Microsoft Office Manager, whereas Office 2000 for Windows includes the Office Shortcut Bar.
- Minor command differences exist in Visual Basic for Applications (VBA) to reflect the slightly different command set available on Windows and the Macintosh, even though many VBA macros and programs can be translated without trouble.

Part
IV

Ch
26

Comparing the Word 98 and Word 2000 Windows Interfaces

Some years ago, when Microsoft introduced Office 4.2 for Windows and later on Office 4.2 for the Macintosh, Microsoft sought to make the Macintosh versions of Word, Excel, and PowerPoint mimic the Windows versions in virtually every detail. The goal was to simplify cross-platform management of Word and Office.

The experiment failed: Macintosh users rebelled against the Windows-like look-and-feel of these Office programs, and many also objected to slow performance on these ported applications. As a result, many Macintosh users are still working with the ancient Word 5.1.

With Word 98 and Office 98 for the Macintosh, Microsoft learned its lesson, carefully restoring most aspects of the Macintosh look-and-feel, along with many of the interface features Word 5.1 users are accustomed to. Although Macintosh users generally seem pleased with the result, Office administrators face platform differences that did not exist previously. Most of these differences are relatively minor and easy to manage—when you understand them.

For example, in Word 98 for the Macintosh (see Figure 26.1), two additional menus appear: the Font menu, which enables users to easily format selected text in any font installed on the system; and the Work menu, which enables users to list the current file so that it is more easily accessible in future sessions. To learn how to add Font and Work menus to Word for Windows, see Chapter 6, "Customizing Word to Your Organization's Needs."

FIGURE 26.1
Word 98 for the Macintosh, running under Mac OS 8.5.

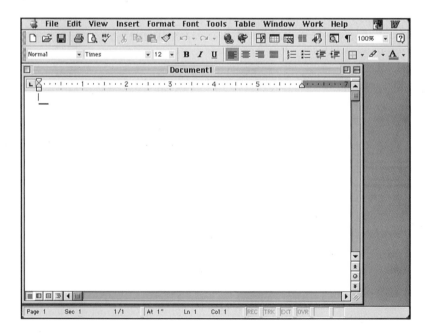

Conversely, several of the user interface innovations in Office 2000 are not available in Office 98 for the Macintosh. In particular, Office 98 lacks the following:

- **Personalized menus and toolbars.** However, you can still use the Customize dialog box to control the items that appear on Office 98 menus and toolbars.
- **Second-generation Office Assistants.** Office 98's Office Assistants don't reflect the subtle improvements that have been made in their appearance and accuracy in Office 2000.

Evaluating Options for Sharing Office 98/ Office 2000 Files

You must consider a number of issues when sharing Microsoft Office files between Macintosh and Windows computers. These issues fall into the following two major categories:

- Can the file be read at all? (Cross-platform networking and removable media issues)
- Can the file be recognized for what it is? (Long filename, filename extension, and Macintosh application/file type issues)

The good news is that file sharing has become significantly easier than it once was, especially if you are running the latest version of the Mac OS (currently, Mac OS 8.1).

Reading Windows Office Files on the Macintosh

If you are running Mac OS 8.1 or later with the PC Exchange extension loaded, your Macintosh recognizes both Windows 95 long filenames and Office filename extensions, such as .doc for Word documents and .xls for Excel workbooks. The Macintosh then automatically assigns the appropriate Macintosh application and document types, which Mac applications use to recognize and open files.

Windows 95/98 long filenames can be as long as 255 characters; Macintosh filenames are limited to no more than 32 characters. As a result, a very long filename in Windows 95 might be truncated when the file is opened on the Macintosh. You can usually distinguish a truncated filename by the presence of the pound (#) symbol.

If you are running Mac OS 7.5x, 7.6x, or 8.0x, PC Exchange still recognizes DOS three-character extensions and assigns correct Macintosh application and file types. These versions of PC Exchange cannot recognize Windows long filenames, however; instead, they use the corresponding 8.3 character alias (short) filename that Windows also generates.

If you are running an earlier version of the Mac OS, consider purchasing DOS Mounter95 from Software Architects, which also offers strong support for Windows long filenames on the Macintosh. A time-limited demo version is available on the Web at `www.softarch.com/us/demofiles/dm95_demo_form.html`.

▶ For information on reading Macintosh files on PCs, **see** "Reading Mac OS Office Files on Windows Computers," later in this chapter on **p. 695**.

Ensuring Accurate Document Types on the Macintosh

Macintosh files consist of two parts: a data fork, which contains the contents of a file that a user might see (such as the text and formatting in a word processing document); and a resource fork, which contains information about the file (including the icon bitmap that should appear with it and the program that should be used to open it). In contrast, in DOS and Windows the file extension identifies the program that should open a file.

One common problem with Office document types occurs when multiple versions of Office are installed on the same computer. If you install an earlier version of Office after you install Office 98, you might find that if you double-click a Word, Excel, or PowerPoint document created in Office 2000, the Macintosh might incorrectly open an earlier Office program, such as Word 6, Excel 5, or PowerPoint 4. This is troublesome because of the changes in file formats between versions of Office. A Word 2000 (or Word 97) file cannot be read in Word 6 unless you download and install a special filter, and even then, newer features embedded in the document can easily be lost.

You might also find that you want to associate other types of documents with Word or Excel; for example, you might want to open text files or WordPerfect files in Word instead of in the application you created them with. Or, you might conceivably want to open HTM or HTML files in Word for editing, instead of opening them in Internet Explorer for viewing.

If you find that filenames are being associated with incorrect applications or document types, or that you want to change the applications associated with specific types of files, you can do so. In Mac OS 8.5, you make these adjustments through the PC Exchange tab of the File Exchange Control Panel (shown in Figure 26.2). In versions of Mac OS prior to 8.5, there is a separate PC Exchange Control Panel. Figure 26.3 shows the Mac OS 8.1 version.

FIGURE 26.2

The PC Exchange tab of the Mac OS 8.5 File Exchange Control Panel.

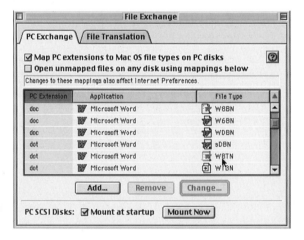

FIGURE 26.3
The PC Exchange
Control Panel in Mac
OS 8.1.

Follow this procedure to change the mapping of a file in Mac OS 8.5:

1. In Mac OS 8.5 or later, open the **Apple** menu, choose **File Exchange** from the list of Control Panel applets, and choose the **PC Exchange** tab.

2. Select a filename extension (PC suffix) you want to change.

3. Click **Change**. The Change Mapping dialog box opens (see Figure 26.4). To show the advanced options at the right, click the **Show Advanced Options** button.

FIGURE 26.4
The Change Mapping
dialog box in Mac OS
8.5, with the advanced
options displayed.

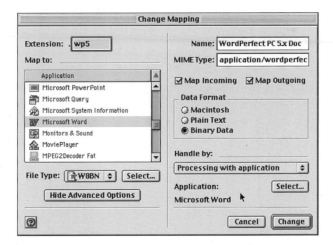

4. From the list of applications at the left, select the application you want to assign to the extension you chose. For example, if you want to assign the extension .wp5 to Microsoft Word, click **Microsoft Word**.

5. Click **Change**. Microsoft Word is now associated with files containing the .wp5 extension.

6. Close the File Exchange Control Panel.

Follow this procedure to change the mapping of a file in Mac OS 8.1:

1. Open the **Apple** menu and choose **PC Exchange** from the list of Control Panels.

2. Select a filename extension (PC suffix) you want to change.

3. Click **Change**. A new dialog box opens (see Figure 26.5).

FIGURE 26.5

Changing the document type associated with a filename extension in Mac OS 8.1.

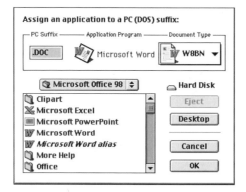

4. In the list of files and folders at the bottom, browse to and select the application you want to assign to the extension you chose. For example, if you want to assign the extension .doc to Word 98, select **Microsoft Word** in the Microsoft Office 98 folder.

5. Click on the current document type and choose a new document type from the list that appears. For example, if you want .doc files to open into Word 98 as documents (and not as templates, for instance), choose **W8BN**.

6. Close the PC Exchange Control Panel.

Table 26.1 lists the most common Office 98 document types.

Table 26.1   Office 97/2000 PC Extensions and Office 98 Macintosh Document Types

PC Extension (Suffix)	Macintosh Document Type
.DIC (Dictionary file)	WDCD
.DOC (Word document)	W8BN
.DOT (Word template)	W8TN
.RTF (Word Rich Text Format)	RTF
.DQY (Microsoft Query file)	DQY
.XLS (Excel Workbook)	XLS8
.XLT (Excel Template)	sLS8
.XLW (Excel Workspace)	XLW8
.XLC (Excel Chart)	XLC
.XLA (Excel Add-In)	XLA8
.PPT (PowerPoint Presentation)	PPT
.PPA (PowerPoint Add-In)	PPPA
.PPS (PowerPoint Slide Show)	PPSS
.POT (PowerPoint Template)	PPOT

Reading Mac OS Office Files on Windows Computers

Windows machines cannot read disks formatted in the Mac OS format. If you need to read disks created on the Macintosh, you have two options. You can format the disks in PC format, either on the Macintosh or on the PC. Alternatively, you can install a third-party program that enables PC floppy disk drives to read Mac OS formatted disks. Such software options include the following:

- MacOpener 3.0 from DataViz (**www.dataviz.com**)
- MacDrive 95 from Media4 Productions (**www.media4.com**)
- Here & Now from Software Architects (**www.softarch.com**)

Note that of these products, MacOpener 3.0 is currently the only one that runs under Windows NT 4.0 (and it also happens to be the least expensive).

Although versions of the Mac OS since 8.1 can store long filenames (up to 32 characters) on PC-formatted disks in a form that can be recognized by Windows, keep in mind that Office and other Macintosh applications typically do not automatically assign extensions to files. This means that Windows systems do not automatically know which programs are associated with a given Macintosh file. You have two options for dealing with this:

- Open the Office (or other application program) first. Display all files in the application's Open dialog box (choose **File**, **Open**, **Files of Type**, **All Files**) so that all files appear whether or not they have the correct extension. Then, choose the file you want to open and click **Open**.
- Require Macintosh users to add DOS and Windows compatible extensions (refer to Table 26.1) to all their document files. If you are running Mac OS 8.1 or later, you can permit long filenames up to 32 characters; otherwise, you should require old-fashioned DOS-style 8.3 filenames.

Networking Windows 95 to Macintosh Peer-to-Peer Solutions

Many small peer-to-peer Ethernet networks are composed of either several PCs with one or a few Macintosh computers, or several Macintosh computers with one or a few PCs. Most of these networks can benefit from simple file-sharing solutions that enable users to share Office files across platforms. Several options exist.

If your network is primarily made up of Macintosh computers with just one or a few PCs, consider PC MacLAN from Miramar Systems (**www.miramarsys.com**). With this Windows software, which enables your PC to speak the AppleTalk networking protocol, Windows PCs can act as file or print servers for Macintosh computers, and vice versa.

If you have one or a few PCs that must access a Macintosh network but it isn't important that the Macintosh computers be able to retrieve information stored on those PCs or print to printers stored on those PCs, consider COPSTalk 2.5 for Windows, recently purchased by

Part

IV

Ch

26

Thursby Software Systems (`www.thursby.com`). After COPSTalk is installed on a Windows PC, Macintosh computers on the Ethernet network appear as part of an Isolated AppleTalk Network available in the Network Neighborhood (shown in Windows Explorer in Figure 26.6).

> **CAUTION**
>
> Note that even with COPSTalk, some characters in Macintosh computer names do not translate accurately in Windows (as the figure shows).

FIGURE 26.6

Macintosh computers are displayed in Network Neighborhood on a Windows PC running COPSTalk.

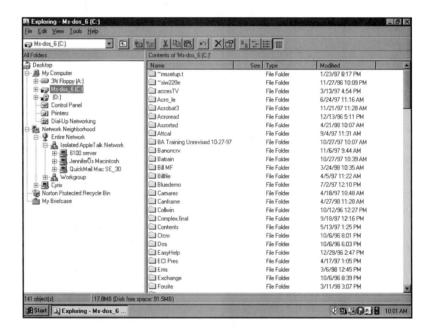

COPSTalk also supports TCP/IP, which means that you can connect your PC to an intranet hosted on a Macintosh server if you've chosen to run TCP/IP alongside (or instead of) the traditional Macintosh AppleTalk protocol. Until recently, COPStalk was a solution strictly for Windows 95/98 computers, but there is now a Windows NT version as well.

If your network is primarily made up of PCs but you have one or two Macintosh computers, consider using Dave 2.1, also from Thursby Software Systems. This software installs on a Macintosh and uses Mac TCP/IP or Windows NetBIOS to connect with Windows 95, 98, NT, or Windows 3.1 PCs. Dave 2.0 enables Macintosh users to see PC drives through the Macintosh Chooser and enables PC users to see Macintosh drives and printers through the Windows Network Neighborhood.

One final option for integrating Macintosh computers and Windows PCs is Timbuktu Pro from Netopia (`www.netopia.com/software/tb2/mac/index.html`), a remote access program that enables Macintosh computers to control Windows PCs (and run Windows software in a window on the Macintosh), or vice versa.

Supporting Macintosh Computers on Windows NT Server Networks

Windows NT Server 4.0 has built-in support for Macintosh clients, making it a natural server solution for cross-platform environments. When you get it running right, Windows NT Server looks like just another Macintosh to the Macintosh client workstations. This section presents a high-level look at what's involved in enabling Macintosh support on Windows NT Server networks. (For a more detailed discussion of connecting Macintosh clients to a Windows NT Server network, see *Using Windows NT Server 4* by Roger Jennings, published by Que Corporation, ISBN: 0-7897-0251-7.)

Start by ensuring that Ethernet is installed and working on all the Macintosh computers you want to connect. If you're not sure, you can check in the AppleTalk Control Panel in Mac OS 7.6 or later (see Figure 26.7).

FIGURE 26.7
The Mac OS 8.5 AppleTalk Control Panel, showing an Ethernet connection.

Of course, be sure the Macintosh computers are physically connected and are connected to the Windows NT Server system you want to use. Finally—and this shouldn't be a problem—be sure that all your Macintosh computers are running at least System 6.07 or later. (Very few of today's business Macintosh computers run Mac OS versions earlier than 7.5x.)

Part
IV

Ch
26

NOTE   Years ago, it was common for low-speed Apple-compatible LocalTalk cards to be installed in PC servers, enabling them to connect with the Macintosh's built-in LocalTalk network connections. However, Ethernet is now virtually universal on Macintosh computers in business, which makes this practice unnecessary.

Occasionally, you might encounter a Laserwriter NTX or a lone Mac SE using its LocalTalk port to connect to the Ethernet through a GatorBox, an earlier product from Cayman Systems (**www.cayman. com**) that is no longer sold. ▦

Next, be sure your Windows NT Server system is up and running properly. It should be updated to the latest Windows NT Service Pack, and it should have at least one partition formatted with NTFS, Windows NT's more sophisticated file system. (In NT Server, NTFS can host Macintosh-accessible volumes; however, old-fashioned FAT partitions cannot.) Using Windows NT's User Manager for Domains utility, create user accounts for the Macintosh users with whom you are working.

Next, install Services for Macintosh on the NT Server system if they are not already installed. On NT Server, choose **Start**, **Settings**, **Control Panel**, and double-click on the **Network** applet. Click the **Services** tab and click **Add**. The Select Network Service dialog box appears (see Figure 26.8). Choose **Services for Macintosh** and click **OK**.

FIGURE 26.8

Beginning the installation of Services for Macintosh on Windows NT Server 4.0.

Windows NT Setup opens, and you're asked to browse to the CD-ROM or network location where the original NT Server disk or files are located. After you copy the files, Windows NT starts the AppleTalk network protocol and asks you to configure it. Depending on the size of your network and whether an AppleTalk router is already present, you might or might not have to enable AppleTalk routing.

When you finish configuring AppleTalk Protocol Properties, you are prompted to restart NT Server. Do so. When NT Server restarts, the Services Control Panel applet lists two new services: File Server for Macintosh and Print Server for Macintosh. In Windows NT Explorer, you also see a new folder installed on your NTFS drive named "Microsoft UAM Volume." This contains the authentication and password encryption software Macintosh computers need to operate securely on an NT network. Later, you will install this software on each Macintosh on your network.

Still on the server, you need to create Macintosh-accessible volumes—shared folders that support Macintosh resource and data forks, as well as the other elements of a typical Macintosh file system. To do so, create and share a new folder using Windows NT Explorer. Next, open NT's Server Manager administration utility; choose the server you're working on; and click **MacFile**, **Volumes**, **Create Volume**. In the **Volume Name** text box, enter the name of the folder you just created and shared. From this dialog box, you can also set security, user limits, and permissions.

After you've done all this, it's time to head back to the Macintosh client workstations. In the Macintosh Chooser, click **AppleShare** to see the network resources available to you. You should see one corresponding to the NT Server system you just set up. Choose that one and click **OK**. Log on with your name and password and browse the available volumes to find **Microsoft UAM Volume**. Click **OK**, and then close the Chooser. A Microsoft UAM Volume icon is now on the Macintosh desktop. Drag it into the System folder. Shut down and restart the Macintosh. Finally, log on again as a Registered User and choose the Macintosh-accessible volume you want to use.

Sending Compressed Files Across Platforms

With the explosion of email, more and more files are transmitted over the Internet—and in many cases, users compress these files first. Unfortunately, Macintosh and Windows compression standards are different. Most Macintosh users work with one of the StuffIt family of products from Aladdin Systems (**`www.aladdinsys.com`**). Most Windows users use the ZIP format originated by PKZIP (**`www.pkzip.com`**) and now most commonly generated by WinZip from Nico Mak Computing (**`www.winzip.com`**).

Aladdin Systems offers a free utility, StuffIt Expander, for both the Macintosh and Windows. This utility is capable of decompressing StuffIt (.sit) files, as well as MacBinary (.bin), BinHex (.hqx), ZIP (.zip), Uuencoded (.uue), and other compressed files. Be sure that your Macintosh uses the latest version of StuffIt available, or you might not be able to unstuff all the .sit files currently being created. If you need to create ZIP files on a Macintosh, consider using the shareware package ZipIt 1.38, available from Tom Brown at **`www.awa.com/softlock/zipit/`**.

Managing Font and Character Set Issues

When moving documents between Windows and the Macintosh, Office administrators need to be aware of issues related to both fonts and character sets.

First, Windows and the Macintosh do not use identical character sets, so a character you type on a Windows machine might not be represented as the same character on a Macintosh, or vice versa. This can especially become a problem if you're creating documents for electronic publishing on the Web or your corporate intranet, where different browsers can interpret the same character differently, even within the same platform. Figure 26.9 shows the characters available in the standard Windows character set. Figure 26.10 shows a document that contains those same characters, as displayed by the Macintosh.

FIGURE 26.9
The Windows character set.

!	"	#	$	%	&	'	(	)	*	+	,	-	.	/	0	1	2	3	4	5	6	7	8	9	:	;	<
=	>	?	@	A	B	C	D	E	F	G	H	I	J	K	L	M	N	O	P	Q	R	S	T	U	V	W	X
Y	Z	[	\	]	^	_	`	a	b	c	d	e	f	g	h	i	j	k	l	m	n	o	p	q	r	s	t
u	v	w	x	y	z	{	|	}	~	¡	¢	£	¤	¥	¦	§	¨	©	ª	«	¬	-	®	¯	°	±	²
³	´	µ	¶	·	¸	¹	º	»	¼	½	¾	¿	À	Á	Â	Ã	Ä	Å	Æ	Ç	È	É	Ê	Ë	Ì	Í	Î
Ï	Ð	Ñ	Ò	Ó	Ô	Õ	Ö	×	Ø	Ù	Ú	Û	Ü	Ý	Þ	ß	à	á	â	ã	ä	å	æ	ç	è	é	ê
ë	ì	í	î	ï	ð	ñ	ò	ó	ô	õ	ö	÷	ø	ù	ú	û	ü	ý	þ	ÿ	Œ	œ	Š	š	Ÿ	ƒ	ˆ
˜	–	—	‘	’	‚	“	”	„	†	‡	•	…	‰	‹	›	™	·										

The best solution is to avoid special characters in cross-platform documents whenever possible. One tip: Choose **Format**, **AutoFormat**, **Options**, click the **AutoFormat As You Type** tab of the AutoCorrect options dialog box, and turn off the **Fractions with Fraction Character** check box.

Other special characters used by Office applications are formatted in the Wingdings TrueType font. Although this font is available on both Windows and Macintosh platforms, many Macintosh users prefer to use the Zapf Dingbats PostScript font instead, especially for documents that are to be printed professionally. Be aware that Wingdings and Zapf Dingbats are different, although a few of the more common characters (such as round bullets) are consistent.

FIGURE 26.10
The characters in the Windows character set as they are displayed on the Macintosh.

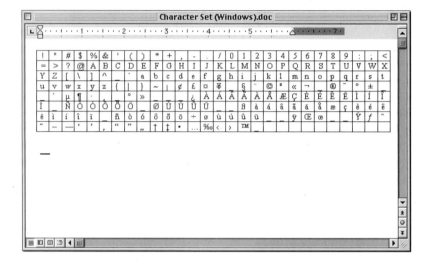

Although Microsoft installs the same TrueType fonts along with both Windows and the Macintosh, other fonts might not be identical across platforms, even if they share the same or similar names. These differences can cause problems in finished documents. If the precise typography of a cross-platform document matters, purchase the identical font from the identical font vendor.

TIP You can find an excellent discussion of differences between the Windows and Macintosh character sets, and their impact on Web pages at **www.hit.net**/**~bobbau**/**platforms**/**specialchars**.

Controlling Font Substitutions Across Platforms

If you move a document across platforms, and a font available on one platform is not available on the other, Word might substitute another font, commonly Times New Roman or Arial. However, you might have another font installed that more closely reflects the appearance you want to display or that uses widths more similar to the original font (and therefore does not increase or decrease your document size as much).

Word enables you to manually control font substitutions in any file where a font substitution has been made. To do so, follow these steps:

1. Choose **Tools**, **Options**, and click the **Compatibility** tab.
2. Click **Font Substitution**. (If this option is grayed out, no fonts are substituted in your current document.) The Font Substitution dialog box opens (as shown in Figure 26.11).
3. Under **Missing document font**, select the missing font for which you want to assign a different substitute.
4. Select the substituted font you prefer to use in the **Substituted font** drop-down box.
5. Click **OK**.

FIGURE 26.11
The Font Substitution
dialog box.

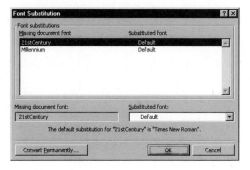

Although the original font name is preserved (in case you move the file back to a computer that contains that font), the document instead displays the substituted font you chose.

TIP   If you never expect to move the document back to its original computer, you can click **Convert Permanently** in the Font Substitution dialog box, and Word reformats any text in the document to use the fonts you have substituted. The original font names are no longer present.

Managing Differences in the Windows and Macintosh Color Palette

If you are using Office applications such as Microsoft Photo Editor for Windows to create images that are used in cross-platform environments, you need to be aware of differences in the color palettes used by the two platforms. This is especially an issue for intranet and Web work, but it can crop up in any application in which you must see accurate colors on the screen in a cross-platform environment.

Only 216 colors are shared between Windows and the Macintosh. If you use other colors, they are dithered and will look different from what you intended—often much worse. None of the Office applications are capable of designing around this 216-color palette. If you use Office applications to generate images for the Web or your corporate intranet and you expect your audience to use both Windows and Macintosh systems, at minimum, check your images in both environments before deploying them.

TIP   For a detailed look at the issue of browser-safe Web color palettes, visit **msdn.microsoft.com/ workshop/design/color/safety.asp**.

If you're serious about color on the Web, consider the shareware package ColorSafe from BoxTopSoft (**www.boxtopsoft.com**), which maps images using millions of hybrid colors formed by combining four pixels of two different colors that are common to both the Macintosh and Windows platforms.

ColorSafe, available for both the Macintosh and Windows, works as a filter plug-in to Adobe Photoshop and a wide variety of image-editing applications that support Photoshop 2.5 plug-ins. These include the low-cost Paint Shop Pro shareware package from Jasc (`www.jasc.com`), as well as Microsoft Image Composer 1.5, a free add-on included with Microsoft FrontPage 98.

Controlling Subtle Differences Between Word 98 and Word 5.1 for the Macintosh

Over the years, Microsoft has made a number of subtle changes to how Word functions, which might not be obvious to even the expert user. Some of these changes might cause documents to behave in unexpected ways. For instance, in Word 5.1 for the Macintosh, small caps appear larger than they do in later versions of Word.

If you have carefully designed a document in an earlier version of Word, such as Word 5.1 for the Macintosh, and you move it to a newer version of Word, you might not want these settings to change. Word enables you to preserve settings such as these through the Compatibility tab of the Options dialog box, shown in Figure 26.12 (choose **Tools**, **Options**, **Compatibility**).

FIGURE 26.12
The Compatibility tab of the Options dialog box.

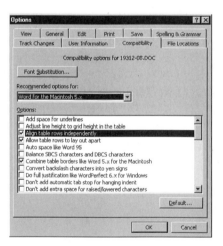

In the **Recommended options for** drop-down box, choose the version of Word with which you want to remain compatible. Word displays the setting changes it makes. You can clear any of the selected check boxes. Click **OK**, and Word reformats the document to reflect these changes.

N O T E   This is not purely a cross-platform feature. You can adjust Word 2000 for Windows documents to reflect Word 2 for Windows formatting just as easily as you can make this change in Word 5.x for the Macintosh. Given the widespread use of Word 5.x for the Macintosh for nearly a decade, however, and the great popularity of Office 2000 for Windows, this feature is likely to prove especially helpful to cross-platform Office administrators. ■

Managing Microsoft Publisher 2000

by Bill Camarda

So far, this book has focused primarily on managing the applications at the heart of Microsoft Office 2000: Word, Excel, Access, PowerPoint, and Outlook. In addition, Chapter 11 covered customizing FrontPage 2000 to meet the needs of your organization.

The next two chapters help you understand and manage several other applications included with some (but not every) edition of Office 2000. This chapter focuses on Microsoft Publisher 2000, a desktop publishing program designed specifically for business users rather than graphic designers, but now enhanced with several important features needed for professional-quality publishing. Microsoft Publisher 2000 is included in all editions of Office 2000 except the Standard Edition.

▶ For more information about working with PhotoDraw and Small Business Tools, **see** Chapter 28, "Managing Microsoft PhotoDraw and Small Business Tools," on **p. 727**.

Evaluating Microsoft Publisher 2000

Microsoft Publisher 2000 offers superior desktop publishing power for mere mortals. It includes built-in wizards for creating newsletters, brochures, flyers, business stationery and forms, awards, certificates, and many other types of publications. Using these wizards, you and your colleagues can create publications in a wide range of styles and formats, doing the "design work" in a matter of minutes. You can even adapt your print publication to serve as a Web site with built-in hyperlinks; this is widely known as *repurposing*.

 TIP Publisher 2000 even comes with Design Sets that make it easy for you to create consistent, matching publications to meet the needs of your entire organization.

As remarkable as Publisher 2000 is, it also has significant limitations you should be aware of as an Office administrator, some of which arise as side effects of its power:

■ *Problem:* Although it's very likely that Publisher's wizards can create publications to meet your needs, if they cannot, you're at a disadvantage because Publisher's "from-scratch" design tools are more limited than those of high-end desktop publishing software. Sophisticated users might find themselves in need of features that aren't available, or you might find that business professionals are spending more time designing newsletters and data sheets than you would like them to.

Recommendation: Establish rules as to how Publisher should and should not be used in your company. For example, you might limit the use of Publisher 2000 to creating in-house newsletters or low-cost "spot color" work, and leave high-end work to your professional designers using QuarkXPress, Adobe PageMaker, or Adobe InDesign. Or, you might provide tested Publisher templates that product managers and marketing professionals can use to quickly create product sheets and other standard documents—thereby leveraging Publisher's simplicity while eliminating the need for extensive custom design.

■ *Problem:* As discussed later in this chapter in the section "Finding Print Resources for Business with Publisher 2000," it can be difficult to find a commercial printer that's willing to work with native Microsoft Publisher files. Commercial color printing is inherently complex. Although Publisher has simplified the design end of the process, your business users might find themselves confronting a complex world of prepress issues they are unfamiliar with, where small errors can quickly become extremely expensive.

Recommendation: If you want to use Publisher for midrange-to-sophisticated design projects, find a printer that's willing to work closely with you on up-front testing to ensure that Publisher's files work as intended. Microsoft has established a program, the *Publisher Service Provider Program*, intended to recruit commercial printers and copy shops to work with native Publisher files. As of June 1999, however, the database of suppliers has not yet been posted, and when it is, it might or might not list any companies in your area. (Check at **www.microsoft.com/office/publisher/default.htm**.) As you will learn in more detail later, you can provide PostScript files as a fallback position, but your printer will not be able to edit these files if a problem is discovered.

■ *Problem:* Although Publisher 2000 offers an exceptionally easy way to create static Web sites, it provides no way to edit HTML source code. When you work in Publisher, your files are stored in the native .pub Publisher format. When you are ready to publish Web pages, you choose **File**, **Create Web Site from Current Publication**. Publisher then builds HTML pages and other graphics from your .pub file. The problem? If you want to make even the smallest change to your site, you must republish all your pages from scratch. (See the section "Assessing the Conversion of Publisher Files to Web Sites," later in this chapter, for some specific issues that can make it necessary to republish pages.)

Recommendation: Limit your Web work in Publisher to low-end or departmental sites (or parts of sites) that rarely need to be updated. Some users create new sites using Publisher and then import them into FrontPage 2000 where they can edit, maintain, and manage the sites. Of course, after the first time you import Publisher's pages to another Web editor, you can no longer work with them in Publisher, which cannot import HTML files.

Depending on the nature of your Publisher print publications, consider finding another technique for repurposing them on the Web, or try saving (or "scanning") print publications in Adobe Acrobat PDF format and creating links to Acrobat pages—making the free Adobe Acrobat reader available to your viewers if they do not already own it.

■ *Problem:* Although Publisher's Web Forms feature is very seductive to users, it requires you or your Internet service provider to install the latest version of FrontPage Server Extensions. FrontPage obviously has the same problem, but many Internet service providers nevertheless do not make FrontPage Extensions available to their customers.

Recommendation: Either limit your Publisher-created sites to those created on servers that use FrontPage Extensions or simply avoid using forms on these sites.

Customizing Publisher 2000 During Installation

The default Publisher 2000 installation includes all Publisher's new commercial printing features. If you do not intend to use Publisher for commercial printing, you can choose Customize in the Publisher Setup program and clear the check boxes associated with the following two features:

■ **Enhanced RGB to CMYK Conversion,** which converts RGB screen colors to CMYK ink colors used in commercial printing

■ **PANTONE libraries,** which provides support for the ink colors used by most commercial printers

By default, two additional features are installed on first use:

■ **Mail Merge,** which adds the capability to run mail merges for printing individually customized brochures, newsletters, and other materials, or for including individual recipients' addresses directly on your printed materials

■ **PaperDirect Previews,** a set of online previews that show how finished publications will look if printed on PaperDirect's specialty papers, which already include color and formatting

Part

IV

Ch

27

By default, Publisher's large library of Background Textures are marked Not Available.

TIP If you need detailed information about specific files in Publisher 2000, download PubInfo.exe from the Office 2000 Resource Kit Toolbox at `www.Microsoft.com/office/ork/2000/appndx/toolbox.htm`.

Working with Publisher 2000

The following sections outline the tools you need to manage Publisher. You'll learn how to perform the following tasks:

- Create a basic publication with Publisher
- Create a custom template you can provide to all your colleagues, thereby helping to standardize your publications companywide
- Use Publisher 2000 and Microsoft Word 2000 together
- Prepare Publisher publications for a commercial service bureau or printer

Creating a Basic Publication with Publisher 2000

When you finish installation, it is extremely easy to create the framework for a publication with Publisher 2000. The following procedure builds the framework of a newsletter:

1. Open Publisher, and Publisher's Catalog of publications appears (see Figure 27.1).

FIGURE 27.1
Microsoft Publisher 2000 provides an extensive choice of publication wizards to streamline production.

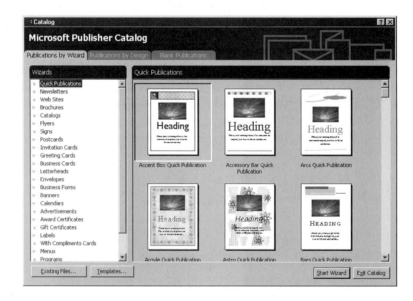

2. In the Wizards scroll box, choose **Newsletters** if it is not already chosen.

3. Scroll through the Newsletters box, and click the newsletter you want to use as your model. Publisher offers 34 options.

4. Click **Start Wizard** to begin the process of customizing your layout. Publisher creates a default newsletter (see Figure 27.2); as you walk through the wizard, Publisher adjusts the newsletter on-the-fly to show you the changes you're making.

FIGURE 27.2
The Newsletter Wizard starts, allowing you to customize the newsletter layout that appears in the Preview window.

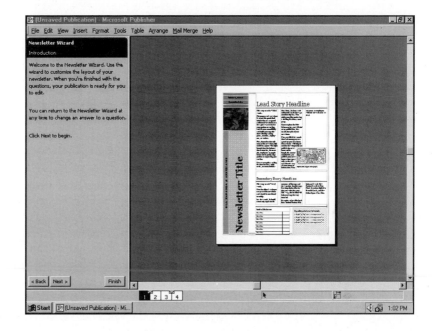

5. If you're using Publisher for the first time, you'll be asked to provide information about yourself and your company (see Figure 27.3). Publisher can automatically use this information in all the publications it creates from now on. You can actually provide four sets of information here: Primary Business, Secondary Business, Other Organization, and Home/Family.

6. Click **Next**.

7. Publisher offers 62 color schemes—sets of colors that are guaranteed to harmonize well (see Figure 27.4). Choose a color scheme and click **Next**.

8. Next, you're asked to specify how many columns your newsletter will have: one, two, or three. Choose the number of columns and click **Next**.

9. Decide whether you want a placeholder for the customer's address, such as whether you want to make space on the back of your newsletter for a mailing label. Choose **Yes** or **No**, and then click **Next**.

10. Choose **Single-sided** or **Double-sided** to indicate whether you will print on one or both sides of the paper, and then click **Finish**.

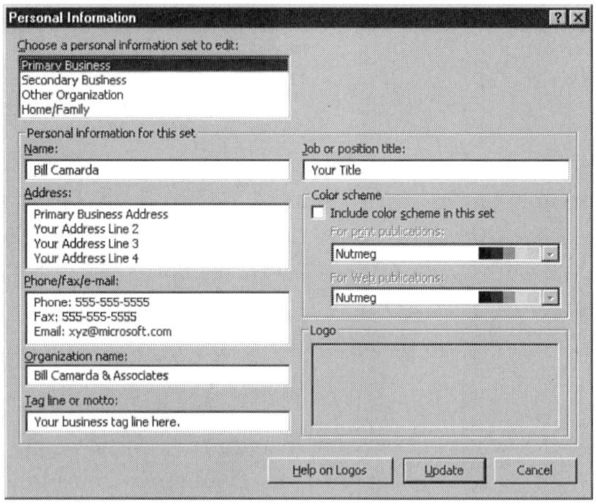

FIGURE 27.3

You can enter information about yourself and your company.

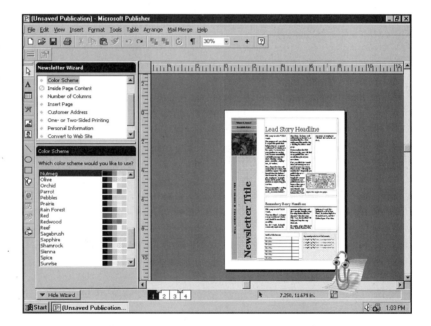

FIGURE 27.4

In this window, you can choose a color scheme from Publisher's 62 available sets of colors.

11. Choose the set of custom information about you and your company that you want to use: the Primary Business information, Secondary Business information, information associated with Other Organization, or Home/Family information.

12. The wizard finishes making changes to your layout and displays the finished layout in the Workspace window.

When the framework for your newsletter is in place, you can edit the publication, replacing default graphics and text with your own.

Notice that Publisher has already placed newsletter titles, volume and issue numbers, tables of contents, captions, callouts, and other copy elements. Before you print the final publication, you'll want to double-check to verify that you've replaced them all with "real" copy and deleted any leftovers.

Replacing a Boilerplate Graphic with a New Graphic

It's easy to select any of the "boilerplate" images Publisher places in your publication and replace it with one of your own. Here's how:

1. Right-click on an image; the shortcut menu appears.
2. Choose **Change Picture**, **Picture**, **From File**. The Insert Picture File dialog box opens.
3. Browse to the file you want to insert and click **OK**. If your new picture is a different size from the one that was there before, Publisher automatically rewraps text to accommodate it.

Replacing Boilerplate Text with New Text

Similarly, it's easy to replace Publisher's boilerplate text with your own newsletter copy. To do so, follow these steps:

1. Click inside any *frame* (section of text) to select all the boilerplate text.
2. Choose **Insert**, **Text File**. The Insert Text File dialog box opens.
3. Browse to the file you want to insert and click **OK**.

If your file is longer than the space available, Publisher offers to AutoFlow it into other text frames or even create new pages as needed.

 TIP
The boilerplate text in each large text frame tells you how many words will fit there, which makes it easier for you to adjust your copy to fit. And if you have time to read the boilerplate text, you'll find useful tips on creating your publication.

Publisher can import text in a variety of formats, including Word 2000/97, Word 6.0/95, RTF, Word 4.0 through 5.1 for the Macintosh, Windows Write, Microsoft Works 3.0 or 4.0 for Windows, WordPerfect 5.x/6.x, WordStar, Microsoft Excel, Lotus 1-2-3, and, of course, other Publisher publications.

Part
IV

Ch

27

Linking and Embedding Material from Other Office Applications into a Presentation

You can also use Object Linking and Embedding to insert part or all of a Word document, Excel worksheet, PowerPoint presentation or other OLE-compatible document into a Publisher presentation. The following steps outline the procedure to use:

1. In the source application, select whatever you want to include.
2. Press **Ctrl+C** to copy it to the Clipboard.

3. Click **Microsoft Publisher** in the taskbar (or load Publisher if it isn't already running).

4. In Publisher, click the frame where you want the item to be pasted.

5. Choose **Edit**, **Paste Special**. The Paste Special dialog box opens (see Figure 27.5).

6. To *embed* the Clipboard contents so they cannot change if the source document changes, click the **Paste** button and click **OK**. (You may also get to choose which form you want the materials to be embedded in.) If you prefer to *link* with the Clipboard contents so your Publisher publication *does* reflect changes made to the source document in the future, click **Paste Link** and click **OK**.

FIGURE 27.5

Linking or embedding material from another Office application.

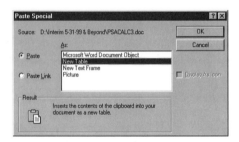

Using Word and Publisher Together

Microsoft Word and Microsoft Publisher are tightly linked. In the section "Replacing Boilerplate Text with New Text" earlier in this chapter, you learned that you can import documents from several versions of Word into Publisher via the **Insert**, **Text File** command. When you do so, Word's styles and most of its Font formatting remain intact.

CAUTION

Not all Word formatting survives. For example, headers and footers are lost, as are the Animation effects available through the Animation tab of Word's Font dialog box.

Conversely, after you import text into Publisher, you might want to edit it with Word—a program truly designed for editing. To do so, follow these steps:

1. Right-click on the text frame. The shortcut menu appears.

2. Choose **Change Text**, **Edit Story in Microsoft Word**. Word opens, displaying Paste Special dialog box the contents of the text frame.

3. Edit the text as desired.

4. When you're finished editing, choose Paste Special dialog box **File**, **Close & Return**. Word closes, and your edits are reflected in your Publisher publication.

Creating Web Pages from Your Publisher Publication

When your publication is ready to go, you can convert it to a set of Web pages with hyperlinks. The quickest way to do this is with the Convert to Web Site Wizard. However, users can also work within Publisher to add their own hyperlinks and create their own Web layouts manually. To run the Convert to Web Site Wizard, follow these steps:

1. Choose **File, Create Web Site from Current Publication**. The Convert To Web Site dialog box opens (see Figure 27.6).

FIGURE 27.6
The Convert To Web Site dialog box.

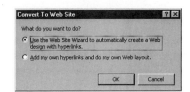

2. Choose **Use the Web Site Wizard to automatically create a Web design with hyperlinks**. Publisher creates a new Publisher document that contains hyperlinks and other Web elements; this new document is based on the existing Publisher print document you have been working on.

    Publisher might replace some standard graphics with animated GIFs that display brief animations when users browse to your page. Publisher might also reformat your page to be narrower because default Web browsers cannot see documents as wide as a typical newsletter or full-size brochure.

3. Choose **File, Save** to save the duplicate file in Publisher. Until you do so, the file is not saved in *any* format and could be lost in the event of a power failure or system crash.

4. The Web Site Wizard appears in the left column (see Figure 27.7). By clicking on the appropriate Wizard item, you can change any of the elements the wizard can control, including the following:

    - Site design
    - Site color schemes
    - Types of forms included (forms require updated FrontPage Server extensions)
    - Types of navigation bars
    - Additional pages not included in the print document
    - Background sounds (in most Web-compatible audio formats, including .wav, .mid, .au, and .aif—but *not* streaming formats such as RealMedia or Microsoft NetShow)
    - Background textures
    - Personal information (about you and your business—as discussed earlier)

FIGURE 27.7
You can make changes in your site with the Web Site Wizard, which appears at the left side of the screen.

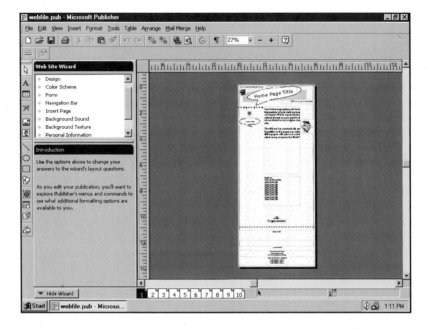

N O T E The Web Site Wizard also contains a Convert to Print option that allows you to reformat your Web site as a print document at any time, creating a duplicate copy with settings designed to work in a print environment.

5. Make any manual adjustments to your Web page that you believe are necessary by using Publisher's editing and formatting tools.

CAUTION

See the following section to learn about some elements that need to be checked and fixed before you convert a Publisher file to HTML.

6. Choose **Tools**, **Design Checker**. Publisher runs the Design Checker (see Figure 27.8), which steps through your Web site one page at a time, identifying potential improvements you could make to your layout, as well as pages that might load too slowly in users' browsers. Choose **Explain** for a detailed explanation of its suggestions.

7. Choose **File**, **Web Properties** to enter information about your site and individual Web pages.

    For example, on the Site tab (see Figure 27.9), you can specify **Keywords** and **Description** that then appear as hidden *metatags*. Web search engines can use these metatags to accurately index your site. You can also specify whether to target your site to people with newer browsers (choose **Microsoft Internet Explorer or Netscape Navigator 4.0+ or later**) or to target a wider range of browsers (choose **Microsoft Internet Explorer or Netscape Navigator 3.0+ or later**).

On the Page tab (see Figure 27.10), you can specify filenames and extensions for each page, as well as the titles that appear in users' browsers when they visit the page. All these site and page settings become part of the HTML code Publisher creates.

FIGURE 27.8
The Design Checker flags possible problems with your design.

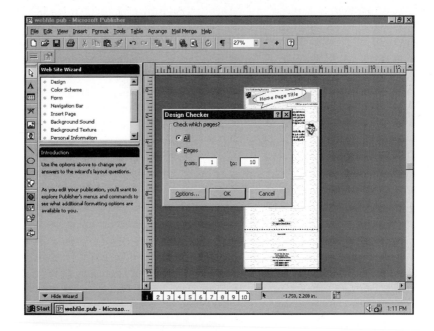

FIGURE 27.9
Specifying properties for your entire site, such as metatags.

8. Choose **File**, **Web Page Preview** to preview either the current page or your entire Web site in Microsoft Internet Explorer (see Figure 27.11). This can take some time because Publisher must actually build new HTML pages to display this preview.

9. When you've finished perfecting your Web pages, choose **File**, **Save as Web Page** (see Figure 27.12) to create the HTML pages, links, graphics, and other elements that will actually be "published" to the Web.

FIGURE 27.10
Specifying properties for individual pages, such as titles and file-names.

FIGURE 27.11
Previewing your pages in Internet Explorer 5.

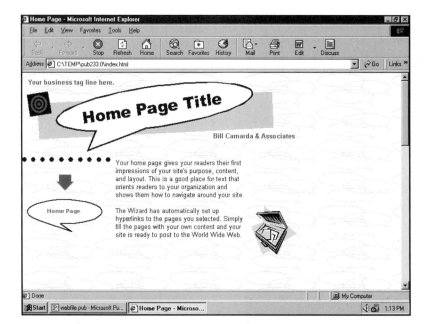

FIGURE 27.12
Saving Publisher files as Web HTML pages, graphics, and hyper-links.

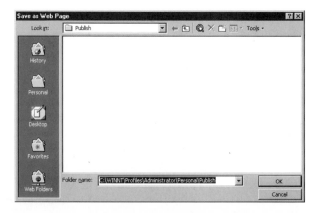

Assessing the Conversion of Publisher Files to Web Sites

If you repurpose Publisher print materials for the Web, you might encounter problems where HTML-based Web pages do not support features in your print design.

For instance, if you use custom line spacing, such as 6 points after paragraphs, this will be lost in Publisher's Web pages. Worse, Publisher can become confused by the inconsistent spacing and might place text hyperlinks slightly higher or lower than they should be placed. The hyperlinks would then fail to work properly.

The solution for this particular problem is to reformat pages with extra lines between paragraphs *before* you convert them to HTML. More broadly, the solution is to check your document manually before conversion to check for potential issues—and then check equally carefully after the conversion.

Table 27.1 lists some specific areas where you might encounter conversion problems, and what to do about them:

Table 27.1   Potential Problems in Publisher 2000 Web Conversions

Feature	Issue
Alignment	Justified text is unavailable in HTML, but you would rarely want to use it, anyway: Most HTML documents look best left-aligned.
Borders/ BorderArt	If you target your Web pages for 4.x browsers, these pages are stored in cascading style sheets; you might want to double-check that they are displayed properly in Netscape Navigator 4.x. If you target for 3.x browsers, Publisher transforms BorderArt into GIF graphics, which preserve your layout but lengthen download times. Use this feature sparingly on Web pages.
Bullets/ Numbered lists	Some advanced options are not supported, but Publisher can create basic numbered and bulleted lists that survive export to HTML.
Columns	HTML doesn't support multiple columns; you might want to manually recast these as tables or separate linked pages.
Drop shadows	These are preserved, but many browsers cannot handle them. In general, do not use drop shadows on text frames in Web pages.
Font effects	HTML doesn't allow for text with any of the following effects: shadowing, small caps, outlining, embossing, engraving, double-underlining, or other custom underlining. Custom underlining is converted to single underlining, which should usually be avoided except for hyperlinks. Use italic or boldface instead.
Font size	Although print-based Publisher documents can be formatted in any type size up to 999 points, HTML supports only seven type sizes. Publisher converts your type size to the closest HTML equivalent. If you must have a large headline, embed the text in a GIF graphic using WordArt or another technique. (In some cases, as when you superimpose your headline over a graphic, Publisher does this for you automatically.)

Part

IV

Ch

27

continues

Table 27.1   Continued

Feature	Issue
Fonts	You can format print documents with any font you want. When you convert your documents to Web pages, Publisher embeds <FONT FACE> commands requesting the same fonts. If those are not available, default fonts will be substituted—which could cause problems with your design. Change unusual fonts to standard fonts such as Arial and Times New Roman before you convert to Web pages. If you must have a non-standard font—possibly for a headline—consider embedding it in a GIF image using WordArt or another technique.
Hyphenation	Forget hyphenating your documents: HTML doesn't support either manual or automatic hyphenation, and different browsers break lines in different ways. If a block of text simply *must* be hyphenated, save it as a GIF graphic.
Indents	HTML doesn't support indents. If you need them, you can change the dimensions of the text frame containing the indented text.
Kerning/tracking	This feature doesn't exist in HTML. If it's absolutely critical that you use it (as in a custom headline), save the headline as a GIF graphic.
Line spacing	As mentioned earlier in this chapter, HTML uses single line spacing; if you do not do the same in your documents, your hyperlinks might not work properly. If paragraphs must be separated, separate them with an extra line of space (using an extra paragraph mark).
Table and object fill colors	If you target your Web pages for 4.x browsers, these pages are stored in cascading style sheets; you might want to double-check that they are displayed properly in Netscape Navigator 4.x. If you target for 3.x browsers, Publisher transforms text with fill colors into GIF graphics, which preserve your layout but lengthen download times.
Tables	Tables translate well, but be sure your users are working with browsers that support them (typically 3.x and later).
Tabs	HTML doesn't recognize tabs, so you'll need to strip them out and organize tabbed text as tables.
Text color	Publisher preserves the text colors you specify, but you should check unusual text colors carefully on a variety of browsers, platforms, and monitors—they might not always appear as you expect.
Text rotation	HTML doesn't support this, so Publisher converts rotated text into GIF graphics.

If you are targeting your site for an intranet, you normally choose whichever browser your intranet uses. For example, if you have installed Internet Explorer 5 throughout your company along with your Office 2000 deployment, you can choose Microsoft Internet Explorer 4.0 or Netscape Navigator 4.0 or later. If you do, Publisher formats your document using Cascading Style Sheets and DHTML.

Be aware that Internet Explorer and Netscape Navigator do not always render CSS/DHTML pages identically. If your audience includes Navigator 4.x (or later) users as well, you should test the pages Publisher generates to see whether they are acceptable.

The alternative setting, Microsoft Internet Explorer or Netscape Navigator 3.0 or later, is the fallback most commonly used when you do not have control over your viewers' browsers—for instance, if you are publishing a public Web site, or an intranet that must serve multiple divisions, or an extranet that reaches selected customers and suppliers.

If you build a Web site targeted for 3.x browsers, Publisher "works around" the absence of CSS/DHTML by transforming text into GIF graphics wherever the text is superimposed on (or very close to) a graphic in your layout. *The result can be that large graphics files download very slowly. Moreover, graphics cannot be indexed by search engines, making it less likely that your pages will appear at search sites.*

You can identify these problems using Design Checker, and in some cases you can manually reformat pages to avoid the problem. However, if you use one of Publisher's built-in wizards, you are likely to find that the problem occurs repeatedly, with no easy fix.

Working with Commercial Printing Firms to Print Your Publisher 2000 Files

If you are preparing a publication for commercial printing, Publisher 2000 provides stronger support than ever before, including new tools for preparing a job for printing. Nevertheless, commercial printing with Publisher remains challenging. In the following sections, you'll learn about:

- The new commercial printing tools Microsoft provides
- How to find a commercial printer that's willing to work with Publisher files (and what to do if you can't)
- Some early problems printers have had working with Publisher 2000 files, and where to find out about the workarounds

Using Publisher 2000 Features and Tools for Successful Commercial Printing

Publisher 2000 contains several new features and tools designed to simplify commercial printing and enhance the results you can achieve. These tools and features include the following:

- **The Pack and Go Wizard,** which makes sure your printer gets all the files needed to print your job correctly.
- **Color separation support,** which is needed for full-color printing involving photography and many other images.

- **Automatic and Manual Trapping,** which allows printers to compensate for slight misalignments ("misregistration") in the printing process by adding slight overlaps that prevent the misalignment from being noticed. (Choose **Tools**, **Commercial Printing Tools**, **Trapping**.)

- **Support for several leading color models,** including PANTONE, CMYK, HSL, and RGB.

- **Graphics and font management tools** (available through the **Tools**, **Commercial Printing Tools** menu) that help you control the contents and elements of your publication.

No matter which tools Publisher provides, however, keep in mind that it is essential for you to consult with a representative from your commercial printing company as early in the process as possible.

Finding Print Resources for Business with Publisher 2000

Unfortunately, as easy as it is to create publications with Microsoft Publisher, it can be equally challenging to find a professional service bureau or printer that works with them. Many Macintosh-oriented service bureaus and printers refuse to work with Publisher files, primarily because those files are unfamiliar, but also because they have in the past occasionally proved troublesome.

Microsoft has committed to providing an online database of firms that work with Publisher files; this database has not been posted yet, but is expected to appear at `www.microsoft.com/office/publisher/default.htm`.

If you find that no service bureau in your area will work with you, the following resources may help:

- Victor Printing Service Bureau, Sharon, PA
  (`www.victorptg.com/service.html`, 800-443-2845)

- Newburyport Press Service Bureau, Newburyport, MA
  (`www.newburyportpress.com/homey.html`, 800-491-4700)

- RAM Offset, White City, Oregon
  (`www.ramoffset.com`, 800-352-6888)

- Megaprint (for oversized graphics only), Holderness, NH
  (`www.megaprint.com`, 800-590-7850)

The national printing chain Sir Speedy (`www.sirspeedy.com`) has many franchisees that work with Publisher files. Two other companies, Printovation (`www.printovation.com`) and Deluxe (`www.deluxe.com`) also print Publisher files but with one major limitation: You must use their predefined templates. Finally, in British Columbia, Canada, Mike Bailey (`www3.bc.sympatico.ca/mikeb/Mikeb.htm`) runs a business that specializes in creating reliable PostScript files from Microsoft Publisher documents.

TIP A detailed guide to preparing Publisher files that output to film well is located at
`http://www.ramoffset.com//mspub.htm`.

Deciding Whether to Send Native Publisher Files or PostScript Files

When you're preparing a project for commercial printing, the most important question your printer can help you answer is this: Should I deliver native Publisher files or PostScript files?

From your standpoint, it is more convenient to deliver native Publisher files. You can then use the Pack and Go Wizard to bundle together all the fonts, graphics, and document files your printer needs—and let the printer worry about the specific document settings needed to output the job properly. In addition, if you provide native Publisher files, your printer can handle minor changes to the source files if that's necessary. For example, if a word needs to be fixed or an image must be replaced at the last minute, the printer can do it without sending the project back to you.

However, as we've said, most printers are unfamiliar with Microsoft Publisher 2000 and might not want to accept files in Publisher format. The fallback position is to provide the files in PostScript format. Adobe PostScript is a standard *page description language* that incorporates all the document information needed to create film and plates, including color and font information, graphics data, positioning, and so forth. Most graphics and desktop publishing programs can create PostScript files, which makes PostScript a common language for the graphics arts world.

Creating PostScript files is not in and of itself difficult; you simply print to a file using a PostScript printer driver, as is described later in the section titled "Creating a PostScript File for Your Printer." However, *you* become responsible for all the document settings and elements that are included in your PostScript file, because your printer has no way to change them. Many of these settings, such as trapping, require detailed guidance from your printer.

Using the Pack and Go Wizard to Deliver Native Publisher Files

When you find a printer or service bureau that works with native Publisher files, you're ready to take the following steps:

1. Consult with your printer on how he or she wants to have the files delivered, and on any special issues associated with graphics, fonts, or printer drivers. Be sure you understand the process and workflow that are used to get your document ready for printing—and the costs.

2. Install the Windows PostScript printer driver your commercial printer wants you to use. This might be a Linotronic 330 printer driver, an Apple LaserWriter NT II printer driver, or a printer driver associated with a specific imagesetter—in which case, your service bureau or printer might provide it. After you've installed the printer driver, select it. You might need to make adjustments in your publication to reflect the slight (or not-so-slight) changes this can cause in layout.

3. Choose **Tools**, **Design Checker** to try to identify any problems that might arise when printing your job, and when problems are identified, fix them (or at least note them for discussion with your printer).

4. Choose **File**, **Pack and Go Wizard**, **Take to a Commercial Printing Service**, and click **Next** to begin working with the Pack and Go Wizard (see Figure 27.13).

FIGURE 27.13

Starting the Pack and Go Wizard.

5. You're asked where you want to store the files; the default location is the A:\ floppy drive. Browse to and select the location you want to use. If you have a removable disk, such as a Zip disk, you'll usually want to use that instead, because print files can often be too large to fit on one floppy—or even several. After you select the location you want to use, click **Next**.

6. You're asked which elements you want to include with your package (see Figure 27.14). In general, you want all three (fonts, linked graphics, and links for embedded graphics) on the disk. If your printer already has up-to-date copies of all the graphics you want to use, clear the check box that says **Create links for embedded graphics** and allow the printer to use their own copies of the graphics.

FIGURE 27.14

Specifying what to include in your Pack and Go package.

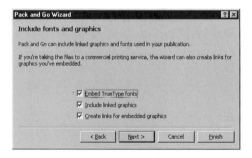

7. Click **Next** and then **Finish**. Publisher compresses your files into a file named Packed01.puz and places that file in the folder you requested. If it must divide the file into several pieces, it names them Packed02.puz, Packed03.puz, and so on. Publisher also places a utility, Unpack.exe, on the same disk. The printer can double-click Unpack.exe to decompress all the files into a single folder that can be used to prepare film and other prepress work.

8. After packing the file, the Wizard asks whether you want to print a composite. This is a single set of pages that show the job as you ultimately want it to appear, including all colors. You might also be asked to print separations—separate sets of pages in each of the four colors that are used in "four-color" (process) printing—Cyan, Magenta, Yellow, and Black. You should print these as well because they can help your printer identify problems by comparing blueprints and film against your "official" version of what each plate should look like.

Delivering PostScript Files Using the Pack and Go Wizard

If your commercial printer has requested that you provide a PostScript file instead of a native Publisher file, follow these steps:

1. Follow steps 1–3 in the previous section (discuss your job with your printer, establish the settings you need, and run the Design Checker to flag potential problems).

2. Choose **File**, **Save As** to display the Save As dialog box. Browse to the location where you want to store the file.

3. From the **Save as Type** drop-down box, choose **PostScript (*.ps)**, and then click **Save**. The Save As PostScript File dialog box opens (see Figure 27.15).

FIGURE 27.15
The Save As PostScript File dialog box.

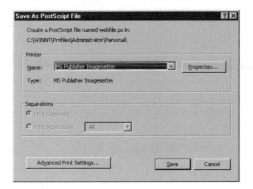

4. Choose the PostScript printer driver you want to use: either MS Publisher Imagesetter or a driver your printer has given you.

5. Click **Advanced Print Settings** and make any changes your printer has requested in the two tabs of the Print Settings dialog box (see Figures 27.16 and 27.17). Click **OK**.

6. When you're returned to the Save As PostScript File dialog box, click **Save**. Microsoft Publisher builds the PostScript file. This might take some time: It is common for PostScript files to be two or three (or more) times as large as the Publisher files they were created from.

Part
IV

Ch
27

FIGURE 27.16

PostScript publication settings are stored in the Publication Options tab of the Print Settings dialog box.

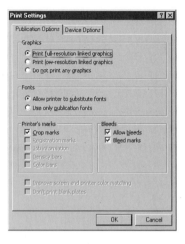

FIGURE 27.17

PostScript printer-related settings are stored in the Device Options tab of the Print Settings dialog box.

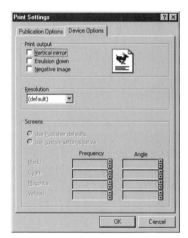

CAUTION

After you create a PostScript file, you cannot make changes to your document's contents. So, be sure the document is correct before you take this step.

Note that if your regular business laser or inkjet printer is not a PostScript printer, there might be slight discrepancies between the file you create for your printer and the files you print on your business printer. Ask your printer to see a proof created on a PostScript printer before you approve a job to be printed. And if you happen to have a PostScript printer available on your network, use it if possible throughout the publication process.

7. Deliver your PostScript file to your printer, either on disk or via modem. (If you use a zip drive or similar device, first be sure your printer has a compatible drive to read it with.)

Reviewing Prepress Problems Reported by Microsoft

Early users of Microsoft Publisher 2000 have reported some problems associated with successfully creating film for printing. These problems and their solutions are discussed at Microsoft's Publisher 2000 Known Issues and Workarounds page (`officeupdate.Microsoft.com/publisher/prepress/issuenavpage.htm`).

In some cases, the solutions require adjustments to Publisher settings that you might be required to make yourself. In other cases, they might require adjustments to settings on the output device your print shop uses. As of September 1999, these issues that were covered included the following:

- Black Separation Plate May Not Print on Scitex Imagesetter
- Composite PostScript Files from Publisher 2000 Are Always RGB
- Errors When Printing Separations to a Panther Pro Imagesetter
- Partially Transparent Bitmaps in EPS Files May Separate Incorrectly
- Preseparated Plate May Print As 16 Plates
- Unwanted Empty Black Plate Prints to Color Separations
- Publisher Can't Trap Adobe Type 1 Fonts on Windows 95 or 98
- Traps Automatically Applied to Text May Be Half of Width Set by User
- Black in WordArt Object Always Overprints
- Pages Shrink When Printed to Some Imagesetters
- Positive/Negative and Emulsion Settings Can't Be Overridden

Be sure that your printer is aware of this page and checks the problems and solutions it contains.

Creating Shared Publishing Templates with Publisher 2000

Whether you are creating print publications or Web pages with Publisher, you might want to standardize your publications so that it's easy for your colleagues to build publications that all look consistent. In Chapter 12, you learned how to create Word templates that made publications more consistent while also streamlining the process of creating publications. You can do much the same thing with Publisher.

Start by creating your publication—most likely by using one of Publisher's many wizards. Add any custom elements you expect to need regularly. For example, if all your newsletters include a letter from the president, set up a page that includes his photo, an appropriate headline and byline, and blank space corresponding to the size of his monthly column.

Replace the generic components of the Wizard's publication with your own; for example, insert your own newsletter title and corporate logo. Make any design adjustments you want; for example, use your company colors and typefaces in the document. Discard boilerplate text you know you'll never need, but leave boilerplate headlines in place to help give the publication its shape.

Part

IV

Ch

27

When you've finished all this, choose **File**, **Save As**. In the Save As dialog box, select the **Template** box and choose **Save**. Publisher saves the file as a template.

To open a new document based on the template, follow these steps:

1. Choose **File**, **New**.
2. Click the **Existing Publications** tab.
3. Click **Templates**. The Open Template dialog box opens, listing all templates stored in the Publications folder.
4. Double-click the template you want. Publisher opens a new publication based on that template.

Creating Shared Folders for Publisher Templates

After you've created successful designs for newsletters, brochures, or other publications, you might want to reuse them repeatedly and share them with colleagues. To do so, you can save them as templates and store them centrally where everyone can access them.

You can establish a shared folder for Publisher templates in two ways: locally, from individual workstations, or centrally, via System Policies. Those approaches are covered in the following two sections.

Establishing a Shared Folder for Publisher Templates (Locally)

If you want to make shared templates available for everyone on your network to use, establish a folder on your network that all your users can access. Then, establish that folder as the location where Publisher searches for templates. You can do this locally, on individual workstations, by following these steps:

1. Choose **Tools**, **Options** and click the **General** tab (see Figure 27.18).

FIGURE 27.18
The General tabof the Options dialog box.

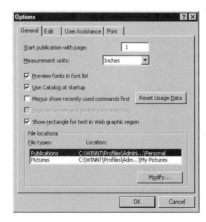

2. In the **File types** window of the General tab, select **Publications** and click **Modify**.

3. Browse to the network location you want to use and click **OK**.

4. If you also want to select a central location for images, select **Pictures** in the **File types** window of the General tab and click **Modify**.

5. Browse to the network location you want to use and click **OK**.

6. Click **OK** again.

Establishing a Shared Folder for Publisher Templates (Through System Policies)

You can also set shared folders for templates and pictures using system policies. To do so, run the System Policy Editor and be sure the Pub9.adm policy template is loaded. Then, click **New**, choose **Default User**, go to **Microsoft Publisher 2000**, and select **Default File Locations**.

Select the **Publication Location** check box and enter the new location in the text box that appears. If you also want to create a shared folder for graphics, select the **Picture Location** check box and enter the new location in the text box that appears.

Save the template and place it in the users' logon folder. For more detailed information about working with the System Policy Editor, see Chapter 37, "Reducing Office 2000's Total Cost of Ownership." ●

Part

IV

Ch

27

Managing Microsoft PhotoDraw and Small Business Tools

by Bill Camarda

In this chapter, you learn what you need to know in order to manage two additional software packages included with many versions of Microsoft Office:

- **Microsoft PhotoDraw** (included in Office Premium and Office Developer's Edition).
- **Small Business Tools** (included in all editions of Office, except Standard). This set of tools includes Direct Mail Manager, Business Planner, Customer Manager, and Small Business Financial Manager.

Understanding and Managing Microsoft PhotoDraw

Both Microsoft Office 2000 Premium Edition and Developer Edition come with a business graphics program called Microsoft PhotoDraw. This program allows business users to create and manipulate virtually any kind of image for both print and Web work.

PhotoDraw integrates bitmap painting and vector drawing tools; image capture and photo retouching tools; 300 business graphics templates; and 20,000 photos, backgrounds, and clip art elements—including the entire Microsoft Clip Gallery. In short, PhotoDraw acts as a business graphics "jack of all trades," delivering key features that might otherwise require several programs, including more expensive packages such as Adobe Photoshop and CorelDRAW.

PhotoDraw installs from Disk 3 of the 4-disk Office 2000 Premium Edition. PhotoDraw uses the old Acme installer instead of the new Windows Installer service used by the rest of Office 2000. The installation options include the Help system, Tutorial, and Graphics filters for the following formats: BMP, CDR, CGM, DRW, DXF, EMF, EPS, FPX (FlashPix), GIF, JPEG, PCD (PhotoCD), PCX, PICT, PNG, and Targa.

N O T E PhotoDraw reads standard EPS files, but it might have trouble with some files generated by versions of Adobe Illustrator after 7.0, which enhance EPS with additional features.

PhotoDraw can also read Photoshop PSD files through version 4.0 but cannot read the slightly different files generated by Photoshop 5.0.

You can separately choose to install the clip art resources on Disk 4, or you can run it from the CD-ROM.

Note that PhotoDraw has the highest system requirements of any Microsoft Office 2000 program. The minimum requirements are outlined here:

- **Pentium 166 or later**
- **32MB RAM** (Microsoft recommends 64MB)
- **200MB of free hard disk space after installation,** for the very large virtual memory swap file PhotoDraw requires. This is not listed as a formal system requirement, but Microsoft makes the recommendation in a recent Knowledge Base article (Q193801).
- **SVGA monitor.** In fact, when PhotoDraw runs for the first time on a system running at 640×480 or at less than True Color, it displays a dialog box telling the user it will run best at 800×600, True Color, as shown in Figure 28.1.

  Depending on how you have configured your hardware and software, you might need to instruct your users to disregard these instructions. In Windows NT, if a user chooses an unsupported video setting, the display could become unreadable, forcing the user to reboot with the VGA option (if he or she even knows how).

  You will probably want to disable this message immediately. To do so, choose **Tools, Options, View.** Clear the **Alert to Change Screen Display Settings on Startup** check box and click **OK.**

FIGURE 28.1

PhotoDraw encourages users to change their Windows display settings.

N O T E Running PhotoDraw at a lower graphics resolution does not significantly improve its performance; PhotoDraw's internal rendering engine always assumes 24-bit graphics, even when it's run at lower resolution or bit depth. ■

N O T E If you want to install PhotoDraw over the network, follow the detailed instructions available on the PhotoDraw CD-ROM in the file NetWrk.wri. ■

 TIP If you intend to use PhotoDraw solely for creating Web graphics, you can achieve better performance by switching to Web mode, which generates lower-resolution graphics and smaller files. (These files would not serve your needs for high-quality hard copy printing, but they are sufficient for the Web.) To switch modes, follow these steps:

1. Choose **Tools**, **Options**, **Picture Quality** (see Figure 28.2).
2. Choose **Web**.
3. Click **OK**.

FIGURE 28.2

Switch to Web mode for better performance in creating Web graphics.

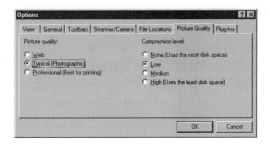

Deciding Who Needs PhotoDraw

Microsoft Office 2000 Premium Edition adds only two programs to Office: FrontPage and PhotoDraw. So, if you've chosen this version of Office, it's quite likely you've already determined that your users need business and Web graphics capabilities. If, however, you purchased Office 2000 Premium Edition solely for FrontPage, you need to decide whether to deploy PhotoDraw to all the same users. Ask yourself the following questions:

■ Who really needs to create or edit business graphics?

■ Do we have a library of Web and other custom graphics already available (so users do not have to reinvent the wheel in PhotoDraw)?

■ Even if users do not create business graphics, will they find PhotoDraw's support for scanning and digital camera downloads useful? Or have we already provided this support through other TWAIN-compliant applications?

N O T E PhotoDraw supports only scanners and digital cameras with TWAIN drivers. ■

Reviewing PhotoDraw Features

PhotoDraw's design goal was to make it possible for businesspeople to create sophisticated business graphics without depending on expensive professionals. To this end, PhotoDraw provides features like these:

■ **Design Templates** (see Figure 28.3) that allow you to walk step by step through creating many categories of Web graphics, business graphics, cards, designer edges, and designer clip art.

FIGURE 28.3
PhotoDraw Design Templates guide users step by step through the process of building Web and business graphics.

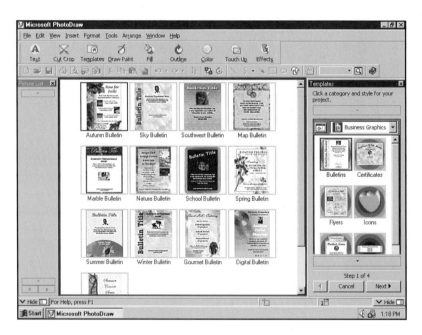

■ The **Save for Use In Wizard** (see Figure 28.4), which guides you through saving files for use on the Web, in documents, in onscreen publications, and elsewhere. For instance, as shown in Figure 28.5, it can show you how a GIF or JPEG will look when saved with different settings, and how long each version would take to download at any speed you choose.

FIGURE 28.4
The Save for Use In Wizard helps users save files in the best possible format for their needs.

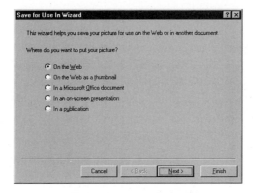

FIGURE 28.5
Determine which *file* compression technique is best for a Web image.

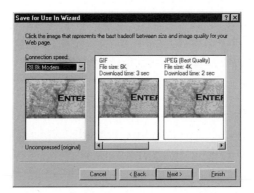

- **Touch Up and Effects filters** that are far easier to control than those in most professional graphics programs. (As an example, Figure 28.6 shows a Fade Out being created.).

Customizing PhotoDraw Options

As with other Microsoft Office programs, most customizations can be found in the Options dialog box (choose **Tools**, **Options**). Note, however, that unlike in other Office 2000 programs, Microsoft provides no system policies template for managing these customizations centrally in PhotoDraw.

This list outlines the customization options available in PhotoDraw's Options dialog box:

- The *View* tab controls several aspects of PhotoDraw's interface, such as whether PhotoDraw displays a list of options at startup and whether it shows Helpful Tips as users work.
- The *General* tab includes the User Name, taken from the Windows Registry; it can be customized here. This tab also includes customizations for how the mouse and keyboard behave and a setting for increasing or decreasing the number of images in the Recently Used File list.

Part
IV

Ch
28

FIGURE 28.6

A Fade Out effect is
created in PhotoDraw.

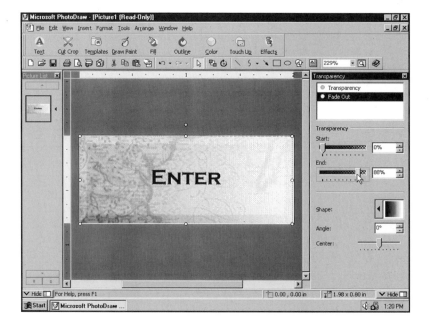

- The *Toolbars* tab allows you to display large icons on toolbars and choose whether to show ScreenTips and whether the ScreenTips should also contain keyboard shortcuts.

- The *Scanner/Camera* tab allows you to manage the behavior of TWAIN devices that PhotoDraw can use for scanning or image retrieval.

- The *File Locations* tab (see Figure 28.7) specifies two folders: a folder where all pictures are stored and a folder that corresponds to PhotoDraw's extensive library of graphics and templates.

  If you want to choose another location, such as a network location, click the **Browse** button next to the <u>L</u>ook for my pictures in this directory text box. Then browse to and select the location you want and click **OK**.

  If you want to store PhotoDraw's library of clip art and templates on the network, copy Disk 4 to a network location that will be accessible to your users. Next, click the **Bro<u>w</u>se** button next to Look for <u>M</u>icrosoft PhotoDraw - Disc 2 in this directory. Browse to and select the location you want and click **OK**.

FIGURE 28.7

The File Locations tab
lets you specify a local
or network location for
the user's pictures and
one for PhotoDraw's
clip art resources and
templates.

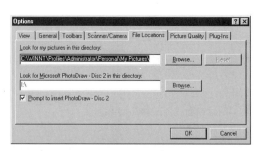

- The *Picture Quality* tab allows you to tell PhotoDraw which applications it should "target" its work for: Web, Typical (Photographic), or Professional (Best for Printing). Professional has the highest memory and CPU requirements; Web has the lowest. Here, you can also set a default compression level for PhotoDraw graphics that can be compressed.

- The *Plug-Ins* tab allows you to specify a second directory, such as a network folder, where Photoshop plug-ins can be stored. The default directory is typically C:\Program Files\Microsoft Office\Office\PhotoDraw\PlugIns.

Understanding and Managing Small Business Tools

All versions of Office 2000 except for Standard Edition come with a set of Small Business Tools that can help streamline many of the tasks small businesses would be more likely to perform if only they were easier. Microsoft Small Business Tools consists of four elements:

- Microsoft Business Planner
- Microsoft Direct Mail Manager
- Microsoft Small Business Customer Manager
- Microsoft Small Business Financial Manager

After they're installed, these tools are accessible by choosing **Start**, **Programs**, **Microsoft Office Small Business Tools**. The following sections briefly describe the tools and provide essential information for managing them.

NOTE Most of the capabilities built into Microsoft Office Small Business Tools are built on other Office applications. For example, Microsoft Small Business Financial Manager works in Excel, using information from your accounting system that has been exported to an Access database. To gain the full benefits of Small Business Tools, you must install the rest of the Office suite, including Internet Explorer 5. ▩

CAUTION

With the possible exception of Microsoft Business Planner, each of these tools relies on sensitive customer information. Use the security tools Microsoft provides to help make sure this information does not fall into unauthorized hands.

Using Microsoft Business Planner

Microsoft Business Planner (shown in Figure 28.8) provides a centralized Web-based interface that integrates the following elements:

- Wizards for building business plans and marketing strategies. You read a series of articles on each element of business planning or marketing strategy and then answer questions. From the answers, the Wizard builds a detailed plan outline, which can be fleshed out into a detailed plan, complete with financial forecasts. Microsoft Business Planner comes with a sample 40-page plan that shows how it can be done.

■ A library of articles, tips, and examples for business planning.

■ Web links to many of the Internet's best business sites.

■ 100+ Word and Excel templates containing worksheets and forms for business planning, tax calculations, and other activities.

■ Links to built-in Microsoft Publisher 2000 business document wizards.

■ Action Plans that offer follow-up information for users, such as recommended reading.

FIGURE 28.8
Microsoft Business Planner.

Using Microsoft Direct Mail Manager

Microsoft Direct Mail Manager (shown in Figure 28.9) is a powerful tool for streamlining the creation of mailings up to 3,500 in size—a tool that can also help you save money by reducing the postage cost of your mailings. Although Direct Mail Manager is included in Microsoft's Small Business Tools, do not assume that it is used solely for small business. It can work equally well for large companies selling niche products. Many companies deliver mailings of 3,500 or less. Of course, if your mailing is slightly larger, you can divide your list and run the software twice.

FIGURE 28.9
Microsoft Direct Mail
Manager.

Using a simple wizard-like interface, Direct Mail Manager starts by importing names and addresses you might already have stored in Outlook address books, Excel worksheets, Word tables, or Access databases (or any ODBC-compliant database). This means you can also use information stored by Microsoft SQL Server, Oracle, and other large database systems.

> **CAUTION**
>
> Because Direct Mail Manager can utilize enterprise data—such as customer data—it raises the following business security issues that you have to manage:
>
> - Who has rights to that data?
> - How will the data be secured after it is exported? (If you use a third-party mailing house, you should also be concerned with their in-house security techniques.)
> - From a technical standpoint, how will you make sure authorized Direct Mail Manager users can access the data?

If you don't have the addresses you need, the software contains hyperlinks to InfoUSA, a leading Web-based list vendor, where you can purchase and download the names immediately. Other list vendors are also available, but they might not be linked directly into Direct Mail Manager.

> **CAUTION**
>
> Keep in mind that many list vendors place significant restrictions on their list. For example, you might be permitted to use a downloaded list only once, preventing you from integrating its names into your own database.
>
> Lists are seeded with dummy names and addresses that find their way back to the list company, so you can count on the dummy names being caught if you use a commercial list in an unauthorized manner.

Part
IV

Ch

28

Assuming you do have your own list, Direct Mail Manager gives you a chance to verify your names. Then, it connects to the Internet and compares each name in your database against the U.S. Postal Service's national ZIP+4 database, inserting the correct ZIP+4 ZIP code and correcting common addressing errors. In many cases, this can make your mailing eligible for significant postage discounts. Running on a 33.6 modem, it processes a little more than one address per second, which translates to roughly 10 minutes per 1,000 names.

When Direct Mail Manager finishes that task, you get another chance to fill in holes, and Direct Mail Manager flags possible duplicate names—helping you save money by mailing fewer pieces. It then creates a merge data file that you can use to print envelopes and merge them with documents created in Microsoft Word or Microsoft Publisher. Working with Word and Publisher's envelope and mail merge features, it can even print envelopes with the correct postal bar code indicias for mailing.

TIP

For more complex mailings, you might want to upgrade to DAZzle Express, the enhanced version of Direct Mail Manager from Envelope Manager Software (**www.EnvelopeManager.com**, 800-576-3279). Unlike the version bundled with Office 2000, the enhanced version can handle the following:

- Mailings of greater than 3,500 pieces
- Discount first-class mail-automation letters and cards (mailings exceeding 500 pieces)
- Presorting for Enhanced Carrier Route discounts
- Nonprofit mailings

For Direct Mail Manager users, the DAZzle Express upgrade costs $195. For more information, see **http://www.envelopemanager.com**.

Using Microsoft Small Business Customer Manager

Microsoft Small Business Customer Manager creates an Access customer database that draws upon (and can parallel) information in your Outlook 2000 Contacts folder (and any other Outlook folder you want). Outlook can also integrate information from these small business accounting systems:

- Money Personal & Business '99
- M.Y.O.B. 6.0 and 7.x
- Peachtree Office 1.1
- QuickBooks 6.0 and 99
- ACCPAC Simply Accounting 6.0

When that database is in place, you can use it to more effectively track and enhance your customer relationships. The following list outlines just some of the tasks Small Business Customer Manager can perform, given up-to-date accounting and contact information:

- Identify your top customers, salespeople, or products
- Sort customers by sales or order volume, time since last order, or product ordered

- Sort products by sales volume, quantity, and time since last ordered
- Sort sales by customer, product, region, salesperson, or time period
- Sort profitability by customer, product, or salesperson

All these items require up-to-date accounting information. Note that this information is not updated automatically via OLE or DDE. When you want to use new accounting information, you must download a new set of data all at once. Typically, you might do this after closing your books each month.

Even if you have not imported accounting data, Small Business Customer Manager can still be useful. Its Activity Tracker feature can keep tabs on all your interactions with specific customers—as well as with companies where you have multiple individual contacts. You can also use Small Business Customer Manager as a centralized front end for other Office tasks, such as these:

- Writing letters to customers using Microsoft Word's Letter Wizard or with one of the built-in Microsoft Word and Publisher letter templates Customer Manager provides. For instance, you might flag all your customers who haven't ordered in some time and send each one a customized version of Customer Manager's "At Risk Customer" letter, using Publisher 2000's mail merge feature.
- Sending faxes using Word's Fax Wizard.
- Creating new messages, appointments, tasks, and journal entries that are stored in Outlook.
- Exporting your analyses to other Office programs, the Internet Explorer Web browser, email, fax, or Microsoft Exchange recipients.

A single customer database can be used by multiple employees, each of whom can draw upon its information and add new data when he or she makes contact with a customer. Of course, this makes it doubly important to be careful about security.

Setting Up Your Small Business Customer Manager Database

Small Business Customer Manager begins with a wizard that walks you through preparing your database (see Figure 28.10), covering the following steps:

1. Establish a user account and password for yourself. After you do this, you can create other user accounts for those who should have access to this sensitive customer data.
2. Choose where to import data from: Outlook folders, small business accounting software, or both.
3. Choose whether you want other users to be able to edit contact records you allow them to import from your customer database.
4. Specify which events you want Customer Manager's Activity Tracker to keep track of. These can include one or both of the following categories:

   Customer Manager Events (such as sending correspondence)

Outlook Events (such as sending email, creating a task, or performing other functions within Outlook that relate to this customer)

5. Name and store your new database. (This process is unfortunately quite slow. A ballpark estimate: It will take 15–20 minutes per 1,000 Outlook contacts.)

FIGURE 28.10
Running the Customer Manager's New Database Wizard.

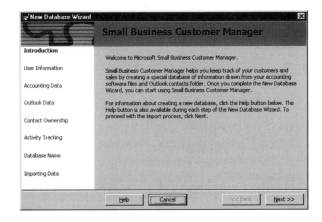

After you create the Customer Manager database and log onto it, you're asked to enter personal information Customer Manager can use whenever it creates documents for you. Customer Manager then opens your database in table format (see Figure 28.11).

FIGURE 28.11
A Customer Manager database in table format.

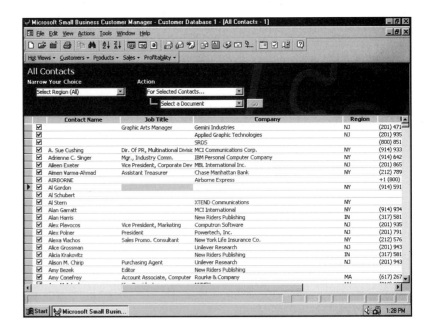

Adding New Users

You can add three types of new users to Small Business Customer Manager:

■ **Basic Users,** who can view only contact detail and activities

■ **Sales Users,** who can view all information in the database except company financials and payroll information

■ **Full Users,** who have access to all information in the database, can add or remove other users, and change user passwords

To add a user, follow these steps:

1. Choose **Tools**, **Security**, **Users**. The User Security dialog box opens (see Figure 28.12).

FIGURE 28.12
The User Security dialog box in Small Business Customer Manager.

2. Click **New User**. The New User dialog box opens (see Figure 28.13).

FIGURE 28.13
The New User dialog box in Small Business Customer Manager.

3. Enter the user's name and password. Then, retype the password in the **Confirm Password** box.

4. Choose the group you want the user to belong to: Basic, Sales, or Full.

5. Click **OK**. If you want to add more users, repeat steps 2 and 3. When you finish, click **Close**.

Part
IV

Ch

28

N O T E Of course, you will also need to store the database in a location accessible to the users you want to have access to it. Folder security (and Windows NT's NTFS file security) give you added opportunities to make sure your crucial customer database does not fall into the wrong hands. ■

CAUTION

Although Small Business Customer Manager does not allow Basic or Sales users to view sensitive financial data, it does allow them to create a backup of the entire customer database to any location they choose. This can represent a substantial security risk.

Using Microsoft Small Business Financial Manager

Small Business Financial Manager (shown in Figure 28.14) imports the financial data you've created in any of several leading desktop PC accounting packages, adding powerful analysis capabilities that give you a clearer sense of where your business stands. Given appropriate source data, Small Business Financial Manager can do these things:

- Perform what-if analyses about issues such as changing your prices, reducing your inventories, changing your cost of sales, or taking out a loan

- Compare your business' financials against a database of more than 100,000 businesses compiled by the nonprofit bank consortium Robert Morris Associates

- Create projections of how your business might look six months or a year from now, based on assumptions you can choose and change

- Create buy-versus-lease analyses

FIGURE 28.14
Small Business
Financial Manager.

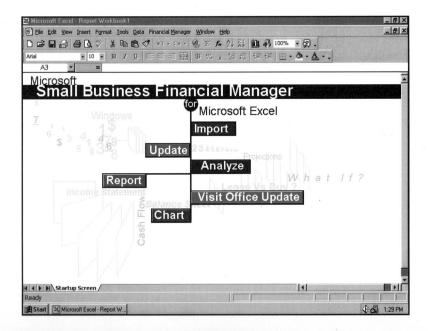

Small Business Financial Manager 2000 can import data from the following accounting packages:

- Money Personal & Business '99 (Business Transactions Only)
- M.Y.O.B. 6.0 and 7.x
- Peachtree Office 1.1
- QuickBooks 6.0 and 99
- ACCPAC Simply Accounting 6.0

N O T E If you want to import data from QuickBooks, one of the most popular PC accounting packages, you should be aware of several important issues.

First, in order to import data from QuickBooks, a registered copy of QuickBooks must be running on the same computer as Small Business Financial Manager.

Second, you must temporarily clear password protection from the file you want to import. Remember to restore password protection after you import the data.

Next, in QuickBooks, enter any "memorized transactions" that should be reflected in your analysis. To do so, first see whether any memorized transactions exist by choosing **Lists**, **Memorized Transactions**. In the Memorized Transaction List dialog box, choose a transaction and click **Enter Transaction**.

Make QuickBooks Reminders unavailable. Choose **File**, **Preferences**. Click **Reminders** in the left-side window and, for each option in the Reminders dialog box, click **Don't Remind Me**.

Finally, be sure no transactions dated more than 12 months ago are still open. (Most accounting software won't permit this, but QuickBooks does.) Choose **File**, **Passwords**. In the Transaction Password area, note the Date through which books are closed: This date should not be more than 12 months prior to the current date. If it is, Small Business Financial Manager will hang while trying to import your data. ■

Small Business Financial Manager 2000 isn't a standalone program; it is an add-in to Microsoft Excel 2000. The results it generates make extensive use of the Excel 2000 PivotTable feature, so anyone who plans to use the program should become familiar with that feature first.

CAUTION

If you used Small Business Financial Manager in Office 97, you cannot work with the same data files: You must reimport your data and rebuild all your what-if analyses.

Small Business Financial Manager *no longer supports* several accounting software formats that were supported in the Office 97 version, but in some cases you might be able to export and save copies of your accounting data in one of the following compatible formats:

- ACCPAC Plus Account 6.1a (DOS)
- BusinessWorks for Windows 9.0 (Windows)
- DacEasy Accounting 5.0 (DOS)
- Great Plains Accounting 8.0, 8.1, 8.2 (DOS)

continues

Part
IV

Ch
28

continued
- MAS 90 Evolution/2 1.51 (DOS)
- One-Write Plus 4.03 (DOS)
- Peachtree Complete Accounting for DOS 8.0 (DOS)
- Peachtree for Windows 3.0, 3.5, 4.0, 5.0 (Windows)
- Platinum Series for DOS and Windows 4.1, 4.4 (DOS/Windows)
- QuickBooks 3.1, 4.0, Pro 4.0, 5.0 (Windows)
- Simply Accounting 3.0, 4.0, 5.0 (Windows)

During the installation process, you're asked to choose the import filter that matches your accounting software and whether you need a U.S. or Canadian version of the package. After you install, either you can double-click on its icon to run it, or you can run Excel and choose its components from the Accounting menu that is added to Excel.

CAUTION

Keep in mind that the information Small Business Financial Manager provides might be sensitive to tax, legal, and accounting changes the software has no way of knowing about. Before you make major decisions based on the analysis you perform here, check it against common sense and/or consult a professional advisor.

To import your existing financial data into Small Business Financial Manager, first run the program. If you're warned that macros are about to run, choose **Enable Macros**. When the program is running, follow these steps:

1. Click **Import**. Screen 1 of the New Database Wizard dialog box opens (see Figure 28.15). Click **Next**.

FIGURE 28.15
Small Business Financial Manager's New Database Wizard.

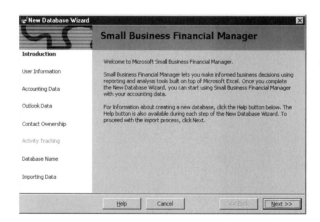

2. Enter your name and a password. Then, type the password again in the **Confirm Password** box. Click **Next**.

3. Financial Manager searches for your accounting files. If this takes too long, you can click **Cancel**, and then browse to and select your accounting data. When you're finished, click **Next**.

4. Select any Outlook folders you want to import and click **Next**.

5. Select the type of activities you want Small Business Financial Manager to track and click **Next**.

6. Name your Financial Manager database. Then, browse to and select a location for the database. Click **Next**.

7. Small Business Financial Manager imports your data. This might take some time. When the program finishes, click **Finish**. You can now work with Small Business Financial Manager.

CAUTION

Small Business Financial Manager does not automatically password protect your financial data. If you're concerned about security, you should add a password yourself by following these steps:

1. Choose **File**, **Save As**.

2. Choose **Options**.

3. In the **Password to Open** text box, enter a password and click **OK**.

4. In the **Confirm Password** text box, retype the password and click **OK**.

5. Click **Save**.

Part

IV

Ch

28

Leveraging Office's Free Mini-Applications

by Bill Camarda

Microsoft Office 2000 comes with a suite of mini-applications that few Office professionals ever fully explore. You might be surprised at how much power is hidden away in these "minor" applications. In this chapter, you walk through the following six applications, discover what each of them can do for your business, and learn how to manage them as effectively as possible:

- Microsoft Clip Gallery
- Microsoft Photo Editor
- Microsoft Equation Editor
- Microsoft System Information
- Microsoft Organization Chart
- Microsoft Map

Using Microsoft Clip Gallery

More and more often, documents contain images and multimedia components. Microsoft Office 2000 for Windows contains a program for managing all the graphics and multimedia resources available to Office users: Microsoft Clip Gallery 5.0.

In the default Office 2000 installation, Clip Gallery is installed, along with two sets of files: AutoShapes and Typical Bullets and Lines. A third set of files, Additional Bullets and Lines, is available to be run from the CD-ROM or the original network installation share point. Each set of files has a corresponding Clip Catalog that contains information and thumbnails associated with each file.

N O T E Office 98 for the Macintosh comes with Clip Gallery 3.0; this feature is covered later in this chapter. ■

To run Clip Gallery from Office 2000, choose **Insert**, **Picture**, **Clip Art** from Word, Excel, PowerPoint, Publisher, or FrontPage. Clip Gallery does not have a menu item in Access, but you can open it from within that program by choosing **Insert**, **Object**, and choosing **Microsoft Clip Gallery** from the **Object Type** list box.

In Office 2000, Clip Gallery 5.0 has been redesigned to resemble a Web browser, as you can see in Figure 29.1. Its revamped interface will be especially comfortable for experienced Web users. For instance, it now contains Back and Forward buttons to enable users to browse through "pages" of images they've already reviewed. Other elements of the Clip Gallery interface have only minor changes from previous versions (for example, it now has a separate tab for each type of media).

FIGURE 29.1

Microsoft Clip Gallery 5.0 for Windows.

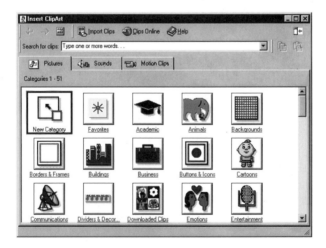

By default, Clip Gallery 5.0 provides 51 categories of images. To review the images in a specific category, click on that category. To select an image, click on it and click the **Insert Clip** button that appears. Alternatively, you can right-click on the image and choose **Insert** from the shortcut menu.

In Clip Gallery 5.0, media resources are organized into the following four categories:

- **Pictures.** This includes both Windows metafiles from the Office 2000 library (called "clip art" in Office 97) and bitmap graphics such as JPGs and BMPs (called "images" in Office 97).

- **Sounds.** Includes Windows WAV and cross-platform MIDI music files; might also include Apple QuickTime files.

- **Motion Clips.** Might include Windows AVI files, Apple QuickTime files, and animated GIFs that can be used on Web or intranet sites.

Clip Gallery doesn't actually contain all the clips. Instead, it contains a database that stores thumbnail previews, category names, and keywords describing the clips. When you add clip art or change categories, as discussed next, you are actually updating this database. In Windows, the default database is a file called Artgal50.cag, which is typically stored in the Windows folder.

N O T E   Although Clip Gallery for Windows has been enhanced, Clip Gallery 3.0—the version that ships with Office 98—more closely resembles the older versions of Clip Gallery that shipped with earlier versions of Office for Windows (see Figure 29.2). This can make switching between platforms slightly less transparent and more complicated than it once was.

FIGURE 29.2
Microsoft Clip Gallery
3.0 for the Macintosh.

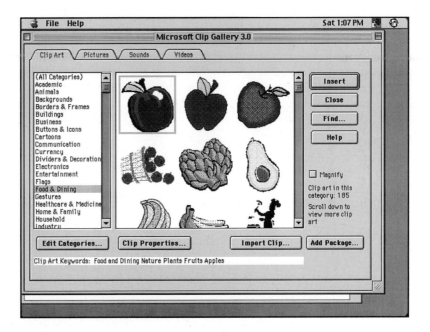

In Clip Gallery 3.0 (Office 98 for the Macintosh), the database is called Clip Gallery User Database and is stored in **System Folder:Preferences**. ■

Importing More Clips into Clip Gallery Folder

Whether you have a new third-party package with 100,000 clip art images or a half-dozen logos and product photos that are specific to your company, you can easily allow your users to access them through Clip Gallery. To add new images to the Clip Gallery database—and create new clip art categories if you choose—follow these steps:

1. Choose **Insert**, **Picture**, **Clip Art** to open the Clip Gallery.

2. Choose **Import Clips**.

3. In the Add clip to Clip Gallery dialog box, browse to and select the clip or clips you want (see Figure 29.3). You can select several consecutive files in a folder by holding down the **Shift** key while clicking to select the first and last files. You can select individual files by holding down the **Ctrl** key while you choose each image.

FIGURE 29.3

Here, you can select one or more clips to add to your Clip Gallery database.

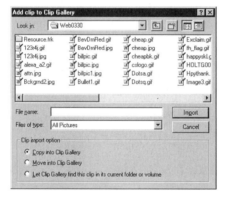

4. Specify where you want the clip file to appear after you import it. You have the following options:

   • **Copy into Clip Gallery** copies the clip file into the default folder Office uses to store all its images. This is typically C:\Program Files\Common Files\Microsoft Shared\Clipart\cagcat50. The advantage of choosing Copy into Clip Gallery is that it helps you keep all your files in the same location. The disadvantage: Because the files are most commonly stored on your C: drive, if you import quite a few files, you might run out of room on that drive—which can cause performance and reliability problems.

   • **Move into Clip Gallery** moves the clip file into the default folder Office uses to store all its images but deletes the original file (unless it is in a read-only folder or CD-ROM).

   • **Let Clip Gallery find this clip in its current folder or volume** leaves the clip art in its original location but adds a pointer to the Clip Gallery database showing where to find it when needed. This option is commonly used for clip art stored on CD-ROMs or removable media, such as zip and Jaz disks.

5. Click **Import**. The Clip Properties dialog box opens, displaying a thumbnail image of the first clip you selected (see Figure 29.4).

FIGURE 29.4
In the Clip Properties dialog box, you can specify information that makes media files easier to find.

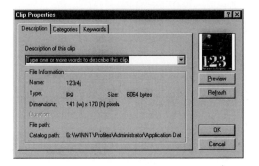

6. Click the **Categories** tab. If you want to create a new category for your clips, click **New Category**, enter a name in the **New Category Name** box, and click **OK**. Otherwise, choose a category from the **Categories** scroll box.

TIP You might want to force a category to appear first in the list of categories—for example, to ensure that users know there are company-specific clip files available to them. To do so, add an asterisk before the name of your new category.

7. Click the **Keywords** tab. In the **Keywords** text box, add any keywords that can help your users find the clip when they search for it.

8. If you want to give all your new files the same keywords and categories, select the **Add All Clips to the Selected Categories** check box.

9. Click **OK**.

Managing Microsoft Clip Gallery Centrally

You might want to give all your users access to the hundreds of megabytes of clip art that come with most versions of Office 2000—but you probably won't want to store copies of that clip art on every single workstation.

Giving workstation users access to a centralized Clip Gallery database is a two-step process that works virtually the same whether you are using Windows or Macintosh servers and workstations. First, you prepare the server. Second, you prepare the user workstations.

Providing Centralized Access to a Custom Clip Gallery Catalog

You might want to give all your users access to Office 2000's large clip art library (or third-party clip art libraries), but you probably won't want to store copies of that clip art on every single workstation.

> **CAUTION**
>
> Be aware of license restrictions that might prevent you from legally networking some CD-ROM graphics packages.

All computers running Clip Gallery have one "primary catalog," which contains information and thumbnails for the clip media files that Clip Gallery has indexed. When users add clips to Clip Gallery with the Import Clips feature, the new information is added to this primary catalog. It's typically named Artgal50.mmc or Artgal50.cag and stored in the following folder:

```
C:\Windows\Application Data\Microsoft\Media Catalog\Artgal50.mmc.
```

or in this folder on Windows NT:

```
C:\WinNT\Profiles\username\Application Data\Microsoft\Media Catalog\Artgal50.mmc
```

where the user's name corresponds to *username*.

As Office administrator, you can set up a supplementary shared read-only Clip Gallery in a network location that's accessible to your Office users. Because the catalog is read only, users need specific access rights to make changes to it; however, they can copy information and clips to the catalogs on their own computers and make changes there.

Creating the Shared Clip Gallery Catalog

Giving Windows workstation users access to a centralized Clip Gallery database is a two-step process. First, you prepare the server. Second, you prepare the user workstations. To prepare the server, follow these steps:

1. On a workstation that has Clip Gallery installed, browse to the Artgal50.mmc file and rename it with a different extension, such as Artgal50.old. This stores the existing Clip Gallery as a backup in case you need it later.

2. Open Clip Gallery as a standalone program—in other words, not from within an Office application. The program is named cag.exe and is typically stored in the \Program Files\Common Files\Microsoft Shared\Artgalry folder. Double-click on **cag.exe**, and Clip Gallery creates a new artgal50.mmc file.

3. From within Clip Gallery, create the categories and import the clip files you want to include in your shared catalog. When you're asked how to import files, use the **Let Clip Gallery Find This Clip in Its Current Folder or Drive** option.

4. When you finish adapting the Clip Gallery catalog to your needs, click **Close** to exit the Clip Gallery.

5. Copy the file to a shared location on your network and rename it in a way that's appropriate for your company—for example, acmeclips.mmc. Don't change the .mmc extension.

6. Right-click on the file and choose **Properties**.

7. In the Properties dialog box, select the **Read-Only** check box.

Now that you've prepared the shared catalog and placed it on your server, you need to configure user workstations so they know where to look for the shared catalog.

Preparing Workstations

Now that your server is ready to deliver information from the shared Clip Gallery database, you need to set up each workstation to do so as well. Usually, you need to do this from the individual workstation. Typically, the most convenient method is to ask each user to follow these steps:

1. Open Clip Gallery.
2. Click on **Import Clips**.
3. Browse to the new Clip Gallery database you just created.
4. Select the new Clip Gallery database and click **Open**.

After a user does this once, Clip Gallery will always look for that database when it opens.

Alternatively, you can send a .reg file to each user via email and ask him or her to double-click it to install the appropriate information in the Windows Registry.

TIP Better yet, if you have a desktop management tool such as Microsoft System Management Server, you can automatically run the .reg file at multiple desktops without the users' involvement.

As always, be extremely careful when editing Registry files; if you make a mistake, you can damage your users' workstations. The .reg file should contain the following text:

```
REGEDIT4

[HKEY_LOCAL_MACHINE\Software\Microsoft\ClipArt
Gallery\3.0\ConcurrentDatabases\MyCatKey]

"CAG"="FullPathToCatalog"
```

MyCatKey should be your catalog's unique name; *FullPathToCatalog* is the full network path to the catalog, as in the following example:

```
"CAG"="K:\centralized\catalogs\clipart\acmeclip.mmc".
```

Using Clip Art Images on the Web

In Office 2000, when you save an Office document containing a Clip Gallery Windows Metafile graphic as a Web page, a copy of the graphic is stored as a separate transparent GIF file in the folder that accompanies the Web page. Later, if you reopen the file, you can still double-click on the image to edit it in Word; when you resave the edited file, a replacement GIF is also created.

N O T E Even though Word has stored keywords about each piece of clip art, these keywords are not automatically used as ALT tags. This means people who visit your Web page with text-only browsers—including many disabled individuals—do not know what your pictures are unless you

continues

continued

add alternate text ("ALT tags"). Many companies make it a policy to require ALT tags on every image on their Web site and/or intranet.

To add alternate text, follow these steps:

1. Right-click on the image you've inserted.
2. Choose **Format Object** from the shortcut menu.
3. Click the **Web** tab.
4. Enter your text in the **Alternative Text** box.
5. Click **OK**. ▨

Using System Policies to Disable the Clips Online Feature

In the default Microsoft Office 2000 setup, users who have Internet access can click the Clips Online button in the Insert ClipArt dialog box to connect to a Microsoft Web site and retrieve additional clip art images. These online clips are retrieved by the Clip Gallery application, stored locally, and reflected in the local computer's Clip Gallery database.

You might want to prevent your users from downloading additional clips with the Clip Gallery, perhaps because you've standardized on a certain set of images or because you don't want to use limited Internet bandwidth in this fashion. To disable Clips Online, run the System Policy Editor associated with Microsoft Office 2000.

> **N O T E** The System Policy Editor is automatically installed if you install the Microsoft Office 2000 Resource Kit. It can also be downloaded as part of the Office Resource Kit Core Tool Set (ORKtools.exe), which is available at **www.microsoft.com/office/ork/2000/appndx/ toolbox.htm**. The tool set also includes Clipgal5.adm, the policy template associated with Clip Gallery 5. ▨

After you open the System Policy Editor, follow these steps:

1. Choose **Options, Policy Template**.
2. Browse to and select the **Clipgal5.adm** policy template.
3. Click **OK**.
4. Double-click on **User Properties** to display the Default User Properties dialog box (see Figure 29.5).
5. Click the + symbol next to Microsoft Clip Gallery 5.0.
6. Select the **Disable Clips Online Access from Clip Gallery** check box.
7. Click **OK**.
8. Choose **File, Save** to save the POL system policy file you've either created or revised.

FIGURE 29.5
The System Policy
Editor's Default User
Properties Policies tab,
with the appropriate
Clip Art Gallery restric-
tion displayed and
checked.

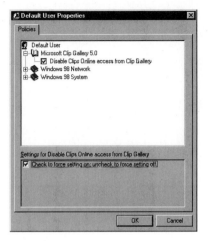

▶ For more detailed information about using system policies to restrict users, including how to
determine where your system policies should be stored, **see** "Running System Policy Editor,"
on **p. 973**.

Using Microsoft Photo Editor

Microsoft Photo Editor 3.01 (see Figure 29.6), which is available for the Windows version of
Office only, is a basic photo-editing program with the following capabilities:

■ Cropping, resizing, rotating, and color-balancing of images (the available choices in the
Image menu).

■ Basic special effects, such as sharpening, embossing, posterizing, and adding textures
(the available choices in the Effects menu).

■ The capability to run any TWAIN-compatible scanner (File, Scan Image). TWAIN is a
widely accepted interface standard for scanners.

N O T E In Office 97, scans and digital camera images could be imported only through Microsoft
Photo Editor. Now, however, Word, Excel, PowerPoint, FrontPage, and PhotoDraw all have
their own Insert, Picture, From Scanner or Camera command, which enables these programs to work
with TWAIN devices whether or not Photo Editor is installed. ■

Microsoft Photo Editor can open and save bitmapped files in the following formats: JPG, GIF,
BMP, TIF, PNG, PCX, and Targa. (It can also open, but not save, files in Photo CD format.
Other formats, such as WMF, can be copied in through the Windows Clipboard.) Because
Photo Editor can work with JPG and GIF files, one of its most common applications is as a
quick and easy way to create and enhance graphics for intranet and Web sites.

FIGURE 29.6

Microsoft Photo Editor 3.01 with an image displayed.

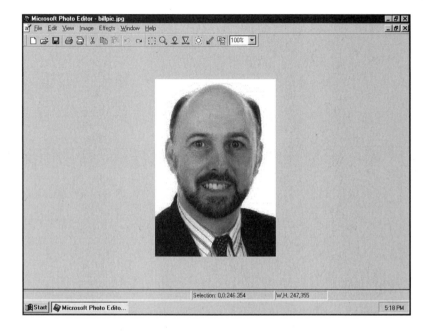

Note that Microsoft Photo Editor is not automatically installed with Office 2000; you must select the Microsoft Photo Editor box in the Office Tools category of Office Setup to install it. You can also enable it as part of a standardized network installation, using the Custom Installation Wizard. If you choose to install it later, you can do so by rerunning the Windows installer to add features.

▶ For more information about network installations using the Custom Installation Wizard, **see** "Understanding What the Office Custom Installation Wizard Does," on **p. 39**.

Some Office administrators might prefer to leave Photo Editor uninstalled for one or both of the following reasons:

- You might not want to provide photo-editing tools to employees whose primary responsibilities have little or nothing to do with graphic design.

- You might have standardized on a different image editor, such as Adobe Photoshop.

TIP If you have purchased Microsoft Office 2000 Premium Edition, you also own Microsoft PhotoDraw 2000, a fast, extremely powerful image-editing package that can handle many of the tasks Microsoft Photo Editor can, as well as many others. Unlike Microsoft Photo Editor, PhotoDraw was designed from the ground up to create images for the Web, such as backgrounds, collages, GIF animations, and more. It even contains a wizard that can help you create well-designed Web buttons in just a few moments.

Assuming Microsoft Photo Editor is installed, you can run it from any Office program (or any other Windows program that supports OLE). Follow these steps:

1. Choose **Insert**, **Object**.
2. Choose **Microsoft Photo Editor 3.0 Photo**.
3. In the New dialog box, choose how you want to get your picture: You can acquire it through a **Scanner**, create a **Blank Picture**, or **Open an Existing Picture** (see Figure 29.7).

FIGURE 29.7
Deciding whether to open, create, or scan an image.

4. If you choose **Blank Picture**, specify the dimensions of your picture in the Blank Picture dialog box.
5. Click **OK**.

You can also run Microsoft Photo Editor as a standalone application. Depending on how it was installed, it might appear as an item in the Start menu, either in the Programs list or in the Programs\Microsoft Office Tools list. Failing that, you can browse for the Microsoft Photo Editor Windows shortcut, which typically appears in the C:\Program Files\Microsoft Office folder.

> **TIP**
> If you (or your colleagues) create images in Microsoft Photo Editor that must be reviewed by others on the network, choose **File**, **Send**. If you're connected to a network and are using Mail Application Programming Interface (MAPI) compatible email, Microsoft Photo Editor will open your email client software with the current image already attached. MAPI is Microsoft's widely accepted standard for sharing email messages across Windows applications.

Using Microsoft Equation Editor

If you are producing documents in a technical environment, you might need to create specialized equations. Office 2000 and Office 98 come with a capable program to do the job: Equation Editor 3.0. These programs are not part of the default Office installation but can be installed by selecting the Equation Editor 3.0 box in the Office Tools category during the Office installation process at the desktop, or while you are creating a custom installation to be run centrally across the network.

N O T E   If you think some of your users will need Equation Editor, install it up-front; don't assume that users can install it themselves later.

Unlike many other "Install on First Run" features in Office 2000, none of the programs in Microsoft Office contains an "Insert Equation" command or any other obvious way to install the feature. (In Word, you can invoke Install on First Run for Equation Editor by choosing **Tools**, **Macro**, **Macros**; choosing **Word commands** from the **Ma̲cros In** drop-down box; choosing **InsertEquation**; and clicking **R̲un**. However, few users are likely to know that.)

Moreover, if you do not install Equation Editor, it does not appear in the list of objects in the Object dialog box, either. Therefore, if you do not include it in your installation, your users are unlikely to know it exists—and will not know how to gain access to it without your assistance—unless it has been left installed from a previous version of Office. ■

To run Equation Editor 3.0 from any Office 2000 or Office 98 application, choose **Insert**, **Object**, and select **Microsoft Equation 3.0**. A blank equation is inserted in your document, and the Equation toolbar appears, as shown in Figure 29.8.

FIGURE 29.8

Equation Editor starts by presenting a blank equation and the Equation toolbar.

When you need to type standard numbers, variables, or standard mathematical operators (for example, plus, minus, or equal signs), do it from the keyboard. When you need a specialized mathematical symbol, click the toolbar button that relates most closely, and then click the symbol that appears. In Figure 29.9, for example, a Greek uppercase letter is being selected from a list of all Greek uppercase letters.

FIGURE 29.9
Choosing an item from an Equation Editor toolbar list.

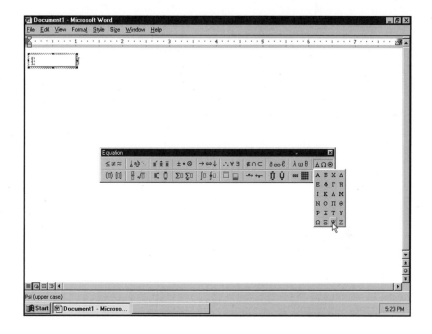

To make an element in a formula superscript, press **Ctrl+H**; to make it subscript, press **Ctrl+L**. To more closely adjust the spacing of a formula, choose **Format**, **Spacing** and work in the Spacing dialog box (shown in Figure 29.10).

FIGURE 29.10
The Spacing dialog box offers precise control over the spacing in an equation.

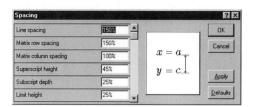

Understanding Spacing Differences Between Equation Editor 2.0 and 3.0

Equations created with earlier versions of Microsoft Equation Editor might be spaced differently after they are opened with Equation Editor 3.0. Occasionally, such equations might be widened beyond Equation Editor 3.0's capability to display them. If that happens, you might receive the following error message:

```
This equation is the maximum size allowed. Please save the equation immediately.
If you want to continue, you must divide it into smaller pieces.
```

Disregard the message and keep clicking **OK** until it goes away. Then, perform the following steps:

1. Double-click on the equation to select it for editing.
2. Choose **Format**, **Spacing**.
3. Scroll to the item marked **Spacing Adjustment** and click inside the text box.
4. Change the 100% setting to **50%**.
5. Click **OK**.
6. Click *outside* the equation.
7. Press **Ctrl+A** and then **F9**. This updates all the fields in your document, including the equations.

Troubleshooting Font Issues in Equation Editor

Equation Editor 3.0 depends on the presence of three TrueType Fonts: Symbol and Times New Roman (which are installed with Windows) and MT Extra (which is installed with Equation Editor). If you copy documents containing equations to a computer where these fonts are not installed, the equations are not displayed or printed properly.

The challenge arises when you need to output equations on a PostScript printer and you do not want to use TrueType fonts. If you have only a few equations in your document, one possible solution is to convert the equations to metafile graphics before sending them into production. Note that line spacing might have to be adjusted after equations are converted into graphics.

> **CAUTION**
>
> Be sure to keep a copy of the document that contains the original equations (not converted into metafile graphics), in case you need to edit them later.

The following Visual Basic for Applications program searches your document for the next equation and converts it to a metafile:

```
Sub FixEqs()
'
' FixEqs Macro
'
    Selection.GoTo What:=wdGoToEquation, Which:=wdGoToNext, Count:=1, Name:=""
    Selection.MoveRight Unit:=wdCharacter, Count:=1, Extend:=wdExtend
    Selection.Copy
    Selection.PasteSpecial Link:=False, DataType:=wdPasteMetafilePicture, _
        Placement:=wdFloatOverText, DisplayAsIcon:=False
End Sub
```

TIP If you're publishing equations as part of a Web page, choose **File**, **Save as HTML**, and Word automatically converts all your equations to GIF files.

TIP If you're planning to use the same equation repeatedly, save it as an AutoText entry. If your colleagues are going to all use the same equations, build a library of AutoText entries and make it available to all of them. Equations inserted via AutoText work—and can be edited—no differently than equations you create manually in Equation Editor 3.0. For more information, see the section in Chapter 12 titled "Using Word Custom AutoText Entries to Provide Standard Copy Blocks."

Understanding Equations on the Web

In Office 2000, when you save an Office document containing an Equation Editor 3.0 equation as a Web page, a copy of the chart is stored as a separate transparent GIF file in the folder that accompanies the Web page. You might encounter minor changes in the appearance of the equation when it is stored as a GIF file.

Later, if you reopen the Web page in Word for further editing, you can still double-click on the organization chart to edit it in Equation Editor 3.0; when you resave the file, a replacement GIF is also created.

Finding More Equation Capabilities

Equation Editor 3.0 is a stripped-down version of MathType, equation software published by Design Science, Inc. (800-827-0685 in the U.S. and Canada; 310-433-0685 elsewhere; **www.mathtype.com**). One especially useful feature that MathType offers is the capability to export equations to TeX, a widely used language for technical publishing.

Using Microsoft System Information

Microsoft System Information (often referred to as MS Info), which is available in Office for both Windows and Macintosh platforms, is a remarkably underappreciated tool for system tracking and troubleshooting.

If you are running Windows NT 4 or Windows 95, Microsoft System Information is installed by default as part of the standard Office installation. If you are running Windows 98, Microsoft System Information is provided as a system tool whether or not you have Office, and the Windows installer does not replace the existing files even though the version shipped with Microsoft Office 2000 is slightly later.

To access Microsoft System Information, choose **Help**, **About Microsoft Word** from within Word (or **Help**, **About** from within any other Office application). In the About Microsoft Word dialog box, click **System Info**. The Microsoft System Information application opens.

TIP Microsoft System Information can also be run as a standalone program. It's typically located in C:\Program Files\Common Files\Microsoft Shared\Msinfo\Msinfo32.exe.

Figure 29.11 shows Microsoft System Information for Office 2000 running in Windows NT 4; Figure 29.12 shows it running in Microsoft Office 98 for the Macintosh under Mac OS 8.1.

FIGURE 29.11

Microsoft System Information for Office 2000, running under Windows 95.

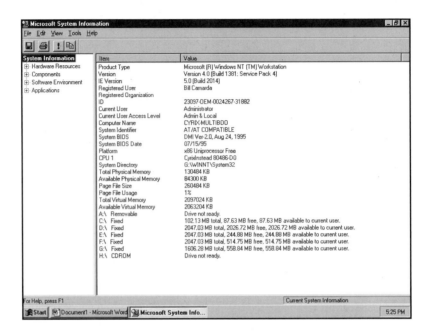

FIGURE 29.12

Microsoft System Information for Office 98, running under Mac OS 8.5.

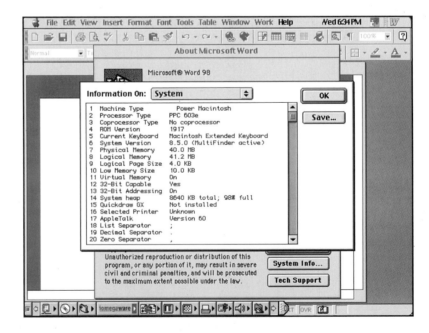

Understanding the Information Provided by Microsoft System Information

Microsoft System Information reports on virtually every aspect of a computer relevant to the operation of Microsoft Office (and most other Windows applications, too). In Windows, it provides detailed information in all the following categories:

- **Windows System Information.** The version of Windows running on the computer, swap files and available disk space, USER and GDI memory in use, printer drivers, and running DLLs.

- **Fonts.** Lists of font substitution settings (for example, Helvetica to MS Sans Serif) and the presence of third-party font managers such as Adobe Type Manager.

- **Proofing.** Registry settings, INI settings (if any), and custom files related to Office proofing tools.

- **Graphics Filters.** Lists of all import and export filters available to Office, with file sizes, version dates, and associated file extensions.

- **Text Filters.** Lists of all import and export filters available to Office, with file sizes, version dates, and associated file extensions.

- **Display.** Current video card and driver.

- **Audio.** WAV, MIDI, CD-Audio, and related settings.

- **Video.** AVI, codecs (software or hardware for compressing and decompressing video files) in use, and related settings.

- **CD-ROM.** Type and speed of system CD-ROM drive, transfer rates, data transfer integrity, and currently loaded CD-ROM.

- **Applications Running.** All applications currently running in the system.

- **OLE Registration.** All OLE applications registered in both the Windows Registry and system INI files.

- **Active Modules.** Program modules currently running in Windows.

Understanding the Mac OS Version of Microsoft System Information

Office 98 for the Macintosh contains a separate version of Microsoft System Information that reports on the following categories of information:

- **System.** Type of Macintosh, hardware, operating system and finder versions, memory usage, system heap, selected printer, AppleTalk version, video output, and more.

- **Disk storage.** Available hard drives, file system, date initialized, free space, number of files and folders.

- **Fonts.** Lists all installed fonts and whether they are TrueType fonts.

- **System Extensions.** Lists all loaded system extensions, with creation dates, size, and version numbers.

- **Application.** Lists the Office application running, with version information.
- **Converters.** Lists text and graphics import and export filters.
- **Proofing Tools.** Lists proofing files, custom dictionaries, and installed languages.

In the Windows version of Microsoft System Information, you can print a copy of your system's current settings by clicking on the **Print** icon. You can also click on **Save** to compile a tab-delimited listing of all the same settings. Either way, it might take Microsoft System Information a few minutes to gather all the information it needs. If you choose to save the file, it is stored in C:\Windows\MSinfo32.txt. On the Macintosh, the default filename is MSInfo Output, and the default storage location is the Microsoft Office 98 folder.

If you don't have a formal desktop management and remote troubleshooting system in place, consider compiling copies of MSinfo32.txt for all the systems you install Office on.

Using Microsoft System Information As a System Management Tool

You can use Microsoft System Information as a handy system management tool for tracking your desktop computing resources. In the Windows version of Microsoft System Information, you can print a copy of your system's current settings by clicking on the **Print** icon. You can also click on **Save** to compile a tab-delimited listing of all the same settings. Either way, it might take Microsoft System Information a few minutes to gather all the information it needs. If you choose to save the file, it is stored in C:\Windows\MSinfo32.txt. On the Macintosh, the default filename is MSInfo Output, and the default storage location is the Microsoft Office 98 folder.

If you don't have a formal desktop management and remote troubleshooting system in place, consider compiling copies of MSinfo32.txt for all the systems you install Office on.

Using Microsoft Organization Chart 2.0

You probably won't want to create the master organization chart for a Fortune 500 company using Microsoft Organization Chart 2.0. For that, you'd want a full-fledged organization chart program such as Broderbund Org Plus.

However, Microsoft Organization Chart 2.0 *is* a valuable tool for the quick-and-dirty org charts needed by departments, workgroups, and on-the-fly "virtual teams." It's also quite useful for planning the structure of small intranets.

To open Microsoft Organization Chart 2.0, perform the following steps:

1. Choose **Insert**, **Object**.
2. In the **Object Type** list box, choose **MS Organization Chart 2.0**, and then click **OK**. (In Office 98 for the Macintosh, choose **Microsoft Organization Chart 2.0**.)

From inside Excel or PowerPoint, choose **Insert**, **Picture**, **Organization Chart**. Whichever method you choose, Microsoft Organization Chart 2.0 appears, with a sample org chart already in place, as shown in Figure 29.13.

FIGURE 29.13
Microsoft Organization
Chart 2.0 opens with a
chart containing a
supervisor and three
subordinates.

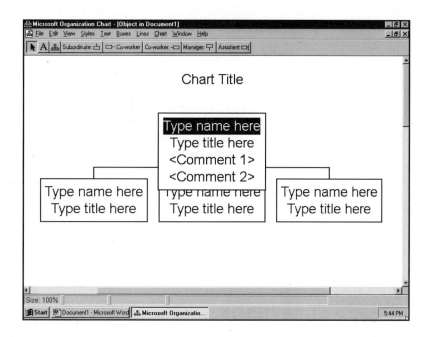

Editing Organization Charts

After your organization chart is open, you can click any existing text (for example, *Type name
here*, *Type title here*, and two comment lines) and enter information about any individual.

You can easily add new individuals to your org chart. To do so, follow these steps:

1. On the icon bar (toolbar), click the box tool corresponding to the type of employee you
   want to add: Subordinate, Co-worker, Manager, or Assistant.

2. Click the existing box with which the new employee has the relationship. If you're
   adding a manager, for example, click the box of someone the manager manages.
   Organization Chart adds a blank box for your manager.

3. Enter the individual's name, title, and two comment lines.

4. When you're finished, click outside the box you just created.

You can change relationships by dragging individual boxes to reflect the new relationships, or
by adding lines using the Custom Drawing Tools for creating new horizontal, vertical, or diagonal lines and rectangles. (If the custom drawing tools aren't visible on the toolbar, choose
View, **Show Draw Tools**.) And if you are downsizing and need to remove someone from the
chart, select his or her box and press the **Delete** key.

Microsoft Organization Chart 2.0 also offers moderate control over formatting. To reformat a
box, follow these steps.

1. Select the box you want to reformat. (To reformat more than one box, hold down the
   Shift key while you select them all, or drag the arrow pointer across all the boxes you

want to select. You can also right-click on the organization chart's background and select the categories of boxes you want to reformat—for example, All Managers or All Assistants, as shown in Figure 29.14.)

FIGURE 29.14
Choosing to reformat only boxes containing Managers.

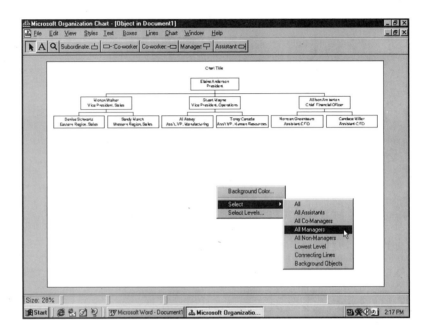

2. After you select the boxes, lines, or objects you want to format, you can choose any of the following tasks you want to perform:

   - Format groups of employees by selecting a format from the **Styles** menu.
   - Format text in boxes by choosing **Text** from the **Font** menu.
   - Format box borders and fills by choosing **Color**, **Shadow**, **Border Style**, **Border Color**, or **Border Line Style** from the **Boxes** menu.
   - Format line **Thickness**, **Style**, or **Color** from the **Lines** menu.
   - Format the chart's **Background Color** from the **Chart** menu.

3. When you finish formatting one or more boxes, click outside them.

N O T E There's one limitation to Microsoft Organization Chart formatting: Organization charts have a way of getting very wide quickly. The only way to limit the size of individual boxes is to reduce the size of text inside them. ■

Adding Your Company Logo to Your Organization Charts

Using Microsoft Organization Chart 2.0, you can place your company's logo (or any other bitmapped image) in the background of your organization charts.

To place an image in your organization chart, open Microsoft Organization Chart 2.0 and follow these steps:

1. Open a bitmapped version of your corporate logo, such as a BMP, PCX, TIF, GIF, or JPG file. (Depending on the format, you can use Microsoft Paint, Microsoft Photo Editor, or another graphics program.)

 TIP If you have only "vector art," such as a CorelDRAW file, you might be able to open it in a program such as Paint Shop Pro and copy it to the Clipboard from there.

2. In your graphics software, select the image (or part of it).
3. Choose **Edit**, **Copy**.
4. Switch to Microsoft Organization Chart 2.0.
5. Click the background of your organization chart (don't click on a box within the chart).
6. Choose **Edit**, **Paste**. The image appears in your organization chart.
7. Drag the image to the location where you want it.

Storing an Image for Use on Your Intranet

Today, one of the most common uses for organization charts is on corporate intranets. Not surprisingly, the native OPX format for organization charts isn't readable on the Web. In Office 2000, when you save an Office document containing an organization chart as a Web page, a copy of the chart is stored as a separate transparent GIF file in the folder that accompanies the Web page. Later, if you reopen the file, you can still double-click on the organization chart to edit it in Microsoft Organization Chart; when you resave the file, a replacement GIF is also created.

Integrating Microsoft Organization Chart 2.0 with Org Plus for Windows

Microsoft Organization Chart 2.0 is actually a stripped-down version of Broderbund's Org Plus for Windows and can open OPX chart files created by the following versions of Org Plus for Windows:

- Version 3.1
- Advanced Versions 4.0, 5.0, 6.0, and 6.01
- Org Plus for Windows Versions 1.0 and 2.0

Org Plus features that do not exist in Microsoft Organization Chart 2.0 will be lost when the file is saved again, so it makes sense to save the file under a new name.

If you save a chart in OPX format, you'll be able to open it in Org Plus for Windows.

Understanding Organizational Chart Features That Are Unavailable in Microsoft Organization Chart 2.0

If you need any of the capability to work with any of the following features, you might want to upgrade to Org Plus for Windows:

- The capability to create bigger charts and squeeze bigger charts into less space
- More control over how individual boxes (or groups of boxes) appear
- Hidden boxes and hidden information
- Images in boxes, such as photos of individuals
- Additional text fields for each individual
- Automatically updatable date stamps and Amount fields
- Find/Replace information in organization chart boxes
- Style sheets for standardizing chart appearance
- Calculations and employee counting features
- The capability to import organization chart information from databases and other software
- More extensive graphics file import/export capabilities

 TIP For information about one additional Office applet, the Microsoft Chart Wizard, see Chapter 11, "Customizing FrontPage to Your Organization's Needs."

Microsoft Map

Office 2000 comes with a mapping applet, Microsoft Map, which can be valuable if you chart sales or other results by state or nation. In a default installation, Microsoft Map should install on first run when invoked from Access or Excel. However, in very late betas, Microsoft Map occasionally did not register properly as an OLE application unless it was fully installed on each workstation (Run on My Computer, not Install on First Run). You might want to test this in your own environment and err on the side of installing Microsoft Map on each workstation you expect to need it.

After Microsoft Map is installed, follow these steps to insert a map in an Excel worksheet:

1. Insert data in Excel that contains labels that correspond to recognized names or initials of geographic locations. (Access can also serve as a data source for Microsoft Map.)

 TIP You can find the formats Microsoft Map recognizes in the Mapstats.xls demographics data worksheet file, which is typically installed in the \Program Files\Common Files\Microsoft Shared\Datamap\Data folder.

2. Select the data you want to map.
3. If the **Map** button appears on your standard toolbar, click it. If it does not appear, choose **Insert, Object**; in the **Create New** tab of the Object dialog box, double-click on **Microsoft Map**.

4. In many cases, Microsoft Map will ask you to choose among multiple maps that fit the data you've selected (see Figure 29.15). If so, select the map you prefer and click **OK**.

FIGURE 29.15
If more than one map in the Microsoft Map library appears to fit your data points, you're asked which one you want to use.

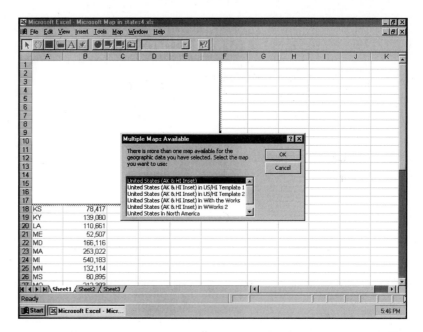

5. If Microsoft Map finds names or data points it cannot interpret, it asks you to fix them (or allows you to delete them). Click **OK** when you're finished. Microsoft Map inserts the map and displays the Microsoft Map Control next to it.

N O T E Microsoft Map is a downsized version of MapInfo Professional, which offers much more sophisticated tools for data analysis. ▉

Customizing Microsoft Map Formats

Microsoft Map offers extensive control over the formatting, content, and behavior of the maps you create. For example, you can do any of the following:

- Add features to your map such as U.S. Airports, Cities, Major Cities, and/or Highways (through **Map**, **Features**).
- Add even more features, such as 5-digit zip code centers (through **Map**, **Add Feature**).
- Change your map's fill color (through **Map**, **Features**).
- Control the number of ranges of shading in a map and how those ranges are defined (accessible by choosing **Map**, **Value Shading Options**, **Value Shading Options**).
- Edit and format the title and subtitle of your map and map legend entries (accessible by choosing **Map**, **Value Shading Options**, **Legend Options**).

- Add labels to individual map features (through **Tools**, **L**abeler).

- Change the map's view (move it, zoom in or out, resize it, or pan to highlight a specific location).

Sharing Custom Map Formats Throughout Your Organization

It's all well and good to customize a single map, but the real value to your organization occurs when you reuse the map and share it with your colleagues. To save a map template, choose **Map**, **S**ave Map Template. The Save Map Template dialog box opens. You can choose to store one or both of the following types of information:

- Map Features (the current list of map features, such as U.S. Highways or 5-Digit zip Code Centers)

- View (how the map has been moved, zoomed, or panned)

Enter a name for the new map template and click **Save**. Microsoft Map creates a new map template file using the first word of the name you assign and the GST extension. The file is stored along with your existing templates in the \Program Files\Common Files\Microsoft Shared\Datamap\Data folder. You can copy this file to the corresponding folder on any other computer to make the same template available there.

After you do so, the new template is listed as an option whenever a user creates a new map that contains data relevant to that template. For example, if you create a template with a map of the 50 U.S. states, that template will appear as an option when a user creates a similar map, but not when a user creates a map of European countries.

Basic Demographic Information Included with Office   If you need basic demographic information to include in your maps—perhaps for high-level market research and planning—Excel and Microsoft Map might come with some of what you need. The file Mapstats.Xls contains the following information (although you should be aware that the data is now four or five years old and was not updated along with the new version of Office):

- World population statistics by nation, including male and female population, population by age, and rural and urban population

- USA population statistics by state, including male and female population and population by age, race, and household income

- Canadian population by province, including male and female population, ethnic background, number and average size of households, household income, and data about renters and homeowners

- Mexican population by province, including male and female population and population by age, household size, household income, and employment by industry

- European population by nation, age, and employment, with annual changes in total population from 1975 through 1993

- A list of counties throughout the United Kingdom and the Republic of Ireland, but no population statistics

- Australian population by state, including male and female population; population by age, ethnic background, and housing; and total businesses and employment
- A list of locations throughout Southern Africa, but no population statistics

Most of the information is now at least a few years old; this file has not been updated for Office 2000. If you need more detailed or more recent data, the file also lists several available sources (although by no means all of them). Another option is to purchase Microsoft MapPoint, Microsoft's new Office-compatible mapping software that was released in spring 1999 at roughly the same time as Microsoft Office 2000.

Using Maps on Web Pages

As with other features discussed in this chapter, if you save an Office 2000 file containing a Microsoft Map as a Web page, a copy of the map will be created in GIF format, and that copy will appear on your Web site. The original map will still, however, be available for editing when necessary.

If you are posting the maps for external consumption, you might want to check them in a browser. The GIFs that Office 2000 creates from maps sometimes have slight gray artifacts. These can easily be eliminated with image-editing software (for example, by using the Brightness and AutoBalance controls in Microsoft Photo Editor). Keep in mind that if you edit the map file and resave the document as a Web page, Office will create a replacement GIF that might have the same problem as the original. ●

Enhancing Office with Third-Party Products

by Bill Camarda

Office is remarkably malleable. It can be extended in many ways with templates and sample files, macros, Visual Basic programs, and Component Object Model (COM) add-ins (fully compiled DLLs) that extend the Microsoft Office environment. This gives software developers significant opportunities to build on Office, delivering features that Microsoft left out, or specialized capabilities unlikely to be made part of a general-purpose office software suite.

Often, these supplementary products give the Office administrator important options for solving business problems or for improving productivity. In this chapter, you learn about the following important categories of products for extending Microsoft Office:

- Supplemental proofing tools
- Third-party Excel worksheets and add-ins
- Enhancements to Microsoft Word
- Voice recognition software
- Vertical market software
- Tools for publishing Help files

In reading this chapter, you might discover that a third-party developer has already streamlined tasks you thought were impossible or impractical with Office, and built those tasks into a product you can purchase off-the-shelf.

Reviewing Specialized Proofing Tools from Spellex

Office 2000 and Word 2000 for Windows ship with standard English-language proofing tools from Microsoft, including a 137,000-word dictionary based on the *American Heritage Dictionary*. You might, however, want to extend Office's proofing capabilities by adding specialized dictionaries for specific disciplines, such as medicine and law. Specialized dictionaries are available from Spellex: 800-442-9673 or `http://www.spellex.com`.

Spellex currently offers the following dictionaries (compatible with the U.S. English version of Office 2000 only:

- **Spellex Medical.** Covers anatomy, anesthesiology, bacteriology, biology, cardiology, dentistry, hematology, immunology, internal medicine, neurology, nursing, oncology, ophthalmology, pathology, psychiatry, radiology, toxicology, veterinary medicine, and many other disciplines

- **Spellex Pharmaceutical.** Covers anesthetics, anti-infective agents, antineoplastic agents, cardiovascular drugs, central nervous system agents, dental agents, diagnostic agents, enzymes, gastrointestinal drugs, oxytopics, serums, vaccines, vitamins, generic and trade names, experimental and investigational drugs, and more

- **Spellex Legal.** Covers administrative law, admiralty law, antitrust, bankruptcy, civil, commercial, computer, constitutional, contract, conveyancing, corporate, criminal, family, immigration, insurance, labor/employment, litigation, patent, trademark/copyright, tax, wills, and other areas of law; integrates with Spellex Medical for legal professionals involved with healthcare, workers' compensation, bodily injury, medical malpractice, and related fields

- **Spellex Dental.** Covers oral pathology, radiography, orthodontics, endodontics, prosthodontics, pedodontics, periodontics, dental pharmacology, general and hospital dentistry, dental surgery, drugs, equipment, and materials

- **Spellex Geographical.** Covers more than 50,000 geographical names, including more than 27,000 U.S. towns and cities; current and ancient place names from world religion, mythology, literature, culture, and more

- **Spellex Technical.** Covers more than 50,000 scientific and engineering terms from astronomy, anatomy, acoustics, architecture, biology, chemistry, chemical engineering, communications, computer science, ecology, electronics, engineering, geology, hydrology, industrial engineering, mapping, mathematics, mechanical engineering, mineralogy, physics, physiology, science and technology, statistics, thermodynamics, virology, zoology, and more

Spellex also provides the Spell-X-Plus subscription, which provides quarterly updates for new medical and pharmaceutical terms.

Simplifying Your Work with Third-Party Worksheets and Functions

Several companies are in the business of developing prebuilt Excel worksheets and functions that simplify the preparation of a wide variety of financial statements and documents. Some of the most widely used solutions are covered in the following three sections.

Worksheet Solutions from VillageSoft

Village Software (www.villagesoft.com) is the company that creates many of the wizards and templates that Microsoft provides as standard with Office 2000. The firm also offers three lines of business products designed to work with Office.

The FastAnswer family of products is designed to offer in-depth, analytical solutions for a wide range of problems.

- **Fast-Cast for Ventures FastAnswer.** Helps prepare detailed financial plans.
- **Ratio Evaluator FastAnswer.** Calculates more than two dozen key financial ratios.
- **Lease vs. Purchase FastAnswer.** Helps evaluate lease versus purchase decisions for a wide range of assets.
- **Stock Investor Plus FastAnswer.** Helps investors make better buy/sell decisions.
- **Stock Investor Plus DataLink FastAnswer.** Imports investment data from online services.
- **Net Worth Builder FastAnswer.** Helps identify an individual's financial strengths and weaknesses.
- **The Money Controller FastAnswer.** Software for budgeting and printing checks.
- **Business Troubleshooter FastAnswer.** Helps small business owners identify and fix five key areas of operating and financial risk.
- **Litigation Budget FastAnswer.** Budgets the potential cost of litigation.
- **401(k) Forecaster FastAnswer.** Analyzes 401(k) or 403(b) plan performance.
- **Retirement Planner FastAnswer.** Determines how much you need to save to meet your retirement goals.
- **Sales Planner FastAnswer.** Plans for higher sales.
- **Weekly Employee Scheduler FastAnswer.** Creates weekly employee schedules.

The FastStart family of products provides electronic forms-based solutions that can help automate your office.

- **FastStart Standard Super Forms Pack.** Create invoices, purchase orders, and other business documents.
- **FastStart Office Super Forms Pack.** Run your business or home office more smoothly.

- **FastStart Necessary Super Forms Pack.** Basic forms for business or home office.
- **FastStart Sales & Marketing Super Forms Packs I and II.** Sales and marketing forms.
- **FastStart Analysis Pack.** Entry-level analytical worksheets for small business.
- **FastStart Human Resources Pack.** Forms to help you organize your workforce more effectively.

The FastPlans family of products helps you create detailed business and financial documents that incorporate analysis, presentation, and text.

- **Business Planning FastPlan.** A Microsoft Office Wizard for writing business plans.
- **Meeting Organizer FastPlan.** A Microsoft Office Wizard for organizing and managing meetings.
- **Proposal and Marketing FastPlan.** Helps create proposals and marketing plans.
- **Report FastPlan.** Helps organize reports more quickly.
- **Client Billing FastPlan.** Helps streamline and organize small business client billing.

Worksheet Solutions from KMT Software

KMT Software Inc. (`www.kmt.com`) offers a wide variety of business and personal forms and templates, including the following

- **Office In Color—Excel Template Collection.** Provides colorful templates for creating company and personal finance worksheets, sales and marketing worksheets, business forms, human resources forms, real estate analysis forms, and personal planners.
- **Excel Results Template Collection.** Includes more than 170 Internet-enabled Excel business and personal form templates for $39.95; another $10 purchases the Office Results Platinum Collection, which also includes 250 Word templates.
- **Amortization Builder.** Creates month-by-month statements for an entire loan period of up to 50 years in an Excel workbook. This product enables you to incorporate added payments and balloon payments and to record each payment as it is made.
- **Ultimate Financial Calculator.** Provides worksheets for solving a wide variety of financial problems, from determining the value of a bond to establishing book and liquidity values; liquidity and activity ratios; debt and profitability rations; net present values; future values; annual and real rates of return; loan payoff amounts; making refinancing decisions; personal safety debt ratios, and more.

N O T E   KMT also does software consulting, and at press time was offering to create new Excel or Word forms for $100 apiece, if you permit KMT to include generic versions of these forms in their future products.

Freeware Worksheets from Baarns Consulting

Baarns Consulting (`www.baarns.com`) has made several of its Excel worksheets available at no charge. To reach these free files, visit `archive.baarns.com/IE4/index_software.asp`.

Next, select Software, and then online catalog, to find a listing of the free files.

These worksheets were created for earlier versions of Excel and have not been tested under Excel 2000. Most of them should work well, although no technical support is available. The no-cost worksheets include the following:

Part IV

Ch 30

- **Added Payment Mortgage.** Shows how much money you can save by paying off more principal on a mortgage early.

- **Biweekly Mortgage Amortization.** Shows how much money you can save by making a biweekly mortgage payment instead of paying once a month.

- **Cost Estimating Form.** Provides template for estimating job costs, based on unit material costs and/or labor hours (see Figure 30.1).

- **Employee Database.** Keeps records of the people working for you, and makes extensive use of Excel's AutoFilter feature to help you track them.

- **Financial Ratio Analysis.** Helps you compare the value of up to four stocks at a time.

- **Inventory Tracker.** Helps you track fast-changing inventory levels, reordering information and related statistics.

- **Mortgage Analysis.** Helps you evaluate the size of the mortgage you can qualify for.

- **Phone Number Names.** Helps you create easy-to-remember words from the phone numbers the telephone company has assigned you.

- **Scheduler.** Helps you set up project activities interactively, somewhat like Gantt or Pert charts.

- **The Baarns Utilities for Microsoft Excel.** Increases your productivity with a collection of tools for Excel. Some of these have since been incorporated into Excel itself.

- **Time Billing Log and Invoice.** Helps manage your small business with a convenient tool. This workbook tracks time and creates invoices for small businesses that bill by the hour.

The Power Utility Pak for Excel

Power Utility Pak (PUP) for Excel 97 and 2000, from JWalk & Associates (`www.j-walk.com`), adds more than 40 functions to Excel, including useful functions such as CREDITCARD, which returns the card type of a credit card number, or returns an "Invalid" notice if the number is not valid. PUP 2000 also adds more than 30 utilities for editing text, formatting, managing worksheets, workbooks, and charts, batch printing, and exporting range selections as graphics or separate files.

FIGURE 30.1

Baarns Consulting's free cost estimating worksheet.

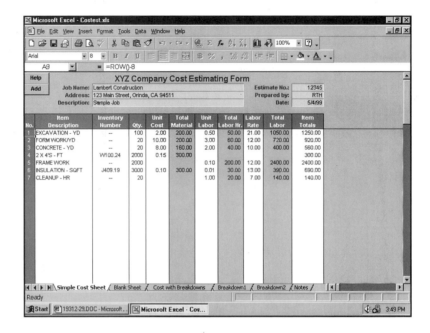

TIP

Power Utility Pak for Excel costs $39.95, but for $59.95 you can purchase an unlocked version that allows you to read the source code—a rare opportunity to learn how real-world Excel Visual Basic for Applications (VBA) programming is done, from an expert.

Improving Excel's Decision Analysis Capabilities

Excel 2000 comes with a variety of analysis tools, including Solver, Goal Seek, and Scenario Manager. But for many sophisticated worksheet users, especially enterprise planners and decision-makers, these tools might be insufficient. Third parties have filled in the gap with a variety of tools, which are discussed next.

Premium Solver Plus: Replacing Excel's Solver

Excel 2000's Solver feature is designed to help you identify the best solutions to a problem given a certain set of facts and assumptions. Some sophisticated users might find that the built-in Solver feature does not provide adequate speed or power. (In particular, the standard Solver limits users to 200 decision variables.)

For these users, you might want to consider Premium Solver Plus 3.5, from Frontline Systems, Inc. (**www.frontsys.com**, 775-831-0300). This is an upwardly compatible Solver extension built by the company that helped create the Solver included in Excel. It is designed to solve much larger problems—including problems with up to 2,000 variables—at speeds from three to several hundred times faster than the standard Solver.

The latest version includes a feature called Evolutionary Solver, which uses genetic and evolutionary algorithms to find good solutions for Excel models that use any standard or user-written functions, even those with IF, CHOOSE, or LOOKUP—functions that often cause Excel's built-in Solver to fail.

After you install Premium Solver, it appears in place of the standard Solver when you choose **Tools**, **Solver**. It provides similar dialog boxes with additional features, and can work with existing Solver models, macros, and custom VBA procedures that your users have already developed.

Risk Assessment Tools

DecisionTools Suite from Palisade Corporation (**www.palisade.com**, 800-432-7475) adds an Excel toolbar providing integrated access to the five following advanced analysis products (which can also be purchased separately).

- **@RISK 3.5.** Adds Monte Carlo simulation to worksheet models. Monte Carlo simulation works like this. First, you represent the uncertainty in your worksheet by selecting a cell and replacing its value with one of 37 @RISK probability distribution functions, including functions such as Beta, Erlang, Binomial, Poisson, Lognormal, Chi-Square, Pareto, and many others. Then, you select the cell(s) with values in which you're interested, and then click **Add Output** in the @RISK toolbar. Next, click **Simulate**. @RISK runs hundreds of thousands of recalculations, each time selecting new random values based on your @RISK functions. Each recalculation shows a possible scenario; when @RISK finishes, it summarizes and displays the results in a new @RISK window. You learn not only what could happen in a given situation, but how likely it is to happen.

- **PrecisionTree.** Designed for anyone faced with a set of complex decisions, PrecisionTree helps you create decision trees and influence diagrams in your worksheets, so you can clarify the relationships between elements of a problem, model sequences of events, and make better decisions. PrecisionTree helps you see the payoff and probability of each alternative path you might take, and then create a full report with statistics that supports the decision you choose. PrecisionTree's sensitivity analysis helps you identify the most important variable in a decision. A more powerful version, PrecisionTree Pro, adds Policy Suggestion Reports that create decision trees showing only the optimal decisions; and Strategy Region Graphs displaying expected values for each decision across the range of one or two variables.

- **TopRank.** Adds more sophisticated what-if analysis to Excel, showing which cells affect results the most and linking them in order of importance.

- **BestFit.** Takes up to 30,000 data points or pairs and tests up to 26 distribution types to find the one that fits best. BestFit accepts three types of data: sample, density, and cumulative. BestFit tests up to 26 distribution types using advanced optimization algorithms.

- **RiskView.** Enables you to view, assess, and create probability distributions.

A competing product, Crystal Ball Pro from Decisioneering (**www.decisioneering.com**, 1-800-289-2550), also works as an Excel add-in and provides sophisticated Monte Carlo simulation.

With Crystal Ball Pro's OptQuest component, Excel can automatically search for an optimal set of decision variables within a simulation model based on the goal you're trying to achieve. Although none of today's decision analysis tools is easy to use, OptQuest provides wizards that simplify things a good deal. Crystal Ball Pro also comes with Extenders that can help you refine your analysis and display the results. These include

- **Tornado Charts.** Helps analyze the impact of individual variables on the target outcome
- **2D Simulation.** Independently accounts for uncertainty and variability in your simulations
- **Correlation Matrices.** Quickly defines and automates the correlation of assumptions
- **Decision Tables.** Evaluates the impact of alternative decisions in your simulation
- **Bootstrap.** Evaluates your forecasts for reliability and accuracy

Reviewing General Word Enhancements

Thanks to VBA—and its predecessor, WordBasic—you can now extend Word with a wide variety of new features.

Woody Leonhard's Pinecliffe International (**www.wopr.com**) specializes in such enhancements, and *WOPR* (*Woody's Office Power Pack*) 2000 is the latest release. WOPR 2000 has dozens of components, but as an Office administrator, you might especially appreciate using (or providing colleagues with) the following:

- **WOPR Enveloper.** Prints envelopes. This more powerful envelope printing utility simplifies the management of multiple custom envelopes.
- **Word 2x4.** Enables users to easily print documents in duplex, 2-up, 4-up, trifold, booklet, and thumbnail formats
- **WOPR Rebuild File.** Reconstructs many corrupted Word documents or templates
- **WOPR Normal Quotes.** Converts "smart quotes" to normal quotes for export to software that can't understand smart quotes

N O T E A free, fully licensed and unrestricted copy of WOPR 2000 is included with each of the following Que *Special Edition* books for Office 2000:

- *Special Edition Using Office 2000*
- *Special Edition Using Word 2000*
- *Special Edition Using Excel 2000*
- *Special Edition Using PowerPoint 2000*
- *Special Edition Using Access 2000*
- *Special Edition Using Outlook 2000*
- *Special Edition Using FrontPage 2000*

Integrating Voice Recognition into Word and Other Office Programs

Slowly but surely, voice recognition software is coming of age. Current voice recognition products support continuous voice recognition, which means users can speak naturally, without inserting artificial pauses between every word. Several of these new packages offer some level of integration with Microsoft Word, enabling automated dictation and control of many Word features.

It's unlikely that you'll implement voice recognition companywide any time soon—especially if you use an open office layout that routinely gets noisy. You might, however, want to provide this software for the following:

- Executives and others with private offices who do extensive dictation
- Employees who do not type or need their hands free
- Physically challenged employees

Be aware of the following two crucial limitations to today's voice recognition systems:

- Hardware requirements are stiff. Typically, 166MHz MMX Pentiums are a bare minimum, and the systems need large chunks of hard disk space. You also need high-quality microphones and a highly Sound Blaster–compatible sound card. In some cases, the audio built into your business PCs might not be sufficiently compatible. Before investing, check the compatibility lists provided by the vendors who make the software you're considering.
- Where users invest time in "training" the system to recognize a specific voice, voice recognition accuracy rates might be as high as 95% or 96%—but that still means one correction every 20–25 words. Moreover, because voice recognition software types only real words, the remaining errors are largely immune to a spelling checker (although a grammar checker might help a bit). Even small differences in performance can make a large difference in the ultimate productivity gains that voice recognition delivers.

Following are three product families that are market leaders in the voice recognition business:

- Dragon Systems' NaturallySpeaking products
- IBM's ViaVoice products
- Lernout & Hauspie's Voice Xpress products

Dragon NaturallySpeaking

Dragon NaturallySpeaking Preferred 3.5 **www.dragonsystems.com** and the rest of the NaturallySpeaking product family are widely acknowledged to offer very strong performance. NaturallySpeaking Deluxe adds macro capabilities, multiple topics (enabling users who dictate on several subjects to improve performance by telling the software which topic they're about to discuss), and access to a larger active dictionary—a dictionary that is immediately available while the user is dictating.

Part

IV

Ch

30

Earlier versions of Dragon NaturallySpeaking, through the 2.x versions, did not integrate with Microsoft Word as smoothly as they might have; it was necessary to download an add-on to NaturallySpeaking, Dragon NaturalWord, to edit by voice from within Word. This is no longer the case; the latest versions offer "Select-and-Say" editing features that do work from within Word.

 TIP Dragon Systems also offers specialized legal and medical voice recognition systems, which are typically configured and sold by resellers.

IBM ViaVoice Products

IBM's ViaVoice Executive and ViaVoice Office (www.ibm.com/viavoice) offer good-quality voice recognition support for voice macros that enable you to insert extensive blocks of text by speaking only a word or two, the ability to dictate into Microsoft Word 2000; some support for controlling Word 2000 menus and formatting commands by voice. ViaVoice Executive and ViaVoice Office come with dictionary supplements for business and finance; other specialized dictionaries, including medical dictionaries, are available for purchase.

Lernout & Hauspie's L&H Voice Xpress Professional Version 4

Lernout & Hauspie's L&H Voice Xpress Professional version 4 (www.lhs.com) enables users to dictate into Word 2000/97/95, Excel 97, PowerPoint 97, Outlook 98, Internet Explorer 4.0 and Windows Explorer. They can also control the software's menus and formatting commands by voice, using a wide variety of voice commands, including variations of a single command such as "bold this word" and "bold that word."

L&H Voice Xpress Professional version 4 supports macros—that is, you can define a short phrase that corresponds to a large block of text that the software automatically inserts, much like an AutoText entry. It also contains speaker profiles that might improve accuracy for men, women, teenagers, and children.

The software also supports the new Speech Application Programming Interface (SAPI) from Microsoft, which could lead to easier integration of voice recognition with future applications. It's worth mentioning that Lernout & Hauspie has made strategic agreements with Microsoft that could eventually result in its base voice recognition technology becoming part of the Windows operating system.

Lernout & Hauspie has recently released three products that include Microsoft Office-integrated speech recognition customized for specific fields, including

- L&H Voice Xpress for Medicine Version 4
- L&H Voice Xpress for Legal Version 4
- L&H Voice Xpress for Safety Version 4 (public safety and law enforcement)

Evaluating Vertical Market Tools

There are specialized tools for Office users in a wide variety of industries. This section presents just a few examples.

Real Estate

Real Estate Investment Analysis, Version 10.0, from RealData (**www.realdata.com**, 203-838-2670) is a comprehensive income-property investment analysis tool for residential or commercial real estate, in the form of an Excel workbook. Each linked module corresponds to a page in the workbook, giving users the flexibility to perform simple or complex analysis.

Part
IV
Ch
30

Corporate Video

For your corporate video department, Indelible, Ink.'s ScriptWright (**www.kois.com/ink/info.html**, 212-255-1956, ext. 301) transforms Word into a dedicated screenplay word processor, with the styles, keyboard, menu, and toolbar customizations and tools that streamline all the mechanics of writing and editing a screenplay. ScriptWright enables you to format your screenplay in three ways: Draft, Master, and Shooting. A stripped-down, free demo version is available at **www.kois.com/ink/**.

Accessing Help File Publishing Tools

Many organizations create manuals and other long documents, and for some, Microsoft Word's built-in tools aren't enough. Even more to the point, what if you want to turn Word files into electronic Help files? Two third-party packages can help.

Doc-to-Help Professional 4.0 from WexTech Systems, Inc.

Doc-to-Help Professional 4.0 from WexTech Systems, Inc. (**www.wextech.com**, 914-741-9700) installs into Microsoft Word and adds features that enable you to build documentation, interactive and Web-based Help at the same time, from a single source file. Doc-to-Help also contains professional, customizable templates that handle virtually all layout details, including headers and footers, tables, crop marks, side heads, even and odd pages, gutters, page numbering, margin notes, and a large part of the work involved in building glossaries and indexes.

After you build your source file, you can create help in virtually any format you want, including print and the following electronic formats:

- Windows 95/Windows NT Help (standard 32-bit Windows help files)
- Windows 3.0 and/or 3.1 Help (standard 16-bit Windows Help files)
- HTML Help (the new, HTML-based Help files from Microsoft)
- Doc-to-Help (creates compiled, ActiveX-enabled or Java-enabled HTML Help)
- Standard HTML (for posting on intranets or Web sites)

Other Help Authoring Tools

Doc-to-Help is by far the market leader and one of the most comprehensive Help authoring solutions available. There are, however, other choices, including

- **RoboHelp Office** from Blue Sky Software (`www.blueskysoftware.com`). This product automatically manages the design and layout of a Help system, enabling you to create multiple types of Help formats, including HTML Help and classic WinHelp, from the same Word documents.

- **EasyHTML/Help** from Eon Solutions, Ltd. (`www.eon-solutions.com`, UK phone: +44 1625 829 037). EasyHTML/Help adds a set of templates, macros, and toolbars to Microsoft Word. If you've built a Word document with heading styles, you can use EasyHTML/Help's AutoTopic feature to transform those headings into pages in your Help file. To add a hyperlink, select the text you want to make into a hyperlink and click **AutoLink**. After you finish adding headings and hyperlinks, click **Process** on the EasyHTML/Help toolbar, and the software creates your Help file.

Reviewing Other Office-Compatible Software

Microsoft has established a program of certification for vendors who want to create *Office-compatible* software, and several vendors have built a good business in this marketplace, notably Visio. Office-compatible products must share nearly identical menu structures, toolbars, shortcut keys, and shortcut menus with Microsoft Office, and provide strong data exchange capabilities with Microsoft Office. In many cases, these applications install toolbar buttons within Microsoft Office applications, providing one-click access to the application.

Visio 2000 from Visio Corporation

Visio 2000 from Visio Corporation (`www.visio.com`) provides comprehensive business drawing tools based on libraries of templates and shapes that eliminate the need for users to create their own graphics from scratch. Visio also works with the Microsoft Office Binder, making it possible to create files that combine Visio pages with text from Word and worksheets from Excel.

Visio 2000 includes extensive flowcharting shapes for total quality management, audit, and data flow diagrams; easier ways to publish diagrams on the Web; new marketing shapes; importing and exporting of diagrams from Microsoft Project; and support for the VBA macro programming language. If you choose, Visio 2000 can install a toolbar button on the Standard toolbar in either Word or Excel, making it especially easy to access from within Office.

Office Advantage from MetaCreations

MetaCreations, best known for graphic design software such as Kai's Power Tools, has released Office Advantage, a software package that runs from within Excel and PowerPoint (versions 97 and 2000), making it easier to build more compelling and visually attractive charts and graphs, helping business people use high-end graphic design techniques without actually having graphic design experience.

In PowerPoint, Office Advantage automatically smoothes text and optimizes spacing, adds drop shadows to titles, cleans up graphics, and makes available slicker video transitions and Web presentation navigation tools. In Excel, Office Advantage adds real-time 3D-chart exploration, including rotation, pan and zoom, data-cutting planes, and adjustable transparency; smoothes out chart titles, and provides more attractive designs than are built into Excel. For more information on Office Advantage, visit `www.metacreations.com/products/advantage`.

Part

IV

Ch

30

More Office Third-Party Resources

A wide variety of Office 2000-compatible products is available, in addition to those covered in this chapter. The following lists three sources for learning about them:

- Microsoft Office Compatible Product Listings, available at

  `www.veritest.com/mslogos/Office/office_prod.htm`

- Softseek's Microsoft Office Add-ons, Tools, and Utilities search page, available at

  `softseek.com/Business_and_Productivity/Microsoft_Office`

- Baarns Consulting's list of Microsoft Office third-party solutions, available at

  `archive.baarns.com/IE4/index_software.asp` ●

Office, the Internet, and Intranets

Deploying an Office-Centered Intranet or Web Site

by Michael A. Larson

When you think of a Web site, you usually think of various combinations of graphics and text embedded into Web pages. With Office 2000, you now have many more tools to simplify the process of adding your Office documents to a Web site. The Save As Web Page feature in Word, Excel, and PowerPoint is much more robust than in earlier versions and, with Internet Explorer 5, allows many more of the features found in Office documents to be displayed as Web pages. The task of posting Web pages is also eased through the use of Web Folders, which are basically shortcuts to Web servers. Office 2000 enables you to collaborate on edits and other comments for documents over the company Web site using the Web collaboration tools found in Word, Excel, and PowerPoint.

FrontPage, now included in several Office bundles, can check hyperlinks between Office documents and Web pages. Office documents can also be easily imported into any FrontPage Web site.

Adding Office content to an Internet, intranet, or extranet site just got easier with Office 2000.

Understanding Internet, Intranets, and Extranets

The Web revolution is now everyday routine. The Internet has evolved as a result of the standardization of a few Web technologies. These Web technologies have created the Internet, and even driven businesses toward incorporating these technologies into their internal networks. Widespread use of these Web technologies has resulted in the rise of the Internet, company intranets, and extranets. These technologies include

- Access via a standardized networking protocol, TCP/IP (Transmission Control Protocol/Internet Protocol) .

- A standard document authoring format, Hypertext Markup Language (HTML), to create Web pages.

- A browser to easily navigate this network and access other Web pages via hyperlinks.

- A Web server to host and serve Web pages via Hypertext Transfer Protocol (HTTP), mostly in response to browser page requests.

Understanding the Internet

An *Internet site* (or Web site) is a group of documents displayed for public access on the Internet network using standard Web technologies. These documents usually consist of Web pages, written in HTML, with content on virtually any topic. These sites are generally public and universally accessible from anywhere in the world where you can find a network connection. Each Web site has its own network address. The network address is often mapped to a common *domain* name, such as **www.microsoft.com**.

Web sites can contain content on any topic. Common business uses for Web sites include

- Product advertising
- Technical support
- Customer feedback forums
- Press releases
- Company information
- Direct sales, also called e-commerce (electronic commerce)

One of the primary advantages of a Web site for a business is the round-the-clock access by anyone from virtually anywhere. Thus, the potential customer base for a business is no longer limited to a given city or locale.

Understanding Intranets

An *intranet* is a network designed for the private use of an organization, but built with the same standards and protocols used by the public Internet. Using an intranet looks and feels like surfing the Web, but rather than visiting multiple public Web sites, you access internal company information. What kind of information? The kind that previously required enormous numbers of printed manuals and brochures such as

- Human resources data, such as company employment and benefit policies
- Product information, such as specification sheets
- Sales and marketing information, such as sample proposals, case studies, and referrals
- Internal directories and contact information

Intranets can be of any size; they can serve an entire company, a division, or even just a work-group. They're especially helpful for cross-functional teams, such as R&D or product development teams, which might need to share the same information even though they are not in the same location. No matter how you use your intranet, however, you leverage the same advantages that are familiar to users of the Web, such as the following:

- Easy point-and-click navigation to any relevant information, wherever it might be stored
- Lower startup costs than previous solutions, and, potentially, lower administrative costs as well
- Improved employee productivity through faster access to relevant information

It's no wonder that many observers see intranets growing even more explosively than the Web has grown.

Understanding Extranets

An *extranet* is a group of cooperative Internet or intranet sites. Businesses within a given sector might need to routinely share information. Typical business relationships might include vendors, suppliers, or subcontractors. Because so much business information is incorporated into intranets and Web sites, extranets have grown as a means for efficiently sharing this information.

Extranets are typically secure Web sites or a combination of secure and public content. Because much of the shared business information would be of great interest to competitors, most content is protected by passwords or encryption. Within this secure environment, participating companies or clients can exchange information quickly and freely, enhancing their competitive edge. The extranet provides the round-the-clock access of an Internet site with the security and specialized capability typically found within an intranet.

Introducing the New and Expanded Web Capability in Office 2000

A host of new Web-related technologies have been built into Office 2000. Microsoft has recognized that the Internet is here to stay and that it now plays a key role in many different business environments. Many of these businesses have standardized on Microsoft Office and have clamored for a more seamless integration of Web capability within Office applications. Office 2000 represents a significant improvement in the application of Web technologies over Office 97. Table 31.1 shows a brief comparison of the Office 97 Web features and the new, improved Web capability found in Office 2000.

Table 31.1 Comparing Office 97 and Office 2000 Web Features

Feature	Office 97	Office 2000
Conversion to HTML	Loss of formatting	Mostly converted
Binary/Web files	One or the other	Interchangeable
Import Web pages	Pages changed	True rendering
Publish Web pages	Complicated Wizard	Web Folders

A brand-new Web feature, Web Collaboration, has been introduced in Office 2000.

Gaining Truer Conversion to Web Pages with Supplemented HTML

One of the shortcomings of HTML is its inability to mimic all the features found in Office applications. HTML was never designed with Office compatibility in mind. The main purpose of HTML was to provide a standard means for displaying basic text and graphical information in browsers on any platform (Windows, UNIX, Macintosh, OS/2, and so on). Office applications are designed to incorporate a large number of functional features for uses in word processing, spreadsheets, presentations, and simple databases.

When the popularity of the Internet exploded, many people wanted to take the content in their Office documents and display it on the Web. Unfortunately, saving feature-laden Office files to simpler HTML often resulted in the loss of formatting and some graphical content. More importantly, the dynamic nature of many Office documents (linked formulas in spreadsheets, for example) could not be reproduced at all by HTML.

By far the most important change in Office 2000 is the improved robustness of the HTML format. Microsoft has cleverly incorporated a wide variety of new Web technologies that have been developed since Office 97 was brought to market. This new alphabet soup of technologies includes XML (eXtensible Markup Language, Cascading Style Sheets (CSS), Vector Markup Language (VML), and JavaScript and Visual Basic Script (VBScript). The following is a short overview of each of these technologies:

■ **XML.** *eXtensible Markup Language* is more robust and extensible, hence its name, than HTML. You can define new tags and their uses at any time and in any way by referencing them in an associated text document. The strength of XML is in using these new tags to identify specific information. For instance, if you're talking about a golf wood on a Web page, your page can include golf-specific tags. This distinguishes your page from the many others that might be dealing with carpentry; those pages would probably use woodworking-specific tags. People who now want to look only for golf wood Web pages can now filter out the woodworking pages or vice versa. This technology vastly improves a user's ability to find specific-subject Web pages and opens the Internet to extensive data mining.

■ **CSS.** *Cascading Style Sheets* are used to define the layout of a document precisely. Style sheets are more powerful than the styles found in Word because style sheets can also specify page layout. A style sheet can be a separate document or embedded in each HTML page. Because browsers have different capabilities in how they interpret these styles, they interpret what they can and ignore the rest; that is, they cascade down in their interpretation and display what they are able to. Netscape Navigator 3 and Microsoft Internet Explorer 2 browsers or earlier cannot read these style sheets. CSS are actually a part of the HTML 4.0 specification.

■ **VML.** *Vector Markup Language* uses text to define geometric shapes, colors, line widths, and so on. These words are then interpreted and displayed as graphical images in browsers that understand VML (currently only Microsoft Internet Explorer 5). No matter what size circle you want to display, you are using the same amount of text to define it.

■ **JavaScript or VBScript.** Both of these script-style programming languages are in common, everyday use on the Web right now. They are both robust. *The vast majority of browsers support JavaScript; VBScript* is supported only by Microsoft Internet Explorer browsers. These languages enable you to program interactivity into Web pages.

▶ For a more complete discussion of these new technologies, their advantages and disadvantages, **see** Chapter 33, "Managing HTML/XML As Your Primary File Format," on **p. 867**.

Part

V

Ch

31

What this means is that many (but not all) of the features in Office 2000 files can be retained in Web pages using HTML combined with all the new technologies shown earlier. Saving an Office file as a Web page causes no loss of features.

Blurring the Line Between Binary and Web Page File Formats

The capability to save all the contents of an Office file as a Web page is called *round tripping*. For instance, if an Excel worksheet is saved as a Web page, the resulting Web page can be viewed in a browser. All the information present in the original Excel binary file might not, however, be displayed by the browser. If the Web page is now loaded back into Excel, all the information present in the original file is displayed in the worksheet. Even if a browser could not render some parts of the worksheet, all the information normally saved to the .xls binary file format is retained in the Web page format.

What this means is that now you can have an Office-centered Web site. When you save your Office documents as Web pages, you no longer lose any information. You no longer have to think differently about Office documents and Web pages; they both contain the same information.

Identifying Specific Web Upgrades to Individual Office Applications

Word, Excel, PowerPoint, and Access have also gained new Web-related capabilities. In Word 2000, you now can

■ Build Web forms

■ Build Web pages with frames

New capabilities in Excel 2000 include

■ Charts that update in the browser as data is updated

■ PivotTable capabilities in Web pages

With PowerPoint 2000, you can now

- Broadcast your presentation over the Internet or an intranet
- Collaborate with others online in real-time on a presentation

Access 2000 now has data access pages. These are linked to Access data, but act like forms inside browsers.

Publishing to the Web with Web Folders

To publish a Web page to a Web server in Office 97, you had to step through the somewhat complicated Web Page Wizard. In Office 2000, this process has been greatly simplified. Web Folders now enable you to work with Web pages directly from the Web server. A *Web server* is the underlying software and hardware platform for servicing requests for Web pages from browsers. All Internet, intranet, and extranet sites are hosted on a wide variety of Web servers. A *Web Folder* is a shortcut to a Web server. Web Folders enable you to save, edit, or delete files directly on a Web server without having to use other software, such as an FTP (File Transfer Protocol) client. A Web Folder is used just like any other folder on your computer or network, and is very easy to set up.

▶ For a more complete discussion of Web Folders and how to build and use them, **see** Chapter 35, "Deploying and Using Office 2000's Web-Collaboration Components," on **p. 895**.

Introducing Web Collaboration

Documents are usually the result of a team effort. Someone writes a document—a report, for instance—and passes the draft around to interested parties for review. The author takes these various revisions and incorporates them into the original document. There might be a second or even a third round of reviews before the report is finalized. This process can be lengthy and must often be manually monitored.

With Office 2000, your team can review and comment on documents using Web collaboration. *Web collaboration* is the process of using a Web server to collect in one place all the given review comments on a given document. The document to be reviewed is posted on a Web server. All interested parties access the draft document on a Web server and leave comments through an easy-to-use discussion interface.

The author can be immediately notified by email using the subscription feature in Web collaboration whenever a review comment is left about the document. Now all the comments are centralized and the author can easily collect, print, and incorporate the comments into the draft report. Monitoring the process is no more complex than checking email.

The Web collaboration capability is added to a Web server by installing Office Server Extensions, which are included with Office 2000.

Advantages of an Office-Centered Web Site

A typical intranet or Internet site is composed almost entirely of Web pages, written in HTML, usually authored in an HTML authoring environment, such as Microsoft FrontPage.

Most of the Web pages are probably authored by Web developers and placed onto Web servers administered by Webmasters. So, how might this process change with Office 2000?

- Anyone can create complete Web pages via Office applications
- No need to convert back and forth between binary and Web page formats for Excel, PowerPoint, and Word
- Anyone can post new content to the Web server using Web Folders
- No extra training for company personnel is required because building Web pages is no different from building any other Office document
- A streamlined document review process using Web-collaboration features

Disadvantages of an Office-Centered Web Site

Although the problems plaguing conversion of Office documents to HTML have been mostly solved, a few problems still persist and a few new ones have come up:

- The Web-page file content is extremely complex and cannot be easily edited by hand. Many Web-page authors like to edit the HTML source directly for optimal control. To do this on Web pages generated by Word, Excel, or PowerPoint, a Web author now has to know HTML, XML, VML, CSS, and the scripting languages, plus how they all interact.
- Even though most of the features present in Office 2000 files are now incorporated into the Web page, not all these features can be displayed or used by current browsers.
- Some features in Office applications are still not implemented in Web pages. These include passwords and versioning.

The browser question is by far the most serious problem, especially for Internet sites. This will go away with time, however, as the older browsers fall into disuse. XML is also gaining momentum and widespread acceptance. For intranet and extranet sites, where everyone can easily standardize on a particular browser version, these disadvantages are more easily manageable.

Planning an Office-Centered Web Site

The planning stage for building a Web site is somewhat different, depending on whether you're building a Web site for an internal intranet, an extranet, or a public Web site. The following sections look at the unique requirements of each.

Planning Your Intranet Site

Building an intranet can be approached in several ways. One approach is to convert all the information you want to publish into HTML files. This offers a powerful advantage: virtually anyone, anywhere, can read an HTML file through an industry-standard browser.

This option is even more attractive now that Web pages saved from Office 2000 applications appear no differently than Office documents saved as .doc, .xls, or .ppt files.

Another approach, which is taking hold among many companies that have standardized on Microsoft Internet Explorer and other Microsoft technologies, is to build a hybrid intranet that incorporates HTML pages wherever it makes sense, but also uses the company's existing Microsoft Office documents. Such an intranet can enable users to view documents in either format. It also enables anyone familiar with a Microsoft Office application to contribute content to the intranet.

Planning Your Internet Site

Because the Internet is global by definition, you have to consider the capabilities of the larger audience. For an intranet, you have some idea of the people who are accessing your site, of their hardware and software capabilities. You know none of this for the Internet. In an intranet, your organization might have standardized on PCs with Windows and Microsoft Office software. On the Internet, however, multiple operating systems are common. Some platforms, such as UNIX, do not even have a Microsoft Office version. Many browser versions are also in common use, some of them quite old and lacking support for some now common HTML features, such as frames.

In this situation, you have to plan your Web site to the lowest common denominator, which is plain vanilla HTML. The Web pages saved from Office 2000 applications, excluding FrontPage, might or might not work on the Internet, especially with the older browsers.

 TIP When you think about how to define the lowest common denominator for browsers to your site, think about your specific audience. If the most important audience is sophisticated and always has the latest browsers, your lowest common denominator might be Microsoft Internet Explorer 5 and Netscape Communicator 5.0. If you want to be sure your content is viewable by everyone, then you might want to use version 3 of both major browsers as your lowest common denominator.

Typically, you shouldn't use Office documents, although you shouldn't rule them out either. For instance, when Microsoft publishes a lengthy document, it often offers a hyperlink to a version of the file in Word .doc format. This is a convenient option for the millions of users who have access to Microsoft Word. Other sites also offer their content in RTF or PDF files.

Planning Your Extranet Site

Each extranet is going to be unique to the business needs driving its existence. The audience and information both are usually highly specialized. Specialty, vertical applications might be in common use, including large databases. The extranet might be hosted on a secure server and require login. Building a site in this situation takes a sophisticated approach and the use of tools that might not be needed when building a Web site or intranet.

N O T E Due to the presence of specialized Web applications and databases, you might need a Web programmer and database developer on the Web-development team for an extranet. ■

Because the audience is specialized, standardization on Web browser types and Office applications can often be counted on. You do not have to design for many different browser versions or types.

Setting Realistic Goals

An important aspect of planning your Web site is to define your goals clearly. You might want to build your Web site in stages, ensuring that each stage offers users a clear new benefit. For instance, your intranet goals might look like this:

Stage 1: Make your department's product data, policy manuals, and company directories available on the intranet.

Stage 2: Provide interactive forms that enable department employees to request vacation time and benefits changes.

Stage 3: Extend the intranet to other departments and locations, and increase its interactivity with more custom scripting and database integration.

Your Internet Web-site goals might look like this:

Stage 1: Provide a clear, straightforward description of the company and its products.

Stage 2: Provide a forum for customers and vendors to contact and provide the company with comments and suggestions.

Stage 3: Make products available for sale on an easy-to-use e-commerce site or provide technical and customer support.

Your extranet Web site goals might be

Stage 1: Provide top-level security for all data exchanges.

Stage 2: Agreement among all parties as to what information to make available.

Stage 3: Provide for technology updates that will improve the quality or speed of data flow.

Identifying Resources and Responsibilities

You might not have to invest much to start an Internet or intranet site, but the time and resources involved in keeping one up-to-date can be substantial. Before you find yourself saddled with the entire task, be sure resources are available to support your efforts. In particular, consider the following:

■ Who is responsible for providing content?

■ On many intranets, virtually anyone can contribute. How can you ensure that the contributions are useful and appropriate? How do you ensure that the people who should make contributions actually do, and that information that is updated on paper is also updated on the intranet?

Except in organizations that are unusually open to new technology, you have to give some thought to promoting the use of your intranet. You might build it, but employees won't necessarily come to your intranet site—even if your content is valuable. Before you start, get answers to questions such as these:

- Will management help you encourage the use of the intranet by using it themselves and posting critical information there?

- Have you encouraged them to do so by demonstrating its value to the company and the money it can save?

- What training will your colleagues need to use the intranet? Are there any special applications they need to learn?

Similar questions and support are required in relation to setting up an Internet Web site:

- Is a Web site integral to the success of the company or is it merely an afterthought?

- Is the company Web site more than just an electronic brochure?

- Is e-commerce important to the Web site? If so, how is it integrated with sales through more traditional channels (stores, TV ads, and so forth)?

Finally, if custom coding is required (for example, scripting or other programming required to integrate the intranet, extranet, or Internet Web site with your company's database), you need to consider yet more questions:

- Who will handle the custom coding?

- What role should your company's IT organization play?

Designing an Office-Centered Internet, Intranet, or Extranet Site

What exactly does it mean to design an Internet or intranet site? It means primarily two things:

- Making it a distinctive site
- Making it easy for users to find everything

Creating a distinctive site is not so much about making an award-winning site as making a site that is distinctive for your company or organization. You want every visitor to your site to know that they are visiting a piece of your company or organization when they come to your Web site. Just as most companies spend time and money on projecting a corporate image through advertising, they need to be sure this same image is projected on the corporate intranet or Internet Web site.

One of the most frustrating experiences for visitors to your Web site is not finding the information they want. Many people come to a Web site with a specific question in mind.

The sooner you can answer that question, the better the impression you leave. So, how can you make it easy for visitors to find things? Two interlocking requirements contribute to a successful Web site:

- Good organization
- An easy-to-use navigation system

Remember, as a Web designer, you have to write to a medium that you cannot completely control or define. People creating print documents have explicit control over their paper and ink, so that they can control every part of their information. TV producers also program to the constant standard of color TV resolution (with a nice decay to the black-and-white standard) and have a high level of control over what their content will look like. The WWW presents a unique challenge for the Web designer: access to the medium from multiple devices with different characteristics. What this means is that your Web page has to be readable and understandable under a variety of conditions. You must have a rugged, simple design to reach the widest possible audience.

So, with your medium in mind, how do you design an effective Web site? Choosing an attractive site theme is a good way to start.

Choosing a Site Theme

Choosing a site theme is the stage where you pour your own personality or your company image into the Web site. If someone visits your Web site and then walks into the front door of your company, he should immediately feel he is in familiar surroundings. You not only want to communicate the hard-wired side of your company or self (logo, product, name, store locations, and so forth) but also those qualities that make your organization unique and any qualities that you are particularly proud of. Your Web site is the place to strut your stuff.

You can use all the tools that HTML has available to project your image onto a Web site. This means selecting the appropriate fonts, colors, and images. For a company, these might revolve around existing objects that are already used in print or other media. For an individual, it might be your favorite colors or the colors of something that means a lot to you, such as your favorite football team. Also, when you think color theme, don't forget black and white.

I highly recommend building and using a template Web page on your Web site. A *template* contains the basic style information you want to use on every page of your Web site, including the following:

- A company logo or other branding image
- Font types (Arial, Roman, and so forth)
- Font color(s)
- Standard font sizes for headings and subheadings
- Background colors or textures
- Sounds, if any
- Standard colors
- Horizontal bar styles

Part
V

Ch
31

- Bullet styles for bulleted lists
- A built-in navigation system, if possible
- Text found on every page, such as disclaimers or email links to the Webmaster

Word and FrontPage are shipped with many predefined themes. If you're building a Web page from scratch, you can choose a theme manually by selecting **Format, Theme** from the menu. This opens an extensive list of themes.

If you want to choose a new theme, just return to the Themes dialog box and choose another theme or turn themes off altogether by choosing the **No Theme** option from the top of the list of themes.

After you've decided on a theme and incorporated other standardized items that you need on every Web page, save your file as a template before proceeding further.

Using a template across your Web site increases its visual appeal. Keep in mind, though, that it is not always essential to use a template file. If you have a large number of documents to place on your site, the time and effort to put them all into a template makes the cost of visual appeal too high. Consider using templates only for major section-header pages. Whichever you choose, be consistent.

Choosing a Navigation System

Having great Web site content is useless if you have an ineffective navigation system. The *navigation system* is a list of topical links, usually on every page, leading to the major subject sections on your Web site. It should be

- Easy to use
- Informative at a glance
- Text-based or, if you use images, clarified by alternative text
- Consistent from page to page or section to section
- Comprehensive
- Attractive

The most common navigation system has a group of text or graphic links down the left side of the page. Any graphical hyperlink with important navigational functionality should be repeated as a text-only hyperlink elsewhere on the page.

 TIP When adding graphics to Web pages, you have the option to add alternative text. This is a good place to briefly describe the graphic or, if the graphic is attached to a hyperlink, describe the destination for the link. A fair number of users typically turn off the images in their browsers to speed up the page download. In this situation, alternative text is displayed in place of the graphic and the users can still find their way around the site.

Some items have to be used cautiously in navigation systems, including

- **Image maps.** *Image maps* are graphics with *hot spots* (hyperlinks), each leading to a different page. Visitors browsing with the images turned off cannot make any sense out of a missing image map; alternative text displays as a ScreenTip only. If you must use an image map, it is a good idea to also include redundant text hyperlinks on the page.

- **Special graphics or animation requiring plug-ins.** Any graphic that requires a plug-in, such as Macromedia Flash or Director animations, shouldn't be used unless backed up with text hyperlinks. Not every visitor has the required plug-in and not all browsers support all plug-ins.

- **Obscured links.** Navigation links should have high contrast and be easy to read against your page background. If you use a background image, will your text be readable if the image is gone?

Adding Office Documents to a Web with FrontPage

FrontPage is a full-fledged HTML editor and Web-site management package, both features required by modern, large and complex Web sites. Typically, building a Web site involves creating HTML pages with their associated files, such as graphics, sounds, other multimedia, or scripting languages. However, given that Office 2000 applications can save existing Office documents as Web pages, you can also add content from Office documents to your Web site. Furthermore, you have the option of using Office documents in their native file formats on your Web site or using their Web page equivalent. Because Office 2000 files support hyperlinks, you can link them to other Web pages or Office documents. FrontPage lets you use native Office 2000 files in your Web site almost as easily as HTML files.

Importing Office Files to Your Web with FrontPage

FrontPage treats Office documents no differently than HTML documents when you place them in your FrontPage Web. To place Office documents into a pre-existing FrontPage Web, choose **File**, **Import** from the menu (Figure 31.1).

FIGURE 31.1
Importing Office files into a pre-existing FrontPage Web.

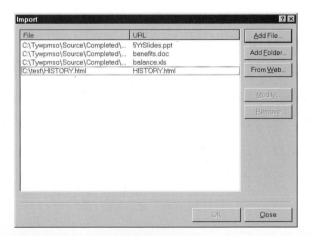

You can add individual files or entire folders containing Office documents. Note that if you choose the **Add Folder** option, both the folder and the files in it are imported to your Web. In other words, the folder will show up as a subfolder under the root of your Web. After you have selected all the files or folders to import to your Web site, you can deselect individual files to exclude them, or you can deselect a group of files using the standard Shift and Ctrl key methods.

To import the selected files, click **OK,** which will be active as long as at least one file is selected. If you click **Close,** FrontPage Explorer retains your file list until you close Explorer, but the files are not imported to your Web.

You can also import files from the Import dialog box by clicking on the **From Web** button. This starts the Import Web Wizard, which lets you get files from a Web (or folder) on your local drive or from the Internet as shown in Figure 31.2.

FIGURE 31.2
Importing Web pages into a pre-existing FrontPage Web.

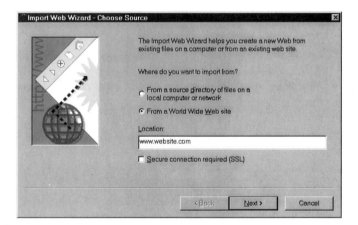

If you choose to add files from a local drive, the next wizard dialog box lists all the files and enables you to exclude any that you don't want in your Web. Clicking **Next** and then **Finish** in the next Wizard dialog box completes the import process.

> **CAUTION**
>
> When any Office 2000 application saves a document as a Web page, the .htm file is saved to the folder you select. Associated files are saved in a newly created subfolder during the save process. This subfolder has the same name as your .htm file with "_files" appended to it. For instance, if you save a worksheet from Excel as Sales.htm, the subfolder is named Sales_files. When you import a Web page created from an Office application, you must also import this subfolder of associated files. FrontPage does not automatically import this subfolder for you.

If you choose to get files from an Internet Web site, the next Wizard dialog box, shown in Figure 31.3, requests information as to how deep and how much of the Web site (in kilobytes) you want to get.

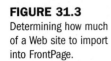

FIGURE 31.3
Determining how much of a Web site to import into FrontPage.

In this Choose Download Amount dialog box, you have to decide

- The number of levels down in the Web site to look for files (up to 100)
- Whether to set a limit in total kilobytes at which to stop downloading
- Whether to limit the file types you import to just images and text

After making these choices and clicking **Next**, click the **Finish** button in the last Wizard dialog box to begin the import process from the Web site. After the Wizard has completed the import, hyperlinks within the files are updated to reflect their new home on your FrontPage Web.

After the files have been imported from their various locations, you can use the views within FrontPage to observe the relationships between the Office documents and other files in your Web. The Hyperlinks view (click the **Hyperlinks** button on the left side) is especially useful. FrontPage can see and display the hyperlinks in native Office documents, as shown in Figure 31.4.

Office documents can be both the source and target of links, just like HTML files. This lets you tightly integrate Office documents into any existing Web.

The decision to use Office documents in their native format must be based on whether your audience can view them. If you know your audience has Office 2000, go ahead and use Office 2000 files. If your users are on multiple platforms or are using earlier versions of Office, however, you need to give them a way to view the Office files. Office file viewers are available for all versions of Windows at

`http://www.microsoft.com/office/000/viewers.htm`

If much of your audience is on non-Windows platforms, you might want to consider saving your Office documents as Web pages for use on your Web site.

FIGURE 31.4

Hyperlinks in Office documents as seen in FrontPage.

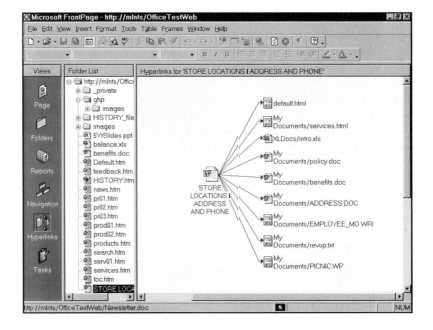

Adding Office Document Content to FrontPage

In the Page view of your FrontPage Web, if you double-click a file that had been imported in its native Office file format, you open the corresponding Office application that created the file. This is also the case if you double-click a Web page that was created by saving an Office document as a Web page. On many computers, you cannot directly edit these formats within FrontPage.

N O T E On some computers, if you right-click a Web page created in an Office 2000 application, choose **Open with** and specify FrontPage to load the Web page into FrontPage 2000. If you do not have the Open with... option on the right-click menu, you can only indirectly edit the Web-page source code in FrontPage 2000 as discussed next. ■

You can, however, import content from Office applications into blank Web pages opened in FrontPage. To bring the content of a Word or Excel file, be sure you have a blank page open; then choose **Insert**, **File** from the menu and browse to the file location. If you selected an earlier (pre-Word 2000) Word document, you will be asked how you want to open the file—as RTF (Rich Text Format), HTML, or text. Use the RTF format to retain most of the Word formatting. Excel worksheets insert as HTML tables.

Hyperlinks are maintained in Word but not in Excel. Any charts or graphics in Excel (and their underlying hyperlinks, if any) are lost using this technique. You have to transfer these to FrontPage via the Clipboard. Graphics (as pictures) are maintained from Word documents;

WordArt or drawing objects are lost unless you convert them to pictures in the Word document first or you insert them later via the Clipboard. After you've inserted the content from the Word or Excel document, it becomes part of the new FrontPage Web page and you can edit it like any other HTML file.

NOTE FrontPage enables you to embed interactive spreadsheet components into Web pages. You can insert a worksheet, a chart, or pivot table. These objects can be viewed only in browsers that accept ActiveX controls, such as Internet Explorer version 4.0 or later or Netscape Navigator with the Ncompass plug-in (**www.ncompasslabs.com**). ■

You can also insert information from Office documents (or from many other types of documents, for that matter) into existing HTML documents using the Windows Clipboard. From within an Office document, copy the information to the Clipboard. In FrontPage, place your insertion point where you want the information to appear, and issue the Paste command. This technique is especially handy for getting Word, Excel, or Access tables translated to HTML tables in your HTML document.

TIP Using the Clipboard to transfer graphics into FrontPage pages makes for a cheap graphics file-format converter. For instance, let's say you have an image document on disk that's not GIF or JPG (say, the company logo), but you want to include it in an HTML document and don't have an image program handy to do the conversion. Just open Word, insert the image as a picture in a blank document (or open a document that already has the company logo), select the image and copy it to the Clipboard, and then paste it into your FrontPage document.

Database information can also be added to pages in FrontPage using the Database Results Wizard. From within this Wizard, you can

- Import an Access database into your FrontPage Web
- Open a path to any database on your network
- Directly issue a SQL query to a database

NOTE It is much easier to build, execute, and then export as Web pages the results of a query from within Access rather than using the Database Results Wizard in FrontPage. This Wizard is most useful if you are conversant in SQL and have a thorough knowledge of the database you are querying. ■

Using FrontPage to Organize Your Office-Based Site

A modern Internet, intranet, or extranet site is a heterogeneous mixture of file formats, including HTML files and associated multimedia files, text files, and Office documents of varying versions. Managing these files can be a time-consuming, administrative headache without the right tools. FrontPage has the Web management tools to

Part
V
Ch
31

- ■ Verify and edit most hyperlinks, except many in Office documents
- ■ Automatically generate a table of contents
- ■ Control access privileges
- ■ Control the structure of your Web
- ■ Look at the relationships between all the files on your Web from a variety of views
- ■ Use shared borders to generate consistent navigation throughout your Web site

Working with Office 97 Hyperlinks Using FrontPage

FrontPage lets you change, edit, or remove hyperlinks from within Office documents. Links to and from Office documents are shown in the same way as typical hyperlinks between HTML documents. To update the status of all the hyperlinks in your FrontPage Web, choose **Tools, Recalculate Hyperlinks** (Figure 31.5).

FIGURE 31.5
Recalculating
Hyperlinks in
FrontPage.

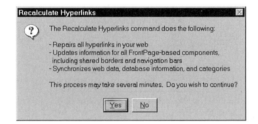

After the hyperlinks have been updated, you can view the status of all the hyperlinks in a FrontPage Web by choosing **View, Reports, Broken Hyperlinks** from the menu (Figure 31.6).

FIGURE 31.6
The Broken Hyperlinks
Report in FrontPage.

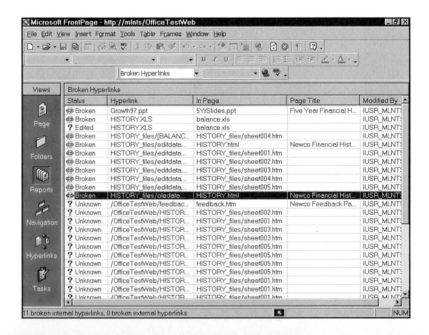

From here, you can edit any broken or unknown hyperlinks in Web pages or Office documents. To fix a broken link, double-click it. The Edit Hyperlink dialog box appears, as shown in Figure 31.7.

FIGURE 31.7
Editing choices in FrontPage for fixing broken hyperlinks in Office documents or Web pages.

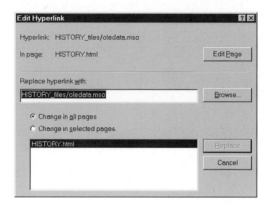

You can use the Edit Hyperlink dialog box to fix broken hyperlinks in Office documents in two ways:

- Click the **Edit Page** button to launch the appropriate Office application (for instance, Word will launch if you're editing a .doc file) and load the document. You can then use tools from within the Office application to edit or remove the hyperlink, and then save the file and return to FrontPage.

- Use the Replace hyperlink with text box. This is the most convenient method of fixing broken hyperlinks in Office documents. If you know the correct location for the broken hyperlink, type it in this text box (or use the Browse button to go to the correct location) and click the **Replace** button. The hyperlink(s) within the Office document is quickly modified and updated without opening any Office applications, and the modified file is saved in its native Office format.

Generating a Table of Contents Using FrontPage

One of the most time-consuming maintenance tasks for a Web site is updating the table of contents. Managing this index can become a full-time job on a large or dynamically changing site. The Table of Contents feature in FrontPage automatically generates a hyperlinked list of all the pages in your FrontPage Web. This table of contents automatically updates as pages are added or deleted during the normal maintenance of your Web site.

N O T E The Table of Contents feature is an ActiveX component. This is viewable only in browsers that support this component, such as Internet Explorer version 4.0 or later or Netscape Navigator with the Ncompass plug-in (**www.ncompasslabs.com**). ■

Part

V

Ch

31

To insert a table of contents, open the page you want to use for the table of contents. Choose **Insert, Component, Table of Contents** from the menu. The Table of Contents Properties dialog box, shown in Figure 31.8, requests the reference point for building the table of contents. The default page is your Web site home page.

FIGURE 31.8
Building a table of contents for your Web site in FrontPage Editor.

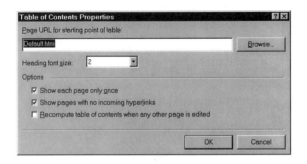

 TIP   You might want to layer your table of contents for a large Web site. Instead of building a megalist of every page from the home page, identify the key topical pages under your home page. Build a table of contents from each of these topical pages. Then, build a top-level table-of-contents page from your home page, leading only to the table of contents for each topical subpage. Do this in as many layers as necessary to allow people to easily navigate through your site.

After choosing the starting or topmost file for your table of contents, you need to make several other decisions about your Table of Contents properties:

- The header size for the *Table of Contents* header text
- Whether to show each page only once
- Whether to show pages containing no hyperlinks from other pages in your Web
- Whether to automatically rebuild the table of contents if any of the pages are edited

After you've made your choices, click **OK** to generate the Table of Contents page. Unfortunately, any Office document included on your Web page is not automatically built into the table of contents; only HTML pages get links in the Table of Contents page. The hyperlinks use the title of the page linked to as the text for the hyperlink. Multiple layers are indented as the list goes deeper into the structure of your Web site. If you want to add Office documents to the table of contents, you have to do so by manually building the hyperlinks.

Managing Web-Site Structure and Access Privileges

Web-site structure can be divided into two types: physical and navigational. The *physical* structure is the actual file-folder structure and location of associated files, such as databases, which might not even physically reside on the Web server. Physical structure usually revolves around some type of logic, such as placing all images in one folder, sounds in another, and scripts in a third, because the scripts folder must have Execute privileges. When FrontPage builds a Web, it automatically adds specialty folders, including a number of hidden folders that cannot be accessed by Web browsers, as well as an images folder. You can add any number of additional folders, public or private, to your Web site as needed.

Part

V

Ch

31

TIP

All hidden folders by default begin with the underscore character—the _private folder, for example—and you can make any folder hidden simply by using an underscore as the first character in its name. You might want to do this if the folder contains files that you don't want visitors to directly access, such as a database.

Navigational structure is, by far, the most important element to organizing your Web site. FrontPage offers a number of features to ease the burden of designing, building, and maintaining a navigational system, including the different views of your Web site in FrontPage, especially Navigation view, shared borders, and the navigation bar.

Viewing Your FrontPage Web Site in FrontPage   FrontPage gives you a number of different ways to view your site, including

- **Page view.** This view shows the Web site as a single list of files.
- **Folders view.** This view shows the actual physical structure of folders and files.
- **Reports view.** This view displays various data about your Web site in the form of reports. As seen in Figure 31.9, a total of 14 reports are available from the View menu.

FIGURE 31.9
Report options available in FrontPage.

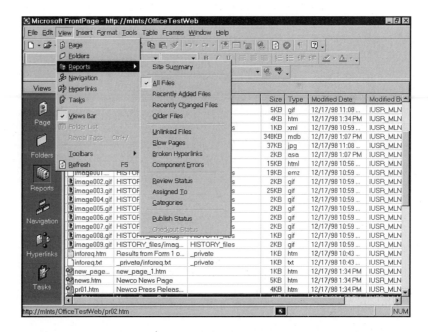

- **Navigation view.** This view is the most useful for designing or changing the navigational structure of your site. See the next section in this chapter, "Using the Navigation View."
- **Hyperlinks view.** This view shows relationships between files based on their hyperlinks. Broken hyperlinks are shown as broken arrows.
- **Tasks view.** This view shows the contents of the prioritized To Do list, along with responsible parties and dates.

Using the Navigation View   Navigation view gives you an easy way to change the relationship between the files on your Web site. You can change your viewpoint by right-clicking over
the right-side pane and choosing various options including Rotate, which offsets your home
page up and to one side, Zoom, and View Subtree Only, which displays only the contents of
the selected subtree. You can create a new folder by selecting the parent folder or clicking
anywhere in the Files pane to create a new folder on the same level as the parent folder and
choosing **File**, **New**, **Folder**. You can drag a file from the Files pane onto a file in the
Navigation pane to associate the two files. When you associate files via drag-and-drop editing,
FrontPage builds a hyperlink into the upper-level (parent) file that targets the lower-level
(child) file.

Using the Navigation Bar and Shared Borders   Navigation view also makes it easy to add a
navigational structure to your Web site as seen in Figure 31.10.

FIGURE 31.10
Navigational view of a
test Web site showing
Web-page interactions.

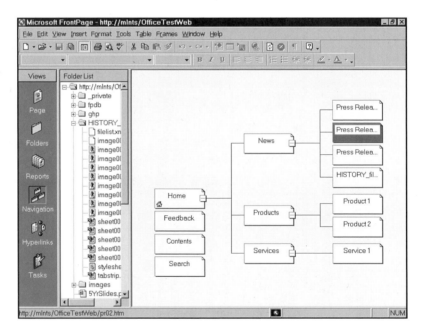

To add a Navigation Bar to all your Web pages, choose **Format**, **Shared Borders** from the
menu. The *Navigation Bar* is a set of text hyperlinks to other pages on your Web site contained in a common content area in each Web page called *shared borders*. FrontPage automatically generates this Bar, adds it to each page, and updates the Navigation Bar as you add or
remove pages. You can change the location of the Navigation Bar on any HTML page by
choosing **Format**, **Shared Borders** in FrontPage. Navigation Bars are not added to Office
documents, but links to Office documents are built and updated in the Navigation Bars. Also,
you cannot associate one Office document with another by using drag-and-drop editing in
Navigation view; you can only associate HTML documents with Office documents. The text
of the hyperlinks built into Navigation Bars is the page title for HTML files; for Office documents, it is the file and folder name.

You can set up your Web site hierarchy and build an almost complete navigation system (totally complete if you don't use Office documents) simply by importing files, adding Navigation Bars to your pages, and using drag-and-drop editing in the FrontPage Navigation view.

Testing an Office-Centered Internet or Intranet Site with Personal Web Server

It is essential to tweak and test all corners of a modern Web site before releasing it into the unforgiving land of the Internet or into the hands of users on your company Intranet. You probably want to first test your Web site offline, that is, on a Web server that cannot be accessed from the Internet or intranet. You can do this easily with *Personal Web Server* (PWS), which you can download from Microsoft's Web site at

`www.microsoft.com/windows/downloads`

This basic Web server installs on Windows 95/98 or Windows NT Workstation 4.0. If you are using Windows NT Server 4.0, I recommend installing the much more sophisticated *Internet Information Server* (IIS) , which is also free.

▶ For complete instructions on installing the Microsoft Web server, **see** "Using Internet Information Server Version 4," on **p. 899**.

Installing the Personal Web Server

Installation for PWS versions for Windows 95, Windows 98, and Windows NT Workstation 4.0 are identical. You cannot install PWS for Windows 98 on a Windows 95 machine unless you have also installed Winsock 2 on your Windows machine (setup will do this for you). PWS for Windows 98 is on the Windows 98 CD-ROM. You can download PWS from the Internet at

`http:/www.microsoft.com/msdownload`

PWS is also included in Windows NT Option Pack 4.0.

N O T E If you have FrontPage on your machine, the PWS has already been installed. If you're uncertain whether the PWS is installed, you can look for a PWS applet in the Control Panel and you should have a PWS folder under Programs from the Windows Start button. ▪

After an opening screen, the PWS installation lets you select a minimum, typical, or custom installation. If you choose the Custom installation, you choose which options to install from the **Select Components** box as shown in Figure 31.11.

FIGURE 31.11
Choosing which components to install when setting up Personal Web Server.

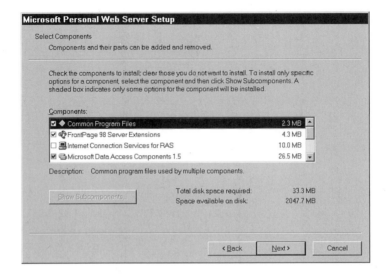

Here is some advice about whether to install the various components of PWS:

- **FrontPage 98 Server Extensions.** You won't need these if you don't plan to use FrontPage with PWS.

- **Microsoft Data Access Components.** I recommend leaving the defaults. This will install ODBC drivers (Open Database Connectivity; essential if you will be using Active Server Pages), ActiveX Data Objects (ADO, another means, more extensible than ODBC, of accessing data), or Remote Data Service (RDS, a Web technology for making database publishing capabilities available to Web applications).

- **Microsoft Message Queue (MSMQ) .** Not installed by default. You won't need this unless you require Web applications to notify one another regarding transactions.

- **Personal Web Server.** All the documentation, management tools, and the Web server itself. You need this one.

- **Transaction Server.** This environment is for Web application development, allowing you to deploy Internet applications. You really don't need this unless you are developing applications.

- **Visual InterDev RAD Remote Deployment Support.** This installs the capability to support the remote deployment of applications to your Web server from within Visual InterDev. This option is also meant for application developers and is otherwise not needed.

After selecting where to install the WWW Service and the Transaction Server files (assuming you elected to install the Transaction Server earlier), setup installs the components you selected and you are asked to reboot your machine. When you do, the Web server is running. You can test it by typing either of the following URLs into a browser address box:

```
http://localhost
```

```
http://YourMachineName
```

Substitute the machine name the Web server is installed on for *YourMachineName* in the previous example. If you don't know the machine name, using //localhost will also work.

N O T E If you're not sure what your machine name is, open **Control Panel**, open the Network applet, and click the **Identification** tab. Your computer name and workgroup are both listed here. ▨

You should now see the default page for your local Web site in your browser. So, where are these local files located? If you have FrontPage installed on your machine, they should be under the root Web folder in /IISSamples/Default/, which you defined when you installed FrontPage (the default is /Inetpub). If you don't have FrontPage, you can usually find them under the WWWRoot subfolder of the WebShare folder on the same drive in which Windows or NT Workstation is installed. It is important to know where your local root Web is so that you can use this location to start from when you test your Web site.

Part

V

Ch

31

Administering the Personal Web Server

To administer the PWS, you use the Personal Web Manager, shown in Figure 31.12. If you used the default folders, the Personal Web Manager can be opened from the Windows Start button, Programs, Microsoft Personal Web Server, Personal Web Manager, or it might be included in the Internet Explorer program folder or listed under Windows NT 4.0 Options Pack. You can also double-click the **Personal Web Server** icon in the Windows System tray in the lower-right corner of the Taskbar to start the Personal Web Manager.

FIGURE 31.12
Administer your Web server with the Personal Web Manager.

Your machine name

Stop/Start the Web server here.

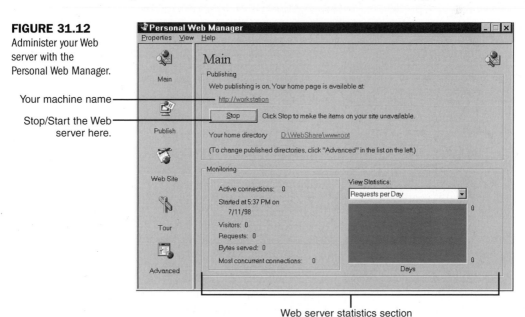

Web server statistics section

The opening Main page of the Personal Web Manager gives the URL for your local machine and the location of your Web root directory, both as hyperlinks. Clicking the URL link opens the default page in Internet Explorer (default.htm); clicking the home directory link opens Windows Explorer at your root directory. You can also stop and start the Web server using the same button (whose name toggles between Stop and Start). The lower half of the window shows some monitoring statistics, including these items:

- Number of active connections
- Time the Web server was started
- Number of unique visitors to your site up to a total of 50 unique addresses
- Requests made to the Web server; also commonly known as hits
- Bytes served to browser requests since the Web server was last started
- The most concurrent connections since the Web server was last started

The lower-right corner of the Main page also shows a graphic representation of any one of these statistics:

- Requests per day
- Requests per hour
- Visitors per day
- Visitors per hour

If this is the first time you've used PWS, the next step is to click **Web Site** on the left side of the Personal Web Manager window and run the Home Page Wizard. Even if you aren't interested in making a home page for your local machine, you need to run this Wizard before you can run the Publishing Wizard. The Home Page Wizard lets you enter the following information via a series of buttons and text boxes:

- Choose a basic template for your home page
- Add a drop-down list box and/or guest book
- Add links
- Enter a page title
- Enter some personal information about yourself
- Enter some subtitles and text paragraphs for whatever content you want to add

Clicking the **Enter New Changes** button builds your home page based on your input and loads it into your default browser. Note that your new home page is now displayed as default.asp. The .asp file displays the time and date in addition to any text or links you added from the Home Page Wizard. You can replace this file with the default.htm file that is also installed in this root when the PWS is installed, although you won't be able to edit default.htm with the Home Page Wizard.

N O T E   The PWS recommends using Internet Explorer 4.0 or later for viewing locally generated pages. It builds your home page using CSS, which are not supported by earlier browser versions. You can also use Navigator 4.0 or later to view pages containing CSS. ▪

The **Advanced** button in the Personal Web Manager gives you the heart of the Web server. From this page, shown in Figure 31.13, you can customize the operation of PWS.

FIGURE 31.13

Customizing the Personal Web Server.

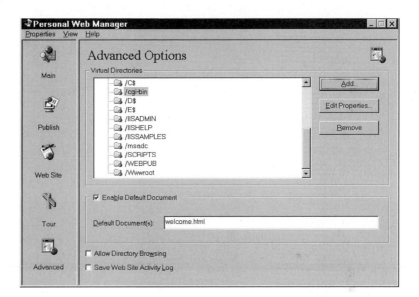

Part

V

Ch

31

The directory listing begins at the Web server root directory and lists all actual and virtual directories. A *virtual directory* is a folder that has been assigned an alias so that it appears to be a part of the Web but actually might be on an entirely different drive. Adding a new virtual directory is as easy as clicking the Add button, browsing to the file folder, choosing an alias, and selecting the access rights. You generally assign access rights to virtual directories as follows:

- ▪ *Read* rights enable visitors to read any files in the folder. You usually set this level of access for HTML files and other files served up by the Web server. Be sure that you don't give Read rights for folders containing executable scripts (CGI, ASP, and so on).

- ▪ *Script* rights should be granted only for folders in which a script engine needs to run—ASP, for instance.

- ▪ *Execute* rights are reserved for running programs from the Web server. Generally, you need to assign both Script and Execute rights to folders that contain scripts for the scripts to operate properly.

You can modify access rights at any time by selecting the folder and clicking the **Edit Properties** button.

TIP You might notice that the root directories of many of the drives on your system are listed under virtual directories. For security, especially if you are putting your Web server up publicly, you should remove the entries pointing to the root directories of the hard drives on your system, unless, of course, you want them accessible. You are still allowed, though, to create virtual directories that point to specific files on these drives.

Three more check boxes in the Advanced Options page add additional functionality to your Web server:

- **Enable Default Document** lets you specify which files are default. Disabling this feature sends an error message to a browser that doesn't specifically list the filename in its URL, unless Allow Directory Browsing is enabled.

- **Allow Directory Browsing** servesup a directory list of files if a visitor specifies a folder and the folder does not contain a default file (default.htm). It is clear by default. This feature is handy if you want to give users access to a group of files to download without having to build or update a list of hyperlinks.

- **Save Web Site Activity Log** writes the log to the \System\LogFiles\W3spc1 directory under Windows (\System32\LogFiles\W3spc1 under Windows NT 4.0). A new log is started each month.

Testing Your Web Site with Personal Web Server

After you have PWS up and running, you can test almost all aspects of your Web site before going live on the Internet or your intranet.

First, if you didn't build your Web site in the Web-root directory of PWS, you need to point to the topmost folder of your Web site by giving your site an alias in a virtual directory. Your Web site must be on a local drive; you cannot map a network drive to a virtual directory. Also, be sure the default document information for your virtual directory is correct. For instance, some Web sites use welcome.html or index.html as their default page. Check that your Web server can find your Web site properly by typing the following into a browser:

```
http://localhost/YourAlias/
```

The home page for your Web site should come up. If it doesn't, check your alias information and be sure that PWS is running. After you've demonstrated that PWS is working properly and serving up your Web site, you can begin to test out your site. Here are some of the items that you can check:

1. Check whether all your images are showing. Blank boxes show up when the path to the graphic is broken.

2. Test your hyperlinks. Be sure you are connected to the Internet before testing whether your URLs point to Internet locations.

> **TIP** HTML editors, such as FrontPage, have hyperlink-checking modules, which make the job of testing large numbers of hyperlinks systematic and bearable. You might not need to try all hyperlinks manually if you've validated your hyperlinks already.

3. Test your scripts (CGI, ASP, IDC, ISAPI, and so on). Troubleshoot any scripts that don't act properly.

4. Test HTML forms by entering dummy information and ensuring you get the proper actions.

5. Test your search engine(s), if present. Be sure any additional software required by your search engine is installed and working.

6. Confirm that your multimedia plays as expected, including animated GIFs, sounds, videos, streaming media, and any specialty items such as Macromedia Flash or Shockwave animations that require plug-ins. Also, be sure you have the necessary links and instructions for getting plug-ins.

7. Check out your Web site with at least the latest versions of Netscape and Microsoft browsers to be sure no HTML tags act improperly or are browser-specific. See how your site looks with images turned off in the browsers. Also, check how your site looks with earlier versions of the major browsers (Internet Explorer and Netscape Navigator), as many people do not regularly upgrade their browsers.

8. If you are using VBScript or JavaScript in your pages, be sure to test all possible conditions—again, using multiple browsers, if possible.

Part

V

Ch

31

After you've tweaked and fixed everything to your satisfaction, you're now ready to publish your files to the Internet or Intranet Web server. Alternatively, you can use PWS to host your Web site. Note, however, that Windows 95 or 98 do not have the sophisticated security of Windows NT Server or UNIX servers.

Publishing Your Site

After you've built and tested a Web, intranet, or extranet site on your local drive, the next step is to upload or publish the site to an active Web server. The Web server used for an intranet or extranet might be located on your company network. A Web server used for a Web site might also be located within your company or your company might be leasing Web server space through a local Internet service provider (ISP) or Web-hosting company. After you've decided which Web server to use, you will need the following information to publish your site:

- The URL of your Web site.
- Write-access to the Web server. You will need to obtain a username and password from the Web-server administrator for your internal network or at the ISP.

■ If you are using FrontPage extensions in your site, you must be sure the Web server also supports these extensions. Your ISP or Web server administrator can tell you this.

■ Sufficient disk space on the Web server to accommodate all the files composing your site, as well as room for anticipated future growth.

After you have an account on the Web server, you can now publish your files using FrontPage or FTP.

Publishing with FrontPage

Publishing your site to a Web server using FrontPage is extremely easy. With the Web you want to publish open in FrontPage, choose **File**, **Publish Web** from the menu. The Publish Web dialog box (Figure 31.14) opens. Click the **Options** button to display all available choices.

FIGURE 31.14

Publishing a FrontPage Web to a Web server.

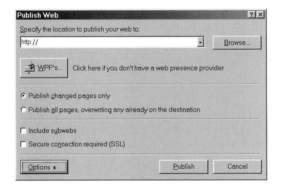

Even though the dialog box opens with a default of http://, you can substitute an ftp path (ftp://) if that is the preferred route to your upload on the Web server. Fill in the complete URL to the Web server. If you don't have a WPP (Web presence provider), click the **WPP**'s button. This opens your browser and takes you to a page on Microsoft's Web site listing WPPs that support FrontPage 2000 extensions. Next, fill in the remaining choices in the Publish Web dialog box, including

■ Publish changed pages only. This uploads only the newest files.

■ Publish all pages, overwriting any already on the destination. This is useful when you've completed a site makeover.

■ Include subwebs. These are other FrontPage Webs imported into your existing Web.

■ Secure connection required (SSL). If you are uploading to a secure server, be sure this is checked.

Click Publish to open a dialog box for your username and password. After you have authenticated, the file upload proceeds. Status boxes listing the files being uploaded will be displayed until the process is complete.

Publishing with FTP

If you don't have FrontPage, you can upload the files for your site using FTP. You have several options here:

- Use a separate FTP client program. Easy-to-use shareware versions are readily available on the Internet. Check out **www.download.com** or **www.filepile.com**.

- All versions of Windows include a command-line version of FTP that operates from an MS-DOS window. Just type **ftp** from any command-line prompt.

Some ISPs and Web-hosting companies have browser-based interfaces for uploading files to the Web server. These are generally easy and convenient alternatives to FTP clients. ●

Using Office 2000 Features to Enhance Your Web Site or Intranet

by Michael A. Larson

Tools for building Web content are built directly into all Office 2000 programs. These tools allow you to perform some of the following tasks:

- Building and editing hyperlinks
- Building HTML forms and editing HTML source code, just like an HTML editor in Word
- Building entire Web sites using wizards in Word or Publisher
- Adding dynamic charts, PivotTables, and spreadsheets to Web pages using Excel
- Building and scheduling a presentation for broadcast over the company intranet using PowerPoint
- Dynamically adding database content to your Web pages using data access pages in Access

For many basic types of Web pages, you can now build your Web pages in familiar Office programs rather than requiring a Web designer to produce the pages for you.

Using Hyperlinks with Office Documents

Why put hyperlinks into native Office documents? Consider these examples:

- A sales report with hyperlinks to more detailed financial reports in Excel, a related PowerPoint presentation, and the latest corporate status report from the CEO in Word
- Financial reports with real-time links to stock quotes
- A technical report with links to other relevant information on the Internet or company intranet

All these hyperlinks would be live from within their respective Office applications; you don't need to crack open a browser. Also, in putting together any of the reports listed previously, you would not have to collect and integrate the disparate documents into a single report. Instead, you can just link to the necessary documents from within your report summary. If you then email your report, you are emailing a much shorter package, reducing network traffic, and the load on the email server.

You do not need to learn HTML to build hyperlinks into any Office document. With a consistent interface for inserting hyperlinks across all the Office applications, all you need to provide is a *Uniform Resource Locator* (URL). The URL can be in the form of a *Transmission Control Protocol/Internet Protocol* (TCP/IP) address, a *Universal Naming Convention* (UNC), or even a file location on your local hard drive.

Behind the scenes, in its most basic form, a *hyperlink* is an HTML tag containing some display text or a path to a graphic and an address. The HTML code for a text hyperlink to Microsoft's home page would look like

```
<a href="http://www.microsoft.com">Microsoft Home</a>
```

Fortunately, you don't have to know HTML to build hyperlinks in Office 2000.

Building Hyperlinks

As I mentioned earlier, hyperlinks are primarily composed of two parts: the display text or graphic (on which you actually click) and the network address, or *URL*.

The same (or very similar) hyperlink dialog box for building and editing hyperlinks is used across all Office applications except Publisher and FrontPage. To build a basic hyperlink in an Office document:

1. From an open Office document, select some text or a graphic.
2. Build a hyperlink from using one of the following options:
   - Choose **Insert Hyperlink** from the menu.
   - Click the **Insert Hyperlink** button (a globe with a chain link) on the standard toolbar.
   - Use the keyboard shortcut, **Ctrl+K**.

The Insert Hyperlink dialog box appears, as shown in Figure 32.1.

FIGURE 32.1
Using the many options in the Insert Hyperlink dialog box to build a hyperlink.

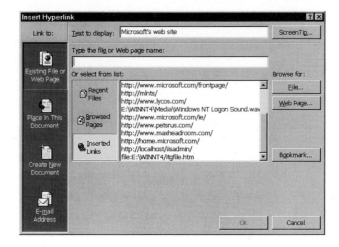

3. The text you selected fills the **Text to display** box at the top. If you chose a graphic, this box is dimmed.

4. In the **Type the file or Web page name**, you can type a URL or UNC.

5. Click **OK** at the bottom and the text or graphic in your Office document is now a hyperlink.

Before building a hyperlink, you do not necessarily have to select the display text. You can start by placing your cursor in the document where you want the hyperlink to be, and then open the Insert Hyperlink dialog box and type the display text into the dialog box.

Of course, you probably noticed many more options in the Insert Hyperlink dialog box. Figure 31.1, shown earlier, shows four buttons running down the left side of the Insert Hyperlink dialog box:

- Existing File or Web Page
- Place in This Document
- Create New Document
- Email Address

Each of these buttons gives you access to different existing lists of files, bookmarks, and email addresses to use as targets when building hyperlinks. Choosing any one of these selections changes the information displayed to the right of it.

CAUTION

Building a hyperlink to a file on your local hard drive might be useful to you, but only to you. Remember, if you email to anyone a document containing a hyperlink to a file on your hard drive (assuming you're not using UNC), or if you use this document with the local hyperlink on another computer, the hyperlink will not lead you or anyone else back to the file on your hard drive.

Part

V

Ch

32

You can also build hyperlinks to refer to specific sections within your current document. This builds a link that enables readers to immediately jump to another section of your document. You can build a hyperlink of this type by clicking the **Place in This Document** button on the left side of the Insert Hyperlink dialog box. Areas to which you can build hyperlinks include the

- Top of the document
- Headings
- Bookmarks (all nonhidden bookmarks in the document)

You can click any of these options and the name of the bookmark or heading is displayed in the **Text to display** box at the top of the dialog box.

You use the Create New Document option to create a brand-new document during the process of creating the hyperlink. In other words, you can link to a file that doesn't yet exist.

Just type your hyperlink display text in the top box and the name of the file to link to. Next, you can choose whether to edit your new file immediately or later.

An email hyperlink opens up and addresses a blank email message. This is an excellent mechanism to give visitors to your document a means of giving you feedback. You can easily build one of these email hyperlinks by clicking on the **Email Address** button at the bottom of the Insert Hyperlink dialog box. Next, type the email address into the Email Address box or choose an email address from the list in the lower part of the screen, which shows any recently used email addresses.

N O T E The text "mailto:" is automatically entered before the email address you type. The word "mailto:" is necessary to make the browser understand this is an email hyperlink.

Change the display text to be anything you choose and fill in the **Subject line** if you want a preaddressed subject line in the email.

Using Hyperlinks in Frames

Hyperlinks between frames require some special code to tell the browser which frame you want to display the target document. You can create frames only in Word, PowerPoint, and FrontPage. Also, when Publisher saves a publication as a Web page, it uses frames.

N O T E FrontPage uses a different set of dialog boxes to create and use frames, which won't be discussed further here. The terminology used later, however, is also used in FrontPage to select frame targets.

Imagine you have two frames—a smaller left frame containing navigation links, whereas the right frame is the main window for displaying your Web pages. You want to click a link in the navigation frame to load a page into the main frame. If you select some text in the left frame, choose **Insert Hyperlink**, and click **Create New Document**, the lower part of this dialog box is now different, as shown in Figure 32.2.

FIGURE 32.2
Building hyperlinks
between frames.

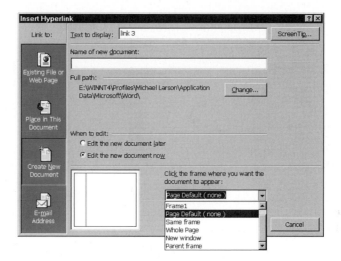

Notice at the bottom of the screen you now have a small representation of your frameset and a list of options under **Click the frame where you want the document to appear:**. You can choose the destination frame by clicking the graphical representation, or you can choose from the list, which contains the following options:

- **Frame name.** The name of each frame is included in the list. As shown previously in Figure 32.2, at the top of the list, you see one of the frame names: Frame1.

- **Page Default.** This option automatically sends the hyperlink to the default frame, if a default is assigned. If none has been assigned, then the word in parentheses after the option is none. If a frame has been assigned, the frame name appears in parentheses. Do not use this option if no page default has been assigned; it opens only a new instance of your browser.

- **Same frame.** The destination is the same frame the link is in. In the navigation scenario in the example, this would be undesirable. This would be useful, though, for links contained in the right, main frame of the example. This keeps your navigation links always displayed.

- **Whole Page.** This option destroys the frameset. In other words, rather than display the page in the right frame, the page is again displayed using the entire browser window. This is useful if you need the whole browser window to display a large graphic or if you go to a part of a Web site that no longer requires the frameset for navigation.

- **New window.** This option is similar to the Whole Page option, except it launches a second instance of your browser and displays the page in it. One copy of the browser now has the unchanged frameset in it and the other new browser is displaying a full page. This keeps your original Web page on the user's desktop even if the user browses elsewhere.

- **Parent frame.** This final option loads the page into whichever frame is defined as the parent frame. If none is defined, this option has the same effect as the Same Frame option.

Inserting Hyperlinks Automatically

Office 2000 includes two ways to build hyperlinks automatically:

- You can type a URL, UNC, or email address directly into the body of your document.
- You can copy and paste as hyperlink between documents or Office applications.

Whenever you type a URL, UNC, or email address into the body of an Office document (excluding Access and Publisher), the application makes it a hyperlink automatically. The display text is the same as the URL, UNC, or email address. You do not need to open the Insert Hyperlink dialog box or do anything extra to create the hyperlink.

Editing and Deleting Hyperlinks

To edit or delete a hyperlink in Word, Excel, or PowerPoint:

1. Right-click anywhere over the text or graphic hyperlink and choose **Hyperlink**, **Edit Hyperlink**. Alternatively, you can use the keyboard arrow keys to place the cursor anywhere in the hyperlink text and choose **Insert**, **Hyperlink** from the menu, toolbar, or using the keyboard shortcut, **Ctrl+K**. You do not need to select all the display text.

2. Figure 32.3 shows you the Edit Hyperlink dialog box. Your display text and original hyperlink are displayed at the top of the box. This dialog box closely resembles the Insert Hyperlink dialog box except for the addition of a Remove Link button at the bottom.

FIGURE 32.3
Editing or deleting a hyperlink from the Edit Hyperlink box.

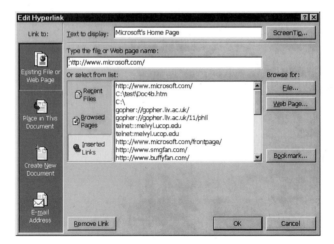

3. To edit the hyperlink, just select the box containing the URL and enter your new URL, or choose a new URL using any of the many techniques already discussed in this chapter.

4. To completely eliminate the hyperlink, click the **Remove Link** button at the bottom. The Insert Hyperlink dialog box disappears and so does your hyperlink, although the display text or graphic is unchanged.

You have more choices when you right-click over a hyperlink and choose the Hyperlink option, including

- **Edit Hyperlink.** Opens the Edit Hyperlink dialog box and you can proceed to edit or remove the hyperlink.
- **Open.** Activates the link and opens the destination.
- **Select Hyperlink.** Selects all the text or graphics in the hyperlink.
- **Open in New Window.** Same as Open, except it opens the destination of the link in a new window (if applicable).
- **Copy Hyperlink.** Copies the display text and URL to the Clipboard. Move your cursor and select Paste to add this hyperlink to another point in your document or into another document.
- **Add to Favorites.** Displays a dialog box that enables you to add the hyperlink to your Favorites list.
- **Remove Hyperlink.** Deletes the hyperlink, but leaves the display text intact. This is the quickest way to delete a hyperlink.

Using Bookmarks in Hyperlinks Between Office Documents

As you saw earlier, it is possible to build hyperlinks to internal markers, such as bookmarks and headings in a Word document. You can use this same idea to build links to similar markers in other Office documents (excluding Publisher), including

- Bookmarks in other Word documents
- Named ranges in Excel spreadsheets
- Specific PowerPoint slides
- Specific Object Pages in Access Databases

To build a hyperlink to an Office document, follow these steps:

1. Before building the hyperlink, be sure you know the name of the Word bookmark, the named range for an Excel worksheet, the PowerPoint slide number, or the Access page.
2. Select your display text, open the **Insert Hyperlink** dialog box, and enter the URL or file path to the Office document.
3. After the URL or file path, type **#**.
4. Type the name of the Word bookmark, the named range for an Excel worksheet, the PowerPoint slide number, or the Access page.
5. Click **OK** to complete your hyperlink.

Following are sample hyperlinks to each of the Office applications:

```
<a href="http://someserver.com/word.doc#bookmark">Link to a Word Bookmark</a>
<a href="http://someserver.com/sheet1.xls#'Sales'!A1">Link to the Sales Data</a>
<a href="http://someserver.com/present.ppt#5>Show the PowerPoint Revenue
➥Chart</a>
<a href="http://someserver.com/data.mdb#ObjectPage>Link to the Access Object
➥Page</a>
```

Part

V

Ch

32

CAUTION

These hyperlinks styles work only from documents loaded into Office applications. They do not work from a browser. In other words, you can jump from a Word document to an Excel worksheet to a PowerPoint slide to an Access page and back. However, if you convert any of these documents to Web pages, load them into a browser, and click the same hyperlinks, they do not work.

Pasting a Hyperlink

You can also create text hyperlinks between Office documents via the Clipboard. First, select a phrase in one document and copy it to the Clipboard (**Ctrl+C** from the keyboard or **Edit**, **Copy**.) Select a second Office document and choose **Edit**, **Paste As Hyperlink**. This pastes the Clipboard text with a link back to your original document. With this method, there are no dialog boxes to fill.

Using Action Buttons, Action Settings, and Slide Master with PowerPoint Hyperlinks

Use Action buttons, slide master, and Action Settings for maximum flexibility in presentations. *Action buttons* are a set of predrawn buttons—you'll find them under **Slide Show**, **Action Buttons**—that allow for a variety of actions, including creating hyperlinks, within a presentation. Adding hyperlinks to the slide master using the standard technique enables you to propagate the same hyperlink throughout your entire presentation. This is useful for building a navigation menu or for providing access to Help at all times. *Action Settings* are found under the Slide Show menu after selecting an object or word in any slide. You can then build a hyperlink to any other slide, show, URL, other PowerPoint presentation, or file. The hyperlink can be set up to be triggered either by the traditional mouse click or just by passing the mouse over it.

Understanding the Hyperlink Data Type in Access 2000

You can add hyperlinks to text and graphics within forms, reports, and pages in Access 2000 using the same techniques as those you use to add hyperlinks in Word, Excel, and PowerPoint. You can't hyperlink text in tables due to database constraints.

You can include hyperlinks in data records by using the Hyperlink data type. The three parts of this data type are

```
displaytext#address#subaddress
```

The pound sign (#) separates each part of the data type. Here is a description of the parts:

- The *displaytext* is the descriptive text for the hyperlink.
- The *address* is the URL or UNC.
- The *subaddress* is the bookmark.

You can build Hyperlink records as the Hyperlink data type by using any of these methods:

- Type the information manually per the definition shown earlier for displaytext and address.
- Use the Insert Hyperlink dialog box.
- Paste hyperlinks from other Office documents.

The **Insert**, **Hyperlink** command becomes active only when you are in a Hyperlink data type field. Type the displaytext first, then choose **Insert**, **Hyperlink**, and then fill out the Insert Hyperlink dialog box.

Understanding the Hyperlink Function in Excel 2000

Excel also contains a Hyperlink function. The syntax is

```
HYPERLINK(Link_location,Friendly_name)
```

Link_location is the hyperlink address and Friendly_name is some descriptive text used to describe the link. Following are several uses of this function:

- `HYPERLINK("http://yahoo.com","Yahoo")` displays the text Yahoo in the cell and jumps to **http://yahoo.com** when clicked.
- `HYPERLINK("[http://yahoo.com/visitors.xls] Sheet1!C3",G4)` displays the contents of G4 in the cell and jumps to cell C3 in Sheet 1 on yahoo.com.
- `HYPERLINK(A5,C5)` displays the contents of cell C5 and jumps to the address referenced in cell A5.

The quotation marks are required for the function to work. Also, as with any function or formula in Excel, enter an equals sign before the function in the cell. The Hyperlink function can be used to build macros that respond to user input. It is also a great way to transform lists of URLs into active links without retyping.

Working with Web Pages from Within Office Applications

In Word, Excel, and PowerPoint, creating a Web page is no different from creating any other Office document. You do not need to open up a special environment or think differently about the contents of your page.

Building a Web Page from Scratch

To begin building from a blank page, just open a new page from the menu or toolbar. If you prefer a page that has some basic formatting, choose from among some preformatted Web page types in Word or FrontPage under **File**, **New** on the menu. You can also add a theme from these applications by clicking **Theme** from the Format menu. You can choose from a very extensive list of preformatted and color coordinated themes.

Building HTML Forms Using the Web Tools Toolbar (Word Only)   A *Web form*, also called an HTML form, is a collection of option buttons, text boxes, list boxes, and so on, designed to pass information (usually filled in by a visitor) to a Web server for additional action. Because Word 2000 does not provide any means to generate Web forms automatically, you need to build any Web form from scratch.

TIP   Publisher and FrontPage both have several canned Web forms. You might want to see if any of these forms closely match what you need to build before building a form from scratch.

The controls for building Web forms in Word are found on the Web Tools toolbar as shown in Figure 32.4.

FIGURE 32.4
Use the Web Tools toolbar to build Web forms in Word.

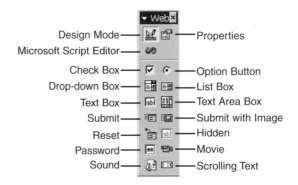

CAUTION

Word 2000 has another toolbar, the Control Toolbox, which contains controls that appear to be identical with those in the Web Tools toolbar. Do not use the controls in the Control Toolbox to build Web forms. Even though the controls (option buttons, list boxes, and so on) look the same, they operate on a different principle and do not work with a Web server.

The Web Toolbox also has a button labeled Design Mode. This button indicates that you will be operating in a WYSIWYG environment when you build your Web form. The first time you select a Web form control, Top of Form and Bottom of Form markers are inserted into your Web page as shown in Figure 32.5. All Web form controls must be placed between these markers to operate properly.

To add a form control to the form, place your cursor where you want the form control to appear and click the appropriate element in the Web toolbar. The form control now appears on your form.

Now that the form control appears in your document, you can select it and drag it to adjust its location or size. With the control selected, choose **Format**, **Control** (or right-click over it and choose Format Control) to display the Format Object dialog box. This dialog box gives you other options for coloring or resizing the control.

FIGURE 32.5
The form boundary
markers in Word.

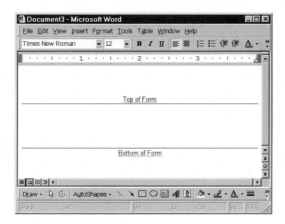

You will usually need to add some descriptive text next to a form control to inform everyone about the information required by that control. After the control has been added and formatted, place your cursor before or after the control and start typing this descriptive text.

N O T E You can use any Word formatting tools to align or place form controls or descriptive text. These include tabs, spacing, justification, and so on. Using a table to organize and align form controls is also a possibility. ■

Periodically, check how your Web form looks in a browser by choosing **File**, **Web Page Preview**.

To view the properties associated with a control, double-click the control on the Web form, right-click over the control and select **Properties**, or with the form control selected, click the **Properties** button on the Web Tools toolbar.

The very top of the Properties window displays the name of the current control. If you click the arrow to the right of the control name, a list of all the form controls in your current document drops down. This is a very convenient way to edit multiple controls without having to click each control separately. You can also access the properties of your current document from this list.

N O T E For all form controls, the first property is always the control's name. Word assigns a name automatically. You can leave that name alone or enter a more descriptive name that makes life easier for those who work with the form control later. This name is not used in data transfer with the Web server. ■

Using Web Scripting Web pages commonly employ scripting languages to define actions and objects accessible from within a browser. In Office applications, the scripting languages available are Jscript (called JavaScript ECMAScript within the program) and Visual Basic Script (VBScript). They are both robust. Microsoft Internet Explorer browsers support only JScript and VBScript. Both of these languages enable you to program interactivity into Web

Part

V

Ch

32

pages without requiring a trip to the Web server (client-side scripts) to execute. Both languages are also capable of supporting server-side scripts that require action from the Web server to execute.

To add scripting code to a Web page, choose **Tools**, **Macro**, **Microsoft Scripting Editor** from the menu (this editor is not available in Access or Publisher). Or, use the keyboard shortcut, **Alt+Shift+F11**. The Microsoft Development Environment (MDE) opens up as shown in Figure 32.6.

FIGURE 32.6
Add script code to Web pages using the Microsoft Scripting Editor.

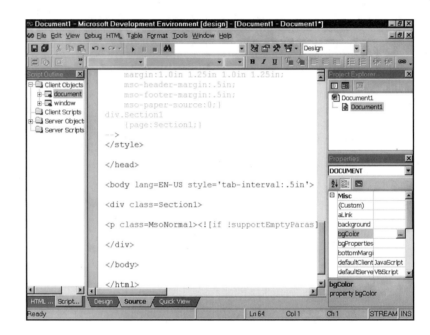

To choose the language in which to write a script, choose **View**, **Property Pages** from the menu (**Shift+F4** from the keyboard). As shown in Figure 32.7, you can choose between either language or client-side or server-side scripts.

Next, you have two choices for how to add code to the Web page: Add a blank scripting container or directly insert script functions. To add a blank script container, choose **HTML**, **Script Block**, **Client** (Server is also available) from the menu. This inserts a blank scripting container into the Web page as shown in Figure 32.8.

If you prefer to select scripting functions from a list, open the Script Outline by choosing **View**, **Other Windows**, **Script Outline** from the menu or **Ctrl+Alt+S** from the keyboard. From the Script Outline, you can double-click any one of the many predefined functions to insert it into your Web page (see Figure 32.9).

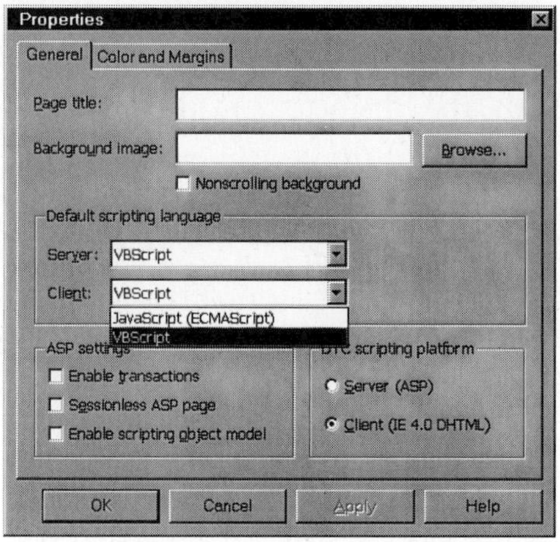

FIGURE 32.7
Choosing the scripting language to use in your Web page.

FIGURE 32.8
Inserting a blank scripting container into a Web page.

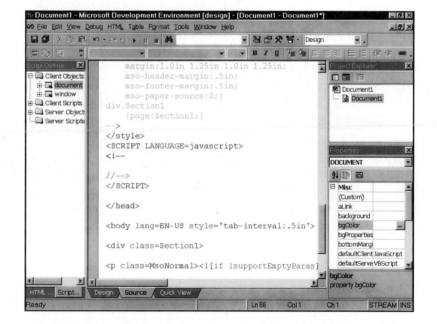

The MDE includes many of the amenities found in sophisticated programming environments such as debugging and the ability to insert breakpoints. You can completely test and debug your script from within the MDE. When the script works to your satisfaction, save the file and exit the MDE to return to your Office application.

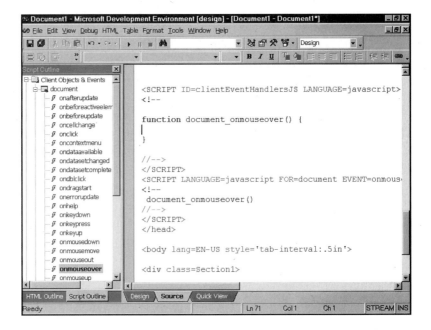

Understanding Web Page Preview and Web Layout View

As you are building your Web page, you can view or preview your Web pages using Web Layout View (in Word only) and Web Page Preview.

Web Layout View (View, Web Layout from the menu) presents your document like a Web Page. Normal view shows your Web page as a series of section breaks similar to an outline. Many of the graphics are not displayed.

Web Page Preview enables you to preview your Web Page in a browser without first having to save the file. Click **File**, **Web Page Preview** on the menu (**File**, **Preview in Browser** in FrontPage) to initiate the process. The file as a Web page is opened in your default browser for viewing.

N O T E   Remember that just because your Web page looks good in one browser doesn't mean it will look good in all browsers. Unless you know everyone will be accessing your Web page with the same browser and version, it is a good idea to test your Web pages with the latest versions of Microsoft and Netscape browsers as well as earlier versions, if possible. Note that if some things do not show up in one browser (for instance, the scrolling marquee is not supported by Netscape browsers), you might need to remove that element or build browser-specific pages. ▪

Saving Web Pages

Whenever you save an Office document as a Web page, you are building a page of HTML source code that can be read by a browser and interpreted by the browser to display the various elements in the Web page. In Office 2000 Web pages (excluding Publisher and FrontPage), traditional HTML code is now being supplemented by four other technologies:

- **XML.** eXtensible Markup Language
- **CSS.** Cascading Style Sheets
- **VML.** Vector Markup Language
- **Scripting languages.** JavaScript and VBScript

This has some plusses and minuses. On the plus side:

- Web pages can now contain almost anything that an Office document can.
- It no longer matters whether you save a file as a binary Office file or as .html; the document looks the same in the Office application that created it as it does in an Internet Explorer 5 Web browser.
- XML greatly improves the organization and ease of searching the Web page.
- VML reduces the bandwidth required to send a graphical image from a Web server to a browser. This improves the browser page load time, improves image quality, and helps to reduce Internet or intranet network congestion.
- By implementing such a complex format, Microsoft is hurrying the market; that is, they are pushing the envelope of Web technologies. VML and XML are very recent additions to Internet technology. CSS has been around longer but is only now beginning to be widely implemented. By making these technologies transparent and easily available to millions of Office users, their quick acceptance into wide usage on the Internet is almost guaranteed.

This souped-up HTML format has a few minuses:

- If you want to edit the HTML code outside of the Office application that created it, you need to be a programmer (that is, be able to understand the markup and scripting languages). Also, rather than just having to know only HTML, you need to understand VML, CSS, and XML, as well as understand how these four technologies interact with one another. This can be daunting even for many experienced Web designers and programmers.
- It might be several years before there is a critical mass of later version browsers (version 5 or later) on the Internet that can properly interpret all the code found in a Web page produced with Office 2000. Telling the Office application to implement Web page features common only to version 4.0 Web browsers helps somewhat, although it reduces the effectiveness of using Office 2000 applications to build Web pages, especially roundtripping ones. (More on how to implement the Web page features common to version 4.0 Web browsers is found later in this chapter in the section "Advanced Web Options.") In the meantime, this technology can be used to its fullest on an intranet or extranet where most people can be motivated or required to have version 5 or later browsers.

▶ For a more detailed discussion of roundtripping, **see** "Blurring the Line Between Binary and Web Page File Formats," on **p. 791**.

Within an Office document, you can embed many elements, such as graphics and sounds, directly into a single binary file, so that you have only one file to worry about. Web pages, however, do not directly embed many of the items that are displayed in browsers. For a graphic,

Part

V

Ch

32

the Web page contains only the path to the image file, not the image file itself. The same is true for sounds, videos, Java applets, and many other items. So, what happens to these associated files when you save a Web page from an Office application? Where do they go? What do you need to do when you want to move your Web page to a different computer or to a Web server? What else do you need to move in addition to the Web page file (.htm or .html)?

Imagine that you're saving a Web page to a local drive under the filename of HomePage.htm. First, the actual Web page, HomePage.htm, is stored in the folder you selected on your local hard drive. Next, a folder called HomePage_Files is created by the Office application under the folder containing HomePage.htm. In the HomePage_Files folder, you will find the following:

- Two files—filelist.xml and header.htm—contain information necessary for roundtripping (that is, for translating HomePage.htm back to its Office binary file). Header.htm is present only if header or footer information is contained in the original document. These files are not used when HomePage.htm is viewed in a browser.

- All the bitmap image files are saved under image001.gif, image002.gif, image001.jpg, and so on.

- Drawing objects are also saved as .gif files.

- Sound and video files are not moved to the HomePage files folder. Although your Web page works on your local hard drive, anyone else accessing it will not receive any audio or video.

Copy audio, video, and Java applets to the HomePage_Files folder before inserting them in your Web page. This ensures that the files remain linked to the saved Web page.

Viewing HTML Source Code

When you save a file as a Web page, the file is saved as an .htm or .html file. The actual code that a browser translates into a Web page is called *HTML source code*. In Office 2000, this not only includes HTML, but also XML, CSS, VML, and the scripting languages. If you want to access this code—for instance to modify the JavaScript—you can access the code from the menu under View, HTML Source. The source code is displayed in an MDE window as shown in Figure 32.10.

As far as the HTML source code is concerned, you can search and edit the HTML source code from within the MDE as desired. To save your changes, just choose **File**, **Exit** from the menu.

Understanding the Web Toolbar

If you used Office 97, you are already familiar with the Web toolbar shown in Figure 32.11. This toolbar has not changed in Office 2000.

FIGURE 32.10
Modifying HTML source code in the Microsoft Development Environment.

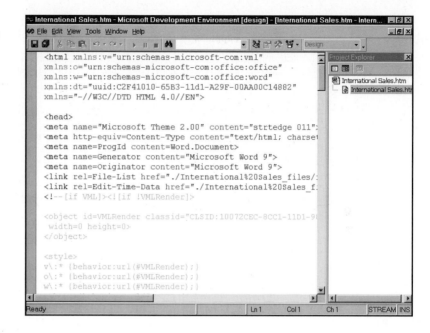

Move Back
Stop
Load Start Page
Favorites List
Web Toolbar Only

FIGURE 32.11
The Web Toolbar in Office 2000 applications.

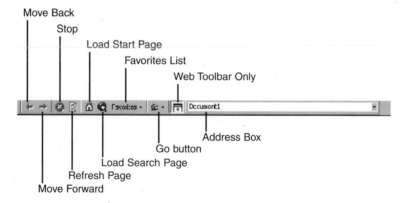

Address Box
Go button
Load Search Page
Refresh Page
Move Forward

Part V
Ch
32

This toolbar contains much of the same functionality as a Web browser toolbar:

- The Move Forward and Move Back arrows take you through your browsing history. Because Word documents and other files can now contain hyperlinks, you can browse through previous Word documents as well as Web pages using these arrows.

- The Stop button stops the loading of a Web page.

- The Refresh button reloads the page into Word.

- Clicking on the Start Page button loads your Start page as it is defined under the Go button on this toolbar.

- The Load Search Page button loads your Search page as it is defined under the Go button on this toolbar.

- The Favorites List is the same list of Internet addresses you see in the Microsoft Internet Explorer Favorites list.

- The Go button enables you to edit your Start and Search pages under Set Start Page and Set Search Page. You can also choose **Open** after clicking this button to pop up an address box. You can enter any Internet address into this address box. The functions of the Load Start Page and Load Search Page are also duplicated here.

- The Web Toolbar Only button toggles between displaying only the Web toolbar and all selected application toolbars.

- You can enter any Internet address, network path, or filename from a local drive in the Address Box. Clicking the arrow to the right of this box displays your browsing history. You can also select from this list to choose a particular file or address.

> **N O T E** If you choose to display several other toolbars while the "Web Only" state is in effect on the Web toolbar, the Office application will display that same set of toolbars the next time the toggle is activated. This lets you display those toolbars of most interest when working with the Web. ■

Using the Web toolbar is a convenient way to browse a set of hyperlinks in Office documents or to launch your browser with your Start page or Search page loaded.

Building Web Sites with Office 2000

Word and Publisher both contain easy-to-use wizards for generating complete Web sites. These include many different page styles and themes. Not only can you generate an entire site, but also at any time, you can change the theme throughout the entire site with only a few clicks. Both wizards also automatically generate a navigation system, connecting all your Web pages together.

Creating a Web Site with the Word Web Page Wizard

You can get to the Web Page Wizard by selecting **File**, **New** from the menu, clicking the **Web Pages** tab and double-clicking **Web Page Wizard**.

Using the Web Page Wizard is a great way to build a small Web site with a consistent theme. It does, however, have two shortcomings:

1. The Web Page Wizard does not have any HTML form page templates. You have to build these yourself completely from scratch.

2. The Wizard does not have any Web-site management tools for dealing with large numbers of files and hyperlinks. If your Web site grows to include more than 10 pages or so, you will benefit from the site-management capabilities built into dedicated HTML editors such as FrontPage 2000.

▶ For more information on building Web forms in Word, **see** the section in this chapter titled "Building HTML Forms Using the Web Tools Toolbar (Word Only)," on **p. 828**.

The next few sections will walk you through the creation of a Web site using the Wizard.

After you start the Wizard, click **Next** to go past the opening screen to the Title and Location screen. Type a title for your Web site into the Web Site Title box. The title becomes the folder name under which all the files and subfolders for your site are saved at the Web-site location. The location for saving your Web page(s) can be any standard place you would normally save a file, such as

- A folder on a local hard drive
- A folder on a network drive
- A Web Folder

A *Web Folder* is a shortcut to a Web server. Web Folders enable you to save, edit, or delete files directly on the Web server without having to use other software, such as an FTP (File Transfer Protocol) client.

▶ For more information about creating and using Web Folders, **see** Chapter 35, "Deploying and Using Office 2000's Web-Collaboration Components," on **p. 895**.

After you choose a title and file storage location, click **Next**. On this Navigation page, you can choose how you want to set up your navigation menu. You can choose to use frames or place the navigation menu on a separate page. Specifically, you have three options to display your navigation menu:

1. **Vertical Frame.** The Navigation Menu is placed in a smaller frame on the left with the contents of the Web page displayed in the larger frame on the right.
2. **Horizontal Frame.** The Navigation Menu is placed in an upper, smaller frame with the contents of the Web page displayed in the lower, larger frame.
3. **Separate Page.** The navigation menu is placed on a separate Web page. Forward and Back hyperlinks are provided on each Web page.

Using frames provides a very convenient and intuitive navigation system.

After you decide what navigation system to use, click **Next** to go to the Add Pages screen. This part of the Wizard allows you to add and remove pages from new site. You can choose from three types of Web pages:

- A blank page
- A template page
- An existing file

If you choose a template page, a selection box, shown in Figure 32.12, appears.

Template pages give you some basic Web-page organization. All you need to do is customize the text and graphics. As you click a template page in the Web Page Templates box, the template is displayed behind the box.

Part V · Ch 32

FIGURE 32.12

Web Page Templates with a background preview of the selected template in the Web Page Wizard.

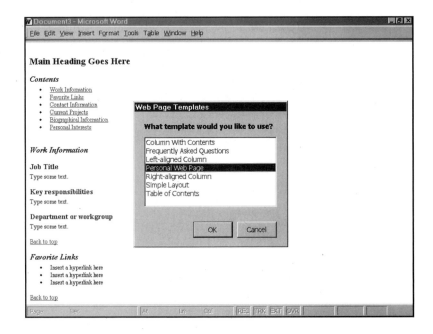

 TIP

Productivity Tip: When you choose files to add to your Web site, they don't necessarily need to be Web pages. You can add any other type of file, such as Office documents. Be aware that if you do choose a non-Web page file to add to your Web site, your machine might respond to that file type very differently from someone else's machine. For instance, if you include an Excel worksheet, when you click it, it opens in Excel on your computer. Someone using UNIX, who clicks on that same link, might be able to download only the file, and might not even be able to view it. Be aware that after you stray from the .htm or .html file formats, you are no longer dealing with universally accessible file formats.

Finally, you can delete pages from your Current List by selecting a given page and clicking **Remove Page**.

Click **Next** when you have all the Web pages you want on your site. On the Organize Pages screen, you can choose the order for your navigation links.

On the next screen, you can add a visual theme to your Web site. To add a theme, select **Add a Visual Theme** and click **Browse Themes**. A list of themes, similar to those shown in Figure 32.13, appears.

Clicking a theme displays a sample of a Web page using that theme. Also notice three additional switches in the lower-left corner:

- **Vivid Colors.** Enables you to toggle the text color for subheadings and hyperlinks.
- **Active Graphics.** Enables you to choose whether to enable animated graphics if the theme uses them.
- **Background Image.** Inserts or removes the background image from your selected theme and replaces it with a background color.

FIGURE 32.13
You can choose a theme for your Web site here.

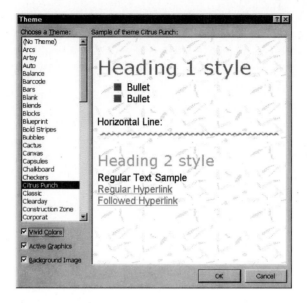

Click **Finish** and the Wizard generates your Web page(s).

A typical Web site might deal with company sales, use frame navigation and a theme, and contain four pages:

- Table of Contents
- Sales Summary
- National Sales
- International Sales

The file structure for this typical Web site would look like Figure 32.14.

FIGURE 32.14
The structure of a typical Web site built with the Web Page Wizard.

In this site, the Wizard creates a folder that corresponds to each Web page. All the Web pages (.htm files) are stored in the root Sales folder. At this point, each of the four folders under the root contains only filelist.xml and the image file from the selected theme for use with the page background. Your home page is named default.htm—by, er, default. Because we're using frames for navigation, default.htm is only the frameset, or container file, for the list of links on the left (TOCFrame.htm) and the Table of Contents (Table of Contents.htm) on the right. Any images or other objects that you add as you edit your Web pages are automatically placed into the correct folder. To edit any of the other Web pages, open them as you would any other file in Word.

Creating a Web Site with Publisher 2000

People who are more comfortable with creating documents using desktop publishing will find Publisher an easy and intuitive choice for building Web sites. A large number of predesigned Web site templates are also available. Publisher offers two means for building a Web site: using one of its many wizards or building it manually, page by page. To invoke a Web Site Wizard, choose **File**, **New** from the menu and choose **Web Sites** from the list of wizards in the Microsoft Publisher Catalog as shown in Figure 32.15.

FIGURE 32.15
Choosing a Web site design from the Publisher Catalog.

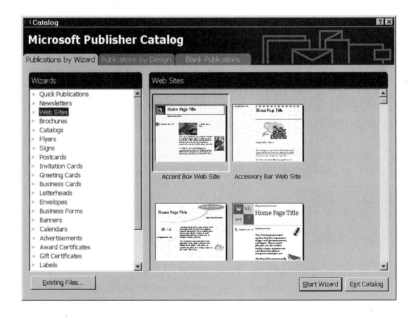

Next, scroll through the large list of Web site designs. When you find a suitable candidate, click the **Start Wizard** button. If this is your first time through, you are prompted for personal information (name, phone number, job title, address, and so on) for use in the Web site. You can also choose a personal or company color scheme to add to your profile. After filling this dialog box out, click **Update** to go to an introductory screen. Proceed next to the Color Scheme page (Figure 32.16).

FIGURE 32.16
Choosing a color scheme for your Web site.

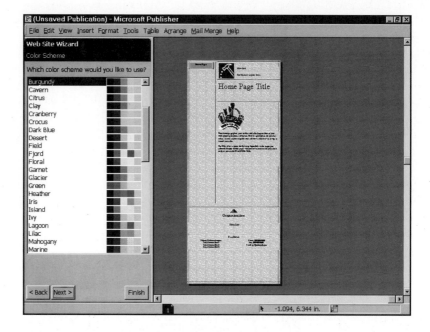

NOTE   If you added a color scheme to your personal information, that scheme will be the selected default color scheme. You can override your personal color scheme from this dialog box.

Each color scheme is named and has colored boxes to its right. Each scheme is color coordinated. The colors of the boxes represent, in no particular order, the colors of the

- Main text
- Hyperlink
- Followed hyperlink
- Color and color accents used for the navigation buttons

Selecting different color schemes changes the appearance of these items on the thumbnail Web page displayed next to the Color Scheme list. Real-time thumbnails are shown for all following screens also. Clicking **Next** lets you add more pages to your Web site. Types of pages listed include

- Story
- Calendar
- Event
- Special offer
- Price list
- Related links

Part

V

Ch

32

After choosing one or more page types, you can proceed to the next screen and choose to add a form to your Web site. Choices include

- Order form
- Response form
- Sign-up form
- None

From the next screen, choose the Navigation bar. This can be

- Both a vertical and horizontal bar
- Just a vertical bar
- None

The next two screens of the Wizard let you add a background sound and background texture. The last screen of the Wizard lets you choose which Personal Information to add, and update it, if desired. Clicking **Finish** generates all the pages you selected and opens the Web site in Publisher, as shown in Figure 32.17.

FIGURE 32.17
A basic Web site created by the Publisher Web Site Wizard.

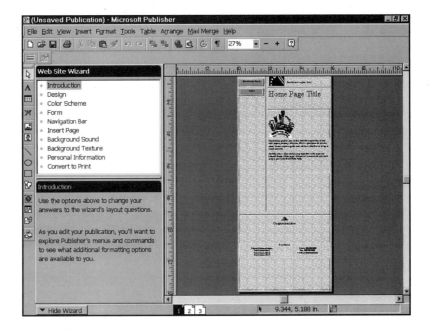

You can edit any of the choices you made earlier in the Wizard and add content specific to your Web site. A small page icon at the bottom of the screen represents each page that you added. To save your publication as Web pages, choose **File**, **Save As Web Page**.

N O T E If you added any forms to your site, you are prompted to add the path and script name that drives the form. It is a good idea to obtain information about how the script works before you build the form, because you might need it to label the data fields in the form. See your Webmaster or ISP for more details. ▓

To create a blank, single Web page without using a wizard, choose **File**, **New** from the menu, click the **Blank Publications** tab at the top of the Publisher Catalog, choose **Web page**, and click **Create**.

Using Excel Spreadsheet, WebChart, and PivotTable Components

New to Excel 2000 is the capability to add interactive components to Web pages. In Excel 97, if you saved your worksheet, PivotTable, or chart to HTML, it became a set of static numbers or a static graphic. Anytime a number changed, you had to regenerate the entire Web page. With the new Excel interactive components, you can change spreadsheet information from within a browser and watch the worksheet, PivotTable, or chart automatically update just as it would from within Excel. You can also add new information, formulas, reformat, and recalculate a worksheet or chart. This feature is entirely interactive and updates in real-time without requiring a trip to the Web server. Excel uses a combination of Dynamic HTML and Component Object Model (COM) objects to provide this interactivity.

Part

V

Ch

32

> **CAUTION**
>
> At this time, the interactive capability of Excel components is supported only by Internet Explorer 4.01 or later with the Microsoft Office Web Components installed. Currently, only Internet Explorer 5 (the version that ships with Office 2000) supports the complete feature range of Excel interactive components.

Using the Interactive Spreadsheet Component

To place spreadsheet interactivity into a Web page, first create a worksheet in Excel. An example is shown in Figure 32.18.

This worksheet displays revenue and profit information for four quarters with a sum formula in the last cell yielding a yearly total. To save this as an interactive Web page, choose **File**, **Save As Web Page** from the menu. This is a typical Save As dialog box except for a small check box labeled _A_dd Interactivity with the Excel logo next to it as highlighted in Figure 32.19. Also note the addition of a _P_ublish button to the Save As dialog box.

FIGURE 32.18
A typical Excel spread-sheet.

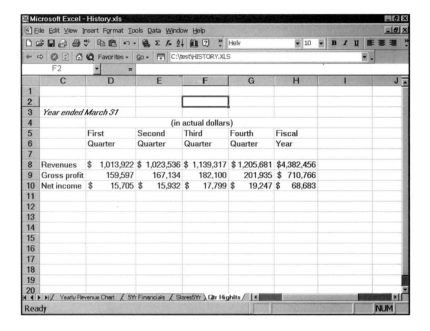

FIGURE 32.19
Saving an Excel work-sheet as an interactive Web page.

This box must be checked to create an interactive worksheet.

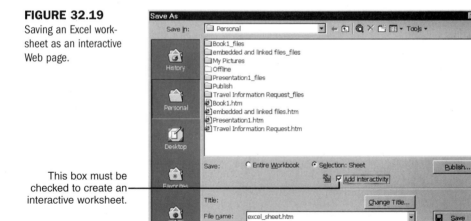

The <u>A</u>dd Interactivity check box must be selected to place the interactive features into the saved Web page. Clicking **Save** saves the worksheet with the selected interactivity. The saved Web page in Internet Explorer 5 is shown in Figure 32.20.

FIGURE 32.20

An interactive worksheet object in the Internet Explorer 5 Web browser.

The Property Toolbox icon

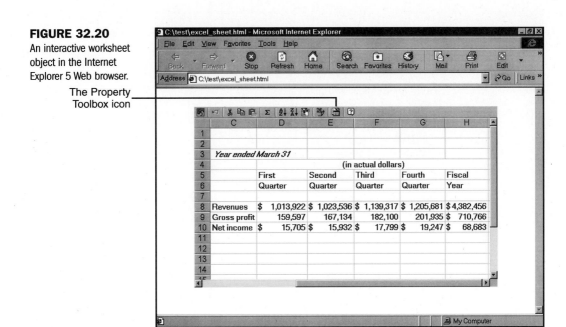

This worksheet is as interactive as a typical worksheet in Excel. A few features are accessible from an abbreviated toolbar across the top. More features can be accessed by right-clicking a cell and choosing Property Toolbox or clicking the Property Toolbox icon. Properties are categorized as shown in Figure 32.21.

FIGURE 32.21

Displaying cell properties and formulas in an Excel interactive worksheet.

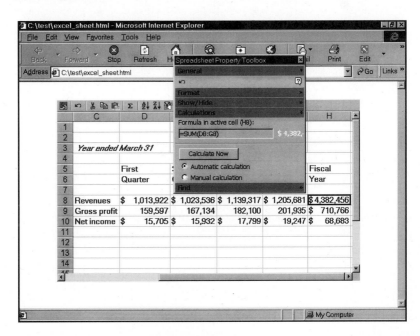

N O T E Note also how the formula for the cell is displayed in the Spreadsheet Property Toolbox. You can edit the formula from here or double-click a cell containing a formula and edit the formula directly in the cell. ▤

Understanding the Interactive WebChart Component

WebChart components update dynamically in a browser just as worksheets do. To place a WebChart component into a Web page, first create a chart in Excel. A sample is shown in Figure 32.22.

FIGURE 32.22
A typical Excel bar chart.

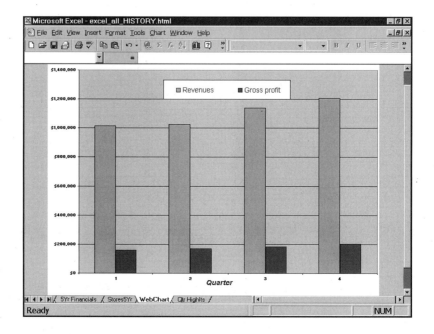

> **CAUTION**
>
> You cannot save a chart that is embedded in a worksheet as an interactive WebChart component. The chart must be saved as a separate sheet in an Excel workbook.

To save this chart as an interactive Web chart, choose **File**, **Save As Web Page** from the menu, click **Selection: Chart** (or **Republish: Chart** if it has been published before), select the **Add Interactivity** check box, and click **Save**. The chart and its accompanying data are both saved and displayed when the Web page is loaded into Internet Explorer 5 (Figure 32.23).

FIGURE 32.23
An Excel chart displayed as an interactive WebChart component in Internet Explorer 5.

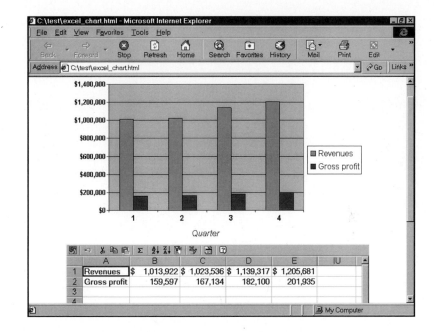

Changing any of the values in the worksheet component updates the chart display in real-time.

Using the Interactive PivotTable Component

The capability to view a complex series of numbers as a PivotTable can now be added to a Web page. Figure 32.24 displays a simple PivotTable in Excel.

FIGURE 32.24
An Excel PivotTable.

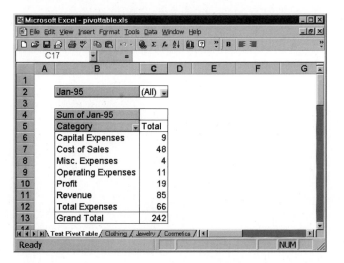

To convert this to a PivotTable in a Web page, choose **File**, **Save As Web Page** from the menu, click **Selection: Sheet** (or **Republish: Sheet** if it has been published before), select the **Add Interactivity** check box, and click **Save**. The resulting interactive Web page in Internet Explorer 5 is shown in Figure 32.25.

FIGURE 32.25
An Excel PivotTable displayed as an interactive PivotTable component in Internet Explorer 5.

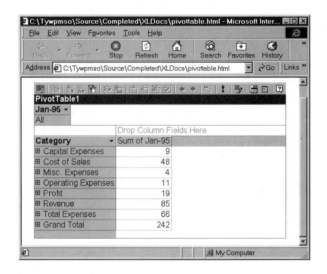

If the word "PivotTable" does not show up at the top of the component in your browser, the PivotTable might have been saved as a worksheet instead. To fix this:

1. Go back to the PivotTable in Excel.

2. Choose **File**, **Save As Web Page** from the menu.

3. Click the **Publish** button to open the Publish as Web page dialog box.

4. Be sure the PivotTable is selected—not the sheet containing the PivotTable—by choosing the appropriate item in the **Choose** drop-down list box, and then selecting the PivotTable in the following list.

5. Be sure the **Add interactivity with** check box is selected.

6. Be sure the list box to the right of the interactivity check box reads "PivotTable functionality" and not "Spreadsheet functionality."

7. Click the **Publish** button.

The completed Publish as Web Page should resemble Figure 32.26.

Publishing Selected Interactive Components from Workbooks

If you have a large workbook containing numerous charts or worksheets that you want to save as interactive components, then you need to choose **File**, **Save As Web Page** from the menu, and then click the **Publish** button from the Save **As** dialog box (refer to Figure 31.26).

This opens the Publish as Web Page dialog box. From here, you can choose which single worksheet, chart, or named range to publish, For each item that you want to publish as an interactive component, you must go through this dialog box and publish it individually.

FIGURE 32.26
Using Publish as Web page to ensure that a PivotTable is saved to a Web page as a PivotTable, not a worksheet.

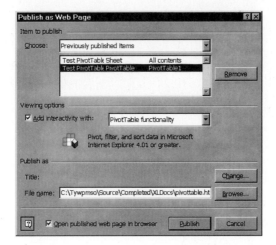

Querying Web-Based Data Sources from Excel

Excel 2000 has a unique capability to dynamically query HTML files or Web search engines or other data compendia and pull that information into a cell in a spreadsheet. This feature is handy for pulling stock quotes off the Internet or for directly querying search engines. You query Web-based data by creating a Web query. A *Web query* is a very simple text file that gives Excel this information:

- Where to go on the Internet or local network
- Which file to access
- How to access the file or which parameters to send to a Web server or search engine

To build a Web Query, choose **Data**, **Get External Data**, **New Web Query**. This opens the New Web Query dialog box (Figure 32.27).

After making your selections, clicking the Advanced button lets you choose how to deal with preformatted text in Web pages and date formats as shown in Figure 32.28.

After you've changed advanced options, click **OK**, and then click **Save Query** to save the Web query as a text file with an .iqy extension. After you've saved the query and clicked **OK** to leave the New Web Query dialog box, you're next prompted for the Excel worksheet and cell location for receiving the results of the query (Figure 32.29).

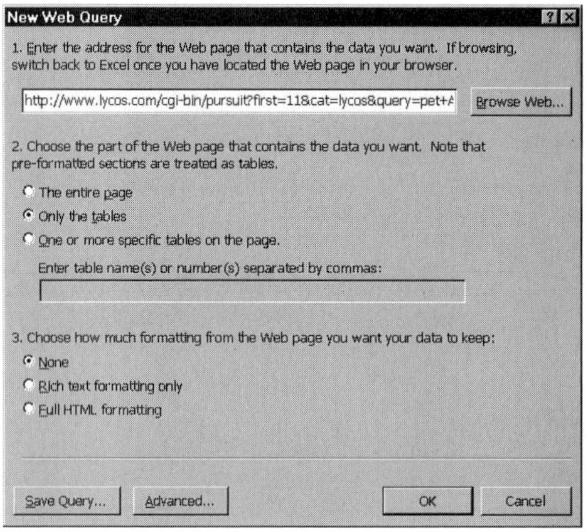

FIGURE 32.27
Building a new Web query.

FIGURE 32.28
Advanced options in building new Web queries.

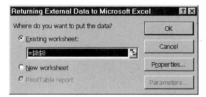

FIGURE 32.29
Choosing the beginning cell and worksheet for placement of data returned by the Web query.

Clicking the **Properties** button opens the External Data Range Properties dialog box, shown in Figure 32.30, which lets you fine-tune your query in several ways:

- Be sure the Save query definition check box is selected to save the query to the worksheet. This gives you the option of refreshing the data at a later time.

- The Enable background refresh check box allows the query to run in the background, so that you can continue to work in Excel while you're waiting for the results.

- The Refresh data on file open check box reruns the query whenever you open the worksheet.

- There are five check boxes under Data formatting and layout; three are probably grayed out. The Adjust column width is self-explanatory. Preserve cell formatting lets you dictate the formatting for the incoming data.

- Below the Data formatting and layout area are three option buttons that enable you to choose what to do if the data table you bring in is larger or smaller than previous query results. Choose whichever option is appropriate.

- The Fill down formulas in columns adjacent to data check box controls the use of formulas that are in cells to the right of the data imported via the query. If this check box is selected, Excel automatically eliminates or adds formulas as the number of rows of imported data shrinks or grows.

FIGURE 32.30

Customizing the results of a Web Query in the External Data Range Properties dialog box.

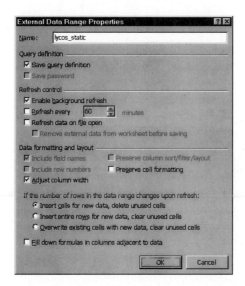

After you've made your selections in the External Data Range Properties dialog box, click **OK** to return to the Returning External Data to Microsoft Excel dialog box. Run the query by clicking **OK** in the Returning External Data to Microsoft Excel dialog box. A small, green rotating globe shows up on the status line of the Excel window as Excel retrieves the data. The query is complete when your Excel worksheet is filled with results (see Figure 32.31).

TIP

You can often obtain Web server syntax to use in a Web query by reading the help files at the search engine site. Alternatively, you can perform a search and then dissect the string passed on to the Web server as it appears in your browser's Address box.

Part

V

Ch

32

FIGURE 32.31
An Excel worksheet containing the results of a Web query search.

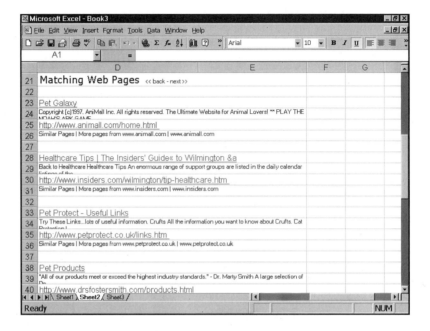

Broadcasting a PowerPoint Presentation over an Intranet

PowerPoint presentations are typically given using digital, overhead, or slide projectors before live audiences. In Office 97, presentations could be saved as Web pages and animations for display over the Internet. In PowerPoint 2000, presentations can be streamed over the company network with accompanying audio and video narration. Any presentation can be broadcast to audiences of 15 or less using software installed with Office 2000.

N O T E If you plan on having 16 or more concurrent connections to your broadcast or if you want to use a video feed, you then need to broadcast the presentation from a NetShow server. The NetShow server is currently free at `http://www.microsoft.com/ntserver/`. The NetShow server installs under Windows 95/98, or Windows NT as a service. ■

Before setting up a presentation for broadcast, be sure the following are available:

- A shared folder on a network server that can be accessed by everyone who will be viewing the broadcast
- Outlook 2000 as your default mail client
- All audience participants have Internet Explorer 4.01 or later
- A time when everyone is available to view the broadcast

To begin setting up the broadcast, open your presentation in PowerPoint.

TIP

You do not have to have your presentation completed before you schedule the broadcast. You can use a blank presentation as a placeholder and replace it with your actual presentation anytime before broadcast.

From the Slide Show menu, click **Online Broadcast**, and then **Set Up** and **Schedule**. Click **Set Up** and schedule a new broadcast from the Broadcast Schedule dialog box and click **OK**. This opens the Schedule a New Broadcast dialog box as shown in Figure 32.32.

FIGURE 32.32
Setting up to broad-cast a PowerPoint presentation.

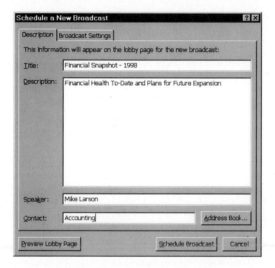

The information you enter under the Description tab of the Schedule a New Broadcast dialog box will be included in an email to your audience. The email will be automatically generated later through Outlook. From the next tab in the Schedule a New Broadcast dialog box, Broadcast Settings, shown in Figure 32.33, you can select:

- Audio and video, whether to use them or not, and their sources
- Options for audience feedback, including email from the audience to the presenter, or chat, if a chat server is also set up
- Whether to record the broadcast for archiving
- Whether viewers can access speaker notes
- Access to server options

To set up the shared folder for the broadcast or the NetShow server, if required, click the **Server Options** button. At a minimum, fill in the location of the shared folder as shown in Figure 32.34.

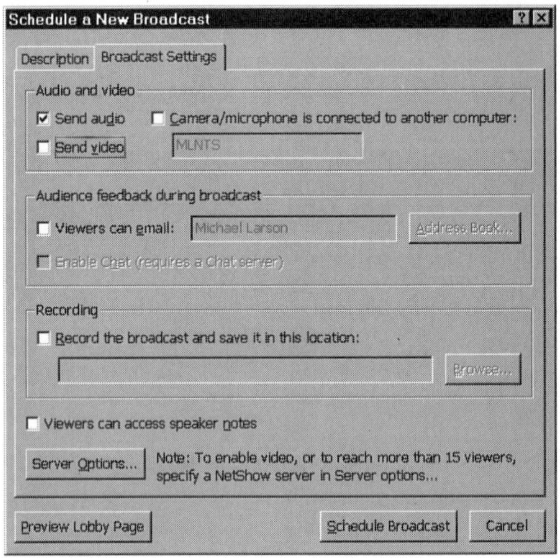

FIGURE 32.33

Changing broadcast
settings for a
PowerPoint broadcast.

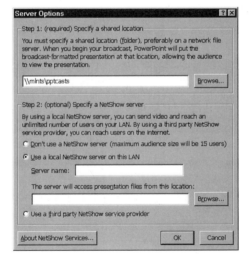

FIGURE 32.34

Setting up the broadcast
server for a PowerPoint
presentation.

The address for the shared folder must be in the form of a network share or UNC address, but PowerPoint will not force this format when you Browse for a network share, so you might need to edit the resulting location. Be sure to use the \\server\share syntax. If you're using a NetShow server, fill in the server location. Clicking **OK** takes you back to the Schedule a New Broadcast dialog box.

Click the **Preview Lobby Page** button. The lobby page is a Web page that the audience will see prior to the start of the broadcast. A sample is shown in Figure 32.35.

FIGURE 32.35
A lobby page in Internet Explorer 5 with a timer counting down to the broadcast of the PowerPoint presentation.

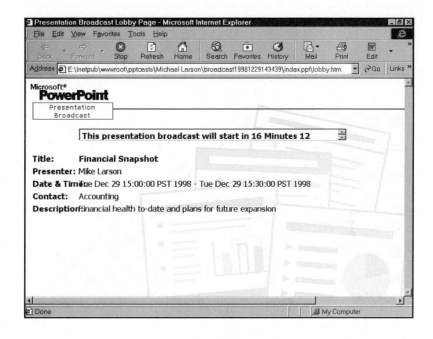

The lobby page is written almost completely in JavaScript; you will need programming skills to modify it.

After previewing the lobby page, close your browser and click the **Schedule Broadcast** button at the bottom of the Schedule a New Broadcast dialog box. This will open up Outlook with a ready-to-send email message showing all the pertinent broadcast information (Figure 32.36).

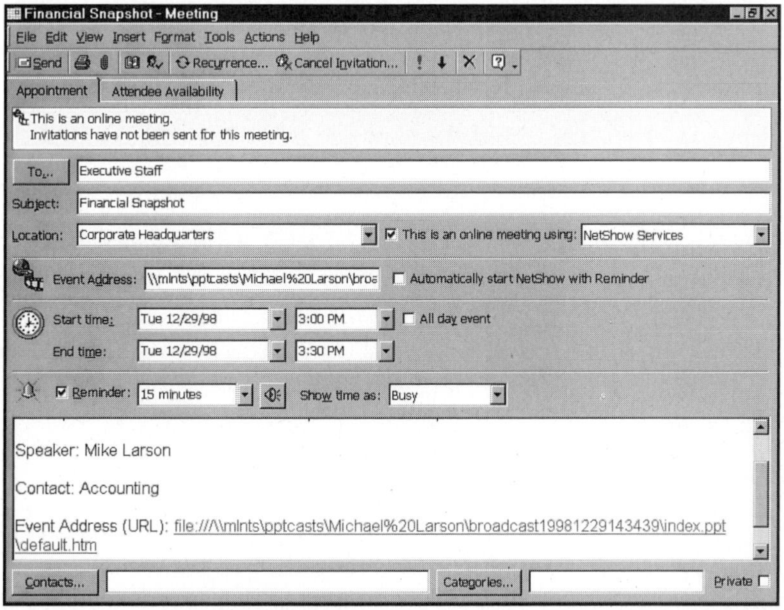

FIGURE 32.36
Sending an email invitation to all parties interested in your PowerPoint broadcast.

Part
V
Ch
32

Select the recipients of the email. Notice that a default time and date have been scheduled for your broadcast. Change this to your actual broadcast start and stop times. After sending the email, close Outlook. The process for setting up the broadcast is now complete.

To edit any settings, just go back to the Slide Show menu, and click **Online Broadcast**, and then **Set Up** and **Schedule**.

To start the actual broadcast process, from the Slide Show menu, click **Online Broadcast**, and then **Begin Broadcast**. The NetShow Encoder will check the broadcast settings and ready itself for broadcast, displaying a countdown timer. Audience members logging into the lobby page will automatically be taken to the event page when the broadcast begins.

Using Data Access Pages to Add Database Content to Web Pages

To date, there have been two primary ways to place Access database content into Web pages:

- Save database objects (tables, query results, and so on) as HTML tables
- Use Open Database Connectivity (ODBC) drivers to connect Active Server Pages to the database

These options are still available with Access 2000. A third option, *data access pages*, is a new capability added in Access 2000. Data access pages are independent Web pages generated from within Access that contain COM controls bound to the database records and Dynamic HTML code. The Web pages can be loaded into Internet Explorer 5 and used interactively to scroll through records and perform standard database operations, such as adding or updating records. Data access pages are very similar in function to Access forms.

> **CAUTION**
>
> Internet Explorer 4 and Netscape Navigator or Communicator browsers are not compatible with data access pages. Even though plug-ins for COM controls (also called ActiveX) are available for Netscape browsers, the Dynamic HTML code used in data access pages is not compatible with Netscape browsers.

Creating Data Access Pages

There are four ways to create data access pages from within Access:

- The Data Access Page Wizard
- AutoPage: Columnar
- Building from scratch
- Modifying existing Web pages

To begin building data access pages using any of these four options, from an open database, choose **Pages** from the list of Objects (Figure 32.37).

FIGURE 32.37
Building data access pages from the list of Pages from database Objects.

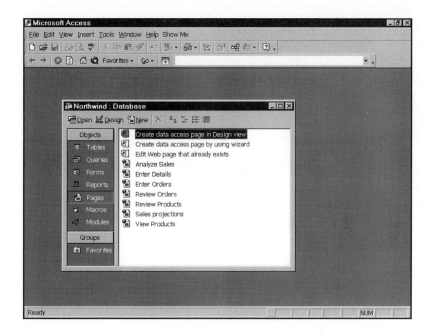

From here, you can build data access pages using the Design view (from scratch), the Wizard, and by editing existing Web pages. You can choose to build your data access pages from one of these choices or click **New** on the database toolbar, **General** tab, **Data Access Page**, **OK** to open the New Data Access Page dialog box as shown in Figure 32.38.

FIGURE 32.38
Ways to build new data access pages.

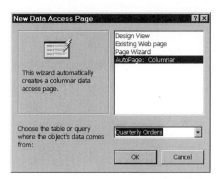

The quickest means to build a data access page, though with the least control, is by using AutoPage. From the New Data Access Page dialog box, click **AutoPage: Columnar**, and then choose a table or query from the drop-down list box at the bottom. Clicking **OK** immediately generates the data access page shown in Figure 32.39.

FIGURE 32.39

Building a data access page using AutoPage.

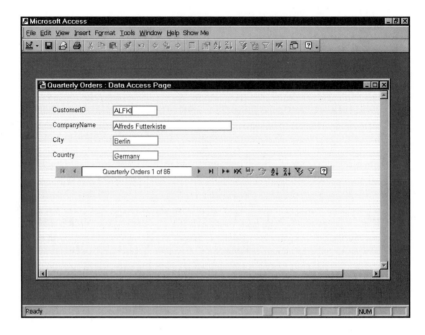

To view the page in a browser (Figure 32.40), select **Web Page Preview** from the File menu.

FIGURE 32.40

A data access page in Internet Explorer 5.

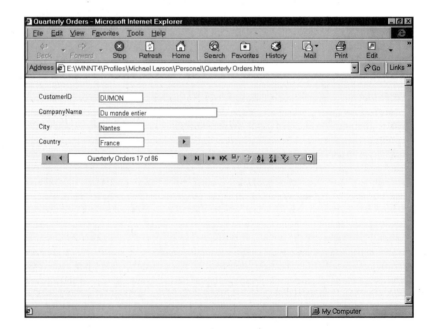

From this data access page in the browser, you can select, sort, filter, add, and delete records. All the functions normally performed using Access forms can now be performed from within a browser using data access pages.

If you want more control over the creation of a data access page, try the Data Access Page Wizard. To find the Wizard, follow the steps for creating an AutoPage, but choose **Page Wizard** instead of AutoPage: Columnar in the New Data Access Page dialog box. From this Wizard, you can also build more complex grouped data access pages. You can select fields for grouping as seen on the second page of the Page Wizard (Figure 32.41).

FIGURE 32.41
Adding groups to a data access page using the Page Wizard.

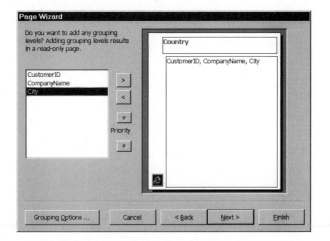

Click **Group Options** to bring up a variety of grouping options (see Figure 32.42).

FIGURE 32.42
Grouping options available for data access pages from the Page Wizard.

Later pages in the Page Wizard let you specify sorting order for records, whether you want to use a theme with the data access page, and whether to add a help option to the page.

Of course, for the ultimate in page control when building data access pages, you can build one from scratch using the Design view. From the blank document that opens, you can add titles, text, and use the Access Toolbox to add any ActiveX control.

Lastly, you can open any existing Web page and add data access capability to it using the Access Toolbox.

Deploying Data Access Pages

Data access pages can be used on intranets, extranets, or on the Internet. The single software requirement for visitors is Internet Explorer 5. Each visitor also needs an Office 2000 license, though not Office 2000 itself, to use data access pages. This probably limits the use of data access pages to intranet or extranet environments.

No special Web server is required for data access pages. Be sure your database has a network address and that the path from the database to data access pages is a network path rather than a disk-file path.

Using Advanced Web Options

Additionally, more advanced Web options can be found in Word, Excel, PowerPoint, and Access. These Web options enable you to change the default display of your Web pages, which languages and features are supported, and how Web pages are saved. From the menu of any of these applications, choose **Tools**, **Options**, click the **General** tab, and finally click the **Web Options** button. The opening Web Options screen from Word is shown in Figure 32.43.

FIGURE 32.43
Setting Web page appearance using Web Options in Word 2000.

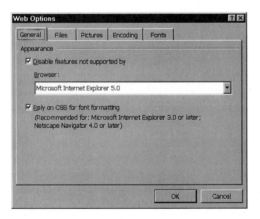

The options available from each tab differ somewhat depending on which application you're in.

Customizing the Appearance of Your Web Page

Under the General tab for Web Options in Word, your first decision is whether to set the lowest common browser version. The **Disable features not supported by** check box is selected by default with the Microsoft Internet Explorer 5 browser selected. What this means is that Word 2000 includes Web-page features that can be read by Microsoft Internet Explorer 5; that is, Microsoft Internet Explorer 5 is the lowest common denominator for browsers. The only other browser option available in the Browser box is Microsoft Internet Explorer 4.0 or Netscape Navigator 4.0 (these are both included in a single option). If the version 4.0

browsers are selected, then Word 2000 will include only Web-page features that can be properly interpreted by version 4.0 browsers. For instance, no VML would be used in Web pages generated by Word 2000 because version 4.0 browsers do not understand VML. If you clear the **Disable features not supported by** check box, then every Web-page feature built into Word 2000 will be utilized without regard for whether any browser version can support it.

The next available choice in Word or Excel is whether to utilize CSS for font formatting. Earlier browsers ignore CSS.

In Excel, two more additional Compatibility check boxes, both selected by default, are available as shown in Figure 32.44.

FIGURE 32.44
Setting Web compatibility options in Excel 2000.

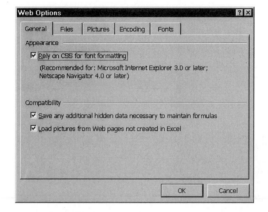

In PowerPoint, the General tab of the Web Options dialog box is completely different from the other applications as shown in Figure 32.45.

FIGURE 32.45
Changing PowerPoint-specific options in the Web Options dialog box.

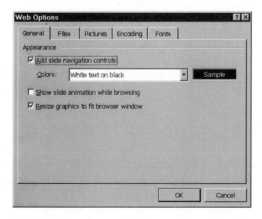

Part
V

Ch
32

From this dialog box, you can change

- Whether to add slide navigation controls to PowerPoint presentations saved as Web pages. You can choose from a limited selection of background/text color combinations. This is selected by default.
- Whether to show animation while browsing. This toggles any slide animations on or off when the presentation is being viewed in a browser. The default is off.
- Whether VML graphics are resized to fit the browser window.

In Access, the General tab of the Web Options dialog box has only options for choosing the hyperlink color, followed hyperlink color, and whether to underline hyperlinks or not.

Selecting Web-Page File Options

From the Files tab of the Web Options toolbox in Word, shown in Figure 32.46, you can change some filename options and make choices about Word 2000 being your default Web-page editor.

FIGURE 32.46

Setting File names and locations and Default editor options using Web Options in Word 2000.

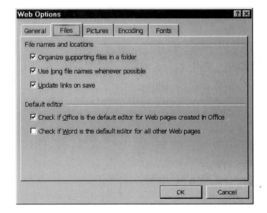

The first check box in the File names and locations section asks whether you want to Organize supporting files in a folder. As was mentioned earlier in this chapter, when Word 2000 saves a Web page, it sends many (although not all) supporting files—such as graphics—to a separate folder. This box should be clear only if you already have a set of folders set up with your Web-page supporting files.

The next check box, Use long file names whenever possible, is selected by default. The only operating system that does not support long filenames is Windows 3.x. Unless you have a large number of people using this operating system, leave this check box clear. The final check box in this section, Update links on save, tracks links to graphics and other supporting files contained in your Web page. With this option selected, Word 2000 checks the links and updates them during the file-saving process.

The File names and location section is also found on the Files tab in Excel and PowerPoint.

Selecting Office Applications As Your Default Web-Page Editor

The Default editor portion of the Files Tab under Web Options enables you to decide whether you want Office to be the default editor for Web pages created in Office (selected by default) and whether you want Word to be the default editor for all Web pages (clear by default). If selected, Word or the Office application displays a message when opening a Web page asking whether you want to make Word or the Office application the default editor. This message will not display if either or both of these check boxes are clear.

N O T E If the Web page you are viewing in Microsoft Internet Explorer was created in another Office 2000 application, such as Excel 2000 or PowerPoint 2000, then initiating the edit sequence opens the Web page in the Office component that originally created it. If the Web page was not created in any Office 2000 application, it is sent to whichever program is designated for editing under Tools, Internet Options, the Programs Tab in Internet Explorer. ▓

Word 2000 does not maintain the HTML source of the original Web page completely (assuming that the page was not created in Word 2000). Word 2000 immediately adds the HTML code it needs to make the Web page being edited suitable for roundtripping. This means that you can save the Web page to file formats other than .htm or as a Word .doc file. This guarantees that the original Web-page formatting is maintained. Any tags in a Web page that Word 2000 does not understand, however, are not changed.

If you do not want Word to add the code for roundtripping, then you should consider editing the Web page using a dedicated Web-page editor, such as FrontPage 2000.

The check box for Office as the default editor is also found in Excel and PowerPoint.

Lastly, in Excel only, there is an Office controls section with a cleared box, Download Office Web Components, and a text box for specifying the location of these components.

Using Specialty File Formats for Graphics

The next tab in the Web Options box in Word, Excel, and PowerPoint, is Pictures, shown in Figure 32.47, and gives you choices on using VML, PNG (another, newer bitmap image format), and target monitors.

The first option under File formats, Rely on VML for displaying graphics in browsers (Recommended for Microsoft Internet Explorer 5.0 or later), is clear by default. Remember, as of the writing of this book, VML is supported only in Microsoft Internet Explorer 5. The next check box, Allow PNG as an output format, is also clear by default. *Portable Network Graphics* (PNG) is a fairly new bitmap file format. It is more complex than GIF or JPG; it can use a reduced-color palette such as GIF but has excellent compression capabilities similar to JPG. This format might become the dominant, single-bitmap format as soon as more browsers support it. For now, only Microsoft Internet Explorer 5 or later supports this new bitmap-graphics file format.

Access does not contain a Pictures tab.

Part
V

Ch
32

FIGURE 32.47

Setting graphic file formats and the target monitor size using Web Options.

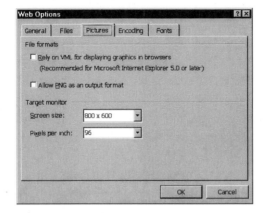

Optimizing the Target Monitor Screen Size

Under the Target monitor section of this page you can choose a Screen Size from 544×376 up to 1,920×1,200. Pixels per inch, supported on the monitors, includes 72, 96, and 120.

The target monitor screen size and pixels per inch are used in Word 2000 whenever a full-page graphic (such as a chart) needs to be converted to a graphic. The larger the screen size and the greater the number of pixels per inch, the larger the output graphic will be. Use the default screen size of 800×600 and 96 pixels per inch unless many people visiting your site might be using smaller monitors with a 640×480-screen resolution.

In PowerPoint, there is no option for specifying pixels per inch for the target monitor.

Changing Language Encoding and Fonts

The next tab, Encoding, the same in Word, Excel, and PowerPoint, shown in Figure 32.48, enables you to choose the language-code page from those installed on your machine. Choose the appropriate code page for the language you are using to build your Web page.

FIGURE 32.48

Choosing the language-code page using Web Options.

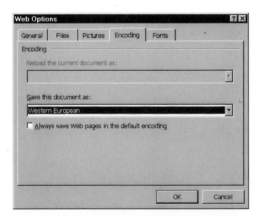

The final tab in the Web Options box, Fonts (shown in Figure 32.49), enables you to choose

- The default fonts, including which default character set to choose from among those installed on your computer
- The default proportional font and font size (in points)
- The default fixed-width font and font size

FIGURE 32.49
Choosing default fonts using Web Options in Word 2000.

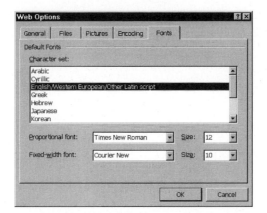

The default fonts are used only if none are specified in the Web page. There is no Fonts tab in Access. This is the final tab in the Web Options dialog box. After you have made your selections, clicking **OK** activates them. ●

Part

V

Ch

32

Managing HTML/XML As Your Primary File Format

by Michael A. Larson

Microsoft has again pushed the envelope by adding several new technologies to Web pages created using Office 2000. These new Web technologies allow Office-built Web pages to display more kinds of information with Internet Explorer version 5. Now most of the information contained in an Office document can be displayed in a Web page and the Web page can be saved back as an Office document. This roundtripping capability gives you the option to select Web pages as your standard company file format.

Web Folders, shortcuts to Web servers, now lets you easily post to or edit files to and from a Web Server just like you're working with another folder on your desktop.

Using Office applications to build and manage Web pages means one less software package to learn and fewer steps to posting Office-built documents to a Web, intranet, or extranet site.

Understanding Office Web Page Component Technologies

Whenever you save an Office document as a Web page, you are building a page of source code. In Office 2000 Web pages, a total of five technologies (four of them new to Office 2000) are being used:

- **HTML.** Hypertext Markup Language
- **XML.** eXtensible Markup Language
- **CSS.** Cascading Style Sheets
- **VML.** Vector Markup Language
- **JavaScript and VBScript.** Visual Basic Script

The addition of these technologies now allows a Web page to truly represent most of the features commonly found in Office documents from within a browser. For instance, complex paragraph styles, including precise positioning information, simply cannot be expressed by HTML alone. With the addition of CSS, this positioning and style information is captured as an Office document and is saved as a Web page. So, now the Office document looks the same whether you're viewing it as a native Office file or as a Web page in a browser. Each of these technologies contributes some functionality to the Office 2000 Web pages.

Evaluating Office 2000 Web Page Technology Roles

So, how does Microsoft use each of these pieces in its Web pages? What role does each technology play and how do they work together?

- **HTML** is still the basis of an Office 2000-generated Web page. All the other languages are generally included between the <HTML> and </HTML> tags; that is, they are all inside or referenced from inside an HTML container. Standard HTML tags are used when needed, but cascading style sheets are used to economize on the number of HTML formatting tags whenever possible.

- **CSS** is used to define text styles, such as fonts and font sizes, page margins, indents, and most other formatting required by any of the text, graphics, or table elements in the Web page.

- **XML** is primarily used in Office 2000 to define which Office application a particular Web page belongs to and which parts of the page relate to specific features within the Office application.

- **VML** is used to define all Microsoft Drawing objects, including lines, geometric shapes, fills, WordArt, and so on. When a page containing a draw object is saved as a Web page, the object is defined as VML. A bitmap image of the object is also saved for use in browsers that don't support VML.

- **JavaScript or VBScript** are used to determine whether any given browser supports the functions in the HTML file—VML, for instance—and send the appropriate data to it.

Hypertext Markup Language

HTML was originally designed to give a simple hierarchical design to text information, such as Header 1, Header 2, and so on, and to provide a means to link documents across a network. HTML pages are simple text pages that you can modify with any basic text editor (such as Notepad) on any computer platform. The heart of HTML is its tags. The tags enable the browser to interpret the data that follows them. Tags are enclosed in angle brackets and generally occur in pairs: an opening tag and a closing tag. For instance, if you want to define some text as header text, it would look like the following:

```
<H1> Some text </H1>
```

In this example `<H1>` and `</H1>` are tags. The slash in the end tag defines the closing tag. Tags can also contain attributes such as

```
<font color="red"> An Important Announcement </font>
```

The text surrounded by the <font> tags would be displayed in red.

> **N O T E** The font or font size that is used to display the Header 1 tag varies from platform to platform. HTML was designed this way so that its other goal of cross-platform use could be met. An unfortunate side effect is that HTML pages can look very different on different platforms or different browsers.
>
> When the Internet was used to deal with strictly technical documents, this was not an issue because fewer people cared about appearance. But now people and companies want complete control over how a Web document looks and want to know that it looks the same no matter where it is viewed. HTML was never designed with this in mind, which has led to the search for other technologies to support HTML. ▓

All Web pages begin with the <HTML> tag and end with the closing </HTML> tag. Web pages have head, title, and body sections denoted by <HEAD>, <TITLE>, and <BODY> tags. That's all. Lists of the HTML tags and their definitions can be found on the Internet in many locations. A good place to start is

```
http://www.ncsa.uiuc.edu/General/Internet/WWW/HTMLPrimer.html
```

Some sample HTML source code is shown in Figure 33.1.

Cascading Style Sheets

Cascading Style Sheets (CSS) can be separate documents, usually with a .css file extension, or defined within the body of an HTML page. CSS can be used to define any text or page formatting that you can normally define using HTML tags. Styles are defined between the <STYLE> and </STYLE> tags. The advantage of using a Style tag over using just HTML tags is that after you have defined a style, you do not need to continually rebuild all the attributes of tags referenced in a style. This usually reduces the size of your HTML page, improving the page load time. This also provides consistent Web page appearance, much as Word's paragraph styles do, giving a much more professional touch to any Web site.

FIGURE 33.1

HTML source code from the beginning of a page about company sales as shown in Notepad.

CSS can also give a Web page designer precise control over the elements on a page using a coordinate system, that is, specifying a horizontal and vertical position for each element on a page. Consider the following style:

```
<STYLE>
BODY {background: #FFFFFF; color: #000000; margin-top: 0.5 in; margin-left: 0.5
in}
H2 {font: 16pt arial black; color: #FF0000}
P {font: 10pt comic sans MS; text-indent: 0.25 in}
A {color: #0000FF}
</STYLE>
```

N O T E Colors in HTML pages are defined using hexadecimal notation (zero through F, base 16) and the *Red-Green-Blue* (RGB) color model. RGB is the way colors are produced on computer monitors. The first two numbers are the red component, the second two, the green component, and the last two, the blue component. For instance, yellow is FFFF00, a mixture of red and green with no contribution from blue. ▓

Based on this style, the Web page body has white text on a black background with half-inch top and left margins. All text surrounded by Header 2 tags—<H2> and </H2> —will be in a red 16-point Arial Black font. Text paragraphs will be in a 10-point Comic Sans MS font and indented one-quarter of an inch from the left margin. Hypertext links—or *anchors*—are blue. CSS works in Web pages just like Word styles do in documents.

After the style is defined, you can then enter your content and it will be formatted according to the style. Browsers earlier than Netscape 4.0 or Microsoft Internet Explorer 3.0 cannot read style sheets properly; they render everything according to their default settings. As these browser versions become increasingly rare, you will see style sheets used more on the Web.

Both HTML and CSS can be used to display and format information, but they give you no internal clues as to the meaning of the content. XML can be used as one way to provide this meaning.

Extensible Markup Language

The primary job of XML, a derivative of *Standard Generalized Markup Language* (SGML), is to define or give meaning to a word or document by enclosing it in a pair of tags. It is a text-based data definition language or even a simple database information language. Unlike HTML, in XML you can create and define your own tags, hence the extensible in its name. XML-enabled browsers or applications can read your definition tags and interpret them as data. For instance, if you have a Web page discussing fruit, you could use the <CHERRIES> and </CHERRIES> tags to surround the paragraph discussing this fruit. You could further define the data in the paragraph using another tag, such as <CHERRY TYPE> bing </CHERRY TYPE>. Now the computer knows the word 'bing' is a cherry and not a singer/comedian.

The capability of a browser to read and properly interpret a tag can now be defined on-the-fly rather than hard coded into the browser as is the case with HTML. XML has nothing to do with page formatting. It is a data workhorse.

N O T E XML is not designed to display information. If you load an XML-only file into a browser, you will see only a blank page (or gibberish). XML is usually embedded in an HTML page. XML does the data definition, but there is no visual indication that XML is even there. XML does the data organization; HTML and CSS take care of the data display. ▪

The tags can be anything. You just need to define which tags you are using and what they mean in a *Document Type Definition* (DTD), which can be a separate text document or embedded in an HTML page. The DTD lists the tag names and their uses.

XML is primarily used in Web pages generated by Office 2000 applications to define metadata.

N O T E *Metadata* is information that is generally not directly related to the display of a Web page. It gives users a more sophisticated tool for labeling key data in a Web page than adding text comments. ▪

Office 2000 applications include XML as a translation dictionary for all the application features incorporated into a Web page. Office applications can correlate this XML metadata (description of data) to a particular application feature.

▶ For more information about the relationship between Office-generated Web pages and Office binary file formats, **see** the section "Roundtripping File Formats" in this chapter on **p. 873**.

It is probable that standards will arise for XML DTDs for any given area or topic. For instance, mathematicians already have their own XML DTD (called *MathML*) with agreed-on definitions for common mathematical concepts incorporated into it. It is not necessary to have agreed-on standards to use XML; you just need to define your tags in a DTD. Building a DTD is not, however, a trivial matter, so it is much easier to use DTDs already in existence.

Vector Markup Language

VML is a way to define line graphical images using textual geometric definitions of the composite parts of the graphic. Graphics defined this way are called *vector graphics*. VML is actually a specialized version of XML and is contained within an HTML page.

> **CAUTION**
>
> Do not confuse VML with VRML (*Virtual Reality Modeling Language*). VRML is used to build three-dimensional objects in Web browsers. It also is a specialized language, but unrelated to VML.

As an example, the VML definition for a circle 54 *points*—points typically define font sizes—in diameter with no color filling is

```
<v:oval id="_x0000_s1024" style='position:absolute; margin-left:95.25pt;margin-
top:69.75pt;width:54.75pt;height:54.75pt;z-index:1'/>
```

The circle is 95.25 points from the left margin and 69 points from the top margin. The z-index is used to determine which objects are on top when multiple objects overlap on the screen. To change the size and position of this circle, all you have to do is change the numbers. Changing the size of the circle does not impact the file size.

NOTE This is in contrast to how bitmap graphics (.gif and .jpg) are defined, which is with a color defined for each pixel and the total number of pixels determining the graphic's size. Increasing the size of a bitmap graphic greatly increases the file size and hence the time it takes to load. ▨

Vector graphics also retain their detail as they are resized, whereas bitmap graphics often lose information and detail if their image size is changed.

Scripting Languages

Office-generated Web pages use scripting languages to define actions and objects accessible from within a browser. The languages used are JavaScript (Microsoft's version is called JScript) or VBScript (Visual Basic Scripting Edition). JavaScript is supported by the vast majority of browsers; VBScript is supported only by Microsoft Internet Explorer browsers. These languages can be used to promote interactivity in Web pages.

NOTE Microsoft's JScript language is not Netscape's JavaScript—it is an implementation of the ECMA-262 specification, which happens to have originated in an early version of Netscape's JavaScript. Any scripting code generated in Office 2000 with the properties set to JavaScript (ECMA) is actually JScript. Be sure to test the script if Netscape browsers might view the Web page. ▨

JScript and VBScript were both developed for use within browsers. Both are structured, non-compiled programming languages. Because they were developed for use in browsers, security concerns played a role in the selection of language functions. For instance, file I/O (input/output) and access to low-level system data are not allowed within either language.

The code for both scripting languages is contained in a script container bounded by <SCRIPT> and </SCRIPT> anywhere in a Web page. The script container defines which language is being used and contains all the functions and definitions typically found in a program. Defined objects or functions can then be referenced from anywhere within the Web page.

Most JavaScript code used in Office-generated Web pages is too lengthy and complex to use in an example here. JavaScript is also commonly used in manually generated Web pages to open another browser instance when a hyperlink is clicked. The code used to define this JavaScript function is shown as follows:

```
<script LANGUAGE="JavaScript">
<!--
function openMaxWin(){
var myWinM = window.open('max_popup_frameset.html','max_win',
➥'width=600,height=300 resizable=yes scrollbars=1')
}
// -->
</script>
```

The following code is included in an image hyperlink to activate the function defined in the previous example:

```
<a href="top_frame_script.html"
onClick="openMaxWin();"
target="header"><img border="0" height="80" name="s4" src="s4.jpg"
alt="text description" width="100"></a>
```

When you click the image hyperlink, a new browser window with the size and features specified in the JavaScript function is opened.

▶ For more information on adding or editing JavaScript or VBScript to Web pages, **see** "Using Web Scripting," on **p. 829**.

Part

V

Ch

33

Roundtripping File Formats

The incorporation of metadata into all Office 2000 Web pages using XML means that almost any Office feature can be defined in a Web page.

▶ For more information on exactly which Office 2000 application features are not displayed in Web pages, **see** the section in this chapter, "Comparing Features of Office Binary Files with Web Pages," on **p. 875**.

In many situations, therefore, it is less important whether you choose to save a document as an Office binary file or as a Web page. Either file format looks the same in both the Office application that created it and a properly equipped browser. All the information normally contained in the Office binary file format is also included in the Web page format and vice versa. This interchangeability of file formats is called *roundtripping* by Microsoft. For example, you can use any Web page created in Word 2000 to completely regenerate the binary .doc format, as long as it does not have a password. This was not possible with Word 97.

The beefed-up Web page format can now display the vast majority of Office application features. These supplementary technologies increase the capability of HTML to display and manage more than is possible by using HTML alone.

> **N O T E** If communication is increasingly performed using Web technologies and Web pages, and Office documents display the same information in browsers as they do in Office 2000 applications, why bother translating back and forth between these two formats? Why not just start saving everything as Web pages? The Web format has most of the same functionality as the binary format. It is up to you as an Office user to decide whether the Web technologies in Office 2000 warrant discarding the binary file format. Microsoft will be watching. ■

Saving As a Web Page

Within a typical Office document, you can embed many elements, such as graphics and sounds, and these are incorporated into a single binary Office file when the document is saved. Web pages, however, do not directly embed many of the items that are displayed. For a graphic, the Web page contains only the path to the image file, not the image file itself. The same is true for sounds, videos, Java applets, and many other items. So, what happens to these associated files when you save a Web page from an Office 2000 application?

Understanding Files Created with Save As Web Page

Imagine that you're saving your Office document as a Web Page to a drive under the filename of HomePage.htm. During the file save operation, first, the actual Web page, HomePage.htm, is stored in the folder you selected on the drive. Next, a folder called HomePage_Files is created by the Office application under the folder containing HomePage.htm. In the HomePage_Files folder, you will find the following:

- Two files—filelist.xml and header.htm—containing information expressing all the Office features used within the file. These files are not used when HomePage.htm is viewed in a browser. Header.htm is present only if header or footer information is contained in the original document.
- All the bitmap image files are saved under image001.gif, image002.gif, image001.jpg, and so on.
- Drawing objects are also saved as .gif files.

TIP Save your Web page before inserting the multimedia elements. This will create the HomePage Files folder. Then, copy the audio, video, and Java applets to the HomePage_Files folder before inserting them in your Web page. This ensures that the files remain linked to HomePage.htm as well as making file management easier.

▶ Office 2000 offers the capability to work directly with files on a Web server using Web Folders. To find out how to create and use Web Folders, **see** Chapter 35, "Deploying and Using Office 2000's Web-Collaboration Components," on **p. 895**.

Because the folder is named after the Web page filename, it is also advisable to not rename the Web page. The Web page will still work properly but it will be more difficult to track its associated files if you ever need to move the Web page to another location.

Comparing Features of Office Binary Files with Web Pages

Roundtripping ensures that Web pages generated by Office applications contain most of the same information as Office documents saved in the Office binary file format. But can all the features present in an Office-generated Web page be displayed in Internet Explorer 5?

NOTE Even though a feature can't be displayed in a browser, the information for that feature is retained in the Office-generated Web page as XML metadata. When you open that Web page in the Office application it was created in, you will see those features. ▨

Word 2000 Features Not Displayed in Internet Explorer 5   Word 2000 still has several weaknesses in its capability to translate all its features to a Web page that can be displayed in Internet Explorer 5. The following Word features are not functional in Internet Explorer 5 if the file is saved as a Web page:

- Versioning is not available.
- Passwords do not protect the document.
- Word file Header/Footers are not displayed in any form.
- Fifteen character formats, including drop-caps and kerned text, cannot be used.
- Four paragraph formats, including negative left indenting, are not available.
- Eight page-layout features, including tabs and page numbering, are not available.
- Graphics surrounded on all sides by wraparound text become left justified.
- Eleven Asian text-formatting elements are not functional.
- Six table formats, including absolute row height, are not available.
- Columns are not maintained, although the text is unaffected.

Information for most of the items that do not display fully or partially in a browser is retained in the Web page file. Passwords and versions are lost, however; you cannot restore them from the Web page.

Excel 2000 Features Not Displayed in Internet Explorer 5   In Excel 97, worksheets and charts are transformed from interactive documents to static tables and images, respectively. With Excel 2000 interactive components, you can add interactive spreadsheets, WebCharts, and PivotTables. These interactive elements allow a user to change spreadsheet information from within a browser and watch the worksheet, PivotTable, or chart automatically update just as it would from within Excel.

▶ To find a more detailed discussion of the interactive components of Excel, **see** "Using Excel Spreadsheet, WebChart, and PivotTable Components," on **p. 843**.

Part
V

Ch
33

Although the interactive elements add more functionality, there are still a number of Excel features that are not displayed in Internet Explorer 5 when Excel files are saved as Web pages:

- Dotted or broken borders are displayed as solid borders.
- Multiple fonts in a single cell are lost; only the font of the first character is used.
- Cell comments are lost.
- Indents for text are not retained.
- Rotated or vertical text is changed to horizontal text.
- Images and pattern fills are lost.
- Password-protected sheets lose their password protection.

PowerPoint 2000 Features Not Displayed in Internet Explorer 5   Many of the custom elements of PowerPoint 2000 presentations are not active when the presentation is saved in a Web browser and viewed in Internet Explorer 5. These include

- Ten animation features don't work, including sound playing through multiple slides and linked or embedded objects aren't active.
- Six action settings don't work, including Run Macro and Object actions.
- Specialized shadowed and embossed font formatting doesn't work.

Access 2000 Features Not Displayed in Internet Explorer 5   Most elements (data tables, queries, forms, and reports) in Access 2000 can be saved as Web pages and display as static data tables. This includes graphics in forms and reports. Access 2000 also has a new capability, data access pages, which are independent Web pages that allow real-time interaction with database records from Internet Explorer 5.

▶ For a more detailed discussion of data access pages, **see** "Using Data Access Pages to Add Database Content to Web Pages," on **p. 856**.

Comparing Office Web Page Compatibility with Other Applications

Being able to transparently generate Web pages from Office applications is a very simple way for anyone to generate Web pages without requiring additional training. But the Web pages generated from Office 2000 applications must be useful in the real world, that is, compatible with many other common applications. Of concern might be compatibility with

- Multiple browser types and versions
- FrontPage 2000
- Office 97
- Other applications

Evaluating Browser Compatibility

Office 2000 applications generate Web pages that have some positive and some negative browser compatibility issues, namely:

- Web pages are almost completely compatible with Microsoft Internet Explorer 5.
- Netscape 4 and earlier do not support XML or VML.
- Netscape 5, however, should support both XML and VML.
- VBScript does not work in any other browser.

N O T E You can alter the compatibility level of Web pages generated from Office 2000 applications by changing Web Options from within any Office application. What this does is set optimal Web page compatibility for version 4 browsers (Netscape and Microsoft) rather than Internet Explorer 5. So, languages not supported by version 4 browsers (such as VML or XML) are not incorporated into Web pages. Roundtripping, however, will be less effective (more Word features will be lost) in this situation. No option is available for setting browser compatibility to version 3 or earlier.

To change Web Options, from within any Office Application except Outlook, FrontPage, and Publisher, select **Tools**, **Options**, click the **General** tab, and click the **Web Options** button. ■

If you are building Web pages for the Internet, you must consider the wide variety of browsers used around the world. You must choose a lowest common denominator browser and build your Web pages accordingly. Remember that Microsoft is including cutting-edge languages in its Web pages built using Office 2000 applications. Given the large number of Office users worldwide, however, this cutting edge might quickly become the norm and browser compatibility might be less of a concern.

Comparing Office 2000 Web Pages with FrontPage 2000

FrontPage 2000 is a powerful HTML editor and Web site management package bundled with Office 2000 in some editions. You can create and publish a complete Web site from within FrontPage 2000. However, can you use FrontPage 2000 to edit Web pages created by the other Office 2000 applications? The answer is mostly no.

If you try to use FrontPage 2000 to open an .htm file created by an Office 2000 application, the Office application that originally generated the Web page is automatically opened with the selected Web page. For instance, if you saved a PowerPoint 2000 presentation as a Web page and then tried to open that .htm file from FrontPage 2000, PowerPoint 2000 launches and loads the presentation. The Web page does not load into FrontPage 2000.

By spawning the associated Office application, the process of modifying Web pages is greatly simplified. Instead of worrying about HTML, CSS, XML, VML, or scripting from within FrontPage 2000, you can simply work on the file using standard Office tools.

Part
V

Ch
33

If you import HTML code from Web pages created in Office 2000 applications into FrontPage 2000 using the Clipboard, the pages usually are not displayed correctly in the Preview window. So, you can't use FrontPage as a WYSIWYG editor for Web pages created in other Office 2000 applications.

TIP

If you really want to edit the HTML source from Web pages saved from Office 2000 applications, your best alternative is to use a plain text editor. You will also have to be familiar with any or all of the technologies used in Office Web pages to effectively edit these files.

Also, from Word 2000 you can choose HTML Source from the **View** menu and edit the HTML source in the *Microsoft Development Environment* (MDE).

Comparing Office 2000 Web Pages with Office 97

The primary Office 97 applications—Word, Excel, and PowerPoint—were designed to both read Web pages and save Office documents as HTML pages. Access could also save some content as HTML files, but also import some HTML content (mostly tables) into Access tables. Word 97 in particular could render Web pages almost as well as a simple browser (except for frames). These Office 97 applications were built before the newer Web technologies (XML, VML, and CSS in particular) were active. So, how do Office 97 applications handle Web pages created in Office 2000 applications?

In reality, Web pages generated by Office 2000 applications might or might not be viewed as Web pages by Office 97 applications. For instance:

- A file containing frames saved as a Web page from Word 2000 is not rendered at all in Word 97 and is simply displayed as HTML source code.

- A simpler Web page saved from Word 2000 might render completely or partially in Word 97.

- A single page worksheet saved from Excel 2000 as a Web page will probably be rendered correctly by Excel 97.

- A multipage workbook saved as a Web page from Excel 2000 opened in Excel 97 might display only a cryptic error message that your browser doesn't support frames.

- PowerPoint 97 will simply distribute the HTML source code from any slide presentation, simple or complex, saved as a Web page from PowerPoint 2000 as text among many slides as shown in Figure 33.2.

The complexity of the technologies used to save Office 2000 Web pages is, for the most part, beyond the capacity of Office 97 applications to interpret. If backward compatibility with Office 97 applications is essential, the Office 2000 Web page format is not the avenue to travel. You will need to save Office 2000 applications as Office 97 binary files for optimal backward compatibility.

FIGURE 33.2
Trying to open a slide presentation saved as a Web page from PowerPoint 2000 in PowerPoint 97.

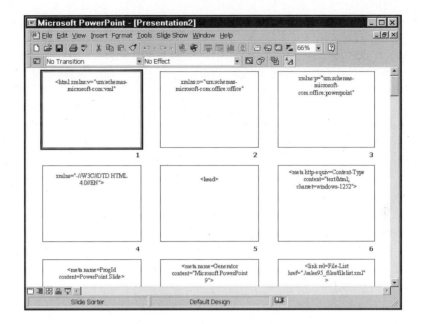

Using Office Web Pages with Other Applications

Many other spreadsheets, word processors, and other applications can read Web pages. It is impossible to catalog the response of these many applications and their varying versions to Web pages generated by Office 2000 applications. There are a few general guidelines, however, that might be useful in gauging how an application might respond when you try to load an Office 2000-generated Web page:

■ Is the application XML-aware or use an XML parser? If not, then the XML content of Office 2000 Web pages will be indecipherable by the application.

■ What is the application response to unknown tags? Most browsers simply ignore tags they don't understand. Other applications, especially HTML editors, try to modify the code or might even stall on unknown tags.

■ Is the application aware of scripting languages, specifically VBScript or JScript?

■ Can the application read Cascading Style Sheets?

In general, most applications created before Office 2000 simply do not know how to handle XML, VML, or CSS and will be unable to respond to these tags embedded in Office 2000 Web pages. These applications will probably respond unpredictably to Office 2000 Web pages and you might end up with jumbled or unusable Web pages when you try to open them. The Office 2000 Web page file format might not be useful outside of Office 2000.

Part
V

Ch
33

Simplifying Web Page File Management with Web Folders

After you have rebooted after installation of Office 2000, a new object appears at the bottom of Windows Explorer on the left side called Web Folders, shown in Figure 33.3.

FIGURE 33.3
The new Web Folders object installed by Office 2000 as seen in Windows Explorer.

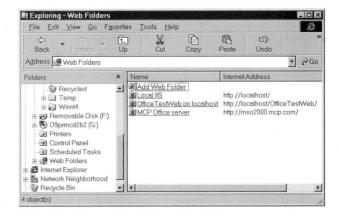

Web Folders are special folders that provide a direct shortcut to an IIS Web server. They enable you to transparently upload files directly to your Web server or even work with your Web pages directly from the Web server.

N O T E For Web Folders to work, the Web server must be properly configured. At this time, the only Web server that supports Web Folders is Microsoft *Internet Information Server* (IIS) 4. ■

In Office 97, you had to invoke a separate process—the Web Publishing Wizard—to upload the Web pages you built in the Office application. This wizard is no longer needed by Office 2000 applications. Now you can see Web Folders in Windows Explorer in the same way that you can see any other folder on your hard drive. Web Folders are now accessible from Office 2000 applications when opening a File List box using the **Open** command from the **File** menu. You can now work with the files on your Web server the same way you work with any other files or folders on your hard drive.

TIP

Using Web Folders is even easier than using *File Transfer Protocol* (FTP) to move files to and from a Web server. You can open a Web Folder to each of the folders on your Web server. You can then use drag-and-drop operations from Windows Explorer or other applications to move files back and forth.

▶ For more information on creating and using Web Folders, **see** Chapter 35, "Deploying and Using Office 2000's Web-Collaboration Components," on **p. 895**.

Using Outlook As an Internet Mail and News Client

by Michael A. Larson

For many businesses, Outlook is the primary client for communicating via email. Outlook 2000 not only manages company email (usually Microsoft Exchange servers) for individual users, but also sends and receives Internet email. Tools are included to easily set up and manage email with your Internet (usually SMTP) server. Also, Outlook can handle encrypted and HTML formatted email.

Businesses also use Outlook as a newsreader for Internet or company newsgroups. This means one less program to learn and support. Everyone can use the familiar Outlook interface to browse newsgroups.

Configuring Outlook to Send and Receive Internet Mail

Outlook makes managing your email easy with features such as message flagging, rules for organizing incoming messages, and junk mail filters. The Outlook Internet mail functionality is fully integrated with its other modules. For example, you can track email messages in the Journal or easily address an email message to a contact. Outlook is also integrated with other Office programs, which include enabling users to designate WordMail as their email editor. Also, because of its new collaboration features, Outlook is a good choice for any user who frequently sends and receives email across the Internet, communicating with one or many other users.

Connecting with Microsoft Exchange

Outlook can send and receive Internet email via Microsoft Exchange Server if Exchange Server is configured with a gateway to the Internet via the Internet Mail Service connector. As with email messages received from within the system, Internet email messages are funneled to the user's Inbox, located on a central Exchange Server computer. The user can then access and download these messages along with internal mail. Similarly, all messages the user sends to the Internet are routed to the central Exchange Server and then sent out through the gateway configured on the server. Therefore, for Outlook to access Internet mail in an Exchange environment, you need only to configure an Internet email information service that downloads email from the user's Inbox and sends email to the Internet Mail Server gateway.

Installing Outlook As an Exchange Server Client   Outlook 2000 must be installed in *Corporate or Workgroup* (CW) mode to connect to Exchange Server via the Internet Email information service. If Outlook is primarily used as an Exchange Server client—to access internal mail, public folders, and group scheduling capabilities—then it's already in CW mode and ready for connecting to the Internet via Exchange Server. If not, you need to add the CW component.

 TIP   Determine which mode Outlook is running in by choosing **Help**, **About Microsoft Outlook**. The mode is listed under Microsoft Outlook 2000.

To activate the CW component, just follow these steps:

1. From the menu select **Tools**, **Options**, choose the **Mail Delivery** tab, and click the **Reconfigure Mail Support** button.

> **CAUTION**
>
> Be sure that Internet Explorer is not in offline mode (**Work Offline** is not selected on the **File** menu).

2. Choose the **Corporate or Workgroup** option from the screen as shown in Figure 34.1.

FIGURE 34.1
Configuring Office
2000 for use in an
Exchange environment.

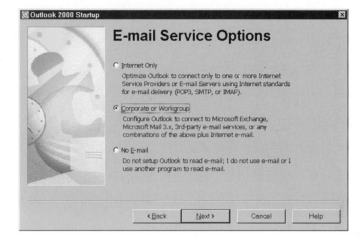

3. Click **Next**. You receive a warning that Outlook will shut down. Click **Yes**. Outlook then closes.

4. Restart Outlook. Be sure your Office 2000 CD-ROM is loaded. Outlook now opens in CW mode.

TIP Because Exchange Server can also function as an Internet Message Access Protocol (IMAP) or Post Office Protocol 3 (POP3) mail server, you don't necessarily have to upgrade to CW mode to use Outlook as an Internet mail client with Exchange Server. Instead, configure Outlook to connect to Exchange Server in the same way as any other mail server (see the upcoming section "Connecting with Non-Microsoft Exchange Environments"). POP3 or IMAP support must be enabled on the Exchange Server computer, however. POP3 and IMAP services are enabled by default. Also, this method doesn't allow Outlook to access other Exchange features, such as group scheduling, groupware, and in POP3 mode, public folders.

Configuring the Internet Email Information Service   When Outlook is running in CW mode, set up the Internet Email information service to connect to Exchange Server by performing the following steps:

1. Choose **Tools**, **Services**.

2. Select the **Internet Email information service** on the Services tab. (If it's not listed, click **Add**, select **Internet Email**, and click **OK**.)

3. Click **Properties**.

4. In the **Mail account** field on the General tab, enter a name for the Internet email information service (see Figure 34.2).

Part
V

Ch
34

FIGURE 34.2

Configuring general properties for the Internet email information service.

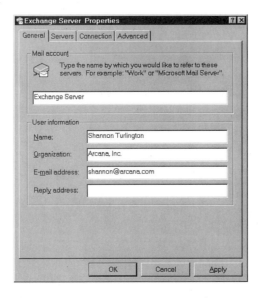

5. Enter the user's full name in the **Name** field.

6. Enter the company name in the **Organization** field (optional).

7. Enter the user's Internet email address in the **E-mail address** field; the email address is usually provided by the Exchange Server administrator and takes the form of `alias_name@organization_name.com`.

8. If desired, enter a different email address in the **Reply address** field where all replies should be sent.

9. Click the **Servers** tab (see Figure 34.3).

FIGURE 34.3

Configuring mail server properties for the Internet email information service.

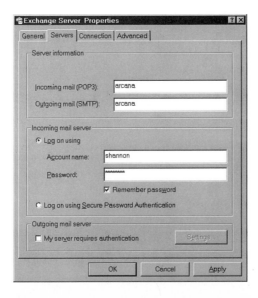

10. In the **Outgoing mail (SMTP)** field, enter the name of the Exchange Server computer running the Internet Mail Service.

11. In the **Incoming mail (POP3)** field, enter the name of the Exchange Server computer that hosts the user's Inbox.

12. Select the **Log on using** button.

CAUTION

Do not select the **Log on using Secure Password Authentication** option, unless directed to do so by the Exchange Server administrator; otherwise, you'll be unable to make the connection.

---

13. Enter the user's Exchange Server Inbox alias name in the **Account name** field.

14. Enter the user's Inbox password in the **Password** field.

15. If the outgoing mail server also requires logon via a username and password, select the **My server requires authentication** check box, click **Settings**, set the username and password as before, and click **OK**.

16. Click the **Connection** tab and choose the appropriate connection type—generally **Connect using my Local Area Network (LAN)** in Exchange environments. If the user connects via remote access, however, choose **Connect using my phone line** and select the appropriate connection from the **Use the following dial-up networking connection** drop-down menu. If the connection is not listed, get the necessary settings from the Exchange Server administrator and click **Add** to create the new connection.

17. Click **OK**.

Connecting with Non-Microsoft Exchange Environments

Outlook 2000 can connect to and download email messages from any Internet mail server that supports IMAP or POP3. The user might set up an email account with a commercial Internet service provider (ISP), or the user might receive email via a mail server running on the company intranet.

NOTE POP3 and IMAP are standard protocols for transferring email over the Internet. POP3 is the most commonly used protocol. Unlike IMAP, POP3 doesn't permit messages to be stored and managed in folders on the mail server; rather, messages are downloaded to the user's computer and stored on the hard drive. This makes IMAP a better choice for users who access email from multiple computers or who have limited storage space. However, because IMAP stores messages on the mail server, IMAP servers are more vulnerable to unauthorized access by anyone with access to the server. ■

Preparing to Set Up Your Internet Mail Account   If Outlook is not operating in an Exchange environment, it should be set up in Internet Only mode. This mode supports connections to an ISP or to an Internet-standard mail server in the enterprise.

Part

V

Ch

34

TIP   If you selected **No E-mail** mode when you installed Outlook, you can still set up an Internet email account and switch to Internet Only mode by following the steps to set up an Internet mail account.

You also need to determine the following (generally provided by the ISP or network administrator):

- Email account information: username, password, and email address
- Type of incoming mail server: POP3 or IMAP
- Incoming (POP3/IMAP) and outgoing (SMTP) mail server domain names or IP addresses
- Type of connection: LAN, Windows dial-up networking, or another dialing program

Setting Up an Email Account   Follow these steps to configure the IMAP or POP3 account:

1. Choose **Tools**, **Accounts** (see Figure 34.4).

FIGURE 34.4
Creating a new Internet mail account.

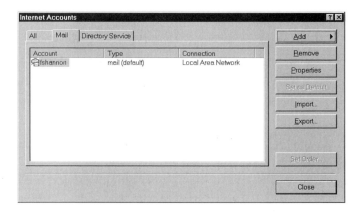

2. On the Mail tab, select **Add** and **Mail**.
3. Enter the name to appear on sent messages in the Display Name field and click **Next**.
4. Enter the user's Internet email address in the **E-mail Address** field and click **Next**.
5. Select **POP3** or **IMAP** next to **My incoming mail server is a** (see Figure 34.5).
6. Enter the IP address or domain name of the IMAP or POP3 server in the **Incoming mail (POP3 or IMAP) server** field.
7. Enter the IP address or domain name of the SMTP server in the **Outgoing mail (SMTP) server** field (often, the incoming and outgoing mail servers are the same). Click **Next**.
8. Select **Log on using**, type the email account's username in the POP3/IMAP Account Name field, and type the account's password in the Password field. Click **Next**.

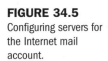

FIGURE 34.5
Configuring servers for the Internet mail account.

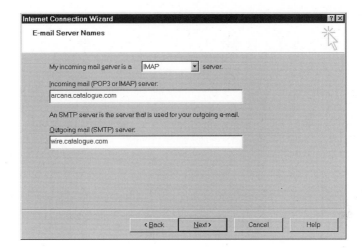

CAUTION

Some ISPs require users to log on using Secure Password Authentication (SPA). If your ISP requires this, select the **Log on using Secure Password Authentication** (SPA) button; you'll be prompted to enter your email account name and password each time you log on. If your ISP doesn't require SPA, be sure the option is *not* selected; otherwise, you'll be unable to make the connection.

---

9. Type a name in the **Internet Mail Account Name** field to identify the new account; this is useful for distinguishing between multiple accounts. Click **Next**.

10. Select the connection type: Connect **Using my phone line**, if using Windows dial-up networking; **Connect using my Local Area Network (LAN)**, if connecting through a network; or **I will establish my internet connection manually**, if using a third-party dialer. Click **Next**.

11. Depending on the connection type you chose, complete the setup with the following steps:

    - If connecting via a LAN or manually, click **Finish**.
    - If connecting via a phone line and the connection has already been set up in Dial-Up Networking, click **Use an existing dial-up connection** and select the appropriate connection. Then, click **Next** and **Finish**.
    - If the dial-up connection has not been set up, select **Create a new dial-up connection** and click **Next**. Fill in the phone number for the connection and click **Next**. Enter the **User name** and **Password** for the Internet access account and click **Next**. Ignore the **Advanced** button unless you know your ISP requires additional settings. Enter a name for the connection in the **Connection name** field, click **Next**, and click **Finish**.

12. Click **Close**.

Part

V

Ch

34

▶ If you're experiencing trouble establishing a connection or sending and receiving Internet mail messages, **see** Chapter 48, "Troubleshooting and Optimizing Outlook," on **p. 1183**.

Configuring Outlook to Retrieve Internet News

A news-only version of Outlook Express functions as a newsreader for Outlook 2000. Newsreaders enable reading and posting of messages to various kinds of newsgroups, including the Usenet network on the Internet and company newsgroups on an intranet. To access the Outlook 2000 newsreader, choose <u>V</u>iew, <u>G</u>o To, New<u>s</u> from the Outlook menu.

 TIP If you're using Outlook in conjunction with an Exchange Server that's hosting newsgroups, you can access them in the same way as any other public folder.

Installing the Outlook Newsreader

If you did not install the newsreader during the original Outlook 2000 installation, you are prompted for the Office 2000 CD-ROM after selecting the News option from the menu for the first time. The newsreader component is then automatically installed and opened.

Configuring the Outlook Newsreader

Before configuring the Outlook newsreader, ask your ISP or network administrator for the domain name or IP address of the news server hosting the user's connection. The news server might also require logon via a username and password. When the Outlook newsreader opens for the first time, the Internet Connection Wizard opens automatically. Follow these steps to configure the Outlook newsreader:

1. Enter the name to appear on newsgroup postings in the **Display Name** field. Click **Next**.
2. Enter the user's Internet email address in the **E-mail Address** field. Click **Next**.
3. Enter the domain name or IP address of the news server in the **Ne<u>w</u>s (NNTP) server** field (see Figure 34.6); if logon with an account name and password is required, select the **My news server requires me to log on** check box.
4. Click **Next**.
5. Click **Finish**.

Now the user can download newsgroups from the news server, choose which groups to subscribe to, and begin reading and posting messages.

If you cannot view any newsgroups or get a news connection error message, double-check the news account's properties against the settings provided by the ISP or network administrator—choose **<u>T</u>ools, <u>A</u>ccounts**, select the news account, and click **Properties**. In particular, be sure that the **Server Name** field on the Server tab matches the NNTP server name provided by the ISP, and find out whether a logon is required. On the Advanced tab, check that the port number in the **News (NNTP)** field matches the one provided by the ISP (most news servers use port 119). Finally, try setting **Server timeouts too long**, because some news servers take more than a minute to establish a connection. If you're still experiencing problems, check with the ISP that the settings are correct and that the news server is up and running.

FIGURE 34.6
Setting up a connection to a news server.

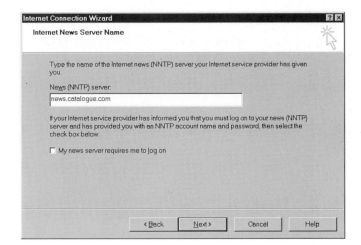

Activating Internet-Specific Email Format Options

Most Internet email is sent as plain text. This yields the greatest compatibility with a multitude of mail systems combined with the lowest bandwidth usage for the massive volume of email sent over corporate LAN systems or the Internet every day. More and more email programs, including Outlook 2000, support other email formats and options including

- Secure, encrypted email
- Email formatted in HTML
- Lightweight Directory Access Protocol (LDAP)

Using Encrypted (S/MIME) Email

For the utmost in security, email from Outlook can be encrypted via S/MIME (Secure Multipurpose Internet Mail Extensions). Before you can send encrypted email from Outlook, you need to acquire a digital certificate. To obtain a digital certificate:

1. From the Outlook menu, choose **Tools**, **Options**, and click the **Security** tab.

2. If you do not have a digital certificate, click the **Get Digital ID** button. This opens your browser and takes you to the Microsoft Web site and a list of digital certificate vendors. Select a vendor and obtain a digital certificate before proceeding.

3. If you have a digital certificate, click the **Import/Export certificate** button to open the screen shown in Figure 34.7.

Part
V

Ch
34

FIGURE 34.7
Importing a digital certificate into Outlook to enable email encryption.

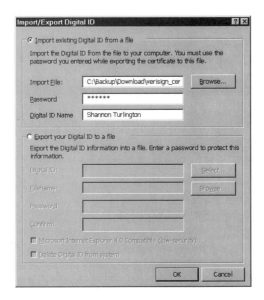

4. Fill in the **Import File** text box with the location of a digital certificate or **Browse** to the file.

 TIP If you're not sure where a digital certificate might be located on your hard drive, the most common file extensions are .epf, .pfx, .p7c, .cer, or .p12. Also check your default browser security screen for the location of your certificate or you might need to export your certificate from your browser to a file before you can use it in Outlook.

5. Click **OK**. You receive a confirmation screen describing the certificate and asking whether you want to add the certificate to the Root Store. Click **Yes**.

The digital certificate has now been imported into Outlook. Repeat this for as many certificates as you want to install.

After you have imported at least one digital certificate, you can use it in Outlook as shown in the following steps:

1. From the Outlook menu, choose **Tools, Options,** and click the **Security** tab (Figure 34.8).

2. Enable encryption by selecting the check box, **Encrypt contents and attachments for outgoing messages**.

3. If you want to include your digital signature, also select the check box, **Add digital signature to outgoing messages**.

N O T E A digital signature is added to an email by the digital certificate to assure the recipient that the email originated from you and was not altered. ▨

FIGURE 34.8
Enabling email encryption in Outlook.

4. Choose the **De̲fault Security Setting** from the drop-down list box.

5. If you want to view or change your security settings, click the **Change S̲ettings** button to display the Change Security Settings dialog box as shown in Figure 34.9.

FIGURE 34.9
Changing email encryption settings in Outlook.

6. Make any changes desired and click **OK**.

7. Click **OK** to return to Outlook.

By default, email sent from Outlook is now encrypted. You can turn off encryption or use of the digital signature for individual email messages, if desired.

Sending HTML Email

Outlook sends email as plain text by default. To send email as HTML, follow these steps:

1. From the Outlook menu, choose **Tools**, **Options**, and click the **Mail Format** tab.
2. From this tab, Figure 34.10, set the message format to HTML.

FIGURE 34.10
Choosing HTML as the default email format in Outlook.

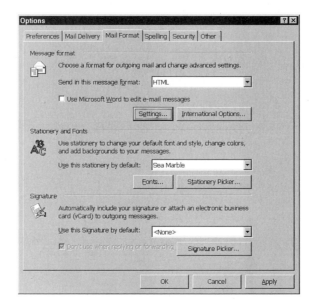

3. Choose a default stationery from the drop-down list box and change fonts, if desired.
4. You can add an HTML signature to each email by clicking **Signature Picker** and browsing to an HTML file.

N O T E   The HTML signature is not the same as the digital signature mentioned in the preceding section of this chapter, "Using Encrypted (S/MIME) Email." The HTML signature is a snippet of customized HTML code (perhaps a URL or link to a graphic) added to the end of your email.

5. If you want to change advanced HTML settings, click the **Settings** button to see the dialog box in Figure 34.11.

FIGURE 34.11
Changing advanced
HTML settings for HTML
email in Outlook.

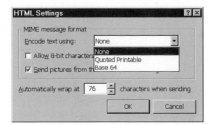

6. You can choose to encode your email using two different MIME message formats: Quoted Printable or Base 64.

N O T E This encoding is not a security encryption. Decoders for these MIME formats are widely available on the Internet or are built into many email packages. Base 64 was originally widely used to transfer binary files or graphics via email. These MIME formats are no longer widely used because most mail servers can now routinely handle binary formats. ▪

7. Select the box labeled **Send pictures from the Internet with messages** if you want to include graphics in the message. If this box is not selected, only a link to the graphic is sent in the email.

8. Click **OK** twice to activate HTML as the default email format in Outlook.

Using Lightweight Directory Access Protocol

LDAP is a relatively new networking protocol. The main use for this new protocol is to provide a means to compare an email address with the existing email address database on an LDAP server. The comparison confirms or denies the existence of a particular email address.

Outlook offers access to several Internet LDAP directory services by default. To view, add to, or modify this list:

1. From the Outlook menu, choose **Tools**, **Accounts**, and click the **Directory Services** tab to view the list of default services in Figure 34.12.

FIGURE 34.12
Viewing the list of
LDAP services avail-
able in Outlook.

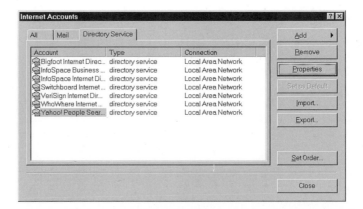

N O T E If the list of LDAP services is blank, click **Add**, **Directory Service** and type the name of an LDAP server, either on your local network or from the Internet. ▩

2. To view or modify the properties of any of the listed services, click **Properties**. The Properties box (Figure 34.13) lists the server name.

FIGURE 34.13

The Yahoo! LDAP server properties.

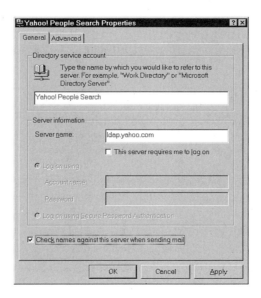

3. Select the check box labeled **Check names against the server when sending mail** if you want to check any email addresses typed in To:, Cc:, or Bcc: in Outlook against the list of email addresses on the selected LDAP server.

N O T E By default, the LDAP servers listed under Directory Services are not searched to verify email addresses. Selecting one or more LDAP servers might significantly slow down the response of Outlook. ▩

4. Click **OK** to apply any changes.

5. To add a new LDAP server, click **Add**, **Directory Service**. Enter the server address and select whether to use the service to verify email. The new server is then added to the list. ●

Deploying and Using Office 2000's Web-Collaboration Components

by Michael Larson

Office 2000 has several tools you can use to work with files on the Web. This chapter introduces you to a tool new to Office 2000: Web Folders, which provides a shortcut to a Microsoft IIS Web server. This chapter also covers two new Web-server based applications: Web discussion and Web subscription. A *Web discussion* enables a group of people to collaborate on a remote document. *Web subscription* enables you to automatically notify anyone by email when a document has been changed or a comment added. Installing and using Internet Information Server Version 4 is also covered. You also learn about installing and configuring OSE, which is required to add Web discussion and Web subscription capability to the Web server. At the end of the chapter, you will find a helpful section on troubleshooting Web-collaboration components.

Introducing Web Folders

Office 2000 introduces a new tool for working with files on a Microsoft Internet Information Server (IIS) Web server: Web Folders. *Web Folders* are special folders that provide a shortcut to a Microsoft IIS Web server. With Web Folders, you can transparently upload files directly to a Web server, or even work with Web pages directly from a Web server.

N O T E   Web Folders do not currently work with other Web servers, such as Apache or Netscape Web servers. ■

In Office 97, you had to invoke a separate process—the Web Publishing Wizard —to upload Web pages to a Web server. This Wizard is no longer needed by Office 2000 applications. You can access Web Folders from within any Office 2000 application using a standard File Open operation. You can now work with the files contained on a Microsoft Web server the same way you work with any other files or folders on your hard drive.

Creating a New Web Folder

After installing Office 2000, a new icon appears near the bottom of Windows Explorer on the left side called Web Folders, shown in Figure 35.1.

FIGURE 35.1
The new Web Folders object installed by Office 2000 as seen in Windows Explorer.

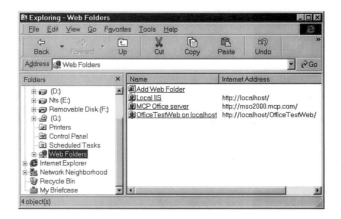

To create a new Web Folder, double-click **Add Web Folder** under Web Folders in Windows Explorer or from My Computer to open the very short Add Web Folder Wizard. The first screen, shown in Figure 35.2, requests the path to the Web server.

This path must lead to a URL accessible by http. It cannot be an FTP or other type of URL. It is optional to begin the address in this dialog box with **http://**. The Web Folder Wizard finds the address without entering **http://** before the address. The Web server for which you are creating the Web Folder must meet two basic criteria:

- It must be a Microsoft IIS Web Server.

- Office Server Extensions (OSE), bundled with Office 2000, must be installed on the Web Server.

- You must also have write access to the Web server.

FIGURE 35.2
Entering the path to your new Web Folder.

N O T E Most people do not normally have write access to a Web server. Your Web server administrator or Webmaster must specifically grant this access to you or anyone else who wants to use a Web Folder for a particular Web server.

▶ For complete instructions on installing the Microsoft Web server, see the later section in this chapter, "Internet Information Server Version 4."

If you save files to any location other than the root of the Web server, you need to add the appropriate subfolder information to the URL. After typing the URL to the Web, click **Next**. The Wizard confirms that the Web server is present, that it contains the OSE, and that you have write access to the Web server.

If any information fails confirmation, you receive an error message and are not able to create the Web Folder. If the information is confirmed, you can then add a descriptive name to the Web Folder, as shown in Figure 35.3.

Click **Finish** to create the new Web Folder. This Web Folder is saved under the descriptive name and is accessible from Windows Explorer and from within any Office 2000 application.

N O T E Web Folders are not available to other Windows non-Office applications.

Using Web Folders to Work with Files on Your Web Server

After the Web Folder is created, you can use it to save or open files. Imagine that you've just created a document in an Office application and you want to save it as a Web page to your Web server. After choosing **File**, **Save as Web Page** from the menu, you see the typical

Part
V

Ch
35

Save As file list dialog box (see Figure 35.4). Clicking the **Web Folders** button in the lower-left corner of this dialog box displays a list of all available Web Folders.

FIGURE 35.3
Adding a descriptive name for the new Web Folder.

FIGURE 35.4
Examining the contents of a Web Folder.

Click **Save** to save the file directly from the Office application to the Web server. You can also use a similar procedure to open files for editing directly from a Web server. From within any Office application, just choose **File, Open** from the menu, click the **Web Folders** button in the lower-left corner of the Open box, double-click the **Web Folder**, select your file, and click **Open**.

After you have set up Web Folders, using them is very similar to using other file folders on your computer. Remember that the speed of copying files is now limited by the speed of your Internet connection.

Using Internet Information Server Version 4

Office 2000 applications now enable you to use two new Web-server based applications: Web discussion and Web subscription. A *Web discussion* enables a group of people to collaborate on a remote document. Each individual can attach comments to the document and comments in turn can be commented on. *Web subscription* enables you to automatically notify anyone by email when a particular document has been changed or a comment left. More information on how to use Web discussions and Web subscriptions can be found in this chapter under the sections titled "Using Web Discussions" and "Using Web Subscriptions."

Web discussion and Web subscription run on a Web server. The Web discussion and Web subscription capabilities are added to a Web server by installing OSE, which comes bundled with Office 2000. More information on installing OSE can be found in this chapter under "Using Office Server Extensions."

OSE must be installed on a Web server in addition to the standard Office 2000 installation. Currently, the only Web server that supports OSE is *Microsoft Internet Information Server* (IIS) version 4 or later. To use OSE, you must have access to a computer running IIS and have installed OSE on the Web server.

The Web server and its associated applications are all contained in the NT 4.0 Option Pack, available as a free download from the Microsoft Web site or available on CD for a nominal price. The Option Pack is also packaged with Office 2000, Premium edition or later. It is very likely that the next version of IIS will be included as part of the next version of Windows NT (Windows 2000). Before installing this package, be sure that you have decided which applications you want to install and that TCP/IP is properly installed on your NT Server.

Understanding Server Specifications

The recommended configuration for a Web server running IIS is

- 90MHz Pentium processor
- 64MB of RAM
- 6X CD-ROM
- 200MB hard drive

The minimum configuration is a 486 running at 66MHz and 32MB of RAM. If you are expecting heavy traffic or plan to run a large number of Web applications through your server, more RAM and a faster CPU are required. At a minimum, you also must have Service Pack 3 for Windows NT installed before proceeding with IIS installation.

Installing Internet Information Server Version 4

After the software (Internet Information Server) and hardware requirements are met, you can begin IIS installation. Choosing the Custom option during Setup gives you the most flexibility in choosing applications. Figure 35.5 shows the installation screen where you make most of your decisions on components to install. Be sure to closely examine the Subcomponent screens, also.

Part

V

Ch

35

FIGURE 35.5

Installing Internet Information Server components.

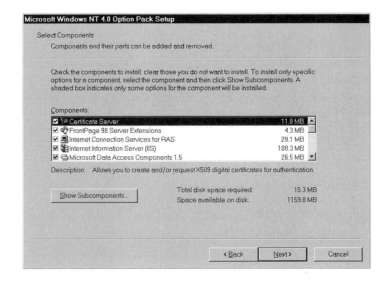

Among the many applications bundled with IIS are the following:

- **Certificate Server.** This server application manages all aspects of digital certificates. *Digital certificates* are used for authentication (both server and client) under Secure Sockets Layer (SSL), secure email, and Secure Electronic Transactions (SET). Certificates are produced in the standard X.509 format.

- **Internet Connection Services for Remote Access Service (RAS).** This collection of applications is designed to help developers set up and use *Virtual Private Networks* (VPN), which are secure networks among groups over the Internet.

- **Transaction Server.** A developer's environment, *Microsoft Transaction Server* (MTS) is used for creating customized server applications using standard programming tools such as C++ or Visual Basic. MTS provides a runtime environment, a graphical user interface, and application programming interfaces for producing enterprise applications.

- **Index Server 2.0.** This application is a text-indexing engine, similar to that used by Internet search engine spiders to index Web sites. It produces an index searchable from a Web page.

- **Microsoft Management Console (MMC).** IIS is managed from the MMC, a stand-alone application that gives administrators access to all parts of the Web server.

- **Site Server Express.** This application is a basic site log analysis tool, containing four tools:

  - Content Analyzer for managing hyperlinks and site structure.
  - Usage Import and Report Writer for generating Web site usage reports.

- Posting Acceptor for managing access by multiple locations to post files to a Web server. This latter option also works with Personal Web Server.
- Web Publishing Wizard for automating the uploading of files to a Web server.

■ **Windows Scripting Host.** This module can be installed and used as a scripting alternative to DOS batch files. Scripts can be run from the desktop and used to automate Web server administrative and routine scheduled tasks.

■ **NNTP newsgroup server and SMTP mail server.** These applications are also part of the IIS package.

After making your choices, click **Next**, choose the drive and folder for the Web site root (Inetpub\wwwroot is the default folder name), and finish the installation. You need to reboot when all is completed.

Testing Internet Information Server Installation

After rebooting, you need to test the installation of the IIS Web server. If you are uncertain whether the Web server services are running, check that the World Wide Web Publishing Service is started in the Services section of the Control Panel. Next, open a browser and type either of the two URLs:

```
http://localhost
```

```
http://YourWebServerName
```

If either or both of these is successful, you should see an introductory page for IIS similar to that shown in Figure 35.6.

You should also try to access the Web server from another computer linked to the Web server over a TCP/IP network using either of the URLs listed previously.

Reviewing Internet Information Server Documentation

IIS has extensive online documentation for all its components. Included are

■ Tutorials

■ Audio and video walkthroughs

■ Sample code

■ Entire sample Web sites demonstrating key features

■ Large amounts of online help

You can search Help through a keyword index or a flexible search engine. The documentation is accessible as a separate item from the Windows Start button (under Windows NT 4.0 Option Pack, Product Documentation) and runs best from within Internet Explorer 4.0 or later.

Part

V

Ch

35

FIGURE 35.6

Testing the Internet
Information Server after
installation.

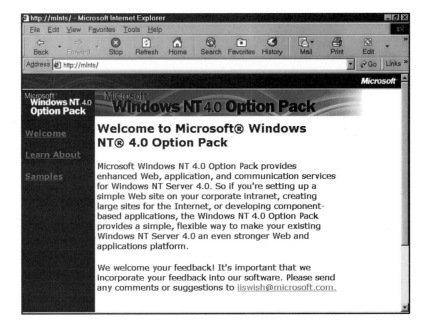

Setting Up the Microsoft Management Console

Administration of the majority of the IIS components is accomplished using the Microsoft
Management Console (MMC) as shown in Figure 35.7. The MMC cannot be launched by
itself from Start. It is launched with a separate snap-in when you launch the Internet Service
Manager, the Index Service Manager, or the Transaction Server Explorer from Start,
Programs, Windows NT 4.0 Option Pack.

The MMC uses the concept of a snap-in. A *snap-in* is an individual component that can be
added to the console. For instance, the Index Server is a snap-in, complete with all the functionality required to manage the Index Server. This means that you can customize the console and also make and save as many console configurations as you want. Adding future
extensions with new capabilities to the console is, well, a snap. Think of the MMC simply as
a terminal or console.

Customizing the MMC by adding or deleting components is easy. Simply choose **Console**
Add/Remove Snap-in from the menu or **Ctrl+M** from the keyboard. This displays the list of
installed snap-ins at the Console Root. Choosing a snap-in and clicking the **Remove** button
eliminates it from the MMC. Choosing the **Add** button brings up a list of all available snap-ins
for addition. You might need to provide some simple information during the addition process,
depending on the snap-in you select. Each snap-in you add shows up in the left pane (also
called the *scope pane*, which displays the *namespace*) of the MMC.

The MMC can be administered remotely. You must have Administrator privileges as a user
on the Web server, however, to gain access to remote administration. Type the URL for the
Web server followed by /iisadmin/ to open the Internet Service Manager, as shown in
Figure 35.8.

FIGURE 35.7
The Microsoft
Management Console
displays the file struc-
ture of your Web
server.

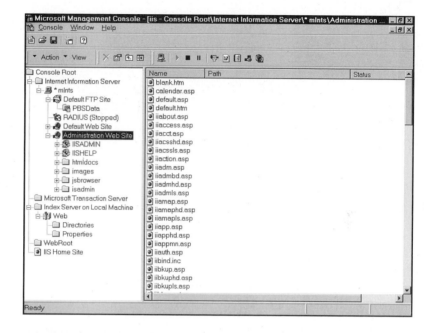

FIGURE 35.8
Performing remote Web
server administration
using the Internet
Service Manager.

Administering Internet Information Server with the MMC

It is easiest to set up and administer the IIS Web server through the MMC. You can begin
basic administration by expanding the IIS snap-in to display the Web server(s). Select the
Web server and right-click to display properties (or choose the Properties button from the
MMC toolbar) and click to open the opening Properties screen, as shown in Figure 35.9.

FIGURE 35.9

Internet Information Server properties available for editing.

From this screen, you can do the following:

■ Edit the WWW or FTP Services to control all aspects of these services.

■ Enable Bandwidth Throttling if you don't want to make the entire network bandwidth available to this Web server.

■ Configure MIME (Multipurpose Internet Mail Extensions) mapping by adding, editing, or removing MIME file types.

If you click the **Edit** button with WWW Service displayed in the Master Properties box, a multitabbed WWW Service Master Properties box for the selected Web server is displayed, as shown in Figure 35.10.

FIGURE 35.10

Editing Web server properties in the Master Properties dialog box.

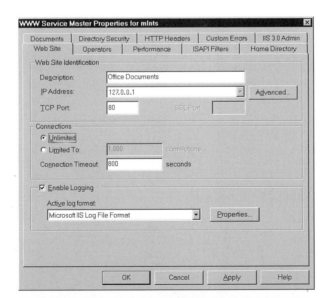

Because the minutiae of Web server administration are beyond the scope of this chapter, this section offers only a general description of which aspects of the Web server each tabbed page in the Master Properties dialog box controls:

- **Web Site.** From this, tab you can:

     Review your IP address information

     Assign a TCP port (if the default of 80 is not suitable)

     Limit the number of connections to the server as well as the connection timeout

     Enable/disable Web server logging and choose your log format

- **Operators.** You can grant Web site operator privileges based on the same Windows NT User Accounts used to grant access privileges to a Windows NT server. An operator can set server access permissions, change default Web pages, and edit content expiration and ratings.

- **Performance.** Performance tuning based on expected daily hits to the Web server can be set at <10,000, <100,000, or >100,000. You can also enable/disable *HTTP Keep-Alives*. HTTP Keep-Alives maintain established connections as enabled under the newer HTTP 1.1 protocol.

- **ISAPI Filters.** You can install/remove ISAPI Filters (such as FrontPage Server Extensions) loaded by the Web server at startup. You can also edit and prioritize each filter.

- **Home Directory.** You can alter the access rights (Read, Write, Execute, and so on) or even change the location of your Web server root Web site directory. Your home directory can be designated as an application (defined as the starting point for all virtual directories involved in a particular application), meaning that all these directories can be involved in items such as Active Server Pages or secure operations.

- **Documents.** You can enable/disable the default document, name the file (usually default.htm), and add more than one file. Alternately, the default document can be reassigned to a different folder.

- **Directory Security.** You can control anonymous access to the Web server and authentication of users, define secure communications using the Key Manager, and restrict access by IP address or domain.

- **HTTP Headers.** With this tab, you can

     Enable content expiration to prevent browsers from loading cached pages after a period of time

     Enable your server to send custom HTTP headers

     Disable/enable/define the content rating for your site

     Edit MIME mappings

- **Custom Errors.** You can customize the error page sent to a browser when a Web server error is encountered. Each error condition and the location of the HTML error page are listed for easy editing.

Part

V

Ch

35

■ **IIS 3.0 Admin.** One last administrative detail involves backward compatibility with IIS 3.0. For applications that install files to the IIS directory, you need to choose the installation location as the Default Web root or the Administrative Web.

Reviewing Security with Internet Information Server

The public nature of most Web servers, whether an internal Web server used for an intranet or a Web server on the Internet, demands the highest possible security. Information on your Web server needs to be protected from alteration and access to other parts of your network restricted from criminal activity.

Security starts with the Windows NT operating system. Access to various folders and drives can be restricted to certain individuals or groups through the Server Manager and the User Manager. Placing the Web server on a volume supporting the NT File System (NTFS) gives you additional control over user access rights through the User Manager.

Some Web server security and rights access settings are controlled through IIS as seen in the preceding section of this chapter. Turning off anonymous access within IIS can enable Web server authentication, or if you require, user authentication under NTFS; this latter option (basic authentication) requires a valid Windows NT user account. Windows NT Challenge/Response can also be used to restrict access, but this option works only with Internet Explorer browsers. Additional authentication can be established using Secure Sockets Layer (SSL) Client Certification, which is supported by IIS. SSL determines the validity of encrypted digital certificates during user login.

Security auditing features under Windows NT track logon attempts and attempts to access restricted areas of the Windows NT Server. The items to monitor via auditing can be determined in the Windows NT User Manager and responses to intrusions (including shutting down the server) can be set up. Your auditing policy should balance user needs with your server security requirements.

Using Office Server Extensions

Installing OSE is required to add Web discussion and Web subscription capability to the Web server. Install OSE from an Office 2000 CD-ROM onto a computer running Windows NT Server with IIS version 4 or later as the Web server. You need to install OSE from the Windows NT console. Here's how:

1. Find the OSE folder on an Office 2000 CD-ROM. The location of OSE will vary depending on which Office 2000 bundle (Basic through Enterprise) you have.

2. Double-click **Setup.exe** to start the installation process. The opening screen of the Office Web Server Wizard requests your name and organization. Click **Next**.

3. On the following screen, you must accept the licensing agreement to proceed. Click **Next**.

4. On the Ready to Install Screen, shown in Figure 35.11, you can change the file locations for the Office Web Server Extensions and documentation. Click **Install Now** to begin installation.

FIGURE 35.11
Changing file locations during Office Server Extension installation.

Installation of the OSE takes several minutes. When installation is done, an Installation Complete screen pops up. Click **Configure** from this screen to start the Server Extensions Configuration Wizard.

Configuring OSE with the Server Extensions Configuration Wizard

The Server Extensions Configuration Wizard starts automatically after OSE installation is complete. To proceed with the OSE configuration, click past the opening screen to the Web Collaboration Database screen, shown in Figure 35.12.

This page might look different depending on whether you have Microsoft SQL Server installed. OSE defaults to using a SQL Server database to store Web discussion information. If you do not have SQL Server installed, OSE installed MSDE (Microsoft Data Engine) and will default to this database for Web discussion information storage. Basically, you just need to name your database and choose an administrative password. Click **Next**.

The next page of the Wizard asks for Access Control parameters. You can choose who has access to Web discussions and subscriptions on the server. Two choices are available in the list box:

- Everyone with a Windows account on this machine
- All users, including those without Windows accounts

Part
V

Ch

35

FIGURE 35.12
Choosing which Web Collaboration features to install and where to store the collaboration information.

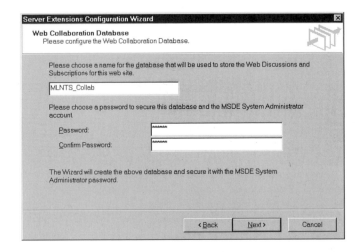

If you choose to restrict access only to users with accounts on the NT server, also make sure the check box, Allow Basic Authentication logins for Collaboration, is checked unless you're sure everyone will be using Internet Explorer for Web discussions. You can also control Directory Browsing from this page. Enabling Directory Browsing allows people to search for the documents in use for Web discussions. Click **Next**.

On the Mail Server screen, you can choose default mail addresses for the Web server (for automated replies) and the Webmaster. You can also enter the name of the mail server to use in conjunction with the Web server or choose to set up the mail server later.

Click **Next** to bring you to a closing screen. Click **Finish** to update the Office Web Server configuration and produce an offer to reboot your machine, which is required for the configuration settings to take effect.

If you are going to use the Web collaboration groups created during OSE installation, be sure to enter the users who will be participating in Web discussions or using Web subscriptions into the User Groups created by the Server Extensions Configuration Wizard. You can find these new groups, prefaced by the Web server name, when you open the User Manager in Windows NT.

Viewing and Searching for Files and Folders on the Web Server

To view or search the file contents of your Web server, using a browser, open a basic administration page installed by OSE and placed under the IIS Web root using either of the following:

```
http://localhost/MSOffice/
```

```
http://yourservername/MSOffice/
```

Click **Browse Web Folders** to receive a report similar to the one shown in Figure 35.13.

FIGURE 35.13
An Explorer-style listing of all the folders on a Web.

This report displays a table of all the folders on a Web. You can click any of the column headings (Name, Size, Date Created, or Date Modified) to sort the list by that criterion. Clicking any of the folders displays all the files and subfolders contained in that folder. Use this listing to make sure all the documents to be discussed are present.

The top of this page contains three buttons:

- **Home.** Takes you back to the administration home page.
- **Up.** Moves the contents of the displayed table up one folder level.
- **Search.** The Search button duplicates the search function displayed on the opening administration page. Clicking Search opens the search page shown in Figure 35.14.

Refining a Search

You can type a keyword into the search box and filter the search further by folder location, file date, or file property.

You can search for files that have been modified, created, or last accessed either today or over a certain number of days, weeks, months, or years. A variety of file properties can be strung together for a very sophisticated search as shown in Figure 35.15.

Part

V

Ch

35

FIGURE 35.14
Searching for files on your Web server.

FIGURE 35.15
Using an extensive array of file properties as the basis for a search of your Web server.

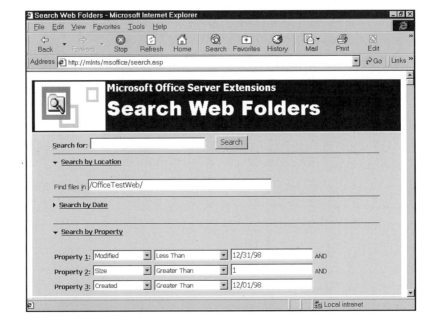

The file properties that can be searched include

- Author
- Category
- Character Count
- Comments
- Company
- Created
- Filename
- Keywords
- Last Accessed
- Last Author
- Last Printed

- Line Count
- Manager
- Modified
- Page Count
- Paragraph Count
- Revision Number
- Size (in bytes)
- Subject
- Title
- Word Count

The logical expressions that can be associated with each file property include

- Equals
- Contains
- Greater Than

- Greater Than or Equal
- Less Than
- Less Than or Equal

As many as three of these search phrases can be strung together for a very specific search.

If the search in Figure 35.15 were run, it would return all files in the OfficeTestWeb folder on this Web that were modified before 12/31/98, were greater than one byte in size, and created after 12/01/98.

Getting Office Server Help

You can access Office Server Help from the Office Server Extensions Start Page by clicking Office Server Help using either of the following

```
http://localhost/MSOffice/
```

```
http://yourservername/MSOffice/
```

From the Office Server Help table of contents, you can learn more about Start Page features.

N O T E   From the OSE Start Page, you can also begin a Web discussion on a document on the current discussion server or on a document on another server. This is convenient if you need a quick update on the status of a document under discussion. ▦

Part

V

Ch

35

Using Web Discussions

After the OSE installation is complete and the discussion server is set up, you are almost ready to hold a Web discussion. You have only three more steps to perform before your discussion can begin:

1. Place the file(s) you want to discuss onto the Web server. The easiest way to do this is via Web Folders. You'll find more information on creating and using Web Folders earlier in this chapter in "Using Web Folders."

2. Notify everyone that the files are now available for comments. Be sure to provide everyone in the discussion a URL to the file. Specify a deadline for the comment period, if necessary.

3. If desired, you can set up Web notification so that you can monitor who is or is not leaving comments, and take appropriate actions (a reminder email, maybe?) as the deadline draws near.

That's it. Your Web discussion is now underway.

> **CAUTION**
>
> If your Web discussion comments are being stored in a Microsoft SQL Server database, any disruption to this application, such as stopping the MSSQLSERVER service, will also stop Web discussions.

The following section shows you how to use the Web Discussion interface to conduct a Web discussion.

Reviewing the Web Discussion Interface

The Web discussion tools enable each user to insert and edit comments for any document under discussion. Figure 35.16 shows the basic Web discussion tools available in Word. Excel and PowerPoint have a slightly more abbreviated toolset available.

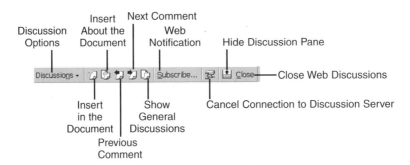

FIGURE 35.16
The Web discussion interface in Word.

This interface (it is not a toolbar, although it looks like one) is activated when **Tools**, **Online Collaboration**, **Web Discussions** are selected from the menu. You find the interface at the bottom of the application window.

N O T E No menu option for Web discussions is available. To use Web discussion features in Internet Explorer 5, click the **Discuss** button on the browser toolbar. If this button is not present, right-click over the toolbar, choose **Customize**, and add the button. ■

Each button has a specific use during a discussion. The leftmost selection, the Discussion Options button, opens a menu of six options, shown in Figure 35.17.

FIGURE 35.17
Selections available from the Discussion button on the discussion interface.

The two top selections, Insert in the Document and Insert about the Document, duplicate other controls with matching icons in the discussion interface and are discussed later in this chapter in "Using the Discussion Creation and Navigation Buttons." The lower four additional choices include

■ **Refresh Discussions.** This command retrieves and displays discussion comments made by anyone else since you loaded the document into your Office 2000 application. Any comments you make are immediately displayed on your view of the document.

■ **Filter Discussions.** Sometimes, it is necessary to filter the comments by creator or for a given time period. The Filter Discussions dialog box, shown in Figure 35.18, enables you to select from the list of comment creators and filter for time intervals ranging from all (anytime) to six months.

FIGURE 35.18
Filtering Web discussion comments by creator or time interval.

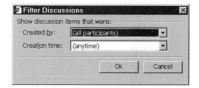

■ **Print Discussions.** Prints a list of all the comments made on a given document. If you filter the discussion comments, only those comments that meet the filter criteria will print. Each comment contains the following information:

The location of the comment by page number and line number

The subject of the comment

The person who wrote the comment

The text of the comment

The date and time the comment was posted

Part
V

Ch
35

A sample printout is shown in Figure 35.19.

FIGURE 35.19

Partial printout from a sample Web discussion.

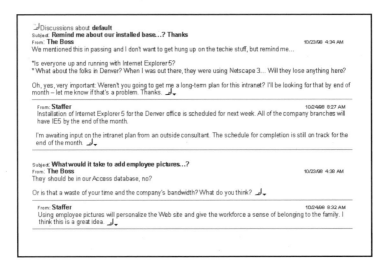

■ **Discussion Options.** From this dialog box (see Figure 35.20), you can select which discussion server to use and choose which information to display in a comment.

Clicking the **Remove** button deletes the displayed discussion server. If you click the **Add** or **Edit** button from the Discussion Options dialog box, you can add a new discussion server or edit the path to an existing server (see Figure 35.21). You do not need `http://` as part of the discussion server address.

NOTE Note that you also need to select SSL (Secure Sockets Layer) if your discussion server is using SSL as security. ■

FIGURE 35.20

Choosing a discussion server and comment display options from the discussion interface.

Using the Discussion Creation and Navigation Buttons

The next five buttons on the discussion interface (see Figure 35.16) are used to actually create or navigate through the discussion comments in Word. The icons on these buttons resemble yellow notes. From left to right, the following list describes these buttons:

FIGURE 35.21
Adding and editing discussion servers.

■ **Insert Discussion in the Document.** Place your cursor where you want to add a comment in a document and click the **Insert in the Document** button. This attaches your comment to that position in the document. An open window for entering a subject and the text for the comment are shown in Figure 35.22.

FIGURE 35.22
Creating a new discussion comment.

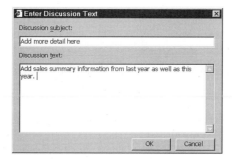

■ **Insert Discussion About the Document.** Use this button to add a general comment about the entire document. These comments enable you to ask general questions ("Where is the section on February sales?") or conversational comments ("Great first draft, Jones"). General comments are scrolled in a lower pane called the *discussion pane* as shown in Figure 35.23.

■ **Previous.** This button works like the browser Back button and selects the comment preceding your current cursor position. Click this button to move you backward through the comments.

■ **Next.** Click this button to move you forward through the comments in the document under discussion.

■ **Show General Discussions.** This button forces the discussion pane to show general document comments (comments that relate to the complete document) rather than comments attached to specific areas.

FIGURE 35.23
The discussion pane showing some general comments about a document.

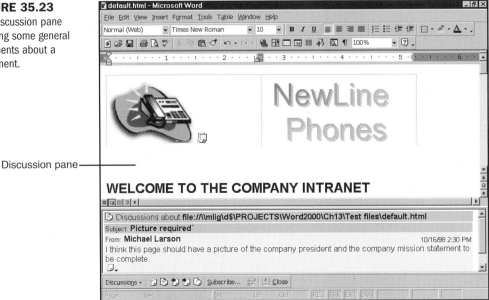

Discussion pane ———

Disconnecting from a Discussion and Removing the Discussion Pane

 On the discussion interface, the next button to the right of Subscribe cancels the connection to the discussion server. This button is active (it has red highlights) only when the connection to the discussion server is active.

 The next button, which has an upward-pointing arrow, toggles the appearance or disappearance of the discussion pane. Toggling the discussion pane off lets you view more of the document.

The last button, Close, closes the discussion interface and eliminates the discussion interface from the screen. The discussion interface for Excel and PowerPoint includes only three of the earlier icons: insert discussion about the document, cancel the connection, and toggle the discussion pane.

Editing, Deleting, or Replying to Existing Comments in a Document

 As you add discussion comments to a document, a yellow placeholder icon appears in the document, marking the location of your comment. A yellow icon also appears in the discussion comment, placed after the text of the comment. If you click this yellow icon, you see three selections on a menu.

- **Reply.** Enables you to respond to an existing comment. When clicked, it opens the same discussion comment box as seen in Figure 35.22. The subject line is automatically filled in with RE: followed by the subject of the original comment. You can type your reply and click **OK**. Your reply is now included in the discussion database.

- **Edit.** Enables the author of a comment to edit his or her own comments. You cannot edit comments placed in a document by anyone else.

- **Delete.** Deletes any comment you've made. You cannot delete comments left by others.

N O T E   Security and user rights on the Web server as related to Web discussions are set in the NT Server user groups and maximized if you use the NTFS file system and basic authentication at a minimum. If you install OSE under NTFS, a special user group, collaborators, is created. Members of this group have the capability to participate in Web discussions but not browse the Web server.

If security is not correctly set up, users might be able to edit or delete one another's comments. ▓

Viewing a Sample Web Discussion

To demonstrate how a Web collaboration might work, use the following assumptions:

- You're the company staffer charged with setting up the content for the company intranet in a small business (about 50 employees).

- The guidelines you've been given are vague (is this too real?): something about adding Human Resource policy and monthly revenue information.

- You've been given only two days to put a draft together. You have never built a Web site in your life.

- You recently installed Office 2000, and read about saving Office files as Web pages, as well as Web discussions.

- You know that you need to include some earlier Office 97 documents on the Web site, too.

- You got the computer department to install OSE on a company IIS Web server.

- You drafted a bare-bones intranet home page in Word 2000 and saved it as a Web page, default.html. You have hyperlinks to a benefits summary document in Word 97 format and an Excel 97 sales summary worksheet.

- You've posted the files to the Web server and emailed the boss that they're ready for comments using Web discussions.

- You turned on Web notification when you posted the files.

- It's now the next day and you have an email from this discussion server that new comments from the boss have been made.

Part

V

Ch

35

Given this scenario, go through the documents and see how a Web discussion might work. Figure 35.24 shows the draft intranet home page, default.html, before any comments were added.

FIGURE 35.24

The draft Web page before any comments have been left via Web discussion.

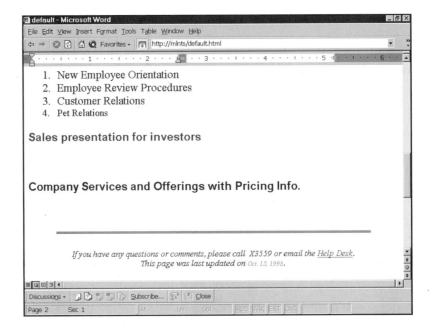

Next, suppose the boss leaves a comment near the heading, Company Services and Offerings with Pricing Info, as shown in Figure 35.25.

FIGURE 35.25

A discussion comment inserted into a draft document.

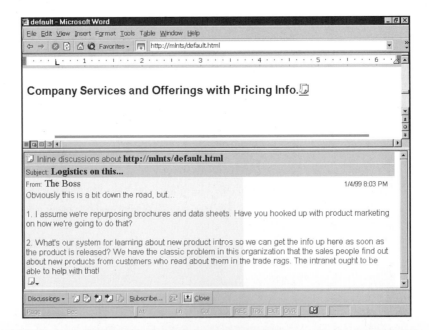

Notice the small, sticky icon after the document section heading. This is the point in the document to which the boss's comment is anchored. The boss entered this comment by clicking the **Insert Discussion in the Document** button on the Web discussion interface and then typing his comments in the Enter Discussion Text dialog box. The comment itself is composed of

- A subject line
- An author name (The Boss)
- A date and time stamp
- The body of the comment
- A small note icon with a downward-pointing arrow

As you view this comment, in your role as the staffer, you will want to post a response to the boss's questions. To do this, click the note icon at the end of the boss's comment and choose **Reply** from the menu. After you pen your reply and click **OK**, your comment is inserted and looks like that seen in Figure 35.26.

FIGURE 35.26
A sample reply to a comment left during a Web discussion.

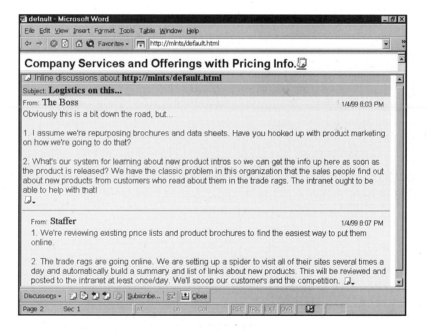

The reply is indented under the original comment and separated from it by a horizontal bar. If the boss wants to respond to your comment, he can click the icon found at the end of it, click **Reply**, and write more comments.

The boss can also make general comments about a draft document. In Figure 35.27, you see a general comment left by the boss in the discussion pane.

Part
V

Ch

35

FIGURE 35.27
A general comment shown in the discussion pane during a Web discussion.

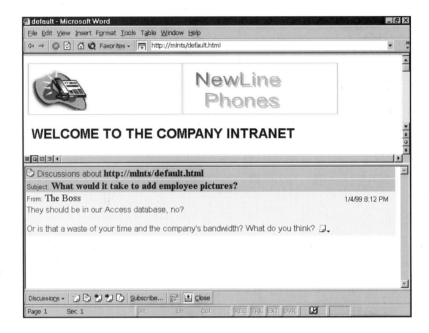

General comments are left by clicking the **Insert Discussion about the Document** button on the Web discussion interface in Word. These comments are not anchored to a particular point in the document. The format for a general comment is identical to comments inserted directly into the document. General comments show up in the discussion pane only. To respond to a general comment, all you do is click the icon at the end of the general comment, click **Reply**, and type your response. After clicking **OK**, you might find that the discussion pane now looks something like Figure 35.28.

TIP

One of the primary advantages of using Web discussions is that the comments are electronic. You do not need to retype the comments if you want to use them. You can cut and paste them directly from the discussion into your original draft document. Therefore, if the boss had left a specific sentence to be entered verbatim into the draft document, it would be very easy for you to do so.

Administering the Discussion Server

You can perform administrative tasks revolving around Web discussions on your Web server via either of the following addresses:

```
http://localhost/MSOffice/MSOAdmin
http://yourservername/MSOffice/MSOAdmin
```

You must have administrator privileges on the Web server to access these features.

You can administer or configure the following Web discussion items from the Microsoft Office Server Administration Home Page.

FIGURE 35.28
A sample reply to a general comment in the discussion pane during a Web discussion.

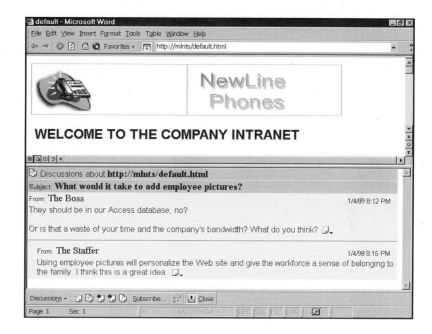

- Configure Web discussion settings
- Manage Web discussions
- Database settings

Configuring Web Discussion Settings   You can configure Web discussion server settings by clicking **Configure Web Discussion Settings**. This opens a screen for configuring Web discussions (see Figure 35.29) and Web subscriptions.

Web discussion options that you can change from here include

- Turning Web discussions on or off
- Allowing Web discussions only on documents located on the Web server or documents anywhere on the WWW
- Enabling the automatic deletion of Web discussions after a set time interval

N O T E   One of the options to configure on the Web server is whether only documents on the server can be reviewed or documents anywhere on the Web can be discussed. If the latter choice is selected, then all participants in a given Web discussion can comment on any page or document on the WWW. Documents reviewed in Web discussions do not have to be present on the Web server containing OSE. ■

Managing Web Discussions   Any document under discussion on the Web server is listed on this page as shown in Figure 35.30.

Part
V

Ch
35

FIGURE 35.29

Changing Web discussion options on your Web server.

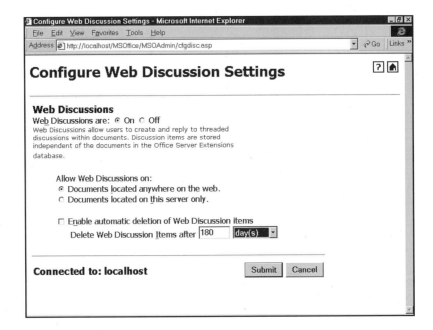

FIGURE 35.30

Using Manage Web Discussions to view and delete existing discussions on the current Web server.

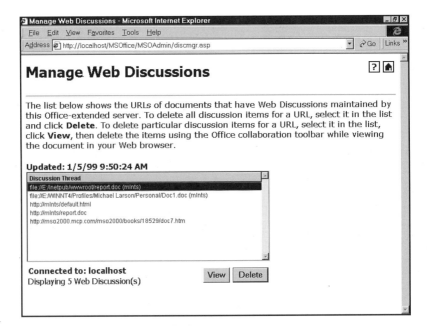

The main use for this screen is to delete discussion threads when they are no longer needed.

Managing the Discussion Database Any comments made on documents residing on the Web server or comments made by someone logged into the local discussion server are stored in the discussion database. This database is either the default Microsoft Data Engine installed during OSE installation or a user selected SQL Server database. By clicking Database Settings on the OSE Administration Page, you can either verify the default database integrity or select a SQL Server to host the discussion database, as shown in Figure 35.31.

FIGURE 35.31
Changing discussion database settings.

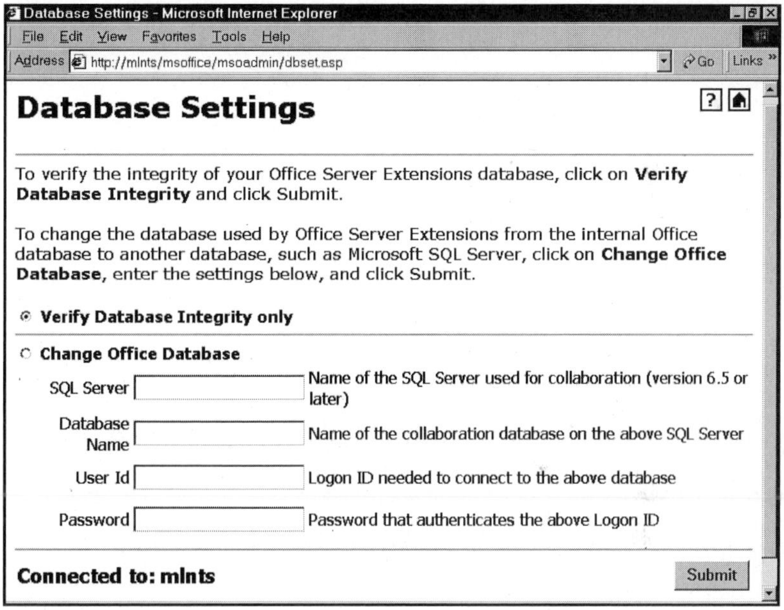

If the default database is used to host discussions on the current Web server, you can select the **Verify Database Integrity only** option button and click **Submit**. The discussion database integrity is verified and the results of the verification are displayed as shown in Figure 35.32.

Archiving Discussion Files

All the comments made during Web discussions from a discussion server are stored in a database. This is either the default MSDE or a SQL Server Database chosen during OSE configuration. These comments are retained by this database unless an expiration date is set during discussion server administration.

Using Web Subscriptions

You can subscribe to any document on a discussion server. You can also subscribe to any document or Web page on the Internet assuming your discussion server is configured to support this. Opening a subscription or Web Notification establishes a request that you be notified by email whenever a comment is left about any document to which you have a subscription.

FIGURE 35.32
The integrity of the default discussion database has been verified.

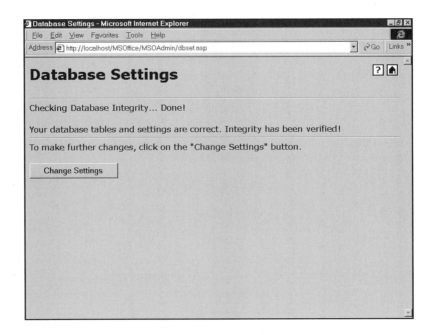

Reviewing the Web Subscription Interface

To subscribe to a document, open the Web discussion interface by choosing **Tools, Online Collaboration, Web Discussions** from the menu in Excel, Word, or PowerPoint. On this interface is a button called Subscribe. Clicking the **Subscribe** button opens the screen shown in Figure 35.33.

FIGURE 35.33
Activating a subscription to monitor document comments.

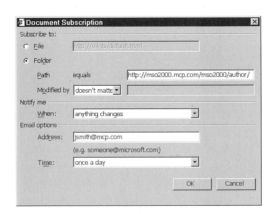

Notice in Figure 35.33 that you can open a subscription to the current document or use the filters under Folder to be notified based on

- All the files in a given folder or path on the discussion server
- Any comments left by anyone changing the document or a specific individual makes a change

You can be notified whenever

- Anything changes
- A new document is created
- A document is modified
- A document is deleted
- A document is moved
- A discussion item is inserted or deleted

Under Email Options, you need totype the email address to which notification should be sent. Time periods of notification include

- When a change occurs
- Once a day
- Once a week

Clicking **OK** places your subscription with the discussion server. Note that for this option to work a valid SMTP (Simple Mail Transport Protocol) server must also be running on the discussion server. SMTP server capability is included in IIS.

Administering Web Subscriptions

You can perform additional administrative tasks for Web subscriptions on a Web server via either of the following addresses:

```
http://localhost/MSOffice/MSOAdmin
http://yourservername/MSOffice/MSOAdmin
```

You must have administrator privileges on the Web server to access these features.

You can administer or configure the following Web subscription items from the Office Server Administration Home Page:

- Configure Web subscription settings
- Manage Web subscriptions

Configuring Web Subscriptions   The Configure Web Subscription Settings page (see Figure 35.34) gives you several options for administering your Web subscriptions.

Items you can change include

- Turning Web subscriptions on or off
- Defining which mail server to use for subscription notification
- Defining email addresses for automatic notification
- Setting security at the document or folder level
- Changing the time interval for sending notifications (not shown in figure)

Part
V

Ch
35

FIGURE 35.34
Changing Web sub-
scription options on
your Web server.

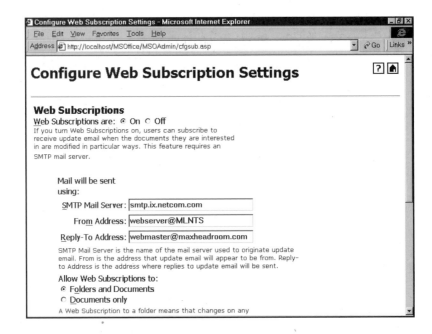

Managing Web Subscriptions   Additional Web subscription administration features can be
found on the Administration home page. Clicking the **Manage Web Subscriptions** link generates a listing of all the subscribers to your Web server (Figure 35.35).

FIGURE 35.35
Managing your list of
Web subscribers.

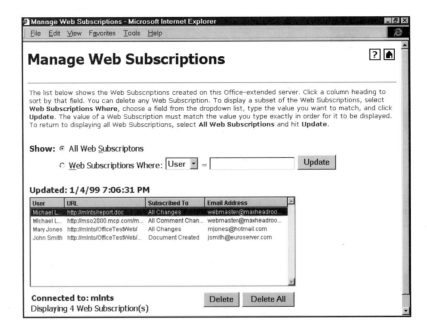

You can sort the list by clicking any of the headers in the subscriber list window. You can also filter the list by User, URL, or email address. The primary purpose of this list is to enable the administrator to delete specific Web subscribers.

Troubleshooting Web-Collaboration Components

When I try to create a Web folder, I get the following error message: "Cannot connect to the Web server server name. The server could not be located, or might be too busy to respond. Please check your typing or check to be sure the Web server is available. For details see drive\folder\wecerr.txt." What do I do?

You might find several problems. After you've double-checked your typing, make sure the URL address points to the Web server http address. The Web server must also support Web Folders. If you're not sure, contact the Webmaster. You also must have a user account established on the Web server.

I installed Option Pack 4 for Windows NT. When I try to install OSE, it says that it requires IIS to proceed. What's wrong?

If you install Option Pack 4 under Windows 95 or 98, a slimmed-down Web server, the Personal Web Server is installed. If Option Pack 4 is installed under Windows NT Workstation, then Peer Web Services is installed. OSE only installs and runs under Windows NT Server with IIS 4.0 installed.

I know a co-worker left some comments on a document on the discussion server, but I can't find them. Where do I look?

If the comments were just recently left, try refreshing the document in your Office application by clicking **Discussions**, **Refresh Discussions** from the Web discussion interface. Comments can also be deleted by whoever created them. Additionally, an expiration date for comments can be set during discussion server administration.

I subscribed to a document on our discussion server. The document was changed, but I never received email notification. What happened?

With your document and the Web discussion interface open, click **Subscriptions**. Choose your discussion server and click **Edit**. Make sure the path to the discussion server and your email address are both accurate. If so, then the problem probably lies with the SMTP server. Either the wrong name for the SMTP server was entered during OSE setup or there are other problems with the SMTP server. ●

Part
V

Ch
35

Deploying Internet Explorer 5 with the Internet Explorer Administration Kit

by Bill Camarda

As Microsoft Office is increasingly integrated with the Web, Office administrators increasingly find themselves managing the Internet Explorer 5 Web browsers as well as traditional office applications. In this chapter, you review the key issues Office administrators face in managing the Internet Explorer 5 Web browser, especially:

- Should you deploy Internet Explorer 5?
- If you do deploy Internet Explorer 5, how can you best manage the deployment process using the new Internet Explorer 5 Administration Kit?

Understanding Internet Explorer 5

Internet Explorer 5 is Microsoft's latest Web browser release, and like previous releases, it actually contains not just a browser, but a comprehensive set of tools for working on the Internet. The following sections review the Microsoft Internet Explorer 5 components and enhancements.

Key Components of Internet Explorer 5

The heart of Internet Explorer 5 is, of course, Microsoft's Web browser, which enables users to visit any Web site on the Internet or your corporate intranet. (Improvements in the browser component of Internet Explorer 5 are discussed in detail in the following sections.)

- In addition to the core browser, Microsoft's full Internet Explorer 5 release encompasses several other distinct components. These include Outlook Express 5, a new version of Microsoft's free mailreader, with new tools for filtering junk mail (if you have standardized on Outlook 2000, you might not want to install this).

- Windows Media Player, which replaces Microsoft's previous media players and includes support for a wide variety of formats, including Real Audio/Real Video 4.0 (but not versions 5.0 or G2); MP3 audio; QuickTime; and more.

- Chat 2.5, a new version of Microsoft's Internet chat client.

- NetMeeting 2.11, a new version of Microsoft's Internet videophone/teleconferencing software.

- FrontPage Express 2.0, a stripped-down version of FrontPage for Web-page editing (if you have standardized on FrontPage 2000 or Word 2000 as your Web editor, or if you do not want users to create pages that require the presence of FrontPage Extensions to work properly, you might choose not to install this).

- Web Publishing Wizard 1.6 for simplifying Web uploads.

- Microsoft Virtual Machine (Microsoft's version of the Java Virtual Machine, which has the advantage of speed and efficiency on Windows platforms, and the disadvantage that you might find yourself and your applications caught in the battle over Java standards between Microsoft and Sun Microsystems).

- The Internet Connection Wizard (primarily for home users; designed to streamline a first-time connection to the Internet using one of a handful of leading Internet service providers).

- The Offline Browsing Pack for enhanced offline Web browsing.

- Microsoft Wallet 3 for secure online shopping (again, often unnecessary in a business environment).

- Agent 2.0 for viewing animation on a relatively small number of Web sites.

- Internet Explorer Help.

- Internet Explorer Core Fonts (Microsoft's Web Core Fonts, including Andale Mono, Webdings, Trebuchet, Georgia, Verdana, Comic Sans, Arial Black, Arial Bold, Impact, Times New Roman, and Courier New). These fonts are also provided with Office 2000, Windows 98, and Windows 2000.

- Dynamic HTML Binding, an add-on that allows client systems to sort information displayed on a page, without connecting again to the page's server.

- Internet Explorer Browsing Enhancements that provide FTP support.

- Virtual Reality Markup Language (VRML) 2.0 Viewer for viewing pages using the VRML 2.0.

- Vector Markup Language (VML) Vector Graphics support (a new vector graphics format).

- AOL Art Image format support.

- DirectAnimation support.

- Visual Basic Scripting: an updated engine for running scripts.

- Radio toolbar for listening to Web-based radio broadcasts.

User Interface Improvements

The Internet Explorer 5 user interface is quite similar to that of Internet Explorer 4.0, simplifying training for companies upgrading from the previous version. Having said this, Microsoft focused much of its investment in user-interface refinements, some of which are intended to bring Office-style automation to the Web browser. Microsoft has made several improvements intended to help users find what they want and achieve their goals on the Web more efficiently. These include

- AutoSearch and Search Assistant, shown at work in Figure 36.1, which allows users to organize their searches of nine different search engines (as well as searches for mailing and email addresses).

- AutoComplete, which (much like Word's AutoComplete feature) attempts to complete lengthy URLs automatically, based on pages users have visited previously. AutoComplete also works within forms, making it faster and easier for users to fill out names, addresses, email addresses, and passwords. (Because AutoComplete can be a security risk, especially on machines shared by multiple users, you might want to turn this feature off. This can be done locally, through Tools, Internet Options, Content, AutoComplete; or centrally at the time of deployment through the Internet Explorer Customization Wizard. To learn how, see the "Customizing System Policies and Restrictions" section, later in this chapter.)

- Tools, Show Related Links, which can speed research by using Alexa technology to list sites on the Web similar to the one you're visiting.

- Simpler adding and organizing Favorites (but it is still practically impossible to reorganize Favorites within a single folder as you create new ones).

- Friendlier error messages: By default, Internet Explorer intercepts standard HTTP error messages and replaces them with friendlier ones that make suggestions about how users might find what they are looking for.

FIGURE 36.1
Internet Explorer 5's
AutoSearch feature.

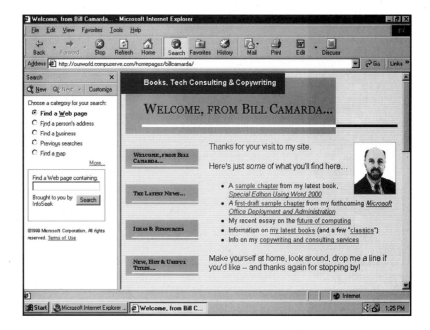

Content Advisor is one more user interface change that you might appreciate as an administrator. Content Advisor gives you highly granular control over the sites your users are permitted to visit, based on language, nudity, sex, and violence. With Content Advisor, you can create lists of sites that are always or never viewable, use Internet-based rating bureaus, and more.

Web Application Development Improvements

As is vividly demonstrated by Office 2000 features such as Web discussions, Web browsers have become a critical infrastructure for building important business applications. Internet Explorer 5 presents the foundation and the plumbing for applications such as these. Highlights include

- Second-generation support for Dynamic HTML and cascading style sheets deliver improved performance, and in some cases, simpler development.

N O T E However, even with the improvements, Internet Explorer 5 and Netscape Communicator 4.7 still handle current Web technology standards differently enough that most developers will still restrict their use to intranets that rely on only one browser, or be forced to develop multiple Web pages for each leading browser. According to Jupiter Communications, nearly two-thirds of the top 100 consumer sites are now built in multiple versions. By one estimate, standards problems add at least 25% to Web development costs.

For a detailed look at Internet Explorer 5 DHTML and CSS standards compliance, see
www.webstandards.org/css/winie/.

- A new Developer Mode that allows site designers and developers to view script and site errors for debugging.

- Nearly complete support for XML 1.0 and the eXtensible Stylesheet Language (XSL) standard for XML style sheets. XML is a markup language that delivers greater structure and flexibility than HTML has provided, allowing developers to create pages with meaning that can be understood by any browser, application, object, or middle-tier server that understands XML. Different vocabularies built on XML are already being used to standardize, streamline, and automate everything from financial communications (The Financial Products Markup Language from J.P. Morgan and PricewaterhouseCoopers) to control of high-end telecommunications equipment (the Call Policy Markup Language from Digital Telecommunications).

N O T E Some XML-related standards—notably the eXtensible Stylesheet Language (XSL) standard for XML style sheets—were still unfinished when Internet Explorer 5 was released, requiring Microsoft to make some best guesses about how XML and the related XSL style sheet language will ultimately work. In addition, some XML experts have objected to certain aspects of Microsoft's implementation. To deliver comprehensive XML support, you can reasonably expect that Internet Explorer 5 will have to be tweaked in the future.

Here are some excellent sources for information about potential inconsistencies between Internet Explorer 5 XML and the official, evolving standard:

- *XML Support in IE5,* by Tim Bray, `www.xml.com/pub/1999/03/ie5/first-x.html`

- *What's the Big Deal with XSL,* by G. Ken Holman,
  `www.xml.com/pub/1999/04/holman/xsl56.html`

- Microsoft's *XSL Working Draft Conformance Notes,*
  `msdn.Microsoft.com/xml/xsl/tutorials/conformance.asp`

When Not to Upgrade to Internet Explorer 5

Not every organization will choose to promptly upgrade to Internet Explorer 5. Reasons to delay or avoid upgrading to Internet Explorer 5 might include

- Your organization has built intranet applications based on specific features in Internet Explorer 4 or Netscape Communicator that might not work identically in Internet Explorer 5, or at minimum, will require extensive testing.

- As Microsoft continues to integrate its browser with the underlying Windows operating system, browser upgrades increasingly replace files that are integral to Windows; you might be reluctant to make these changes until you can be confident that they do not affect unrelated applications you depend on.

- Your installed base of hardware cannot handle the higher system requirements of Internet Explorer 5 (system requirements are discussed in the following section).

Internet Explorer 5 Resource Requirements

Microsoft's minimum system requirements for Internet Explorer 5 are shown in the following list; as usual, you can expect that acceptable system performance will require somewhat more powerful systems.

- **Processor:** 486DX/66MHz or higher processor.
- **Operating System:** Windows 95, Windows 98, or Windows NT 4.0 Service Pack 3 or later (the English version of Internet Explorer 5 is not compatible with the Hebrew or Arabic versions of Windows 98).
- **Memory:** 16MB RAM (Windows 95/98); 32MB RAM minimum (Windows NT); note that Microsoft has not yet published Internet Explorer 5 memory requirements for Windows 2000, but the base requirement for Windows 2000 Professional is 64MB.
- **Disk space:** Minimum install (browser only) 27MB; Typical install 55MB; Full install 80MB. During the installation process, Internet Explorer 5 requires additional space for temporary files: 15MB additional for minimum and typical installation, and 30MB additional for full installation.
- **Other requirements:** Mouse, modem, or Internet connection; CD-ROM drive if installing from CD-ROM disk. Additional requirements might apply if you are using some optional features of Internet Explorer 5; for example, NetMeeting video-conferencing requires a video source, such as a video camera.

Deploying Internet Explorer 5 with the Internet Explorer Administration Kit

Users whose PCs do not already contain Internet Explorer 5 are offered a chance to install it as part of the standard Office 2000 installation. As with other aspects of the Office 2000 installation, you can choose to centrally control whether (and how) Internet Explorer 5 is installed.

Microsoft provides a powerful tool, the Internet Explorer Administration Kit (IEAK), to help you deploy Internet Explorer 5 in the most effective way for your organization. If you deploy Internet Explorer 5 along with Office 2000, you can run the Internet Explorer Administration Kit as you build your custom Office installation. (See the section of Chapter 2 titled "Customizing Internet Explorer 5 Installation Options.") If you plan to deploy Internet Explorer 5 before or after the rest of Office 2000, you can run IEAK whenever you are ready.

IEAK allows you to customize virtually every aspect of how Internet Explorer 5 is installed, including the following:

- Customized Links bar and Favorites lists that give your users immediate access to important locations on your corporate intranet or the Web.
- Customized Internet Explorer options settings, including home page, language support, content restrictions, digital certificates and other security settings, preconfigured Internet connections, programs associated with HTML editing, email, other Internet-related tasks, and more.

■ Setup customizations that control how much (or how little) users need to be involved in the setup process.

You customize Internet Explorer 5 installation using the Microsoft Internet Explorer Customization Wizard, which (like all Microsoft wizards) guides you through the complex process, step-by-step. In the following sections, you walk through using the Internet Explorer Customization Wizard to build and deploy Internet Explorer 5. To stress a point made earlier, you can follow these steps either as part of your Office 2000 deployment, or before, or afterward.

NOTE Leave yourself significant time for customization. As you'll see in the following pages, running the Internet Explorer Customization Wizard is a lengthy process. Moreover, it's unusual for your settings to be perfect the first time: Expect to perform significant testing and to rerun the Wizard at least once or twice, making adjustments to your settings based on issues your testing turns up. ■

Preparing to Use the Internet Explorer 5 Customization Wizard

You need to perform several steps before you begin working with the Internet Explorer 5 Customization Wizard.

1. Get and install the IEAK. If you have the Microsoft Office 2000 Resource Kit, the IEAK can be found in the following folder of the accompanying CD-ROM:
   `O9ork\Pfiles\Orktools\Tools\Ciw_ieak\Ieak`
   Otherwise, you can download the IEAK at the following location:
   `www.microsoft.com/windows/ie/Business/ieak.asp`.

2. Register with Microsoft at
   `www.microsoft.com/windows/ieak/en/licensing/default.asp`
   to get the 10-digit code you need to run the Internet Explorer Customization Wizard. You'll need to give Microsoft information about yourself, your company, and the number of users you intend to customize Internet Explorer for.

3. Get Microsoft's Corporate Deployment Guide at
   `www.microsoft.com/windows/ieak/en/deploy/Corp/default.asp`
   This 142-page book includes comprehensive information on deploying Internet Explorer, including several pages of detailed checklists on information you should gather before deployment.

4. Be sure you've installed Internet Explorer 5 on the system from which you plan to run the Internet Explorer Customization Wizard.

5. Working with the Corporate Deployment Guide, gather the information you need to deploy Internet Explorer 5. This information falls into the following categories:
   - On which platforms you plan to distribute Internet Explorer (although most administrators distribute for Windows 9.x and Windows NT, versions are also available for Windows 3.x and UNIX, and a separate version of IEAK is available for the Macintosh).

- Whether you will distribute from an intranet, a LAN, via CD-ROMs, or via multiple floppy disks.

- How much involvement you want your users to have in the installation process.

- Whether (and how) you want to customize IE's installation screens, welcome screen, and browser interface.

- What URLs you want to use as your home page, Favorites lists, and Links bar.

- What dial-up settings, Internet, and proxy server connections you want to use.

- Whether you want to use Outlook Express as your mailreader, and if so, which email and Lightweight Directory Access Protocol (LDAP) directory settings you want to use.

- Digital certificate and related security settings, including certificate authorities you want to use to manage signed code.

- Any Active Desktop channels you want to use to provide regular updates to users via push technology.

- User Agent String information that allows servers to track which browsers visitors are using.

- Custom components you want to install along with Internet Explorer 5, such as ActiveX components and Java applets.

6. Finally, be sure you run the Internet Explorer Customization Wizard from a computer with a high-speed Internet connection: partway through you are asked to download current copies of all Internet Explorer 5 files that you do not have—a download that can easily be 70MB or more.

Running the Internet Explorer 5 Customization Wizard

After you've installed the Internet Explorer 5 Administration Kit, you can run it by choosing **Start**, **Programs**, **Microsoft IEAK**, **Internet Explorer Customization Wizard**. The welcome screen opens. Click **Next** twice to display the Company Name and Customization Code window (see Figure 36.2).

Entering Your Name and Customization Code   Enter your company name and customization code. After you've done so, you'll be prompted to identify yourself as a Content Provider/Developer, Service Provider, or Corporate Administrator. The choice you make here shapes the choices that the Customization Wizard gives you later on.

 If you haven't received a customization code from Microsoft yet, you can click **Get Customization Code** to open Internet Explorer 5 and go to Microsoft's licensing Web page. However, you'll have to wait at least a few minutes for Microsoft to email the code to you.

When you're finished, click **Next**. The Platform Options window opens (see Figure 36.3).

FIGURE 36.2
The Company Name
and Customization
Code window.

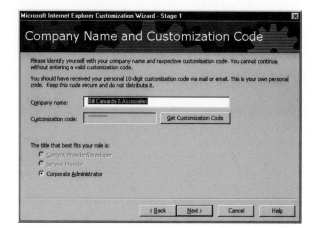

FIGURE 36.3
The Platform Options
window.

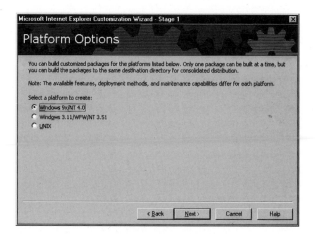

Specifying Platform Options   In the Platform Options window, you can choose the plat-
form(s) for which you want to create customized packages: Windows 9.x or Windows NT 4.0;
Windows 3.11/ Windows for Workgroups (WFW); Windows NT 3.51; or UNIX. If you are
preparing packages for Windows 2000, use Windows 9.x/Windows NT 4.0. The UNIX versions of Internet Explorer are certified to run only on Solaris 2.5.1 and 2.6, not Linux or other
prominent versions of UNIX.

CAUTION

Setting up customized Internet Explorer packages for UNIX requires some different techniques. To learn
more, click **Help**, **Building Customized IEAK Packages for UNIX**.

When you're finished, click **Next**. The File Locations window opens (see Figure 36.4).

FIGURE 36.4

The File Locations window.

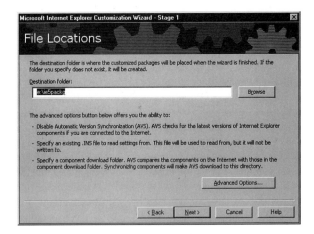

Specifying File Locations   In the File Locations window, you specify a folder where your customized Internet Explorer package will be stored. If you plan to have a large number of users install over a corporate LAN or intranet, be sure the folder is accessible to them and that the network connection and server you use have sufficient power and bandwidth to support multiple concurrent downloads. If you haven't prepared the appropriate folder yet, you can store it elsewhere and copy it to your deployment server(s) whenever you are ready.

To choose a new folder, click **Browse**, and then browse to and select the folder you want to use.

Controlling Advanced File Location Options   Microsoft provides several advanced file locations options. Clicking **Advanced Options** displays the Advanced Options dialog box (see Figure 36.5).

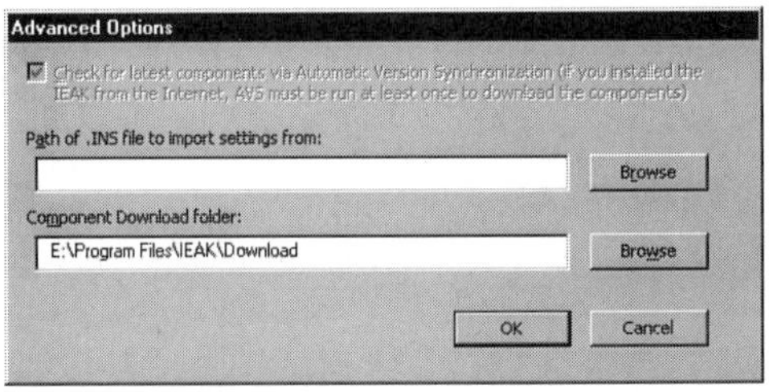

FIGURE 36.5

The Advanced Options dialog box.

Using the Advanced Options dialog box, you can

- Determine whether to use Automatic Version Synchronization to ensure you include the most recent components of Internet Explorer 5 in your customized package. Later in the process, the Customization Wizard accesses the Microsoft Web site to download the newest versions of each component you want to provide.

- Point the Customization Wizard to an INS file that contains predefined settings you want to provide to all your users. (These files can be created using a separate program called the Internet Explorer Administration Kit Profile Manager, which installs with the

IEAK. To run it, choose **Start, Programs, Microsoft IEAK, Internet Explorer Administration Kit Profile Manager.** You can run the Profile Wizard only when the Customization Wizard is not running.)

■ Specify where to store the components you download.

TIP Some administrators find it more convenient to build all their settings in a custom profile and simply import the profile, rather than building the settings a step at a time in the Customization Wizard.

When you're finished, click **OK,** and then click **Next.** The Language Selection window opens.

Choosing a Language for Your Custom Internet Explorer Browser In the Language Selection window, you can choose a language from the 26 target languages Microsoft currently provides. The IEAK creates a subfolder containing the language files that correspond to the version you choose. English language files are stored in a subfolder named EN.

N O T E If you want to create more than one version of Internet Explorer, each localized with a different language, you must rerun the Wizard. If you want to use the same settings for each language version of Internet Explorer you create, use the same destination folder for each version. (IEAK will create a separate subfolder for each language within that destination folder.) ▧

When you've finished, click **Next.** The Media Selection window opens (see Figure 36.6).

FIGURE 36.6
The Media Selection window.

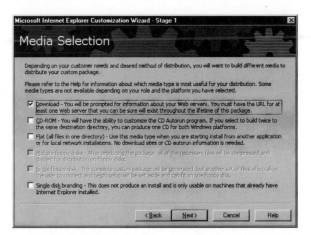

Specifying the Media from Which You Want to Deploy Internet Explorer In the Media Selection window, you can choose among several options for delivering Internet Explorer to your users:

■ **Download** allows you to set up Internet Explorer to install from a Web server on your intranet or Web site. The majority of Office administrators are likely to choose this, and Download is the default setting. If you choose **Download**, you need to know the URL for the location you intend to use. The coverage of the Internet Explorer Connection Wizard that follows assumes you have chosen **Download**.

- **CD-ROM** assumes you'll provide a CD-ROM to all your users. Internet service providers who want to create custom versions of Internet Explorer for their subscribers most commonly use this. It might also be used by companies that want to make customized versions of Internet Explorer available to far-flung employees and telecommuters who might not have consistent access to the corporate intranet.

- **Flat** places all the files in a single directory on a network server. This option is for those who do not have an intranet, but want to deploy Internet Explorer 5 from a traditional LAN server.

- **Multiple Floppy Disks and Single Floppy Disk** are available only to administrators deploying Internet Explorer 5 to Windows 3.x and Windows NT 3.51 systems. Multiple Floppy Disks allows you to create a version of Internet Explorer across multiple floppy disks. (Each floppy disk image is stored in a separate, numbered folder in an \Mfloppy subfolder IEAK creates. You then manually copy the disk images to multiple disks for reproduction.) Single Floppy Disk creates an Internet Explorer package that is stored on your network server, and a separate floppy disk containing only the files users need to connect to your network server and download from there.

- **Single Disk Branding** enables you to customize a version of Internet Explorer 5 (or Internet Explorer 4.01, Service Pack 1 or later) with the features and settings you desire (but not with custom components).

When you're finished, click **Next**. The Feature Selection window opens (see Figure 36.7).

FIGURE 36.7
The Feature Selection window.

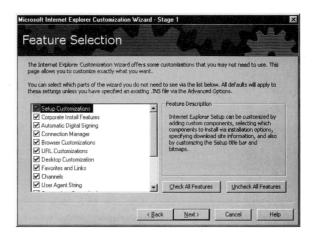

Choosing the Features You Want to Customize   By default, Internet Explorer Customization Wizard allows you to customize 16 more aspects of Internet Explorer beyond those you have already reviewed. Most companies won't need to customize all 16, however. In fact, many companies choose to customize only a few. In the Feature Selection window, you can clear check boxes corresponding to screens you don't want to customize. The Wizard uses default settings for each of these areas, unless you have pointed it to an INS file containing different settings that you want to use, instead.

Each of these features is described in the following sections of this chapter, and a brief description appears in the Feature Selection window when you select any feature. However, it's worth pointing out several check boxes that many Office administrators are likely to clear:

- **Automatic Digital Signing** can be cleared if you haven't (and do not intend to) purchased a unique digital certificate to secure the code you create. Digital certificates, however, represent a powerful security technique for protecting the code you distribute. You might want to seriously consider using them.

- **Desktop Customization** allows you to customize the Windows desktop with components, toolbars, and folder WebViews. Many organizations have opted not to use these Active Desktop features, however.

- **Channels** options are used primarily by companies that have implemented Microsoft's push technology to automatically send information to desktops at regular intervals. You can, however, use the Channels window to delete any channels users might have already installed with previous versions of Internet Explorer.

- **User Agent String** allows you to customize the small block of text that browsers send to the servers they visit. Many companies choose not to customize this information, because they do not want other companies to use it to track their users.

- **Certificate Customization**, like Automatic Digital Signing, is relevant only if you have deployed digital certificates.

- **Outlook Express Customization** is relevant only if you choose to deploy Outlook Express.

When you've finished removing features, click **Next**. You've just completed Stage 1 of the Internet Explorer Customization Wizard; you now move on to Stage 2, in which you specify where you download your official Internet Explorer components from, as well as other components you might want to include in your installation. Click **Next** again. The Microsoft Download Site window opens.

Selecting a Download Site and Running Automatic Version Synchronization   In the Microsoft Download Site window, you select the Microsoft download site from which you want to use to retrieve components. At press time, only one download site was available: Conxion. To select it, choose **Next**. The Automatic Version Synchronization Window opens (see Figure 36.8), and Microsoft checks to see which Internet Explorer 5 files you need to update.

If you installed Microsoft Internet Explorer 5 over the Internet, you'll have to update them all. After a minute or two, a list appears. Click **Synchronize All**, and the Wizard downloads current versions of all the files you need. As this download might be 70MB or more, this might take some time.

CAUTION

You might have to disable virus checking before you download these components. If so, a message appears to warn you. If the message does not appear, you can leave virus checking turned on.

FIGURE 36.8

The Automatic Version Synchronization window.

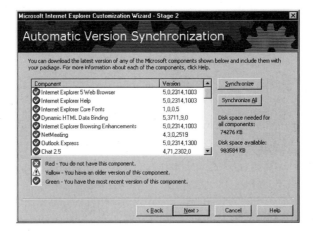

After you've downloaded all the files you need, click **Next**. The Add Custom Components window opens (see Figure 36.9).

FIGURE 36.9

The Add Custom Components window.

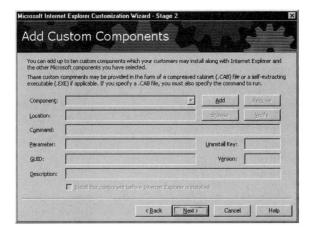

Adding Custom Components to Your Internet Explorer Deployment   In the Custom Components window, you're offered the opportunity to add up to ten custom components that your company might have developed to accompany Internet Explorer 5. You can use compressed cabinet (.cab) files, or in the case of Windows 9.x/Windows NT/Windows 2000, you can also use self-extracting executable (.exe) files. In a Windows environment, every component must have a Globally Unique Identifier (GUID); normally, your developers would create this when they build the component, and you should enter that GUID in the GUID box. If one does not exist, IEAK creates one automatically.

CAUTION

Especially if you plan to have users install Internet Explorer from the Internet, your developers should use digital certificates with their custom code, and you should use the Verify feature to ensure that the custom code has not been tampered with since it was created. If you are using your own digital signature to sign the other components you are providing, IEAK signs this custom component with your signature as well, giving those who install it greater confidence that it actually came from you, without tampering.

After you've added any custom components to your package, click **Next**. This completes Stage II of the Internet Explorer Customization Wizard; you now move into Stage III, where you control how Setup itself looks and works when your users run it. Click **Next** again to display the Customize Setup window (see Figure 36.10).

FIGURE 36.10
The Customize Setup window.

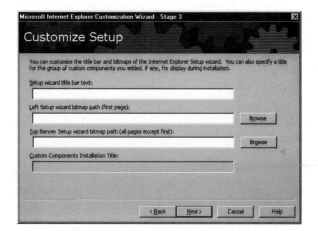

Customizing Internet Explorer Setup for Your Users   In the Customize Setup window, you begin the process of customizing how Setup looks and works for the users who install Internet Explorer 5 with it. You can customize

- Setup Wizard title bar text with text that identifies your company
- Bitmap graphics at the left side and top edge of the Setup Wizard (for detailed information about the format of these bitmaps, see Help or the *Internet Explorer 5 Corporate Deployment Guide*)
- Custom components installation title that describes the custom components your users are installing as they are being installed

After you've finished with these Setup customizations, click **Next** to display the Silent Install window (see Figure 36.11).

FIGURE 36.11
The Silent Install
window.

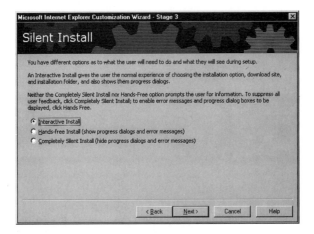

Specifying an Interactive or Silent Install for Internet Explorer 5   The conventional installation is called *interactive*: Users are given the opportunity to make choices and view
progress messages. In this window, you can choose an **Interactive Install** or one of two
forms of *Silent* installs, which automate installation and reduce or eliminate user involvement.

If you choose **Hands-Free Install**, users see progress messages but are given no opportunities to take action: All settings reflect the choices you make throughout the Internet Explorer
Customization Wizard. If you choose **Completely Silent Install**, no messages are provided
even if the install fails. **Completely Silent Install** is often chosen when you are automatically
pushing software to the user's desktop at night or on the weekend, using a desktop management tool such as Microsoft System Management Server.

If you choose a silent install, you will be able to specify only one installation site. If you choose
an interactive install, you can choose up to ten sites, to balance the load among servers.

After you've made your choice, click **Next**. The Installation Options window appears (see
Figure 36.12).

FIGURE 36.12
The Installation Options
Window.

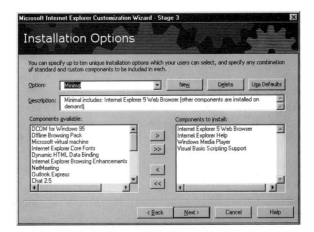

Setting Installation Options   If you've given users the right to make decisions about their Internet Explorer installation, you can use the Installation Options window to define which Internet Explorer components they can choose from, and which components are to be included in a Minimal, Typical, and Full installation. You can also define and describe up to seven additional types of custom installation; you might, for example, provide a Notebook install, a Sales Department install, and so forth.

You can choose only among the components you have already downloaded from Microsoft and the custom components you have already specified earlier in the Wizard.

After you've made your choices, click **Next**. If you earlier decided to create an installation that requires users to download from a Web site, the Component Download Sites window appears (see Figure 36.13).

FIGURE 36.13
The Component
Download Sites
window.

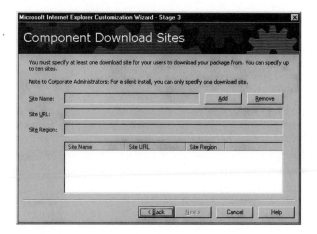

Specifying Component Download Sites   In this window, you can specify a URL corresponding to the Web or intranet location your users will download from. You must use a location served by a Web (HTTP) or FTP server. If you earlier specified an interactive installation, you can choose up to nine additional backup locations; if you chose a silent install, you cannot choose backup locations.

> **CAUTION**
>
> The Wizard won't check to make sure the address you use is a working address, and it won't copy your Internet Explorer package files there. You'll have to do that yourself, later, manually.

After you've made your choices, click **Next**. The Component Download window appears (see Figure 36.14).

FIGURE 36.14
The Component
Download window.

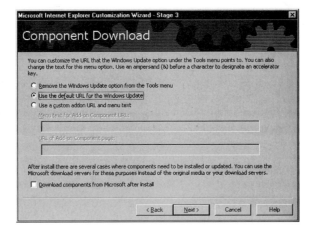

Determining How to Handle Component Updates After Installation   In the Component
Download window, you can specify how (or whether) users can automatically update Internet
Explorer components after they've installed them.

- Choose **Remove the Windows Update option from the Tools menu** if you do not
  want users to update the components you have given them.
- Choose **Use The Default URL for the Windows Update** if you want users to be able
  to update Internet Explorer using the same URL they originally installed it from. You
  need to be sure the location remains available throughout the useful life of Internet
  Explorer 5.
- Choose **Use a custom addon URL and menu text** if you want users to get their
  updates from a different location that you control.
- Check **Download components from Microsoft after install** if you want to send
  users to Microsoft's official download site for new components after they've installed
  Internet Explorer 5 for the first time. This gives you less control over their updates, but
  also reduces the load on your servers.

After you've made your choices, click **Next**. The Installation Directory window appears (see
Figure 36.15).

Specifying an Installation Directory   You can use the Installation Directory window to
specify where Internet Explorer will be installed on your users' computers. You can specify
installation in a specific subfolder within the Windows folder; within the Program Files folder;
or elsewhere.

If you maintain tight control over a large number of very similar PCs, standardizing the install
folder can simplify support, maintenance, and software inventorying down the road. However,
be aware of some potential problems. For example, if you require users to install on their C:
drives, some users might find themselves running out of space—which causes reliability
problems on Windows systems. Conversely, you might have an installed base where some
users have several drives to choose from, and others have only C: drives. In this case, complete standardization becomes impossible.

FIGURE 36.15

The Installation
Directory window.

After you've made your choices, click **Next**. The Corporate Install Options window appears
(see Figure 36.16).

FIGURE 36.16

The Corporate Install
Options window.

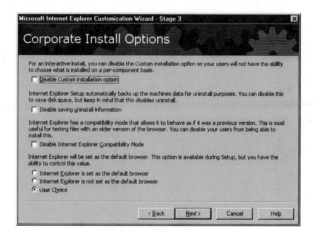

Specifying Corporate Install Options   Corporate Install Options gives you a little more control over how you deploy Internet Explorer on user desktops.

For example, if you've allowed users an interactive install, you can still disable the Custom
installation option so they cannot choose exactly which components to install. If you know
disk space is tight, you can reduce the size of an Internet Explorer installation by disabling
Uninstall, which would otherwise save the older Internet Explorer files you might be
replacing. In the standard install, Internet Explorer 5 provides a Compatibility Mode, in which
it behaves like Internet Explorer 4; you can turn this off. Finally, you can control whether
Internet Explorer 5 registers itself as the default browser on a system; decide whether to give
users the option of choosing their browser; and decide whether Windows Media Player will
be used as the default multimedia player on your users' systems.

After you've made your choices, click **Next**. The Advanced Installation Options window appears (see Figure 36.17).

FIGURE 36.17

The Advanced
Installation Options
Window.

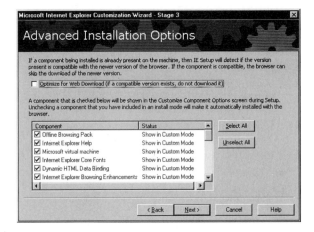

Specifying Advanced Installation Options   In the Advanced Installation Options window, you can control two more aspects of how Setup works. You can potentially reduce the time it takes for Setup to download files from your Web server by instructing it to skip downloading any files it already finds on a user's computer (Optimize for Web download). You can also prevent users from customizing specific components that would otherwise appear in the Custom Installation window. By default, users cannot customize any components; place a check mark next to any component you do want to allow users to customize.

After you've made your choices, click **Next**. The Components on Media window appears (see Figure 36.18).

FIGURE 36.18

The Components on
Media Window.

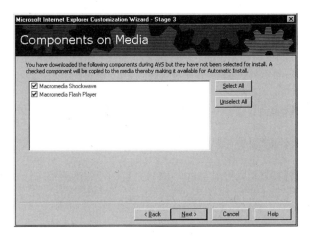

Adding More Components to the Installation   In the Components on Media window, you see a list of components you have downloaded from Microsoft but not yet given users an opportunity to install. These might include Macromedia Flash and Macromedia Shockwave, two very widely used plug-ins for multimedia Web sites, which should be provided to users in virtually every case. Foreign language support files might also be included on the list. These are more than 20MB in size, so you might want to avoid providing them as part of a download unless you have reason to believe that your users need them.

After you've made your choices, click **Next**. The Connection Manager Customization window appears (see Figure 36.19).

FIGURE 36.19
The Connection
Manager Customization
window.

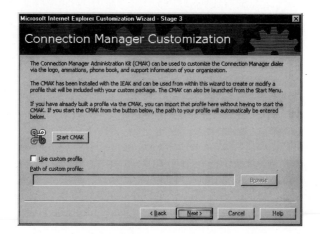

Including a Connection Manager Profile   If you choose, you can customize the Internet connection that your users make, creating a *service profile* that reflects Dial-Up Networking entries, virtual private network settings, logon procedures, special bitmapped graphics, and more. You don't have to create a custom service profile, but if you have a complex network where users cannot configure their own Internet connections, you'll probably want to do so.

To create a service profile, you must use a separate program called the Connection Manager Administration Kit. This program comes with the IEAK; you can run it from this window by clicking **Start CMAK**. For detailed information about using the Connection Manager Administration Kit, see Appendix B of the *Internet Explorer 5 Corporate Deployment Guide*. If you've already created a service profile with the Connection Manager Administration Kit, you can access it by clicking **Browse**, browsing to the profile (an EXE file), and selecting it.

After you've finished creating or choosing a service profile, click **Next**. The Windows Desktop Update window appears.

Incorporating Windows Desktop Update in Your Internet Explorer 5 Installation   As mentioned earlier, Microsoft has aggressively sought to integrate its Web browser with the underlying Windows operating system. One way it has done so is via the Active Desktop, which in Microsoft's words "makes the desktop and folders look and work more like the Web." Users with Windows 98 already have the Active Desktop, but Windows 95 and Windows NT users do not. If you choose **Yes** in this window, the Windows Desktop Update is deployed along with Internet Explorer 5. Microsoft points out that this can help you standardize your desktop, but many companies are likely to forego the privilege. After you've made your choice, click **Next**. The Digital Signatures window appears (see Figure 36.20).

FIGURE 36.20
The Digital Signatures window.

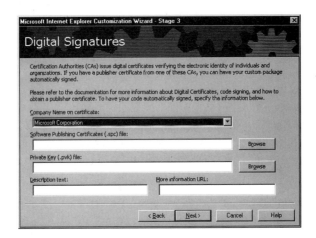

Incorporating Digital Signatures into Your Files   If your company has digital signatures that verify its identity, then you probably want to include them with each of the Internet Explorer files you distribute. Before you use Digital Signatures, you must prepare them using the Certificate Manager Import Wizard, which is a component of Internet Explorer 5. Assuming you have already installed Internet Explorer 5 on your system, you can double-click the digital signature SPC file, or run Internet Explorer by choosing **Tools**, **Internet Options**, **Content**, **Certificates**, **Import**.

After your digital signature is prepared, return to the Digital Signatures window, click **Browse**; then find and select the digital signature. You also need to find and select an accompanying Private Key (PVK) file.

The Description Text box enables you to provide text that appears on the dialog box that users will see when they attempt to install your signed components; the More Information URL enables you to give users an address where they can get more information about you and your signed components.

After you've included your Digital Signatures in your package, click **Next**. You now move into Stage 4 of the Internet Explorer Customization Wizard: customizing the browser itself. Click **Next** again, and the Browser Title window appears (see Figure 36.21).

FIGURE 36.21
The Browser Title window.

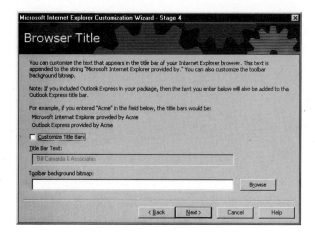

Customizing the Browser's Title In the following three screens, you can choose to customize your browser's title, add custom toolbar buttons, and replace Microsoft's animated and static logos with logos of your choice.

In the Browser Title window, if you want to add your company name to Internet Explorer's title bar, select the **Customize Title Bars** check box, and enter a new name in the **Title Bar Text** box. Doing so adds your company name to Microsoft's product name, as in the following example:

```
Microsoft Internet Explorer provided by Smith & Co.
```

You can also specify a bitmap to use as a watermark that adds a light image in the background behind Internet Explorer's toolbar buttons. Click **Browse** to find the image you want to use; be sure you use one that won't make it difficult for users to work with the toolbar buttons. When you're finished, click **Next**.

Customizing Internet Explorer Toolbar Buttons In the Browser Toolbar buttons window, you're given the opportunity to add custom toolbar buttons that perform specific tasks customized to your company. For example, you might want to include an icon that runs a specific program or takes users to a specific Web location. If you want to add buttons to the browser, click **Add**. The Browser Toolbar Button Information dialog box appears (see Figure 36.22).

You'll need to provide four pieces of information:

- **Toolbar caption**. A word or two of text you want to appear beneath the toolbar button
- **Toolbar Action**. A script or executable file you want to run when users click the button
- **Toolbar color icon**. A color version of the icon you want to appear when users hover the mouse pointer over the button
- **Toolbar grayscale icon**. A grayscale version of the same icon that appears when users are not hovering the mouse pointer over the icon, and always appears on monochrome monitors

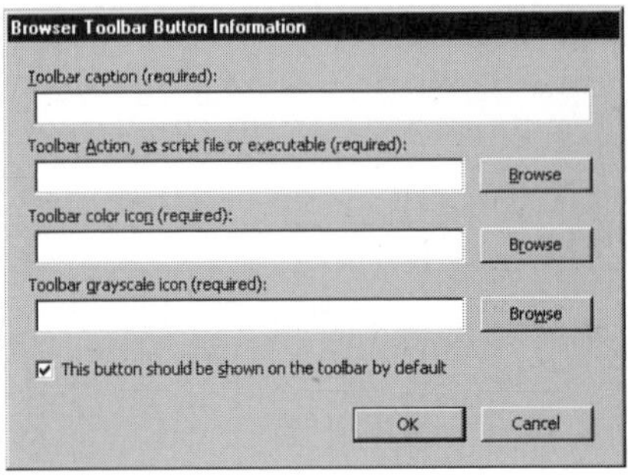

FIGURE 36.22

The Browser Toolbar Button Information dialog box.

When you've finished adding the button, click **OK**. When you've added all the buttons you want to add, click **Next**.

Customizing Internet Explorer's Logos   In the Animated Logo window, you're given the opportunity to replace Microsoft's standard Internet Explorer animated logos with your own. You'll need two logos, one sized at 22×22 pixels, the other at 38×38 pixels. Each has very specific formatting requirements; see the *Internet Explorer 5 Corporate Deployment Guide* for details.

The easiest way to build compliant animated logos is to use two command-line tools provided with the IEAK: Makebmp.exe (for compiling the logos) and Animbmp.exe (for previewing the logos). In a default installation of the IEAK, these might be found in the following folder:

\Program Files\IEAK\Toolkit\Graphics\Tools.

After you've created the logos, browse to and select each of them. After you've finished, click **Next**. The Static Logo window appears. Here, you can choose corresponding (nonanimated) bitmap graphics files to replace Microsoft's static 22×22 and 38×38 logos.

After you've provided customized logos, click **Next**, to display the Important URLs window (see Figure 36.23).

FIGURE 36.23

The Important URLs window.

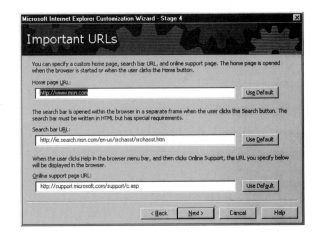

Specifying a Custom Home Page, Support Page, and Search Page   On the Important URLs window, you can customize three key pages:

- You can replace the default home page, **www.msn.com**, with a corporate portal that gives all your users a starting point with the specific information you want them to get whenever they go online

- You can replace the support page that users see when they choose **Help**, **Online Support**, with a Web or intranet location that gives them help customized to their specific needs

- You can provide another HTML page to replace the Infoseek search page that appears when users click **Search** on the Internet Explorer toolbar

When you're done customizing your home page, support page, and search page, click **Next** to display the Favorites and Links window (see Figure 36.24).

FIGURE 36.24
The Favorites and Links window.

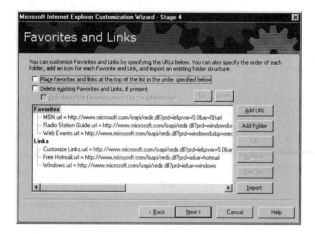

Adding Custom Favorites and Links   In the Favorites and Links window, you can add Favorites and Links that deliver information relevant to your users.

To add a URL, first click either **Favorites** or **Links** to specify where you want the URL to go; then, click **Add URL** to identify the URL. To add a folder, first click either **Favorites** or **Links**, and then click **Add Folder**. To remove a link or folder, select it and click **Remove**. To rearrange URLs or folders, select one or more, and click the **Up** or **Down** button until it appears in the list where you want it to go.

TIP   If you plan to provide many links, set them up in Internet Explorer in advance, and click **Import** to import them all at once.

If you check **Place favorites and links at the top of the list in the order specified below**, your custom Favorites and Links appear before any others. If you select **Delete existing Favorites and Links,** if present, users' existing favorites and links will be eliminated; consider using this feature only if you're redeploying PCs to new users.

When you've finished customizing Favorites and Links, click **Next** to display the Channels window. Here, you can specify any custom channels you might have set up to push information to users' desktops. Channels are used by relatively few organizations. Click **Next** to display the Welcome Page window.

For more information about creating and working with channels, see Que's *Special Edition Using Internet Information Server 4.* For more information about including channels in your customized Internet Explorer package, see the *Internet Explorer 5 Corporate Deployment Guide.*

Customizing the Welcome Page By default, the first time Microsoft Internet Explorer 5 runs, it displays a special Microsoft welcome page, not the Home page. If this is what you want, leave the default setting. If you don't want a custom home page, choose Do Not Display a Welcome Page. If you want to provide a Welcome Page of your own, choose Use a Custom Welcome Page, and then specify the URL you want to use. When you're finished, click **Next** to display the Folder WebView page.

Providing Folder WebViews If you chose to install the Windows Desktop Update in an earlier window, Microsoft now gives you the opportunity to add custom Folder WebViews (custom Web page backgrounds) that appear when users open the My Computer or Control Panel folders on their Windows systems. The easiest way to do so is to carefully edit copies of the existing Folder WebView files on your computer. Be sure not to edit the JavaScript code in these files unless you know how. (These files are present only if you are running the Active Desktop yourself.) Use Notepad to carefully edit the following files:

- Mycomp.htt (My Computer)
- Controlp.htt (Control Panel)

After you've edited them, browse to and select the copies of the Folder WebView HTT files you want to use. Then, click **Next** to display the User Agent String window.

Customizing the User Agent String You can track the number of visits users make to your site with your custom browser by including a custom string of text that the browser sends whenever it visits a server. This is called the User Agent String, and can be entered in the User Agent String window, in the Custom String text box. Be aware, however, that this string will be sent to all sites, not just the ones you control—so anyone, including your competitors, will be able to track traffic to their site generated by your custom browser. Providing a custom string is optional. When you're finished, click **Next** to display the Connection Settings window (see Figure 36.25).

Customizing Connection Settings In the Connection Settings window, you can provide standard settings for users' Internet dial-up and LAN connections, if you choose. If you do not have standard settings, or plan to provide them in another way, leave the default choice: Do not customize Connection Settings. If the settings your own computer is using are the same settings (or similar to those) you want everyone else to use, click **Import the current Connection Settings**. Make any changes you need by clicking the **Modify Settings** button. If you want to clear existing settings on your users' computers, choose **Delete existing Connection Settings, if present**. When you're finished, click **Next** to display the Automatic Configuration window (see Figure 36.26).

FIGURE 36.25
The Connection
Settings window.

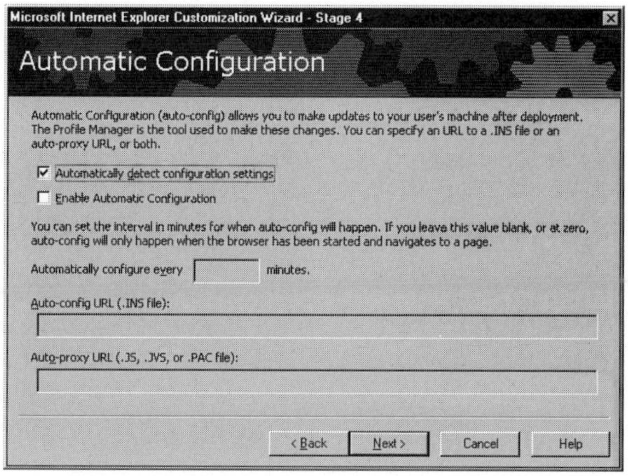

FIGURE 36.26
The Automatic
Configuration window.

Customizing Automatic Configuration   If you want to give yourself the option of centrally reconfiguring users' browsers after they install them, the Automatic Configuration window makes this possible. Select **Enable Automatic Configuration**, and specify an Auto-Config URL containing the INS file that contains the service profile you want users to work with. Or, if you have a JavaScript or JScript file that can automatically configure your browser, specify its URL in the Aut**o**-Proxy URL text box.

After you specify **Enable Automatic Configuration**, your browser automatically searches for configuration information at the URL you specify; you can use the **Automatically configure every** text box to specify how often you want this to happen.

By default, Internet Explorer 5 can use the configuration setting information stored on network servers using Domain Name System (DNS) and Dynamic Host Configuration Protocol (DHCP). If you do not want this to occur, clear the **Automatically detect configuration settings** check box. When you're finished, click **Next** to display the Proxy Settings window (see Figure 36.27).

FIGURE 36.27

The Proxy Settings window.

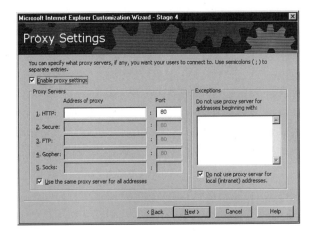

Customizing Proxy Settings If you rely on proxy servers for enhanced security and performance, you can now specify which ones to use and where they can be found. You can also specify exceptions: Web addresses that should be visited directly, not through proxy servers. (By default, proxy servers are not used for intranet addresses within your firewall.)

Most commonly, you'll use the same proxy server for all the Internet services you need to access, including HTTP, secure HTTP, FTP, Gopher, and Socks. But if you need to specify a different proxy server for one service, clear the **Use the same proxy server for all addresses** check box, and enter each of the specific proxy server addresses you need. When you're finished, click to display the Security window (see Figure 36.28).

FIGURE 36.28

The Security window.

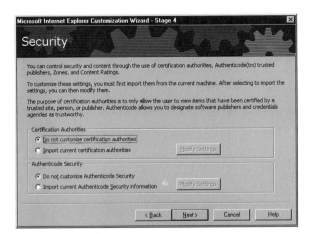

Customizing Security In the Security window, Microsoft provides opportunities to import and customize Certification Authorities and Authenticode Security Information. Certification Authorities are independent online credentials agencies that can certify who you are and that the code you are providing is actually unaltered. Authenticode is a Microsoft technology that allows developers to digitally sign their code, so users can verify that it has not been tampered with before they run it. If you choose to import either Certification Authorities or Authenticode Security Information, click the corresponding **Modify Settings** button to get the specific information you need to include. After you've finished customizing security, click **Next** to display the Security Settings window (see Figure 36.29).

FIGURE 36.29
The Security Settings window.

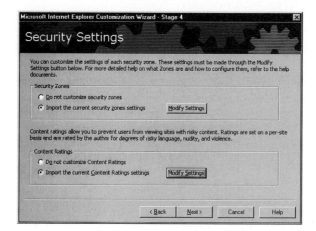

Establishing Security Settings   Here, if you choose, you can control two aspects of how Internet Explorer 5 handles security: Security Zones and Content Ratings.

Security Zones refers to Internet Explorer's capability to provide different levels of security depending on the location users are visiting. You can set four levels of security for each of the following zones:

- Internet
- Local intranet
- Trusted Sites
- Restricted Sites
- My Computer (locations on the user's own computer)

To set security levels, click **Modify Settings** (in the Security Zones area). You see the current settings on your own computer, which you can now adjust as needed for inclusion in the custom version of Internet Explorer you're creating. If you do not customize Security Zones, Microsoft's default settings are used.

Content Ratings refers to Internet Explorer's capability to prevent users from reaching certain sites based on ratings provided by you or independent authorities, such as the Recreational Software Advisory Council on the Internet (RSACi). To set Content Ratings, click **Modify Settings** (in the Content Ratings area). Again, you'll see the current settings on your own computer; adjust them as you want. If you do not customize Content Ratings, no restrictions are imposed.

When you're finished, click **Next**. You've now moved into the final stage of the Internet Explorer Customization Wizard, Customizing Components.

Understanding the Final Stage of Customization   In the final stage of customization, the Internet Explorer Customization Wizard allows you to customize additional options for components you've chosen to include, such as

- Which programs the Wizard will use for which tasks
- Any system policies and restrictions you want to impose

Some of these customizations apply to Outlook Express; these are covered only in passing, because most Office administrators use the full version of Outlook 2000 as their email client.

Click **Next** again to display the Programs window.

Customizing the Programs to Be Used for Each Task   From the Programs window, you can choose which Internet Explorer and Microsoft Office program is used for each Internet-related task. If you choose **Do Not Customize Program Settings**, users are presented with Microsoft's default settings, and permitted to make changes. If you want to set your own defaults, choose **Import the Current Program Settings**, and click **Modify Settings**. The Internet Properties dialog box opens (see Figure 36.30).

FIGURE 36.30
The Internet Properties dialog box.

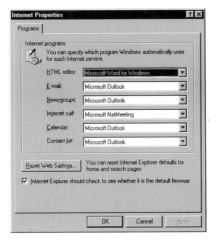

The settings in this dialog box are those on the computer you're currently using. Change them to reflect the settings you want your users to work from, and click **OK**; then click **Next**. In the next six windows Outlook displays, you can configure Outlook Express and its email and newsreader services. As mentioned earlier, we'll skip this because most Office 2000 administrators configure these services in other ways, and use Outlook 2000 instead of Outlook Express as their email and newsgroup clients.

After you're through these windows, you arrive at System Policies and Restrictions (see Figure 36.31).

FIGURE 36.31
The System Policies
and Restrictions
window.

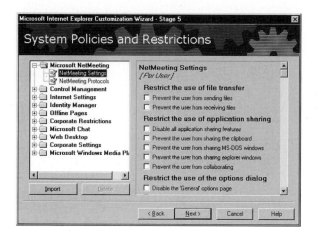

Customizing System Policies and Restrictions   From the System Policies and Restrictions window, you can impose a wide range of settings covering each component of Internet Explorer package, including the Web browser; NetMeeting; Chat, and more. You can also customize Active Desktop settings that go far beyond the Internet, including settings for the Desktop, Start Menu, Shell, Printers, and the System. In other words, you can use the Internet Explorer Customization Wizard to strengthen your control over user workstations with surprising thoroughness. Following are a few of the settings you might establish:

- To limit network traffic, prevent NetMeeting users from sending video (Microsoft NetMeeting, NetMeeting Settings, Prevent the User from Sending Video)

- To prevent access to inappropriate material, prevent users from changing ratings settings (Corporate Restrictions, Content Page, Disable Changing Ratings Settings)

- To ensure that users always start at your customized corporate portal, prevent users from changing their home pages (Corporate Restrictions, General Page, Disable Changing Home Page Settings)

- To ensure that users always start at your customized corporate portal, prevent users from changing their home pages (Corporate Restrictions, General Page, Disable Changing Home Page Settings)

- To prevent security breaches that might occur when unauthorized people see which documents others have been working on (Web Desktop, Start Menu, Do Not Keep History of Recently Opened Documents)

- To prevent security breaches that might occur when unauthorized people use AutoComplete to enter others' passwords (Internet Settings, AutoComplete Settings, clear Use AutoComplete for User Names and Passwords on Forms)

Needless to say, any restrictions you impose should have a clear rationale and be consistent with your corporate culture and goals.

N O T E Most settings you impose here are stored in the Registry. Depending on how you have configured your desktops, users who are familiar with the Registry might be able to override them.

▶ For more information about working with system policies, **see** Chapter 37, "Reducing Office 2000's Total Cost of Ownership," on **p. 963**.

After you've finished establishing system policies and restrictions, click **Next**; you've arrived at the final screen of the Wizard. You might want to use the **Back** navigation control to double-check your settings. After you've finished, click **Next** again, and the Internet Explorer Customization Wizard generates and compresses custom package files, storing them in the location you specified earlier. This might take a few minutes. ●

Superior Techniques for Managing Office

37 Reducing Office 2000's Total Cost of Ownership   963

38 Maximizing Office 2000 Security   981

39 Supporting Microsoft Office 2000   1005

40 Finding Office Training and Self-Help Solutions   1037

41 Managing Mobile Office Users   1051

42 Using Office in a Global Environment   1079

43 Making Office More Accessible to People with
Disabilities   1093

Reducing Office 2000's Total Cost of Ownership

by Bill Camarda

In the wake of independent studies from the Gartner Group and others, which estimated the total cost of owning, managing, and maintaining PCs at $15,000 or more per machine per year, business customers have become increasingly worried about the total costs of desktop computing. These costs take many forms, including the cost of hardware and software, training and help desk services, and custom software development, to name a few.

Microsoft began focusing on these *total cost of ownership* (TCO) issues in Office 97 with limited success. Installation became more flexible than it had been, but still required hand editing of complex STF files. The Zero Administration Kit for Windows made it possible to create limited-feature sets for users with minimal needs, it but proved extremely difficult to deploy—and even more difficult to customize.

As is often the case with Microsoft products, however, a poor first attempt has been followed with dramatic improvements. Microsoft has provided a series of tools that now make Office 2000 easy to deploy and maintain. Some of these tools, such as the Custom Installation Wizard, are covered elsewhere in the book.

▶ For detailed coverage of the Custom Installation Wizard, **see** Chapter 2, "Automating and Customizing Office Installations Across the Network," on **p. 27**.

Others, such as the System Policy Editor, Custom Maintenance Wizard, and Office Profile Wizard, are mentioned briefly elsewhere, but deserve more coverage. These tools are covered in greater depth in this chapter.

N O T E Most of the tools covered in this chapter are available as part of the Office 2000 Resource Kit Toolbox, available for free download at **www.microsoft.com.office/ ork/2000/appndx/toolbox.htm**. Throughout this chapter, it is assumed that you have downloaded and installed these tools. ■

Introducing the Office Profile Wizard

Over time, users establish a wide variety of settings as they work with Office 2000: custom templates, spelling dictionaries, personal preferences for Office's user interface, and so forth. As Office administrator, you too might have preferences for how Office works, and you might want these preferences to be reflected in how Office behaves on all the workstations in your workgroup or organization, without investing time and money in manually configuring every computer.

When you deploy new computers, or provide notebook PCs to users who also have desktop workstations, or replace a crashed hard disk, you might want to be sure all these Office customizations are available on the new or repaired systems—again, without costly, time-consuming manual reconfiguration. Similarly, if you reassign a computer to a new employee, you might want to restore its original settings without reinstalling Office from scratch.

One tool can support all these scenarios: the Office Profile Wizard, which can store all the elements of an existing Office configuration, and restore them—to the same computer, or to a different computer.

Saving an Existing Office Configuration

To store an existing Office configuration with the Office Profile Wizard, follow these steps:

1. Choose **Start**, **Programs**, **Microsoft Office Tools**, **Microsoft Office 2000 Resource Kit Tools**, **Profile Wizard**. The Profile Wizard runs (see Figure 37.1).
2. Click **Next**. The Save or Restore Settings dialog box appears.
3. In the **Save the Settings from This Machine** text box, enter the path and filename you want to use for your settings (OPS) file.
4. Click **Finish**. Office compiles your Office customizations, registry settings, templates, shortcuts, and related files into a new binary file.
5. Click **Exit** to close the Office Profile Wizard.

Note that OPS files might be several megabytes in size. (They are, however, typically quite compressible via utilities such as WinZIP—especially if they contain many user templates.) You might consider capturing an OPS file at each user workstation and storing it locally, as a way of simplifying the restoration process in the event that Office must be reinstalled on a specific workstation. Or, to restore the original customizations you made during deployment, without preserving user changes made later, you might provide copies of the original OPS file you created to deploy from.

FIGURE 37.1
The Office Profile Wizard's opening window.

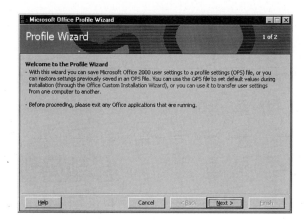

N O T E Of course, the Office Profile Wizard must be installed on any computer you want to run it on. ■

Restoring a Saved Office Configuration

To restore a configuration you previously saved with the Office Profile Wizard, follow these steps:

1. Choose **Start**, **Programs**, **Microsoft Office Tools**, **Microsoft Office 2000 Resource Kit Tools**, **Profile Wizard**. The Profile Wizard runs.

2. Click **Next**. The Save or Restore Settings dialog box appears.

3. Click **Restore Previously Saved Settings**. The path and filename associated with the most recent OPS file you created at this workstation appears. If this is not the OPS file you want to use, browse to and select a different one.

4. If you want to restore Office's original defaults before superimposing your OPS file's customizations, select the **Reset to Defaults Before Restoring Settings** check box. You might want to select this option if, as discussed earlier, you are reassigning a computer to a new user.

5. Click **Finish**. Office restores your Office customizations, Registry settings, templates, shortcuts, and related files.

6. Click **Exit** to close the Office Profile Wizard.

Controlling the Profile Wizard from the Command Line

The Office Profile Wizard can be set to create or restore profiles with little or no user involvement. You might, for example, decide to store current profiles for each workstation every six months. Or, you might want to automatically restore all the computers in a department to their original Office settings, perhaps after a reorganization that moves people around.

The Office Profile Wizard might be controlled from the command line, or by including a line in a batch file that runs when a user logs onto the network. Table 37.1 shows the switches available for use with the Wizard.

Table 37.1   Office Profile Wizard Command-Line Options

Option	Does This
/d	First resets Office 2000 to default settings before superimposing any settings in the OPS file.
/e	Displays error messages but no progress indicators.
/i *filename*	Sets the name of an INI file that contains settings associated with the OPS file. If you do not use /i, the settings are stored in Proflwiz.ini.
/p	Displays progress indicators but no error messages.
/q	Runs the Wizard silently, without error messages or progress indicators. Can be used with /s or /r, but cannot be used with /p or /e.
/r *filename*	Restores settings from a path and filename you specify.
/s *filename*	Saves settings to a path and filename you specify.

For example, the following command restores the settings from an OPS file c:\My Documents\Settings1.ops:

```
proflwiz.exe /r "c:\My Documents\Settings1.ops"
```

If you want this to occur silently, with no user involvement, add the /q switch:

```
proflwiz.exe /q /r "c:\My Documents\Settings1.ops"
```

Introducing the Custom Maintenance Wizard

In September 1999, Microsoft delivered its long-promised Custom Maintenance Wizard (CMW), which streamlines and centralizes several key Office administration tasks that previously required complex scripting or expensive add-ons such as Systems Management Server 2—if they could be performed at all.

The Custom Maintenance Wizard walks administrators through the creation of a feature state file, which can be distributed to the desktop via email. A client component reads the file and works with the Windows Installer to apply changes to Office 2000 at the desktop without further user or administrative involvement. For administrators, the Wizard should enable

■ **Simpler staged rollouts.** For example, many organizations would like to deploy most of Office, but defer deployment of Outlook 2000 until later, as part of an overall messaging system upgrade. According to Microsoft, the Custom Maintenance Wizard makes it possible to centrally deliver new Office applications to a workstation already running Office 2000.

■ **Centralized changes to feature states.** If administrators determine that users need access to additional features of an Office application, they can send a small file to each user; when the user double-clicks the file, the features are enabled or installed. Similarly, the Wizard could be used to change default file locations if a new server is deployed.

The Custom Maintenance Wizard is available for download at the Microsoft Office Resource Kit Toolbox site, `www.microsoft.com/office/ork/2000/appndx/toolbox.htm`. After you've downloaded Maintwiz.exe, follow these steps to create Office 2000 customizations that can be deployed to workstations from a central location:

1. In Windows Explorer, double-click **Maintwiz.exe**; the first window of the Custom Maintenance Wizard opens (see Figure 37.2).

FIGURE 37.2
The opening window of the Custom Maintenance Wizard.

2. Click **Next**. The Open the MSI File window appears (see Figure 37.3).

FIGURE 37.3
The Open the MSI File window.

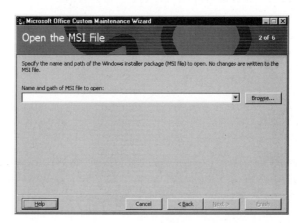

3. Browse to, and select, the Data1.msi package file that comes with Office 2000, and specifies Office 2000's standard settings. You can find this file in one of two places. It appears in the main folder of Disk 1 of the Office 2000 CD-ROM; if you installed Office

2000 across the network from a central server, it can be found in the network Administrative Installation Point folder you created before installation. The Custom Maintenance Wizard does not change this MSI file.

4. Click **Next**. The Open the CMW File window appears (see Figure 37.4). From here, you can browse to and select a CMW file that already includes customizations you might already have made. If you're using the Custom Maintenance Wizard for the first time, you probably won't have a CMW file. That's not a problem; you'll create one later in this Wizard.

FIGURE 37.4

The Open the CMW File window.

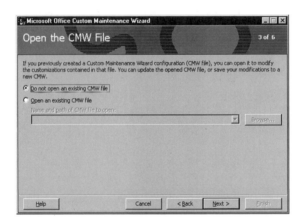

5. Click **Next**. The Select the CMW File to Save window appears (see Figure 37.5). Here, you can change the name and location of the CMW file you are creating; the default name is New Maintenance Data File.CMW.

FIGURE 37.5

The Select the CMW File to Save window.

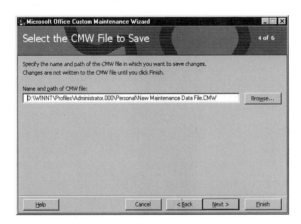

6. Click **Next**. The Set Feature Installation States window appears (see Figure 37.6). Here, you can set one of four feature installation states for each feature component of Office 2000. (See the Appendix for a detailed list of the feature components that can be customized here.)

FIGURE 37.6
The Set Feature Installation States window.

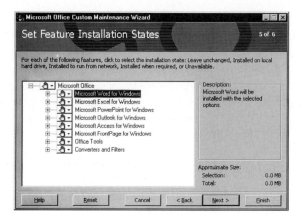

The feature installation states are as follows:

- **Leave Feature's Installation State Unchanged.** Whatever setting is currently found on an individual workstation is left intact.

- **Run from My Computer (Installed on Local Hard Drive).** Installs the feature on the local hard drive of whatever individual workstation you apply this settings file to.

- **Run from Network.** Sets the feature to run from a network location, rather than from a local hard drive. If the feature is already installed, this setting tells the local workstation to look for the feature on the network instead.

- **Installed on First Use.** Sets the feature to be installed locally the first time a user tries to work with it. If the feature is already installed, this setting removes the local files until the next time the user seeks to work with the feature, at which time the files will be reinstalled.

- **Not Available.** Sets the feature to be unavailable. If the feature is already installed, this setting removes the local files and prevents the user from adding them again.

N O T E If you make a feature unavailable, you might want to eliminate its corresponding menu command, if any. This can often be done through system policies, as discussed later in this chapter. ▨

7. After you're finished setting feature states, click **Next**. The next window of the Custom Maintenance Wizard appears.

8. If you want to double-check your settings, click **Back** to review them again. When you're finished, return to the final window, and click **Finish**. The Custom Maintenance Wizard writes the settings to your CMW file.

In its final window (see Figure 37.7), the Custom Maintenance Wizard displays the command line you can adapt and provide to your users.

FIGURE 37.7
The final window of the
Custom Maintenance
Wizard.

To install your
customizations on
user workstations,
copy and adapt this
command line.

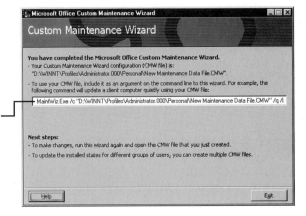

When they run the command line (as part of a DOS batch file or a Windows shortcut you can email to them), the Custom Maintenance Wizard runs and applies the changes you make. If you use logon scripts, you can automatically run the Wizard without users' intervention, the next time they log onto the network.

N O T E   Be sure to include the correct path to your copy of the MaintWiz.Exe file on your network server. Also note that two switches are set by default in the command line that Custom Maintenance Wizard creates for you:

- /q runs the Custom Maintenance Wizard in quiet mode, without user involvement or feedback.
- /l creates a log file, cmw_log.txt, and stores it in the user's local c:\temp folder. (You can specify a different location.) ■

N O T E   You can create multiple CMW files to serve the custom needs of different departments or types of users. If you have deployed different versions of Office 2000 (for example, Office 2000 Premium Edition and Office 2000 Standard Edition), you must create separate CMW files for each. ■

Using System Policies with Office 2000

System policies remain a key tool for Office administrators who want to tighten their control over Office in the enterprise. First introduced in Windows 95 and available in Windows NT 4.0, system policies are files that control aspects of a program's behavior by changing entries in the Windows Registry.

You can deploy system policies on a server and run them at logon from individual Windows 95/98 or NT Workstation 4.0 workstations. (They are not available for Macintosh computers, even those running on NT Server networks.)

System policies give the Office administrator a way to control the behavior of Office for the following:

- Individual workstations
- Individual users sharing a workstation
- Groups of users
- Every user at once

You can implement system policies at any time, although if you're planning to impose highly restrictive policies, it's usually best to do so at the same time you deploy Office 2000. If you don't, you'll face the challenge of users who want to know why restrictions have suddenly become necessary.

N O T E System policies run at logon only if you choose the correct primary network logon for each workstation. In NT Server and/or Windows 2000 networks, you must use Client for Microsoft Networks, and define an appropriate Windows NT domain on each workstation.

In NetWare networks, System policies are easiest to implement if you use Microsoft Client for NetWare, specifying a preferred server for logon. If you prefer to use Novell's client software, you must manually download system polices from a mapped drive on each computer. For detailed directions on doing this, see Chapter 15 of the Windows 95 Resource Kit.

Microsoft has provided several versions of the system policy Editor over the past few years. However, the only one you should use with Office 2000 is the one that comes with the Microsoft Office 2000 Resource Kit

`www.microsoft.com.office/ork/2000/appndx/toolbox.htm`

N O T E The same policy templates work on Windows 2000, Windows NT 4.0, Windows 98, and Windows 95. However, to create a policy file for Windows 95 or Windows 98, you must be running System Policy Editor on a Windows 95 or Windows 98 computer. To create a policy file for Windows NT Workstation, you must run System Policy Editor on an NT Workstation system.

> **CAUTION**
>
> If you created system policies for Office 97, you will have to re-establish them for Office 2000: Your existing policies cannot be migrated.

The system policies Microsoft provides for Office 2000 control virtually every behavior Office administrators are concerned with. Some enable you to tighten your control of Office (and presumably reduce your cost of ownership). Others are primarily intended to give you more flexibility in deploying Office to users throughout your network. Many correspond to settings that users would otherwise set individually in the Tools, Options dialog boxes of individual Office applications.

Part
VI

Ch
37

Outside of Office, you can use other Policy templates to place restrictions on the rest of the Windows environment. For example, you can use the Windows 98 system policy template windows.adm, available in the Reskit\Netadmin folder of the Windows 98 CD-ROM, to limit individual users to running specific applications, such as Word. (The setting to do this is Default User\Windows 98 System\Restrictions\Only Run Allowed Windows Applications.)

> **CAUTION**
>
> If you're planning to use the policy Only Run Allowed Windows Applications, be sure to include Poledit.exe (System Policy Editor) as one of those applications, or you might not be able to change the settings later.

Reviewing Improvements on System Policies in Office 2000

Although system policies were available in Office 97, Microsoft has extended them and made them more flexible in Office 2000. The improvements include

- **Policies are easier to enforce.** If you use system policies to restrict an element of the user interface, the element is grayed out so it cannot be used, and (unlike Office 97), your system policy cannot be manually overridden.

- **Policies are restored when an application is restarted.** In Office 97, policies were read and enforced only when the computer logged onto the network; in Office 2000, they are read and enforced every time a user starts an Office application.

- **A broader range of policies exists.** In Office 97, Microsoft made available a select group of policies that it believed would be most useful to system administrators. In Word and Excel 2000, nearly all the options available through the Tools, Options dialog box are subject to centralized system policies, including settings formerly stored in the Word Settings and Excel Settings Registry subkeys. Most of the remaining exceptions are settings that apply only to individual documents.

- **Now, policies can be undone.** In Office 97, if you decided to stop enforcing a policy, the policy's settings would remain intact until a user changed them. Now, you can clear a policy setting, and the application reverts either to its default setting or a setting the user created earlier.

- **Now, policies can incorporate environment variables.** Environment variables can substitute for values that might vary among computers, such as paths, filenames, and usernames. This change enables you to set a variable and have each computer read the variable to reflect the correct information for that computer.

N O T E For a list of Office 2000 policies that support environment variables, see the following page in the Office 2000 Resource Kit: Office 2000 System Policies That Accept Environment Variables. ▪

In connection with these changes, Microsoft has centralized storage of Office-related system policies in a new HKCU\Software\Policies Registry subkey. Policies that are in effect are no longer scattered throughout workstation registries in subkeys associated with each individual Office application.

Understanding Policy Templates

System policies are created with Microsoft's System Policy Editor, using *policy templates*. Policy templates are ADM files that contain all the Microsoft predefined policy settings. To establish the policies you want, you open the appropriate ADM template file from within System Policy Editor; create a policy file based on these templates; and save the file with a POL extension.

The ADM templates associated with Office 2000 are listed in Table 37.2.

Table 37.2   Policy Templates for Office 2000 Applications

To Control This Application	Use This Policy Template
Access 2000	Access9.adm
Clip Gallery 5	Clipgal5.adm
Excel 2000	Excel9.adm
FrontPage 2000	Frontpg4.adm
Office 2000 (common settings that apply across multiple applications)	Office9.adm
Outlook 2000	Outlk9.adm
PowerPoint 2000	Ppoint9.adm
Publisher 2000	Pub9.adm
Windows Installer	Instlr1.adm
Word 2000	Word9.adm

N O T E   No system policy template is available for Microsoft PhotoDraw. ▪

Running System Policy Editor

Assuming you've installed System Policy Editor with the Office Resource Toolbox, you can run it as follows:

1. Choose **Start, Programs, Microsoft Office Tools, Microsoft Resource Kit Tools**, and then **System Policy Editor**. The System Policy Editor opens (see Figure 37.8).

Part

VI

Ch

37

FIGURE 37.8

The System Policy
Editor window.

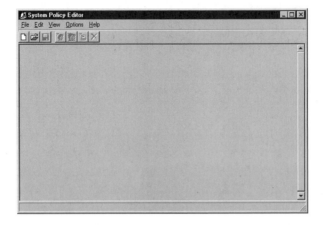

2. Choose **Options**, **Policy Template**. The Policy Template Options dialog box opens, listing any current Policy templates already installed. If no Policy templates are installed, click **Add** to display the Open Template File dialog box. This lists the Policy templates available (but not installed) in the Policy folder. (Figure 37.9 shows this dialog box with several standard Policy templates listed.)

FIGURE 37.9

The Policy Template
Options dialog box lists
currently installed
policy templates.

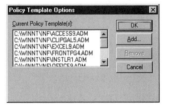

N O T E   When a Policy template is listed in the Policy Template Options dialog box, the settings contained within it are available for customization (see steps 5 and 6). If a Policy template is not listed in this dialog box, its settings are not available. So, for example, if you want to control general Windows 95 settings, you need to find and install the admin.adm template file, which contains them. ▨

3. Click **OK** again. The blank System Policy Editor window returns.

4. Click the **New** button or choose **File**, **New Policy**. As shown in Figure 37.10, the System Policy Editor window now displays two icons: Default Computer, which controls System policies related to an entire computer (or computers); and Default User, which displays System Policies associated with a specific user (or group of users).

FIGURE 37.10
The System Policy Editor window after you've chosen a template to work from.

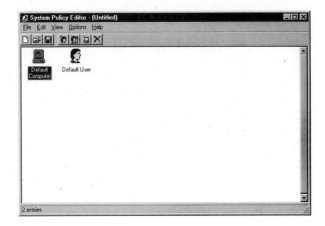

N O T E Some system policies for Microsoft Outlook and the Windows Installer affect all users on a specific computer; these are accessible through Default Computer. All the others can be attached to individual users, even if multiple users share the same computer. These are accessible through Default User.

To set policies for individual users, you must first enable User Profiles on their workstations, if User Profiles are not already enabled. To do this in Windows 95 or Windows 98, start the Passwords applet in the Control Panel, click the **User Profiles** tab, and select the option button labeled **Users Can Customize Their Preferences and Desktop Settings**. ▓

5. Click the icon associated with the System policies that you want to work with (Default User or Default Computer). The Default User Properties or Default Computer Properties dialog box appears, listing the categories of System policies available for editing (see Figure 37.11).

FIGURE 37.11
The Default User Properties dialog box, with some of Office 2000's suitewide settings displayed.

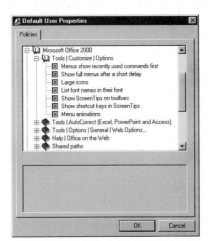

6. Scroll down to the policy you want to change, and make the selection you want. For each policy, you have several choices:

- **Grayed.** The system policy leaves local settings alone; the user can decide which setting to use.
- **Selected.** The policy always goes into effect as soon as the user logs onto the network or runs an Office application.
- **Cleared.** The setting is always turned off when the user first logs onto the network or runs an Office application.

In Office 2000 system templates, you can enforce a policy—that is, prevent a user from overriding it— by selecting or clearing an additional check box that appears at the bottom of the dialog box after you select a policy (see Figure 37.12). Selecting this second check box forces the setting on while clearing the check box enforces the setting off.

FIGURE 37.12

You can use the additional check box at the bottom of the Policies tab to enforce a setting, preventing users from overriding it.

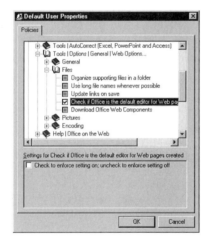

7. When you finish changing settings, click **OK**. You return to the System Policy Editor window with its Default Computer and Default User icons. If you want to make changes to the category of settings you haven't worked with yet, click its icon and repeat steps 5 and 6.

8. When you finish, click the **Save** button or choose **File, Save**. The Save As dialog box appears.

9. Enter a name for your policy—**Ntconfig.pol** if you're setting a policy for NT Workstation systems, or **Config.pol** for Windows 95/98 systems.

10. Browse the network to the NetLogon folder on the Primary Domain Controller that controls your user logons, and click **Save**. The new Policy is saved with the .pol extension. (If your users log onto a NetWare network, instead save the POL file to the Sys\Public folder on their preferred server.)

Specifying Policies for Individuals or Groups

When you create system policies for the Default User, those System policies affect all users except those for whom you have created separate policies. Similarly, when you create System policies for Default Computer, those affect all computers that do not have System policies to the contrary.

The real benefits of system policies come when you customize them to the needs of specific groups within your organization. You might, for example, have a roomful of computers that are used by account executives during the day and telemarketers at night. You might provide your account executives access to Excel to help them prepare high-level proposals, but limit your telemarketers to the software they need to take orders and check on order status.

Part

VI

Ch

37

To create system policies for a specific group, first open the System Policy Editor, and then follow these steps:

1. If you already have a system policy file (Config.pol or Ntconfig.pol), choose **File**, **Open** to open it. If not, choose **File**, **New** to create a new system policy file.

2. Choose **Edit**, **Add Group**. The Add Group dialog box appears. Enter the name of the group that you want to add.

N O T E   The groups you add in System Policy Editor should correspond to groups recognized by your network server. If you are running on a Windows NT Server network, for example, use the group names you have established in User Manager for Domains. ▓

3. Click **OK**. The new group appears as a separate icon next to Default Computer and Default User.

4. Double-click the new icon to display the policies available for editing.

5. Make your edits, click **OK**, and save your policy file.

Reviewing Selected Office 2000 System Policies

As mentioned earlier, the Office 2000 Policy templates can customize hundreds of settings throughout Office. Chapters 6 through 11 discuss system policies for individual Office applications, and Chapter 42 covers system policies for customizing Office to the needs of international environments. The next sections focus on some additional Office-wide system policies you might want to pay attention to in your role as Office administrator.

Office 2000 Web-Related Policies   The following Microsoft Office 2000\Tools|Options| General|Web Options settings help control the way Office 2000 creates Web pages and integrates with your Internet connections:

■   **Rely on CSS for Font Formatting.** Tells Office that it can rely on cascading style sheets to store font information on Web pages. Keep in mind that cascading style sheets are supported only by Internet Explorer 3.0 and later, and Netscape Navigator 4.0 and later; and that each browser platform might render CSS style sheets slightly differently. Consider enforcing this setting off if you create pages for users using multiple browsers and versions.

- **Organize Supporting Files in a Folder.** By default, when you save an Office file as a Web page, Office creates a folder with the same name as the Web page, and places all associated graphics and XML data files there. You can specify that Office not create these folders by enforcing this setting off.

- **Use Long File Names Whenever Possible.** Some Web servers cannot properly understand Windows long filenames, including filenames with four-character extensions. If your Web server has this limitation, you can require old-fashioned 8.3 filenames by enforcing this setting off.

- **Update Links on Save.** By default, Office updates all hyperlinks to supporting files (such as graphics) whenever you save a Web page.

- **Check Whether Office Is the Default Editor for Web Pages Created in Office.** Some companies might create Web pages in Word or other Office applications, but then import them into another Web design tool, such as Macromedia Dreamweaver or Adobe GoLive, for further editing. By default, if another program is registered as owning the HTM or HTML extension, when you save an Office file as HTML, you're asked whether you would like to change the association of the HTM or HTML file back to the Office application that created it. If you've set another Web tool as your primary editor, this can be annoying and confusing. Enforcing this setting off eliminates the dialog box.

- **Download Office Web Components.** This setting enables you to specify where updated Office Web Components might be retrieved.

- **Rely on VML for Displaying Graphics in Browser.** VML is a proposed Web standard currently supported only by Internet Explorer 5. Unless all your users work with Internet Explorer 5, consider enforcing this setting off.

- **Allow PNG As an Output Format.** PNG is a fast and efficient graphics format, but it is currently only a proposed Web standard currently supported only by Internet Explorer 4.0b1 and Netscape Navigator 4.04 and later. Unless all your users work with very recent browsers, consider enforcing this setting off.

- **Target Monitor.** If your installed base of monitors is largely or entirely consistent in size, you can consider optimizing the Office Web pages you create for that size of monitor. To specify screen resolution or pixels per inch, set this policy.

- **Default or Specific Encoding.** By default, Web pages are saved with Western European encoding. If you want to use a different encoding scheme, or prevent users from changing the encoding scheme you've standardized upon, set this policy.

- **Help|Office on the Web|Office on the Web URL.** When users choose Help, Office on the Web, this policy enables you to set a destination other than Microsoft's Web site.

Commonly Changed Office 2000 Default User Policies   The following settings help control the way Office 2000 runs for individual users:

- **Shared Paths\User Templates.** Specifies where a user's templates are stored. By default, the location is c:\Windows\Profiles\Username\Application Data\Microsoft\Templates.

- **Shared Paths\Shared Templates.** Specifies an additional location, typically on a network server, where a user can store additional Word, Excel and/or PowerPoint templates beyond those installed locally.

- **Shared Paths\Shared Themes.** Specifies where a workgroup's shared Web themes are stored, typically on a network server.

- **Shared Paths\Web Queries.** Specifies where a workgroup's shared Web queries are stored, typically on a network server.

Customizing Other Useful System Policy Settings

The following miscellaneous settings might also be worth your time to customize:

- **Microsoft Office 2000|Graph Settings|Graph Gallery Path.** Specifies where custom graphs are stored; can be set to a network location to help ensure all users work with the same customized graph formats.

- **Microsoft Clip Gallery 5.0|Disable Clips Online Access from Clip Gallery.** Prevents users from using Clip Gallery to download new clip art from Microsoft's Clip Gallery Live. (They can still, however, access Clip Gallery Live manually, unless you limit their Internet connections.)

- **Windows Installer|Search Order.** Enables you to control the order in which Office applications search for Office files when they need to install new features across the network, or fix damaged files through Detect and Repair. ●

Part
VI

Ch
37

Maximizing Office 2000 Security

by Bill Camarda

A key to managing Office in today's organizations is ensuring that business-critical Office documents remain secure and get into the hands only of people authorized to see them. This means designing a multilayered security strategy that takes advantage of the following:

- Security features built into Office applications, including password protection, macro security, and digital certificates
- Third-party security solutions, such as up-to-date antivirus software
- Security built into the network operating system of your choice, such as access controls

This chapter reviews each of these topics, beginning with the precautions built into Office.

Adding Passwords and Encryption in Microsoft Word

Word and Excel 2000/97 (and Word/Excel 98 for the Macintosh) enable you to protect documents with passwords. When documents are protected with passwords, they are encrypted using a relatively powerful algorithm called RC4. This is a more secure encryption algorithm than was provided in earlier versions of Office, such as Office 95.

Excel and Word files that are encrypted cannot be indexed by either the Microsoft Office Server Extensions (OSE) search engine or the Office Find Fast feature.

CAUTION

If you save a password-protected Word 2000 document to an earlier version of Word, such as Word 6/95, password protection is lost, and you have to reapply it in the earlier version of Word. This is true even though Word 6 and Word 95 also offered password protection.

N O T E   RC4 password protection is illegal in France. If Regional Settings are set to French in the Windows Control Panel, Word users cannot open password-protected Word 2000 documents. If Regional Settings are reset to another locale, the files can be opened. ▪

Password-Protecting an Entire Word Document

To protect an entire document, follow these steps:

1. Choose **File**, **Save As**.

2. In the Save As dialog box, click **Tools**, **General Options**. The Save options dialog box opens (see Figure 38.1).

FIGURE 38.1
You can enter passwords to open or modify files in Word's Save dialog box.

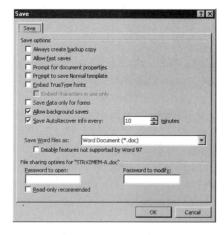

3. If you want to require a password for opening the file, enter the password in the **Password to open** text box.

4. If you want to require a password for modifying the file, enter the password in the **Password to modify** text box.

5. Click **OK**.

6. Re-enter the password or passwords in the confirmation boxes Word displays, and click **OK**.

7. Click **Save** to save the file.

CAUTION

If you forget your password, you will not be able to be open your document. Even more serious, if one of your colleagues forgets a password, or leaves the company and does not share the password with someone, you will not be able to open his documents. If your workgroup uses passwords, be sure copies of these passwords are stored securely—ideally, in a locked, fireproof, waterproof safe—where the company can access them in an emergency.

Using Word's Read-Only Recommended Option

If you need less security than password protection, but nonetheless want to discourage users from overwriting or changing specific files, use the **Read-only recommended** option in the Save options dialog box. Selecting this option provides very light security: When this box is selected, Word displays a dialog box when a file is opened, encouraging the user to open the file as read-only. If the user does so, and then makes edits, the file must be saved under a different name.

Read-Only recommended can be selected whether or not you set a password for the document.

Protecting Elements of a Word Document

In some cases, you might want to permit changes to a document, but only within carefully prescribed parameters. For example, you might want to permit changes for the following:

- Only with the Track Changes feature turned on (that is, so all changes will be tracked)
- Only to permit Comments (annotations), but not to add or remove text from the document
- Only to allow users to fill out electronic forms—or sections of forms—but not make changes to the text, layout, or formatting of the underlying form itself

To set any of these restrictions, choose **Tools**, **Protect Document**. The Protect Document dialog box opens (see Figure 38.2). Select how you want to allow users to edit the document. If you want, enter a password. Click **OK**. If you've entered a password, you'll be asked to confirm it; do so and click **OK** again.

FIGURE 38.2

Choosing how to protect portions of your document.

N O T E   When a document is protected in this fashion, the user can open and read it, but not make changes other than those you have permitted. If you don't specify a password, your document is still protected, but a user can turn off the protection simply by choosing **Tools**, **Unprotect Document**, clearing the selected button, and clicking **OK**. ■

If your document has more than one section, and you want to protect it for forms, you can protect only certain sections. Choose the **Forms** option button, and click **Sections**. The Section Protection dialog box appears (see Figure 38.3). Clear the check boxes associated with any sections you do not need to protect.

FIGURE 38.3

The Selection Protection feature enables you to protect only certain sections of a document for forms.

This feature enables you to incorporate a form that cannot be changed into a document that includes other, editable components.

TIP   You can use Word's document passwords and protection together. For example, you can specify a password that is required to open a document, and also restrict users to make only tracked changes even after they open the document, unless they present a different password.

Using Excel's Worksheet and Workbook Protection Tools

Like Word, Excel offers two types of password protection, both of which use RC4 encryption (except in France, where it is not legal).

- You can require a password to open a workbook, modify a workbook, or both.
- You can protect a specific worksheet, an entire workbook, or specific elements within a worksheet or workbook

Password-Protecting an Entire Excel Workbook

To protect an entire Excel 2000/98 workbook, follow these steps:

1. Choose **File**, **Save As**.

2. In the Save As dialog box, click **Tools**, **General Options**. The Save Options dialog box opens (see Figure 38.4).

FIGURE 38.4
You can enter passwords required to open or modify Excel workbooks in Excel's Save Options dialog box.

3. If you want to require a password for opening the file, enter the password in the **Password to open** text box.

4. If you want to require a password for modifying the file, enter the password in the **Password to modify** text box.

5. Click **OK**.

6. Re-enter the password or passwords in the confirmation boxes Excel displays, and click **OK**.

7. Click **Save** to save the file.

As in Word, you can discourage users from overwriting or changing an Excel worksheet by selecting the **Read-only recommended** check box in the Save Options dialog box. When this box is selected, Word displays a dialog box as a file is opened, encouraging the user to open the file as read-only. If the user does so, and then makes edits, the file must be saved under a different name. Otherwise, the user can edit the worksheet at will.

Read-only recommended can be selected whether or not you have set a password for the document.

Password-Protecting Elements of an Excel Workbook

In some cases, you might want to limit changes to an Excel workbook, but not prevent them altogether. You might want to permit changes only in a specific worksheet within a workbook, for example, or you might want to protect only certain aspects of your workbook. You might want to prevent others from adding or deleting worksheets. Excel 2000 and Excel 98 give you this flexibility.

Password-Protecting an Individual Worksheet

To password-protect one worksheet in an Excel 2000/98 workbook, perform the following steps:

1. Display the worksheet you want to protect.

Part
VI

Ch
38

2. Choose **Tools**, **Protection**, **Protect Sheet**. The Protect Sheet dialog box opens (see Figure 38.5).

FIGURE 38.5
The Protect Sheet dialog box.

3. Select the boxes associated with the elements you want to protect. (All three boxes are selected by default.)

- Checking **Contents** protects the values and text in cells from editing, and ensures that the contents and appearance of charts remain unchanged.

  After a sheet is protected, you can also hide a formula in a cell so it doesn't appear in the formula bar when a user selects the cell. To do so, protect the sheet; select the cell(s); choose **Format**, **Cells**; click the **Protection** tab; check the **Hidden** check box, and click **OK**.

- Checking **Objects** prevents unauthorized users from moving, editing, deleting, or resizing graphics in a worksheet or a chart.

- Checking **Scenarios** prevents unauthorized users from changing the definitions associated with Excel scenarios.

4. If you choose, enter a password, and click **OK**.

5. If you entered a password, re-enter it and click **OK** to confirm the password. The document is now protected.

CAUTION

You can't protect a workbook after you've shared it, except by turning off sharing—which deletes all the change histories Excel might have been tracking. You can, however, password-protect elements of a worksheet or workbook, and then share it with the protections intact.

▶ For more information about shared workbooks, **see** Chapter 12, "Standardizing Document Production with Word and Excel," on **p. 311**.

Protecting a Workbook's Structure and Windows

Even if you require a password to open or modify a workbook, you can superimpose a second level of protection for the structure and windows contained in that workbook.

Protecting a workbook's structure prevents individual worksheets from being added, deleted, moved, hidden, unhidden, or renamed. Protecting its windows prevents users from closing, hiding, unhiding, resizing, or moving them. This tactic can be especially helpful if you've used

Excel to create an interactive presentation with clickable buttons where you want the windows to display in a specific way.

To protect the structure or windows in a workbook, or both, perform the following steps:

1. Choose **Tools**, **Protection**, **Protect Workbook**. The Protect Workbook dialog box opens (see Figure 38.6).

FIGURE 38.6
The Protect Workbook dialog box.

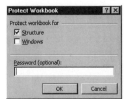

2. Select the **Structure** and/or **Windows** check boxes.
3. If you want to use a password, enter it in the Password text box.
4. Click **OK**.
5. If you have entered a password, confirm it and click **OK** again. The workbook is now protected as you specified.

Protecting Against Office Macro Viruses

According to a 1996 study by the National Computer Security Association, 98% of large North American organizations have encountered virus infections, and 90% of sites with more than 500 PCs encountered significant virus incidents at least once a month. Significant incidents were those "in which a minimum of 25 PCs, floppy disks, or files were infected by the same virus at relatively the same time." In the same study, NCSA determined that the chances of a virus infection were 1 per 100 PCs per month.

Of late, the mix of viruses has shifted dramatically—toward macro viruses designed specifically to run in Microsoft Office. Macro viruses are undesired programs that attach themselves to a template or document created in any program that uses a macro language. As the most widely used business application, Word has attracted the most virus authors, by far. Excel viruses are reasonably common; PowerPoint and Access viruses are possible though rarely seen; and (as the recent Melissa virus showed), attachments to email opened in Outlook can be extremely susceptible.

In Office 2000, macro viruses are written in Visual Basic for Applications (VBA). Not only does Office expose virtually all its functionality to VBA macros, VBA can control Windows as well. Therefore, hostile virus authors can wreak havoc with their victims' computers, up to and including destroying all the data and programs on a hard drive. Moreover, because VBA macros can be stored in both templates and documents, they are extremely easy to spread.

In all honesty, this relatively uncontrolled power is a disaster waiting to happen—one that can be prevented only by vigilant administrators and users.

Part
VI

Ch
38

N O T E Because the Melissa virus is likely to serve as a model for many virus infections in the future, it's worth discussing in a bit more detail. The Melissa virus was transmitted in the form of an infected Word document attached to an email message that included a name known to the recipient in the Subject header. When opened in either Word 97 or Word 2000, the virus contained in the attachment would run—but only if macros were enabled to run on the user's system, or the user chose to enable the macros contained in this particular document.

Assuming the user or administrator enables macros and opens the infected document, Melissa runs, doing the following:

1. Melissa lowers Word's macro security settings so that all macros will run from now on. This enables Melissa to run undetected in the future.

2. Next, the macro reads the system Registry, looking for the key:

    HKEY_Current_User\Software\Microsoft\Office\Melissa?

    If it cannot find this key, or if the key is present but has a value other than "... by Kwyjibo," the virus looks for Microsoft Outlook and an Outlook MAPI address book. If it finds one, it sends a copy of the infected file to the first 50 names in the address book. Because Outlook address book entries can include entire mailing lists, not just individual names, Melissa can automatically send to all the names on these mailing lists—so a single infected computer can infect far more than 50 other computers.

3. Then, the macro virus writes the value "...by Kwyjibo" to the HKEY_Current_User\Software\ Microsoft\Office\Melissa? Registry key. As long as this Registry key is present, the macro virus does not send any more infected email, but if the Registry key is removed for any reason, the next time the virus runs, it sends new messages and writes the Registry key again.

4. Next, the macro infects Normal.dot, the template used by all Word documents. Having done so, it can infect any other Word document you create.

Several points about Melissa and its imitators are worth keeping in mind:

- If a user or administrator disables macros on a system, or if the recipient of the message fails to open it, or if the recipient chooses to open it without enabling macros, the virus cannot automatically spread from that computer. However, the infected file can remain stored on that computer. If manually opened or forwarded later, from Word or any other email client that uses Word as an editor, it can still cause infection.

- The virus is incapable of automatically sending messages if the user does not have Microsoft Outlook installed and configured to send email. Outlook Express cannot automatically forward Melissa's messages on either the Windows or Macintosh platform; neither can any other email client software.

- Although the Melissa virus did not damage data, in many organizations it caused so much email traffic that it effectively made it impossible for email servers to function. In these organizations, it had the same effect as a deliberate *denial of service* attack, in which a hostile entity attempts to disrupt a server by overwhelming it with requests.

- After infecting Normal.dot, Melissa is capable of using any Word document as a host and sending that document to others. Obviously, if the host document it chooses contains sensitive data, you risk a serious security breach.

Other common symptoms of macro viruses include the following:

- In Word, you cannot save a file except by saving it as a template.
- Odd error messages appear—for example, STOP ALL FRENCH NUCLEAR TESTING IN THE PACIFIC.
- Odd, unexplained edits appear in your document; or certain blocks of text are inexplicably replaced with unusual replacement text.

When a user opens an Office file infected with a virus, the macro is executed and the virus runs, installing itself on the user's system. In Word, the virus usually runs immediately; one reason is that some viruses use a macro name Word sets aside for automatic execution, such as AutoOpen.

Office Features That Can Limit the Risk of Macro Virus Infection

Part

VI

Ch

38

Although Word, Excel, PowerPoint, and Outlook still have no built-in virus detection, Microsoft has provided three partial solutions for limiting the risk of infection. These are

- Trusted Sources and Code Signing
- Setting Security Levels
- The Anti-Virus API

Each of these is covered next.

Understanding Trusted Sources and Code Signing

Microsoft Office and Internet Explorer each base their security on *digital certificates* and *trusted sources*.

Developers of macros and other programs might purchase a digital certificate from a certificate authority such as VeriSign (`www.verisign.com`) or Thawte (`www.thawte.com`), and then attach that certificate to their programs. When a user attempts to run these programs, Office programs check the certificate by using public key cryptography. By doing so, they can verify that the program

- Originated from where it claims
- Has not been tampered with since it was digitally signed

Depending on the security settings you choose, the user might be shown a dialog box specifying where the macro originated, and asked whether to accept it as secure (see Figure 38.7). If the user chooses **Yes**, the macro runs.

FIGURE 38.7

A digital certificate, displayed in Word.

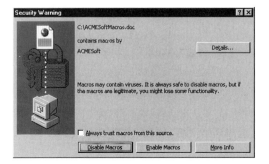

It is important to understand what digital certificates guarantee—and what they do not guarantee:

- They guarantee the source of a macro only if that source has successfully protected its private key against theft. If the source's key was stolen, digital signatures could be forged.

- They might identify the source accurately, but cannot guarantee the source is actually honorable, or that the code is virus-free. Although the presence of a signature certainly makes a virus traceable, nothing prevents a developer from creating a virus and then digitally signing it—or, more likely, from signing a file that has been infected inadvertently. To reduce this risk, digital signatures have expiration dates, and can be revoked if a certificate authority discovers that they have been used maliciously.

- Finally, a digital signature certainly does not guarantee that code was competently written.

In short, you must trust the source, not just the accuracy of the identification.

Despite these limitations, digital certificates have proven to be an extremely valuable security technique—arguably the best available to Microsoft Office users. There have been very few reported incidents of stolen digital certificates, or of virus-infected signed code.

CAUTION

For digital signatures to work, users must have Microsoft Internet Explorer 4.0 or later installed on their computers. In fact, digital certificates on individual computers are managed through Internet Explorer.

On systems running Internet Explorer 4.x, they are managed through the Content tab of the View, Internet Options dialog box. On systems running Internet Explorer 5.x, they are managed through Tools, Internet Options, Content, Certificates.

Office 2000 comes with Internet Explorer 5, so most organizations will not have a problem with the requirement to use Internet Explorer. However, some organizations have standardized on Netscape browsers and might prefer not to use IE. These organizations are unable to utilize Office 2000's support for digital signatures.

Instead, Office 2000 applications work much like Office 97 applications did: By default, users are warned about the presence of macros, and given the option to enable or disable them, without regard to any digital signatures that might be present.

CAUTION

Excel 2000 workbooks containing Excel 4.0 macros cannot be digitally signed. If you copy Excel 4.0 macros into a signed Excel 2000 workbook, and save the workbook, Excel removes your digital signature even if your digital certificate is properly installed and available.

Setting Security Levels for Running VBA Macros

Digital certificates work in tandem with the security settings built into Word, Excel, PowerPoint, and Outlook. In any of these programs, you can set fairly granular security policies, either at individual workstations or through system policies. To set security at an individual workstation, choose **Tools**, **Macro**, **Security**, and click the **Security Level** tab (see Figure 38.8). Then, choose **High**, **Medium**, or **Low**.

FIGURE 38.8
The Security Level tab of the Security dialog box in Word, Excel, PowerPoint, or Outlook.

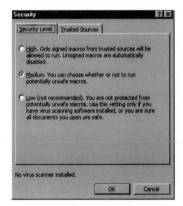

Part
VI

Ch
38

Table 38.1 shows how Office applications treat macros of various kinds, depending on the Security Level you choose.

Table 38.1   How Office Handles Macros at Each Security Level

Type of Macro	High Security	Medium Security	Low Security
Unsigned	The macro is automatically disabled, and then the document is opened.	The user is asked whether to enable or disable the macro.	The macro is enabled and the document is opened.
Signed by a trusted source, with a valid signature.	The macro is enabled, and the document is opened.	The macro is enabled, and the document is opened.	The macro is enabled, and the document is opened.

continues

Table 38.1   Continued

Type of Macro	High Security	Medium Security	Low Security
Signed with a valid signature by a source you haven't yet trusted.	Office displays information about the source and the digital certificate. Users can enable macros if they trust the source and the company that provided the digital certificate.	Office displays information about the source and the digital certificate. Users can enable macros if they trust the source and the company that provided the digital certificate.	The macro is enabled, and the document is opened.
Signed, but with an invalid signature, indicating possible tampering.	Office displays a warning about the possibility of a virus, and automatically disables macros.	Office displays a warning about the possibility of a virus, and automatically disables macros.	The macro is enabled, and the document is opened.
Signed, but Office cannot tell whether the signature is valid.	Office displays a warning that the signature cannot be confirmed, and automatically disables macros.	Office displays a warning that the signature cannot be confirmed, and asks the user whether she wants to enable the macros.	The macro is enabled, and the document is opened.
Signed, but after the digital certificate expired or was revoked.	Office displays a warning that the signature has expired or been revoked, and automatically disables macros.	Office displays a warning that the signature has expired or been revoked, and asks the user whether he wants to enable the macros.	The macro is enabled, and the document is opened.

> **CAUTION**
>
> In Word 97, if a document once contained macros but they have been removed, support structures for those macros remain. These support structures might trigger the Word 2000 macro warning dialog box. The only ways to eliminate the warnings are to save the file as an RTF file or copy its contents to a new file.

Working with Trusted Sources

When a user is prompted to decide whether a digitally signed macro should be enabled, she can decide at the same time to accept all future macros from the same source, by selecting the **A̲lways trust macros from this source** check box. This adds the source to the list of

Trusted Sources shown in Figure 38.9. If you decide later that you do not trust a Trusted Source after all, you can remove a listing by selecting it and clicking **Remove**.

FIGURE 38.9

The Trusted Sources tab of the Security dialog box in Word, Excel, PowerPoint, or Outlook.

Trusting All Installed Add-Ins and Templates

On the Trusted Sources tab, you'll find a check box that enables users to Trust all installed add-ins and templates. This box is selected by default, for the convenience of users. Many templates, add-ins, and COM add-ins—surprisingly, including some of Microsoft's—are not digitally signed. Similarly, templates placed in Excel's XLSTART folder could generate a security warning as soon as users start Excel.

If Office applications flagged files such as these, many users would find themselves besieged with unnecessary security warnings. However, if you choose to leave this box selected, you are taking a significant risk. Be careful to use precautions, such as access controls, to prevent these possible areas of infection:

■ Add-in and template files being replaced by identical versions with the same names

■ Infected files being placed in Office application startup or template folders, where they will be ignored if this check box is selected

If at all possible, consider clearing this check box, and signing all the custom templates and add-ins you use.

Preventing Outlook from Running Macros in Mail Attachments

As mentioned earlier, Office administrators face increasing risks from viruses attached to email messages. Because Microsoft Outlook integrates with other Office applications, reading a Word document or Excel worksheet attached to an email message can also run any macros hidden in that document. To prevent macros from automatically running when attachments are open, open Outlook, and follow these steps:

1. Choose **Tools**, **Options**.
2. Click the **Security** tab (see Figure 38.10).

3. Click **Attachment Security** (see Figure 38.11).

4. Be sure **High** is selected, and choose **OK**.

Users are now warned whenever they attempt to open an attachment containing a macro.

FIGURE 38.10
The Security options tab in Outlook 2000.

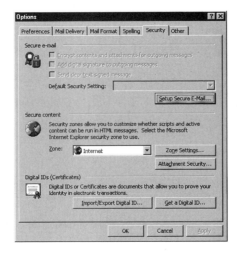

FIGURE 38.11
Setting Attachment Security to **High**.

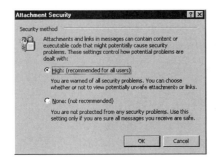

CAUTION

Users are warned, but not prevented from doing so. You still need to educate your users to never open a macro unless they are confident of its source.

Controlling Security Levels and Trusted Sources via System Policies

You can also control security levels and trusted sources centrally, through System Policies.

1. Run the **System Policy Editor**.

2. Choose **Options**, **Policy Template**.

3. Select the Office9.adm policy template (if necessary, first browse to it, and add it to the list); click **OK.**

4. Click the **New** button, and double-click **Default User.**

5. Double-click the application you want to set security for.

6. Go to **Tools, Macro, Security.**

7. To set the Security Level, select the **Security Level** check box, and choose the Security Level from the drop-down box that appears below.

8. To specify that add-ins and templates not be automatically trusted, select the **Trust All Installed Add-Ins and Templates** check box. The **Check to Enforce Setting On, Uncheck to Enforce Setting Off** check box appears below. Leave this box cleared.

9. If you want to control security settings for another Office application, double-click it and follow steps 6-9 again.

10. Choose **OK.**

11. Choose **File, Save** to save the POL policy file you just created.

12. Copy the policy file to a location on your network where it can be added to the network logon script for users who will be affected by it.

▶ The System Policy Editor is part of the Office 2000 Resource Kit Toolbox, downloadable at **www.microsoft.com/office/ork**. For more information about working with the System Policy Editor, **see** "Controlling Security Levels and Trusted Sources via System Policies," earlier in this chapter on **p. 994.**

N O T E Unfortunately, no system policy setting exists for preventing email attachments from being opened with macros in Outlook. ■

Prompting Word to Save the Normal Template

Because viruses typically infect the Normal.dot template that all Word documents depend on, one additional security measure is to specify that users confirm changes to Normal.dot instead of having them saved automatically whenever Word saves any other file. If users have done nothing that would lead to a change in Normal.dot, and find that it has changed anyway, they might have reason to suspect a virus infection, and can abandon the changes rather than saving them.

You can require confirmation of changes to Normal.dot at a client workstation by choosing **Tools, Options, Save**, and select the **Prompt to Save Normal Template** check box. From the System Policy Editor, go to Microsoft Word 2000, **Tools, Options, Save, Prompt to Save Normal Template.**

Keep in mind, however, that most changes to Normal.dot—such as changes to Word's default margins or new AutoText entries—are, in fact, desirable. Moreover, most users are not familiar enough with Word's inner workings to understand whether they should save Normal.dot, when asked.

Using Antivirus Software

The hard reality is that the best virus protection is to purchase and install antivirus software on individual workstations and network servers, and to update it regularly—at least weekly—with new virus definition files downloaded from the Web. Table 38.2 lists software packages that protect networks against Word 2000 and Excel 2000 macro viruses.

CAUTION

Office 2000 makes it doubly important to upgrade your virus definitions. Although Word, Excel, and PowerPoint's file formats are largely unchanged from Office 97, there are subtle differences in how VBA code is incorporated in these files. In many cases, antivirus software that handles Office 97 files will catch viruses in Office 2000—but some might slip through, due to the slight format changes. (And, of course, newer viruses might slip through because your older definitions don't include them.)

Table 38.2   Network Antivirus Software

Product Name	Web Site
Computer Associates Inoculate-IT	`www.cai.com`
Network Associates VirusScan, Total Virus Defense	`www.nai.com`
Symantec Norton AntiVirus 5.0	`www.symantec.com`
Trend Micro OfficeScan Corporate Edition	`www.trendmicro.com`

In selecting antivirus software, obviously your number one concern has to be effectiveness: Does the software recognize all or virtually all macro viruses, and is it updated at least weekly to reflect new viruses? There are, however, other issues to consider as well:

- You will also want a product that enables you to distribute updates to individual workstations from a central location, avoiding the necessity of visiting every workstation to apply updates every month (or even more).
- Network antivirus software can vary in its impact on your server performance, and should be tested on a lab server if possible.
- Some antivirus software developers, such as Symantec, have begun to charge for updates after a specific number of free updates. Take into account the cost and management effort required to pay for these updates.

The Office 2000 Antivirus Application Programming Interface

Although most leading antivirus solutions can recognize macro viruses in Office 2000 documents, more timely and thorough virus checking would be welcome. To this end, Microsoft has introduced an Antivirus Application Programming Interface (API) that enables antivirus software vendors to embed hooks from their software directly into Office.

For instance, antivirus software that supports this API could automatically check every document a user opens from the File, Open dialog box in an Office application. The antivirus software could also provide more detailed and informative messages than those included in Office itself.

Be aware, however, that the mere presence of this API is no guarantee that your antivirus software uses it. At press time, two vendors—Network Associates and Trend Micro—had announced their plans to support this API, but had not yet actually released products with this support. Two other vendors, Symantec and Computer Associates, had not yet publicly announced their plans.

If virus software installed on a workstation supports the Antivirus API, the words Virus Scanner(s) Installed appear at the bottom of the Security dialog box. Otherwise, the words No Virus Scanner Installed appear (refer to Figure 38.9)—even if you are running a conventional virus scanner that is perfectly capable of catching Office 2000 viruses.

Part
VI

Ch
38

How Office Applications Handle VBA Macros Saved with Web Pages

When a user saves a binary Office document (such as a DOC file) that contains macros as a Web page, the macros are stored in a separate data file in the same folder as the HTML file. This data file is named EDITDATA.MSO. Earlier antivirus software might not be able to recognize that macro viruses are present in EDITDATA.MSO—yet another reason to be sure your antivirus protection is absolutely up-to-date.

If the Web page is subsequently opened in a browser, the macros cannot run. However, if a user opens the file for editing in a Microsoft Office application (for example, by choosing **Edit, Edit with Microsoft Word for Windows**), the macros run unless prevented from doing so by your existing security settings.

Securing Access Databases

Microsoft Access provides several complementary means of limiting access to databases. These include the following:

- Restricting user access through startup options
- Requiring a password to open a database
- Protecting the source code in a database by saving it as an MDE file
- Encrypting a database to prevent it from being viewed with a text or disk editor
- Setting user-level security similar to that provided for files and folders in NT Server and other network operating systems

Each of these options is covered briefly in the following text. They represent all the security many organizations will ever need. If database security is truly business-critical to your organization, however, you might want to read the following quote from a Microsoft-published paper titled *Microsoft Access for Windows 95 Security*:

"Microsoft Access is designed to be the most secure desktop database management system you can buy. However, it has no security rating with the U.S. government or any other certifying body, and it is not guaranteed by Microsoft to be secure. Skilled hackers with enough time and computing resources, and a desire to break into your database, could crack Microsoft Access security. If you have applications that require absolute security, you should consider using a server database such as Microsoft SQL Server on the Microsoft Windows NT operating system, and a compiled application programming language such as Microsoft Visual C/C++."

Restricting User Access Through Startup Options

If your security needs are not extensive, and you aren't protecting your database against sophisticated users, one option is to use startup options. You can use these to restrict access for the following:

- Default menus
- Toolbars
- The database window
- Special keys

The following procedure assumes that you have created a startup form and custom menu bar that includes the commands to which you do want users to have access.

To restrict user access through startup options, follow these steps:

1. Choose **Tools**, **Startup**.
2. Choose the startup form you want to use from the Display Form drop-down box.
3. Choose the custom menu bar you want from the Menu Bar drop-down box.
4. Click the **Advanced** button (see Figure 38.12).
5. Clear these check boxes:
   - Allow Full Menus
   - Allow Default Shortcut Menus
   - Display Database Window
   - Allow Built-in Toolbars
   - Allow Toolbar/Menu Changes
   - Use Access Special Keys
6. Click **OK**.

CAUTION

Users who are familiar with Access can still bypass these settings by pressing **Shift** as Access loads the database. You can set the database's Visual Basic property AllowBypassKey to **False** to prevent this.

FIGURE 38.12
Controlling Access
Startup to enhance
security.

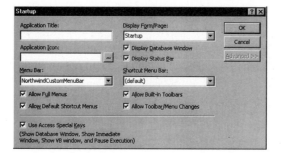

Requiring a Password to Open an Access Database

Like Word and Excel, Access enables you to password-protect a database, thereby preventing users from opening it unless they have the password.

> **N O T E** Unlike Word and Excel, Access' password-protection feature does not control the rights users have to modify a database. This is done with user-level security features, as described later. ▨

To password-protect a database, open the database and follow these steps:

1. Choose **Tools**, **Security**, **Set Database Password** (see Figure 38.13).
2. Enter your password in the **Password** box, and click **OK**.
3. Confirm your password in the **Verify** box, and click **OK**.

FIGURE 38.13
Controlling Access
startup to enhance
security.

> **CAUTION**
>
> Although it is always important that your organization have a secure way to access passwords used by individuals who work there, this is even more critical with Access databases, which almost always store information of critical value to large numbers of people.

Protecting Access Database Source Code

In Access 2000, you can save a database as an MDE file that contains all the information but none of the Visual Basic source code that you might want to protect. Working in an MDE file, users have access to tables, queries, relationships, and macros. However, users cannot view, modify, create, import, or export reports, forms, or modules.

Microsoft points out that creating an MDE file could make it more difficult to keep data consistent; users might be entering different information in MDB and MDE files, which would then have to be reconciled. As a result, Microsoft suggests using MDE files as front ends to applications where the data is stored in a single database on the back-end database server.

To create an MDE file from an existing database, perform the following steps:

1. Choose **File**, **Close** to close the database.
2. Choose **Tools**, **Database Utilities**, **Make MDE File**. The Save As MDE dialog box opens.
3. Browse to and select the database from which you want to create an MDE file.
4. Click the **Make MDE** button. The Save MDE As dialog box opens (see Figure 38.14).
5. Enter a filename and click **MDE Files(*.mde)** in the **Save as type** drop-down list box.

FIGURE 38.14
Creating an Access
MDE file.

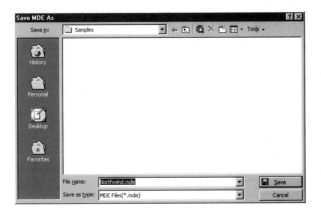

CAUTION

Because it's likely that you'll need to edit reports, forms, or modules, be sure you keep a current backup of the database.

MDE files are not runtime files: They still require the presence of Access 2000 to run. However, if you want to provide database information to a user who does not have Access 2000 installed, such as a user of Microsoft Office Standard Edition or Small Business Edition, you can do so in two ways. Using tools in Microsoft Office 2000 Professional Edition, you can create a runtime file from an MDE file. You also can use the Access Snapshot Viewer, as is covered in the following section.

Using the Access Snapshot Viewer

Using the Access Snapshot Viewer, distribute a *static snapshot* of an Access report containing only the specific data you want to share. By default, the Access Snapshot Viewer installs on first run. To use it, open the database and follow these steps:

1. Click the name of the report you want to take a snapshot of.
2. Choose **File**, **Export**.
3. Choose **Snapshot Format** in the Save as type dialog box.
4. Browse to, and select, the location where you want to save the snapshot.
5. Enter the snapshot's filename in the **File name** text box.
6. Click **Save**.

Encrypting Access Databases

Access databases can be encrypted using the same RC4 encryption algorithm available to other Office applications, except in France where RC4 is illegal. When encrypted, a text editor or any other utility cannot read Access databases.

As with most security precautions, there is a tradeoff; in this case, it's a performance penalty of approximately 15%. Keep in mind that encryption is useful only if you have already secured your database with passwords or other techniques: Otherwise, users can simply open the encrypted database and get access to all its data and code, just as if it were not encrypted.

To encrypt a database, you must either own the database or be a member of its Admin group. Choose **Tools**, **Security**, **Encrypt/Decrypt Database** to display the Encrypt/Decrypt Database dialog box. Here, you select the name of the database you want to encrypt, and choose **OK**. The same dialog box appears again, with a new database name listed in the File name box. Edit the name as needed, and click **Save**. Access creates a separate, encrypted copy of your original database.

If you choose to save the encrypted database with the same name and in the same location as the original, Access first proceeds through the entire encryption. After encryption has been successful, it deletes the original unencrypted file.

Providing User-Level Security

Access 2000 provides both share-level and user-level security. Share-level security assigns passwords to individual databases, as you've already seen. In Access 2000, user-level security looks a lot more like the rights and permissions you might expect to use with folders and files on a Windows NT Server (or NetWare)-based network.

As an Office administrator, you can grant specific permissions to individuals or groups of users for specific actions they can take on specific objects. When the user logs onto Access, he enters a name and password. Then, every time he attempts to perform an action—such as reading data or modifying the database design—Access checks its internal workgroup information file, to see whether the user has the right to perform this action. If so, the user can keep working; if not, the user encounters a message box stating that permission is denied. By default, all users have rights to perform all actions on all objects, unless you specify otherwise.

To secure a database with user-level security, choose **Tools**, **Security**, **User-Level Security Wizard**. The User-Level Security Wizard runs. By default, this is an Install on First Run feature, so Office might need to install it first. The Wizard walks you through the process of identifying which users and groups needs to work with your database; and which database objects you want to secure. After you've done so, it creates a new, secured copy of your database, with restricted permissions to those objects.

Combining Operating System Security with Application Security

You can enhance all the security mechanisms built into specific Office applications by using the security built into your network operating system.

Suppose that you are running Windows NT Server and you have a shared folder containing files to be used by your entire workgroup. One of these files, however, perhaps next year's salary projections, needs to be kept strictly confidential. If the file is stored on a network drive formatted with the NTFS file system (rather than FAT), you can set up file permissions so that only the individuals who should access that file can do so.

To limit a file's permissions to a specific user, perform the following steps:

1. Right-click the file in Windows NT Explorer.

2. Click **Properties**. The Properties dialog box opens, listing the properties associated with the file.

3. Click **Security** to display the Security tab (see Figure 38.15).

FIGURE 38.15
Setting the security for a file stored on an NTFS drive.

4. Click **Permissions**. The File Permissions dialog box opens (see Figure 38.16) showing that everyone currently has permission to access the file. (Windows NT doesn't know about any Word, Excel, or Access passwords that might be built into the file itself.)

FIGURE 38.16
Specifying exactly who
has access to a file on
an NTFS drive.

5. Be sure the **Everyone** group is selected, and click **Remove**. Now, nobody has access to the file.

6. Click **Add**. The Add Users and Groups dialog box opens.

7. Click **Show Users** to display a list of the users on your network.

8. Select the name of the user you want to have access to the file.

9. Choose **Full Control** from the Type of Access drop-down box.

10. Click **OK** three times.

In NetWare 4.x, 5.x and IntranetWare 4.x, you can achieve much the same result by setting file system trustee rights using the NetWare Administrator Windows-based utility.

Part
VI

Ch
38

Integrating Office with Document Management Systems

Yet another way to improve the security of Office documents is to integrate Office with an Open Document Management (ODMA)-compatible Document Management System. Systems such as these typically replace the Open and Save dialog boxes in Office applications, providing more sophisticated options, including security features such as the following:

■ More control over accessing, moving, or removing documents

■ Mechanisms that enable documents to be checked out and returned

■ Locks on documents

■ Security mechanisms that follow distributed documents

N O T E FrontPage 2000 offers check-in/check-out features for Web pages, but these are easily evaded. ■

Suppliers of ODMA-compliant Document Management Systems include the following:

■ Documentum, Inc. (888-362-3767, **www.documentum.com**)

■ Novell Groupwise (801-222-6000, **www.novell.com/groupwise**)

■ PC DOCS, Inc. (800-937-3627, **www.pcdocs.com**)

■ Saros (800-827-2767, **www.saros.com**) ●

Supporting Microsoft Office 2000

by Bill Camarda

No sizable organization on Earth can succeed with Microsoft Office 2000 without providing quality support to its users. Support means ensuring that users can get reliable answers on a timely basis. It also means anticipating their problems with quality up-front help and training so that they can accomplish their tasks more effectively and become increasingly confident in the tools they depend on.

This chapter covers key support techniques associated with building a quality Office help desk, including new Office 2000 features that enable you to build customized program Help.

NOTE In Chapter 40, "Finding Office Training and Self-Help Solutions," you learn about resources and techniques for helping users train themselves and solve their own problems. ■

Defining the Office Help Desk: A Brief Overview

A help desk exists to serve the needs of technology users. Whether your organization is large or small, you probably have some incarnation of a help desk; perhaps it consists of one part-time volunteer (who already has a full-time job), or perhaps you have a full-time support department. Your help desk might exist as a phone number for users to call when they are having trouble, or it might include a live person who comes to users' aid. The sole purpose of a help desk is to get the user of technology productive again, as soon as possible.

Who Pays for Help Desk Support?

To keep things in perspective, remember that a help desk is usually considered overhead in an organization. The cost of maintaining a help desk comes right out of company profits, and businesses typically attempt to minimize such costs. Unfortunately, with the growing complexity of applications such as Microsoft Office, the help desk is needed now more than ever. And this issue is not unique to a particular business—the escalating costs of support are affecting businesses in all industries.

Help desks must cover a wide range of subjects, from basic hardware to detailed feature levels of program applications. This chapter suggests ways to make Office support and the associated administrative functions a little bit easier.

Common Goals for All Help Desks

The purpose of a help desk is to assist users in resolving difficulties that arise while using their computers. Effective assistance includes good communication, the ability to solve problems, and a system that incorporates the knowledge and experience that you have gained from solving past problems. After you have a help desk in place, you'll want to measure its effectiveness, but before you can do that, you'll need to define your goals.

Common help desk goals include the following:

- **Provide users with a single, centralized source for the help they need.** In organizations without help desks, the costs of help are buried organizationwide, as users get help wherever they can find it: from power users, long wasteful Internet searches, or other means. A centralized help desk can deliver solutions faster, without the inefficiency of catch-as-catch-can help.

- **Provide the organization with detailed, centralized information on the problems users are having.** The best way to reduce support costs is to understand in greater depth the problems your users are encountering and to provide practical means for users to solve their own problems.

- **Provide expert coverage of targeted subject material.** Becoming an expert on all features of a given product might not be possible, but the help desk should always be an expert on the products and features required by your organization. Technical reference material should be readily available (several are recommended later in this chapter), including Microsoft TechNet and the Knowledge Bases.

- **Provide quick problem resolution.** When a problem comes to the attention of the help desk, it should be resolved within set time parameters or guidelines. Tracking tools are usually required to maintain consistency and measure

- **Minimize involvement of help desk personnel.** Also known as *call avoidance*, this strategy attempts to make all users self-sufficient. Doing so requires training of users in the required applications, availability of self-help resources, and—often— implementation of policies and procedures.

- **Reduce actual visits of a support technician.** Having a technician walk over and assist a user is usually the most expensive method of support (although the most preferred by users). Software tools are available for controlling the user's computer screen from a remote location, enabling you to talk them through a problem without visiting them in person.

- **Build on existing talent and knowledge base.** If your users have previously been trained in WordPerfect, respect that knowledge and encourage them to use the WordPerfect help features in Word. If you notice users developing specialized skills, encourage them to be a resource for peers.

N O T E For more information about building and maintaining quality help desks, **see** Philip Verghis' Help Desk FAQ at **www.philverghis.com/helpdeskfaq.html**. If you're serious about getting involved with help desks, you should also read *Support Management* Magazine, accessible at **www.supportmanagement.com**. ▨

Strategies for Improving Your Help Desk

These common-sense strategies can help you build a much more effective help desk:

- **Set clear goals for your help desk.** This isn't as obvious as it sounds. For example, do you want your help desk staffers to focus on solving a user's problem as quickly as possible, or on helping the user understand the problem, so he or she can avoid it next time? These are both laudable goals, but they conflict. Be sure your support staff understands your true priorities.

- **Respect the challenge of delivering quality support.** Competent support people are rare and highly sought after. To keep yours from leaving, provide competitive pay and opportunities for advancement. Perhaps equally important, try to avoid burnout by providing diversity: Rotate job functions and tasks as much as possible, and be sure your best people get challenges worthy of their skills.

- **Next time you're ready to hire, look in nontraditional locations.** For instance, try colleges and universities. Also, be conscious of overcoming the high-tech industry's traditional aversion to hiring older employees.

- **Be sure you give your support people the support they need.** Provide detailed technical resources, preferably online, in the most convenient possible way.

■ **Use the feedback you get from users.** If users keep tripping over the same problem, offer them a global solution—a shortcut, a macro, a special help page on your intranet, a weekly email tip. Whatever the best option, be proactive—so your support staff won't have to keep solving the same problems repeatedly.

One Size Does Not Fit All

Particular needs of any organization vary, and so will the organization's underlying support structure. The most effective help desk is designed according to business requirements. The amount of staffing might range from less than a single individual with general knowledge to a fully supervised and managed department of technical specialists.

From a business perspective, the best help desk is lean and mean, with the fewest number of dedicated technicians able to cover the widest range of problems.

Help desks large enough to appear on the company organizational chart usually start with a minimum of one to three generalists, and with three or more, they develop a hierarchy of specialty and supervisory responsibility. Larger organizations often specify minimum support headcount ratios, such as one support person for every 40–50 users, but suggesting a recommended ratio outside the context of your particular business is meaningless. At a minimum, management should observe the effectiveness and potential of the help desk and allocate resources accordingly.

Outsourcing is a method of supplementing, or replacing, your help desk function. When you *outsource*, you pay an external organization to provide technical support to yours. Support implementation might include software tools, telephone numbers to call, or even onsite technicians. Sometimes, a company turns to outsourcing when the help desk fails to meet expectations.

Change with the Times

Your help desk should be flexible. Understand your business operations and the nature of tasks performed; try to provide the required training to get the tasks accomplished. After establishing this base knowledge, you can quickly move on to advanced support. Actually, you'll have no choice, because support requirements change as users become more proficient—they start asking more complex questions.

A new installation of Office requires support on basic Office functions, such as file creation, saving, and importing of existing information. When the dust settles, users start asking about formatting features, integrating other applications, and so on. Experienced users start demanding more complex training on advanced features, and the help desk is charged with meeting this demand.

Know Your Target Audience

To run an effective help desk, you have to know your audience. Understand your users' priorities and what they need from technology. Users don't always have the time for you to ask such questions, but you can observe the tasks they accomplish and determine the role of technology in your organization.

The *80:20 rule* applies well to the help desk. This rule suggests that 80% of your time and effort will be spent satisfying 20% of your user population. This group includes both your brightest workers and your novices, who stand out because of some particular requirement the majority of your users either never notice or choose to ignore. Come up with a strategy in advance to handle this 20%, and you can save yourself many headaches.

These are the people who impact your support efforts the most:

- Busy people who have no time for training classes but expect personal service at their convenience. You'll waste time repeating material previously available in class. *Strategy*: Schedule training classes at a variety of times; provide alternative forms of education; give them easy access to self-help tools.

- Fearful people who tend to avoid technology (fear of breaking something, fear of public display of their ignorance, and so on). They stick with what they know, avoiding features or methods that might make their lives easier. *Strategy*: Demonstrate tasks with recordings; provide help via remote-control programs; find them a technology mentor; start a support group.

- Stubborn people who believe they are experts, refuse to listen to others, and in the end do things their own way. They tend to ignore procedures and policies they don't understand. *Strategy*: Implement System Policies for Office (see Chapter 37); educate them in the value of standardization; convince them they are part of the ultimate solution.

- People who simply don't care and are probably in the wrong job. They aren't consistent in how they use technology and don't care about the resulting impact on others. *Strategy*: Suggest that computer skills are valuable for anyone; demonstrate the impact of not following standards in the organization; ask management for assistance with these individuals.

When the Help Desk Fails

If you don't handle these individuals properly, they're likely to have a negative impact on your company. Errant users tend to stray from the imposed standards created for efficiency. For example, one standard might state that Word documents are to be created with consistent styles to foster workgroup productivity and document reuse. If people ignore this simple rule, they nullify any productivity gains from Word features, such as the table of contents or authorities in the later stages of document construction, and their work might require hours of cleanup effort. A single poorly constructed document can have a chain-reaction effect that impacts other employees, managers, executives, administrative assistants, and support staff (even temporary staffing agencies) and might even result in missed deadlines and lost business.

Measuring Help Desk Effectiveness

When an organization invests in an official help desk, it then wants to know whether it's getting its money's worth. One way to measure effectiveness is to record the frequency and outcome of a particular activity. A common example is the number of help desk phone calls answered per day. In itself, this number might not hold much information (you don't know the nature of the call, whether the user was actually helped, and so on), so refine your measurements until they align with your intended goals.

- How many calls are related to Word versus Excel or Access?
- How long does it take to solve the average page-formatting problem?
- How many users have called about a troublesome template?
- Is a particular department demanding a disproportionate amount of the help desk resources?
- Are users beginning to ask about a rarely used feature? Perhaps the technology needs of your users have changed. If so, the help desk must adapt accordingly to maintain effectiveness.

A successful help desk continually asks itself these types of questions, and acts accordingly. When the help desk is comfortable that it can provide a guaranteed level of support, it communicates this information to the users in what is known as a service-level agreement.

A service-level agreement is, in essence, a contract between the help desk and the users. The help desk agrees, for example, to return all calls within an hour. This simple agreement sets expectations for everyone. Now your users know they can call the help desk, leave a message, and expect a response in a reasonable time period. User satisfaction with the help desk typically increases after you establish minimum service-level agreements. However, a help desk that does not live up to published agreements can quickly become perceived as ineffective. In this example, if the help desk fails to respond within an hour, the users will want to know why they aren't getting the attention they deserve.

Other examples of service-level agreements include

- Designation of supported and nonsupported applications (making it easier for the help desk to say "no")
- Definitions of what is considered an emergency call versus merely high or low priority (removing the politics from assigning call priority)
- Off-hour and weekend support availability
- Guaranteed closure to all calls within a given time period

Creating and Tracking Trouble Tickets   Most organizations benefit from maintaining a record of solved help desk problems. One option for doing this is to create a printed help-desk ticket, or *trouble ticket*, for each incident. At a minimum, a trouble ticket should include the time and date, who asked for help, and the problem resolution. If you gather such information, anyone can sort through it to determine how well the help desk is performing.

CAUTION
Unfortunately, the trouble ticket doesn't always provide the whole story. The best measure of a help desk's effectiveness is not the quantity of tickets you process, but the quality of the solutions you provide.

A better system than the printed trouble ticket is a paperless database. A database is easy enough to create, and it provides the obvious benefits of letting you sort, track, and maintain online trouble tickets. Furthermore, you can analyze the data to track trends and measure the effectiveness of the help desk. You can also let users access the database so they can search for solutions on their own.

To start your paperless system, create an online trouble ticket. Depending on your needs and skills, you can design your trouble ticket by using Word, Excel, Access, Outlook (or any combination of these applications), and then save it as a template or form. Here are the key elements typically included:

- Automated data and time field
- User identification from a pop-up list
- Subject category for problem from a pop-up list
- Urgency checklist
- Data entry fields for problem details
- Data entry fields for problem tracking and resolution

You can purchase help desk software in all sizes, prices, and configurations. On one end are simple desktop systems such as WN Help Desk from Wickett.Net, which integrates with Office—its system is based on the Access 97 database engine, and you can send work orders to Microsoft Outlook task lists, and track service statistics with Microsoft Excel. At the other extreme are enterprisewide systems such as Remedy Help Desk 4.0 (`www.remedy.com/itsm/ helpdesk.htm`) that can pass along trouble tickets from help desks in one time zone to another, to help you provide 24-hours-a-day, 7-days-a-week support worldwide.

Building Your Own Trouble Ticket Software with Access and Excel   If your needs are not especially complex, you can create your own help desk software using Office 2000. You might build it in Access, possibly by adapting the Service Call Management Wizard (although this Wizard seems designed more for onsite service calls, such as might be made by an appliance repair company).

Another solution is to use the Template Wizard with Data Tracking in Microsoft Excel. With this Wizard, you can use a new copy of a Help Desk form every time you need one. When you create the wizard, Excel automatically creates a companion Excel worksheet or Access database; then, whenever you save a new form, the information is automatically transferred into the database.

First, create your form. Use techniques such as list boxes and combo boxes to streamline data entry: The more you can simplify filling out the form, the more likely it will actually be filled out in detail, and the more useful it will become in tracking. Figure 39.1 shows a basic data entry form created in Excel.

FIGURE 39.1

A typical data entry form created in Excel.

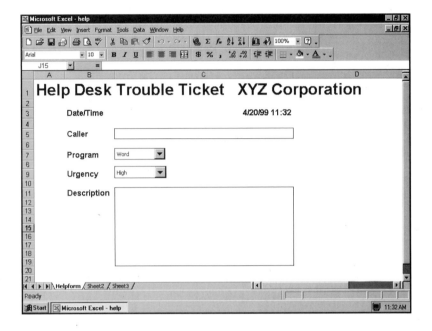

Next, choose **Data, Template Wizard**. The Template Wizard with Data Tracking opens (see Figure 39.2). In the following steps, you'll walk through using this Wizard:

FIGURE 39.2

The Template Wizard with Data Tracking.

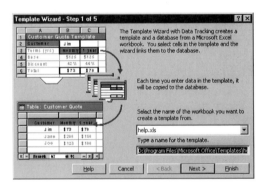

1. In step 1 of the Wizard, specify from which open workbook you want to create the template, and then name the template. Click **Next** to continue.

2. In step 2 of the Wizard, specify whether you want to create your database in Excel or Access, and where you want it to go. Click **Next** to continue.

3. In step 3 of the Wizard (see Figure 39.3), specify the cells in your worksheet that contain the data you want to use; and the cells in your worksheet that correspond to the field names you want to use in your database. In our example, the field names are Date/Time, Caller, Program, Urgency, and Description. When you're finished, click **Next** to continue.

4. In step 4 of the Wizard, you're given the option of including data from existing workbook files that are already organized the same way as the template you're creating. If you have these files, click **Yes**; specify the files, and click **Next** to continue. If you do not have any such files, click **Next** now.

5. Click **Finish** to complete the Wizard and create the template or database you want to build.

FIGURE 39.3
Specifying cells corresponding to data and field names.

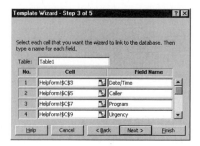

After you create your template, store it on a network share available to the help desk staff, and start using it. You'll find that taking advantage of your form's time and date stamp, user information, subject categories, and notes about problem resolution will improve your accuracy and save you a lot of time.

If your users are cooperative, you might even ask them to fill in and track their own online trouble tickets. They might prefer this option to calling the help desk, especially if you include some sort of automated immediate response informing them you're receiving and processing their call. Once again, make it as easy as possible to include all necessary information without any hassle. The user can choose the most appropriate problem category from a list in the form and describe the necessary details. The benefit of letting the users fill in the form is that they become more involved in problem resolution. If your form includes links to the support site on your intranet, users might even be able to find the information they need without even submitting the ticket.

Training Users for an Office Upgrade

The more time and resources you have invested in your previous office software, the more challenging it can become to prepare users for the switchover to Microsoft Office. Most people don't take change lightly, especially change that affects the tools they use every day to make a living. The only solution is careful planning and a thorough understanding of your users' real needs.

Understanding the Previous Work Environment

If you are migrating from an earlier version of Microsoft Office, some of your training is already done: The latest versions share much of the user interface of their predecessors. If you are migrating from non-Microsoft office applications, such as WordPerfect, or from non-PC environments, the impact of the change can be more significant, and productivity is at greater risk.

Planning begins with understanding the previous work environment. Be sure to allow enough time to do the appropriate research. You'll be much closer to a smooth migration when you can answer these questions for your users:

- Where is our previous work stored? Can we still use it?
- How do we create new work?
- Where should we store things? How can we find our work after we create it?

Soon after the initial panic, users become aware that many of the old familiar features also exist in the new applications, but they don't know how to use them. Be sure that you don't bombard users with all the features of Office 2000 at once. Analyze how work was accomplished previously, and break it down into discrete tasks. Now convert each task into a set of steps that use comparable features in Office. You might need to prepare lots of these new tasks, and different users in your organization might require completely different tasks, but users will be much happier when they have a proven solution to follow.

Demonstrating the New Office Environment to a Pilot Group

Successful rollouts of Office require careful planning. Getting early feedback from selected users, such as a pilot group, is an effective way to ensure that you are staffed to provide the required training and assistance. The sooner you can expose yourself and your users to the new Office environment, the less likely you are to forget something important, such as required filters, templates, accessible storage locations, and so on. Perhaps you can set up a computer, or a whole training room of computers, with the Office suite to allow users to experience the new environment before it is imposed on them. You can start winning their support and confidence with actions such as these:

- Demonstrate how tasks are accomplished in Office 2000. Be sure to include any custom toolbar buttons you have designed to make life easier.
- Use language they can relate to (such as "We used to press this key combination; now we click this button.")
- After demonstrating a task, do it again, and this time pretend you've forgotten what to do next, so you can demonstrate how to use all the available help to finish the task.
- Start exposing them to new ways of doing things, and ask their opinion on whether various features are valuable. Be sure to include the exciting stuff such as Find and Replace, AutoCorrect, or how to customize the Office bar to clean up a desktop full of shortcuts.

Don't expect your users to love Office immediately. For example, users coming to Word from a WordPerfect background might be terror-stricken when they realize there is no Reveal Codes. You can, of course, explain the alternatives to Reveal Codes in Word, but this change and some others require a period of adjustment on the part of your users.

Create a plan for handling bugs and software glitches. Users need to understand the value of the AutoSave feature in Office products, and they need to know how it works. (For example, they need to know that documents that were open when an application crashed will be labeled as Recovered the next time they start the application.) The possibility always exists that documents, workbooks, presentations, and databases will become corrupted and require repair. The ideal repair procedure is specific to your organization. You should document it and make it available to all users.

Promoting Awareness of Available Help

You don't want to beswamped with support issues, so publicize every avenue of technical assistance available to your users. Built-in Office help features should be among the first training items on your agenda. Getting a user to try the help features is more than half the battle. Users typically get the answer they are looking for from the Office Assistant on their first attempt, and if they try to construct their questions to the Office Assistant more carefully, their likelihood of success increases dramatically. If they don't like the Office Assistant, you can customize it to suit their preferences.

Planning for an Office Upgrade

As a technical support professional, you want the migration to Microsoft Office to be as smooth as possible. This book, together with the downloadable Office 2000 Resource Kit, should provide most of the planning documentation you will need. The next sections discuss the most important upgrade-related issues.

Preparing Your Support Professionals

If you lead a team of professionals who support Office 2000, your first goal is to be sure they understand the software well enough to help users solve their problems. One option is to train and certify your support professionals as *Microsoft Office User Specialists* (MOUS).

The program offers three levels of certification:

- **Master Certification** indicates that a user has a comprehensive understanding of all five key Office 2000 programs: Word, Excel, PowerPoint, Access, and Outlook.

- **Expert Certification** indicates that a user has a thorough understanding of the advanced features of one key Office 2000 program: Word, Excel, PowerPoint, Access, or Outlook.

- **Core Certification** indicates that a user has a thorough understanding of the core features of one key Office 2000 program: Word, Excel, PowerPoint, Access, or Outlook.

You can use these certifications to provide targeted staffing support for individual programs, or use the certifications as a way of providing an escalation path, with Expert Level and Master Level help desk staffers taking the toughest problems.

NOTE The MOUS program started in early 1998 and is not yet as popular as other Microsoft training programs, such as MCSE and MCSD training. As a result, you might find it difficult to hire MOUS-certified professionals. The program might best be used to ensure that your onstaff help desk personnel and trainers have the skills they need to support users. ■

N O T E To help your colleagues prepare for MOUS certification, consider the following books
from Que:

- *Microsoft Word 2000 MOUS Cheat Sheet*
- *Microsoft Excel 2000 MOUS Cheat Sheet*
- *Microsoft Access 2000 MOUS Cheat Sheet* ▓

Supporting the Migration Process

If you are migrating to Office from another product, computer system, or mainframe, you
need to be sure users can still access the work they created under the old system. You have
a few choices for handling this issue:

- **Convert all old work to new Office 2000 files before allowing any users to
  access it.** This requires a lot of up-front work, but eliminates most user problems
  relating to conversion and compatibility.

- **Leave old work where it is and allow users to access it directly, using Office
  2000 products.** You can install Office with the appropriate filters to automatically
  open and convert most existing formats.

- **Convert as much work as you can, and leave the remainder in the previous
  format.** For instance, convert everything created in the last year, and leave the rest
  to be converted on an as-needed basis.

The nitty-gritty of file conversions is covered in Chapter 18, "Migrating from or Coexisting
with Legacy Applications," and Chapter 19, "Managing Multiple Versions of Office."

Gather as much information as you can about how users created work on the old system.
This helps you decide which features and tools to make available when you roll out Office.

Supporting the Transition from WordPerfect

If your company is converting from WordPerfect, you might explore some of Word's features
designed to make the transition easier. To access these features, double-click the **WPH** box
on the status bar, or choose **Help, WordPerfect Help**. The Help for WordPerfect Users
dialog box opens.

N O T E By default, WordPerfect Help is installed on demand the first time users request it. If you
are migrating from WordPerfect, consider installing it locally on all workstations so users
don't have to waste time retrieving it. For more information about customizing Office 2000 installation, see Chapter 2, "Automating and Customizing Office Installations Across the Network." ▓

The Command Keys scroll box includes a list of WordPerfect for DOS Command keys. When
you select a command key, Word displays a description of how to accomplish the same task in
Word 2000. If Word offers additional help for any key submenus, the Command Key is followed by an ellipsis. You can view the additional information by clicking on **Help Text**. When

you've arrived at the bottom level of information, you can click **Help Text** again, and Word displays the help information over your document window so you can view the information and perform the task at the same time.

TIP If your users are coming from a WordPerfect background, they are likely to be more comfortable with keyboard shortcuts than the mouse. And anyone who can speed type usually avoids the mouse at all costs. Publish the keyboard shortcuts found on the Help Topics Index tab (search for *shortcut keys*) and click the Print button. They'll thank you for it.

Word can also provide demonstrations of equivalent features when a user types a recognized WordPerfect for DOS key combination. To see these demos, choose **Help**, **WordPerfect Help**. Click **Options** to display the Help Options dialog box, and select the **Help for WordPerfect Users** check box. Word now monitors the keyboard, and if it catches you pressing a WordPerfect key combination, it automatically demonstrates the new way to do it in Word. While this option is selected, the WPH box on the status bar is highlighted.

Depending on the speed of your computer, you might find these feature demonstrations run either too quickly or too slowly. You can change the speed by opening the **Help Options** dialog box and choosing **Fast**, **Medium**, or **Slow** in the Demo Speed drop-down box.

The Help Options dialog box also contains a Navigation Keys for WordPerfect Users check box. If you select this option, the functions of the Page Up, Page Down, Home, End, and Esc keys change to their WordPerfect equivalents.

▶ For information about using Word's Compatibility options to control how WordPerfect documents are imported into Word, **see** Chapter 18, "Migrating from or Coexisting with Legacy Applications," on **p. 481**.

Part
VI

Ch
39

Strategies for Minimizing Support Problems

Even under the best of circumstances, you're likely to have continuing support issues with an Office installation. Although there are no magic answers, some of these tips might help you minimize problems:

- **Create a feedback mechanism to receive information and complaints from your users.** If you're getting a lot of calls on a particular feature or function, publicize the method or solution to everyone. You can post solutions in Outlook folders, or modify training classes to incorporate new information.

- **Get the training required to support your users.** If you can't attend traditional classes, consider alternative education, such as Web training, videos, or interactive CD-ROM courseware.

- **Communicate with your users.** Try to use as many different ways to get computer know-how into their heads as you can—different users respond to different methods. Some methods you might use include informal luncheon workshops, published newsletters, internal and external training classes, books, recordings, and videos.

■ **Obtain the necessary support tools, whether books, videos, or software.**
Several of each are discussed later in this chapter.

N O T E　When you understand the needs of your users, customize the Office products yourself.
Create simpler toolbars by eliminating buttons that are rarely used, or try creating new
toolbars that focus on a custom business process and name them accordingly. For example, you
might create a toolbar called Billing that contains custom buttons for choosing templates, inserting
AutoText entries, and saving and printing. Users can later learn how to customize and expand their
own toolbars, as their experience and skills grow. ■

Customized Help for Forms

If you are developing any custom forms, databases, or applications within your Office environment, put in the extra effort to include custom Help files. Word and Excel make two levels of help available for form fields: status bar and help key. Status Bar help displays a line of context-sensitive guidance (up to 83 characters) in the status bar when the user activates the form field. The Help Key feature displays help text (up to 255 characters) for the active form field when the user presses the **F1** key.

To add help to your form fields, follow these steps:

1. Double-click the desired form field.
2. In the Form Field Options dialog box, click the **Add Help Text** button.
3. If you want context-sensitive help to appear on the status bar, click the **Status Bar** tab.
4. To use an AutoText entry for the help text, click the **AutoText Entry** option button and select the entry from the drop-down box.
5. To type the help text, click the **Type Your Own** option button and type the text in the large text area.
6. If you want context-sensitive help to appear when the user presses F1, click the **Help Key (F1)** tab and follow steps 4 and 5.
7. Click **OK** when you finish.
8. Lock the form by using the **Protect Form** button on the Forms toolbar.

You can use both help features together. For example, if you have constructed an expense account form, you might create Status Bar help for a form field that says, "Enter total meal cost—press **F1** to list allowable meal expenses by city." You can then create Help Key text for the same form field, listing the allowable meal expenses by city.

Customizing Built-In Error Messages

If you support Office, the following might be a common scenario: A user sits down at a new PC that hasn't yet been configured with a local printer, creates a new document, and then clicks the Print button. Instead of printing, the computer beeps and displays an error message indicating that a problem exists with the current printer. The error message might provide some generic advice, as shown in Figure 39.4, but that advice is often insufficient to help the user solve his or her own problem. For example, even if a user could figure out how to connect a network printer, she would be unlikely to know where on your network the printers are located, or what names you've given them.

FIGURE 39.4
A typical Office 2000 error message.

What happens next? In previous versions of Office, the answer was pretty much inevitable: you would get an expensive help desk call. In Office 2000, you might be able to head off that help desk call by providing specific enough information to users that they really can solve problems like these themselves.

Creating your own custom error messages is a four-step process:

- Assemble the codes that identify each error message, application, and language for which you want to create custom messages
- Build Web pages with the information you want your users to see
- Create Active Server Page (ASP) scripts for your custom error messages
- Enable custom error messages before or after you deploy Office 2000

N O T E   You must run your custom error messages on a Web server that supports Active Server Pages. This typically limits you to using Internet Information Server 4 running on Windows NT Server. However, if your requirements are light, you might try Personal Web Server for Windows 98 or Windows NT Workstation 4.0.

If it makes business sense, you can keep running other intranet or Web services on the server of your choice, while creating a separate Web server for supporting Microsoft Office. One possible strategy: to set aside a single NT Server system running IIS4 to handle support tasks and also Web document collaboration, using the new Office Server Extensions.

If you do set aside a separate server for these purposes, you might consider assigning it a private IP address that cannot route through the Internet, for security purposes. IP addresses set aside for this purpose include

10.0.0.0–10.255.255.255

172.16.0.0–172.31.255.255

192.168.0.0–192.168.255.255 ▦

Part

VI

Ch

39

Assuming your Web server is up and running, your first step is to gather the information and make the decisions you need to successfully customize your error messages. The following sections walk you through each step of the process.

Collecting Office Error Codes and Deciding Which Ones to Customize

Begin by determining which error messages you want to customize, and finding the error message numbers for each of these messages. This information can be found in the Excel workbook Errormsg.xls, which is included in the Office 2000 Resource Kit and downloadable at **www.microsoft.com/office/ork/2000/appndx/toolbox.htm**.

If you install Errormsg.xls as part of the Office 2000 Resource Kit toolkit, it can be reached from the Desktop by choosing **Start**, **Programs**, **Microsoft Office Tools**, **Microsoft Office 2000 Resource Kit Documents**, **Customizable Alerts**. Figure 39.5 shows this file displayed in Excel 2000.

FIGURE 39.5

The Errormsg.xls file, displaying error messages from Word 2000.

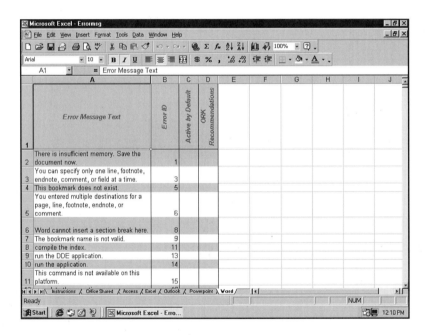

In the fourth column, ORK Recommendations, Microsoft suggests which error messages might be worth customizing. Microsoft's recommendations for Word, Access, Excel, and PowerPoint are summarized in Tables 39.2 through 39.5. Microsoft recommends no customizations for Outlook or for Office Shared components. You can, of course, review Errormsg.xls and choose to customize any messages you want. Many Office administrators are likely to customize relatively few, perhaps limiting the customization to certain categories of problems, such as printing or file access.

Table 39.1   Word Error Messages Microsoft Suggests Customizing

Error Message	Error ID
There is a serious disk error on file [Name of file]	23
The file [Name of file] is not available.	24
The document name or path is not valid. Try these suggestions...	25
The password is incorrect. Word cannot overwrite the document.	39
Cannot print. There is no printer installed.	44
Windows cannot print due to a problem with the current printer setup. Try one or more of the following...	46
There is a printer error.	120
No printers are installed. To install a printer, point to **Settings** on the Windows Start menu, click **Printers**, and then double-click **Add Printer**. Follow the instructions in the wizard.	121
There is an unrecoverable disk error on file [Name of file]. The disk you're working on has a media problem that prevents Word from using it. Try the following...	190
Word cannot display this picture format.	245
The graphics filter was unable to convert this file.	286
The password is incorrect. Word cannot open the document.	312
The disk drive is not valid. The drive letter is incorrect or inaccessible. Check the disk drive letter or network drive you want to use, and then enter the correct drive letter in the path.	314
You do not have network permissions for this action.	360
A file error has occurred. Try one or more of the following...	364
The password is incorrect.	399
The active document is not a valid mail merge main document.	397
The network drive cannot be accessed without a password.	425
The network path is not valid.	426
The network password is not valid.	427
Could not successfully convert the picture metafile into drawing objects.	444
The file cannot be opened with write privileges.	458
Cannot print because there is no default printer selected. Please select a printer.	474
There has been a network or file permission error. The network connection may be lost.	486
Word could not merge the main document with the data source because the data records were empty or no data records matched your query options.	535

continues

Table 39.1   Continued

Error Message	Error ID
Could not open [Name of file] because it didn't contain a valid database...	553
Word could not merge these documents or insert this database.	566
Cannot make the requested network connection.	592
Word has lost data due to a bad network connection or missing floppy. Documents relying on this data are going to be saved and then closed.	719
No registered converter supports saving files in this format.	784
Word cannot bring up the properties dialog because the printer returned an error.	832
No registered converter supports reading files in this format.	843
Word cannot display this picture format because the correct graphics filter was not found.	871
Word could not load the e-mail envelope. This could be caused by a network connection problem or a problem with your Office installation.	934
Word cannot save [Format] files. The converter for this format can only open files.	32935
The current drive is not valid. A network connection may have been lost, the floppy drive door may be open, or the floppy drive may contain the wrong disk. Choose the **Yes** button to retry.	33022
Word failed reading from this file [Name of file]. Please restore the network connection [Name of connection] or replace the floppy disk and retry...	33121

Table 39.2   Access Error Messages Microsoft Suggests Customizing

Error Message	Error ID
The password you entered is incorrect.	20
The changes you made can't be saved. The save operation may have failed due to the temporary locking of the records by another user. Click **OK** to try again...	21
...doesn't support the format of the file [Name of file], so it can't load the picture...	24
...has encountered an error in compiling the Visual Basic code. You don't have permission to edit code; inform someone who does have permission about this error...	2155
There was a problem retrieving printer information... The object may have been sent to a printer that is unavailable...	2201
You must install a printer before you design, print, or preview...	2202
The dynamic-link library Commdlg failed: error code 0x [Error code]. The printer driver for the selected printer may be incorrectly installed...	2203
The default printer driver isn't set up correctly...	2204

Error Message	Error ID
The default printer driver isn't set up correctly...	2205
...couldn't print your object. Make sure that the specified printer is available...	2212
... can't open the file [Name of file]...	2220
The database [Name of database] needs to be repaired or isn't an Access 2000 database file...	2239
The file name you specified in the Picture property for a command button or toggle button can't be read. The file you specified may be corrupted...	2244
An error occurred while sending data to the OLE server (the application used to create the object). You may have tried to send too much data...	2260
...can't save your changes to this bound OLE object. Either you don't have permission to write to the record in which the object is stored, or the record is locked by another user...	2278
...can't write to the file. The network may not be working. Wait until the network is working, and then try again...	2284
...can't create the output file. You may be out of disk space on the destination drive. The network might not be working. Wait until the network is working, and then try again...	2285
...can't close the file. The network may not be working. Wait until the network is working, and then try again...	2286
...can't open the mail session. Check your mail application to make sure that its working properly...	2287
...can't attach the object; the message was not sent. The network may not be working. Wait until the network is working, and then try again...	2294
Unknown message recipient(s); the message was not sent...	2295
The password is invalid; the message wasn't sent...	2296
...can't output data now. The network may not be working. Wait until the network is working, and then try again...	2303
...can't save output data to the specified file. Make sure that you have enough free disk space on your destination drive...	2304
Errors were encountered during the save operation...	2395
...can't find the module...	2516
Lotus .wks file formats aren't supported in the current version of Access. Convert your .wks file to a more recent format, such as .wk1...	2527
...can't delete [Name of database] after compacting it. The compacted database has been named [Name of database]. If you compact a database using the same name, Access creates a new compacted database and then deletes the original database. In this case, however, the original database wasn't deleted because it is read-only...	2549

Part
VI

Ch
39

continues

Table 39.2   Continued

Error Message	Error ID
...can't delete [Name of database] after encrypting it. The encrypted database has been named [Name of database]...	2550
...can't delete [Name of database] after decrypting it. The decrypted database has been named [Name of database]...	2551
You can't encrypt a database that you didn't create or don't own. See the owner of the database or your workgroup administrator...	2552
You can't decrypt a database that you didn't create or don't own. See the owner of the database or your workgroup administrator...	2553
...can't open or convert this previous version database. The database was created in an earlier version of Access. You don't have appropriate security permissions to open or convert databases created in earlier versions...	2567
Access can't delete [name of database] after enabling it. The enabled database has been named [name of database]...	2569
This database is in an unexpected state; Access can't open it...	2572
You don't have permission to read [name of object]. To read this object, you must have Read Design permission for it...	2601
You don't have permission to modify [name of object]. To modify this object, you must have Modify Design permission for it... If the object is a table, you must also have Delete Data and Update Data permissions for it.	2602
You don't have permission to run [name of object]. To run this object, you must have Open/Run permission for it...	2603
You can't view this objects permissions. To view or change permissions for this object, you must have Administer permission for it...	2604
You don't have permission to cut [name of object]. To cut this object, you must have Modify Design permission for it... If the object is a table, you must also have Delete Data permission for it...	2607
You don't have permission to copy [name of object]. To copy this object, you must have Read Design permission for it... If the object is a table, you must also have Read Data permission for it...	2608
You don't have permission to delete [name of object]. To delete this object, you must have Modify Design permission for it... If the object is a table, you must also have Delete Data permission for it...	2609
You don't have permission to rename [name of object]. To rename a database object, you must have Modify Design permission for the object.	2613
You don't have permission to insert this form into another form. To insert a form into another form as a subform, you must have Read Design permission for the form being inserted...	2614
You don't have permission to change the owner of [name of object]. To change the owner of a database object, you must have Administer permission for it...	2615

Error Message	Error ID
You can't change permissions for [name of object]. To change permissions for this object, you must have Administer permission for it...	2616
You don't have permission to import, export, or link to [name of object]. To import, export, or link to this object, you must have Read Design and Read Data permissions for it.	2617
You can't change permissions for [name of object] in a replica. may only be changed in the Design Master for the replica set.	2619
The password you entered in the Old Password box is incorrect. Please enter the correct password for this account.	2620
Access can't communicate with the OLE server. The OLE server may not be registered. To register the OLE server, reinstall it.	2691
The connection with the OLE server was lost, or the OLE server encountered an error while you were using it. Restart the OLE server, and then try the operation again.	2699
Access can't find an OLE server or a dynamic-link library (DLL) required for the OLE operation. The OLE server or DLL may not be registered. To register the OLE server or DLL, reinstall it.	2700
Access can't read the object because communication was interrupted. If the OLE server application is located on a network server, make sure your computer is connected to it. General data object error.	2703
Access can't open the file containing the OLE object.	2707
The OLE object you tried to edit is busy. Try again later.	2729
An error occurred while accessing the OLE server. The OLE server may not be registered. To register the OLE server, reinstall it.	2731
Access can't read the object. Communication between Access and the OLE server was interrupted. Make sure your computer is connected to the network server on which the OLE server is located...	2732
The OLE object you tried to edit can't be accessed. You don't have permission to change the object, or another user opened and locked the object.	2733
You can't save the object now. The OLE server is running an operation, or another user opened and locked the object. Try to save the object again later.	2734
This disk is write-protected. You can't save the object to it.	2735
An error occurred during the operation with an OLE object. The object is in use.	2739
Your computer ran out of disk space while Access was saving the changes you made to the object...	2741
The user-supplied function named [Name of database], the program to assist you in resolving conflicts, could not be found. Contact the author of this customized database application...	7702
The process failed because there is no printer installed...	7796
You don't have permission to modify the design of this table...	7907

continues

Table 39.2   Continued

Error Message	Error ID
Access can't find the module [name of module] referred to in a macro expression or Visual Basic code. The module you referenced may be closed or may not exist in this database, or the name may be misspelled.	7961
Access can't open the file [name of module]. It may not be a database, or it may be a database you are unable to open…	7970
An error occurred while saving the output of the form.	7982
Access failed to create the Visual Basic module [name of module]. If your database is on a network drive, check your network connection, and then try again.	29002
Access couldn't create storage space for a Visual Basic module. If your database is on a network drive, check your network connection, and then try again…	29008
Access couldn't open the storage space for a Visual Basic module. Your computer may be low on disk space…	29009
Another user has modified this database. To see the current version, close the database and open it again.	29020
The current user account doesn't have permission to convert or enable this database…	29024
The database that you are trying to open or convert is currently in use, or you do not have permission to open it exclusively…	29026
Access can't establish a reference to the specified database. The referenced database can't be found, or it's locked exclusively by another user so it can't be opened…	29030
Access can't create or open the requested database now. The database may be locked exclusively by another user.	29031
The current user account doesn't have permission to make an MDE file from this database…	29051

Table 39.3   Excel Error Messages Microsoft Suggests Customizing

Error Message	Error ID
Your formula contains an invalid external reference to a worksheet. Verify that the path, workbook, and range name or cell reference are correct, and try again.	196644
Reference is not valid. Reference must be a simple external reference to a worksheet.	196647
Cannot access directory [Name].	196656
[Name] cannot be accessed. The file may be read-only, or you may be trying to access a read-only location. Or, the server the document is stored on may not be responding.	196657

Error Message	Error ID
The disk is full.	196661
Unable to read file.	196662
The file could not be accessed. Try one of the following.	196663
[Name] file format is not valid.	196665
Document is not completely saved.	196670
Your file could not be printed due to an error on [Name]. There are several possible reasons…	196681
There is a problem with the printer driver…	196748
File error: data may have been lost.	196749
Microsoft Excel cannot display some of the graphics in this file because the [Name] graphics filter is not installed…	196751
Cannot save [Name] because the volume is locked.	196760
The password you supplied is not correct. Verify that the CAPS LOCK key is off and make sure to use the correct capitalization.	196762
Cannot open protected file.	196847
File format is not valid.	196853
Operation failed. [Name] is write reserved.	196862
Sheet is protected with password. File format cannot be used.	196883
References in object formulas must be external references to worksheets.	196913
This file is not in a recognizable format…	196937
Cannot print file.	196982
An error occurred while importing this file.	197041
Document not saved.	197046
Document not saved. Any previously saved copy may have been deleted.	197047
You tried to open a Lotus 1-2-3 FMT or FM3 file created by the Impress add-in. Microsoft Excel uses these files for formatting information, but cannot open them directly. Instead, open the WK1 or WK3 file associated with the FMT or FM3 file you want. The corresponding FMT or FM3 file information will be incorporated when the file is opened in Microsoft Excel.	197091
Cannot open PivotTable source file [Name].	197107
The PivotTable field name is not valid. To create a PivotTable, you must use data that is organized as a list with labeled columns. If you are changing the name of a PivotTable field, you must type a new name for the field.	197108
Microsoft Excel could not open or read this query file. Either the file has been damaged or the file format is not valid.	197300
Unexpected file lock by [Name]. Please try again, and then if necessary, use the Share Workbook command (Tools menu) to turn off sharing.	197405

continues

Table 39.3   Continued

Error Message	Error ID
This file has been locked by [Name] for reading. Try again later.	197415
This file has been locked by [Name] for saving. Try again later.	197416
This file is locked. Try the command again later.	197417
You are no longer connected to this file. Another user may have removed you from it, or saved over it. To preserve your unsaved work…	197418
The file [Name] cannot be found.	197419
No printers are installed. To install a printer…	197520
Cannot load the mail service. Check your mail installation.	197530
Mail system failure. Check your mail installation.	197531
Current printer is unavailable. Select another printer.	197565

Table 39.4   PowerPoint Error Messages Microsoft Suggests Customizing

Error Message	Error ID
PowerPoint can't read the outline from [Name]. No text converter is installed for this file type.	65536
There was an error accessing the disk containing [Name].	65537
The disk containing [Name] is full. Please save to another disk.	65540
This file has an older format that isn't supported.	65542
The disk containing [Name] is no longer available.	65551
No printers are installed. To install a printer…	65561
Windows cannot print due to a problem with the current printer setup. Try one or more of the following.	65562
There's a problem with this printer's setup. Please select a different printer.	65563
An error occurred while printing.	65599
There was an error accessing [Name].	65601
PowerPoint couldn't translate this file.	65625
One or more files have unsupported formats:	65629
PowerPoint can't export the slide(s) because no installed converter supports this file type.	65699
The printer [Name] does not exist or is unavailable.	65712
The printer name, device driver, or port for this print job were not specified or are invalid.	65713
The printer is currently busy or the printer queue is full. Try to print again at a later time.	65739
Either there isn't enough memory to print, or the connection to the printer has been lost.	65790
[Name]The network connection has been lost.	65793

Error Message	Error ID
There is no graphics filter that can read [Name].	131075
[Name] is damaged and can't be read.	131076
PowerPoint was unable to import the file because of a file error.	131079
There was a network error ([Name]) accessing the file.	131082
PowerPoint can't print to [Name]. It's not a valid printer type.	131106
Write failed (disk full?) to [Name].	131111

N O T E Now's the time to analyze your help desk records to see whether there are problems that recur constantly in your organization, and can be solved through custom Help pages. Involve your help desk professionals in planning which error messages to customize. ▪

Collecting Office Program GUIDs

In the previous sections, you've learned how to collect Office error codes and decide which ones to customize. As you customize error codes, remember that because the same error code number might be used by more than one Windows program, every application contains a Globally Unique Identifier (GUID) that specifies which application generated the error message. GUIDs for Office 2000 applications are shown in the following list, and can also be found at **officeupdate.microsoft.com/info/Office2000/GUIDlist.htm**.

- **Access:** {CC29E96F-7BC2-11D1-A921-00A0C91E2AA2}
- **Excel:** {CC29E963-7BC2-11D1-A921-00A0C91E2AA2}
- **Outlook®:** {CC29E94B-7BC2-11D1-A921-00A0C91E2AA2}
- **PowerPoint®:** {CC29E967-7BC2-11D1-A921-00A0C91E2AA2}
- **Word:** {CC29EA4B-7BC2-11D1-A921-00A0C91E2AA2}
- **Graph:** {CC29E975-7BC2-11D1-A921-10A0C91E2AA2}
- **Office Shared:** {CC29E943-7BC2-11D1-A921-00A0C91E2AA2}

Part VI

Ch 39

Identifying Country Codes

If you are working in a global environment, you can create separate custom help pages for each language your people work in, by assigning a Country Code to each custom error message. You can find a detailed list of Office 2000 country codes in Aspscrpt.xls, another Excel worksheet file that is placed in the Customizable Alerts folder when you install the Office Resource Kit. (As you'll see later, this is the same worksheet file that will help you build Active Server Pages for your customized help.)

N O T E If you are customizing Help only for the U.S. and English-speaking Canada, you do not need to include country codes, and you can skip this section. ▪

Creating Web Pages That Serve As Custom Help

Now that you've defined which Office features will invoke custom Help, you can use Word or FrontPage to create HTML Web pages that present the help you want users to receive. From a content standpoint:

■ If you place several answers on the same page, be sure to add hyperlinks for each one, and add a convenient navigation mechanism within the page. Place related answers near one another; for example, create a section that responds to all file access questions.

■ Be sure the answers really answer the questions, and are clear and simple enough to be understood by your average user. If you use jargon, you'll find the results counter-productive. If you can't have your text edited by a professional writer or editor, at least have it read and commented upon by a typical user within your organization.

■ Include links to other help resources on your intranet, or Web-based resources you've found to be especially useful.

■ Create a failsafe page that will be used if Office cannot find a more specific link, or if the correct link is for some reason not working. This page might include alternative contact information.

■ Either on the failsafe page or on every page, include mailto: links or other contact information that helps users reach you if the Web page's answers do not solve their problems.

As part of the Customizable Alerts resources included in the Microsoft Office 2000 Resource Kit, Microsoft provides two simple Web HTML pages you can use as a starting point. These are ALERT.HTM, which contains two questions and answers, as well as predefined links to a Help Desk; and NYI.HTM, a page that simply reports that other information (including the Help Desk link) has not been implemented. You can adapt these pages as a starting point. Here are two other places you might start in order to streamline the task of building support pages:

■ For simple pages, use the Frequently Asked Questions Web Page template included in Word 2000.

■ For more complex sites, use the Customer Support Web Wizard included in FrontPage 2000.

A sample Help page is shown in Figure 39.6.

Now that you've created your HTML file or files, copy them to your Web server. If you are using Office Server Extensions, you can create a Web folder and store it there. If you are using FrontPage 2000, you can use File, Publish Web (Figure 39.7), and specify the Web address where your server pages are to be stored. You will then be asked for the Administrator password.

FIGURE 39.6
Sample Help Page based on FrontPage 2000 Customer Support Template.

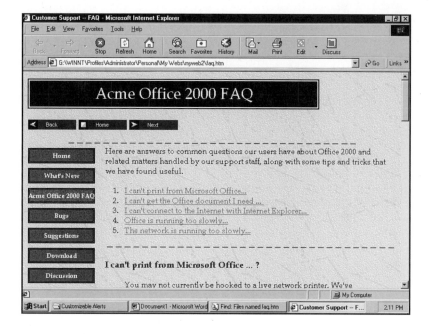

FIGURE 39.7
Publishing your Help pages to the Web in FrontPage 2000.

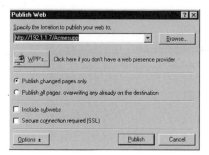

Write down the specific location on your Web server for each file you copy. You'll need this information shortly when you create the ASP file Internet Information Server uses to handle user requests from within Office applications.

Creating Active Server Pages That Link to Your Custom Help

Your custom Web help pages have now been posted, but they're not yet working. You have two more steps to follow. The first is to create an Active Server Page (ASP) that's in charge of responding when a user clicks Web Help from within a dialog box that displays an error message. Microsoft provides three ways to create an ASP page:

- If you know very little about ASP, and you need to create no more than a dozen separate error messages, Microsoft provides an Excel worksheet, **aspscrpt.xls**, that will build your ASP page for you. (Using aspscrpt.xls will be covered in the next section.)

- If you have some knowledge of ASP, you can modify the sample ASP page that Microsoft provides, **alert.asp**, to reflect your own Web page locations, GUID codes, error message codes, and country codes.

- If you are a sophisticated ASP developer, you can write your own ASP page from scratch, using either JavaScript or Visual Basic Scripting Edition. This is, of course, more complex, but you can perform more advanced tasks as well. For instance, you might write code that automatically tracks the problems your users report, and then generates a log file that helps you identify the most common ones.

▶ If you're interested in a complete course in building Active Server Pages, **see** *Sams Teach Yourself Active Server Pages 2.0 in 24 Hours*, by Christoph Wille, June 1999.

Creating Active Server Pages Automatically with Aspscrpt.xls

The easiest way to create Active Server Pages is to use the aspscrpt.xls worksheet to build them for you. To work with this script, first install the Office 2000 Resource Kit tools, downloadable at **www.microsoft.com/office/ork/2000/appndx/toolbox.htm**. After you've installed them, choose **Start**, **Programs**, **Microsoft Office Tools**, **Microsoft Office 2000 Resource Kit Documents**, **Customizable Alerts**. The Customizable Alerts folder appears; double-click **aspscrpt.xls** to open it in Excel. Click the **Enable Macros** button to allow Microsoft's built-in macros to run. The workbook opens, displaying sample data (see Figure 39.8).

FIGURE 39.8
The Aspscrpt.xls workbook displaying sample data.

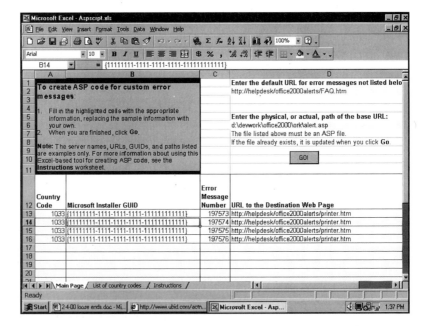

Working in the Main Page worksheet, you now need to replace the sample data with the live information you've gathered:

- In cell D2 (Enter the default URL for error messages not listed below), enter the complete Web address of the page users should see in the event a more specific link cannot be found.

> **CAUTION**
>
> This is typically a Web address that includes your Web server's IP address followed by the path from wwwroot to the specific page. Do not use a traditional network path.

- In cell D6 (Enter the physical, or actual, path of the base URL), enter an actual network path to the location where you want to store the ASP file you're about to create, including the filename you want to use (with an ASP extension).
- Starting on Row 13, enter the correct information for each custom error message you want to create:
  - Change the country code (only if the default 1033, representing U.S. and Canada, is not what you want).
  - Change the Microsoft Installer GUID to the 32-digit number associated with the specific Office application, which is generating the error message. (A list of GUIDs appears earlier, in the Collecting Office Program GUIDs section of this chapter.)
  - Change the Error Message Number to correspond to the error message dialog box you want to link with.
  - Change the URL to the Destination Web Page to correspond to the Web address that contains the Help page you want users to see.
- Repeat the process for each separate error message you want to create, including multiple error messages that connect to the same Web page. If some rows of generic information still appear, select and delete them. Figure 39.9 shows how the worksheet might look when you're finished. Save the Excel file; then, click **Go** to run the built-in macros that create the Web page and store it in the location you selected. The final ASP file is shown in Figure 39.10.

Activating Custom Error Messages Through the Windows Registry

Now that you have your custom error messages, you're almost ready to use them, but there's one final, crucial step. You need to be sure the Windows Registry on every computer on your network is updated to use them. You can do this before you deploy Office, through the Custom Installation Wizard. Or, you can do this after you've deployed Office, using the System Policy Editor.

If you haven't yet deployed Office 2000, you can include the appropriate Registry entry as you work with the Custom Installation Wizard. When you reach the Add Registry Entries screen, click **Add**; the Add/Modify Registry Entry dialog box appears).

FIGURE 39.9
An example of how aspscrpt.xls might look when you finish editing it.

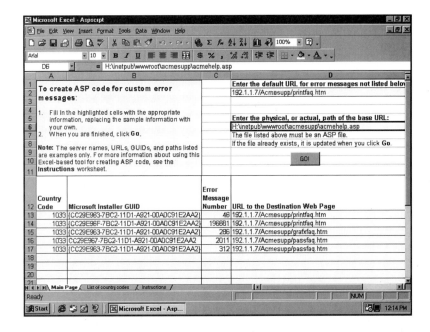

FIGURE 39.10
The ASP file Excel creates from the data in Figure 39.9.

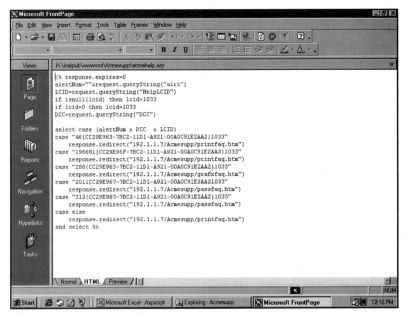

Enter the following Registry entry:

```
Root: HKEY_CURRENT_USER
Data type: REG_SZ
Key: Software\Microsoft\Office\9.0\Common\General
Value Name: CustomizableAlertBaseURL
```

In the Value Data text box, enter the URL of the ASP page you created, with a question mark at the end of it. For example:

```
192.1.17/acmesupp/acmehelp.asp?
```

Click **OK**, and continue customizing your Office installation. Later, when you deploy Office across the network, your help pages will appear instead of the Microsoft Office Update page when users click Web Help in a dialog box.

Using the System Policy Editor to Activate Custom Error Messages

If you've already deployed Office, you can establish a system policy that uses the same Registry key, through the System Policy Editor. Working with the System Policy Editor is covered in depth in Chapter 37, but briefly, if you've installed the System Policy Editor as part of the Office Resource Kit Toolkit, you can run it by choosing **Start**, **Programs**, **Microsoft Office Tools**, **Microsoft Office Resource Kit Tools**, **System Policy Editor**.

If you haven't created system policies before, choose **Options**, **Policy Template**; then, choose **Office9.adm** and click **OK**. Click the **New** button, and double-click **Default User**. The Default User Properties dialog box opens.

Go to Microsoft Office 2000\Customizable Error Messages, and select the **Base URL** check box (see Figure 39.11). Then, enter the Web address of the ASP page you created, followed by a question mark, and click **OK**. Choose **File**, **Save** to save the policy file.

Finally (as discussed in Chapter 37), include the policy file as part of your user's network logon.

Part
VI

Ch
39

FIGURE 39.11
Adjusting the default user properties to reflect your custom help messages.

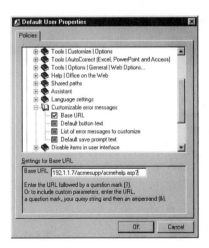

Finding Office Training and Self-Help Solutions

by Bill Camarda

Let's face it: Most users ignore the built-in help features of most application programs. Microsoft has created an impressive collection of help tools and has done its best to make them interesting enough for users to try. However, getting your users to work with the help tools in earnest is up to you. In the following sections, you'll briefly review Office 2000's Help, and ways that you can encourage your users to take greater advantage of it.

Understanding the Revamped Office Assistant

In Office 2000, the primary mechanism for users to get online Help is by asking English-language questions of the *Office Assistant*. As in Office 97, the default Office Assistant is Clippit—but this version of Clippit (see Figure 40.1) might rub fewer users the wrong way than the Office 97 version, with its legendary attitude.

FIGURE 40.1

Clippit, the default Office 2000 Office Assistant, ready to answer your questions.

> **N O T E** Later, you'll learn how to change the Office Assistant, or enable users to do so. ■

Using the Office Assistant

With the Office Assistant, users can ask questions in plain English, and Office points you to the Help pages that are most likely to contain the answers. Office Assistant isn't perfect. Sometimes, users still have to rummage around in Help because Office Assistant's suggestions prove to be irrelevant. But more than half the time, Office Assistant points them in the right direction, and it appears to be a bit more effective in Office 2000 than it was in Office 97. To use Office Assistant:

1. If the **Office Assistant** is displayed, click it; or press **F1**; or click the **Office Assistant** icon at the far right of the Standard toolbar; or choose **Microsoft Office Help** from the Help menu.

2. In the What would you like to do? text box, enter your question.

3. Click **Search**. Office Assistant displays a list of the Help pages it finds most relevant to your question.

4. Click the one you would like to view, or enter a different question and search again.

Changing the Way the Office Assistant Works

Help is a very personal matter. Some users don't like to get help from cute creatures and prefer an old-fashioned Help table of contents and index. Others find the Office Assistant's default settings a bit too intrusive (for example, Office Assistant can offer help without being asked). Others simply don't like paperclips. Office enables you—or individual users—to control precisely how the Office Assistant works.

To control Office Assistant from a workstation running Office, click the **Office Assistant**, and then click the **Options** button. The Office Assistant dialog box opens (see Figure 40.2).

FIGURE 40.2
The Options tab of the Office Assistant dialog box.

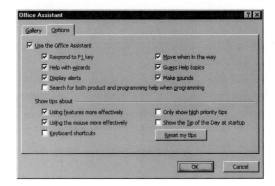

Turning Off the Office Assistant   Some users might not want to use the Office Assistant at all. To eliminate it, clear the **Use the Office Assistant** check box. Then, when a user clicks the Help button, press **F1**, or choose **Help**, **Microsoft Office Help**, Office's three-tab Help system appears. The user can

- Type an English-language question in the **Answer Wizard** tab (as shown in Figure 40.3)
- Click **Contents** to see Help's table of contents
- Click **Index** to see an index of all Help's contents

FIGURE 40.3
Using Microsoft Office Help rather than an animated Office Assistant.

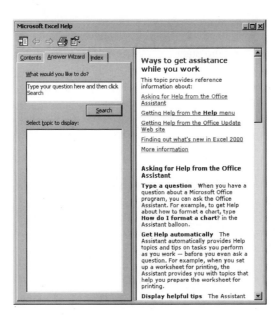

Modifying the Office Assistant's Capabilities   Perhaps your users basically like the Office Assistant, but find it a bit too intrusive. You can use settings in the Options tab of the Office Assistant dialog box (refer to Figure 40.2) to adjust it a bit.

By default, the Office Assistant appears when you start a Wizard; if you prefer otherwise, clear the **Help with wizards** check box.

By default, the Office Assistant appears when Office displays an alert. If you prefer old-fashioned dialog boxes, clear the **Display alerts** check box.

By default, the Office Assistant provides audio feedback (for example, if you use Rocky, the dog, he barks on occasion). To turn that off, clear the **Make sounds** check box.

By default, the Office Assistant displays tips when it thinks it knows a better way to perform a task. To turn this off, clear the **Using features more effectively** check box and the **Using the mouse more effectively** check box. You can also limit the number of times the Office Assistant displays tips by checking the **Only Show high priority tips** check box.

N O T E   Conversely, if you're trying to learn keyboard shortcuts, select the **Keyboard shortcuts** check box. ▓

Choosing a Different Office Assistant   If you don't like Office's default Office Assistant, you can specify a different Office Assistant from the library of assistants Office provides. Click the **Office Assistant, Options**, and then click **Gallery**. The Gallery of Office Assistants appears (see Figure 40.4).

FIGURE 40.4
Replacing Clippit with a different Office Assistant.

Click **Next** repeatedly to view each of Office Assistant's possible personalities, including

- Clippit, the paper clip
- The Dot (a smiling red ball)
- F1 the Robot
- The Genius (an Einstein look-alike)

- The Office Logo (animated)
- Mother Nature (a gently spinning Earth)
- Links, the cat
- Rocky, the dog
- The Office Logo (not animated: better for low-performance systems, and for users running Office from Windows terminals)

When you've selected the Office Assistant you want, click **OK**, and that assistant replaces the one you've been using. Note that when you change the Office Assistant (or its behavior) in one Office application, the change applies to the entire Office suite.

N O T E Only Clippit is installed with the default Office 2000 installation; the others are set to Install on First Run. This means Office searches the local hard drive or the network installation point for the additional Assistant files it needs; if these are not available, users will not be able to change their assistants.

As part of the Custom Installation Wizard, you might choose to install all the Assistant files on each user's local computer from the outset. ■

Understanding the What's This? Command

Here's a quick tip you can share with users to help them understand parts of the Office interface they don't understand. Office contains a What's This? feature that explains anything a user clicks on.

To use What's This?, press **Shift+F1**, or choose **What's This?** from the **Help** menu. The mouse pointer changes into a question mark. Click whatever you are interested in, and Office displays an explanation (see Figure 40.5). When you're finished with What's This?, press **Esc**. The Help text disappears and your mouse pointer returns to normal.

For example, in Word, if a user isn't sure how a block of text is formatted, you can click the **What's This?** mouse pointer on the text, and Office shows a detailed description of all the direct formatting and styles that have been applied. This is fairly similar to WordPerfect's classic Reveal Codes feature, which many WordPerfect users have come to depend upon heavily.

Part
VI

Ch
40

FIGURE 40.5
The What's This? pointer can display text formatting or any element of the Office interface.

Accessing Microsoft's Help on the Web

Microsoft provides free and current help information on all Office applications via its Web site. Users might find this resource helpful because they can access it precisely when they need it, without having to leave the Office application in which they are working. To access Microsoft help on the Web:

1. From an Office application, choose **Help**, **Office on the Web**.
2. Click any of the Web resources in the submenu that appears. The Help files you access are dynamic and might be updated automatically during or after your visit.
3. If you like, you can tile your Web browser and Office application so that you can see both of them at the same time.

Disabling or Redirecting Microsoft Web-Based Help

Help on the Web obviously requires users to have an Internet connection. In fact, the feature is automatically disabled if a user's computer does not contain a browser that has been registered in the Windows Registry.

However, many organizations that do have Internet connections and browsers prefer that users get their Office guidance from sources other than the Microsoft Web site. If you want, you can disable Help on the Web for individual applications or for all applications.

The individual Web links in Microsoft Office Help files are stored in separate *Compiled HTML* (CHM) files from the rest of Office's Help. The files are typically stored in \Program Files\Microsoft Office\Office\1033 (in the U.S. and Canada; in other locales, the four-digit country code would be different). If you do not want users to have access to the Web links, you can delete these files or choose not to install them in the first place. The files are listed in Table 40.1.

Table 40.1   Compiled HTML Files Containing Links to Microsoft's Office on the Web Support Site

This File	Contains Links to the Web from These Help Files
Acweb9.chm	Access Help files
Olweb9.chm	Outlook Help files
Ppweb9.chm	PowerPoint Help files
Wdweb9.chm	Word Help files
Xlweb9.chm	Excel Help files

Redirecting Office on the Web Help Links to Your Intranet

Microsoft says you can also edit the Help links to redirect them to your own intranet. Be aware, however, that doing so requires significant skills with HTML and Microsoft HTML Help application (which is provided as part of the downloadable Office Resource Kit toolbox). In brief, the process is as follows:

1. Open the correct CHM file in HTML Help. (Be sure to only work with the CHM files previously listed, not the main program Help files.)

2. Use HTML Help's decompiler feature to break the CHM file into its component HTML pages and other elements.

3. Open each HTML page in an HTML editor. (You can use HTML Help or FrontPage. You can also use the HTML source editor built into the Microsoft Development Environment that comes with Office. This is the same editor that appears when you choose **View**, **Source** to review the source code associated with a Web page you're editing.

4. Carefully edit the links on the page so that they point to the page you want. Also, edit page titles and the text associated with links, if necessary. Be careful not to damage any of the surrounding HTML, JavaScript, or VBScript code on these pages.

5. When you've finished editing every page, open HTML Help and recompile the pages into a new CHM Help file. Before doing so, be sure that indexes, tables of contents, CSS files, and all other components are available for compilation.

Disabling the Help, Office on the Web Menu Command

If you want, you can also use the System Policy Editor to disable the Help, Office on the Web menu item, so users cannot use it to access Microsoft's Help resources (of course, this has no impact on their ability to use a Web browser to access the Microsoft site). You must disable Help on the Web in each Office application separately by following these steps:

1. Choose **Start**, **Programs**, **Microsoft Office Tools**, **Microsoft Office 2000 Resource Kit Tools**, **System Policy Editor**.

2. Choose **Options**, **Policy Template**, and be sure the appropriate policy template files are present (Access9.adm, Excel9.adm, Frontpg9.adm, Office9.adm, and so forth).

3. Click the **New** button to create a new policy file.

4. Double-click **Default User**.

5. In the Default User dialog box, double-click the Microsoft Office application you want to customize.

6. Go down to **Disable Items in User Interface**, and then to **Predefined**.

7. Check the **Disable Command Bar Buttons and Menu Items** check box. A list of predefined menu items appears below.

8. Check **Help**, **Office on the Web**.

9. Click **OK**.

10. Choose **File**, **Save** to save the policy file.

11. Include the Policy file in your users' network logon script.

If you have a location you want to use instead of Microsoft's Web site, don't disable the Help on the Web menu item. Instead, point your users to the location of your choice. To do so, follow steps 1-4 listed previously; then, go to Microsoft Office 2000, Help|Office on the Web, Office on the Web URL. Select the **Office on the Web URL** check box. A new text box appears where you can insert your Office on the Web URL. Do so; then click **OK**, save the policy file, and include it in your users' network logon script.

Applying Just-in-Time Training Techniques

Often good advice goes in one ear and out the other, without sticking around in memory. Experts explain that humans don't retain knowledge very efficiently if they can't understand how to apply that knowledge. You've probably attended a technical seminar that had a great teacher and interesting subject matter, but because you had no immediate use for the information, you can hardly remember any of it.

You can help your new Office users avoid similar frustrations by applying some just-in-time training techniques—training solutions that stay unnoticed until they are needed, at which time users receive targeted information to solve the problem at hand. If the training works, the user generally retains the knowledge, which in turn makes your life easier.

Using Camcorder AVI Files for Office 2000 Training

Here's a simple way to communicate good Office techniques, and it's also fun. The Microsoft Camcorder is a free program you can use to record your actions on the computer screen, including mouse movements, menu pull-downs, and so on. You save this recording to a file, and then anyone can play it back and watch the same events replayed. Camcorder movies can include a sound track, so you might include voice narration to describe the actions onscreen.

N O T E Camcorder can record in Windows 95 or 98, but not in Windows NT 4.0. However, movies recorded by Camcorder can be viewed in Windows NT 4.0. ■

You can use Camcorder to create computer demonstrations or training sessions. Most business functions can be reduced to a simple set of repetitive tasks. Each set of tasks has a right way—and many wrong ways—of being accomplished. You choose the best way, record yourself performing the task as a model, and then distribute the Camcorder file to your users. Make it available so they can view it conveniently when they need it the most. You can save Camcorder movies as AVI or EXE files, although the EXE files are much larger because they include the Camcorder player (this enables you to play the movie on a computer that doesn't have the Camcorder player installed). Figure 40.6 shows the opening screen of a Camcorder movie.

FIGURE 40.6
Camcorder files can show your users the correct way to perform a task.

Start the recording by clicking the red **Record** button. You can record mouse movements as well as keystrokes. When you've finished the actions you want to record, press **Esc** (or the key you've set as the stop key in Camcorder preferences). You can play back the movie by clicking the **Play** button. If it meets your satisfaction, save the file by choosing **File**, **Save As** or **File**, **Create Standalone Movie**. If you need to make basic changes in how Camcorder functions, such as choosing audio settings or an alternate stop key, you'll find them in **Camcorder Movie**, **Preferences** (as shown in Figure 40.7).

Part
VI

Ch
40

FIGURE 40.7
Improve your sound settings in the Camcorder preferences.

Don't go crazy. These files can get big quickly. Your network could get bogged down if many users are accessing long recordings. Camcorder is best for creating short, concise exercises that are available when needed, just in time to prevent a call to the help desk. You can even include suggestions in your recordings about when it's appropriate to call the help desk.

When you have a large selection of your best help desk recordings, you might want to burn a CD-ROM (or several) to store them all. This type of CD-ROM can make a great training tool; you can lend it out as needed, and human resources can make it required material for new employees.

Camcorder was provided on the Office 97 ValuPack, but is not on the Office 2000 CD-ROMs or on Microsoft's Web site. If you need it, however, one source for downloading it is: **www.windowsmagazine.com/software/1997/0301/03share.htm#a8**.

Here are tips for creating an award-winning recording:

- Record your movie at the same screen resolution in which you plan to view it. If your audience has varied resolution settings, record at a lower screen resolution, such as 640×480.

- For the highest-quality movie, be sure Camcorder has plenty of memory to draw on. It's a good idea to quit programs you're not using before you record your movie. If you have low or insufficient memory available, Camcorder displays an alert.

- Properly introduce the segment. Provide a title, and perhaps a summary at the end. You can have multiple programs running while you run Camcorder, so why not use PowerPoint to create an impressive title and description, and keep PowerPoint running in the background? During your recording, you can toggle between the PowerPoint slides and the task at hand. If Camcorder disappears during a recording, just press **Alt+Tab** or click the Camcorder taskbar button to bring it to the front.

- Rehearse your movie before you record. Practice the steps you want to capture, so your movements are smooth and natural while recording. Camcorder records six frames per second, so moving your mouse slowly and steadily results in the smoothest playback.

- Camcorder normally displays the Stop button to enable you to stop recording easily, but you can hide the Stop button if you prefer. Choose **Movie**, **Preferences** and select the **Hide stop button while recording** check box. You can then specify which keys you want to press to stop a recording.

- Keep it short. Multiple short segments are better than one long recording. You'll be more likely to keep the attention of your audience, and you'll save on storage space as well.

Providing Network and Intranet-Based Office 2000 Training

Because all your users are likely to be networked and have a Web browser installed, you've got what's needed for creating and providing Intranet-based education for them. To create your Intranet training site, you can simply gather your support documentation, save the files in HTML format, and store them in a shared folder on the network. You might want to create a title page in Word to organize your site. You might also let users search your help desk database from the site.

You can also purchase training materials you can deliver through your network. To use these products, you need to purchase a license for your site, install the materials on a server, and allow your users to access them. A brief sampling of products is shown in the following list, but you'll also want to explore the Web to find out what's currently available.

- *Que Education and Training* publishes teaching materials for corporate training. To see what's available, visit its Web page at **www.mcp.com/resources/education**.

- *Microsoft Office 2000 Professional Essentials* (ISBN 1-57576-787-2), by Laura Acklen, Linda Bird, Robert Ferrett, Donna Matherly, John Preston, Sally Preston, Michele Reader, Rob Tidrow, Thomas Underwood, and Suzanne Weixel, includes data disks and instructors' disks that further develop the written text.

- *Learn On-Demand*, from PTS Learning Systems and Que E&T, provides interactive applications training. For more information, visit **www.mcp.com/learning**.

- *Complete Office 2000* (ISBN 1-58076-015-5) and *Complete Office 2000 Annotated Instructor's Edition* (ISBN 1-58076-132-1) feature full-semester applications with a business emphasis.

- *MOUS Essentials Series,* by Jane Calabria and Dorothy Burke. Microsoft has certified this courseware for the Microsoft Office User Specialist (MOUS) program. The included Student Test Preparation Guide provides general exam information, including how and where to register.

 TIP

For information about authorized training for Office, call 800-SOLPROV (800-765-7768) for a referral to a local Microsoft Solution Provider Authorized Technical Education Center (ATEC), or call the Microsoft Fax Server at 800-727-3351 and request document number 10000256 for the location of the Authorized Academic Training Program (AATP) site nearest you. Microsoft ATECs and Microsoft AATPs offer Microsoft Official Curriculum delivered by Microsoft Certified Trainers to educate computer professionals on Microsoft technology.

Providing Interactive CD-ROM Instructional Products

Another good source of training material is interactive CD-ROM courseware. These products require the use of a computer and usually a local CD-ROM drive, although several of the products can also be installed and shared over a network. Most are produced using multimedia and provide excellent graphics and sound accompaniment.

This class of products appeals to the user who needs a quick response to a specific question. Typically, a start menu provides direct access to various topics, and then directs the user to specific lessons and objectives. The user can control the pace and the order of the topics. These products are helpful both as primary instruction and as refreshers.

Providing Instructional Video Products

You might want to offer self-study training to users who can't attend a traditional class or who have special needs. Many training companies have created literally hundreds of self-study products from which to choose. These products generally fall into two categories: video courseware and interactive computer courseware (or a combination of both).

To provide training that does not require the use of computers, try the large market of video products. In general, these products are recorded instruction sessions taught by an expert and professionally produced.

 TIP The range of subject material available in video will boggle your mind, as will the quality. Be sure to do research and check the return policies before you spend company money on a video training session.

Videos, by nature, tend to be a passive experience. The user watches the video and observes instruction. Then, you hope, the user returns to the work environment and applies that knowledge effectively. If some of it sticks, that's good, and you can consider the investment worthwhile. Unfortunately, many users have short attention spans and expect to be entertained, not engaged. Many videos try to accommodate this group by providing lively instructors and interesting instruction.

Most video products are available on VCR, but some Web-accessed streaming video products are starting to emerge. You might find the same titles offered both in video and via the Web. The rules are the same; stick with a reliable company that has provided you with good service in the past.

What are appropriate uses of these products?

- In a company conference room turned into a "learning room"
- As part of a checkout system for employee home use
- As an extension of training or support staff
- As a required part of human resource development for all employees

Video products have a downside (even the very best ones) if they are used incorrectly:

- The students typically have no control over the pace of instruction or the order of material (especially in a group setting). With long exposure, this can become frustrating for all but the most disciplined students.
- If students do not sense that they need this information immediately, they'll have a strong tendency to forget the material quickly.
- Users needing information in a panic might become frustrated if the exact solution is not presented on the particular video.
- These same users might also be in a panic if they have difficulty locating a specific subject by fast-forwarding and rewinding through a tape. The material is linear and is usually intended to be viewed that way.

■ The material on the video might describe a procedure or policy not consistent with your own. For instance, a Word video might tell users they can easily modify templates, but your company might restrict access to templates. In this case, the video sends the wrong message, and users might start questioning the appropriateness of other material.

Suggested Web-Based Training

If users in your organization can't afford any time out of the office to take training, suggest one of the many online courses available on the Web. The good ones cost money, but the cost is much less than you'd pay for live instruction and associated travel expenses. Plus, Web-based training is convenient. You schedule and take the classes at the best time for your users.

Search the Web for the latest online training resources. The two resources listed are established companies that provide excellent training in both Office products and administration topics.

■ *Microsoft Online Institute* (`moli.microsoft.com`). MOLI offers online technical Microsoft product training for computer professionals.

■ *ZD University* (`www.zdu.com`). ZD Education publishes computer-training products and services for users at every level (see Figure 40.8).

FIGURE 40.8
Save travel time and expense by using your Web browser to experience online education.

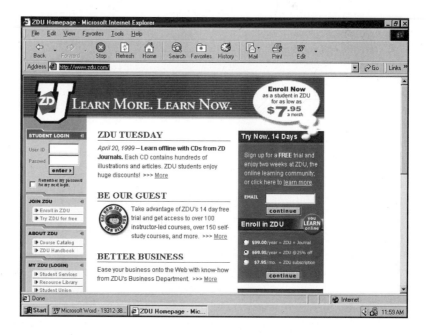

Part

VI

Ch

40

Accessing Macmillan Computer Publishing's Personal Bookshelf

Customized online libraries are becoming more popular, and Macmillan Computer Publishing offers a valuable one. Hundreds of online books are available for checkout after registering your interests at the Web site. To view a book, you access your personal bookshelf via the Personal Bookshelf home page (**www.mcp.com/personal**), enter your email address, click the **Bookshelf** button, and then click the **View Book** button.

TIP You can review your current Macmillan online book inventory at **www.mcp.com/personal/ebooklist.html**.

Ninety days is the longest time a book can be checked out. After the expiration date, a book loses its View Book button. At that time, you can either check out another book or check out the same book again.

After you gain access to your personal bookshelf, you can change your interest areas by clicking the **Modify Interest Areas** button near the top of your personal bookshelf page. Fill out and submit the form that appears, and your new preferences will take effect the next time you visit your personal bookshelf.

Help Desks are all well and good, but your real goal should be to prevent calls to the help desk: to help users solve their own problems—by themselves.

Managing Mobile Office Users

by Deb Shinder

Our world is becoming increasingly mobile, and in today's business environment, our work often goes with us wherever we go. Executives take Excel worksheets home for revision; salespeople take PowerPoint presentations on the road; and managers on business trips work on Word documents in their hotel rooms.

Computers are getting smaller in size and less expensive as they grow more powerful. Laptops, notebooks, and handheld systems are becoming affordable for those at all levels of the organization. Portable computing, once considered a luxury, is fast becoming a necessity.

Employees expect the same standards of productivity from their equipment and software, regardless of where they are. When things don't work, they call you. The Office 2000 administrator must be prepared to support Office applications both inside the company's walls and via long distance phone lines. This chapter offers some tips for enhancing the productivity of on-the-go office users, and creative ways of overcoming the obstacles peculiar to their mobile situations.

Conserving Disk and Memory Resources on Mobile Computers

As portable computers become more and more powerful, the difference between working on a desktop machine and a laptop or notebook computer diminishes. Unfortunately, though, miniaturized components still cost significantly more than their space-consuming counterparts. Consequently, most of us still find that when we "go mobile," we end up working with systems that are scaled down not only in size, but in processor power, memory, and hard drive capacity as well.

Office 2000 is a feature-rich suite of programs, and its hardware requirements are greater than earlier versions. But there are ways to optimize the Office applications to run more efficiently on the small systems.

Office 2000 also includes special features designed specifically to enhance the productivity of mobile users, and if you are running the software on Windows 2000 Professional, there are operating system enhancements that provide better support to those who take their computers on the road.

Installing Office 2000 Using Minimal Hard Disk Space

To conserve hard disk space, you can customize the Office 2000 installation process. The setup program uses the new Windows installer technology and gives you two choices of installation (see Figure 41.1). If you choose **Install Now**, Office installs a "typical" configuration. To optimize the installation for a laptop or notebook machine, click **Customize**.

FIGURE 41.1
The Office 2000 Setup Wizard lets you customize the installation process for optimum performance with a portable computer.

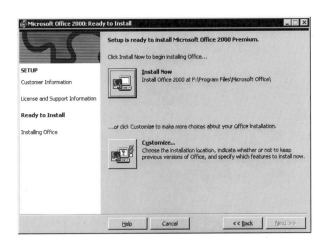

Using the Custom installation option, you can choose to install only the specific applications, components, and features you need.

Choosing Which Components to Leave Out   First assess whether you need to install the entire suite of applications (see Figure 41.2). If you use the laptop for word processing and giving presentations, but rarely or never work with worksheet or database files, you can save a great deal of disk space by installing Word and PowerPoint, but not Access or Excel.

FIGURE 41.2
Setup lets you select exactly which features are installed.

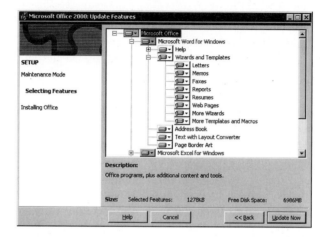

Another way to save space is to leave out the Help files (or remove them after installation). In Office 2000, these consist of files with the .hlp or the .chm extension (the latter is compiled HTML Help). If you are already familiar with how to use the programs and rarely consult the Help files, consider not installing them.

Other components you might consider leaving out include wizards and templates that you don't use, text and graphics converters for less common formats, Office tools you can do without (such as the Office Assistant, language settings tool, Web components, themes, and the clip art gallery).

Remember that if you find later that you need one of these features, you can run Setup again and add it.

Performing Maintenance Duties to Conserve Hard Disk Space   Performing periodic maintenance and "housekeeping" duties on your hard disk helps you to keep from running out of space. For instance:

- Remove programs you don't use, including Windows components such as WordPad and HyperTerminal.
- Delete the files in your Temp folder regularly.
- Set the Windows Recycle Bin to use a smaller percentage of disk space (default is 10 percent of the drive).
- Clear out your Web browser cache and history folders often.

Part
VI

Ch

41

- Move files from your laptop to your desktop machine if you no longer need to access them away from the office, or back up older, seldom-accessed files to floppy, tape, CD-ROM or other backup media and remove them from the portable's hard disk.

- Consider compression. If you are using Windows NT or Windows 2000 and the NTFS file system, you can compress data on a file-by-file basis without the dangers associated with earlier methods of compression.

Using Viewers to Display Documents   It is not necessary to install Word if all you need to be able to do from your notebook computer is read Word documents. The same is true for the other Office 2000 programs. You can just install the appropriate viewer, which uses considerably less disk space and system resources to display the contents of the files. For instance, you can view a PowerPoint slideshow without having PowerPoint installed on your computer, by using the PowerPoint 97/2000 Viewer.

Viewers have other advantages: They're free, and you don't have to have a license for each instance as you do for applications. The viewer does not enable users to edit files, but it can be used to copy information from a document to other applications (copy and paste).

The Viewer software is available for download from Microsoft's "Office on the Web" site at `http://officeupdate.microsoft.com`. You can also access the Web site by selecting **Office on the Web** from the **Help** menu in any Office 2000 application.

Installing the Viewer Software   To install the Word 97/2000 Viewer:

1. Download the file from Office Update by clicking the **Download Now!** at the top left of this page and following the instructions in the dialog boxes.

2. Double-click the **wd97vwr32.exe** program file on your hard disk to start the Setup program.

3. Word Viewer 97 Setup prompts you for a folder in which to install Word Viewer. The default folder location for Word Viewer is *<drive>*:\Program Files\WordView on a Windows 95/98 system (*<drive>*:\WordView on Windows NT 3.51).

4. Click the large **Install** button to install Word Viewer 97/2000.

If Word Viewer Setup detects Word version 6.x or later on your system, Setup prompts you to determine which application should open Word documents by default, as shown in Figure 41.3. The default application is used to open files with .doc file extensions when they are double-clicked.

Choosing **Open with Word** means that Word for Windows will be used by default to open Word files.

Choosing **Open with Viewer** means that the Word Viewer will be used by default to open Word files.

FIGURE 41.3

If you have Word installed on your computer, the Viewer setup program asks you to select a default method for opening Word documents.

N O T E If you select the **Open with Word** option and you want to restore Word as the default Word document handler, you have to uninstall Word Viewer and then restart Word so that it can restore its Registry information. For more information, see "Installation and Maintenance" in the Readme.doc installed with the viewer. ■

The process is the same for the other Office Viewers.

Using the Viewer Software   After you install the Viewers, they appear on your Start menu and can be selected like any other program. If you've chosen to set the Viewer as the default application to open documents, double-clicking an Office document with the appropriate extension opens the Viewer (In other words, .doc for the Word Viewer, .ppt for the PowerPoint Viewer, and .xls for the Excel Viewer).

Using Word and Excel Viewers   The Viewers have the same look and "feel" as the applications themselves. Word and Excel documents display almost identically to the full applications.

The Word Viewer provides the same views as the full-featured Word application: Normal, Page Layout, Outline, and Master Document. The Viewer also includes Online Layout view, which corresponds to Word 2000's Web Layout view.

Although you can copy from the Viewer document and paste into other documents, you cannot edit the document in the Viewer. If Word is also installed on the machine, you can select **Open for Editing** in the **File** menu of the Viewer to open the document in Word.

There are a variety of options that can be set for viewing and printing documents with the Viewer. Select **View**, **Options**, and you'll see the dialog box shown in Figure 41.4.

Figure 41.5 shows an Excel spreadsheet displayed in the Excel Viewer. Again, you'll note that it is almost identical to the display in Excel itself.

Part

VI

Ch

41

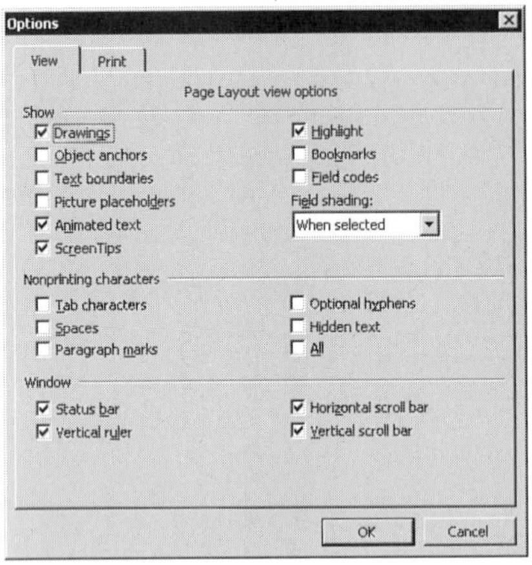

FIGURE 41.4
Use the Options settings dialog box to configure the Viewer's features and optimize performance.

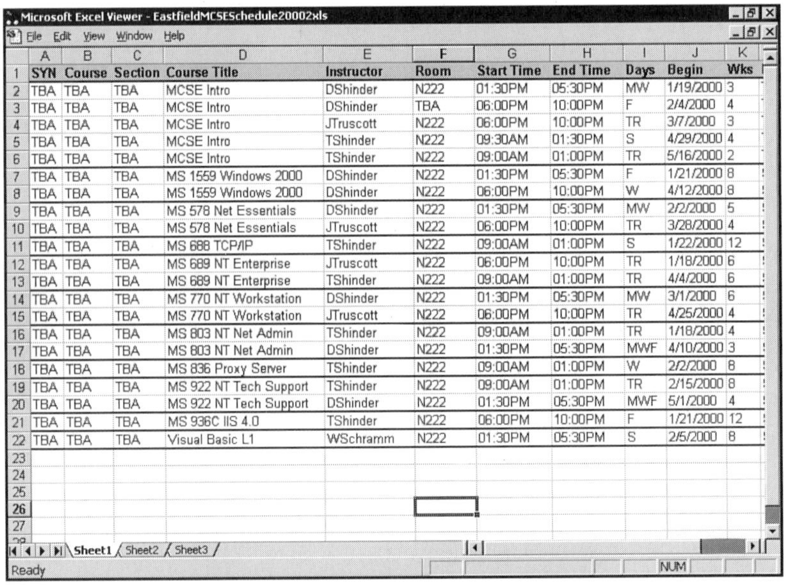

	A	B	C	D	E	F	G	H	I	J	K
1	SYN	Course	Section	Course Title	Instructor	Room	Start Time	End Time	Days	Begin	Wks
2	TBA	TBA	TBA	MCSE Intro	DShinder	N222	01:30PM	05:30PM	MW	1/19/2000	3
3	TBA	TBA	TBA	MCSE Intro	DShinder	TBA	06:00PM	10:00PM	F	2/4/2000	4
4	TBA	TBA	TBA	MCSE Intro	JTruscott	N222	06:00PM	10:00PM	TR	3/7/2000	3
5	TBA	TBA	TBA	MCSE Intro	TShinder	N222	09:30AM	01:30PM	S	4/29/2000	4
6	TBA	TBA	TBA	MCSE Intro	TShinder	N222	09:00AM	01:00PM	TR	5/16/2000	2
7	TBA	TBA	TBA	MS 1559 Windows 2000	DShinder	N222	01:30PM	05:30PM	F	1/21/2000	8
8	TBA	TBA	TBA	MS 1559 Windows 2000	DShinder	N222	06:00PM	10:00PM	W	4/12/2000	8
9	TBA	TBA	TBA	MS 578 Net Essentials	DShinder	N222	01:30PM	05:30PM	MW	2/2/2000	5
10	TBA	TBA	TBA	MS 578 Net Essentials	JTruscott	N222	06:00PM	10:00PM	TR	3/28/2000	4
11	TBA	TBA	TBA	MS 688 TCP/IP	TShinder	N222	09:00AM	01:00PM	S	1/22/2000	12
12	TBA	TBA	TBA	MS 689 NT Enterprise	JTruscott	N222	06:00PM	10:00PM	TR	1/18/2000	6
13	TBA	TBA	TBA	MS 689 NT Enterprise	TShinder	N222	09:00AM	01:00PM	TR	4/4/2000	6
14	TBA	TBA	TBA	MS 770 NT Workstation	DShinder	N222	01:30PM	05:30PM	MW	3/1/2000	6
15	TBA	TBA	TBA	MS 770 NT Workstation	JTruscott	N222	06:00PM	10:00PM	TR	4/25/2000	4
16	TBA	TBA	TBA	MS 803 NT Net Admin	TShinder	N222	09:00AM	01:00PM	TR	1/18/2000	4
17	TBA	TBA	TBA	MS 803 NT Net Admin	DShinder	N222	01:30PM	05:30PM	MWF	4/10/2000	3
18	TBA	TBA	TBA	MS 836 Proxy Server	TShinder	N222	09:00AM	01:00PM	W	2/2/2000	8
19	TBA	TBA	TBA	MS 922 NT Tech Support	TShinder	N222	09:00AM	01:00PM	TR	2/15/2000	8
20	TBA	TBA	TBA	MS 922 NT Tech Support	DShinder	N222	01:30PM	05:30PM	MWF	5/1/2000	4
21	TBA	TBA	TBA	MS 936C IIS 4.0	TShinder	N222	06:00PM	10:00PM	F	1/21/2000	12
22	TBA	TBA	TBA	Visual Basic L1	WSchramm	N222	01:30PM	05:30PM	S	2/5/2000	8

FIGURE 41.5
The Excel 97/2000 Viewer displays an Excel workbook in the same format as the full Excel application.

Using the PowerPoint Viewer With the PowerPoint Viewer, as shown in Figure 41.6, you have slightly different options. As you can see, you are able to preview the slide presentation before playing it as a slideshow. You can choose to advance the slides manually, or use the automatic timings, if they are set in the presentation.

If you click the **Options** button, you will see the dialog box shown in Figure 41.7, with which you can choose to use or override the settings saved with the file, and configure Viewer settings for mouse and screen behavior.

FIGURE 41.6
The PowerPoint 97/2000 Viewer gives you a preview prior to displaying the slideshow.

FIGURE 41.7
With the PowerPoint Viewer, you can choose to use or override the settings saved with the .ppt file.

Using the Access Snapshot Viewer   The Access SnapShot Viewer is also a little different. Before you can view Access database files with the SnapShot Viewer, you must save it in SnapShot format. To do this, open the database file (it will have an .mdb extension) and select **File, Save As** in the Save As Type drop-down box. Now it can be viewed with the Access Snapshot Viewer, even on a computer that does not have the Access application installed, as shown in Figure 41.8.

The Snapshot Viewer provides fully functioning data controls and scrollbars, and you can print the report from the **File** menu.

> **N O T E**   The version of Quick View that comes with Windows 98 and Windows 2000 will display Word 97/2000 documents. The Quick View that comes with Windows 95 and Windows NT can display many file types, including Word 95 documents, but it cannot display Word 2000 documents. If you use these operating systems, you can purchase or buy Quick View Plus Version 5, which supports Word 2000 documents (and other file types, such as .gif images, that cannot be displayed by the Windows Quick Viewer). For more information, see `http://www.jasc.com/download.html`.

Part
VI

Ch
41

FIGURE 41.8
You can use the Access Snapshot Viewer to display Access reports that have been saved in snapshot format.

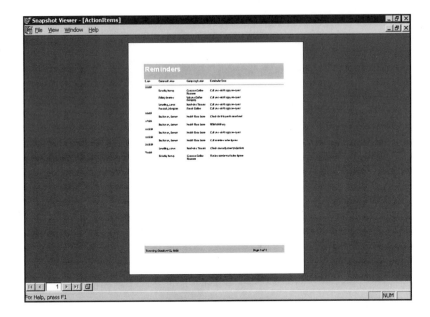

Working with Reduced Processor Power and Memory Resources

Although laptops and notebooks are now being made with powerful processors and memory capacity that comes close to that of desktop machines, the financial outlay for a portable with hardware resources equivalent to your desktop will be considerably higher. Due to this cost factor, you might find that affordability requires you to work with diminished hard disk capacity, less installed physical memory (RAM), and a slower microprocessor.

For this reason, it's a good idea to reduce the need for memory and processor resources, to the extent possible, when working with Office 2000 on a portable system. Some suggestions include:

- Run fewer applications simultaneously.

- Disable Active Desktop if you are using Windows 98 or Windows 2000, or if you have Microsoft Internet Explorer 4.0 installed on Windows 95 or Windows NT.

- On each Office 2000 application (Access, Excel, PowerPoint, and Word), perform the following:

  Select **Tools, Customize, Options**. Select **None** for the Menu Animation option, as shown in Figure 41.9.

- Application features that are always on and running in the background by default (for instance, the automatic spelling and grammar checking in Word) require more system resources, so consider disabling them for optimal performance.

FIGURE 41.9
Setting menu animation to None on Office 2000 applications reduces the load on system resources.

Working Handheld and Palm-Sized Computers Using Windows CE

Computers keep getting smaller. Mobile users want portability, but they also demand functionality that's comparable to their desktop or tower systems.

The terminology can be confusing. What's the difference between a handheld and a palm-sized computer?

■ **Handheld.** Basically a scaled-down version of the ever-shrinking notebook PC. Most handhelds have keyboards, although depending on size and design, some are more usable than others. Handhelds have wider screens, are more expandable, and generally cost more than palm-sized systems.

■ **Palm-sized.** Palm-sized PCs usually have a stylus for handwritten input, but also use an onscreen "soft keyboard" for data entry. Palm-sized PCs are smaller, and work well for retrieving email, scheduling, and quick capture of data.

N O T E Microsoft has also announced Windows CE for the Auto PC, a voice-activated computer system for the car. For more information about this and other Windows CE news, visit the Microsoft Windows CE homepage at **www.microsoft.com/windowsce/**. ■

The problems inherent to smaller physical design, which we've discussed in the preceding sections (less memory, less powerful processors, and smaller hard disks), apply to an even greater degree to the new handheld and palm-sized computers that fit into a pocket. Microsoft built an operating system specifically designed for these miniature devices.

Windows CE is the "lite" member of the Microsoft Windows operating system family. It runs on handheld machines and includes stripped-down but fully functional versions of the Microsoft Office applications (called *pocket* versions). Best of all, the data you create on a Windows CE device can be synchronized with your Windows-based desktop computer so that both are always current.

Today's palm-sized PCs include such features as handwriting input, voice recorders, soft keyboard, and the familiar Outlook Inbox, Contacts, Calendar, and Task List.

The Windows CE operating system cannot be purchased by itself; it is available preinstalled in Read-Only Memory (ROM) only in handheld and palm-sized computing devices. In order to synchronize your miniature computer's data with your desktop's data, the desktop (or a powerful laptop or notebook, for that matter) can run the Windows CE Services software, which enables it to communicate with the CE device.

N O T E Microsoft provides downloadable add-ons for Windows CE, as well as product guides, tips, news, and support information for Windows CE users at
`http://www.microsoft.com/windowsce/products/`. ▪

The exact procedure for setting up your handheld device to synchronize with your desktop computer varies depending on the manufacturer of the device. Follow the directions that come with your Windows CE device or download the vendor's instructions from the Web.

In general, the first step is to attach the CE device to your desktop computer with a serial cable (this is usually provided with the device). Then, you install the Windows CE Services software from CD-ROM onto the desktop system. The CE Services program should automatically detect the presence of the handheld device and update the data continuously when connected.

N O T E Instead of using a serial cable, palm-sized PCs running Windows CE can communicate with your desktop machine through their wireless infrared features if your desktop system supports IR communication. ▪

Using ActiveSync to Update Information

The process of installing CE services creates a "partnership" between the desktop and the CE device so they can use the ActiveSync process to update information. During this process, files that are stored in the Synchronization File folder on each of the computers are compared, and the software ensures that the most recent version of each file is stored in both locations.

 TIP ActiveSync 3.0 supports Microsoft Windows 95 and Windows 98—including Second Edition—and Windows NT 4.0 Workstation and Windows 2000 Professional. ActiveSync 3.0 also supports Microsoft Office 95, Office 97, and Office 2000. Version 3.0 is an upgrade that works with devices running Windows CE 2.0 and later.

You can view or change the ActiveSync options from the desktop computer by performing the following steps:

1. On the desktop computer, from the **Start** menu, select **Programs, Microsoft Windows CE Services, Mobile Devices**.

2. Choose **Tools, ActiveSync Options**. If you want to manually synchronize the files on the two systems, click **Synchronize Now**.

3. If you want to schedule the synchronization, select the appropriate option from this list:

   - **Automatic.** Files will be synchronized continuously when the two computers are connected.

   - **Continuous.** Only changed files will be synchronized, at the time there is a change.

   - **Manual.** You must initiate synchronization.

4. Click **OK** and then click **Close**, and close the Mobile Devices window.

Understanding Windows CE Features

The programs that are included with the CE operating system depend on the type of CE device you use. Handheld devices run a version of CE that provides enhancements over the palm-sized version. Also note that some manufacturers provide for upgrading to a later version of the CE operating system, whereas others do not. A typical Windows CE desktop is shown in Figure 41.10.

FIGURE 41.10
Windows CE offers scaled-down versions of most of the familiar Office applications, and can be synchronized with Office 2000.

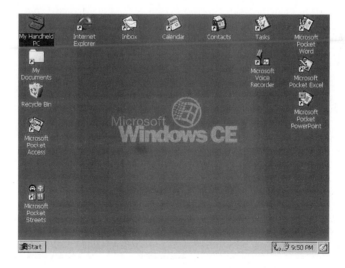

Part
VI

Ch
41

Using Pocket Office   Windows CE includes its own suite of basic application for handheld and palm-sized computers, designed for the scaled-down hardware platform. These include

- **Pocket Word.** Simple document processing, including review, editing, and printing.
- **Pocket Excel.** Simple spreadsheet activity.

- **Pocket PowerPoint.** Presentation graphics (can be attached to an external VGA display).
- **Pocket Outlook.** Email, calendaring, contacts, and task management.

N O T E The Windows CE Handheld PC Professional Edition software runs on Handheld PC version 2.0 devices (not palm-sized PCs). Version 3.0 includes the new Pocket Access and enhanced versions of Pocket Word, Pocket Excel, Pocket PowerPoint, Pocket Internet Explorer, and Pocket Outlook. ▪

Using Pocket Word   The Pocket version of Microsoft Word maintains much of the functionality of Word 2000, but is designed with features that mobile users are most likely to need. It does not include some of the advanced features, such as headers and footers, tracking changes, comments, sections, and page setup information.

Because those who use Pocket Word will almost certainly be using it in conjunction with desktop systems and its "big brother" application, it is important to know how to convert document files between the two.

To convert a Word 2000 document to Pocket Word format, first start the Windows CE Services program on the desktop computer. From the **File** menu, choose **Open**. Select the Word document and save as a Pocket Word file (using the .pwd extension for documents and .pwt for templates).

Now perform a manual ActiveSync synchronization, and then open the document on the mobile device.

> **CAUTION**
> Some formatting might be changed or removed during the conversion process.

To convert a Pocket Word document to Word, run ActiveSync to move the document to your desktop computer's hard disk. Open the file in the Windows CE Services window on the desktop computer, and save it as a Word document (.doc extension) or as a Rich Text Format file (.rtf extension).

 TIP   The conversion process uses conversion filters installed by Office. If you receive an error message indicating that a particular converter cannot be found, run the Office 2000 setup on the desktop computer, select **Add/Remove Components**, and install the missing conversion filter(s).

There are templates and sample files for the Pocket programs in the My Handheld PC\Programs\Office\Templates folder on both the desktop computer and the handheld or palm-sized device.

Using Pocket Excel You can convert a Microsoft Excel workbook (.xls extension) or template (.xlt) to Pocket Excel format with Windows CE Services. Pocket Excel files use the .pxl and .pxt file extensions.

Pocket Excel doesn't support macros and some advanced formatting features, but most worksheets display well. Any formatting features that are not supported are stripped out (you will not receive any warning messages). For example, the following is removed:

- Text boxes
- Drawing objects
- Pictures
- Controls
- Chart objects

Hidden worksheets become visible, and pivot table data is converted to values.

There are limitations to the size of Pocket Excel worksheets; only 16,384 rows areallowed, as opposed to more than 65,000 rows with Excel 2000.

Using Pocket PowerPoint Pocket PowerPoint works a little differently from its companion applications. For instance, a Pocket PowerPoint file (.ppv extension) cannot be converted to a PowerPoint 2000 file (.ppt). When you copy a PowerPoint file from the desktop computer to the Windows CE device, it is automatically converted to Pocket PowerPoint format. Unfortunately, this means it loses some features, such as animation and slide transitions.

Although Pocket PowerPoint is handy for "spur of the moment" presentations and situations in which you don't have access to a more powerful computer, it sacrifices some performance and visual quality for portability.

Due to the limited memory resources of the miniature devices, you can expect Pocket PowerPoint to be significantly slower than PowerPoint 2000 running on a desktop or a modern laptop or notebook. Additionally, you are not able to use high resolutions for optimal visual impact. Pocket PowerPoint supports compact, 640×480, and 800×600 output, but as you increase the resolution, you also increase the file size and slow performance.

Using Pocket Access Pocket Access is available only on the handheld version of Windows CE. With Windows CE 2.1, it enables you to drag Microsoft Access database (.mdb) files from the desktop to your Windows CE device. Another new feature is the capability to synchronize Pocket Access Databases with Microsoft SQL Server.

Using Pocket Outlook The Pocket version of Microsoft Outlook makes it possible for you to check your email, read and compose messages, and manage your mail no matter where you are.

To configure Pocket Outlook to access your email account, close all the windows on your handheld PC screen and follow these steps:

1. Double-click the **Inbox** icon on your desktop. This opens the Inbox window for Pocket Outlook.

2. Click the **Compose** menu and choose **Options**. This opens the Options dialog box.

3. Click the **Delete** tab to display the configuration dialog box shown in Figure 41.11.

FIGURE 41.11
The Options box is used for configuring Pocket Outlook to access email.

4. Choose the **Upon exit** and **Upon disconnect** buttons. This tells the Inbox to remove messages you have deleted as soon as you exit the Inbox program or you disconnect from the Internet.

5. Click the **Services** tab. You see the screen depicted in Figure 41.12.

FIGURE 41.12
You must add a service to provide Pocket Outlook with information about your email account and server.

6. Click the **Add** button to add a new Service profile for your mailbox. Choose **Internet Mail**, as shown in Figure 41.13, and then click **OK**.

FIGURE 41.13
Add the Internet Mail service to Pocket Outlook.

7. You are prompted to enter a name for your new service, as shown in Figure 41.14.

8. Enter the name of your mail service and click **OK** to continue. The first page of the Service Definition dialog box appears. You need the following information from your email provider:

   • Fully qualified domain name or IP address of your POP3 Host (used for accessing and downloading your email).

FIGURE 41.14

Enter a name to identify the mail account.

- Fully qualified domain name or IP address of your SMTP Host (this is used for sending email, and is optional).
- User ID assigned by your email provider (this will be the first part of your email address, preceding the @ sign).
- Your email password (you can check the check box to enable Outlook to save your password so you don't have to enter it every time you access your email).
- Your return address (this is optional; it is the address that is used when another sender uses "reply to" in responding to your message).

Complete all of the fields carefully. Be sure that your **User ID** is in lowercase letters and that your password is correct. Also be sure to enter your correct email address into the **Return Address** text box.

9. Check all the information for accuracy and click **Next.** You then see the General Preferences dialog box, which gives you the following options:
   - Disconnect services after actions are performed (select this box if your connection time is metered).
   - Check for mail every {x} min. (select this box if you want the program to automatically check your email, and specify an interval setting in minutes).
   - When new mail arrives: play a sound and/or display a message box (if you want to be notified in one or both ways, select the appropriate box).
   - Address Book: in the Contacts database, get addresses from {specify email fields}.

10. Click **Next** to display the final page of the Wizard, Inbox Preferences. If you want to read the full email message when you download it from the mail server, choose the **Full Copy of All Messages** radio button. If not (and for faster download), select the **Message Headers Only** button.

11. Click the **Finish** button to return to the Services dialog box.

12. Click the **OK** button to return to the Options dialog box.

13. Click the **OK** button to return to the Inbox.

You can now receive and send email with your handheld PC.

Part

VI

Ch

41

Using Pocket Internet Explorer The Pocket version of Microsoft's popular Internet Explorer Web browser lets you access a Web site via your Windows CE device. It provides the following features:

- Security enhancements to encrypt data sent across the Internet for online transactions.
- Support for "cookie" technology.
- Capability to save images, HTML pages, and source code for later viewing in Pocket Word.
- Caching to speed up access to revisited Web pages.

Understanding Other Windows CE Features Windows CE support for the standard TCP/IP, serial line interface protocol (SLIP), and point-to-point protocol (PPP) are built in to facilitate connection to your Internet service provider.

N O T E Microsoft has released mobile terminal services client software, with which you can use your CE device to connect to a terminal server running Windows NT 4.0 Terminal Server Edition or a Windows 2000 server running Terminal Services. ■

Addressing Windows CE Security Issues Windows CE Services uses the Dial-Up Networking (DUN) connection feature of Windows 95 and Windows 98 when synchronizing data between a PC Companion device and the desktop over a serial link (infrared, serial cable, direct dialup).

Windows CE Services requires a RAS Server to be opened and running the first time a partnership is set up, as well as whenever Windows NT Workstation (version 4.0 and 5.0) is synchronizing with a PC companion device over a serial link (infrared, serial cable, and direct dialup).

> **CAUTION**
>
> Having an open RAS server on the network might pose security concerns in some environments. This might need to be discussed with senior network administrators and/or with the company's upper management.

Troubleshooting Windows CE Services If you are having problems with the communication or synchronization between the CE device and the desktop computer, and believe that it is related to the ActiveSync desktop connectivity software, do the following:

Open the Mobile Devices folder (icon located on your desktop screen), select the **Help** pull down menu, and click either the **Windows CE Services Help Topics** or **Communications Troubleshooter** for assistance. The Help menu also provides pointers to a number of online resources by clicking **Microsoft on the Web**.

For more information on using Windows CE, try the following resources:

- Windows CE newsgroup: post questions and answers about Windows CE on the `microsoft.public.windowsce` newsgroup, using the `msnews.microsoft.com` news server.

- FAQ: The Windows CE Frequently Asked Questions page is maintained at `http://windowsce.kensai.com/faq`.

- Chris Herrera's CE Web site: `www.cewindows.net`.

Using Office 2000 When Mobile

Office 2000 includes features that are designed to make life easier for mobile users. The Microsoft Windows operating systems also have features built in to support mobile users, which you can use in conjunction with your Office applications.

These include the Pack-and-Go feature for PowerPoint users, Offline Files for Windows 2000 users, and the Briefcase for users of Windows 95/98/2000 and Windows NT.

Using PowerPoint 2000's Pack-and-Go Component

Mobile computers and PowerPoint presentations are made for each other. Slideshows are often designed to go "on the road," and as presentations get more sophisticated (incorporating more animation and sounds and other disk-hungry components), their files might grow too large to fit on a floppy disk.

This is where PowerPoint's Pack-and-Go feature comes in. PowerPoint 2000 enables you to pack all the files and fonts used in your presentation onto a disk or network location, using the Pack-and-Go Wizard. You can include linked files, TrueType fonts, and even the PowerPoint Viewer if the computer on which the slideshow will run doesn't have PowerPoint installed.

Pack-and-Go compresses the data to make more efficient use of disk space. It spans floppy disks if necessary, embedding special commands that decompress and reunite the split files when the presentation is unpacked to run on another computer.

Packing a Presentation   Follow these steps to pack your presentation using Pack-and-Go:

1. Open the presentation you want to pack.
2. On the **File** menu, click **Pack and Go**.
3. Follow the instructions in the **Pack and Go Wizard**, shown in Figure 41.15. Click **Next** to begin.
4. Choose **Active presentation** if the presentation you want to pack is already open. Or select **Other presentation(s)** to pack a presentation that is not currently open, and

Part
VI

Ch
41

type or browse to the file location (see Figure 41.16). You can pack multiple presentations by selecting more than one filename; just hold down the Ctrl key while you click on the filenames. Click **Next**.

FIGURE 41.15

The Pack-and-Go Wizard walks you through the process of packing up a PowerPoint presentation so you can take it on the road.

FIGURE 41.16

Select the PowerPoint presentation(s) to be packed.

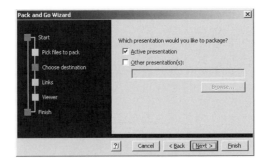

5. Choose the destination for the packed files (choose **A:\drive** if you want to save the presentation on a floppy disk), as shown in Figure 41.17. Click **Next**.

FIGURE 41.17

The Wizard prompts you to select a destination for the packed files.

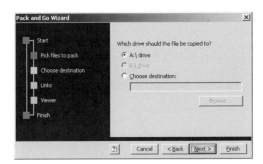

6. Select whether to embed TrueType fonts and/or include linked files, as shown in Figure 41.18, and then click **Next**.

FIGURE 41.18
You can choose to include linked files or embed TrueType fonts in your packed presentation.

7. In the next box, you are given the option to include the PowerPoint Viewer. Make your selection and click **Next** and you will see the message shown in Figure 41.19.

FIGURE 41.19
The Wizard instructs you how to complete the compression.

Congratulations! After you click **Finish**, it takes a few moments for PowerPoint to compress the files and write them to the selected disk. When it is done, you see a message informing you that Pack-and-Go has successfully packed your presentation. Now you're ready to go.

TIP

The PowerPoint Viewer is a large file, and consumes more than the space of one floppy by itself. Don't include it in your packed presentation unless you need it.

Unpacking a Presentation on the Destination Computer

N O T E   Before you can perform this procedure, you must have used the Pack-and-Go Wizard to pack your presentation. ■

Follow these steps to unpack your presentation:

1. Insert the disk or connect to the network location to which you packed the presentation.

2. In Windows Explorer, go to the location of the packed presentation, and then double-click **Pngsetup**.

3. Enter the destination you want to copy the presentation to.

TIP To run the slideshow later, locate the presentation in the folder you unpacked it to, right-click the presentation and then click **Show** on the shortcut menu. If the **Show** command is not available, neither Microsoft PowerPoint nor the PowerPoint Viewer is installed on this computer. Pack your presentation again and include the Viewer.

Using Email and Scheduling on the Road

Outlook 2000 provides a way for you to easily check your email and keep your calendar up-to-date whether you are at home or on the road.

Accessing Email with Outlook 2000   You can set up Outlook 2000 on your portable computer to connect to your email server(s) so you can access your mail accounts on the road just as you do at the office or at home. Configuring your email access on the mobile system uses the same settings you use on your desktop PC—with a few possible exceptions.

Leaving Mail on the Server   You like to download and read your email while you're on the go, but this can cause some problems. You might not have time to reply to those messages until you get back home or to the office, and then they're on the portable's hard drive, although you'd prefer to answer them from the desktop computer.

Of course, you can save the messages and then fire up the laptop and transfer them to the desktop machine using floppy disks, networking, or a direct cable connection. But there is an easier way. On the portable computer only, do the following:

1. Open Outlook 2000, and from the **Tools** menu, select **Services**. The Services dialog box will be displayed (see Figure 41.20).

FIGURE 41.20
Select the Internet email account you want to configure from the Services dialog box in Outlook 2000.

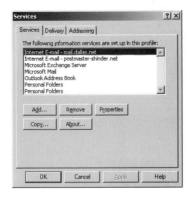

2. Double-click the name of your Internet mail account.
3. Go to the **Advanced** properties sheet, and select the **Leave a copy of messages on server** check box.

4. Click **OK,** and then click **OK** again to close the Services dialog box.

5. You'll see a message informing you that you must exit and log off before the changes take effect.

Now when you check your email from the portable computer, a copy of each message you download stays on the server, and it can be downloaded again to your desktop machine when you return.

Using Remote Mail   If you set up your computer with a modem, a telephone, dial-up networking software, and a mail delivery service to use Remote Mail, you don't have to download all the messages to your laptop at all. After you're set up, you connect and download only the message headers to screen out the messages you don't want to download. Mark the headers to download, copy, or delete specific messages. Then, reconnect and download your messages.

Keeping your Calendar Up-to-Date   You can access and update your Outlook 2000 calendar when you're away from the office, and then synchronize the calendars on your office and portable computers when you return. This is done by using personal folders.

TIP
Outlook stores all your email, calendar, and other data in personal folder files with a .pst file extension. It is possible to just copy a .pst file from one computer to another, but this is not the best way to make your desktop information available on your portable computer. One problem with this is the size of a typical .pst file; because it contains all your email (as well as messages that are in the deleted items box), it is often very large.

If you need to take only your calendar on the road, you can create a new personal folder and copy only your calendar into it (or you might want to also copy your contacts and/or task list). This results in a much smaller file, which will probably fit on a floppy disk.

Creating a New Personal Folder for Your Calendar   To create a .pst for your calendar, follow these steps:

1. Open Outlook 2000. From the **Tools** menu, select **Services**.

2. The **Services** dialog box displays (refer back to Figure 41.20). Click the **Add** button.

3. When the **Add** dialog box is displayed, choose **Personal Folders**. Click **OK**.

4. In the **Create/Open Personal Folders** dialog box, type a name for this new personal folder (it is best to identify it with your name or initials, rather than just calling it Calendar.pst. This is to avoid confusion with someone else's personal folder).

5. Click **Open** to display the **Personal Folders** dialog box. Type a name that will be used to display the folder in Outlook. You can password-protect the folder if you want. Click **OK**, and then **OK** again to exit the Services dialog box.

You must exit and log off before your new folder appears.

Part
VI

Ch
41

Copying Your Calendar to the New Personal Folder   To copy the calendar, follow these steps:

1. Open Outlook. Right-click your original calendar folder in the Folder list.
2. Choose **Copy Calendar** from the context menu.
3. In the Copy Calendar dialog box, select the name of the personal folder you created in the preceding section.

Now you should delete the original calendar folder, to make it easier and less confusing for you to use only the calendar in the new personal folder.

> **CAUTION**
>
> Be sure the calendar copied correctly to the new personal folder before you delete the original.

Your email will still be delivered to the original personal folder, and your calendar will reside in the new personal folder.

N O T E   If you also want to take your contacts and task list on the road with you, follow the same procedure with those folders, copying each to the new personal folder (.pst file), and then deleting the originals. ▪

Copying the Calendar to your Portable Computer   To make your new personal folder appear in Outlook 2000 on your portable computer, follow these steps:

1. Open Outlook on the portable.
2. From the **File** menu, select **Open Special Folders**, **Personal Folder**.
3. In the Connect to Personal Folder dialog box, locate the personal folder (.pst) file. If you are using the Briefcase to transfer files, it is located in your Briefcase.
4. Select the new .pst file, and then click **OK**. This loads the file into the current Outlook profile on the portable computer.

N O T E   If you are using the Briefcase for synchronization, before starting Outlook each time on the portable computer, right-click the Briefcase and choose **Update** to ensure that you have the most current copy of your calendar. ▪

Synchronizing Your Outlook Calendars   You can synchronize the calendars on your portable and desktop computers using the Briefcase or, if you are running the Windows 2000 operating system, using Offline Files (see the following sections on Offline files and the Briefcase).

Using Windows 2000's Offline Files Feature

Windows 2000 has a new feature that lets you make network files available while working offline on a portable computer. Any shared network files or folders, including program files and Web pages, can be made available offline.

First, you must set up your computer to use offline files and then make your files available for offline use. This makes it possible for you to disconnect your computer from the network and the files are still available for use on your computer just as though you were still connected.

When you return your portable computer to its docking station, or when your network connection is otherwise restored, any changes you made to the files on your computer while you were disconnected will be synchronized with those on the network.

Setting Up Your Windows 2000 Computer to Use Offline Files   To set up your computer to use offline files, follow these steps:

1. Open **My Computer** by double-clicking the icon on your desktop.
2. On the **Tools** menu, click **Folder Options**.
3. On the **Offline Files** tab, shown in Figure 41.21, be sure that the **Enable Offline Files** check box is selected.

FIGURE 41.21
Use the Folder Options settings to enable offline files in Windows 2000.

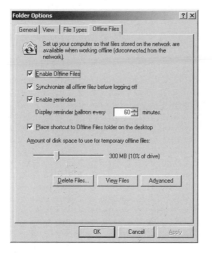

Part

VI

Ch

41

N O T E   Select **Synchronize all offline files before logging off** if you want a full synchronization. Leave it unselected for a quick synchronization. ▪

Making a File or Folder Available Offline   To make a file or folder available offline, follow these steps:

1. In **My Computer** or **My Network Places**, click the shared network file or folder that you want to make available offline.

TIP   You need to map a network drive letter to the file or folder you want to make available offline.

2. On the **File** menu, click **Make Available Offline**. You see the dialog box shown in Figure 41.22.

FIGURE 41.22
Select whether to make the folder and all its subfolders available offline, or only the folder itself.

N O T E   The **Make Available Offline** selection appears on the **File** menu only if your computer has been set up to use offline files (see the preceding section). ▨

To make an offline file or folder unavailable offline, right-click the item and click **Make Available Offline** again to remove the check mark from the selection.

Synchronizing Files with Briefcase

You can use the Briefcase, built into Windows 95/98/2000 and Windows NT, to synchronize your portable computer's files with their counterparts on your main computer when you finish working on them.

When you reconnect your laptop or notebook computer to your main computer (or insert a removable disk containing the modified files), Briefcase automatically updates the files on your main computer to the modified versions. You do not need to move modified files out of Briefcase or delete the existing copies on your main computer.

N O T E   To use Briefcase to copy files from your main computer to your portable computer, you must connect the two computers over a network or by a direct cable connection. ▨

Creating a New Briefcase   Creating a new Briefcase is simple:

1. On the desktop, right-click **My Computer**, and then click **Explore**.
2. Click the folder in which you want to create the new Briefcase.
3. On the **File** menu, point to **New**, and then click **Briefcase**.

TIP To make a new Briefcase directly on the desktop, just right-click in any clear area of the desktop, and then select **New, Briefcase.**

Using the Briefcase   You can check the synchronization status of each file in the Briefcase by opening it, and choosing **View, Details.** This tells you whether the file is up-to-date or needs updating.

You can also select a Briefcase, choose **File, Properties,** and click the **Update Status** tab, shown in Figure 41.23. This tab also contains the **Find Original** button, which you can click to locate the original file.

FIGURE 41.23

You can find the original file or split the Briefcase file from the original by using the Update Status tab on the file Properties sheet.

If you want to separate a Briefcase file from its original (when you remove it from the Briefcase because you no longer need it to be synchronized), click **Split From Original** in the **Update Status** tab shown in Figure 41.23.

Choosing Which to Use: Briefcase or Offline Files   Briefcase is designed to transfer files between computers using a direct cable connection or a removable disk. Briefcase lets you synchronize the files you modified on another computer with their counterparts on your main computer. You can keep your files organized by creating multiple briefcases.

Offline files are the best choice for working with shared files on a network. Offline files let you make changes to shared files while you are disconnected from the network and then synchronize them the next time you are connected to the network.

Of course, you will have the offline files choice only if you are using the Windows 2000 operating system. Windows 95/98 and Windows NT offer only the Briefcase file synchronization method.

Getting Connected with Remote Access

Taking your portable computer on the road doesn't have to mean remaining disconnected from the office network or the Internet until you return. Thanks to the dial-up networking and remote access components built into modern Windows operating systems, mobile users are no longer limited to working in an isolated environment.

There are two basic ways in which you can connect your mobile machine to another network over the telephone lines: in remote control mode, or as a remote node.

- **Remote control**: In this mode, your computer takes control of the remote system, and the display you see on your monitor is identical to the monitor of the remote machine. When you type keyboard commands or move the mouse, the text appears or the cursor moves on the remote system's screen.

- **Remote node**: As a remote node, your computer becomes another node on the network. You are able to access files and other resources on the remote machine(s), but you do not control their desktops and applications. The only difference between a computer that is attached over the phone line as a remote node and a computer that is cabled to the office network onsite is *access speed*; connection via analog phone lines and modem is much slower.

Understanding How and When to Use Remote Control

Remote control capability is not built into the Windows desktop operating systems. In order to dial up another computer and take over its functions completely from a remote location, you need special software, such as Symantec's PC Anywhere or Laplink 2000.

The software must be installed on both computers. One becomes the remote node and the other becomes the host. You can establish the connection either by using the remote computer's modem to dial up the modem of the host computer, or by going through the Internet if both computers have Internet connections.

Remote control is appropriate if an administrator needs to dial up and administer a server, or if you need to connect to your home computer from your hotel room and check your email. One drawback to remote control is that only one remote user at a time can control the host's desktop; this is not a good solution if you have multiple users who need access to the network from remote locations.

Establishing a Remote Node Session

Connecting to your company network as a remote node gives you the same functionality you have as a member of the local area network at the office.

You log on to the network in the same way (using the same username and password, if your account has been given dial-in permissions) and you can access any resources your user account has been granted permissions to use. You can even print to a printer on the company network from your remote node. The only drawback to a remote node connection is the speed limitations of analog phone lines (this is overcome if you are able to connect over high-speed digital lines such as ISDN or DSL).

Setting up the remote node link is more difficult than installing and using remote control software. You must first create a dial-up networking connection to the network, and you must configure your computer's local area network connection properties to use the appropriate protocols and addressing information.

Using Office 2000 with Remote Access

Microsoft recommends that you not attempt to run Office applications over low-speed analog phone lines. Office 2000 should be installed on your portable computer; you can then access your Word documents, Excel spreadsheets, and other Office data that is stored on the company network over the dial-up connection.

Understanding Virtual Private Networking

Dialing up the company network directly is not the only way to access resources there, however. In many cases, it might be more efficient and cost-effective to go through the Internet to get to your files back on the office machine. This is now feasible and relatively easy, using a solution called *virtual private networking* (VPN).

When a mobile user dials up the company server's modem from a hotel room in another city, someone (the employee or the company) is going to end up paying long distance charges for whatever amount of time the connection lasts. This can become quite expensive if the remote user needs to transfer large files or perform many actions while online.

However, there is a way to save money and still have all the time you need to get your work done from a distance. Virtual private networking (VPN), which uses *tunneling protocols* to establish a connection to a private network through the Internet, is becoming a popular alternative.

But what about security? You certainly don't want to expose your organization's data to everyone on the Internet. Well, with VPN technology, you don't have to worry about that. Using *encryption* (methods for scrambling data with a secret code) and *encapsulation* (placing data packets inside other packets to travel across the network), VPNs provide secure communication from one point to another.

Windows 95/98 and Windows NT all have built-in support for the Point-to-Point Tunneling Protocol (PPTP) and Windows 2000 comes with both PPTP and L2TP (Level 2 Tunneling Protocol), a newer and more sophisticated version. No extra software or hardware is required to create a VPN connection (assuming you have a modem or other way of connecting to your Internet service provider). The only restriction is that both computers must be connected to the Internet.

Part

VI

Ch

41

So, the mobile user in a distant city can dial up a local ISP and attach to the company's server, which has a dedicated ISDN connection to the Internet, hundreds of miles away. There is no need to make a long distance call. You can see how this can result in thousands of dollars saved per year.

Using Office in a Global Environment

by Deb Shinder

As communications technology improves, more and more business is conducted across national and international boundaries. As this happens, it becomes more likely that you will be called on to support Office applications in a multilanguage environment.

Microsoft Office 2000 was designed with the global user in mind. The powerful multilingual features included in the software give you a lot of flexibility in configuring Office for international use. In previous versions of Microsoft Office, you had to use a separate version of Office for each language. Office 2000 still offers localized versions, but it can combine support for all languages into one version, using the MultiLanguage Pack. This gives you the capability of customizing multilanguage features to fit your needs.

In this chapter, we discuss some of the key elements of providing support in a global environment, including

- Multiple language support in Office 2000
- International versions of Office 2000
- Language settings in Office 2000
- Using multiple languages in Office 2000 applications
- Unicode character support in Office 2000

We will also discuss how to find and use foreign language fonts, how to use international currency formats, and how to use Office 2000's international features in conjunction with the Windows 2000 operating system.

Understanding Multiple Language Support in Office 2000

International and multiple language support occurs at two layers within Office: the Office layer and the Document layer.

Recognizing the Function of the Office Layer

Settings in the *Office layer* define the language of the user interface and Help in Office applications. Settings in this layer also specify which languages the user can enter into documents. Changes in the Office layer affect only Office applications and only within the user account in which they are made.

Recognizing the Function of the Document Layer

The *document layer* defines the language settings and tools that are used in a specific Office document. Any changes you make in this layer are stored within the individual document and do not affect any other documents. (For example, you can set the language of a single paragraph in a Word document to German).

Microsoft Office 2000 supports multiple languages in several ways:

- The MultiLanguage Pack
- Localized versions of Office 2000
- Multilingual features

Using the MultiLanguage Pack

The Microsoft Office 2000 MultiLanguage Pack enables users to change the language of their Office user interface and online Help. It includes the Microsoft Office 2000 Proofing Tools, which provide spelling checkers, grammar checkers, and other tools for editing in different languages.

Office 2000 with the MultiLanguage Pack provides the basic Office core functionality combined with language-specific features designed to make it easier for your international users to benefit from the suite's many features.

Supporting Far East Languages   The MultiLanguage Pack Proofing Tools include utilities that are particularly useful for Office 2000 users who work with Asian languages:

- Translator for Simplified Chinese and Traditional Chinese translator
- Korean converter for Hangul and Hanja

NOTE   Information about user interface and Help features and a list of proofing tools available for each language is included on the LPK and PTK Language Components worksheets in the Excel workbook Multilpk.xls. ■

Installing the MultiLanguage Pack   The MultiLanguage Pack provides full plug-inlanguage capability in Office 2000.

 N O T E   The MultiLanguage Pack and Office 2000 are installed from different CD-ROMs. The MultiLanguage Pack has its own Setup program. The installation procedure is the same as the procedure for installing Office 2000. The MultiLanguage Pack is also included in the Office 2000 Resource Kit. ■

When you install the MultiLanguage Pack, you can make language files available to users on demand, instead of copying files to users' computers, or you can copy the language files to users' hard disks. The MultiLanguage Pack uses the Windows installer to install the necessary files for a particular language only when users run Office 2000 with that language configuration.

TIP   You can enable functionality for working with certain languages regardless of whether the MultiLanguage Pack is installed. For example, by selecting Korean as an editing language, you enable Asian and Korean features in Word, regardless of whether Korean proofing tools from the MultiLanguage Pack are available.

Changing the Language for the Office User Interface   The MultiLanguage Pack must be installed before you can perform the following:

1. On the Windows **Start** menu, point to **Programs**, point to **Microsoft Office Tools**, and then click **Microsoft Office Language Settings**, as shown in Figure 42.1.

FIGURE 42.1
Select **Microsoft Office Language Settings** from the **Microsoft Office Tools** menu after installing the MultiLanguage Pack.

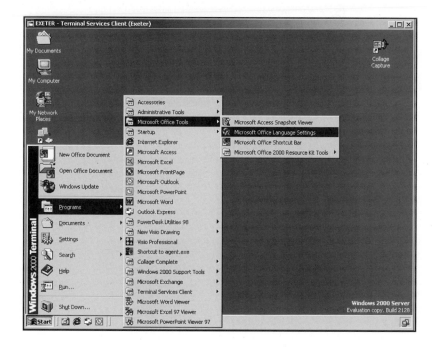

Part
VI

Ch
42

2. On the **Enabled Languages** tab (see Figure 42.2), check whichever languages you want Office to recognize.

FIGURE 42.2

Choose the language(s) you want to enable for editing of Office 2000 documents.

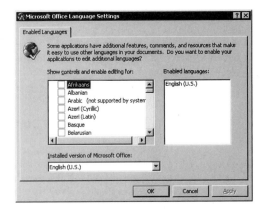

In addition to the features that are installed with the Microsoft Office 2000 MultiLanguage Pack Setup program, you can install other features from subfolders in the Extras folder on the MultiLanguage Pack CD-ROM. The Extras include

- Excel add-ins that enable users to run localized add-ins.
- Excel object libraries, for running multilingual macros created in Excel 95 or Excel 5.0.
- MSIE user-interface languages, which enable users to change the language of the Web browser interface in MSIE 5.0.
- Input Method Editors (IMEs), which enable users to enter text in Asian languages.
- Microsoft Jet 4.0 user-interface languages, with which users can change the language of the Access 2000 database engine interface.
- Outlook forms, with which users can use localized Electronic Forms Designer files to open forms.

CAUTION

If you are going to install the localized Excel add-ins, do not install English add-ins. If English add-ins are already installed, remove them before installing the localized add-ins.

Using Localized Versions of Office 2000

The MultiLanguage Pack is a handy tool—it enables you to change the user interface and Office Help to any supported language you choose, and it includes proofing tools for more than 80 languages. But in some situations, you might want to use a localized version of Office 2000.

Not all Office features have plug-in language capability. However, Office 2000 comes in localized versions for many languages so that users can still benefit from all of Office 2000's features in their own languages. These localized versions of Office 2000 are compatible with Office 2000 with MultiLanguage Pack, so users of one language version can share files created in other language versions.

Understanding Multilingual Features

Office 2000 applications use Unicode (discussed later in this chapter) to provide support for editing and viewing documents in more than 80 languages. Although you might have a particular language version of Office 2000, you still have multiple language functionality through the following multilingual features:

- **Automatic language detection.** The United States English version of Office 2000 comes with proofing tools not only for English, but also for Spanish and French. If you open a document or enter text into a document, Word 2000 can automatically detect the language of the text and use the appropriate spelling and grammar dictionaries and punctuation rules for the language you use.

- **Date, time, number style.** When you enter dates, times, and numbers, the Office 2000 application programs can format them in the correct style for different languages.

- **Dual font support.** Access 2000 data that includes both English-language characters and Asian-language characters can be displayed correctly in datasheets, forms, and reports.

Using and Modifying Language Settings in Office 2000

Office 2000 provides you with the capability to customize language settings in a granular fashion. For instance, with the MultiLanguage Pack installed, you can change the language in which the online Help is displayed without changing other language settings, or you can change the user interface without affecting the Help content.

N O T E   The language that appears in menus, dialog boxes, and wizards is called the *user-interface language.*

Changing the Default Language in Word

To specify the default language, from the **Tools** menu, select **Language**, and choose the language you want to set as the default. Then, click the **Default** button. You will see a message as shown in Figure 42.3.

Part
VI

Ch
42

FIGURE 42.3
You can change the
default language for
Word documents.

Click the **Yes** button, and new Word documents based on the `Normal.dot` template will use
the new default language.

Changing the Online Help Language

The MultiLanguage Pack enables you to change the online Help language in Office 2000.
When you do so, the Help content is displayed in the new selected language, but the Help
user interface is still shown in the language for which the Office user interface is set. Also,
some parts of the Help user interface (such as the Contents tab, the Options menu, and
toolbar ScreenTips) will always be in English.

> **N O T E**   When you change the Help content language, the language must have code page support
> from your operating system, or the Help topics listed in the **Contents** tab will be unintelli-
> gible. If this occurs, you can use the **Answer Wizard** and **Index** tabs to find Help topics, but you must
> display online Help in a language that the Answer Wizard supports. ▨

Reviewing Languages Supported in the Answer Wizard

The following languages are supported by the Office Answer Wizard. You can find Help
topics by asking questions in your own words using the Office Assistant or by using the
Answer Wizard tab in the **Help** dialog box.

- Arabic
- Chinese
  (Simplified and Traditional)
- Czech
- Danish
- Dutch
- English
- Finnish
- French
- German

- Italian
- Japanese
- Korean
- Norwegian
- Polish
- Portuguese (Brazil and Portugal)
- Russian
- Spanish
- Swedish
- Thai

Setting the Language for Selected Text

To set the language for a selected portion of text in a Word 2000 document, select **Tools,**
Language, Set Language. You will see the dialog box shown in Figure 42.4.

FIGURE 42.4
You can use the spelling and grammar checker and other proofing tools in a specified language to check selected text.

Now, the proofing tools will use the dictionaries of the selected language (if they are available).

Enabling Right-to-Left Language Features

You can enable the right-to-left features in Microsoft Word 2000 only if you are running a 32-bit Microsoft Windows operating system that has right-to-left support, such as the Arabic version of Microsoft Windows 95.

Installing the Keyboard Layout

Some languages, such as Asian right-to-left languages, have special system requirements you must meet to type characters for those languages in Office programs. For most other languages, you can install the appropriate keyboard layout for that language, by following these steps:

1. On the Windows **Start** menu, point to **Settings,** and then click **Control Panel**.

2. Double-click the **Keyboard** icon.

3. If you are running Microsoft Windows 95 or later, click the **Language** tab. If you are running Microsoft Windows NT version 4.0 or Windows 2000, click the **Input Locales** tab, shown in Figure 42.5.

FIGURE 42.5
Use the **Keyboard Properties** applet in **Control Panel** to add languages to the input locales list.

4. Click **Add**.

5. If you are running Windows 95 or later, click the language you want in the **Language** list, and then click **OK**. If you are running Windows NT 4.0 or Windows 2000, click the language you want in the **Input locale** list, and then click **OK**.

6. If you want to be able to switch keyboard layouts by using the Windows taskbar, be sure the **Enable indicator on taskbar** check box is selected.

N O T E The Microsoft Windows operating system uses an indicator on the taskbar to display the current keyboard language. ▓

Using Multiple Languages in Office 2000 Applications

In a global organization, you can use Office 2000's multiple language support in many ways.

Determining Which Language Format to Apply to Text

To select the current language and change the language format, use the **Language** box on the **Formatting** toolbar.

To add the **Language** box to the **Formatting** toolbar:

1. Click **More Buttons** on the **Formatting** toolbar.

2. Click **Add or Remove Buttons**.

3. Click **Language**.

Using AutoText with MultiLanguage Support Enabled

If you have enabled automatic language detection, the entries on the **AutoText** submenu and the **AutoText** toolbar will be in the language of the text where your insertion point is positioned. The entries listed on the **AutoText** tab (**Insert** menu, **AutoText** submenu, **AutoText** command), however, will use the language used by the Normal template.

If you want to insert AutoText entries in the language you're typing in, you must use the **AutoText** submenu or the **AutoText** toolbar. If you want to insert AutoText entries in the language that corresponds to the version of Word that you are using, use the **AutoText** tab.

N O T E If you insert an AutoText field by using the **Field Options** dialog box (**Insert** menu, **Field** command, **Options** button), the **Field Options** dialog box, like the **AutoText** tab, will use the language version of Word that you have installed, rather than the language you are typing in. ▓

Translating Words to Other Languages

You can translate from one language to another by doing the following:

1. Select the word in the document.

2. Point to **Language** on the **Tools** menu, and click **Dictionary**. If you want to use the dictionary to look up a word that is not in the document, point to **Language** on the **Tools** menu, click **Dictionary**, and then type the word in the **Look Up** box.

3. Click **Translate**.

TIP

To replace a word with another word, select a word from the **Replace with Translation** box, and then click **Replace**.

Understanding Unicode Character Encoding Support in Office 2000

Microsoft Office 2000's multiple-language support is based on the Unicode text-encoding standard. This enables Office programs to display documents correctly regardless of the language they are written in (so long as the operating system supports the characters specific to that language).

Office 2000's Unicode support enables users to copy multilingual text from most Office 97 documents and paste it into an Office 2000 document, and the text will be displayed correctly. In general, this works the other way as well: Multilingual text copied from an Office 2000 document can be pasted into a document created in an Office 97 application. (The only exception is Access 97.)

The Unicode 2.1 standard defines the character encoding of approximately 40,000 characters, covering the world's major languages.

The Arial Unicode MS font, which comes with Office 2000, is a full Unicode font. It contains all 40,000 alphabetic characters, ideographic characters, and symbols defined in the Unicode 2.1 standard.

CAUTION

Because of its large size and the typographic compromises that were necessary to create such a font, you should use Arial Unicode MS only if you aren't able to use multiple fonts tuned for different writing systems.

To install the Arial Unicode MS font if you didn't install it when you installed Office 2000:

1. Run the Office 2000 Setup CD.

2. Choose **Add or Remove Features**.

3. Click the plus sign (+) next to **Office Tools**.

4. Click the plus sign next to **International Support**.

5. Click the icon next to **Universal Font**, and then choose the installation option you want.

Installing the Unicode Font

1. On the **Select Features** panel in Office Setup, select the **Office Tools\International Support** feature.

2. Select the **Universal Font** feature, and then set the installation state to **Run from My Computer**.

Resolving Unicode Printing Problems

Some printers are not able to print Unicode text properly. If text is not printing correctly, first try updating the printer driver. If this doesn't work, you can edit the Registry to provide a workaround for most printers. This might degrade the print quality, however.

> **CAUTION**
>
> Editing the Registry can affect your entire system and should be done only by administrators. Follow directions exactly.

To set the Registry so that extended characters are printed correctly, do the following:

1. From the **Start** menu, select **Run** and type **Regedit** (Windows 95 or 98) or **Regedt32** (Windows NT or Windows 2000).

2. Go to the following Registry subkey: `HKEY_CURRENT_USER\Software\Microsoft\Office\9.0\Word\Options` (see Figure 42.6).

FIGURE 42.6
You can edit the Windows Registry to provide a workaround for Unicode printing problems on most printers.

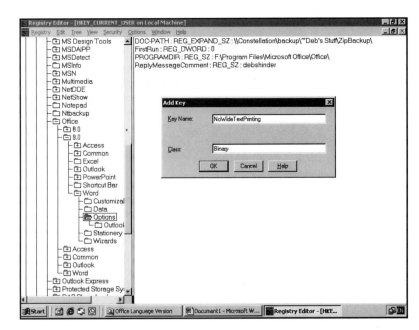

3. Add a new entry to the subkey, consisting of the value name **NoWideTextPrinting** and the binary value data of **1**.

Installing Foreign Language Fonts

Office 2000 provides foreign language fonts that enable users to view and edit documents in different languages. Some of these fonts are installed along with Office 2000, and more are available in the MultiLanguage Pack.

The fonts included in the MultiLanguage Pack support particular character sets. Office 2000 also includes a complete Unicode font, which supports all characters in all the languages supported by Office.

Office 2000 supports Asian fonts for Japanese, Korean, Simplified Chinese, and Traditional Chinese languages. For you to edit or read documents in these languages, you must install the appropriate Asian fonts. To do so, follow these steps:

1. On the **Selecting Features** panel in Office Setup, choose the **Office Tools\International Support** feature.

2. For each Asian font you want to use, select the font and set the installation state to **Run from My Computer**.

TIP Some non-Asian printers cannot properly print Asian documents because the size of the Asian font is too large for the printer's memory. You might need to install additional memory in these printers.

Using the International Currency Formats

Microsoft Word 2000 has full support for displaying and entering the euro currency symbol. If you use Microsoft Windows 95 or Microsoft Windows NT Workstation version 4.0, you might need to add Microsoft euro currency support to your system.

To add euro currency support, see Microsoft's euro support Web site at `http://www.microsoft.com/technet/euro/` to download the necessary files.

To change the display of currency to the euro on a Windows 2000 computer, from the **Start** menu select **Settings**, **Control Panel**, **Regional Options**, and **Currency** tab (see Figure 42.7). Change the currency symbol to the euro.

FIGURE 42.7
You can change the symbol displayed for currency to the euro in the **Regional Options Settings** from **Control Panel** on a Windows 2000 computer.

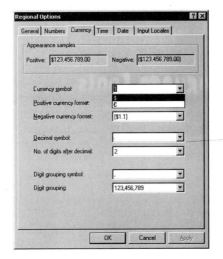

Operating System Support for Global Users

Windows 95/98, Windows NT 4.0, and Windows 2000 all provide support for the international features of Microsoft Office 2000. However, Microsoft recommends that if your users work with Asian or right-to-left languages (Arabic, Farsi, Hebrew, and Urdu), Windows 2000 is your best operating system choice.

In any event, the operating system must be configured to support multiple languages, in addition to Office itself. The way this is done differs slightly, depending on which operating system you use.

Understanding MultiLanguage Support in Windows 2000

Windows 2000 offers the best support for multiple languages, especially those using Asian characters or that read from right to left. Windows 2000 enables you to set both the system and input locales to use different languages.

Specifying System and Input Locales The *system locale* determines which code pages and associated bitmap font files are used as defaults for the operating system. These code pages and fonts enable non-Unicode applications to run in the same way as they would on the version of the operating system written for that language.

This means that if you set the system locale to German on an English version of Windows 2000 (or Windows NT), non-Unicode applications will run as if they were running on a German version of Windows.

N O T E Unicode applications are not affected by the system locale setting. See the section on Unicode encoding for more information. ■

In the Windows 95 and 98 operating systems, the system locale is fixed according to the language version, and you cannot change it. But if you use Windows NT 4.0 or Windows 2000, you have more control. The system locale defaults to the language version of the operating system, but you can change it by clicking **Regional Options** in **Control Panel**.

TIP   You must have administrator privileges to change the system locale in Windows NT or 2000.

Don't confuse the *system locale* with the *input locale*. The latter specifies the keyboard layout. An input locale is a combination of an input language and an input method.

The input locale describes the language being entered and how it is being entered. You can install more than one input locale and switch between them when you are entering text. In this way, you can create multilingual documents.

TIP   Under Windows 2000, only those system locales and input locales for which the appropriate language groups have been installed are available in the settings dialog boxes.

Configuring System Locale Settings   To set the system locale in Windows 2000:

1. In **Control Panel**, double-click **Regional Options** and click the **General** tab.
2. Click **Set default**. You will see the dialog box shown in Figure 42.8.

FIGURE 42.8
Windows 2000 enables you to change the system locale using the **Regional Settings** in **Control Panel**.

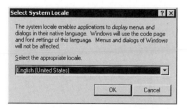

3. Select the system locale and click **OK**.

Configuring Input Locale Settings   To set the input locale(s) in Windows 2000:

1. In **Control Panel**, double-click **Regional Options** and click the **Input Locales** tab.
2. In the **Installed Input Locales** box, select the input locale or click **Add** to add a new language, as shown in Figure 42.9.
3. To change the specific keyboard layout for the locale, select the input language and click **Properties**.

TIP   Office 2000 MultiLanguage Pack and Office 2000 Proofing Tools include the Microsoft Visual Keyboard. This tool can display multiple-language keyboard layouts, making it easy to switch the input locale and type in different languages.

Part
VI

Ch
42

FIGURE 42.9
You can install multiple input locales in Windows 2000.

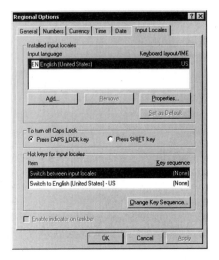

Understanding MultiLanguage Support in Windows 95 and 98

If you want to be able to enter characters for Baltic, Central European, Cyrillic, Greek, and Turkish languages in Microsoft Office 2000 programs running on Windows 95 or 98, follow these steps:

1. On the Windows **Start** menu, point to **Settings**, and then click **Control Panel**.
2. Double-click the **Add/Remove Programs** icon.
3. Click the **Windows Setup** tab.
4. In the **Components** list, click **Multilanguage Support**, and then click **Details**.
5. Select the check boxes next to the languages you want to use. ●

Making Office More Accessible to People with Disabilities

by Bo Williams

Many users face distinct challenges when performing certain computing tasks. Fortunately, efforts to make computers as accessible as possible for everyone have progressed substantially. Often, making relatively simple changes to a computing environment can make a big difference. For example, enlarging or simplifying a display can help users who have impaired vision. Also, alternative input methods can help other users who have difficulty using a mouse.

Microsoft Office includes several accessibility features that make it easier for people with disabilities to use the software. Additionally, Windows 95/98, Windows NT, and Windows 2000 include other accessibility features that can help. These features change the computing environment so that users can work both inside and outside of Microsoft Office. This chapter explores some of these accessibility features, and points to additional resources for further exploration on topics such as Microsoft Active Accessibility development tools and third-party accessibility aids.

N O T E This chapter provides basic coverage of some accessibility features included with the Windows operating system, such as high-contrast displays and mouse customizations. The Windows features covered are closely related to Office accessibility features. For more information on other accessibility features in the operating system, consult your Windows documentation or the Microsoft Accessibility Web site at `http://www.microsoft.com/enable/`.

Improving the Visibility of the Display

Assorted display changes to Office can help users with visual challenges work more effectively. The Zoom, Black and White Pictures, and High Contrast features can help users who might have difficulty seeing fine print or are color blind.

Changing the Zoom Level

One of the quickest ways to make an Office document easier to see is to increase its zoom level. To increase the zoom level, click **View**, and then **Zoom**. Choose a zoom level, and click **OK** (see Figure 43.1).

FIGURE 43.1
The Zoom dialog box controls the zoom level of Office documents.

Displaying Pictures in Black and White

Many users, most often men, have some degree of color blindness. Viewing the screen in black and white can frequently help make sense of a colorful picture. When the picture is converted from color, similar shades are often resolved and made distinct from one another. To display a picture in black and white, display the Picture toolbar, and click **Black and White** from the **Image Control** button.

If a picture contains a lot of color information that is important for comprehension (for example, a color-coded population density map), then converting the picture to black and white might not be enough for a color-blind user to fully comprehend the picture. If it's important that a color-blind user understand such a picture, consider color-neutral alternatives, such as converting the picture's colors into fill patterns.

N O T E   Some users have disabilities that can cause epileptic seizures upon exposure to certain light or color patterns. These disabilities are comparatively rare, and users with them typically make changes at an operating system level (a black-and-white color scheme, for example) to minimize risk. However, if you have concerns, you can recommend a black-and-white display for all Office document pictures. ■

Using High Contrast

Windows provides options for using a high-contrast display. High-contrast displays can ease screen reading for users with impaired vision.

To enable High Contrast:

1. Double-click **Accessibility Options** in Control Panel. The Accessibility Properties dialog box appears.
2. Click the **Display** tab (see Figure 43.2).
3. Select **Use High Contrast**.
4. Click **Settings** to configure the high-contrast display scheme.
5. Click **OK**.

FIGURE 43.2
The Display tab of the
Accessibility Properties
dialog box enables you
to choose a high-
contrast display.

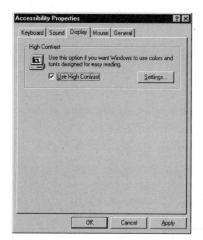

NOTE   You can also specify a high-contrast display by choosing one on the Appearance tab of
the Display Properties dialog box.

As mentioned previously, some users have disabilities that can cause epileptic seizures upon exposure to certain light or color patterns. If you have such users, ask them about potential problems
before deploying a high-contrast display scheme.

Making the Mouse More Accessible

Some users have difficulties using the mouse. To help these users, the Microsoft IntelliMouse
can be configured to zoom and scroll. With MouseKeys, the numeric keypad can replace the
mouse altogether.

Scrolling and Zooming with the Microsoft IntelliMouse

The Microsoft IntelliMouse enables zooming and scrolling with the wheel button. For many
users, this is easier than using onscreen controls to zoom and scroll. Microsoft Office is
IntelliMouse-aware. If the IntelliMouse software is properly installed, then no further configuration is necessary to use IntelliMouse functions in Office applications.

- To scroll manually, rotate (without clicking) the wheel button up and down as desired.
- To scroll automatically, click the wheel button. Automatic scrolling begins. To scroll down, move the scroll indicator below the midpoint on the side scrollbar. To scroll up, move the scroll indicator above the midpoint on the side scrollbar. The further the scroll indicator from the midpoint (in either direction), the more quickly the document scrolls. To stop automatic scrolling, either click or rotate the wheel button.
- To zoom, hold Ctrl while rotating (without clicking) the wheel button. Clicking up increases the zoom level; clicking down decreases the zoom level.
- To pan, click and hold the wheel button while moving the mouse. The further the pointer from the origin indicator, the more quickly the document pans. To stop panning, release the wheel button.

Using the Numeric Keypad for Mouse Functions

Windows enables the use of the numeric keypad as a substitute for the mouse. This substitution, MouseKeys, can be an excellent candidate for rapid deployment in your organization. Because it mimics mouse activity, MouseKeys provides a way for a user who has difficulty using a mouse to be productive quickly.

To enable MouseKeys:

1. Double-click **Accessibility Options** in Control Panel. The Accessibility Properties dialog box appears.
2. Click the **Mouse** tab (see Figure 43.3).
3. Select **Use MouseKeys**.
4. Click **Settings** to configure MouseKeys.
5. Click **OK**.

FIGURE 43.3
The Mouse tab of the Accessibility Properties dialog box enables you to choose MouseKeys.

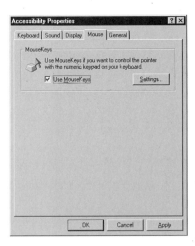

Making the Keyboard More Accessible

Keyboard changes to Office applications can help users who have coordination difficulties. For example, a user might have trouble double-clicking, or might have difficulty following the mouse pointer on the screen. Some users become more effective when they ignore the mouse completely. Fortunately, extensive accessibility capabilities for the keyboard are delivered with both Office and the Windows operating system.

Using the Keyboard Instead of the Mouse

The keyboard can capably duplicate almost any mouse function. Like most Windows applications, Office delivers two kinds of ready-to-use keyboard functions: mnemonic keys and keyboard shortcuts. *Mnemonic keys* enable selection of menu items without using the mouse. For example, rather than clicking **File**, and then **Open**, you can type **Alt**, **F**, **O**. The menu opens and the command is executed, just as with the mouse.

A *keyboard shortcut* is a keystroke or combination of keystrokes that performs a function. For example, to Copy in any Office application, type **Ctrl+C**, and the highlighted data is copied to the Clipboard. Unlike mnemonics, when you use a shortcut, the menu doesn't appear.

You can find keyboard shortcuts for most commands listed directly on the menus. You can also print lists of all shortcut keys from Help in any Office application.

Creating Customized Keyboard Shortcuts in Microsoft Word

Microsoft Word contains other keyboard shortcut functions. For example, you can create custom keyboard shortcuts, print a list of all keyboard shortcuts in Microsoft Word, and change basic keyboard actions.

To create custom keyboard shortcuts:

1. Click **Tools**, and then **Customize**.
2. Click **Keyboard**. The Customize Keyboard dialog box appears (see Figure 43.4).
3. In the **Save changes in** list, choose the document or template in which you want to save the customized shortcuts.
4. In the **Categories** box, choose the category that contains the command (or other item) for which you want to create a keyboard shortcut.
5. In the **Press new shortcut key** box, type the key combination you want to assign to the command.
6. Click **Assign**.

FIGURE 43.4
The Customize
Keyboard dialog box
enables you to create
custom keyboard
shortcuts.

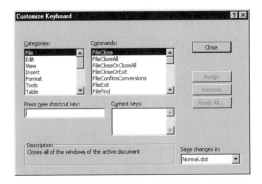

The custom shortcut is created and becomes available whenever you use the document or template in which you saved it. Microsoft Word enables you to print a list of all Word keyboard shortcuts:

1. Choose **Tools**, **Macro**, **Macros**. The Macros dialog box appears (see Figure 43.5).

2. In the **Macros in** dialog box, choose **Word commands** from the drop-down list.

3. In the **Macro name** box, click **ListCommands**. Click **Run**.

4. In the List Commands dialog box, click **Current menu and keyboard settings**.

5. Choose **File**, **Print**.

FIGURE 43.5
The Macros dialog box
enables you to run the
ListCommands macro.

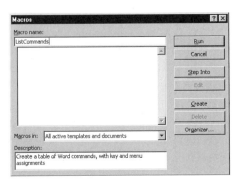

The shortcut list prints. The shortcut list contains all shortcuts delivered with the program, as well as any custom shortcuts created.

Changing Keyboard Behavior

Windows provides some basic accessibility options for keyboard control. These options can help users who can use a keyboard, but with some difficulty.

- *StickyKeys* enables the use of "hold" keys, such as Shift and Ctrl, by pressing one key at a time.

■ *FilterKeys* makes Windows more forgiving of repeated keystrokes.

■ *ToggleKeys* plays a tone when Caps Lock, Num Lock, or Scroll Lock is pressed.

To enable these options:

1. Double-click **Accessibility Options** in Control Panel. The Accessibility Properties dialog box appears.

2. Click the **Keyboard** tab (see Figure 43.6).

3. Use the check boxes to turn the features on and off.

4. Use the **Settings** buttons to configure feature parameters.

5. Click **OK**.

FIGURE 43.6
The Keyboard tab of Accessibility Properties enables you to choose and configure custom keyboard actions.

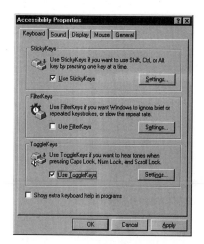

Reducing Keyboard Use with Automatic Text Processing

Office includes several automatic text-processing features that can substantially reduce keyboard use—a plus for users who have difficulty typing. AutoCorrect enables correction of typographical errors, and AutoComplete automatically completes commonly used words and phrases.

Using AutoCorrect to Minimize Typing

The AutoCorrect feature, available in Word, Excel, PowerPoint, and Access, automatically corrects typing errors. Several options for correcting capital letter usage are delivered, as are options for correcting common typographical errors. For example, you can set AutoCorrect to automatically capitalize days of the week, as well as to automatically change "byt he" into "by the." When AutoCorrect is enabled, these changes are made on-the-fly.

To set AutoCorrect options:

1. Choose **Tools**, **AutoCorrect**. The AutoCorrect dialog box appears (see Figure 43.7).

2. Select the options you want to enable.

3. Click **OK**.

To add AutoCorrect entries for typographical errors:

1. Choose **Tools**, **AutoCorrect**. The AutoCorrect dialog box appears (see Figure 43.7).

2. Select **Replace text as you type**.

3. In the **Replace** box, type the typographical error (for example, **Chicaog**).

4. In the **With** box, type the text you want to automatically substitute for the error (for example, **Chicago**).

5. Click **Add**. If you have additional entries, return to step 3.

6. Click **OK**.

FIGURE 43.7
The AutoCorrect dialog box enables you to configure automatic corrections.

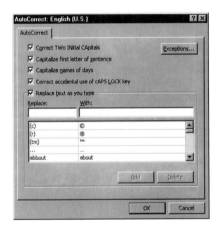

Using AutoComplete to Minimize Typing

The AutoComplete feature, available in Word, automatically completes commonly used words and phrases called *AutoText*. For example, AutoComplete can automatically complete the current date, standard salutations such as "To Whom It May Concern," and commonly used names. When AutoComplete believes it recognizes an AutoText entry, a pop-up tip appears near the insertion point. The tip contains the AutoComplete guess of the word or phrase currently being typed. To accept the guess, press Enter, and the guess appears in the document. To ignore the guess, simply ignore the tip.

To enable AutoComplete:

1. Choose **Insert**, **AutoText**, **AutoText**. The AutoText dialog box appears (see Figure 43.8).

2. Select **Show AutoComplete tip for AutoText and dates**.

3. Click **OK**.

To add AutoComplete entries:

1. Choose **Insert, AutoText, AutoText**. The AutoText dialog box appears (see Figure 43.8).
2. Type the new AutoText entry in the **Enter AutoText entries here** box.
3. Click **Add**. If you have additional entries, return to step 2.
4. Click **OK**.

FIGURE 43.8
The AutoText dialog box enables you to configure and customize automatic word completion.

You can also display the AutoText toolbar, which enables you to select AutoText entries directly from cascading menus without typing at all.

Customizing Toolbars and Menus to Enhance Accessibility

When you make changes to Office toolbars and menus, you are changing both the appearance and input method. You can enlarge toolbar buttons, as well as create custom toolbars with your own choice of buttons.

N O T E   Some toolbar customizations, such as hiding the Standard and Formatting toolbars, affect all Office 2000 applications. ■

Enlarging Toolbar Buttons

You can enlarge toolbar buttons to make them easier to see in any Office application. To enlarge toolbar buttons, choose **View, Toolbars, Customize**. On the Options tab, select **Large Icons**. The toolbar buttons increase to approximately four times normal size.

Customizing Toolbars

Custom toolbars, available in all Office applications, can ease some navigational frustrations of users with certain types of physical challenges. Microsoft Office is a large suite of products with many different capabilities, and for some people, it isn't always easy to navigate to a particular function or set of functions. In many cases, the user uses only a limited number of functions anyway, and a custom toolbar can contain all those functions in one place.

To create a custom toolbar:

1. Choose **Tools**, **Customize**.
2. Click the **Toolbars** tab.
3. Click **New**.
4. Choose a name for the new toolbar, as well as the template to which you want to make the new toolbar available.
5. Click **OK**. The new (empty) toolbar appears.
6. Click the **Commands** tab (see Figure 43.9).
7. Drag commands from the displayed menu replicas onto the new toolbar. You can drag icons, descriptions, or both.
8. Click **Close**.

FIGURE 43.9
Drag icons and/or descriptions from the menu replicas onto the new toolbar.

The new custom toolbar can be manipulated in exactly the same ways as any other Office toolbar. You can dock it, make it float, increase its size, change its orientation, and so on.

To edit items on existing (delivered or custom) toolbars:

1. Choose **Tools**, **Customize**.
2. Click the **Toolbars** tab.
3. Select the toolbar you want to edit. The toolbar appears.
4. Click the **Commands** tab.

5. Drag items to and from the toolbar.

   To add an item, drag it from the displayed menu replicas and drop it onto the toolbar. To delete an item, drag it from the toolbar and drop it (anywhere).

6. Click **Close**.

Finally, you can also move items from one toolbar to another. This can be helpful when a delivered toolbar already contains most of the commands needed.

To move items from one toolbar to another:

1. Choose **Tools**, **Customize**.
2. Click the **Toolbars** tab.
3. Select the source and destination toolbars.
4. Drag items from the source toolbar to the destination toolbar.
5. Click **Close**.

Introducing Microsoft's Active Accessibility Development Tools

Active is a Microsoft-developed set of technologies that makes software and accessibility aids work better together. It is not an individual software program that can be purchased and installed. Rather, it is built into the operating system (in Windows 98 and Windows 2000), software program (in Office 2000 and Internet Explorer), and accessibility aids (such as keyboard enhancement utilities) at a core level. Active Accessibility has no user interface.

Active Accessibility enables hardware and software accessibility aids, such as screen readers and voice input utilities, to work better with software. A program using Active Accessibility can automatically output information about a graphics-heavy user interface that enables a screen reader, for example, to access the presented information reliably. The technology can provide information about dialog boxes, icons, and other controls on the interface just as they appear. Before Active Accessibility, the best answer for such scenarios was often to convert everything to text—not always a desirable, or even feasible, solution.

Furthermore, Active Accessibility enables development of accessible applications without compromising design or functionality. Because the Active Accessibility development tools are freely available from Microsoft, software developers can easily use the technologies. A growing number of accessibility aid vendors and other software vendors are including Active Accessibility in their products.

With Active Accessibility built into so many current Microsoft offerings, chances are good that you're awash in it. If you have users with disabilities, it's worth checking for Active Accessibility when you purchase accessibility aids.

Finding Accessibility Aids Beyond Microsoft Products

Accessibility aids are software and/or hardware products that provide additional accessibility beyond what is available in Windows and in Office.

- **Keyboard enhancement utilities** enable users to accelerate keyboard operations. Simple accelerations, such as one-touch use of Alt and Ctrl, are either included in or available for the operating system at no charge. More complex accelerations, such as word anticipation and abbreviation expansion, are available from third parties.

- **Onscreen keyboard utilities** enable users with motion impairment to select keys from an onscreen keyboard. The onscreen keyboard can be a graphic representation of the standard keyboard, a collection of custom graphic keys that execute macros, or both.

- **Screen enlarger utilities** enlarge a portion of the screen to help users with low vision. Magnifier, a simple screen enlarger program, is included in Windows 98 and Windows 2000.

- **Screen review utilities** work in conjunction with hardware, such as dynamic Braille displays, to make visual information available to blind users.

- **Voice input utilities** enable users to speak directly to the computer to execute commands, bypassing both the mouse and the keyboard entirely.

Your current software supplier might stock accessibility aids (most larger suppliers do). You can also investigate the following Web sites for further information.

Using Additional Resources

There are many resources to help users with disabilities get the most out of Office.

Discovering Microsoft Office 2000, a document delivered with Office 2000, contains an appendix with further information on Microsoft accessibility solutions.

The Microsoft Accessibility Web site

`http://www.microsoft.com/enable`

is an excellent place to explore the latest accessibility news and downloads, including operating system accessibility upgrades. Microsoft also provides links to vendors of accessibility aids, as well as advice for maximizing the effectiveness of these aids with Office.

WebABLE!

`http://www.webable.com/`

provides a comprehensive, often-updated list of accessibility resources available on the Internet.

Recording for the Blind & Dyslexic

`http://www.rfbd.org/`

is a leading provider of audio reference materials (including technical and computer titles) for people with visual disabilities.

The Trace Research & Development Center

`http://www.trace.wisc.edu/`

is a treasure trove of readings and guidelines on information technology accessibility efforts. ●

Part
VI

Ch
43

PART VII

Troubleshooting and Optimizing Office

Troubleshooting and Optimizing Word

by Bill Camarda

Bad things happen to good software, and if that software is Microsoft Word, odds are it's going to be your problem. In this chapter, you'll walk through the key elements of Word troubleshooting: what to do when Word won't start, won't keep running, or corrupts the documents and templates that your business depends on. You'll also take a quick look at some settings that can help optimize Word for the systems you're running it on.

Keeping Word Up-to-Date

Although Microsoft makes little pretense that its service releases fix *all* the bugs in Word (or any other program), they do fix many of the problems Microsoft has found it easiest to reproduce. Therefore, it usually makes sense to qualify and deploy Word service releases as quickly as possible.

As this book is being written, Microsoft has not yet issued any service releases for Office 2000, although it seems likely that at least one will be released.

For the Macintosh, Microsoft has released the Combined Office 98 Updater, which provides several bug fixes and security updates, as well as better support for Mac OS 8.5.

For those running Office 97 for Windows, Microsoft has issued two Service Releases, each of which includes fixes that are relevant to Word. Among the most important problems largely solved by service releases are the following:

- Loss of graphics data, with Word displaying a red X in place of graphics (fixed in SR-1).
- Corrupted documents when saving to a hard disk with less than 20MB free space (improved in SR-1, but Word still works more reliably with more free space).
- Problems with headers and footers containing field codes; invalid page faults (IPFs) when saving such documents as RTF files (fixed in SR-1).
- In GroupWise and Document Management System environments, problems with reopening files that are closed after copying large amounts of text (fixed in SR-2).

Troubleshooting Damaged Documents in Word 2000/98/97

What could be worse than going through the trouble of building a complex document and then finding that document corrupted? When this happens to you—or to a panicked colleague—the first step is to calm down.

> **NOTE** It will be a lot easier to calm down if you know you have a recent backup. Ensuring that you have a reliable system for backing up files is one of the most important things you can do as an Office administrator. ▓

The second step is to do some basic troubleshooting, intended to rule out causes that are external to the document:

- Does the problem occur only in this document? (Try opening other documents, especially documents containing similar elements.)
- Is the problem related to the template that is attached to the document? (Try attaching a different template via the **Tools**, **Templates** and **Add-Ins** dialog box.)
- Is the problem specific to this computer? (Try opening the file on another computer.)

- Is the problem specific to Word? (Try running other programs to see if the problem recurs.)

- Does the problem occur only when you are using a specific printer driver? (Try switching printers and printer drivers.)

- Is the problem video-related; in other words, are there unreadable characters on screen? (In Windows, try running Windows with the standard `Vga.drv` video driver.)

If, after this, it appears that the problem is actually with the document, try the steps discussed in the next section.

Recovering a Damaged Word 2000/98 Document

If your document opens but does not work properly, you have several options for recovering all or most of the information stored in it:

- First, try to copy everything in the document except for the last paragraph mark into a new document. Word stores a great deal of information in paragraph marks, and the last paragraph mark in the document contains even more information, including critical section and style data. If the document corruption is contained there, copying everything else into a new document could solve the problem.

- Save the entire document to another format, such as Word 6.0/95, RTF, or in Word 2000—HTML. Often, this solves the problem, but you might lose document elements that are supported only in the Word 2000/97 document format. In addition, saving to the older format sometimes causes graphics in your document to be resized.

- Copy chunks of your document into a new document, a piece at a time—saving the new document after each copy. You might be able to figure out roughly where in your document the corruption exists, and copy all the other elements before and after the corruption. Often, you'll find that the problem is in a damaged image, which you can then delete and replace. Or, it might be in a specific paragraph; you might then be able to copy the contents of that paragraph, except for the paragraph mark at the end of the paragraph.

- Use **Insert**, **File** to insert the damaged file into a new document.

- Try viewing the file in Draft mode. Choose **Tools**, **Options**, click the **View** tab, select the **Draft Font** check box, and click **OK**.

The preceding techniques are intended to preserve both text and formatting. If these fail, you might still be able to preserve most of the text in your document by saving the file as Text Only or by opening it in another word processor, such as WordPad, and copying blocks of text into Word. You'll have to reformat the document, but it's better than losing everything.

NOTE Special reliability issues might arise if you are using files that were originally created in WordPerfect and then imported using Word's WordPerfect import filters. Many of these issues are covered in "Migrating from or Coexisting with Legacy Applications," in Chapter 18. You might also want to read the Microsystems white paper, *Making the Change from WordPerfect to Word in a Legal Environment*, available at **www.microsystems.com/expert.htm**.

Using the Recover Text Filter

If a Word file appears to be damaged, you can also try opening the file using the **Recover Text from Any File** filter, which strips everything except text from any formatted file. Follow these steps:

1. Choose **File**, **Open**.
2. Choose **Recover Text from Any File** in the **Files of Type** drop-down box.
3. Browse to and select the file you want to open.
4. Click **Open**.

If Word's Fast Save feature was turned on when you last saved this file successfully, you might find that the text is not displayed in proper order. Still, most or all of it should be there—*somewhere*.

You might be able to mix and match these techniques. You could, for example, copy formatted text from your original file wherever possible, and copy unformatted text from a copy of the file recovered using the **Recover Text from Any File** filter.

> **CAUTION**
> Be careful to reset the **Files of Type** setting to your original setting when you are finished working with **Recover Text from Any File**. Otherwise, Word processes the next document you open with the Recover Text filter.

> **N O T E** In Word 2000, the Recover Text from Any File filter installs as part of the default installation. If it is not present, you can run a maintenance install to install it. You'll find this filter in the **Converters and Filters/Text Converters** category of installation options. ■

Using the Word AutoRecover Feature

Word's AutoRecover feature can help reduce the risk that your users will lose documents in the event of a power failure or system crash. By default, Word creates a new AutoRecover file every 10 minutes. You can ensure AutoRecover is turned on at a user's workstation by choosing **Tools**, **Options**, **Save**, and selecting the **Save AutoRecover Files Every** check box. You can also change the interval Word uses to create AutoRecover files; for example, if your computers are relatively fast, you might double AutoRecover file creation to every 5 minutes.

This setting might also be established centrally, via the System Policy Editor: go to **Default User**, **Microsoft Word 2000**, **Tools**, **Options**, **Save**, **Save AutoRecover Info**. For more information on using the System Policy Editor, see Chapter 37, "Reducing Office 2000's Total Cost of Ownership."

> **CAUTION**
> *AutoRecover is no substitute for saving files*, if for no other reason than that users will still lose data created since the last AutoRecover.

N O T E AutoRecover cannot create recovery files for master documents, but it can create them for individual subdocuments. ■

New AutoRecover files are created with the filename <document name>.asd. By default, the files are stored in the \Windows\Application Data\Microsoft\Word folder, or if profiles are in use, the Windows\Profiles*username*\Application Data\Microsoft\Word folder. If necessary, you can change this location through **Tools, Options, File Locations** (or via **System Policies** by going to **Default User, Microsoft Word 2000, Tools, Options, File Locations, AutoRecover Files**). However, it usually makes sense to keep AutoRecover files stored locally in case the problems that caused the system to crash were network-related.

In the event Word crashes or the entire computer crashes, the next time Word is opened, it looks for the AutoRecover files and attempts to open them. If the user had many files open, many AutoRecover files might be displayed. The user can then resave each file under its original filename.

Part

VII

Ch

44

> **CAUTION**
>
> Before resaving over their original files, users should always open and check those original files. If a user has manually saved a file very recently, that file could be more recent than the AutoRecover file—and resaving over it might actually lead to *losing* recent work.

If a user does not choose to save the AutoRecover file, Word renames it using the WBK extension and leaves it in the same subfolder where it was originally placed. You might find many WBK files are placed there over time.

In fact, if for some reason Word does not open an AutoRecover file when you expected it to, you can browse to this folder from within Word's Open dialog box and look for it. In some cases, it will have the WBK extension; in other cases, it will still have the ASD extension. If you find the file, open it and resave it with a DOC extension.

Creating and Opening Backup Files

Word enables users to preserve their most recently saved versions of a file when they save again. For users who are in the good habit of saving regularly, this ensures that a recent copy of their file exists even if AutoRecover cannot restore it. Backup copies are not created by default; to instruct Word to create them, choose **Tools, Options, Save**, and select the **Always Create Backup Copy** check box. When you turn this feature on, Word turns off the **Allow Fast Saves** features because it is incapable of creating backups and doing fast saves at the same time.

You can also control this feature centrally, via **System Policies**, by going to **Default User, Microsoft Word 2000, Tools, Options, Save, Always Create Backup Copy**. If you want to force users to create backup copies even if they might prefer otherwise, also select the **Check to Enforce Setting On** check box that appears at the bottom of the Default User Properties dialog box in the System Policy Editor. (For more information on using the System Policy Editor, see Chapter 37.)

After Always Create Backup Copy is turned on, Word creates a backup file named `Backup of filename.wbk` whenever the user saves a DOC file. The backup is stored in the same folder as the original file. When the user saves the file yet again, the original backup is replaced by a newer backup, so there is always one backup file, and the backup is always one version behind the current file. If the user needs to open the WBK file, she can do so by choosing it either in the **File Open** dialog box or through **Windows Explorer**.

If the user chooses to work from the Open dialog box, she must choose **All Files as Files of Type** to view the WBK files. To prevent extraneous files from being displayed, Word does not show WBK files when All Word Documents is selected (as it is by default).

> **CAUTION**
>
> Word's Always Create Backup Copy feature does *not* create backup copies of documents stored as Web pages.

NOTE   Backup files use the WBK extension in Word 2000, 97, and 95; previously, they used the BAK extension. ■

Always Create Backup Copy can help ensure that users never lose much data; however, it has three drawbacks from a management standpoint.

- It reduces system performance a bit, especially because it also turns off Fast Saves.
- It roughly doubles the amount of disk space needed for document storage.
- You need to educate users that the backup files are not current; rather, they are one version behind. Users who are familiar with the term "backup" might well expect otherwise.

Finding a Lost or Misplaced File

In some cases, you will find that users lose files simply by inadvertently storing them in the wrong folder. Here are some ways in which this can happen:

- You expect users to store files in a network location, but Word defaults to the Personal folder on the user's local workstation, and the user begins storing files there (or vice versa).
- The user expects files to be located in My Documents, as in Word 97, but the files are instead placed in Word 2000's Personal folder.
- Files are stored with the wrong extension, or the Files of Type setting is inadvertently changed to exclude the files the user needs.
- The user stores a file in a custom folder, and then creates a new file and saves it without realizing that the new file is also stored in that custom folder.
- Network drive mappings change without users realizing it, and they save files to the wrong networked drive.

Before assuming a file has been permanently lost, check these possibilities and any other similar "confusions" that have been reported in your organization.

TIP If Recover Text from Any File and Save as Text still do not work, you can still try opening the file in another text editor, such as WordPad or Notepad, and copying blocks of text into Word. This is really a last resort. The text will be interspersed with nontext characters and is difficult to read. However, if you simply must learn the contents of a file, this is worth trying.

Troubleshooting Protection Faults and Startup Problems in Word 2000

So far, this chapter has focused on troubleshooting Word documents. Now, we turn to troubleshooting Word itself. In the following sections, you'll learn what to do if Word doesn't run as reliably as it should, won't start, or doesn't deliver the performance you expect.

TIP If Word has never started properly, your Office installation might have failed. For more information about fixing failed Office installations, refer to Chapter 5, "Troubleshooting Office 2000 Installations."

Using Detect and Repair

Word 2000 (and all other core Office applications except PhotoDraw) now has a powerful tool for fixing a wide variety of problems: Detect and Repair. When Office 2000 is installed, a new Windows installer is also installed on your system. The installer keeps track of files on a user's computer and checks at startup to determine whether any essential files have been deleted or corrupted. However, to reduce start time, this "self-check" is limited and will not catch every potential problem.

If the installer does find a problem, it can find replacement files (if they remain accessible) and copy them to the appropriate location, often without any involvement by the user.

If Word or another Office application that supports Detect and Repair begins to misbehave, you can run a more detailed Detect and Repair process manually. To do so, follow these steps:

1. Choose **Help**, **Detect and Repair**. The Detect and Repair dialog box appears (see Figure 44.1).

2. Click **Start**. The Windows Installer runs. If you installed Office locally from CD-ROM or if the network location is unavailable, you'll be asked to browse to the disk.

3. The Windows installer continues to work, checking each Office file and restoring original copies if it finds any that are damaged. This can easily take 15 minutes or more.

FIGURE 44.1
The Detect and Repair dialog box.

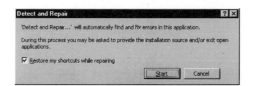

> **N O T E** Detect and Repair works only if the Internet Explorer 4.0/5 and/or Windows 98 Active Desktop is installed. However, Active Desktop does not have to be in use for Detect and Repair to work. ▪

> **N O T E** Although users can run Detect and Repair, they might encounter errors, especially in Microsoft Access, if they do not have sufficient administrative rights. Detect and Repair, however, fixes other problems it finds that are not subject to rights restrictions. ▪

Troubleshooting Word 2000 Startup Problems

If Word 2000 has run properly before, but now consistently crashes at startup, your first step should be to run **Detect and Repair**, as previously described.

> **N O T E** Even if you run it from another Office application, it attempts to fix any problems it finds in Word. If only Word is installed on your system, or if all Office applications are failing to run properly, you can also run Detect and Repair by choosing **Microsoft Office 2000** in the **Install/ Uninstall** tab of the **Add/Remove Programs** applet in the **Control Panel**. ▪

If running Detect and Repair does not work, your problem might lie elsewhere, in one of these places:

- ▪ The Normal.dot global template
- ▪ A damaged global template or damaged (or badly programmed) add-in that loads at startup
- ▪ A damaged Tahoma font, which Word 2000 uses to display dialog boxes and menus

> **N O T E** Some of the troubleshooting recommendations made throughout the remainder of this section can take a significant amount of time to perform. As an Office administrator, you might decide that it is a better use of your time to simply uninstall and reinstall Office and/ or Windows.

If you do decide to reinstall Office, it's best to remove all traces of the existing installation first. To do so, run the Microsoft Office Removal Wizard (Offlcn9.exe), which removes components that Setup sometimes leaves behind, including components from earlier versions of Office. The Office Removal Wizard can be downloaded as part of the Microsoft Office Resource Kit Toolbox, at **www.microsoft.com/office/ork**. ▪

Begin troubleshooting by starting Word without the items that normally run at startup. Follow these steps:

1. Choose **Start, Run**.
2. In the **Run** dialog box, enter Word's path and file name, along with the **/a** switch. In a typical installation, the command is

```
C:\Program Files\Microsoft Office\Microsoft Word /a
```

> **CAUTION**
>
> When you run Word with the **/a** switch, any changes that you make to **Tools**, **Options** settings or to
> `Normal.dot` during that session are lost when you exit Word.

If Word starts properly, you know that the problem is in `Normal.dot`, a global template or
add-in, or data stored in Word's Registry key. To determine whether the problem is in
Normal.dot, perform the following steps:

1. Exit Word.
2. Rename `Normal.dot`, typically stored in the `C:\Program Files\Microsoft`
   `Office\Template` folder. (Note that there might be more than one `Normal.dot` on your
   computer, especially if you've retained an earlier copy of Word. Be sure you rename the
   correct one.)
3. Run Word again (without using the **/a** switch).

If Word runs properly, the problem is in `Normal.dot`. Word regenerates a new `Normal.dot`
with no custom settings. You can then use the **Organizer** to copy all or most macros, toolbars, AutoText entries, and styles from the renamed `Normal.dot` to the new one.

If Word still does not run normally, check whether the problem is with global templates or
add-ins that load at startup.

1. Run Windows Explorer and browse to Word's startup folder, typically `C:\Program`
   `Files\Microsoft Office\Office\Startup`.
2. If any DOT or WLL files are there, move them to another folder outside of the
   Microsoft Office folder.
3. Run Word again.

If Word runs properly, the problem is in one of the global templates or add-ins. To discover
which one, you can restore them one at a time until the problem recurs. If the problem still
exists, it might be with the Data key associated with Word in the Windows Registry. You might
be able to solve the problem by deleting the Data key, using the Registry Editor (`regedit.exe`).

> **CAUTION**
>
> As always, be extremely careful with the Registry Editor; if you delete or edit the wrong information, you
> could render your computer inoperable. Be aware that deleting the Word 2000 Data key clears a variety of
> custom settings, notably the settings accessible through the Tools, Options dialog box.

You can delete the Data key as follows:

1. Exit Word (including any instance of Word running with Outlook email).
2. Choose **Start, Run**.
3. In the **Run** dialog box, type **regedit** and click **OK**.

4. Navigate to the following key:
   ```
   HKEY_CURRENT_USER\Software\Microsoft\Office\9.0\Word\Data.
   ```

5. Be sure the Data folder is selected in the left pane of the Registry Editor, and press the **Delete** key.

6. Click **Yes** to confirm that you want to delete the Data key.

7. Exit the Registry Editor.

8. Run Word (without the /a switch).

If Word runs normally, you've solved the problem, although you might have to recustomize Word's Registry settings.

If none of this works, the problem might be with the Tahoma font that Word uses to display dialog boxes and menus; try reinstalling it from the Office 2000 CD-ROM or your Windows CD-ROM.

Troubleshooting Other Word-Related Protection Faults

If you are experiencing an unacceptable number of system crashes (invalid page faults) while working in Word 2000, the following troubleshooting steps can help you identify and solve the problem.

When the invalid page fault occurs, click **Details** to see where it occurred. If you find that a printer or video driver is at fault, concentrate your efforts there. For example, switch from your video driver to the basic Vga.drv video driver in Windows, or check your printer or video card vendor's Web site to see whether a more recent driver is available for the device in question. It's common for IPFs related to printer or video drivers to occur while you are printing or formatting a document, but they can happen at other times, as well.

You can install a printer driver in Windows and select it in Word regardless of whether you actually have the corresponding printer (although, of course, you will not actually be able to send the print job to be printed). To simulate printing (and therefore see whether Word and the file can actually be printed), install the test print driver to the FILE: port instead of to a parallel port such as LPT1 or LPT2.

> **N O T E** When you change the printer driver, be sure you switch to a printer that does not use the same core minidriver. Most HP-compatible printers use Unidrv.dll, and most PostScript printers use Pscript.drv. To ensure that you fully test your printer driver, if you've been working with a PostScript printer driver, switch to an HP-compatible printer driver—or vice versa. ▪

> **N O T E** Printer or video drivers might also be at fault if Word hangs on exit. In some cases, a DLL file called Msgsrv32.dll might receive an incomprehensible error message from a Windows driver, leading it to stop responding. In Windows 95/98, press **Ctrl+Alt+Del** once to display the Close Program list of currently running tasks, and look for the line Msgsrv32.dll (Not responding). If it's there, try swapping print or video drivers. ▪

If the module that causes the system crash is a DLL file that is part of Word or Windows, the file might be damaged. You've already seen that running Detect and Repair can fix components associated with Office.

If the file is part of Windows, you might want to run a maintenance setup in Windows or run the Windows 98 System File Checker utility. To do so, run Microsoft System Information by choosing **Start, Programs, Accessories, System Tools, System Information**. Then choose **System File Checker** from the **Tools** menu.

Part
VII
Ch
44

If the problem persists after running Detect and Repair and appears to be in `Winword.exe`, the main Word program file, either replace the file or continue your troubleshooting to see which interactions are actually causing the problem. Try to determine whether all the problem documents have the same element in common. These elements might include the following:

- **The same font.** Create a new document using the same fonts and systematically reduce the number of fonts in the document one at a time until the problem disappears. If it does disappear, the last font you removed might be damaged, and you should reinstall it from its original disk.

- **The same graphic.** Again, remove graphics one at a time to see whether the problem disappears. If you find a damaged graphic, replace it with one that is intact.

- **Links to the same documents.** Check whether there is any damage to one of the linked documents that you can fix.

- **The same custom template.** Try attaching the document to a different template.

If none of this works, the problem could be with Word's automatic features or proofing tools. Whenever a user presses the spacebar to end a word, Word's background spelling and proofreading tools go to work, checking your custom dictionaries (DIC files) and AutoCorrect lists (ACL files). If any of these files is damaged, Word might crash. To troubleshoot these files, exit Word, and then rename the files with a different extension. (Do *not* rename `Mso1033.acl`.)

Restart Word and work in a few documents. If the problem disappears, a DIC or ACL file might have caused it. If the problem remains, it might be that your spelling or grammar tools are at fault.

To find out, turn off background spell checking and grammar checking through the **Spelling & Grammar** tab of the **Tools**, **Options** dialog box . If Word now works properly—and especially if you can cause the protection fault by running the spell checker manually—the solution might be to remove and reinstall the proofing tools via a maintenance install of Word or Office. (You must remove them in one maintenance install and then reinstall them in a second.)

If none of these steps work, and you've already upgraded Office 2000 to the latest service release, the problem might be with Windows, or you might need to upgrade your hardware:

- Troubleshoot Windows by loading it in Safe Mode (in Windows 95, press **F8** at startup, and then choose **Safe Mode** from the list of options; in Windows 98, press and hold the **Ctrl** key during startup, and choose **Safe Mode**). This loads Windows without any unnecessary drivers or options. Run Word and see whether the problem goes away. If it does, the problem might be with another Windows driver or optional feature. Try running a maintenance installation of Windows.

■ If you have been running Word 2000 on a machine with only 16MB or 24MB RAM or with very little free hard drive space, stop running simultaneous programs and clean up your hard drive to create more space. If this does not help, either add memory or hard disk space and see whether this solves the problem.

Troubleshooting Performance Problems

If you are running Word on a low-powered computer, you might be able to make some adjustments to improve speed. Each of the following adjustments has trade-offs, which might or might not be acceptable in your environment, but all of them can make Word perform at least a little bit better.

Adjustments to Hardware

■ Add memory. Office 2000 needs a bare minimum of 32MB under Windows 95 or 98; it will run better with 64MB. Running under Windows NT 4.0 Workstation, it needs a bare minimum of 64MB and will run better with 96MB or 128MB.

Adjustments to Windows

■ Defragment your hard drive using the built-in Disk Defragmenter in Windows 95 or 98 (choose **Start**, **Programs**, **Accessories**, **System Tools**, **Disk Defragmenter**). If you are running Windows 98, the Disk Defragmenter can relocate Word to the fastest area on your hard drive.

■ If your computer has more than one drive, consider adjusting the virtual memory settings in Windows 95/98 to place the swap file on a local drive that has more space available or that is significantly faster than your boot drive.

■ Use fewer fonts.

■ Use lower color depth—in other words, use 16 or 256 colors instead of millions of colors.

■ Don't use wallpaper.

■ Disable screen savers, especially while printing.

■ Install Word locally, not on a network server.

■ Run Word and store your documents on uncompressed drives, not drives that use DriveSpace.

Adjustments to Word features

■ Turn off **Check Spelling As You Type** and **Check Grammar As You Type** in the **Spelling & Grammar** tab of the Options dialog box.

■ Turn off other automatic features, including all the check boxes in the **AutoFormat As You Type** and **AutoCorrect** tabs of the **AutoCorrect** dialog box.

■ Use **Normal** view instead of Page Layout view whenever possible.

■ Select **Picture Placeholders** (in the **View** tab of the Options dialog box) to display boxes instead of images whenever possible. And in text-only documents in which formatting is not a constant worry, select **Draft Font** to display text in the Windows built-in system font.

- When precise formatting doesn't matter, speed printing by using the **Draft Output** option (in the **Print** tab of the Options dialog box).
- In documents converted from Word 6.0 or Word 95, in which slight changes in page layout are acceptable, improve scrolling speed by clearing the check box labeled **Use Printer Metrics to Lay Out Document** in the **Compatibility** tab of the Options dialog box.

Adjustment to Office

- If the Journal feature in Microsoft Outlook is set to track every Word document when it is closed or saved, turn this feature off.

Troubleshooting Word 98 for the Macintosh

If you support Word 98 for the Macintosh, you might be called upon to troubleshoot system errors that occur while Word is running. You can try several things to identify and solve the problem.

Reproducing the Problem

As with all troubleshooting, see whether you can reproduce the problem: Does it always occur when you perform a specific task or only on a system configured in a specific way? What message do you get? (For example, does the Macintosh consistently display a Type 1 or Type 3 message?)

Also consider whether the problem happens only (or mostly) in Word. If so, you might have a Mac OS system problem or, much less likely, a hardware problem.

N O T E Be aware that errors such as Type 1 and Type 3 are common on the Macintosh. It's likely they will happen occasionally no matter what you do. This troubleshooting process is intended to help when you are getting an unacceptable number of errors or when they happen consistently at certain times.

As Apple has upgraded the Mac OS, it has taken steps to reduce the number of system errors and their severity. Most Macintosh users agree that Mac OS 8.6, the current version at the time of this writing, is the most stable version of Mac OS. If you are having consistent problems and your other software is compatible with Mac OS 8.6, consider an upgrade.

Troubleshooting Macintosh Extensions

Now that you (hopefully) know what kind of problem you have, try to determine whether the cause is a conflict with a specific *extension*—a file loaded into the Macintosh's memory at startup to add specific capabilities to the Mac OS.

Shut down the Macintosh and restart it with extensions off. To do this, press the **Shift** key as you start the Macintosh and hold it down until the Macintosh reports that extensions are turned off. Next, run Word and see whether the error still occurs. If not, chances are that a conflict exists between Word and an extension.

Now, you need to start the trial-and-error process of trying to figure out which extension is causing the problem. Double-click the **Extensions Manager** in the **System** folder's **Control Panel** to display a list of extensions currently running. One at a time, clear an extension, click **Restart** to restart the Macintosh, load Word, and see whether the problem still exists.

In Mac OS 8.*x*, you can streamline the process of testing by choosing the Mac OS Base set of extensions from the list of extension sets in the Selected Set box, as shown in Figure 44.2. The Mac OS Base set represents the minimum number of extensions your Macintosh needs to run properly. If Word runs correctly with the Mac OS Base set of extensions, you can begin loading additional extensions one at a time to see which one caused the problem.

FIGURE 44.2

Choosing the Base set of extensions in Mac OS 8.5's Extension Manager.

Selecting Base Settings

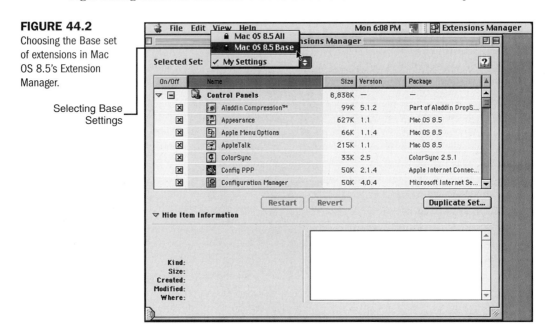

You can see that, even under the best of circumstances, that troubleshooting extension conflicts can be a lengthy process. Fortunately, a third-party program, Conflict Catcher 8 from Casady & Greene at **www.casadyg.com/products/conflictcatcher/8/default.html** might be able to help.

Conflict Catcher helps identify and resolve potential conflicts, especially those that occur at startup when all the Macintosh's extensions and resources first load into memory. It also provides more powerful tools than the built-in Extension Manager for creating extension sets designed to serve particular purposes. (If you know that you're planning to work extensively with Word, for example, you can build a set that doesn't include the extensions you don't need, reducing the likelihood of conflicts.)

NOTE Some extensions are necessary to the operation of your Macintosh; you have no choice but to run them. If one of these has caused the conflict, see whether Apple or the third party who provided it has updated the extension. In other cases, you might be able to disable an extension permanently and never notice the difference. ■

Rebuild the Desktop File

The Macintosh contains a hidden desktop database that tracks program locations, icons, file types, comments stored in Get Info windows, and more. Over time, this database can either become corrupted or become disorganized so that it does not run as well. If you are having unexplained problems with Word, try rebuilding it (this process is usually called *rebuilding the desktop*).

Restart the Macintosh while pressing the **Command** and **Option** keys. After all extensions load, the Finder asks whether you want to build the startup disk (the disk containing the Macintosh's working system folder). Click **OK**. Depending on the size of your disk, rebuilding the desktop might take several minutes. When Mac OS finishes, if you have more than one disk, you'll be asked whether you want to rebuild the next one; choose **OK**. When you're finished, restart the Macintosh again and run Word to see whether the problem has disappeared.

 TIP Many Mac OS experts recommend routinely rebuilding the desktop once a month.

Replacing the Word Settings File

In Word 98, a wide variety of settings are stored in the Word Settings (8) file, including many of the settings that would be stored in the Registry in Windows 95, 98, or NT. Word Settings files can be damaged, preventing Word for the Macintosh from working properly. The easiest solution is to quit Word and then drag your settings file out of the System Folder:Preferences folder onto the Macintosh desktop. Now, restart Word. Word looks for its settings file and, not finding one, creates a new copy.

If Word works properly now, you have solved the problem, but you will have to manually re-enter any custom settings in the Tools, Options dialog box.

NOTE Previous versions of Word for the Macintosh have corresponding files, such as Word Settings (6) and Word Settings (5). ■

Troubleshooting OLE on the Macintosh

When you install Office for the Macintosh, OLE support is also added, allowing OLE-compliant programs to link and embed one another's data. OLE is native to Windows; the approximate Macintosh equivalent is Publish and Subscribe, also supported in Word 98 for the Macintosh. You might occasionally run into trouble with OLE on the Macintosh. When you choose **Insert, Object**, for example, Word might not display the program containing the data you want to embed or link with. Assuming that the program is also OLE compliant, try taking these steps:

1. If possible, reinstall the program in question to "reregister" it in the OLE database.

2. If this is impractical, run that application; in most cases, this should reregister it. Note that some OLE applications must be run from within Word or another OLE-compatible program.

3. If neither of the first two methods works, delete the Office Registration Cache file and allow Office to rebuild it.

4. As an absolute last resort, delete the Registration Database and PPC Registration Database files. This eliminates all OLE information on your computer, including information related to non-Office programs such as Adobe PageMaker. It also has some effects within Office. You might, for example, have to reregister the Clip Art Gallery and reset the Custom dictionary. ●

Troubleshooting and Optimizing Excel

by Laura Stewart

To help you take full advantage of the inherent power in Excel, this chapter discusses how to design the most efficient Excel workbooks and solve the most common problems that affect Excel's performance and accuracy. In this chapter, you

- Learn ways to optimize Excel components
- Create custom number formats
- Standardize worksheet appearance with styles
- Protect cells, worksheets, and workbooks from inadvertent errors
- Optimize inaccurate worksheet calculations
- Optimize Excel workbook performance problems
- Build faster, more efficient workbooks
- Troubleshoot startup problems
- Troubleshoot Excel for the Macintosh

Optimizing Excel's Basic Components

Understanding how Excel is structured enables you to optimize the program and troubleshoot problematic behavior. At the core of Excel's architecture is the *workbook*, the primary document type used in Excel. All other components are based on or tied to a workbook. Although the workbook is the most widely used Excel file type, there are several other file types that can be extremely beneficial when employed in a business environment. For example, you can use a template to create standard company worksheet forms that automatically feed information into a database. A group of related workbooks can be opened simultaneously by creating a workspace. Macros and Visual Basic for Applications (VBA) code can be used to automate routine tasks.

N O T E   Most people drop the "work" from workbooks and worksheets, and simply refer to them as *books* and *sheets*. ▇

Understanding Basic Excel Components

The four main components or document types in Excel are workbooks, templates, workspace files, and add-in programs. Most users create only workbooks, because that is the component with which they are most familiar. Unfortunately, they do not often employ these other useful components because they are unaware that these components exist. The next few sections describe the four components and offer you examples of their use.

Excel Workbooks   The most common type of document used in Excel is a workbook. Excel workbooks are designed like loose-leaf notebooks and can contain any number of worksheets. Sheets can be added to or removed from the book, rearranged in any order in the book, and moved (or copied) to entirely separate books. A common feature of business workbooks is the consolidation of data into summary sheets, such as year-to-date running totals. This is accomplished through calculations that create links across sheets. Figure 45.1 shows an example of this type of workbook, where sales and expense information is used in a formula to calculate net income.

You can also create calculations that link across books. Information stored in regional workbooks can feed into workbooks summarizing national data, which in turn can feed into workbooks summarizing international data.

In addition to worksheets, workbooks can also contain graphic chart sheets, PivotChart sheets, and modules:

■   **Graphic chart sheets.** When a chart is created in Excel, it can either be embedded in the same worksheet as the data it is based on, or it can be placed on its own sheet in the workbook. When a chart is placed on its own sheet, Excel actually creates a new sheet, called a *chart sheet,* and inserts the new sheet in the active workbook. Like worksheets, chart sheets have a default name with a number—Chart1, Chart2, and so on.

■ **PivotChart sheets.** New in Excel 2000, PivotCharts are interactive graphic charts based on PivotTable data. Like PivotTables, you can change and arrange the data plotted with a few simple mouse clicks. When the PivotTable data is updated, the PivotCharts are automatically updated. Figure 45.2 shows an example of a PivotChart.

■ **Modules.** Used to store recorded macros and code in VBA, which automate repetitive tasks, modules are associated with specific workbooks. When a workbook containing modules is open, the VBA modules can be shared with other open workbooks. Visual Basic 6.0, the latest version of VBA, is included with Office 2000. VBA 6.0 includes features such as modeless user forms and support for additional ActiveX controls. VBA modules can be viewed and modified using the Visual Basic Editor (VBE). You access the VBE by selecting **Tools, Macros, Visual Basic Editor**. Figure 45.3 shows a module in the VBE.

FIGURE 45.1
When your formulas
link to other sheets,
the sheet names
appear in the formula.

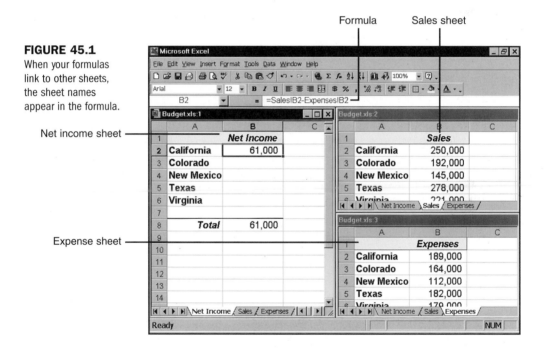

You might encounter other elements from earlier versions of Excel. Excel 4.0 stored macros on sheets. Prior to incorporating VBA into Excel, macros were created in Excel's earlier, functional-style macro language XML. If you are converting VBA and XLM macros from earlier versions of Excel, you should be able to run them in Excel 2000. However, you cannot record new XLM macros in Excel 2000. New macros can be recorded in Excel 2000 and then edited in the VBE, or you can write them directly in the VBE.

FIGURE 45.2
When you create a
PivotChart, Excel auto-
matically creates a
PivotTable.

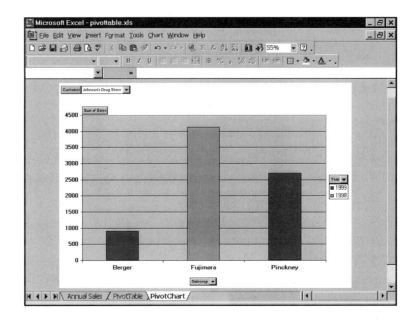

FIGURE 45.3
Edit macros using
the VBE.

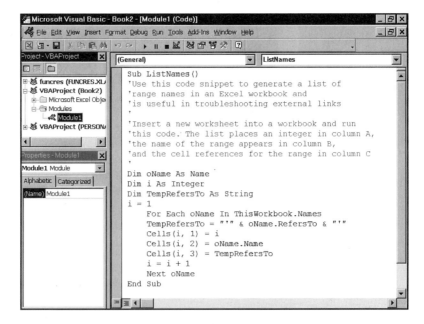

```
Sub ListNames()
'Use this code snippet to generate a list of
'range names in an Excel workbook and
'is useful in troubleshooting external links
'
'Insert a new worksheet into a workbook and run
'this code. The list places an integer in column A,
'the name of the range appears in column B,
'and the cell references for the range in column C
'
Dim oName As Name
Dim i As Integer
Dim TempRefersTo As String
i = 1
    For Each oName In ThisWorkbook.Names
    TempRefersTo = "'" & oName.RefersTo & "'"
    Cells(i, 1) = i
    Cells(i, 2) = oName.Name
    Cells(i, 3) = TempRefersTo
    i = i + 1
    Next oName
End Sub
```

N O T E If you are developing Excel application solutions that will be used across several versions
of Excel, be sure they are written in the lowest-common-denominator code. For example,
if some of the people in your organization are using Excel 2000 but others are still using Excel 5.0,
the code should be written in Excel 5.0.

In this type of environment, it might be necessary for some developers to use Excel 4.0 macro functions. Help for these macros is not available through the Excel 2000 Help screens. However, you can download the Macro Function Help files (`Macrofun.hlp`) from the Microsoft Knowledge Base article titled `XL:Macrofun.exe File Available on Online Services`. You can see this article at the following Web location:

> `http://support.microsoft.com/support/kb/articles/q128/1/85.asp` ▪

Another element you might encounter is *dialog sheets*. In Excel 5.0 and Excel 95, custom dialog boxes appeared as sheets in workbooks. Since Excel 97, custom dialog boxes (called *user forms*) are created in the VBE. If your organization has workbooks that contain dialog sheets, they should run in Excel 2000 without the need to change them. To create a custom dialog box in Excel 97 or 2000, access the VBE and choose **Insert**, **UserForm**.

Excel Templates   A *template* is a special type of workbook file that is used as a master, or blueprint, for a file that is created frequently, such as an invoice form or a standard company chart. There are two types of templates: ordinary templates and autotemplates. *Ordinary templates* are workbooks or worksheets that you create to serve as the basis for similar workbooks. Users can create ordinary templates while working in Excel. An *autotemplate* is a workbook that is automatically created when Excel starts. Autotemplates are used to change the default formats for new, blank workbooks. Autotemplates are used to standardize settings for workbooks that can't be set in the Options dialog box (select **Tools**, **Options**). This includes the default print options, such as the header and footer that appear on printed files, or the default column width and row height.

You can create workbook templates and worksheet templates (which include chart sheet templates). A sheet template is simply a workbook that contains only one sheet; all the extra sheets must be removed before the workbook is saved as a template. You can then insert a specific type of sheet (based on the template) into an existing workbook through the **File**, **New** command.

Figure 45.4 shows a form type of template used to provide price quotes, which include any discounts and applicable tax. There are three controls in this form—two combo boxes and a spinner.

▶ **See** "Using Templates to Customize Excel," on **p. 168**.

Workspace Files   *Workspace* files are pointers to a group of Excel workbooks. When a workspace is opened, the files the workspace points to are all opened. The most common use for workspaces is when there is a series of linked workbooks, or when a person is working on project involving several workbooks that need to be open at the same time. By creating and using workspace for the linked files, when the workspace is opened the links are updated—which is imperative when dealing with three or more workbooks.

FIGURE 45.4

Excel templates provide an easy method to collect data.

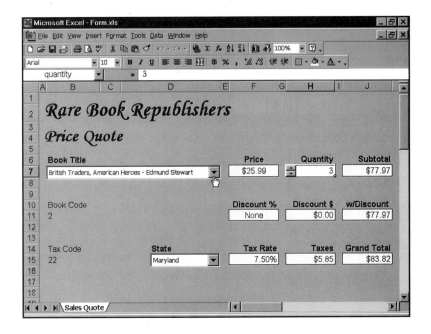

A workspace file keeps track of the filenames, their locations, and the positions of the windows on the screen. Because a workspace is merely a pointer to a set of files, creating a workspace does not preclude you from opening the files individually. You can distribute a workspace file to other users as long as the workbooks in the workspace are stored on a shared network drive.

▶ For step-by-step instructions on creating a workspace, **see** "Organizing a Project with Workspace Files," on **p. 178**.

 TIP

Encourage workgroup members to place the workspace file in their startup or alternative startup folder; the workspace will be opened automatically when Excel is started.

CAUTION

If the individual workbooks in a workspace are moved or renamed, the workspace file won't be able to locate the files. Whenever possible, save the workspace file in the same folder as the individual workbooks.

Excel Add-Ins   Add-ins are a good way to distribute automated solutions created for Excel. *Add-ins* are hidden, read-only files in which Visual Basic, XLM, or C code has been compiled to provide supplemental and specialized functionality to Excel workbooks. When an add-in file is opened, the macros and other functionality (such as menu options, toolbar buttons, and worksheet functions) are available to use in Excel. Excel comes with a group of add-ins (which are described in Chapter 7), several add-ins are available commercially, or you can create custom add-ins for your organization. Add-ins are created by first creating an Excel workbook that contains the code or features you want.

CAUTION

Regardless of whether you or a developer is creating the add-in, be sure that the workbook is saved as a standard Excel workbook *before* it is saved as an add-in file.

Add-ins can't be converted back to a standard workbook. If changes to the add-in are necessary, you need to make the changes to the standard workbook, resave the standard workbook, and then save the workbook as an add-in.

Add-in files are opened when Excel starts and, as a result, might slow down how quickly Excel starts. If the add-ins are no longer needed, you should unload them to speed up starting Excel. Unloading an add-in removes its features and commands from Excel, but does not remove it from your computer. If you are having trouble opening Excel, one cause might be an add-in. You can isolate the problem by using the /automation switch in the Target text box.

▶ For more information about creating, loading, and unloading add-ins, **see** "Working with Add-Ins," on **p. 201**.

▶ For more information about creating, loading, and unloading startup switches, **see** "Using Excel Startup Switches," on **p. 199**.

Storing Information in Worksheet Cells

There are two types of cell entries in Excel: constant values and formulas. Anything that is not a formula is a constant value. This includes text, numeric values (such as Social Security numbers), or alphanumeric entries (such as part numbers or street addresses). *Constant values* are the data that is used in calculations or other information used for display purposes, such as titles and headings.

Formulas are Excel expressions that perform calculations. The most common form of a calculation is one that uses the cell references of the constant values. There are two styles of cell references that can be used in Excel:

- A1 style references
- R1C1 style references

In Excel, you can designate the rows and columns of your worksheet by either A1 or R1C1 style references. *A1 style references* use letters of the alphabet to identify columns and numbers to identify the rows. A1 style references always list the column and then the row. For example, C10 is the cell at the intersection of the third column and tenth row of a worksheet. *R1C1 style references* use numbers to identify both the rows and columns. R1C1 style references always list the row number and then the column number. For example, R10C3 is the cell at the intersection of the tenth row and third column.

The default cell reference style, A1, is the standard for most modern spreadsheet applications.

TIP There are times when it is handy to use the R1C1 reference style. For example, you might want to set a VBA range object variable using the Cells (RowNumber, ColumnNumber) syntax. That's a lot easier to do if, on the worksheet, you see a number at the head of a column instead of trying to figure out the number of column EH. Some users also prefer the R1C1 style when debugging worksheet formulas.

You can easily change back and forth between the two styles. To change to the R1C1 cell reference style, choose **Tools**, **Options** and click the **General** tab. Mark the R1C1 Reference Style check box and click **OK**.

The flexibility behind worksheet formulas lies in the use of cell references in formulas, instead of the actual worksheet values. By using cell references in a formula, when the worksheet values change the formula results are automatically updated. Additionally, when you create a formula that contains cell references, the formula can be copied to other cells in the worksheet.

Using cell references in formulas can save you a tremendous amount of time creating and updating worksheets. There are three types of cell references you can use in formulas:

- **Relative cell references.** Formulas containing relative cell references adjust when copied to other locations.

- **Absolute cell references.** Typically used in only part of a formula, absolute cell references do not adjust when you copy a formula. The dollar symbol ($) is used as a code to tell Excel not to adjust that portion of the formula. Absolute cell references are used quite often in advanced formulas that use range names and functions. You'll also see them in formulas that reference cells in other worksheets or workbooks.

- **Mixed cell references.** When part of a cell reference is absolute reference and part is relative (for example, **$B3**) you are creating a mixed cell reference. Mixed references are typically used to create a formula that you want to copy both down a column and across a row.

TIP It's inconvenient to type or remove the dollar signs in absolute or mixed cell references. Instead, use the F4 key to cycle through the cell reference types. Suppose the cell reference is C5:

Press **F4** once to make both references absolute (C5).

Press **F4** again to display mixed references—with a relative column and absolute row (C$5).

Press **F4** again to display mixed references—with an absolute column and relative row ($C5).

Press **F4** again to make both references relative (C5).

If you press F4 once again, it cycles back to make both references absolute.

Another very useful alternative to using cell references in formulas is to use range names. This option is discussed in the next section.

Using Range Names in Worksheet Cells

Range names are textual names given to one or more cell references that describe the cell or range. Range names are used for the following:

- To quickly move around to different parts of a large worksheet or workbook—use F5 or the Name Box in the Formula Bar to select the name and jump from range to range.

- To designate a select group of cells for printing—similar to a print area, but with the print area feature, you are limited to identifying one area at a time. You can have unlimited range names.

- To make it easier to read and work with complex formulas.

This last bullet is the most popular use of range names, and there are several distinct advantages to using range names in formulas. First, a descriptive name in the formula makes it easier to understand the formula. Suppose you create a formula such as **=SUM(B2:B13)**, where cells **B2:B13** represent your business revenue. For most people, the formula is more meaningful if you create the range name **Revenue** for the cell references and substitute the name in the formula. The result would be **=SUM(Revenue)**. Range names make the meaning of a formula's result immediately apparent. Secondly, range names are absolute cell references. An absolute cell reference is especially useful when you freeze a cell reference in formula and then copy the formula.

Part
VII

Ch
45

There are specific requirements used for naming ranges. Use the following guidelines when creating range names:

- Use a letter or an underscore for the first character in a range name; the remaining characters can be letters, numbers, periods, and underscores.

- The maximum length of a range name is 255 characters.

- Range names cannot contain spaces. You can run the words together—for example, **AmountDue** or **Sales1999**. You also can use a period or underscore to separate words—for example, **Amount.Due** or **Sales_1999**.

- Names can contain uppercase and lowercase letters, although Excel does not distinguish between them. Therefore, you cannot create two names—**Expenses** and **expenses**—in a workbook, even if they are for different worksheets in the workbook.

- Range names that are the same as a cell reference, such as **F111** or **B52** (designating military aircraft), are not allowed. If you must have a name that is like a cell reference, use an underscore as the first character of the name (**_F111**).

There are several methods you can use to create range names. The two most common are using the Name Box on the Formula Bar, and using the **Insert**, **Name**, **Define** command. The Name Box is by far the more convenient method. To create a range name using the Name Box, follow these steps:

1. Select the cell or cells you want to name.

2. Click in **Name Box** on the left side of the Formula Bar.

3. Type the range name (using the preceding guidelines) and then press Enter.

To delete a range name, choose **Insert**, **Name**, **Define**. In the Define dialog box, select the range name you want to remove and click the **Delete** button. Then, click **OK**.

It's possible to define so many names that it becomes difficult to remember all of them. While you're building or editing a formula, you can use the F3 key to display the list of range names in the active workbook.

TIP   Suppose that you already have a number of formulas in a worksheet. You can still change existing cell references in your formulas to range names. Create all the range names you want to use in your formulas. Then, choose **Insert**, **Name**, **Apply**. The range names will replace their associated cell references in all the formulas in your workbook.

There are two broad classes of range names: sheet-level range names and book-level range names. When you create a range name in a worksheet, you are creating a *book-level range name*. To create a *sheet-level range name*, you need to include the name of the sheet in the range name. For example, if you type **Sheet1!JanSales**, the **JanSales** range name will be available in **Sheet1**. You always identify the worksheet name by typing an exclamation point immediately after the name.

N O T E   The Name Box on the Formula bar displays all book-level range names and any sheet-level names associated with the active sheet. ■

Although range names can be extremely useful in creating and interpreting worksheet formulas, they have their downside. See the section "Troubleshooting Inaccurate Calculations" later in this chapter.

Applying Formatting and Styles to Your Worksheet

Each cell in an Excel workbook contains a collection of formatting attributes. Through the **Format**, **Cells** command, you can either apply the built-in formats or create new custom formats for worksheet cells. Excel contains six types of formats: number formatting, data alignment (within and across cells), font formatting, cell border formatting, cell background color and pattern formatting, and cell protection.

In addition to applying individual formats to cells, you can also create *styles* to apply to worksheet cells. Like styles in Word, you can use Excel styles to standardize the appearance of common elements in your company worksheets. For example, you can create styles for worksheet titles, column headings, row headings, currency, summary calculations, and so forth to provide a uniform appearance to the worksheets.

Most people are unaware of the styles feature in Excel, because it is not available on the default toolbars. You can access styles from the **Format** menu or customize a toolbar (to place a drop-down choice similar to the font drop-down) for quick access to styles you create.

Creating custom number and style formats is discussed in the next two sections.

Custom Number Formats   There are times when you need to create a custom number, date, or special format. Perhaps your organization has a particular way it wants to see dates, or you need a special format that displays leading zeros for part or order numbers. You can accomplish this by creating a custom number format. Each format can contain four format codes:

positive numbers, negative numbers, zero values, and text. If you specify only two codes, the first is used for positive numbers and zeros, and the second is used for negative numbers. The codes are separated by semicolons. If you need a format for only positive numbers and text, you can skip the format for negative numbers by including a semicolon that indicates there isn't a code for that format. Table 45.1 lists number format codes you can use, and Table 45.2 shows examples for these number format codes.

Table 45.1 Excel Number Format Codes

Format	Description
# (pound sign)	Displays only the digits entered. Does not display leading or trailing zeros.
0 (zero)	Displays leading or trailing zeros if a number has fewer digits than there are zeros in the format.
? (question mark)	Displays a space for leading or trailing zeros on either side of the decimal point (or fraction such as 3 1/16), so that decimal points (or fraction forward slash) align when formatted with a fixed-width font, such as Arial or Times New Roman.

Table 45.2 Excel Number Format Code Examples

Use This Code	To Display These Numbers
###.##	123.456 as 123.46 or 123.40 as 123.4
#,###	15000 as 15,000
#	15000 as 15
#.000	4.5 as 4.500 or 5.67 as 5.670
0.#	.777 as 0.8 or 1.55 as 1.6
#.0#	25 as 25.0 or 123.453 as 123.45
0.0,,	7200000 as 7.2
???.???	4.5, 100.75, and 2.543, with decimals aligned
# ???/???	2.25 as 2 1/4 and 7.7 as 7 7/10, with forward slashes aligned
[Blue]0.#;[Red]0.#	Positive numbers in blue and negative numbers in red

N O T E There are eight colors to choose from. The color name must appear in square brackets and be the first item in the code. The color choices are Black, Blue, Cyan, Green, Magenta, Red, White, and Yellow. ■

You can also create custom format codes that include both text and numbers in a cell by enclosing text in double quotation marks in the format. For example, type the format

```
# ??/??" Increase";# ??/??" Decrease"
```

to display a negative amount as "2 5/8 Decrease."

There are several characters you can use in these formats that don't require the double quotation marks:

$ - + / ( ) : ! ^ & ~ { } = < > ' '

Custom Style Formats   As discussed previously, Excel enables you to format individual cells and ranges directly. However, to have consistent formatting in your workbooks, use styles to apply formats systematically. Excel comes with a few built-in styles, but these simply mimic the currency and comma formats available on the Formatting toolbar. You will probably want to create your own styles. After you create a style, you can apply that style to cells and ranges throughout your workbook to achieve quick and consistent formatting, without having to remember or individually apply all the formatting options that make up the style.

To create a group of styles:

1. Create a new, empty workbook.
2. Enter sample data, such as labels, headings, number values, and formulas.
3. Apply the desired formatting to each part of the sample data.
4. Select the cell(s) that contain the formatting for the first style.
5. Choose **Format**, **Style** or press **Alt+'** (apostrophe); the Style dialog box appears.
6. Type a name for the style in the Style Name text box.
7. Click **Add**, and then click **Close**.
8. Repeat steps 3–7 for each style you want to create.
9. Save the workbook and name it **"Styles"** in case you want to add or modify styles in the future.

After you have the styles created, you can apply them to any sheet in the *active* workbook. However, they are not available to other workbooks. To share styles with other workbooks, you have several choices:

- You can copy the styles from one open workbook to another workbook. This method is useful when you want to use the newly created styles in existing workbooks. To copy styles between two open workbooks, activate the destination workbook and choose **Format**, **Style** (or press **Alt+'**) to display the Style dialog box. Click **Merge**, select the source workbook, and choose **OK**.

- You can include the styles in an autotemplate (discussed earlier in this chapter). This is the best option when you want to have the styles available in each new workbook created. Copy the styles to the workbook that will be used for the autotemplate before you save it as the autotemplate. To share standardized styles companywide, be sure every user has the autotemplate installed.

> **TIP** You should probably modify the autotemplate toolbars to include a style drop-down button for easy access to the styles.

Creating and Sharing Custom Charts in Excel

When you create a chart in Excel, a separate application (Microsoft Graph) starts and a Wizard takes you through the steps to create a chart. On the final step of the Wizard, you have the option of embedding the chart as an object in the same worksheet as the data it is based on, or the chart can be placed on a sheet of its own. When a chart is placed on its own sheet, Excel actually inserts a chart sheet in the active workbook.

Embedding is useful when you have a small amount of data and want to see the data and chart simultaneously. Placing the chart on its own sheet makes it easier to display and print the chart, independent of the source data and other worksheets in the workbook.

The Chart Wizard contains an option of creating custom charts. If you want to generate uniform-looking charts, it's worth the short time it takes to create and save the charts as custom charts. To create a custom chart type based on an existing chart, follow these steps:

Part
VII

Ch
45

1. Display the chart that you want to use as a custom chart type. If the chart is embedded in a worksheet, select the chart. If the chart is on a chart sheet, make it the active sheet.

2. Choose **Chart**, **Chart Type** from the menu. In the Chart Type dialog box, select the **Custom Types** tab.

3. Click the **User-Defined** option button; then, click the **Add** button.

4. The Add Custom Chart Type dialog box appears. Enter a name and description for the new custom chart (see Figure 45.5). Then, choose **OK**.

FIGURE 45.5

Type a name and a description that clearly defines the custom chart.

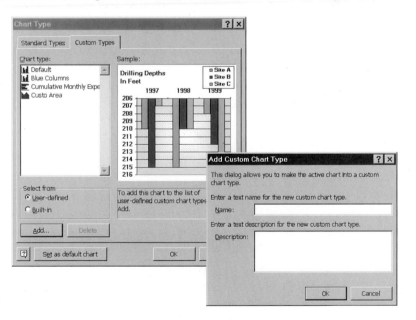

5. The new chart is added to the User-Defined chart list and the description appears in the lower-right corner when that chart type is selected.

6. Close the dialog box.

After you've created a custom chart type, you can share it with other people so that it can be used as a template. All user-defined custom chart types are stored in the `xlusrgal.xls` file, which is located in the Windows folder in Office 2000:

`C:\Windows\Application Data\Microsoft\Excel\xlusrgal.xls`

Before you share these custom chart types, you should be aware of the following:

■ You are, in fact, replacing the `xlusrgal.xls` file on someone else's machine with the one from your machine. Any custom chart types the other machine's user had will be lost. If that person has not created custom chart types, this does not present a problem. However, if the other user wants to preserve any custom charts he or she has created, it would be better to create a sample workbook containing the custom charts you want to give the user. Using the steps outlined in the previous section, he or she can add your custom charts to existing files. When working with less-experienced Excel users, consider creating a macro that performs these steps and adding a macro button to the sample workbook.

■ Use Windows Explorer to copy the `xlusrgal.xls` file to the appropriate folder (listed previously). Because you are replacing the existing file, a dialog box appears, confirming the replacement.

■ Although Excel can be open when you copy the `xlusrgal.xls` file to your machine, it's better to close it. If Excel is open and you have created a chart during the active session, you won't be able to copy the `xlusrgal.xls` file. When you create a chart, the `xlusrgal.xls` file is automatically opened, and you can't copy over an open file. Even if you close the Excel workbook that contains the chart, the `xlusrgal.xls` file remains open until you terminate the active Excel session.

N O T E   You can also share the `xlusrgal.xls` with users who still have Excel 97. However, it is located in a different folder:

`C:\Program Files\Microsoft Office\Office\` ▨

Storing and Distributing Macros

Excel's primary macro language is VBA. When you record a macro, it is coded in VBA. The macro modules are not visible directly in the workbook, but are viewed in the Visual Basic Editor (VBE) by choosing **Tools**, **Macro**, **Visual Basic Editor**.

VBA macros can be stored in modules in workbooks, templates, and add-ins. You can distribute macros by sharing the files containing the macros with other users. When a file containing VBA modules is open, the modules can be used and easily shared with other open workbooks.

If you are working with Excel 95 or earlier, refer to the previous section titled "Excel Workbooks" for information about how macros and XML are handled in Excel 2000.

If you're unfamiliar with macros or VBA, I recommend the following book: *Sams Teach Yourself Excel Programming in 21 Days,* by Matthew Harris, published by Sams (ISBN: 0-6723-1543-2).

Securing a Workbook and Its Components

Microsoft Excel includes several features for protecting workbooks, individual worksheets, and cells. The security features can be password-protected, preventing others from changing the parts of the workbook you have secured. Protecting the data and formats from inadvertent changes is especially important when many people have access to critical organizational files. Because security settings are stored with the workbook, you must open the workbook and unprotect it before you can change any security settings.

Protecting Your Worksheet   To apply protection at the worksheet level, choose **Tools, Protection, Protect Sheet**. The Protect Sheet dialog box appears. You can check any or all of the following protection options:

- **Contents.** Prevents users from deleting or editing cells in the worksheet, to prevent viewing of hidden rows, columns, and formulas, or from making changes to chart sheets.
- **Objects.** Prevents users from editing, moving, resizing, or deleting embedded objects on a sheet, such as drawings, ActiveX controls, or embedded charts.
- **Scenarios.** Preventsusers from changing scenarios saved with the workbook.

Unless you also type a password in the Protection dialog box, anyone can remove the protection you have enabled. To make changes to the protection, a user will need to know the password.

When protected, any type of change to the worksheet is prevented. To remove protection from a sheet, choose **Tools, Protection, Unprotect Sheet**. If you used a password when you protected the sheet, you must enter the password at this time to unprotect the sheet.

Locking and Unlocking Cells   All cells in a worksheet are locked initially, but the actual locking doesn't take effect until you protect the sheet *contents* (described previously). Most organizations want users to be able to enter data but need to protect a worksheet's text and formulas. To do this, individual cells can be unlocked *before* the sheet contents are protected.

To unlock individual cells:

1. Be sure the worksheet is not protected.
2. Select the cells in which you want to allow data entry and choose **Format, Cells**. The Format Cells dialog box appears.
3. Click the **Protection** tab.
4. Clear the Locked check box to unlock the cells and choose **OK**.

Protecting Your Workbook   There are several ways to protect a workbook. The **Tools**, **Protection**, **Protect Workbook** command provides limited protection for the workbook. In the Protect Workbook dialog box, select either or both of the protection options:

- ■ **Structure.** Prevents users from changing the structure of the workbook by adding, deleting, moving, renaming, hiding, or unhiding any *sheets* in the workbook. However, it does not prevent users from performing the same operations on rows, columns, or cells. Nor does it prevent them from saving their changes.

- ■ **Windows.** Prevents the user from moving, resizing, hiding, unhiding, or closing the workbook *window.*

Unfortunately, unless you also protect the worksheet contents, users can wreak havoc on your worksheets.

The other alternative is to restrict access to the workbook entirely. In Office 2000, this feature is buried in the Save As dialog box. Choose **File**, **Save As** and click the **Tools** option on the dialog box toolbar. Select **General Options**. The Save Options dialog box appears (as shown in Figure 45.6), in which you can require a password to open the workbook, to modify the workbook, or both.

FIGURE 45.6

Use different passwords for open and modify options for the best security.

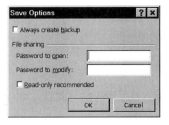

N O T E   Passwords are case-sensitive. You must remember your password exactly to be able to remove the protection from a worksheet or workbook. ■

Storing Custom Toolbars and Lists

There are reasons for developing and sharing custom toolbars and lists. Organization-specific worksheet solutions, styles, or other enhanced features might be easier for users to access from toolbar buttons than from menu commands. Standardized lists, where a series of text fragments must always appear in a specific order, can be created to expedite generating worksheets. Excel comes with several built-in lists that you have probably already worked with: the months of the year and days of the week. In your own company, there are probably similar lists: department names, a product series, store numbers, and so forth.

You can customize the Excel toolbars and list settings, and then make the customizations available to all workbooks or share the customizations with other users.

To customize the toolbars, choose **Tools**, **Customize**. You can modify the existing toolbars or create new toolbars.

▶ For more information about customizing toolbars, **see** "Personalizing Your Menus and Toolbars," on **p. 132**.

There are several ways to create custom lists. You can use a list you already have or you can create the list from scratch:

- ■ If the list already exists, select the cells containing the list. Choose **Tools**, **Options** and click the **Custom Lists** tab (see Figure 45.7). Then, click the **Import** button. The list then appears in the List entries box. Click **OK**.

- ■ If you need to create the list from scratch, choose **Tools**, **Options** and click the **Custom Lists** tab. Click in the **List entries** text box and type each item, pressing **Enter** after each item. When the list is complete, click **Add**. Click **OK** to close the dialog box.

FIGURE 45.7
You can import a list that you have selected or type one from scratch.

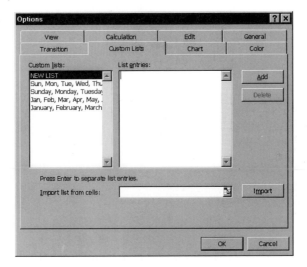

Toolbar and list customizations are stored in a file with an .xlb extension. Depending on the version of Excel you are using, this file will be stored in different locations. In Excel 2000, the file is called Excel.xlb and is typically located in this folder:

`C:\Windows\Application Data\Microsoft\Excel\`

If you are using other versions of Excel, the file is stored in

`C:\Windows`

N O T E   If you can't locate the Excel.xlb file, use the **Find** command in Windows Explorer to locate any files using the .xlb extension. Depending on how your system is set up (and especially if you are running Windows NT) the filename might actually be your name or your organization's name followed by the extension. ■

Toolbars attached to VBA modules are stored in the workbook file.

The toolbar and list customizations you create can be shared throughout a workgroup, further extending their convenience. To share your custom toolbars and lists within a workgroup:

1. In a new workbook, create the custom toolbar or list you want to share.

2. Save the workbook on a network drive shared by your workgroup.

3. When users open the workbook, the custom toolbars are added to their Excel.xlb file.

4. Close Excel and the Excel.xlb file is saved to reflect the new toolbars and lists.

After the custom lists and toolbars are added, they are available to you (and the other users) whenever Excel is started.

Optimizing Inaccurate Worksheet Calculations

The main function of a spreadsheet is to perform numeric calculations, so accurate calculations are imperative. To ensure the accuracy of your calculations, you need to understand how Excel stores and displays data, and the options you have for locating and resolving errors.

Comparing Displayed Values with Stored Values

Numeric data in a cell is stored as a floating-point number, with 15 digits of accuracy. This might differ from the displayed value in the cell, which is controlled by the cell's number formatting. When performing calculations, Excel uses the stored value, not the displayed value. The results displayed in the worksheet can be misleading if you are not careful.

Consider the example shown in Figure 45.8. The cells in this worksheet are displayed in the general number format, the default format for new workbooks. The formulas in column D calculate a net price by subtracting a 33.33 percent discount from the original unit prices in column B. Cell D6 displays the sum of the net prices, and the answer displayed is the one we would expect. Of course, the results aren't displayed in a common currency or percent format, so the next natural step is to apply some number formatting.

FIGURE 45.8

Before the data is formatted, the Net column adds properly.

	D2			=B2-(B2*C2)		
	A	B	C	D	E	F
1		Price	Discount	Net		
2	Item 1	1	0.3333	0.6667		
3	Item 2	1	0.3333	0.6667		
4	Item 3	1	0.3333	0.6667		
5						
6	Total			2.0001		
7						
8						

Figure 45.9 shows the result of applying two-digit number formatting to columns B and D. Note that the result will be the same whether you use a currency format or a decimal format. Now a problem seems to appear—0.67 + 0.67 + 0.67 should be 2.01, not 2.00. The apparent error occurs because cells D2 through D4 still contain the true result of the calculations, which is 66 2/3 cents (or .6667). Because the currency and decimal formats automatically round to the decimal place you designate, the answer is technically correct; however, the visual effect of the sum appears to be an error.

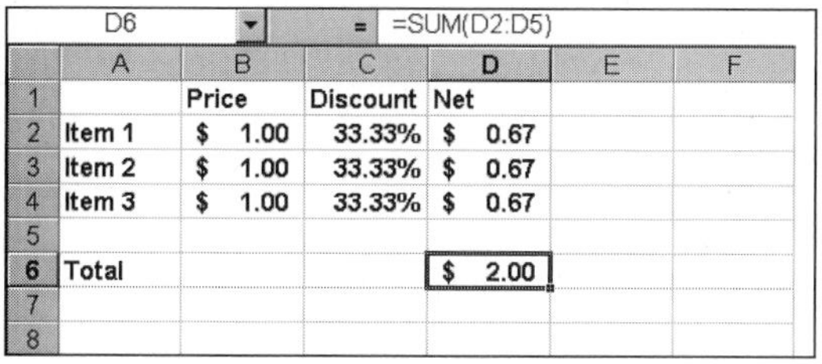

FIGURE 45.9
The number formatting displays only two decimals, resulting in a perceived problem with the total.

Because formatting is often useful to control the appearance of the numbers and calculations in your worksheets, you need to be able to accommodate this type of precision conflict. To resolve the conflict, you can use Excel's rounding functions in your calculations, or you can use Excel's Precision As Displayed option. The next two sections explain how to use these two options.

Controlling Rounding with Worksheet Functions

A common solution to precision conflicts is to use the ROUND, or other related worksheet functions, to clarify the accuracy of the calculations in your worksheets. In the discount example discussed in the previous section, the solution is to round the prices to the nearest cent when the individual discount is applied. Then, when the net prices are summed, the total displays the expected result.

The syntax for each of the rounding functions is similar:

```
=ROUND(number,num_digits)
=ROUNDUP(number,num_digits)
=ROUNDDOWN(number,num_digits)
```

The *number* argument is any number that you want rounded. The *num_digits* argument is the number of digits to which you want the number rounded.

The difference between the three rounding functions is obvious: The ROUND function rounds up numbers greater than or equal to 5 and rounds down numbers less than 5, ROUNDUP always rounds up, and ROUNDDOWN always rounds down.

When you specify the number of digits, keep the following in mind:

■ If the number of digits is greater than 0 (zero), the number is rounded to the right of the decimal point. For example, **ROUND(2390.149, 2)** displays 2390.15, rounding to the second place to the right of the decimal.

- If the number of digits is 0, the number is rounded to the nearest integer. For example, **ROUND(2390.149, 0)** displays 2390.

- If the number of digits is less than 0, the number is rounded to the left of the decimal point. For example, **ROUND(2390.149, -2)** displays 2400.

There are several instances when you might use ROUNDUP or ROUNDDOWN. Suppose you are performing calculations to track when employees are entitled to additional vacation days. At two years, each employee gets two additional vacation days. If an employee has been with the company 1.6 years, formatting and the ROUND function rounds this up to two years, making the employee eligible long before the employee is entitled. ROUNDDOWN rounds down the years until the employee actually reaches or surpasses the two-year mark.

Figure 45.10 shows the use of the ROUND function. In cell D2, the net price is calculated to the nearest penny. The ROUND function requires two arguments, or input values. The first argument is the value that needs to be rounded—in this case, the expression B2-(B2*B3), which calculates the net price. For the second argument—the number of digits—the value 2 is used, which rounds the net price to the nearest hundredth, or cent.

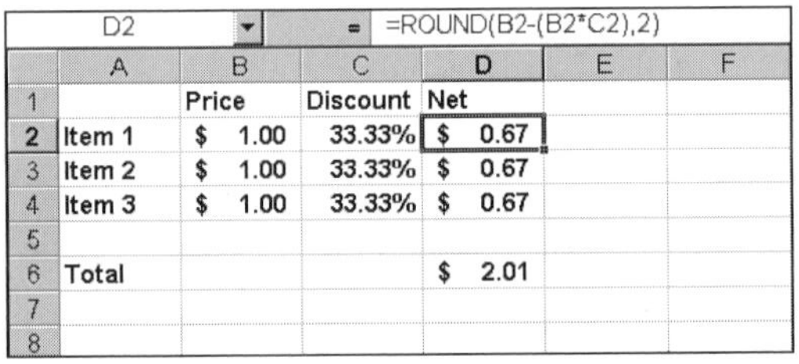

FIGURE 45.10

Use the ROUND function to alter the displayed results of calculations.

	A	B	C	D	E	F
		Price	Discount	Net		
1						
2	Item 1	$ 1.00	33.33%	$ 0.67		
3	Item 2	$ 1.00	33.33%	$ 0.67		
4	Item 3	$ 1.00	33.33%	$ 0.67		
5						
6	Total			$ 2.01		
7						
8						

D2 = =ROUND(B2-(B2*C2),2)

Number formatting changes the cell's display but not the value used in calculations. When you use one of the ROUND functions, the rounded value is used in all further calculations, so the total now yields the expected value, $2.01.

Several other functions perform actions similar to the ROUND functions, depending on your requirements. Some of the ones you might find useful are

- **INT.** Truncates a number to the integer. For example, **INT(4.8) = 4**, and **INT(4.4) = 4**.

- **TRUNC.** Truncates a number to the designated decimal place. For example, **TRUNC(4.5,0) = 4**, and **TRUNC(15.875,1) = 15.8**.

- **CEILING.** Adjusts the result up to a number of significance, moving away from zero. For example, to round a price to the next higher nickel, you can use **CEILING(0.23,0.05)**, which returns 0.25 as a result.

- **FLOOR.** Adjusts the result down to a number of significance, moving closer to zero. For example, to round a price to the next lower nickel, you can use **FLOOR(0.23,0.05)**, which returns 0.29 as a result.

By carefully considering the precision requirements of your spreadsheet application, you can select the appropriate rounding function to provide the desired accuracy.

Controlling Numeric Precision in Calculations

Excel provides another solution for controlling numeric precision in calculations—the Precision As Displayed option. This option is turned off by default, but can be turned on for individual workbooks. When you turn on Precision As Displayed, Excel uses the formatted precision of cell contents in calculations. Excel performs the calculations based on the data as displayed, rather than the underlying data. In the earlier price discount example, using the Precision As Displayed option gives the correct answer of $2.01 without requiring any rounding functions.

To activate this option, choose **Tools, Options**. Then, click the **Calculation** tab and select the **Precision As Displayed** check box. When you click **OK**, a warning message, Data will permanently lose accuracy," displays with an option for you to cancel activating Precision As Displayed. This is a reminder that Excel permanently changes any values to the precision as displayed in the cells. If you later choose to calculate with full precision, the original underlying values *cannot* be restored.

Although turning on Precision As Displayed is clearly less work than entering the various rounding functions into your worksheet, the precision option is less flexible and could be dangerous if you're not careful. You should use this option only for very simple and uniform applications.

Optimizing Excel Workbook Performance Problems

Excel is a high-performance analytical application that can perform thousands of calculations on very large amounts of data. As your workbooks become larger and more complex, you might notice a decrease in performance. Several strategies are available to maximize performance when working in Excel.

Optimizing Hardware for Excel

Another option is to upgrade your hardware. The two hardware factors most important to Excel are the processor speed and the amount of memory you have installed.

Because most Excel workbooks perform lots of calculations, the processor speed has a direct bearing on performance. If you are buying a new computer, be sure you test it to be certain the processor is fast enough to handle Excel and your most complex workbooks. Many earlier computers can be upgraded with replacement processors and motherboards if a new computer is not feasible.

As memory prices continue to fall to all-time lows, adding more memory to your system is often the most cost-effective and simplest upgrade available. Because Excel sometimes needs to keep large amounts of data in memory, increasing this resource can greatly improve Excel's performance. The amount of memory you should install depends on the complexity of your workbooks. If you have access to others' computers, try your workbooks on a computer with more memory to see whether this has a significant effect on performance.

Upgrading earlier video cards can improve Excel's performance, especially if you use a lot of charts. In addition, today's larger, high-resolution displays enable you to display significantly more data at one time. You'll see a big difference between Excel's appearance on a 14-inch display versus a 20-inch—or larger—display. Most video cards enable you to use the Display tool in the Windows Control Panel to adjust the screen resolution and the number of colors you can see. Depending on the overall performance of your system, you might be able to improve performance by choosing a lower display resolution and fewer colors.

Installing a larger and faster hard drive in your system generally results in some improvement in overall performance, although this is usually not as critical to Excel as to database applications, such as Access or FoxPro. With a faster drive, your workbooks load and save faster. If you have a large amount of unfragmented free space on your hard drive, you can increase the amount of virtual memory used by Windows, which improves performance somewhat. However, adding more physical memory usually has a greater impact on performance in Excel than increasing virtual memory.

Delaying Calculation Updates

With complex workbooks that contain a large number of formulas, consider disabling the feature in Excel that instantly recalculates formulas when data values change. You can disable this feature by choosing **Tools**, **Options** and selecting the **Calculation** tab in the Options dialog box. The default setting under Calculation is Automatic. Select **Manual** instead. Then, when you have made all the corrections or additions to the data values in your workbook, press F9 to update the calculations in the entire workbook, or return to the Options dialog box and select the **Calc Sheet** button to update just the calculations on the active worksheet.

Improving Startup Performance Through Add-Ins and *XLSTART* Files

If you have add-ins (such as the Analysis ToolPak that comes with Excel), you might notice a degradation in the speed at which Excel starts. The add-ins are loaded when Excel starts. If you no longer need an add-in, you can disable it by choosing **Tools**, **Add-Ins**. Clear the add-in name check box and click **OK**.

Likewise, workbooks you place in the XLSTART folder are opened when Excel starts. By removing files you no longer need from this folder, you will notice an increase in start speed when Excel opens.

Building Faster, More Efficient Workbooks

You can also use several spreadsheet design strategies to maximize Excel's performance. By getting into the habit of employing these strategies, your workbooks will take optimal advantage of Excel's power on your hardware platform.

Organizing Your Worksheets Efficiently

Sometimes, improving your workbook's design can have a significant effect on its performance. There are several strategies to organize your Excel workbooks for best performance. Combine the ideas in the following list to create the best overall solutions:

- Excel works most efficiently when data is organized in consistent tables in the upper-left corner of the sheet. Many spreadsheet designers are in the habit of storing different tables of unrelated data on a single sheet. This is especially true of earlier spreadsheets that have been upgraded from other applications or earlier versions of Excel that supported the use of only one sheet at a time.

- If your spreadsheet has many tables, put each table in a separate sheet in the workbook. You can use formulas and range names to look up data on any sheet in the workbook.

- If you have large amounts of data that are not referenced often, store them in a separate workbook. Then, open the second workbook only when needed, speeding up the process by creating a workspace file to open several workbooks at once.

- If possible, formulas should refer to cells above them in the spreadsheet. In this case, Excel performs its calculations from top to bottom, which is more efficient than left to right.

- Use the simplest formulas possible to perform your calculations. For example, if you use a constant number instead of a calculated value, your formulas will calculate faster.

- The Data Table feature can have a large impact on performance. Setting the table to calculate manually instead of automatically improves the overall performance of workbooks with data tables.

- Only cells with equal signs (=) recalculate. You can temporarily suspend the calculation of a range of cells by replacing the equal signs with another unique string. Then, restore the equal signs for only those cells you need to recalculate.

- Starting with Excel 97, the default number of sheets in a book is 3. If you are using an earlier version of Excel, or workbooks created in an earlier version, there are probably additional sheets in the workbooks that are not being used. Even though the sheets are empty, they do have to be accounted for by Excel. Empty sheets waste precious storage space on your hard drive and memory when opened onscreen. Deleting unused sheets will make loading and storing your workbooks more efficient.

Part VII

Ch 45

Changing the Number of Excel's Undo Levels

You can change the number of undo levels Excel uses by modifying the Windows Registry. Excel stores up to 16 levels of undo actions by default. There is a trade-off to changing the number of undo levels. Setting the undo level to a higher number reserves more memory for undoing operations, which has a negative impact on performance. Microsoft recommends keeping the undo level at 100 or lower.

> **CAUTION**
>
> It's a *very* good idea to create a backup copy of your Registry before modifying it. Mistakes made to the Registry can disable your entire computer. To back up a copy of your Registry, access the **Registry Editor** from the Registry Editor menu bar and choose **Registry, Export Registry File Command**.

If you are familiar with the Registry editing tools for Windows, you can change the following Registry key:

Hkey_CURRENT_USER\Software\Microsoft\Office\9.0\Excel\Microsoft Excel

Create a new DWORD value in this key named **UndoHistory**. Set the value to a number from 0 to 100.

Troubleshooting Excel Application Errors

Aside from the hardware and performance suggestions outlined earlier in this chapter, there are problems that you might encounter with the application itself. A new feature (Detect and Repair) added to Excel 2000 makes it easier to fix program file errors, and you can use Excel's startup switches to isolate problems with starting Excel. Additionally, Microsoft periodically releases updates or patches to features that don't work properly.

Introducing Detect and Repair

The Microsoft Windows Installer has the capability of determining whether essential files are missing when Excel is started. It automatically checks the Registry entries for missing or corrupted files. If files are missing, it reinstalls them. If files are corrupted, it repairs them. This self-repairing activity requires little or no intervention by you, but it does require that you have the Office CD loaded in your CD-ROM drive or that you have access to the program files online, such as on a company network server.

If you encounter problems while working in Excel, try selecting **Help**, **Detect and Repair**. This new Excel 2000 feature scans the noncritical Excel files and fixes discrepancies between the original installation and the current software setup.

Troubleshooting Excel 2000 Startup Crashes

The switches described in Chapter 7 can be used to troubleshoot problems starting Excel. It is possible that corrupt files are preventing a proper startup. To help isolate the problem, try both the /automation switch and the /s switch.

The /automation switch starts Excel without any ancillary files and is referred to as a *clean boot*. Add-ins, files in the XLSTART folder, and files in the Alternate Startup File Location are not loaded. If Excel starts properly when this switch is used, you have narrowed the problem to one of these four items.

Use the /s switch to start Excel in the Safe Mode. The words Safe Mode actually appear in the Excel title bar. Several startup triggers are reset as if this were the first time Excel had been started. You might be prompted to enter your workgroup name and initials, and the Office Assistant introduces itself to you. The files listed in the XLSTART folder and the Alternate Startup File Location are ignored. Add-ins, however, are loaded. If Excel starts using this switch, you have isolated the problem to the add-ins. You can determine which add-ins are loading by looking at the list under **Tools**, **Add-Ins**. By removing them one at a time and checking the startup again, you can determine which is the culprit. If Excel does not start properly, the problem lies in the files in the XLSTART folder or the Alternate Startup File Location. As with the add-ins, by removing the files one at a time, you should be able to locate the problem.

Getting the Latest Service Releases for Excel

Microsoft provides a myriad (although sometimes it might seem like a maze) of support and product information online. As new releases of Excel come out, invariably there are minor bugs or glitches that Microsoft needs to fix. Typically, these are provided to users who have authorized copies of Excel in the form of Service Releases. These can easily be downloaded from the Microsoft Web site:

http://officeupdate.microsoft.com/

You also can contact Microsoft and they will send your organization a CD-ROM containing the Service Release to make it easier to deploy the fixes in your organization.

Recovering Data

There are several methods that you can use to recover information from damaged or corrupted files, including

- Use external references to link to the corrupted file.
- Open the file and save it in the SYLK (Symbolic Link) format. Then, open the SYLK file in Excel.
- Use the **Revert to Saved Document** command. Choose **File**, **Open** and select the name of the file. A dialog box appears with the message Revert to Saved Document? Click **OK**; the file you are editing reverts to the last saved version of the file.
- Use the Microsoft Excel File Recovery Macro. Part of the Office Resource Kit, this macro re-creates Excel worksheets, XLM macro sheets, and module sheets in a new workbook.
- Open the file in Microsoft Word or the Microsoft Excel Viewer.

For more information on these methods, see the Knowledge Base article at this URL:

http://support.microsoft.com/support/kb/articles/q179/8/71.asp

Finding Known Excel 2000 Bugs and Workarounds

There are several known problems and deficiencies in Excel 2000 that you should be aware of. Microsoft publishes a series of Knowledge Base articles that describe the problems and deficiencies in detail.

Limits of the Microsoft Office Spreadsheet Component   One of the deficiencies is the limited capability of the Microsoft Office Spreadsheet Component. The Spreadsheet Component provides the capability of incorporating a spreadsheet onto a Web page. Although the Office Spreadsheet Component offers much of the same basic functionality of Microsoft Excel, there are certain functions that are not available, and array formulas will not calculate accurately in the Office Spreadsheet Component. See the Knowledge Base article at this URL:

`http://support.microsoft.com/support/kb/articles/q216/5/78.asp`

Year 2000 Date Migration   Four date migration add-in tools are available for you to use with Excel 97 and Excel 2000. These add-ins help you prepare dates in Excel workbooks for transitioning from earlier versions of Excel, or for auditing workbooks for the year 2000. See the Knowledge Base article at this URL:

`http://support.microsoft.com/support/kb/articles/q211/3/99.asp`

Troubleshooting Excel for the Macintosh

Many of the troubleshooting techniques described previously in this chapter work for both the PC and the Macintosh. There are several known problems with Excel that you might encounter; these are documented here.

Natural Language Formulas

Natural language formulas enable you to use column and row labels that are part of tables you create without having to define range names. When creating these formulas, you might receive an error message, such as That name is not valid or you might see the #NULL! error displayed. There are several reasons why this problem might occur:

- The workbook contains a function with a name that is identical to one of the labels in the formula.

- The workbook contains a reference to another workbook that contains a function with a name that is identical to one of the labels in the formula.

- The workbook contains a globally defined name that is identical to one of the labels in the formula, or the worksheet in which you are entering the formula contains a locally defined name that is identical to one of the labels in the formula.

One way to fix this problem is to modify the formulas and enclose the labels in apostrophes ('). For example, you change this formula:

`=California Sales`

to this formula:

```
='California' 'Sales'
```

The result of enclosing labels in apostrophes is they do not conflict with the names of subroutines, functions, and defined range names.

Garbled or Sluggish Text

Because of the way in which Excel works with the system Memory Manager library on Power Macintosh, you might encounter a problem when you type data in a cell. The text might appear very slowly or might be garbled. This problem occurs when the cell is formatted for a TrueType font with a bold format, before you enter the text. You can fix this problem easily by simply applying the bold format *after* you enter the text into the cell. This problem occurs only on the Power Macintosh platform.

Part
VII
Ch
45

Sorting Merged Cells

When you attempt to sort a range on a worksheet, you might receive this message: `This operation requires the merged cells to be identically sized`. There are a few rules you must follow to successfully sort data in merged cells:

- All cells in the list you are attempting to sort must be merged. You cannot sort a list where some of the cells are merged and some are not.
- The merged cells all need to be the same size. Each merged cell in the range must occupy the same number of rows and columns as the other merged cells in the range.

Hyperlink Problems

You might have trouble when you click on hyperlinks, such as the **Help**, **Help On The Web** menu command or hyperlinks in a worksheet. These problems might occur because of errors in files in the `System Folder:Preferences` folder. There is a detailed Knowledge Base article describing this problem and the workarounds:

```
http://support.microsoft.com/support/kb/ARTICLES/Q181/5/08.asp
```

Microsoft Query Errors

If you have both Microsoft Query 1.0 and 8.0 installed on the computers, you might see an error message when you use the **Data**, **Get External Data**, **Create New Query** command. You need to remove Microsoft Query version 1.0 and reinstall Microsoft Query version 8.0. ●

Troubleshooting and Optimizing PowerPoint

by Bill Camarda

In this chapter, you review what you need to know to troubleshoot problems that can arise with PowerPoint presentations, and with PowerPoint itself. You learn how PowerPoint files are structured, how to retrieve data from files that have been damaged, and how to change system settings that might be causing problems.

Understanding PowerPoint's Presentation Architecture

In order to understand what can go wrong with PowerPoint presentations, it helps to first understand how they are structured.

Slides are the basic building blocks of PowerPoint presentations, and each slide might contain many different *objects*, each with its own formatting. These objects can include some or all of the following:

- **A background.** Even a blank slide has a background; it's blank. If a slide is created with a presentation template, it has a graphical background, filled with color and often clip art and drawn images.

- **Text boxes.** Title slides have a title text box and a subtitle text box, where text can be placed. Other slides, based on different AutoLayouts, might have two or three text boxes. Users can add more manually, as needed.

- **Clip art.** You can insert any installed Office image through the Microsoft Clip Gallery. You can also add clip art from a variety of other sources, including the Internet, CD-ROM collections, or other software on your computer. When using clip art or other graphic images found on the Internet, be sure that they are not copyrighted images and that you use only images that are considered public domain. PowerPoint can insert graphic files in most common formats. The number of file formats your installation of PowerPoint can recognize depends on which graphic filters you included when you installed Office 2000. As is discussed later in this chapter, PowerPoint 2000 and PowerPoint 97/98 handle some graphics differently than their predecessors, which can lead to surprising changes in file size for organizations that work with a mix of PowerPoint versions.

- **Charts.** You can add a variety of graphs and organization chart types to individual slides through Microsoft Graph and Microsoft Organization Chart, shared applications included with Office, which run within PowerPoint. When you insert a graph or chart, the program becomes embedded in the slide, displayed as the created chart.

- **Drawn objects.** Using PowerPoint's Drawing toolbar, you can draw simple geometric shapes, elaborate AutoShapes, or lines and arrows. You can then fill these objects with solid colors, patterns, textures, or pictures, and you can apply 3D effects and/or shadows to them.

- **Word tables and Excel worksheets.** Users can insert a table directly in a PowerPoint slide, using the **Insert Table** button on the Standard toolbar, or embed an existing Word table or Excel worksheet in a slide. Having done so, they can edit the text and numbers directly or double-click on the table to activate Word or Excel, if one of these programs created the cells in the table.

- **Hyperlinks.** You can insert a hyperlink to link to another presentation, Office document (or a document from any other Windows application), or Web address.

Objects might be manually formatted with attributes, such as specific fonts, colors, or animation. They might also be formatted consistently automatically, as is discussed in the next section.

Understanding How PowerPoint Controls Presentationwide Formatting

PowerPoint contains two features designed to help users build consistent presentations:

- *Slide Masters*, which specify graphics, text formatting, background colors, special effects, and layout for every slide in a presentation. Slide masters also control the contents of footers, including date and time stamps, and slide numbering. (For title slides, which often need to look significantly different from the rest of the presentation, PowerPoint provides a separate *Title Master*, which controls only the title page. In some cases, as you'll see, a master might become corrupted, preventing users from working with the presentation—in these cases, exporting the individual slides and rebuilding (or reattaching a separate copy of) the master might solve the problem. Figure 46.1 shows the Slide Master view in PowerPoint 2000.

- *AutoLayouts*, which specify locations for text and graphic elements on individual slides. Unless PowerPoint's default settings have been changed, users are asked to choose an AutoLayout when they enter a new slide (see Figure 46.2). AutoLayouts are built into PowerPoint's user interface and cannot be changed, although you can change them manually and create duplicate slides that use the revised layout.

Part

VII

Ch

46

FIGURE 46.1
Use Slide Master view to make global changes to both the content and appearance of all the slides in a presentation.

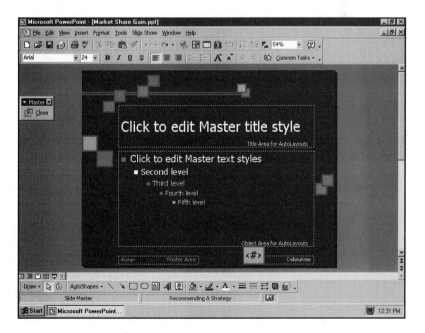

FIGURE 46.2
Users can select from
24 AutoLayouts for indi-
vidual slides.

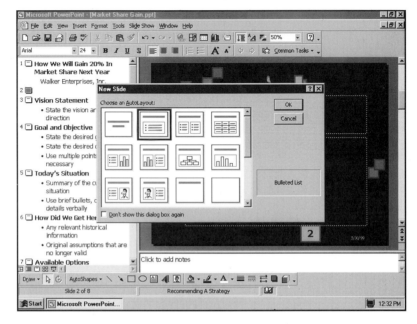

At a higher level, most presentations are created using a *template*, which specifies both masters and color schemes. Templates might also contain pre-existing text, graphics, charts, tables, multimedia elements, and more. In fact, existing presentations might be saved as templates, saving users the trouble of re-creating boilerplate information and visuals. As with masters, PowerPoint's original template files can become damaged; one solution is to reinstall them using Office 2000's Detect and Repair feature. If a custom template you create becomes damaged, replace it with a backup copy of the template. You can also create a new copy of the template from a backup copy of a working presentation that uses the same template.

Other presentations are created using the AutoContent Wizard, which enables users to specify the content structure of their presentation, and chooses a template for the user automatically.

Troubleshooting Presentations That Won't Open or Work Properly

In some cases, PowerPoint 2000 presentations might become damaged. Users find either they cannot open the presentations at all, or that they can open them, but PowerPoint crashes soon afterward. You might see messages such as the following:

- Invalid Page Fault
- General Protection Fault
- Illegal Instruction error

- Out of Memory error
- Low System Resources error
- This is not a PowerPoint Presentation

In the following sections, you learn techniques that can help you troubleshoot problems such as these.

N O T E This is a good time to remind you that the #1 solution for avoiding productivity loss is to scrupulously maintain regular backups and to encourage users to save regularly. ■

Determining Whether the Problem Is Limited to One Presentation

As with most troubleshooting, your first goal is to narrow down the problem. Often, a single damaged object—a damaged graphic or master, for instance—might make an entire presentation unusable.

Does PowerPoint crash consistently when you display or attempt to edit a specific slide? If so, the problem might be a graphic or other object on that slide.

On the same computer that is having the problem, attempt to open similar presentations, such as those using the same slide master or graphics. If these also fail to open, try opening presentations that are different.

If many or all presentations cause problems, you might have one or more damaged PowerPoint files. Run **Help**, **Detect and Repair** to restore PowerPoint's original files.

N O T E One indication of damaged original PowerPoint files is your inability to open or create presentations from PowerPoint's Open or New dialog boxes. Until you fix the problem by running **Detect and Repair**, you might be able to open files by double-clicking them in Windows Explorer, or by dragging them to the PowerPoint icon in Windows Explorer. ■

Part

VII

Ch

46

Determining Whether the Problem Is Limited to One Computer

In some cases, you might find that a presentation that fails to work properly on one computer will work perfectly on another. This is sometimes a symptom of printer or video driver problems on the source computer, as discussed in the previous section. However, if you open and resave a presentation on a different computer, you can sometimes fix whatever was wrong with the individual file—and then use it reliably on either system.

When you open a presentation on a second computer, display each slide one at a time. If you find any blank object placeholders where images should be, try deleting the placeholders. Resave a copy of the presentation, and try reopening the copy on the first computer.

▶ Images might disappear from presentations for reasons other than file corruption. For more information on disappearing images, **see** "Troubleshooting Other Graphics and Layout Problems," on **p. 1162**.

TIP If your damaged file was created in Windows and you have a Macintosh available—or vice versa—you might sometimes have success by opening and resaving your presentation on the opposite platform. You can open PowerPoint 2000 and PowerPoint 97 files using PowerPoint 98 for the Macintosh.

If your Macintosh is running PowerPoint 4.*x*, you can still open PowerPoint 2000/97 for Windows files if you first download and install the PowerPoint 97/98 filter for the Macintosh. This filter is available at **www.microsoft.com/macoffice/freestuff/powerpoint/impconv.htm**.

If you find yourself still having problems with PowerPoint presentations, you might have a driver problem. Check the following:

- Be sure your computer has a working, active printer driver. If you have never configured a printer driver (as is common on notebook PCs that might never need to print) or if the driver has become damaged, PowerPoint might crash, especially while you are running slideshows.

- Be sure your computer has a working, active video driver. Try switching to the standard 640×480 VGA driver that comes with each version of Windows 9*x* and NT, and see whether this eliminates the problem. If so, check with your video card's manufacturer to see whether there is a more recent driver that works more reliably with PowerPoint.

If you are running PowerPoint on Windows 95/98, one way to determine whether defective drivers are at fault is to reboot in Safe Mode and attempt to open presentations that did not work correctly. If the presentations work properly in Safe Mode, it's likely you have a driver problem.

To run in Safe Mode, follow these steps. In Windows 95, shut down and restart your computer; as soon as the words Starting Windows 95 appear, press **F8**. In Windows 98, press **Ctrl** as soon as the computer identifies its drives (before the Windows logo splash screen appears). In either case, the Startup menu appears. Choose either **Safe Mode** or **Safe Mode with Network Support**.

TIP Microsoft Knowledge Base articles Q164519 and Q190517 contain detailed techniques for troubleshooting Office application errors in Windows, especially invalid page faults that might occur in the Kernel32.dll module, a file that's absolutely critical to both Windows 95 and 98.

Certain video cards and drivers, especially earlier ones, can use upper memory blocks that conflict with Windows 95 or 98. In PowerPoint, this can cause presentations with imported graphics to crash. If you encounter this problem, see whether your video driver has placed a line in your Windows 95/98 config.sys file similar to the following:

```
device=emm386.exe noems
```

Most contemporary video cards do not place any entry in `config.sys` files. If you *do* find such an entry, however, you might be able to eliminate the conflict by adding the following to the end of the line:

```
x=a000-c7ff
```

In short, the line should read something like this:

```
device=emm386.exe noems x=a000-c7ff
```

When you're finished, resave `config.sys`; then shut down and restart your computer.

Retrieving Data from a Presentation You Can Open

It is common for a presentation to contain one damaged element, but otherwise be intact. In such cases, it is often possible to copy all or nearly all the presentation into a new PPT file, leaving only the need to rebuild the damaged portion. You can do this manually, or by using a little-known add-in Microsoft has provided on its Web site.

To import slides manually, follow these steps:

1. Open a blank presentation (or a new presentation based on the template you want to use).
2. Open the damaged presentation.
3. Choose **Window**, **Arrange All**, to view both presentations at once.
4. Click **Slide Sorter View** in each window to display all the slides in each presentation.
5. Select and drag slides from the existing presentation to the new one.

Although you can select and move all or many slides at once, you might prefer to move slides one at a time, saving the new presentation after each new slide is imported. This can help you determine which slide, if any, contains a damaged graphic or other object.

If all the slides import properly, save the new presentation and reapply the correct master (if you haven't done so already). It's better to reapply a master from a file that you know works. To apply a master from another file, follow these steps:

1. Make a copy of your undamaged presentation.
2. Working in the copy, choose **Format**, **Apply Design Template**.
3. Browse to and select the presentation containing the master you want to use.
4. Click **Apply**.

Occasionally, the master you need might exist only in the damaged file. In this case, after you import slides into a new, undamaged copy, try applying the master from the damaged file. Sometimes, this will work; if so, the problem in the source file was not related to the master. Other times, importing a master from a damaged file imports the problems as well. If this occurs, you have to re-create the master manually.

Part
VII

Ch
46

Using Microsoft's *Cloneme.ppa* Add-In

If you must rebuild or salvage large presentations, you might want to use Microsoft's new PowerPoint add-in for cloning active presentations. The add-in automates the process of copying slides from an existing presentation to a new one. To install it, download `Cloneme.exe` at the following location:

`http://support.microsoft.com/download/support/mslfiles/Cloneme.exe`.

Double-click on the downloaded file to extract it. Copy it into the folder where your other PowerPoint add-ins are stored and set it up as follows:

1. Choose **Tools, Add-Ins**.
2. Click **Add New**.
3. Browse to and select **CloneMe.ppa**.
4. Click **OK**.

After `CloneMe` is installed, you can use it by opening the damaged presentation and choosing **Tools, Clone Presentation**.

N O T E   Clone Presentation won't clone presentations you can't open. ■

Using PowerPoint's AutoRecover Feature

As in Microsoft Word, PowerPoint offers an AutoRecover feature that can help reduce the risk that your users will lose presentations in the event of a power failure or system crash. By default, PowerPoint creates a new AutoRecover file every ten minutes. You can be sure AutoRecover is turned on at a user's workstation by choosing **Tools, Options, Save** and selecting the **Save AutoRecover Files Every** check box. You can also change the interval PowerPoint uses to create AutoRecover file; for example, if your computers are relatively fast, you might double AutoRecover file creation to every five minutes.

This setting might also be established centrally, via the System Policy Editor: Go to **Default User, Microsoft PowerPoint 2000, Tools | Options, Save, Save AutoRecover Info**. For more information on using the System Policy Editor, see Chapter 37, "Reducing Office 2000's Total Cost of Ownership."

> **CAUTION**
>
> *AutoRecover is no substitute for saving files*, if for no other reason than that users will still lose data created since the last AutoRecover.

New AutoRecover files are stored by default in the `\Windows\Temp` folder. In the event PowerPoint crashes, or the entire computer crashes, the next time PowerPoint is opened, it looks for the AutoRecover files and attempts to open them. If the user had many files open, many AutoRecover files might be displayed. The user can then resave each file under its original filename.

> **CAUTION**
>
> Before resaving over their original files, users should always open and check those files. If a user has manually saved a file very recently, that file could be more recent than the AutoRecover file—and resaving over it might actually lead to *losing* recent work.

If for some reason PowerPoint does not open an AutoRecover file when you expected it to, you can sometimes open it manually from the `\Windows\Temp folder` and then resave it with a `.ppt` extension.

> **N O T E**   On PowerPoint 98 for the Macintosh, damaged AutoRecover files can sometimes prevent PowerPoint from starting. For more information, see "Troubleshooting PowerPoint 98 for the Macintosh," later in this chapter. ▨

Saving a Damaged Presentation to Another File Format   If you can open a damaged presentation, saving it in a different format can sometimes solve problems with the file. Keep in mind, of course, that saving to a format other than PowerPoint 2000/97 or HTML can eliminate presentation features that are not supported in that format.

Here are some options for resaving damaged PowerPoint files, in rough order of desirability:

- **Save to HTML.** If you save to HTML and then resave the HTML file to PPT format, you can preserve nearly all your presentation's features while eliminating some of the problems that can cause PPT files to fail.

- **Save to dual PowerPoint 97/95 format.** This saves two copies of your presentation together, one for each format. If one of them works, you can open and resave the presentation in the older version of PowerPoint that opens it.

- **Save to PowerPoint 95 or PowerPoint 4.** If you can save to an earlier version of PowerPoint, you can retain most of the features in your presentation, but you will lose those that did not exist in the previous version. Of course, the earlier the version, the more features you will lose.

- **Save to a graphics format.** If you never expect to edit the presentation, it might sometimes be sufficient to export graphics files for display in a Web browser. PowerPoint can export GIFs, JPGs, and PNGs, as well as BMP, WMF, TIF, and Targa files. Note that these can vary in quality; for example, GIFs and JPGs can often be blurrier than the original slides they were created from.

- **Save to RTF.** If all you need is text, or if all else fails, you can save to RTF. You will lose all slide formatting; however, you will retain all text, tagged with styles and character formats. These files resemble outlines in Word. RTF files can be reopened in PowerPoint from the Open dialog box; you must first choose **All Outlines** in the Files of Type drop-down box to display them. Once reopened, you can reapply the formatting, masters, and templates you need.

Troubleshooting Disappearing Graphics

PowerPoint 97 was notorious for disappearing graphics: Many users encountered slides with small red Xs where their images were supposed to be. Many of the program bugs that caused this problem were fixed in Service Releases 1 and 2. If some of your users are still using PowerPoint 97 with no immediate plans to upgrade, be sure they are using SR-2.

In both PowerPoint 2000 and PowerPoint 97, pictures might disappear from files where users have chosen to link images rather than store them in the file, and then have moved the file to another location or computer without using the Pack and Go feature. PowerPoint tracks image (and other) links with absolute file references that include drive name, folder, and filename. If the entire path is no longer accurate, the linked file cannot be displayed.

To solve this problem, PowerPoint experts Brian Reilly and Steve Rindsberg wrote a PowerPoint VBA add-in that edits the links to specify only a filename, without drive and folder references. To download `FIXLINKS.ZIP`, visit **www.rdpslides.com/ftp/FIXLINKS.ZIP**. For information on using this add-in, visit Rindsberg's excellent PowerPoint FAQ at **www.rdpslides.com/pptfaq.htm**.

Understanding Unexpected Changes in File Size

To keep file sizes manageable, PowerPoint 97 and 2000 automatically compress photos, scans, and other bitmapped images. However, previous versions of PowerPoint, such as PowerPoint 95 and PowerPoint 4, saved images as BMP files, which can be much larger.

In other words, if you save a presentation to a previous version of PowerPoint, and that presentation contains images, your file sizes can balloon. This problem also occurs if you save in the combined PowerPoint 97-2000 and 95 format, which stores presentations in each format within a single file. The more compressible your images, the more they will grow when decompressed. JPGs and screen captures are often the worst offenders.

If you support users who still work with PowerPoint 97, they might also encounter ballooning graphics file sizes when they use Pack and Go. To solve the problem without upgrading the users to PowerPoint 2000, apply Microsoft Office 97 Service Pack 1, which contains an updated version of the Pack and Go utility that can create and read PowerPoint 97 compressed images without decompressing them. (While you're at it, you might as well apply Service Pack 2 also, which fixes other problems.)

Troubleshooting Other Graphics and Layout Problems

Graphics and layout problems in PowerPoint can also surface when slides are printed. Incomplete printouts and printer errors often occur when the PowerPoint slides' printable content exceeds the capability of your printer—namely, its memory.

The following are some additional problems that you might experience:

- **Colors onscreen don't match what's printed.** This, of course, applies only to color printers. Your monitor's display of colors invariably differs from the colors on your printout. If this is a chronic problem, contact your printer manufacturer—it might have a newer printer driver that improves color matching.

- **The printout is missing clip art, charts, or text.** If the missing items have thick lines or borders in or on them, try making them thinner. Many times, this change is all it takes to make an item reappear. If this doesn't work, try resetting your printer's spool settings through your printer's Properties dialog box. Open your **Printers** folder and right-click the printer icon. Choose **Properties** from the shortcut menu and click the **Details** tab. Click the **Spool Settings** button and select an alternate spool data format, if any. Try printing with the new setting. If the problem persists, return to your default setting and try reinserting the missing slide object and printing again.

- **Slow printing.** This normally happens if there are too many demands on your system resources, and you might notice other functions slowing down, too. Try turning off background printing. Background printing enables your print job to spool and then print while you continue to work in PowerPoint or any other program. To turn this feature off, choose **Tools**, **Options**, click the **Print** tab, and clear the **Background Printing** check box.

- **PowerPoint shuts down during a print job.** If you can determine that the print job was the culprit (by restarting PowerPoint and trying to print again), you probably have a corrupt element in one of your slides, and graphics (clip art, photos, and so on) are usually to blame. If a particular slide doesn't make it through the printer on each of your attempts, try deleting each graphic element on that slide and attempting to print after each deletion. The process of elimination, in most cases, shows you which graphic is corrupt. You can try reinserting it or substituting another graphic file.

Layout problems are normally due to problems with how you've composed your slides. The most common errors are placing too many elements on a slide, adding graphics or text to the master that conflicts with existing elements on individual slides, and placing elements too close to the edge of the slide (when slides will be printed).

Here are some layout do's and don'ts:

- **Keep text to a minimum.** Don't try to list eight bullet points on one slide. No more than five bullets, each on a single line, is a good rule of thumb.

- **Don't crowd the slide.** Keep your charts and clip art images sparse. It's better to have more slides than a few crowded ones.

- **If you want to print your slides, keep the slide elements clear of the slide edges.** To keep elements from getting cut off, you should keep them at least a half-inch from the edge of the slide. The required distance between the edge of the slide and the paper's edge varies by printer.

■ **Be prepared to adjust the master.** If you've added your company logo or some repeated text or graphic on every slide via the master, you might find that the item's placement interferes with charts, clip art, or text on some of your slides. Placing the master item as far out of the main slide area as possible and keeping it small helps mitigate the problem. Consider placing your logo on the slide as a watermark (a lightly shaded object behind your slide content) instead.

Troubleshooting Audio Problems

In some cases, users might encounter problems with audio in their presentations. Here are a few pointers for troubleshooting audio presentations:

■ Check to be sure the computer contains a working audio card or built-in audio on the motherboard.

■ If the problem occurs only when presenting online, keep in mind that Microsoft's NetMeeting software takes precedence in using your computer's audio capabilities (allowing the presenter to have audio conversations with viewers). As a result, presentations must run silently.

■ Recorded narrations in a presentation override embedded sounds and sounds that play along with animated effects. Such embedded sounds will not be heard. You will, however, hear sounds associated with slide transitions.

■ If you encounter one of the following messages in Windows 95 or 98, check that the proper Windows CODECs (compressor/decompressor) are installed:

```
Your audio hardware cannot play files like the current file.

Mmsystem326 No wave device that can play files in the current format is
installed.

Error Starting Program! A required .DLL file, Msacm32.dll, was not found

Mmsystem296 The file cannot be played on the specified MCI device.

The file may be corrupt, or not in the correct format.
```

Microsoft Knowledge Base article Q133365 presents detailed instructions for installing or reinstalling missing CODECs in Windows 95 or 98.

Troubleshooting Other PowerPoint Problems

PowerPoint is notorious for running slowly and crashing on systems without enough memory. If you are often running PowerPoint with other Office or large-scale applications, you might find that PowerPoint "locks up" and ceases to respond, eventually resulting in a message from Windows stating that the program is no longer responding. The following are some warning signs that PowerPoint is about to crash:

- Screen refreshes don't work. When you switch from Slide view to Slide Sorter view, you can see your slide through the mosaic of slides in the sorter window.
- Clicking on and activating embedded objects—such as charts, tables, and work-sheets—takes longer than usual.
- Your fonts change to Courier or some other system font.
- Your graphics don't show.
- Your slideshow (onscreen) takes longer than usual, and the transitions between slides are choppy or halting.

When any of these symptoms appears, save your work and shut down PowerPoint. This avoids an unceremonious crash that results in lost work. After shutting down, consider closing any other applications that you're not using in tandem with PowerPoint. Then restart PowerPoint.

Changing System Settings That Have Been Reported to Cause Problems

Over the years, two PowerPoint settings from the Options dialog box have been associated with occasional file corruption. Although most users have no problems with these settings, and it is too soon to tell whether the problems continue in PowerPoint 2000, you might want to adjust the settings to be on the safe side. The settings are

- **Allow Fast Saves (Save tab).** With this option checked, PowerPoint records all the changes to your document together, at the end of the presentation file—usually reducing the time it takes to save files. On occasion, PowerPoint performs a full save, integrating all the changes throughout your presentation. However, if a file becomes damaged, it might become impossible for PowerPoint to integrate these changes, and more difficult to recover them.

  Some organizations also view Allow Fast Saves as a security risk, because deleted text can remain in a presentation until PowerPoint performs its next full save. In the original version of PowerPoint 97 (prior to service packs), Allow Fast Saves was associated with lost Notes Pages and a host of other problems. Consider using the System Policy Editor to turn this feature off permanently. To find this setting, run the System Policy Editor, open the **Default User** tab, and go to **Microsoft PowerPoint 2000, Tools | Options, Save, Allow Fast Saves**. For more information about using the System Policy Editor, see Chapter 37.

- **Maximum Number of Undos (Edit tab).** This is set to 20 by default. Some users have found that reducing the number of undos to 10—or even 5—might improve PowerPoint's reliability, especially on systems with 32MB or less.

Part
VII

Ch
46

Troubleshooting PowerPoint Presentation Broadcasts

Given that many users are only starting to experiment with PowerPoint's online presentation broadcasting features, you might find yourself spending more time than you expect in supporting this feature. Here are some things you should know about online presentations:

■ For online broadcasts to work, each participant's computer must have Windows' TCP/IP network protocol installed and configured properly. Third-party TCP/IP stacks do not work.

■ Participants must also have a TEMP folder where temporary presentation files can be stored. On Windows 95 and 98 systems, you can add a TEMP folder by adding a line such as the following to the user's AUTOEXEC.BAT file:

```
Set Temp=C:\Temp
```

Of course, be sure the TEMP folder actually exists; if it doesn't, create the folder.

■ Users must have sufficient disk space to store temporary files. If a user runs out of disk space, he or she might not only lose access to the presentation, but also cause the presenter's computer to stop responding properly.

■ Online presentations might not work properly if either the presenter or an audience member uses a computer with a name longer than 15 characters, or one that contains uppercase characters, spaces, or symbols such as the following: $,@,#,!,^,&,*,<,>,?,_)

■ Online presentations might fail if the presentation file itself is damaged, as discussed earlier in this chapter.

■ If a user cannot connect to the presenter or server to view a broadcast presentation, check to be sure the user can connect to the same network location for other purposes. If the user does not have appropriate rights, or if the network is not configured properly, this might be the problem. Often, outside viewers such as customers or suppliers will not have adequate rights to reach folders on your internal servers.

■ Network problems (including misconfiguration and overloaded servers) can also make it impossible to connect to a NetMeeting directory server. Similarly, users might be able to reach a server, but no names will be visible in the Place a Call box, preventing them from connecting to an online meeting.

■ If the first 15 users connect properly, but the 16th does not, you have exceeded the capabilities of PowerPoint working on a standalone basis: You need to install Microsoft NetShow Server.

Troubleshooting PowerPoint 98 for Macintosh

Many of the same issues that apply to troubleshooting presentations on Windows also apply on PowerPoint 98 for the Macintosh, especially the techniques described for recovering data in a damaged presentation.

> **CAUTION**
>
> One exception: PowerPoint 98 does not offer round-trip HTML support, so you might want to save damaged presentations to an earlier PowerPoint format rather than saving them to HTML.

If you encounter one of the following messages or events, the cause might be a damaged presentation file:

- Type 11 or Type 1 error
- Bad f-line error
- Out of Memory error, even in small presentations
- `This is not a PowerPoint Presentation` message
- PowerPoint hang
- Your Macintosh hang

There are, however, some Macintosh-specific issues and troubleshooting techniques you should be aware of.

Part VII

Ch 46

Using Alternative Methods to Open Files

If you cannot open a PowerPoint presentation by double-clicking on its icon from the Finder, it is possible that the Macintosh cannot recognize the file as a PowerPoint presentation. This can happen with PowerPoint for Windows files that no longer have PPT extensions, for example. Try opening the file from within PowerPoint's Open dialog box.

Conversely, if you cannot open a file from within PowerPoint, try double-clicking on its filename in the Finder or dragging it to a PowerPoint program icon. It is possible that the thumbnail image PowerPoint stores with its first slide has become damaged; without that image, the Open dialog box cannot show the file.

Troubleshooting PowerPoint-Related System Conflicts

Two common causes of PowerPoint crashes on the Macintosh are corrupted desktop databases and extension conflicts. (These problems can cause other applications to crash as well.)

Deleting Damaged AutoRecover Files   In some cases, damaged AutoRecover files can keep PowerPoint from starting or opening presentations properly. These files are typically stored in the Preferences folder, within the System folder. Using the Finder, browse to this location, and drag all files named

```
PowerPoint temp file x
```

(where *x* is a number) to the Trash. Or, if you suspect you might need these files, drag them elsewhere, outside your System folder. Now, try opening your presentation again. If this fails, continue to the next section(s).

Rebuilding the Macintosh Desktop Database   As mentioned earlier, it is common for the Macintosh *desktop database*—the file that stores desktop icons and important file information—to become corrupted. To rebuild your desktop database, follow these steps:

1. Restart the Macintosh with the **Shift** key pressed; this turns all extensions off.
2. After the Startup screen confirms that extensions are off, release the **Shift** key, and press **Option+Command**. You'll see a dialog box asking to confirm whether you want to rebuild the desktop database.
3. Click **Yes**. The Macintosh rebuilds the desktop database.
4. Reboot, this time allowing all extensions to load normally.

Restoring Factory PRAM Settings   If you have encountered a series of system crashes, either while using PowerPoint or another application, you might have corrupted critical system data stored in your Macintosh's Parameter RAM (PRAM) chip. To restore the PRAM to its factory settings, follow these steps:

1. Reboot your Macintosh and press the following keys as it starts up again: **Command+Option+P+R**.
2. After the Macintosh starts up, repeat step 1.

TIP   If you support many Macintosh computers, and want a faster way to rebuild desktop files and "zap" PRAMs, download TechTool (or purchase TechTool Pro) from Micromat (**www.micromat.com**).

Starting the Macintosh Without Unnecessary Extensions   Most Macintosh trouble-shooters are familiar with the technique of starting the Macintosh without extensions and then loading one extension at a time until the one that is causing a conflict can be identified. With PowerPoint, however, there's a twist: PowerPoint will not load if the following four extensions have not loaded at startup:

- Microsoft Component Library
- Microsoft Structured Storage
- Microsoft OLE Automation
- Microsoft OLE Library

You need to be sure these extensions, and no other nonessential extensions, load at startup. To do so, follow these steps (on Mac OS 8.5):

1. From the Apple menu, choose **Control Panels**, **Extensions**. The Extensions Manager opens (see Figure 46.3).

FIGURE 46.3
Mac OS 8.5 Extensions Manager.

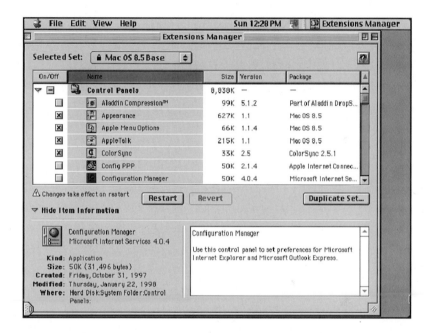

2. Choose **Mac OS 8.5** Base from the Selected Set drop-down box. This selects only the extensions the Macintosh itself needs in order to work properly.

3. Click the **Duplicate Set** button.

4. In the Duplicate Set dialog box, enter the name of your duplicate set—Apple suggests **Test Set**—and click **OK**. You've now created and activated another set of extensions you can use for testing purposes.

5. Select the check boxes to the left of each of the four Microsoft extensions listed previously. When you make a change, two additional buttons become available: Restart and Revert.

6. When you're finished, click **Restart**. The Macintosh restarts, using the Test Set you've just created.

7. After the Macintosh restarts, try to run the presentations that caused problems earlier. If they work, you probably have a conflict with one of the extensions you disabled. You can now return to the Extensions Manager and start the process of adding one extension at a time, rebooting and retesting PowerPoint to eventually identify the conflict.

Part
VII

Ch
46

N O T E If you find yourself encountering extension conflicts you cannot troubleshoot with the Extensions Manager, consider purchasing Casady & Greene's Conflict Catcher 8 (`www.casadyg.com/products/conflictcatcher/8/default.html`). Conflict Catcher 8 provides far more control over your extensions, as well as a detailed database of information on potential conflicts.

Troubleshooting and Optimizing Access

by Paul Kimmel

Access is a computer program. Like any computer program, sometimes things go wrong. Access, however, is a unique breed of program because you use Access to develop other programs. Software development tools are more complex in that they and you can inadvertently introduce problems to your system while you're using them.

This chapter provides you with a road map of the objects in Access that can be problematic. After reading this chapter, you will be better prepared to find your way around Access and identify and resolve problems that Access objects can introduce. The chapter begins by reviewing the objects in Access and discussing the kinds of problems you are likely to encounter—such as the need to increase virtual memory or compact a database, if you are low on system resources—and follows up with an appropriate resolution to the problem encountered. By the time you are finished, you will be able to diagnose the Access patient, inside and out, and keep things running smoothly.

Understanding Access Database Objects

Unlike most other desktop database products, Access bundles almost all its objects into one file. Although this concept might initially take some getting used to, the convenience of having all the elements of your application in one file quickly becomes obvious.

With the exception of command bars, all the major objects within Access are accessible through the database container.

Tables

Access tables are the repositories of your data. In other database systems, each Access table might be a separate file (that is, each table would be the equivalent of a .dbf file in a database). One major advantage of Access, due in part to the fact that all the data tables are contained in one file, is the capability of graphically establishing all the table relationships (including referential integrity and cascading deletes and updates) without the necessity of writing any code.

All elements of a table's design—field names, data types, indexes, relationships, and so on—are contained with the .mdb file.

You Cannot Undelete a Record

In some database packages, you have access to the delete flag and can undelete a record by changing this flag. Access does not expose the way it flags a record as being deleted; therefore, you cannot undelete a record.

Queries

Queries can be thought of as equivalent to views in server-based database systems, such as Microsoft SQL Server or Oracle. Although Access queries are built on the use of SQL statements, the graphical query builder does such a good job of hiding this that many users never realize the role that SQL plays in developing their queries. Figure 47.1 shows how the Employees Sales by Country query from the Northwind database is represented in the graphical query builder, and Figure 47.2 shows the same query in SQL view. Experienced developers often design a query in the query building window, and then switch to SQL view to either tweak the code or copy the SQL statements to use elsewhere in their project.

FIGURE 47.1
The design of the Employees Sales by Country query, using the query building window.

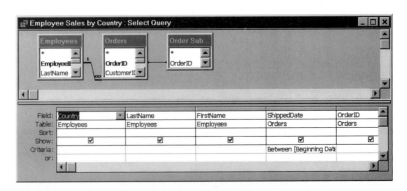

FIGURE 47.2

The design of the Employees Sales query by Country query, using the SQL design window.

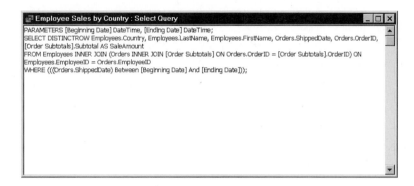

```
Employee Sales by Country : Select Query                          _ □ ×
PARAMETERS [Beginning Date] DateTime, [Ending Date] DateTime;
SELECT DISTINCTROW Employees.Country, Employees.LastName, Employees.FirstName, Orders.ShippedDate, Orders.OrderID,
[Order Subtotals].Subtotal AS SaleAmount
FROM Employees INNER JOIN (Orders INNER JOIN [Order Subtotals] ON Orders.OrderID = [Order Subtotals].OrderID) ON
Employees.EmployeeID = Orders.EmployeeID
WHERE (((Orders.ShippedDate) Between [Beginning Date] And [Ending Date]));
```

Within the internals of Access, queries and tables are very similar—to the point where queries automatically inherit any relationships defined for the member tables. You can however, create additional relationships for queries, and even delete the inherited relationships, without affecting the underlying table relationships.

Forms

Forms provide the heart of the user interface for an Access application, offering a controlled view into the application's data. You can write code to support form events and perform other tasks by associating a module with a form.

Reports

Just as Access internally treats tables and queries very similarly, it does the same thing with forms and reports. Almost any control that can be placed on a form can be placed on a report. Reports can also contain their own class modules.

Pages

Pages are the only major objects that are not saved within an Access .mdb file. Pages are designed in the same manner as Forms, but an HTML document is created; the Pages are stored externally because a browser, such as Internet Explorer, reads them. Due to Microsoft's increasing emphasis on the Internet, pages were essentially retrofitted into Access, starting with Access 97.

Macros

Macro is probably something of a misnomer for these objects, because they are not really the same as the old Excel or Word macros. Initially, they were going to be called *scripts* and are still referred to by that terminology in some of the Access internals. Generally, macros should be avoided, in favor of VBA code, due to speed and the lack of any error-trapping capability. At this point in the evolution of Access, there is really very little that macros can do that can't be done in some other way. In earlier versions of Access, one of the major functions of macros was to build menus, but starting with the introduction of the command bar object, in Access 97, even that use has diminished.

Modules

Modules are the repositories of the VBA code in Access. Although Access has always had its own dialect of Basic, it hesitantly joined the VBA family with Access 97; but with the inclusion of the VBA integrated development environment (IDE) in Access 2000, it is now a full-fledged family member.

Troubleshooting Damaged Databases

The easiest way to troubleshoot damaged databases is to avoid the damage to begin with. As with any database system, your Access .mdb file will periodically need some sort of internal housecleaning. As you develop your Access applications—adding and deleting objects and making changes to existing objects—your .mdb file becomes fragmented on your hard drive. Additionally, when you delete an object, Access internally marks the object as deleted, but does not actually release the disk space that the object used. The same holds true for any records that have been deleted—they are marked as deleted, but they are not physically removed from the database file.

Access provides a Compact and Repair utility, which performs all these tasks and more. Specifically, the Compact and Repair utility

- Removes all deleted and temporary database objects (including table records), reducing the size of the .mdb file and improving performance.

- Resets AutoNumber fields so that the next value used will be one more than the highest value actually used for an undeleted record.

- Recalculates all table statistics and query execution plans to reflect the current composition of the data in the tables (number of records, indexes, and so on) and flag all queries to be recompiled the next time they are run. This can result in significantly improved performance in an application where records are frequently added and deleted.

- Rewrites the .mdb file, creating a contiguous file containing contiguous data pages. If the .mdb file is on a local drive, defragmenting your drive before you compact your database helps ensure a completely contiguous file.

Have You Used Other Database Packages?

The compact function in Access provides functionality similar to the reindex or pack functionality found in other database packages, such as Paradox or dBASE.

Although frequent use of the Compact and Repair utility aids in avoiding damaged database files, Access is primarily a desktop database and occasional corruption is possible. Unfortunately, determining the source of corruption can be a difficult task.

Finding Causes of Corruption

The most common source of corruption is a user, with an active connection to the database, improperly shutting down his or her machine. This includes when the machine has frozen and the user is forced to reboot. If corruption is random and infrequent, this might be the most likely source of corruption. If corruption is a persistent problem, you need to look for other possibilities.

The first thing to check would be the workstations of the application users:

- Run ScanDisk, or a similar program, to check the integrity of the local workstation.
- Verify that each workstation has sufficient free space for Access to create the necessary temporary files. Check the temp directory to be sure it is not cluttered with old temporary files (an indication that the user might not be properly shutting down his or her machine).
- Run a disk defragmenter to provide a large contiguous block of free space.
- Check the workstation's Network Interface Card and LAN wire to be sure that they are not faulty.

If you cannot identify a workstation-related cause for your corruption, you need to look at your network environment, perhaps using network-monitoring software:

- Is there sufficient free space on your server?
- Is the load on your server (either processor or disk reads/writes) too heavy?

Another source of troubleshooting information can be the associated .ldb file. The .ldb file keeps track of the record locks for the .mdb file—it also includes the workstation and username of everyone using the .mdb file.

Part VII

Ch 47

The first user to access an .mdb file creates the associated .ldb file, and each subsequent user adds a record to the existing file. When a user is no longer accessing the .mdb file, that user's record is deleted; when the last user's record is deleted, the .ldb file itself is deleted. If an .ldb file exists for an .mdb file that is not being used, something is not right. If you can view the file and identify a username and workstation, you might help narrow the scope of your problem resolution.

Additionally, Access occasionally will not allow users to open an .mdb file, indicating that it might be locked or corrupted. If you compact the database and the problem persists, the problem might actually be caused by a corrupted .ldb file. Deleting any .ldb files that exist after all users have exited the application can solve this problem.

LDB View Utility

Microsoft provided an unsupported utility for Access 97 to make it easier to read the .ldb file and determine the locks used by each user in the database. Although such a utility did not exist for Access 2000 at the time this book was being written, it is reasonable to assume that Microsoft will provide a similar utility in the future.

Using the New Compact and Repair Utility

In prior versions of Access, Compact and Repair were two separate utilities, which could be run independently of each other. After Access 97 was released, it was discovered that the Jet 3.5 Repair utility could actually cause damage to an .mdb file in certain situations. In response to this problem, Microsoft released Jet 3.51, which fixed the Repair problem and also combined the repair functionality into the Compact utility. Because Access 97 showed the utilities as separate menu choices, many people were not aware that the two utilities had actually been combined when they upgraded to Jet 3.51. In Access 2000, this combined utility is formally recognized and there is only one menu choice.

To Compact and Repair the currently opened database, select the **Tools** menu, choose **Database Utilities**, and then choose **Compact and Repair Database**, as shown in Figure 47.3. Access immediately closes your database, compacts it, and reopens it. If your database has an Autoexec macro, it is run when the database is reopened. If you don't want the Autoexec macro to run, you should hold down the **Shift** key when you choose **Compact and Repair Database.**

FIGURE 47.3

Compact your database by using the **Tools** menu.

You can also Compact and Repair a database that is not opened, by using the same procedure—the only difference is that Access displays a dialog box to enable you to choose the database to compact and a dialog box to specify the file that you want to compact to.

If Access tries to open a database that it believes is corrupted, it displays a message that your database is corrupted and needs to be repaired. You click the **OK** button, and Access attempts to compact and repair your database.

Compacting Databases Automatically

Access 2000 introduced a new feature called Compact on Close. If this option is selected for a database, it automatically compacts itself when the application closes. You can select this feature for an application by selecting **Tools**, **Options** from the menu and then selecting the box in the lower-left corner, as shown in Figure 47.4.

FIGURE 47.4
Access 2000 provides you with the ability to automatically compact your database when it closes by selecting **Compact on Close**.

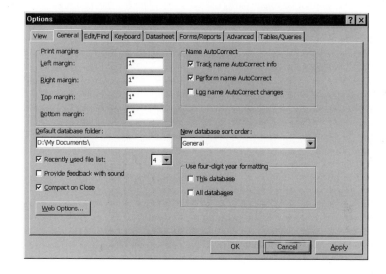

Restoring a Database If Compact and Repair Doesn't Solve the Problem

Generally, the attempt to repair the database will be successful. In cases in which it is not successful, you need to restore a backup of your database.

If you don't have a backup of your database, you should take a sheet of paper and write 50 times—"I will always make a backup." After that, you should try the following procedure.

To save a database that cannot be repaired:

1. Create and open a new blank database.
2. From the **File** menu, select **Get External Data**, **Import**.
3. From the Import dialog box, select the corrupted Access mdb file.
4. From the Import Objects dialog box (see Figure 47.5), select an object and then click the **OK** button to import that object to your new database.
5. Repeat the preceding step for each object in the corrupted database.

FIGURE 47.5
Import objects from a corrupted database.

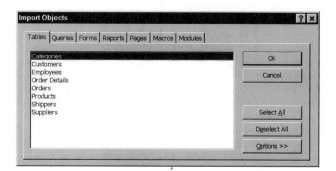

It is quite possible that you will not be able to import all the objects from the corrupted database. However, if you don't have a backup, saving some of the objects is better than starting your application from scratch.

As a last resort, there are some companies that offer recovery services for Access database files.

Saving Databases to Earlier Formats

Each major release of Access has changed the format of the .mdb file to implement enhancements and new features. Although there has been some backward compatibility, to the extent that you could attach/link to tables from an earlier version, there has never been a mechanism to convert an .mdb file to a prior version of Access. Access 2000, however, provides the functionality to convert an entire .mdb file back to Access 97.

To convert an Access 2000 database to Access 97, from the menu, select **Tools, Database Utilities, Convert Database, To Prior Access Database Version**. Although the conversion does not completely handle everything, it is impressive and a big improvement over past versions.

One problem that is likely to be encountered is illustrated by the dialog box shown in Figure 47.6. This dialog box tells you that your current machine does not contain the necessary files for Access 2000 to convert the current Access 2000 references to the Access 97 versions. Most likely, the machine is missing the Access 97 object type library or the Jet 3.5 DLLs.

FIGURE 47.6
The current machine does not contain the necessary type libraries or DLLs needed to fully convert the .mdb file to Access 97.

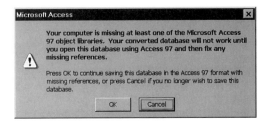

Using Performance Analyzer

The performance of almost any application can be improved if you take the time to review its construction and look for the right things. Performance Analyzer is a tool, included with Access, that can help developers with this review. The tool analyzes the objects in an Access database and makes suggestions on how to improve the application's performance. This handy tool can even implement some of its suggestions.

To use the Performance Analyzer:

1. From the menu, select **Tools, Analyze, Performance** to display the Performance Analyzer dialog box, as shown in Figure 47.7. (You will be prompted to install this feature the first time you attempt to use it; the Performance Analyzer is not part of the initial installation and setup process.)

FIGURE 47.7
Using the Performance
Analyzer to analyze
your database.

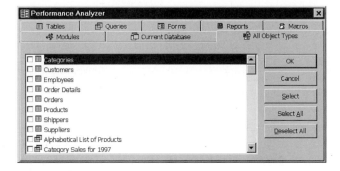

2. Select the objects that you want to analyze.

3. Click **OK**, and the analyzer reviews the object you have selected.

When the performance Analyzer has finished, the result appears as shown in Figure 47.8.
The Performance Analyzer breaks its findings into Suggestions, Ideas, and
Recommendations. All items should be reviewed for appropriateness.

FIGURE 47.8
The results of using
the Performance
Analyzer to analyze
your database.

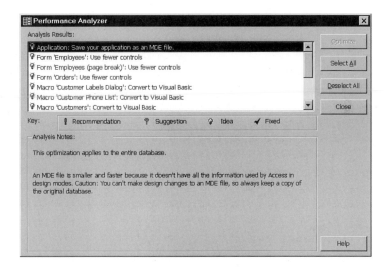

Part
VII

Ch
47

Creating More Efficient Tables

Poorly designed tables can severely degrade the performance of your application. If you are
going to develop Access applications (or any applications using a relational database), it is
important that you understand the principles of normalization and how to implement them. A
discussion of normalization is beyond the scope of this text, but normalization can be briefly
described as the process by which your data is structured to remove duplication and ensure
logical table construction.

When designing tables, keep the following points in mind:

- Choose the correct data type for your table fields. Access will default to a data type of `double` for numeric fields, but if the only values that you will be storing in the field are from 0 to 25, a `byte` data type would be more appropriate.

- Establish your indexes carefully. Too few indexes result in poor query performance, and too many indexes slow down record updates and inserts. Be sure that fields, which are often used as selection or sort criteria, are appropriately indexed.

Improving Query Speed

Access queries are very powerful and easy to create—unfortunately, it is easy to create queries that are not as efficient as they could be. When designing queries, keep the following points in mind:

- Although it is tempting to simply drag the * from the table to the query grid, you should include only the fields that you need in the output of your query.

- Complex query operations might run faster if you use two queries instead of one. An example of this would be a query that selects a limited number of records from a large population and performs grouping and totaling. Your overall execution time might be longer using a query that performs all operations rather than using one query that selects the desired records and a second query that groups and totals the output of the first query.

- When returning a count of records, use **Count(*)** rather than **Count([ColumnName])**. The difference might not be apparent with smaller amounts of test data, but the difference can be substantial with large amounts of data.

- Although the ability to use functions in a query to perform complex calculations is very powerful, it also extracts a high overhead. Keep the use of complex calculations to a minimum and, if possible, use them in the later queries when using nested queries.

- Avoid the use of domain type functions (`DMax`, `DSum`, and so on).

- Be sure that fields, which are often used as selection or sort criteria, are appropriately indexed.

Solving Performance Issues

Three areas affect the overall performance of an Access application:

- Windows issues
- Network issues
- Access-specific issues

Windows Issues

To the extent that your PC is optimized for the best Windows performance, all applications (not just Access) will perform better. However, there are some key Windows performance areas that will have a significant affect on Access.

Memory and Machine   The power and flexibility that Access provides definitely come at a price. Access likes memory and powerful machines—with the emphasis on memory. Do not run Access applications with less than 32MB of memory or a 133MHz Pentium, as an absolute minimum. Although Microsoft has dramatically improved the performance of the Jet Engine, Access 2000 can still benefit from larger amounts of memory.

Virtual Memory   The standard Windows 9x installation enables Windows to manage Virtual Memory (Virtual Memory is the equivalent of the Swap File in Windows 3.x). Changing your Virtual Memory to a fixed size generally improves the performance of both Windows 9.x and Access. As a rule of thumb, you should set the size of your Virtual Memory to two to three times the size of your machine's actual memory. You should also experiment with various settings, under different conditions, because in some infrequent instances, setting your virtual memory to a fixed size can decrease performance.

To change your Virtual Memory management:

1. Go to your desktop and right-click on the **My Computer** icon.
2. Select **Properties** from the pop-up menu.
3. In the System Properties dialog box, select the **Performance** tab and then select **Virtual Memory** from the Advanced Settings.
4. In the Virtual Memory dialog box (see Figure 47.9), select the option **Let me specify my own virtual memory settings**. Then, set the Minimum and Maximum size to the same number (the number is in MB).
5. When you click **OK**, you are presented with a dialog box that asks you to confirm that you want to change your settings. After you confirm the change, you should click **OK** to close the System Properties dialog box.
6. Your changes do not take effect until you restart your system. When you are asked whether you want to restart your system, click **OK**.

One of the changes that you should see is a dramatic decrease in the seemingly random disk drive activity that is characteristic of Windows 9.x. By setting your Virtual Memory to a large, fixed size, Windows does not need to continually manage it and will be more responsive to your users' actions in your application.

Hard Drive   You should periodically defrag your hard drive for optimal performance. Windows 9.x comes with a defrag application, which is accessible from the **Start** menu, **Programs**, **Accessories**, **System Tools**. There are also third-party tools available that provide a greater degree of control over the defrag process.

Part
VII

Ch
47

FIGURE 47.9
Changing virtual
memory settings.

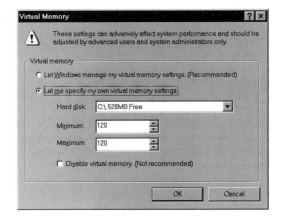

Your hard drive should have plenty of temporary space, and you should periodically check that the old temporary files are being deleted (the default location for temporary files is in `C:\Windows\Temp`).

Network Issues

Without going into the many issues that can affect network performance, suffice it to say that if your network is not up to par, the performance of your network-based Access applications can suffer.

Whenever possible, Access should not be installed on a network drive; performance will be significantly faster if Access is installed on a local drive. If your application's data does not need to be shared by others, your application should also be placed on a local drive. ●

Troubleshooting and Optimizing Outlook

by Gordon Padwick

To troubleshoot and optimize anything, you first have to understand how that thing works. That's why this chapter starts by reminding you how Outlook organizes its data in items, forms, and profiles. Subsequently, the chapter draws your attention to various resources you can use for troubleshooting and optimizing Outlook, and then gives you some tips on solving some specific Outlook troubleshooting problems.

NOTE The information in this chapter applies principally to Outlook's Corporate/Workgroup service option because this is the option appropriate for people who share information in a corporate environment. ■

Understanding Outlook's Architecture

Microsoft Outlook enables users to manage electronic mail, calendar, and other information in a single application. All these capabilities are provided under a single system of data management, which exists at three levels:

- **Item.** A single unit of information, such as an email message, a calendar appointment, a contact entry, or a journal entry. Each type of item contains various fields of information.
- **Folder.** Items are stored in folders, and each folder can hold a particular type of item, such as task items or journal items.
- **Information Store.** On a user's computer, folders are contained in one or more files, which might be Personal Folders or Offline Folders files. When Outlook is used as a client for an Exchange Server, folders are contained within the Exchange store on the server.

You can work with Outlook items in two environments:

- **Views.** You can use views to control how Outlook displays items in a folder. You can define many views for each folder, each view showing certain fields for several items, and activate the view with which you want to display items in either a sorted order or filtered so that only certain items appear.
- **Forms.** Outlook associates one form with each folder. You can use the form associated with a folder to display the contents of many fields in one item at a time. You can create your own forms, based on the forms supplied with Outlook, and select which form you want to associate with each folder.

N O T E You can use views and forms to display the content of Outlook items. To create new Outlook items, or to edit existing items, you primarily use forms. However, you can set up Outlook so that some types of items can be created and edited in views. ▓

Because Outlook is fundamentally a messaging system, it complies with the Messaging Application Programming Interface (MAPI) , which is a standard interface for communication between clients and messaging servers such as Microsoft Exchange Server. Outlook uses MAPI profiles on your computer to define which messaging systems, address books, and personal folders you have available. Profiles enable you to exchange messages and other data with many systems, such as Exchange Server, Microsoft Mail, Microsoft Fax, the MSN network, Internet mail, and other email systems.

Understanding Outlook Items

You can store six types of items in Outlook folders:

- **Mail items.** Email messages.
- **Appointment items.** Meetings, appointments, and events. Appointment items can be recurring or nonrecurring.
- **Contact items.** Information, such as names, addresses, phone, fax numbers, and much more.

- **Journal items.** Information you can use to track the date and times of phone calls, email messages, and many other activities.

- **Note items.** Simple text that you can organize any way you like.

- **Task items.** To-do information, such as when a task is due, its priority, and who owns it. Tasks can be recurring or nonrecurring.

With the exception of Note items, you can insert files and other Outlook items into any Outlook item.

NOTE A new capability in Outlook 2000 is to be able to create distribution lists that consist of a collection of Contact items. Distribution lists are saved, by default, in your Contacts folder. You can use distribution lists to send email messages (including task requests and meeting requests). You can send distribution lists to other people.

If you've used a Personal Address Book to create distribution lists with previous Outlook versions, you can import those distribution lists into your Contacts folder.

In addition to viewing the contents of Outlook folders, you can also use Outlook to view the contents of file folders on your computer's disk drives. Used in this way, Outlook becomes an enhanced version of Windows Explorer.

Exporting an Outlook Item

You can save an Outlook item as a separate file in these formats:

- **Text files.** Can be opened in any text editor, such as Windows Notepad.

- **Rich text (RTF) files.** Includes common formatting, such as fonts. Many word processors, including Word and Windows WordPad, can open and edit RTF files.

- **Message format.** Retains all the properties of the item. If the item is an email message, you can open it in the Microsoft Exchange Client (also known as Windows Messaging). Other item types can be opened only in Outlook.

- **Outlook templates.** Can be used to create other Outlook items of the same type.

- **vCard files.** You can save a contact item as a vCard file and send that file as an attachment to an email message. vCards provide a convenient way to share contact information using email over the Internet.

- **vCalendar files.** You can save a Calendar item as a vCalendar file, which you can send as an attachment to an email message to request a meeting.

- **iCalendar files.** You can save a Calendar item as an iCalendar file, which you can send as an attachment to an email message. This format is used to exchange free/busy information.

To export an Outlook item to a file, follow these steps:

1. Select the Outlook item that you want to save in a different format.

2. Choose **File**, **Save As**. The Save As dialog box appears, shown in Figure 48.1.

FIGURE 48.1
Use the Save As dialog box to select a location, filename, and file type for an exported Outlook item.

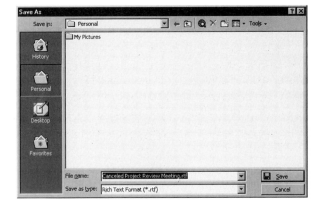

3. Open the drop-down **Save in** list and navigate to the folder in which you want to save the file.

4. Enter a filename for the item in the **File name** text box and select the file type in the **Save as type** drop-down list.

N O T E The file types available in the drop-down box depend on the type of item you're trying to save. For example, vCard is available only if you're saving a Contact item. Also, in the case of Message items, RTF is available only for messages created using the RTF format; HTML is available only for messages created in the HTML format. You can, though, save RTF and HTML messages as Text Only files. ▓

5. Choose **Save** to save the file.

Understanding Outlook Folders

Outlook provides a standard set of folders that contain the different types of items you can create in Outlook. These folders are created automatically:

- **Calendar folder.** Holds Appointment items.
- **Contacts folder.** Holds Contact items and distribution lists.
- **Inbox folder.** Holds mail items. By default, Outlook is configured to store all newly received email messages in the Inbox folder.
- **Journal folder.** Holds Journal items.
- **Notes folder.** Holds Note items.
- **Outbox folder.** Holds email items. By default, Outlook stores newly created messages in the Outbox folder until they are sent to your email server. When a message is sent, it is automatically deleted from the Outbox folder.
- **Sent Items folder.** Holds mail items. By default, Outlook stores copies of the messages you have sent in this folder.

- **Tasks folder.** Holds Task items, which can be tasks you've assigned to yourself, tasks you've asked another person to accept, or tasks someone has assigned to you.

- **Deleted Items folder.** Holds items of any type. When you delete an item, Outlook moves that item to the Deleted Items folder. You can undelete an item by moving it from the Deleted Items folder back to its original folder. After you empty the Deleted Items folder, you cannot recover the items that were previously stored there.

- **Drafts folder.** Holds mail items. New messages that you have begun composing but have not sent to the Outbox are stored here so that you can edit them later before sending them.

If you are using Outlook as a client for an Exchange Server, you can also work with Exchange public folders. Public folders work much like Outlook folders, but their contents are stored centrally on the Exchange Server. The person who creates an Exchange Server public folder can set specific access privileges on the folder, controlling who can view, edit, or create new items in the folder. The Exchange administrator gives individual users the privilege of creating public folders.

Understanding Outlook Views

Outlook provides a variety of views to display the contents of folders. A view determines the appearance of items in a folder and controls how much data is displayed. All Outlook views are based on five view types:

- **Card view.** Displays information much like a card file. The Detailed Address Cards view, shown in Figure 48.2, is an example of a Card view.

FIGURE 48.2
The Detailed Address Cards view shows Outlook contact information.

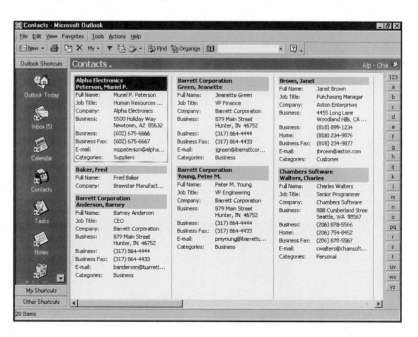

Part

VII

Ch

48

■ **Day/Week/Month view.** Used with calendar items to arrange appointment items by day, work week, week, or month. Outlook's Day/Week/Month view, shown in Figure 48.3, is an example of the Day/Week/Month type.

FIGURE 48.3

The Day/Week/Month view shows appointments and meetings in a calendar layout, in this case for a week.

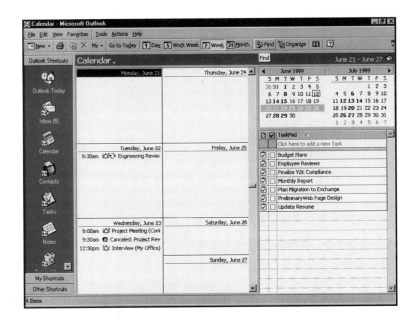

■ **Icon view.** Uses icons to represent items or files. In Figure 48.4, Note items are displayed in Icons view.

FIGURE 48.4

The Icons view displays Outlook Note items as icons.

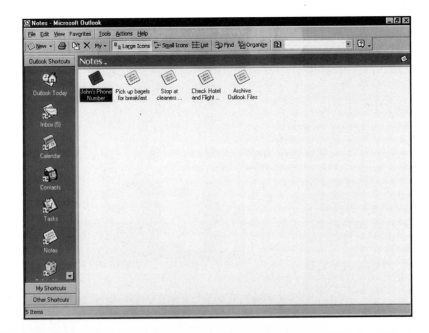

■ **Table view.** Displays a folder's information in a grid of rows and columns. The Phone List view of Contact items, shown in Figure 48.5, is an example of a Table view.

FIGURE 48.5
The Phone List view displays information about Contact items in rows and columns.

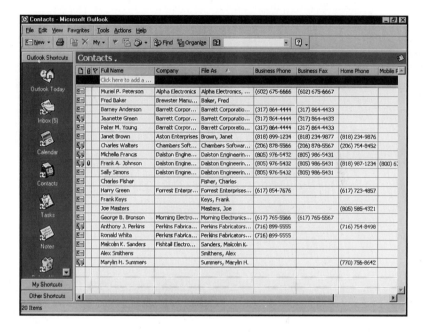

■ **Timeline view.** Displays the date and time for items of various types. The E-mail message Timeline view, shown in Figure 48.6, is an example of a Timeline view.

FIGURE 48.6
The E-mail message Timeline view, shown here with the E-mail message expanded, displays the date and time messages were sent and received.

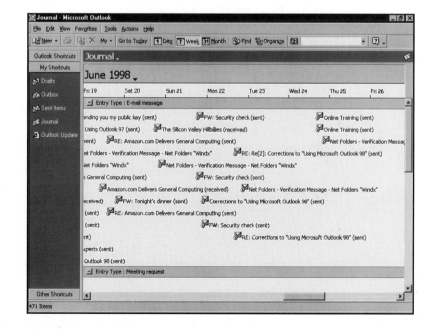

Each folder has a variety of views associated with it. You can select any existing view at any time, by choosing **View**, **Current View**, and selecting from the list of views available. You can also create custom views.

Optimizing Outlook Backups

To back up data in Outlook, you must first understand where Outlook data is stored. Outlook items are stored in folders, but these are not the same kind of folders that you can view in the Windows Explorer. Where the folders are stored depends on how Outlook is used on each computer.

For computers on a network that are directly connected to a messaging system, such as Microsoft Exchange Server or Microsoft Mail, the primary storage location is the message store of the mail system. For example, the items created by Outlook users on an Exchange Server system are stored in the Exchange Server message store. Exchange Server provides utilities the Exchange administrator can use to back up the message store, and to perform additional maintenance of this data.

Users who work only while connected to the messaging system do not require any additional storage and do not need to back up any files that are on their hard drives or personal storage areas on the network. Networked users might still want to use personal folders, however, so that they can use Outlook even if the network is not available.

Understanding Personal Folders

You can create personal folders to provide more options for storing and organizing your Outlook items. Personal folders are displayed in the Outlook folders list, along with Outlook's standard folders. You can further customize your personal folders by creating subfolders within each folder.

Personal folders are stored in a Personal Folders (.pst) file on your local hard drive or on a network drive. Personal folders provide a place for storing Outlook items when your computer is not connected to the messaging system. Users who use Outlook only as an information manager, without using any email services, store their Outlook items in personal folders. By default, a single Personal Folders file contains all your Outlook folders, so it can grow to be a very large file.

Before you can create personal folders, you have to be sure that the Personal Folders information service is installed at least once in your profile. To do so, take these steps:

1. Customize your profile by opening the **Mail** icon in the Windows Control Panel or by choosing **Tools**, **Services** in Outlook. In either case, the Services dialog box appears, as shown in Figure 48.7.

FIGURE 48.7
Use the Services dialog box to install and configure messaging services for use with Outlook.

2. If Personal Folders is not listed, or if you want to have an additional Personal Folders service, choose the **Add** button to add a service to your profile. The Add Service to Profile dialog box appears, as shown in Figure 48.8.

FIGURE 48.8
Select **Personal Folders** to add the Personal Folders service.

3. Select **Personal Folders** and then choose **OK**. The Create/Open Personal Folders File dialog box appears, as shown in Figure 48.9.

FIGURE 48.9
Enter the name and location of the Personal Folders file.

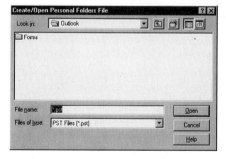

4. Open the **Look in** drop-down list and navigate to the folder in which you want to save the new Personal Folders file.

5. Enter a filename (such as your name or initials) for the Personal Folders file and choose **Open**. The Create Microsoft Personal Folders dialog box appears, as shown in Figure 48.10.

FIGURE 48.10

Use the Create MicrosoftPersonal Folders dialog box to customize the settings for your new Personal Folders file.

N O T E A Personal Folders file has two names, one of which is its Windows filename—the name you supplied in step 5. The other name, supplied in step 6, is the name used within Outlook, such as in the Outlook folders list; by default, Outlook proposes to use "Personal Folders" for this name. It's usually best to replace the default name with a more specific name so that you can readily identify the file.

6. Replace the default name with a name that identifies the Personal Folders file.

7. Select an encryption setting. You can't change the encryption setting after you have created the Personal Folders file. The compressible encryption setting enables your Personal Folders file to be compressed by compression software that you have installed on your computer.

8. Add a password if you want to add a level of security to the use of your personal folders. After you do so, Outlook prompts you for your password each time you start Outlook or connect to the Personal Folders file, unless you mark the Save this password in your password list check box.

9. Choose **OK** to save the new Personal Folders file.

If you have more than one Personal Folders file or more than one messaging system installed, you can designate where your incoming messages are to be delivered. If you are using Outlook as a client for an Exchange Server, for example, you can choose to have your messages delivered to your personal folders instead of to the Exchange store. If you do that, each time you connect to the Exchange Server, the messages in your Exchange Server inbox are moved to your personal folders Inbox; Exchange Server does not keep a copy of the messages. This option is useful for users who work primarily via a laptop computer, and who are responsible for their own backups. Because Exchange Server doesn't keep a copy of the messages, the Exchange administrator's routine backup procedures do not back up these users' messages.

To have your messages delivered to your personal folders, follow these steps:

1. Choose **Tools**, **Services** and then select the **Delivery** tab in the Services dialog box, as shown in Figure 48.11.

FIGURE 48.11
Use the Delivery tab to select the delivery destination for your messages.

2. Open the drop-down **Deliver new mail to the following location** list and then select the destination for your mail delivery.

3. Choose **OK**.

Archiving Outlook Data

You can archive the data in your personal storage files by copying older items to a separate personal storage file. Archiving prevents your primary personal storage file from growing too large, which slows Outlook's performance. You can use archiving with a Personal Folders file or with your Microsoft Exchange mailbox. You can archive any Outlook folder, and all its subfolders, at any time:

1. Choose **File**, **Archive**. The Archive dialog box appears, as shown in Figure 48.12.

FIGURE 48.12
Select the folder you want to archive in the Archive dialog box.

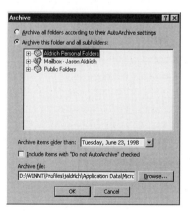

2. Select a folder to be archived and adjust the settings for how old items should be before they are archived.

3. Type the name of the archive file you want to use, or choose the **Browse** button to browse the folders on your computer or network. You can also choose to accept the default filename, **Archive.pst**.

4. Choose **OK** to begin the archiving process.

Archiving can take a long time, depending upon the size of the folder branch you have selected and the speed of your disk drives or network. However, Outlook archives in the background, so you can continue using Outlook during the archiving process.

You can configure Outlook to perform archiving on a regular basis. To do so, follow these steps:

1. Choose **Tools**, **Options**, select the **Other** tab, and choose **AutoArchive**. The AutoArchive dialog box appears, as shown in Figure 48.13.

FIGURE 48.13
Use the AutoArchive dialog box to set your archive options.

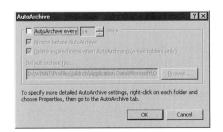

2. Mark the **AutoArchive every x days** check box and enter the number of days between AutoArchive sessions. Select **Prompt before AutoArchive** if you want Outlook to ask for permission to execute the archive according to schedule. Select **Delete expired items when AutoArchiving (e-mail folders only)** to move expired email messages from your Inbox folder to the Deleted Items folder.

3. Enter the filename for the AutoArchive file, or choose the **Browse** button to browse the folders on your computer or network.

4. Choose **OK**.

When Outlook performs AutoArchiving, it follows the AutoArchiving properties of each Outlook folder. To view the properties for a folder, select the folder in the Folder List, choose **File**, **Folder**, and then select **Properties** for the folder. Select the **AutoArchive** tab to view and modify the AutoArchiving settings for the folder. You can choose the age after which items will be archived, whether to move the items to an archive file, or whether to delete them. AutoArchiving does not affect items in your Contacts folder.

Exporting and Importing Data with Personal Folder Files

You can export the contents of any Outlook folder and its subfolders to a Personal Folders file. This provides an easy mechanism for transferring Outlook items between two or more computers, because you can also import the contents of a personal folder file into Outlook.

The Outlook Import and Export Wizard helps you through the steps of exporting items to a Personal Folders file. Take the following steps:

1. Choose **File, Import and Export**. The Import and Export Wizard appears.
2. Select **Export to a File** and choose **Next >**.
3. Select **Personal Folder File (.pst)** and choose **Next >**.
4. Select the folder from which you want to export. If you want to export items in that folder's subfolders, mark the **Include Subfolders** check box.
5. To filter the items so that not all items are copied, choose the **Filter** button. Use the options in the Filter dialog box to select items based upon date ranges, names of email recipients, or contents of the items. Choose **OK** in the Filter dialog box to return to the wizard and choose **Next >**.
6. Enter the filename for the personal folder file that you want to create, or choose **Browse** to search your disk drives or network folders. If you are exporting to a Personal Folders file that already contains items, select the option you prefer for handling duplicate items.
7. Choose **Finish**. Outlook creates the Personal Folders file or opens the existing file, and copies the selected items to that file.

The Import and Export Wizard also helps with importing Outlook items from a personal folder file:

1. Choose **File, Import and Export**. The Import and Export Wizard appears.
2. Select **Import from Another Program or File** and choose **Next>**.
3. Select **Personal Folder File (.pst)** and choose **Next>**.
4. Enter the filename for the personal folder file from which you want to import items, or choose **Browse** to search your disk drives or network folders. Select the option you prefer for handling duplicate items and choose **Next >**.
5. Outlook displays the folder structure of the file from which you are importing. Select the folder from which you want to import items, and specify whether to include subfolders.
6. To filter the items so that not all items are copied, choose the **Filter** button. Use the options in the Filter dialog box to select items based upon date ranges, names of email recipients, or contents of the items. Choose **OK** in the Filter dialog box to return to the wizard.
7. Select the destination folder location and then choose **Finish** to complete the importing operation.

Using Offline Folders with Microsoft Exchange

Offline folders are available only if you're using Outlook as a client for an Exchange Server. These folders, located on your local hard disk, contain copies of Outlook items saved in the Exchange Server store. As explained later in this section, the original items in the Exchange store and the copies of those items on your hard drive are compared from time to time so that they are up-to-date in both places, a process known as *synchronization*.

Part

VII

Ch

48

N O T E   Offline folders are quite similar to personal folders. The principal difference is that each offline folder has a matching folder in the Exchange store, whereas a personal folder does not. Offline folders are contained in a file with a filename extension of `.ost`; personal folders are contained in a file with a filename extension of `.pst`.

Offline folders have two principal uses:

■ They provide a means for people who travel with a laptop to work with their Outlook items while the computer is physically disconnected from the server.

■ They provide a means for people to continue working with their Outlook items if the server or LAN is unavailable.

Follow these steps to configure Outlook to use offline folders:

1. Choose **Tools**, **Services** and select **Microsoft Exchange Server**. Choose **Properties** to view and modify the settings for Exchange Server.

2. Select the **Advanced** tab, as shown in Figure 48.14.

FIGURE 48.14
Use the Advanced tab of the Microsoft Exchange Server dialog box to enable offline use.

3. Choose **Offline Folder File Settings** to display the dialog box shown in Figure 48.15.

FIGURE 48.15
Use the Offline Folder File Settings dialog box to customize your offline folders.

4. Enter the filename for the Offline Folder file, or choose **Bro<u>w</u>se** to browse the folders on your computer. After you have an Offline Folder file active, you can't change the name or location of the file.

5. Select an encryption setting for the Offline Folder file. You can't change the encryption setting after you have created the file. The compressible encryption setting enables your file to be compressed by compression software installed on your computer.

6. Choose **OK** to return to the Advanced tab.

7. Check **Enable offline <u>u</u>se**.

The next time you start Outlook, your offline folders are opened automatically. When you connect to Exchange Server, either via modem or by logging onto the Exchange Server, Outlook synchronizes the contents of your offline folders with your Exchange Server folders.

The following are two other operations you can perform while the Offline Folder File Settings dialog box is open:

■ Choose **<u>C</u>ompact Now** to reduce the size of your offline folder, recovering the space that was used by items that you have deleted. This operation is usually not necessary, because Outlook and Exchange routinely compact the offline folders during normal use.

■ Choose **<u>D</u>isable Offline <u>U</u>se** to turn off the use of offline folders. The next time you start Outlook, the offline folder file is not opened.

Troubleshooting Outlook

I'd like to be able to tell you Outlook 2000 has evolved into such a mature product that you're unlikely to experience problems. Unfortunately, I can't do that. Although Outlook 2000 is significantly less troublesome than earlier versions, there are likely to be many times when you, as well as the people you support, experience problems.

NOTE Outlook, like other Office 2000 applications, is self-repairing. When you launch Outlook, it automatically determines whether any critical files are missing or corrupted. If that's the case, those files are automatically reinstalled if they're available on the network; if the required files are not available, the user is prompted to supply the Office 2000 CD-ROM so that the files can be reinstalled.

Sometimes, Outlook might start normally and then run into problems because a noncritical file, such as a font file or template, is missing. Problems of this type can often be corrected by choosing **Help**, **Detect and Repair**. The built-in Detect and Repair utility scans noncritical files to find discrepancies between the original and current files, and corrects such problems wherever possible. ■

The first place to look for help in solving Outlook problems is in online Help. As you know if you've worked with other Office 2000 applications, you can use the Office Assistant to help you find information or you can use the traditional way of accessing online Help information. As an administrator, you'll probably prefer to move the Office Assistant out of the way. To do that, choose **<u>H</u>elp**, **Hide the <u>O</u>ffice Assistant**.

With the Office Assistant hidden, choose **Help, Microsoft Outlook Help** and select the **Index** tab. Enter **troubleshoot** in the Type Keywords box, choose **Search**, and you'll see a list of 47 major troubleshooting topics. When you select one of these topics, Outlook displays a list of subtopics, usually eight to ten of them. As you see, there's a lot of built-in troubleshooting help available within Outlook itself.

Another valuable resource for troubleshooting information is the Microsoft Knowledge Base. On the day this chapter was written (which happened to be the day Microsoft officially released Office 2000), the Knowledge Base already contained many articles about Outlook 2000. Among the particularly useful Knowledge Base articles are

- Troubleshooting Synchronization Problems (Q195875)
- Troubleshooting Forms That Don't Run on Other Computers (Q201083)
- Troubleshooting MSN 2.5 and Outlook 2000 (Q195866)
- Synchronizing Offline with Network Card Installed (Q195871)
- Outlook Rules Wizard Troubleshooting (Q197496)
- Troubleshooting Outlook Configuration Problems (Q195714 and Q195795)
- Troubleshooting Security Issues in Outlook (Q195843)
- How to Troubleshoot Mail Stuck in the Outbox (Q195922)

N O T E That's just a small sampling of the troubleshooting information that was available in the Knowledge Base at the time this book was written. ▦

Another valuable resource for Outlook information, available on the Internet, is the Slipstick Systems Exchange Center, which contains much information not available elsewhere and comprehensive references to othersources of information. You can access this site at

`http://www.slipstick.com`

I'm not going to attempt to summarize all the information available in these resources. Instead, I'll provide some tips that I've found particularly useful.

N O T E When looking for information about solving Outlook problems, don't limit yourself to sources of information only about Outlook 2000. You might well find something in a topic about Outlook 98 (or even Outlook 97) that applies to Outlook 2000 or gives you a strong hint about something that applies to Outlook 2000. ▦

Other valuable resources for solving Outlook problems are the various newsgroups hosted by Microsoft. At the time this book was written, these newsgroups were

- `microsoft.public.outlook`
- `microsoft.public.outlook.Calendaring`
- `microsoft.public.outlook.Contacts`
- `microsoft.public.outlook.Fax`

- `microsoft.public.outlook.General`
- `microsoft.public.outlook.installation`
- `microsoft.public.outlook.interop`
- `microsoft.public.outlook.printing`
- `microsoft.public.outlook.Program_Addins`
- `microsoft.public.outlook.program_forms`
- `microsoft.public.outlook.Program_VBA`
- `microsoft.public.outlook.teamfolders`
- `microsoft.public.outlook.ThirdPartyUtil`

There might well be additional newsgroups by the time you read this book. You can submit questions to these newsgroups and, most of the time, you'll get a fast response from one of your peers.

Troubleshooting Startup Problems

In a corporate environment in which people use Outlook as a client for an Exchange Server, it's usual for people to save all their Outlook items in the Exchange store. This has several benefits over saving items on local hard disks:

- Items can easily be shared among users.
- Local hard disks aren't filled with Outlook items.
- Archiving is taken care of at the server level.

All this is fine until the day arrives when a user attempts to launch Outlook and sees the message

`Your Microsoft Exchange Server is unavailable.`

This message box contains three buttons: Retry, Work Offline, and Help. If the Exchange Server is really unavailable, choosing **Retry** won't do anything for you. Choosing **Work Offline** is not much help if your Outlook items are on the unavailable Exchange Server.

If several users have this problem, the problem is likely to be with Exchange Server, the server computer, the server operating system, or the network. However, if an individual user has this problem, one possibility is that the Microsoft Exchange Server information service on that person's computer has become corrupted or perhaps has been accidentally deleted. You can solve the problem by creating a new profile, as follows:

1. In the Windows desktop's taskbar, choose **Start**, **Run** to display the Run dialog box.
2. In the Open box, enter **Outlook.exe /profile** and choose **OK**. Outlook opens and displays the Choose Profile dialog box.
3. Choose **New**. Outlook displays the first Outlook Setup Wizard dialog box, shown in Figure 48.16.

FIGURE 48.16
You can use this Wizard window to select the information services you want in the new profile.

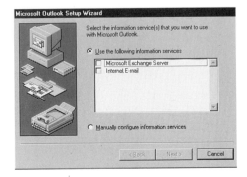

4. To create a profile that provides access to the Exchange Server, check Microsoft Exchange Server and then choose **Next** > to display the second Wizard dialog box, as shown in 48.17.

FIGURE 48.17
This Wizard window asks you to provide a name for the new profile.

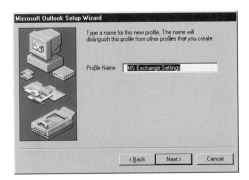

5. Replace the default name with the name for the new profile and then choose **Next** > to display the third wizard window, shown in Figure 48.18.

FIGURE 48.18
Use this Wizard window to identify the server and a mailbox on that server.

6. Enter the name of the server and the name of the mailbox and then choose **Next** > to display the fourth wizard window, shown in Figure 48.19.

FIGURE 48.19
This Wizard window asks whether you want to be able to work with Outlook while your computer doesn't have a connection to the server.

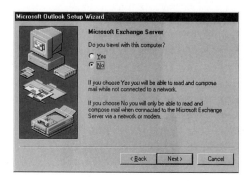

7. In this example, you re-establish a connection to the server. Accept the default **No** and then click **Next** > to display the final wizard window, which states you are ready to use Outlook as a client for Exchange Server. Choose **Finish** to display the Choose Profile dialog box with the name of the new profile selected. Choose **OK** to open Outlook with a connection to the Exchange Server.

Resolving Missing File Errors

When you try to start Outlook, or while you're using it, you might see error messages about missing files. As mentioned previously, Outlook automatically detects and reinstalls critical files. You might run into problems, though, with missing or corrupted add-in files. Table 48.1 contains a complete list of the files required to use the add-ins supplied with Outlook. If you see an error message relating to a problem with an add-in, you can often solve the problem by reinstalling the appropriate file.

Table 48.1   Add-In Filenames

Add-In	Filename
Delegate Access	dlgsetp.ecf
Exchange Extensions Commands	Outex.ecf
Exchange Extensions Property Pages	Outex2.ecf
NetMeeting Extensions	Nmexchex.ecf
TeamStatus Form	Olmenu.ecf
Rules Wizard	Rwiz1.ecf
Mail 3.0 Extensions	Mail3.ecf
Deleted Item Recovery	Dumpster.ecf
Server Scripting	scrtxtn.ecf
Internet Mail	Minet.ecf
Net Folders	Fldpub.ecf
Fax Extension	Faxext.ecf

Part
VII

Ch
48

continues

Table 48.1   Continued

Add-In	Filename
cc:Mail Menu Extension	Ccmxp.ecf
Digital Security	Etexch.ecf
Microsoft Fax	Awfext.ecf
Microsoft Mail 3.x Menu Extensions	Msfsprop.ecf
Schedule+	Msspc.ecf
The Microsoft Network	Msn.ecf
CompuServe E-mail	Cserve.ecf
Outlook Forms Redirector	Frmrdrct.ecf
Windows CE Support	Pmailext.ecf

Troubleshooting Outlook Mail Problems

After you send an email message, you might receive a message in your Inbox from the system administrator with this text:

```
No transport provider was available for delivery to this recipient.
```

There are several reasons why you might receive this message:

- Your Personal Folder file might be damaged. Remove the Personal Folder from your profile and create a new one. You can then import the old Outlook items from the old Personal Folder file into the new file.

- You have no mail transport service in your profile. Use the Mail icon in the Windows Control Panel to add the mail transport service you want to install.

- You upgraded your MSN mail to POP3/SMTP format. Change your email type to SMTP by following these steps:

  1. Open a contact, right-click the email address, and then select **Properties**.

  2. Type **SMTP** in the E-mail Type box and choose **OK**.

  3. Choose **Save and Close**.

- The Contact item might be damaged. Delete and re-create the contact.

- You might have an apostrophe in your computer name. Open the **Network** icon in the Windows Control Panel. On the Identification tab, type a new name for your computer.

- Your offline folders are not configured. Connect to your Microsoft Exchange Server and re-establish your offline folder file.

Troubleshooting Outlook Mail File Attachment Problems

Many users send email messages with attached files created in other applications, such as Word documents, Excel workbooks, graphics, and many other types of files. Although this method of transferring files is extremely convenient and fast, some problems can arise.

Solving Disconnection Problems   When you send mail with an attachment from Outlook through an ISP, you might be disconnected from the ISP. This can happen if your attachment exceeds the maximum allowable size for attachments supported by the ISP. Contact your ISP to verify the maximum attachment size and inquire about the availability of alternative mail servers to handle larger attachments.

If you are sending the attached files in their original size, consider using a file-compression program to reduce the file size before attaching the files. If you are sending a message with several attached files, you might need to break the message into several messages, one for each attachment.

Solving Missing File Attachment Problems   If your ISP or mail system appears to be sending the message properly, but some of your recipients are not able to receive the attachments, ask them to check with their ISP or their company's email administrator to verify any limitations on the size and number of attachments.

Double-Clicking an Attachment Generates an Error Message   If you receive an email message with an attached file, you might get the following message:

```
The file <file name>, does not have a program associated with it for this
action. To create an association, double-click My Computer on your desktop.
On the View menu, choose Options, then choose File Types.
```

This message indicates that the attachment doesn't match any entries in your Windows file associations. The attachment might not have an extension, or its extension might not be associated with a program on your computer.

If the file has an extension, and you want to register the file type for future use, follow the instructions in the message that was presented.

To prevent sending messages without extensions, follow these steps:

1. Double-click **My Computer** on the Windows Desktop.
2. Choose **View, Options** (or **Folder Options** in Windows 98) and choose the **View** tab.
3. Clear the check box labeled **Hide MS-DOS File Extensions for File Types That Are Registered** (or **Hide File Extensions for Known File Types** in Windows 98) and choose **OK**.

Finding Out Why Outlook Keeps Accessing the Floppy Drive

Outlook might seem to unnecessarily access your floppy drive. Here are some reasons why Outlook might be accessing the floppy drive:

- Outlook might be looking for a Personal Folder file. Check the locations for your Personal Folder files by choosing **Tools, Services**. One at a time, select your Personal Folder files, and choose **Properties** to verify the path to the files.
- Outlook might be attempting to save archive information to the floppy drive. Choose **Tools, Options**, select the **Other** tab, and choose **AutoArchive**. Check the path to the default AutoArchive file.

- Reminders might be trying to access a sound file on the floppy drive. Choose **Tools**, **Options**, select the **Other** tab, choose **Advanced Options**, and then choose **Reminder Options**. Check the path for the Reminder sound.

- If you're using Word as your email editor, Word might be searching for a template on the floppy drive. Choose **Tools**, **Options** and select the **Mail Format** tab. If you have selected **Use Word as your E-mail editor**, check the path to the template.

Taking a Systematic Approach to Troubleshooting

Outlook is probably the most complex application in the Windows suite because it embraces much of what's in all the other applications and deals with so many information protocols. Most of the time, Outlook behaves very well, but when troubles occur they can be quite difficult to solve.

I hope you'll find some of the suggestions I've made in the preceding pages useful, but I know I haven't provided solutions to more than a few of the problems you'll encounter.

When you encounter a problem with Outlook, be very systematic in looking for a solution. Be careful to note exactly what happens on the computer that has problems. Compare all the settings on the problem computer with those on another computer that does not experience the same problems.

If you can't immediately solve the problem yourself, send a message to one of the Outlook newsgroups explaining *exactly* the computer's configuration and the *complete* details of the problem. It's quite likely someone else has experienced—and solved—the same problem and will take the time to help. Always remember, though, that people who are generous enough to spend their time answering your questions know only what you tell them about your settings and your problems. The more details you provide, the more likely you are to get the answer you need. ●

Troubleshooting and Optimizing FrontPage

by Brady P. Merkel

Now that FrontPage has been added to the Microsoft Office suite, you are likely to spend more time with FrontPage publishing and managing your Web sites. Sometimes, you might encounter problems with FrontPage, and other times you might want to know how to make FrontPage perform better for you. In this chapter, you find some hints and tips to troubleshoot FrontPage, as well as some guidelines to optimize the application.

Troubleshooting FrontPage

As you use FrontPage more and more, you grow increasingly familiar with the online Help and quite possibly the Microsoft support Web site (**http://support.microsoft.com**). Sometimes, however, those resources do not provide a troubleshooting overview that can resolve some of your most challenging problems efficiently. In this section, we cover the areas of FrontPage that seem to cause the most frustration when trouble arises.

Problems with Editing Pages

FrontPage provides a sophisticated WYSIWYG editing environment, but sometimes you might run into difficulty. Although FrontPage is an application in the Office suite, you might find the editing environment somewhat restrictive and confusing, especially when compared to Microsoft Word or Publisher. Use the following troubleshooting hints and tips to understand and resolve those occasional edit frustrations.

Use HTML View   Perhaps the most useful troubleshooting tip is to use the FrontPage HTML view of your page when you encounter a problem editing in the Normal view. Sometimes the Normal view can prevent you from making fine adjustments that are easier to do by editing the HTML itself.

Additionally, use **Edit**, **Replace** in HTML view to make global changes that you cannot make in Normal view. For example, if you want to change the color of several cells within an HTML table, use **Edit**, **Replace** to find all occurrences of the current color and replace it with your new color. Be sure to click the **Find in HTML** check box.

TIP   If you do not know the hexadecimal color code you need, type some text in your page in Normal view, select it, and click the **Font Color** toolbar button. Next, choose **More Colors** and use the More Colors dialog box (see Figure 49.1) to choose the color and learn its hexadecimal code. The benefit of using the colors displayed in the More Colors dialog box is that they are *Web-safe*—derived from a palette that displays the same on most platforms, such as Windows and Macintosh systems.

Cannot Position the Mouse Between Elements   When editing pages in Normal view, occasionally you might find yourself unable to position the mouse cursor between two elements to divide them or type new text. This commonly occurs when you nest a table within another and cannot insert text before the internal table at the top of a cell of the outer table.

One solution is to go to HTML view, find the location where you want to insert, and type the HTML code for a nonbreaking space there (also known as an *HTML entity*)—type ** **. The reason you need a nonbreaking space is that HTML ignores regular spaces and new lines. If you simply type a space, FrontPage will ignore it.

FIGURE 49.1
Choose **Web-safe colors** in the More Colors dialog box.

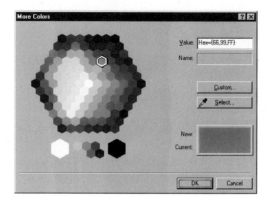

Cannot Display a Cell with Nothing in It   HTML Tables are powerful elements to use for displaying tabular information, as well as laying out your pages. Unfortunately, browsers display empty table cells differently from other cells—especially visible when using tables with borders and cell spacing. To avoid this unsightly occurrence, you must put something into the offending cell. Use the nonbreaking space entity—in HTML view, type ** ** into the cell and browsers display the cell with the borders as expected.

View the Source from a Browser   When you save pages to a Web server equipped with the FrontPage Server Extensions (or Office Server Extensions), the Server Extensions perform some editing of your pages—replacing components with their proper HTML, making substitutions, adding validation scripts, including pages, and so on. Sometimes, this transparent editing can be confusing, because the formatting of the included text can conflict with the formatting you prefer. To see how the Server Extensions affect your page, view the page with a browser and view the HTML source there. You can see how the resulting HTML was saved by the Server Extensions and learn how to compensate within your own content.

Align Shared Borders   If you use Shared Borders on your Web site, you might encounter difficulty when you try to align content within the borders with one another. For example, you want the content in the Top and Bottom borders to align with information in the Left border. The way the borders are assembled by the Server Extensions makes it difficult to attain exact alignment, but it is possible using the following hints. For more information about Shared Borders, see "Using Shared Borders," later in this chapter.

First, use a browser to view the HTML source of one of your Shared Border pages to see how the Server Extensions assembled the page. When using a left Shared Border, you'll notice that the Server Extensions add an adjacent cell of 32 pixels wide. That additional width can help you align elements with the Top and Bottom borders. Furthermore, you'll notice that only the body portion of the shared borders is included in the assembled page.

Second, edit the borders individually, rather than from within a single page that references them. FrontPage maintains the shared border contents in separate files in the _borders folder. To edit the HTML of the shared borders, open the files in the _borders folder. If you cannot see the _borders folder, choose **Tools**, **Web Settings** and click the **Advanced** tab. Select the **Show documents in hidden directories** check box and click **OK**.

Part
VII

Ch
49

Invalid Pages Found with Search Form Component   The Search Form component provides a quick and easy way to add a search engine to your Web site, enabling users to perform keyword searches and find documents. When you add the Search Form component to your Web site, the Server Extensions construct an index to all of your Web site's content. Normally, the Server Extensions keep the index up-to-date whenever pages change within the Web site. Sometimes, however, this index can get out-of-date and users might find documents that no longer exist on the Web site. To manually regenerate the index, choose **Tools**, **Recalculate Hyperlinks**.

Scheduled Components Not Updating   If you use the Scheduled Include Page or Scheduled Picture Component to modify the content of your Web site automatically, you might find that the content does not change when the scheduled time expires. These components check their start and end time only when a user modifies the current Web in some way using the Server Extensions, such as by using one of the FrontPage form handlers. To update the content manually, choose **Tools**, **Recalculate Hyperlinks** from within FrontPage.

Running Out of Disk Space   To improve performance, FrontPage maintains its own separate cache of Web files on your system. This can spell trouble if left unchecked—because the cache of temporary files can consume valuable disk space. If you find that your system is getting low on disk space, choose **Tools**, **Web Settings** and clickthe **Advanced** tab. Click **Delete Files** to clean out the cache.

Problems with Publishing

When using FrontPage to author Web content, you have two basic modes of operation: Connect directly to the host Web server, or use a staging server to develop the content and then publish the Web to the host Web server when ready. The preferred method usually is to connect directly with the host Web server so your changes become live immediately. However, the staging server mode is useful in some circumstances, too—your link performance might be too slow for a direct connection, the host Web server does not employ the FrontPage Server Extensions, or you prefer to stage the content first and post the changes only when they are approved. Unfortunately, a few problems canoccur when you publish your Web.

Files Not Updated   When you publish your Web site to another server, FrontPage can perform an incremental update—posting only the files that have changed since the last update. Sometimes, however, some files might not be updated. This occurs when files are updated on the host Web server outside the FrontPage environment. When you publish your Web, FrontPage does not update files on the host Web server that have more recent time stamps. To update the files, go to Reports view and use the Publish Status report to identify the pages that should not be published again. Choose **File**, **Publish Web**, and choose **Publish All Pages** to force the update of the files even though they have earlier time stamps than those on the host Web server.

Broken Links   As content authors develop their pages, sometimes they embed absolute links to other pages within the site. When you publish the files to the host Web server, these links can remain pointed to the original location. Use FrontPage's Broken Hyperlinks Report to identify the links and affect repairs. Remember to fix them on the staging Web server.

Custom CGI Script Doesn't Work   As you become more adept at creating Web content, you might become curious to try out some server-side common gateway interface (CGI) programs. There are plenty of CGI scripts available on the Web that can add a new dimension to your Web site. Unfortunately, if you use custom CGI scripts, you might encounter problems when you publish the Web to the Web site hosting service—the script might no longer function. For example, the CGI script will not execute when referenced by a form.

The reason is simple: For security reasons, most Web site hosting services restrict CGI scripts from executing within the content area of a Web site. You might have to move the custom CGI program to another area of the host Web server that will allow programs to run, such as in the `/cgi-bin` or `/scripts` folders. Contact your Web site administrator for help.

Problems with Web Server

FrontPage supports many different Web servers, from Microsoft's own Internet Information Server and Personal Web Server to those found on UNIX systems, such as Apache and Netscape Commerce Server. When using FrontPage with a Web server equipped with the FrontPage Server Extensions, you might not notice a difference between them. However, there are some occasional problems you might encounter.

Cannot Use Security Features   If you are using the FrontPage Server Extensions with Microsoft's Personal Web Server or Internet Information Server on a disk volume with a FAT (file allocation table) or FAT32 file system, you cannot use the security features of FrontPage to restrict content from being viewed. The security features do not work because of the lack of file security features in FAT and FAT32. To use the security features, you must upgrade to Windows NT and use an NTFS volume instead.

Maximum Number of Users Encountered   If you are using Microsoft's Internet Information Server (also known as Personal Web Server) on a Windows NT Workstation, you might discover that when others browse your Web site, some get an error page that asserts that the maximum number of users has exceeded. This is an intentional strategy on Microsoft's part to coerce you to upgrade to the costlier Windows NT Server. The Windows NT Workstation version of IIS is restricted to only 10 simultaneous connections, but IIS on Windows NT Server has no user limitations.

Cannot Send Email from Form Handler   One of the new FrontPage features enables you to send an email message from the Web server when a user submits an HTML form. The message can be sent to the user or to a recipient within the organization. For example, you could set up a simple suggestion box soliciting comments about your Web site—use FrontPage's Send to E-mail Address feature to forward the suggestion to you so you can properly act on the comments. However, to use the feature, the host Web server must employ the FrontPage Office Server Extensions, and they must be installed and configured properly for sending email. Contact the administrator of your Web server to install or update the Office Server Extensions Resource Kit to fix the problem.

▶ For more information on the Office Server Extensions, **see** Chapter 35, "Deploying and Using Office 2000's Web-Collaboration Components," on **p. 895**.

Part
VII

Ch
49

Optimizing FrontPage

FrontPage is a sophisticated application that, at first, can appear daunting and confusing. Although it is an Office application, FrontPage is different from the typical Office tools that you might already be familiar with, such as Microsoft Word, Excel, and PowerPoint. Many of the complex features are there to save you time and money when developing and managing Web sites. To get the most productivity out of FrontPage, consider the following optimizations.

Using a Web Site Equipped with Server Extensions

Perhaps the most important suggestion for optimizing FrontPage is to use a Web server that employs the FrontPage Server Extensions (or the Office Server Extensions). The Server Extensions are used when you develop Web pages and when users browse your Web. The Server Extensions support searching your Web content, incrementing hit counters, coordinating interactive discussion groups, updating dynamic page components, and performing live connections to databases. Microsoft provides the Server Extensions free for more than 20 Web server platforms, including most popular Windows- and UNIX-based Web servers.

N O T E The Office Server Extensions include the FrontPage Server Extensions and some added functionality to support the new Office 2000 Web-collaboration features—namely, subscriptions and discussion groups. Unfortunately, the Office Server Extensions are supported only on Microsoft's Internet Information Server version 4 Web server. ■

The Server Extensions can also help when you publish your Web files to the Web server. The extensions assist FrontPage with file and link management, and can duplicate many of your actions on your staging Web server, such as deleting, renaming, or moving files. For example, if you rename a file on your staging Web server, when you publish the Web files, the Server Extensions also rename the file on the host Web server.

N O T E Occasionally, Microsoft releases updates to the Server Extensions—for more information, see `http://officeupdate.microsoft.com/frontpage/wpp/platforms.htm`. ■

If you use FrontPage with a Web server that does not employ the Server Extensions, you must publish your Web another way and many interactive capabilities will not be available to you. For instance, you will not be able to use some of FrontPage's most powerful features, such as automated form handling, database integration, team collaboration, discussion groups, user registration, hit counters, or the interactive search form.

TIP If you must use a Web-site hosting service that does not support the FrontPage Server Extensions, you might be able to use some custom CGI scripts that perform similar tasks. For more information, see

`http://dynamicnet.net/support/fp/cgialternatives.htm`.

Using SubWebs to Manage Different Areas

FrontPage 2000 provides the capability of designating folders in a Web site as *subWebs*—independent Webs that can have their own shared borders, theme, and security permissions. Another reason to use subWebs is if your Web site grows too large to manage all the content within one Web. If it takes more than five minutes to connect to your Web server and download the list of files, consider designating some of your folders as subWebs.

To create a subWeb, right-click on a folder in the Folder List and choose **Convert to Web**. Then, double-click on the new **subWeb** icon to open a FrontPage window connected to the new Web. By default, the subWeb will inherit the settings from the parent Web, but you can manage the subWeb differently. For example, you can grant author permission to a different set of people.

Using a Theme

As your Web site grows larger, you will find that maintaining a consistent look and feel across all the Web pages becomes a challenge. When you use a Theme, and apply it to your entire Web site, the battle is half over. When you use a Theme, you can save much of the time used for formatting a new page—let FrontPage and the Theme perform that for you.

▶ If you do not like any of the standard Themes that Microsoft supplies, use the FrontPage 2000 integrated Theme Designer to customize your own design. For information, **see** Chapter 11, "Customizing FrontPage to Your Organization's Needs," on **p. 295**.

Using Shared Style Sheets

As with using a Theme, you can also use cascading style sheets (CSS) to create consistent styles. Using FrontPage, you can create an external CSS style sheet and link it to all your pages automatically. When you change a style in the external style sheet, all your pages inherit the new settings. This can save you time formatting your pages. Choose **Format**, **Style Sheet Links** and use the Link Style Sheet dialog box to link a style sheet to all pages within your Web site.

> **CAUTION**
>
> FrontPage enables you to apply multiple external style sheets to a page—the styles cascade and produce a combined effect. Beware: When you link multiple style sheets to a page, the order can affect how styles combine formatting. If you have conflicting formatting associated with the same style, the formatting of the last (not the first) style sheet linked to the page takes precedence.

Part
VII

Ch
49

Using Shared Borders

FrontPage provides a feature called *Shared Borders*, which enables you to design and maintain common top, bottom, left, and right sections to your Web pages. You can use Shared Borders to build a consistent layout to your Web pages and simplify changes to the shared content throughout your Web site. If you do not use Shared Borders, any time you want to make a simple change, such as adding a new navigational link, you must edit each page individually, which can take a lot of time.

When you edit pages that use Shared Borders, FrontPage displays the shared areas with dashed lines, and you can edit the border contents as you would normally. When you save the page, the Shared Border is also saved, and all other pages that reference that border are updated with the new content.

Using the Navigation View, Navigation Bar, and Page Banner Components

Using the FrontPage Navigation view and Navigation bar components, you can save yourself time when you change the navigational structure of your site. You place the Navigation bar within your pages, or better yet, in a Shared Border, and you move icons in the Navigation view. As you make changes to the view, your changes are reflected in all the pages with the Navigation bar—all without editing a single page. You can literally alter the entire structure and navigation hierarchy of your Web site within a few minutes.

Additionally, if you use the Page Banner component in your pages, you can change the names of your pages from within the Navigation view—again without editing the page itself. A word of warning though—keep the names short and simple, because they are used for the Navigation bar, too, and long names tend to create unsightly navigation links.

 TIP Apply a Theme to your Web site to create graphical buttons in the Navigation bar and graphical banners in the Page Banner components.

Finding Microsoft and Third-Party Online Resources for Office Administrators

by Bill Camarda

The Internet has rapidly become a critical source of up-to-date technical information for those who manage and support Microsoft Office 2000. In this chapter, you review key Internet resources available to you, both from Microsoft and from independent sources, including

- Microsoft online support resources
- Web sites and publications
- Newsgroups

NOTE Remember that Web addresses might change.

Discovering Microsoft Web Sites and Online Publications for Office Administrators

Microsoft offers extensive online support resources for Office professionals, including

■ The Microsoft Personal Support Center

■ Microsoft TechNet CD Online

■ Microsoft Seminars Online

■ The online version of the Office 2000 Resource Kit

Each resource is covered in the following sections.

The Microsoft Personal Support Center

Microsoft has redesigned its online Office support center several times; the most recent version brings together nearly all these resources at the Microsoft Personal Support Center for Microsoft Office. You can think of this page as your personal portal to support help for Office. To reach this page, go to **www.microsoft.com/office** and click **Support** (see Figure 50.1).

FIGURE 50.1

The Microsoft Personal Support Center for Microsoft Office.

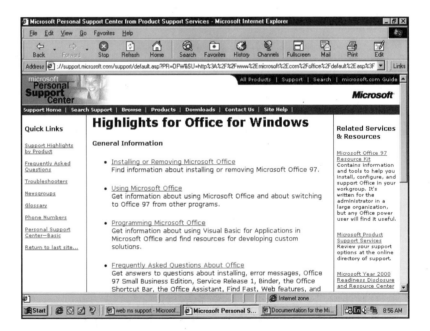

The main support page includes links to information Microsoft believes is especially useful to Office administrators and users. It also contains links to Microsoft's other Office help resources. For example, you can

■ Click **Newsgroups** at the left to access Microsoft's public newsgroups (covered later in this chapter).

- Click **Frequently Asked Questions** for Microsoft's FAQ on commonly discussed Office issues.

- Click **Troubleshooters** to view a set of interactive troubleshooting tools for Office, Windows, and other Microsoft products.

- Click **Microsoft Office 2000 Resource Kit** to access Microsoft's Office 2000 Resource Kit, the same one you'd normally pay $59.99 for, except the online version is updated more regularly—and it's free. (The Office 2000 Resource Kit is covered in the next section.)

- Click **Search Support** to search Microsoft's entire Knowledge Base, library of troubleshooting wizards, and downloadable files. You might then want to click **Advanced View**, which gives you more control over how you search (see Figure 50.2). Clicking **Search Support** provides a different set of support options than clicking **Support** at the top of the Microsoft Office home page (as discussed earlier).

FIGURE 50.2
The Advanced View of Microsoft's Office search page.

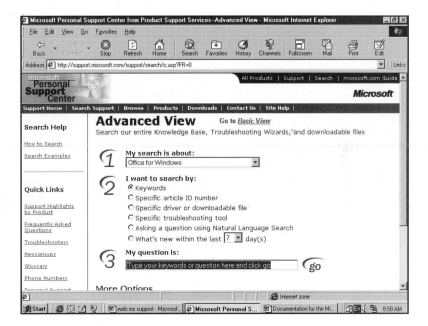

Microsoft TechNet

Microsoft TechNet brings together extensive resources for IT professionals covering Office, Windows, and other Microsoft products. For several years, these resources have been available through a CD-ROM subscription costing approximately $300 per year. Microsoft has recently made most of these resources available free on the Web at **www.technet.microsoft. com/cdonline/default.asp** (see Figure 50.3).

When you fill out the free registration form, you have access to an extensive library that includes

- Microsoft Office 2000 white papers
- Technical notes

- Supplemental drivers and patches
- Application notes
- More than 55,000 Microsoft Knowledge Base articles
- Troubleshooting tips
- Usage and optimization techniques

FIGURE 50.3
TechNet CD Online: free access to extensive Microsoft technical support resources.

Microsoft Seminars Online

If you'd rather listen than read, Microsoft has posted several online seminars for deploying and administering Office, accessible at **www.microsoft.com/Seminar**. Each seminar consists of a series of PowerPoint slides that run automatically, with audio commentary from a product manager or other subject matter expert. Seminars currently available include

- Microsoft Office 2000: Hot Ownership Topics
- Microsoft Office 2000: New Application Horizons
- Microsoft Office 98, Macintosh Edition, Product
- Microsoft Outlook 2000 (Messaging and Collaboration)
- New Development Features in Microsoft Outlook 2000
- Why Web Professionals Can Love FrontPage 2000

A typical seminar is shown in Figure 50.4.

FIGURE 50.4
Viewing an audio-and-
PowerPoint seminar
on Microsoft's Seminar
Online Web site.

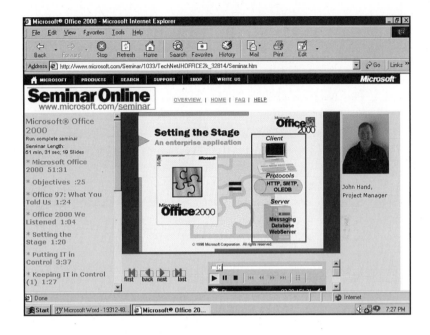

Microsoft's Online Office Resource Kit

Microsoft's online Office 2000 Resource Kit (`www.microsoft.com/office/ork/2000/ one/05ct_1.htm`) is an invaluable resource for any Office administrator. The Office 2000 Resource Kit contains extensive information for trouble-shooting, deploying, and configuring Microsoft Office 2000. Microsoft has organized the Office 2000 Resource Kit into six parts:

- Part 1, *The Office 2000 Environment*, presents coverage of the hardware and Windows environments in which Office 2000 can run, including server issues, OS service packs, and BackOffice.

- Part 2, *Deploying Office 2000*, is Microsoft's official guide to planning for and installing Office 2000. It covers the Office Custom Installation Wizard, Profile Wizard, Systems Management Server, and installation in an international environment.

- Part 3, *Managing and Supporting Office 2000*, covers Microsoft techniques for managing Office, including locking down configurations, customizing Help, using the System Policy Editor, and enhancing security.

- Part 4, *Upgrading to Office 2000*, covers migration techniques for organizations using previous versions of Office, including information on the Microsoft Office Converter Pack, batch file conversion, and Y2K issues.

- Part 5, *Office 2000 and the Web*, presents Microsoft's official guide to Office 2000's Web and intranet features, including Web discussions and Office Server Extensions.

- Part 6, *Using Office 2000 in a Multinational Organization,* covers configuring Office for use in multinational environments, including the MultiLanguage Pack, global help and user interfaces, international proofing tools, Unicode character sets, and more.

An Appendix, available at **www.microsoft.com/office/ork/2000/appndx/toolbox.htm**, contains the latest versions of a wide range of Office support tools, including the Office Custom Installation Wizard and Profile Wizard.

Discovering Online Newsgroups and Forums

Often, there's no substitute for asking a live human being your question—or better yet, an entire community of live Microsoft Office experts. Internet newsgroups and similar online forums enable you to do just that: Post a question to the world in the reasonable likelihood that someone who knows the answer will post a response within a couple of days.

There are four sizable communities of Office users and experts on the Web, and if you're responsible for supporting or managing Office, you should get to know at least some of them. In the following sections, you learn about

- ▪ microsoft.public Internet newsgroups
- ▪ WOPR forums
- ▪ MSN Computing Central forums
- ▪ Private CompuServe forums

Microsoft's Public Newsgroups

Microsoft hosts more than 100 newsgroups covering a wide range of products and technologies. Some are host to large groups of active participants; others generate little traffic and might not ever be visited by anyone who can answer your question. Note that Microsoft employees do not necessarily visit these newsgroups, and posting a question here might not get you an "official" answer. Figure 50.5 shows a typical newsgroup, the microsoft.public. office newsgroup, viewed with Internet Explorer's newsreader:

FIGURE 50.5

The microsoft. public.office newsgroup.

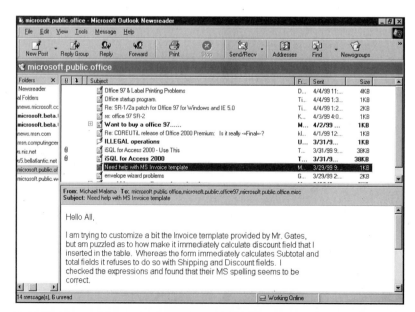

Microsoft newsgroups that might be of special interest to Office professionals include the following:

Access Newsgroups

- ■ microsoft.public.access
- ■ microsoft.public.access.3rdpartyusrgrp
- ■ microsoft.public.access.activexcontrol
- ■ microsoft.public.access.chat
- ■ microsoft.public.access.commandbarsui
- ■ microsoft.public.access.conversion
- ■ microsoft.public.access.customcontrols
- ■ microsoft.public.access.developerstoolkitode
- ■ microsoft.public.access.forms
- ■ microsoft.public.access.gettingstarted
- ■ microsoft.public.access.interopoledde
- ■ microsoft.public.access.macros
- ■ microsoft.public.access.modulesdaovba
- ■ microsoft.public.access.queries
- ■ microsoft.public.access.replication
- ■ microsoft.public.access.reports
- ■ microsoft.public.access.security
- ■ microsoft.public.access.setupconfig
- ■ microsoft.public.access.tablesdbdesign

Excel Newsgroups

- ■ microsoft.public.excel
- ■ microsoft.public.excel.123quattro
- ■ microsoft.public.excel.charting
- ■ microsoft.public.excel.datamap
- ■ microsoft.public.excel.interopoledde
- ■ microsoft.public.excel.links
- ■ microsoft.public.excel.macintosh
- ■ microsoft.public.excel.misc
- ■ microsoft.public.excel.printing
- ■ microsoft.public.excel.programming

- `microsoft.public.excel.setup`
- `microsoft.public.excel.templates`
- `microsoft.public.excel.worksheetfunctions`

FrontPage Newsgroups

- `microsoft.public.frontpage.client`
- `microsoft.public.frontpage.extensions.unix`
- `microsoft.public.frontpage.extensions.windowsnt`

PowerPoint Newsgroups

- `microsoft.public.powerpoint`
- `microsoft.public.powerpoint.mac`

Word Newsgroups

- `microsoft.public.word`
- `microsoft.public.word.conversions`
- `microsoft.public.word.dos`
- `microsoft.public.word.general`
- `microsoft.public.word.mac`
- `microsoft.public.word.oleinterop`
- `microsoft.public.word.printingfonts`
- `microsoft.public.word.programming`

Other Office-Related Newsgroups

- `microsoft.public.office`
- `microsoft.public.office.binders`
- `microsoft.public.office.misc`
- `microsoft.public.office.setup`
- `microsoft.public.office.shortcutbar`
- `microsoft.public.outlook98`
- `microsoft.public.project`
- `microsoft.public.publisher`

Relevant BackOffice Newsgroups

- `microsoft.public.exchange`
- `microsoft.public.exchange.admin`
- `microsoft.public.exchange.applications`

- microsoft.public.exchange.clients
- microsoft.public.exchange.connectivity
- microsoft.public.exchange.misc
- microsoft.public.exchange.setup
- microsoft.public.sms.admin
- microsoft.public.sms.inventory
- microsoft.public.sms.misc
- microsoft.public.sms.netmon
- microsoft.public.sms.microsoft.public.sms.sms.rcdiags
- microsoft.public.sms
- microsoft.public.sms.sms.setup
- microsoft.public.sms.sharedapps
- microsoft.public.sms.sitecomm
- microsoft.public.sms.swdist
- microsoft.public.sms.tools

TIP One way to find information in Microsoft's myriad newsgroups is to run a search for specific terms at **www.dejanews.com**, which maintains archives of all public newsgroups.

Woody's Office Portal and Lounge

Woody Leonhard, well-known Office expert, publisher of the Woody's Office Power Pack add-on Office enhancements, and author of *Woody Leonhard Teaches Microsoft Office 2000*, published by Que, now also offers a free Web site with extensive Office information resources, **www.wopr.com**. Within this site, at **www.wopr.com/lounge/splitbbs.html**, you'll find The WOPR Lounge—a thriving discussion forum that many top Office experts visit regularly (see Figure 50.6).

The Lounge even has a search feature that enables you to narrow the search, so you can review all messages about tables in Word posted within the last month.

N O T E Woody Leonhard provides several additional resources for Office professionals. Perhaps most valuable is Woody's Office Watch, a weekly email newsletter that has consistently broken important Office news (and identified urgent Office bugs) long before Microsoft or traditional news sources have publicized them. To subscribe, visit **www.wopr.com** and provide your email address.

FIGURE 50.6

Discussion in The
WOPR Lounge.

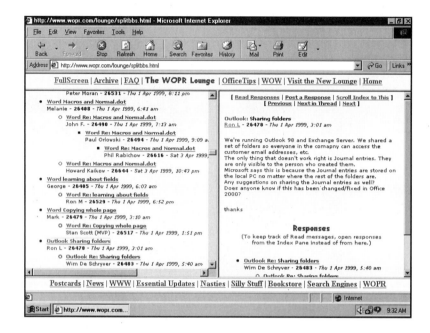

Microsoft's Computing Central Newsgroups

Another ongoing discussion about Office topics is accessible through the Microsoft Network (MSN). Visit **computingcentral.msn.com/newsgroups/default.asp** and choose the **PC Applications** newsgroup; your newsreader will open and display all recent messages in the newsgroup msn.computingcentral.pcapplications.general. Typically, the majority of these messages are related to Microsoft Office—and most of the answers are quite well-informed.

CompuServe's Office-Related Forums

CompuServe was once the best and only source for discussion about Microsoft Office and other computer-related topics. Then came the Internet, and the majority of CompuServe's tech-savvy users fled to other Internet service providers. But not all. The CompuServe forums on Microsoft Office are still quite good (although you must be a CompuServe member to access them). They are currently managed by WUGNET, the Windows User Group Network.

TIP CompuServe currently offers a $9.95/month limited access plan, so you can gain access to these forums at low cost even if you already use another Internet service provider.

Figure 50.7 shows a CompuServe forum, displayed through CompuServe's optional Web interface.

FIGURE 50.7
The CompuServe
Office forum,
displayed with
CompuServe's
Web interface.

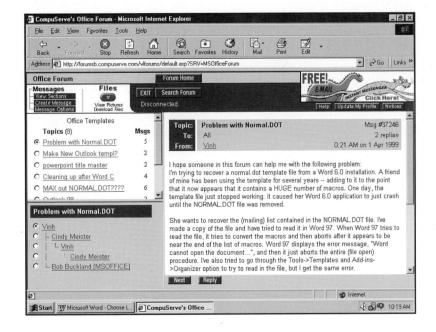

The following are especially helpful CompuServe forums:

- GO MSOFOR (Microsoft Office forum)
- GO MSWORD (Microsoft Word Forum)
- GO MSEXCEL (Microsoft Excel Forum)
- GO MSACCESS (Microsoft Access Forum)
- GO MSDESK (Assorted Microsoft Desktop applications, including PowerPoint, FrontPage, Project, and Publisher)

TIP

CompuServe members who use the Web browser interface might find it easier to access these forums from the links at **www.wugnet.com/compuserve** than to wade through several layers of pages at **www.compuserve.com**. Of course, after you reached the forum, you can create a shortcut or bookmark for it.

Exploring BugNet

Is anyone out there keeping track of all the bugs in today's rushed-to-market software? Well, yes, there are the manufacturers, who tend not to share the information unless quite necessary. There's also BugNet, which for several years has been collecting, testing, tracking, and publicizing software and hardware bugs on the Internet.

BugNet provides some high-profile information at no cost (see Figure 50.8). For instance, BugNet currently displays a free monthly top-ten list of the most dangerous, comic, or widespread bugs currently affecting PCs.

FIGURE 50.8

BugNet reporting on a new Internet Explorer 5 bug.

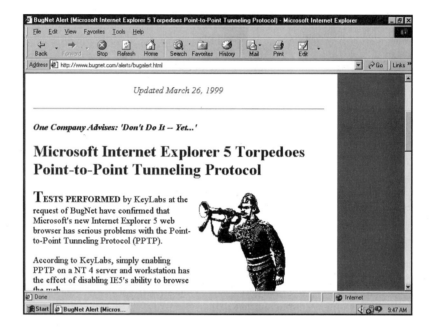

However, most BugNet information is available by subscription only. Many Office administrators, especially those working in organizations that use many other software packages as well, will find BugNet to be worth the price. BugNet subscriptions include

- **BugNet newsletter.** An online newsletter discussing glitches, bugs, and incompatibilities
- **BugNet database.** An online database with bugs and fixes
- **BugNet yearbook.** Thousands of bugs and fixes for your own system
- **BugNet alert.** Special bulletins for serious problems

BugNet's annual subscription fees vary depending on the type of organization you represent; renewals are less expensive:

- For home noncommercial use: $65
- For home business (commercial) use: $100
- For small business (12 employees or less) use: $150
- For other business (more than 12 employees) use: $250
- For nonprofit organization use: $200
- For consultants/outsourcers: $2,500

Exploring Other Windows Resources

When you need a solution to an Office-related problem, you'll often find yourself looking for information about the underlying Windows operating system Office is running on. To assist, the following sections provide information on some of the Web's best Windows-related information resources.

Frank Condron's World O'Windows

Frank Condron's World O'Windows (**www.worldowindows.com**) brings together an extensive collection of news, resources, and helpful tips about both Office and Microsoft's multiple versions of Windows, including Windows 95, Windows 98, Windows NT, and Windows CE. The Microsoft Office area, shown in Figure 50.9, contains these and other resources:

- Discussion Newsgroups
- Updates and Patches
- Links to current Microsoft resources, patches, and free add-on software

FIGURE 50.9
Frank Condron's
World O'Windows has
a separate area for
Office information
and discussions.

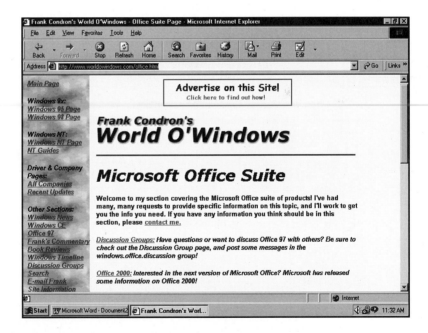

TIP

Frank Condron also hosts a newsgroup discussion on Microsoft Office, at `windows.office.discussion`, although this forum is less widely utilized than the ones mentioned elsewhere in this chapter.

John Savill's Windows NT/Windows 2000 FAQ

If you're running Microsoft Office in a Windows NT environment, you'll find John Savill's NT FAQ (**www.ntfaq.com**) to be an invaluable resource. Updated once a week, NT FAQ now contains several hundred questions and answers, many of them quite relevant to deploying and supporting Office. Every week, Savill also compiles his entire site into a downloadable Help file (traditional Windows Help or HTML Help), so you can have access to current information without going online.

Baarns, Your Microsoft Office Resource Center

Baarns Consulting has extensive experience in building and deploying custom applications with Microsoft Office. Although the company has moved its primary focus to Web application development, it still maintains an extensive Office-related Web site at **http://archive.baarns.com** containing over 500 pages of FAQs and solutions, including a collection of free and low-cost add-ins for Excel and Word.

> **CAUTION**
>
> Be aware, however, that not all these software resources have been tested for Office 2000.

Microsoft MVP Resources

Microsoft has honored several Microsoft Office users and developers as "Most Valuable Professionals" (MVPs) for their contributions to the community of Office users. There are MVPs for each leading Office application and several MVPs for Visual Basic application development.

Many of these MVPs are active on the newsgroups covered earlier in this chapter; quite a few also maintain Web sites that include valuable information or resources for Office administrators and developers. Although MVPs are generally not available to answer private questions, you might find it useful to browse the information they have posted publicly. A list of MVP site links might be found at **www.mvps.org/links.html**.

Office Computing Magazine Online

Ziff-Davis' *Office Computing Magazine* Web site brings together a wide variety of projects that walk Office professionals step-by-step through building basic VBA projects that solve a wide range of business problems. You can find the magazine and the projects at **www.zdnet.com/pccomp/oc**.

 TIP If you are interested in Office information targeted at serious developers, visit **www.advisor.com/ wHome.nsf/wPages/AVmain** and sign up for the free (but private) newsgroup associated with *Access * Office * VB Advisor* Magazine.

Integrating Office 2000 with Windows 2000

by Bill Camarda

Microsoft has invested heavily in integrating its key offerings so that each of them works better when the others have also been installed. Office 2000 and Windows 2000 are a case in point. Organizations that upgrade to Windows 2000 Server and Active Directory on the server side and Windows 2000 Professional on the client side have several Office 2000 management options unavailable to those who do not.

This chapter offers a high-level overview of the capabilities Windows 2000 brings to the Microsoft Office 2000 administrator. Coverage includes

- User data management features for storing user data safely in network locations, while making the data appear "local" at all times to users, even if they are working offline

- Software installation and maintenance features for streamlining the installation, configuration, repair, and removal of Office 2000 and any other package that uses the new Windows Installer

- User settings management features for centrally controlling how Office 2000 works across sites, domains, or organizational units

- Seamless HTML file copying, which automatically copies any support files associated with an HTML document whenever a user copies the HTML document alone

- Other Windows 2000 enhancements, including Distributed File System (Dfs) support, Windows Terminal Services, disk quotas, Unicode filename support, and more

NOTE Migrating to Windows 2000 is a complex task, and taking advantage of these features requires careful planning and deployment. You might find the following books valuable:

- *Special Edition Using Microsoft Windows 2000 Server,* by Roger Jennings (Que)
- *Special Edition Using Microsoft Windows 2000 Professional,* by Bob Cowart (Que)
- *Microsoft Windows 2000 Server Unleashed,* by Chris Miller and Todd Brown (Sams)
- *Microsoft Windows 2000 Professional Unleashed,* by Paul Cassel (Sams)
- *Practical Microsoft Windows 2000 Professional,* by Ed Bott (Que)
- *Microsoft Windows 2000 Professional Installation and Configuration Handbook,* by Jim Boyce (Que)
- *Microsoft Windows 2000 Registry Handbook,* by Jerry Honeycutt (Que) ▧

Controlling Client Workstations with IntelliMirror

IntelliMirror is Microsoft's term for a collection of features scattered throughout Windows 2000 that make it possible to store data, software, and settings centrally, and deliver this information seamlessly to users wherever they go on the network—or even if they disconnect from the network and work offline.

IntelliMirror requires Windows 2000 Server and client computers running Windows 2000 Professional. In particular, some IntelliMirror features make extensive use of Microsoft's new Active Directory and group policies. *Active Directory* is a directory that enables administrators to centrally review and manage virtually all their networks' key information and resources. *Group policies* extend Windows system policies to centralize control over desktop computers for groups of users throughout a single site, domain, or organizational unit.

Potential benefits of IntelliMirror to Office 2000 administrators include the following:

- Better central control of data, without compromising user flexibility and autonomy
- Stronger control over desktop workstations and how they are used
- Simpler deployment of new software and computers
- Easier disaster recovery and repair of damaged software
- Better support for mobile computer users

The key elements of IntelliMirror are described in the following sections.

IntelliMirror User Data Management Features

IntelliMirror's *user data management features* store user data safely in network locations, while making the data appear "local" at all times to users, even if they are working at home on disconnected notebook PCs.

One easy way to take advantage of IntelliMirror user data management is to provide *offline folders*. With offline folders, when the network is available, Windows 2000 saves the file to the appropriate network location and then stores a copy on the local workstation. When the network becomes unavailable (for example, when a user disconnects a notebook PC to work on an airplane), the local "cached" version of the file is used. When the computer is connected to the network again, Windows 2000 handles synchronization in the background.

The result: The most recent version of each file in folders marked Make Available Offline is always stored safely on the network—and at the same time available locally to the user.

N O T E   Offline folders can be implemented on networks that do not use Active Directory or group policies, but they require servers that use the Windows server message block (SMB) protocol. ■

To make a folder available offline, follow these steps:

1. From the server, right-click on the folder and choose **Sharing** (see Figure 51.1).
2. In the Sharing tab of the Properties dialog box, click **Share this folder**.

FIGURE 51.1

The Sharing tab of the Properties dialog box.

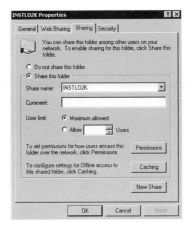

3. Click **Caching**. In the Caching Settings dialog box (see Figure 51.2), be sure the **Allow caching of files in this shared folder** check box is selected.
4. Choose **Automatic Caching for Documents** from the Settings drop-down box and click **OK**.

Part
VII

Ch
51

FIGURE 51.2

The Caching Settings dialog box.

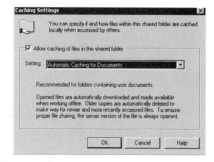

5. From the user workstation, right-click on the shared folder and choose **Make Available Offline** from the shortcut menu. The Offline Files Wizard appears (see Figure 51.3).

FIGURE 51.3

The Offline Files Wizard.

6. Click **Next >**. The window shown in Figure 51.4 appears.

FIGURE 51.4

Choosing to synchronize offline files automatically.

7. Select the **Automatically synchronize the Offline Files when I log on and log off my computer** check box and click **Next**. The window shown in Figure 51.5 appears.

FIGURE 51.5
Controlling reminders
and shortcuts.

8. If you want Windows 2000 to remind the user he or she is working offline, leave the Enable reminders check box checked. If you want a shortcut to the Offline Files folder to appear on the desktop, select the **Create a shortcut to the Offline Files folder on my desktop** check box.

9. Click **Finish**.

IntelliMirror Software Installation and Maintenance Features

Several IntelliMirror features are designed to streamline the installation, configuration, repair, and removal of a wide variety of software. These features rely heavily on group policies, together with the Windows Installer feature that was introduced with Office 2000 and is built into Windows 2000.

You can use these features to provide Office 2000 to users on a "just-in-time" basis, instead of deploying to every user at once. Client computers get the same Start menu shortcuts and file associations they would have if Office 2000 were fully installed, but Office isn't installed until they actually need it. When a user chooses the application from the Start menu—or double-clicks a file that requires it—the Windows Installer automatically installs the application across the network, from the administrative installation point. (For more information about Office 2000 network installations, see Chapter 2, "Automating and Customizing Office Installations Across the Network.") Similarly, you can

- **Publish an application.** Enables users to install it through the Add/Remove Programs control panel applet whenever they're ready to use it

- **Assign an application.** Installs the application across the network automatically and prevents users from uninstalling it (if they do, the application reinstalls itself the next time the user logs on)

Before using these features, create an Administrative Installation Point for Office 2000 on your network server. The Administrative Installation Point contains the files and instructions that will be used to automate installations across the network. "Instructions" include an MSI file that contains the generic directions for installing Office, an MST ("transforms") file that includes customizations that differ from the generic installation, and optionally, an OPS profile that contains user settings, templates, and additional files you want to include. If you want to use OPS profiles, also follow the steps in the preceding two sections, "Installing Office 2000 on a Client Workstation" and "Running the Office Profile Wizard."

▶ To learn about preparing an administrative installation point, **see** "Creating an Administrative Installation Point," on **p. 34**.

After you create Administrative Installation Point, instruct Windows 2000 Server as to where and how it should install Office across the network. To do this, you need to establish a group policy for the application and define which group(s) the policy should apply to.

Group policies are controlled through the Active Directory Users and Computers snap-in of the Microsoft Management Console. To access it, choose **Start**, **Programs**, **Administrative Tools**, **Active Directory Users and Computers**. Figure 51.6 shows a simple Active Directory with Windows 2000's default groups, as well as several additional Organizational Units (Finance, Manufacturing, Marketing, R&D, and Sales). Follow these steps to create a policy that installs Office 2000 from the Administrative Installation Point you've already established:

FIGURE 51.6

A sample Active Directory, with Users and Computers displayed.

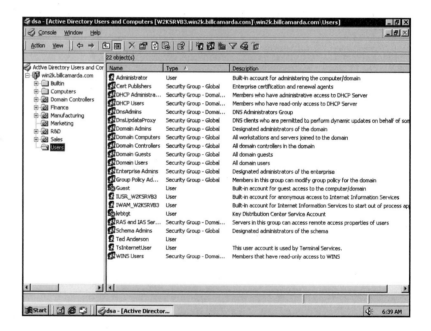

1. Right-click on the group or organizational unit you want to create a policy for; then choose **Properties** from the shortcut menu and click the **Group Policy** tab (see Figure 51.7).

Part
VII

Ch
51

FIGURE 51.7
The Group Policy tab; no group policies are displayed yet.

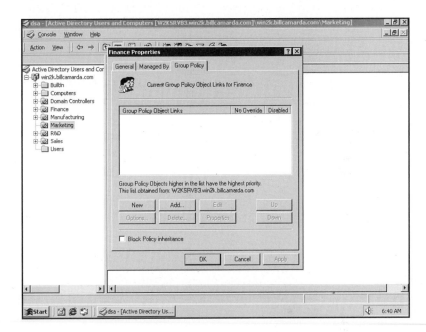

2. Click **New** to create a new group policy. The policy name appears in the Group Policy Object Links column. You can rename it to whatever name is appropriate; for example, **Office 2000 Default Install**. When you've renamed the group policy, press **Enter**.

3. With the group policy selected, click **Edit**. The Group Policy snap-in of the Microsoft Management Console appears (see Figure 51.8).

4. Click to expand **User Configuration**; then click to expand **Software Settings**.

5. Select **Software Installation** and choose **New**, **Package** from the Action menu.

6. Browse to the folder you established as your Administrative Installation Point, choose the MSI file associated with Office (typically **data1.msi**), and click **Open**. You might be asked to confirm that the path is available from a network share; if so, click **Yes**. The Deploy Software dialog box opens (see Figure 51.9).

FIGURE 51.8

The Group Policy snap-in of the Microsoft Management Console.

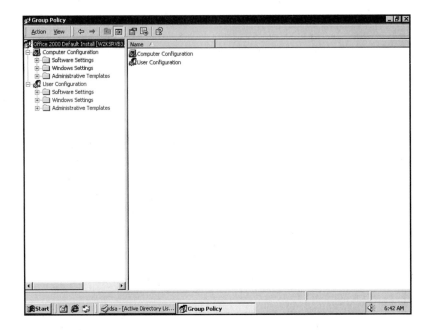

FIGURE 51.9

The Deploy Software dialog box.

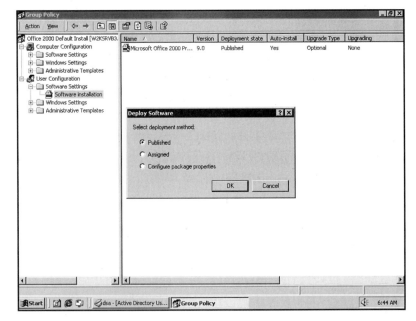

7. To assign Office 2000 with default settings (requiring users to have it and preventing them from uninstalling it), choose **Assigned**. Typically, however, you'll want more control over how Office installs; if so, choose **Configure package properties**. Click **OK**. The Microsoft Office 2000 Premium Properties dialog box opens (see Figure 51.10). This box enables you to customize several aspects of how Office installs:

FIGURE 51.10

The Microsoft Office 2000 Premium Properties dialog box.

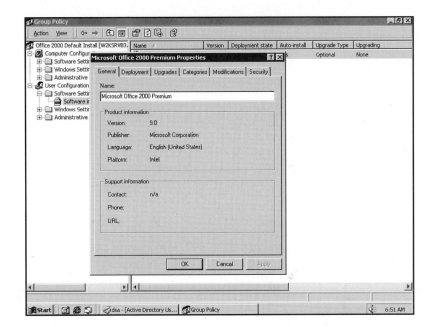

- The General tab shows the name of the product you plan to install and enables you to customize the Name.

- The Deployment tab enables you to control whether Office is Assigned or Published, how and when it is uninstalled, how much feedback users will get during installation, and whether users will be able to install Office through the Add/Remove Programs control panel.

- The Upgrades tab enables you to specify which versions of Office are to be upgraded and any packages that might be considered upgrades to Office 2000.

- The Categories tab enables you to specify categories the application will be listed under in the Add/Remove Programs control panel, if any.

- The Modifications tab enables you to specify any Transforms (MST) files you have created to customize how Office 2000 installs.

- The Security tab enables you to control the permissions required for groups of users to install Office 2000.

8. When you've finished setting the Properties for this group policy, click **OK**. The policy will appear in the Group Policy snap-in window of the Microsoft Management Console. The policy will also appear listed in the Group Policy tab of the Properties dialog box associated with the group or organizational unit you associated it with.

IntelliMirror User Settings Management Features

Previous versions of Windows supported *system policy templates*, which enabled administrators to centrally control many aspects of how Office works, especially most of the settings in the Options dialog box of each Office application—settings that would otherwise have to be controlled directly, through the Registry. (Chapter 37 covers system policies in depth, and Chapters 6 through 11 include detailed coverage of system policies associated with each major Office 2000 application.) Windows 2000 extends system policies in a variety of ways:

- Most important, although Windows NT 4 system policies were applied domainwide, with filtering via user security group membership, group policies can be set at the site level, domain level, or organizational level (and also filtered through security group membership). The result is greater flexibility for the administrator.

- Windows 2000 group policies are more secure. They are stored in specific Windows 2000 group policies trees in the Windows 2000 Registry, which cannot be changed except by administrators.

CAUTION

Use Office 2000 administrative template files designed for Windows 2000, not those designed for Windows NT 4 or Windows 9.x. Earlier administrative template files might work, but might write policies throughout the Registry, in locations that are not secured from change by local users.

- Windows 2000 group policies are more effective in mobile and fast-changing environments. Where users move among computers, temporary and local computer information no longer roams with the user; rather, it is dynamically regenerated at the user's new workstation as needed. Users still get a consistent experience, but there's less network traffic.

The Office 2000 Resource Kit includes Administrative Template (ADM) files designed for use with group policies on systems running Windows 2000 Professional. Note that Windows NT 4.0 system policies do not migrate to Windows 2000 when a system is upgraded.

Copying HTML Files Seamlessly

In Office 2000, HTML is a companion file format nearly equivalent in capabilities to Office binary formats, such as DOC (Word) and XLS (Excel). When a user saves a file to HTML format in an Office 2000 application, Office creates a text-only HTML file, as well as a separate folder with the same name (excluding extensions). The accompanying folder contains all graphics and other files that are needed by the HTML file in order to display the full page as intended.

In Windows 95, 98, and NT 4.0 (and earlier), when a user manually copies an HTML file—perhaps to a floppy disk for work at home—only the HTML file is copied. Unless the user manually copies the folder containing support files, the HTML file will not display properly when loaded on another computer.

In Windows 2000, however, if a user copies the HTML file, the corresponding folder is copied automatically (if it exists). If a user moves, copies, or deletes the HTML file, Windows 2000 does the same automatically with the corresponding folder. The same is true in reverse: If a user copies, moves, or deletes a folder containing supporting files, Windows 2000 will also copy, move, or delete the individual HTML file that goes with it.

Part
VII

Ch
51

CAUTION

This feature does not work with HTML files created by FrontPage 2000 or stored in Web Folders.

N O T E   This feature can be turned off through the Windows 2000 Registry. To do so, run
Regedit and browse to the **HKEY_CURRENT_USER\Software\Microsoft\Windows**
CurrentVersion\Explorer subkey. Add a DWORD value entry named **NoFileFolderConnection** there.
Set its value to **1**. If you later want to reactivate the feature, change the value to **0** or delete the
NoFileFolderConnection entry altogether. ■

Understanding Other Windows 2000 Changes

The following list brings together information about several new Windows 2000 Server and Windows 2000 Professional features that might affect how you administer Office 2000 and how your users work with it:

■ Windows 2000 provides full support for Microsoft's Distributed File System (Dfs), which enables you to combine separate, network-connected volumes into one logical volume that looks and acts as if it were a single disk. This gives you several opportunities. First, if you are deploying Office 2000 on hundreds of thousands of workstations in a short period of time, you can use Dfs to create a single logical volume that corresponds to several Office 2000 distribution servers. Users can log on with a single path from anywhere in your organization, making installation simpler—while you balance the load among as many server resources as necessary, enhancing network performance.

You can use Dfs to move and change network resources without changing the share names users must know to reach their data. You can also provide seamless access to your Office (or other) intranet servers even when they must go down for scheduled maintenance, by moving the information to another drive to another server in the same logical volume. Note, however, that Dfs requires careful planning and can increase network traffic. Moreover, although more limited versions of Dfs were available as NT4 add-ons, widespread Dfs implementation is practical only in all-Windows 2000 environments.

■ Windows 2000's IntelliMirror features enable remote operating system installation, which enables you to reload Office 2000 (along with Windows 2000 Professional itself) on replacement computers, complete with a user's customized settings.

■ Windows 2000 provides for disk quotas that enable you to restrict the amount of server space provided to each user on your network, and to warn users when they are nearing their quota limits, encouraging them to eliminate old files. Enforcing disk quotas gives the administrator a powerful way to control the cost of server storage. However, disk quotas should be used with care, especially in organizations that plan to make extensive use of the HTML file format. Files that contain graphics and are saved in HTML tend to be significantly larger than files saved in the traditional binary formats Office has used previously. (Unicode support, introduced in most Office applications with Office 97, also ballooned the size of files—so those upgrading from Office 95 or earlier versions will see even greater file size increases. Note that quotas are available only on drives formatted with the NTFS 5 file system included with Windows 2000 Server.)

■ In earlier versions of Windows, Office 2000 users can publish a file to the Web or a corporate intranet by saving it to a Web folder. Web folders appear as separate items in the Look In drop-down box in the File, Open and File, Save dialog boxes. In Windows 2000, however, Web Folder objects are replaced by the My Network Places object, which stores shortcuts to folders published on the Web, connections to computers on the same LAN, and universal naming convention shortcuts to drives on networked computers.

■ In Windows 9x, users cannot use Unicode characters in filenames, even though Office 2000 provides full Unicode support. In Windows 2000 and Windows NT 4.0, they can. If files are to be shared between Windows NT/2000 and Windows 9x systems, however, you might want to keep avoiding Unicode filenames, as you have in the past.

■ Windows 2000 Server now provides Terminal Services as a built-in feature (you no longer need to purchase a separate copy of Windows NT Terminal Server). This might give you the flexibility to extend Office 2000 applications to selected terminals, older workstations, and even Macintosh and UNIX systems that might not have been viable candidates for Office 2000 previously. If you intend to use Terminal Services on a Windows NT Server system that has other responsibilities, carefully test its impact on overall server performance before you go into production. Also, pay close attention to the complex licensing issues associated with using Terminal Server; each client must have its own valid client license, separate from any Windows license already purchased for that client system. ●

Components of a Default Office 2000 Premium Installation

by Bill Camarda

The following pages present the contents of a default Office 2000 Premium installation (excluding PhotoDraw, which is installed separately).

Boldfaced text represents a top-level application selection. Components are installed locally unless otherwise specified as Install on 1st Run, Run from CD-ROM, or Not Available.

Microsoft Word for Windows
- Help
  - Help for WordPerfect users (Install on 1st Run)
- Wizards and Templates
  - Letters
  - Memos
  - Faxes
  - Reports (Install on 1st Run)
  - Résumés
  - Web Pages
  - More Wizards (Install on 1st Run)
  - More Templates and Macros (Install on 1st Run)
- Address Book
- Text with Layout Converter (Install on 1st Run)
- Page Border Art

Microsoft Excel for Windows

    Help

    Spreadsheet Templates (Install on 1st Run)

        Invoice Template (Install on 1st Run)

        Expense Report Template (Install on 1st Run)

        Purchase Order Template (Install on 1st Run)

    Add-Ins

        Access Links (Install on 1st Run)

        ODBC Add-In (Install on 1st Run)

        Template Utilities (Install on 1st Run)

        Analysis ToolPak (Install on 1st Run)

        AutoSave (Install on 1st Run)

        Euro Currency Tools (Install on 1st Run)

        Lookup Wizard (Install on 1st Run)

        Report Manager (Install on 1st Run)

        Internet Assistant VBA

        Conditional Sum Wizard (Install on 1st Run)

        Solver (Install on 1st Run)

        Template Wizard with Data Tracking (Install on 1st Run)

        Update Links (Install on 1st Run)

    Sample Files

    Quattro Pro 5.0 Converter (Not Available)

    Microsoft Map (Install on 1st Run)

Microsoft PowerPoint for Windows

    Help

    Tutorial (Run from CD-ROM)

    Design Templates

        Typical Design Templates

        Additional Design Templates

    Content Templates

        Typical Content Templates

        Additional Content Templates (Install on 1st Run)

    Presentation Broadcasting (Install on 1st Run)

Presentation Translators (Install on 1st Run)

PowerPoint 4.0 Export (Install on 1st Run)

Harvard Graphics 3.0 for DOS (Install on 1st Run)

Lotus Freelance 1.0–2.1 for Windows (Install on 1st Run)

Animation Sound Effects

Genigraphics Wizard (Install on 1st Run)

Pack and Go Wizard (Install on 1st Run)

Viewer for Pack and Go

Microsoft Outlook for Windows

Help

Importers and Exporters

Stationery (Install on 1st Run)

Junk E-mail

Net Folders (Install on 1st Run)

Visual Basic Scripting Support

Collaboration Data Objects (Not Available)

Electronic Forms Designer Runtime (Not Available)

Symantec Fax Starter Edition (Internet Mail Only Configuration) (Install on 1st Run)

Integrated File Management

Microsoft Access for Windows

Help

Typical Wizards

Additional Wizards (Install on 1st Run)

Sample Databases (Install on 1st Run)

Northwind Database (Install on 1st Run)

Northwind SQL Project File (First)

Address Application (Install on 1st Run)

Contact Application (Install on 1st Run)

Household Inventory (Install on 1st Run)

Snapshot Viewer (Install on 1st Run)

Database Replication (Install on 1st Run)

Calendar Control

Client Server Visual Design Tools

Microsoft FrontPage for Windows

Tutorial

Help

Samples

Server Extensions Resource Kit (Not Available)

Server Extensions Admin Forms (Not Available)

Additional Themes (Install on 1st Run)

Office Tools

Clip Gallery

Clip Files

AutoShapes

Typical Bullets and Lines

Additional Bullets and Lines (Run from CD-ROM)

Clip Catalogs

AutoShapes

Typical Bullets and Lines

Additional Bullets and Lines

Digital Signature for VBA Projects (Install on 1st Run)

Equation Editor (Install on 1st Run)

Find Fast Control Panel

HTML Source Editing (Install on 1st Run)

Web Scripting (Install on 1st Run)

International Support

Core Support Files

Extended Support Files (Not Available)

Bidirectional Support (Install on 1st Run)

Universal Font (Not Available)

Japanese Font (Install on 1st Run)

Korean Font (Install on 1st Run)

Traditional Chinese Font (Install on 1st Run)

Simplified Chinese Font (Install on 1st Run)

Language Settings Tool (Install on 1st Run)

Lotus VIM Mail Support (Not Available)

Microsoft Binder (Not Available)

    Help (Not Available)

Microsoft Graph

    Help

Microsoft Office Shortcut Bar (Install on 1st Run)

Microsoft Photo Editor (Not Available)

Microsoft Query (Install on 1st Run)

Office Assistant

    Rocky (Install on 1st Run)

    Dot (Install on 1st Run)

    MotherNature (Install on 1st Run)

    Genius (Install on 1st Run)

    Logo (Install on 1st Run)

    F1 (Install on 1st Run)

    Clippit

    Links (Install on 1st Run)

Office Server Extensions Support

    Web Discussions

    Web Publishing

Office Web Components

Organization Chart (Install on 1st Run)

Proofing Tools

    Spelling Checker

    Grammar/Style Checker

    Hyphenation (Install on 1st Run)

    Thesaurus

    Find All Word Forms (Install on 1st Run)

Proofing Tools (French) (Install on 1st Run)

    Spelling Checker (Install on 1st Run)

    Grammar/Style Checker (Install on 1st Run)

    Hyphenation (Install on 1st Run)

    Thesaurus (Install on 1st Run)

    Find All Word Forms (Install on 1st Run)

Proofing Tools (Spanish) (Install on 1st Run)

    Spelling Checker (Install on 1st Run)

    Grammar/Style Checker (Install on 1st Run)

    Hyphenation (Install on 1st Run)

    Thesaurus (Install on 1st Run)

    Find All Word Forms (Install on 1st Run)

Scanner and Camera Add-In (Install on 1st Run)

System Information

Themes

    Typical Themes

    Additional Themes (Install on 1st Run)

Visual Basic Help (Install on 1st Run)

Converters and Filters

    Text Converters

        WordPerfect 6.x Converter (Install on 1st Run)

        WordPerfect 5.x Converter (Install on 1st Run)

        Microsoft Excel Converter (Install on 1st Run)

        Word 97–2000 & 6.0/95 RTF Converter (Install on 1st Run)

        Word 6.0/95 Export Converter

        Word for Macintosh 4.0–5.1 Converter (Install on 1st Run)

        Word for Windows 2.0 Converter (Install on 1st Run)

        Works for Windows 4.0 (Install on 1st Run)

        Recover Text Converter

        Converters for Search Tools (Install on 1st Run)

            Find Fast Search Engine (Install on 1st Run)

        Word 97 for Windows/Word 98 Macintosh (Install on 1st Run)

        Word 6.0/95 for Windows/Macintosh (Install on 1st Run)

        Lotus 1-2-3 Converter (Install on 1st Run)

    Graphics Filters

        Tag Image File Format Import

        Encapsulated PostScript

        FPX Import (Install on 1st Run)

        Windows Bitmap Import

        Enhanced Metafile Import (Install on 1st Run)

Computer Graphics Metafile Import (Install on 1st Run)

PC Paintbrush PCX Import (Install on 1st Run)

CorelDRAW Import (Install on 1st Run)

WordPerfect Graphics Filters (Install on 1st Run)

Windows Metafile Support

Kodak Photo CD Import (Install on 1st Run)

PNG File Format Import (Install on 1st Run)

Macintosh PICT Import

GIF (Graphics Interchange Format)

JPEG Interchange Format ●

Index